ELEVENTH EDITION

HUMAN SEXUALITY
Diversity in Contemporary Society

William L. Yarber

INDIANA UNIVERSITY

Barbara W. Sayad

CALIFORNIA STATE UNIVERSITY, MONTEREY BAY

McGraw Hill

HUMAN SEXUALITY: DIVERSITY IN CONTEMPORARY SOCIETY, ELEVENTH EDITION

Published by McGraw Hill LLC, 1325 Avenue of the Americas, New York, NY 10019. Copyright ©2022 by McGraw Hill LLC. All rights reserved. Printed in the United States of America. Previous editions ©2019, 2016, and 2013. No part of this publication may be reproduced or distributed in any form or by any means, or stored in a database or retrieval system, without the prior written consent of McGraw Hill LLC, including, but not limited to, in any network or other electronic storage or transmission, or broadcast for distance learning.

Some ancillaries, including electronic and print components, may not be available to customers outside the United States.

This book is printed on acid-free paper.

1 2 3 4 5 6 7 8 9 LWI 26 25 24 23 22 21

ISBN 978-1-260-88859-1 (bound edition)
MHID 1-260-88859-2 (bound edition)
ISBN 978-1-260-71887-4 (loose-leaf edition)
MHID 1-260-71887-5 (loose-leaf edition)

Portfolio Manager: *Jason Seitz*
Product Developer: *Miranda Hency*
Marketing Manager: *Olivia Kaiser*
Product Development Manager: *Dawn Groundwater*
Content Project Managers: *Melissa M. Leick, Katie Reuter*
Buyer: *Sandy Ludovissy*
Content Licensing Specialists: *Shawntel Schmitt*
Cover Image: © *Hi Brow Arabia/Alamy Stock Photo; ©Rawpixel.com/Shutterstock*
Compositor: *Straive*

All credits appearing on page or at the end of the book are considered to be an extension of the copyright page.

Library of Congress Cataloging-in-Publication Data

Names: Yarber, William L. (William Lee), 1943- author. | Sayad, Barbara
    Werner, author.
Title: Human sexuality: diversity in contemporary society / William L.
    Yarber, Indiana University, Barbara W. Sayad, Califorornia State
    University, Monterey Bay.
Description: Eleventh edition. | New York, NY : McGrawHill, [2022] |
    Includes bibliographical references and index.
Identifiers: LCCN 2021031263 | ISBN 9781260888591 (hardcover ; alk. paper)
Subjects: LCSH: Sex. | Sex customs. | Sexual health.
Classification: LCC HQ21 .S8126 2022 | DDC 306.7–dc23
LC record available at https://lccn.loc.gov/2021031263

mheducation.com/highered

Dedication

This book is dedicated to two courageous and visionary women who have made pronounced contributions to advancing sexual health.

Betty Dodson, PhD, a feminist icon and sex-positive educator, was an outspoken advocate for women's right to sexual knowledge and pleasure, and taught generations of women how to masturbate through workshops, videos, and books. For over five decades, she helped millions of women embrace their bodies and orgasms through self-pleasuring and use of the vibrator. Her book, *Liberating Masturbation: A Mediation on Selflove* (1974), is considered a feminist classic, and her *Sex for One* (1987) text sold over a million copies and was translated into 25 different languages. She received numerous awards including the Masters & Johnson Award in 2012 from the Society for Sex Therapy and Research, and was recently named one of the top 10 sexual revolutionaries by *Cosmopolitan* magazine. In 2020, she was named among the 50 top sexual and gender health revolutionaries worldwide by the Program in Human Sexuality, University of Minnesota Medical School. Dr. Dodson died on October 31, 2020, at age 91.

Joycelyn Elders, MD, has been career-long outspoken physician who challenged public health taboos. She courageously and frankly advocated for the sexual and reproductive health education and health care for young persons. Despite frequent opposition, Dr. Elders defended young people's "right to know" about their sexual health. Dr. Elders became Surgeon General of the United States in 1993 but her term was ended in 1994 when she suggested that our youth need to be taught about masturbation as a means for keeping them from engaging in more risky sexual behaviors. She is currently Professor Emeritus of Pediatrics at the University of Arkansas for Medical Sciences. Dr. Elders has received numerous expressions of praise and admiration. *Time* magazine named her one of the top 100 most influential women in the world during the past century. The Rural Center for AIDS/STD Prevention in the Indiana University School of Public Health-Bloomington awarded her the Ryan White Distinguished Leadership Award 2020.

—W. L. Y.

To Lucca and Adrian, who embody joy and hope, and to the rest of my family whose love and support are the sustenance of my life.

—B. W. S.

Brief Contents

Mc Graw Hill | connect McGraw Hill Education Psychology APA Documentation Style Guide

Contents

1 Perspectives on Human Sexuality 1

Peopleimages/iStock/Getty Images

2 Studying Human Sexuality 28

Hero/Corbis/Glow Images

3 Female Sexual Anatomy and Physiology 60

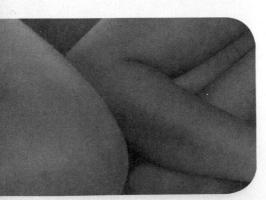

Ingram Publishing/SuperStock

4 Male Sexual Anatomy and Physiology 87

Dennis Grasse/EyeEm/Getty Images

5 Gender, Gender Roles, and Sexuality 104

©Jeff Gross/Getty Images

WeAre/Shutterstock

Laura Doss/Image Source/Getty Images

Tom Merton/Getty Images

Mark Wragg/Getty Images

10 Variations in Sexual Behavior 282

11 Contraception and Abortion   308

Rafe Swan/Cultura/Getty Images

12 Conception, Pregnancy, and Childbirth 343

13 The Sexual Body in Health and Illness 376

14 Sexual Function Difficulties, Dissatisfaction, Enhancement, and Therapy   406

Radius Images/Alamy Stock Photo

Peter Dazeley/Getty Images

15 Sexually Transmitted Infections 449

16 HIV and AIDS 489

MANDEL NGAN/Getty Images

©Mario Mitsis/Alamy Stock Photo

17 Sexual Assault and Sexual Misconduct 530

18 Sexually Explicit Materials, Sex Workers, and Sex Laws 573

©David Angel/Alamy Stock Photo

 McGraw Hill Education Psychology APA Documentation Style Guide

Guide to Diversity, Equity, and Inclusion

Chapter 1 Perspectives on Human Sexuality:

- Inclusive terminology: Sexual orientation and identity
- Media portrayals of gender
- LGBTQ+ individuals in film and television
- Cross-cultural comparison of sexual interests
- Cross-cultural comparison of sexual orientation
- Cross-cultural comparison of gender
- The Declaration of Sexual Rights and the right to sexual and reproductive health

Chapter 2 Studying Human Sexuality:

- Sexual stereotyping and ethnocentrism
- Underrepresentation of ethnic groups, gender identity, and sexual orientations in sampling and surveys
- Researchers broadening the study of sexual activity and behaviors
- Accurately measuring gender identity and sexual orientation of non-binary and non-conforming individuals in surveys
- Feminist scholarship in human sexuality
- The feminist perspective in sex therapy
- Insights and perspectives from feminist, gay, lesbian, bisexual, transgender, and queer research
- Contemporary studies documenting sexual minority students

Chapter 3 Female Sexual Anatomy and Physiology:

- Cross-cultural data on women's genital perceptions
- Female genital mutilation/cutting as a cultural custom
- Cross-cultural attitudes toward menstruation
- Ethnicity and the use of cosmetic procedures

Chapter 4 Male Sexual Anatomy and Physiology:

- Phallic symbols and identity across cultures
- Cultural and religious associations for circumcision

Chapter 5 Gender and Gender Roles:

- International data on binary gender classifications
- Nonbinary gender identity and expression
- Gender-neutral pronouns
- Cross-cultural data on sex, gender and sexual fluidity
- Influence of media on gender
- Gender equality and same-sex couples
- Sex, gender, and sexual orientation continuum
- Transgender issues and experiences
- Gender dysphoria and gender-confirming treatments
- Anti-sex and anti-gender discrimination advocacy and laws

Chapter 6 Sexuality in Childhood and Adolescence:
- Sexual orientation and gender identity during adolescence
- Homophobia and LGBTQ+ youth
- Cross-cultural data on teenage pregnancy and births
- Analysis of what Latinx and lower income students wish to know about sex and sexuality
- Comprehensive sexuality education for youth

Chapter 7 Sexuality in Adulthood:
- Development of sexual orientation models
- Prevalence of sexual minorities
- The identity process for LGBTQ+ individuals
- Singlehood in sexual minority dating communities
- Same sex marriage and anti-discrimination laws
- Sexuality and stereotypes of aging

Chapter 8 Love and Communication in Intimate Relationships:
- A global perspective on gender equality
- Gender and cultural differences related to love
- Frequency of sex and orgasm among heterosexual and LGBTQ+ individuals
- Sex and gender differences in the context of jealousy
- Sexual communication and LGBTQ+ individuals

Chapter 9 Sexual Response and Expression:
- Cross-cultural data on sexual attractiveness
- Sexual fantasizes of men and women
- Research on same-sex sexual attraction
- Levels of sexual desire in same-sex and mixed-sex relationships
- Frequency and duration of sex in mixed-sex and same-sex relationships
- International data on declining birth rates
- International data on romantic kissing
- Sexual behavior in mixed- and same-sex couples
- Diversity in photo-realistic representations of individuals and couples by skin-tone, body type, gender, physical ability, and age during solo masturbation and partnered sex
- Sexual intimacy for people who use a wheelchair

Chapter 10 Variations in Sexual Behavior:
- Individuals with transvestism versus transgender individuals
- Pedophilia sexual orientation versus pedophilic disorder
- Difference between paraphilic sexual interest and paraphilic disorder
- Higher prevalence of paraphilic behavior among men
- Frequency of paraphilic behaviors and desire among females and males

Chapter 11 Contraception and Abortion:
- Reproductive justice and access to contraception

- Cross-cultural data on teen birth rate
- Barriers to contraceptive services for underserved populations
- Cross-cultural data on women and abortions

Chapter 12 Conception, Pregnancy, and Childbirth:
- Cross-cultural and international data on infant and maternal mortality
- Adverse pregnancy outcomes among women of color
- Impact of COVID-19 on racial and ethnic minorities
- Same-sex couples and use of artificial insemination
- Longevity of relationships and families in same-sex and mixed-sex couples

Chapter 13 The Sexual Body in Illness and Health:
- Eating disorders in racial and sexual minorities
- Alcohol use and sexual violence and victimization on college campuses
- Sexuality and people with disabilities
- Sexuality and people with chronic illnesses
- Sexual rights of people with disabilities
- Cervical cancer among women of color
- Cross-cultural and international data on prostate cancer

Chapter 14 Sexual Function Difficulties, Dissatisfaction, Enhancement, and Therapy:
- DSM-5 and nonphysiological aspects of female sexuality
- Differences in sex therapy for LGBTQ+ individuals
- Impact of internalized and societal homophobia on LGBTQ+ individuals
- Strategies of dealing with differences in sexual desire among persons of diverse sexual orientations in long-term relationships
- Importance of context in women's sexual arousal
- Similarities of the components of "magnificent" sex among men and women and persons young and old, heterosexual, LGBTQ+, disabled or chronically ill
- Percentage of sexually satisfied men and women versus those dissatisfied who indicated that they had done different activities to improve their sex life
- Diversity in photo-realistic representations of mixed-sex and same-sex couples doing activities to deal with sexual function problems

Chapter 15 Sexually Transmitted Infections:
- Gender and sexual orientation disparities in the incidence of STIs
- Rates of chlamydia, syphilis, and gonorrhea among racial and ethnic minorities
- Impact of poverty, marginalization, and limited health services on treatment of STIs in racial and ethnic minorities
- International data on benefits and risks of male circumcision
- Repercussions of the Tuskegee Syphilis Study on African American communities
- CDC recommendations for HIV/STI testing for adults by gender, age, pregnancy status, sexual orientation, and injection drug users.

Chapter 16 HIV and AIDS:

- Epidemiology of HIV and AIDS in the United States by transmission group, age and race and ethnic minorities
- Social and economic factors limiting HIV prevention and treatment services among injection drug users
- HIV/AIDS as a health crisis for African Americans
- HIV among gay, bisexual, and queer men in the U.S. South as "America's Hidden H.I.V. Epidemic"
- Prevalence of HIV/AIDS in the Hispanic/Latinx community
- HIV/AIDS as a public health issue among Asian Americans, Native Hawaiians and other Pacific Islanders, and American Indians and Alaskan Natives
- HIV/AIDS in the gay community
- HIV infection and AIDS among women of color
- HIV prevalence among transgender individuals, particularly transgender women

Chapter 17 Sexual Harassment and Sexual Misconduct

- Incidence of sexual harassment on colleges for sexual minorities
- Street harassment among LGBTQ+ individuals
- Campus nonconsensual sexual contact experienced by men, women, transgender women, transgender men, gender non-conforming, and queer individuals
- Female and male similarities and differences in giving consent to intimate sexual behavior
- Diversity in drawing representations of mixed-sex and same-sex couples doing activities to deal with sexual function problems
- Forms of heterosexual bias
- Negative outcomes of anti-gay prejudice, cross-cultural findings
- Violence against sexual minorities in the United States.
- Sexual assault of men by women
- Sexual orientation equality laws to protect sexual minority individuals
- Supreme Court ban of discrimination based on sexual orientation and gender identity
- Campus nonconsensual sexual contact experienced by sexual minorities, data

Chapter 18 Sexually Explicit Materials, Sex Workers, and Sex Laws

- Censorship of books featuring transgender individuals, gay marriage, and questions of gender identity
- Research on male sex workers and their clients
- The prevalence of HIV/AIDS among sex workers
- The focus of heterosexual-centered, gay and lesbian-centered, and feminist-values sexually explicit videos
- Representation of female and male orgasms in mainstream sexually explicit videos
- Barriers sex workers face in accessing HIV services
- Criminalization and decriminalization of same-sex behavior
- Legalization of same-sex marriage in the United State in 2015

Celebrating Sexual Diversity in Contemporary Society

Since the first edition, *Human Sexuality: Diversity in Contemporary Society* has presented students with a nonjudgmental and affirming view of human sexuality while encouraging them to embrace their own sexuality. More recently, our discussion of human sexuality has increasingly cited research studies and writings from countries beyond America, thus broadening student understanding of the diverse meanings and expressions of human sexuality.

Eleven editions later, *Human Sexuality: Diversity in Contemporary Society* continues to be a pioneering text. The sexual affirmation approach encourages students to become proactive in and about their own sexual well-being and includes an emphasis on the importance of embracing intimacy, pleasuring, and mutual satisfaction in sexual expression. It also strives to represent the contemporary, diverse society that students encounter inside and outside the classroom. And with McGraw Hill Education Connect for Human Sexuality, students embark on a personalized digital learning program, which allows them to study more effectively and efficiently.

Health and Well-Being

As one fundamental component of the human condition, sexuality can impact personal well-being. When balanced with other life needs, sexuality contributes positively to personal health and happiness. When expressed in destructive ways, it can impair health. We believe that studying human sexuality is one way of increasing the healthy lifestyle of students. Integrated into all chapter are discussions, research, questions, and prompts that interrelate students' well-being and their sexuality.

Thinking Critically About Human Sexuality

Each chapter contains multiple **Think About It** features that prompt students to think critically about topics in sexuality such as am I normal, the science of love, hooking up, what behaviors constitute having had sex, orgasm and pleasure, and how college students indicate and interpret consent to have sex.

think about it

Those Who Experience "Magnificent Sex": What They Say That Makes It Happen

Sex is not just some bonus activity in life. It can define who we are, where we're going and what we're capable of being.
—Peggy Kleinplatz and A. Dana Menard

What makes sex magnificent? Sex researchers and therapists Peggy Kleinplatz and A. Dana Menard (2020) state that they have found that many people and couples in new relationships say that their sex life is "satisfactory" or "functional" yet they suspect that it could be better. Kleinplatz and Menard believe that great sex is desired and available, but many people do not know how to get it. So they conducted a study to identify the components of what can be called "great," "remarkable," "wonderful," and/or "memorable" partnered sex. The goal of their study was to learn what makes some sex magnificent in hope that the information can be valuable to individuals and couples who desire more pleasurable, intimate, and rewarding sex. The results of their study were presented in their book *Magnificent Sex: Lessons from Extraordinary Lovers* (2020).

respect for and trust in their partner. Words often used were "synchronicity," "merger," "bridging the gap," "electricity," and "energy." One woman stated, "At that moment, there was no one else in the world" (p. 24).

Deep Sexual and Erotic Intimacy

A major component of magnificent sex declared by nearly everyone was the intensity and depth of the intimacy shared with their partner and mutual respect. Some noted that optimal sex cannot be separated from the relationship in which it occurs.

Extraordinary Communication and Deep Empathy

Having extraordinary communication with one's partner was a recurring theme. Being able to share oneself completely with another person—that is, revealing parts of themselves not usually shared—

Speaking Practically about Human Sexuality

The **Practically Speaking** feature asks students to examine their own values and the ways they express their sexuality. Topics include sexual communication, effective condom use, having sex again after sexual assault, and a glossary on sex, gender, and gender variation terms. These features help students apply the concepts presented in the book to their own lives.

practically speaking

A Quick and Evolving Glossary of Sexual Identity and Sexual Orientation

Our knowledge and understanding about sexuality, gender, gender identity, and gender variations along with the nomenclature to describe each are evolving. For example, we now recognize that gender diversity extends well beyond variation in masculinity or femininity such that both government institutions and social media platforms like Facebook and Tinder have adopted over 30 different self-identifying gender terms that go well beyond the social constructs of man and woman (Whyte et al., 2018). Though subject to opinions and differences, this document represents a partial list of current terminology used for sexual and gender identities and variations and sexual orientation. The comprehensive list is, undoubtedly, much longer. To learn of the other current terms, one can seek information from professional sexuality organizations, especially those that focus on sexuality and gender-related issues. Over time, there will be additions and corrections to this

Gender confirming treatment A means for those who find it essential and medically necessary to establish congruence with their gender identity. Also referred to as *gender affirming treatment* or *gender reassignment surgery.*

Gender diverse An umbrella term used to describe an ever-evolving array of labels people may apply when their gender identity, expression, or perception does not conform to the norms and stereotypes of others. Replaces the former term gender nonconforming.

Gender dysphoria A clinical symptom and psychiatric diagnosis which has focus on the distress that stems from the incongruence between one's expressed or experienced gender and the gender assigned at birth. Previously called gender identity disorder.

Gender fluid(ity) People whose gender expressions and/or identity is not static; that is, it is not the same all the time.

The Significance of Ethnicity

Until relatively recently, Americans have ignored race and ethnicity as a factor in studying human sexuality. We have acted as if being white, African American, Latino, Asian American, or Native American made no difference in terms of sexual attitudes, behaviors, and values. But there are significant differences, and it is important to examine these differences within their cultural context. Ethnic differences, therefore, should not be interpreted as "good" or "bad," "healthy" or "deficient," but as reflections of the diversity in our culture. Our understanding of the role of race and ethnicity in sexuality, however, is a still evolving area of research.

Celebrating sexual diversity, however, is only part of the story. Through an integrated, personalized digital learning program, students gain the insight they need to study smarter and improve performance. McGraw Hill Education Connect is a digital assignment and assessment platform that strengthens the link between faculty, students, and course work, helping everyone accomplish more in less time. Connect for Human Sexuality includes assignable and assessable animations, quizzes, exercises, and interactivities, all associated with learning objectives.

A Personalized Experience that Leads to Improved Learning and Results

How many students think they know everything about human sexuality but struggle on the first exam? Students study more effectively with Connect and SmartBook.

- Connect's assignments help students contextualize what they've learned through application, so they can better understand the material and think critically.

- Connect reports deliver information regarding performance, study behavior, and effort so instructors can quickly identify students who are having issues or focus on material that the class hasn't mastered.

- SmartBook helps students study more efficiently by highlighting what to focus on in the chapter, asking review questions, and directing them to resources until they understand.

- SmartBook creates a personalized study path customized to individual student needs.

SmartBook is now optimized for mobile and tablet and is accessible for students with disabilities. Content-wise, it has been enhanced with improved learning objectives that are measurable and observable to improve student outcomes. SmartBook personalizes learning to individual student needs, continually adapting to pinpoint knowledge gaps and focus learning on topics that need the most attention. Study time is more productive and, as a result, students are better prepared for class and coursework. For instructors, SmartBook tracks student progress and provides insights that can help guide teaching strategies.

Powerful Reporting

Whether a class is face-to-face, hybrid, or entirely online, McGraw Hill Connect provides the tools needed to reduce the amount of time and energy instructors spend administering their courses. Easy-to-use course management tools allow instructors to spend less time administering and more time teaching, while reports allow students to monitor their progress and optimize their study time.

- The **At-Risk Student Report** provides instructors with one-click access to a dashboard that identifies students who are at risk of dropping out of the course due to low engagement levels.

- The **Category Analysis Report** details student performance relative to specific learning objectives and goals, including APA learning goals and outcomes and levels of Bloom's taxonomy.

- The **SmartBook Reports** allow instructors and students to easily monitor progress and pinpoint areas of weakness, giving each student a personalized study plan to achieve success.

Preparing Students for Higher-Level Thinking

Available in McGraw Hill Connect, **Power of Process** guides students through the process of critical reading, analysis, and writing. Faculty can select or upload their own content, such as journal articles, and assign analysis strategies to gain insight into students' application of the scientific method. For students, Power of Process offers a guided visual approach to exercising critical thinking strategies to apply before, during, and after reading published research. Additionally, utilizing the relevant and engaging research articles built into Power of Process, students are supported in becoming critical consumers of research.

At the Apply and Analyze level of Bloom's taxonomy, Scientific Reasoning Exercises offer in-depth arguments to sharpen students' critical thinking skills and prepare them to be more discerning consumers regarding information in their everyday lives. For each chapter, there are multiple sets of arguments related to topics in the Human Sexuality course, accompanied by autograded assignments that ask students to think critically about claims presented as facts. These exercises can also be used as group activities or for discussion.

New to this edition and found in Connect, **Writing Assignments** offer faculty the ability to assign a full range of writing assignments to students) with just-in-time feedback.

You may set up manually scored assignments in a way that students can

- automatically receive grammar and high-level feedback to improve their writing before they submit a project to you;
- run originality checks and receive feedback on "exact matches" and "possibly altered text" that includes guidance about how to properly paraphrase, quote, and cite sources to improve the academic integrity of their writing before they submit their work to you.

The new writing assignments will also have features that allow you to assign milestone drafts (optional), easily re-use your text and audio comments, build/score with your rubric, and view your own originality report of student's final submission.

And McGraw Hill Education Psychology's APA Documentation Style Guide helps students properly cite and document their writing assignments.

Inform and Engage on Psychological Concepts

At the lower end of Bloom's taxonomy, **Concept Clips** help students comprehend some of the most difficult concepts in human sexuality. Colorful graphics and stimulating animations describe core concepts in a step-by-step manner, engaging students and aiding in retention. Concept Clips can be used as a presentation tool in the classroom or for student assessment. Clips cover topics such as attraction, mate selection, and learning gender roles.

Interactivities, assignable through Connect, engage students with content through experiential activities. Topics include first impressions and attraction.

New to the 11th edition, **Application-Based Activities** are highly interactive, automatically graded exercises built around course learning objectives. These online learn-by-doing exercises offer students a safe space to apply their knowledge and problem-solving skills to real-world scenarios as well as practice vocabulary and identify examples. Feedback is provided throughout the activity to support learning and improve critical thinking skills. Topics explored in this edition include Ethics in Research, Sexual Anatomy, Gender Identity, Types of Love, and Homologous Structures.

New videos demonstrate psychological concepts in action and provide the opportunity to assess students' understanding of these concepts as they are brought to life. New to this edition are: Weird Facts About the History of Birth Control, Alexander Tsiaras: Conception to Birth, History of the word "Gay," My Girlfriend Is Now My Husband, Myths About IUDs, Sarah Barmak: The Uncomplicated Truth about Women's Sexuality, Talking to Kids About Sex is a Good Thing, The Cases For and Against Circumcision, The Heartbreak Of Not Having A Vagina, The Origin of Gender, Tiny Husband: Larger Than Life Couple Shows Love Knows No Bounds, Why was Pink for Boys and Blue for Girls, Can a Child have more than Two Parents?

Through the connection of human sexuality to students' own lives, concepts become more relevant and understandable. Located in Connect, **NewsFlash** is a multi-media assignment tool that ties current news stories, TedTalks, blogs and podcasts to key psychological principles and learning objectives. Students interact with relevant news stories and are assessed on their ability to connect the content to the research findings and course material. NewsFlash is updated twice a year and uses expert sources to cover a wide range of topics including: emotion, personality, stress, drugs, COVID-19, disability, social justice, stigma, bias, inclusion, gender, LGBTQ+, and many more.

Online Instructor Resources

The resources listed here accompany *Human Sexuality: Diversity in Contemporary Society,* eleventh edition. Please contact your McGraw Hill representative for details concerning the availability of these and other valuable materials that can help you design and enhance your course.

- **Instructor's Manual:** Broken down by chapter, this resource provides chapter outlines, suggested lecture topics, classroom activities and demonstrations, suggested student research projects, essay questions, and critical-thinking questions.

- **PowerPoint Slides:** The PowerPoint presentations, now with improved accessibility, highlight the key points of the chapter and include supporting visuals. All of the slides can be modified to meet individual needs.

Test Bank and Test Builder Organized by chapter, the questions are designed to test factual, conceptual, and applied understanding; all test questions are available within Test Builder. Available within Connect, Test Builder is a cloud-based tool that enables instructors to format tests that can be printed, administered within a Learning Management System, or exported as a Word document of the test bank. Test Builder offers a modern, streamlined interface for easy content configuration that matches course needs, without requiring a download.

Test Builder allows you to:

- access all test bank content from a particular title.

- easily pinpoint the most relevant content through robust filtering options.

- manipulate the order of questions or scramble questions and/or answers.

- pin questions to a specific location within a test.

- determine your preferred treatment of algorithmic questions.

- choose the layout and spacing.

- add instructions and configure default settings.

Test Builder provides a secure interface for better protection of content and allows for just-in-time updates to flow directly into assessments.

Remote Proctoring & Browser-Locking Capabilities Remote proctoring and browser-locking capabilities, hosted by Proctorio within Connect, provide control of the assessment environment by enabling security options and verifying the identity of the student.

Seamlessly integrated within Connect, these services allow instructors to control students' assessment experience by restricting browser activity, recording students' activity, and verifying students are doing their own work.

Instant and detailed reporting gives instructors an at-a-glance view of potential academic integrity concerns, thereby avoiding personal bias and supporting evidence-based claims.

Supporting Instructors with Technology

With McGraw Hill Education, you can develop and tailor the course you want to teach.

 With Tegrity, you can capture lessons and lectures in a searchable format and use them in traditional, hybrid, "flipped classes," and online courses. With Tegrity's personalized learning features, you can make study time efficient. Its ability to affordably scale brings this benefit to every student on campus. Patented search technology and real-time learning management system (LMS) integrations make Tegrity the market-leading solution and service.

 Easily rearrange chapters, combine material from other content sources, and quickly upload content you have written, such as your course syllabus or teaching notes, using McGraw Hill Education's Create. Find the content you need by searching through thousands of leading McGraw Hill Education textbooks. Arrange your book to fit your teaching style. Create even allows you to personalize your book's appearance by selecting the cover and adding your name, school,

and course information. Order a Create book, and you will receive a complimentary print review copy in three to five business days or a complimentary electronic review copy via email in about an hour. Experience how McGraw Hill Education empowers you to teach your students your way at http://create.mheducation.com.

Trusted Service and Support

McGraw Hill Education's Connect offers comprehensive service, support, and training throughout every phase of your implementation. If you're looking for some guidance on how to use Connect or want to learn tips and tricks from super users, you can find tutorials as you work. Our Digital Faculty Consultants and Student Ambassadors offer insight into how to achieve the results you want with Connect.

Integration with Your Learning Management System

McGraw Hill integrates your digital products from McGraw Hill Education with your school learning management system (LMS) for quick and easy access to best-in-class content and learning tools. Build an effective digital course, enroll students with ease and discover how powerful digital teaching can be.

Available with Connect, integration is a pairing between an institution's LMS and Connect at the assignment level. It shares assignment information, grades, and calendar items from Connect into the LMS automatically, creating an easy-to-manage course for instructors and simple navigation for students. Our assignment-level integration is available with Blackboard Learn, Canvas by Instructure, and Brightspace by D2L, giving you access to registration, attendance, assignments, grades, and course resources in real time, in one location.

Annual Editions: Human Sexualities

This volume offers diverse topics on sex and sexuality with regard to the human experience. *Learning Outcomes, Critical Thinking* questions, and *Internet References* accompany each article to further enhance learning. Customize this title via McGraw Hill Create at http://create.mheducation.com.

Taking Sides: Clashing Views in Human Sexuality

This debate-style reader both reinforces and challenges students' viewpoints on the most crucial issues in human sexuality today. Each topic offers current and lively pro and con essays that represent the arguments of leading scholars and commentators in their fields. *Learning Outcomes,* an *Issue Summary,* and an *Issue Introduction* set the stage for each debate topic. Following each issue is the *Exploring the Issue* section with *Critical Thinking and Reflection* questions, *Is There Common Ground?* commentary, *Additional Resources,* and *Internet References* all designed to stimulate and challenge the student's thinking and to further explore the topic. Customize this title via McGraw Hill Education Create at http://create.mheducation.com.

Chapter-by-Chapter Changes

The research on sexuality is ever increasing, thereby providing the material to allow this new edition to be current and relevant. Not only does our book incorporate the latest research on sexual diversity and expression, but it also reflects current social and cultural trends in sexuality that impact the development of a healthy and pleasurable sexuality. Below are listed the major additions and changes to the eleventh edition of *Human Sexuality: Diversity in Contemporary Society.*

Chapter 1: Perspectives on Human Sexuality

- New *Practically Speaking:* "A Quick and Evolving Glossary of Sexual Identity and Sexual Orientation"
- Revised *Think About It:* "Online Dating: No Longer a Last Attempt"
- A new look at sexting
- Updated data and figures on media use

Chapter 2: Studying Human Sexuality

- Expanded discussion of the Kinsey heterosexual-homosexual rating scale.
- New material on how gender identity of gender non-binary and non-conforming individuals can be more accurately assessed on research questionnaires and other surveys.
- New *Practically Speaking:* "Spotting Flawed Research"
- Discussion of the findings of the latest Centers for Disease Control and Prevention Youth Risk Behavior Survey.
- Discussion of the findings of the latest American College Health Association on research on college student sexual behavior.
- Presentation the major findings of the 2015 Sexual Exploration in America Study, which assessed the prevalence and appeal of over 50 diverse sexual behaviors.

Chapter 3: Female Sexual Anatomy and Physiology

- New discussion on the role and grooming of pubic hair for all genders
- Revised *Think About It:* "My Beautiful/Ugly Genitals: What Women are Saying"
- New research on the safety of monthly menstrual cycles and the safety of menstrual products
- Models of the sexual response cycle have been moved to Ch. 9, where all genders' responses are discussed
- New *Think About It:* "Body Modification: You're Doing What? Where?"

Chapter 4: Male Sexual Anatomy and Physiology

- Updated *Think About It:* "The Question of Male Circumcision"
- Revised *Think About It:* "Does Penis Size Matter?"
- Updated evidence regarding supplemental testosterone for adult men

Chapter 5: Gender, Gender Roles, and Sexuality

- New *Think About It:* "Why Gender-Neutral Pronouns Matter"
- Updated *Think About It:* "Sexual Fluidity: Women's and Men's Variable Sexual Attractions"
- Revised and updated material on gender differences in patterns of sexual behavior
- New material on society's changing views of family
- A new look at the gender binary as it relates to sexual behavior, along with the challenges and costs in maintaining it
- New sex and gender continuum is presented and discussed
- Updated and expanded discussion on transgender youth

Chapter 6: Sexuality in Childhood and Adolescence

- Expanded discussion on young people talking about sex with their parents
- New material on what young people wish to learn about sexual behaviors

- New *Think About It:* "Does First Sex 'Just Happen?' Reflections from College Students About Their First Sexual Activity"
- Updates on teen pregnancy, birth rates, and racial, ethnic, and economic disparities
- New *Think About It:* "Are Young People Really Having Less Sexual Activity?"
- Expanded discussion on views of comprehensive sexuality education
- New *Think About It:* "Promoting Positive Sexual Health Among Teens"

Chapter 7: Sexuality in Adulthood

- Introduction to the sexual configurations theory and its relationship to sexual identities and attractions
- An exploration of "mostly straight" as a distinct sexuality
- Updated *Think About It:* "'Hooking Up' Among College Students: As Simple as One Might Think?"
- Expanded discussion and updates on the social context of singlehood
- Updates on why people marry and cohabitate
- New Happiness Index describing what "perfectly happy" couples look like
- New *Think About It:* "Singles in America: Dating Trends, Social Media & Fatigue"
- New material on how sexual interactions differ by the length of a relationship
- New research on sexual activity, concerns, perspectives, and satisfaction among older adults
- New perspectives on menopausal hormone therapy

Chapter 8: Love and Communication in Intimate Relationships

- New research on gender differences, sexual orientation, and orgasm
- Broadened perspectives on individuals who identify as asexual
- New taxonomy on Sternberg's triangular theory of love.
- Expanded discussion on how social media can induce jealousy in romantic relationships
- A new and expanded discussion of consensual nonmonogamy, its types, and demographics of who engages in polyamory
- New *Think About It:* "Making Love Last: A New Path to Romance"
- New discussion on how socializing can revitalize a partnership
- New research on sexual communication and sexual functioning

Chapter 9: Sexual Response and Expression

- Expanded discussion of erotophilia-erotophobia
- Expanded discussion of repeated orgasms among women
- New *Practically Speaking:* "Clitoral Self-Stimulation Scale"
- Renamed and updated *Think About It:* "Factors that Prompt and Inhibit Men's Sexual Desire"
- New material on the findings of a national study of sexual fantasies of adults in America and a similar study conducted in Canada
- Updated information on the prevalence of solo masturbation, penile-vaginal intercourse, and anal penetration among American adults
- Additional photo-realistic representations of solo masturbation and partnered sex among diverse couples.

Chapter 10: Variations in Sexual Behavior

- Expanded discussion of several paraphilias such as exhibitionism, frotteurism, BSDM, and cross-dressing.
- Discussion of the World Health Organization's new definition of "too frequent sexual behavior"
- New *Practically Speaking:* "Sexual Novelty Scale"
- New research on the prevalence of having sex with someone in a public place
- New *Think About It:* "College Students Making Out: Sometimes an Audience is Needed"
- Updated discussion of autoerotic asphyxia

Chapter 11: Contraception and Abortion

- Complete updates throughout the chapter on pregnancy, unintended pregnancies, contraception, and abortion
- New data on current contraceptive status by age
- New *Think About It:* "Factors that Influence College Students' Contraceptive Use"
- Introduction to the social determinants of health and barriers that prevent use of family planning services
- Expanded discussion on Title X and its impact on women's reproductive health
- A new discussion on how the COVID-19 pandemic has influenced reproductive health care

Chapter 12: Conception, Pregnancy, and Childbirth

- Expanded discussion on environmental concerns as they relate to fertility, pregnancy, and births
- Rapidly-evolving research on COVID-19 and pregnancy and pregnancy outcomes
- Updates on infertility, including causes, treatments, and outcomes
- Clarification and updates regarding stages of childbirth and phases of labor
- Updates on labor and delivery, along with data on episiotomies, labor induction, and C-sections
- New to this chapter *Think About It:* "Are Same-Sex Couples and Families Any Different from Heterosexual Ones?"

Chapter 13: The Sexual Body in Health and Illness

- Expanded discussion on body image and eating disorders as they relate to race/ethnicity and age
- New material on marijuana use and sexuality
- New *Practically Speaking:* "Screening Guidelines for the Early Detection of Prostate Cancer"
- New material on polycystic ovary syndrome
- New research and discussion on COVID-19 and sexuality
- New *Practically Speaking:* "COVID-19 and Sexuality: It's Complicated"

Chapter 14: Sexual Function Difficulties, Dissatisfaction, Enhancement, and Therapy

- Updated *Think About It:* "Sexual Desire: When Appetites Differ"
- Expanded discussion of dealing with sexual desire discrepancy among couples

- New *Practically Speaking:* "The 'Pelvic Swing' During Penile-Vaginal Intercourse Facilitates Sexual Arousal and Orgasm in Women"
- Expanded discussion of orgasm difficulties among women
- New research on strategies couples use to maintain sexual passion
- New *Think About It:* "Those Who Experience 'Magnificent Sex': What They Say Makes It Happen"
- Updated discussion of a painful sex
- Additional photo-realistic representations of partnered sex addressing sexual function difficulties among diverse couples.

Chapter 15: Sexually Transmitted Infections

- Updated data on the prevalence, incidence, and medical information of major sexually transmitted infections
- New *Think About It:* "Are Persons Knowledgeable About STIs and Worried They Might Become Infected? Results of a National Study"
- New discussion on a short gap between partners and sexual delay discounting
- Expanded discussion on the role of male condoms, female condoms, and dental dams in STIs
- Updated research on the efficacy of male circumcision on preventing HIV and other STIs
- New *Practically Speaking:* "Which STI Tests Should I Get and What Should I Do If I Test Positive?"

Chapter 16: HIV and AIDS

- Updated information on the prevalence and incidence of HIV/AIDS in the United States and worldwide
- Results of a 2019 Kaiser Family Foundation national poll of percent of persons believing that HIV/AIDS is a serious issue, a serious concern for people they know, and how concerned they are about acquiring HIV.
- New *Practically Speaking:* "How to Negotiate Condom Use and What to Say When Your Partner Refuses"
- Updated and expanded discussion of HIV/AIDS among minority races/ethnicities and sexual minorities such as transgender individuals
- Expanded discussion of pre-exposure prophylaxis and new material on post-exposure prophylaxis
- New *Practically Speaking:* "Want to Become More Confident in Using Condoms and Experience More Sexual Pleasure? Try Self-Guided Practice at Home"
- New and updated information on HIV/AIDS testing, diagnosis, and treatment

Chapter 17: Sexual Assault and Misconduct

- Expanded discussion and updated research on the prevalence of sexual assault and misconduct on college campuses
- New *Think About It:* "An Unexplored Form of Sexual Violence: Women Forcing Penile Penetration"
- New and expanded discussion of sexual harassment in school and college, in the workplace, and in public places
- Renamed and updated *Think About It:* "Drug-facilitated Sexual Assault: An Increasing Threat"

- Updated information on harassment and discrimination of LGBTQ+ persons and state laws and policies to protect LGBTQ+ individuals from discrimination.
- Expanded discussion on sexual consent
- New *Think About It:* "Are College Students Verbally and Unambiguously Affirming Sexual Consent? Research Shows That Rarely Happens"

Chapter 18: Sexually Explicit Materials, Sex Workers, and Sex Laws

- New research on the percentage of adults who report having watched sexually explicit videos and the impact of viewing
- Results of research on viewing sexually explicit videos during the COVID-19 pandemic
- New *Practically Speaking:* "Pornography Usage Measure"
- New *Think About It:* "The Representation of Female and Male Orgasms in Mainstream Sexually Explicit Videos: Realistic or Fantasy?"
- Updated *Think About It:* "Should Sex Work Be Decriminalized and Legalized?"
- New *Think About It:* "Tourist Women as Buyers of Sex from Men: Inequalities of Power and Socioeconomics"
- Update on the number of countries that have legalized same-sex marriage

Acknowledgments

Feedback from instructor reviews were instrumental in guiding this revision. Special thanks to the following:

Gretchen Blycker, *University of Rhode Island*
Meghan Brodie, *Valencia College*
Christina Goldpaint, *California State University, Long Beach*
Kate Halverson, *Des Moines Area Community College*
Lisa Hoopis, *Rhode Island College*
Nathan Matza, *California State University, Long Beach*
Danielle McAneney, *Southwestern College*
Robyn Moreland, *Eastern Kentucky University*
Amy Popillion, *Iowa State University*
Brent Powell, *California State University, Stanislaus*
Melissa Schreiber, *Valencia College*
Banafshe Sharifian, *California State University, Long Beach*
Laurie Wagner, *Kent State University*
Jay Warden, *Cape Cod Community College*
Michelle Worley, *Saddleback College*
Sarah E. Wright, *University of South Carolina*

We would also like to thank our team at McGraw Hill Education: Senior Portfolio Manager Jason Seitz, Product Development Manager Dawn Groundwater, Marketing Manager Olivia Kaiser, Content Production Manager Melissa Leick, and Content Licensing Specialist Shawntel Schmitt. Special thanks to Joni Fraser, Product Developer and person who makes us better writers, and to Karly Beavers, input editor, who provides the skill and positive attitude that helps to make this work enjoyable.

"Our bodies silently plead for sex that makes us feel alive and engaged in one another's embrace. . ."

—Peggy Kleinplatz & A. Dana Menard

We have found that when students first enter a human sexuality class, they may feel excited, nervous, and uncomfortable, all at the same time. These feelings are common; the more an area of life is judged "off limits" to public and private discussion, the less likely it is to be understood and embraced. Yet sex surrounds us and impacts our lives every day from the provocative billboard ad on the highway, to the steamy social media images of the body, to men's and women's fashions, and to prime-time television dramas. People *want* to learn about the role and meaning of human sexuality in their lives and how to live healthy psychologically and physically, yet they often do not know whom to ask or what sources to trust. In our quest for knowledge and understanding, we need to maintain an intellectual curiosity. Author William Arthur Ward observes, "Curiosity is the wick in the candle of learning."

As you can see from the title of this book, a focus on diversity has been a central theme of our research and writing as well as the photos and illustrations that accompany this text. Because we believe that sexual expression and behavior develop within a social context, it has been our intention to provide a broad range of perspectives to help enrich your understanding of human sexuality. Over the eleven editions of this textbook, we have made every effort to integrate both national and international studies that relate to aspects and expressions of sexual diversity - from the evolving language that we use, to the cultural perspectives that are shared, and to the broad range of photos that have been chosen. This can be most visibly seen in Chapter 9, where the photo-realistic representations effectively capture the wide expression of sexuality that exists among diverse individuals. Our hope and intention are to provide you, the student, with a broader perspective of what it means to be a sexual person.

Students begin studying sexuality for many reasons: to gain insights into their sexuality and relationships, to become more comfortable with their sexuality, to learn how to enhance sexual pleasure for themselves and their partners, to explore personal sexual issues, to dispel anxieties and doubts, to validate their sexual identity, to consent for sex and avoid and resolve traumatic sexual experiences, and to learn how to avoid STIs and unintended pregnancies. Many students find the study of human sexuality empowering: They become more free to explore and discover their sexuality, they become better communicators about their sexual desires, they focus more on giving and receiving pleasure rather than on performance, and they develop the ability to make intelligent sexual choices based on reputable information and their own needs, desires, and values rather than on stereotypical, unreliable, incomplete, or unrealistic information; guilt; fear; or conformity. They learn to differentiate between what they have been told about their own sexuality and what they truly believe; that is, they begin to own their sexuality and develop a sexuality that fits them. Those studying human sexuality often report that they feel more appreciative and less apologetic, defensive, or shameful about their sexual feelings, attractions, and desires.

The study of human sexuality calls for us to be open-minded: to be receptive to new ideas and to various perspectives; to respect those with different experiences, values, orientations, ages, abilities, and ethnicities; to seek to understand what we have not understood before;

to reexamine old assumptions, ideas, and beliefs; and to embrace and accept the humanness and uniqueness in each of us.

Sexuality can be a source of great pleasure. Through it, we can reveal ourselves, connect with others on the most intimate levels, create strong bonds, and bring new life into the world. Paradoxically, though, sexuality can also be a source of shame, guilt and confusion, anger and disappointment, a pathway to infection, and a means of exploitation and aggression. We hope that by examining the multiple aspects of human sexuality presented in this book, you will come to understand, embrace, and appreciate your own sexuality and the unique individuality of sexuality among others; to learn how to make healthy sexual choices for yourself; to integrate and balance your sexuality into your life as a natural health-enhancing component; and to express your sexuality with partners in pleasurable, sharing, nonexploitive, and nurturing ways.

William L. Yarber
Barbara W. Sayad

About the Authors

WILLIAM L. YARBER is senior scientist at The Kinsey Institute and Provost Professor in the Indiana University School of Public Health–Bloomington. He is also senior director of the Rural Center for AIDS/STD Prevention, affiliated faculty member in the Department of Gender Studies at IU, and adjunct professor in the Indiana University-Bloomington School of Medicine.

In 2020, Dr. Yarber was selected as one of the recipients of the first-ever 50 Distinguished Sexual and Gender Health Revolutionaries award given by the Program in Human Sexuality, University of Minnesota Medical School. Chosen from nominies throughout the world, this award recognizes fifty scientists, activists, thought leaders, scholars, and writers who have made positive and significant contributions to revolutionize the sexual and gender health climate of the world.

Dr. Yarber, who received his doctorate from Indiana University, has authored and co-authored numerous scientific reports on sexual risk behavior and AIDS/STD prevention in professional journals and has received federal and state grants to support his research and prevention activities. He is a member of the international Kinsey Institute Condom Use Research Team that has, for over two decades, investigated male condom use errors and problems and developed behavioral interventions designed to improve correct and consistent condom use that aligns with sexual pleasure.

William L. Yarber
Charles Rondot/Indiana University

At the request of the U.S. Centers for Disease Control and Prevention, Dr. Yarber authored the country's first secondary school AIDS prevention education curriculum, *AIDS: What Young People Should Know* (1987, 1989). He is founder and co-editor of the *Handbook of Sexuality-Related Measures, Fourth Edition* (2019). Dr. Yarber and Dr. Sayad's textbook, *Human Sexuality: Diversity in Contemporary Society* (McGraw Hill), which is used in colleges and universities throughout the United States, was published in 2012 by the Beijing World Publishing Company as the most up-to-date text on human sexuality published in China in the past half century. Also in 2012, the text was published in South Korea and in 2018 it was published in Taiwan where the text was considered the beginning of reformed sexuality education.

Dr. Yarber chaired the National Guidelines Task Force, which developed the *Guidelines for Comprehensive Sexuality Education: Kindergarten–12th Grade* (1991, 1996, 2004), published by the Sexuality Information and Education Council of the United States (SIECUS) and adapted in six countries worldwide. Dr. Yarber is past president of The Society for the Scientific Study of Sexuality (SSSS) and a past chair of the SIECUS board of directors. His awards include the SSSS Distinguished Scientific Achievement Award; the Professional Standard of Excellence Award from the American Association of Sex Educators, Counselors, and Therapists; the Indiana University President's Award for Distinguished Teaching; and the inaugural Graduate Student Outstanding Faculty Mentor Award at Indiana University.

Dr. Yarber has been a consultant to the World Health Organization Global Program on AIDS as well as sexuality-related organizations in Brazil, China, Jamaica, Poland, Portugal, Taiwan, and Venezuela. He regularly teaches undergraduate and graduate courses in human sexuality. He was previously a faculty member at Purdue University and the University of Minnesota, as well as a public high school health science and biology teacher. Dr. Yarber endowed at Indiana University, for perpetuity, the world's first professorship in sexual health, the *William L. Yarber Endowed Professor in Sexual Health* and the annual *Ryan White & William L. Yarber Lecture.*

Barbara Werner Sayad
Barbara Werner

BARBARA WERNER SAYAD is a teacher, trainer, writer, and consultant in the field of human sexuality and public health. As a retired faculty member from California State University, Monterey Bay, Dr. Sayad has taught a wide variety of courses ranging from human sexuality to multi-cultural health education and promotion. Her work among students and in the classroom has earned her several teaching awards, each of which she is most proud. Additionally, she has chaired university committees, spoken at dozens of university-related events, trained and collaborated with other faculty members and colleagues, and helped to raise monies for both national and international non-profit organizations.

Dr. Sayad has presented her work at a variety of institutions, the most significant of which has focused on comprehensive sexuality education. One that she is most proud of is her alliance with Aibai, the largest LGTBQ organization in China, where she twice traveled to present to the Asian Conference on Sexual Education in Beijing and Chengdu. There she also led workshops and roundtables with and for American delegates and Chinese scholars at the U.S. Embassy, U.S. State Department, and UNESCO and was invited to present at Xixi, the equivalent of a TED Talk, in Shanghai. Most recently, Dr. Sayad helped to facilitate a trip to Cuba, where she collaborated with colleagues and met with delegates from CENESEX, Cuba's government-sponsored sexuality education and gender equity organization.

The vast majority of Dr. Sayad's career has been connected to issues of social justice: women's reproductive rights, sexuality education and advocacy, and health access. Her commitment to social justice has fueled all of her professional work, including her contributions to health-related texts, curricular guides, publications, training programs and conference presentations.

Dr. Sayad holds a Bachelor of Science degree in Foods and Nutrition, a Master's degree in Public Health, and a PhD in Health Services.

Above all, Dr. Sayad is most proud of her three children, two young grandchildren, and extended family. She is also eternally grateful and happy to be married for 40 plus years to Dr. Robert Sayad.

1

Perspectives on Human Sexuality

Peopleimages/iStock/Getty Images

CHAPTER OUTLINE

Studying Human Sexuality

Sexuality, Popular Culture, and the Media

Sexuality Across Cultures and Times

Societal Norms and Sexuality

Student Voices

"The media, especially magazines and television, has had an influence on shaping my sexual identity. Ever since I was a little girl, I have watched the women on TV and hoped I would grow up to look sexy and beautiful like them. I feel that because of the constant barrage of images of beautiful women on TV and in magazines young girls like me grow up with unrealistic expectations of what beauty is and are doomed to feel they have not met this exaggerated standard."

—21-year-old female

"The phone, television, and Internet became my best friends. I never missed an episode of any of the latest shows, and I knew all the words to every new song. And when Facebook entered my life, I finally felt connected. At school, we would talk about status updates: whom we thought was cute, relationship status, and outrageous photos. All of the things we saw were all of the things we fantasized about. These are the things we would talk about."

—23-year-old female

"Though I firmly believe that we are our own harshest critics, I also believe that the media have a large role in influencing how we think of ourselves. I felt like ripping my hair out every time I saw a skinny model whose stomach was as hard and flat as a board, with their flawless skin and perfectly coifed hair. I cringed when I realized that my legs seemed to have an extra 'wiggle-jiggle' when I walked. All I could do was watch the television and feel abashed at the differences in their bodies compared to mine. When magazines and films tell me that for my age I should weigh no more than a hundred pounds, I feel like saying, 'Well, gee, it's no wonder I finally turned to laxatives with all these pressures to be thin surrounding me.' I ached to be model-thin and pretty. This fixation to be as beautiful and coveted as these models so preoccupied me that I had no time to even think about anyone or anything else."

—18-year-old female

"I am aware that I may be lacking in certain areas of my sexual self-esteem, but I am cognizant of my shortcomings and am willing to work on them. A person's sexual self-esteem isn't something that is detached from his or her daily life. It is intertwined in every aspect of life and how one views his or her self: emotionally, physically, and mentally. For my own sake, as well as my daughter's, I feel it is important for me to develop and model a healthy sexual self-esteem."

—28-year-old male

"Nature is to be reverenced, not blushed at."

—Tertullian (c. 155 CE–c. 220 CE)

Sᴇxᴜᴀʟɪᴛʏ ᴡᴀs ᴏɴᴄᴇ ʜɪᴅᴅᴇɴ from view in our culture: Fig leaves covered the "private parts" of nudes; poultry breasts were renamed "white meat"; censors prohibited the publication of the works of D. H. Lawrence, James Joyce, and Henry Miller; and homosexuality was called "the love that dares not speak its name." But over the past few generations, sexuality has become more open. In recent years, popular culture and the media have transformed what we "know" about sexuality. Not only is sexuality *not* hidden from view; it often seems to surround and embed itself into all aspects of our lives.

In this chapter, we discuss why we study human sexuality and examine popular culture and the media to see how they shape our ideas about sexuality. Then we look at how sexuality has been conceptualized in different cultures and at different times in history. Finally, we examine how society defines various aspects of our sexuality as natural or normal.

● Studying Human Sexuality

"Educating the mind without educating the heart is no education at all."

—Aristotle (384 BCE–322 BCE)

The study of human sexuality differs from the studies of accounting, plant biology, and medieval history, for example, because human sexuality is surrounded by a vast array of taboos, fears, prejudices, and hypocrisy. For many, sexuality creates ambivalent feelings. It is linked not only with intimacy and pleasure but also with shame, guilt, and discomfort. As a result, you may find yourself confronted with society's mixed feelings about sexuality as you study it. You may find, for example, that others perceive you as somehow "unique" or "different" for taking this course. Some may feel threatened in a vague, undefined way. Parents, partners, or spouses (or your own children, if you are a parent) may wonder why you want to take a "sex class"; they may want to know why you don't take something more "serious"—as if sexuality were not one of the most important issues we face as individuals and as a society. Sometimes this uneasiness manifests itself in humor, one of the ways in which we deal with ambivalent feelings: "You mean you have to take a *class* on sex?" "Are there labs?" "Why don't you let me show you?"

Ironically, despite societal ambivalence, you may quickly find that your human sexuality text or ebook becomes the most popular book in your dormitory or apartment. "I can never find my textbook when I need it," one of our students complained. "My roommates are always reading it. And they're not even taking the course!" Another student observed: "My friends used to kid me about taking the class, but now the first thing they ask when they see me is what we discussed in class." "My friends gather around when I open up my online sexuality course, waiting for a glimpse of photos or new information."

As you study human sexuality, you will find yourself exploring topics not ordinarily discussed in other classes. Sometimes they are rarely talked about even among friends. They may be prohibited by family, religious, or cultural teaching. For this reason, behaviors such as masturbation and sexual fantasizing are often the source of considerable guilt and shame. But in your human sexuality course, these topics will be examined objectively. You may be surprised to discover, in fact, that part of your learning involves *unlearning* myths, factual errors, distortions, biases, and prejudices you learned previously.

Sexuality may be the most taboo subject you study as an undergraduate, but your comfort level in class will probably increase as you recognize that you and your fellow students have a common purpose in learning about sexuality. Your sense of ease may also increase as you and your classmates get to know one another and discuss sexuality, both inside and outside the class. You may find that, as you become accustomed to using the nuanced sexual vocabulary, you are more comfortable discussing various topics. For example, your communication with a partner may improve, which will strengthen your relationship and increase sexual satisfaction for both of you. You may never before have used the word *masturbation, clitoris,* or *penis* in a class setting or any kind of setting, for that matter. But after a while, using these and other terms may become second nature to you. You may discover that discussing sexuality academically becomes as easy as talking about computer science, astronomy, or literature. You may even find yourself, as many students do, sharing with your friends what you learned in class while on a bus or in a restaurant, as other passengers or diners gasp in surprise or lean toward you to hear better!

Studying sexuality requires respect for your fellow students. You'll discover that the experiences and values of your classmates vary greatly. Some have little sexual experience, while others have a lot of experience; some students hold progressive sexual values, while others hold conservative ones. Some students are lesbian, gay, bisexual, transgender, queer, questioning, intersex, asexual, or another identity (LGBTQ+). This plus sign represents inclusiveness of all identities. Most students are young, others middle-aged, some older—each in a different stage of life and with different developmental tasks before them. Furthermore, the presence of students from any of the numerous religious and ethnic groups in the United States reminds us that there is no single behavior, attitude, value, or sexual norm that encompasses sexuality in contemporary society. Finally, as your sexuality evolves you will find that you will become more accepting of yourself as a sexual human being with your own "sexual voice." From this, you will truly "own" your sexuality.

Taking a course in human sexuality is like no other college experience. It requires that students examine their sexual beliefs and behaviors in the context of a wide variety of social and cultural factors and incorporate this new perspective into their sexual lives and well-being.

Andersen Ross/Getty Images

"Words do not have inherent meaning, they are signifiers of meaning and these meanings shift across time."

—Morgan Lev Edward Holleb (1989–)

● Sexuality, Popular Culture, and the Media

Much of sexuality is influenced and shaped by popular culture, especially the mass media. Popular culture presents us with myriad images of what it means to be sexual. But what kinds of sexuality do the media portray for our consumption?

Media Portrayals of Sexuality

What messages do the media send about sexuality to children, adolescents, adults, and older people? To people of varied races, ethnicities, and sexual orientations? Perhaps as important as what the media portray sexually is what is not portrayed—masturbation, condom use, and older adults' sexuality, for example.

Media are among the most powerful forces in people's lives today. Adults ages 18 and over spend more time engaging with media than in any other activity—an average of 12 hours per day, 7 days per week (see Figure 1). Watching TV, playing video games, texting, listening to music, and searching the Internet provide a constant stream of messages, images, expectations, and values about which few (if any) of us can resist. Whether and how this exposure is related to sexual outcomes is complex and debatable, depending on the population studied. However, data that are available may provide an impetus for policymakers who are forming media policies, parents who are trying to support their children's identity and learning, and educators and advocates who are concerned about the impact of media on youth and who wish to underscore the potential impact of media in individuals' lives. For those concerned about promoting sexual health and well-being, understanding media's prominence and role in people's lives is essential.

Mass-media depictions of sexuality function not only to entertain and exploit, but also in some cases to educate. As a result, the media often do not present us with "real" depictions of sexuality. Sexual activities, for example, are usually not explicitly acted out or described in mainstream media. The social and cultural taboos that are still part of mainstream U.S. culture remain embedded in the media. Thus the various media present the social *context* of sexuality; that is, the programs, plots, movies, stories, articles, newscasts, and vignettes tell us *what* behaviors are culturally most appropriate, *with whom* they are appropriate, and *why* they are appropriate.

Probably nothing has revolutionized sexuality the way that access to the Internet has. A click on a website link provides sex on demand. The Internet's contributions to the availability and commercialization of sex include live images and chats, personalized pages and ads, and links to potential or virtual sex partners. The spread of the web has made it easy to obtain information, solidify social ties, and provide sexual gratification.

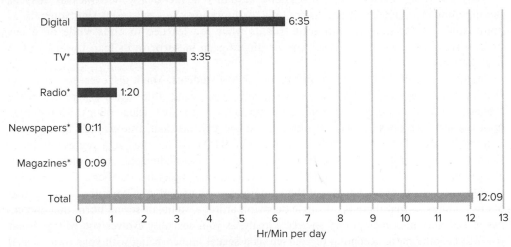

Note: Includes all time spent with that medium, regardless of multitasking; for example, 1 hour of multitasking on TV while listening to radio is counted as 1 hour for TV and 1 hour for radio; *excludes digital

● **FIGURE 1**

Average Time Spent Per Day With Media by Persons in the United States, Ages 18 and Over, 2019.

Source: www.eMarketer.com [April 2019]

A Quick and Evolving Glossary of Sexual Identity and Sexual Orientation

Our knowledge and understanding about sexuality, gender, gender identity, and gender variations along with the nomenclature to describe each are evolving. For example, we now recognize that gender diversity extends well beyond variation in masculinity or femininity such that both government institutions and social media platforms like Facebook and Tinder have adopted over 30 different self-identifying gender terms that go well beyond the social constructs of man and woman (Whyte et al., 2018). Though subject to opinions and differences, this document represents a partial list of current terminology used for sexual and gender identities and variations and sexual orientation. The comprehensive list is, undoubtedly, much longer. To learn of the other current terms, one can seek information from professional sexuality organizations, especially those that focus on sexuality and gender-related issues. Over time, there will be additions and corrections to this evolving nomenclature.

Agender Those who do not identify with any gender.

Anatomical sex Refers to physical sex: gonads, uterus, vulva, vagina, penis, etc.

Androgyny A combination of masculine and feminine traits or nontraditional gender expression. May be referred to as *genderqueer* or *gender fluid*.

Asexuality Lack of sexual attraction.

Assigned sex An assignment that is made at birth, usually male or female, typically on the basis of external genital anatomy but sometimes on the basis of internal gonads, chromosomes, or hormone levels.

Bisexuality An emotional and sexual attraction to two or more genders or someone who is attracted to people, regardless of their gender. (See also *pansexuality*.)

Cisgender Someone whose gender identity aligns with the gender assigned at birth.

Disorders of sex development (DSD) Considered by some to pathologize gender variations, the diagnosis may be used to describe congenital conditions in which the external appearance of the individual does not coincide with the chromosomal constitution or the gonadal sex. The term DSD is no longer used by the World Health Organization. Also known as *differences of sex development* or *intersex*.

Gender The socially constructed roles, behaviors, activities, and attributes that a society considers appropriate for a sex.

Genderqueer A spectrum of identities that are not exclusively masculine or feminine. Rather, a person identifies with neither, both, or a combination of male or female genders.

Gender binary The idea that gender is an either-or option of male or female. Many who question their gender are uncertain, unwilling to state, or feel limited by those neatly fitting categories.

Gender non-binary or *genderqueer* is a spectrum of gender identities that are not exclusively masculine or feminine.

Gender confirming treatment A means for those who find it essential and medically necessary to establish congruence with their gender identity. Also referred to as *gender affirming treatment* or *gender reassignment surgery*.

Gender diverse An umbrella term used to describe an ever-evolving array of labels people may apply when their gender identity, expression, or perception does not conform to the norms and stereotypes of others. Replaces the former term gender nonconforming.

Gender dysphoria A clinical symptom and psychiatric diagnosis which has focus on the distress that stems from the incongruence between one's expressed or experienced gender and the gender assigned at birth. Previously called gender identity disorder.

Gender fluid(ity) People whose gender expressions and/or identity is not static; that is, it is not the same all the time.

Gender identity A person's internal sense or perception of being male, female, or blend of both, or neither.

Gender roles Attitudes, behaviors, rights, and responsibilities that particular cultural groups associate with our assumed or assigned sex.

Gender variant Anyone who deviates from the historical norms of masculinity and femininity. Also known as *transgender, gender diverse, gender non-binary,* or *genderqueer*.

Genetic sex Chromosomal and hormonal sex characteristics.

Heteroflexible Individuals who identify as heterosexual or mostly heterosexual but report moderate same-sex behavior and attraction.

Heteronormativity The belief that heterosexuality is normal, natural, and superior to all other expressions of sexuality.

Heterosexuality Emotional and sexual attraction between persons of the other sex. Also referred to as *straight*.

Homosexuality Emotional and sexual attraction between persons of the same sex. Also referred to as *gay* or *queer*.

Intersex A variety of conditions that may occur during fetal development and lead to atypical development of physical sex characteristics. These conditions can involve the external genitals, internal reproductive organs, sex, and sex-related hormones. May also be known as *disorders of sex development* (DSD).

Pansexuality Emotional and sexual attraction regardless of gender identities and expressions.

Queer Those whose identified gender or sexual identity is non-conforming, that is, not heterosexual or cisgender.

Sex Consists either of the two main categories (male and female) into which humans and most other living things are divided on the basis of their reproductive functions.

Sexual and gender minority A group including, but not limited to, individuals who identify as lesbian, gay, bisexual, asexual, transgender, two-spirit, queer, and/or intersex.

Individuals with same-sex or -gender attractions or behaviors and those with a difference in sex development are also included.

Sexual orientation A multidimensional construct composed of sexual identity, attraction, and behavior.

Transgender An umbrella term for those whose gender expression or identity is not congruent with the sex assigned at birth. This includes those who identify as *genderqueer or gender fluid, gender nonconforming, intersex,* and *trans.*

Transsexual A somewhat outdated term for someone who is not the gender they were assigned at birth. Often implied is a medical transition. *Transgender* is now the preferred term.

Transvestism Wearing of clothes of the other sex for any one of many reasons, including relaxation, fun, and sexual gratification. Often referred to as *cross-dressing.*

Images of sexuality permeate our society, sexualizing our environment. Think about the sexual images you see or hear in a 24-hour period. What messages do they communicate about sexuality?

John Violet/Alamy Stock Photo

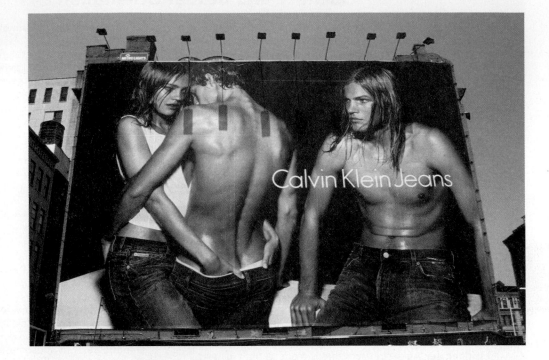

It's common knowledge that most of us have thoroughly integrated all forms of media into our lives. In spite of being heavy users of media, more than half of those aged 13–17 are worried that they spend too much time on their cellphones, while a similar percent have tried to limit their use of social media or video games (Pew Research Center, 2018). Though high school males spend more time on the computer than high school females, teenagers spend most of their media/communications time watching TV and videos (Rideout & Robb, 2019). For school-aged children and adolescents, the American Academy of Pediatrics [AAP] (2016) suggests that parents teach young people to balance media use with other healthy behaviors; no small endeavor considering the powerful draw and influence of the media.

The music industry is awash with sexual images and messages too. Contemporary pop music, from rock 'n' roll to rap, is filled with lyrics about sexuality mixed with messages about love, rejection, violence, and loneliness. Research has found that women are frequently sexualized and objectified within music videos, with sexual references including women engaging in implicit sexual behaviors, sex is seen as a priority for men, and women are defined by having a man (American Psychological Association [APA], 2018). As a result, there is increasing evidence that exposure to sexual content in music may be impacting young people's identity and gender role development, most significantly related to stereotypical gender role attitudes, ideals, and expectations. Because of censorship issues, the most overtly sexual music is not played on the radio but is more often streamed through the Internet via YouTube, Pandora, Spotify, and other sites.

Magazines, tabloids, and books contribute to the sexualization of our society as well. It's important to note that sexualization is not the same as sex or sexuality; rather **sexualization** is a form of sexism that narrows a frame of a person's worth and value. The sexualization of individuals sees value and worth only as sexual body parts for others' sexual pleasure. For example, popular romance novels and self-help books disseminate ideas and values about sexuality and body image. Men's magazines have been singled out for their sexual emphasis. *Playboy, Men's Health,* and *Maxim,* with their Playmates of the Month, sex tips, and other advice, are among the most popular magazines in the world. *Sports Illustrated's* annual swimsuit edition alone draws 63 million adult users in the United States (Sports Illustrated, 2020).

It would be a mistake to think that only male-oriented magazines focus on sex. Women's magazines such as *Cosmopolitan* and *Elle* have their own sexual content. These magazines feature romantic photographs of lovers to illustrate stories with such titles as "Sizzling Sex Secrets of the World's Sexiest Women," "Making Love Last: If Your Partner Is a Premature Ejaculator," and "Turn on Your Man with Your Breasts (Even If They Are Small)." Preadolescents and young teens are not exempt from sexual images and articles in magazines such as *Seventeen* and *J-14*. Given these magazines' heavy emphasis on looks, it's not surprising that those who read a lot of women-focused magazines are more likely to have internalized the thin ideal, have negative views of their appearance, engage in restricted eating and bulimic behaviors, and experience negative psychological health (Northrup, 2013; Swiatkowski, 2016).

In the absence of alternative resources to guide their decisions concerning sexual relationships, college students often rely on sexual scripts conveyed through mass media (Hust et al., 2014). Since the majority of men's magazines seem to promote men as sexual aggressors, it's easy to understand how many men internalize this message. As a result, readers of men's magazines report lower intentions to ask their sexual partner for consent for sexual activity and are less likely to adhere to sexual consent decisions by their partner (Hust et al., 2014). A recent meta-analysis from 59 studies revealed that exposure to sexual media had a small but significant effect on sexual attitudes and behaviors, with effects being stronger for adolescents than emerging adults. Additionally, the effects were stronger for boys than girls and for white individuals compared with Black individuals (Coyne et al., 2019). Regarding women's exposure to women's magazines, Ward (2016) found that their exposure was positively associated with their ability to refuse unwanted sexual activity.

Advertising in all media uses the sexual sell, promising sex, romance, popularity, and fulfillment if the consumer will only purchase the right soap, perfume, cigarettes, alcohol, toothpaste, jeans, or automobile. In reality, not only does one *not* become "sexy" or popular by consuming a certain product, but the product may actually be detrimental to one's sexual well-being, as in the case of cigarettes or alcohol.

Throughout the world, the media have assumed an increasingly significant role in shaping perspectives toward gender and sexual roles. In a review of 135 peer-reviewed studies in the United States between 1995 and 2015, the findings found consistent evidence that both laboratory exposure and everyday exposure to mainstream media are directly associated with higher levels of body dissatisfaction, greater **self-objectification**, or evaluating oneself based on appearance; greater support of sexist beliefs; and greater tolerance of sexual violence toward women (Ward, 2016). In addition, experimental exposure to media has led society to have a diminished view of women's competence, morality, and humanity. This evidence, however, varies depending on the genres of media we consume and our preexisting beliefs, identities, and experiences.

Though much research has focused on the impact of media on female development, media undoubtedly has an impact on men as well. What has been found is that men's frequent consumption of sexually objectifying media (i.e., TV, films, and videos) was associated with greater objectification of their romantic partners, which in turn was linked to lower levels of relationship and sexual satisfaction (Zurbriggen et al., 2011).

Reality shows, such as *The Bachelorette* and *90 Day Fiancé* frequently highlight idealized and sexual themes. What are some of the most popular reality shows? Do they differ according to race/ethnicity?

Raymond Hall/GC Images/Getty Images

Media images of sexuality permeate a variety of areas in people's lives. They can produce sexual arousal and emotional reactions, provide social connection, entertain, increase sexual behaviors, and be a source of sex information. On the other hand, unmonitored Internet access among youth raises significant concerns about its risks. Since 2006, the **Me Too movement** (or #MeToo) in social media has helped to create more gender and racial equality and inclusion, as well as safer working environments. Though it originally addressed sexual harassment and sexual assault, its scope has expanded to an international movement for justice for people in marginalized communities. However, there is still work to be done. Though sexual harassment has decreased and the voices of women are being heard, it doesn't mean that we can cease our awareness or actions around social justice and empowerment issues.

Given the fact that teens now spend an average of more than seven hours per day on screen media for entertainment, it's clear that media consumption and exposure play a significant role in their lives (Rideout & Robb, 2019). Currently, the total time spent on screen media beats time spent eating and drinking, socializing, and grooming.

Of concern around adolescents' heavy media use is their viewing of sexually explicit videos. Because of its easy access along with the potential risks associated with its use, understanding its implications is important for parents, partners, as well as the rest of us.

Television and Digital Media

Among all types of media, television and digital (online and mobile) have been the most prevalent, pervasive, and vexing icons, saturating every corner of public and private space, shaping consciousness, defining reality, and entertaining the masses (see Figure 2). While the frequency of online videos has been increasing, so has been the number of sexual references in programming. While narratives that provide educational information regarding the risks and consequences of sexual behavior are frequently missing from television shows, sexual violence and abuse, casual sex among adults, lack of contraception use, and failure to portray consequences of risky behaviors are common. Because reality programs (e.g.,

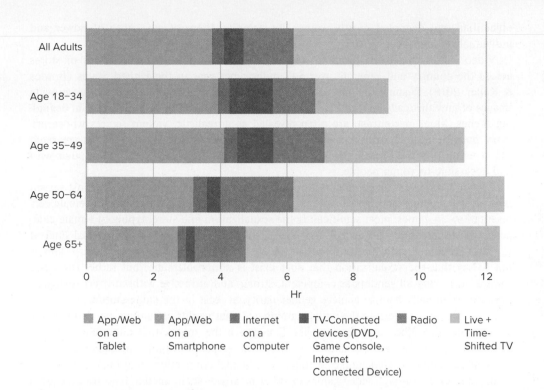

• FIGURE 2

**Amount of Time of Daily Media Use,
By Age, 2019.**

Source: The Nielsen Company, 2019

Chart legend:
- App/Web on a Tablet
- App/Web on a Smartphone
- Internet on a Computer
- TV-Connected devices (DVD, Game Console, Internet Connected Device)
- Radio
- Live + Time-Shifted TV

Temptation Island and *Are You The One?*), and screen media feature "real" people (as opposed to actors), it is possible that exposure to their objectifying content can have even a more significant impact than other types of programming. Considering the variety of media genres, including music videos, advertising, video games, and magazines, it becomes apparent that sexualized images are often the dominant way that young people learn about sex.

While it is apparent that exposure to television does not affect all people in the same way, it is clear that the sexual double standard, or judging heterosexual men and women differently for the same sexual behavior, taps into our national ambivalence about sex, equality, morality, and violence. It accomplishes this in ways that are both subtle and blatant, leaving some viewers confused, others angry, and still others reinforced around their views of the other sex. Other programs seek to normalize non-heterosexual behaviors as well as gender varia-tions (Kinsler et al., 2018). With no shortage of dramas, comedies, movies, or specials available we now see queer characters in a variety of mainstream venues including those in *Schitt's Creek, Grace and Frankie,* and *Everything's Gonna Be Okay.* Additionally, television is making strides to educate teens and young adults about sexuality and parenting. Programs such as *Teen Mom, 13 Reasons Why,* and *Sex Education* have consulted with professional organizations to help educate viewers. This type of alliance is good for all of us.

Unlike the film industry, which uses a single ratings board to regulate all American releases, television has been governed by an informal consensus. In 1997, networks began to rely on watchdog standards and practices departments to rate their shows; however, these divisions have few, if any, hard-and-fast rules. While the Federal Communication Commission (FCC) does not offer clear guidelines about what is and is not permissible on the airwaves, the agency does permit looser interpretations of its decency standards for broadcasts between 10 P.M. and 6 A.M.

Music and Game Videos   MTV, MTV2, VH1, BET, and music video platforms such as Vimeo and YouTube are very popular among adolescents and young adults. Unlike audio-recorded music, music videos play to the ear and the eye. With this, artists have brought energy, sexuality, and individualism to the young music audience, while others have

"The vast wasteland of TV is not interested in producing a better mousetrap but in producing a worse mouse."

—Laurence Coughlin

Watching female icons such as Cardi B and Megan Thee Stallion dance in a provocative manner has become mainstream in most music videos.

(a) Scott Legato/Getty Images; (b) Tommaso Boddi/Getty Images

objectified and degraded mostly women by stripping them of any sense of power and individualism and focusing strictly on their sexuality.

Video games that often promote sexist and violent attitudes fill the aisles of stores across the country and generate over $43 million per year in the United States (Bowles & Keller, 2019). Pushing the line between obscenity and amusement, games often provide images of unrealistically shaped and submissive women mouthing sexy dialogues in degrading scenes. Men, in contrast, are often revealed as unrealistic, violent figures whose primary purpose is to destroy and conquer. Though many of these video games are rated "M" (mature) by the Entertainment Software Ratings Board, they are both popular with and accessible to young people.

Recently, however, the gaming industry has been challenged by an outcry against sexism in both video games and in the workplace that produces them. The nature of female representations in games, most significantly the sexualization and stereotyping of female characters, has decreased. The decline has been attributed to an increasing universal interest in gaming coupled with the heightened criticism directed at the gaming industry. This is not to say that the sexualization that does exist is nonproblematic, but rather the trend toward portraying all genders as competent, strong, and attractive without overt sexualization may eventually help to achieve gender parity, at least in the game culture.

An additional concern in the online gaming and chat worlds, including the chat features on consoles like Xbox and services like Steam, are the spaces that allow children and adults to interact. Sexual predators can meet young people online through multiplayer video games and chat apps and, over time, make virtual connections that build trust. Their goal, whether it's through video games or other means of social media, is to trick children into sharing sexually explicit photos and videos of themselves, which they use as blackmail for more imagery or to humiliate or exact revenge; a practice known as **sextortion** (Bowles & Keller, 2019; De Santisteban & Gamez-Guadix, 2018). Though there are tools to detect abuse content, scanning for new images is difficult. Parents need to know what their children are playing and what tools are available to help protect them. Parents who suspect a problem should react carefully when their children report encounters as punishing children by prohibiting video games or social media could backfire and drive children to even more secrecy.

Feature-Length Films

From their very inception, motion pictures have dealt with sexuality. In 1896, a film titled *The Kiss* outraged moral guardians when it showed a couple stealing a quick kiss. "Absolutely disgusting," complained one critic. "The performance comes near being indecent in its emphasized indecency. Such things call for police action" (quoted in Webb, 1983). Today, in contrast, film critics use "explicit," a word independent of artistic value, to praise a film. "Explicit" films are movies in which the requisite "sex scenes" are sufficiently titillating to overcome their lack of aesthetic merit. What is clear is that movies are similar to television in their portrayal of the consequences of unprotected sex, such as unplanned pregnancies or sexually transmitted infections (STIs), including HIV/AIDS.

The notion of "true love" in dramas and romantic comedies has come to represent the idealized belief of some that love conquers all. Stories about love, including those in books, magazines, music, television, and the Internet, are often so stereotypical and idealized that it is difficult for people to separate these unrealistic representations from what is healthy and reasonable in their romantic relationships. (For more information about styles of love, see Chapter 8.) To help balance these notions, it is important to have authentic personal experiences, mentors in one's life, honesty with oneself, and peers who will reveal that sex is often imperfect and that disagreements and communication difficulties are typical.

Lesbian, Gay, Bisexual, Transgender, and Queer People in Film and Television

Lesbian, gay, bisexual, transgender, and queer (LGBTQ+) individuals are slowly being integrated into mainstream films and television. However, when queer people do appear, they are frequently defined in terms of their sexual orientation or gender identity, as if there were nothing more to their lives. Though the situation is changing, gay men are generally stereotyped as effeminate or flighty or they may be closeted. Lesbian women are often stereotyped as either super-feminine or super-masculine. And queer individuals often appear as odd.

"Coming out" stories are now the standard for television programs that deal with gay characters. However, what has recently changed is that the age of these characters has become younger. Teen coming-out stories seem relevant in that they reflect the identity issues of being gay, transgender, queer, questioning, or unsure about their sexual identity and expose the vulnerability most young people in junior high and high school feel about being bullied. Different from stories in which queer people are marginalized and stereotyped, the messages in many of the shows for younger audiences are quite consistent: that you will be accepted for who you are. Still, media have a long way to go in terms of normalizing any type of healthy sexual relationships. The biggest hurdle remains in showing adults, particularly two males, kissing on screen as their heterosexual counterparts would. While teen shows may have somewhat overcome this barrier, most "adult" programs have not.

More frequent in movies is what has been referred to as **queerbating**, a marketing technique used to describe media where the creators integrate homoeroticism between two characters to lure in same sex and liberal audiences, yet never fully include actual representation for fear of alienating a wider audience. For example, in Disney's remake of *Beauty and the Beast* in 2017, there's a momentary shot that shows Le Fou dancing with another man, along with coded words about his feelings for Gaston. This bait-and-switch technique leaves many LGBTQ+ fans disappointed not to see themselves represented in meaningful ways that shed light on their lives and relationships.

In the film, *Bombshell*, a group of women take on Fox News head Roger Ailes for the toxic environment he presided over.
Axelle/Bauer-Griffin/FilmMagic/Getty Images

Online Social Networks

Using the Internet is a major recreational activity that has altered the ways in which individuals communicate and carry on interpersonal relationships. Though social theorists have long been concerned with the alienating effects of technology, the Internet appears quite

Writers in television and film are finally giving gay characters prominence beyond their sexuality. These programs include *The L Word, Generation Q, Pose, Betty, & Dear White People*.
TCD/Prod.DB/Alamy Stock Photo

For anyone with a computer, social networks provide readily accessible friends and potential partners, help maintain friendships, and shape sexual culture.

Dean Mitchell/Getty Images

different from other communication technologies. Its efficacy, power, and influence, along with the anonymity and depersonalization that accompany its use, have made it possible for users to more easily obtain and distribute sexual materials, images, and information, as well as to interact sexually in different ways.

Social networking sites like Facebook, Instagram, and Twitter are well integrated into the daily lives of most people around the world. Their popularity cannot be underestimated: Facebook alone reports to have nearly 2.5 billion global users (Statista, 2019.1a). Add this to the 500 million Americans who are daily active users on Instagram and the one billion monthly active users worldwide (Statista, 2019.1b), and it's obvious that the digital landscape has taken over the globe.

Social networking sites provide an opportunity for many to display their identities: religious, political, ideological, work-related, sexual orientation, and gender identity, to name a few. While doing so, individuals can also gain feedback from peers and strengthen their bonds of friendship. At the same time, social networking can be a place of "relationship drama." By posting details or pictures from a date on a social networking site such as Instagram or Snapchat, individuals share every gory detail of their relationship with anyone willing to take the time to view or read about it. While many who use the Internet to flirt with others have largely positive opinions and experiences, significant numbers of other users have negative ones. Many social networking users report having unfriended or blocked someone who was flirting in a way that made them feel uncomfortable, while others have unfriended someone they are no longer dating. Some have also used these sites to check up on someone they previously dated or to research potential romantic partners. **Ghosting**, or withdrawing from a person's life without notice and by ignoring their communications following a date or relationship, is another problem that may be more common among online dating. Not surprising, many realize that these sites can serve as an unwanted reminder that relationships have ended and, maybe worse, that their previous beloved one is now dating someone else. There is also increasing concern about the potential link between social media use and mental health and well-being in young people. A British study involving more than 10,000 youth, ages 13 to 16, found a clear connection between increased social media use and symptoms of psychological distress in girls. The link was not clear among boys (Viner et al., 2019). Though sites such as Instagram and Facebook did not directly cause mental health issues, nearly 60% of the impact on psychological distress in girls was attributed to social media disrupting their sleep and exposing them to **cyberbullying**, the use of electronic communication to bully, intimidate, or threaten a person.

With thousands of sexual health sites maintained online, new forms of media are also powerful tools for learning. When credible sources are located, these media have become convenient avenues by which people can get important sexual health information. There are, however, two significant concerns associated with using media to learn about sexuality and sexual health: the possibility that the information is inaccurate or misleading and the possibility that those who turn to the media may turn away from real people in their lives.

For many users, the Internet provides a fascinating venue for experiencing sex. For some users, however, porn consumption gets them in trouble: maxed-out credit cards, neglected responsibility, and overlooked loved ones. There are both online and community resources for those who desire counseling. While searching for such sources, however, consumers and professionals must be aware of the differences between therapy, consultation, and entertainment. Additionally, because entrepreneurs can make more money from hype and misinformation than from high-quality therapy and education, consumers must remain vigilant in assessing the background of the therapist and the source of the information.

One occurrence associated with the drastically changing culture of interpersonal communication is what is called **sexting** —the sending or receiving suggestive or explicit texts, photos, or video messages via computers or mobile devices. The wide array of accessible media provides the opportunity for choosing different purposes for sending and receiving sexts, including sexual self-expression, experimentation, self-definition, and education. At the same time, it has become clear that expectations of privacy in the digital world are being challenged related to ownership of sexual messages and images, sharing and trafficking of sexual material

think
about it

Online Dating: No Longer A Last Attempt

The popularity and accessibility of digital media and technology have allowed individuals to present themselves publicly in ways that were previously never possible. No longer is online dating seen as a last attempt for the lonely and desperate, nor is it stigmatized by the general public. After all, almost half of U.S. online users have met or known someone who has met a romantic partner on a dating website or app (Statista, 2019.1c). Dating sites such as Match.com, Tinder, Plenty of Fish, and Grindr, along with platforms such as Facebook, Instagram, Twitter, and Snapchat enable individuals to find potential partners in just minutes with the simple swipe of an app or a click on a website. Social media facilitate communication and support, play a prominent role in navigating and documenting romantic relationships, provide an outlet for sexual exploration and expression and, for a small minority, are a means to exploit another. Using technology, individuals negotiate over when, with whom, and how to meet and interact.

Over time, traditional sites and avenues for meeting singles, including universities, clubs, gyms, and workplaces, have been partially replaced by the Internet, thereby allowing people to meet and form relationships with others with whom they have no knowledge or social connections. But just how successful or risky are these sites and apps? Once the work of creating a profile is complete, can getting a date really be that difficult? To some degree, that depends on what it is that people want—to hook up or have casual sex, to date casually, or to date as a way of actively pursuing a relationship. In early 2019, 49% of dating app users stated that they were using online dating services to look for an exclusive romantic partner.

An additional 20% used online dating for non-exclusive romantic partners and 33% stated that they used online dating apps and services specifically for sexual encounters (Statista, 2019.1c). The same survey found that dating platform or app users were predominately male and younger in age (see Figure 3). Combined, the online dating audience size is approximately 34 million, amounting to approximately $555 million in revenue in 2018 (Statista, 2019.1c).

No doubt, the Internet, including dating sites, is a means of communication which not only brings new contexts for socialization and interaction, but provides a means of expressing identity and sexuality that might otherwise feel more threatening than a face-to-face contact. It's common knowledge that technology can enhance one's ability to find a date, and in doing so, fulfill their desire to flirt, date, and in some cases, find a suitable partner. For the isolated, marginalized, underrepresented, and disenfranchised individuals, many of whom hide their gender or sexual identities from others, Internet dating sites may play an even more prominent and useful role in navigating romantic relationships because it allows them to be honest about who they are. When the experiences with online dating are examined, almost half of users reported having had a very or somewhat positive experience with it. Men report having a better time with dating apps than women, with only 10% of male users reporting somewhat or very negative experiences, whereas 29% of women reported negative experiences (Statista, 2019.1c).

Dating apps are not without their detractors and caveats. One pitfall of online dating is the view that in the endless array of online partners, one can be less satisfied with their choice. This could be

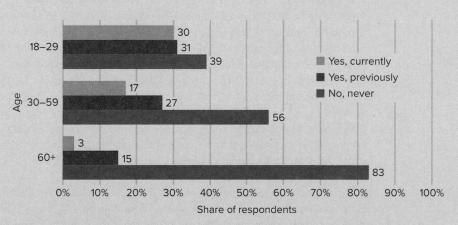

• FIGURE 3

Percentage of Internet Users in the United States Who Have Used Online Dating Sites or Apps as of 2017, by Age Group.

Source: Statista, 2020

compared to going to a frozen yogurt shop, seeing the 15 delicious options, choosing 1 or 2, and feeling less satisfied because of all the flavors they could have had instead. Outcomes related to this level of frustration include the belief that technology has made finding a mate more difficult, and in doing so may delay or even suppress the desire to establish a deeper relationship. As a result, both the selection process and the process of self-presentation have, in some people's experience, brought about a kind dating-app fatigue or weariness. What might underscore this fatigue is that of the 1.6 billion swipes a day on Tinder, there are just 26 million matches (Julian, 2018). It appears that the overwhelming majority of matches don't lead to either a two-way text exchange, much less a date, or sex for that matter. Additional concerns associated with online dating are that some users feel uncomfortable meeting someone who might pose a danger, having to block or report someone for personal or legal reasons, or having requests for or being sent unsolicited photos. The phenomenon of ghosting appears to occur among one-fourth of dating respondents (Henderson, 2018). In the past when partners met through peer groups, for example, ghosting was perhaps not as prevalent because of the social stigma associated with it. Today, because of the anonymity the Internet provides and possible isolation of its users, individuals don't have to incur such costs.

Based on these and other factors, many online dating users have taken measures before personally meeting someone to first search their name on social media profiles as well as search their phone number online. Additionally, it's always wise to meet someone for the first time in a public place and let a friend or colleague know in advance about your plans. Despite the risks associated with dating apps and sites, most customers view them as welcome agents in their search for companionship, love, sex, and intimacy (Hobbs et al., 2016). For those who are still waiting for that perfect date, if what you're doing doesn't work, then change your strategy.

Think Critically

1. Would you consider participating in or have you posted or created a dating site? If so, how did you describe yourself? Were you completely honest? If you would not consider using a dating site, what prevents you from doing so?
2. Do you believe that Internet sites should be censored? Why or why not?
3. What are some actions you might take to protect yourself from being uncomfortable and remaining safe when using a dating site?

without consent, and potential social and psychological health consequences of shared texts (Garcia et al., 2016).

When looking at the relationship status of those who send and receive sexts, the landscape is quite varied. Three common scenarios for sexting are: (1) the exchange of images solely between two romantic partners, (2) exchanges between a partner and someone outside the relationship, and (3) exchanges between people who are not yet in a relationship but at least one person hopes to be. When surveyed about their reasons for sending sexts, most stated that they wanted to give their partner a sexy present, use it to enhance their relationship, or respond to a sext that was given to them (Champion & Pedersen, 2015).

The most damaging aspect of the sharing of sexts occurs when they go beyond the intended recipient and are trafficked to others for whom they were not intended. Sexting can hurt one's reputation, career, self-esteem, and current relationships and friendships. It can also cause shame and guilt to the victim of such a transgression. And the potential of sextortion, or coaxing victims into taking explicit photos and videos and then threatening to distribute them to others if they don't pay them, is becoming increasingly common among scammers. Complicating this problem is the offenders' utilization of privacy protection networks to obscure their identities. These sites enable offenders to route all of their incoming and outgoing Internet traffic through a number of different locations anywhere in the world, so that law enforcement cannot use traditional means to locate them (Pittaro, 2019). Additionally, the utilization of encryption can protect offenders' identities as well as the exploitation materials they create, share, and collect from observation by law enforcement. It probably comes as no surprise that some individuals, particularly women and very young persons, are more susceptible to being victimized because they are perceived to be more vulnerable to calculating offenders.

In response to teen sexting, some states have brought felony charges under child exploitation laws, while in other places prosecutors can require young people to take courses on the dangers of social media instead of charging them with a crime. The struggle to reconcile digital eroticism with real-world consequences is inherent when using technology to facilitate human interactions. Instead of looking at sexting as objectifying and inherently dangerous, another perspective is that sexting can be sexually liberating. That is, the self-portrayal of the body that occurs in sexting can facilitate individuals' exploration of their bodies and help them reclaim and liberate themselves from society's view of the ideal. An indicator of this sexual liberation is acceptance with nudity. Two researchers recently assessed the contrasting views of sexting, that being objectifying versus liberating, and found that sexting is both of these (Liong & Cheng, 2019). That is, while sexting involves showing one's bare body or body parts to another person can encourage objectification, sexting for all genders can be a form of liberation from the everyday restrictions placed upon the body. The authors concluded with the need for sex(t) education that could help youth develop awareness to explore their unique bodies, accept that no one must be subjected to the desires of others, and if they choose to sext, do so responsibly and consensually.

Because of the high volume of sexual discussions and material available on the Internet, there is an increasing demand for government regulation. In 1996, Congress passed the Communications Decency Act, which made it illegal to use computer networks to transmit "obscene" materials or place "indecent" words or images where children might read or see them. However, courts have declared this legislation a violation of freedom of speech.

While one might argue that it is unwise to confuse entertainment with education, media use is not without its negative consequences on health. Studies find that high levels of media use among young people is associated with academic problems, sleep deprivation, obesity, risky behaviors, and more (American Academy of Pediatricians [AAP], 2016). Recognizing the ubiquitous role of media in children's lives, AAP has released policy recommendations to help families maintain healthy media usage, which includes the following:

Congressman Anthony Weiner resigned from the House of Representatives in 2011 after sending to multiple women sexually suggestive pictures of himself.

Archive PL/Alamy Stock Photo

- Avoid use of screen media except video chatting among children younger than 18 months
- Locate high-quality programming beginning at around 18–24 months of age and watch it with their children
- Allow one hour of high-quality programming per day for children aged 2–5 years
- Limit time and type of media for children 6 and older, along with media-free times together and ongoing communication about online citizenship and safety.

● Sexuality Across Cultures and Times

What we see as "natural" in our culture may be viewed as unnatural in other cultures. Few Americans would disagree about the erotic potential of kissing. But other cultures perceive kissing as merely the exchange of saliva. To the Mehinaku of the Amazon rain forest, for example, kissing is a disgusting sexual abnormality; no Mehinaku engages in it (Gregor, 1985). The fact that others press their lips against each other, salivate, *and* become sexually excited merely confirms their "strangeness" to the Mehinaku.

Culture takes our **sexual interests**—our incitements or inclinations to act sexually—and molds and shapes them, sometimes celebrating sexuality and other times condemning it. A brief exploration of sexual themes across cultures and times will give you a sense of the diverse shapes and meanings humans have given to sexuality.

Sexual Interests

All cultures assume that adults have the *potential* for becoming sexually aroused and for engaging in sexual intercourse for the purpose of reproduction. But cultures differ considerably in terms of how strong they believe sexual interests are. These beliefs, in turn, affect the level of desire expressed in each culture.

The Mangaia Beginning at a young age, the Mangaia of Polynesia emphasize both the pleasurable and procreative aspects of sex (Marshall, 1971). At about age 7, a Mangaian boy first learns about masturbation and at about age 8 or 9, he may begin to masturbate. Around age 13 or 14, following a circumcision ritual, boys are given instruction in the ways of pleasing a girl: erotic kissing, cunnilingus, breast fondling and sucking, and techniques for bringing her to repeated orgasms. After 2 weeks, an older, sexually experienced woman has sexual

"Sex is hardly ever just about sex."
—Shirley MacLaine (1934–)

intercourse with the boy to instruct him further on how to sexually satisfy a woman. Girls the same age are instructed by older women on how to be orgasmic: how to thrust their hips and rhythmically tighten their vagina in order to experience repeated orgasms. A girl finally learns to be orgasmic through the efforts of a "good man." If the woman's partner fails to satisfy her, she is likely to leave him; she may also ruin his reputation with other women by denouncing his lack of skill. Young men and women are expected to have many sexual experiences prior to marriage.

This adolescent paradise, however, does not last forever. The Mangaia believe that sexuality is strongest during adolescence. As a result, when the Mangaia leave young adulthood, they experience a rapid decline in sexual desire and activity, and they cease to be aroused as passionately as they once were. They attribute this swift decline to the workings of nature and settle into a sexually contented adulthood.

The Dani In contrast to the Mangaia, the New Guinean Dani show little interest in sexuality (Schwimmer, 1997). To them, sex is a relatively unimportant aspect of life. The Dani express no concern about improving sexual techniques or enhancing erotic pleasure. Extra-relational sex and jealousy are rare. As their only sexual concern is reproduction, sexual intercourse is performed quickly, ending with male ejaculation. Female orgasm appears to be unknown to them. Following childbirth, both mothers and fathers go through 5 years of sexual abstinence. The Dani are an extreme example of a case in which culture, rather than biology, shapes sexual attractions.

Victorian Americans In the nineteenth century, white middle-class Americans believed that women had little sexual desire. If they experienced desire at all, it was "reproductive desire," the wish to have children. Reproduction entailed the unfortunate "necessity" of engaging in sexual intercourse. A leading reformer wrote that in her "natural state" a woman never makes advances based on sexual desires, for the "very plain reason that she does not feel them" (Alcott, 1868). Those women who did feel desire were "a few exceptions amounting in all probability to diseased cases." Such women were classified by a prominent physician as suffering from "Nymphomania, or Furor Uterinus" (Bostwick, 1860).

Whereas women were viewed as asexual, men were believed to have raging sexual appetites. Men, driven by lust, sought to satisfy their desires by ravaging innocent women. Both men and women believed that male sexuality was dangerous, uncontrolled, and animal-like. It was part of a woman's duty to tame unruly male sexual impulses.

The polarized beliefs about the nature of male and female sexuality created destructive antagonisms between "angelic" women and "demonic" men. These beliefs provided the rationale for a "war between the sexes." They also led to the separation of sex from love. Intimacy and love had nothing to do with male sexuality. In fact, male lust always lingered in the background of married life, threatening to destroy love by its overbearing demands.

The Sexual Revolution Between the 1960s and the mid-1970s, significant challenges to the ways that society viewed traditional codes of behavior took place in the United States. Dubbed the "sexual revolution," or "sexual liberation," this period of rapid and complex changes invited individuals and society to confront the sexually repressive Victorian era and begin to recognize a separation and autonomy in what was thought to be unexamined decisions and regulations. This counterculture movement questioned previously established rules, regulations, and decisions in these areas:

- *Individual self-expression and autonomy.* Previously structured around the collective good of the family and community, the counterculture found meaning and purpose in supporting the individual rights of men and women, including the right to sexual expression and pleasure.

- *Women's rights.* The traditional, stereotypical role of the man being breadwinner and of the woman being the homemaker were challenged by roles whereby individuals could choose according to their needs. It became acceptable for women to express their inherent sexuality and for men to be their emotional and authentic selves. It was during this period that abortion became legal, and widespread accessibility and dissemination of birth control became available.

- *Relationship status.* No longer was marriage the only context within which couples could express their sexuality, love, and commitment for one another.
A new philosophy of sex, referred to as "free love," allowed individuals to broaden and act on their sexual desires without marriage, judgment, or contempt.

- *Sexual orientation.* Overriding previous dogma from church and state, there has been a broader acceptance of homosexuality. This was reinforced in 1973 when the American Psychiatric Association removed homosexuality from its list of diagnosable mental disorders. More recently in 2015, the U.S. Supreme Court ruled same-sex marriage legal in all states.

- *Sexuality education.* Though a handful of sexuality education programs had been introduced prior to the 1960s, few were uniformly embraced or included in school curriculums until SIECUS: Sex Ed for Social Change became a vocal force in education and policy.

Although a significant amount of time has passed since the end of the Victorian era and the counterculture's attempt to shift values and attitudes about sexuality, many traditional sexual beliefs and attitudes continue to influence us. These include the belief that men are "naturally" sexually aggressive and women sexually passive, the sexual double standard, and the value placed on women being sexually inexperienced. While the media continue to push boundaries about what is acceptable and desirable in sexual expression, so do most Americans continue to adapt their thinking about what is acceptable, desirable, "normal," and tolerable.

Sexual Orientation

Homosexuality, more commonly referred to as **gay**, is an emotional and sexual attraction to individuals of the same sex or gender. Some people who have same-sex attractions or relationships may identify as **queer**, or for a range of reasons may choose not to identify with those or any labels. **Bisexuality** is an emotional and sexual attraction to two or more genders or someone who is attracted to people regardless of their gender. Individuals who identify as heterosexual or mostly heterosexual, but report some same-sex behavior and attraction are referred to as **heteroflexible**. There is significant debate about whether **asexuality**, a state of having no sexual attraction to anyone or low or absent interest in sexual activity, is a sexual orientation. There is a lack of consistent methods for defining and assessing sexual orientation, making it difficult to assess the populations who experience sexual orientation-related disparities. Nevertheless, now that **same-sex marriage** has been legalized in the United States, full social legitimacy and dignity have been granted to persons who marry a person of the same sex. This view of marriage is currently shared by 29 other countries.

In ancient Greece, the highest form of love was that expressed between males.

Ancient Greece In ancient Greece, the birthplace of Western civilization, the Greeks accepted same-sex relationships as naturally as Americans today accept heterosexuality. For the Greeks, same-sex relationships between men represented the highest form of love.

The male-male relationship was based on love and reciprocity; sexuality was only one component of it. In this relationship, the code of conduct called for the older man to initiate the relationship. The youth initially resisted; only after the older man courted the young man with gifts and words of love would he reciprocate. The two men formed a close emotional bond. The older man was the youth's mentor as well as his lover. He introduced the youth to men who would be useful for his advancement later; he assisted him in learning his duties as a citizen. As the youth entered adulthood, the erotic bond between the two evolved into a deep friendship. After the youth became an adult, he married a woman and later initiated a relationship with an adolescent boy.

Greek male-male relationships, however, were not substitutes for male-female marriage. The Greeks discouraged exclusive male-male relationships because marriage and children were required to continue the family and society. Husbands regarded their wives primarily as domestics and as bearers of children (Keuls, 1985). (The Greek word for woman, *gyne,* translates literally as "child-bearer.") Husbands turned for sexual pleasure not to their wives but to *hetaerae* (hi-TIR-ee), highly regarded courtesans who were usually educated slaves.

The Sambians Among Sambian males of New Guinea, sexual orientation is very malleable (Herdt & McClintock, 2000). Young boys begin with sexual activities with older boys, move to sexual activities with both sexes during adolescence, and engage in exclusively male-female activities in adulthood. Sambians believe that a boy can grow into a man only by the ingestion of semen, which is, they say, like mother's milk. At age 7 or 8, boys begin their sexual activities with older boys; as they get older, they seek multiple partners to accelerate their growth into manhood. At adolescence, their role changes, and they must provide semen to boys to enable them to develop. At first, they worry about their own loss of semen, but they are taught to drink tree sap, which they believe magically replenishes their supply.

During adolescence, boys are betrothed to preadolescent girls, with whom they engage in sexual activities. When the girls mature, the boys give up their sexual involvement with other males. They become fully involved with adult women, losing their desire for men.

Gender

Gender, or the socially constructed roles, behaviors, activities, and attributes that a society assigns to a person, is not as straightforward as one might believe. For many, it is not possible to extract gender from our feelings and experiences because it is imposed on us by society. For those who do not ascribe to gender "normative" behaviors or expressions, the umbrella term of **transgender** is used. This broad term describes those whose gender expression or identity is not congruent with the sex assigned at birth. (For a discussion about gender and related topics, see Chapter 5.)

Transgender people reside in many cultures, crossing age, religion, and social status.

Maciej Dakowicz/Alamy

Our sex appears solidly rooted in our biological nature. But is being any gender *really* biological? The answer is yes *and* no. Having male or female genitals is anatomical. But the possession of a penis does not always make a person a man, nor does the possession of a clitoris and vagina always make a person a woman. Men who consider themselves women, "women with penises," are accepted or honored in many cultures throughout the world (Bullough, 1991). Thus culture and a host of other factors help shape aspects of masculinity and femininity, while biology defines men and women. But this is not the case in all regions of the world.

Two-Spirited People   A Native American tradition involving the existence of cross-gender roles, the male-female, the female-male is what is called the **two-spirit** person (Laframboise & Anhorn, 2008). These individuals often expressed their gender through dress and work roles; however, they were celibate and so did not convey it through their sexual behaviors. Two-spirit people were often visionaries, healers, medicine people, nannies of orphans, and caregivers. They were respected as fundamental components of the Native American culture and societies. However, since European colonization and persecution by the church to eradicate these individuals, the two-spirit community is now often viewed as perverted, untraditional, or untrustworthy. As such, two-spirit people have lost their place in society and their dignity.

In South Asian society, the third gender is known as the *hijra*. Regarded as sacred, they perform as dancers or musicians at weddings and religious ceremonies, as well as providing blessings for health, prosperity, and fertility (Nanda, 1990). It is almost always men who become two-spirits, although there are a few cases of women assuming male roles in a similar fashion (Blackwood, 1984). Two-spirits are often considered shamans, individuals who possess great spiritual power.

Among the Zuni of New Mexico, two-spirits are considered a third gender (Roscoe, 1991). Despite the existence of transgender people and those born with disorders of sexual development (e.g., two testes or two ovaries but an ambiguous genital appearance), Westerners tend to view gender as only biological, an incorrect assumption. The Zuni, in contrast, believe that gender is socially acquired.

American Indian two-spirits were suppressed by missionaries and the U.S. government and were considered "unnatural" or "perverted." As a result of cultural genocide and other factors, some Native American communities now regard homophobia and sexism as common. This relatively new and unfortunate set of beliefs makes some who identify as Native American and queer feel both isolated and unsupported (Laframboise & Anhorn, 2008).

In some cultures, men who dress or identify as women are considered shamans. We'wha was a Zuni two-spirit who lived in the nineteenth century.

History Archives/Alamy Stock Photo

Crossing Gender Normative Categories   In a few non-Western cultures, **androphilic** males, those who are attracted to and aroused by adult males, often cross-gender normative categories to assume roles that are usually associated with women (VanderLaan et al., 2015). (Note that the term **gynephilia** refers to sexual attraction to and arousal by adult females.) These include, but are not limited to, the *woubi* of the Ivory Coast, the *xanith* of Oman, the *kathoey* of Thailand, and the *muxas* of Mexico. In Samoa, a person self-identified as *fa'afafine,* meaning "in the manner of a woman," report elevated willingness to invest time in raising their nieces and nephews, a responsibility typically designed for Samoan women. Most fa'afafine enjoy a high level of acceptance both within their families and Samoan society. From a Western culture perspective, a fa'afafine would be viewed as transgender male; a term not used in the Samoan culture to describe this phenomenon.

● Societal Norms and Sexuality

The immense diversity of sexual behaviors across cultures and times immediately calls into question the appropriateness of labeling these behaviors as *inherently* natural or unnatural, normal or abnormal. Too often, we give such labels to sexual behaviors without thinking about the basis on which we make those judgments. Such categories discourage knowledge and understanding because they are value judgments or personal evaluations of right and wrong. As such, they are not objective descriptions about behaviors but statements of how we feel about those behaviors.

Natural Sexual Behavior

How do we decide if a sexual behavior is natural or unnatural? To make this decision, we must have some standard of nature against which to compare the behavior. But what is "nature"? On the abstract level, nature is the essence of all things in the universe. Or, personified as nature, it is the force regulating the universe. These definitions, however, do not help us much in trying to establish what is natural or unnatural.

When we asked our students to identify their criteria for determining which sexual behaviors they considered "natural" or "unnatural," we received a variety of responses, including the following:

- "If a person feels something instinctive, I believe it is a natural feeling."
- "Natural and unnatural have to do with the laws of nature. What these parts were intended for."
- "I decide by my gut instincts."
- "I think all sexual activity is natural as long as it doesn't hurt you or anyone else."
- "Everything possible is natural. Everything natural is normal. If it is natural and normal, it is moral."

When we label sexual behavior as "natural" or "unnatural," we are typically indicating whether the behavior conforms to our culture's sexual norms. **Heteronormativity** is the most pervasive view of sexuality: the belief that heterosexuality is normal, natural, and superior to all other expressions of sexuality. Our sexual norms appear natural because we have internalized them since infancy. These norms are part of the cultural air we breathe, and, like the air, they are invisible. We have learned our culture's rules so well that they have become a "natural" part of our personality, a "second nature" to us. They seem "instinctive."

Normal Sexual Behavior

"The greatest pleasure in life is doing what people say you cannot do."

—Walter Bagehot (1826–1877)

Closely related to the idea that sexual behavior is natural or unnatural is the belief that sexuality is either normal or abnormal. More often than not, describing behavior as "normal" or "abnormal" is merely another way of making value judgments in the ways in which people perceive and appraise sexuality. Psychologist Sandra Pertot (2007) quips, "Normal today means that a person should have a regular and persistent physical sex drive, easy arousal, strong erections and good control over ejaculation for males, powerful orgasms, and a desire for a variety and experimentation [for women]" (p. 13). Normal has often been used to imply "healthy" or "moral" behavior. **Normal sexual behavior** is behavior that conforms to a group's

think
about it

Am I Normal?

The question "Am I normal?" seems to haunt many people. For some, it causes a great deal of unnecessary fear, guilt, and anxiety. For others, it provides the motivation to study the literature, consult with a trusted friend or therapist, or take a course in sexuality.

What is normal? We commonly use several criteria in deciding whether to label different sexual behavior "normal" or "abnormal." According to professor and psychologist Leonore Tiefer (2004), these criteria are subjective, statistical, idealistic, cultural, and clinical. Regardless of what criteria we use, they ultimately reflect societal norms.

- *Subjectively "normal" behavior.* According to this definition, normalcy is any behavior that is similar to one's own. Though most of us use this definition, few of us will acknowledge it.

- *Statistically "normal" behavior.* According to this definition, whatever behaviors are more common are normal; less common ones are abnormal. However, the fact that a behavior is not widely practiced does not make it abnormal except in a statistical sense. Fellatio (fel-AY-she-o) (oral stimulation of the penis) and cunnilingus (cun-i-LIN-gus) (oral stimulation of the female genitals), for example, are widely practiced today because they have become "acceptable" behaviors. But years ago, oral sex was tabooed as something "dirty" or "shameful."

- *Idealistically "normal" behavior.* Taking an ideal for a norm, individuals who use this approach measure all deviations against perfection. They may try to model their behavior after Christ or Gandhi, for example. Using idealized behavior as a norm can easily lead to feelings of guilt, shame, and anxiety.

- *Culturally "normal" behavior.* This is probably the standard most of us use most of the time: we accept as normal what our culture defines as normal. This measure explains why our notions of normalcy do not always agree with those of people from other countries, religions, communities, and historical periods. Men who kiss in public may be considered normal in one place but abnormal in another. It is common for "deviant" behavior to be perceived as dangerous and frightening in a culture that rejects it.

- *Clinically "normal" behavior.* The clinical standard uses scientific data about health and illness to make judgments. For example,

the presence of the syphilis bacterium in body tissues or blood is considered abnormal because it indicates that a person has a sexually transmitted infection. Regardless of time or place, clinical definitions should stand the test of time. The four criteria mentioned previously are all somewhat arbitrary—that is, they depend on individual or group opinion—but the clinical criterion has more objectivity.

These five criteria form the basis of what we usually consider "normal" behavior. Often, the different definitions and interpretations of "normal" conflict with one another. How does a person determine whether he or she is normal if subjectively "normal" behavior—what that person actually does—is inconsistent with his or her ideals? How could our ideas about what we consider to be "normal" sexual functioning be altered if we knew that diversity, not homogeneity, was more characteristic of real-life sexual behavior? Such dilemmas are commonplace and lead many people to question their normalcy. However, they should not question their normalcy as much as their *concept* of normalcy.

Think Critically

1. How do you define "normal" sexual behavior? What criteria did you use to create this definition?

2. How do your sexual attitudes, values, and behaviors compare to what you believe are "normal" sexual behaviors? If they are different, how do you reconcile these? If they are similar, how do you feel about others who may not share them?

3. In Nepal, some young women are isolated for one week during their first menses, whereas in Brazil, it is common to see men embrace or kiss in public. What are your thoughts about how other cultures define normality?

Source: Tiefer, L. (2004).

typical patterns of behavior. Normality has nothing to do with moral or psychological deviance. Rather, the term is often used when one is critical of one's partner and wants to "wheel in the heavy artillery of 'you're not normal. I'm normal'" (Klein, 2012).

Ironically, although we may feel pressure to behave like the average person (the statistical norm), most of us don't actually know how others behave sexually. People

Kissing is "natural" and "normal" in our culture. It is an expression of intimacy, love, and passion for young and old, and persons of all sexual orientations.

(Female couple lying together on couch) Thinkstock/Getty Images; (Senior man kissing his wife) Ronnie Kaufman/Blend Images; (interracial kissing) Christopher Kerrigan/McGraw-Hill Education; (Couple kissing) Stockbyte/Getty Images

don't ordinarily reveal much about their sexual activities. If they do, they generally reveal only their most conformist sexual behaviors, such as **sexual intercourse**, or the movement of bodies while the penis is in the vagina; sometimes penis-anus behavior is considered sexual intercourse. They rarely disclose their masturbatory activities, sexual fantasies, or anxieties or feelings of guilt. All that most people present of themselves—unless we know them well—is the conventional self that masks their actual sexual feelings, attitudes, and behaviors.

The guidelines most of us have for determining our normality are given to us by our friends, partners, and parents (who usually present conventional sexual images of themselves) through stereotypes, media images, religious teachings, customs, and cultural norms. None of these, however, tell us much about how people *actually* behave. Because we don't know how people really behave, it is easy for us to imagine that we are abnormal if we differ from our cultural norms and stereotypes. We wonder if our desires, fantasies, and activities are normal: Is it normal to fantasize? To masturbate? To enjoy erotica? To be attracted to someone of the same sex? Some of us believe that everyone else is "normal" and that only we are "sick" or "abnormal" (or vice versa). The challenge, of course, is to put aside our cultural indoctrination and try to understand sexual behaviors objectively.

Because culture determines what is normal, there is a vast range of normal behaviors across different cultures. What is considered the normal sexual urge for the Dani would send most of us into therapy for treatment of low sexual desire. And the idea of teaching sexual skills to early adolescents, as the Mangaia do, would horrify most American parents.

think
about it

Declaration of Sexual Rights

Sexuality is an integral part of the personality of every human being. Since health is a fundamental human right, so must sexual health be recognized, promoted, respected, and defended by all societies and through all means. Sexual health is the result of an environment that recognizes, respects, and exercises these rights.

1. **The right to equality and nondiscrimination.** Everyone is entitled to enjoy all sexual rights set forth in this Declaration without distinction of any kind.

2. **The right to life, liberty, and security of the person.** This right cannot be arbitrarily threatened, limited, or taken away for reasons related to sexuality. These include: sexual orientation, consensual sexual behavior and practices, gender identity and expression, or because of accessing or providing services related to sexual and reproductive health.

3. **The right to autonomy and bodily integrity.** Everyone has the right to control and decide freely on matters related to their sexuality and their body. This includes the choice of sexual behaviors, practices, partners, and relationships with due regard to the rights of others.

4. **The right to be free from torture and cruel, inhumane, or degrading treatment or punishment.** This right includes traditional practices, forced sterilization, contraception, or abortion; and other forms of torture, cruel, inhumane, or degrading treatment perpetrated for any reason.

5. **The right to be free from all forms of violence and coercion.** This right includes rape, sexual abuse, sexual harassment, bullying, sexual exploitation and slavery, trafficking for purposes of sexual exploitation, virginity testing, and violence.

6. **The right to privacy.** Everyone has the right to privacy related to sexuality, sexual life, and choices regarding their own body and consensual sexual relations and practices without arbitrary interference and intrusion.

7. **The right to the highest attainable standard of health, including sexual health; with the possibility of pleasurable, satisfying, and safe sexual experiences.** This requires the accessibility to quality health services and access to the conditions that influence health including sexual health.

8. **The right to enjoy the benefits of scientific progress and its application.** This right is inclusive of sexuality and sexual health.

9. **The right to information.** Everyone shall have access to scientifically accurate and understandable information related to sexuality, sexual health, and sexual rights through diverse sources.

10. **The right to education and the right to comprehensive sexuality education.** Comprehensive sexuality education must be age appropriate, scientifically accurate, culturally competent, and grounded in human rights, gender equality, and a positive approach to sexuality and pleasure.

11. **The right to enter, form, and dissolve marriage and other similar types of relationships based on equality and full and free consent.** All persons are entitled to equal rights entering into, during, and at dissolution of marriage, partnership, and other similar relationships without discrimination or exclusion of any kind.

12. **The right to decide whether to have children, the number and spacing of children, and to have the information and means to do so.** To exercise this right requires access to the conditions that influence and determine health and well-being.

13. **The right to freedom of thought, opinion, and expression.** Everyone has the right to express their own sexuality with due respect to the rights of others.

14. **The right to freedom of association and peaceful assembly.** Everyone has the right to peacefully demonstrate and advocate, including about sexuality, sexual health, and sexual rights.

15. **The right to participation in public and political life.** Everyone is entitled to an environment that enables active, free, and meaningful participation in all aspects of human life.

16. **The right to access to justice, remedies, and redress.** This right requires effective, adequate, accessible, and appropriate educative, legislative, judicial, and other measures.

Think Critically

1. What are your reactions to the "Declaration of Sexual Rights"? For whom should these rights be promoted? Would you delete, edit, or add rights to this list?

2. Why do you suppose such a declaration is necessary and important?

3. What (if any) consequences should there be for governments, cultures, or individuals who do not follow these rights?

Are there behaviors, however, that are considered essential to sexual functioning and consequently universally labeled as normal? Not surprisingly, **reproduction**, or the biological process by which individuals are produced, is probably one shared view of normal sexual behavior that most cultures would agree upon. All other beliefs about sexual expression and behavior develop from social context.

Sexual Behavior and Variations

Sex researchers have generally rejected the traditional sexual dichotomies of natural/unnatural, normal/abnormal, moral/immoral, and good/bad. Regarding the word *abnormal,* sociologist Ira Reiss (1989) writes:

> We need to be aware that people will use those labels to put distance between themselves and others they dislike. In doing so, these people are not making a scientific diagnosis but are simply affirming their support of certain shared concepts of proper sexuality.

Instead of classifying behavior into what are essentially moralistic normal/abnormal and natural/unnatural categories, researchers view human sexuality as characterized by **sexual variation**—that is, sexual variety and diversity. As humans, we vary enormously in terms of our sexual orientation, our desires, our fantasies, our attitudes, and our behaviors. This variation was noted by Alfred Kinsey and his colleagues (1948) who succinctly stated: "The world is not to be divided into sheep and goats."

Researchers believe that the best way to understand our sexual diversity is to view our activities as existing on a continuum. On this continuum, the frequency with which individuals engage in different sexual activities (e.g., sexual intercourse, masturbation, and oral sex) ranges from never to always. Significantly, there is no point on the continuum that marks normal or abnormal behavior. In fact, the difference between one individual and the next on the continuum is minimal (Kinsey et al., 1948; Kinsey et al., 1953). The most that can be said of a person is that their behaviors are more or less typical or atypical of the group average, whatever that group may be. Furthermore, nothing can be inferred about an individual whose behavior differs significantly from the group average other than their behavior is atypical. Except for engaging in sexually atypical behavior, one person may be indistinguishable from any other.

Many activities that are usually thought of as "deviant" or "abnormal" sexual behavior—activities diverging from the norm, such as exhibitionism, voyeurism, and fetishism—are engaged in by most of us to some degree. We may delight in displaying our bodies on the beach (exhibitionism) or in "twerking" in crowded clubs. We may like watching ourselves having sex, viewing erotic scenes, or seeing our partner undress (voyeurism). Or we may enjoy kissing our lover's photograph, keeping a lock of his or her hair, or sleeping with an article of his or her clothing (fetishism). Most of the time, these feelings or activities are only one aspect of our sexual selves; they are not especially significant in our overall sexuality. Such atypical behaviors represent nothing more than sexual nonconformity when they occur between mutually consenting adults and do not cause distress.

"Imagination is more important than knowledge."

—Albert Einstein (1879–1955)

The rejection of natural/unnatural, normal/abnormal, and moral/immoral categories by sex researchers does not mean that standards for evaluating sexual behavior do not exist. There are many sexual behaviors that are harmful to oneself (e.g., masturbatory asphyxia—suffocating or hanging oneself during masturbation to increase sexual arousal) and to others (e.g., rape, child molestation, and obscene phone calls). Current psychological standards for determining the harmfulness of sexual behaviors center around the issues of coercion, potential harm to oneself or others, and personal distress.

We, the authors, believe that the basic standard for judging various sexual activities is whether they are between consenting adults and are expressed in sharing, enhancing, and nonexploitive ways. Understanding diverse sexual attitudes, motives, behaviors, and values will help deepen our own value systems and help us understand, accept, and appreciate our own sexuality and that of others.

Peopleimages/iStock/Getty Images

Sexuality can be a source of great pleasure and profound satisfaction as well as a source of guilt and means of exploitation. Popular culture both encourages and discourages sexuality. It promotes stereotypical sexual interactions but fails to touch on the deeper significance sexuality holds for us or the risks and responsibilities that accompany it. Love and sexuality in a committed relationship are infrequently depicted, in contrast to casual sex. The media often ignore or disparage the wide array of sexual behaviors and choices—from masturbation to gay, lesbian, bisexual, transgender, and queer relationships—that are significant in many people's lives. They discourage the linking of sex and intimacy, contraceptive responsibility, and the acknowledgment of the risk of contracting sexually transmitted infections.

What is clear from examining other cultures is that sexual behaviors and norms vary from culture to culture and, within our own society, from one time to another. The variety of sexual behaviors even within our own culture testifies to diversity not only between cultures but within cultures as well. Understanding diversity allows us to acknowledge that there is no such thing as inherently "normal" or "natural" sexual behavior, but behaviors that are typical or atypical in a group. Sexual behavior is strongly influenced by culture—including our own.

Summary

Studying Human Sexuality

- Students study sexuality for a variety of reasons. Examining the multiple aspects of this fascinating topic can help students understand, accept, and appreciate their own sexuality and that of others.

Sexuality, Popular Culture, and the Media

- The media are among the most powerful forces in people's lives today. Mass-media depictions of sexuality are meant primarily to entertain and exploit, not to inform.

- The Internet's contributions to the availability and commercialization of sex and sexuality information have made it easy for individuals to obtain information, strengthen social ties, and provide sexual gratification.

- Digital media and television are the most prevalent and pervasive media. At the same time, the risks and responsibilities that accompany this programming remain disproportionate to the sexual images that are portrayed.

- The popularity and accessibility of digital media and technology, including Internet social networking sites (SNS), have allowed individuals to present themselves publicly in ways that were previously never possible.

Sexuality Across Cultures and Times

- One of the most powerful forces shaping human sexuality is culture. Culture molds and shapes our *sexual interests.*

- The Mangaia of Polynesia and the Dani of New Guinea represent cultures at the opposite ends of a continuum, with the Mangaia having an elaborate social and cultural framework for instructing adolescents in sexual technique and the Dani downplaying the importance of sex.

- Middle-class Americans in the nineteenth century believed that men had strong sexual drives but that women had little sexual desire. Because sexuality was considered animalistic, the Victorians separated sex and love. The sexual revolution brought significant changes to previous assumptions about sexuality.

- *Sexual orientation* is a complex, multidimensional construct composed of sexual identity, attraction and behavior. In contemporary America, *heterosexuality,* or emotional or sexual attraction between men and women, is the only sexual orientation that receives full societal legitimacy. *Homosexuality* refers to emotional and sexual attraction to an individual of the same sex or gender, *bisexuality* involves emotional and sexual attraction to two or more genders, and *asexuality* is a state of having no sexual attraction to anyone, or low or absent sexual activity.

- In ancient Greece, same-sex relationships between men represented the highest form of love. Among the Sambians of New Guinea, boys have sexual contact with older boys, believing that the ingestion of semen is required for growth. When the girls to whom they are betrothed reach puberty, adolescent boys cease these same-sex sexual relations.

- The socially constructed roles, behaviors, activities, and attributes that a society assigns to a person is called *gender*. While culture helps shape masculinity or femininity, biology defines men and women.

- A *two-spirit* is a person of one sex who identifies with the other sex; in some communities, such as the Zuni, a two-spirit is considered a third gender and is believed to possess great spiritual power.

Societal Norms and Sexuality

- Sexuality tends to be evaluated according to categories of natural/unnatural, normal/abnormal, and moral/immoral. These terms are value judgments, reflecting social norms rather than any quality inherent in the behavior itself.

- *Heteronormativity* is probably the most pervasive view of sexuality. It is the belief that heterosexuality is normal, natural, and superior to all other expressions of sexuality.

- There is no commonly accepted definition of natural sexual behavior. *Normal sexual behavior* is what a culture defines as normal. We commonly use five criteria to categorize sexual behavior as normal or abnormal: subjectively normal, statistically normal, idealistically normal, culturally normal, and clinically normal.

- Human sexuality is characterized by *sexual variation*. Researchers believe that the best way to examine sexual behavior is on a continuum. Many activities that are considered deviant sexual behavior exist in most of us to some degree. These include exhibitionism, voyeurism, and fetishism.

- Behaviors are not abnormal or unnatural; rather, they are more or less typical or atypical of the group average. Many of those whose behaviors are atypical may be regarded as sexual nonconformists rather than as abnormal or perverse.

Questions for Discussion

- At what age do you believe a young person should be given a smartphone? What, if any, type of education should accompany it?

- To what extent do you think your peers are influenced by the media? How does it affect you?

- While growing up, what sexual behaviors did you consider to be normal? Abnormal? How have these views changed now that you are older?

Sex and the Internet
Sex and the Media

With hundreds of millions of sexuality-related websites available, you might wonder about the issues and laws associated with access to cyberspace. Though the following sites each deal primarily with intellectual freedom, they also contain information and links to other sites that address issues of sex and the media. Select one of the following:

- Electronic Frontier Foundation **https://www.eff.org**

- Entertainment Software Rating Board **https://www.esrb.org/**

- National Coalition for Sexual Freedom **https://ncsfreedom.org**

- Pew Research Internet Project **https://www.pewresearch.org/internet/**

Go to the site and answer the following questions:

- What is the mission of the site—if any?

- Who are its supporters and advocates?

- Who is its target audience?

- What is its predominant message?

- What current issue is it highlighting?

Given what you have learned about this site, how do your feelings about sex and the Internet compare with those of the creators of this website?

Suggested Websites

National LGBTQ Task Force
www.thetaskforce.org
Helps to build the grassroots power of the LGBTQ+ community by training activists, organizing campaigns, and providing research and policy analysis to support equality.

Savvy Cyber Kids
www.savvycyberkids.org
Focused on online safety and available for families and educators.

SIECUS: Sex Ed for Social Change
www.siecus.org
Educates, advocates, and informs about sexuality and sexual and reproductive health.

World Association for Sexual Health
www.worldsexualhealth.net
Promotes sexual health throughout the world by developing and supporting the field of human sexuality and sexual rights for all.

Suggested Reading

Airton, L. (2018). *Gender: Your guide.* Adams Media. An accessible guide to understanding and engaging in gender conversation.

Dines, G., Humez, J. M., Yousman, W. E., & Bindig, L. B. (2017). *Gender, race, and class in media: A critical reader* (5th ed.). Sage Publishing. An analysis of media entertainment culture.

Francoeur, R. T., & Noonan, R. (Eds.). (2010). *The continuum complete international encyclopedia of sexuality.* Oxford University Press. The foremost reference work on sexual behavior throughout the world.

Holleb, M. L. E. (2019). *The A–Z of gender and sexuality: From ace to ze.* Jessica Kingsley Publishers. An accessible and engaging text of the evolving terminology used to navigate gender, sexuality, and the relationships between them.

Rosewarne, L. (2016). *Intimacy on the Internet: Media representations of online connections.* Routledge. Media representations are categorized and analyzed to explore what they reveal about the intersection of gender, sexuality, technology, and the changing mores regarding intimacy.

Sales, N. J. (2016). *American girls: Social media and the secret lives of teenagers.* Vintage Books. Though limited by its single-gender focus, the author discusses the ways in which the sexual behavior of teenagers is being changed and shaped by new technology, including the influence of online porn.

Strasburger, V. C., Wilson, B. J., & Jordan, A. B. (2014). *Children, adolescents, and the media* (3rd ed.). Sage. Explores mass media, including the sexual messages the media convey and their impact on adolescents.

Tiefer, L. (2004). *Sex is not a natural act and other essays* (2nd ed.). Westview Press. A revised collection of provocative essays on sex and its many meanings in our culture.

chapter

2

Studying Human Sexuality

CHAPTER OUTLINE

Sex, Advice Columnists, and Pop Psychology

Thinking Objectively About Sexuality

Sex Research Methods

The Sex Researchers

Contemporary Research Studies

Hero/Corbis/Glow Images

Student Voices

"I've heard about those sex surveys, and I wonder how truthful they are. I mean, don't you think that people who volunteer for those studies only report behaviors that they deem socially acceptable? I just don't think people who lose their virginity, for instance, at age 12 or age 30, would actually report it. Besides, no sex study is going to tell me what I should do or whether I am normal."

—21-year-old male

"I took a sex survey once, during my undergraduate years. I found that the survey was easy to take, and the process of answering the questions actually led me to ask myself more questions about my sexual self. The survey was detailed, and I was encouraged to answer truthfully. Ultimately, every answer I gave was accurate because I knew that the research would benefit science and it was completely anonymous."

—22-year-old female

"I feel that sexual research is a benefit to our society. The human sexuality class I took my sophomore year in college taught me a lot. Without research, many of the topics we learned about would not have been so thoroughly discussed, due to lack of information. Sexual research and human sexuality classes help keep the topic of sex from being seen as such a faux pas by society."

—20-year-old female

"I think sex research is great because it helps remove the taboo from the topic. Sex, in this country, is on TV, on the Internet, and in movies all the time, but people do not want to seriously discuss it, especially adults with children. Sex research, when made public, can help ease the tension of discussing sex—especially when it reveals that something considered abnormal actually is normal and that many people practice the specific behavior."

—24-year-old male

"A NEW UNIVERSITY STUDY FINDS that many college students lie to a new sexual partner about their sexual past . . . but first, a message from. . . ." So begins a commercial lead-in on the news, reminding us that sex research is often part of both news and entertainment. In fact, most of us learn about the results of sex research from television, the newspapers, the Internet, and magazines rather than from scholarly journals and books. After all, the mass media are more entertaining than most scholarly works. And unless we are studying human sexuality, few of us have the time or interest to read the scholarly journals in which scientific research is regularly published.

But how accurate is what the mass media tell us about sex and sex research? In this chapter, we discuss the dissemination of sexuality-related information by the various media. Then we look at the critical-thinking skills that help us evaluate how we discuss and think about sexuality. When are we making objective statements? When are we reflecting biases or opinions? Next, we examine sex research methods because they are critical to the scientific study of human sexuality. Then we look at some of the leading sex researchers to see how they have influenced our understanding of sexuality. Next, we discuss five national studies as examples of important research that has been conducted. Finally, we examine feminist scholarship.

"Discovery consists of seeing what everybody has seen and thinking what nobody has thought."

—Albert Szent-Györgyi (1893–1986)

"Science gathers knowledge faster than society gathers wisdom."

—Isaac Asimov (1920–1992)

● Sex, Advice Columnists, and Pop Psychology

As we've seen, the mass media convey seemingly endless sexual images. Besides various television, film, Internet, and advertising genres, there is another genre, which we might call the **sex information/advice genre**, which transmits information and norms, rather than images, about sexuality to a mass audience to both inform and entertain in a simplified manner. For many college students, as well as others, the sex information/advice genre is a major source of their knowledge about sex. This genre is ostensibly concerned with transmitting information that is factual and accurate. In addition, on an increasing number of college campuses, sex columns in student-run newspapers have become popular and sometimes controversial, as some college administrators have been concerned that the information provided is too explicit.

Information and Advice as Entertainment

Newspaper columns, Internet sites, syndicated radio shows, magazine articles, and TV programs share several features. First, their primary purpose is financial profit. This goal is in marked contrast to the primary purpose of scholarly research, which is to increase knowledge. Even the inclusion of survey questionnaires in magazines asking readers about their sexual attitudes or behaviors is ultimately designed to promote sales. We fill out the questionnaires for fun, much as we would crossword puzzles or anagrams. Then we buy the subsequent issue or watch a later program to see how we compare to other respondents.

Second, the success of media personalities rests not so much on their expertise as on their ability to present information as entertainment. Because the genre seeks to entertain, sex information and advice must be simplified. Complex explanations and analyses must be avoided because they would interfere with the entertainment purpose. Furthermore, the genre relies on high-interest or bizarre material to attract readers, viewers, and listeners. Consequently, we are more likely to read, view, or hear stories about unusual sexual behaviors or ways to increase sexual attractiveness than stories about new research methods or the negative outcomes of sexual stereotyping.

Third, the genre focuses on how-to information and often on morality. Sometimes it mixes information and normative judgments. How-to material tells us how to improve our sex lives. Advice columnists often give advice on issues of sexual morality: "Is it all right to have sex without commitment?", "Yes, if you love the person," or "No, casual sex is empty," and so on. These columnists act as moral arbiters, much as ministers, priests, and rabbis do.

Fourth, the genre uses the trappings of social science and psychiatry without their substance. Writers and columnists interview social scientists and therapists to give an aura of scientific authority to their material. They rely especially heavily on therapists, whose background is clinical rather than academic. Because clinicians tend to deal with people with problems, they often see the problematic aspects of sexuality.

The line between media sex experts and advice columnists is often blurred. This line is especially obscure on the Internet, where websites dealing with sexuality have proliferated. Most of these sites are purely for entertainment rather than education, and it can be difficult to determine a site's credibility. One way to assess the educational value of a website is to investigate its sponsor. Reputable national organizations like the American Psychological Association (http://www.apa.org) provide reliable information.

The Use and Abuse of Research Findings

To reinforce their authority, the media often incorporate statistics from a study's findings, which are key features of social science research. Further, the media may report the results of a study that are contradicted by subsequent research. It is common, particularly in the medical field, for the original results not to be replicated when continued research is conducted (Tanner, 2005). For example, a review of major studies published in three influential medical journals from 1990 to 2003 found that one third of the results are not confirmed (Ionannidis, 2005). But, of course, changes in "current knowledge" also happen in behavioral research. For example, an assertion that is often presented in the media as definitive is that the consumption of alcohol always leads to risky sexual behaviors. However, studies have found that among young people the relationship between alcohol use and risky sexual behaviors is complex, and often the research findings are inconsistent or inconclusive (Cooper, 2006). An alternative explanation is that a high proportion of young people take more risks than other young people in several areas such as cigarette use, drug use, alcohol use, driving, and sex and have certain personality traits such as impulsivity. That is, there is a clustering of risk behaviors representing high sensation seeking, and alcohol use alone does not cause risky sex but both are part of the total risk behavior pattern (Charnigo et al., 2013; Coleman, 2001; Coleman & Cater, 2005).

Western University sex researcher and psychologist John Sakaluk (2016) states that concerns about the replicability of social science and medical research have increased and that replication of studies is the cornerstone of good science. Sexual scientists not only conduct research to discover knowledge but also because they highly value applied science that can

"If you believe everything you read, don't read."

—Chinese proverb

"If we knew what it was we were doing, it would not be called research, would it?"

—Albert Einstein (1879–1955)

think about it

Does Sex Have an Inherent Meaning?

Some people are afraid that if sex has no inherent meaning and they do not salute it, they won't behave ethically.

—Marty Klein (1950-)

Renowned sex therapist and author Marty Klein addresses a commonly believed idea that sex has inherent meaning by provocatively stating that "sex has no inherent meaning" (Klein, 2012). He states that individuals can make their sexual experiences meaningful but that sex is meaningless until and unless they give it meaning. Klein continues by noting that many people give sex too much meaning and often the wrong type of meaning. When sex has too much meaning, too much is riding on each sexual encounter, producing both pressure and anxiety that interferes with pleasurable and rewarding sexual expression.

The meanings of sexuality are derived from the religious, political, ethical, and legal interpretations of sexuality, reflecting how culture describes why we have sex. Some meanings or distinctive purposes of human sexual expression commonly held include the following:

- What individuals do when they love each other
- The ultimate expression of love
- A divine gift to humans
- A validation of our identities as a person
- A supreme gift to another person
- A method of strengthening a relationship
- A way of fulfilling desire

Historically, the naming and categorization of sexual behaviors have reflected efforts to "normalize" specific sexual behavior and to label unsanctioned behavior as abnormal, resulting in many persons being stigmatized. The variation of sexual expression was not recognized or endorsed. An example of efforts to attach meaning to sexuality is the "invention of heterosexuality" and heterosexual-homosexual dichotomization of sexual orientation.

In her book *Straight: The Surprisingly Short History of Heterosexuality,* author Hanne Blank (2012) states that the term *heterosexuality* first appeared in the medical literature in 1869, offering a way to validate and support the religious priorities of heterosexual marriage and to be a synonym of "sexually normal." Blank contends that normal is not a mode of eternal truth but a mechanism to describe commonness and conformity to expectations. She continues by noting:

> The original creation of "heterosexual" and "homosexual" had nothing to do with scientists or science at all. Nor did it have anything to do with biology or medicine. There is, biomedically speaking, nothing about what human beings do sexually that requires that something like what we now think of as "sexual orientation" exists. Virtually everyone alive today, especially in the developed world, has lived their entire lives in a culture of sexuality that assumes that "heterosexual" and "homosexual" are objectively real elements of nature (Blank, 2012, pp. xiv–xvi).

As described in this chapter, Alfred C. Kinsey ordered individuals on a 0–6 scale instead of the binary heterosexual-homosexual model or triad model of homosexual, bisexual, and heterosexual. His scale shifted the perspective and conversation about the classification of sexual behavior toward a focus on multiple varieties and combinations of sexual desire, behavior, and fantasy, resulting in variation being more culturally, scientifically, and politically determined to be normal (Drucker, 2014). In speaking about the diversity of sexual orientation, Kinsey said:

> Males [similarly for females] do not represent two discrete populations, heterosexual and homosexual. The world is not to be divided into sheep and goats. Not all things are black and white. It is a fundamental of taxonomy that nature rarely deals with discrete categories. Only the human mind invents categories and tries to force facts into separated pigeon-holes. The living world is a continuum in each and every one of its aspects. The sooner we learn this concerning human sexual behavior the sooner we shall reach a sound understanding of the realities of sex (Kinsey et al., 1948, p. 639).

Klein contends that when people believe that sex has inherent meaning they want to experience sex that fulfills the meaning, and if they don't, they assume there is something wrong with them or their partner. Some worry that they are not fulfilling some duty to "honor" sex, such as avoiding having sex "like animals." He purports that we should not be serving sex but sex should be serving us: This perspective enables one to experience a huge range of sexual feelings and meanings. Klein states:

> If we think that sex has inherent meaning and that it's our job to both find and conform to that meaning, we won't be able to see sex freshly, we won't be motivated to perceive or act counterintuitively, and we'll accept arbitrary, outside limits on our erotic activities. If you want to give sex meaning, go ahead. At the same time, remember to enjoy the freedom of playful, amoral (not immoral, *amoral*) sex (p. 157).

Think Critically

1. Do you agree with Klein's contention that sex has no inherent meaning? Explain your rationale.
2. Does sex have an inherent meaning to you? If so, what is that meaning and how did you learn it?
3. Can one believe that sex has no inherent meaning yet express sex ethically?

improve the sexual experiences of persons. Sakaluk encourages sexual scientists to begin creating ways to increase replication and replicability of studies, such as having data repositories, and then to take the initiative to implement them. He continues by stating that "The result of doing so will be more replicable sexual science that can inspire greater trust in research findings, among both scientists and lay-public alike" Replication leads to self-correction in science.

The media frequently quote or describe social science research, but they may do so in an oversimplified or distorted manner. An excellent example of distorted representation of sex-related research was some of the media coverage of the research on ram sheep by Charles Roselli, a researcher at the Oregon Health and Science University. Roselli searched for physiological explanations of why 8% of rams exclusively seek sex with other rams instead of ewes. His research was funded by the National Institutes of Health and published in major scientific journals. Following media coverage of his research, animal-rights activists, gay advocates, and others criticized the studies. A *New York Times* article in January 2007 noted that his research drew outrage based on, according to Roselli and his colleagues, "bizarre misinterpretation of what the work is about." The researchers contended that discussion of possible human implications of their findings in their reports differed from intentions of carrying the work over to humans. Critics claimed that the research could lead to altering or controlling sexual orientation. According to the *Times* article, *The Sunday Times* in London asserted, incorrectly, that Dr. Roselli found a way to "cure" homosexual rams with hormone treatment, adding that critics feared the research "could pave the way for breeding out homosexuality in humans." John Schwartz, author of the *Times* article, concluded that "the story of the gay sheep became a textbook example of the distortion and vituperation that can result when science meets the global news cycle" (Schwartz, 2007). As this example illustrates, scholars tend to qualify their findings as tentative or limited to a certain group, and they are very cautious about making generalizations. In contrast, the media tend to make results sound generalizable.

● Thinking Objectively About Sexuality

Although each of us has our own perspective, values, and beliefs regarding sexuality, as students, instructors, and researchers, we are committed to the scientific study of sexuality. Basic to any scientific study is a fundamental commitment to **objectivity**, or the observation of things as they exist in reality as opposed to our feelings or beliefs about them. Objectivity calls for us to suspend the beliefs, biases, or prejudices we have about a subject in order to understand it.

Objectivity in the study of sexuality is not always easy to achieve, for sexuality can be the focal point of powerful emotions and moral ambivalence. We experience sex very subjectively. But whether we find it easy or difficult to be objective, objectivity is the foundation for studying sexuality.

Most of us think about sex, but thinking about it critically requires us to be logical and objective. It also requires that we avoid making value judgments; put aside our opinions, biases, and stereotypes; and not fall prey to common fallacies such as egocentric and ethnocentric thinking.

Value Judgments Versus Objectivity

For many of us, objectivity about sex is difficult because our culture has traditionally viewed sexuality in moral terms: Sex is moral or immoral, right or wrong, good or bad, normal or abnormal. When examining sexuality, we tend, therefore, to make **value judgments**, evaluations based on moral or ethical standards rather than objective ones. Unfortunately, value judgments are often blinders to understanding. They do not tell us about what motivates people, how frequently they behave in a given way, or how they feel. Value judgments do not tell us anything about sexuality except how we ourselves feel. In studying human sexuality, then, we need to put aside value judgments as incompatible with the pursuit of knowledge.

How can we tell the difference between a value judgment and an objective statement? Examine the following two statements and determine which is a value judgment and which is an objective statement:

- College students should be in a committed relationship before they have sex.
- The majority of students have intimate sexual behavior with another person sometime during their college careers.

The first statement is a value judgment; the second is an objective statement. There is a simple rule of thumb for telling the difference between the two: Value judgments imply how a person *ought* to behave, whereas objective statements describe how people *actually* behave.

There is a second difference between value judgments and objective statements: Value judgments cannot be empirically validated, whereas objective statements can be. That is, the truth or accuracy of an objective statement can be measured and tested.

Opinions, Biases, and Stereotypes

Value judgments obscure our search for understanding. Opinions, biases, and stereotypes also interfere with the pursuit of knowledge.

"Don't believe everything you think."
—Byron Katie (1942–)

Opinions An **opinion** is an unsubstantiated belief or conclusion about what seems to be true according to our thoughts. Opinions are not based on accurate knowledge or concrete evidence. Because opinions are unsubstantiated, they often reflect our personal values or biases and rarely change unless we are open to verifiable facts.

Biases A **bias** is a personal leaning or inclination that reflects a prejudice in favor of or against a person, group, or thing in contrast to another. Biases lead us to select information that supports our views or beliefs while ignoring information that does not. We need not be victims, however, of our biases. We can make a concerted effort to discover what they are and overcome them. To avoid personal bias, scholars apply the objective methods of social science research.

"The human understanding when it has once adopted an opinion . . . draws all things else to support and agree with it."
—Francis Bacon (1561–1626)

Stereotypes A **stereotype** is a set of simplistic, rigidly held, overgeneralized beliefs about a particular type of individual or group of people, an idea, and so on. Stereotypical beliefs are resistant to change. Furthermore, stereotypes—especially sexual ones—are often negative.

The problem with stereotypes is that they are incomplete. They make one story the only story.
—Chimamanda Ngozi Adichie (1977–)

Common sexual stereotypes include the following:

- Men are always ready for sex.
- "Nice" women are not interested in sex.
- Women need a reason for sex; men need a place.
- Virgins are uptight and asexual.
- The relationships of gay men never last.
- Lesbian women hate men.

Psychologists believe that stereotypes structure knowledge. They affect the ways in which we process information: what we see, what we notice, what we remember, and how we explain things. Or as humorist Ashleigh Brilliant said, "Seeing is believing. I wouldn't have seen it if I hadn't believed it." A stereotype is a type of **schema**, a way in which we organize knowledge in our thought processes. Schemas help us channel or filter the mass of information we receive so that we can make sense of it. They determine what we will regard as important. Although these mental plans are useful, they can also create blind spots. With stereotypes, we see what we expect to see and ignore what we don't expect or want to see.

Sociologists point out that sexual stereotyping is often used to justify discrimination. Targets of stereotypes are usually members of subordinate social groups or individuals with limited economic resources. Sexual stereotyping is especially powerful in stigmatizing racial/ethnic populations and lesbian, gay, bisexual, transgender, and queer individuals.

"Re-examine all that you have been told. Dismiss that which insults your soul."
—Walt Whitman (1819–1892)

Ethnocentrism is the belief that one's own culture or ethnic group is superior to others. Although child marriage is prohibited in our society, it is acceptable in many cultures throughout the world, including India.

STRDEL/AFP/Getty Images

"A great many people think they are thinking when they are merely rearranging their prejudice."

—William James (1842–1910)

"All universal judgments are weak, loose, and dangerous."

—Michel de Montaigne (1533–1592)

"Be curious, not judgmental."

—Walt Whitman (1819–1892)

We all have opinions and biases, and most of us to varying degrees think stereotypically. But the commitment to objectivity requires us to become aware of our opinions, biases, and stereotypes and to put them aside in the pursuit of knowledge.

Common Fallacies: Egocentric and Ethnocentric Thinking

A **fallacy** is an error in reasoning that affects our understanding of a subject. Fallacies distort our thinking, leading us to false or erroneous conclusions. In the field of sexuality, egocentric and ethnocentric fallacies are common.

The Egocentric Fallacy   The **egocentric fallacy** is the mistaken belief that our own personal experience and values generally are held by others. On the basis of our belief in this false consensus, we use our own beliefs and values to explain the attitudes, motivations, and behaviors of others. Of course, our own experiences and values are important; they are the source of personal strength and knowledge, and they can give us insight into the experiences and values of others. But we cannot necessarily generalize from our own experience to that of others. Our own personal experiences are limited and may be unrepresentative. Sometimes, our generalizations are merely opinions or disguised value judgments.

The Ethnocentric Fallacy   The **ethnocentric fallacy**, also known as ethnocentrism, is the belief that our own ethnic group, nation, or culture is innately superior to others. **Ethnocentrism** is reinforced by opinions, biases, and stereotypes about other groups and cultures. As members of a group, we tend to share similar values and attitudes with other group members. But the mere fact that we share these beliefs is not sufficient proof of their truth.

Ethnocentrism has been increasingly evident as a reaction to the increased awareness of ethnicity, or ethnic affiliation or identity. For many Americans, a significant part of their sense of self comes from identification with their ethnic group. An ethnic group is a group of people distinct from other groups because of cultural characteristics, such as language, religion, and customs, that are transmitted from one generation to the next.

Although there was little research on ethnicity and sexuality until the 1980s, evidence suggests that there are significant ethnic variations in sexual attitudes and behavior. When data are available, the variations by ethnicity will be presented throughout this book.

Ethnocentrism results when we stereotype other cultures as "primitive," "innocent," "inferior," or "not as advanced." We may view the behavior of other peoples as strange, exotic, unusual, or bizarre, but to them it is normal. Their attitudes, behaviors, values, and beliefs form a unified sexual system that makes sense within their culture. In fact, we engage in many activities that appear peculiar to those outside our culture.

● Sex Research Methods

One of the key factors that distinguish the findings of social science from beliefs, prejudice, bias, and pop psychology is the field's commitment to the scientific method. The **scientific method** is the method by which a hypothesis is formed from impartially gathered data and tested empirically. The scientific method relies on **induction**—that is, drawing a general conclusion from specific facts. The scientific method seeks to describe the world rather than evaluate or judge it.

Although sex researchers, sometimes called **sexologists**, use the same methodology as other social scientists, they are constrained by ethical concerns and taboos that those in many other fields do not experience. Because of taboos surrounding sexuality, some traditional research methods are inappropriate (Schick et al., 2014).

Sex research, like most social science research, uses varied methodological approaches. These include clinical research, survey research (questionnaires and interviews), observational research, and experimental research. And as in many fields, no single research approach has emerged in sexual science. Further, sex researchers strive to conduct methodologically strong studies that can make their conclusions defendable. Certain standards guide their study, but it may difficult for the persons who do not conduct research to identify which standards were not adequately applied. To aid in identifying stronger from weaker studies, see Practically Speaking "Spotting Flawed Research."

Research Concerns

Researchers face two general concerns in conducting their work: (1) ethical concerns centering on the use of human beings as subjects and (2) methodological concerns regarding sampling techniques and their accuracy. Without a representative sample, the conclusions that can be drawn using these methodologies are limited.

A couple is being interviewed by a sex researcher. The face-to-face interview, one method of gathering data about sexuality, has both advantages and disadvantages.

sturti/Getty Images

Ethical Issues   A fundamental principle of research is informed consent. **Informed consent** means that people are free to decide, without coercion, whether to participate in a research study. This occurs following the full disclosure to an individual of the study purpose and the potential risks and the benefits of being a participant in the research project. Studies involving children and other minors typically require parental consent. Once a study begins, participants have the right to withdraw at any time without penalty.

Each research participant is entitled to protection from harm. All colleagues and universities have institutional review boards (IRBs), sometimes called human subject committees. A major role of the IRB committee is to minimize risk and ensure that the research procedures and topic studied will not cause harm to participants. The identity of research participants are kept confidential and participants are guaranteed anonymity. Some sex researchers have experienced difficulties in acquiring IRB approval for some research topics, thus potentially impeding scientific inquiry in human sexuality. For example, some IRBs have deemed research dealing with "sensitive topics" such as trauma and sexual activity as potentially high risk to participants, thus require more scrutiny from the IRB. However, an increasing number of studies have shown that participants in trauma and other sex-related research were not emotionally distressed by such research and, in fact contrary to some assumptions, participants found the study to be enjoyable, interesting, and valuable (Rinehart et al., 2017; Yeater et al., 2012).

Sampling   In each research approach, the choice of a sample—a portion of a larger group of people or population—is critical. To be most useful, a sample should be a **random sample**—that is, a sample collected in an unbiased way, with the selection of each member of the sample based solely on chance. Furthermore, the sample should be a **representative sample**, with a small group representing the larger group in terms of age, sex, ethnicity, socioeconomic status, sexual orientation, and so on. With a random sample, information gathered from a small group can be used to make inferences about the larger group. Samples that are not representative of the larger group are known as **biased samples** (Crosby et al., 2006).

Using samples is important. It would be impossible, for example, to study the sexual behaviors of all college students in the United States. But we could select a representative sample of college students from various schools and infer from their behavior how other college students behave. Using the same sample to infer the sexual behavior of Americans in general, however, would mean using a biased sample. We cannot generalize the sexual activities of American college students to the larger population.

"Anything more than truth would be too much."

—Robert Frost (1874–1963)

Most samples in sex research are limited for several reasons:

- They depend on volunteers. Because these samples are generally self-selected, we cannot assume that they are representative of the population as a whole. Volunteers for sex research are often more likely to be male, sexually experienced, liberal, and less religious and to have more positive attitudes toward sexuality and less sex guilt and anxiety than those who do not choose to participate (Bouchard et al., 2019; Strassberg & Lowe, 1995; Wiederman, 1999).

- An online study assessed men's and women's willingness to participate in 15 different sex research scenarios. Participants were more likely to be willing to participate in research in which they remained clothed versus being undressed with genitals exposed. Both men and women with the most positive attitudes about sexuality indicated willingness to participate in unclothed research. However, personality factors generally did not account for difference in willingness or not to expose genitals during a research study (Bouchard et al., 2019).

- Most sex research takes place in a university or college setting with student volunteers. Their sex-related attitudes, values, and behaviors may be very different from those of other adults.

- Some ethnic groups are generally underrepresented. Representative samples of African Americans, Latinos, Native Americans, Middle Eastern Americans, and some Asian Americans, for example, are not easily found because these groups are often underrepresented at the colleges and universities where subjects are generally recruited.

- The study of gay men, lesbian women, and bisexual and transgender individuals presents unique sampling issues. Are gay men, lesbian women, and bisexual individuals who have **come out**—publicly identified themselves as gay, lesbian, or bisexual— different from those who have not? How do researchers find and recruit subjects who have not come out (Dawson et al., 2019)?

Because these factors limit most studies, we must be careful in making generalizations from studies.

Clinical Research

Clinical research is the in-depth examination of an individual or group that goes to a psychiatrist, psychologist, or social worker for assistance with psychological or medical problems or disorders. Clinical research is descriptive; inferences of cause and effect cannot be drawn from it. The individual is interviewed and treated for a specific problem. At the same time the person is being treated, he or she is being studied. In their evaluations, clinicians attempt to determine what caused the disorder and how it may be treated. They may also try to infer from dysfunctional people how healthy people develop. Clinical research often focuses on atypical, unhealthy behaviors, problems related to sexuality (e.g., feeling trapped in the body of the wrong gender), and sexual function problems (e.g., lack of desire, early ejaculation, erectile difficulties, or lack of orgasm).

A major limitation of clinical research is its emphasis on **pathological behavior**, or unhealthy or diseased behavior. Such an emphasis makes clinical research dependent on cultural definitions of what is "unhealthy" or "pathological." These definitions, however, change over time and in the context of the culture being studied. For example, in the nineteenth century, masturbation was considered pathological. Physicians and clinicians went to great lengths to root it out. In the case of women, surgeons sometimes removed the clitoris. Today, masturbation is viewed more positively.

Survey Research

Survey research is a method that uses questionnaires or **interviews** to gather information. Questionnaires offer anonymity, can be completed fairly quickly, and are relatively inexpensive to administer; however, they usually do not allow an in-depth response. A person must respond with a short answer or select from a limited number of options. The limited-choices

"One of the great tragedies of life is the murder of a beautiful theory by a gang of brutal facts."

—Benjamin Franklin (1705–1790)

Answering a Sex Research Questionnaire: Motives for Feigning Orgasms Scale

To measure variables related to human sexuality, many sex researchers use standardized questionnaires; that is, those that are reliable (the questionnaire provides the same results every time it is used) and valid (the questionnaire measures what it intends to measure). One such measure is the Motives for Feigning Orgasms Scale (MFOS), which assesses motives for feigning (i.e., pretending, faking) orgasms among men and women (Seguin et al., 2015, 2020). The researchers who developed MFOS state most recent studies have focused exclusively on women and the predictors of this behavior. In the development of the questionnaire 43% of women and 17% of the men indicated that they had pretended to have an orgasm with their relationship partner. The mean age of the sample was 25 years.

The MFOS is presented below and can be valuable in determining if there are differences in pretending motives between groups of individuals (e.g., female and male, different ages, and varied sexual orientations and gender racial/ethnic groups). Furthermore, the MFOS can be taken by an individual to identify his or her pretending motives. The MFOS is designed for persons who are currently in a sexual relationship and who are feigning orgasm. If you have pretended an orgasm with a past partner, you might find the MFOS insightful. If you have never had sex nor pretended an orgasm with a partner, it still might be interesting for you to go through the questionnaire imagining in what circumstances you might pretend, thus learning what motivations you might have. Throughout the text other sexuality-related scales will be presented for you to complete.

Directions

From 1 = "not at all important" to 7 = "extremely important," please rate how important each of the following reasons were in influencing your decision to pretend to have an orgasm with your current partner (from the first time to the most recent time you pretended to have an orgasm with your current partner). Make an "x" through the chosen number.

	1 = not at all important		7 = extremely important				
MOTIVE							
I had too much to drink	1	2	3	4	5	6	7
I was too drunk	1	2	3	4	5	6	7

I was too intoxicated	1	2	3	4	5	6	7
I wanted my partner to think s/he did a good job	1	2	3	4	5	6	7
I wanted my partner to feel good about himself/herself	1	2	3	4	5	6	7
I wanted to boost my partner's self-esteem	1	2	3	4	5	6	7
I wanted to make my partner happy	1	2	3	4	5	6	7
I wanted to avoid hurting my partner's feelings	1	2	3	4	5	6	7
I felt uncomfortable with my partner	1	2	3	4	5	6	7
The sex was awkward	1	2	3	4	5	6	7
I regretted my choice of partner	1	2	3	4	5	6	7
My partner was unskilled	1	2	3	4	5	6	7
I was not in the mood	1	2	3	4	5	6	7
I did not feel like having sex	1	2	3	4	5	6	7
I felt tired and wanted to sleep	1	2	3	4	5	6	7
I wanted to avoid discussing my not having an orgasm	1	2	3	4	5	6	7
My partner seemed ready to have an orgasm	1	2	3	4	5	6	7
My partner's orgasm seemed imminent	1	2	3	4	5	6	7
I wanted to avoid appearing frigid	1	2	3	4	5	6	7
I wanted to feel or appear sexy	1	2	3	4	5	6	7
I wanted to avoid appearing abnormal or inadequate	1	2	3	4	5	6	7
I wanted to add a bit of excitement to our lovemaking	1	2	3	4	5	6	7
I wanted to avoid losing my partner	1	2	3	4	5	6	7
I wanted to reinforce a sexual technique that my partner used	1	2	3	4	5	6	7

format provides a more objective assessment than the short-answer format and results in a total score. For example, see Think About It "Answering a Sex Research Questionnaire: Motives for Feigning Orgasms Scale." Interview techniques avoid some of the shortcomings of questionnaires, as interviewers are able to probe in greater depth and follow paths suggested by the participant.

Although surveys are important sources of information, the method has several limitations, such as people may be poor reporters of their own sexual behavior:

- Some people may exaggerate their number of sexual partners; others may minimize their casual encounters. Research has suggested that normative gender role expectations for both men and women influence self-reported sexual behavior more than reports of other types of behavior. That is, people tend to lie to match cultural sexual behavior expectations about how men and women should behave. For example, men tend to overrepresent and women tend to underrepresent their number of lifetime sex partners. Both men and women reported less behaviors that are considered negative for their gender. However, gender differences in self-reporting of sexual behaviors were less likely when the individuals were pressured to be honest (Alexander & Fisher, 2003; Fisher, 2013; "Men, women lie about sex to match gender role expectations," 2013).

- Respondents generally underreport experiences that might be culturally considered deviant or immoral, such as bondage and same-sex experiences.

"Facts do not cease to exist because they are ignored."
—Aldous Huxley (1894–1963)

- Some respondents may feel uncomfortable about revealing information—such as about masturbation or fetishes—in a face-to-face interview.

- The accuracy of one's memory may fade as time passes, and providing an accurate estimation, such as how long sex lasted, may be difficult. One study found that when self-reported information from individuals is sought, persons can identify each instance of behavior when recalling low frequencies of behaviors and small number of sexual partners. However, when persons recall high frequencies of behaviors, they usually give general impressions or rate-based estimates of behavior frequency. The researchers recommended for valid and reliable assessment that researchers should ask respondents to recall sexual behavior in small chunks through the use of an interview or other specific prompts (Bogart et al., 2007).

- Individuals of some ethnic groups and sexual orientations may be reluctant to reveal sexual information about themselves. For example, a study of sexual and gender minority youth ages 14–17 who completed an online survey of their sexual behavior and sexual and gender minority status found that most would not have participated in the study if guardian permission was required. They cited negative parental attitudes about adolescent sexuality and sexual and gender minority issues and currently not being "out" about their identity as reasons for their hesitancy (Macapagal et al., 2017). However, this reluctance changes if these and similar groups begin to feel safer in providing personal data. For example, research has shown that policies recognizing same-sex relationships, such as hospital visitation and domestic partnerships, may encourage women to report a sexual minority orientation (Charlton et al., 2016).

- Interviewers may allow their own preconceptions to influence the way in which they frame questions and to bias their interpretations of responses.

- The interviewer's sex, race, religion, age, or sexual orientation may also influence how comfortable respondents are in disclosing information about themselves. To test this, college men and women were asked to anonymously report their sexual behavior after being interviewed by either a male or female assistant and after reading a fictitious statement about gender differences in sexuality. With female research assistants (but not with male assistants), men reported a greater number of past sexual partners when they were told that women are now more sexually permissive than men (Fisher, 2007).

- Because of vague terminology sometimes used by sex researchers in assessing sexual behavior, such as "How many sex partners did you have in the past year?", research participants may not be sure how to respond. To learn more about the challenges researchers face in choosing terminology, see Think About It, "A Challenge Facing Sex Researchers: Selecting the Best Way to Measure Sexual Behavior, Sexual Orientation, and Gender Identity."

A Challenge Facing Sex Researchers: Selecting the Best Way to Measure Sexual Behavior, Sexual Orientation, and Gender Identity

If you were asked on a sex questionnaire if you have had "sex" in the past year or to indicate your sexual orientation and gender identity, how would you answer? Maybe you have a clear understanding of these terms, but not all persons may have the same interpretation. Though these and other sexuality-related terms are commonly used in survey research in human sexuality, they are not always defined by the researcher nor understood by the research participant. The terminology used in sex research to measure sexual behavior and sexual orientation, sexual attraction, and gender identity is often ambiguous, incomplete, and open to interpretation, and may be misunderstood, especially among those with lower levels of reading comprehension and language barriers.

One study of 34 graduate and undergraduate university students' views on and perspectives with choosing sexual orientation (SO) and gender identity (GI) labels in the health care setting. Nearly half of the participants indicated that they used different labels to describe their SO or GI on health care forms, depending on the context. They also reported that choosing a term that was not congruent to their lived experience was not only inaccurate but could also be alienating and painful (Scheffey et al., 2019). Because of these possible barriers, respondents may not provide an answer that accurately reflects their sexuality, thus threatening the validity of the study findings. Studies of the same research issue may not use similar terminologies or definitions of sexual behavior, making the comparisons of study findings from different studies problematic (Wolff et al., 2016). Here are some examples of the issues sex researchers face in measuring sexual behavior:

- Studies have shown that even though the vast majority of persons consider penile-vaginal or penile-anal intercourse as "having sex," other behaviors such as oral sex and manually stimulating genitals were considered as "having sex" by some respondents (Randall & Beyers, 2003; Sanders et al., 2010; Sanders & Reinish, 1999; Schick et al., 2016; Sewell & Strassberg, 2015). Often the responses differed by gender, age, and sexual orientation. Gay men from the United States and those from the United Kingdom reported differing opinions of what constitutes "having sex" (Hill et al., 2010). In one study of adults residing in Indiana, many more women than men considered oral sex as having "had sex" (see in Chapter 9 Think About It, "You Would Say You 'Had Sex If You . . .'") (Yarber et al., 2007).

- Accurately responding to sexual behavior questions may be difficult for sexual minority groups given the heteronormative standard that real "sex" is defined as penile-vaginal intercourse. For example, these women may not interpret using a sex toy during sex play as actually "having sex" (Malacad & Hess, 2011).

- Vague terms such as *sex, sexual relations, sexual contact,* and *foreplay* are sometimes not defined (Malacad & Hess, 2011). Research has shown that adolescents often find sexual behavior terms, such as *sexual contact,* confusing when they are not defined (Austin et al., 2007). Some individuals, including

non-LGBTQ+ respondents, those of lower educational level, and non-native English speaking persons, may not know what the term *heterosexual* means and even though being heterosexual they may indicate "other" for sexual orientation (Berg & Lien, 2006; Ridolfo et al., 2012).

- Researchers present a time frame when asking the respondent if they participated in a certain sexual behavior: for example, during most recent sexual event, in the past 30 days, in the past 12 months, during lifetime. The time frame chosen by the researchers may result in an inaccurate response. For example, because some individuals report a fluidity of their sexuality (Diamond, 2008), asking the person the sex of their most recent sexual partner may not reflect their sexuality over time. Thus, a possible misclassification of that individual could occur.

One of the most difficult challenges faced by sex researchers is the measurement of sexual orientation and sexual attraction, both complex and multidimensional constructs.

- Researcher Margaret Wolff and colleagues (2016) found inadequate and inconsistent measures of sexual orientation, resulting in misunderstanding of sexual minority status. This, in turn, may result in public health resources being inadequately allocated to these groups. A one-dimensional measurement of sexual orientation can result in erroneous conclusions of sexual identity, attraction and behavior, and associated health outcomes (Badgett, 2009; Meyer & Wilson, 2009). Sexual attraction is a particularly complicated phenomenon; hence, research that measures sexual attraction should expand beyond assessing attractions toward people identifying as binary or a single identity (Fu et al., 2019).

- An Institute of Medicine (IOM) report on LGBTQ+ health (2011) recommends the development and standardization of sexual orientation measures that is usually utilized in the public health and social science literature; that is, sexual orientation has three components: sexual identity, sexual attraction, and sexual behavior.

- In the past, the gender question was binary; that is, the person had to make a choice between male/man and female/woman. This approach to assessing gender excluded individuals who identify as non-binary (i.e., not exclusively male or female) and does not distinguish cisgender persons from gender minorities, such as transgender, non-binary, and gender non-conforming persons (Diamond et al., 2011; Haupert et al., 2020; IOM, 2001; Joel et al., 2014; Kuper et al., 2012). Two standardized measures have been published that are designed to capture gender minorities and they are briefly described here to give you an idea of how these scales address gender. The New Multidimensional Sex/Gender Measure (Bauer et al., 2017) has three core items that assess sex assigned at birth, gender identity, and lived gender which is completed only by the participants that do not indicate male-male or female-female on the first two items. Also, an optional write-in item for indicating personal gender identity may be included. Another measure, An Inclusion Gender

Identity Measure (Haupert et al., 2020), assessed gender identity to indicate "do not know" or "choose not to answer." Utilization of questionnaires such as these communicates to participants that the researcher or organization acknowledges varied gender identities and the importance of having an inclusive and accurate assessment of participant's sexuality.

As we have seen, accurately measuring sexual behaviors, sexual orientation, and gender identity is an ongoing challenge. Sex researchers have called for further guidance and improved methods for incorporating better assessment of sexuality-related variables (Lerum & Dworkin, 2015; Fu et al., 2019). Such advances would improve sex research, the results being more valid, better accepted by the public, and more valuable in shaping sexual health education and policy.

Think Critically

1. Have you ever taken a scientific sex questionnaire? If so, did you have to answer questions about sexual behaviors and orientation that you found were ambiguous or unclear? Explain.
2. How would you define, for example, "having sex," "sexual contact," "sexual relations," "foreplay," "heterosexual," and "homosexual"?
3. How would you feel, no matter your sexual orientation, about reporting your sexual identity, sexual behavior, and sexual attraction on a sex questionnaire?

Despite these limitations of self-reporting of sexual behavior, a review of seven population-based surveys of adults in the United States concluded that self-reported data may not be as unreliable as generally assumed. The study examined the consistency in the number of sexual partners reported in seven national studies and found a remarkable level of consistency among the studies. The researchers concluded that the findings show promise for research that relies on self-reported number of sexual partners (Hamilton & Morris, 2010).

Some researchers use computers to improve interviewing techniques for sensitive topics. With the audio computer-assisted self-interviewing (audio-CASI) method, the respondent hears the questions over headphones or reads them on a computer screen and then enters his or her responses into the computer. Audio-CASI, an increasingly popular method of data collection, apparently increases feelings of confidentiality and accuracy of responses on sensitive topics such as sexual risk behaviors. Even though the use of audio-CASI has advantages, research has found that the use of the audio part by respondents was limited and that gains in more candid responses from the audio component are modest relative to text-only CASI (Couper et al., 2009).

Other types of computer-based technology being used for data collection include: (1) computer-assisted telephone interviewing, involving a telephone interviewer administering a scripted questionnaire and then entering the participant's responses directly into the computer and (2) computer-assisted personal interviewing, during which a face-to-face interviewer administers a scripted questionnaire and enters the responses of the participant directly into the computer. Such technologies, which include smartphones, have several advantages, including convenient data entry and the ability to enter information about sexual-related variables (e.g., attitudes and behaviors) at a specified time such as soon after a sexual episode with a partner (McCallum & Peterson, 2012; Schick et al., 2014).

Another technology technique is the use of the Internet to administer questionnaires and conduct interviews. Since the mid-1990s, the use of the Internet has become a popular and useful method of survey research (Catania et al., 2015), largely because of its ability to collect data quickly and to eliminate the costs of other methods such as travel expenses for interviews, office space for interviews, printing and mailing of written questionnaires, and the software for audio-CASI. The use of the Internet can also result in larger samples. For example, a British Internet study on sexuality and gender had about 255,000 participants (Reimers, 2007). Because of the large number of Internet websites, social networks, and chat rooms that serve particular populations such as sexual minorities, the Internet also facilitates access to hard-to-reach groups as well as geographically isolated persons. For example, stigmatized groups such as transgender individuals may feel more comfortable participating via the Internet. While an advantage of the Internet is the perceived anonymity by the participant, resulting in greater levels of disclosure of sexual behavior and attitudes, it can be a disadvantage in that a researcher is not present to clarify survey instructions or questions or to verify that the participant is the person he or she claims to be (Schick et al., 2014). Further, an investigation of the use of the web data collection method in a large national study found that for only about one third of the questions, the anonymity of the web led to greater reporting of sensitive behaviors and less socially desirable opinions. The researchers concluded that the greater anonymity afforded by the web data collection may not necessarily result in greater levels of disclosure (Burkill et al., 2016).

Daily data collection, using a **sexual diary**, or personal notes of one's sexual activity, can increase the accuracy of self-reported data and make possible the analysis of any specific sexual-related event (Crosby et al., 2006). Often, research participants make daily diary entries online or by phone, for example, about sexual variables such as interest, fantasies, and behavior. Or they may be requested to make entries only after a certain sexual activity has occurred, such as intercourse. Most research suggests that event-specific behaviors such as condom use during sex will be more accurately recalled in diaries than by retrospective methods such as self-report questionnaires and interviews (Fortenberry et al., 1997; Gilmore et al., 2001; Graham & Bancroft, 1997; McAuliffe et al., 2007). Among a sample of men and women college students, sex researchers Malachi Willis and Kristen Joskowski (2018) assessed reporting differences between sexual behavior collected via daily diary and retrospective estimates using smartphones. Like previous research, they found that students significantly over-reported how often they engaged in penile-vaginal intercourse on retrospective studies compared to daily diaries. The study also provided evidence this trend was in similar direction for making out, breast stimulation, manual genital stimulation, and oral-genital stimulation. The researchers concluded that smartphones are a promising tool for collecting sexual health data among college students as reporting appears to be more accurate. However, they caution that smartphone use may be problematic for other groups of people, such as older persons, whom may have fewer technology skills and familiarity.

Observational Research

Observational research is a method by which a researcher unobtrusively observes and makes systematic notes about people's behavior without trying to manipulate it. The observer does not want his or her presence to affect the subject's behavior, although this is rarely possible. Because sexual behavior is regarded as significantly different from other behaviors, there are serious ethical issues involved in observing people's sexual behavior without their knowledge and consent. Researchers cannot observe sexual behavior as they might observe, say, flirting at a party, dance, or bar, so such observations usually take place in a laboratory setting. In such instances, the setting is not a natural environment, and participants are aware that their behavior is under observation.

Participant observation, in which the researcher participates in the behaviors he or she is studying, is an important method of observational research. For example, a researcher may study prostitution by becoming a customer or may study anonymous sex between men in public restrooms by posing as a lookout (Humphreys, 1975). There are several questions raised by such participant observation: How does the observer's participation affect the interactions being studied? For example, does a prostitute respond differently to a researcher if he or she tries to obtain information? If the observer participates, how does this affect his or her objectivity? And what are the researcher's ethical responsibilities regarding informing those he or she is studying?

"Ignorance is like a delicate exotic fruit; touch it and the bloom is gone."
—Oscar Wilde (1854–1900)

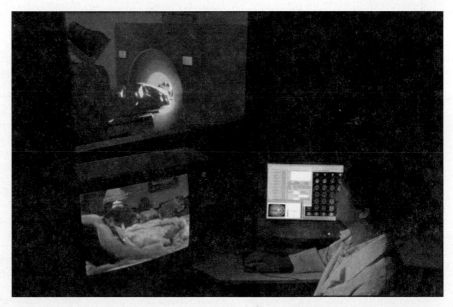

Sex researchers are using electronic techniques within a private laboratory setting to assess sexual arousal and body changes during the viewing of explicit videos.

Antonio RIBEIRO/Gamma-Rapho via Getty Images

practically speaking

Spotting Flawed Research

"That which can be asserted without evidence can be dismissed without evidence."

—Christopher Hitchens (1949–2011)

For many people, determining which research studies in human sexuality, particularly those reported in the media, are good studies and those which are questionable is difficult. Most persons do not have the academic preparation to be able to determine which studies are of high quality, yet may wonder which ones they can believe. Even journalists who report sexuality studies face the same problem: One study found that 53% of journalists surveyed indicated that they were "not very" or just "somewhat confident" in distinguishing high-quality studies from questionable ones (Ordway, 2019).

Below are listed some questions to ask yourself when reading either media reports of research or published studies in professional journals (Farnam Street Media, 2020; Ordway, 2017). You may not be able to answer all the questions, but they may give you a general idea of the strengths and weaknesses of the research and what criteria are used by academic reviewers of the study. Before you begin, a caveat: No research is perfect; researchers strive to minimize and eliminate as many limitations as possible by adhering to high research standards (Crosby et al., 2006).

Was the research peer-reviewed? Peer-review, a detailed critique by a small number of qualified researchers, is a standard process in academic publishing. Though not perfect, this process is designed to assess the quality and accuracy of new research such as the methodology and statistical analysis. Only those receiving positive reviews are published. If the study has not been peer-reviewed there is a possibility that flawed research with incorrect or exaggerated conclusions will be published, resulting in false news. For example, early in the coronavirus epidemic, Stanford University researchers published a paper on the online server, medRxiv, which distributes unpublished research that has not been peer-reviewed. The paper described the results of exposure to COVID-19 in 3,300 Santa Clara, California residents. The researchers concluded that cases were actually substantially higher than detected, meaning that fatality rates were much lower than previously thought. Many aspects of the study, such as the study design and statistical methodology, were quickly questioned by scientists and errors were identified. The rush to publish research on COVID-19 and an overwhelming number of papers submitted has made more it likely some published studies would be flawed, resulting in the possibility that questionable findings could influence the development of ineffective or harmful public health policy (Eisen & Tibshirani, 2020). Sometimes an academic journal retracts a previously published paper because it was subsequently found to be flawed. For example, a public health journal retracted a paper that advocated use of homeopathy to combat the coronavirus pandemic (Oransky, 2020).

Do the authors have expertise and background in the field? One may not be able to determine if the researchers have the credentials to conduct quality research, but if they represent legitimate and respected universities and organizations, and have published in the past in the area of the study they are more likely to be sound researchers and scholars.

Was the research published in a reputable academic journal? Journals that are considered top-tier are more likely to publish high-quality research as they typically have more rigorous peer-review and are more selective in which papers to publish. Although somewhat controversial, one measure used to gauge a journal's ranking is its Impact Factor, a calculation of the average number of times a journal's articles are cited in subsequent published research. The higher the Impact Factor score (range of 0–10+) the higher the journal is ranked. Most journals have an Impact Factor score which is typically listed on their website.

Do the researchers have a possible conflict of interest? Sometimes studies are funded by companies whose products are related to the study. For example, a study might determine if a newly developed vaginal spermicide by the funding company is more effective than another company's spermicide. This type of arrangement could lead to suspicion of whether or not the researchers had something to gain from the study findings, particularly if the findings were favorable to the funding company's product. Most academic journals require research authors to declare any "conflict of interest."

Did the study use a reasonable, representative sample? Using a random sample, in which each person of a group has an equal chance of participating in the study, is the best method to ensure an unbiased sample. Because of challenges in getting random samples, most survey studies are not based on a random sample although many researchers take steps to minimize biases in sampling. Also, research based on larger samples usually result in more accurate findings than studies having smaller samples. For experimental studies, the best design is the double-blind method in which neither the participants nor the researchers do not know who are in the control or experimental group.

Are the conclusions supported by the findings? Researchers must make the study conclusion based on what the data suggests, and be careful not to exaggerate or minimize their findings or conclude that a positive correlation between two variables shows causation. One should be skeptical of research in which its "promises" appear to be a bit too amazing or dramatic, or states that its study results are proof that something is true or occurs. Science is about finding evidence, not proof. Usually, a single study in itself is just the starting point of discovery. Replication of the same study is valuable in that it leads to self-correction. Media reports of research have sometimes sensationalized the findings with headlines like "New research points to HIV vaccine available soon" yet none has been developed since the emergence of HIV/AIDS in the early 1980s.

Experimental Research

Experimental research is the systematic manipulation of individuals or the environment to learn the effects of such manipulation on behavior. It enables researchers to isolate a single factor under controlled circumstances to determine its influence. Researchers are able to control their experiments by using **variables**, or aspects or factors that can be manipulated in experiments. There are two types of variables: independent and dependent. **Independent variables** are factors that can be manipulated or changed by the experimenter; **dependent variables** are factors that are likely to be affected by changes in the independent variable.

Because it controls variables, experimental research differs from the previous methods we have examined. Clinical studies, surveys, and observational research are correlational in nature. **Correlational studies** measure two or more naturally occurring variables to determine their relationship to each other. Because these studies do not manipulate the variables, they cannot tell us which variable *causes* the other to change. But experimental studies manipulate the independent variables, so researchers *can* reasonably determine what variables cause the other variables to change.

Much experimental research on sexuality depends on measuring physiological responses. These responses are usually measured by **plethysmographs** (pluh-THIZ-muh-grafs)—devices attached to the genitals to measure physiological response. Two of the most frequently used methods of penile plethysmograph assessment is the measurement of the penis circumference using a **strain gauge** (a device resembling a rubber band that fits around the penis) and the measurement of the volume of the penis using an airtight cylinder and cuff placed on the base of the penis. The device measures penile engorgement but not necessarily sexual desire or sexual arousal, as we know that men can experience erections, such as awakening from sleep with an erection. The vaginal plethysmograph is about the size of a menstrual tampon and is inserted into the vagina like a tampon. The device measures the amount of blood within the vaginal walls, which increases as a woman becomes sexually aroused (Chivers et al., 2014). The device may not be a good indicator of female sexual arousal as studies have shown poor correlations between women's self-reported sexual desire and device readings (Chivers et al., 2010).

Suppose researchers want to study the influence of alcohol on sexual response. They can use a plethysmograph to measure sexual response, the dependent variable. In this study, the independent variable is the level of alcohol consumption: no alcohol consumption, moderate alcohol consumption (1–3 drinks), and high alcohol consumption (3+ drinks). In such an experiment, subjects may view an erotic video. To get a baseline measurement, researchers measure the genitals' physiological patterns in an unaroused state, before participants view the video or take a drink. Then they measure sexual arousal (dependent variable) in response to erotica as they increase the level of alcohol consumption (independent variable).

● The Sex Researchers

It was not until the nineteenth century that Western sexuality began to be studied using a scientific framework. Prior to that time, sexuality was the domain of religion rather than science, the subject of moral rather than scientific scrutiny. Treatises, canon law, and papal bulls, as well as sermons and confessions, cataloged the "sins of the flesh." The early researchers of sexuality were concerned with the supposed excesses and deviances of sexuality rather than its healthy functioning. They were fascinated by what they considered the pathologies of sex, such as fetishism, sadism, masturbation, and homosexuality—the very behaviors that most religions condemned as sinful. Alfred Kinsey ironically noted that nineteenth-century researchers created "scientific classifications . . . nearly identical with theological classifications and with moral pronouncements . . . of the fifteenth century" (Kinsey et al., 1948).

As we will see, however, there has been a liberalizing trend in our thinking about sexuality. Both Richard von Krafft-Ebing and Sigmund Freud viewed sexuality as inherently dangerous and needing repression. But Havelock Ellis, Alfred Kinsey, William Masters and Virginia Johnson, and many other more recent researchers have viewed sexuality more positively; in fact, historian Paul Robinson (1976) regards these later researchers as modernists, or "sexual

"We don't see things as they are, we see them as we are."
—Anais Nin (1903–1977)

"Judge a man by his questions rather than by his answers."
—Voltaire (1694–1778)

Richard von Krafft-Ebing viewed most sexual behavior other than marital coitus as a sign of pathology.

Imagno/Getty Images

enthusiasts." Three themes are evident in the work of modernists: (1) they believe that sexual expression is essential to an individual's well-being, (2) they seek to broaden the range of legitimate sexual activity, including homosexuality, and (3) they believe that female sexuality is the equal of male sexuality.

Sex researchers and reformers Karl Heinrich Ulrichs, Karl Maria Kertbeny, Magnus Hirschfeld, Evelyn Hooker, and Michel Foucault attempted to understand homosexuality. These individuals presented homosexuality as inborn or socially constructed and a normal variant of sexual expression. This view contrasted with most physicians and moralists of their time who condemned same-sex sexual behavior as both pathological and immoral. In studying sexual activities between men, medical researchers "invented" and popularized the distinction between heterosexuality and homosexuality (Blank, 2012; Gay, 1986; Gray & Garcia, 2013; Weeks, 1986). As a result of the rejection of the psychopathological model, social and behavioral research on sexual minority individuals has moved in a new direction. For example, research no longer focuses on the causes and cures of homosexuality, and the vast majority of contemporary research approaches homosexuality in a nonjudgmental manner.

As much as possible, sex researchers attempt to examine sexuality objectively. But, as with all of us, many of their views are intertwined with the beliefs and values of their times. This is especially apparent among the early sex researchers, some of the most important of whom are described here.

Richard von Krafft-Ebing

Richard von Krafft-Ebing (1840–1902), a Viennese professor of psychiatry, was probably the most influential of the early researchers. In 1886 he published his most famous work, *Psychopathia Sexualis,* a collection of case histories of fetishists, sadists, masochists, and homosexuals. (He invented the words *sadomasochism* and *transvestite.*)

Krafft-Ebing traced variations in Victorian sexuality to "hereditary taint," to "moral degeneracy," and, in particular, to masturbation. He intermingled descriptions of fetishists who became sexually excited by certain items of clothing with those of sadists who disemboweled their victims. For Krafft-Ebing, the origins of fetishism and murderous sadism, as well as most variations, lay in masturbation, the prime sexual sin of the nineteenth century. Despite his misguided focus on masturbation, Krafft-Ebing's *Psychopathia Sexualis* brought to public attention and discussion an immense range of sexual behaviors that had never before been documented in a dispassionate, if erroneous, manner. A darkened region of sexual behavior was brought into the open for public examination.

Karl Heinrich Ulrichs

Karl Ulrichs (1825–1895) was a German poet and political activist who in the 1860s developed the first scientific theory about homosexuality (Kennedy, 1988). As a rationalist, he believed reason was superior to religious belief and therefore rejected religion as superstition. He argued from logic and inference and collected case studies from numerous men to reinforce his beliefs. Ulrichs maintained that men who were attracted to other men represented a third sex, whom he called *Urnings.* Urnings were born as Urnings; their sexuality was not the result of immorality or pathology. Ulrichs believed that Urnings had a distinctive feminine quality about them that distinguished them from men who desired women. He fought for Urning rights and the liberalization of sex laws.

Karl Maria Kertbeny

Karl Maria Kertbeny (1824–1882), a Hungarian physician, created the terms "heterosexuality" and "homosexuality" in his attempt to understand same-sex relationships (Feray & Herzer, 1990). Kertbeny believed that "homosexualists" were as "manly" as "heterosexualists." For this reason, he broke with Ulrich's conceptualization of Urnings as inherently "feminine" (Herzer, 1985). Kertbeny argued that homosexuality was inborn and thus not immoral. He also maintained what he called "the rights of man" (quoted in Herzer, 1985):

The rights of man begin . . . with man himself. And that which is most immediate to man is his own body, with which he can undertake fully and freely, to his advantage or disadvantage, that which he pleases, insofar as in so doing he does not disturb the rights of others.

Sigmund Freud

Few people have had as dramatic an impact on the way we think about the world as the Viennese physician Sigmund Freud (1856–1939). In his attempt to understand the **neuroses**, or psychological disorders characterized by anxiety or tension, plaguing his patients, Freud explored the unknown territory of the unconscious. If unconscious motives were brought to consciousness, Freud believed, a person could change his or her behavior. But, he suggested, **repression**, a psychological mechanism that kept people from becoming aware of hidden memories and motives because they aroused guilt, prevents such knowledge.

To explore the unconscious, Freud used various techniques; in particular, he analyzed dreams to discover their meaning. His journeys into the mind led to the development of **psychoanalysis**, a psychological system that ascribes behavior to unconscious desires. He fled Vienna when Hitler annexed Austria in 1938 and died a year later in England.

Freud believed that sexuality begins at birth, a belief that set him apart from other researchers. Freud described five stages in psychosexual development. The first stage is the **oral stage**, lasting from birth to age 1. During this time, the infant's eroticism is focused on the mouth; thumb sucking produces an erotic pleasure. Freud believed that the "most striking character of this sexual activity . . . is that the child gratifies himself on his own body; . . . he is autoerotic" (Freud, 1938). The second stage, between ages 1 and 3, is the **anal stage**. Children's sexual activities continue to be autoerotic, but the region of pleasure shifts to the anus. From age 3 through 5, children are in the **phallic stage**, in which they exhibit interest in the genitals. At age 6, children enter a **latency stage**, in which their sexual impulses are no longer active. At puberty, they enter the **genital stage**, at which point they become interested in genital sexual activities, especially sexual intercourse.

The phallic stage is the critical stage in both male and female development. The boy develops sexual desires for his mother, leading to an **Oedipal complex**. He simultaneously desires his mother and fears his father. This fear leads to **castration anxiety**, the boy's belief that his penis will be cut off by his father because of jealousy. Girls follow a more complex developmental path, according to Freud. A girl develops an **Electra complex**, desiring her father while fearing her mother. Upon discovering that she does not have a penis, she feels deprived and develops **penis envy**. By age 6, boys and girls have resolved their Oedipal and Electra complexes by relinquishing their desires for the parent of the other sex and identifying with their same-sex parent. In this manner, they develop their masculine and feminine identities. But because girls never acquire their "lost penis," Freud believed, they fail to develop an independent character like that of boys.

In many ways, such as in his commitment to science and his explorations of the unconscious, Freud seems the embodiment of twentieth-century thought. But in recent times, his influence among American sex researchers has dwindled. Two of the most important reasons are his lack of empiricism and his inadequate description of female development.

Because of its limitations, Freud's work has become mostly of historical interest to mainstream sex researchers. It continues to exert influence in some fields of psychology but has been greatly modified by other fields. Even among contemporary psychoanalysts, Freud's work has been radically revised.

Havelock Ellis

English physician and psychologist Havelock Ellis (1859–1939) was the earliest important modern sexual theorist and scholar. His *Studies in the Psychology of Sex* (the first six volumes of which were published between 1897 and 1910) consisted of case studies, autobiographies, and personal letters. One of his most important contributions was pointing out the relativity

Sigmund Freud was the founder of psychoanalysis and one of the most influential European thinkers of the first half of the twentieth century. Freud viewed sexuality with suspicion.

Chronicle/Alamy Stock Photo

Havelock Ellis argued that many behaviors previously labeled as abnormal were actually normal, including masturbation and female sexuality. For example, he found no evidence that masturbation leads to mental disorders, and he documented that women have sexual drives no less intense than those of men.

Hulton-Deutsch Collection/Corbis/Getty Images

of sexual values. In the nineteenth century, Americans and Europeans alike believed that their society's dominant sexual beliefs were the only morally and naturally correct standards. But Ellis demonstrated not only that Western sexual standards were hardly the only moral standards but also that they were not necessarily rooted in nature. In doing so, he was among the first researchers to appeal to studies in animal behavior, anthropology, and history.

Ellis also challenged the view that masturbation was abnormal. He argued that masturbation was widespread and that there was no evidence linking it with any serious mental or physical problems. He recorded countless men and women who masturbated without ill effect. In fact, he argued, masturbation had a positive function: It relieved tension.

In the nineteenth century, women were viewed as essentially "pure beings" who possessed reproductive rather than sexual desires. Men, in contrast, were driven by such strong sexual passions that their sexuality had to be severely controlled and repressed. In countless case studies, Ellis documented that women possessed sexual desires no less intense than those of men.

Ellis asserted that a wide range of behaviors was normal, including much behavior that the Victorians considered abnormal. He argued that both masturbation and female sexuality were normal behaviors and that even the so-called abnormal elements of sexual behavior were simply exaggerations of the normal.

He also reevaluated homosexuality. In the nineteenth century, homosexuality was viewed as the essence of sin and perversion. It was dangerous, lurid, and criminal. Ellis insisted that it was not a disease or a vice but a congenital condition: A person was *born* homosexual; one did not *become* homosexual. By insisting that homosexuality was congenital, Ellis denied that it could be considered a vice or a form of moral degeneracy, because a person did not *choose* it. If homosexuality were both congenital and harmless, then, Ellis reasoned, it should not be considered immoral or criminal.

Magnus Hirschfeld

In the first few decades of the twentieth century, there was a great ferment of reform in Europe. While Havelock Ellis was the leading reformer in England, Magnus Hirschfeld (1868–1935) was the leading crusader in Germany, especially for homosexual rights.

Hirschfeld was a gay man and possibly a transvestite (a person who wears clothing of the other sex). He eloquently presented the case for the humanity of transvestites (Hirschfeld, 1991). And in defense of homosexual rights, he argued that homosexuality was not a perversion but rather the result of the hormonal development of inborn traits. His defense of homosexuality led to the popularization of the word *homosexual*. Hirschfeld's importance, however, lies not so much in his theory of homosexuality as in his sexual reform efforts. In Berlin in 1897, he helped found the first organization for homosexual rights. In addition, he founded the first journal devoted to the study of sexuality and the first institute of sex research, where he gathered a library of more than 20,000 volumes.

Evelyn Hooker

As a result of Kinsey's research, Americans learned that same-sex sexual relationships were widespread among both men and women. A few years later, psychologist Evelyn Hooker (1907–1996) startled her colleagues by demonstrating that homosexuality in itself was not a psychological disorder. She found that "typical" gay men did not differ significantly in personality characteristics from "typical" heterosexual men (Hooker, 1957). The reverberations of her work continue to this day.

Earlier studies had erroneously reported psychopathology among gay men and lesbian women for two reasons. First, because most researchers were clinicians, their samples consisted mainly of gay men and lesbian women who were seeking treatment. The researchers failed to compare their results against a control group of similar heterosexual individuals. (A **control group** is a group that is not being treated or experimented on; it controls for any variables that are introduced from outside the experiment, such as a major media report related to the topic of the experiment.) Second, researchers were predisposed to believe that homosexuality was in itself a sickness, reflecting traditional beliefs about homosexuality. Consequently, emotional problems were automatically attributed to the client's homosexuality rather than to other sources.

Magnus Hirschfeld was a leading European sex reformer who championed homosexual rights. He founded the first institute for the study of sexuality, which was burned when the Nazis took power in Germany. Hirschfeld fled for his life.

Keystone-France/Gamma-Keystone via Getty Images

Alfred Kinsey

Alfred C. Kinsey (1894–1956), a biologist at Indiana University and America's leading authority on gall wasps, destroyed forever the belief in American sexual innocence and virtue. He accomplished this through the publications of the results of over 18,000 face-to-face interviews in two books, *Sexual Behavior in the Human Male* (Kinsey et al., 1948) and *Sexual Behavior in the Human Female* (Kinsey et al., 1953). These two volumes statistically documented the actual sexual behavior of Americans. In massive detail, they demonstrated the great discrepancy between *public* standards of sexual behavior and *actual* sexual behavior. Kinsey discovered that many sexual behaviors traditionally considered deviant or perverse commonly occurred. Many of the Kinsey findings remain relevant today even though his books were published seven decades ago.

Kinsey believed that sex was as legitimate a subject for study as any other and that the study of sex should be treated as a scientific discipline involving compiling and examining data and drawing conclusions without moralizing. He challenged the traditional medical field's dominance of sexual research, leading to the field becoming open to many more disciplines (Bullough, 1994).

In the firestorm that accompanied the publication of Kinsey's books (popularly known as the *Kinsey Reports*), many Americans protested the destruction of their cherished ideals and illusions. Kinsey was highly criticized for his work—and that criticism continues even today (Allen et al., 2017). Many people believed that his findings were responsible for a moral breakdown in the United States. Eminent sex researcher Vern Bullough (2004) stated that:

> few scholars or scientists have lived under the intense firestorm of publicity and criticism that he did but even as the attacks on him increased and as his health failed, he continued to gather his data, and fight for what he believed. He changed sex for all of us.

Alfred C. Kinsey photographed by William Dellenback, 1953. Kinsey shocked Americans by revealing how they actually behaved sexually. His scientific efforts led to the termination of his outside research funding because of political pressure.

Arthur Siegel/The LIFE Images Collection/Getty Images

"We are the recorders and reporters of facts—not judges of the behavior we describe."

—Alfred C. Kinsey (1894–1956)

"I don't see much of Alfred anymore since he got so interested in sex."

—Clara Kinsey (1898–1982)

Sexual Diversity and Variation   What Kinsey discovered in his research was an extraordinary diversity in sexual behaviors. He declared that all types of sexual behavior—even those that occur infrequently—are simply variants on the complex continuum of human behavior. A fundamental tenet of Kinsey was his commitment to be objective in research, refraining from traditional and religious judgments and from suggesting that persons participating in variant behavior should change their behavior (Drucker, 2014). Among men, he found individuals who had orgasms daily and others who went months without orgasms. Among women, he found individuals who had never had orgasms and others who had them several times a day. He discovered one male who had ejaculated only once in 30 years and another who ejaculated 30 times a week on average. "This is the order of variation," he commented dryly, "which may occur between two individuals who live in the same town and who are neighbors, meeting in the same place of business and coming together in common social activities" (Kinsey et al., 1948).

A Reevaluation of Masturbation   Kinsey's work aimed at a reevaluation of the role of masturbation in a person's sexual adjustment. Kinsey made three points about masturbation: (1) it is harmless, (2) it is not a substitute for sexual intercourse but a distinct form of sexual behavior that provides sexual pleasure, and (3) it plays an important role in women's sexuality because it is a more reliable source of orgasm than heterosexual intercourse and because its practice seems to facilitate women's ability to become orgasmic during intercourse. Indeed, Kinsey believed that masturbation is the best way to measure a woman's inherent sexual responsiveness because it does not rely on another person.

"You shall know the truth and the truth shall make you mad."

—Aldous Huxley (1894–1963)

Sexual Orientation   Prior to Kinsey's work, an individual was identified as homosexual if they had ever engaged in any sexual behavior with a person of the same sex. Kinsey found, however, that many people had sexual experiences with persons of both sexes. He reported that 50% of the men and 28% of the women in his studies had had same-sex experiences and that 38% of the men and 13% of the women had had orgasms during these experiences (Kinsey et al., 1948; Kinsey et al., 1953). Furthermore, he discovered that sexual attractions

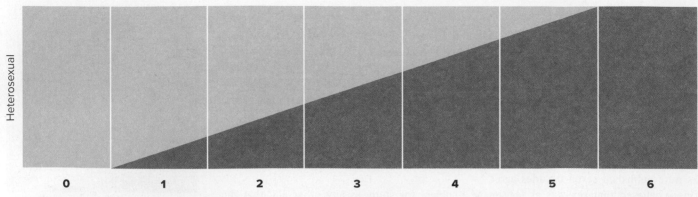

| 0 | 1 | 2 | 3 | 4 | 5 | 6 |

Based on other-sex and/or same-sex sexual behaviors and psychosexual reactions such as sex dreams and fantasies in the person's sexual history, individuals rate as follows:

| Exclusively heterosexual with no homosexual | Predominately heterosexual, only incidentally homosexual | Predominately heterosexual, but more than incidentally homosexual | Equally heterosexual and homosexual | Predominately homosexual, but more than incidentally heterosexual | Predominately homosexual, but incidentally heterosexual | Exclusively homosexual |

● **FIGURE 1**

The Heterosexual-Homosexual Rating Scale. This scale illustrates the continuum of sexual expression.

could change over the course of a person's lifetime. Kinsey's research led him to conclude that it was erroneous to classify people as either heterosexual or homosexual. A person's sexuality was significantly more complex and fluid. Actually, he found that very few people identified as either exclusively heterosexual or homosexual.

Kinsey wanted to eliminate the concept of heterosexual and homosexual *identities*. He did not believe that homosexuality, any more than heterosexuality, existed as a fixed psychological identity. Instead, he argued, there were only sexual behaviors, and behaviors alone did not make a person gay, lesbian, bisexual, or heterosexual. It was more important to determine what proportion of behaviors were same-sex and other-sex than to label a person as gay, lesbian, or heterosexual.

He devised the Heterosexual-Homosexual Rating Scale to represent the proportion of an individual's sexual behaviors and psychosexual reactions with the same or other sex (see Figure 1). The scale charts sexual behavior and psychosexual reactions exclusively directed toward either persons of the same or the other sex and along a continuum of both sexes. By conceptualizing human sexuality as a spectrum and fluid, Kinsey radicalized the categorization of human sexual expression (Drucker, 2014; McWhirter, 1990). Since this contribution seven decades ago, our understanding of sexuality and gender, in their varied forms, has increased. Kinsey's scale describes sexual attraction as either male or female, and does not account for persons outside the male/female binary, such as non-binary and genderqueer (Smith, 2019). There are now over 200 scales designed to measure and describe sexual orientation (see Chapter 7 to learn more about other models).

Rejection of Normal/Abnormal Dichotomy As a result of his research, Kinsey insisted that the distinction between normal and abnormal was meaningless. Like Ellis, he argued that sexual differences were a matter of degree, not kind. Almost any sexual behavior could be placed alongside another that differed from it only slightly. His observations led him to be a leading advocate of the acceptance of sexual diversity.

Michel Foucault

One of the most influential social theorists in the twentieth century was the French thinker Michel Foucault (1926–1984). A cultural historian and philosopher, Foucault explored how society creates social ideas and how these ideas operate to further the established

Michel Foucault (1926–1984) of France was one of the most important thinkers who influenced our understanding of how society "constructs" human sexuality.

AFP/Getty Images

order. His most important work on sexuality was *The History of Sexuality, Volume I* (1978), a book that gave fresh impetus to scholars interested in the social construction of sex, especially those involved in gender and gay and lesbian studies.

Foucault challenged the belief that our sexuality is rooted in nature. Instead, he argued, it is rooted in society. Society "constructs" sexuality, including homosexuality and heterosexuality. Foucault's critics contend, however, that he underestimated the biological basis of sexual impulses and the role individuals play in creating their own sexuality.

William Masters and Virginia Johnson

In the 1950s, William Masters (1915–2001), a St. Louis physician, became interested in treating sexual function difficulties—such problems as early ejaculation and erection difficulties in men and lack of orgasm in women. As a physician, he felt that a systematic study of the human sexual response was necessary, but none existed. To fill this void, he decided to conduct his own research. Masters was joined several years later by Virginia Johnson (1925–2013).

Masters and Johnson detailed the sexual response cycles of 382 men and 312 women during more than 10,000 episodes of sexual behavior, including masturbation and sexual intercourse. The researchers combined observation with direct measurement of changes in male and female genitals using electronic devices. (Their four-phase sexual response cycle will be discussed in Chapter 9.)

Human Sexual Response (1966), their first book, became an immediate success among both researchers and the public. What made their work significant was not only their detailed descriptions of physiological responses but also the articulation of several key ideas. First, Masters and Johnson discovered that, physiologically, male and female sexual responses are very similar. Second, they demonstrated that women experience orgasm primarily through clitoral stimulation. Penetration of the vagina is not needed for orgasm to occur. By demonstrating the primacy of the clitoris, Masters and Johnson destroyed once and for all the Freudian distinction between vaginal and clitoral orgasm. (Freud believed that an orgasm a woman experienced through masturbation was somehow physically and psychologically inferior to one experienced through sexual intercourse. He made no such distinction for men.) By destroying the myth of the vaginal orgasm, Masters and Johnson legitimized female masturbation.

In 1970, Masters and Johnson published *Human Sexual Inadequacy,* which revolutionized sex therapy by treating sexual problems simply as difficulties that could be treated using behavioral therapy. They argued that sexual problems were not the result of underlying neuroses or personality disorders. More often than not, problems resulted from a lack of information, poor communication between partners, or marital conflict. Their behavioral approach, which included "homework" exercises such as clitoral or penile stimulation, led to an astounding increase in the rate of successful treatment of sexual problems. Their work made them pioneers in modern sex therapy.

Feminist Scholarship

The initial feminist research generated an immense amount of groundbreaking work on women in almost every field of the social sciences and humanities. Feminists made gender and gender-related issues significant research questions in a multitude of academic disciplines, with the goal of producing useful knowledge that can be valuable to individual and societal change (Harding & Norberg, 2005; Letherby, 2003). In the field of sexuality, feminists expanded the scope of research to include the subjective experience and meaning of sexuality for women; sexual pleasure; sex and power; erotic material; risky sexual

William Masters and Virginia Johnson detailed the sexual response cycle in the 1960s and revolutionized sex therapy in the 1970s.

Bettmann/Getty Images

Judith Butler is an American philosopher and gender theorist who developed gender performativity theory, which has had significant influence on feminist and queer scholarship.

Target Presse Agentur Gmbh/Getty Images

behavior; and issues of female victimization, such as rape, the sexual abuse of children, and sexual harassment.

There is no single feminist perspective; instead, there are several. For our purposes, **feminism** is "a movement that involves women and men working together for equality" (McCormick, 1996). Feminism centers on understanding female experience in cultural and historical context—that is, the social construction of gender asymmetry. **Social construction** is the development of social categories, such as masculinity, femininity, heterosexuality, and homosexuality, by society.

Feminists believe in these basic principles:

- *Gender is significant in all aspects of social life.* Like socioeconomic status and ethnicity, gender influences a person's position in society.

- *The female experience of sex has been devalued.* By emphasizing genital sex, frequency of sexual intercourse, and number of orgasms, both researchers and society ignore other important aspects of sexuality, such as kissing, caressing, love, commitment, and communication. Sexuality in lesbian women's relationships is even more devalued. Until the 1980s, most research on homosexuality centered on gay men, making lesbian women invisible.

- *Power is a critical element in male-female relationships.* Because women are often subordinated to men as a result of our society's beliefs about gender, women generally have less power than men. As a result, feminists believe that men have defined female sexuality to benefit themselves. Not only do men typically decide when to initiate sex, but the man's orgasm often takes precedence over the woman's. Some women even believe that male sexual pleasure is more important than their own; for example, female orgasm is not vital for women's satisfaction during sex with a male partner (Salisbury & Fisher, 2014). The most brutal form of male expression of sexual power is rape.

- *Ethnic and cultural diversity must be addressed.* Women of color, feminists point out, face a double stigma: being female *and* being from a minority group. Although an inadequate number of studies exist on ethnicity and sexuality, feminists are committed to examining the role of ethnicity in female sexuality (Amaro et al., 2001).

Despite its contributions, feminist research and the feminist approach have often been marginalized. However, the feminist perspective in sex research has expanded in recent years, and many more women are making important contributions to the advancement of sexual science. As one consequence, the research literature has increased, resulting in an expansion of our understanding of all sexualities and gender identities. For example, renowned sex researchers Charlene Muehlenhard of the University of Kansas and Zoe Peterson and Kristen Jozkowski at The Kinsey Institute at Indiana University have developed a body of research that has defined the field of women's experiences with sexual coercion. They have addressed controversial issues such as token sexual resistance and have challenged researchers to clarify their conceptualizations of wanted and unwanted sex, particularly among young women (Muehlenhard, 2011; Muehlenhard et al., 2016; Muehlenhard & Peterson, 2005; Peterson & Muehlenhard, 2007).

● Contemporary Research Studies

Several large, national sexuality-related studies have been conducted in recent years. We briefly describe five national surveys here to illustrate research on the general population of men and women, adolescents, and college students. These studies, largely directed to determine the prevalence of certain behaviors, give little or no attention to factors that help explain the findings. Further, they represent only the tip of the sexuality-related research pertinent to the topics covered in this textbook. Sex research continues to be an emerging field of study. Most studies are not national projects but are smaller ones dealing with special populations or issues and focus on examining factors that are related to or influence sexual behavior. Even though these studies may be smaller in scope, they provide valuable information for furthering our understanding of human sexual expression. Throughout the book, we cite numerous studies to provide empirical information about the topic.

Before describing these studies, it is important to note that, just as in the days of Alfred Kinsey, these are difficult times in which to conduct sex research. For example, some federal government officials, members of Congress, and conservative groups are attacking the value of certain sex research topics, even those related to HIV prevention. The result has been a chilling effect on sex research. Funding for sex research has become more limited, and sexuality-related grant applications to the National Institutes of Health that have been approved by peer review have been questioned (Allen et al., 2017). Sex research is a relatively young area of study when compared to longer and better-established fields such as psychology, and the number of researchers specializing in sexuality-related study is small. Hopefully, these efforts to limit and discredit sex research will not discourage the next generation of researchers from becoming sex researchers. (To read a brief discussion about the controversy surrounding sex research, see Think About It, "Sex Research: A Benefit to Individuals and Society or a Threat to Morality?")

The National Health and Social Life Survey

In 1994, new figures from the first nationally representative survey of Americans' sexual behavior were released, showing us to be in a different place than when Kinsey did his research a half century earlier. The study, conducted by researchers at the University of Chicago and titled the National Health and Social Life Survey (NHSLS) involved 3,432 randomly selected Americans aged 18–59, interviewed face-to-face (Michael et al., 1994; Laumann et al., 1994). Even though this study was conducted in 1992 and had some sampling limitations, sexual scientists regard it as one of the most methodologically sound studies. The survey contradicted many previous findings and beliefs about sex in America. The NHSLS findings remain basically the same that are found in more contemporary research although some specific results of current studies may differ. For example, the National Survey of Sexual Health and Behavior (see below) found greater diversity in sexual behaviors than discovered by the NHSLS. In general, the NHSLS found, for example, that Americans are generally sexually exclusive, have sex about once a week, and have fairly traditional sexual behaviors. Orgasms appeared to be the rule for men but the exception for women. Extramarital sex is the exception. Also, homosexuality was not as prevalent as originally believed. Specific study findings will be cited in other parts of this text.

The National Survey of Family Growth

Periodically, the National Center for Health Statistics (NCHS) conducts the National Survey of Family Growth (NSFG) to collect data on marriage, divorce, contraception, infertility, and the health of women and infants in the United States. In 2011, the NCHS published *Sexual Behavior, Sexual Attraction, and Sexual Identity in the United States: Data from the 2006–2008 National Survey of Family Growth,* which presents national estimates of several measures of sexual behavior, sexual attraction, and sexual identity among males and females 15–44 years of age in the United States. In-person, face-to-face interviews and audio-CASI were used with a nationally representative sample of 13,495 males and females in the household population of the United States. Important findings for this sample include the following:

- Sexual behaviors among males and females aged 15–44, based on the 2006–2008 NSFG, were generally the same as those reported in a similar report of 2002.

- Among adults aged 25–44, about 98% of females and 97% of males ever had sexual intercourse, 89% of females and 90% of males ever had oral sex with an other-sex partner, and 36% of females and 44% of males ever had anal sex with an other-sex partner.

- For men aged 15–44, the mean number of lifetime female partners was 5.1 and for women 3.2 lifetime male partners.

Sex Research: A Benefit to Individuals and Society or a Threat to Morality?

Socrates said, **"There is only one good, knowledge, and one evil, ignorance."** This philosophy has been a core tenet in the growth of humankind and cultures since it was first written sometime between 469 BCE and 399 BCE. But in one area of life, human sexuality, some espouse that there is one good, ignorance, and one evil, knowledge. In our culture, the value of sexual knowledge is debated. One way this ambivalence manifests itself is through criticism and barriers to research on human sexuality (Yarber, 1992; Yarber & Sayad, 2010).

Sex research faces many issues that other areas of scientific inquiry do not, largely because human sexuality in our culture is too often surrounded by fear and denial, and its expression is often accompanied by shame, guilt, and embarrassment. These discomforts, particularly the fear of sexual knowledge, have fueled efforts to refute sex research. Some opposed to sex research believe that it has little value, and the research may be discredited. As such, the researchers may face public scorn, as Alfred Kinsey did. In fact, because of public outcry, Alfred Kinsey lost foundation funding for his research following the publication of his first book on male sexuality. The National Health and Social Life Survey (Laumann et al., 1994) conducted in the 1990s had to seek funding from foundations and private donors after a large federal grant was withdrawn following political pressure. Even today, federal government funding of sexuality-related areas is limited primarily to the study of HIV/STI risk behavior and prevention, which means researchers must search for nongovernment funding sources for topics outside this area. For example, a study of relationships between masturbation and mental health among older adults who no longer have a partner would most likely not be federally funded. The National Survey of Sexual Health and Behavior (Herbenick et al., 2010), a national study of Americans' sexual behavior conducted in 2010, was funded by a condom manufacturer.

A major test of academic freedom within the university occurred over 70 years ago when Alfred Kinsey's research was heavily criticized and outside pressure was exerted upon Indiana University (IU) to end Kinsey's work (Capshew, 2012). Herman B Wells, president of IU then, defended Alfred Kinsey by declaring that the search for truth is an important function of a university and that a fundamental university tenet and core value is that a faculty member is free to conduct research on any subject in which the person has competence. Wells (1980) unequivocally articulated the tenet that ". . . a university that bows to the wishes of a person, group, or segment of society is not free." Wells's support of Alfred Kinsey's research is considered a landmark victory for academic freedom and helped pave the way for sex research at other universities (Clark, 1977). William Masters stated that without Kinsey's work and the support it received from IU, Virginia Johnson and he would not have been able to conduct their observational research on sexual response and dysfunction (Maier, 2009).

In the face of criticism, sex research has shown value—many individuals and society have benefited in so many ways from the deeper understanding of human sexual expression that research brings. But not all people agree. Here are just three examples of the cultural ambiguity surrounding sex research and sexual knowledge:

- Some persons believed that Kinsey's research was destructive, leading to the sexual revolution of the 1960s and the breakdown of traditional mores. However, renowned sexologists consider Kinsey's scientific findings profound, making it possible for individuals, couples, and the public to talk about sex as well as freeing many persons from the stigma of abnormality (Bullough, 2004; Gagnon, 1975).

- Some persons were outraged upon learning that Masters and Johnson actually observed persons having sex, believing that such research had gone too far. However, Masters and Johnson's laboratory observation and measurement of the sexual responses of men and women led to the development of effective behavioral therapy for sexual function problems that have benefited many individuals and couples (Masters & Johnson, 1970).

- Some individuals and evangelical religious groups support abstinence-only education and contend that sexuality education that discusses methods of preventing HIV/STIs and pregnancy other than abstinence leads to sexual behavior among young persons outside of marriage. However, research has shown that abstinence-only sexuality education is largely ineffective in delaying the onset of sex and that comprehensive approaches, which include information about HIV/STIs and pregnancy prevention methods, postponed the initiation of first vaginal intercourse, reduced the number of sexual partners and frequency of sex including returning to abstinence, and increased condom and contraception use. Further, the comprehensive approach did not encourage students to have sex (Boskey, 2019; Grossman et al., 2014; Kirby, 2007, 2008; Stanger-Hall & Hall, 2011).

Supporters of sex research contend that we all suffer and the public loses when sex research is hampered. They believe that a fundamental principle of a democracy is at stake: the individual right to know. One way of making it possible for people to learn more about sexuality is through sex research's goals to increase people's knowledge about sexuality and its various components and to show them the positive impact that a rewarding and health-enhancing sexuality can have. But many opponents believe that sex research is harmful to society and should be limited or even eliminated.

Think Critically

1. For human sexuality, was Socrates right or wrong when he said, "There is one good, knowledge, and one evil, ignorance"?

2. Do you believe that sex research benefits individuals and society, has no impact, or that it leads to moral decay? Explain.

3. Should researchers at colleges and universities have the academic freedom to conduct any type of sex research? Defend your answer.

4. Given that the vast majority of federal government-funded sexuality-related research deals with HIV/STI risk behavior, do you think that other areas of human sexuality should be funded? If so, what areas? If not, why?

- For ages 15–44, 21% of men and 8% of women reported 15 or more lifetime sexual partners.

- For ages 15–44, 12.5% of women and 5.2% of men reported any same-sex contact in their lifetimes, and 9.3% of women and 5% of men reported oral sex with a same-sex partner.

- For ages 15–44, for sexual identity, 92.8%, 1.0%, and 3.5% of women self-identified as heterosexual (straight), homosexual (gay or lesbian), and bisexual, respectively. For men, 95.0%, 1.6%, and 1.1% self-identified as heterosexual (straight), homosexual (gay or lesbian), and bisexual, respectively.

- Of sexually active people aged 15–24, 63% of females and 64% of males had oral sex.

- Among teenagers aged 15–19, 7% of females and 9% of males had oral sex with an other-sex partner, but no vaginal intercourse.

For a full copy of the report, see the National Center for Health Statistics website: http://www.cdc.gov/nchs/data/nhsr/nhsr036.pdf.

The Youth Risk Behavior Survey

The Youth Risk Behavior Survey (YRBS), conducted biannually by the Centers for Disease Control and Prevention (CDC), measures the prevalence of six categories of health risk behaviors among youths through representative national, state, and local surveys using a self-report questionnaire. Sexual behaviors that contribute to unintended pregnancy and sexually transmitted infections, including HIV, are among those assessed. Starting in 2015, the YRBS has provided the first national estimates of the percentage of high school students who self-identify as a gay male, lesbian female, or bisexual person or are not sure of their sexual identity as well as the percentage of high school students who have had sexual contact with only the same sex or with both sexes. The 2019 survey contains 99 questions assessing health-related behaviors. The report describes overall trends in health-related behaviors during 1991–2019 and the percentage of students who report a specific sexual orientation, as presented below. The 2019 report includes a national school-based survey of 13,677 students in grades 9–12 from 136 in 44 states, three territories, and two tribal governments (CDC, 2020.2).

- Thirty-eight percent of students (38% of females and 39% of males) reported ever having had sexual intercourse, a decrease from 54% in 1991.

- Ten percent of students (8% of females and 12% of males) reported having had sexual intercourse with four or more partners during their life, a decrease from 19% in 1991.

- Three percent of students (2% of females and 4% of males) reported having had sexual intercourse for the first time before age 13, a decrease from 10% in 1991.

- Twenty-eight percent of students (28% of females and 26% of males) reported having had sexual intercourse with at least one person during the 3 months before the survey, a decrease from 38% in 1991.

- Fifty-four percent of students (50% of females and 60% of males) who reported being currently sexually active (29%) also reported using a condom during their most recent sexual intercourse, an increase from 46% in 1991.

- Twelve percent of students (13% of females and 10% of males) who reported being currently sexually active (29%) did not use any method of contraception to prevent pregnancy during their last intercourse, a decrease from 17% in 1991.

- Twenty-one percent of students (19% of females and 24% of males) who reported being currently sexually active (29%) also reported using alcohol or drugs prior to their most recent sexual intercourse, a decrease from 22% in 1991.

- Seven percent of students (11% of females and 4% of males) reported ever being forced to have sexual intercourse, a decrease from 8% in 2001.

- Among the 68% of students who dated or went out with someone during the 12 months prior to the survey, 11% of students (17% of females and 5% of males) had been kissed, touched, or physically forced to have sexual intercourse when they did not want to by someone with whom they were dating or going out, a decrease from 10% in 2017.

- Nine percent of students (10% of females and 9% of males) reported ever having been tested for HIV (not counting being done while donating blood), a decrease from 12% in 2005.

- Nine percent of students (11% females and 6% males) reported ever having been tested for STIs.

- Nationwide, 84% of students (78% females and 91% males) identified as heterosexual, 2.5% (2.9% female and 2.1% of male) identified as gay or lesbian, 9% (14% female and 3% male) identified as bisexual, and 5% (6% female and 3% male) were not sure of their identity.

- Nationwide, 45% (41% female and 50% male) had had sexual contact with only the other sex, 2% (1.8% female and 1.4% male) had had sexual contact with only same sex, and 5% (8.4% female and 2.3% male) had had contact with both sexes.

Most high school students cope with the transition from childhood through adolescence to adulthood successfully and become healthy and productive adults. However, this report documented that some subgroups of students defined by sex, race/ethnicity, grade in school, and sexual minority status have a higher prevalence of many health-risk behaviors that might place them at risk for unnecessary or premature mortality, morbidity, and social problems. Sexual minority students in particular struggle because of the disparities in health-related behaviors documented in this report, including violence-related behaviors and alcohol and other drug use that can be compounded by stigma, discrimination, and homophobia. Because many health-risk behaviors initiated during adolescence often extend into adulthood, they might have life-long negative effects on health outcomes, educational attainment, employment, housing, and overall quality of life. Schools have a unique and an important role to play in addressing these issues.

See https://www.cdc.gov/mmwr/volumes/67/ss/ss6708a1.htm for more information on the 2019 YRBS.

The National College Health Assessment

Since the year 2000, every fall and spring terms the American College Health Association has conducted research at colleges and universities throughout the United States to assess students' health behaviors in nine areas: general health; disease and injury prevention; academic impacts; violence, abusive relationships, and personal safety; alcohol, tobacco, and other drug use; sexual behavior; nutrition and exercise; mental health; and sleep. The data reported below is from the Spring 2019 report representing 54,497 undergraduate students at 98 U.S. campuses (American College Health Association, 2019). Findings from the sexual health questions include:

- Within the last 12 months, 62% of college males and 66% of college females had at least one sexual partner. Most had one sexual partner—39% of males and 42% of females—although 11% of males and 9% of females had four or more partners. (See Figure 2 for the percentage reporting having oral, vaginal, and anal intercourse in the past 30 days and the percentage who used protection during these behaviors.)

- Among sexually active students, birth control pills (58% males and 55% females), male condoms (66% males and 58% females) were the most common birth control methods used to prevent pregnancy by the students or their partner the last time they had vaginal intercourse. Twenty-seven percent of males and 34% of females reported using withdrawal.

- Seventy-two percent and 62% reported receiving the vaccination against hepatitis B and against human papillomavirus, respectively.

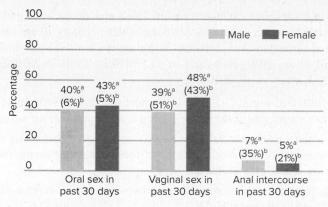

• FIGURE 2

Percentage of Undergraduate College Students Who Reported Having Oral Sex, Vaginal Sex, and Anal Intercourse in the Past 30 Days and the Percentage Reporting Using a Condom or Other Protective Barrier, Spring 2019.

Source: American College Health Association National College Health Assessment II: Undergraduate Students Reference Group Executive Summary, Spring 2019.

[a]Percentage reporting the behavior.

[b]Percentage of sexually active students reporting using a condom or other protective barrier during the specific sexual behavior within the past 30 days.

- Within the last 12 months, students reported sexual touch without their consent (14% of females and 5% of males), sexual penetration attempt without their consent (5% of females and 1% of males), sexual penetration without their consent (4% of females and 1% of males), and a sexually abusive intimate relationship (4% of females and 1% of males).

- Among sexually active students, 18% reported using (or reported their partner used) emergency contraception (the "morning-after pill") within the last school year.

- One percent of students who had vaginal intercourse within the last 12 months reported experiencing an unintended pregnancy or got someone pregnant within the last 12 months.

- Thirty-three percent of males reported performing a testicular self-exam in the last 30 days.

- Thirty-four percent of females reported performing a breast self-exam in last 30 days.

- Thirty-seven percent of females reported having a routine gynecological exam in the past 12 months.

- Twenty-six percent reported ever being tested for human immunodeficiency virus (HIV).

- One hundred percent of males and females were assigned that sex at birth.

- Among males, 87% described their sexual orientation as straight/heterosexual, 1% as asexual, 6% as gay, and 4% as bisexual.

- Among females, 80% described their sexual orientation as straight/heterosexual, 2% lesbian, 11% as bisexual, 1% as asexual, and 2% as pansexual or questioning.

- One-hundred percent of men described their gender identity as man and 100% of women described their gender identity as woman.

- None of both men and women indicated that they identified as transgender.

See https://www.acha.org/documents/ncha/NCHA-II_SPRING_2019_UNDERGRADUATE_REFERENCE_GROUP_DATA_REPORT.pdf for more information on the Spring 2019 Undergraduate Report of the National College Health Association.

The National Survey of Sexual Health and Behavior

The National Survey of Sexual Health and Behavior (NSSHB), a nationally representative study, was published in 2010, 16 years following the first nationally representative study, the 1994 National Health and Social Life Survey (NHSLS), described earlier. The NSSHB, a study based on Internet reports from 5,865 American adolescents and adults aged 14–94, provides a needed and valuable updated overview of Americans' sexual behavior and reveals an increase in sexual diversity since the NHSLS.

"The good thing about science is that it's true whether you believe it or not."

—Neil deGrasse Tyson (1958–)

The NSSHB provides data on masturbation (solo and partnered), oral sex (given and received), vaginal intercourse, and anal intercourse, categorized by 10 age ranges. These data will be highlighted throughout the textbook. Major generalized NSSHB findings include the following (Dodge et al., 2010; Herbenick et al., 2010.2a, 2010.2b, 2010.2c; Reece et al., 2010.2a, 2010.2b; Sanders et al., 2010):

- A large variability of sexual repertoires of adults was found, with numerous combinations of sexual behaviors described at adults' most recent sexual event.

- Men and women participated in diverse solo and partnered behaviors throughout their life course, yet in spite of lower frequency of these behaviors among older adults, many reported active, pleasurable sex lives.

- Masturbation was common among all age groups but more common among men than women and individuals aged 25–29.

- Vaginal intercourse occurred more frequently than other sexual behaviors from early to late adulthood.

- Partnered noncoital behaviors—oral sex and anal intercourse—were well-established components of couple sexual behavior and were reported in greater numbers than in the NHSLS.

- Among adults, many sexual episodes included partnered masturbation and oral sex, but not intercourse.

- Fewer than 1 in 10 men and women self-identified as a gay man, lesbian woman, or bisexual person, but the proportion of study participants having same-gender interactions sometime in their lives was higher.

- Masturbation, oral sex, and vaginal intercourse were prevalent among all ethnic groups and among men and women throughout the life course.

- During a single sexual event, orgasm among men was facilitated by vaginal intercourse with a relationship partner, whereas women's orgasm was facilitated by varied sexual behaviors.

- Higher rates of condom use during most recent vaginal intercourse were found compared to other recent studies, and condoms were used more frequently with casual partners than relationship partners.

2015 Sexual Exploration in America Study

The Internet-based, U.S. nationally representative probability survey, the 2015 Sexual Exploration in America Study (SEAS), surveyed a broad range of sexual behaviors among 2,021 adults (975 men and 1,046 women ages 18–70+) (Herbenick et al., 2017). The study expanded our understanding of more diverse adult sexual behaviors than previously U.S. nationally representative probability surveys. Lifetime and recent sexual behaviors and appeal of 50+ sexual behaviors were assessed. Major 2015 SEAS findings are listed below. Further findings will be presented in this and other chapters.

- About 91% of respondents identified as heterosexual, with more women identifying as bisexual (3.6%) compared to lesbian (1.5%) and more men identifying as gay (5.8%) compared to bisexual (1.9%).

- Most of the respondents (n = 1,421) who were in relationships reported being entirely monogamous.

- Twelve percent of partnered respondents were currently in exclusive but sexless relationships.

- About 46% of men and 41% of women had masturbated in the last month and about 8% of men and 22% of women reported never masturbating in their lifetime.

- Most respondents reported lifetime vaginal sex and oral sex.

- Common lifetime sexual behaviors included wearing sexy lingerie/underwear (75% women, 29% men), sending/receiving digital nude/semi-nude photos

(54% women, 65% men), reading erotic stories (57% participants), and watching sexually explicit videos/DVDs. Less common behaviors included having engaged in threesomes (10% women, 18% men).

- More participants identified behaviors as "appealing" than had engaged in them. Romantic/affectionate behaviors were among those most commonly identified as appealing for both men and women.

- The appeal of particular behaviors was associated with greater odds that the individual had ever engaged in the behavior.

Final Thoughts

Hero/Corbis/Glow Images

Popular culture surrounds us with sexual images, disseminated through advertising, music, television, film, video games, and the Internet, that form a backdrop to our daily living. Much of what is conveyed is simplified, overgeneralized, stereotypical, shallow, sometimes misinterpreted—and entertaining. Studying sexuality enables us to understand how research is conducted and to be aware of its strengths and its limitations. Richard von Krafft-Ebing, Sigmund Freud, Havelock Ellis, and Magnus Hirschfeld are among the early sex researchers and reformers. Alfred Kinsey, William Masters, Virginia Johnson, Evelyn Hooker, and Michel Foucault are more contemporary noted researchers who have expanded our understanding of sexual expression. In recent years, several large national studies have been conducted to determine the prevalence of sexual behaviors and attitudes among the general population of men and women. Traditional sex research has been expanded in recent years by feminist, gay, lesbian, bisexual, transgender, and queer research, which provides fresh insights and perspectives. Although the study of sexuality and ethnicity has yet to reach its full potential, it promises to enlarge our understanding of the diversity of attitudes, behaviors, and values in contemporary America.

Summary

Sex, Advice Columnists, and Pop Psychology

- The *sex information/advice genre* transmits information to both entertain and inform; the information is generally oversimplified and sometimes distorted so that it does not interfere with the genre's primary purpose, entertainment. Much of the information or advice conveys dominant social norms.

Thinking Objectively About Sexuality

- *Objective statements* are based on observations of things as they exist in themselves. *Value judgments* are evaluations based on moral or ethical standards. *Opinions* are unsubstantiated beliefs based on an individual's personal thoughts. *Biases* are personal leanings or inclinations. *Stereotypes*—rigidly held beliefs about the personal characteristics of a group of people—are a type of *schema,* which is the organization of knowledge in our thought processes.

- *Fallacies* are errors in reasoning. The *egocentric fallacy* is the belief that others necessarily share one's own values, beliefs, and attitudes. The *ethnocentric fallacy* is the belief that one's own ethnic group, nation, or culture is inherently superior to any other.

Sex Research Methods

- Ethical issues are important concerns in sex research. The most important issues are *informed consent, protection from harm,* and confidentiality.

- In sex research, *sampling* is a particularly acute problem. To be most meaningful, samples should be representative of the larger group from which they are drawn. But most samples are limited by volunteer bias and dependence on college students.

- The most important methods in sex research are clinical, survey, observational, and experimental. *Clinical research* relies on in-depth examinations of individuals or groups who go to the clinician seeking treatment for psychological or medical problems. *Survey research* uses questionnaires, interviews, or diaries, for example, to gather information from a representative sample of people. *Observational research* requires the researcher to observe interactions carefully in as unobtrusive a manner as possible. *Experimental research* presents subjects with various stimuli under controlled conditions in which their responses can be measured.

- Experiments are controlled through the use of *independent variables* (which can be changed by the experimenter) and *dependent variables* (which change in relation to changes in the independent variable). Clinical, survey, and observational research efforts, in contrast, are *correlational studies* that reveal relationships between variables without manipulating them. In experimental research, physiological responses are often measured by a *plethysmograph.*
- Accurately measuring sexual behaviors is an ongoing challenge to sex researchers.

The Sex Researchers

- Richard von Krafft-Ebing was one of the earlies sex researchers. His work emphasized the pathological aspects of sexuality.
- Karl Heinrich Ulrichs believed that men who are attracted to other men represented a third sex when he called Urnings. Ulrich advocated for Urning rights and the liberation of sex laws.
- Karl Maria Kertheny created the terms "heterosexuality" and "homosexuality. He argued that homosexuality was inborn, thus not immoral.
- Sigmund Freud was one of the most influential thinkers in Western civilization. Freud believed there were five stages in psychosexual development: the *oral stage, anal stage, phallic stage, latency stage,* and *genital stage.*
- Havelock Ellis was the first modern sexual theorist and scholar. His ideas included the relativity of sexual values, the normality of masturbation, a belief in the sexual equality of men and women, the redefinition of "normal," and a reevaluation of homosexuality.
- Alfred Kinsey's work documented enormous diversity in sexual behavior, emphasized the role of masturbation in sexual development, and argued that the distinction between normal and abnormal behavior was meaningless. The Kinsey scale charts sexual behaviors and psychosexual reactions along a continuum ranging from exclusively other-sex behaviors to exclusively same-sex behaviors.
- William Masters and Virginia Johnson detailed the physiology of the human sexual response cycle. Their physiological studies revealed the similarity between male and female sexual responses and demonstrated that women experience orgasm largely through clitoral stimulation. Their work on sexual inadequacy revolutionized sex therapy through the use of behavioral techniques.

Contemporary Research Studies

- The National Health and Social Life Survey (NHSLS) in 1994 was the first nationally representative survey of Americans' sexual behavior, and its findings contradicted many prior findings and beliefs about sex in America.
- The National Survey of Family Growth (NSFG) is a periodic survey that collects data related to marriage, divorce, contraception, infertility, and the health of women and infants in the United States. A 2011 NSFG is a comprehensive survey of the prevalence of certain sexual behaviors in the general population.
- The Youth Risk Behavior Study (YRBS), conducted biennially since 1991, is a large, national, school-based study of the health behaviors of adolescents. Behaviors related to sexuality and risk taking are assessed. Beginning in 2015, the YRBS provides the first national estimate of the percentages of high school students' self-identified sexual orientation and sexual identity, and whether they had sexual contact with only the same sex, the other sex, or both sexes.
- The American College Health Association's National College Health Assessment has conducted research on campuses throughout the United States since 2000 to determine students' health and sexual behaviors.
- The National Survey of Sexual Health and Behavior (NSSHB), conducted in 2010, was a nationally representative Internet study of adolescents and adults aged 14-94, an age range much greater than in other studies. The NSSHB provided an update on Americans' sexual behavior, showing an increase in sexual diversity since the NHSLS.
- The 2015 Sexual Exploration in America Study (SEAS) surveyed a broad range of sexual behaviors among U.S. adults, ages 18-70+. Lifetime and recent sexual behaviors and appeal of 50+ sexual behaviors were assessed. The study expanded our understanding of more diverse adult sexual behavior than prior U.S. national representative probability surveys.
- Most feminist research focuses on gender issues, maintains that female sexuality has been devalued and that power is a critical element in female-male relationships, and explores the experience of being a person other than heterosexual.

Questions for Discussion

- Is sex research valuable or necessary? If you feel that it is, what areas of sexuality do you think need special attention? Which, if any, areas of sexuality should be prohibited from being researched?
- Alfred Kinsey was, and continues to be, criticized for his research. Some people even believe that he was responsible for eroding sexual morality. Do you think his research was valuable, or that it led to the sexual revolution in the United States, as many people claim?
- Would you volunteer for a sex research study? Why or why not? If so, what kind of study?

Sex and the Internet

The Kinsey Institute

Few centers that conduct research exclusively on sexuality exist in the world. One of the most respected and well-known centers is The Kinsey Institute (KI) at Indiana University, in Bloomington, Indiana. The institute bears the name of its founder, Alfred C. Kinsey, whose research was described earlier in this chapter. Visit the institute's website (www.kinseyinstitute.org

- The mission and history of KI

- A chronology of events and landmark publications

- The KI research staff and their publications

- KI's current research projects

- KI's exhibitions, services, and events

- KI's library and special collections

- Graduate education in human sexuality at KI and Indiana University

- Links to related sites in sexuality research

Suggested Websites

Advocates for Youth

www.advocatesforyouth.org

Focuses on teen sexual health; provides valuable data on issues related to teen sexual health.

Centers for Disease Control and Prevention

http://www.cdc.gov

A valuable source of research information about sexual behavior and related health issues in the United States.

Gallup Poll

http://www.gallup.com

Provides results of current surveys, including those dealing with sexuality-related issues.

International Academy of Sex Research

http://www.iasr.org

A scientific society that promotes research in sexual behavior; provides announcements of IASR conferences and abstracts of its journal's recent articles.

Society for the Scientific Study of Sexuality

http://www.sexscience.org

A nonprofit organization dedicated to the advancement of knowledge about sexuality; provides announcements of the ssss conferences and other meetings.

Suggested Reading

Allen, J. A., Allinson, H. E., Clark-Huckstep, A., Hill, B. J., Sanders, S. A., & Zhou, L. (2017). *The Kinsey Institute: The first seventy years.* Indiana University Press. The book looks at the work Alfred Kinsey began over 70 years ago and how the institute continued to make an impact on understanding human sexual expression. Over 65 images of Kinsey and the institute's collection are included.

Bancroft, J. (Ed.). (1997). *Researching sexual behavior.* Indiana University Press. A discussion of the methodological issues of large-scale survey research in studying human sexuality.

Bullough, V. L. (1994). *Science in the bedroom: A history of sex research.* Basic Books. A comprehensive history of sex research of the twentieth century.

Drucker, D. J. (2014). *The classification of sex: Alfred Kinsey and the organization of knowledge.* University of Pittsburgh Press. A detailed description of Alfred Kinsey's early research of the gall wasp, which provided the scientific foundation for this assembling, analysis, and publication of the research of over 18,000 personal sexual behavior histories.

Garton, S. (2004). *Histories of sexuality: Antiquity to sexual revolution.* Routledge. A comprehensive historical review of major figures, from Havelock Ellis to Alfred Kinsey, and an exploration of such topics as the "invention" of homosexuality in the nineteenth century and the rise of sexual sciences in the twentieth century.

Maier, T. (2009). *Masters of sex.* Basic Books. An unprecedented look at Masters and Johnson and their pioneering work together that highlights interviews with both.

Meezen, W., & Martin, J. I. (Eds.). (2006). *Research methods with gay, lesbian, bisexual and transgender populations.* Harrington Park Press. Discusses the unique issues in sexuality-related research among gay, lesbian, bisexual, and transgender populations and provides suggestions for doing this research.

Oliffe, J. L., & Greaves, L. J. (Eds). (2011). *Designing and conducting gender, sex, and health research.* Sage Publications. This book provides the first resource dedicated to critically examining gender and sex study designs, methods, and analysis in health research.

Female Sexual Anatomy and Physiology

Ingram Publishing/SuperStock

CHAPTER OUTLINE

ALTHOUGH ALL GENDERS are similar in many more ways than they are different, we tend to focus on the differences rather than the similarities. Various cultures hold diverse ideas about exactly what it means to be female or male, but virtually the only differences that are consistent are actual physical differences, most of which relate to sexual structure and function. This chapter introduces the sexual structures and functions of women's bodies, including hormones and the menstrual cycle. In Chapter 9, we describe models of sexual arousal and response, and the relationship of these to women's and men's experiences with sex and the role of orgasm. Because this and the next chapter's focus is on anatomy and physiology, we shall use the terms male and female to discuss their similarities and differences.

● Female Sex Organs: What Are They For?

Anatomically speaking, all embryos are female when their reproductive structures begin to develop (see Figure 1). If it does not receive certain genetic and hormonal signals, the fetus will continue to develop as a female. In humans and most other mammals, the female, in addition to providing half the genetic instructions for the offspring, provides the environment in which it can develop until it becomes capable of surviving as a separate entity. She also nourishes the offspring, both during gestation (the period of carrying the young in the uterus) via the placenta and following birth via the breasts through lactation (milk production).

In spite of what we do know, we haven't yet mapped all of the basic body parts of women, especially as they relate to the microprocesses of sexual response. Such issues as the function of the G-spot, the role of orgasm, and the placement of the many nerves that spider through the pelvic cavity still are not completely understood. Add to these puzzles the types, causes, and treatments of sexual function problems, and one can quickly see that the science of sexual response is still emerging.

Clearly, the female sex organs serve a reproductive function. But they perform other functions as well. Significant to nearly all females are the sexual parts that bring them pleasure; they may also attract potential sexual partners. Because of the mutual pleasure partners give each other, we can see that sexual structures also serve an important role in human relationships. People demonstrate their affection for one another by sharing sexual pleasure and form enduring partnerships at least partially on the basis of mutual sexual sharing. (See Chapter 9, Sexual Response and Expression.) Let's look at the features of human female anatomy and physiology that provide pleasure to women and their partners and that enable women to conceive and give birth.

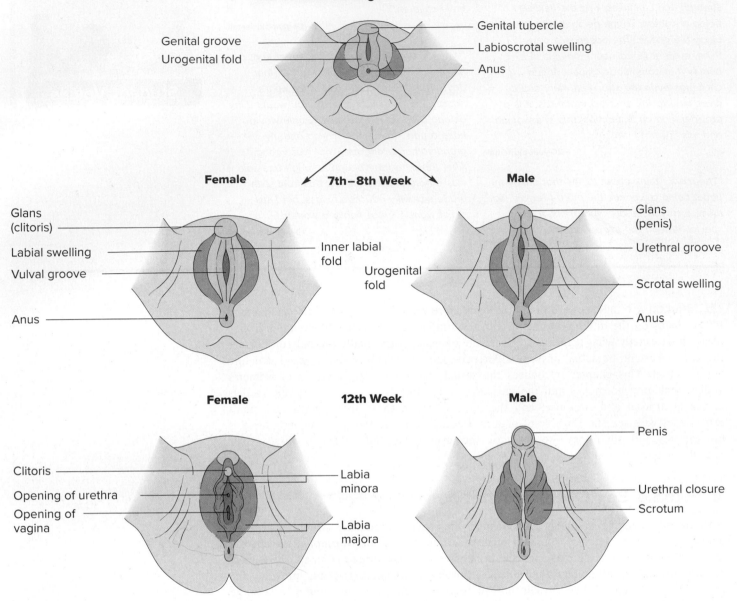

Undifferentiated Stage Prior to 6th Week

Genital groove
Urogenital fold

Genital tubercle
Labioscrotal swelling
Anus

Female — **7th–8th Week** — **Male**

Glans
(clitoris)
Labial swelling
Vulval groove
Anus

Inner labial
fold

Glans
(penis)
Urogenital
fold
Urethral groove
Scrotal swelling
Anus

Female — **12th Week** — **Male**

Clitoris
Opening of urethra
Opening of
vagina

Labia
minora
Labia
majora

Penis
Urethral closure
Scrotum

● **FIGURE 1**

**Embryonic-Fetal Differentiation of the
External Reproductive Organs.** Female
and male reproductive organs are
formed from the same embryonic
tissues. An embryo's external genitals
are female in appearance until certain
genetic and hormonal instructions signal
the development of male organs.
Without such instructions, the genitals
continue to develop as female.

*"People will insist on treating the mons
veneris as though it were Mount
Everest."*

—Aldous Huxley (1894–1963)

*"Really that little dealybob is too far
away from the hole. It should be built
right in."*

—Loretta Lynn (1935–)

External Structures

The sexual and reproductive organs of humans are called **genitals**, or genitalia, from the Latin
genere, "to beget." The external female genitals are the mons pubis, the clitoris, the labia
majora, and the labia minora, collectively known as the **vulva** (see Figures 2 and 3). (People
often use the word *vagina* when they are actually referring to the vulva. The vagina is an
internal structure.) For more about the external genitals, see Think About It, "The Grooming
of Pubic Hair" and "My Beautiful/Ugly Genitals."

The Mons Pubis   The **mons pubis** (pubic mound), or **mons veneris** (mound of Venus), is
a pad of fatty tissue that covers the area of the pubic bone about 6 inches below the navel.
Beginning in puberty, the mons is covered with pubic hair. Because there is a rich supply of
nerve endings in the mons, caressing it can produce pleasure in most women.

The Clitoris   The **clitoris** (KLIH-tuh-rus) is considered the center of sexual arousal.
It contains a high concentration of sensory nerve endings and is exquisitely sensitive to

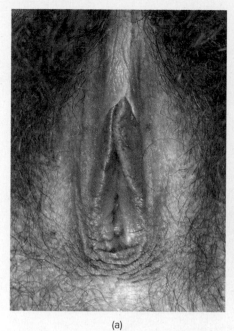 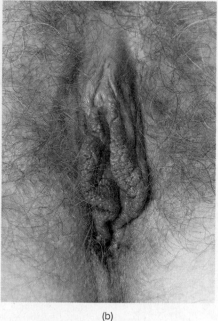 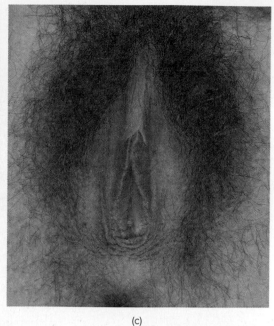

(a)   (b)   (c)

The external female genitals
(vulva) can assume many different
colors and shapes.

(a) Daniel Sambraus/Science Source; (b) H. S.
Photos/Science Source; (c) Daniel Sambraus/
Science Source

stimulation, especially at the tip of its shaft, the **glans clitoris**. A fold of skin called the **clitoral hood** covers the glans when the clitoris is not engorged. Although the clitoris is structurally analogous to the penis (it is formed from the same embryonic tissue), its sole function is sexual arousal. (The penis serves the additional functions of urine excretion and semen ejaculation.) The clitoris is a far more extensive structure than its visible part, the glans, would suggest (Bancroft, 2009). The shaft of the clitoris is both an external and an internal structure. The external portion is about 1 inch long and a quarter inch wide. Internally, the shaft is divided into two branches called **crura** (KROO-ra; singular, *crus*), each of which is about 3.5 inches long, which are the tips of erectile tissue that attach to the pelvic bones. The crura contain two **corpora cavernosa** (KOR-por-a kav-er-NO-sa), hollow chambers that fill with blood and swell during arousal. The hidden erectile tissue of the clitoris plus the surrounding muscle tissue all contribute to muscle spasms associated with orgasm. When stimulated, the clitoris enlarges initially and then retracts beneath the hood just before and during orgasm. With repeated orgasms, it follows the same pattern of engorgement and retraction, although its swellings may not be as pronounced after the initial orgasm.

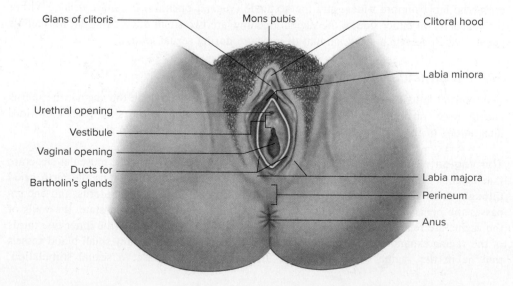

Glans of clitoris — — Mons pubis — — Clitoral hood

— Labia minora

Urethral opening —

Vestibule —

Vaginal opening —

Ducts for
Bartholin's glands — — Labia majora

— Perineum

— Anus

● **FIGURE 2**

External Structures of the Female Genitals

• FIGURE 3
Internal Structures of the Female Genitals

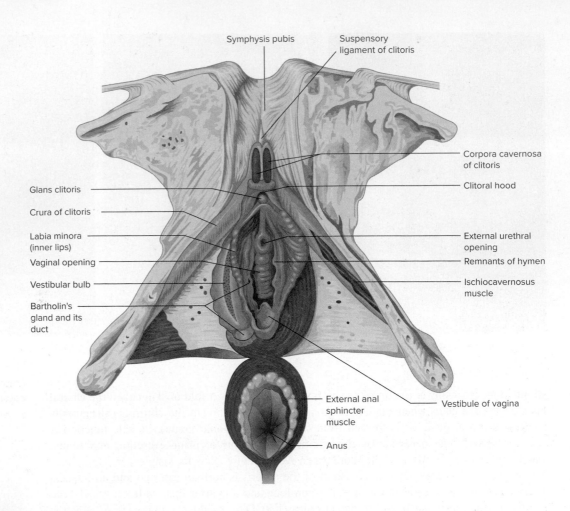

Artwork often imitates anatomy, as can be seen in this painting titled *Black Iris* (Georgia O'Keeffe, 1887–1986).

Tomas Abad/AGE Fotostock

The Labia Majora and Labia Minora   The **labia majora** (LAY-be-a maJOR-a) (outer lips) are two folds of spongy flesh extending from the mons pubis and enclosing the labia minora, clitoris, urethral opening, and vaginal entrance. The **labia minora** (inner lips) are smaller folds within the labia majora that meet above the clitoris to form the clitoral hood. The labia minora also enclose the urethral and vaginal openings. They are smooth and hairless and vary quite a bit in appearance from woman to woman. Another rich source of sexual sensation, the labia are sensitive to the touch and swell during sexual arousal, doubling or tripling in size and changing in color from flesh-toned to a deep wine-red hue. The area enclosed by the labia minora is referred to as the **vestibule**. During sexual arousal, the clitoris becomes erect, the labia minora widen, and the vestibule (vaginal opening) becomes visible. Within the vestibule, on either side of the vaginal opening, are two small ducts from the **Bartholin's glands**, which secrete a small amount of moisture during sexual arousal.

Internal Structures

The internal female sexual anatomy and reproductive organs include the vagina; the uterus and its lower opening, the cervix; the ovaries; and the fallopian tubes. (Figure 4 provides illustrations of the front and side views of the female internal sexual anatomy.)

The Vagina   The **vagina**, from the Latin word for "sheath," is a flexible, muscular structure that extends 3–5 inches back and upward from the vaginal opening. It is the **birth canal** through which an infant is born, allows menstrual flow to pass from the uterus, and encompasses the penis or other object during sexual activity. In the unaroused state, the walls of the vagina are relaxed and collapsed together, but during sexual arousal, the inner two thirds of the vagina expand while pressure from engorgement causes the many small blood vessels that lie in the vaginal wall to produce lubrication. In response to sexual stimulation,

think
about it

The Grooming of Pubic Hair: Nuisance or Novelty?

Whether influenced by the chatter in social media, glances in the locker room, and/or sexually explicit websites, the "grooming" of women's and men's pubic hair has become an accepted, if not expected, social norm. Given the time and effort that it takes to maintain this practice, one might ponder whether it enhances sexual response, is hygienic, or even desirable by all genders? Why do we even have pubic hair?

What we know about pubic hair is still somewhat limited. It's well recognized that pubic hair patterns vary widely according to a person's stage of development, race, and individuality. Pubic hair functions as a physical barrier to protect the skin, it traps bacteria and other pathogens, and it retains humidity which helps the vulvar skin. Additionally, as each pubic hair is attached to a nerve, tugging during sex may increase sexual stimulation (Gunter, 2019.3a). In all individuals, the presence of pubic hair is thought to relate to pheromones or scents that the body produces which can be sexually stimulating to others. When pheromones get trapped in the pubic area, as well as underarm hair, the resulting scent may act as an erotic aid.

The practice of grooming, the shaving, waxing, trimming, or dyeing of pubic hair, is not new. Throughout time, there is evidence that humans have modified their hair, including that in their pubic region. For instance, among the Ancient Egyptians in the fifteenth century it was common for women in particular to shave their pubic hair as a defense against lice. In the nineteenth century, some British people would cut off a portion of their pubic hair and give it to a lover who would then affix it to their hat (Padden, 2014). The modern trend of pubic hair removal is likely to have originated in South America (hence the term *Brazilian* is used for complete hair removal). It has gained popularity most likely because of the increased prevalence of sexually explicit websites that depict bare or partially shaved genital areas as being normal or desirable and as such, is frequently associated with a positive body image and amplified and varied sexual activity.

Just how widespread the practice is in the United States varies, depending on the study. Approximately 80% of women ages 18 to 65 report they remove some or all of their pubic hair (Gunter, 2019.3b). Among college-age women in one study, the practice was almost universal (98%) (Luster et al., 2019). Grooming is most prevalent among young, white, adult women with high levels of income and education. Men also participate in this practice. An earlier study reviewing the grooming practices of 7,600 men and women, aged 18–65, found that of the 74% who reported grooming their pubic hair, 66% were men and 84% were women, the majority of whom were between the ages of 18 and 24 (Osterberg et al., 2016). Among women, there is some concern that the hairless, almost prepubescent female genitalia that is an accepted norm among some teens and women may be further narrowing the standards of genital beauty and acceptability among all women.

Partner preferences and expectations also play a role in the motivations for why women in particular groom. Research has shown that women were more likely to groom if their partner also groomed and if their partner expressed a preference for it. Women were also significantly more likely to report their status as hair-free, and men were significantly more likely to prefer a hair-free sexual partner (Butler et al., 2015; Rowen et al., 2016).

Apart from sexual situations, some women have reported the need to groom before visiting a health care professional. While the reasons for this are unclear, it suggests that women are self-conscious about their appearance even in nonsexual settings. It may also signal the likelihood that among women, hair removal is associated with personal hygiene. This perception troubles Tami S. Rowen, an obstetrician and gynecologist who states, "Many women think they are dirty and unclean if they haven't groomed" (cited in Hoffman, 2016).

Though relatively safe, pubic hair removal has its medical risks. Approximately 27% of women who reported removing their pubic hair had sustained an injury and 2.5% reported needing surgical intervention (Gunter, 2019.3b). Additionally, there can be itching, burns from waxing, contamination of tools which can lead to infection, or lack of hygiene during the procedure.

Removing pubic hair is a cosmetic choice that can be performed at home and safely. A few guidelines include the following (Healthline, 2019):

1. Soak in the bathtub for at least 5 minutes to soften the skin and pubic hair.

2. Apply shaving cream or gel with aloe vera or another soothing agent over all the areas you plan to shave.

3. Use a new/sharp razor; for women, a "bikini" razor.

4. Hold the skin tight and shave slowly and gently in the direction that your hairs grow.

5. Rinse your razor after each swipe.

Pubic hair can also be removed or shaped by tweezing, trimming, using over-the-counter depilatories, and waxing as well as medically by a licensed and well-reviewed clinic that specializes in these procedures. If abnormal symptoms, such as itchiness, ingrown hairs, redness, swelling, or other problems occur and don't start healing in a few days, a person should see a doctor.

While a growing number of individuals are beginning to embrace their body hair, for others the choice to groom is about their desire to feel in control of their bodies and their definitions of beauty.

Think Critically

1. Have you or do you groom or remove your pubic hair? If so, how often and in what circumstances do you groom? If not, why not?

2. If sexually active, does your partner have any influence on whether or not you groom? Which, if any, sexual behaviors are affected by your grooming?

3. Would you consider a sex partner who has groomed or removed their pubic hair more or less sexually attractive? Or does grooming make any difference?

The Vagina Museum, located in London, is the world's first institution dedicated to gynecological anatomy.

Stephen Bell/Alamy Stock Photo

● **FIGURE 4**

Internal Female Sexual Structures.

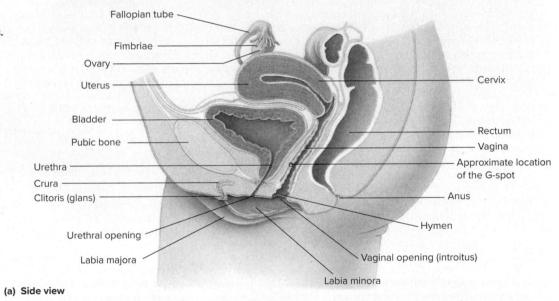

Fallopian tube

Fimbriae

Ovary

Uterus

Bladder

Pubic bone

Urethra

Crura

Clitoris (glans)

Urethral opening

Labia majora

Cervix

Rectum

Vagina

Approximate location of the G-spot

Anus

Hymen

Vaginal opening (introitus)

Labia minora

(a) Side view

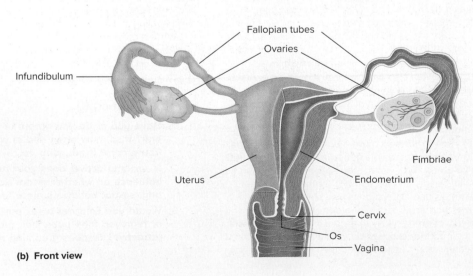

Fallopian tubes

Ovaries

Infundibulum

Uterus

Endometrium

Fimbriae

Cervix

Os

Vagina

(b) Front view

lubrication can occur within 10–30 seconds. The majority of sensory nerve endings are concentrated in the **introitus** (in-TROY-tus), or vaginal opening. This part of the vagina is the most sensitive to erotic pressure and touch. In contrast, the inner two thirds of the vagina has virtually no nerve endings, which makes it likely that a woman cannot feel a tampon when it is inserted deep in the vagina. Although the vaginal walls are generally moist, the wetness of a woman's vagina can vary by woman, by the stage of her menstrual cycle, and after childbirth or at menopause. Lubrication also increases substantially with sexual excitement. This lubrication serves several purposes. First, it increases the possibility of conception by alkalinizing the normally acidic chemical balance in the vagina, thus making it more hospitable to sperm, which die faster in acid environments. Second, it can make penetration more pleasurable by reducing friction in the vaginal walls. Third, the lubrication helps prevent small tears in the vagina, which, if they occur, can make the vagina more vulnerable to contracting HIV and some other STIs.

Before reaching puberty, the acid/base balance (otherwise known as pH) of the vagina is neutral. Once a female reaches puberty and then for the rest of her life, the pH becomes somewhat acidic and stays that way until she reaches menopause, when it becomes almost neutral again. The acidity of a woman's vagina is important in helping to prevent infections and reduce inflammation.

Prior to first intercourse or other form of penetration, the introitus is partially covered by a thin membrane containing a relatively large number of blood vessels, the **hymen**, named for the Roman god of marriage. The hymen typically has one or several perforations, allowing menstrual blood and mucous secretions to flow out of the vagina and generally allowing for tampon insertion. In many cultures, it is (or was) important for a woman's hymen to be intact on her wedding day. Blood on the nuptial bedsheets is taken as proof of her virginity. The stretching or tearing of the hymen may produce some pain or discomfort and possibly some bleeding. Usually, the partner has little trouble inserting the penis or other object through the hymen if they are gentle and there is adequate lubrication. Prior to first intercourse, the hymen may be stretched or ruptured by tampon insertion, by the woman's self-manipulation, by a partner during noncoital sexual activity, by accident, or by a health care provider conducting a routine pelvic examination. Hymenoplasty, a controversial procedure that reattaches the hymen to the vagina, is now sought by some women, particularly in Muslim countries where traditionalists place a high value on a woman's virginity, to create the illusion that they are still virgins. Hymen repair, also referred to as "revirgination," may also be performed for women who have been abused or those from cultures who risk a violent reaction from their partners. In spite of its availability, the American College of Obstetricians and Gynecologists (ACOG, 2020) has issued strong warnings to women that there is no evidence cosmetic genital surgery is safe or effective.

First identified during the time of *Kama Sutra,* considered to be a standard guide about human sexual behavior, and published in 400 BCE, scholars have proposed the existence of a sexually sensitive area inside the vagina and around the urethra, homologous to a "female prostate." While some researchers have not defined this region as a distinct anatomical entity, others have identified it as the Skene's glands, also called the paraurethral glands or the **Gräfenberg spot** (**G-spot**), a name derived from Ernest Gräfenberg, a gynecologist who discussed its erotic significance. Some women report that the G-spot is an erotically sensitive area located on the anterior or front wall of the vagina midway between the pubic bone and the cervix. The spot varies in size from a small bean to half a walnut (see Figure 5). The region can be located by pressing one or two fingers and about two knuckles deep into the front wall of the vagina. Coital positions such as rear entry, in which the penis makes contact with the spot, may also produce intense erotic pleasure (Ladas et al., 1982; Whipple & Komisaruk, 1999). Women who report orgasms as a result of stimulation of the G-spot describe them as intense and extremely pleasurable (Perry & Whipple, 1981; Whipple, 2002). Though an exact gland or site has not been found in all women, nor do all women experience pleasure when the area is massaged (Kaya & Caliskan, 2018), it has been suggested that the orgasm occurring in the area called the G-spot could be caused by the contact and connection of the richly innervated internal clitoris and the anterior vaginal wall (Foldes & Buisson, 2009; Gunter, 2019.3a). More specifically, by using special instruments and photography that

• FIGURE 5

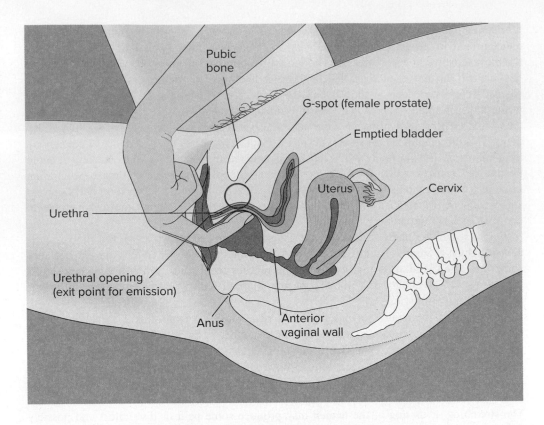

measure changes in the vagina, it was found that the displacement of the anterior vaginal wall that occurs with pressure of the finger on this site, along with movement of the engorged and enlarged clitoris that occurs during sexual arousal, could provide close contact between the internal root of the clitoris and the anterior vaginal wall and thereby lead to what is known as a G-spot orgasm.

A variety of responses to G-spot stimulation have been reported by women. Initially, a woman may experience a slight feeling of discomfort or the need to urinate, but shortly thereafter, the tissue may swell and a pleasurable feeling may occur. Additionally, a fluid that is either urine or vaginal fluid may squirt out of the urethra. This type of ejaculation often increases sexual pleasure. For a woman to ejaculate during orgasm, the Skene's glands, located on either side of the urethra, may be involved, as the ducts open into the urethra. These small glands are also referred to as the female prostate because their secretions contain small amounts of prostate-specific antigen (PSA), a protein found in the male prostate (Gunter, 2019.3a). The Skene's glands can secrete a small amount of fluid during sexual activity. Another explanation for women who report ejaculate is that the urinary bladder is being emptied.

Despite the discussion that still exists concerning the presence of the G-spot, many women would agree that having another area of erotic arousal is sexually liberating and, as such, expands sexual enjoyment beyond the clitoris. In fact, some women who are concerned about their lack of ability to experience orgasm during vaginal intercourse have sought out G-spot amplification, also referred to as genital augmentation or enhancement, in which collagen is injected into the vicinity of the G-spot to increase its size and sensitivity. Because there is a lack of data to support the effectiveness and safety of genital cosmetic surgical procedures, The American College of Obstetricians and Gynecologists [ACOG], (2020), recommends that surgery or procedures to alter sexual appearance or function, excluding those that are medically indicated, not be performed.

The Uterus and Cervix   The **uterus** (YU-te-rus), or womb, is a hollow, thick-walled, muscular organ held in the pelvic cavity by a number of flexible ligaments and supported by several muscles. It is pear-shaped, with the tapered end, the **cervix**, extending down and opening into the vagina. If a woman has not given birth, the uterus is about 3 inches long

think
about it

My Beautiful/Ugly Genitals: What Women are Saying

Given that there is no such thing as a "normal" looking vulva, we know that viewing surgically modified genitals, as can happen when we watch sexually explicit material on the Internet, alters the perception of how we regard women's genitals. In an era of so-called "designer" vaginas, elective female cosmetic genital surgeries are increasing, resulting in the normalization of altered aspects of women's genitalia.

Let's start with what "normal" female genitals look like. We have long recognized that the appearance of genitals differs depending on a person's ethnicity, age, weight, hormonal status, type of skin, and genetic predisposition. However, just how similar or different are women's genitals? Swiss researchers recently sought to answer this question by measuring and providing detailed data on age-related dimensions and descriptions of the external female genitals (Kreklau et al., 2018). Specifically, they measured the labia majora and minora, clitoris, vaginal opening, and perineum of 650 white women between the ages of 15 and 84. The authors concluded that there's so much variety in what a healthy vulva looks like that a so-called "normal" vulva doesn't actually exist.

Given the increasing number of cosmetic procedures done in the United States, we know that all genders are concerned about their appearance, including that of their genitals. In order to help understand how women's genital self-perceptions impact their attitudes and behaviors and to increase our understanding of the complexities of women's experiences, researchers Miranda C. Fudge and E. Sandra Byers (2017) surveyed and interviewed 20 women, ages 19 to 35, regarding their feelings about their genitals. On average, women felt moderately positively about their genitals. Additionally, five themes emerged from this study:

1) Women's global genital self-perceptions are diverse. Regardless of how much they had thought about their genitals, the majority of the women indicated that they held positive perceptions of their genitals. Nevertheless, these perceptions ranged in intensity and clarity. For example, some women described their feelings about their genitals as "happy," "content," or "good," while others described them as "weird," "foreign," or "creepy-looking."

2) Each woman has mixed specific genital self-perceptions. That is, when asked to describe their perceptions of specific genital parts and characteristics, each woman discussed a personal pattern of positive and negative thoughts and feelings. For example, one woman stated: "I feel like they're normal," whereas that same woman alluded to the fact that she did not like her pubic hair. The aspects of their genitals most commonly seen as problematic to women were their smell and

taste, and the appearance of pubic hair. Many also shared their concern about the reactions of others to their genitals.

3) Women's genital self-perceptions fluctuated across situations and people. Many women were affected by the degree to which their genitals were visible to another person, particularly physicians and partners.

4) Women's genital self-perceptions evolved over time. Almost half of women revealed that their self-perceptions had become more positive over time; they saw this transformation as a kind of "journey," or "aha moment." In spite of this, some felt that they still slipped back to more negative self-perceptions from time to time.

5) Negative genital self-perceptions can have consequences for women. More than half who described feelings of self-consciousness about their genitals stated that these concerns had negatively impacted their behavior and/or life experiences. Uneasiness about the smell of their genitals and/or the amount of discharge they experienced caused some women to hide their genitals in both public and private sexual situations, limit sexual activities, and engage in special hygiene practices.

The authors concluded that while women's genital self-perceptions are multi-faceted and malleable, the "prevalence of negative genital self-perceptions among women is problematic in and of itself. However, it is even more concerning that women's negative thoughts and feelings about their genitals can be associated with behavioral consequences" (Fudge & Byers, 2017, p. 359).

Empowering women with knowledge about how their body works and when and how to look for help if something seems off is necessary if we are to overcome the biases and misrepresentations that keep women frightened about their own "normal" body and bodily functions.

Think Critically

1. How do you feel about the appearance of your genitals? How might you describe them?

2. Have your feelings and concerns about your genitals changed over time? If so, how? If not, why do you suppose this is true?

3. How do your feelings about your genitals influence your sexual behaviors?

and 3 inches wide at the top; it is somewhat larger in women who have given birth. The uterus expands during pregnancy to the size of a volleyball or larger, to accommodate the developing fetus. The inner lining of the uterine wall, the **endometrium** (en-doe-MEE-tree-um), is filled with tiny blood vessels. As hormonal changes occur during the monthly menstrual

practically speaking

Performing a Gynecological Self-Examination

While reading this material, some females may wish to examine their own genitals and discover their unique features. In a space that is comfortable for you, take time to look at your vulva, or outer genitals, using a mirror and a good light. The large, soft folds of skin with hair on them are the outer lips, or labia majora. The color, texture, and pattern of this hair vary widely among women. Inside the outer lips are the inner lips, or labia minora. These have no hair, vary in size from small to large, and may protrude. They extend from below the vagina up toward the pubic bone, where they form a hood over the clitoris. The glans may not be visible under the clitoral hood, but it can be seen if a woman separates the labia minora and retracts the hood. The size and shape of the clitoris, as well as the hood, also vary widely among women. These variations have nothing to do with a woman's ability to respond sexually. You may also find some cheesy white matter under the hood. This is called smegma and is normal.

Below the clitoris is a smooth area and small opening, the urethral opening. Below the urethral opening is the vaginal opening, which is surrounded by rings of tissue. One of these, which you may or may not be able to see, is the hymen. Just inside the vagina, on both sides, are the Bartholin's glands. These may secrete a small amount of mucus during sexual excitement, but little else of their function is known. If they are infected, they will be swollen, but otherwise you won't notice them. The smooth area between your vagina and anus is called the perineum.

You can also examine your inner genitals, using a speculum, flashlight, and mirror. A speculum is an instrument used to hold the vaginal walls apart, allowing a clear view of the vagina and cervix. You should be able to obtain a speculum and information about doing an internal exam from a clinic that specializes in women's health or family planning, or online.

It is a good idea to observe and become aware of what your normal vaginal discharges look and feel like. Colors vary from white to gray, and secretions change in consistency from thick to thin and clear (similar to egg white that can be stretched between the fingers) over the course of the menstrual cycle. Distinct

Examining your genitals can be an enlightening and useful practice that can provide you with information about the health of your body.

agefotostock/Alamy Stock Photo

changes or odors, along with burning, bleeding between menstrual cycles, pain in the pelvic region, itching, or rashes, should be reported to a health care provider.

By inserting one or two fingers into the vagina and reaching deep into the canal, it is possible to feel the cervix, or tip of the uterus. In contrast to the soft vaginal walls, the cervix feels like the end of a nose: firm and round.

In doing a vaginal self-exam, you may initially experience some fear or uneasiness about touching your body. In the long run, however, your patience and persistence will pay off in increased body awareness and a heightened sense of personal health.

Once you're familiar with the normal appearance of your outer genitals, you can check for any changes, especially unusual rashes, soreness, warts, or parasites, such as pubic lice, or "crabs."

cycle, this tissue is built up and then shed and expelled through the cervical **os** (opening), unless fertilization has occurred. In the event of pregnancy, the pre-embryo is embedded in the nourishing endometrium.

In addition to the more or less monthly menstrual discharge, mucous secretions from the cervix also flow out through the vagina. These secretions tend to be somewhat white, thick, and sticky following menstruation, becoming thinner as ovulation approaches. At ovulation, the mucous flow tends to increase and to be clear, slippery, and stretchy, somewhat like egg white.

The Ovaries On each side of the uterus, held in place by several ligaments, is one of a pair of ovaries. The **ovary** is a **gonad**, an organ that produces **gametes** (GA-meets), the sex cells containing the genetic material necessary for reproduction. Female gametes are called **oocytes** (OH-uh-sites), from the Greek words for "egg" and "cell." Oocytes are commonly referred to as eggs or **ova** (singular, **ovum**). Technically, however, the cell does not become an egg until it completes its final stages of division following fertilization. The ovaries are the size and shape of large almonds. In addition to producing oocytes, they serve the important function of producing hormones such as estrogen, progesterone, and testosterone. (These hormones are discussed later in this chapter.)

At birth, the female's ovaries contain about half a million oocytes. During childhood, many of these degenerate; then, beginning in puberty and ending after menopause, about 400 oocytes mature and are released during a woman's reproductive years. The release of an oocyte is called **ovulation**. The immature oocytes are embedded in saclike structures called **ovarian follicles**. The fully ripened follicle is called a vesicular or Graffian follicle. At maturation, the follicle ruptures, releasing the oocyte. After the oocyte emerges, the ruptured follicle becomes the **corpus luteum** (KOR-pus LOO-tee-um) (from the Latin for "yellow body"), a producer of important hormones; it eventually degenerates. The egg is viable for about 24 hours.

The Fallopian Tubes At the top of the uterus are two tubes, one on each side, known as **fallopian tubes**, uterine tubes, or oviducts. The tubes are about 4 inches long. They extend toward the ovaries but are not attached to them. Instead, the funnel-shaped end of each tube (the **infundibulum**) fans out into fingerlike **fimbriae** (fim-BREE-ah), which drape over the ovary but may not actually touch it. Tiny, hairlike **cilia** on the fimbriae become active during ovulation. Their waving motion, along with contractions of the walls of the tube, transports the oocyte that has been released from the ovary into the fallopian tube. (The process of ovulation and the events leading to fertilization are discussed later in this chapter.)

Other Structures

There are several other important anatomical structures in the genital areas of both men and women. Although they may not serve reproductive functions, they may be involved in sexual activities. In women, these structures include the urethra, anus, and perineum. The **urethra** (yu-REE-thra) is the tube through which urine passes; the **urethral opening** is located between the clitoris and the vaginal opening. Between the vagina and the **anus**—the opening of the rectum, through which feces passes—is a diamond-shaped region called the **perineum** (per-e-NEE-um). This area of soft tissue covers the muscles and ligaments of the **pelvic floor**, the underside of the pelvic area extending from the top of the pubic bone (above the clitoris) to the anus.

The anus consists of two sphincters, which are circular muscles that open and close like valves. The anus contains a dense supply of nerve endings that, along with the tender rings at the opening, can respond erotically. In sex play or intercourse involving the anus or rectum, care must be taken not to rupture the delicate tissues. This may occur because of the lack of adequate lubrication or very rough anal sex play. Anal sex, which involves insertion of the penis or other object into the rectum, is potentially unsafe, unlike vaginal sex, because abrasions of the tissue provide easy passage for pathogens, such as HIV, to the bloodstream. To practice safer sex, partners who engage in anal intercourse should use a latex condom with a water-based lubricant.

The Breasts

With the surge of sex hormones that occurs during adolescence, the female breasts begin to develop and enlarge (see Figure 6). The reproductive function of the breasts is to nourish offspring through **lactation**, or milk production. A mature female breast, also known as a **mammary gland**, is composed of fatty tissue and 15–25 lobes that radiate around a central protruding nipple. Around the nipple is a ring of darkened skin called the **areola** (a-REE-o-la). Tiny muscles at the base of the nipple cause it to become erect in response to touch, cold, or sexual arousal.

• FIGURE 6

The Female Breast. Front and
cross-sectional views.

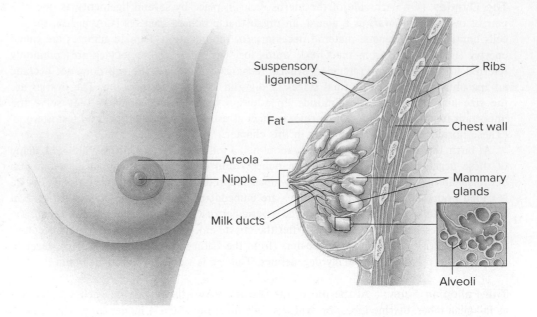

When a woman is pregnant, the structures within the breast undergo further development. Directly following childbirth, in response to hormonal signals, small glands within the lobes called **alveoli** (al-VEE-a-lee) begin producing milk. The milk passes into ducts, each of which has a dilated region for storage; the ducts open to the outside at the nipple. During lactation, a woman's breasts increase in size from enlarged glandular tissues and stored milk. Because there is little variation in the amount of glandular tissue among women, the amount of milk produced does not vary with breast size. In women who are not lactating, breast size depends mainly on fat content, which is determined by hereditary factors.

think about it

Female Genital Mutilation/Cutting: Human Rights Violation or Cultural and Social Norm?

In African countries, some parts of Asia and the Middle East, young females may undergo *female genital mutilation/ cutting (FGM/C)*, a procedure that intentionally alters the female genital organs for nonmedical reasons. Often performed on girls between infancy and age 15, it is estimated that more than 200 million girls and women in 30 countries worldwide have undergone this cultural tradition (World Health Organization [WHO], 2018).

Since the late 1970s, the term female genital mutilation has been used by the World Health Organization to emphasize that the act violates women's human rights, alters or causes injury to the female genital organs, and has no health benefits. Though other organizations don't dispute these findings, the United Nations Children's Fund and the United National Population Fund use the somewhat less judgmental expression

"female genital mutilation/cutting." For the sake of this discussion, we will adopt the term female genital mutilation/cutting (FGM/C), which the WHO (2018) has classified into four major types as follows:

■ Type I: Partial or total removal of the clitoris (clitoridectomy).

■ Type II: Partial or total removal of the clitoris and the labia minora with or without excision of the labia majora (excision).

■ Type III: Narrowing of the vaginal opening through the creation of a covering seal by cutting and repositioning the labia minora or labia majora with or without removal of the clitoris (infibulation).

■ Type IV: All other harmful procedures to the female genitals for nonmedical purposes, for example, pricking, piercing, incising, scraping, and cauterizing the genital area.

Classification of Female Genital Mutilation / Cutting

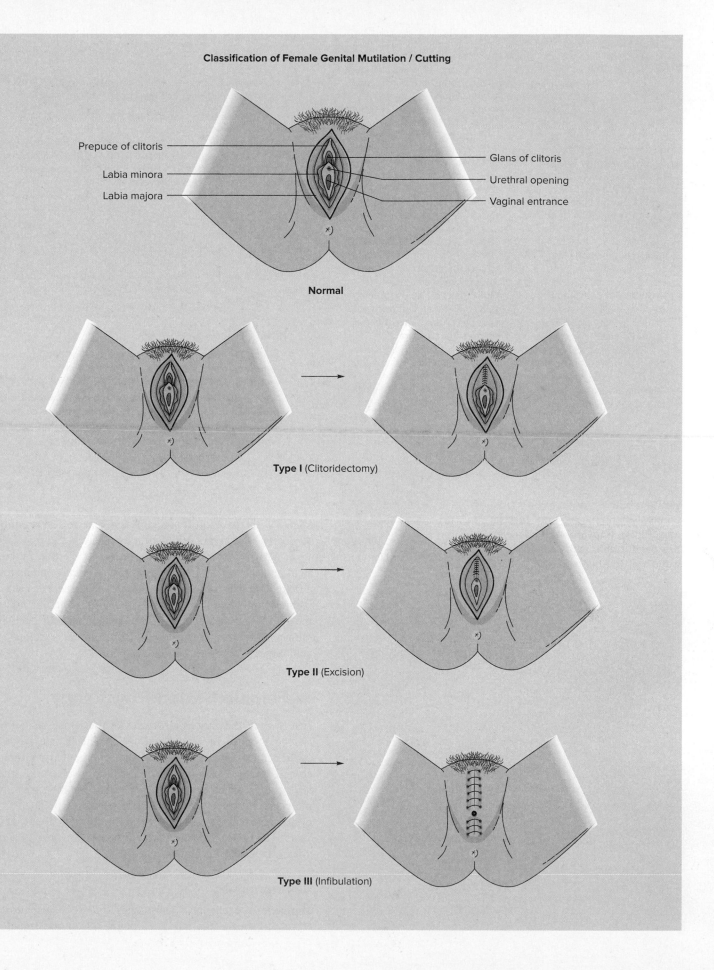

Prepuce of clitoris

Labia minora

Labia majora

Glans of clitoris

Urethral opening

Vaginal entrance

Normal

Type I (Clitoridectomy)

Type II (Excision)

Type III (Infibulation)

These procedures are generally performed in unsanitary conditions, with a knife, razor, or a piece of broken glass, without medical anesthesia; antiseptic powder or concocted pastes may be applied. The effects of the devastatingly painful operations include bleeding, infections, infertility, scarring, the inability to enjoy sex, and, not uncommonly, death. Upon marriage and to allow for intercourse or to facilitate childbirth, a practice known as deinfibulation may be performed whereby the sealed vaginal opening is cut in a woman who has been infibulated. Women who have undergone FGM/C and their babies are more likely to die during childbirth (WHO, 2018).

This ancient procedure, practiced mainly in Africa, is difficult for outsiders to understand. Why would loving parents allow this to be done to their daughter? As with many other practices, including male circumcision in our own culture, the answer is "tradition." Many cultures consider FGM/C a part of raising a girl. Motivated by beliefs about what is considered acceptable sexual behavior, parents who choose to have their girls cut believe it helps to ensure premarital virginity and marital fidelity as well as helping her resist extra-relational sex. Some also maintain that being cut increases marriageability and is associated with ideals of femininity and modesty. No religious scripts prescribe the practice.

Though progress has been made in curtailing FGM/C through international responses and resolutions, research shows that if communities themselves decide to abandon FGM/C, the practice could be eliminated very rapidly (WHO, 2018). Additionally, the World Health Organization recommends efforts to eliminate FGM/C, including:

- Strengthening the health sector's response by providing guidelines, tools, training, and policy to ensure medical care and counseling for those living with FGM/C.

- Generating knowledge about the causes and consequences of the practice.
- Increasing advocacy by developing materials and tools for international, regional, and local efforts to eliminate FGM/C.

In spite of a growing demand for clitoral reconstruction or restoration on the part of women who have FGM/C, the World Health Organization (2018) states that there is insufficient evidence to support its safety or effectiveness. For those who still seek out this surgery, the organization advises against raising women's unrealistic expectations, especially among those who seek sexual improvement.

International efforts to end cutting have been somewhat successful, but the practice still persists. The U.S. government prohibits FGM/C for girls under the age of 18 unless it is performed for medical purposes by a licensed practitioner (Equality Now, 2019). Though the practice has been declining over the past 3 decades, strongly held customs are difficult to change and there remains an urgent need to raise awareness of this problem.

Think Critically

1. **Which is the better term: *female genital cutting, female genital mutilation,* or *female genital mutilation/cutting*? Why do you feel this way?**
2. **Should FGM/C be eliminated worldwide, or should it be permitted in countries where it is an important custom?**
3. **Does FGM/C violate the human rights of girls and women? If so, in what ways? If not, why?**

Western culture tends to be ambivalent about exposed breasts and nudity. Most people, however, are comfortable with artistic portrayals of the nude female body.

Anthony Saint James/Getty Images

In the Western culture, women's breasts capture a significant amount of attention and serve an erotic function. Most women find breast stimulation intensely pleasurable, whether it occurs during breastfeeding or sexual contact. Partners tend to be aroused by both the sight and the touch of women's breasts. Nipple stimulation trips a brain area that overlaps with the area that interprets sensations coming from the clitoris (Gunter, 2019.3a). There is no basis to the belief that large breasts denote greater sexual responsiveness than small breasts. (Table 1 provides a summary of female sexual anatomy.)

● Female Sexual Physiology

Just how do the various structures of the female anatomy function to produce the menstrual cycle? The female reproductive cycle can be viewed as having two components, although, of course, multiple biological processes are involved: (1) the ovarian cycle, in which eggs develop, and (2) the menstrual, or uterine cycle, in which the womb is prepared for pregnancy. These cycles repeat approximately every month for about 35 or 40 years. The task of directing these processes belongs to a class of chemicals called hormones.

Sex Hormones

Hormones are chemical substances that serve as messengers, traveling within the body through the bloodstream. Most

TABLE 1 ● Summary Table of Female Sexual Anatomy

External Structures

Mons pubis (mons veneris)	Fatty tissue that covers the area of the pubic bone
Clitoris	Source of sexual arousal
Clitoral hood	Covers the glans clitoris when the clitoris is not engorged
Crura (singular, crus)	Tips of erectile tissue that attach to the pelvic bones
Corpora cavernosa	Hollow chambers that fill with blood and swell during sexual arousal
Labia majora (outer lips)	Two folds of spongy flesh that extend from the mons pubis and run downward along the sides of the vulva
Labia minora (inner lips)	Smaller, hairless folds within the labia majora that meet above the clitoris to form the clitoral hood
Vestibule (vaginal opening)	Area enclosed by the labia minora
Bartholin's glands	Glands that secrete a small amount of moisture during sexual arousal

Internal Structures

Vagina (birth canal)	Flexible, muscular structure in which menstrual flow and babies pass
Introitus	Vaginal opening
Hymen	Thin membrane that partially covers the introitus and contains a large number of blood vessels
Gräfenberg spot (G-spot)	Located on the upper front wall of the vagina, an erotically sensitive area that may produce intense erotic pleasure and a fluid emission in some women
Uterus (womb)	Hollow, thick-walled muscular organ in which a fertilized ovum implants and develops until birth
Cervix	Lower end of the uterus that extends down and opens to the vagina
Endometrium	Inner lining of the uterine wall to which the fertilized egg attaches; partly discharged (if pregnancy does not occur) with the menstrual flow
Os	Opening to the cervix
Ovary (gonad)	Organ that produces gametes (see below)
Gametes	Sex cells containing the genetic material necessary for reproduction; also referred to as oocytes, eggs, ova (singular, ovum)
Ovarian follicles	Saclike structures that contain the immature oocytes
Corpus luteum	Tissue formed from a ruptured ovarian follicle that produces important hormones after the oocyte emerges
Fallopian tubes (oviducts)	Uterine tubes that transport the oocyte from the ovary to the uterus
Infundibulum	Funnel-shaped end of each fallopian tube
Fimbriae	Fingerlike projections that drape over the ovary and help transport the oocyte from the ovary into the fallopian tube
Cilia	Tiny, hairlike structures that provide waving motion to help transport the oocyte within the fallopian tube to the ovary
Ampulla	Widened part of the fallopian tube in which fertilization normally occurs

Other Structures

Urethra	Tube through which urine passes
Urethral opening	Opening in the urethra, through which urine is expelled
Anus	Opening in the rectum, through which feces passes
Perineum	Area that lies between the vaginal opening and the anus
Pelvic floor	Underside of the pelvic area, extending from the top of the pubic bone (above the clitoris) to the anus

hormones are composed of either amino acids (building blocks of proteins) or steroids (derived from cholesterol). They are produced by the ovaries and the endocrine glands—the adrenals, pituitary, and hypothalamus. Hormones assist in a variety of tasks, including development of the reproductive organs and secondary sex characteristics during puberty, regulation of the menstrual cycle, maintenance of pregnancy, initiation and regulation of childbirth,

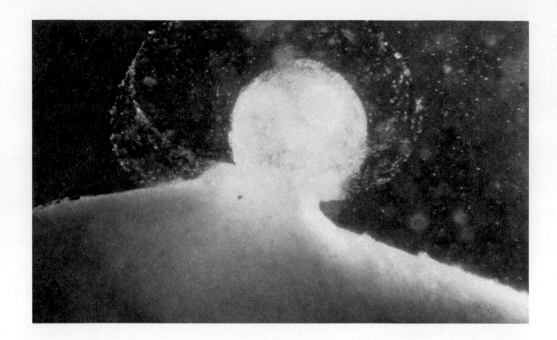

During ovulation, the ovarian follicle swells and ruptures, releasing the mature oocyte to begin its journey through the fallopian tube.

Petit Format/Science Source

initiation of lactation, and to some degree, the regulation of **libido** (li-BEE-doh), or sex drive or interest. Hormones that act directly on the gonads are known as **gonadotropins** (go-nad-a-TRO-pins). **Kisspeptin**, a hormone made by the hypothalamus, starts the secretion of gonadotropin-releasing hormone at puberty.

On the first day of the menstrual cycle, **gonadotropin-releasing hormone (GnRH)** is released from the hypothalamus, which in turn, stimulates the pituitary to produce **luteinizing hormone (LH)** and **follicle-stimulating hormone (FSH)**. These hormones regulate the levels of **estrogen**, which affect the maturation of the reproductive organs, menstruation, and pregnancy, and **progesterone**, which helps maintain the uterine lining until menstruation occurs. A negative feedback loop is controlled by the hypothalamus, pituitary, and ovaries, which are responsible for the drops in hormones preceding menstruation. The pituitary also produces prolactin and oxytocin. (The principle hormones involved in a woman's reproductive and sexual life and their functions are described in Table 2.)

The Ovarian Cycle

The development of female gametes is a complex process that begins even before a female is born. In infancy and childhood, the cells develop into ova (eggs). During puberty, hormones trigger the completion of the process of **oogenesis** (oh-uh-JEN-uh-sis), literally, "egg beginning" (see Figure 7). The **oocyte**, otherwise referred to as germ cell or immature ovum, marks the start of mitosis, the process by which a cell divides, creating two daughter cells. Oogenesis results in the formation of both primary oocytes, before birth, and as secondary oocytes after it and as part of ovulation. This process, called the **ovarian cycle**, continues until a woman reaches menopause.

The ovarian cycle averages 28 days in length, although there is considerable variation among women, ranging from 21–40 days. In their own particular cycle length after puberty, however, most women experience little variation. Generally, ovulation occurs in only one ovary each month, with only a fifty-fifty chance of releasing an egg from the opposite ovary as the month before. If a single ovary is removed, the remaining one usually begins to ovulate every month. The ovarian cycle has four phases: menstrual, follicular (fo-LIK-u-lar), ovulatory (ov-UL-a-toree), and luteal (LOO-tee-ul). As an ovary undergoes its changes, corresponding shifts occur in the uterus. Menstruation marks the end of this sequence of hormonal and physical changes in the ovaries and uterus.

TABLE 2 ● Female Sex Hormones

Hormone	Where Produced	Functions
Estrogen (including estradiol, estrone, estriol)	Ovaries, adrenal glands, placenta (during pregnancy)	Promotes maturation of reproductive organs, development of secondary sex characteristics, and growth spurt at puberty; regulates menstrual cycle; sustains pregnancy; maintains libido
Progesterone	Ovaries, adrenal glands, placenta	Promotes breast development, maintains uterine lining, regulates menstrual cycle, sustains pregnancy
Gonadotropin-releasing hormone (GnRH)	Hypothalamus	Promotes maturation of gonads, regulates menstrual cycle
Follicle-stimulating hormone (FSH)	Pituitary	Regulates ovarian function and maturation of ovarian follicles
Kisspeptin	Hypothalamus	Initiates secretion of GnRH at puberty
Luteinizing hormone (LH)	Pituitary	Assists in production of estrogen and progesterone, regulates maturation of ovarian follicles, triggers ovulation
Human chorionic gonadotropin (HCG)	Embryo and placenta	Helps sustain pregnancy
Testosterone	Adrenal glands and ovaries	Helps stimulate sexual desire and maintenance and repair of reproductive tissues and bones
Oxytocin	Hypothalamus	Stimulates uterine contractions during childbirth and possibly during orgasm, promotes milk let-down
Prolactin	Pituitary	Stimulates milk production
Prostaglandins	All body cells	Mediates hormone response, stimulates muscle contractions

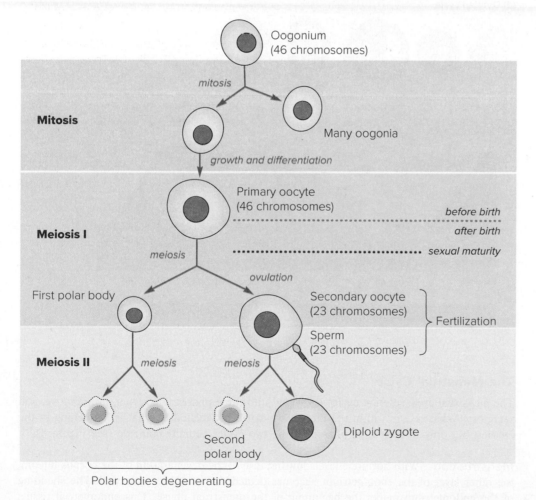

● FIGURE 7

Oogenesis. This diagram charts the development of an ovum, beginning with embryonic development of the oogonium and ending with fertilization of the secondary oocyte, which then becomes the diploid zygote. Primary oocytes are present in a female at birth; at puberty, hormones stimulate the oocyte to undergo meiosis.

Changes During the Menstrual Cycle.
This chart shows the influence of the
brain on the levels of hormones in
the blood and their impact on the
menstrual cycle.

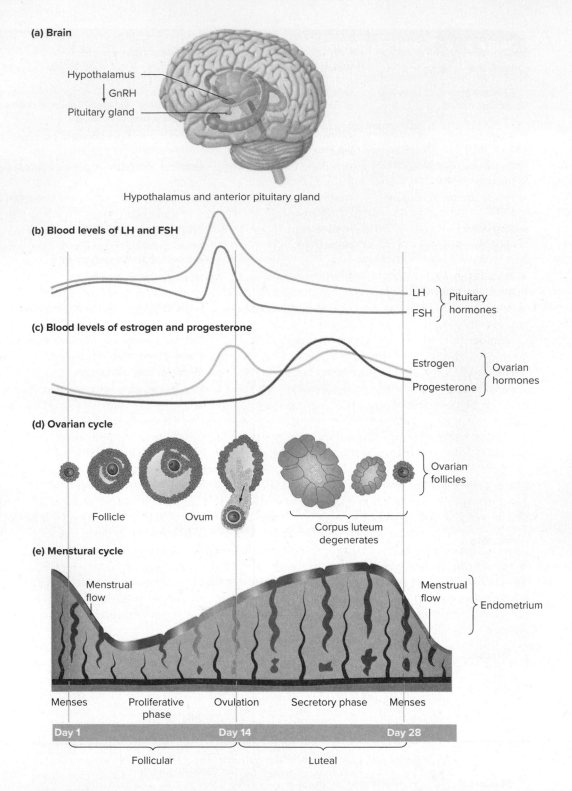

(a) Brain

Hypothalamus

↓ GnRH

Pituitary gland

Hypothalamus and anterior pituitary gland

(b) Blood levels of LH and FSH

LH ⎱ Pituitary
FSH ⎰ hormones

(c) Blood levels of estrogen and progesterone

Estrogen ⎱ Ovarian
Progesterone ⎰ hormones

(d) Ovarian cycle

Ovarian
follicles

Follicle   Ovum

Corpus luteum
degenerates

(e) Menstural cycle

Menstrual
flow

Menstrual
flow

Endometrium

Menses   Proliferative   Ovulation   Secretory phase   Menses
           phase

Day 1   Day 14   Day 28

Follicular   Luteal

The Menstrual Cycle

The **menstrual cycle** (uterine cycle) is divided into three phases: menstrual, proliferative, and
secretory. What occurs within the uterus is inextricably related to what is happening in the
ovaries, but only in their final phases do the two cycles actually coincide (see Figure 8).

Menstruation   With hormone levels low because of the degeneration of the corpus luteum,
the outer layer of the endometrium becomes detached from the uterine wall. The shedding
of the endometrium marks the beginning of the menstrual phase. This endometrial tissue,

along with mucus, other cervical and vaginal secretions, and a small amount of blood (2–5 ounces per cycle), is expelled through the vagina. The menstrual flow, or **menses** (MEN-seez), generally occurs over a period of 3–5 days. FSH and LH begin increasing around day 5, marking the end of this phase. A girl's first menstruation is known as **menarche** (MEH-nar-kee).

The Proliferative Phase   The **proliferative phase** lasts about 9 days. During this time, the endometrium thickens in response to increased estrogen. The mucous membranes of the cervix secrete a clear, thin mucus with a crystalline structure that facilitates the passage of sperm. The proliferative phase ends with ovulation.

The Secretory Phase   During the first part of the **secretory phase**, with the help of progesterone, the endometrium begins to prepare for the arrival of a fertilized ovum. Glands within the uterus enlarge and begin secreting glycogen, a cell nutrient. The cervical mucus thickens and starts forming a plug to seal off the uterus in the event of pregnancy. If fertilization does not occur, the corpus luteum begins to degenerate, as LH levels decline. Progesterone levels then fall, and the endometrial cells begin to die. The secretory phase lasts approximately 14 days, corresponding with the luteal phase of the ovarian cycle. It ends with the shedding of the endometrium.

Menstrual Synchrony   Women who live or work together sometimes report developing similarly timed menstrual cycles (Cutler, 1999). Termed **menstrual synchrony**, or period syncing, this phenomenon appears to be related to the sense of smell—more specifically, a response to **pheromones**, or chemicals that the body produces that can be sexually stimulating or impact the behavior of others. There is some controversy among researchers as to whether the phenomenon actually exists, with research leaning towards the conclusion that menstrual cycles do not sync between women who spend a lot of time together (FIGO, 2017).

Menstrual Effects   American women have divergent attitudes toward menstruation. For some women, menstruation is a problem; for others, it is simply a fact of life that creates little disruption. For individual women, the problems associated with their menstrual period may be physiological, emotional, or practical. The vast majority of menstruating women notice at least one emotional, physical, or behavioral change in the week or so prior to menstruation. Most women describe the changes negatively: breast tenderness and swelling, abdominal bloating, irritability, cramping, depression, or fatigue. Some women also report positive changes such as increased energy, heightened sexual arousal, or a general feeling of well-being. For most women, changes during the menstrual cycle are usually mild to moderate; they appear to have little impact on their lives.

Menstrual Period Slang: that time of the month, monthlies, the curse, female troubles, a visit from my friend, a visit from Aunt Flo, a visit from George, on the rag, on a losing streak, falling off the roof

The combination of cultural expectations combined with taboos surrounding menstruation creates negative attitudes toward menstruation in many parts of the world. In some communities, these taboos are rooted in cultural mythology and have led to a range of restrictions on menstruating girls and women: from sleeping outside the house to forbidding entrance to kitchens and temples (Preiss, 2016). This practice, known as menstrual seclusion, is still widespread in regions of western Nepal and Southeast India. Though the tradition of banishing girls and women from society while they are menstruating is forbidden in Nepal, the practice is difficult to eradicate because many people still believe that a menstruating female who breaks the rules risks angering the gods and inviting misfortune on her family.

While these views are extreme, the common negative attitudes and stereotypes of menstruating girls and women still prevail. Since a monthly period is not a requirement for good health, some women are turning to means to stop menstruation, including oral contraceptives, the Mirena IUD, and birth control shot. Hormonal contraceptives can be taken continuously, meaning a woman can stay on the pill and skip the placebo week of pills when she would otherwise have a period. This method of using hormonal contraception to stop a period is completely reversible (Gunter, 2019.3c). (For more about contraception, see Chapter 11.)

Menstrual Problems

Premenstrual Syndrome   A group of physical and psychological changes that may occur 7–14 days before a women's menstrual period is known as **premenstrual syndrome (PMS)**. These symptoms disappear after the start of menstrual bleeding. Though the precise causes of PMS are still unclear, the phenomena seem to be linked to alterations in ovarian hormones and brain chemicals, or neurotransmitters. Some other possible causes include low levels of vitamins and minerals, eating large amounts of salty foods, which can cause a woman to retain water, and drinking alcohol and caffeine, which may alter a woman's mood and energy levels ("Premenstrual syndrome," 2017).

Most women have at least one sign of PMS each month ("What is PMS?," 2019). Common emotional symptoms include but are not limited to depression, angry outbursts, irritability, poor concentration, insomnia, and anxiety. Physical changes can include thirst and appetite changes, breast tenderness, bloating, headache, and fatigue. Many women also experience a decreased libido. Most PMS symptoms are not usually severe and the majority of women cope well with them. For example, women may make changes in their diet, sleep, and exercise routine.

Pre-Menstrual Dysphoric Disorder   Far less common than PMS, accounting for 2%–5% of cases, is **pre-menstrual dysphoric disorder (PMDD)**, a term used as a diagnosis category by the American Psychiatric Association (2013) in its *Diagnostic and Statistical Manual of Mental Disorders (DSM-5)*. What differentiates PMDD from PMS is that PMDD is more severe, characterized by a combination of distinct symptoms, and is persistent, occurring during most menstrual cycles and over a period of a year. This diagnosis category remains controversial in that some argue that it represents a medicalization of women's menstrual experiences and that the scientific basis for PMDD is nonexistent. We have, however, learned that while those with PMDD have normal hormone levels, for some reason their bodies are more sensitive to these hormones than those who do not have this disorder (Dubey et al., 2017). This biological cause holds hope for improved treatment.

Menorrhagia   At some point in her menstrual life, nearly every woman experiences heavy or prolonged bleeding during her menstrual cycle, also known as **menorrhagia**. Although heavy menstrual bleeding is common among most women, only a few experience blood loss severe enough for it to be defined as menorrhagia. Signs and symptoms may include a menstrual flow that soaks through one or more sanitary pads or tampons every hour for several consecutive hours, the need to use double sanitary protection throughout the menstrual flow, menstrual flow that includes large blood clots, and/or heavy menstrual flow that interferes with a person's regular lifestyle. Though the cause of heavy menstrual bleeding is unknown, a number of conditions may cause menorrhagia, including hormonal imbalances, uterine fibroids, having an IUD, cancer, or certain medications. Among adolescents with heavy menstrual periods, the most common reason is what is called anovulatory bleeding, or a cycle in which no ovulation has occurred but hormones cause continued bleeding (Klass, 2020). Over time, a young woman's cycles should become more regular and the bleeding should decrease. Excessive or prolonged menstrual bleeding can lead to iron deficiency anemia and other medical conditions; thus, it is advisable for women with this problem to seek medical care and treatment.

Dysmenorrhea   While menstrual cramps are experienced by some women before or during their periods, a more persistent, aching, and serious pain sufficient to limit a woman's activities is called **dysmenorrhea**. There are two types of dysmenorrhea. Primary dysmenorrhea is not associated with any diagnosable pelvic condition. It is characterized by pain that begins with (or just before) uterine bleeding when there is an absence of pain at other times in the cycle. It can be very severe and may be accompanied by nausea, weakness, or other physical symptoms. In secondary dysmenorrhea, the symptoms may be the same, but there is an underlying condition or disease causing them; pain may not be limited to the menstrual phase alone. Secondary dysmenorrhea may be caused by pelvic inflammatory disease (PID), endometriosis, endometrial cancer, or other conditions that should be treated.

The effects of dysmenorrhea can totally incapacitate a woman for several hours or even days. Once believed to be a psychological condition, primary dysmenorrhea is now known to be caused by high levels of **prostaglandins** (pros-ta-GLAN-dins), natural substances made by cells in the endometrium and other parts of the body. When excessive amounts are produced, the woman may have extreme pain with her menstrual cycle along with headaches, nausea, vomiting, and diarrhea. Prostaglandin production can be decreased with over-the-counter drugs such as aspirin or ibuprofen. Birth control pills, Depo-Provera, or the hormonal intrauterine device (IUD), can also be used to prevent ovulation and thus decrease the thickness of the endometrium, where the prostaglandins are produced.

Amenorrhea   When women do not menstruate for reasons other than aging, the condition is called **amenorrhea** (ay-meh-neh-REE-a). Principal causes of amenorrhea are pregnancy and breastfeeding. Lack of menstruation, if not a result of pregnancy or nursing, is categorized as either primary or secondary amenorrhea. Women who are older than 16 and have never menstruated are diagnosed as having primary amenorrhea. It may be that they have not yet reached their critical weight, when an increased ratio of body fat triggers menstrual cycle–inducing hormones, or that they are hereditarily late maturers. But it can also signal hormonal deficiencies, abnormal body structure, or an intersex condition or other genital anomaly that makes menstruation impossible. Most primary amenorrhea can be treated with hormone therapy.

Secondary amenorrhea exists when a previously menstruating woman stops menstruating for several months. If it is not due to pregnancy, breastfeeding, or the use of hormonal contraceptives, the source of secondary amenorrhea may be found in stress, lowered body fat, heavy physical training, cysts or tumors, disease, or hormonal irregularities. Anorexia is a frequent cause of amenorrhea. If a woman is not pregnant, is not breastfeeding, and can rule out hormonal contraceptives as a cause, she should see her health care practitioner if she has gone 3 months without menstruating.

Lifestyle changes or treatment of the underlying condition can almost always correct amenorrhea, unless it is caused by a congenital anomaly. Because there is no known harm associated with amenorrhea, the condition is corrected when an underlying problem presents itself or it causes a woman psychological distress.

Menstrual Products   Most American women who menstruate use sanitary pads, panty liners, or tampons to help absorb the flow of menstrual blood. While pads and panty liners are used outside the body, tampons are placed inside the vagina. For a wide variety of reasons, including environmental concerns, comfort, chemical residues, and **toxic shock syndrome (TSS)**, a rare bacterial infection that can occur in menstruating women who use tampons and cause her to go into shock, many women are turning to alternative means for catching menstrual flow. More women talking publicly about menstruation, requesting sanitary supplies in schools and offices, and demanding a repeal of tampon taxes, represents a change in the way society addresses and manages menstruation. While some Americans may question the use of alternative products, across time and cultures a wide variety of methods have been used to absorb the flow of blood.

For those desiring to wear something internally, reusable, or disposable, menstrual cups are another alternative to tampons. The cup is inserted inside the vagina a few inches below the cervix and is held in place by the muscles of the lower vagina. When put into place properly, the cup should not be felt. Two types of menstrual cups are available. The cup is designed to collect, instead of absorb, menstrual blood and can be safely worn up to 12 hours. Additionally, the cups don't contain chemicals, bleaches, or fibers and can be used during intercourse because they can prevent the menstrual blood from flowing outside the body. Some women find the cups more difficult to insert and remove than tampons and many feel uncomfortable with cleaning the reusable cups (Rabin, 2019).

Research on the safety of menstrual cups is sparse. Some research has found menstrual cups to be linked to toxic shock syndrome (TSS) because they can introduce oxygen into the vaginal canal. In the presence of oxygen, *Staphylococcus aureus,* the bacteria behind most cases of TSS as well as the toxin that the bacteria produces, can multiply to high enough levels to produce the toxin (Nonfoux et al., 2018). Some women have used the diaphragm

(a)

(b)

An array of choices that collect and absorb menstrual flow are now available to women.
(a) Tampons come in a variety of sizes and are worn internally to help absorb the flow of menstrual blood. Most have a small cotton string that hangs outside the body to allow for easy removal;
(b) Sanitary pads, napkins, and other products may come in different shapes and sizes and range from light to high absorbency to handle each stage of a female's period. The menstrual cup is worn similarly to a tampon to catch and collect the flow. The decision to use one menstrual product over another is a personal one.

(a) drmicrobe/123RF; (b) Editorial Image, LLC/ Alamy Stock Photo

or cervical cap in a similar manner; that is to collect the menstrual blood during sexual intercourse, however there is also risk of TSS using these devices.

Reusable sea sponges are not recommended to absorb the flow of blood because their large surface area is ripe for bacterial growth. Additionally, their numerous air pockets, super-absorbency potential, and swell could potentially cause micro-trauma to the vagina (Gunter, 2019.3c). Since there is no data to prove that they are safe, it's illegal to sell sea sponges for menstrual use in the United States.

The sheer magnitude of feminine care products marketed to women each year ($3 billion in the United States; $37 billion worldwide) (Statista, 2019) has given reason for women to question their safety as well as their environmental impact. This public concern has pushed Congress to approve funding for research on their ingredients and safety. As a result, a few companies are beginning to list the ingredients in some their feminine hygiene products. This legislation does not address the environmental impact of disposal of these products. While this agenda will continue to be pursued, the next progressive wave will occur when feminine hygiene products become exempt from sales tax in all states.

Most likely, the majority of American women will continue to rely on more widely available and advertised tampons or sanitary pads; however, alternatives to these provide women with additional options for how they address their menstrual flow and, in some cases, the environmental impacts of that decision.

Sexuality and the Menstrual Cycle   Although studies have tried to determine whether there is a biologically based cycle of sexual interest and activity in women that correlates with the menstrual cycle such as higher interest around ovulation, the results have been varied. There is also variation in how people feel about sexual activity during different phases of the menstrual cycle.

Research has found that sexual activity may positively affect the immune response in healthy women (Lorenz et al., 2018). Although we know that the female immune system defends against pathogens, we've recently learned that sexual activity may serve as a trigger to modulate the immune system's response, thus promoting a defense during non-fertile times and allowing a more permissive environment for pregnancy during ovulation.

There has been a general taboo in our culture, as in many others, against sexual intercourse during menstruation. This taboo may be based on religious or cultural beliefs. Among Orthodox Jews, for example, women are required to refrain from intercourse for seven days following the end of menstruation. They may then resume sexual activity after a ritual bath, the *mikvah*. Contact with blood may make some people squeamish. Some women, especially at the beginning of their period, feel bloated or uncomfortable; they may experience breast tenderness or a general feeling of not wanting to be touched. Others may find that sexual activity helps relieve menstrual discomfort.

For some couples, merely having to deal with the logistics of bloodstains, bathing, and laundry may be enough to discourage them from intercourse at this time. For many, however, menstrual blood holds no special connotation. While it is perfectly safe to have sex during a woman's period if not HIV infected, only 15% of women on their period engage in their usual sexual activity ("Condom Use. . . ," 2018). Many women who are comfortable with menstrual sex view it as just another part of a committed intimate relationship. Although it is unusual, conception *can* occur during menstruation. Some women find that a diaphragm or menstrual cup can collect the menstrual flow. Menstrual cups, however, are not a contraceptive. A woman should not engage in intercourse while a tampon is inserted because of possible injury to the cervix. And inventive lovers can, of course, find many ways to give each other pleasure that do not require putting the penis or other object into the vagina.

practically speaking

Vaginal and Menstrual Health

Many factors can influence the way we experience the changes that occur over the course of the menstrual cycle. While the vast majority of women feel few and minor changes, others experience changes that are uncomfortable and debilitating. The variations can be significant in any one woman and from month to month. For women, recognizing their menstrual patterns, learning about their bodies, and recognizing and dealing with existing difficulties can be useful in heading off or easing potential problems. Different remedies work for different women. We suggest that you try varying combinations of them and keep a record of your response to each. A variety of apps are now available to help track your menstrual cycle. Following are some common changes that occur during the menstrual cycle and self-help means to address them.

For Vaginal Changes

The mucous membranes lining the walls of the vagina normally produce clear, white, or pale yellow secretions. These secretions pass from the cervix through the vagina and vary in color, consistency, odor, and quantity, depending on the phase of the menstrual cycle, the woman's health, and her unique physical characteristics. It is important for you to observe your secretions periodically and note any changes, especially if symptoms accompany them. Because self-diagnosis of unusual discharges is inaccurate over half the time, it is wise to go ahead with self-treatment only after a diagnosis is made by a health care practitioner. Call a health professional if you feel uncertain or suspicious and/or think you may have been exposed to a sexually transmitted infection.

Most "vaginal health" products are bogus (Vaughn, 2020). Nevertheless, here are some guidelines that may help a woman avoid getting vaginal infections (vaginitis):

1. Avoid douching and vaginal deodorants, especially deodorant suppositories or deodorant tampons. The vagina is a clean environment and does not need to be washed. Douching upsets the natural chemical balance of the vagina.

2. Maintain good genital hygiene by washing the labia and clitoris regularly (about once a day) with mild soap.

3. After a bowel movement, wipe the anus from front to back, away from the vagina, to prevent contamination with fecal bacteria.

4. Wear cotton underpants with a cotton crotch. Nylon does not "breathe," and it allows heat and moisture to build up, creating an ideal environment for infectious organisms to reproduce.

5. If you use a vaginal lubricant, be sure it is water-soluble. Oil-based lubricants such as Vaseline encourage bacterial growth.

For Premenstrual Changes

1. Consume a well-balanced diet, with plenty of whole-grain cereals, fruits, and vegetables.

2. Moderate your intake of alcohol, avoid tobacco, and get sufficient sleep.

3. Exercise at least 30–45 minutes a day. Aerobic exercise brings oxygen to body tissues and stimulates the production of endorphins, chemical substances that help promote feelings of well-being.

For Cramps

1. Relax and apply heat by using a heating pad or hot-water bottle (or, in a pinch, a cat) applied to the abdominal area may help relieve cramps; a warm bath may also help.

2. Get a lower-back or other form of massage, such as acupressure or Shiatsu.

3. Take prostaglandin inhibitors, such as aspirin and ibuprofen, to reduce cramping of the uterine and abdominal muscles. Aspirin increases menstrual flow slightly, whereas ibuprofen reduces it. Stronger antiprostaglandins may be prescribed by your health care practitioner.

4. Having an orgasm (with or without a partner) is reported by some women to relieve menstrual congestion and cramping.

When symptoms are severe, further medical evaluation is needed.

think
about it

Body Modification: You're Doing What? Where?

Have you ever wondered if your genitals were normal? Desired to modify a part of your body? Had a procedure done that somewhat altered your appearance? Though the majority who seek plastic and cosmetic surgery do so to increase their attractiveness or improve their body image, we still might wonder about the motivations of those who seek these changes, especially if the modifications are to otherwise healthy parts of their body.

When people think of cosmetic surgery, they often think of middle-age white women seeking to enhance their physical attractiveness. To a great extent this remains true; however, a broader cross-section of society is increasingly seeking to modify or alter their appearance. In spite of their different motivations, many in midlife are embracing the "Mommy Makeover" or "Daddy Do-Over." Still, gender plays a role in who gets surgery with females accounting for 92% or nearly 15 million cosmetic procedures. Males obtained 8% or 1.3 million surgeries; an amount representing a 29% increase among men since 2000 (American Society of Plastic Surgeons [ASPS], 2019).

More men are having cosmetic surgery, most likely the result of increased exposure to an ideal body image and greater acceptance of cosmetic surgery. A variety of cosmetic procedures are requested by men, the majority of which involve nose reshaping, eyelid surgery, and liposuction. Men also seek out breast augmentation and lifts, breast implant removals, buttock implants and lifts, and pectoral implants, to name a few. Penis enlargement procedures, including vacuum pumps, pills that some manufacturers claim will increase penis size, and surgical practices are available for men who believe that augmentation would increase their sexual performance or self-esteem. Only rarely is a man's penis considered by a partner to be too small; a more common problem is that partners complain that the penis is too large.

Ethnicity also plays a role in who seek surgeries. The vast majority of those who sought out cosmetic procedures were Caucasian (12.4 million), followed by Hispanics (1.9 million), African Americans (1.6 million), and Asian Americans (1.2 million) (ASPS, 2019). The growing interest in esthetic surgeries among people of color reflects a newfound prosperity as well as widespread acceptance of these procedures. But this demand has posed a problem for surgeons whose training has been directed toward Caucasian standards of beauty. For all races and genders, though some of these procedures may be necessary for the patient's health and well-being, the appeal for surgery is not.

Breast augmentation is the top cosmetic surgical procedure for women and has been since 2006 (ASPS, 2019). If someone is unhappy with the size of their breasts, a breast lift, breast implant, or fat transfer breast augmentation can be performed. Less often, a breast reduction can provide relief for some women whose breasts size compromises posture and/or causes physiological or physical discomfort. In the case of breast reconstruction after mastectomy or injury, breast implants can be inserted. Silicone implants account for 88% of all breast augmentation procedures, while saline implants are used in 12% of procedures. For those who prefer to avoid implants, fat grafting can be done.

Though breast implants undergo extensive testing to establish their safety and effectiveness, there are risks associated with each type. Given new evidence and the rapid increase in the demand for cosmetic breast surgeries, The Food & Drug Administration (FDA) (2019) has undertaken a review of their safety and effectiveness. In the meantime, researchers continue to site warnings including their association with lymphoma as well as a variety of systemic symptoms that can occur with the devices (Roberts et al., 2019; Swanson, 2019).

Of concern among physicians and others is the increasing number of young girls, who express an interest in cosmetic surgery, to improve, for example, the appearance of their breasts and vulva. Unrealistic expectations are often associated with cosmetic surgery. Additionally, lack of knowledge about the wide variation in appearance of anatomy along with a misunderstanding about healthy growth and development may be fueling young women's concerns. Fortunately, those between the ages of 13 and 19 make up the lowest percent and number of cosmetic procedures—only 1% of the total or approximately 227,000 surgeries per year (ASPS, 2019).

Perhaps as a result of women who have experienced genital shame or fear of aging, there has been an increase in the number of surgeries that "rejuvenate" or "renew" genitals, in particular, the labia (Gunter, 2019.3a). The usual goal is to reduce the length of the labia so that it appears smaller and, for some, can no longer chaff or pull against clothing. In spite of the long-term medical implications, including the impact of labial reduction on sensation or sexual functioning, in 2018 there were over 10,000 labiaplasties performed in the United States (ASPS, 2019). Jan Gunter, obstetrician and gynecologist and author warns: "Surgically reducing the labia should be considered the exact same thing as surgically reducing the size of the penis" (2019.3a, p. 206). If a woman is concerned about the normalcy of her genitals and wants surgery, she should seek two medical opinions and opt for the smallest reduction.

If you are unhappy with certain parts of your anatomy, talk to a professional health care provider. If you are in a relationship, talk to your partner. In most cases, you will learn that size is usually not an important issue. However, intimacy, communication, mutual respect, and acceptance of your body and sexuality are.

Think Critically

1. Have you ever been rejected by a sexual partner because they were dissatisfied with parts of your body? Have you ever rejected a sexual partner for the same reason?

2. Is there a cosmetic procedure that you would consider? If so, why? If not, what contributes to this feeling?

3. What could you do to help a sexual partner feel more comfortable about accepting their body?

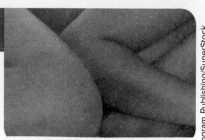

Ingram Publishing/SuperStock

Another chapter will discuss the anatomical features and physiological functions that characterize men's sexuality. The information in these two chapters should serve as a basis for understanding the material that follows.

Summary

Female Sex Organs: What Are They For?

- All embryos appear as female at first. Genetic and hormonal signals trigger the development of male organs in those embryos destined to be male.

- Sex organs serve a reproductive purpose, but they perform other functions also: giving pleasure, attracting sex partners, and bonding in relationships.

- The external female *genitals* are known collectively as the *vulva*. The *mons pubis* is a pad of fatty tissue that covers the area of the pubic bone. The *clitoris* is the center of sexual arousal. The *labia majora* are two folds of spongy flesh extending from the mons pubis and enclosing the other external genitals. The *labia minora* are smooth, hairless folds within the labia majora that meet above the clitoris.

- The internal female sexual structures and reproductive organs include the *vagina*, the *uterus*, the *cervix*, the *ovaries*, and the *fallopian tubes*. The vagina is a flexible, muscular organ that encompasses the penis or other object during sexual expression and is the *birth canal* through which an infant is born. Prior to first intercourse or other intrusion, the opening of the vagina, the *introitus*, is partially covered by a thin, perforated membrane, the *hymen*.

- Though controversy exists about the presence of the exact site, many women report the existence of an erotically sensitive area, the *Gräfenberg spot* (*G-spot*), or female prostate on the anterior (front) wall of the vagina midway between the introitus and the cervix.

- The *uterus*, or womb, is a hollow, thick-walled, muscular organ; the tapered end, the *cervix*, extends downward and opens into the vagina. The lining of the uterine walls, the *endometrium*, is built up and then shed and expelled through the cervical *os* (opening) during menstruation. In the event of pregnancy, the pre-embryo is embedded in the nourishing endometrium. On each side of the uterus is one of a pair of *ovaries*, the female *gonads* (organs that produce *gametes*, sex cells containing the genetic material necessary for reproduction). At the top of the uterus are the *fallopian tubes*, or uterine tubes. They extend toward the ovaries but are not attached to them. The funnel-shaped end of each tube (the *infundibulum*) fans out into fingerlike *fimbriae*, which drape over the ovary. Hairlike *cilia* on the fimbriae transport the ovulated *oocyte* (egg) into the fallopian tube.

The *ampulla* is the widened part of the tube in which fertilization normally occurs. Other important structures in the area of the genitals include the *urethra, anus,* and *perineum.*

- The reproductive function of the female breasts, or *mammary glands,* is to nourish the offspring through *lactation,* or milk production. A breast is composed of fatty tissue and 15–25 lobes that radiate around a central protruding nipple. *Alveoli* within the lobes produce milk. Around the nipple is a ring of darkened skin called the *areola.*

Female Sexual Physiology

- *Hormones* are chemical substances that serve as messengers, traveling through the bloodstream. Important hormones that act directly on the gonads (*gonadotropins*) are *follicle-stimulating hormone* (*FSH*) and *luteinizing hormone* (*LH*). Hormones produced in the ovaries are *estrogen,* which helps regulate the menstrual cycle, and *progesterone,* which helps maintain the uterine lining, until menstruation occurs.

- At birth, the human female's ovaries contain approximately half a million *oocytes,* or female gametes. During childhood, many of these degenerate. In a woman's lifetime, about 400 oocytes will mature and be released, beginning in puberty when hormones trigger the completion of *oogenesis,* the production of oocytes, commonly called eggs or ova.

- The *menstrual cycle* (uterine cycle), like the ovarian cycle, is divided into four phases. The shedding of the endometrium marks the beginning of the *menstrual phase.* The menstrual flow, or *menses,* generally occurs over a period of 3–5 days. Endometrial tissue builds up during the *proliferative* or *follicular phase*; it produces nutrients to sustain an embryo in the *secretory phase.*

- Menstrual problems have been attributed to *premenstrual syndrome* (*PMS*), a cluster of physical, psychological, and emotional symptoms that may occur 7–14 days before the menstrual period. Some women experience very heavy bleeding (*menorrhagia*), while others have pelvic cramping and pain during the menstrual cycle (*dysmenorrhea*). When women do not menstruate for reasons other than aging, the condition is called *amenorrhea.* Principal causes of amenorrhea are pregnancy and nursing.

- An array of choices are available for menstrual products, the number of which have given women reason to question their safety, effectiveness, and impact on the environment.

Questions for Discussion

- Are changes in mood that may occur during a woman's menstrual cycle caused by biological factors, or are they learned? What evidence supports your response?

- Given the choice between the environmentally friendly menstruation products and commercial products, which would you choose for yourself (or recommend to a woman), and why?

- What are your thoughts and reactions to learning about the Gräfenberg spot? Do you believe it is an invented erotic spot for some women or a genuine gland or erogenous zone?

- How important is it to you that *both* you and your partner enjoy sexual pleasuring and pleasure?

- For women only: What is your response to looking at your genitals? For men only: What is your response to viewing photos of women's genitals? Why is it that women are discouraged from touching or looking at their genitals?

- How do you feel about the idea of having sex during a woman's menstrual period? Why do you feel this way?

Sex and the Internet

Sexuality and Ethnicity

Of the 332 million people living in the United States, nearly 168 million are women. Many of these women are in poor health, use fewer reproductive health services, and continue to suffer disproportionately from premature death, disease, and disabilities. In addition, there are tremendous economic, cultural, and social barriers to achieving optimal health. To find out more about the reproductive health risks of special concern to women, go to the Office on Women's Health website: https://www.womenshealth.gov/a-z-topics. From the menu, select one topic and report on the following:

- One reproductive health concern

- Barriers women may encounter that would prevent them from obtaining services

- Potential solutions to this problem

Suggested Websites

American College of Obstetricians and Gynecologists
http://www.acog.org
A professional association with information about women's reproductive health, including pregnancy and childbirth.

Centers for Disease Control and Prevention
http://www.cdc.gov/women/
Provides a wide variety of specific information and links related to all aspects of women's health and well-being.

Clue
https://helloclue.com/articles/sex
A menstrual tracking app, encyclopedia, health resource, and more.

#HappyPeriod
http:/hashtaghappyperiod.org
A social movement providing menstrual hygiene kits to those who would otherwise go without.

International Society for the Study of Women's Sexual Health
www.isswsh.org
A multidisciplinary, academic, and scientific organization that provides opportunities for communication among scholars, supports ethics and professionalism, and provides the public with accurate information about women's sexuality.

National Organization for Women (NOW)
http://www.now.org
An organization of women and men who support full equality for women in truly equal partnerships.

National Women's Health Network
http://www.nwhn.org
Provides clear and well-researched information about a variety of women's health- and sexuality-related issues.

North American Menopause Society (NAMS)
http://www.menopause.org
Promotes women's health during midlife and beyond through an understanding of menopause.

Suggested Reading

Bergner, D. (2013). *What do women want? Adventures in the science of female desire.* HarperCollins. Recaps studies and gives a fresh perspective to this lifelong question.

Bobel, C. (2019). *The managed body: Developing girls and menstrual health in the global south.* Palgrave/Macmillan. A critique of the menstrual hygiene management movement to support menstruating girls in the Global South.

Gunter, J. (2019). *The vagina bible: The vulva and the vagina – Separating the myth from the medicine.* Kensington Publishing Corp. A wise and informative guide to female health and well-being.

Komisaruk, B. R., Whipple, B., Nasserzadeh, S., & Beyer-Flores, C. (2010). *The orgasm answer guide.* Johns Hopkins University Press. Provides a broad overview of women's orgasm and men's orgasm, their anatomy and physiology, and their connection to relationships and health.

Meston, C. M., & Buss, D. M. (2009). *Why women have sex.* Henry Holt. Combines psychology and biology to help uncover women's sexual motivations.

Nagoski, E. (2015). *Come as you are.* Simon Schuster. An exploration of why and how women's sexuality works that is based on research and brain science.

Male Sexual Anatomy and Physiology

Dennis Grasse/EyeEm/Getty Images

CHAPTER OUTLINE

Male Sex Organs: What Are They For?

Male Sexual Physiology

Student Voices

"Behold—the penis mightier than the sword."

—Mark Twain (1835–1910)

C LEARLY, MALE SEXUAL STRUCTURES and functions differ in many ways from those of females. What may not be as apparent, however, is that there are also a number of similarities in the functions of the sex organs. In the previous chapter, we learned that the sexual structures of both females and males derive from the same embryonic tissue (see Chapter 3). But when this tissue receives the signals to begin differentiation into a male, the embryonic reproductive organs begin to change their appearance dramatically.

● Male Sex Organs: What Are They For?

Like female sex organs, male sex organs serve several functions. In their reproductive role, a man's sex organs manufacture and store gametes and can deliver them to a woman's reproductive tract. Some of the organs, especially the penis, provide a source of physical pleasure for both the man and his partner.

External Structures

The external male sexual structures are the penis and the scrotum.

The Penis   The **penis** (from the Latin word for "tail") is the organ through which both semen and urine pass. It is attached to the male perineum, the diamond-shaped region extending from the base of the scrotum to the anus.

The penis consists of three main sections: the root, the shaft, and the head (see Figure 1). The **root** attaches the penis within the pelvic cavity; the body of the penis, the **shaft**, hangs free. At the end of the shaft is the head of the penis, the **glans penis**, and at its tip is the **urethral opening**, for semen ejaculation or urine excretion. The rim at the base of the glans is known as the **corona** (Spanish for "crown"). On the underside of the penis is a triangular area of sensitive skin called the **frenulum** (FREN-you-lem), which attaches the glans to the foreskin (see Figure 2). The glans penis is particularly important in sexual arousal because it contains a relatively high concentration of nerve endings, making it especially responsive to stimulation.

A loose skin covers the shaft of the penis and extends to cover the glans penis; this sleevelike covering is known as the **foreskin** or *prepuce* (PREE-pews). It can be pulled back

"There is nothing about which men lie so much as about their sexual powers. In this at least every man is, what in his heart he would like to be, a Casanova."

—W. Somerset Maugham (1874–1965)

• FIGURE 1

External Male Sexual Structures.

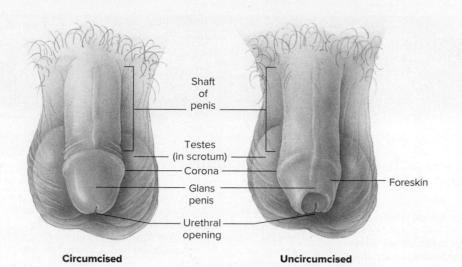

Shaft
of
penis

Testes
(in scrotum)

Corona

Glans
penis

Urethral
opening

Foreskin

Circumcised　　　　**Uncircumcised**

easily to expose the glans. The foreskin of a male infant can sometimes be surgically removed by a procedure called **circumcision**. As a result of this procedure, the glans penis is left exposed. The reasons for circumcision seem to be rooted more in tradition and religious beliefs (it is an important ritual in Judaism and Islam) than in any firmly established health principles, although some scientific evidence has shown that circumcision can help prevent HIV and other sexually transmitted infections. Beneath the foreskin are several small glands that produce a cheesy substance called **smegma**. If smegma accumulates, it thickens, produces a foul odor, and can become granular and irritate the penis, causing discomfort and infection. Uncircumcised males should periodically retract the skin and wash the glans and penile shaft to remove the smegma.

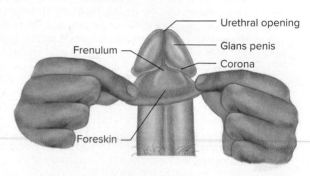

Urethral opening

Glans penis

Corona

Frenulum

Foreskin

• FIGURE 2

Underside of the Penis.

　　The shaft of the penis contains three parallel columns of erectile tissue (see Figure 3). The two that extend along the front surface are known as the **corpora cavernosa** (KOR-por-a kav-er-NO-sa; cavernous bodies), and the third, which runs beneath them, is called the **corpus spongiosum** (KOR-pus spun-gee-OH-sum; spongy body), which also forms the glans. At the root of the penis, the tips of the corpora cavernosa form the **crura** (KROO-ra), which are anchored by muscle to the pubic bone. The **urethra**, a tube that transports both urine and semen, runs from the bladder through the prostate and corpus spongiosum, to the tip of the penis, where it opens to the outside. Inside the three chambers are a large number of blood vessels through which blood freely circulates when the penis is flaccid

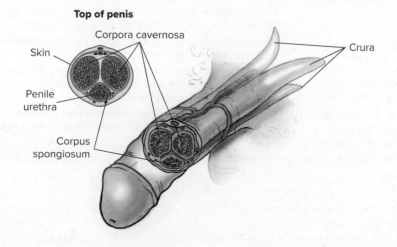

Top of penis

Corpora cavernosa

Skin

Penile
urethra

Corpus
spongiosum

Crura

• FIGURE 3

Interior Structure of the Penis with Cross Section.

think
about it

The Question of Male Circumcision

Who shall decide when doctors disagree?
—Alexander Pope (1688–1784)

In 1975, when about 93% of newborn boys in the United States were circumcised, the American Academy of Pediatrics and the American College of Obstetricians and Gynecologists issued a statement declaring there is "no absolute medical indication" for routine circumcision. Since that time, the American Academy of Pediatrics has undergone a series of debates and has concluded: "the health benefits of newborn male circumcision outweigh the risks" (AAP, 2015.4a). The Centers for Disease Control and Prevention (CDC) has concurred (Morris et al., 2017).

This procedure, which involves slicing and removing the sleeve of skin (foreskin) that covers the glans penis, is the most common procedure performed on newborns. The national rates of newborn circumcision have over time both fluctuated and declined, so that now approximately 65–75% of newborn boys born in the United States get circumcised each year (Eisenberg et al., 2018). Though this procedure has been performed for thousands of years for both religious and medical reasons, there remain questions and controversy, particularly regarding its efficacy in reducing HIV and other genital issues. (For more information about circumcision and HIV/STI prevention, see Chapter 15.) Some of the health benefits to routine circumcision at birth include (AAP, 2015.4a; Carroll, 2016; Eisenberg et al., 2018; Jewell, 2018):

1) Lower rates of urinary tract infection (UTI)—Studies have shown that circumcised penises have lower levels of yeast and bacteria, both of which contribute to UTIs.

2) Lower rates of transmission of HIV—Rate reductions of 1–2% have been seen in Africa over 1 to 2 years. That is, for every 10 to 20 males circumcised, one fewer man might contract HIV over a lifetime.

3) Lower acquisition rates of herpes simplex virus (HSV) and lower transmission rates of syphilis and human papillomavirus (HPV).

4) Lower rates of penile cancer—Uncircumcised men have a three times greater chance of developing penile cancer.

5) Lower rates of bacterial vaginosis (BV) in female partners—Bacterial vaginosis is an infection caused by having too much of a certain type of bacteria among women. While there's no way for men to get BV, experts are still unsure about whether men can spread BV to female partners.

Circumcision is a permanent surgical procedure with both benefits and risks. Some report that the lack of randomized trials along with the reliance on observational studies have contributed to mixed recommendations regarding whether it should be routinely performed (Eisenberg et al., 2018). Here's what we know about some of the complications and concerns that are associated with the procedure:

1) Surgical complications—Most contemporary studies report complication rates below 0.5%. Pain is also a concern, however medication is available to prevent this. Evidence exists to both support and rebut the notion that infants recover quickly.

2) Sexual functioning and satisfaction—We know that the foreskin, like much of the penis, contains numerous nerve endings. It also protects the head of the penis from chafing. In measuring penile sensitivity in circumcised and uncircumcised men, there appears to be no real difference. Circumcision has also been found to be unrelated to premature ejaculation, erectile dysfunction, or difficulty achieving orgasm.

3) Ethical issues—Some argue that circumcision is akin to a form of "genital mutilation/cutting" inflicted on children for no legitimate reason. Given the lack of consent involved, some maintain that parents should wait until boys are old enough to make a decision for themselves. A number of factors make that option difficult though, as circumcision is a more complicated, risky, and painful procedure when done later in life.

Given the cultural and religious associations, particularly in the Jewish and Muslim faiths, along with evidence for its risks and benefits, the decision to circumcise a baby boy is a personal one which is best left to the parents.

Think Critically

1. Given the evidence about circumcision, would you have your son circumcised? Why or why not?

2. How important would data be in deciding whether to have your son circumcised?

3. If you have ever had a male sex partner, did you notice whether he was circumcised or not? Would it make a difference to you?

4. Do you believe that male circumcision is akin to female genital mutilation/cutting? Why or why not?

(not erect). During sexual arousal, these vessels fill with blood and expand, causing the penis to become erect. (Sexual arousal, including erection, is discussed in greater detail later in Chapter 9.)

In men, the urethra serves as the passageway for both urine and semen. Because the urethral opening is at the tip of the penis, it is vulnerable to injury and infection. During sexual activity, the sensitive mucous membranes around the opening may be subject to abrasion and can provide an entrance into the body for infectious organisms. Condoms, properly used, can provide an effective barrier between this vulnerable area and potentially infectious organisms.

In an unaroused state, the *average* penis is slightly under 3 inches long, although there is a great deal of individual variation. When erect, penises become more uniform in size, as the percentage of volume increase is greater with smaller penises than with larger ones. The mean erect penis length is about 5.5 inches, while the mean erect penis circumference is 4.8 inches (Herbenick et al., 2013). Cold air or water, fear, and anxiety, for example, often cause the penis to temporarily be pulled closer to the body and to decrease in size. When the penis is erect, the urinary duct is temporarily blocked, allowing for the ejaculation of semen. But erection does not necessarily mean sexual excitement. A man may have erections at night during REM sleep, the phase of the sleep cycle when dreaming occurs, or when he is anxious.

Myths and misconceptions about the penis abound, especially among men. Many people believe that the size of a man's penis is directly related to his masculinity, aggressiveness, sexual ability, or sexual attractiveness. Others believe that there is a relationship between the size of a man's penis and the size of his hands, feet, thumbs, or nose. In fact, the size of the penis is not specifically related to body size or weight, muscular structure, race or ethnicity, or sexual orientation; it is determined by individual hereditary factors. Except in very rare and extreme cases, there is no relationship between penis size and a man's ability to have sexual intercourse or to satisfy his partner. (For more about this, see Think About It: "Does Penis Size Matter?")

"My brain. It's my second favorite organ."

—Woody Allen (1935–)

The Scrotum Hanging loosely at the root of the penis is the **scrotum**, or scrotal sac, a pouch of skin that holds the two testes. The skin of the scrotum is more heavily pigmented than the skin elsewhere on the body; it is sparsely covered with hair and divided in the middle by a ridge of skin. The skin of the scrotum varies in appearance under different conditions. When a man is sexually aroused, for example, or when he is cold, the testes are pulled close to the body, causing the skin to wrinkle and become more compact. The changes in the surface of the scrotum help maintain a fairly constant temperature within the testes (about 93°F). Two sets of muscles control these changes: (1) the dartos muscle, a smooth muscle under the skin that contracts and causes the surface to wrinkle, and (2) the fibrous cremaster muscle within the scrotal sac that causes the testes to elevate.

(a)

(b)

The penis is a prominent symbol in both ancient and modern art. Here we see (a) contemporary phallic sculpture in Frogner Park, Oslo, Norway, and (b) a phallic statuette offering at the Chao Mae Tuptim shrine in Bangkok.

(a) John Henderson/Alamy Stock Photo
(b) Medicimage Ltd/age fotostock

think about it

Does Penis Size Matter?

Forget smile, abs, or haircut; penis size matters a whole lot to most men, regardless of their age. For many, penis size is a symbol of masculinity and power and has a significant impact on self-esteem and sexual function. With the belief that "bigger is better," the way in which some men assess their self-worth is by their penis length.

Across time and culture, **phallic identity**, the tendency of males to seek their identity in their penis, and **phallocentrism**, the idea that the penis is central to identity and symbolically empowered, are concepts that have been deeply embedded into the psyche of men. Examples can be seen among the Karamoja tribe in Uganda who use weights to increase the length of their penis. Historic drawings and sculptures of ancient Romans and Greeks also reveal the significance of an enlarged penis size.

The fact is most boys and men fall within the "normal" range of penile length, with variability depending on the measuring technique. Occasionally a parent worries about the size of their son's penis. The vast majority of parents who bring up this issue with their pediatricians are assured that their boy's penis falls within the normal range (Klass, 2016). A baby's or toddler's penis can look small, especially when the child himself is larger. Additionally, the penis can be buried in the fat pad that sits in front of the pubic bone and can remain hidden until the body completes puberty. This condition can also occur in adulthood when among obese men, losing weight will reveal more of the hidden shaft that is buried beneath belly fat. And in some cases, an anatomical condition causes the shaft to retreat and only the skin or the foreskin, in an uncircumcised boy, to be visible. There is also a condition called micropenis that can be diagnosed in the newborn and can reflect a variety of disruptions of the hormone system during pregnancy.

With the ease of access and abundance of sexually explicit media (SEM) available on the Internet, there is a growing concern that unrealistic depictions of nude bodies and body parts, including genital size, may cause individuals to feel vulnerable to its standards of "normalcy." A recent experimental investigation explored whether exposure to SEM influenced consumers' self-esteem as well as genital specific self-esteem (Skoda & Pedersen, 2019). Researchers found that among male participants (but not female participants), exposure to SEM imagery had a significant negative effect on their satisfaction with the appearance of their genitalia, specifically about the size and appearance of their genitals. Why the difference between the sexes is unclear, however the researchers hypothesized that body image among men is distinct from that of women. Among men, body image centered more on performance and function, rather than appearance, and exposure to highly sexualized, female-focused media is so commonplace that it has been shown to have a significant negative effect on body- and genital-specific self esteem among men only (Koda & Pedersen, 2019).

Some average-size men become obsessed with the belief that their penis is too small, a medical diagnosis called penile dysmorphic disorder (PDD); a variant of body dysmorphic disorder. This is similar to the distorted body image that those with anorexia experience when they think they are fat no matter how thin they actually are. People with PDD do not have an unusually small penis. Instead, they are severely anxious about their penis size and often suffer

from shame and anxiety. This concern over penis endowment typically emerges during adolescence and is triggered by comparisons among men rather than by the fear of not satisfying a partner (Littara et al., 2019). When an adult male brings this issue of penis size up with his physician he is almost always assured that it is perfectly normal.

Relative to the degree of pleasure for the sexual partner, there is little evidence that a longer penis provides a greater advantage. Research on more than 52,000 heterosexual men and women found that 85% of women were satisfied with the size of their partner's penis. Rather, penis girth (width) rather than length is more concerning for women (cited in Apostolou, 2015). In comparison, only 55% of men were satisfied with their penis size (Veale et al., 2015). Though other studies have been conducted on whether "size matters" to partners, the results have been mixed in that for some, penis size doesn't matter, while for others, it plays a part in their sexual satisfaction.

In the quest for the perfect body, surgery to augment penile length or girth has become increasingly common. Some of the unproven options to increase penis size include a vacuum pump, injections with silicone, injections of hyaluronic acid, and fat transplantation. Complications include scarring, buildup of fat, and movement of materials that can lead to sexual function difficulties, decreased sensation, and penile deformity (Furr et al., 2018). Penile enhancement surgery is experimental and dermal fillers (hyaluronic acid) are not approved by the Food and Drug Administration (FDA) for this purpose. One surgery that has been approved by the FDA is the use of a penile implant called Penuma. The procedure comes with both caveats and risks. As a last resort to improve a man's dissatisfaction, cosmetic penis enlargement/augmentation may improve the man's self-esteem and improve the quality of his sex life (Furr et al., 2018). However, no major medical organization currently approves of cosmetic penile enlargement surgery (Mayo Clinic Staff, 2018).

Men who are dissatisfied with the appearance of their penis should consider all medical factors before seeking augmentation for purely cosmetic reasons. In the end, creative and satisfying sexual expression comes from how a man uses his imagination and communicates with his partner about sexual pleasure. And when he embraces his sexuality from this perspective, the size of his penis won't matter.

Think Critically

1. If you are a male, how do you feel about the size of your penis? What is your source of reference for this observation?

2. If you have a male partner, does the size of his penis make a difference to you?

3. Have you ever been or ever rejected a sexual partner because of his penis size?

4. Would you ever consider obtaining or would you support your partner getting a penis-enlargement/augmentation surgery?

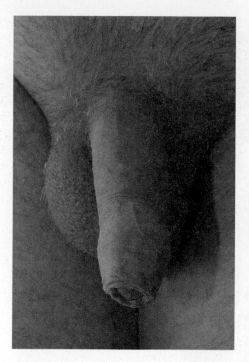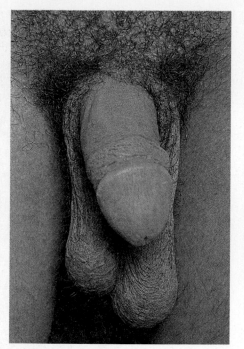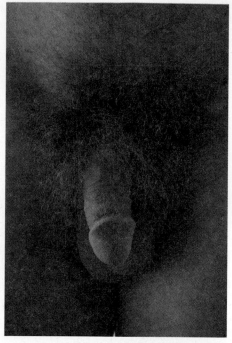

Internal Structures

Male internal reproductive organs and structures include the testes (testicles), seminiferous tubules, epididymis, vas deferens, ejaculatory ducts, seminal vesicles, prostate gland, and Cowper's (bulbourethral) glands (see Figure 4).

The Testes   Inside the scrotum are the male reproductive glands, or gonads, which are called **testes** (singular, *testis*), or **testicles**. The testes have two major functions: sperm production and hormone production. Each olive-shaped testis is about 1.5 inches long and 1 inch in diameter and weighs about 1 ounce; in adulthood and as a male ages, the testes

There is great variation in the appearance, size, and shape of the penis. Note that the penis on the left is not circumcised, whereas the other two are.

(a) John Henderson/Alamy Stock Photo;
(b) Medicimage Ltd/age fotostock;
(c) Medicshots/Alamy Stock Photo

"Nowhere does one read of a penis that quietly moseyed out for a look at what was going on before springing and crashing into action."

—Bernie Zilbergeld (1939–2002)

● **FIGURE 4**

Internal Side View of the Male Sex Organs.

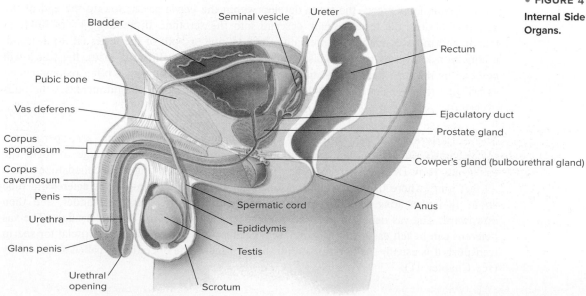

• FIGURE 5

Cross Section of a Testis.

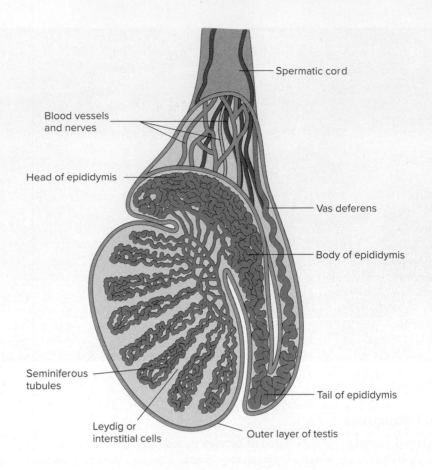

decrease in size and weight. The testes are usually not symmetrical; the left testis generally hangs slightly lower than the right one. Within the scrotal sac, each testis is suspended by a **spermatic cord** containing nerves, blood vessels, and a tube called the vas deferens (see Figure 5). Within each testis are around 1,000 **seminiferous tubules**, which are tiny, tightly compressed tubes 1–3 feet long (they would extend several hundred yards if laid end to end). Within these tubes, **spermatogenesis**—the production of sperm—takes place. (Spermatogenesis is discussed in greater detail later in the chapter.)

As a male fetus grows, the testes develop within the pelvic cavity; toward the end of the gestation period, the testes usually descend into the scrotum. In about 3–4% of full-term infants and more commonly in premature infants, one or both of the testes fail to descend, a condition known as **cryptorchidism**, or undescended testis. In most cases, the testes will descend by the time a child is 9 months old. If they do not, surgery is often recommended as bringing the testes into the scrotum maximizes sperm production and increases the odds of fertility.

The Epididymis and Vas Deferens   The epididymis and vas deferens carry sperm from the testes to the urethra for ejaculation. The seminiferous tubules merge to form the **epididymis** (ep-e-DID-i-mes), a comma-shaped structure consisting of a coiled tube about 20 feet long, where the sperm mature. Each epididymis drains into a **vas deferens**, a tube about 18 inches long, extending into the abdominal cavity, over the bladder, and then downward. The vas deferens joins the seminal vesicle to form the **ejaculatory duct**. The vas deferens can be felt easily in the scrotal sac. Because it is accessible and is crucial for sperm transport, it is usually the point of sterilization for men. The operation is called a vasectomy (see Chapter 11).

The Seminal Vesicles, Prostate Gland, and Cowper's Glands At the back of the bladder lie two glands, each about the size and shape of a finger. These **seminal vesicles** secrete a fluid that makes up about 70% of the seminal fluid (semen). Encircling the urethra just below the bladder is a small, muscular gland about the size and shape of a chestnut called the **prostate gland**, which produces about 30% of the seminal fluid that nourishes and transports sperm. These secretions flow into the urethra through a system of tiny ducts. The prostate gland is located in front of the rectum, and stimulation of this and nearby structures can be very pleasing. Some men who enjoy receiving anal sex experience erotic sensations when the prostate is gently stroked; others find that contact with the prostate is uncomfortable. Men, especially if they are older, may be troubled by a variety of prostate problems, ranging from relatively benign conditions to more serious inflammations and prostate cancer (see Chapter 13).

Below the prostate gland are two pea-sized glands connected to the urethra by tiny ducts. These are **Cowper's glands**, or **bulbourethral** (bul-bo-you-REE-thrul) **glands,** which secrete a thick, clear mucus prior to **ejaculation**, the process by which semen is forcefully expelled from the penis. This fluid may appear at the tip of the erect penis; its alkaline content helps buffer the acidity within the urethra and provides a more hospitable environment for sperm. Fluid from the Cowper's glands may contain sperm that have remained in the urethra since a previous ejaculation or that have leaked in from the ejaculatory duct. Consequently, it is possible, although rare, for a pregnancy to occur from residual sperm even if the penis is withdrawn before ejaculation. Hence, in order to prevent an unintended pregnancy, condoms or another form of birth control should be used from the first moment of genital contact.

Other Structures

Male anatomical structures that do not serve a reproductive function but may be involved in or affected by sexual activities include the breasts, buttocks, rectum, and anus.

Although the male breast contains the same basic structures as the female breast—nipple, areola, fat, and glandular tissue—the amounts of underlying fatty and glandular tissues are much smaller in men. Our culture appears to be ambivalent about the erotic function of men's breasts, but it does appear to place emphasis on their appearance. We usually do not even call them breasts, but refer to the general area as the chest or "pecs." Some men find stimulation of their nipples to be sexually arousing; others do not. **Gynecomastia** (gine-a-ko-MAS-tee-a), the swelling or enlargement of the male breast, is triggered by a decrease in the amount of testosterone compared with estrogen. This condition can occur during adolescence or adulthood. In puberty, gynecomastia is a normal response to hormonal changes. In adulthood, its prevalence peaks again between the ages of 50 and 80 and affects at least one in four men. Its causes may include the use of certain medications, alcoholism, liver or thyroid disease, and cancer. Not surprising, in our perfection-driven society, is the rise in pectoral implants among men who wish to have sculpted chests. Though still a niche market, some men are finding these semisolid silicone implants to be a confidence booster. The medical risks of the procedure are similar to those of female implant procedures, such as migration, infection, and loss of feelings around the nipple.

An organ used primarily for excretion, the anus can be stimulated during sexual activity. Because the anus is kept tightly closed by the external and internal anal sphincters, most of the erotic sensation that occurs during anal sex is derived from the penetration of the anal opening. Beyond the sphincters lies a larger space, the rectum. Because the anus and rectum do not provide significant amounts of lubrication, most people use water-based lubricant for penetrative sexual activity. All genders may enjoy oral stimulation of the anus ("rimming"), or the insertion of fingers, a hand ("fisting"), a dildo, or a penis into the rectum, all of which may bring erotic pleasure to both the receiver and the giver. (Table 1 provides a summary of male sexual anatomy.)

Male breasts, which are usually referred to euphemistically as "the chest" or "pecs," may or may not be considered erotic areas. Men are allowed to display their breasts in certain public settings. Whether the sight is sexually arousing depends on the viewer and the context.

Purestock/Getty Images

TABLE 1 ● Summary Table of Male Sexual Anatomy

External Structures

Penis	Organ through which both semen and urine pass
Root of penis	Attaches the penis within the pelvic cavity
Shaft	Body of the penis that hangs free
Glans penis	Head of the penis
Corona	Rim at the base of the glans
Frenulum	Triangular area of sensitive skin that attaches the glans to the foreskin
Foreskin (prepuce)	Loose skin or sleevelike covering of the glans; the removal of the foreskin in male infants is called circumcision
Corpora cavernosa	Two parallel columns of erectile tissue that extend along the front surface of the penis
Corpus spongiosum	One of three parallel columns of erectile tissue that run beneath the corpora cavernosa, surround the urethra, and form the glans
Crura	Root of the penis that is anchored by muscle to the pubic bone
Urethra	Tube that transports both urine and semen and runs from the bladder
Scrotum	Pouch of loose skin that holds the two testes

Internal Structures

Testes (testicles)	Male reproductive glands, or gonads, whose major functions are sperm and hormone production
Spermatic cord	Located within the scrotal sac; suspends each testis and contains nerves, blood vessels, and a vas deferens
Seminiferous tubules	Tiny, highly compressed tubes where the production of sperm takes place
Epididymis	Merged from the seminiferous tubules, a comma-shaped structure where the sperm mature
Vas deferens	Tube that extends into the abdominal cavity and carries the sperm from the testes to the urethra for ejaculation
Ejaculatory duct	One of two structures within the prostate gland connecting to the vas deferens
Seminal vesicle	One of two glands at the back of the bladder that together secrete about 70% of the seminal fluid
Prostate gland	A walnut-sized gland that secretes about 30% of the seminal fluid (ejaculate) responsible for nourishing and protecting sperm
Cowper's glands	Also called bulbourethral glands; secrete a clear, thick, alkaline mucus prior to ejaculation

Other Structures

Urethral opening	Opening in the urethra, through which urine and semen are expelled
Anus	Opening in the rectum, through which excrement passes
Perineum	Area that lies between the scrotum and anus
Pelvic floor	Underside of the pelvic area, extending from the top of the pubic bone to the anus

● Male Sexual Physiology

The reproductive processes of the male body include the manufacture of hormones and the production and delivery of sperm. Although men do not have a monthly reproductive cycle comparable to that of women, they do experience regular fluctuations of hormone levels although there is also some evidence that men's moods follow a cyclical pattern (American Psychological Association, 2011).

Sex Hormones

"Women say it's not how much men have, but what we do with it. How many things can we do with it? What is it, a Cuisinart? It's got two speeds: forward and reverse."

—Richard Jeni (1957–2007)

Within the connective tissues of a man's testes are **Leydig cells** (also called interstitial cells), which secrete **androgens** (male hormones). The most important of these is **testosterone,** which triggers sperm production, regulates the sex drive, and is associated with the development of secondary sex characteristics. Other important hormones in male reproductive physiology are gonadotropin-releasing hormone (GnRH), follicle-stimulating hormone (FSH), and

TABLE 2 ● Male Reproductive Hormones

Hormone	Where Produced	Functions
Testosterone	Testes, adrenal glands	Stimulates sperm production in testes, triggers development of secondary sex characteristics, regulates sex drive, bone mass, fat distribution, and muscle mass
Gonadotropin-releasing hormone (GnRH)	Hypothalamus	Stimulates pituitary during sperm production
Follicle-stimulating hormone (FSH)	Pituitary	Stimulates sperm production in testes
Luteinizing hormone (LH)	Pituitary	Stimulates testosterone production in interstitial cells within testes
Inhibin	Testes	Regulates sperm production by inhibiting release of FSH
Oxytocin	Hypothalamus, testes	Stimulates contractions in the internal reproductive organs to move the contents of the tubules forward; promotes touch, affection, and relaxation
Relaxin	Prostate	Increases sperm motility

luteinizing hormone (LH). In addition, men produce the protein hormone inhibin, oxytocin, and small amounts of estrogen. (Table 2 describes the principal hormones involved in sperm production and their functions.)

Testosterone   Testosterone is a steroid hormone synthesized from cholesterol. Testosterone is made by both sexes—by women mostly in the adrenal glands (located above the kidneys) and ovaries and by men primarily in the testes. Furthermore, the brain converts testosterone to estradiol, a female hormone. The variability of the hormone makes the link between testosterone and behavior precarious.

During puberty in males, besides acting on the seminiferous tubules to produce sperm, testosterone targets other areas of the body. Testosterone causes the penis, testes, and other reproductive organs to grow and is responsible for the development of **secondary sex characteristics**, those changes to parts of the body other than the genitals that indicate sexual maturity. In men, these changes include the growth of pubic, facial, underarm, and other body hair and the deepening of the voice. In women, estrogen and progesterone combine to develop secondary sex characteristics such as breast development, the growth of pubic and underarm hair, and the onset of vaginal mucous secretions. Testosterone also influences the growth of bones and increase of muscle mass and causes the skin to thicken and become oilier, leading to acne in many teenage boys.

Though numerous studies have attempted to understand the impact of testosterone on personality, findings are mixed. What complicates the research is that testosterone levels vary according to what specific components of testosterone were measured and that levels are rarely stable. Consequently, if a man suspects he has a testosterone deficiency, he would be wise to have his testosterone level assessed in the morning when it is at its peak (Brambilla, 2009). Research is emerging about the role of a particular form of estrogen known as estradiol, which is especially crucial to male sexuality (Healthline, 2019). It's this hormone that needs to stay in balance with testosterone to help moderate the sex drive, experience an erection, and produce sperm. Testosterone naturally decreases as men age, while estrogen increases. For most men, this usually not a cause for concern. However, if a man suspects he has abnormal hormone levels, he should see a doctor.

The increasing focus on testosterone and its derivatives, the anabolic-androgenic steroids, has fueled a market for those seeking anti-aging therapies, desiring athletic bodies and performance, and feeling entitled to unfailing and lifelong sexual prowess and fulfillment.

Testosterone therapy (TT) consists of supplemental testosterone for adult men with age-related low testosterone. However, for all of the changes that have been associated with age, there is inadequate evidence that testosterone therapy helps to treat the myriad of symptoms associated with it, including low sex drive, depression, fatigue, reduced muscle mass, erectile dysfunction, and irritability (American College of Physicians [ACP], 2020). There are many other possible reasons for these symptoms, including the aging process. For generally healthy

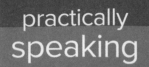

Sexual and Reproductive Health Care: What Do Men Need?

Men's sexual health is directly related to their general health. However, because men do not get pregnant or give birth to children, and because condoms are available without a prescription, men's sexual and reproductive health needs are not as obvious as women's and as such, are often ignored. In recent years, however, such issues as the high incidence of HIV and other sexually transmitted infections (STIs), prevalence of sexual function problems, and concerns regarding the role of males in teenage pregnancies and births have begun to alter this trend. Clearly, a movement toward a holistic and broad-based approach to sexual and reproductive health care for men is needed, one that embraces the full range of men's physical and emotional capacities and needs.

Here are some facts all people should know about the sexual health of men (Besera et al., 2016; CDC, 2016a; Guttmacher Institute, 2017; Planned Parenthood, 2017):

- Men have several birth control options: abstinence, condoms, sex play without penile penetration into a vagina, vasectomy, and withdrawal. The male condom is the most common method used by couples.

- Testicular cancer is the most common cancer among men aged 20–34. If treated early, it is usually curable.

- Only 9% of those who receive services by the Title X Family Planning Program, a program that prioritizes the health care needs of low-income families and individuals, are men.

- STIs, including syphilis, chlamydia, and gonorrhea, all of which can be cured with antibiotics, are common. Gay, bisexual, and queer men and young people are particularly affected by these infections. Each of these infections can be prevented by consistent and effective use of the condom.

From adolescence on, most men need information and referrals for their sexual and reproductive concerns. Understanding men's perspectives is necessary in order to engage men in their own sexual and reproductive health care. To achieve optimal sexual health, men need the following (Marcell et al., 2017):

1. Information and education about contraceptive use, pregnancy, childbirth, and STI prevention and treatment. Information about where to obtain and how to use condoms correctly.

2. Counseling and support regarding how to talk about these and other sexuality-related issues with partners.

3. Surgical services for vasectomies, screening and treatment for reproductive cancers, particularly prostate and testicular cancer, and counseling and treatment for sexual function difficulties and infertility.

4. Assurances from health care providers that services will be confidential, affordable, respectful, and nonjudgmental.

5. Role models in the media, support from families, and availability of professionals and friends. Especially needed are those who can speak honestly and knowledgeably about masculine sexual scripts, self-risk assessments, and fear and stigmas associated with care.

Additionally, development of skills related to self-advocacy, risk assessment and avoidance, resistance to peer pressure, communication with partners, fatherhood, and role expectations is both needed and desired.

The complex relationships between race/ethnicity, poverty, high-risk behaviors, and poor health outcomes are undeniable. Helping men lead healthier sexual and reproductive lives is a goal that is garnering attention and legitimacy.

men with declining testosterone levels later in life, it is not clear if or when the problem should be treated. Medical testing can determine if a man is at or below a clinical and laboratory definition of testosterone deficiency, at which point TT may be an option. The only area where there is some benefit to TT is in treating sexual function problems. As for safety, the overall research suggests that testosterone therapy does not raise the risks of heart-related problems, blood clots, or prostate cancer. Based on current evidence, ACP, endorsed by the American Academy of Family Physicians, has developed new recommendations for adult men with age-related low testosterone, the most significant of which is that clinicians not initiate TT in men with age-related low testosterone to improve energy, vitality, physical function, or cognition.

Male Cycles   Studies comparing men and women have found that both sexes experience hormonal cycles resulting in changes in mood, behavior, and sexual desire (Law, 2011). Whereas such changes in women are often attributed, rightly or wrongly, to monthly menstrual cycle fluctuations, men's testosterone levels appear to cycle throughout the day, month,

Though changes in sexual functioning are a common occurrence, men (and women) can, as they age, maintain their physical and psychological vitality through a healthy lifestyle.

Caia Image/Glow Images

and possibly season. On a daily basis, men's testosterone levels appear to be lowest in the evening and highest in the morning. Levels of testosterone also decline with age.

Throughout the night, specifically during REM sleep, men experience spontaneous penile erections. (Women experience labial, vaginal, and clitoral engorgement during REM sleep.) These erections are sometimes referred to as "battery-recharging mechanisms" for the penis, because they increase blood flow and bring more oxygen to the penis. Typically, men have penile engorgement during 95% of REM sleep stages (Komisaruk et al., 2010). If a man has erectile difficulties while he is awake, it is important to determine whether he has normal erections during sleep. If so, his problems may have to do with something other than the physiology of erection. Approximately 90% of men and nearly 40% of women have ever experienced **nocturnal orgasms**; for men, these are often referred to as "wet dreams" or orgasm accompanied by erotic dreams while asleep (Kinsey et al., 1948; Wells, 1986).

Spermatogenesis

Within the testes, from puberty on, spermatogenesis, the production of the male gametes, or **sperm**, is an ongoing process. Every day, a healthy, fertile man produces several hundred million sperm within the seminiferous tubules of his testes (see Figure 6). After they are formed in the seminiferous tubules, which takes 64–72 days, immature sperm are stored in the epididymis. It then takes about 20 days for the sperm to travel the length of the epididymis, during which time they become fertile and motile (able to move). Upon ejaculation, sperm in the tail section of the epididymis are expelled by muscular contractions of its walls into the vas deferens; similar contractions within the vas deferens propel the sperm into the urethra, where they are mixed with seminal fluid, creating semen, and then expelled, or ejaculated, through the urethral opening.

The sex of the **zygote**, the fertilized egg cell that results from the union of egg (ovum) and sperm, is determined by the chromosomes of the sperm. The ovum always contributes a female sex chromosome (X), whereas the sperm may contribute either a female or a male sex chromosome (Y). The combination of two X chromosomes (XX) means that the zygote will develop as a female; with an X and a Y chromosome (XY), it will develop as a male. In some cases, combinations of sex chromosomes other than XX or XY occur, causing sexual development to proceed differently (see Chapter 5).

Between 100 million and 600 million sperm are present in the semen from a single ejaculation. Typically, following ejaculation during intercourse fewer than 1,000 sperm reach the fallopian tube, where an ovulated oocyte may be present. Though many sperm assist in helping dissolve the egg cell membrane, typically only one sperm ultimately achieves fertilization.

CNRI/Science Source

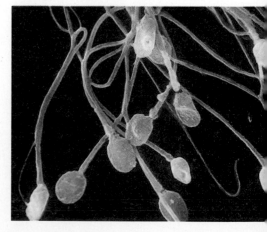

Spermatogenesis. This diagram shows the development of spermatozoa, beginning with a single spermatogonium and ending with four complete sperm cells. Spermatogenesis is an ongoing process that begins in puberty. Several hundred million sperm are produced every day within the seminiferous tubules of a healthy man.

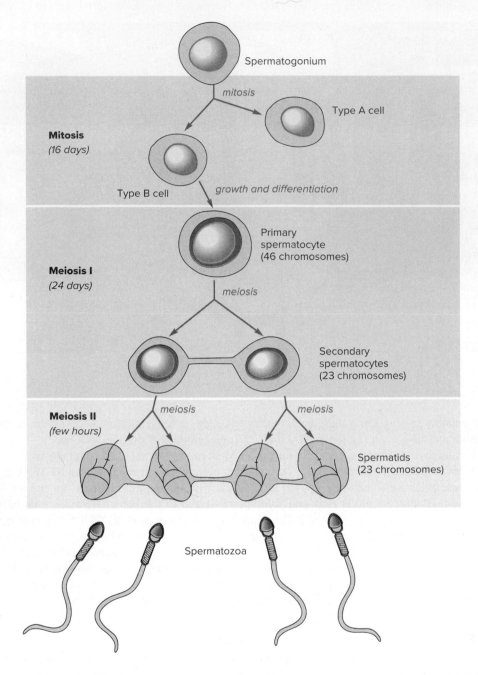

"The sex organ has a poetic power, like a comet."

—Joan Miró (1893–1983)

"Men always want to be a woman's first love—women like to be a man's last romance."

—Oscar Wilde (1854–1900)

Semen Production

Semen, also known as **seminal fluid**, is a fluid that contains spermatozoa. The function of semen is to nourish sperm and provide them with a hospitable environment and means of transport if they are deposited within the vagina. Semen is mainly made up of secretions from the seminal vesicles and prostate gland, which mix together with sperm and are ejaculated through the urethra. Immediately after ejaculation, the semen is somewhat thick and sticky from clotting factors in the fluid. This consistency keeps the sperm together initially; then the semen becomes liquefied, allowing the sperm to swim out. Semen ranges in color from opalescent or milky white to yellowish or grayish upon ejaculation, but it becomes clearer as it liquefies. Normally, about 2–6 milliliters (about 1 teaspoonful) of semen is ejaculated at one time; this amount of semen generally contains between 100 million and 600 million sperm. In spite of their significance, sperm occupy only about 1% of the total volume of semen; the remainder consists of secretions from the seminal vesicles (70%) and the prostate gland (30%). Fewer than 1,000 sperm will reach the fallopian tubes. Most causes of male infertility are related to low sperm count and/or low motility.

Recent research has found, however, that taking fish oil supplements may improve sperm quality in healthy young men (Jensen et al., 2020). Researchers studied 1,679 Danish men whose average age was 19 and found that compared to those who took none, men who took fish oil supplements for at least 60 days during the previous 3 months had a higher sperm count, a greater proportion of normal sperm cells, higher average semen volume and larger average testicular size. It's important to note, however, that this latest study cannot prove a cause-and-effect link between fish oil and the improvements in sperm counts and testosterone levels.

Homologous Organs

Each of the male sexual structures has a **homologous structure**, or similar characteristic, that is developed from the same cells in the developing female fetus. The presence of a Y chromosome in a male produces testosterone in greater amounts. Without this Y chromosome, the fetus would become a female. (See Figure 7 for the homologous structures of males and females.)

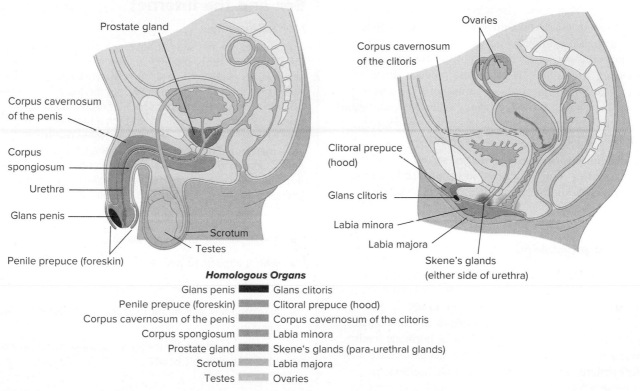

Homologous Organs

Glans penis	Glans clitoris
Penile prepuce (foreskin)	Clitoral prepuce (hood)
Corpus cavernosum of the penis	Corpus cavernosum of the clitoris
Corpus spongiosum	Labia minora
Prostate gland	Skene's glands (para-urethral glands)
Scrotum	Labia majora
Testes	Ovaries

● **FIGURE 7**

Homologous Structures of Male and Female Genitalia. Note that males and females share many of the same structures since they developed from the same cells during fetal development.

Final Thoughts

In this chapter and the last, we have looked primarily at the physical characteristics that designate us as male or female. But as we discover, there's more to gender than mere chromosomes or reproductive organs. How we feel about our physical selves (our male or female anatomy) and how we act (our gender roles) also determine our identities as human beings.

Moof/Cultura /Getty Images

Summary

Male Sex Organs: What Are They For?

■ In their reproductive role, a man's sex organs produce and store gametes and can deliver them to a woman's reproductive tract. The *penis* is the organ through which both sperm and urine pass. The *shaft* of the penis contains two *corpora cavernosa* and a *corpus spongiosum,* which fill with blood during arousal, causing an erection. The head is called the *glans penis;* in uncircumcised men, it is covered by the *foreskin.* Myths about the penis equate its size with masculinity and sexual prowess. The *scrotum* is a pouch of skin that hangs at the root of the penis and holds the *testes.*

■ The paired testes, or testicles, have two major functions: sperm production and hormone production. Within each testis are about 1,000 *seminiferous tubules,* where the production of sperm takes place. The seminiferous tubules merge to form the *epididymis,* a coiled tube where the sperm finally mature, and each epididymis merges into a *vas deferens,* which joins the *ejaculatory duct* within the *prostate gland.* The *seminal vesicles* and prostate gland produce *semen,* or *seminal fluid,* which nourishes and transports the sperm. Two tiny glands called *Cowper's glands* or *bulbourethral glands* secrete a thick, clear mucus prior to *ejaculation,* whereby semen is forcefully expelled from the penis.

■ Male anatomical structures that do not serve a reproductive function but that may be involved in or affected by sexual activities include the breasts, *urethra,* buttocks, rectum, and anus.

Male Sexual Physiology

■ The reproductive processes of the male body include the manufacture of hormones and the production and delivery of *sperm,* the male gametes. Although men do not have a monthly reproductive cycle comparable to that of women, they do experience regular fluctuations of hormone levels; there is also some evidence that men's moods follow a cyclical pattern. The most important male hormone is *testosterone,* which triggers sperm production and regulates the sex drive. Other important hormones in male reproductive physiology are GnRH, FSH, LH, inhibin, and oxytocin.

■ Sperm carry either an X chromosome, which will produce a female zygote, or a Y chromosome, which will produce a male.

■ *Semen* is the ejaculated liquid that contains sperm. The function of semen is to nourish sperm and provide them with a hospitable environment and means of transport if they are deposited within the vagina. It is mainly made up of secretions from the seminal vesicles and prostate gland. The semen from a single ejaculation generally contains between 100 million and 600 million sperm, yet only about 1,000 make it to the fallopian tubes.

Questions for Discussion

■ **Make a list of what you have heard about men's sexuality. Identify the myths and compare them with information from the text.**

■ **What do you think gets in the way of men seeking and getting sexual and reproductive health care? What might you say to encourage a man to reach out for sexual health care?**

■ **Do you believe that men have cycles, similar to women's menstrual cycles? If so, what might contribute to this phenomenon? If not, why not?**

Sex and the Internet

Men's Sexuality

Try to locate Internet sites about men's sexuality. You'll find that, apart from those relating to erectile dysfunction, AIDS, and sexually explicit materials, few sites address this topic. What does this say about men? About the topic of men and sexuality? Because of this absence of reputable content-specific sites, it is necessary to search a broader topic: men's health. Go to the Men's Health Network (https://www.menshealthnetwork.org) and, in the Library section, either select one of the more popular topics on the website or conduct your own search. When you find a topic that interests you, see if you can find the following:

■ Background information about the topic

■ The incidence or prevalence of the issue/problem

■ Who it impacts or affects

■ The causes and potential solutions

■ A related link that might broaden your understanding of this topic

Last, what recommendations might you make to someone who identified with this issue?

Suggested Websites

American Sexual Health Association
https://www.ashasexualhealth.org/sexual-health/mens-health/
Created to help men (and their partners) understand how their sex organs work together.

American Urological Association
https://auanet.org
Provides a variety of information on adult sexual functioning and infertility.

Harvard Health Publications: Men's Sexual Health

https://www.health.harvard.edu/topics/mens-sexual-health

Trusted advice for men's health and healthy sexuality.

Male Health Center

https://www.malehealthcenter.com

Provides information on a wide variety of issues related to male genital health, birth control, and sexual functioning, from the male perspective.

WebMD

https://www.webmd.com/men/

Focuses on a variety of health topics, including men's sexuality.

Suggested Reading

Almeling, R. (2020). *GUYnecology: The missing science of men's reproductive health.* University of California Press. The book describes why individuals are reluctant to talk about men's reproductive health and how this void influences reproductive health policy.

Danoff, D. S. (2017). *Ultimate guide to male sexual health.* (2nd ed.). Beyond Words. Written by a physician, the book is an insightful and educational guide to many sexual health concerns of men.

Fine, C. (2017). *Testosterone rex: Myths of sex, science and society.* Norton. A comprehensive factbook about testosterone.

Murray, S. H. (2019). *Not always in the mood: The new science of men, sex, and relationships.* Rowman & Littlefield. Challenges the myths that society holds about men and their sexual desire.

Natterson, C. (2020). *Decoding boys: New science behind the subtle art of raising sons.* Ballantine Books. Provides parents with tools to engage their sons in ways that they can become caring and independent men.

Spitz, A. (2018). *The penis book: A doctor's complete guide to the penis–from size to function and everything in between.* Rodale. A urologist writes in both a humorous and knowledgeable way about what most would like to know about the penis.

Zilbergeld, B. (1999). *The new male sexuality.* (Rev. Ed.). Bantam Books. A classic in the field of male sexuality; the author provides an explanation of both male and female anatomy and sexual response, plus communication, sexual problem solving, and much more.

5

Gender, Gender Roles, and Sexuality

©Jeff Gross/Getty Images

CHAPTER OUTLINE

Studying Gender, Gender Roles, and Sexuality

Gender-Role Learning

Contemporary Gender Roles and Scripts

Gender Variations

Student Voices

"As early as preschool I learned the difference between boy and girl toys, games, and colors. The boys played with trucks while the girls played with dolls. If a boy were to play with a doll, he would be laughed at and even teased. In the make-believe area, once again, you have limitations of your dreams. Girls could not be police, truck drivers, firefighters, or construction workers. We had to be people that were cute, such as models, housewives, dancers, or nurses. We would sometimes model ourselves after our parents or family members."

—23-year-old female

"I grew up with the question of 'why?' dangling from the tip of my tongue. Why am I supposed to marry a certain person? Why do I have to learn how to cook meat for my husband when I am a vegetarian? Why can't I go out on dates or to school formals? The answer was the same every time: 'Because you're a girl.' Being that she is such a strong woman, I know it tore a bit of my grandmother's heart every time she had to say it."

—19-year-old female

"My stepfather and I did not get along. I viewed him as an outsider, and I did not want a replacement father. Looking back, I feel like I overcompensated for the lack of a male figure in my life. I enlisted in the Navy at 18, have a huge firearm collection, and play ice hockey on the weekends. All of these activities seem to be macho, even to me. I guess it's to prove that even though a woman raised me, I'm still a man's man."

—27-year-old male

"I was in fifth grade, and my parents put me on restriction. My mom inquired where I got the [Playboy] magazine. I told her we found it on the way home from school. She wanted to know where. I lied and said it was just sitting in somebody's trashcan and I happened to see it. She wanted to know where. I said I forgot. My sexual identity was being founded on concealment, repression, and lies. Within my family, my sexual identity was repressed."

—27-year-old male

HOW CAN WE TELL the difference between a man and a woman? While most distinguish their sex by the appearance of their genitals, others rely on their gender identity. As accurate as this answer may be academically, it is not particularly useful in social situations. In most social situations—except in nudist colonies or while sunbathing au naturel—our genitals are not visible to the casual observer. We do not expose or may not disclose our identity or ask another person to do so for gender verification. We are more likely to rely on secondary sex characteristics, such as breasts and body hair, or on bone structure, musculature, and height. But even these characteristics are not always reliable, given the great variety of shapes and sizes we come in as human beings. And from farther away than a few yards, we cannot always distinguish these characteristics. Instead of relying entirely on physical characteristics to identify an individual's gender, we often look for other clues.

Culture provides us with an important clue for recognizing a person's gender: dress. In almost all cultures, female and male clothing differs to varying degrees so that we can usually identify a person's gender. Some cultures, such as our own, may accentuate secondary sex characteristics, especially for females. Traditional feminine clothing, for example, emphasizes a woman's gender: dress or skirt, a form-fitting or low-cut top, high heels, and so on. Most clothing, in fact, that emphasizes or exaggerates secondary sex characteristics is female. Makeup—lipstick, mascara, eyeliner—and hairstyles also mark or exaggerate the differences between males and females. Even smells—perfume for women, cologne for men—and colors—blue for boys, pink for girls—help distinguish females and males.

Clothing and other aspects of appearance further exaggerate physical differences. And culture encourages us to accentuate or invent psychological, emotional, mental, and behavioral differences. Should the United States follow Germany to allow "undetermined" as a gender type for newborn babies? Legislation enacted in 2013 in Germany specifies that babies born without gender-defining physical characteristics can be registered as having an "undetermined" gender on their birth certificate. Multiple countries have followed by legally recognizing non-binary or third gender classifications. While a biological understanding of

"There is no essential sexuality. Maleness and femaleness are something we are dressed in."

—Naomi Wallace (1960–)

gender identity remains somewhat of a mystery, medical, ethical, and parental recommendations are being created to respond to the growing number of individuals who see gender variance as an alternative to psychiatric diagnoses and a normal part on the wide continuum of gender expression.

In this chapter, we look at the connection between our genitals; our identity as female, male, transgender, or none of these; and our feelings of being feminine, masculine, or a mixture or absence of these identities. We also examine the relationship between femininity, masculinity, and sexual orientation. Then we discuss how feminine and masculine traits result from both biological and social influences. Next, we focus on theories of socialization and how we learn to behave in our culture. Then we look at traditional, contemporary, and androgynous gender roles. We examine gender variation—including gender dysphoria—along with disorders of sex development. Finally, we address coming to terms with gender variations.

● Studying Gender, Gender Roles, and Sexuality

Let's start by redefining some key terms, to establish a common terminology. (Note that some of these terms were listed in the Practically Speaking glossary in Chapter 1.) Keeping these definitions in mind will make the discussion clearer.

Sex, Gender, and Gender Roles: What's the Difference?

Assigned sex is a determination of sex that is made at birth, usually male or female, typically on the basis of external anatomy but sometimes on the basis of internal gonads, chromosomes, or hormone levels. **Genetic sex** refers to one's chromosomal and hormonal sex characteristics, such as whether one's chromosomes are XY or XX and whether estrogen or testosterone dominates the hormonal system. **Anatomical sex** refers to physical sex: gonads, uterus, vulva, vagina, penis, and so on.

Although "sex" and "gender" are often used interchangeably, gender is not the same as biological sex. **Gender** relates to femininity or masculinity, the social and cultural characteristics associated with biological sex. Whereas **sex** is rooted in biology, gender is rooted in culture. When a baby is born, someone looks at the genitals and exclaims, "It's a boy!" or "It's a girl!" With that single utterance, the baby is transformed from an "it" into a "male" or a "female."

Gender roles are the attitudes, behaviors, rights, and responsibilities that particular cultural groups associate with our assumed or assigned sex. Age, race, and a variety of other factors further define and influence these. A **gender-role stereotype** is a rigidly held, oversimplified, and overgeneralized belief about how each gender should behave. Stereotypes tend to be false or misleading, not only for the group as a whole (e.g., women are more interested in relationships than sex) but also for any individual in the group (e.g., Eric may be more

"Whatever women do they must do twice as well as men to be thought half as good. Luckily, this is not difficult."

—Charlotte Whitton (1896–1975)

The interaction of biological, cultural, and psychosocial factors contributes to the development of gender.

Katrina Wittkamp/Digital Vision/Getty Images

interested than Carla in sex than relationships). Even if a generalization is statistically valid in describing a group average (e.g., males are generally taller than females), such generalizations do not necessarily reflect specific traits of individuals (e.g., whether Roberto will be taller than Andrea).

Sex and Gender Identity

Gender identity is a person's internal sense of being male, female, a blend of both, or neither. We develop our gender through the interaction of its biological, cultural, and psychosocial components. When addressing the biological component, the term **cisgender** is used to describe a person whose gender identity aligns with the biological sex they were assigned at birth. The cultural component creates gender distinctions, while the psychosocial component includes assigned gender and gender identity. Because these dimensions are learned together, they may seem to be natural. For example, if a person looks like a girl (biological), believes she should be feminine (cultural), feels as if she is a girl (psychological), and acts like a girl (social), then her gender identity and role are congruent with her anatomical sex.

Our culture emphasizes that there are only two genders, otherwise referred to as the gender binary, whereby gender is an either-or option of female or male. Many who question their gender, are uncertain, are unwilling to state, or feel limited by these categories are said to be gender variant. On the other hand, a spectrum of gender identities that are not exclusively masculine or feminine are referred to as **gender variant**, **gender non-binary**, or **genderqueer**. Diagnostic terms that are used for gender non-binary or genderqueer include *gender-atypical behavior or gender dysphoria.* Gender variations, still often stigmatized, are now being reexamined, evaluated, and viewed as natural and "normal" on the spectrum of gender expression. As a result, an increasing number of parents and professionals are finding that molding children's gender identity is not as important as allowing them to be who they are, regardless of what their genitals may tell them.

The nuances and controversies inherent in gender studies force many of us to think about our assumptions and biases about those whom we regard as different or variant. When trying

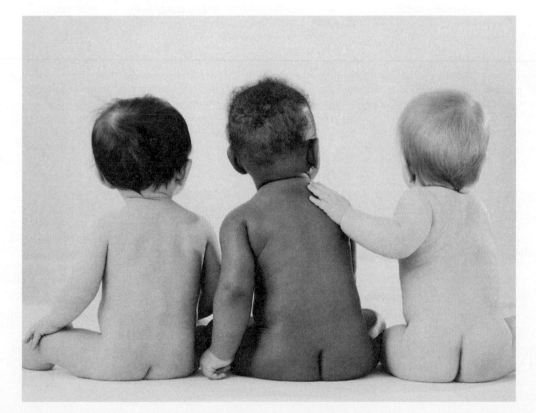

Although strangers can't always readily tell the sex of a baby, once they learn the sex, they often respond with gender stereotypes and expectations.

Jamie Grill/JGI/Getty Images

think
about it

Why Gender-Neutral Pronouns Matter

What pronouns do you use to identify yourself: he, she, they, ze/zir? Something other? While language has been expanding to become more inclusive, keeping up with these changes has not been as simple. Words are powerful and our cultural priorities are reflected in the language that we use (Holleb, 2019). Unlike Chinese or Persian, which doesn't assign nouns a gender or already has gender-neutral form, languages such as English and French are based exclusively on binary or male or female options. To some degree this changed in 2019, when the Merriam-Webster Dictionary added "they" as the pronoun to use for a "single person whose gender identity is non-binary" and named it Word of the Year in 2019. But language is evolving, and for people of Latin American descent, the word Latinx (pronounced la-TEEN-ex) is meant to be a broad, inclusive term that considers transgender and non-binary people, instead of the binary of Latino (male) and Latina (female). As social factors change, the language has also changed for some companies and institutions that have both led and followed the still-expanding language. This includes, for example, American Airlines, which in 2019 provided non-binary gender options, including "U" or "X" for customers during the booking process. By early 2021, 19 states plus the District of Columbia also now grant the right to label oneself non-binary on their driver's license. Using gender-neutral language can be validating for those who do not subscribe to the two gender categories. The authors of this text acknowledge that there are various terms used for gender-neutral language, including gender inclusive, gender sensitive, non-binary, and gender variant. Though these terms can often be used interchangeably, we shall use the term gender-neutral here and in most other parts of the book.

Over time, gender-related terms are expanding the ways in which we regard gender. The process of educating all of us has occurred as LGBTQ+ activists and linguists have championed more inclusive language, both by creating new terms and by revising existing words. Pronouns are a political part of speech. When, for example, we use the feminine, "she/her" when referring to a person of unspecified gender, we may consciously be refuting patriarchy. As with everything political, the use of gender-neutral pronouns has been subject to controversy. Some argue that to respect a person's choice of pronoun underscores their basic rights; the other perspective may disagree with what they perceive as an excess of sensitivity or political correctness. According to Teresa Bejan (2019), professor of political theory at the University of Oxford, "The logic with pronouns is that if individuals—not grammarians or society at large—have the right to determine their own gender, shouldn't they get to choose their own pronouns, too?"

Among the institutions that are helping us re-think language, university writing centers across the United States are teaching students, for example, that gendered nouns are easy to spot and replace with more neutral language, even in the context where readers expect a gendered noun. For example, instead of saying "man," an alternative such as person or individual can be used; a policeman can be referred to as a police officer, etc. When you are not sure of someone's gender, or wish to use gender-neutral language, it might be helpful to imagine a diverse group of people reading your research paper with gendered pronouns and ask yourself: Would each reader feel respected? By envisioning your audience and focusing on gendered language, the use of gender-neutral terms can help you make a stronger, more effective paper or presentation that will be both inclusive and persuasive to a variety of readers. (See Table 1 for some examples of gender-neutral language that can be integrated into writing and conversation.)

TABLE 1 ● **Examples of Gender-Neutral Pronouns**

		Gender Pronouns		
Subjective	**Objective**	**Possessive**	**Reflexive**	**Examples**
He	Him	His	Himself	He is walking. It belongs to him. The record is his. He bought himself a Coke.
She	Her	Hers	Herself	She is walking. It belongs to her. The record is hers. She bought herself a Coke.
They	Them	Theirs	Themself	They are walking. It belongs to them. The record is theirs. They bought themself a Coke.
Ze	Hir/Zir	Hirs/Zirs	Hirself/Zirself	Ze is walking. It belongs to hir. The record is zirs. Ze bought hirself a Coke.
Ve	Ver	Vis/Vers	Verself	Ve is walking. It belong to ver. The record is vers. Ve bought verself a Coke.

Think Critically

1. How important is it that people and cultures begin to shift the language to be more inclusive?
2. What are your thoughts about university centers and businesses educating their students or employees about gender-neutral terms? How comfortable are you using gender-neutral language?
3. Have you ever felt hurt or insulted when another person incorrectly stated your gender? How did you respond?
4. What, if anything, are you doing to learn and practice more gender-neutral language?

to make sense of gender, Jack Drescher (2014), psychiatrist and expert in the field of gender variations, cuts across lives and cultures when he reflects:

> The closest I have come to an overview of the subject is the image of six blindfold scientists in white coats trying to describe an elephant. Each of them, touching only one of six parts (trunk, horn, tail, ear, leg, flank), understandably mistakes the part for the whole. I have come to appreciate that any understanding of this subject requires a capacity to hold complexity and tolerate the anxiety of uncertainty.

It will become clear in the following pages that though little is known about the causes of gender, gender identity, and gender variations, many of us will often fall back on our opinions and biases about this subject. Instead, the goal of this discussion is to help raise awareness about those who are gender variant.

Assigned Gender   When we are born, we are assigned a gender based on anatomical appearance. **Assigned gender** is significant because it tells others how to respond to us. As youngsters, we have no sense of ourselves as female or male. We learn that we are a girl or a boy from the verbal responses of others. "What a pretty girl," or "What a good boy," our parents and others say. We are constantly given signals about our gender. Our birth certificate states our sex; while our name, such as Jarrod or Felicia, is often gender-coded. Our clothes, even in infancy, may also reveal our assigned gender.

By the time we are 2 years old, we are probably able to identify ourselves as a girl or a boy based on what we have internalized from what others have told us coupled with factors not yet understood. We might also be able to identify strangers as "mommies" or "daddies." But we don't really know why we are a girl or a boy. We don't associate our gender with our genitals. In fact, until the age of 3 or so, most children identify girls or boys by hairstyles, clothing, or other nonanatomical signs. At around age 3, we begin to learn that the genitals are what make a person male or female.

By age 4 or 5, children have learned a wide array of social stereotypes about how boys and girls should behave. Consequently, they tend to react approvingly or disapprovingly toward each other according to their choice of sex-appropriate play patterns and toys. Fixed ideas about adult roles and careers are also established by this time.

"Roles come with costumes and speeches and stage directions. In a role, we don't have to think."
—Ellen Goodman (1941–)

Gender Identity   By about age 2, we internalize and identify with our gender. We think we are a girl or a boy. This perception of our femaleness, maleness, a blend of both or neither is our gender identity. For most people, gender identity is permanent and is congruent with their sexual anatomy and assigned gender. Sometimes, however, a person rejects the female-male option of gender identity and expression and embraces a non-binary option. Other terms for this include **agender,** *bigender, genderqueer,* **gender fluid,** or *pangender.* Once again, this may be suggestive of greater acknowledgment of gender fluidity.

As non-binary identity has been slowly seeping into societal conscious, it's still impossible to identify how many non-binary people there are in the United States (Bergner, 2019). The problems in relying on numbers related to gender are both reliability and terminology. An abundance of labels, including **transgender**, an umbrella term for those whose gender expression or identity is not congruent with the sex assigned at birth, may introduce complexity in categorizing people and producing demographics. While data are scarce, an analysis of two federal public-health surveys conducted by phone in 2014–2015 suggests that the number of transgender-identified adults age 18 and over is approximately 1.4 million, or approximately 0.6% of adults (Flores et al., 2016). Differences exist by age, with younger adults more likely to identify as transgender than older adults. These estimates have doubled from a decade ago; a figure that may be attributed to greater visibility, social acceptance, reporting, and education.

Some cultures recognize that sex and gender are not always divided along binary lines, such as male and female or homosexual and heterosexual (World Health Organization [WHO], 2015). In some East African societies, for example, a male child is referred to as a "woman-child"; there are few social differences between young boys and girls. Around age 7, the boy undergoes male initiation rites, such as circumcision, whose avowed purpose is to "make" him into a man. Such ceremonies may serve as a kind of "brainwashing," helping the young male make the transition to a new gender identity with new role expectations. Other cultures allow older males to act out a latent female identity with such practices as the couvade, in which husbands mimic their wives giving birth. And in our own society, into the early twentieth century, boys were dressed in gowns and wore their hair in long curls until age 2. At age 2 or 3, their dresses were replaced by pants, their hair was cut, and they were socialized to conform to their anatomical sex. Children who deviated from this expected conformity were referred to as sissies (boys) or tomboys (girls) and ridiculed to conform to gender stereotypes. More recently, there is both debate and discussion among professionals concerning how to best counsel families whose child does not conform to gender norms in either clothing or behavior and has identified intensely with the other sex.

Masculinity and Femininity: Opposites, Similar, or Blended?

Each culture determines the content of gender roles in its own way; however, cultural norms fluctuate and change with time and across cultures. Among the Arapesh of New Guinea, for example, members of both sexes possess what we consider feminine traits. Both men

"Men are taught to apologize for their weaknesses, women for their strength."

—Lois Wyse (1926–2007)

Cultural norms vary over time, resulting in changes in gender stereotypes and expectations.

kali9/E+/Getty Images

and women tend to be passive, cooperative, peaceful, and nurturing. The father as well as the mother is said to "bear a child"; only the father's continual care can make the child grow healthily, both in the womb and in childhood. Eighty miles away, the Mundugumor live in remarkable contrast to the peaceful Arapesh. "Both men and women," Margaret Mead (1975) observed, "are expected to be violent, competitive, aggressively sexed, jealous, and ready to see and avenge insult, delighting in display, in action, in fighting." Biology creates males and females, but it is culture that creates our concepts of masculinity and femininity and its inherent fluidity and complexity.

In the traditional Western view of masculinity and femininity, men and women have been seen as polar opposites. Our terminology, in fact, reflects this view. Women and men refer to each other as the "opposite sex." But this implies that women and men are indeed opposites, that they have little in common. We use "other sex" in this book. Our gender stereotypes have fit this pattern of polar differences: men are aggressive, whereas women are passive; men embody **instrumentality** and are task-oriented, whereas women embody **expressiveness** and are emotion-oriented; men are rational, whereas women are irrational; men want sex, whereas women want love; and so on.

Changes in gender stereotypes and related expectations have been occurring over the past decades such that as women have moved into the workforce and taken on occupations previously ascribed to men; their self-views and perceptions have also evolved and expanded. While the male stereotype in recent decades has not significantly changed, one might argue that the female stereotype has become more fluid. These changes in gender stereotypes are most likely linked to global shifts in culture, politics, and economics (Lips, 2014).

Gender-role stereotypes, despite their depiction of men and women as opposites, are usually not all-or-nothing notions. Most of us do not think that only men are assertive or only women are nurturing. Stereotypes merely reflect *probabilities* that a person will have a certain characteristic based on their gender. When we say that men are more independent than women, we simply mean that there is a greater probability that a man will be more independent than a woman.

Though the majority of men still seem governed by traditional standards of male behavior, a survey of 1,000 women and men conducted by the editors of *Gentlemen's Quarterly (GQ)* (2019) found that 97% said that their expectations for male behavior have changed in the last decade. While 48% of men described themselves as comfortable with these changes in the past decade, 27% of them were uncomfortable. The authors concluded: ". . . we'd have a lot to feel hopeful about if more men could extend their most closely held values outward, projecting compassion and respect for others in the public sphere as well as the private one."

Sexism, discrimination against people based on their sex rather than their individual merits, is often associated with gender stereotypes and may prevent individuals from expressing their full range of emotions or seeking certain vocations. A different and more hostile form of prejudice is **misogyny**, or the hatred of or disdain for women. Sexism may, for example, discourage a woman from pursuing a career in math or inhibit a man from choosing nursing as a profession. Children may develop stereotypes about differences between men and women and carry these into their adult lives.

We now recognize that our sexual and gender identities are a combination of nature and nurture. It is through new technology that researchers can observe brains in the act of cogitating, feeling, or remembering. In fact, many differences and similarities that were once attributed to learning or culture have been found to be biologically based. Add to this our individual choices, sense of identities, environmental factors, and life experiences, and we begin to get a picture of what contributes to making each person unique. (To learn more about sexual fluidity, see Think About It, "Sexual Fluidity: Women's and Men's Variable Sexual Attractions.")

Media is increasingly reporting celebrities who have left their heterosexual partners for same-sex ones.

Jason LaVeris/FilmMagic/Getty Images

"The main difference between men and women is that men are lunatics and women are idiots."

—Rebecca West (1892–1983)

think about it

Sexual Fluidity: Women's and Men's Variable Sexual Attractions

People can change. We've seen this, for example, among celebrities who have left their other-sex partner and become involved with a same-sex one (or vice versa), while others claim to be "straight" yet have lovers who are of the same sex. Actresses Ann Heche left Ellen DeGeneres for a man, Lauren Morelli, writer of *Orange is the New Black,* left her husband and married actress Samira Wiley, and Miley Cyrus identifies as pansexual and states that she is "open to every single thing that is consenting and doesn't involve an animal and everyone is of age." So, what's the story? Are these incidents simply flukes? Are individuals confused? Bisexual? On the "down low"?

Though each person has the right to identify and label their own sexual desires and behaviors, for some, using the term "sexual fluidity" may describe their sexual desires and attractions as situation-dependent in sexual responsiveness (Diamond, 2008). Based on her research and analysis of animal mating and women's sexuality coupled with reviews of other studies, Lisa Diamond, professor of psychology and gender studies at the University of Utah, suggests that female desire may be dictated by both intimacy and emotional connection. She further states that for women, sexual desire is malleable, embedded in the nature of female desire, and cannot be captured by asking women to categorize their attractions.

Some researchers have suggested that the key difference between sexual fluidity and bisexuality is the type of changes in the attraction: Bisexuality is a consistent pattern of sexual responsiveness to more than one gender, whereas situational fluidity is a capacity for variation in responsiveness across different contexts (Diamond et al., 2017). However, other researchers have suggested that sexual fluidity is simply an extension of bisexuality, noting that bisexual orientations are more "open" and flexible than exclusive or other-sex orientations. Yet, do the different experiences of sexual attraction and behavior over time represent the same thing? To help us understand this, Lisa Diamond and colleagues sought to explore the forms of sexual variability and how they might relate to one another. The researchers sampled 76 women of diverse sexual orientations to explore the nature of sexual fluidity, revealing four major forms (Diamond et al., 2019):

1. *An overall responsiveness to a less-preferred gender.* This most strongly resembles the construct of bisexuality.

2. *A variability in erotic responsiveness across different situations.* In this form of fluidity, a woman would respond erotically to her "less-preferred" gender in the laboratory, but not in everyday life.

3. *A discrepancy between the gender patterning of sexual attractions and that of sexual partnering.* For example, in a specific situation, a self-identified lesbian woman might pursue sex with men or self-identified heterosexual woman might pursue sex with women.

4. *Instability over time in day-to-day attractions.* This form highlights the variability of all individuals over time but takes a different form for "highly fluid" individuals who are less likely to revert to their original pattern of attraction. What remains a contentious question is whether a sexual orientation adequately describes the experiences and interpretations that are distinct from a category (e.g., heterosexual, bisexual, homosexual).

With the exception of the 1st and 4th form, the authors concluded that the four types of fluidity did not correlate with one another as each showed a different pattern of sexual expression. It is apparent that the link between sex drive and different forms of fluidity need further clarification (Diamond et al., 2019).

Though less is known about male sexual fluidity, we now realize that sexual identity and attraction undergo changes throughout a person's life. We also recognize that men are often stigmatized while women are fetishized for their thoughts or actions outside of traditional sexual boxes. In viewing sexual orientation on a spectrum, from "straight" to "same-sex preference," males, in general, tend to fall onto one or the other side of the spectrum: either "straight" or gay (Kaestle, 2019). A study of nearly 7,000 individuals ranging in age from mid-teens to late 20s found substantial changes in self-reported sexual orientation throughout adulthood. Many men who said they were heterosexual and had sex with other men did not identify as gay or bisexual. The study concluded that men, it seems, can "compartmentalize an aspect of their sex lives in a way that prevents it into blurring into or complicating their more public identities" (Singal, 2016). This study expands our knowledge about how humans interpret complex questions of sexual orientation, identity, and desire, and reconcile them with cultural expectations. We're learning that men's sexuality isn't necessarily as rigid as we may think, nor does one's stated sexual orientation determine who one is attracted to (Schrieber, 2018).

Whether sexual fluidity is a generic term that can be used by anyone or takes on nuanced meanings depending on the sex is revealed in the work of Diamond and her colleagues who suggest that indeed male's and female's sexual orientations differ in several important ways (Bailey et al., 2016):

1. *Women are more likely than men to report a bisexual orientation.* That is, they are more open than men to the possibility of same- and other-sex attractions.

2. *Men's sexual orientation is linked to their sexual arousal of female or male erotic stimuli.* In other words, men tend to be more comfortable identifying as either homosexual or heterosexual, as opposed to bisexual or sexually fluid.

3. *Women appear to experience same-sex attraction in close affectionate relationships.* For men, sexual attraction can be congruent with or follow a close psychological connection.

4. *Women's patterns of sexual attraction appear more likely to change over time.* That is, women can embrace various forms of sexual expression over time and in context to their relationships.

What remains a contentious question is whether a sexual orientation adequately describes the experiences and interpretations that are distinct from a category (e.g., heterosexual, bisexual, homosexual). Though tremendous strides have been made to foster greater acceptance of a diversity of sexual expression, sexual minorities remain isolated and unsupported. Textbooks, media, and culture continue to assume that there is a fixed model of same-sex sexuality though many individuals know differently. Although the notion of sexual fluidity may be confusing, frightening, or threatening to some, it does offer one or more variables to the broad spectrum of sexual expression of which humans are capable and can celebrate. Still, the question of whether sexual expression is a biological or cultural phenomenon remains a mystery. According to Charles Blow (2015), a *New York Times* Op-Ed columnist, "Attraction is attraction, and it doesn't always wear a label."

Think Critically

1. Is sexual orientation innate and/or fixed? How has your understanding of sexual orientation changed over time? Or has it?

2. Have you experienced sexual fluidity? If so, what were your feelings and reactions?

3. What would you do if your same-sex or other-sex best friend told you that he or she was romantically interested in you?

Gender and Sexual Orientation

Gender, gender identity, and gender roles are conceptually independent of sexual orientation. But in many people's minds, these concepts are closely related to sexual orientation. Our traditional notion of gender roles assumes that heterosexuality is a critical component of femininity and masculinity. That is, a "masculine" man is attracted to women and a "feminine" woman is attracted to men. From this assumption follow two beliefs about same-sex behavior: (1) if a man is gay, he cannot be masculine, and if a woman is lesbian, she cannot be feminine; and (2) if a man is gay, he must have some feminine characteristics, and if a woman is lesbian, she must have some masculine characteristics. What these beliefs imply is that same-sex behavior is somehow associated with a failure to fill traditional gender roles. A "real" man is not gay; therefore, gay men are not "real" men. Similarly, a "real" woman is not a lesbian; therefore, lesbian women are not "real" women. These negative stereotypes, which hold that people fall into distinct genders, with natural roles, and are presumed to be heterosexual, are referred to as **heteronormativity** or *heterocenterism*.

"Stereotypes fall in the face of humanity . . . this is how the world will change for gay men and lesbians."
—Anna Quindlen (1953–)

• Gender-Role Learning

As we have seen, gender roles are socially constructed and rooted in culture. So how do individuals learn what their society expects of them as males or females?

Theories of Socialization

Definitions and concepts of how gender emerges come from a wide variety of theoretical perspectives. Theories influence how we approach sexuality research, practice, education, and policy. Two of the most prominent theories are cognitive social learning theory and cognitive development theory. In the study of sexuality, a growing body of literature uses a social constructionist theory on gender, including queer theory.

Cognitive social learning theory is derived from behavioral psychology. In explaining our actions, behaviorists emphasize observable events and their consequences, rather than internal feelings and drives. According to behaviorists, we learn attitudes and behaviors as a result of social interactions with others—hence the term *social learning* (Bandura, 1977).

The cornerstone of cognitive social learning theory is the belief that consequences control behavior. Behaviors that are regularly followed by a reward are likely to occur again; behaviors that are regularly followed by a punishment are less likely to recur. Thus girls are rewarded for playing with dolls ("What a nice mommy!"), but boys are not ("What a sissy!").

"The war between the sexes is the only one in which both sides regularly sleep with the enemy."
—Quentin Crisp (1908–1999)

This behaviorist approach has been modified to include cognition—mental processes that intervene between stimulus and response, such as evaluation and reflection. The cognitive processes involved in social learning include our ability to: (1) use language, (2) anticipate consequences, and (3) make observations. By using language, we can tell our child that we like it when they do well in school and that we don't like it when they hit someone. A person's ability to anticipate consequences affects behavior. A boy doesn't need to wear lace stockings in public to know that such dressing will lead to negative consequences. Finally, children observe what others do. A girl may learn that she "shouldn't" play video games by seeing that the players in video arcades are mostly boys.

We also learn gender roles by imitation, through a process called modeling. Most of us are not even aware of the many subtle behaviors that make up gender roles—the ways in which individuals use different mannerisms and gestures, speak differently, use different body language, and so on. Initially, the most powerful models that children have are their parents. As children grow older and their social world expands, so does the number of people who may act as their role models, including siblings, friends, teachers, athletes, and media figures. Children sift through the various demands and expectations associated with the different models to create their own unique selves.

In contrast to cognitive social learning theory, **cognitive development theory** (Kohlberg, 1966) focuses on children's active interpretation of the messages they receive from the environment. Whereas cognitive social learning theory assumes that children and adults learn in fundamentally the same way, cognitive development theory stresses that we learn differently depending on our age. At age 2, children can correctly identify themselves and others as boys or girls, but they tend to base this identification on superficial features such as hair and clothing: Girls have long hair and wear dresses; boys have short hair and wear pants. Some children even believe they can change their gender by changing their clothes or hair length. As they age, children develop the stereotypic conceptions of gender they see around them.

Social construction theory examines the development of jointly-constructed understandings of society that help form our shared assumptions about reality. We can use it, for example, to view gender as a set of practices and performances that occur through language and a political system (Bartky, 1990; Butler, 1993; Connell, 1995; Gergen, 1985). Social constructionists suggest that gendered meanings are only one vehicle through which sexuality is constituted.

Another way of viewing gender is through the lens of **queer theory**, which identifies gender and sexuality as systems that are not gender neutral and cannot be understood by the actions of heterosexual males and females (Parker & Gagnon, 1995). Queer theory views the meaning and realities associated with sexuality as socially constructed to serve political systems. They furthermore underscore the role of institutional power in shaping the ideas of what is normal, deviant, natural, or essential. Thus, a social constructionist approach to gender would inquire about ways in which males and females make meaning out of their experiences with their bodies, their relationships, and their sexual choices, while queer theorists would challenge the notion of gender as fixed and seek to reframe it as being socially constructed and hence varying with context.

Gender-Role Learning in Childhood and Adolescence

It is difficult to analyze the relationship between biology and personality because learning begins at birth. In our culture, infant girls are usually held more gently and treated more tenderly than boys, who are ordinarily subjected to rougher forms of play. The first day after birth, parents may characterize their daughters as soft, fine-featured, and small and their sons as strong, large-featured, big, and bold. When children feel they may not measure up to these expectations, they may stop trying to express their authentic feelings and emotions.

Parents as Socializing Agents During infancy and early childhood, children's most important source of learning is the primary caregiver, whether the mother,

Parents' influence on children is fundamental to their healthy development.

Image Source

father, grandmother, or someone else. Many parents are not aware that their words and actions contribute to their children's gender-role socialization. Nor are they aware that they treat their daughters and sons differently because of their gender. Although parents may recognize that they respond differently to sons than to daughters, they usually have a ready explanation: the "natural" differences in the temperament and behavior of girls and boys.

Increasingly, parents are blurring gender lines when naming their newborns. Non-binary names such as Sam, Alex, Emery, Cori, and Ari are predicted to be among the most popular gender-neutral baby names in 2020 (Parade, 2020). In a time when most merchandisers of children's toys and wear have done away with pink and blue aisles, some toy manufacturers are expanding their collection of dolls to be more reflective of the diversity that exists among all of us.

Children are socialized in gender roles through several very subtle processes (Oakley, 1985):

- *Manipulation.* Parents manipulate their children from infancy onward. They treat a daughter gently, tell her she is pretty, and advise her that nice girls do not fight. They treat a son roughly, tell him he is strong, and advise him that big boys do not cry. Eventually, most children incorporate their parents' views in such matters as integral parts of their personalities.

- *Channeling.* Children are channeled by directing their attention to specific objects. Toys, for example, are differentiated by sex. Dolls are considered appropriate for girls, and cars for boys.

- *Verbal appellation.* Parents use different words with boys and girls to describe the same behavior. A boy who pushes others may be described as "active," whereas a girl who does the same is usually called "aggressive."

- *Activity exposure.* The activity exposure of girls and boys differs markedly. Although both are usually exposed to a variety of activities early in life, boys are discouraged from imitating their mothers, whereas girls are encouraged to be "mother's little helper."

Raising children, of course, requires talking with them. One of the easiest ways to start is to ask children questions about their experiences, about the pressures they may feel, as well as about their favorite activity or book. Over time, they learn that parents can be trusted to both listen and help them manage life.

As children grow older, their social world expands, and so do their sources of learning. Throughout this time and despite any embarrassment parents might have, they may wish to increase the frequency of conversations with their children about sexuality as well as consider the content of these discussions. Around the time children enter day care or kindergarten, teachers, and peers become important influences.

Teachers as Socializing Agents Day-care centers, nursery schools, and kindergartens are often children's first experience in the world outside the family. Teachers become important role models for their students. Because most day-care workers and kindergarten and elementary school teachers are women, children tend to think of child-adult interactions as primarily the province of women. In this sense, schools reinforce the idea that women are concerned with children and men are not. In fact, the teaching profession has slowly become even more female over the past several decades, with women consisting of approximately 76% of the workforce (National Center for Education Statistics, 2016). What is also concerning is the lack of racial diversity in the teacher workforce. Beyond this concern are the educational outcomes of children and how they compare by sex. According to the National Assessment for Educational Progress (NAEP) (2017), a congressionally mandated assessment project representative of fourth- and eighth-grade students in the nation, the average math scores in 2017 were slightly higher for boys in both fourth and eighth grades; however boys continue to lag in reading. In school districts that are mostly rich, white, and suburban, boys are more likely to outperform girls in math. Based on 260 million standardized test scores, local norms appear to influence how children from an early age perform in school, and it appears that boys are more influenced by these norms than are girls (Reardon et al., 2018).

"Behavior is the mirror image in which everyone shows their image."
—Johann Wolfgang von Goethe (1749–1832)

"What are little girls made of? Sugar and spice and everything nice. That's what little girls are made of. What are little boys made of? Snips and snails and puppy dogs' tails. That's what little boys are made of."
—Nursery rhyme

"The beautiful bird gets caged."
—Chinese proverb

It has also been observed that teachers and parents may shame males into conforming to the traditional image of masculinity. For example, males are taught to hide their emotions, act brave, and demonstrate independence. Even though males may get good grades and be considered normal, healthy, and well-adjusted by peers, parents, and teachers, they may also report feeling deeply troubled about the roles and goals of their gender.

Gender bias often follows students into the college arena and can be witnessed both in and outside the classroom. This environment coupled with high rates of sexual violence has resulted in impediments to academic success, lower graduation rates, health problems, and mental health issues (Office on Women's Health, 2018). In recognition of this campus and public health concern, there is a nationwide movement to develop and enforce policy and programming that reflect intolerance for sexual bias and violence across its continuum—from sexist statements to sexual harassment to sexual assault.

Peers as Socializing Agents   Children's age-mates, or peers, become especially important when they enter school. By granting or withholding approval, friends and playmates influence what games children play, what they wear, what music they listen to, what TV programs they watch, and even what cereal they eat. Peers provide standards for gender-role behavior in several ways:

- Peers provide information about gender-role norms through play activities and toys. Though this is slowly changing, girls often play with dolls that cry and wet themselves or with glamorous dolls with well-developed figures and expensive tastes. Boys often play with video games in which they kill and maim in order to dominate and win.

- Peers influence the adoption of gender-role norms through verbal approval or disapproval. "That's for boys!" or "Only girls do that!" is a strong negative message to the boy playing with dolls or the girl playing with a football.

- Children's perceptions of their friends' gender-role attitudes, behaviors, and beliefs encourage them to adopt similar ones to be accepted. If a girl's same-sex friends play soccer, she is more likely to play soccer. If a boy's same-sex friends display feelings, he is more likely to display feelings.

Even though parents tend to fear the worst in general from peers, they can provide important positive influences. It is within their peer groups, for example, that adolescents learn to

develop intimate relationships. Because of these peer-driven influences, sexual communication, including the use of peer educators to transmit accurate sexual health information to adolescents, can also support positive sexual decision making, particularly among non-sexually-active adolescents (Ragsdale et al., 2014).

Media Influences   Media and the public benefit when a broad range of voices are included; however, much of television and video programming promotes or condones negative stereotypes about gender, ethnicity, age, ability, sexual orientation, and gender identity. Female characters on television typically are under age 30, well-groomed, thin, and attractive. In contrast, male characters are often aggressive and constructive; they solve problems and rescue others from danger. Indeed, all forms of media glorify stereotypical gender norms. With 24/7 access to media, beginning as early as 3 years of age or younger, the influence of media cannot be understated or ignored.

Gender categorizing in children's toys, clothes, costumes, and other merchandise has been used by the media to target children and their parents. Princess dresses and kitchen items for girls, and action figures and video games for boys have helped fuel the $27 billion toy industry, which historically has relied on these gender-based stereotypes (Toy Association, 2020). Radical shifts, however, have taken place among manufacturers and retailers, including Target, Amazon, and Mattel, who have responded to parents' pushback by no longer segregating toys along gender lines. Though there may still be some differences in what toys girls and boys prefer, the gender lines that previously existed have begun to blur.

Gender Schemas: Exaggerating Differences

Actual differences between females and males are minimal, except in anatomy, levels of aggressiveness, and visual/spatial skills, yet culture exaggerates these differences or creates differences where few otherwise exist. One way that culture does this is by creating a schema: a set of interrelated ideas that helps us process information by categorizing it in a variety of ways. We often categorize people by age, ethnicity, nationality, physical characteristics, and so on. Gender is one such way of categorizing.

Psychologist Sandra Bem (1983) observed that although gender is not inherent in inanimate objects or in behaviors, we treat many objects and behaviors as if they were masculine or feminine. These gender divisions form a complex structure of associations that affects our perceptions of reality. Bem referred to this cognitive organization of the world according to

"That's not me you're in love with. That's my image. You don't even know me."

—Kelly McGillis (1957–)

"Women need a reason to have sex. Men just need a place."

—Billy Crystal (1948–)

Over time, Barbie dolls have become more diverse and representative of the larger population.

Sipa USA/Alamy Stock Photo

gender as a **gender schema**. We use gender schemas in many dimensions of life, including activities (nurturing, fighting), emotions (compassion, anger), behavior (playing with dolls or action figures), clothing (dresses or pants), and even colors (pink or blue), considering some appropriate for one gender and some appropriate for the other. Fortunately, these lines are blurring as rigid gender roles are diminishing.

Processing information by gender is important in cultures such as ours, for several reasons. First, gender-schema cultures make multiple associations between gender and other non-sex-linked qualities such as affection and strength. Our culture regards affection as a feminine trait and strength as a masculine one. Second, such cultures make gender distinctions important, using them as a basis for norms, status, taboos, and privileges. These associations, however, often undermine and undervalue the uniqueness of individuals.

● Contemporary Gender Roles and Scripts

In the past several decades, there has been a significant shift toward more egalitarian gender roles. Although women's roles have changed more than men's, men's are also changing, and these changes seem to affect all socioeconomic classes. Members of conservative religious groups still tend to adhere most strongly to traditional gender roles. Despite the ongoing disagreement, it is likely that the egalitarian trend will continue.

Traditional Gender Roles and Scripts

As has been previously discussed, much of what we believe about men and women come from stereotypes and the popular media. Cartoons that depict the male brain as filled with nothing other than fantasies of sex and that depict women as obsessing and conniving to obtain love are so prevalent that they are barely entertaining. Since we now know that endorsement and enactment of gendered sexual roles and scripts (boys are filled with sexual prowess whereas girls are expected to have sexual modesty) are negatively related to sexual and mental health, what purpose, if any, do these roles serve (Emmerink et al., 2016)?

The Traditional Male Gender Role   What does it take to be a man? What is a real man? Everybody has beliefs about how men should behave. One can simply go online to find stereotypical jokes, images, and lyrics to demonstrate what this looks like. The real answer to this question, however, is complex, multifaceted, dynamic, and dependent on a variety of factors.

Central personality traits associated with the traditional male role—no matter the race or ethnicity—may include aggressiveness, emotional toughness, independence, feelings of superiority, and decisiveness. Males are generally regarded as being more power-oriented than females, and they exhibit higher levels of aggression, especially violent aggression, dominance, and competitiveness. Although these tough, aggressive traits may be useful in the corporate world, politics, and the military (or in hunting saber-toothed tigers), they are rarely helpful to a man in his intimate relationships, which require understanding, cooperation, communication, and nurturing.

What perpetuates the image of the dominance of men, and what role does it serve in a society that no longer needs or respects such an image? It may be that a human's task is not to define gender roles but rather to redefine what it means to be human. Despite the fact that boys and men are overrepresented in a variety of psychological and social problems (e.g., bullying, school suspensions, and aggression), many boys and men do not receive the support they need. Socialization practices that teach boys to be self-reliant, strong, and to manage their problems on their own often result in adult men who are less willing to seek mental health treatment; that is a sense that if things aren't okay, they are not shared with others (APA, 2018). These internal secrets and conflicts can have tragic outcomes: For example, men are 3.5 times more likely to die by suicide than women, have more academic challenges, receive harsher punishments in school settings, and are the victims of 77% of homicides (and commit 90% of them). Understanding how boys and men experience masculinity and teaching them how to navigate their feelings has important implications for all of us.

Male Sexual Scripts   Different from a role, which is a more generalized behavior, a **script** consists of the specific behaviors, rules, and expectations associated with a particular role. It is like the script handed out to an actor. Unlike most dramatic scripts, however, social scripts allow for considerable improvisation within their general boundaries. We are given many scripts in life according to the various roles we play. Among them are **sexual scripts** that outline how we are to behave sexually when acting out our gender roles. Sexual scripts and gender roles for heterosexuals may be different from those for sexual minorities. Perceptions and patterns in sexual behavior are shaped by sexual scripts, especially among adolescents. Research is still needed to identify the dominant sexual scripts for varied sexual attractions among both men and women.

Psychologist Bernie Zilbergeld (1992) suggested that the mostly heterosexual male sexual script includes the following elements:

- *Men should not have (or at least should not express) certain feelings.* Men should not express doubts; they should be assertive, confident, and aggressive. Tenderness and compassion are not masculine emotions.

- *Performance is the thing that counts.* Sex is something to be achieved, to win at. Feelings only get in the way of the job to be done. Sex is not for intimacy but for orgasm.

- *The man is in charge.* As in other realms, the man is the leader, the person who knows what is best. The man initiates sex and gives the woman her orgasm. A real man doesn't need a woman to tell him what women like; he already knows.

- *A man always wants sex and is ready for it.* No matter what else is going on, a man wants sex; he is always able to become erect. He is a machine and no "real man" would ever turn down sex.

- *All physical contact leads to sex.* Because men are basically sexual machines, any physical contact is a sign for sex. Touching is seen as the first step toward sexual intercourse, not an end in itself. There is no physical pleasure other than sexual pleasure.

- *Sex equals intercourse.* All erotic contact leads to sexual intercourse. Foreplay is just that: warming up, getting one's partner ready for penetration. Kissing, hugging, erotic touching, and oral sex are only preliminaries to intercourse.

- *Sexual intercourse leads to orgasm.* The orgasm is the "proof in the pudding." The more orgasms, the better the sex. If a woman does not have an orgasm, she is not sexual. The male feels that he is a failure because he was not good enough to give her an orgasm. If she requires clitoral stimulation to have an orgasm, she has a problem.

Common to all these myths is a separation of sex from love and attachment. Sex is seen as performance. One cause for these views, the APA guidelines suggest, is "traditional masculinity" itself—the Western concept of manliness that relies on dominance, aggression, stereotypes, and competitiveness (APA, 2018). Yet, recent research shows that men's sexual desire is more relationship focused than previously thought, that many men desire to be "an object of desire," and that they consistently report their primary motivation to having sex is to pleasure their female partner (Murray, 2019; Murray et al., 2016). (To learn more about these studies see Think About It, "Factors that Prompt and Inhibit Men's Sex Desire" in Chapter 9).

The Traditional Female Gender Role   Though there are striking ethnic and individual differences, traditional female roles are expressive, or assume emotional or supportive characteristics. They emphasize passivity, compliance, physical attractiveness, and being a partner or wife and mother.

Though gender differences in patterns of sexual behavior have been decreasing, the sexual double standard, which implies that female and male sexual behavior should be judged by different standards, still exists. One can see this in discussions about casual sex, which many believe as acceptable for men but not for women. A survey of nearly 700 self-identified heterosexual men, mean age 37, found that overall, men expressed disapproval of sexually assertive women, perceiving them as non-conformist and judging them less positively than women who expressed sexual timidity (Klein et al., 2019). The authors found that gender-role conformity was held for women, but not for men, and there was an overall conservative attitude toward sexually assertive behavior of women.

In recent years, the traditional role has been modified to include work and marriage. Work roles, however, are still clearly subordinated to marital and family roles. Upon the birth of the first child, the woman may be expected to both work and parent or, if economically feasible, to become a full-time mother.

Female Sexual Scripts   Whereas the traditional male sexual script focuses on sex over feelings, the traditional female sexual script focuses on feelings over sex, on love over passion. The traditional mostly heterosexual female sexual script cited by psychologist and sex therapist Lonnie Barbach (2001) includes the following elements:

- *Sex is good and bad.* Women are taught that sex is both good and bad. What makes sex good? Sex in marriage or a committed relationship. What makes sex bad? Sex in a casual or uncommitted relationship. Sex is "so good" that a woman needs to save it for her husband or for someone with whom she is deeply in love. Sex is bad—if it is not sanctioned by commitment, love or marriage, a woman will get a bad reputation.

- *It's not OK to touch themselves "down there."* Girls are taught not to look at their genitals, not to touch them, and especially not to explore them. As a result, some women know very little about their genitals. They are often concerned about vaginal odors and labia size, making them uncomfortable about oral sex.

- *Sex is for men.* Men want sex; women want love. Women are sexually passive, waiting to be aroused. Sex is not a pleasurable activity as an end in itself; it is something performed *by* women *for* men.

- *Men should know what women want.* This script tells women that men know what they want even if women don't tell them. The woman is supposed to remain pure and sexually innocent. It is up to the man to arouse the woman even if he doesn't know what she finds arousing. To keep her image of sexual innocence, she does not tell him what she wants.

- *Women shouldn't talk about sex.* Many women are uncomfortable talking about sex because they are expected not to have strong sexual feelings. Some women (and men) may know their partners well enough to have sex with them but not well enough to communicate their needs to them.

- *Women should look like models.* The media present ideally attractive women as beautiful models with slender hips, supple breasts, and no fat or cellulite; they are always young, with never a pimple, wrinkle, or gray hair in sight. As a result of these cultural images, many women are self-conscious about their physical appearance. They worry that they are too fat, too plain, or too old. Because of their imagined flaws, they often feel awkward without clothes on.

- *Women are nurturers.* Women give; men receive. Women give themselves, their bodies, their pleasures to men. Everyone else's needs come first: his desire over hers, his orgasm over hers.

- *There is only one right way to have an orgasm.* Women often "learn" that there is only one "right" way to have an orgasm: during sexual intercourse as a result of penile stimulation.

Changing Gender Roles and Scripts

Contemporary gender roles are evolving from traditional hierarchical gender roles, in which one sex is subordinate to the other, to more egalitarian roles, in which both sexes are treated equally, and to androgynous roles, in which both sexes display the traits of instrumentality and expressiveness previously associated with only one sex. Thus, contemporary gender roles often display traditional elements along with egalitarian and androgynous ones. Furthermore, they operate on cultural, intrapersonal, and interpersonal levels, each one influencing the others to impact the individual's sexual beliefs and behaviors (Masters et al., 2013).

"I don't know why people are afraid of new ideas. I am terrified of the old ones."

—John Cage (1912–1992)

It is disheartening to note that over the past several decades, gender equality has stalled among all ages (New York University, 2020). This, however, may not be true for many same-sex couples, who appear to be having happier and more satisfying marriages (Garcia & Umberson, 2019). Researchers asked 756 midlife U.S. couples from gay, lesbian, and heterosexual marriages to provide daily accounts of their marital difficulties. What they found was that women in heterosexual marriages experienced the most significant amount of distress, while men in same-sex marriages reported the lowest levels. Heterosexual couples conveyed a stress level more in the middle. The researchers underscored the value of partnership inventories for psychological well-being by both spouses, especially for the well-being of women in other-sex marriages.

Megan Rapinoe won gold with the U.S. national team in the 2019 FIFA Women's World Cup, also winning the Golden Ball for the tournament's best player and the Golden Boot for its top scorer. She's just the 4th woman to receive the Sports Illustrated Person of the Year award, which is an acknowledgment of her remarkable athletic achievement and a reflection of entrenched gender biases.

lev radin/Shutterstock

Stephanie Coontz, author, historian, and professor of family studies, has been reviewing the literature for decades concerning society's changing views of family (Coontz, 2020). She has outlined the traditional reasons heterosexual marriages as compared to same-sex relationships are vulnerable to stress, miscommunication, and resentment. What she found was that sharp disparities in the responsibilities and authority of its partners contributed to higher stress in relationships. Prior to 1992, married couples seemed satisfied to have the wife do most of the housework and childcare. However, a study released in 2006 revealed that the most sexually satisfied and content couples were those who shared family tasks, including childcare. For example, while men assume about half the housework, women have double amount of child and adult care. This compares to lesbian and gay parents, who are more likely to share in the care of their children. Coontz, however, recognizes that same-sex couples don't have all the answers when it comes to marriage. Most couples face obstacles in figuring how to navigate relationships and how to replace traditional gender and marriage rules. Coontz notes, "Indeed, sharing domestic tasks has become an increasingly important component of marital stability, and lack of sharing an increasingly powerful predictor of conflict."

Contemporary sexual scripts include the following elements for all genders:

- Sexual expression is positive and healthy.

- Sexual activities involve a mutual exchange of erotic pleasure.

- Sexuality is equally involving, and both partners are equally responsible.

- Sexual activities are not limited to sexual intercourse but include a wide variety of sexual expression.

- Sexual activities may be initiated by either partner and should always be consensual.

- Both partners have the freedom to accept sexual pleasure and experience orgasm, no matter from what type of stimulation.

These contemporary scripts can support intimacy and satisfaction by allowing individuals to better understand gender-related issues and their impact on relationships. This deepened understanding along with the celebration of the uniqueness of each individual can assist couples in recognizing and freeing themselves from ineffectual and limiting stereotypes.

● Gender Variations

For many of us, there is no question about our gender: We know we are female or male. We may question our femininity or masculinity, but rarely do we question being female or male. For gender-variant individuals, or those who see themselves as part of a normal phenomenon with a right to self-definition and actualization in regard to sexual identity, "What gender am I?" is a dilemma. Their answer to this question reinforces the fact that little is known about the origins of a gender identity, whether cisgender or transgender (Drescher, 2014; Hyde et al., 2018). What is reported is that psychosexual development is influenced by multiple factors, including exposure to androgens, sex chromosome genes, and brain structure, as well as social circumstances and family dynamics.

Over the past two decades, many have challenged the **gender binary** or the view that humans comprise only two types of persons: women and men. This is due, in part, to the expanded research in neuroscience and psychological science, research on the experiences of transgender individuals, and social activism (Hyde et al., 2018). A global movement is gaining momentum to help us better understand sex and gender, with laws and language trying to keep pace. This expanded way of thinking is challenging the ways we regard the genders and our tradition of dividing people into two distinct groups. For example, in order to keep up with the non-categorization of gender, at the printing of this book, *Facebook* offered its users 58 gender options, including agender, androgyne, androgynous, bigender, and cisgender. Though some of the terms are still not yet found in standard dictionaries or thesauruses, they are part of a language that is still evolving. For many persons, the terms male and female are too limiting.

Because our culture views sexual anatomy as a female/male dichotomy, it is difficult for many to accept another view of gender variation (see Figure 1). While most transgender individuals are familiar with gender-variant expressions, there are many forms of gender variance, including but not limited to drag queens, drag kings, faeries, and others who use a variety of terms to self-identify. It's important to note, however, that since some terms are only for use within a community, it may not be appropriate to use them if you are not part of that group. Acknowledging other forms of gender-variant expressions and cross-gender identities can provide an important context to understanding human behaviors. Nevertheless, none of the forms of gender variance necessarily contribute to or define sexual orientation.

Researchers have reviewed empirical findings spanning multiple disciplines that question the gender binary (Hyde et al., 2018). They have concluded that although it is premature to identify a replacement to the gender binary, the results of the studies help to broaden our understanding of gender as it relates to sexual behavior:

1) Though distinct from one another, gendered and sexual behavior are intertwined such that sexuality cannot be studied without consideration of gender, and studies of gender can benefit from considering sex. The use of the term gender and sex (sometimes referred to as sex/gender) may be helpful in expressing this interconnection.

2) Gender and sex are multidimensional and each component is dynamic and responsive to both internal forces (biological, psychological) as well as external forces (cultural, social).

3) Individuals show variability across the different components of gender/sex that may not all align in a single category of the gender binary.

4) Thinking of oneself and others in terms of gender and sex is not fixed. Rather, the tendency to view gender and sex as a meaningful, binary category is both culturally determined and malleable.

In addition to the challenges of understanding gender and sex, researchers have stressed the costs in maintaining the gender binary, both in research as well as in the denial and marginalization of individuals whose bodies or identities fall outside of or between the binary categories. Because the complex, multidimensional, and fluid nature of gender and sex cannot be captured by two categories, the researchers suggest that the gender binary be replaced by multiple categories that are not mutually exclusive (one can identify as more than one gender), are fluid (identity can change over time), and view gender as irrelevant to the sense of self.

Transgender Issues and Experiences

Over time, there has been a major shift in the gender world. Upsetting old definitions and classification systems, a visible community that embraces the possibility of numerous genders and multiple social identities has emerged.

As previously stated, an estimated 0.6% of adults in the United States, or 1.4 million people, identify as transgender (Flores et al., 2016). These estimates have doubled from a decade ago and may be attributed to greater visibility, education, social acceptance, and expanded Medicare coverage for transgender people.

Billy Porter's fashion often blurs the lines between male and female.

Kathy Hutchins/Shutterstock

Sex

| Male | Intersex | Female |

Gender Identity

| Man/Boy | Transgender/Genderqueer Two-spirited/etc. | Woman/girl |

Gender Expression

| Masculine | Androgynous | Feminine |

Sexual Orientation

| Attracted to women | Attracted to all/both/none | Attracted to men |

• FIGURE 1

Sex and Gender Continuum. In contrast to the traditional gender binary view, the concepts of sex, gender and sexual orientation are complex and multidimensional. How people identify and express themselves can change, as can their pattern of sexual attraction.

In December 2020, Elliot Page, formerly Ellen Page, the Academy Award nominated star of *Juno* as well as *Inception* and *The Umbrella Academy,* announced he is transgender and would like to be identified as he/they.

Warren Toda/EPA-EFE/Shutterstock

"Treat people as if they were what they ought to be and you help them become what they are capable of being."

—Johann Wolfgang von Goethe
(1749–1832)

As the familiarity of gender identity grows, terminology and definitions are also evolving. The umbrella term transgender is a name used to capture all the identities that fall outside of traditional gender norms. Terms such as *androgynous, genderqueer,* and *gender fluid* are also used to describe the variations that exist on the gender spectrum. **Androgyny** refers to a combination of masculine and feminine traits or a nontraditional gender expression. (The term is derived from the Greek *andros,* "man," and *gyne,* "woman.") An androgynous person combines the trait of instrumentality traditionally associated with masculinity with the trait of expressiveness traditionally associated with femininity.

As of 2019, the World Health Organization (WHO) no longer categorizes being a transgender person as having a "mental disorder." According to the revised version of the International Classification of Diseases (ICD-11), "gender identity disorders" have been reframed as "gender incongruence," and gender nonconformity is now included in a chapter on sexual health, rather than being listed with mental disorders (WHO, 2018). Additionally, the American Psychiatric Association removed "gender identity disorder" from its previous *Diagnostic and Statistical Manual* (DSM-4) to help destigmatize transgender people. These are important developments for transgender adolescents and adults who may seek medical care without being diagnosed as having a mental disorder. According to Jack Drescher, psychiatrist and a member of the ICD-11 working group, "There is substantial evidence that the stigma associated with the intersection of transgender status and mental disorders contributes to precarious legal status [and] human rights violations" (Human Rights Watch, 2019).

The trans community along with its allies challenge binary categorizations of gender identity (see Figure 1). People who do not identify with any of the gender categories, whose gender expression or identity is not congruent with the sex assigned at birth, or do not favor one gender over another may identify as transgender, genderqueer, genderfluid, agender, or gender nonconforming.

Like cisgender individuals, transgender individuals can be attracted to their same sex, the other sex, or all sexes/genders in their sexual orientation and may represent their sexual orientation in non-binary ways, such as queer or pansexual. Many individuals may wish to represent their attractions in ways that do not specifically reference their own sex or gender, which may be in transition, fluid, or not fully captured by a label.

Support is aimed at affirming a unique transgender identity and role. To help in understanding and respecting transgender people, the Gay & Lesbian Alliance Against Defamation (GLAAD) (2018) has developed "Tips for Allies of Transgender People," which include the following:

1. Respect the terminology transgender persons use to describe their identity.
2. Don't make assumptions about a person's sexual orientation. Understand the differences between "coming out" as a lesbian, gay, or bisexual person and "coming out" as a transgender person.
3. If you don't know what pronouns to use, listen first, and if it's not apparent ask how the person identifies.
4. Don't ask about a transgender person's genitals, surgical status, or sex life.
5. Don't ask a person what his or her "real name" is.
6. Avoid backhanded compliments or "helpful" tips.
7. You can't tell if someone is transgender just by looking; ask how they identify.

This is not an exhaustive list nor does it include all of the "right" things to say, but it can begin to help change the culture for those who challenge or violate gender expectations.

Transgender Youth Gender is one of the central categories that help to organize a child's social world (Gulgoz et al., 2019). While patterns of gender development are well-documented among cisgender children, they are less understood among transgender children, who, in early childhood, identify and live as a gender different from their assigned sex. For those who do not identify with either gender or feel they are somewhere in between or have no gender, it may be natural for parents to ask if it is "just a phase" (American Academy of

Pediatrics [AAP], 2019). Research cited from AAP suggests that gender is something that we are born with and, as such, underscores the need for parents to love and accept their children for who they are. Others may argue this point, suggesting that gender development is a process in which we are socialized by others, however all agree that children need to be supported as they grown and evolve.

A variety of theories and approaches relating to gender development and standards of care for gender-nonconforming children and youth have emerged. Traditional approaches to addressing gender variations among children can include interventions that block puberty, provide cross-sex hormones and/or perform surgery to "correct" the variation. The Human Rights Campaign (HRC), supported by the United Nations treaty bodies and three former U.S. Surgeon Generals, condemn unnecessary surgeries on the grounds that they can cause pain, scarring, loss of sexual function, and the need for life-long hormone therapy replacement and maintenance surgery. They suggest that any medically unnecessary or elective surgeries should not be performed on children too young to participate in the decision (HRC, 2016). Instead, many professionals are using what's called the "watchful waiting approach" for gender-diverse children. That is, when children who are "insistent, persistent, and consistent" in expressing a gender other than the one assigned at birth, parents are encouraged to allow that child to decide if and when to socially transition (Ehrensaft, 2017). When a child's gender identity is unclear, this approach would give the family time to develop a broader understanding of the child's needs. This view was corroborated by evidence of psychosocial harm that is done through elective genital intervention especially when parents are not given informed consent before their child undergoes treatment (Roen, 2019). A research article that appeared in the *Proceedings of the National Academy of Sciences of the United States of America* (Gulgoz et al., 2019) suggests that early sex assignment and parental rearing based on that sex assignment do not always define how a child identifies or expresses gender later in life. If followed, this approach would minimize some of the traditional interventions, including medically unnecessary surgeries, until a child could participate in the decision about which gender best matches their gender identity. (For more about interventions for transgender individuals, see Think About It, "Gender-Confirming Treatment: Psychological and Physiological Needs.")

Citing the health and rights of transgender children, the Human Rights Watch (2019) emphasizes the need for access to care. They call particular attention to transgender children's heightened risk of anxiety, depression, and suicidal thoughts and provide evidence that acceptance of gender identity is associated with better physical and mental health outcomes. Experts suggest that transgender children be protected from bullying and harassment at school, have access to confidential counseling and support, and have the health care they need. Lawmakers should ensure that they are protected from discrimination based on gender identity. How to best support gender-nonconforming children, youth, and their families needs to be founded in medical science and psychology and tailored to each child's needs because we know that gender-diverse children thrive when their feelings are explored and validated.

Gender Dysphoria

Gender dysphoria is a diagnosis in *The Diagnostic and Statistical Manual-5 (DSM-5),* the American Psychiatric Association's (APA) classification and diagnostic tool (APA, 2013). The emphasis for the diagnosis is placed on the individual's distress that stems from the incongruence between their expressed or experienced gender and the sex and gender assigned at birth. Gender dysphoria is not the same as transgender. As previously stated, transgender is an umbrella term that refers to those whose gender expression or identity is not congruent with the sex assigned at birth. Though a trans person may not be distressed by their cross-gender identification, they may suffer from the stigma and discrimination that others impose on them.

Gender dysphoria has replaced the psychiatric diagnosis termed *gender identity disorder* and is meant to be a more inclusive category. The category consists of one overarching diagnosis with separate developmentally appropriate criteria for children and adolescents. Additionally, it is separate from *DSM-5* chapters on sexual dysfunction and paraphilia disorders.

"The fact that we are all human beings is infinitely more important than all the peculiarities that distinguish humans from one another."

—Simone de Beauvoir (1908–1986)

"If you don't like a certain behavior in others, look within yourself to find the roots of what discomforts you."

—Bryant McGill (1969–)

think about it

Gender-Confirming Treatment: Psychological and Physiological Needs

Now, more than at any time in history, there is an increasing need for accessible and affordable care for transgender individuals. Why? Because data indicates that, in addition to other psychological and physiological needs, gender-confirming treatments, also referred to as gender-confirming surgeries or gender or sex reassignment surgeries, have risen 20% between 2015 and 2016 alone. This translates to an increase of more than 3,200 gender-confirming surgeries per year (American Society of Plastic Surgeons [ASPS], 2017). These treatments are focused on helping individuals address the incongruity between the appearance of their bodies and their gender identity. The American Medical Association and the American Psychological Association have joined ASPS to endorse gender-confirming surgery as a safe option for those experiencing gender dysphoria. At the same time, it's important to note that not all trans people want or seek hormones and/or surgery, as having such treatments/interventions do not define whether someone is trans.

Changes in Gender Expression and Role

Experiencing life as a different gender from the one assigned at birth isn't easy. Lack of validation and support along with bullying take a toll. Also difficult for some but essential is living part- or full-time in another gender role that is consistent with one's gender identity. Such subtle gender clues such as mannerisms, voice, inflections, and body movement, learned in early childhood, need to be altered.

Psychotherapy

Transgender individuals experience more mental distress than cisgender people due to anxiety and tension, discrimination, sexual assault, and lack of support (Haelle, 2016). Too often this results in higher rates of unemployment and poverty, substance dependence, psychiatric conditions, and suicide.

Now more than ever, validation and support of gender variations are needed from family, friends, peers, media, and health professionals. Many individuals, couples, and families find that psychotherapy can be helpful in exploring gender identity, role, and expression; addressing the negative impact of gender dysphoria and stigmas; alleviating internalized transphobia, a negative attitude toward trans people; enhancing social and peer support; improving body image; and promoting resilience. If a person seeks gender-confirming surgery, Standards of Care (SOC) available through The World Professional Association for Transgender Health (2012) recommend that one referral from a qualified mental health professional be required for breast/chest surgery, while two referrals from qualified mental health professionals be required for genital surgery. Until people understand gender dysphoria, education, guidance, and support from professionals may be among the best tools we have to combat stereotypes and ignorance.

Hormone Therapy

Feminizing/masculinizing hormone treatment is a medically necessary intervention for many trans people. Hormone therapy takes two forms: puberty suppression, which pauses the hormonal changes that activate puberty in young adolescents and allows more time to make decisions about hormonal interventions, and hormone therapy to feminize or masculinize the body. Both the administration and the suppression of hormones can facilitate a physicality that is more congruent with a patient's gender identity.

When physicians administer androgens (testosterone) to an assigned female at birth (AFAB) to male patients, and estrogens, progesterone, and testosterone-blocking agents to an assigned male at birth (AMAB) to female patients, that person will experience changes that occur over the course of 2 years. Note that AFAB and AMAB are newer terms and sometimes preferred in trans and queer communities. They may be used to replace MtF (male to female) or FtM (female to male). Hormone therapy can precede gender-confirming surgery and can provide an intervention to individuals who do not wish to make a social gender-role transition or are unable or do not choose to undergo surgery.

Gender-Confirming Surgery

For those who find it psychologically and medically necessary to establish congruence with their gender identity, gender-confirming surgery (GCS) can change the primary and/or secondary sex characteristics. It is a treatment that has proven to have beneficial effects on selective individual's sense of well-being, body image, and sexual functioning. Of the 27,000 transgender and gender-nonconforming Americans responding to a 2015 U.S. Transgender Survey, 25% had undergone one or more gender-confirming surgeries (Lane et al., 2018). The average age for any procedure was 30, the majority of which were among higher-earning employed people. At the same time, one size does not fit all. A range of medical interventions and options are possible, and different people choose different interventions.

For AMAB to female individuals, penile inversion vaginoplasty involves the removal of the testicles and construction of the labia majora from the scrotal skin. The nerves to the sensitive glans penis and skin are used to form a clitoris, while the skin of the penis along with additional skin grafts from the scrotum are used to construct a vagina. The urethra is shortened and placed in the female position. Another technique, known as rectosigmoid vaginoplasty, uses a piece of the colon instead of skin grafts or inverted penile tissue to construct a vagina. This technique allows the creation of a deep and lubricated vagina. A third technique used to create the vagina uses "full thickness" skin grafts. These grafts are obtained from the penile skin to create the labia minora, while the scrotum skin creates the labia majora. A clitoris fully supplied with nerve endings can be formed from part of the glans of the penis. To prevent the

are only mild signs and no symptoms. The presence of the Y chromosome designates a person as male. It causes the formation of small, firm testes and ensures a masculine physical appearance. However, the presence of a double X chromosome pattern, which is a female trait, interferes with male sexual development, often preventing the testes from functioning normally and reducing the production of testosterone. At puberty, traits may vary: tallness, gynecomastia (breast development in men), sparse body hair, and/or small penis and testes (see Figure 3). XXY boys may also have learning or language problems (NIH, 2020.5). Because of low testosterone levels, there may be a low sex drive, an inability to experience erections, and infertility. Consequently, individuals may need testosterone replacement therapy and breast reduction surgery. In vitro techniques can allow some men to become biological fathers.

Prenatal Hormonal Variations Prenatal hormonal anomalies may cause males or females to develop physical characteristics associated with the other sex.

Androgen Insensitivity Syndrome When a person who is genetically male (has XY chromosomes) is unable to respond to male hormones or androgens, he is said to have **androgen insensitivity syndrome (AIS)** (MedlinePlus, 2020.5b). As a result, the person with this condition is genetically male but because their bodies are unable to respond to certain male sex hormones, they have mostly female sex characteristics or signs of male and female sexual development. This syndrome is divided into three categories: complete, partial, and mild, with 2 to 5 per 100,000 infants born with complete androgen insensitivity. Complete AIS prevents the development of the penis and other male body parts. Thus a person with complete AIS appears to be female but has no uterus. They are usually raised as females and have a female gender identity. Persons with partial or mild forms of AIS have a broader range of symptoms, including infertility, and breast development in men. Those with partial androgen insensitivity may be raised any gender.

Most people with complete AIS are not diagnosed until they fail to menstruate or have difficulties becoming pregnant. Treatment and corrective surgery can be a very complex issue and must be individualized. This may involve removal of the undescended testes to reduce the risk of cancer and estrogen replacement therapy to prevent osteoporosis.

Congenital Adrenal Hyperplasia **Congenital adrenal hyperplasia (CAH)** refers to a group of inherited disorders of the adrenal gland and can affect both males and females. People with congenital adrenal hyperplasia lack an enzyme needed by the adrenal gland to make the hormones cortisol and aldosterone. At the same time, the body produces more androgen, a type of male sex hormone (MedlinePlus, 2020.5c). Thus a genetic female (XX) is born with ovaries and a vagina but develops externally as male. This condition occurs in about 1 in 15,000 children.

Symptoms in both boys and girls vary, depending on the type of congenital adrenal hyperplasia and the age in which the symptoms were diagnosed. Children with milder forms may not have signs or symptoms and thus may not be diagnosed until adolescence. Females with more severe forms at birth will often have atypical genitals and may be diagnosed before symptoms appear. Males with a more severe type at birth will appear to have enlarged genitalia. Both, however, will soon experience poor feeding ability, vomiting, dehydration, and abnormal heart rhythm. Girls with the milder form will usually have normal female reproductive organs, but as they mature they may experience abnormal menstrual periods or failure to menstruate, have an early appearance and/or excessive amount of pubic or facial hair growth, and notice some enlargement of the clitoris. As boys with the milder form enter puberty, symptoms may include a deepening voice, early appearance of pubic or armpit hair, enlarged penis but normal testes, and well-developed muscles. Both boys and girls will be taller as children but as they mature will be much shorter than average adults.

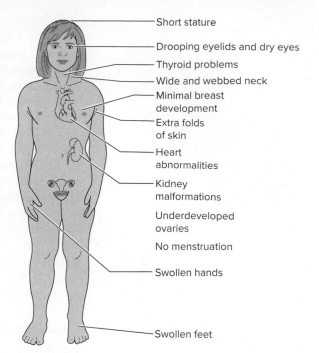

Short stature

Drooping eyelids and dry eyes

Thyroid problems

Wide and webbed neck

Minimal breast development

Extra folds of skin

Heart abnormalities

Kidney malformations

Underdeveloped ovaries

No menstruation

Swollen hands

Swollen feet

• FIGURE 2

Characteristics of Turner Syndrome.

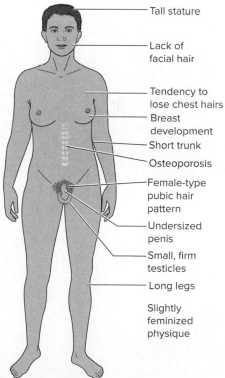

Tall stature

Lack of facial hair

Tendency to lose chest hairs

Breast development

Short trunk

Osteoporosis

Female-type pubic hair pattern

Undersized penis

Small, firm testicles

Long legs

Slightly feminized physique

• FIGURE 3

Characteristics of Klinefelter Syndrome.

Treatment for congenital adrenal hyperplasia is aimed at returning the hormone levels to normal by taking steroids that replace the low hormones. Additionally, the health care provider will check the chromosomes to help determine the genetic sex of the baby. Girls with male-appearing genitals may, during infancy, need surgery if, for example, changes in the genitals affect urine flow.

5-Alpha Reductase Deficiency **5-Alpha reductase deficiency** is a condition whereby a genetic male (XY) does not produce enough of a hormone called dihydrotestosterone (DHT) (MedlinePlus, 2020.5d). Given DHT's significant role in male sexual development, a shortage of this hormone in utero disrupts the formation of the external sex organs before birth, causing individuals to be born with external genitalia that appear female. In other cases, the external genitalia do not look clearly male or clearly female and are sometimes referred to as ambiguous genitalia. Still other affected infants have genitalia that appear primarily male, often with an extremely small penis (micropenis) and the urethra opening on the underside of the penis (hypospadias). Because of the rarity of this condition, there is no available estimate about how often it occurs. Children with 5-alpha reductase deficiency are often raised as girls, about half of whom adopt a male gender role in adolescence or early adulthood. Most affected males are infertile.

Coming to Terms With Differences

Everyone wishes and deserves to be loved, accepted, and supported. At the same time, most societies have a difficult time with differences. Western society is not exempt, especially when these differences are complex, are not understood, and/or may challenge the traditional or religious notions of "normal." Because rejection and loss are common concerns for individuals facing gender transition, some may feel their only choice is transition or suicide. When the real or perceived risk of loss and rejection is too great a price to pay, many will choose suicide. This may result when families and communities avoid discussing children's gender differences or sharing their own gender identity history. Most professionals, however, acknowledge that the more one educates oneself and talks about these issues, the easier it gets. And when transgender children and youth are emotionally supported, that is affirmed in their gender identities in all aspects of their lives, and receive timely and appropriate interventions and care, their health and wellness becomes more achievable (Olson et al., 2016).

On May 13, 2016, the U.S. Departments of Education and Justice released joint guidance to help provide educators the information they need to ensure that all students, including transgender students, attend school in an environment free from discrimination based on sex.

The guidance answers questions that schools may have, with a goal to ensure that all students be treated equally consistent with their gender identity. A school may not require transgender students to have a medical diagnosis, undergo any medical treatment, or produce a birth certificate or other identification before treating them consistent with their gender identity. Additionally, it is the schools' obligation to:

1. Respond promptly and effectively to sex-based harassment of all students;
2. Treat students consistent with their gender identity even if the school records or identification documents indicate a different sex;
3. Allow students to participate in sex-segregated activities and access sex-segregated facilities consistent with their gender identity; and
4. Protect students' privacy related to their transgender status.

Many parents, schools, and districts have raised questions about this area of civil rights laws; however, these documents are available to help navigate what may be new terrain for many.

Self-acceptance, beginning with an understanding and appreciation of our physical appearance and the expectations that come with our preferred gender, can be a gateway to building intimacy in personal relationships. Pleasure and satisfaction can be strengthened when individuals have a better understanding of gender issues and differences. Because people sometimes react negatively to variations simply because they are fearful or ignorant, educating others about non-binary individuals, or those who don't conform to society's expectations of masculinity and femininity, may help reduce their fear and ignorance and the stigmatization that accompanies both. While societies, laws, and some individuals may remain closed to accepting and supporting the wide variability in sexuality differentiation, gender, and expression, progress can be seen when education, advocacy, and open communication occur. It's this kind of work that will help all of us embrace our full humanity.

An important function among schools and campuses across the country is to provide a safe space for all students. This includes LGBTQ+ and ally students who wish to share their thoughts and experiences in a social environment that is supportive, fun, and friendly. Such a student group can be the first point of contact for individuals during the coming-out process, a time when many feel doubt, fear, and shame. Often an LGBTQ+ and ally group works to educate and advocate on behalf of equal rights. As such, the goals and purposes of the organization need to be communicated to potential members and to the administration, and partnerships need to be built with departments and services, including that of the counseling offices to address the mental health needs of the group. In addition to supporting advocacy groups, universities and schools across the country are slowly responding to gender equity mandates articulated in **Title IX**, an education amendment that protects people from discrimination based on sex in education programs or activities that receive federal financial assistance.

To further advance anti-sex and anti-gender discrimination laws and expand Title VII of the Civil Rights Act of 1964, which prohibits discrimination "because of sex," the Supreme Court in 2020 ruled that gay and transgender employees can no longer be fired because of their sex or gender. Prior to this change, judges for 50 years had interpreted Title VII's prohibition on discrimination because of sex to mean only that employers could not treat women worse than men. This revision now makes it illegal for businesses across the nation to fire employees based on their sexual orientation or gender identity. As a result, approximately 8.1 million people (ages 16 and older), are protected from discrimination and, if necessary, have recourse available through the federal courts (Human Rights Watch, 2020). The ruling is particularly important for LGBTQ+ employees in states that lack state protection. This ruling does not address how housing, religious employers, or sports would be affected, but it does underscore what many already believe, which is that discrimination against LGBTQ+ people is both unfair and illegal.

Though much of the attention around this anti-gender discrimination law is centered on combating sexual assault, there are a number of best practices to support transgender and other non-binary students, including the following (Beemyn, 2015):

1. Add the phrase "gender identity or expression" to the institution's nondiscrimination policy.

2. Ask "gender identity" on college forms and surveys. This would mean changing options from male and female to woman, man, trans woman, trans man, and a range of non-binary gender identities.

3. Enable students to change their gender and use a chosen name on campus records and documents. This can prevent a student from being "outed" as transgender when an instructor takes attendance or when someone sees a student's identification card.

4. Offer gender-inclusive bathrooms and adopt a policy that enables students to use the campus restrooms that are in keeping with their gender identity and expression.

5. Offer gender-inclusive housing, which enables two or more students to share a multiple-occupancy room, suite, or apartment, in mutual agreement, regardless of the students' gender assignment or gender identity.

6. Enable insurance coverage for trans-related psychotherapy, hormone replacement therapy, and gender-affirming surgeries.

Caitlyn Jenner stunned the world when she made it clear that her self-identity allows her to finally be her own person.
MediaPunch/Shutterstock

Many people take their gender for granted. The making of gender, however, is a complex process involving biological, cultural, environmental, and psychological elements. Biologically, the majority of us are male or female in terms of genetic and anatomical makeup. Psychologically, most of us identify as male or female in terms of our assigned gender and our gender identity. More often, what concerns us is related to our gender roles: am I sufficiently masculine? Feminine? For others, living as a gender-nonconforming person is an important part of their identity. What it means to be feminine, masculine, or another gender variation differs from culture to culture. Although femininity and masculinity are generally regarded as opposites in our culture, there are relatively few significant inherent differences between the sexes aside from males impregnating and females giving birth and lactating. The majority of social and psychological differences are exaggerated or culturally encouraged. All in all, persons of all gender variations are more similar than different. The more that we as individuals and as a society do to educate ourselves, the more likely the shame and stigmatization that accompany sexual and gender variations will be reduced.

Summary

Studying Gender, Gender Roles, and Sexuality

- *Assigned sex* is the assignment made at birth. *Gender* encompasses the social and cultural characteristics associated with biological sex. Normal gender development depends on biological, cultural, and psychological factors. Psychological factors include assigned gender and gender identity. *Gender roles* tell us how we are to act with our assumed or assigned sex in a particular culture. *Gender variations* occur among those who cannot or choose not to conform to societal gender norms.

- Although our culture encourages us to think that men and women are "opposite" sexes, they are more similar than dissimilar. Innate gender differences are generally minimal; differences are primarily encouraged by socialization.

- We develop our gender through the interaction of its biological, cultural, and psychosocial components. The term used by some for a person whose gender identity matches the biological sex they were assigned at birth is *cisgender.* Our culture emphasizes that there are only two genders, otherwise referred to as the *gender binary,* whereby gender is an either-or option of male or female. Many who are questioning their gender, are uncertain, unwilling to state, or feel limited by these categories are said to be gender variant, or *gender nonconforming. Transgender* is the umbrella term used to describe individuals whose gender expression or identity is not congruent with the sex assigned at birth.

Gender-Role Learning

- *Cognitive social learning theory* emphasizes learning behaviors from others through cognition and modeling. *Cognitive*

development theory asserts that once children learn gender is permanent, they independently strive to act like "proper" girls and boys because of an internal need for congruence.

- *Social construction theory* views gender as a set of practices and performances that occur through language and a political system. *Queer theory* views gender and sexuality as systems that cannot be understood as gender neutral or by the actions of heterosexuals.

- Though the stereotypes are somewhat outmoded, children still learn their gender roles from parents through manipulation, channeling, verbal appellation, and activity exposure. Parents, teachers, peers, and the media are the most important agents of socialization during childhood and adolescence.

- A *gender schema* is a set of interrelated ideas used to organize information about the world on the basis of gender. We use our gender schemas to classify many non-gender-related objects, behaviors, and activities as male or female.

Contemporary Gender Roles and Scripts

- The trait most associated with the traditional male gender role is *instrumentality.* Traditional male roles emphasize aggression, emotional toughness, and independence. Traditional male sexual *scripts* include the denial of the expression of feelings, an emphasis on performance and being in charge, and the belief that men always want sex and that all physical contact leads to sex.

- The trait most associated with the traditional female gender role is *expressiveness.* Traditional female roles emphasize passivity, compliance, physical attractiveness, and being a wife and mother. Female sexual scripts suggest that sex is good and bad (depending on the context); genitals should not be touched; sex is for men; women shouldn't talk about sex; women should look like models; and there is only one "right" way to experience an orgasm.

- Important changes affecting today's gender roles and sexual scripts include increasing questioning of values and expectations around parenting, dating, and careers.

- Contemporary gender scripts are more egalitarian than traditional ones and include the belief that sex is positive, that it involves a mutual exchange, and that it may be initiated by either partner.

Gender Variations

- For most of us, there is no question about our gender. However, for many others, gender-variant expressions are an important means of identity.

- As our understanding of gender identity grows, so do the terminology and definitions expand. Under the umbrella term of transgender, often referred to as trans, a term used to capture all the identities that fall outside of traditional gender norms, terms such as androgynous, genderqueer, and gender fluid are ways to capture the variations that exist on the gender spectrum. *Androgyny* refers to a combination of masculine and feminine traits or a nontraditional gender expression.

- *Gender dysphoria* is a medical diagnosis that reflects an individual's distress that stems from the incongruence between their expressed or experienced gender and the gender assigned at birth. Those who find it essential and medically necessary to establish congruence with their gender identity may seek *gender-confirming treatment.*

- *Disorders of sex development (DSD),* also referred to as differences of sexual development, or *intersex,* is a diagnosis used to describe congenital conditions in which the external appearance of the individual does not coincide with their chromosomal constitution or the gonadal sex.

Questions for Discussion

- **How have gender stereotypes and roles influenced your views of your sexuality and the ways in which you relate to others?**

- **If you had an infant born with ambiguous genitalia, would you opt for surgery? Inhibit the onset of puberty with drugs? What gender would you raise the child? If surgery were chosen, when the child was old enough, would you inform him or her about this treatment? Or would you not choose surgery and instead leave the decision to the individual at a later time?**

- **Do you believe that your gender identity was biologically or socially determined? Who or what most influenced your gender identity? In what ways?**

Sex and the Internet

Working for LGBTQ+ Equal Rights

The number of education and advocacy groups working around sexual orientation and gender has increased tremendously in recent years. Go to the Human Rights Campaign (http://www.hrc.org). From there, click "Explore," identify two topics of interest, and read what they have to offer. Once you have read about two issues, answer the following questions:

- How does the new information you have gathered influence the way you think about gender and/or sexual orientation?

- What was one specific aspect of this subject that most interested you?

- What is one point you still have questions about?

- What have you learned as a result of this research?

Suggested Websites

Accord Alliance

https://www.accordalliance.org
Information, referrals, and support for those who are seeking information and advice about disorders of sex development.

Asexual Visibility & Education Network (AVEN)

https://www.asexuality.org
Hosts the world's largest online asexual community as well as a large archive or resources on asexuality.

Disorders of Sex Development

https://dsdguidelines.org
Handbooks for clinicians and patients about the diagnosis, treatment, education, and support of children with disorders of sex development.

Endocrine Society

https://www.endocrine.org
Provides information and training around a variety of endocrine-related problems as well as updates and recommendations for transgender health.

Focus Foundation

https://thefocusfoundation.org
Seeks to increase awareness and early detection of X and Y disorders and to discover innovative treatments for recovery.

GATE: Trans, Gender Diverse and Intersex Advocacy in Action

https://transactivists.org
An international organization that works to educate and support those who have gender identity, sex characteristics, or bodily diversity issues.

Gender Spectrum

https://www.genderspectrum.org

Provides education, training, and support to help create a gender-sensitive and inclusive environments for children and adults.

Interact: Advocates for Intersex Youth

Interactadvocates.org

Uses innovative legal and other strategies to advocate for the human rights of children born with intersex traits.

My Pronouns

www.mypronouns.org

Provides helpful, practical tips to help navigate different pronouns.

National Center for Transgender Equality

https://www.transequality.org

Dedicated to advancing the equality of transgender people through advocacy, collaboration, and empowerment.

PFLAG: Our Trans Loved Ones

www.pflag.org/ourtranslovedones

Questions and answers for parents, families, and friends of people who are transgender and gender expansive.

Translifeline

www.translifeline.org

A national trans-led organization aimed at improving the quality of trans people's lives and fighting the epidemic of trans suicide.

Trans Awareness Project

www.transawareness.org

Sponsored by the University of Minnesota, a campaign that attempts to challenge stereotypes and cultivate an environment that celebrates and respects people of all genders.

Trevor Project

https://www.thetrevorproject.org

Provides crisis and suicide prevention services for LGBTQ+ people under age 25.

United Nations Inter-Agency Network on Women and Gender Equality

www.unwomen.org/en

Gateway to information and resources to help advance the promotion of gender equality.

World Professional Association for Transgender Health (WPATH)

https://www.wpath.org

A professional organization that provides evidence-based care, education, research, and advocacy in transgender and transsexual health.

Suggested Reading

Airton, L. (2018). *Gender: Your guide.* Adams Media. A primer on all things gender: how gender works in everyday life, how to use accurate terminology, and how to talk knowledgeably and compassionately about gender diversity.

Baron, D. (2020). *What's your pronoun? Beyond he & she.* Liveright Publishing Company. Addresses the untold story of how we got from he and she to zie and hir and singular-they.

Brill, S., & Kenney, L. (2016). *The transgender teen. A handbook for parents and caregivers supporting transgender and non-binary teens.* Cleis Press. Helps parents and others to come to terms with the possibility that their child/patient may be transgender.

Diamond, L. M. (2008). *Sexual fluidity: Understanding women's love and desire.* Harvard University Press. Offers insight into the context-dependent nature of female sexuality.

Holleb, M. L. E. (2019). *The A-Z of gender and sexuality: From Ace to Ze.* Morgan Lev Edward Holleb. A glossary of trans and queer words that, when used, will help dispel anxiety around using the 'wrong' words. Also includes an in-depth look at queer history and culture.

Lips, H. (2014). *Gender: The basics.* Routledge. An examination of gender theories, research, and issues, highlighting the fact that there is more to gender than biological sex.

Savin-Williams, R. C. (2017). *Mostly straight: Sexual fluidity among men.* Harvard University Press. Explores the phenomenon of young men who identify as "mostly straight" and what that means for our understanding of sexual orientation, sexual identity, and sexual behavior.

6

Sexuality in Childhood and Adolescence

WeAre/Shutterstock

CHAPTER OUTLINE

Sexuality in Infancy and Childhood (Ages 0 to 11)   Sexuality in Adolescence (Ages 12 to 19)

"I cannot say that I am sexually attracted to females, but I get lost in their looks and their angelic energy. I love to kiss girls and have close relationships with them. There is a liberating and beautiful trust that I find between certain women and myself that I have not shared with a man. I am, however, sexually attracted to men and love to be affectionate and have relationships with them."

—22-year-old female

"For most of college, I dated several women, but I never found the right one. Sex is special to me, and although at times I feel like just

doing it with anyone, like all my friends, I don't. However, the first time that I did have actual intercourse was in my sophomore year with a random person. I was almost 20 years old and living in my fraternity house. Constantly, I was bombarded with stories of the conquests of my fraternity brothers. Why was I different? I had remained a virgin for so long, and up until then I was pretty secure about it. But during that time, not only did I give up my virginity, but I also slipped in life. This represented a major down time for me."

—25-year-old male

A S WE CONSIDER the human life cycle from birth to death, we cannot help but be struck by how profoundly sexuality weaves its way through our lives. From the moment we are born, we are rich in sexual and erotic potential, which begins to take shape in our sexual curiosity and experimentations in childhood. As children, we are only partly formed, but the world around us helps shape our sexuality. In adolescence, our education continues as a random mixture of learning, yearning, and experimenting with new behaviors.

In this chapter, we discuss both the innate and the learned aspects of sexuality, from infancy through adolescence. We examine both physical development and **psychosexual development**, which involves the psychological aspects of sexuality. We see how culture, family, media, and other factors affect children's feelings about their bodies and influence their sexual feelings and activities. We look at how the physical changes experienced by teenagers affect their sexual awareness and sexual identity. And we discuss adolescent sexual behaviors, teenage pregnancy, teenage parenthood, and sexuality education.

● Sexuality in Infancy and Childhood (Ages 0 to 11)

Our understanding of infant sexuality is based on observation and inference. It is obvious that babies derive sensual pleasure from stroking, cuddling, bathing, and other tactile stimulation. Ernest Borneman, a researcher of children's sexuality, suggested that the first phase of sexual development be called the cutaneous phase (from the Greek *kytos,* "skin"). During this period, an infant's skin can be considered a "single erogenous zone" (Borneman, 1983).

The young child's healthy psychosexual development lays the foundation for further stages of growth. Psychosexual maturity, including the ability to love, begins to develop in infancy, when babies are lovingly touched all over their bodies, which appear to be designed to attract the caresses of their elders.

Infants and young children communicate by smiling, gesturing, crying, and so on. Before they understand the language, they learn to interpret movements, facial expressions, body language, and tone of voice. Humans' earliest lessons are conveyed in these ways. Infants begin to learn how they "should" feel about their bodies. If a parent frowns, speaks sharply, or slaps an exploring hand, the infant quickly learns that a particular activity—touching the genitals, for example—is wrong. The infant may or may not continue the activity, but if they do, it will be in secret, probably accompanied by feelings of guilt and shame.

Infants also learn about the gender role they are expected to fulfill (Bussey & Bandura, 1999). While there is evidence of inborn influences on sex-typed toy preferences (Jadva et al., 2008), much of what children experience is reinforced by parental and societal upbringing. In our culture, baby girls are often handled more gently than baby boys, are dressed up more, and are often given soft toys and dolls to play with. Baby boys, in contrast, are often expected to be "tough." Their dads may roughhouse with them and speak more loudly to

"Conscience is the inner voice which warns us that someone may be looking."

—H. L. Mencken (1880–1956)

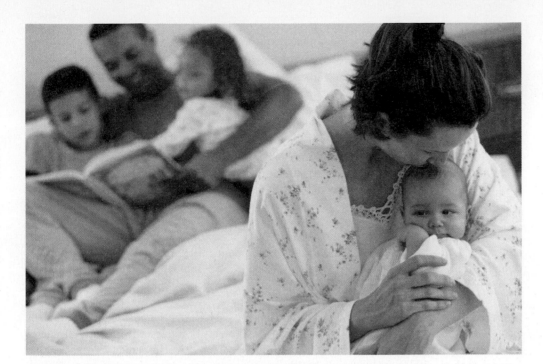

Kissing and cuddling are essential to an infant's healthy psychosexual development.

Lisette Le Bon/Purestock/SuperStock

them than to baby girls. Most are still given "boy toys"—blocks, cars, and action figures. This gender-role learning is usually reinforced as the child grows older.

Infancy and Sexual Response (Ages 0 to 2)

Infants can be observed discovering the pleasure of genital stimulation soon after they are born. However, the body actually begins its first sexual response even earlier, in utero, when sonograms have shown that boys have erections. This begins a pattern of erections that will occur throughout their lives. Signs of sexual arousal in girls, though less easily detected, begin soon after birth and include vaginal lubrication and genital swelling. In some cases, infants have been observed experiencing what appears to be an orgasm. Obviously, an infant is unable to differentiate sexual pleasure from other types of enjoyment, so viewing these as sexual responses are adult interpretations of these normal reflexes and do not necessarily signify the infant's desire or interest. What it does reveal is that the capacity for sexual response is present soon after conception (DeLamater & Friedrich, 2002). Following birth, the accumulation of a wide range of physical, emotional, and intellectual experiences begins.

Childhood Sexuality (Ages 3 to 11)

Children become aware of sex and sexuality much earlier than many people realize. They generally learn to disguise their interest rather than risk the disapproval of their elders, but they continue as small scientists—collecting data, performing experiments, and attending "conferences" with their colleagues. In fact, as part of normative childhood sexual behavior, children engage in self-stimulatory behavior, demonstrate interest in sexual topics, reveal their bodies and sexual parts to adults and children, and show interest in viewing the bodies of others (Friedrich et al., 1998; Thigpen, 2009, 2012).

"I do not think that there is even one good reason for denying children the information which their thirst for knowledge demands."

—Sigmund Freud (1856–1939)

Curiosity and Sex Play   Starting as early as age 3, when they begin interacting with their peers, children begin to explore their bodies together. They may masturbate or play "mommy and daddy" and hug and kiss and lie on top of each other; they may play "doctor" so that they can look at each other's genitals. Author and social justice activist Letty Cottin Pogrebin (1983) suggested that we think of children as "students" rather than "voyeurs." It is important for them to know what others look like in order to feel comfortable about themselves.

Physician and noted sexuality educator Mary Calderone (1983) stressed that children's sexual interest should never be labeled "bad" but that it may be deemed inappropriate for certain times, places, or persons. According to Calderone, "The attitude of the parents should be to socialize for privacy rather than to punish or forbid." If children's natural curiosity about their sexuality is satisfied, they are likely to feel comfortable with their own bodies as adults.

Children who participate in sex play generally do so with children of their own sex. In fact, same-sex activity is probably more common during the childhood years. Most go on to develop heterosexual orientations; some do not. But whatever a person's sexual orientation, childhood sex play clearly does not *create* the orientation. The origins of sexual orientation are not well understood; in some cases, there may indeed be a biological basis. Many LGBTQ+ individuals say that they first became aware of their attraction to the same sex during childhood, but many heterosexual people also report attraction to the same sex during this time. These feelings and behaviors appear to be quite common and congruent with healthy psychological development in heterosexual, as well as among sexual minorities (DeLamater & Friedrich, 2002). (See Table 1 for common childhood sexual behaviors.)

"A good thing about masturbation is that you don't have to dress up for it."
—Truman Capote (1924–1984)

Masturbation and Permission to Feel Pleasure   Most of us masturbate; most of us also were raised to feel guilty about it. In fact, by the end of adolescence, nearly all males and many females have masturbated (Friedrich et al., 1998; Herbenick et al., 2010.6; Laumann et al., 1994). Virtually all health professionals consider masturbation a normal, harmless, and common childhood behavior. But the message "If it feels good, it's bad," is often internalized at an early age, which sometimes leads to psychological and sexual difficulties in later life. Virtually all psychologists, physicians, child development specialists, and other professionals agree that masturbation is healthy. Negative responses from adults only magnify the guilt and anxiety that a child is taught to associate with this behavior.

Children often accidentally discover that playing with their genitals is pleasurable and continue this activity until reprimanded by an adult. Male infants have been observed with erect penises a few hours after birth. A baby boy may laugh in his crib while playing with his erect penis. Baby girls sometimes move their bodies rhythmically, almost violently, appearing to experience orgasm. By the time they are 4 or 5, children have usually learned that adults consider this form of behavior "nasty." Parents generally react negatively to masturbation, regardless of the age and sex of the child. Later, this negative attitude becomes generalized to include the sexual pleasure that accompanies the behavior. Children thus learn to conceal their masturbatory play. Although children vary in the age

Age Group	Behavior	% of Boys	% of Girls
2–5 Years	Stands too close to people	29	16
	Touches own sex parts when in public places	27	44
	Touches/tries to touch mother's or other woman's breast	42	44
	Touches genitals at home	60	44
	Tries to look at people when they are nude or undressing	27	27
6–9 Years	Touches own genitals at home	40	21
	Tries to look at people when they are nude or undressing	20	21
10–12 Years	Is very interested in the other sex	24	29

TABLE 1 ● Childhood Sexual Behaviors Witnessed by at Least 20% of Parents, by Age Group and Gender

Source: Adapted from Table 3, Friedrick, W. N. (2003). Studies of Sexuality of Nonabused Children. In Bancroft, J. (Ed.), *Sexual development in childhood*. Indiana University Press.

Children are naturally curious about bodies. It is important that these kinds of explorations are seen as normal and not be labeled "bad."

Christine DeVault Mendes/Buena Vista Photography

at which they begin to conceal their sexuality, it appears to occur between the ages of 6 and 10 (Bancroft, 2009).

Children need to understand that pleasure from masturbation is normal and acceptable. But they also need to know that masturbation is something that we do in private.

The Family Context

Family styles of physical expression and feelings about modesty, privacy, and nudity vary considerably.

Family Nudity   Some families are comfortable with nudity in a variety of contexts: bathing, swimming, sunbathing, dressing, or undressing. Others are comfortable with partial nudity from time to time, for example, when sharing the bathroom or changing clothes. Still others are more modest and carefully guard their privacy. Most researchers and therapists would agree that styles of modesty can be compatible with the formation of sexually well-adjusted children, as long as some basic guidelines are observed:

- *Accept and respect a child's body and nudity.* If 4-year-old Chantel runs naked into her parents' dinner party, she should be greeted with friendliness, not horror or harsh words. If her parents are truly uncomfortable, they can help her get dressed matter-of-factly, without recrimination.

- *Do not punish or humiliate a child for seeing his or her parents naked, going to the bathroom, or being sexual with each other.* If the parent screams or lunges for a towel, young Antonio will think he has witnessed something wicked or frightening. He can be gently reminded that mommy or daddy wants privacy at the moment.

- *Respect a child's need for privacy.* Many children, especially as they approach puberty, become quite modest. It is a violation of the child's developing sense of self not to respect his or her need for privacy. If 9-year-old Jeremy starts routinely locking the

"Learning about sex in our society is learning about guilt."

—John Gagnon (1931–2016) and William Simon (1927–2000)

bathroom door or 11-year-old Sarah covers her chest when a parent interrupts her while she is dressing, it is most likely a sign of normal development. Children whose privacy and modesty are respected will learn to respect that of others.

Expressing Affection   Families also vary in the amount and type of physical contact in which they engage. Some families hug and kiss, give back rubs, sit and lean on each other, and generally maintain a high degree of physical closeness. Some parents extend this closeness to their sleeping habits, allowing their infants and small children in their beds each night. In many cultures, this is the rule rather than the exception. Other families limit their contact to hugs and tickles. Variations of this kind are typical and normal. Concerning children's needs for physical contact, we can make the following generalizations:

- *All children (and adults) need freely given physical affection from those they love.* Although there is no prescription for the right amount or form of such expression, its quantity and quality affect both children's emotional well-being and the emotional and sexual health of the adults they will become.

- *Children should be told, in a nonthreatening way, what kind of touching by adults is "acceptable" and what is "not acceptable."* Children need to feel that they are in charge of their own bodies, that parts of their bodies are "private property," and that no one has the right to touch them with sexual intent.

- *It is not necessary to frighten a child by going into great detail about the kinds of bad things that others might do to them sexually.* A better strategy is to instill a sense of self-worth and confidence in children so that they will not allow themselves to be victimized.

- *We should listen to children and trust them.* Children need to know that if they are sexually abused it is not their fault. They need to feel that they can tell about it and still be worthy of love.

● Sexuality in Adolescence (Ages 12 to 19)

Puberty is the biological stage of human development when the body becomes capable of reproduction. For legal purposes (e.g., laws relating to child abuse), puberty is considered to begin at age 12 for girls and age 14 for boys. As will be discussed later, the actual age of puberty in girls and boys varies, depending on a wide host of factors. **Adolescence** is the social and psychological state that occurs between the beginning of puberty and acceptance into full adulthood.

Psychosexual Development

Adolescents are sexually mature (or close to it) in a physical sense, but they are still learning about their gender and social roles, and they still have much to learn about their sexual scripts. They may also be struggling to understand the meaning of their sexual feelings for others, their gender identity, and their sexual orientation.

Physical Changes During Puberty   Though the mechanisms that activate the chain of development that occurs during puberty are not fully understood, researchers have observed that as the child approaches puberty, typically beginning between the ages of 8 and 13 for girls and 9 and 14 for boys, the levels of hormones begin to increase. This period of rapid physical changes is triggered by the hypothalamus, which plays a central role in increasing secretions that cause the pituitary gland to release large amounts of hormones into the bloodstream. The hormones, called gonadotropins, stimulate activity in the gonads and are chemically identical in boys and girls. In girls, they act on the ovaries to produce estrogen; in boys, they cause the testes to increase testosterone production. These higher levels of male and female hormones result in the development of specific external signs of male and

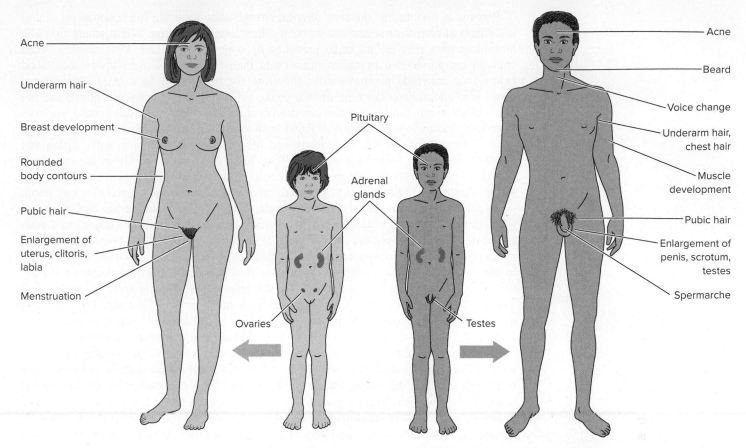

Acne

Underarm hair

Breast development

Rounded
body contours

Pubic hair

Enlargement of
uterus, clitoris,
labia

Menstruation

Pituitary

Adrenal
glands

Ovaries

Testes

Acne

Beard

Voice change

Underarm hair,
chest hair

Muscle
development

Pubic hair

Enlargement of
penis, scrotum,
testes

Spermarche

• **FIGURE 1**
**Physical and Hormonal Changes
During Puberty.**

female sexual maturation, known as secondary sex characteristics, including the onset of menstruation in girls, and **spermarche** in boys, the development of sperm in the testicles (see Figure 1).

The first sign of puberty in girls, between the ages of 8 and 13, is breast development. This is also the beginning of a girl's growth spurt, which is followed by the growth of pubic and underarm hair and the onset of vaginal mucus secretion. Menarche, the onset of menstruation, follows within 2–3 years after the development of breast buds. The average age for menstruation in the United States is 12, although this can vary, depending on the sequence and time frame of events that occur (Biro et al., 2018). Some data over the past several decades regarding timing of puberty have shown that girls are experiencing earlier breast development that is associated with an elevated body mass index (BMI), however more research is needed on this.

Precocious puberty refers to the appearance of physical and hormonal signs of pubertal development at an earlier age than is considered typical: before age 8 in girls and before age 9 in boys (WebMD, 2019). About 1 in 5,000 children, most of whom are girls, are affected. Sometimes, precocious puberty stems from a structural problem in the brain or a brain injury, an infection, or a problem in the ovaries or thyroid gland. However, for the majority of girls there is no underlying medical problem; they simply start puberty earlier than what is considered typical. In boys, the condition is less common and more likely to be associated with an underlying medical problem or, for a small percentage, inherited from father to son.

When puberty ends, growth in height stops. Because their skeletons mature and bone growth stops at an earlier age than typical, children with precocious puberty usually don't achieve their full adult height potential. The goal of treating precocious puberty is to halt or even reverse sexual development and stop the rapid growth and bone maturation that can result in short stature.

Perhaps as troubling as the early physical changes that occur are the potential psychological effects of premature sexual development. The concern, of course, is that young girls who look older than they are might be pressured by others to act older. Unfortunately, when children are bombarded by sexual images and their bodies push them toward adulthood before they are ready psychologically, they lose the freedom to be a child. The cultural pressure to short-circuit the time when a young girl is developing her sense of self and her place in the world can set a dangerous precedent for later behavior. Additionally, society's relentless pressure to sexualize girls is found in all forms of media. Because hormonal changes often stoke the fires of sexual curiosity and behavior in young people, early dating and possible progression toward sexual activity may begin at a young age. Given the many psychological components that are involved in sexual activity, if a young person is not prepared for being sexual with another person, social, psychological, and emotional issues may result.

As previously stated, puberty generally begins later in boys, at an average age of 9 to 14 years, though the age at which puberty is construed legally is 14. It usually takes 3 to 4 years for a boy's body to experience the hormonal changes that transition his body into that of a man's body; this process may continue until he is 20 years old. The first sign is an increase in the size of the testicles, followed by the growth of pubic hair. Physical changes continue, including a growth spurt; hand and foot growth; muscle-mass growth; voice deepening; and hair growth on the face, underarms, and sometimes other parts of the body. The penis also grows larger. Some boys reach puberty around age 12; others, not until their later teens. Generally, however, they lag about 2 to 3 years behind girls in pubertal development.

The scarcity of research on early orgasm is apparent in contemporary sexology. However, we do know that at puberty boys begin to ejaculate semen which accompanies the experience of orgasm they may have been having for some time. Just as girls often do not know what is happening when they begin to menstruate, many boys are unnerved by the first appearance of semen as a result of masturbation or **nocturnal emissions** during sleep ("wet dreams"). By age 12, about 20% of girls and 40% of boys recall orgasms from masturbation (Larsson & Svedin, 2002). Like menstruation for girls, the onset of ejaculation is a sexual milestone for boys; it is the beginning of their fertility. Alfred Kinsey called first ejaculation the most important psychosexual event in male adolescence (Kinsey et al., 1948).

Influences on Psychosexual Development   Besides biological forces, numerous factors are known to increase or decrease teen sexual behavior. Though teens' behaviors cannot necessarily be controlled, parents and other concerned adults can attempt to affect the factors that influence teens' sexual decisions in order to facilitate the development of a healthy sexuality.

Parental Influence   Children and young adults learn a great deal about sexuality from their parents, including family expectations, societal values, and role modeling of sexual

Rites of passage are built into the traditions of most cultures. Among them are the (a) Jewish Bar and Bat Mitzvahs, (b) Indian Navjote ritual, and (c) South African Xhosa initiation rite.

(a) Rob Melnychuk/Getty Images; (b) Natasha Hemrajani/Hindustan Times/Getty Images; (c) Mujahid Safodien/AFP/Getty Images

(a)

(b)

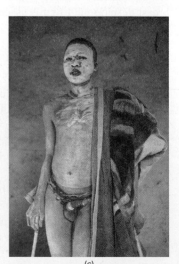
(c)

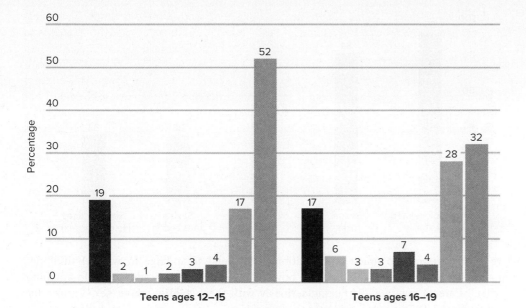

• **FIGURE 2**

Who Teenagers Say Most Influences Their Decisions About Sex.

Source: Power to Decide (formerly The National Campaign to Prevent Teen and Unplanned Pregnancy). (2016). *Survey Says: Parent Power.* Washington, DC.

Who Most Influences

■ Don't know/ refused ■ Someone else ■ Teachers & educators ■ Siblings ■ Religious leaders ■ Media ■ Friends ■ Parents

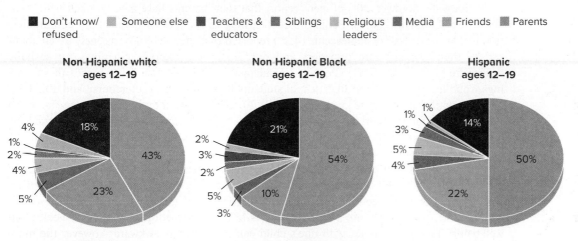

health and risk-reduction strategies (Flores & Barroso, 2017) (see Figure 2). Parents are ideal sex educators because they can reach youth early to provide ongoing information that is responsive to the adolescent's needs and questions. For the most part, however, children learn not because their parents set out to teach them but because they are avid observers of their parents' behavior and family dynamics and characteristics. Much of what they learn involves the connection, or lack of, they have with their parents.

A literature review of 116 articles from 2003–2015 focusing on child-parent communications about sex identified concerns unique to parenting (Flores & Barroso, 2017). What became apparent from the studies was that factors that contributed to communication about sex were established long before individuals became parents. For example, gender dynamics, communication style, religiosity, comfort level, and parental attributes, including their levels of knowledge about sexuality, were among the factors that played significant roles in both the message and ways in which parents communicated them to their children (see Figure 3).

As they enter adolescence, young people are especially concerned about their own sexuality, but they are often too embarrassed to ask their parents directly about these "secret" matters. And many parents are ambivalent about their children's developing sexuality. Parents often underestimate their children's involvement in sexual activities, even as their children progress through adolescence, and so perceive less need to discuss sexuality with them. They are often fearful that their children, daughters especially, will become sexually

"Most mothers think that to keep young people from love making it is enough not to speak of it in their presence."

—Marie Madeline de la Fayette
(1634–1693)

• FIGURE 3

Percentage of Parents Who Talked About Selected Sexuality Issues With Their Adolescent, Aged 12–17, United States, 2020.

Source: Evans, R., et al. (2020). Gender differences in parents' communication with their adolescent children about sexual risk and sex-positive topics. *Journal of Sex Research,* 57(2), 177–188.

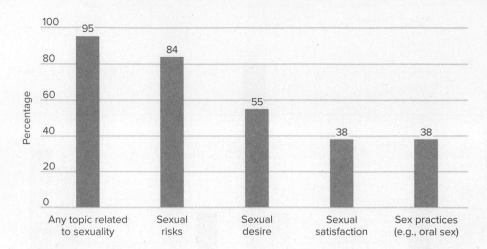

"Children are educated by what the grown-up is and not by his talk."

—Carl Jung (1842–1896)

active if they have "too much" information. They tend to indulge in wishful thinking: "I'm sure Jenny's not really interested in boys yet"; "I know Jose would never do anything like that." Parents may put off talking seriously with their children about sex, waiting for the "right time." Or they may bring up the subject once, make their points, breathe a sigh of relief, and never mention it again. Still, teens continue to say that parents most influence their decisions about sex.

Nationwide, however, 30% of teens report that their parents have never spoken with them about sex (Lohmann, 2018). Perhaps as concerning as the lack of parent-child communication is that nearly half of adolescents (45%) reported that they were not routinely asked about sex by their primary care providers and only 13% were offered screenings for sexually transmitted infections (STIs) (Pediatric Academic Societies, 2018). What makes these findings troubling is that 40% of high school students have had sexual intercourse and 10% have had sex with four or more partners (CDC, 2018.6a). (For additional data, see Table 3.) Parents and children not talking about sex-related issues can have serious consequences, leaving adolescents vulnerable to other sources of unhealthy information and opinions, including that from media and peers.

Because self-esteem plays an important role in adolescent sexuality, parents can indirectly contribute to their teen's positive sexual health by fostering an open and honest relationship with them. These connections are often characterized by high levels of warmth, closeness, and support, all of which are protective factors in relation to adolescent's sexual health and well-being. Talking about sex with one's child can be extremely awkward, however the more frequently the conversations occur, the more natural they will become. Being authentic, straightforward, and real will help young people know that they can rely on you for information. In addition, lightening the conversation with humor or a story to illustrate a point—but not necessarily about you as young people often don't want to hear about their parent's sexual experiences—might also help. If a topic arises that you don't want to hear or discuss, it's important not to shame or silence your child. Instead and depending on the age of the child, let them know how special actually connecting with another person can be. Peggy Orenstein (2016, 2020), author of *Girls and Sex* and *Boys and Sex,* sums up the need for honesty and openness in conversations between adults and teens by saying:

> What if we went the other way? What if we spoke to kids about sex more instead of less, what if we could normalize it, integrate it into everyday life and shift our thinking in the ways that we (mostly) have about women's public roles? Because the truth is, that more frankly and fully teachers, parents and doctors talk to young people about sexuality, the more likely kids are both to delay sexual activity and to behave responsibly and ethically when they do engage in it.

Peer Influence No doubt, adolescents receive a lot of information about sex from peers, especially same-sex peers. With this, they may put pressure on each other to carry out traditional gender roles. Boys encourage other boys to be sexually active even if they are

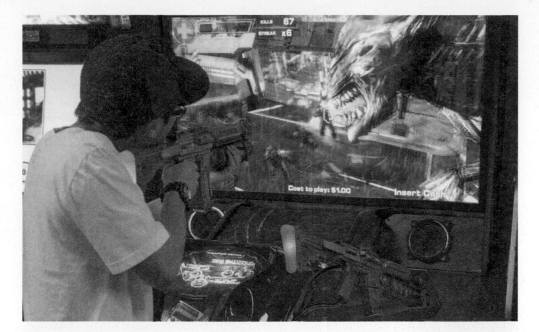

In addition to biological factors, social forces strongly influence young teenagers. Because certain types of violence and aggression are considered "manly" in our culture, the boy in this photograph (top) takes great pleasure in a video game featuring simulated violence. For adolescent girls, the physical and social changes of puberty often result in a great deal of interest, some would say obsession, with personal appearance, including the selection of makeup, clothing, and shoes.

unprepared or uninterested. They must camouflage their inexperience with bravado, which increases misinformation; they cannot reveal sexual ignorance. Girls, on the other hand, are encouraged to be sexually modest and passive. When both girls and boys endorse and enact the heterosexual double standard prescribing sexual prowess for boys and sexual modesty for girls, they are at risk of poor sexual functioning and lower sexual satisfaction (Emmerink et al., 2016).

Even though many teenagers find their early sexual experiences less than satisfying, they may still seem to feel a great deal of pressure to conform, which means becoming or continuing to be sexually active. The social effects on teen sexuality can be strong. Teens are more likely to be sexually active if their best friends and peers are sexually active and are older, use alcohol or drugs, or engage in other risky behaviors (Kirby, 2007). Similarly, simply having a romantic partner increases the chances of sexual activity, especially if that partner is older.

The Media As discussed previously, erotic portrayals—nudity, sexually provocative language, and displays of sexual passion—are of great interest to the viewing public. This public includes many curious and malleable children and adolescents who don't just absorb mass media representations but respond to them in various ways.

Although some people would protect young viewers by censoring what is shown on television or the Internet, or played on the radio or on YouTube, a more viable solution to sexual hype in the media is to balance it with information about real life. It's also important to remember that the media also offer positive and informative sexual messages and outcomes that can be instrumental in educating young people about sexuality.

Adolescent Sexual Orientation and Gender Identity

During adolescence and early adulthood, sexual orientation becomes a salient issue for many youth. In fact, and for many reasons, few adolescents experience this period of their life as trouble- or anxiety-free. Many young people have sexual fantasies involving others of their own sex; some engage in same-sex play. For many, these feelings of sexual attraction are a normal stage of sexual development, and for 2–10% of the population, the realization of a romantic attraction to members of their own sex will begin to grow (Chandra et al., 2011; Laumann et al., 1994). And as acceptance of LGBTQ+ teens has risen, the average age of coming out has dropped from 25 to 16 (Institute of Medicine, 2011). While some gay, lesbian, and queer individuals acknowledged that they began to be aware of their "difference" in middle or late childhood, others reported that they were simply not sure about their sexual orientation. Sometimes, the term questioning is used to describe those individuals who are examining their sexual orientation during this time of life. Gay, lesbian, and queer adolescents usually have heterosexual dating experiences, and some engage in intercourse during their teens, but they often report ambivalent feelings about them.

Because of the increased media attention and social awareness on LGBTQ+ issues, it might be easy to assume that now must be a better time than ever to be a sexual minority. Unfortunately, for many, this is not the case. Society, in general, has difficulty dealing with adolescent sexuality. Accepting lesbian, gay, bisexual, transgender, or queer adolescent sexuality has been especially problematic.

In 1973, the American Psychiatric Association (APA) removed homosexuality from its list of psychological disorders in its *Diagnostic and Statistical Manual of Mental Disorders (DSM-II)*. The APA decision was reinforced by similar resolutions by the American Psychological Association and the American Sociological Association. In 1997 at its annual meeting, the American Psychological Association overwhelmingly passed a resolution stating that there is no sound scientific evidence on the efficacy of reparative therapies for gay men and lesbian women. This statement reinforced the association's earlier stand that, because there is nothing "wrong" with homosexuality, there is no reason to try to change sexual orientation through therapy. In 1998, the APA issued a statement opposing reparative therapy, thus joining the American Psychological Association, the American Academy of Pediatrics, the American Medical Association, the American Counseling Association, and the National Association of Social Workers.

Research has suggested that sexual minorities who endorsed a sexual minority orientation (lesbian/gay/queer, bisexual, mostly heterosexual) or reported same-gender sexual behavior in early adolescence may be at greater risk for adverse mental and physical health outcomes than sexual minorities who reach sexual minority milestones in late adolescence or young adulthood (Katz-Wise et al., 2017). These same authors found that earlier age of sexual minority status was linked to childhood maltreatment among females and victimization and depression among sexual minority males, perhaps because those who reach sexual minority milestones early in their life may not have the skills needed to cope effectively with minority stress.

The assumed heterosexuality, or what some refer to as heteronormativity, of society has resulted in a collective **homophobia**, the irrational or phobic fear of sexual minorities, such that the phrase "That's so gay"—used as a derogatory statement—is part of mainstream and youth vernacular. Teachers, parents, and administrators also perpetuate homophobia by ignoring and/or contributing to the harassment of sexual minorities. One study found that though there has been a continued decline in biased language over the years, LGB high school students (trans and queer students were not identified in the study) are far more likely than their classmates to be raped or assaulted in a dating situation (CDC, 2016.6a). Additionally, STI and HIV infections and pregnancy occur more frequently among sexual minority students who had sexual contact with only the same sex or with both sexes than students who had sexual contact with only the other sex. The research has found that gay teens, as compared with straight teens, were far more likely to have attempted suicide and taken illegal drugs. Many LGBTQ+ youth also struggle with stigma, discrimination, bullying and violence, family disapproval, and social rejection (see Table 2). It is extremely important that those who are feeling alone connect with others and with resources that will support them. A safer school climate directly relates to the availability of LGBTQ+ school-based resources and support, including Gay-Straight Alliances, an inclusive curriculum, supportive school staff, and comprehensive and enforced anti-bullying policies.

Very few lesbian and gay, bisexual, or queer teens feel that they can talk to their parents about their sexual orientation. Many, especially boys, leave home or are kicked out because their parents cannot accept their sexuality. A significant number of our children are forced into lives of secrecy, suffering, and shame because of parents' and society's reluctance to openly acknowledge the existence of same-sex attractions.

Evidence suggests a positive association between coming out to oneself and feelings of self-worth. Those who are "out" to themselves and have integrated a sexual identity with their overall personal identity are usually more psychologically well adjusted than individuals who have not moved through this process (Savin-Williams, 2017). Support groups such as the Gay-Straight Alliance network and the "It Gets Better" Project can help adolescents attracted to their own sex or who are gender non-conforming deal with the discrimination and difficulties they face.

Developing a mature identity is a more formidable task for LGBTQ+ individuals who also face issues of color. The racial or ethnic background of a youth may be both an impediment and an advantage in forming a sexual identity. Though racial, ethnic, and cultural communities can provide identification, support, and affirmation, all too often families and peer groups within the community present youths with biases and prejudices that undermine the process of self-acceptance as a lesbian, gay, bisexual, transgender, or queer person. The individual may have to struggle with the question of whether sexual orientation or identity or ethnic identification is more important; in some instances, the individual may even have to choose one identity over the other.

"Nowadays the polite form of homophobia is expressed in safeguarding the family, as if homosexuals somehow came into existence independent of families and without family ties."

—Dennis Altman (1943–)

TABLE 2 ● Percentage of Heterosexual and LGB Students, Grades 9–12, Who Indicated They Had Experienced Selected Events		
	Heterosexual Students	**Lesbian/Gay/ Bisexual Students**
Skipped school because of a safety concern in the last 30 days	6.1%	10%
Physically forced to have unwanted intercourse	5.4%	21.9%
Attempted suicide in the last 12 months	5.4%	23%
Experienced sexual dating violence in the last 12 months	5.5%	15.8%
Seriously considered suicide in the last 12 months	13.3%	47.8%
Bullied on school property in the last 12 months	17.1%	33%
Electronically bullied	13.3%	27.1%
Felt sad or hopeless	27.5%	63%

Note that the study included a "not sure" category that is not represented in this chart.

Source: Adapted statistics from the Centers for Disease Control & Prevention. (2018.6c). Youth risk behavior surveillance—United States, 2017. *Morbidity & Mortality Weekly Report, 67*(8).

In 2010, Dan Savage and his husband, Terry Miller, created a movement called It Gets Better, focused on uplifting, empowering, and connecting LGBTQ+ youth.

ZUMA Wire Service/Alamy

Adolescent Sexual Behavior

Hormonal changes during puberty bring about a dramatic increase in sexual interest. Whether this results in sexual activity is individually determined.

Masturbation   One activity that nearly all adolescents engage in is masturbation, a normal activity that is a natural extension of a child's exploration of their body. As teens experience puberty, they become more curious about their bodies and will explore it in this pleasurable and healthy way. In a national sample of young people aged 14–17, reports of ever having masturbated increased with age with more males reporting masturbating than females (74% vs. 48%) (Guttmacher Institute, 2019). Rates of masturbation appear to be affected by

TABLE 3 ● Trends Among 9th–12th Graders in the Prevalence of Sexual Behaviors (%): 1991–2017		
Sexual Behaviors	**1991** **%**	**2017** **%**
Ever had sexual intercourse	54	40
Had sexual intercourse before age 13 (for the first time)	10	3
Were sexually active (sex in the past 3 months)	38	29
Have had four or more partners (during their life)	19	10
Used alcohol or drugs at last sexual intercourse	22	19
Were ever tested for HIV (not counting blood donations)	—	9
Contraceptive Behaviors		
Used a condom at last sexual intercourse	46	54
Used the birth control pill at last sexual intercourse	21	21
Did not use any method to prevent pregnancy	17	14

Source: Adapted statistics from the Centers for Disease Control & Prevention. (2018.6c). Youth risk behavior surveillance—United States, 2017. *Morbidity & Mortality Weekly Report, 67*(8), 1–114.

a wide range of factors. In addition to providing release from sexual tension, masturbation gives us the opportunity to learn about our sexual functioning; knowledge that can also be shared with a sex partner.

When boys reach adolescence, they no longer regard masturbation as ambiguous play; they know that it is sexual. Data reveal that many males begin masturbating between ages 13 and 15, whereas among females it typically occurs later (Bancroft, 2009). Additionally, among those adolescents who do masturbate, prevalence is higher in males than females in all age groups (Robbins et al., 2011).

Gender differences may be the result of social conditioning, culture, and communication. Though both boys and girls may feel guilt and shame for engaging in a behavior that their parents and other adults indicate is wrong or bad, most boys discuss masturbatory experiences openly with one another, whereas girls seldom talk about their own sexuality, including masturbatory activities.

Motivations for Sexual Activity   As most of us know, the motivations for sexual experimentation and activity are numerous and complex: curiosity, pleasure, and desire, to name a few. In spite of these strong drives and feelings, why teens are indeed waiting longer to have sex for the first time is not clear. What we do know is that although teen pregnancy and birth rates have been declining since the early 1990s, rates of unplanned pregnancies in the United States are still higher than those in other developed countries (CDC, 2017.6a). The decline in pregnancy rates are across all races and ethnicities.

"My sexuality has never been a problem for me, but I think it has been for other people."
—Dusty Springfield (1939–1999)

Sexuality researchers have been able to target and cluster several important factors that predispose teenagers to sexual behavior: social/environmental factors, which include community, family structure, peers, and romantic partners, and individual characteristics. Being in a relationship appears to be important among those who have had sexual experience in their teens, with 74% of females and 51% of males reporting that their first sexual experience was with a steady partner (CDC, 2017.6a). The most common reason that teens have given for not having had sex was that it was "against my religion or morals" followed by "I don't want to get (a female) pregnant" and "I haven't found the right person yet."

Most young people in the United States learn about and engage in sexual behavior in high school. However, despite what we know about young people's sexual behaviors and where they learn about sex, little is known about what they want to know. Examining young people's questions about sex can provide us with their knowledge gaps, perceptions of risk, and what they are curious about. A content analysis of anonymous questions about sex ($N = 655$) among predominantly lower-income and Latinx ninth-grade students was conducted to learn about what they want to know about sex and sexuality but perhaps were afraid to ask (Pariera & McCormack, 2017) (see Table 4). The authors concluded that though many young people were misinformed on a variety of topics, they were anxious to learn more about their sexuality, especially how to use birth control and prevent pregnancy. It is apparent that in order to develop a safe and healthy sex life, youth need accurate and comprehensive sexuality education, including information that dispels myths and provides a realistic view of the risks and responsibilities associated with sexuality.

First Intercourse   Sexuality is a core aspect of being human and sexual activity is a basic component of human development. We know that during adolescence, many young people develop romantic and intimate relationships and engage in a range of sexual behaviors (Guttmacher Institute, 2019). With the advent of the "sexual revolution" in the 1960s, adolescent sexual behavior began to change. The revolution, otherwise called sexual liberation, challenged traditional sexual behaviors, including acceptance of sex outside of heterosexual, monogamous relationships, the use of contraception, public nudity, and legalization of abortion. Between that time and now, the explosion of the Internet has both altered and sharpened the attention given to sexuality, resulting in vast changes in the ways in which we view ourselves and others. One notable change is the percentage of teens, aged 15–19, who have ever had sex: 42% of teen females and 44% of teen males. These percentages have gradually declined since 1988, when the numbers were 51% of female teens and 60% of male teens (CDC, 2017.6a).

TABLE 4 ● Types of Anonymous Questions by 9th Grade Students (*N* = 655).

	Sample questions	*n*	%
Procedural questions about birth control	"Does a girl take the pill after or before you have sex?"	131	20.3
	"How do you know the condom is on right?"		
Understanding risk of pregnancy	"Can you get pregnant while you're on your period?"	122	18.9
	"Which method is most effective besides abstinence?"		
What happens during sex	"Is it possible to pee during sex?"	114	17.7
	"What happens when you have oral sex and you swallow their precum and sperm?"		
Pain/pleasure	"Is sex painful?" "Does a girl bleed during sex?"	34	5.3
What happens during pregnancy and childbirth	"What can happen [to the baby] if a woman gets pregnant on birth control?"	48	7.4
	"If you have sex with a pregnant girl, when her cervix opens up does it touch the baby?"		
Resources and access	"Where do you get the Plan B pill?"	42	6.5
	"Which prescription method is least expensive?"		
Understanding risk of sexually transmitted infections	"Will two virgins get an STD if they have sex?"	37	5.7
	"How do you even get STDs from having oral sex?"		
Slang terms	"What is a cherry pop?"	32	5.0
	"What is blue balls? Explain."		
Understanding others' behaviors	"Why do people like to suck dick?"	29	4.5
	"When a girl moans, does that mean it feels good?"		
Bodies (nonsexual)	"Why do you get cramps?"	28	4.3
	"How deep is the vagina?"		
Guidance on norms	"What age do people normally start having sex?"	27	4.2
	"How much does the average girl and guy masturbate?"		
Legal/ethical	"What is the legal age for sex?"	25	3.9
	"Is abortion a good idea?"		
Communication	"How do I tell my mom I am pregnant?"	10	1.6
	"How do you approach a girl if they want to have sexual intercourse?"		

Source: Pariera, K. L., & McCormack, T. A. (2017). "Why can't we just have sex?": An analysis of anonymous questions about sex asked by ninth graders. *American Journal of Sexuality Education, 12*(3), 277–296.

The proportion of young people who have had sexual intercourse increases rapidly as they age through adolescence. Among adolescents aged 15–19 who had penile-vaginal sex, 75% of females and 48% of males reported that it occurred with a steady partner and most men (71%) and half of women (51%) described the experience as wanted (Guttmacher Institute, 2019). However, among 6.5% of women, or 1 in 16 women, their first sexual experience was rape (Hawks et al., 2019). The average age which rape occurs is 15, with the perpetrator often several years older. Initiation of sexual intercourse in adolescence is also associated with an increased risk of STIs, including HIV/AIDS, and unintended pregnancy (Santelli et al., 2017).

Since 1988, there has been a downward trend in the percentage of teens, ages 15–19, who have had intercourse at least once; from an average of 54% in 1991 to an average of 40% in 2013 (CDC, 2018.6c). This trend reflects increased numbers of young people who are choosing not to have sex until a later age and when they do, they more often have their first experience of sexual intercourse with a steady partner.

Just what constitutes having "had sex" is debatable and context-specific. For example, age group, gender, and factors such as orgasm and giving/receiving stimulation may affect whether a person recognizes a behavior as "having sex." Perhaps even more ambiguous is

"Before she said, 'I do . . .' she did."

—Bill Margold (1943–2017)

For most teens, increased commitment is accompanied by increased likelihood of sexual intimacy.

J.Hardy/PhotoAlto

the expression "hooking up," which depending on the person using it, can describe behaviors ranging from kissing to oral sex to intercourse. There also exist inconsistent attitudes concerning hookups or casual sex, ranging from endorsement to blame, regardless of whether individuals participate in it or not. As young people negotiate the culture of casual sex, it means navigating between fun and uncertainty, risk-taking and feeling carefree (Orenstein, 2016).

The experience of first sexual intercourse, sometimes also referred to as **sexual debut**, often carries enormous personal and social meaning, often symbolizing an important milestone of adolescent development. (See Figure 4 for percentages of adolescents and young adults who have had sexual intercourse by each age.) While public health organizations and researchers have devoted considerable attention to the implications of first intercourse, few studies have explored how young people view and experience their sexual debut.

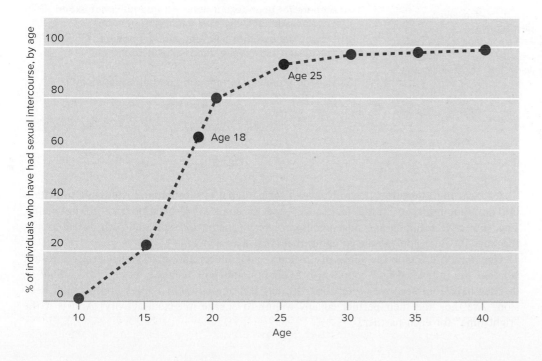

• **FIGURE 4**

Sexual Intercourse Among Young People in the United States.

Source: Guttmacher Institute. (2019). Adolescent and sexual and reproductive health in the United States.

think about it

Does First Sex "Just Happen?" Reflections from College Students About Their First Sexual Activity

Do you recall your first sexual experience? If so, was it planned? Under what circumstances or conditions did it occur? What type of discussion or planning took place ahead of time? When these questions were put before a group of first- and second-year college students (N = 74) in exploratory focus groups, some surprising results occurred (Lieberman et al., 2017). We do know that having sex for the first time is a major transition for most young people. With that, many might assume that first sex largely happens spontaneously or simply "happens." It's worth noting that the mean age of first sex (as defined by participants) was 16 and by the time students graduated high school, 89% of them had experienced intercourse (Lieberman et al., 2017).

Ideally, a discussion (or two) precedes having sex, including discussions about contraception and STIs. Beyond these topics, other related issues have implications for healthy sexuality and relationships, including expectations, pleasure, and risks. Researchers have found that how a person experienced their sexual debut has an impact on both the experience itself and subsequent encounters. The following represent the conclusions of how some college students reflected on their first sexual experience (Symons et al., 2014):

1. When college students reflected on the amount and nature of planning involved in their first sexual experience, they reported elements of anticipation, willingness, and/or intent to have sex.

2. Though women were more likely than men to report that their first sexual experience was spontaneous, many recalled having chosen or desired a particular partner and discussed sex with that person.

3. Opportunity played a role in the time of sex and, when planned, condoms were part of that discussion.

4. Among LGBQ+ participants, though most reported not using protection during their first sex, discussions about readiness, planning, and choice of partners were similar to those among straight individuals.

5. Stereotypical gender differences, for example, about whether it is okay to plan for or want sex, carry condoms, readiness for sex, and choosing or not choosing sex partners, suggest engrained messages about people's roles with respect to sex.

The researchers concluded that planning, forethought, and anticipation are characteristics of first sex among men and women and among those who identify as both heterosexual and LGBQ+. These findings have significant implications for school-based sexuality education in that waiting until after first sex represents a missed opportunity for intervention, planning, and referrals. Additionally, programs may miss the chance to help young people focus on whether, when, and under what circumstances they are ready for sex. The authors of this study conclude by saying:

> Young people should be encouraged to critically examine when and under what conditions they want to have sex, and be provided, in a timely manner, with decision-making models and expectations that increase the likelihood that it will be planned, and in the context of relationships, intimacy, and mutual pleasure and safety.

Adapted from: Lieberman et al. (2017). Does first sex really "Just happen?" A retrospective exploratory study of sexual debut among American adolescents. *American Journal of Sexuality Education, 12*(3), 237–256.

Think Critically

1. In addition to the lead-in questions to this TAI box, what, if anything, might you have done to better prepare for your sexual debut? If you have not experienced sexual activity, how might you plan for it?

2. Do you believe that different genders address their first sexual experience differently? If so, how? If not, why not?

3. How do planning, forethought, and anticipation influence the outcomes of first sex?

It's clear that the cultural significance of sexual debut is substantial, including a transition into adulthood, loss of "sexual innocence," and for some an association with marital status. This subjective meaning and interpretation of sexual debut is associated with differences in the ways in which individuals go about their first experience.

One way to examine the subjective meaning and interpretation of sexual debut is to ask whether the individual and couple are "sexually competent" (Palmer et al., 2017). That is, do they have contraceptive protection? Do they feel autonomy or unpressured in their decision? Are they and their partner equally willing to engage in sexual activity? And is it the "right time" for each partner?

For many, the traditional ways in which adolescents evaluate psychological or emotional factors of their sexuality, such as sexual pleasure and communication with their partner, have not changed. Research has revealed that adolescents generally believe that men are more likely than women to feel pleasure due to differences that include biology, understanding of their body, and control over partnered sexual behavior (Saliares et al., 2017). Inequalities in the acceptance of received pleasure were observed as typical among both young men and women. Though adolescents expressed motivation to communicate with partners about sexual pleasure, their responses to statements have suggested that they often lack the skills to do so. The authors reported that it was the quality of a relationship coupled with a positive sexual self-concept that were important determinants of experiencing sexual pleasure and enjoyment (Saliares et al., 2017).

Teenage Pregnancy and Birth Rates

Over the past two decades, teen pregnancy and birth rates have declined dramatically such that they are at a historic low (see Figure 5). The teen pregnancy rate includes pregnancies that end in a live birth, and in abortion or miscarriage. About 77% of teen pregnancies are unplanned with an estimated 61% resulting in a live birth, 15% ending in a miscarriage, and 25% ending in abortion. In 2018, there were 17.4 births for every 1,000 females ages 15–19, accounting for 5% of all births in the United States that year (Pew Research Center, 2019). Nearly 9 in 10 of these births occurred outside of marriage and 1 in 6 births were to females who already had one or more children (U.S. Department of Health & Human Services, 2019). Still, the teen birth rate in the United States remains higher than that in many developed countries, including Canada and the United Kingdom.

What accounts for these declining trends in teen pregnancies and birth rates? One possible factor is the economy (Pew Research Center, 2019). Given the economic ruin following the 2008–2009 recession coupled with the devastating toll that coronavirus has had on the economy and people's lives, this downward trend may continue. Additionally, having less intercourse, use of more effective contraception and more information about pregnancy prevention may also contribute to the lower rates of teen pregnancy, births, and abortion.

Race and ethnicity along with education, family dynamics, and economics also play a role in teen pregnancy and birth rates. Not only are Black and Hispanic teens more likely to be

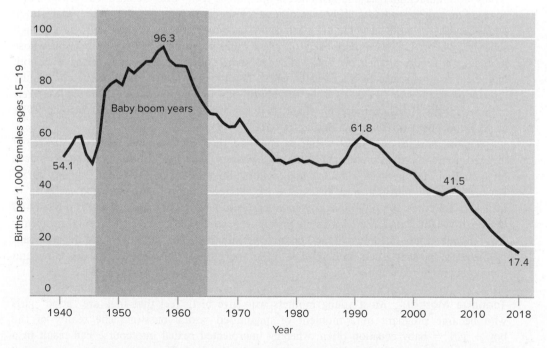

• **FIGURE 5**

Births per 1,000 Females Ages 15–19, United States, 2019.

Source: Pew Research Center. (2019). Why is the teen birth rate falling?

Note: Data labels shown are for 1940, 1957, 1991, 2008, and 2018. Teens younger than 15 not included. Data only accounts for live births and does not include miscarriages, stillbirths or abortions.

• FIGURE 6

Births per 1,000 Female, Ages 15–19, United States, 2018.

Source: Pew Research Center. (2019). Why is the teen birth rate falling?

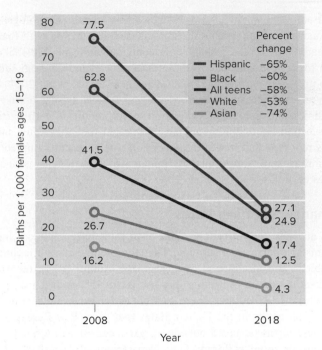

Note: Teens younger than 15 not included. Data only accounts for live births and does not include miscarriages, stillbirths, or abortions. Hispanics are of any race. Racial categories are based on single race classifications. Blacks and whites include only non-Hispanics. Asians include Pacific Islanders. Following the conventions used in the 2008 NCHS births report, Asians include Hispanics. Percentage changes are based on unrounded numbers.

sexually active than white teens, their birth rates are also higher (see Figure 6). All races and ethnicities living in poverty also have disproportionately high teenage birth rates. These rates do not occur in a vacuum but are the result of a myriad of factors at the individual, family, community, and state levels. For example, those teens who are enrolled in school and engaged in activities are less likely than other adolescents to have a child. At the family level, adolescents with mothers who gave birth as teens and/or whose mothers only have a high school degree or GED are more likely to have a child before age 20 than those teens whose mothers were older at their birth and attended some college. Additionally, living with both biological parents at age 14 is associated with a lower risk of a teen birth. At the community level, adolescents who live in wealthier neighborhoods with strong employment are less likely to have a baby than are those in which there are limited employment and income levels (U.S. Department of Health & Human Services, 2019).

Teen pregnancies trap most young parents and their children in a downward spiral of lowered expectations, economic hardship, and poverty. Only 50% of young adults who gave birth in their teenage years hold a high school diploma or GED (Child Trends, 2018). Because of poor nutrition and inadequate medical care during pregnancy, babies born to teenagers are twice as likely to lack prenatal care and have higher rates of preterm birth and low birth weight, which are responsible for numerous physical and developmental problems. Also, many of these children will have disrupted family lives, absent fathers, and the attendant problems of poverty, such as poor diet, violent neighborhoods, limited health care, and limited access to education.

Teenage Mothers Most young mothers who give birth feel that they are "good" girls who became pregnant in a moment of unguarded sexual passion. The reality of the boy + girl = baby equation often, whereby unprotected sexual intercourse can result in a pregnancy, may not sink in until pregnancy is well advanced. This lack of awareness coupled with increasingly lack of access to abortion services makes it difficult emotionally and physically, if not impossible, for those who might otherwise choose to do so to have an abortion.

Teenage mothers have special needs, the most pressing of which are health care and education. Improving preconception health and regular prenatal care are essential to monitor fetal growth and the mother's health, including diet, possible STIs, and possible alcohol or drug use. Babies born to young mothers are more likely to have childhood health problems and to be hospitalized than those born to older mothers. After the birth, both mother and child need continuing care. The mother may need contraceptive counseling and services, and the child needs regular physical checkups and immunizations. Graduation from high school is an important goal of education programs for teenage mothers because it directly influences their employability and ability to support or help support themselves and their children. Some teenage mothers need financial assistance, at least until they complete their education. Government programs such as is provided by Supplemental Nutrition Assistance Program (SNAP), Medicaid or the Affordable Care Act, and the Special Supplemental Nutrition Program for Women, Infants, and Children (WIC), which provides coupons for essential foods, are often crucial to the survival of young parents and their children. Even with programs such as these in place, most young families need additional income and emotional support in order to thrive.

Teenage Fathers   The rate of teenage fatherhood has also significantly declined over the past decade. Nevertheless, 8 out of 10 teen dads don't marry the mother of their child, teen dads are less likely to finish high school than their peers, and absent fathers pay less than $800 annually for child support (DoSomething.org, 2017b). Teen fatherhood is not a function of any single risk factor. Living in poverty, having certain expectations and values about early childbearing, having poor school achievement, and engaging in delinquent behavior seem to be pathways leading to adolescent fatherhood. Such circumstances may prompt some men to react by avoiding marriage or rejecting the responsibilities of fatherhood.

Adolescent fathers typically remain physically or psychologically involved throughout the pregnancy and for at least some time after the birth. It is usually difficult for teenage fathers to contribute much to the support of their children, although most express the intention of doing so during the pregnancy. Most have a lower income, less education, and more children than men who postpone having children until age 20 or older. They may feel overwhelmed by the responsibility and may doubt their ability to be good providers. Though many teenage fathers are the sons of absent fathers, most do want to learn to be fathers. Teen fathers are a seriously neglected group who face many hardships. Policies and interventions directed at reducing teen fatherhood will have to take into consideration the many factors that influence it and focus efforts throughout the life cycle.

Teen Mom focuses on the often challenging terrain of navigating teen pregnancy while also coming of age, getting educated, and dealing with relationships.
Theo Wargo/Getty Images

Sexuality Education

For over 40 years, **abstinence-only sexuality education**, a form of sex education that teaches not having sex outside of marriage, has been a focal point in school sexuality education policy and curriculum in the United States. This approach began in 1981 when, during the Reagan administration, federal policymakers began pouring taxpayer money into a form of sexuality education that excluded all types of sexual and reproductive health education and focused exclusively on abstinence from sexual behaviors until marriage. During the administration of George W. Bush, the federal government spent $1.5 billion on programs that encouraged teens to delay sex until marriage. Critics cited that it was grounded in conservative and religious doctrine, was ineffective, and failed to educate teens about condoms in the age of sexually transmitted infections (STIs). These programs were fully rescinded under President Obama in 2016 and replaced with teen pregnancy prevention programs focusing on age-appropriate, evidence-based education that address life skills. The goal of these programs is to provide information and support needed to become sexually healthy adults. Healthy development requires complete and accurate information, open and honest conversations, and guidance for decision making about sex and relationships (Santelli et al., 2017).

As noted above, sexuality education has changed a lot over the past decades. We've learned, for example, that the implementation of high-quality evidence-based **comprehensive**

think about it

Are Young People Really Having Less Sexual Activity?

Changing attitudes toward premarital sex, economic factors, stress and anxiety, and access to dating apps and social media are among the factors that may be driving down the numbers of young people who are engaging in sexual activity. And for those whoever had any sexual activity, the frequency among young people in the United States has decreased over time (Scott et al., 2020; Ueda et al., 2020). Contrary to popular media conceptions of a "hookup generation" more likely to engage in frequent casual sex, nearly 20% of 18- to 29-year-olds reported having no sex at all in 2016; a 50% rise over those who were celibate in 2000 (General Social Survey, 2019) (see Figure 7).

When we consider that sexual health and satisfaction are key components of health and well-being and that sexual relationships can positively influence life satisfaction and happiness, it may be surprising to learn that sexual inactivity in the United States increased predominantly among younger people (ages 18–24), such that approximately 31% of men and 19% of women reported being sexually inactive in the past year (Ueda et al., 2020). Sexual activity also increased among men and women ages 25 to 34, with the increase among men mainly occurring among unmarried individuals. It's important to note that the increase in sexual inactivity was observed only among men who identified as heterosexual.

In the era when social stigma around premarital sex is gone, hookups are not stigmatized, technological assists are widely available, including access to pornography and dating apps, what contributes to the declining rates of sexual activity? A variety of hypotheses for why individuals engage in less sexual activity have

been proposed including (Klein, 2016; Luscombe, 2018; Twinge et al., 2017; Ueda et al., 2020):

1. *Stress, anxiety, and depression.* Whether it's economic pressures, use of psychiatric medications, school and work overload, concern around COVID-19, or unrealistic expectations, many young people suffer psychological consequences which can lead to low desire. Exhaustion also puts a damper on sex.

2. *Physical health and body image.* Many types of illnesses or maladies and medications used to treat them can affect the libido. Body imagine and feelings of being unattractive can also cause many to refrain from sex. There are additional concerns, particularly among obese men, who may also be impotent.

3. *Heavy use of the Internet.* Since 2000 when the Internet gained in access and popularity, there have become many ways to entertain oneself, besides having sex. Given that 40% of individuals bring an Internet-connected device to bed with them, this distraction can be a deterrent to the kindling of sexual arousal.

4. *Sexually explicit videos.* Though most health specialists say that sexually explicit videos (SEV) are harmless, there is controversy among some on its effect on people's sex lives. Though SEVs may be a way to get couples to talk or use as an arousal technique, others say they can sometimes get in the way of communication or drive a wedge between a couple.

5. *Changing conversation about consent.* The increased emphasis on consent along with the #MeToo movement has led some to initiate sex less or at the least, add a layer of

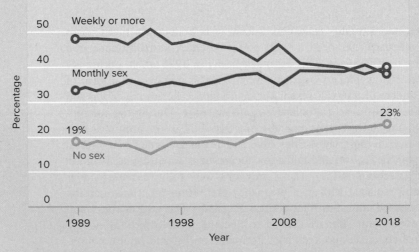

• **FIGURE 7**

Frequency and Percent of Young People, Ages 18–29 Who Report Having Sex.

complexity to a subject that many couples are already bad at talking about.

6. *Living with parents.* There is a declining rate of having a steady romantic partner, especially if one is unemployed and living at home. When one does find a partner, many who are living in their parent's home find it difficult to bring that person into their bedroom.

7. *Dishonesty and unrealistic expectations.* Whether personal uncertainty about sex comes from the lack of comprehensive sexuality education, absence of communication with parents or a partner, peer pressure, or sexually explicit videos, it is common, especially among youth. Those who suppress their feelings about their preferences and desires to avoid conflict or to preserve romantic partnerships are often unrealistic about how this will impact their relationships.

8. *Lower income or part-time or no employment.* Men with little or no employment were more likely to be sexually inactive as were men and women who were students. The decreased appeal in the mating market was especially true for men.

Whatever the causes of the decline in sexual activity among young people, the solutions don't change: Realistic expectations with oneself and honest communication with one's partner can alter how we feel about ourselves and the ways in which we express our sexuality.

Think Critically

1. Do you believe that young people are having less sex? From what sources do you base these feelings?

2. What, in your opinion, is leading to a decrease in sexual activity among young people? Do you feel that these factors differ as one ages?

3. What are three things that would you tell your own children about sex?

sexuality education, a method that aims to give students the knowledge, attitudes, skills, and values to make appropriate and healthy choices in their sexual lives, can help shape healthy growth across adolescence and young adulthood. Despite great advancements in evidence-based models, deeply rooted cultural and religious norms along with political ideologies around adolescent sexuality have impeded their implementation as well as the delivery of services to youth.

In spite of advocating for harmful and ineffective abstinence-only programs, the past administration shifted its thinking and funding to a perspective which is coined the Teen Pregnancy Prevention Program (TPPP). Making no mention of years-long campaign for abstinence-only programming, this curriculum highlights the importance of holistic, "optimal health" for adolescents, and emphasizes the significance of access to high-quality and teen-friendly health care (Guttmacher Institute, 2020.6). Sexuality education has the potential to shape the way individuals view their own and others' sexuality and because of this, we need policies in place that will ensure that young people receive accurate and complete sexuality education. Whether this new programming will be successful will rest largely on who receives the grants and how that money is used (Guttmacher Institute, 2020.6). While some may continue to argue the merits of the abstinence-only approach, leading public health and professional organizations support comprehensive sex education, that is a scientific and broad developmental view that includes the possibility of a positive framework for understanding and advocating for a realistic adolescent sexuality education (Hall, 2016; Santelli et al., 2017; Yarber & Sayad, 2010).

An important tenant of a broad comprehensive approach is that sexuality education should prepare young people for the healthy expression of their sexuality. This not only addresses unintended pregnancies and STIs but also sexual pleasure, masturbation, sexuality and society, sexual orientation, and gender identity. To engage youth, implementation for these must use a variety of modes of communication, including peers, digital and social media, and gaming. We know that the vast majority of adults in the United States support this view. These programs are also required to address life skills that help teens make responsible decisions that lead to safe and healthy lives.

Expanding Views of Comprehensive Sexuality Education Sexuality education is a lifelong process. From the time we are born, we learn about love, touch, affection, and our bodies. As young people grow, the messages continue from both our families and the social environment, with school-based programs complementing and augmenting these primary sources of information. Additionally, governments need to support medically accurate, evidence-based, and scientifically justified approaches to sexuality education for young people.

think about it

Promoting Positive Sexual Health Among Teens

Programs are useless unless they are linked to all the things that make young people whole.

—Michael Carrera

Adolescence is a crucial time in one's life for the development of sexuality, which involves not only body changes, sexual behaviors, and new health care needs but also nurturing emotional maturity, building relationship skills, and supporting a healthy body image. Adolescence is also a time when individuals and society swing between viewing teens as innocent and uninterested in sex in contrast to them being judged and acting out in ways that are physically and mentally harmful. In light of this, can teens and young adults ever become sexually healthy adults? What does it even mean to be a sexually healthy teen?

As previously noted, sexual health has been defined by the World Health Organization (WHO, 2006) as a "state of physical, emotional, mental, and social well-being in relation to sexuality." The American College of Obstetricians and Gynecologists (2017) defines sexuality as "a broad range of expressions of intimacy and is fundamental to self-identification, with strong cultural, biologic, and psychologic components." In order for young people to achieve this, comprehensive sexuality education coupled with ongoing and honest conversations about sex will need to occur.

So, how do we as individuals, families, and culture move from an historically sex-negative society, where risks and scare tactics are central to the dialogue and teachings, to a place where we can discuss sexuality as a way to connect with another, and experience intimacy, joy, and pleasure? Adults have many roles to play including that of being supportive of positive sexual health for young people, being role models, supporting sexual health programming, and becoming involved in communities that engage in youth development. Changing the narrative about sexuality often involves examining our own thinking about sexuality and avoiding assumptions and judgments about others. Being sex positive can shift the conversion from that of facts, scare tactics, shame and guilt to a broader view which embraces the joys of sexuality and relationships, gender diversity, consensual expressions of sexuality, skills for health and well-being, pleasure, and variations of sexual behaviors, all at age-appropriate levels. At the same time, addressing risks and responsibilities associated with sexuality involves risk-reducing practices and, if sexually active, being screened regularly for STIs (Kantor, 2020; Pitts & Greene, 2020).

The redefining about what it means to be a sexually healthy young person should not solely be left to young people and their peers who, with 24/7 access to the Internet, are susceptible to many unhealthy sexuality-related messages. In addition to the necessary role that parents and adults play in young people's lives, communities should maximize the use of information and communication through technology, utilize a positive, broad-based approach to sexuality education that is beyond problem focus, and address funding issues such as easier access to health insurance. Author Peggy Orenstein (2020) underscores this message by saying:

All young people need ongoing discussion and education that addresses pleasure, mutuality, safety, love, intimacy, and self-discovery. They need to understand the potential to be either the perpetrator or the victim of intimate partner violence and sexual assault. They need to have agency over their bodies. Adult denial puts young people at risk of physical and emotional trauma.

In order to address some of the inequities and inadequacies that exist in health, researchers have identified four themes: the importance of adolescents: (a) having connections via school, friends, and others; (b) having a well-maintained physical space to thrive; (c) changing procedures to proactively offer STI testing and ask specific screening questions to assess adolescent's context; and (d) promoting partnerships and collaboration across multiple sectors to better serve adolescents' needs (Garrido et al., 2019). Connections to programs and services and support for the relationships in which adolescents live, learn, and play can help advance adolescent health outcomes.

Think Critically

1. How would you define a sexually healthy teen? How did you arrive at this?

2. What are the roles of parents in communicating and modeling a definition of sexual health? What topics should be included in this discussion? What (if anything) should be omitted?

3. Do you consider yourself to be a sexually healthy person? What has contributed to this? What might you do to become a sex-positive person?

For 17 years, the Sexuality Information and Education Council (SIECUS), rebranded as Sex Ed for Social Change, has been providing an in-depth and up-to-date look at the state of sexuality education in all 50 states, the District of Columbia, Puerto Rico, and the other U.S. territories and associated states (SIECUS, 2020). In 2004, SIECUS developed the *Guidelines for Comprehensive Sexuality Education* the first national model for sexuality education (SIECUS, 2004). These guidelines, the most widely recognized and implemented framework for comprehensive sexuality education in the United States and several countries worldwide, along with the National Sexuality Education Standards published by the *Journal of School Health* (2012), have used evidence-based research to suggest age-appropriate topics and methods.

Since that time, a variety of comprehensive sexuality education programs, including those from the Sex Information & Education Council of Canada (SIECCAN) and the United Nations Educational Scientific and Cultural Organization (UNESCO), have been adopted in a wide range of populations. Key features of these include identifying key educators and settings that have roles in ensuring equitable access, adopting technology as a means to transform how people learn and communicate about sexuality, providing relevant programs tailored to the learning needs of LGBTQ+ populations, addressing the topic of consent, and expanding the enhancement of sexual health and well-being (SIECCAN, 2019; UNESCO, 2018). These curricula, along with others that support healthy sexual development, frame sex as a positive and healthy aspect of life, rather than a strictly risky activity. Programs such as these serve as models for educators and those they teach and inspire.

According to the Guttmacher Institute (2020.6), an expansive and inclusive curriculum would:

"...give young people skills and information related to contraception, healthy relationships, sexual pleasure, consent, and sexual agency and autonomy. Further, the sexual health information provided should be age appropriate as well as responsive to and respectful of a range of cultural backgrounds, sexual orientations, and gender identities."

Investing in adolescents will yield a triple benefit today, into adulthood, and the next generation of children. Most individuals, communities, and professionals agree that young people, guided by their parents and community and armed with knowledge and self-confidence, can make informed decisions and become sexually healthy adults.

Final Thoughts

WeAre/Shutterstock

From birth, humans are rich in sexual and erotic potential. As children, the world around us begins to shape our sexuality and the ways that we ultimately express it. As adolescents, our education continues as a random mixture of learning and yearning. With sexual maturity, the gap between physiological development and psychological development begins to narrow and emotional and intellectual capabilities begin to expand. Responses to and decisions about sexuality education, sexual activity, sexual orientation, gender identity, STI protection, and pregnancy begin to emerge. Each of these presents a challenge and an opportunity to more fully evolve into the sexual beings that we are.

Summary

Sexuality in Infancy and Childhood (Ages 0 to 11)

- *Psychosexual development* begins in infancy, when we begin to learn how we "should" feel about our bodies and our gender roles. Infants need stroking and cuddling to ensure healthy psychosexual development.

- Children learn about their bodies through various forms of sex play. Their sexual interest should not be labeled "bad" but may be deemed inappropriate for certain times, places, or persons. Children need to experience acts of physical affection and to be told nonthreateningly about "good" and "bad" touching by adults.

Sexuality in Adolescence (Ages 12 to 19)

- *Puberty* is the biological stage when reproduction becomes possible. The psychological state of puberty is *adolescence,* a time of growth and often confusion as the body matures faster than the emotional and intellectual abilities. The traits of adolescence are culturally determined.

- Pubertal changes that result in secondary sex characteristics in girls begin between ages 8 and 13. They include a growth spurt, breast development, pubic and underarm hair, vaginal secretions, and menarche (first menstruation). Pubertal changes in boys generally begin between 9 and 14. They include a growth spurt, a deepening voice, hair growth, development of external genitals, and spermarche. *Precocious puberty* refers to the appearance of pubertal signs at an earlier age than is considered typical. Preparing young people for these changes is helpful.

- Children and adolescents often learn a great deal about sexuality from their family dynamics and characteristics. A strong bond between parent and child reduces the risk of early sexual involvement and pregnancy.

- Peers provide a strong influence on the values, attitudes, and behavior of adolescents. They are also a source of much misinformation regarding sex.

- The media present highly charged images of sexuality that are often out of context. Parents can counteract media distortions by discussing the context of sexuality with their children and balancing it with information about real life.

- Young sexual minorities are largely invisible because of society's assumption of heterosexuality. They may begin to come to terms with their sexual orientation and gender identity during their teenage years. Because of society's reluctance to acknowledge homosexuality and gender identity, most LGBTQ+ teens suffer a great deal of emotional pain.

- Most adolescents engage in masturbation. Gender differences in rates of masturbation may be the result of social conditioning and communication.

- The pregnancy and birth rates among teens ages 15–19 are at a historic lows for the nation. Various factors including the economy and access to effective contraception are fueling this change.

- Most teenagers have pressing concerns about sexuality, and most parents and the public favor *comprehensive sexuality education* for children. National and international organizations have designed and are using evidence-based comprehensive sexuality education programs.

Questions for Discussion

- **Who or what taught you the most about sexuality when you were a child and teenager? What lessons did you learn? What would have made the transition from childhood to adolescence easier?**

- **Should masturbation in young children be ignored, discouraged, or encouraged? What effect might each of these responses have on a child who is just beginning to learn about themself?**

- **To what do you attribute the decline in teen pregnancy rates? What are some ways to reduce the rates of unintended teenage pregnancy?**

Sex and the Internet

Unplanned Pregnancy and Young People

Despite historic declines in the rates of teen and unplanned pregnancy, there is still plenty of work to do to ensure that young people, regardless of their circumstances, have the power to decide if, when, and under what circumstances to get pregnant. One of the most helpful and thorough websites that educate and advocate for sexual health information, including data about contraceptive methods, is Power to Decide. To see what this site offers and does to achieve these goals, go to Powertodecide.org. From the top menu bar, select "Sexual Health" and then "Articles about Sexual Health." Search for several topics of interest. For each topic you choose, respond to the following questions:

- What did you learn from this article?

- Which fact was the most surprising to you? Least surprising?

- In what ways do many young people, especially those who are economically disadvantaged or marginalized, feel they lack the power to decide about if, when, and under what circumstances to get pregnant? What are some ways in which these challenges can be addressed?

- Would you recommend this site to a friend? Why or why not?

- If you had unlimited resources, how might you go about solving the problem of unplanned pregnancy?

Suggested Websites

ACT for Youth
Actforyouth.net
Connects research to practice in the areas of positive youth development and adolescent sexual health.

Advocates for Youth
http://www.advocatesforyouth.org
Champions efforts to help young people make informed and responsible decisions about their reproductive and sexual health.

Amaze
amaze.org
Created for young people, teachers, and parents, the site envisions and promotes a world that recognizes child and adolescent sexual development as natural and healthy.

American Academy of Pediatrics

http://www.aap.org

A wealth of information about the physical, mental, and social health and well-being of infants, children, adolescents, and young adults.

Bedsider

Bedsider.org

Especially for teens, provides information about birth control and a birth control reminder.

GLSEN

http://www.glsen.org/

Mission is to ensure that every member of every school community is valued and respected regardless of sexual orientation, gender identity, or gender expression.

"It Gets Better" Project

http://www.itgetsbetter.org

Spreads the message that everyone deserves to be respected and denounces hate and intolerance.

Our Whole Lives

https://www.uua.org/re/owl

An inclusive and sex-positive K-adulthood sexuality curriculum developed by the Unitarian Universalist church. Particularly useful for some students who think religion is always anti-sex or who are religious.

Scarleteen

http://www.scarleteen.com

Staffed by volunteers, some of whom are young adults, the site provides sexuality education for a young adult population.

Suggested Reading

Alderton, M., Fellman, D., Hilton, M., LaBarr, J., & Planned Parenthood of the Rocky Mountains (2019). *In case you're curious: Questions about sex from young people with answers from the experts.* Planned Parenthood Federation of America. A book to help ensure that young people have access to the sexuality information they need, when they need.

Belge, K., & Bieschke, M. (2019). *Queer: The ultimate LGBTQ guide for teens.* (2nd ed.). Zest Books. Written for LGBTQ+ teens, this approachable book addresses such topics as dating, coming out, safe sex, and standing up for one's rights.

Corinna, H. (2016). *s.e.x. the all-you-need-to-know sexuality guide to get you through your teens and twenties.* (2nd ed.) Da Capo Press. A comprehensive sexuality book for parents, teachers, mentors, and other people who care about teens and emerging adults.

Damour, L. (2017). *Untangled: Guiding teenage girls through the seven transitions into adulthood.* Ballantine. Provides parents with intelligent and compassionate advice for anticipating challenges and encouraging growth in their daughters.

Orenstein, P. (2016; 2020). *Girls & sex* and *Boys & sex.* HarperCollins. Insightful looks into the complicated sexual worlds that girls and boys face and the complex ways in which they navigate it.

Steinberg, L. D. (2019). *Adolescence.* (12th ed.). McGraw-Hill. A comprehensive, research-based examination of adolescent development within the context of environmental and social relationships.

7

Sexuality in Adulthood

CHAPTER OUTLINE

Laura Doss/Image Source/Getty Images

"By looking at me, no one would know that I am as sexual as I am. I see many interesting things out there and when the time is right, I will try them. I think it's fine for a virgin (like me) to be sexual and be with someone without sex, until they become familiar and comfortable with one another."

—19-year-old female

"Sexuality has to have a place in my life because it is how I connect with a person and show my partner that I am a human who has feelings, whether it be giving affection or receiving it. Sexuality allows me to be free with my feelings, thereby allowing myself to open up and become a better partner for my mate."

—25-year-old male

"My skills and experience as a sexual person are limited compared to other people my age. I got married young and the fact that I was practically brainwashed as a child has greatly reduced my sexual partners. I have had intercourse with three people and oral sex with only one person (another female). . . . Just because I don't have a lot of sex doesn't mean I can't satisfy others sexually."

—23-year-old female

"Staying happily married isn't easy. Children, workload, financial issues, and a host of other factors create difficult circumstances that often put my relationship on the back burner. If someone came along with a magic panacea that would help to ignite our marriage and our sexuality, I would take it."

—51-year-old female

As WE ENTER ADULTHOOD, with greater experience and understanding, we develop a potentially mature sexuality. We establish our sexual identity and sexual orientation; we integrate love and sexuality; we forge intimate connections and make commitments; we make decisions regarding our fertility; and we develop a coherent sexual philosophy. Then in our middle years, we redefine the role of sex in our intimate relationships, accept our aging, and reevaluate our sexual philosophy. Finally, in later adulthood we reinterpret the meaning of sexuality in accordance with the erotic capabilities of our bodies. We come to terms with the possible loss of our partner and our own eventual decline. In all these stages, sexuality weaves its bright and dark threads through our lives.

In this chapter, we continue the exploration and discussion of sexuality over the human life cycle. We begin with an examination of the developmental concerns of young adults, further explore the establishment of sexual orientations and gender identity, turn to singlehood and cohabitation, then to middle adulthood, continuing to focus on developmental concerns, relational and nonrelational sexuality, and separation and divorce. Next, we look at sexuality in late adulthood, examining developmental issues, stereotypes, and differences and similarities in aging and sex between men and women and among gay and queer couples. Finally, we examine the role of the partner in sustaining health.

"The good life is one inspired by love and guided by knowledge."

—Bertrand Russell (1872–1970)

• Sexuality in Early Adulthood

Like other life passages, the one from adolescence to early adulthood offers potential for growth if one is aware of and remains open to the opportunities this period brings (see Figure 1).

Developmental Concerns

Several tasks challenge young adults as they develop their sexuality (Gagnon & Simon, 1973):

- *Establishing sexual orientation.* Children and adolescents may engage in sexual experimentation, such as playing doctor, kissing, and fondling, with members of both sexes, but they do not necessarily associate these activities with sexual orientation. Instead, their orientation as heterosexual, lesbian, gay, bisexual, or queer is in the process of emerging.

● **FIGURE 1**

Sexual and Reproductive Time Line: Mean Age of Major Events.

Source: Finer, L. B., & Philbin, J. M. (2014). *Trends in ages at key reproductive transitions in the United States*, 1951–2010. *Women's Health Issues, 23*(3), e1–e9; Pew Research Center. (2018). Population Reference Bureau. (2018).

Women	Age	Men
	10	
Menarche 12.3	15	14.0 Spermarche
First sex 17.8		18.1 First sex
	20	
First serious relationship 22.4	25	23.7 First serious relationship
First marriage 26.5		
First birth 27.0		
	30	29.8 First marriage
		29.5 First birth

"Let's face it, a date is like a job interview that lasts all night."

—Jerry Seinfeld (1954–)

Critical life questions, such as those involving relationships, personal skills, sexual behavior, and health, often arise during the college-age years when young people begin to live independently and away from their parents.

Stockbyte/Getty Images

■ *Integrating love and sex.* Traditional gender roles call for men to be sex-oriented and women to be love-oriented. In adulthood, this sex-versus-love dichotomy should be addressed. Instead of polarizing love and sex, people need to develop ways of uniting them.

■ *Forging intimacy and making commitments.* Young adulthood is characterized by increasing sexual experience. Through dating, courtship, and cohabitation, individuals gain knowledge of themselves and others as potential partners. As relationships become more meaningful, the degree of intimacy and interdependence increases. Sexuality can be a means of enhancing intimacy and self-disclosure, as well as a source of physical and emotional pleasure. As adults become more intimate, most desire to develop their ability to make relationship commitments.

■ *Making fertility/childbearing decisions.* Becoming a parent is socially discouraged during adolescence, but it becomes increasingly legitimate for some people when they reach their 20s. Fertility issues are often critical but sometimes unacknowledged, especially for single young adults.

■ *Practicing safer sex to protect against sexually transmitted infections (STIs).* An awareness of the various STIs and ways to best protect against them must be integrated into the communication, values, and personal behaviors of young adults.

■ *Evolving a sexual philosophy.* As individuals move from adolescence to adulthood, they reevaluate their ethical standards, moving from decision making based on authority to standards based on their personal principles of right and wrong, caring, and responsibility. They become responsible for developing their own moral code, which includes sexual issues. They also need to differentiate between what they have been taught about sexuality and what they truly believe about themselves. This is an important step in "owning one's own sexuality." In doing so, they need to evolve a personal philosophical perspective to give coherence to sexual attitudes, behaviors, beliefs, and values. They need to place sexuality within the larger framework of their lives and relationships.

Establishing Sexual Orientation and Gender Identity

A critical task of adulthood is establishing one's sexual orientation and gender identity. Most people develop a heterosexual identity by adolescence or young adulthood. Their task is simplified because their development as heterosexuals is approved by society. But for those who are attracted to the same or both sexes, identify as queer or are unsure, their development features more doubt and anxiety. Because those who are attracted to the same, or both sexes are aware that they are questioning remaining

think
about it

Why College Students Have Sex

What is the Earth? What are the body and soul without satisfaction?

—Walt Whitman (1819–1892)

The reasons people have sex may appear obvious and simple when, in fact, they are actually quite complex and diverse. Add gender differences to this mix, and the number of reasons for having sex begins to mount. Researchers Cindy Meston and David Buss (2007), in a 5-year study, sought to identify an array of potential reasons that motivate people to engage in sexual intercourse and to classify reasons by gender. Meston suggests these findings have "refuted a lot of gender stereotypes that men only want sex for the physical pleasure and women want love." Meston and Buss found that college men and women seek sex for mostly the same reasons: attraction, pleasure, affection, love, romance, emotional closeness, experience, connection, curiosity, and opportunity. Women and men were not found to be very different on many counts: 20 of the top 25 reasons given for having sex were the same for both. Though expressing love and showing affection were in the top 10 for both women and men, the clear number-one reason was "I was attracted to the person." Wanting to experience the physical pleasure was the second reason for women and third for men.

The researchers began with 444 women and men—ranging in age from 17 to 52—and a list of 237 reasons people have sex (Meston & Buss, 2007). From the same list of reasons, the researchers asked 1,549 college students to rank the reasons. The analysis of the rankings found four categories of reasons to have sex:

Physical

- *Stress reduction* "I wanted to release anxiety/stress," "I thought it would relax me"
- *Pleasure* "I wanted the pure pleasure," "It's exciting and adventurous"
- *Physical desirability* "The person was too physically attractive to resist," "The person smelled nice"
- *Experience seeking* "I wanted to improve my sexual skills," "I wanted to see what it would be like to have sex with another person"

Goal Attainment

- *Resources* "I wanted to make money," "I wanted to reproduce"
- *Social status* "I thought it would boost my social status," "I was competing with someone else to 'get the person'"
- *Revenge* "I wanted to even the score with a cheating partner," "I wanted to break up another's relationship"
- *Utilitarian* "The person had taken me out for an expensive dinner," "I wanted to get a favor from someone"

Emotional

- *Love and commitment* "I wanted to express my love for the person," "I wanted to increase the emotional bond by having sex"
- *Expression* "I wanted to say 'thank you,'" "I wanted to lift my partner's spirits"

Insecurity

- *Self-esteem boost* "I wanted to feel attractive," "I wanted my partner to notice me"
- *Duty/pressure* "I felt like I owed it to the person," "I didn't know how to say 'no'"
- *Mate guarding* "I was afraid my partner would have an affair if I didn't have sex with him/her," "I didn't want to 'lose' the person"

In general, men, significantly more than women, cited reasons for having sex centered on the physical appearance and desirability of a partner. Additionally, they indicated experience-seeking and mere opportunity as factors. Women exceeded men in endorsing certain emotional motivations for sex, such as wanting to express love and realizing they were in love.

Psychologist Leif Kennair and colleagues (2015) assessed sex and mating strategies of 1,327 Norwegian college students for having sexual intercourse, based on the research of Meston and Buss. The researchers found similar results as Meston and Buss in that the students were most strongly motivated to have sex by the desire for pleasure, with feelings of love and commitment and the physical desirability of one's partner tying for the second most-cited reasons. Both men and women were relatively more focused on their partner's attractiveness than on feelings of love and commitment for short-term relationships.

University of Guelph sex researchers Jessica Wood, Robin Milhausen, and Nicole Jeffery (2014) focused on over 200 lesbian, bisexual, queer, and questioning women's reasons why they have sex in romantic relationships. Their results showed that reasons for sex may be consistent across varied sexual orientations. The most common reasons for the women were related to pleasure and love/commitment. The number-one reason for the four groups of women was, "It feels good." The women participants in both long-term and short-term relationships did not report significant differences for having sex. However, University of Ottawa researchers (Armstrong & Reissing, 2015) found a contrary outcome among 510 women of same-sex and same-sex/bisexual attraction: Relationship type affected motivation for sex; that is, for casual sex the major reasons to have sex were related to physical outcomes such as pleasure, and for committed relationships the major reasons reflected emotional aspects such as the expression of love and commitment. No differences were found in motivation between women reporting same-sex attraction and those who did not. Further, women reporting having bisexual attraction and identified as being lesbian, bisexual, or another sexual minority indicated no significant differences in motivation for sex with male or female partners.

taboos by some members of society, it can take them longer to confirm and accept their sexual orientation. It may also be difficult and dangerous for them to establish a relationship.

"Somewhere in the mounting and mating, rutting and butting is the very secret of nature itself."

—Graham Swift (1949–)

Models of Sexual Orientation Sexual orientation is an area of human sexuality that has been clouded by misunderstanding, myth, and confusion. To help explain the complex nature of sexual orientation, psychologists and researchers in sexuality have developed various models (see Figure 2). Much as our views of gender, masculinity, and femininity have changed, so have conceptualizations of sexual orientation, although these are different phenomena. It is important to note that sexual orientation labels do not constitute the entirety of sexual orientations (Savin-Williams, 2014). Though discrete categories are more easily understood and conveyed, this labeling disguises variability and complexity within a sexual orientation. According to Cornell University researcher and gender specialist Ritch C. Savin-Williams (2014), "sexual orientation is a continuously distributed characteristic of individuals, and all decisions to categorize it into discrete units, regardless of how many, are ultimately external impositions placed on individuals' experiences."

Until the research of Alfred C. Kinsey and his colleagues, sexual orientation was dichotomized into "heterosexual" and "homosexual"—that is, a person could be one or the other. As shown in Model A in Figure 2, some researchers considered a third category, bisexuality, although others believed that a bisexual individual was a homosexual person trying to be

● **FIGURE 2**

Three Models of Sexual Orientation.

Source: Adapted from Sanders, S. A., et al. (1990). Homosexuality/heterosexuality: An overview. In McWhirter, D. P., et al. (Eds.), *Homosexuality/heterosexuality: Concepts of sexual orientation*. Oxford University Press.

Model A: Dichotomous—psychoanalytic

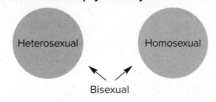

Model B: Unidimensional—bipolar (Kinsey)

Model C: Two-dimensional—orthogonal (Storms)

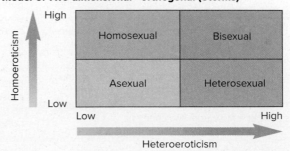

heterosexual, or that an individual was merely "confused" about their sexual identity. One of Kinsey's most significant contributions was his challenge to this traditional model. Research by Kinsey and others showed that same-sex sexual behavior was not uncommon. They also found that participation in both same- and other-sex behavior was not uncommon. This led them to conclude that sexual orientation is a continuum from exclusively heterosexual to exclusively homosexual, as depicted in Model B, and that a person's sexual behavior pattern can change across a lifetime. Since that time, this continuum has been widely utilized in sexuality research, education, and therapy.

The Kinsey continuum has been criticized for its implication that the more heterosexual a person is the less homosexual he or she must be, and vice versa. Sex researchers Sanders et al. (1990) note that some researchers have modified the Kinsey scale by using bipolar ratings of heterosexuality and homosexuality; that is, indicators such as sexual behavior, sexual fantasies, the person one loves, and feelings about which sex is more "attractive" can each be assessed independently. Storms (1980, 1981) suggested that homoeroticism—feelings of sexual attraction to members of the same sex—and heteroeroticism are independent continua (Model C). A bisexual individual is high on both homoeroticism and heteroeroticism dimensions, a heterosexual person is high on heteroeroticism and low on homoeroticism, and a homosexual individual is high on homoeroticism and low on heteroeroticism. A person low on both dimensions would be considered asexual.

Because definitions of sexual orientation vary, it is important to distinguish sexual orientation from other combinations and degrees of identity and behavior. Using a one-dimensional measurement of sexual orientation can result in erroneous conclusions about sexual identity, attraction, and behavior (Badgett, 2009.7a; Meyer & Wilson, 2009). Physician and sex researcher Charles Moser (2015) suggests understanding diverse partner sexuality by looking at the following:

1. *Sexual identity*—how individuals define themselves sexually. It may not describe their actual sexual behavior, fantasy content, or to which sexual stimuli they respond.

2. *Sexual interests/attraction*—what individuals want to do, whether or not they actually do it.

3. *Sexual behavior*—what individuals actually do, whether or not their behavior is consistent with their sexual identity or sexual interests.

4. *Sexual orientation*—a distinct type of an intense sexual interest.

The combinations and degrees to which individuals experience these components help define sexual orientation. For example, how much sexual interest and identity does a person have with individuals of the same or other sex before they declare their sexual orientation? Is a person whose sexual interests are with both men and women but who have not had a same- or other-sex behavior considered to be bisexual? What about individuals who, for religious or other reasons, do not acknowledge sexual interests or behaviors? Are they asexual, true to their spiritual beliefs, or simply repressed? These multidimensional perspectives broaden the definitions for sexual orientation by taking into consideration the complexity and ambiguity of human behavior (Moser, 2015).

Given that sexual orientation is the single most important feature of a person's sexual identity, it's important to move beyond an exclusive reliance on sexual orientation based solely on biological sex; that is people with male or female genitalia. Another way of looking at sexual orientation is in terms of sexual attraction to one gender or another. For example, if one is sexually attracted to men, does that mean that one is attracted to penises? Social identities? Interactions? What about attractions to feminine men? Sexual configurations theory (SCT) takes into consideration the multidimensional aspects of people's sexualities and reflects upon the diversity of sexual identities and attractions based on biological *and* gender characteristics (van Anders, 2015). That is, sexual attraction is based on the biological sex of a desired partner as well as the gender characteristics (i.e., degrees of masculinity and femininity, transgender, genderqueer). Sex researcher and psychologist van Anders has proposed a sexual configuration consisting of four parameters of partnered

"Sex lies at the root of life, and we can never learn to revere life until we know how to understand sex."

—Havelock Ellis (1859–1930)

sexuality: (1) gender/sex (orientation to male and/or female sexes and/or genders), (2) partner number (erotic interest in some but nurture other partners), (3) sexual parameter (eroticism and nurturance), and (4) partnered sexuality, which is connected to the previous three identity(ies), their combination and/or intersectional factors. Notably, the introduction of non-binary attractions makes the theory applicable and inclusive of a wide range of sexual behaviors otherwise left out and considered difficult to locate on the sexual orientation continuums and provides a multidimensional model tailored to each person's individuality or uniqueness.

Prevalence of Sexual Minorities More people than ever before in the United States identify as something other than heterosexual. Data from YouGov, an international Internet-based market research and data analytics firm from the United Kingdom, revealed that one-third of 18 to 34-year-olds did not identify as heterosexual and those who did identify other than heterosexual are steadily rising (YouGov, 2017). This may be due in part because data collection assessing sexual orientation has been increasing to include sexual minority persons who may feel safer disclosing their orientation.

Still, we do not know the exact numbers of those who identify as heterosexual, gay, lesbian, bisexual, queer, or transgender. In large part, this is because same-sex attractions and behaviors are often stigmatized. LGBTQ+ individuals are often reluctant to reveal their identities in research surveys for reasons of personal hesitancy as well as conceptual problems surrounding what constitutes sexual orientation.

According to a 2017 Gallup poll, the portion of American adults identifying as LGBTQ+ increased to 4.5%, implying that more than 11 million adults now identify as a sexual minority in the United States (Newport, 2018). Identification was highest for millennials, those born between 1980 and 1998 (8.2%) and among women (5.1%), Asians (4.9%), and Latinx (6.4%). As noted previously, self-identification as LGBTQ+ represents only one way of measuring sexual orientation and gender identity. Various structural and individual barriers, including internalized guilt and shame, can dramatically alter the rates.

Every 10 years the U.S. Census Bureau attempts to count everyone in the United States, regardless of their nationality or sexual orientation. Though the Census has not previously tabulated measures of alternative living arrangements, such as civil unions or domestic partnerships, the 2020 Census provided individuals with the option to categorize a relationship as same-sex (2020 Census: LGBTQ+). At the same time, the Census will not inquire about individuals' sexual orientation and gender identity. Gathering data about those who identify as a sexual minority, an historically undercounted community, would provide reliable statistics to help inform policymakers, researchers, and others about the needs and issues related to this population.

In part, the variances that exist in the literature regarding prevalence of diverse sexual orientations may be explained by different methodologies, interviewing techniques, sampling procedures, definitions of sexual orientation, random response errors, and differences in the way questions are framed. Stigma and discrimination may also prevent some from disclosing their sexual orientation, particularly if they feel judged. Finally, because sexuality is varied and can change over time, its expression at any one time is not necessarily the same as at another time or for all time. (For more about measuring sexual behaviors, see Think About It, Chapter 2: "A Challenge Facing Sex Researchers: Selecting the Best Ways to Measure Sexual Behavior, Sexual Orientations, and Gender Identity.")

The Lesbian, Gay, Bisexual, Transgender, or Queer Identity Process As previously discussed, the vocabulary we use to describe sexual orientation falls short of the complex reality of many people's lives. Given that sexual orientation involves a variety of attributes, including attraction, sexual activity, and self-identification, focusing on just one component can oversimplify sexual identities, sexual behavior, or romantic experiences (Institute of Medicine, 2011). Actually, many sexual health professionals question whether we need to give a categorical name to many aspects of sexuality, including sexual orientation. Often, the categories result in persons in a particular category feeling stigmatized and marginalized.

"Love is sacred, and sex is sacred too. The two things are not apart; they belong together."

—Lame Deer, Lakota Indian holy man (1903–1976)

Identifying oneself as a lesbian, gay, bisexual, transgender, or queer (LGBTQ+) person often takes considerable time and, for some, may involve multiple paths. The most intense phase in the development of one's sexual identity is during late adolescence and early adulthood. College graduates are more likely to identify themselves as LGBTQ+ while they are attending college because postsecondary education tends to engage students with issues of pluralism, diversity, and self-evaluation. Same-sex attraction typically precedes same-sex sexual behavior by several years.

Gay pride commemorates the LGBTQ+ rights movement both in the United States and abroad.
jvnimages/Alamy Stock Photo

How does one arrive at their sexual orientation? Does it really matter if one is born heterosexual or homosexual, for example, whether an orientation comes later, or whether it varies over time? For some, the awareness of being or feeling something other than heterosexual occurs in phases. The first phase is marked by the initiation of a process of self-discovery and exploration, including becoming aware of one's sexual attractions, questioning whether one may be a lesbian, gay, bisexual, transsexual, or queer (LGBTQ+) person, and having sex with members of the same sex. The second phase, identity integration, is a continuation of sexual identity development as individuals integrate and incorporate the identity into their sense of self. Engaging in LGBTQ+-related social activities, addressing society's negative attitudes, and feeling more comfortable about disclosing one's identity to others are part of this process. Difficulties in developing an integrated sexual identity often cause distress and may have particularly negative implications for the psychological adjustment of sexual minority youth. At the same time, the categorization of individuals as gay, straight, bisexual, trans, or queer does not consider that some may move back and forth among sexual identities (Diamond, 2008). (See Think About It, Chapter 5: "Sexual Fluidity: Women's and Men's Variable Sexual Attractions.")

New in the U.S. Department of Health and Human Services' *Healthy People 2020* report is the goal to improve the health, safety, and well-being of sexual minorities. Research suggests that LGBTQ+ individuals face health disparities linked to social stigma, discrimination, and denial of their civil and human rights (Williams Institute, 2020). Discrimination against LGBTQ+ persons is also associated with high rates of psychiatric disorders, substance abuse, higher rates and long-lasting effects of violence and victimization, and suicide. Eliminating disparities and enhancing efforts to improve sexual minorities' mental and physical health are necessary to ensure that they, like everyone else, can lead long, healthy lives.

"Bisexuality immediately doubles your chances for a date on a Saturday night."

—Rodney Dangerfield (1921–2004)

Publicly acknowledging one's same-sex attraction, commonly called coming out, is a major decision because it may jeopardize relationships, but it is also an important means of self-validation and self-affirmation. By publicly acknowledging a lesbian, gay, bisexual, queer, or other sexual minority orientation, a person begins to reject the stigma and condemnation associated with it.

Sexual minorities are often "out" to varying degrees. Generally, coming out to others occurs in stages involving family members and friends. Some are out to no one, not even themselves, while others are out only to selected individuals and lovers, and others come out to close friends but not to their families or employers. Because of fear of reprisal, dismissal, or public reaction, many LGBTQ+ professionals are not out to their employers, their co-workers, or the public.

Mostly Straight   When we consider sexual attraction and behavior, we may not consider or include those who identify as "mostly straight." An exploration of mostly straight people derives from Ritch C. Savin-Williams (2019), psychologist and professor emeritus at Cornell University, who surveyed nonexclusive heterosexuality among 160 ethnically and racially diverse men between the ages of 17 and 27. His research found mostly straight young men to be different from straight and bisexual men in their sexual and romantic profiles. Rather than being halfway between straight and bisexual, those who self-identified as mostly straight on a sexual/romantic continuum were considerably closer to the straight man than the bisexual man. For example, a typical straight man is 0% attracted to men; a typical mostly straight man is 10% sexually attracted to men, and a typical bisexual man is 50% sexually attracted to men. Additionally, mostly straight men varied little from straight men in their attraction to women—nearly 100% were attracted to women. Other findings might suggest the existence of mostly straight as a distinct sexuality:

1. Mostly straight men have a distinguishing *physiological arousal pattern.* That is, mostly straight men responded to female stimuli exactly as straight men do, with an enlargement of the penis and eye pupils. However, they were more aroused by male stimuli than straight men but less so than bisexual men.

2. The *prevalence rate* of mostly straight males ranged from 2% to 9% of the population. Among college students, the prevalence rate was found to be about 7%. Whether fewer men than women are mostly straight is uncertain as fewer men than women report it. What we do know about women is that many acknowledge a degree of sexual attraction and/or behavior with other women yet identify as straight because it is the closest identity option available on most surveys. If they were given more non-straight options, such as mostly straight, pansexual, queer, fluid, questioning, or asexual, women might feel these options would more adequately reflect their sexuality and gender preferences.

3. The identification as mostly straight is fairly *stable* over time. If a mostly straight man's self-perception of his sexuality is persistent over time, rather than a result of experimentation, then this would support his actual sexual and romantic point on a continuum. A mostly straight identity among men appears to be less stable over time than a straight identity but is more constant than a bisexual identity.

4. Mostly straight has *subjective relevance or personal meaningfulness* for young men. The unique integrity of being mostly straight is corroborated in the lives and stories of those who share it.

Savin-Williams suggests that if mostly straight is a true sexual and romantic orientation, it should then be based on the same biological and environmental factors that might determine all sexual orientations.

Bisexuality Still debated is whether bisexuality consists of heterosexual and homosexual orientations in the same person or whether it is a sexual orientation and a sexual interest (Moser, 2015). Recognizing that gender is on a spectrum that includes various gender identities from cisgender to non-binary and transgender, bisexual people are attracted to people of more than one gender. We know that bisexuality is not new or rare. Those who are attracted to, engage in sexual behavior with, and love other individuals regardless of gender actually outnumber exclusively homosexual individuals (Bostwick & Dodge, 2019).

Though additional sexual orientations have been proposed, including asexuality (lack of sexual attraction), and polyamory (having more than one loving intimate relationship at a time), it's clear that figuring out a way to accurately define specific sexual minorities may be an impossible challenge.

Asexuality Controversy exists about whether **asexuality,** or lack of sexual attraction, is a sexual orientation, a sexual dysfunction or symptom of a sexual dysfunction, or a paraphilia (Brotto & Yule, 2017). Most professionals have ruled out the latter two classifications: sexual dysfunction or paraphilia. Using the definition of sexual orientation as attraction to members of one's own gender, another gender or both genders it might be argued that lack of attraction to another could also be an orientation. Complicating research about this understudied population is lack of an operational definition of asexuality, with some considering it to be a lack of sexual activity while others, a lack of sexual desire, little to no sexual attraction and/or self-identifying as being asexual. Distinct from abstinence, also known as chastity, studies have reported that a relatively small minority of the population (ranging between 0.4% and 1%) lacks sexual attraction toward another person. Other researchers have found that asexuality could be as high as 1.5% of men and 3.3% of women (Bulmer & Izuma, 2018). Attitudes toward sex also vary among those who identify as asexual, ranging from simply lacking interest in sex to being disgusted by it. Separate from sexual attraction or intimacy, the majority of asexual individuals report that they desire emotionally intimate relationships with others (The Trevor Project, 2020).

Many of those who identify as a sexual minority experience some of the same negative attitudes toward homosexuality as their heterosexual counterparts. **Internalized homophobia** is a set of negative attitudes and affects toward homosexuality in other persons and toward same-sex attraction in oneself. Growing up in a heterosexual world that condones only one way of sexual expression and reproduction, many LGBTQ+ individuals learn to believe that heterosexuality is the only option and that homosexuality is a perversion. Such self-hatred can significantly impede the self-acceptance process that many sexual minorities go through in order to come out and embrace their sexuality.

Being Single

In recent decades, there has been a staggering increase in the numbers of unmarried adults (never married, divorced, or widowed) in America. Most of this increase has been the result of individuals, especially young adults, marrying later.

The College Environment The college environment is important not only for intellectual development but also for social development. The social aspects of the college setting— classes, dormitories, fraternities and sororities, parties, clubs, and athletic events—provide opportunities for meeting others. For many, college is a place to search for or find mates.

Dating in college is similar to high school dating in many ways. It may be formal or informal ("getting together" or "hooking up"); it may be for recreation or for finding a mate. Features that distinguish college dating from high school dating, however, include the more independent setting away from home, with diminished parental influence, the increased maturity of partners, more role flexibility, and the increased legitimacy of sexual interactions. For most college students, love and dating become qualitatively different during emerging adulthood, with more focus on sexuality as it relates to developing one's own identity.

The college social setting provides opportunities for students to meet others and establish relationships.

Digital Vision/Getty Images

think about it

"Hooking Up" Among College Students: As Simple as One Might Think?

Hookups have been damned, praised, and dismissed in the popular press, feeding a debate about whether we should applaud or condemn the "hookup" generation, drawing out prescriptions for students' sex lives from both the right and the left.

—Lisa Wade (2017)

"Hooking up," is a term used by some to describe casual sexual encounters, ranging from kissing to intercourse, between two persons with no clear mutual expectation of further interactions or a committed relationship (Black et al., 2019). A similar mating strategy is having "friends with benefits" or "fuck buddies," or making "booty calls," which involve explicit or implicit solicitation of a non-long-term sex partner. Whether that hookup results in positive or negative outcomes depends on how individuals interpret or make meaning of their hookup experiences. Research on factors related to hooking up has revealed some conflicting findings including those cited below:

- *Well-Being* A study of college freshmen and juniors found the relationship between hooking up and well-being was both positive and negative depending on age, gender, and hookup definition. However, when gender differences in well-being were found, hookups were associated with higher well-being for women than for men (Vrangalova, 2015). From 22 universities and colleges, women, more than men, reported being negatively judged for hooking up (Kettrey, 2016).

- *Feelings/Emotions/Reactions* For their most recent hookup, college students reported more positive feelings than negative feelings about it, but men reported more positive feelings and lower negative feelings than women did. Actually, the vast majority of these students indicated that they wanted to have their most recent hookup experience (Lewis et al., 2012).

- *First-Year Students* For first-year college students, hookup behavior was associated with experiencing depression, sexual victimization, and STIs. Hookups that involved penetrated sex increased psychological distress for first-year female students but not for first-year male students. Most first-year college women reported at least one benefit of their most recent hookup; including sexual pleasure, exploration, and intimacy; fun/enjoyment; increased confidence; and clarification of feelings; meeting the needs for social connection (Shepardson et al., 2016).

- *Unprotected Sex/Drinking* One-third of students from three universities reported having unprotected sex during a hookup (Napper et al., 2016). Another study found that less than one-half of college students reported using a condom during their most recent hookup. Among students from 22 colleges and universities binge drinking and marijuana use prior or during a hookup was associated with increased risk of unprotected sex and other substance use (Kuperberg & Padgett, 2017).

- *Sexual Behavior* Both men and women college students reported being comfortable with touching above and below the waist during hookups, but only men were comfortable with oral sex and intercourse behaviors. Further, for the same students, both men and women did not experience orgasm as frequently as desired during hookups, but the gap was greater for female students than male students.

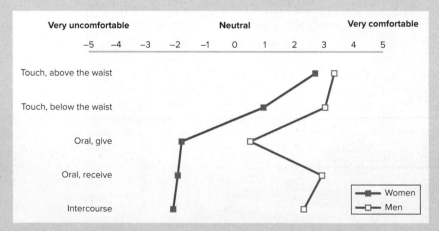

● **FIGURE 3**

Comfort Levels of College Men and Women with Various Hookup Behaviors.

Source: Adapted from Reiber, C., & Garcia, J. R. (2010). Gender differences, evolution, and pluralistic ignorance. *Evolutionary Psychology, 8,* 390–404.

Although acceptance of sex outside of marriage is widespread among college students, there are more boundaries placed on women. If a woman has sexual intercourse, some people still believe it should take place in the context of a committed relationship. Women who "sleep around" or "hook up" are often morally censured. Reflecting the continuing sexual double standard, men are not usually condemned as harshly as women for having sex without commitment.

For those who identify as a sexual minority, the college environment is often liberating because campuses tend to be more accepting of sexual diversity than society at large. College campuses often have LGBTQ+ organizations that sponsor social events and get-togethers and advocate for sexual minority rights. There, individuals can freely meet others in open circumstances that permit meaningful relationships to develop and mature. Although prejudice against those who are different continues to exist in some colleges and universities, college life has been an important haven for many.

Hooking Up and College Students   Today, college students and other young adults have their own form of casual sex, commonly called **hooking up.** Though there isn't a consistent definition of hooking up, many use it as an umbrella term for a variety of casual sex relationships (see Figure 4). This term, analogous to one-night stands of previous generations, consists of sexual interactions between two people who may or may not know each other nor necessarily expect a subsequent sexual encounter or a romantic commitment. With the increasing use of dating websites and apps, access to birth control, and readily available emergency contraception, hooking up is easier than ever.

The hook-up culture isn't new. By the 1970s, the sexual revolution was in full swing and many college students were experimenting with casual sex. What has changed since that time are both the attitudes and technology associated with it. While bars and fraternities are still

"I must paint you."
—Paul Gauguin, pick-up line (1848–1903)

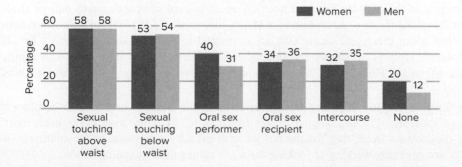

● **FIGURE 4**

Percentage of College Women and Men Reporting Participation in Hookup Behaviors.

Source: Reiber, C., & Garcia, J. R. (2010). Gender differences, evolution, and pluralistic ignorance. *Evolutionary Psychology, 8,* 390–404.

the places of choice for many young people to find a potential hookup partner, apps like Tinder have provided additional options for those interested in pursuing hookups as a lifestyle.

A common experience for many university students, hooking up has been reported to occur among as many as 70–85% of undergraduate students at some point during the time they are in college (Black et al., 2019). It's been noted that certain personality traits, including being an extrovert and open to new experiences, are among the characteristics shared by those who engage in it. According to sociology professor Lisa Wade (2017), who extensively researched hooking up on college campuses, hooking up is not only what some people do, it's also seen as a cultural phenomenon, or in this case, a set of routines built into the institution of higher learning. Wade states:

> (for those).."who are unsure of whether they want to participate, hookup culture has a way of tipping the scales. Its logic makes both abstaining from sex and a preference for sex in committed relationships difficult to justify, and its integration into the workings of higher education makes hooking up hard to avoid.

Wade (2017) found there to be both careless and carefree components of hooking up, especially as it relates to (a lack of) emotions. Hooking up implies casual sex with no expression of tenderness. Separating hookups from "making love," some acknowledge that cuddling is for people you love and that if you hold hands or make eye contact during sex, you are "making love."

Though hooking up is common on college campuses, it's also customary for some to report mixed or negative feelings about having casual sex. While many enjoy hooking up and adapt to hookup culture's views for calling for fun and casual sex, about a third of students opt out, finding hookup culture unappealing (Wade, 2017). For some, hookup culture is a problem not because it promotes casual sex, but because it makes what some view as a destructive form of casual sex feel compulsory. As a result, those who resist getting involved in casual sex may endure a kind of punishment emotionally where caring for others seems inappropriate while carelessness and sometimes even cruelty are allowed or encouraged. Hooking up may also heighten risks that students will become either perpetrators or victims of sexual crimes. However, some forms of sexually aggressive behaviors might be seen by both men and women as normal in the hookup culture and are not identified as sexual violence.

When asked why young adults choose to hook up, 34 first-year students in a qualitative study cited how perceptions of costs and rewards influenced their decisions (Anders et al., 2020). Specifically, four themes emerged when students described it as a rewarding experience: (a) having fun, (b) fulfilling sexual desires, (c) gaining a sense of status or accomplishment, and (d) the potential to develop a relationship. Participants also described the costs of hooking up both for themselves and others: (a) regrets/mistakes, (b) ambiguity, (c) increased sexual risk, and (d) loss of respect. Gender differences in the costs and implications on hooking up were prevalent, with females having more favorable views of committed dating relationships compared to men. The feelings of regret discussed by many women might be representative of a continued "sexual double standard" wherein expectations for men and women differed, with women's sexuality judged more harshly. In the vast majority of hookups, alcohol was involved, which influenced the perceptions of the costs versus rewards and altered the individual preferences, such as attractiveness of the partner.

In spite of the high incidence of hooking up on college campuses, many college students are still looking for love. According to a Match.com study (2019), 75% of singles are hopeful that love is out there, and nearly 60% are motivated to find romantic love and a long-term companion. Only 9% of singles are looking to date casually. (For more about this topic, see Think About It: "Hooking Up Among College Students: As Simple as One Might Think?")

The Singles World Men and women involved in the singles world tend to be older than college students, typically ranging in age from 25 to 40. They have never been married, or if they are divorced, they usually do not have primary responsibility for children. Single adults are generally working or looking for a job rather than attending school.

Although dating in the singles world is somewhat different from dating in high school and college, there are similarities. Singles, like their counterparts in school, emphasize recreation and entertainment, sociability, and physical attractiveness.

The isolation many single people feel can be quite overwhelming. In college, students meet each other in classes or dormitories, at school events, or through friends. There are many meeting places and large numbers of eligibles. Singles who are working may have less opportunity than college students to meet available people. For single adults, the most frequent means of meeting others are introductions by friends, Internet, dating sites, parties, and social groups.

Sexual experimentation and activity are important for many singles. Although individuals may derive personal satisfaction from sexual activity, they must also manage the stress of conflicting commitments, loneliness, and a lack of connectedness. To fill the demand for meeting others, the singles world has spawned a multibillion-dollar industry—bars, resorts, clubs, housing, and Internet sites dedicated solely to them. A large percent of U.S. adult singles rely on online dating sites such as Bumble, Hinge, Hornet, and Match. Additionally, many utilize social networking apps such as Tinder to advertise their "status" and to solicit interest from potential partners.

The New Social Context of Singlehood   A wide range of traits exists among unmarried young adults in America, regardless of whether a person is straight or part of a sexual minority. These include but are not limited to the following:

- *Greater sexual experience* Those who marry later are more likely to have had more partnered sexual experience and sex partners than individuals from previous generations who married younger. Nonmarital sex has become the norm among many adults.

- *Increased number of singles, or those who have never married, are divorced, or are widowed* Of all Americans, 51% of those between the ages of 18 and 34 are single (General Social Survey, 2019) and in 2017, 42% of American adults did not live with a spouse or a partner (Pew Research Center, 2017). Many factors, including financial instability, societal acceptance of singlehood, and personal preference are among the factors that contribute to these percentages.

- *Widespread acceptance of cohabitation* As young adults are deferring marriage longer and cohabitation is seen as a viable living arrangement, it has become an integral part of adult life. Among young adults ages 18 to 44, a larger share has cohabited than have been married (59% vs. 50%). Additionally, most Americans (69%) say cohabitation is acceptable even if a couple doesn't plan to get married (Pew Research Center, 2019.7a).

- *Women are having fewer children and having them at older ages* Whether partnered or not, women are having fewer children and are older when they do have them. Being part of a single-parent family is also increasing. These trends hold across races and for urban and rural areas (CDC, 2019.7).

- *The median age of first marriage is increasing* Among those who have never married but are open to it, most say that the reason for not being married is that they haven't found the right person (Pew Research Center, 2017). In 2019, the median age of marriage for women was 28 and for men was 30. This compares to a median age at first marriage of 25 for women and 29 for men in 2000 (U.S. Census Bureau, 2019).

- *Being unemployed* The share of non-partnered Americans is higher among those unemployed (54%) as compared with those who are employed (32%) (Bonos & Guskin, 2019).

- *Greater numbers of separated and divorced people* In Western cultures, more than 90% of people marry by age 50, however about 40–50% of married couples in the U.S. divorce. The divorce rate for subsequent marriages is even higher (American Psychological Association, 2020).

- *Increased number of same-sex couples* It is estimated that the number of same-sex married couples has increased by almost 70% since 2014. During this same period, the number of unmarried same-sex couples has also dramatically increased (Schneider, 2020).

While many of those who identify as a sexual minority choose to have or adopt children, **some individuals still argue** about what constitutes "family."

JGI/Tom Grill/Getty Images

The world that unmarried young adults inhabit is one in which greater opportunities for exploring intimate relationships exists more than ever before. The American household is changing: It is smaller, more diverse, and more likely to be made up of single adults or non-married partners than married couples.

Being Single and a Sexual Minority   In the late nineteenth century, as a result of the stigmatization of homosexuality, groups of gay men and lesbian women began congregating in their own clubs and bars. There, in relative safety, they could find acceptance and support, meet others, and socialize. Today, there are neighborhoods in most large cities that are identified with LGBTQ+ individuals. These communities feature not only openly LGBTQ+ bookstores, restaurants, coffeehouses, and bars, but also places of worship, clothing stores, medical and legal offices, hair salons, and so on.

During the decade of 2010-2020, a range of historical events transpired that changed the landscape of gay single and partnered life. These include the legalization of marriage and increased social acceptance of sexual minorities. At the same time, there has been a rapid increase in national data sources that have provided greater understanding of the issues facing LGBTQ+ individuals which could lead to greater acceptance and support. For example, research has shown that relative to heterosexual and cisgender peers, sexual minority youth experience less support and more strain from their families, are less likely to report closeness or attachment, are less likely to disclose personal problems, and more likely to report conflict with parents than their heterosexual counterparts (Reczek, 2020). As a result of these and additional social stressors, including prejudice and stigma, verbal bullying, violence, and harassment, more depressive symptoms and diagnoses have been reported among sexual minorities than in their heterosexual counterparts (Krueger et al., 2018).

As we learn more, researchers have found that cultural norms often differ in sexual minority dating communities as compared to heterosexual ones. For example, though LGBTQ+ adults may adhere to normative heterosexual romantic relationship values (e.g., romantic love ideology), as young adults, they are less likely to value exclusivity and lifelong commitment than heterosexual young adults (Reczek, 2020). In one of the few studies on transgender dating experiences, the additional effort transgender individuals take to find a romantic partner was significant, especially given the stigmatization and violence experienced by trans people in the United States (Belawski & Sojka, 2014).

Cohabitation

Cohabitation, the practice of living together and having a sexual relationship without being married, is on the rise in the United States (Pew Research Center, 2019.7b). As more U.S. adults are delaying marriage or forgoing it altogether, roughly 7% are living with an unmarried partner. While the share of adults who are currently cohabiting remains smaller than the share who are married, the percent of those ages 18 to 44 who have ever lived with an unmarried partner (59%) has surpassed the share who has ever been married (50%). What has accompanied the rise cohabitation is the percentage of people who are accepting of it. While older adults are more likely to see societal benefits in marriage, young adults are particularly accepting of cohabitation, with 78% of those ages 18 to 29 accepting an unmarried couple living together even if they don't plan to get married (Pew Research Center, 2019.7b).

Like married couples, most of those who cohabitate cite love and companionship as major reasons why they decided to move in or get married to a partner (Pew Research Center, 2019.7b). Additional reasons include financial, convenience, and wanting children (see Figure 5). Still, most married adults (66%) who lived with their spouse before they were married, and who were not engaged when they moved in together, say they viewed cohabitation as a step toward marriage when they first started living with their now-spouse.

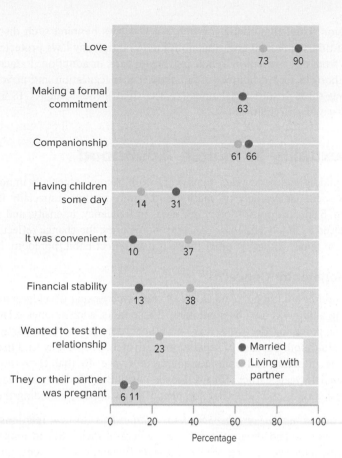

● **FIGURE 5**

Why Get Married? Percentage of American Adults Saying Each Reason is a Very Important Consideration to Marry.

Source: Pew Research Center (2019). Key findings on marriage and cohabitation in the United States.

With more accepting attitudes toward nonmarital sex, Americans' sexual behaviors have also changed (Twenge et al., 2015). For many, cohabitation is a practical decision (e.g., split rents and household expenses) and for others, it is a matter of convenience (e.g., no more driving between apartments). It is also a significant legal, financial, and emotional step. Decisions such as whether to permanently combine finances or co-sign for credit cards, how to pare down possessions, and when screen time is allowed need to be discussed. Talking about "what if" scenarios can help ensure that living together is the right move.

The concept of **domestic partnership**, which refers to the rights of unmarried adults who choose to live together in the same manner as married couples, has led to laws granting some of the protections of marriage to all people. For others, permanence is increasingly replaced by **serial monogamy**, a succession of relationships or marriages.

Same-Sex Marriage

For LGBTQ+ and heterosexual individuals, intimate relationships provide love, romance, satisfaction, and security. There is one important difference, however: Many of those involved in lesbian, gay, and queer relationships resist the traditional heterosexual provider/homemaker roles. Among heterosexual couples, these divisions are often gender-linked as male or female. In same-sex couples, however, tasks are often divided pragmatically, according to considerations such as who likes cooking more (or dislikes it less) and who works when. Most gay couples are dual-worker couples; neither partner supports or depends on the other economically. And because partners in lesbian, gay, bisexual, and queer couples are or may be the same sex, the economic discrepancies based on greater male earning power are often absent. Although gay couples emphasize egalitarianism, if there are differences in power, they are attributed to personality; if there is an age difference, the older partner is usually more powerful.

In 2020, a major civil rights decision by the U.S. Supreme Court ruled that federal law protects workers from job discrimination based on a person's sexual orientation or

"To deny people their human rights is to challenge their very humanity."

—Nelson Mandela (1918–2013)

Lesbian women, including celebrities such as Ellen DeGeneres and her wife, Portia de Rossi, are increasingly accepted into mainstream media.

Lumeimages.com/123RF

"Seldom, or perhaps never, does a marriage develop into an individual relationship smoothly and without crisis; there is no coming to consciousness without pain."

—Carl Jung (1875–1961)

"Setting a good example for your children takes all the fun out of middle age."

—William Feather (1889–1981)

expression. Until that ruling, 27 states lacked laws banning such discrimination. In spite of this, the federal government has not codified any laws protecting transgender people from discrimination in housing, health care, or adoption. In fact, at the writing of this book, a record number of anti-transgender legislation and policies are making their way through state legislatures (ACLU, 2020). (See Chapter 18 for more details on anti-gay discrimination.)

● Sexuality in Middle Adulthood

In the middle-adulthood years, family and work become especially important. Personal time is spent increasingly on marital and family matters, especially if a couple has children. Sexual expression often decreases in frequency, intensity, and significance, to be replaced by family and work concerns. Sometimes, the change reflects a higher value placed on family intimacy; other times, it may reflect habit, boredom, or conflict.

Developmental Concerns

In the middle-adulthood years, some of the psychosexual developmental tasks begun in young adulthood may be continuing. These tasks, such as ones related to intimacy issues or parenting decisions, may have been deferred or only partly completed in young adulthood. Because of separation or divorce, people may find themselves facing the same intimacy and commitment tasks at age 40 that they thought they had completed 15 years earlier (Cate & Lloyd, 1992). But life does not stand still; it moves steadily forward, and other developmental issues appear, including the following:

- *Redefining sex in marital or other long-term relationships.* In new relationships, sex is often passionate and intense; it may be the central focus. But in long-term relationships, habit, competing family and work obligations, finances, fatigue, and unresolved conflicts often erode the passionate intensity associated with sexuality. Sex may need to be redefined as more of an expression of intimacy more than performances and caring. Individuals may also need to decide how to deal with the possibility, reality, and meaning of extramarital or extrarelational sex.

- *Reevaluating one's sexuality.* Single women and single men may need to weigh the benefits and costs of sex in casual or lightly committed relationships. In long-term relationships, sexuality may become less than central to relationship satisfaction, as nonsexual elements such as communication, intimacy, and shared interests and activities become increasingly important. Women who desire children and who have deferred their childbearing begin to reappraise their decision: Should they remain child-free, race against their biological clock, or adopt a child? Some people may redefine their sexual orientation and identity. One's sexual philosophy continues to evolve.

- *Accepting the biological aging process.* As people age, their skin wrinkles, their waistline increases, their flesh sags, their hair turns gray or falls out, their vision blurs—and they become, in the eyes of society, less attractive and less sexual. By their 40s, their physiological responses have begun to slow. By their 50s, society begins to "neuter" them, especially women who have gone through menopause. The challenge of aging is to come to terms with its biological changes.

Sexuality in Marriage and Established Relationships

When people marry, they may discover that their sex lives are very different from what they were before marriage. Sex is now more morally and socially sanctioned. It is in marriage that the great majority of sexual interactions take place, yet as a culture, we feel ambivalent about marital sex. On the one hand, marriage is traditionally the only relationship in which sexuality is legitimized. On the other, marital sex is an endless source of humor and ridicule.

Sexual Frequency Ask any long-term couple about their patterns of lust over time, and you'll no doubt find wide variations, from no sex to large fluctuations in desire and activity.

We're also learning that sexual frequency is declining among American adults by about nine episodes per year, based on tallies between the late 1990s and the early 2010s (Twenge et al., 2017). This was true for individuals, regardless of their gender, race, marriage status, or the region in which they lived. Declines in sexual frequency were largest among those in their 50s, those with school-age children, and those who did not watch sexually explicit videos. More recently, a survey study found that from 2000 to 2018, sexual inactivity increased among U.S. men such that approximately 1 in 3 men aged 18 to 24 reported no sexual activity in the past year. Sexual inactivity also increased among men and women aged 25 to 35 years (Ueda et al., 2020). Not having a partner, a decrease in sexual frequency for those who do have partners, and the coronavirus are contributing to this decline. Biological aging also influences the sex drive. Or, for still others, it could be the way our brains adapt from the initial surge of dopamine that prompts romance and desire to the relative quiet of an oxytocin-induced attachment. Oxytocin is a hormone that produces a feeling of connectedness and bonding. For many, a decrease in sexual frequency may simply mean that one or both partners are too tired. For dual-worker families and families with children, stress, financial worries, fatigue, and lack of private time may be the most significant factors in this decline.

The demands of parenting may diminish a couple's ability to be sexually spontaneous.

Noel Hendrickson/Digital Vision/Getty Images

Many couples don't seem to feel that declining frequency in sexual intercourse is a major problem if their overall relationship is good. Intimate sexual behavior is only one erotic bond among many in committed relationships. There are also kisses, caresses, nibbles, massages, candlelight dinners, hand-in-hand walks, and intimate words, for example, that can increase a couple's sense of connectedness. Research indicates that quality of time is more important than quantity among the most sexually happy couples (Klenplatz & Menard, 2020).

Sexual Satisfaction and Pleasure Higher levels of sexual satisfaction and pleasure typically occur in marriage than in singlehood or extramarital relationships (Laumann et al., 1994). In fact, 83% of American adults, age 21+ reported being "happy" in their romantic relationships with a partner or spouse, according to an eHarmony report (2019) involving over 2,300 online interviews of heterosexual and LGBTQ+ adults. Those who were the happiest tended to be in love, have a healthy sex life, and have an equal balance of power. They were also most likely to be younger (between the ages of 25–44), have two children, an income of $75,000 or more, and have a higher education than their counterparts (see Figure 6) (eHarmony, 2018).

The Happiness Index

What does the self-described "perfectly happy" couple look like?

Have open communication with partner

Much more likely than average to have had relationship therapy

Younger than average, at 25–44 years

They have a wide circle of friends

Personality traits: optimistic, creative, confident, sociable

More likely to have 2+ kids living in their household

They are more likely than average to be married, and tend to be on their first marriage

Likely to be the same age as their partner

Like to have regular date nights and hold hands when out together

More likely to live in the city or an urban area

Have sex much more frequently than average

Have completed a higher level of education (post grads Index highest!)

More likely than average to be first to compromise

They love activities like camping or going to the gym together

• **FIGURE 6**

The Happiness Index.

Source: eHarmony (2019). 83 percent of Americans report being "happy" in their relationship.

"Good Enough Sex": The Way to Lifetime Couple Satisfaction

Sex provides a buffet of experiences: at times, sex is enthusiastic, cheerful, erotic, gratifying and at other times uninspiring.
—Metz and McCarthy (2011)

Renowned sex therapists and authors Michael Metz and Barry McCarthy, in their book *Enduring Desire: Your Guide to Lifetime Intimacy* **(2011), challenge the current cultural models of "perfect sex" and "perfect intercourse" with an alternative concept for long-term, committed couples, the "Good Enough Sex" (GES) model.** They contend that prevailing beliefs that sex should always be perfect are toxic and can lead to disappointment and disillusionment. Unrealistic expectations about sex precipitate a sense of failure as "great sex" in committed relationships, particularly, is uneven and variable. Metz and McCarthy state that the GES model with its physical, psychological, and interpersonal dimensions is not a cop-out that leads to mediocre, boring, or mechanical sex but rather a "roadmap to a lifetime of terrific, meaningful sex, a guide to help you feel sexually satisfied, not in a fantasy world but in real life." They note that research suggests that regular, variable, and flexible couple sex that is fully integrated into real life is the best couple sex. The GES model does not lead to disappointing compromise or feelings of "selling out" but rather to feelings of relief, affirmation, and inspiration; it seeks *realistically great sex* grounded on an appreciation that variations in couple sex over time are both healthy and necessary.

The GES approach works best when one develops realistic, flexible, accurate, and positive beliefs about GES's three dimensions, what great sex is and is not, and what sex can be for "oneself." GES partners embrace concepts such as:

- Sexual satisfaction varies from one experience to the next.
- Achieving high-quality sex is a lifelong process.
- Sexual function difficulties are opportunities for increased cooperation and intimacy.
- Satisfied couples cooperate as an intimate team.
- Quality sex is flexible: You adapt to the inevitable variability and difficulties.

- Sex fits real life, and real life should be brought into the sexual relationship.
- The best sex involves being intimate and erotic partners.
- Quality sex is cooperative relationship sex.

There are numerous benefits of "Good Enough Sex." One feels self-assured and proud of being a sexual person knowing that positive, realistic expectations decrease embarrassment and shame about one's body and sexuality. A person will view sex as a normal, real, and positive part of an honest and genuine life. One adopts beliefs that sex is "decent" and wild and that passionate couple sex is "good." One accepts that sex is variable and creates flexible ways to integrate variability into the couple's life situation to enhance mutual pleasure. Partners form an intimate team to discover the meanings of sexuality and to balance eroticism and intimacy. Metz and McCarthy state that "no longer bound by shame, no longer having to be different than who you are, no longer anxiously fearing failure, and no longer pursuing perfection, you feel self assured, confident, and content."

Think Critically

1. In what ways does society stress "perfect sex"?
2. Do you think by adopting the "Good Enough Sex" approach one would be settling for mediocre and boring sex? Explain your response.
3. Is the "Good Enough Sex" approach realistic for college-age students? Why or why not?
4. If you have been in a sexual relationship, have you experienced "great sex" or "uninspiring sex"? If so, how did you deal with that? Is the "Good Enough Sex" approach a good way to deal with the variability of sex?

Adult love relationships often have numerous expectations including emotional stability, shared time and values, personal enrichment, security, and support. An essential ingredient to this mix is sex. In the eHarmony report (2019) happy couples reported having sex often and of those that did, the majority reported being very satisfied with their sex life. Couples who described being most happy placed importance on the connection that occurs from both sex and quality time together. Many acknowledged that being open-minded to new activities in the bedroom facilitated happiness. Additionally, those who made a commitment to learning each other's sexual likes and dislikes and were sensitive to the other's needs reported the greatest relational satisfaction. These feelings were shared by both heterosexual and same-sex couples.

Life Behaviors of a Sexually Healthy Adult

In 1996, the Sexuality Information and Education Council of the United States (SIECUS) published the first national guidelines for comprehensive sexuality education in kindergarten through 12th grade. These guidelines, updated in 2004, covered the life behaviors of a sexually healthy adult in six areas.

Behaviors of the Sexually Healthy Adult

1. Human development:

   a. Appreciate one's own body.
   b. Seek further information about reproduction as needed.
   c. Affirm that human development includes sexual development, which may or may not include reproduction or sexual experience.
   d. Interact with all genders in respectful and appropriate ways.
   e. Affirm one's own sexual orientation and respect the sexual orientation of others.
   f. Affirm one's own gender identities and respect the gender identities of others.

2. Relationships:

   a. Express love and intimacy in appropriate ways.
   b. Develop and maintain meaningful relationships.
   c. Avoid exploitative or manipulative relationships.
   d. Make informed choices about family options and relationships.
   e. Exhibit skills that enhance personal relationships.

3. Personal skills:

   a. Identify and live according to one's own values.
   b. Take responsibility for one's own behavior.
   c. Practice effective decision making.
   d. Develop critical thinking skills.
   e. Communicate effectively with family, peers, and romantic partners.

4. Sexual behavior:

   a. Enjoy and express one's sexuality throughout life.
   b. Express one's sexuality in ways congruent with one's values.
   c. Enjoy sexual feelings without necessarily acting on them.
   d. Discriminate between life-enhancing sexual behaviors and those that are harmful to oneself and/or others.
   e. Express one's sexuality while respecting the rights of others.
   f. Seek new information to enhance one's sexuality.
   g. Engage in sexual relationships that are consensual, nonexploitative, honest, pleasurable, and protected.

5. Sexual health:

   a. Practice health-promoting behaviors, such as regular checkups, breast and testicular self-exams, and early identification of potential problems.
   b. Use contraception effectively to avoid unintended pregnancy.
   c. Avoid contracting or transmitting an STI, including HIV.
   d. Act consistent with one's values in dealing with an unintended pregnancy.
   e. Seek early prenatal care.
   f. Help prevent sexual abuse.

6. Society and culture:

   a. Demonstrate respect for people with different sexual values.
   b. Exercise democratic responsibility to influence legislation dealing with sexual issues.
   c. Assess the impact of family, cultural, religious, media, and societal messages on one's thoughts, feelings, values, and behaviors related to sexuality.
   d. Critically examine the world around them for biases based on gender, sexual orientation, culture, ethnicity, and race.
   e. Promote the rights of all people to have access to accurate sexuality information.
   f. Avoid behaviors that exhibit prejudice and bigotry.
   g. Reject stereotypes about the sexuality of different populations.
   h. Educate others about sexuality.

Think Critically

1. Is it possible for young people to enact or achieve all of the behaviors? If so, how? If not, why not?
2. Which of the behaviors would seem to be the most difficult to achieve? Why?
3. Which of the behaviors do you believe change over the life span?
4. What life behaviors related to sexuality are missing from the list?

Source: National Guidelines Task Force. (2004). *Guidelines for Comprehensive Sexuality Education: Kindergarten–12th Grade* (3rd ed.). Sexuality Information and Education Council of the United States. Reprinted with permission.

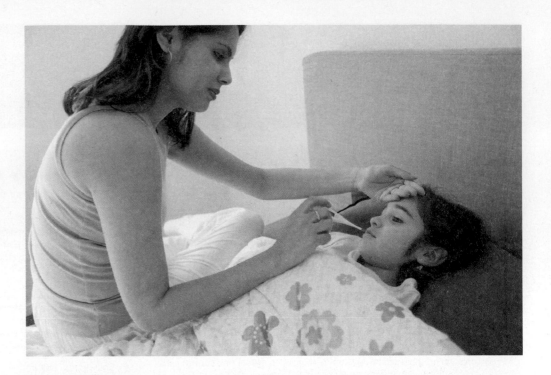

Because of their child-rearing responsibilities, single parents are often not part of the singles world.

PNC/Digital Vision/Getty Images

Divorce and After

Divorce has become a fact of life for many American families. A quick observation of demographics in this country points to a growing way of life: post-divorce singlehood. Contrary to divorce trends in the twentieth century, in recent decades the divorce rate has actually dropped. In 1990, the divorce rate was 7.2 per 1,000; in 2000, it was 6.2; and in 2018, the rate dropped to 2.9 (CDC/National Vital Statistics, 2019.7). And so while the divorce rate has been dropping among all ages, there's one exception: older people, often referred to as "gray divorce." Divorce rates have doubled among people age 50 and older in the past two decades. As the average life span lengthens, challenges negotiating later in life transitions can lead to stress and emotional turmoil. These, in turn, can cause couples to drift apart and eventually divorce. Still among those who get divorced, 40% will eventually remarry (Pew Research Center, 2017.7d). Many reasons for the declining divorce rate have been noted, including increased rates of cohabitation, later marriages, and birth control.

Scholars suggest that divorce represents not a devaluation of marriage but, oddly enough, an idealization of it. We would not divorce if we did not have such high expectations for marriage's ability to fulfill various needs. Our divorce rate further tells us that we may no longer believe in the permanence of marriage. Instead, many remain married only as long as the marriage is rewarding or until a potentially better partner comes along.

Outcomes of Divorce on Children Slightly over half of all divorces involve children. Differences between children with divorced parents and those with continuously married parents are modest and individual; thus, one should not assume that children of divorced parents have or will develop adjustment problems (Kuehnle & Drozd, 2012). In fact, encouraging views emerge from studies (see Ahrons, 2004; Amato, 2003, 2010) that demonstrate the majority of children whose parents have divorced do not suffer long-term consequences simply because of the divorce. Rather, the consequences of divorce for children and adults are contingent on the quality of family relationships prior to marital dissolution. In most cases, the way the children think and feel about the important relationships in their families are not significantly altered. In fact, most of these children grow up to be well-adjusted adults who sustain family connections and commitments.

Single Parenting In 2018, 40% of unmarried women aged 15 to 50 had a birth in the past 12 months (Martin et al., 2019). Several demographic trends have affected the shift from two-parent to one-parent families, including a larger proportion of births to unmarried women, the delay of marriage, and the increase in divorce among couples with children.

think about it

Singles in America: Dating Trends, Social Media & Fatigue

We shouldn't be surprised to know that singles of all ages in America have a lot to say about sexuality, particularly as it relates to trends around dating, gender roles, and of all things dating fatigue. Over the course of nearly a decade, Match.com (2019) has released nine large-scale studies involving adults ages 18–70+. New data from 5,000+ single men and women living across the U.S. reveal current trends, including how America's singles are searching for romance yet at the same time are fatigued by the process. The study also uncovered the sexual habits of Gen X (ages 39–54) and Millennials (ages 22–38), and how men are responding to the #MeToo movement. The results provide the most comprehensive study ever on American singles. What may not be surprising to learn is that, according to Helen Fisher, biological anthropologist and Chief Scientific Advisor to Match (2019):

Modern love, sex, and romance are thriving in America—from Millennials to seniors. The current fear that the young don't care about love and commitment is just plain wrong. They are simply having a hard time finding it and feeling burnt out by the search.

One recent trend reported from singles of all generations was dating burnout, described as "fatigue" from searching for a relationship. While 83% of respondents felt that love is hard to find, 43% believed that technology has made finding love even more difficult. When asked their feelings about today's dating world, single's responses included: "overwhelming" and "unkind." Still the vast majority of singles (75%) were hopeful that love was accessible, and nearly 60% were motivated to find romantic love and a long-term companion. Only 9% were looking to date casually (Match.com, 2019).

According to Justin Garcia, Executive Director of The Kinsey Institute and scientific advisor to this Match.com study, dating rituals and gender roles are fully integrated into society which helps explain the gap between what individuals say they want and what they do on dates. For example, who pays for the meal and who initiates the first or second date? Although women are still fighting for equality in most areas of life, many still want men to initiate a date. Additionally, many still feel bound by traditional courtship rituals. For example, 73% of young men are comfortable when a woman first says "hello" on a dating app, yet only 29% of young women take the lead. And 83% of young men would be happy if a woman initiated the first kiss, but only 23% of young women often do. When asked about #MeToo and dating, half of men said that the #MeToo movement has caused them to act differently, nearly 40% stated that they are more reserved towards female colleagues at work, and 34% said that because of the movement they act more reserved or cautious on a date. Only 14% have found the #MeToo movement has made dating more challenging.

Some recent trends in dating are not only shifting gender norms and dating rituals, they are also revealing the challenges presented by social media and technology. Courtship is taking on a renewed significance and singles of all ages are looking at dating in broader ways:

- 40% of young singles feel they need self-acceptance before they seek love, 23% say they need to reach a certain point in their career, and 20% feel they must reach a certain income level before committing to a serious relationship. Economics was an important issue for 33% of young singles who say that their financial situation has held them back from pursuing romance.

- Most singles are now meeting through dating apps. More than half of young singles have created a dating profile and 68% say they carefully evaluate profiles.

- Disturbing behavior is still something that singles are dealing with. For example, among young singles who have dated in the last year, 40% have been "ghosted" (relationship has ended without communication or an explanation), 21% have believed that a relationship was exclusive when it was not, and 28% had someone try to initiate a sexual liaison.

Though a "sex drought" has been reported in the literature, the survey revealed that 49% of Gen Z (ages 18–22) and Millennials are motivated to find a sex partner. Most reported being sexually active within the last week. When asked how often they'd like to have sex the majority of Gen Z and Millennials said 2 to 3 times per week.

Research on dating is not limited only to straight persons. In another study Match (2016) surveyed 1,000 LGBTQ+ singles between the ages of 18 and 70+ across the United States. The study findings revealed that dating online plays a significant role in 56% of LGBTQ+ singles' lives (Match, 2016). Transgender singles used online dating sources 65% of the time. Assuming nonprescribed gender roles among trans people, issues such as initiating dates, "first moves," and who pays for the date were individual's choices, not prescribed by gender. On the first date, 57% of LGBTQ+ singles expected a kiss, while 25% expected deep, passionate kissing. Only 9% expected sexual intercourse (16% of gay men and 2% of lesbian women). Thirty percent don't expect any physical activity at all.

When it comes to dating, what is clear, according to Justin Garcia, is that:

. . .an enthusiastic, caring, and communicative partner are the key ingredients for a pleasurable sexual experience, which further emphasizes that affirmative consent and mutual respect and engagement are paramount to good sex.

Think Critically

1. Can you relate to any of these results? If so, explain.
2. If you are single and dating, what in your dating experience has been positive and negative? Regardless of your dating status, how comfortable are you communicating your desires and opinions?
3. Have you experienced dating fatigue? What might have caused it? How might you resolve it?

Source: Adapted from Match.com (2016, 2019). Singles in America: March releases ninth annual study on U.S. single population and Match releases new study on LGBTQ+ single population.

Single parents are not often a part of the singles world, which involves more than simply not being married. It generally requires leisure and money, both of which single parents, especially women, generally lack because of their family responsibilities.

Dating Again   A first date after years of marriage and subsequent months of singlehood evokes some of the same emotions felt by inexperienced adolescents. Separated or divorced men and women who are beginning to date again may be excited and nervous; worry about how they look; and wonder whether it's OK to hold hands, kiss, or be sexual. They may believe that dating is incongruous with their former selves, or they may be annoyed with themselves for feeling excited and awkward. Furthermore, they may know little about the norms of postmarital dating.

Sexual activity is an important component in the lives of separated and divorced individuals. Engaging in sexual behavior with someone for the first time following separation may help some people accept their newly acquired single status.

● Sexuality in Late Adulthood

Sexual feelings and desires continue throughout the life cycle. Though many of the standards of activity or attraction are constant, it may be necessary for each of us to overcome the taboos and stereotypes associated with sex and aging in order to create a place for its expression in our lives.

Developmental Concerns

Many of the psychosexual tasks older Americans must undertake are directly related to the aging process, including the following (Das et al., 2012; DeLamater & Sill, 2005):

- *Biological changes.* As older men's and women's physical abilities change with age, their sexual responses change as well. As men and women continue to age, their sexuality tends to be more diffuse, less genitally oriented, and less insistent. Chronic illness, hormonal changes, vascular changes, and increasing frailty understandably result in diminished sexual activity. These considerations contribute to the ongoing evolution of the individual's sexual philosophy.

- *Death of a partner.* One of the most critical life events is the loss of a partner. After age 60, there is a significant increase in spousal deaths. Because having a partner is the single most important factor determining an older person's sexual interactions, the absence of a sexual partner signals a dramatic change in the survivor's sexual interactions.

- *Psychological influences.* Given America's obsession with youth and sexuality, it is not surprising that many people consider it inappropriate for older men and women to continue to be sexually active. To the contrary, many older persons have a fulfilling and pleasurable sex life. Such factors as lack of sexual information, negative attitudes toward sexual expression, and mental health problems, including depression or dementia (along with the treatments that remedy them), may interfere with older individuals' ability or willingness to see themselves as sexual beings.

Older adults negotiate these issues within the context of continuing aging. Resolving them as we age helps us accept the eventuality of our death.

Stereotypes of Aging

Our society stereotypes aging as a lonely and depressing time, but most studies of older adults find that, relative to younger people, they express high levels of satisfaction and well-being. However, poverty, loneliness, and poor health can also make old age difficult. Even so, older people have a lower poverty rate than younger adults and children. More importantly and depending on their age, many older people experience few restrictions on their activities because of health.

"You have to accept the fact that part of the sizzle of sex comes from the danger of sex."

—Camille Paglia (1947–)

"The bed: A place where marriages are decided."

—Anonymous

Regardless of our age, sexual behavior is part of being human.

Jean Mounicq/Roger-Viollet/The Image Works

The sexuality of older Americans tends to be invisible, as society discounts it. Many older adults themselves have internalized negative stereotypes about their sexuality, because, in part, they have been denied important sexual health information and legitimization of their sexual interests. A narrow definition of sex, which focuses almost exclusively on intercourse, also contributes to this problem. The outcome for many older adults is a reported disinterest or sexual function difficulties for themselves and/or a dislike of their partner's interest in sex (Foley, 2015).

Sexuality and Aging

Older adults nonetheless are interested in sex, have sex, and enjoy sex. However, cultural attitudes along with health appear to influence whether sex among older individuals is encouraged or discouraged. Sexual expression has historically been viewed in the United States as an activity reserved for young and newly partnered people. However, this viewpoint is not universally accepted. Cross-cultural studies show that in many countries sexual activity is not only accepted but also expected among older adults.

"You only possess what will not be lost in a shipwreck."

—Al Ghazali (1058–1111)

For many older adults, sex remains important and a source of pleasure and because of this knowledge, many older individuals share the view that sex extends beyond coitus. Dispelling the belief that "having sex" is strictly limited to vaginal or anal penetration allows adults to share in mutual pleasure and touch. This knowledge can take the pressure off performance to allow individuals to experience the breadth of behaviors that are inherent in sexuality. In fact, partnered individuals aged 57–85 demonstrated that although sexual frequency may decline with age, the frequency of noncoital sexual activities, such as kissing, caressing, and cuddling, was not associated with age (Waite et al., 2009).

We know that sexual behavior is a natural part of being human, but what we may not yet totally understand is how sexual interactions differ by the length of the relationship, life's circumstances, and the perspectives that individuals bring to it. A University of Michigan (2018) study consisting of more than 1,000 Americans found that 40% of those between ages 65 and 89 are sexually active (see Table 1). And regardless of whether or not they had a partner, two-thirds of respondents acknowledged that they were interested in sex and more than half said that sex was important to their quality of life. What satisfying sex means differs from person to person and can evolve over time. For example, some older adults may be less concerned with sexual intercourse than with the feelings of closeness, erotic connection, and self-validation that accompany sex. This may be especially true for those who have physical limitations that make certain sexual behaviors and expectations a challenge. What changes for many is that pleasure and pleasuring may take precedence over sexual performance or orgasm. (See Table 6 in Chapter 9 to learn the incidence of sexual behaviors among persons ages 70 and older.) All of these factors may help explain why over 70% of the respondents in the University of Michigan study (2018) said they felt satisfied with their sex lives. Differences in responses between women and men were noteworthy, with men more likely to report being interested in sex, acknowledging that it was important to their quality of life. Women, on the other hand, were more likely to report that they were satisfied with their sex lives.

As the number of Americans aged 50 and older increases, sexual interests and health need to be discussed. Sexual health is associated with quality of life, positive relationships, and physical and mental well-being (Forbes et al., 2017). Given that much of the empirical literature on sexual expression in later life is focused on function and dysfunction, it's important to know how sexual wellness is defined and measured by those in middle and older adulthood. In a study involving 373 participants, ages 50 or older (mean age 60) researchers asked individuals what sexual wellness meant to them, both in middle and older adulthood (Smith et al., 2019) (see Tables 1 and 2). The researchers examined three themes of sexual wellness: biological/behavioral (i.e., sexual response and sexual risk), psychological (i.e., cognition, emotions, and feelings), and social (i.e., quality, commitment level, and type of relationship). A clear message emerged from the data which was that participants' sexual wellness

TABLE 1 ● Sexual Activity, Functioning, and Concerns and Satisfaction in Relation to Enjoyment of Life Among Older Adults		
	Men (n = 3,045) ± SEM Yes, %	**Women (n = 3,834)** ± SEM Yes, %
Sexual activity		
Any sexual activity in the past year	76.9	57.8
Frequent sexual intercourse[†]	45.9	49.3
Frequent kissing, petting, or fondling[†]	64.3	67.1
Frequent masturbation[†]	42.0	15.0
Sexual function		
Erectile difficulties	42.7	—
Difficulty becoming sexually aroused[‡]	—	33.1
Difficulty achieving orgasm[‡]	17.5	26.4
Sexual health concerns		
Concerned about. . .		
Level of sexual desire	13.5	7.6
Frequency of sexual activities[†]	13.7	8.2
Ability to have an erection	14.6	—
Ability to become sexually aroused[‡]	—	8.2
Orgasmic experience[‡]	12.1	6.7
Sexual satisfaction		
Emotionally close to partner[§]	94.4	92.0
Satisfied with overall sex life[§]	78.6	87.3

[†]In participants reporting any sexual activity in past year.

[‡]In participants reporting any sexual activity in past month.

[§]In participants reporting any sexual activity with a partner in the past 3 months.

Source: Smith, et al. (2019). Sexual activity is associated with greater enjoyment of life in older adults. *Sexual Medicine, 7*(11), 11–18.

TABLE 2 ● Sexual Intercourse Frequency, Gender Gaps, and Sexual Satisfaction Among Older Adults

	Sex is an important part of a romantic relationship at any age (n = 989)	Sex is important to my overall quality of life. (n = 989)	How would you describe your interest in sex? (n = 979)	How satisfied are you with your sex life? (n = 959)
	Percent that strongly agreed or agreed	Percent that strongly agreed or agreed	Percent that were extremely or very interested	Percent that were extremely or very interested
All respondents	76%	54%	30%	37%
Age				
65–70	78%	57%	34%	38%
71–75	72%	52%	28%	37%
76–80	77%	50%	19%	36%
Gender				
Male	84%	70%	50%	31%
Female	69%	40%	12%	43%
Relationship status				
Married/Partnered/In a relationship	76%	61%	34%	40%
Not in a relationship	75%	36%	19%	30%
Physical health				
Excellent/Very good/Good	77%	56%	32%	40%
Fair/Poor	71%	49%	21%	28%
Sexually active				
Yes	92%	83%	52%	49%
No	66%	35%	16%	29%

Margin of error ± 3 to 8 percentage points.

Source: University of Michigan (2018). National poll on healthy aging.

was impacted by a number of diverse factors. These included biological and physical functioning, that took into consideration natural changes in sexual response, cognitive flexibility, including an open and a flexible outlook, and sexual self-esteem, or feelings of being desirable and capable of being involved in sexual practices and outcomes. Partnerships also exerted significant influence on sexual wellness as there are limited opportunities for relationships in later life, particularly for women. The findings suggest that flexibility and being adaptive are key traits in experiencing rewarding sexual experiences.

Even though the frequency of sexual activity declines from ages 50–80, it by no means disappears. Since many older adults are now living into their 80s and beyond, it will become increasingly important to provide education about and support for the sexual vitality that exists in all of us, regardless of our age.

Among older LGBQ+ couples, as well as heterosexual ones, the happiest are those with a strong commitment to the relationship. The need for intimacy, companionship, and purpose transcends issues of sexual orientation and gender identity.

Women's Issues   Beginning sometime in their 40s, most women start to experience a normal biological process resulting in a decline in fertility. This period of gradual change and adjustment is referred to as perimenopause. During this time, the ovaries' production of estrogen and progesterone varies greatly. As a result, menstruation and ovulation become irregular and eventually stop, usually between the ages of 45 and 55. But this transition can also happen anytime from the 30s to the mid-50s or later. Perimenopause usually occurs over a period of about 7 years, but can last up to 14 years. The average age of **menopause**, a point in time 12 months after a woman's last menstrual period, is 51 (National Institute on Aging, 2017.7a). A woman can also undergo menopause as a result of a **hysterectomy**, the surgical removal of the uterus, if both ovaries are also removed. In postmenopausal women, estrogen levels are about one tenth of those in premenopausal women, and progesterone is nearly absent. Most women experience some physiological or psychological symptoms during menopause including (Gunter, 2019; National Institute of Aging, 2017):

- *Changes in menstrual period.* Periods may be shorter or last longer, and bleeding can be more or less than usual.

- *Hot flashes.* These are the result of falling estrogen levels, which cause the body's "thermostat" in the brain to trigger dilation (expansion) of blood vessels near the skin's surface, producing a sensation of heat. Red blotches may accompany the hot flashes, along with heavy sweating and sometimes cold shivering. Hot flashes typically last from 15 seconds to 1 hour in length. While hot flashes usually diminish within 2 years of the menopausal transition, many women experience them for more than 7 years.

- *Vaginal and vulvar changes.* Dropping levels of estrogen may cause the skin of the vulva and vagina to become thinner, the labia minora to reduce in size, and vaginal dryness to occur. Approximately 50% of women report symptoms of **genitourinary syndrome** which consists of various menopausal symptoms and involving genital irritation (dryness and burning), sexual issues (discomfort or pain and impaired function), and urinary problems (urgency, painful or leaking or incontinence).

- *Changes in sleep.* A common occurrence, changes in patterns of sleep may be related night sweats or hot flashes experienced as heavy perspiration that occur during sleep.

- *Sex.* Either increased or less interest in sex can occur. After 1 year without a period, a woman can no longer become pregnant; however, she can still be at risk for STIs or HIV infection.

- *Mood changes.* While it is unclear why some women are more moody or irritable during menopause, mood changes may be related to an "empty nest," declining health, depression, or feeling tired.

- *Changes in the body.* Some women's waist size increases, muscle mass declines, skin becomes thinner, memory problems may occur, and joints and muscles may feel stiff or achy.

The physical effects of menopause may be reduced by a diet low in saturated fat and high in fiber, calcium, and vitamin D to reduce risk of osteoporosis; weight-bearing exercise; maintenance of a healthy weight; topical lubricants to counteract vaginal dryness; and Kegel exercises to strengthen pelvic floor muscles. Frequent masturbation by oneself or partner may help maintain vaginal moistness and well-being. For women who smoke, quitting provides many benefits as does the avoidance of trigger foods, including alcohol and caffeine (North American Menopause Society, 2020).

Menopausal Hormone Therapy Menopause is a normal part of life, not a disease that needs to be treated. However, for approximately 9% of women, the effects are severe enough to use menopausal hormone therapy (North American Menopause Society, 2020).

Some women seek help from a physician to relieve the symptoms of menopause. As a result, they may be prescribed **menopausal hormone therapy (MHT)**, also called hormone therapy or hormone replacement therapy. This involves the use of estrogen or a combination of estrogen with progesterone, or progestin in its synthetic form. As you recall, these hormones normally help regulate a woman's menstrual cycle.

Over time, two competing perspectives have been presented about menopausal hormone therapy: take hormones to stay young and stave off menopause-related problems, or avoid hormones because they will cause breast cancer and other diseases. A consensus is that hormone therapy is considered to be good for some but not all women. The North American

Menopause Society (2020), the American Society for Reproductive Medicine (2020), and the Endocrine Society (2016) state that most healthy, recently menopausal women can use hormone therapy for relief of their symptoms of hot flashes and vaginal dryness. The optimal intervention, however, depends on the woman, the severity of her symptoms, and whether she also needs birth control.

Today, more options than ever exist for hormone treatment that include pills, skin patches, and vaginal delivery products, the latter of which is effective for treating vaginal dryness that interferes with sexual intercourse. While some women may choose bioidentical hormones, which are similar to those that the body makes, there is no evidence for their safety or effectiveness (Gunter, 2019).

Different from low-dose vaginal estrogen, systemic estrogen is an option for postmenopausal women who don't get sufficient relief from vaginal atrophy, or thinning, drying, or inflammation of the vaginal walls (WebMD, 2018). Systemic hormone therapy contains either estrogen alone or estrogen plus progesterone. Estrogen alone is used for postmenopausal women who have had a hysterectomy as taking estrogen alone raises the risk of uterine cancer. Low-dose vaginal products, including creams, tablet or ring form, minimize the amount of estrogen absorbed by the body and are used to treat vaginal and urinary symptoms. Adding progestin protects against the risk of uterine cancer; hence estrogen and progestin taken together are used for postmenopausal women who still have their uterus.

Depending on the form of delivery (i.e., pill, vaginal delivery), dosage, woman's age, medical history, and personal preferences, there are benefits and risks of hormone therapy, including (MedlinePlus, 2018; WebMD, 2018):

Benefits:

- Relieves hot flashes and night sweats
- Helps with sleep
- Eases vaginal dryness and itching, which can also make sex less painful
- Helps prevent fractures caused by osteoporosis (thinning bones)
- Lowers risk of blood clots and strokes if applied to the skin or low-doses of estrogen pills are taken

Marital satisfaction and emotional health foster the desire for emotional intimacy. The greatest determinants of an older person's sexual activity are the availability of a partner and health.

Purestock/PunchStock

Risks:

- Endometrial cancer, if estrogen is taken without progestin (a synthetic version of progesterone) and a woman still has her uterus
- Heart disease
- Blood clots (primarily among those who take oral preparations)
- Stroke
- Breast cancer

Because systemic hormone therapy has been associated with increased risks of severe health outcomes, especially among older women and with longer duration of use, it is recommended that women take the lowest possible dose for the shortest amount of time to relieve symptoms of menopause (North American Menopause Society, 2020).

Men's Issues Changes in male sexual responsiveness begin to become apparent when men are in their 40s and 50s, a period of change referred to as the male climacteric, andropause, or sometimes manopause. For a minority of men, these physical changes of aging including hair loss, weight gain, and decreased muscle mass and strength may be accompanied by experiences such as fatigue, an inability to concentrate, depression, loss of appetite, and a decreased interest in sex. As a man ages, his frequency of sexual activity declines, attaining erection requires more stimulation and time, and the erection may not be as firm. Ejaculation takes longer and may not occur every time the penis is stimulated; also, the force of the ejaculation is less than before, as is the amount of ejaculate; and the refractory period is extended up to 24 hours or longer in older men. Approximately 80% of men ages 40 to 75 have erectile difficulties (ED) to some degree, with nearly 50% of men 75 or older unable to have an erection sufficient for intercourse (Harvard Health Publishing, 2020). However, sexual interest and enjoyment generally do not decrease, as witnessed by the frequency and variety of sexual activity reported by older men. Although some of the changes are related directly to age and a normal decrease in testosterone production, others may be the result of diseases and conditions associated with aging. Poor general health, obesity, urinary tract infections, diabetes, atherosclerosis, and some medications can contribute to sexual function problems.

Slower responses are a normal aspect of aging in men and are unrelated to the ability to give or receive sexual pleasure. "The senior penis," wrote Bernie Zilbergeld (1999), "can still give and take pleasure, even though it's not the same as it was decades ago." (Prescription drugs that aid men in getting erections are available, and are discussed in more detail in Chapter 14.)

About half of men over age 50 are affected to some degree by **benign prostatic hyperplasia (BPH)**, an enlargement of the prostate gland. The healthy prostate is about the size of a walnut and as a man ages, it can grow to the size of a lemon. By age 70, almost all men have some prostate enlargement. BPH is not linked to cancer and does not raise a man's chance of getting prostate cancer, yet the symptoms of BPH and prostate cancer can be similar. The enlarged prostate may put pressure on the urethra, resulting in difficulty urinating and the frequent and urgent need to urinate. It does not affect sexual functioning. BPH symptoms do not always get worse. At the same time, BPH cannot be cured, but drugs can often relieve its symptoms. If the blockage of the urethra is too severe, surgery can correct the problem (Harvard Men's Health Watch, 2019).

Testosterone Supplementation As you may recall, testosterone plays an important role in puberty and throughout a man's life. Although it is the main sex hormone of men, women also produce small amounts of it. Testosterone production is the highest in adolescence and early adulthood and declines as a man ages. But the chance that a man will ever experience a major shutdown of hormone production similar to a woman's menopause is remote. Most older men maintain a sufficient amount for normal functioning.

As men age, changes such as less energy and strength, decreased bone density, and erectile difficulties may occur; these changes are often erroneously blamed on decreasing testosterone levels. Because of changes like these—particularly sexual declines—many older men consider taking supplemental testosterone. Though many middle-aged and older men take testosterone supplements because they feel it will improve their sex life, recent guidelines from the American College of Physicians suggest that clinicians not initiate testosterone treatment in men with age-related low testosterone to improve energy, vitality, physical function, or cognition (Qaseem et al., 2020). It is still unclear whether changes in nonspecific signs and symptoms associated with age-related low testosterone, including sexual functioning difficulties, decreases in energy and muscle mass, mood disturbances, and cardiovascular disease are a consequence of age-related low testosterone or the result of other factors such as chronic illnesses or concomitant medications. Consumers should be aware that testosterone supplementation may increase the risk of heart attacks and strokes. Until more rigorous scientific studies are conducted, indiscriminate use of testosterone by men whose levels of testosterone are low-normal is not warranted.

Final Thoughts

Laura Doss/Image Source/Getty Images

As this chapter has shown, psychosexual development occurs on a continuum rather than as a series of discrete stages. Each person develops in his or her own way, according to personal and social circumstances and the dictates of biology. In early adulthood, tasks that define adult sexuality include establishing sexual orientation, making commitments, entering long-term intimate relationships, and deciding whether or not to have children. None of these challenges is accomplished overnight, nor does a task necessarily end as a person moves into a new stage of life.

In middle adulthood, individuals face new tasks involving the nature of their long-term relationships. Often, these tasks involve reevaluating these relationships. As people enter late adulthood, they need to adjust to the aging process—to changed sexual responses and needs, declining physical health, the loss of a partner, and their own eventual death. Each stage is filled with its own unique meaning, which gives shape and significance to life and to sexuality.

Summary

Sexuality in Early Adulthood

- Several tasks challenge young adults as they develop their sexuality, including establishing a sexual orientation, integrating love and sex, and making fertility/childbearing decisions.

- As our views of gender, masculinity, and femininity have changed, so have the ways that we conceptualize sexual orientation.

- The increase in the number of single adults in the United States has resulted in more sexual experience and sex partners and a widespread acceptance of cohabitation.

- For sexual minorities, the college environment is often liberating because of greater acceptance.

- Among single men and women not or no longer attending college, meeting others can be a problem. Singles often meet via the Internet and at work, clubs, events, and housing complexes.

- Racism, homophobia, and transphobia result in critical and disproportionate disparities among sexual minorities of color.

- *Cohabitation* has become more widespread and accepted in recent years. *Domestic partnerships* provide some legal protection for cohabiting couples in committed relationships.

Sexuality in Middle Adulthood

- Developmental issues of sexuality in middle adulthood include redefining sex in long-term relationships, reevaluating one's sexuality, and accepting the biological aging process.

- In marriage and long-term partnerships, sexual activity tends to diminish in frequency the longer a couple is partnered or married. Most partnered couples don't feel that declining frequency is a major problem if their overall relationship is good.

- Divorce rates in the United States have steadily declined. Single parents are usually not a part of the singles world, because the presence of children constrains their freedom.

Sexuality in Late Adulthood

- Many of the psychosexual tasks older Americans must undertake are directly related to the aging process, including changing sexuality and the loss of a partner. Most studies of older adults find that they express relatively high levels of satisfaction and well-being. Older adults' sexuality tends to be invisible because society associates sexuality and romance with youthfulness and procreation.

- Although some physical functions may be slowed by aging, sexual interest and satisfaction remain high for many older people. Diminished sexual activity for both men and women is primarily due to health issues and/or loss of a partner.

- In their 40s, women's fertility begins to decline. Generally, between ages 45 and 55, *menopause,* cessation of menstrual periods, occurs. Other physical changes occur, which may or may not present problems. *Menopausal hormone therapy* (*MHT*) may be used to treat these symptoms, though a woman should evaluate the benefits versus the risks.

- Slower responses are a normal aspect of aging in men and are unrelated to the ability to give or receive sexual pleasure. It is not recommended that testosterone treatment be given to men to improve energy, vitality, physical function, or cognition.

Questions for Discussion

- **The text describes some of the challenges faced by people who choose to live together without marrying. Should society support cohabitation regardless of sexual orientation by providing tax benefits or acknowledging domestic partnerships? If so, how? If not, why not?**

- **Given the three models of sexual orientation (see Figure 2), which model do you think is most accurate? Can you find a place for yourself within each model?**

- **Many changes have taken place in marriage policies, and there has been liberalization of divorce laws. Has it become too easy to get divorced? What factors do you feel contribute to long-term partnerships?**

Sex and the Internet

Sexuality in Early Adulthood

Go Ask Alice! is the health question-and-answer Internet service produced by Alice!, Columbia University's Health Promotion Program, a division of its Health Services. This site has three primary features: It provides recently published inquiries and responses, lets you find health information by subject via a search of the ever-growing Go Ask Alice! Archives, and gives you the chance to ask and submit a question to Alice, a team of Columbia University health promotion specialists.

To access the site, go to http://www.goaskalice.columbia.edu and follow the link to "Health Answers." From there, go to "Sexual and Reproductive Health" and select two topics. In each one of these, prepare a summary of what you have learned. Would you recommend this site to others? Why or why not? Would you feel comfortable entering your own response? What position did you take on the issue that you investigated?

Suggested Websites

AARP, Inc. (formerly American Association of Retired Persons)

AARP.org

A nonprofit organization with a mission to enhance the quality of life for all as they age. Offers information and advocacy around many topics, including sexuality.

American College Health Association

https://www.acha.org

Provides advocacy, education, and research for and about college-age students.

American Institute of Bisexuality

https://www.bi.org/en

Encourages, supports, and assists research and education about bisexuality.

National Institute on Aging

https://www.nia.nih.gov

Leads the federal government's efforts on aging research.

North American Menopause Society (NAMS)

www.menopause.org

Promotes the health and quality of life of women during midlife and beyond through education about menopause and healthy aging. Sponsors a free mobile app (MenoPro) that can calculate a woman's 10-year risk of disease and lifestyle modifications to reduce hot flashes and other problems associated with menopause.

Singles in America
https://www.singlesinamerica.com
Comprehensive studies produced by Match.com that focus on relationships, desires, love, and other topics related to single Americans.

The Williams Institute
https://williamsinstitute.law.ucla.edu
Advances sexual orientation law and public policy through research.

Suggested Reading

Bell, L. C. (2013). *Hard to get: 20-something women and the paradox of sexual freedom.* University of California Press. Three archetypes of women, the sexual, relational, and desiring women are examined in light of the cruel paradox that young women face.

Doskow, E., & Hertz, F. (2018). *Making it legal: A guide to same-sex marriage, domestic partnerships & civil unions.* (5th ed.). NOLO. Answers many questions, including those about taxes, family, and a living trust, that same-sex couples should discuss before getting married.

Hertz, F., & Guillen, L. (2020). *Living together: A legal guide for unmarried couples.* (17th ed.). NOLO. Written by two attorneys, a trusted source of the how, when, where, and why of the laws and protections for those who live together.

Savage, D. (2013). *American Savage: Insights, slights, and fights over faith, sex, love and politics.* Plume. The advice columnist and talk show personality provides a thought-provoking collection of essays about sexuality and life.

Traister, R. (2016). *All the single ladies.* Simon & Schuster. Traces the history of single women in America and the social, economic, and political means necessary to advance them.

Zilbergeld, B., & Zilbergeld, G. (2010). *Sex and love at midlife: It's better than ever.* Crown. A guide for couples who wish to maintain a passionate relationship.

chapter

8

Love and Communication in Intimate Relationships

Thinkstock/Getty Images

CHAPTER OUTLINE

Student Voices

"Because my mother was both a raving drug addict and a loving warm mother, I grew up with a very dualistic look at women. I can be madly in love with them and bitterly hate them at the same time. This affects all of my relationships with women. I truly love them and can feel so connected to them one day, but other days I am so distant from them that I begin to wonder if I am there myself."

—22-year-old male

"My grandfather, being a Hindustani priest, talks to me a lot about love. It was not through a lecture but through stories he told from the Gita [somewhat like an Indian Bible]. Spending time with him, I learned to respect sex, even though he never plain-out meant it; he described how marriage is a love bond between two people who share mind, body, and soul with each other and no one else. These stories like Kama Sutra and Ramayan sound so beautiful. Because of his influence,

I want to try my best to wait to have sex until I meet my soulmate."

—19-year-old female

"I have difficulty trusting women. Getting close to my girlfriend has been difficult. My first reaction in most instances is to wonder what her ulterior motive is. Being intimate is tough for me because most of those I have trusted have betrayed me. Sometimes I feel like I am alone for the simple fact that I don't know how to act when I am with people."

—23-year-old male

"Through high school and college, my relationship with my father grew. . . . During the time I lived with my father, I noticed his inability to express his emotions and his closed relationships with others. Thankfully, I have not yet noticed this rubbing off on my relationships or me."

—20-year-old male

L OVE IS ONE of the most profound human emotions, and it manifests itself in various forms across all cultures. In our culture, love binds us together as partners, parents, children, and friends. It is a powerful force in the intimate relationships of almost all individuals, regardless of their sexual orientation, and it crosses all ethnic boundaries. We often make major life decisions, such as whether or not to have children, based on love. We make sacrifices for it, sometimes giving up even our lives for those we love. We may even become obsessed with love. Popular culture in America glorifies it in music, films, and print and on the Internet and television. Individuals equate romantic love with marriage and often assess the quality of their partnerships by what they consider love to be.

Love is both a feeling and an activity. We can feel love for someone and act in a loving manner. But we can also be angry with the person we love, or feel frustrated, bored, or indifferent. This is the paradox of love: it encompasses opposites. A loving relationship includes affection and anger, excitement and boredom, stability and change, bonds and freedom. Its paradoxical quality makes some ask whether they are really in love when they are not feeling "perfectly" in love or when their relationship is not going smoothly. Love does not give us perfection, however; it gives us meaning. In fact, as sociologist Ira Reiss (1980) suggests, a more important question to ask is not if one is feeling love, but "Is the love I feel the kind of love on which I can build a lasting relationship or marriage?"

Communication is the thread that connects sexuality and intimacy. The quality of the communication affects the quality of the relationship, and the quality of the relationship affects the quality of the sexual interaction. Good relationships tend to feature good sex; bad relationships often feature bad sex. Sexuality, in fact, frequently serves as a barometer for the quality of the relationship. The ability to communicate about sex is important in developing and maintaining both sexual and relationship satisfaction. People who are satisfied with their sexual communication also tend to be satisfied with their relationships as a whole. Effective communication skills do not necessarily appear when a person "falls in love"; they can, however, be learned with practice.

"Love doesn't make the world go round. Love is what makes the ride worthwhile."

—Franklin P. Jones (1853–1935)

At the start of a romantic relationship, it is often impossible to tell whether one's feelings are infatuation or the beginning of love.

Fuse/Getty Images

"A friend may well be reckoned a masterpiece of nature."

—Ralph Waldo Emerson (1803–1882)

"Familiar acts are beautiful through love."

—Percy Bysshe Shelley (1792–1822)

Most of the time, we don't think about our ability to communicate. Only when problems arise do we consciously think about it. Then we become aware of our limitations in communicating or, more often, our perceptions of the limitations of others: "You just don't get it, do you?" or "You're not listening to me." And as we know, communication failures are marked by frustration.

In this chapter, we examine the relationship between sex, love, and communication and look at the always perplexing question of the nature of love. Next, we explore sex outside of committed relationships and examine the ways that social scientists study love to gain new insights into it. We then turn to the darker side of love—jealousy—to understand its dynamics. We see how love transforms itself from passion to intimacy, providing the basis for long-lasting relationships. We then examine the characteristics of communication and the way different contexts affect it. We discuss forms of nonverbal communication, such as touch, which are especially important in sexual relationships. Then we look at the different ways we communicate about sex in intimate relationships and explore ways we can develop our communication skills in order to enhance our relationships. Finally, we look at the different types of conflicts in intimate relationships and at methods for resolving them.

● Friendship and Love

Friendship and love breathe life into humanity. They bind us together, provide emotional sustenance, buffer us against stress, and help preserve our physical and mental well-being.

What distinguishes love from friendship? Research has found that, although love and friendship are alike in many ways, some crucial differences make love relationships both more rewarding and more vulnerable (Davis & Todd, 1985). Best-friend relationships are similar to spouse/lover relationships in several ways: levels of acceptance, trust, respect, confiding, understanding, spontaneity, and mutual acceptance. Levels of satisfaction and happiness with the relationship are also similar for both groups. What separates friends from lovers is that lovers have much more fascination and a greater sense of exclusiveness with their partners than do friends. Though love has a greater potential for distress, conflict, and mutual criticism, it runs deeper and stronger than friendship.

Friendship appears to be the foundation for a strong love relationship. Shared interests and values, acceptance, trust, understanding, and enjoyment are at the root of friendship and a basis for love. Adding the dimensions of passion and emotional intimacy alters the nature of the friendship and creates new expectations and possibilities.

With individuals marrying later than ever before, close friendships are more likely to be a part of the tapestry of relationships in their lives. In fact, increased happiness levels that have been found to be linked with marriage are also true for best-friend couples who lived together, even if they weren't married (Brodwin, 2015). The happiness described by these couples was tied to their friendship. Regardless of their living situation, almost half of mixed-sex friends experience romantic attraction at some point (Flora, 2016). At the same time, best friends report that the friendship is not necessarily weakened or doomed because of this attraction. When one individual feels a sense of attraction, the friends may need to reaffirm the importance of their bond and possibly renegotiate the terms of their friendship. For those individuals who enjoy the support of good friends outside their romantic relationship, partners need to also communicate and seek understanding regarding the degree of emotional closeness they find acceptable. Boundaries should be clarified and opinions shared. Many couples find friendships acceptable and even desirable. Like other significant issues involving partnerships, success in balancing a love relationship and other friendships depends on the ability to communicate concerns, the maturity of the people involved, and willingness to understand the mix of friendship and love as it affects marital satisfaction.

For many, friends are their primary partners through life: the ones that support them when they are moving out of bad relationships, encourage them during job interviews and stressful days, and support them through births and deaths. As so many millions of young people remain unmarried for longer periods of their lives, friends play an increasingly significant role in people's lives.

● Love and Sexuality

Love and sexuality are intimately intertwined. Although marriage was once the only acceptable context for sexual intercourse, for some people today, love legitimizes sexuality outside of marriage. With the "hookup" or "friends with benefits" standard of sexual expression, many persons use individualistic rather than social norms to legitimize sexual behavior with others. Our sexual standards may have become personal rather than institutional. This shift to personal opportunity makes love important in sexual relationships. In fact, love still remains most Americans' top reason to marry (Pew Research Center, 2019.8).

We can see this connection between love and sex in our everyday use of words. Think of the words we use to describe sexual interactions. When we say that we "make love," are "lovers," or are "intimate" with someone, we generally mean that we are sexually involved; hence, overtones of caring or love. Such potential meanings are absent in such technically correct words as "sexual intercourse," "fellatio," and "cunnilingus," as well as in such slang words as "fuck," "screw," and "hook up."

People in relationships who share power equally are more likely to be sexually involved than those in inequitable relationships. Using global data, researcher and professor Roy Baumeister (2011) found that there's more sexual activity in countries with higher gender equality than in those with less. The countries ranking highest in gender equality are Iceland, Norway, Finland, and Sweden, while the United States ranks 53rd in gender equality (World Economic Forum, 2019). Women in countries where females are at a significant disadvantage educationally and politically may withhold or reserve sex, while men may use their resources to barter for sex. The reverse, that of men withholding or reserving sex and women using their available resources to barter for sex, does not seem to occur. Much of this exchange may be unconscious or unnoticeable (Baumeister, 2011).

Environmental factors involving both the physical and the cultural setting play a role in the level of sexual activity. In the most basic sense, the physical environment affects the opportunity for sex. Because sex is a private activity, the opportunity for it may be precluded by the presence of parents, friends, roommates, or children. The cultural environment also affects the decision of whether to have sex. The values of one's parents or peers may encourage or discourage sexual involvement. Furthermore, a person's subculture—such as the university environment, a social club, or the singles world—exerts an important influence on sexual decision making.

Men, Women, Sex, and Love

Though men and women share more similarities than differences, they tend to have somewhat different perspectives on love and sex, as previously discussed. For example, men, in general are more likely than women to separate sex from affection. Studies consistently show that, for the majority of men, sex and love can be easily separated (Blumstein & Schwartz, 1983; Laumann et al., 1994).

A factor that some heterosexual men see as evidence of sexual interest and intensity in a romantic relationship is assertive, forceful, and even aggressive behavior by the woman. Rather than viewing this behavior as inappropriate or threatening, men more often find it to be desirable. This contrasts with the perceptions of some heterosexual women, who more often perceive forceful behavior by men as related to power; these overtures may seem threatening and dangerous rather than sexually arousing. Women see

"Sex is a momentary itch. Love never lets you go."

—Kingsley Amis (1922–1995)

"Love has as few problems as a motorcar. The only problems are the driver, the passengers, and the road."

—Franz Kafka (1883–1924)

"The Eskimos had fifty-two names for snow because it was important to them. There ought to be as many names for love."

—Margaret Atwood (1939–)

Though many values and ideals are shared, men and women may have different perspectives on love and sex.

Kirk Weddle/Getty Images

For LGBTQ+ individuals, love is an important component in the formation and acceptance of their sexual orientation. The public declaration of love and commitment is a milestone in the lives of many couples.

Creatas/Getty Images

"There is hardly any activity, any enterprise, which is started with such tremendous hopes and expectations and yet fails so regularly as love."

—Erich Fromm (1900–1980)

"Love is the irresistible desire to be irresistibly desired."

—Robert Frost (1874–1963)

sexual activity as being more appropriate and desirable when their romantic partner engages in behavior that inspires trust and confidence.

The theory that there are gender differences in love—that love is central to a woman and peripheral to a man—persists in literature and popular culture, including social media. This theory upholds all gender differences in behavior as instinctual or psychological, thereby perpetuating the notion that men and women have both different views about and different desires within relationships. However, research has shown not only that demographics, such as ethnicity, race, and social class, explain variations in views and desires, but also that cultural differences override gender differences (Sprecher & Toro-Morn, 2002). In fact, across three studies testing the accuracy of gender differences in love, the only stable and robust gender difference that emerged was a desire for relationship support, expressed more by women than by men (Perrin et al., 2011).

Traditionally, women were labeled "good" or "bad" based on their sexual experiences and values. "Good" women were virginal, sexually naïve, and passive, whereas "bad" women were sexually experienced, independent, and passionate. This perception is sometimes altered as individuals age, and when societies accept and embrace all people's sexuality. In spite of changing gender norms, however, our society still remains ambivalent about sexually active and experienced women.

There is a notable difference between heterosexual men and women in terms of frequency of orgasm during sex, with men experiencing orgasm during sexual activity much more frequently than women. Further, lesbian women experience orgasm more frequently than heterosexual women and heterosexual men experience orgasm more frequently than lesbian women (Garcia et al., 2014).

When researchers asked over 5,000 men who had sex with men (MSM) about their frequency of sex, they found that younger age, shorter relationship duration, and a primary (vs. casual) partner to be positively associated with sexual frequency When comparing the sex frequency of MSM to heterosexual men, their rates were similar. In fact, patterns of sexual frequency between MSM and other couples appear to have more similarities than differences in terms of relationship duration, race, and partner type (Wall et al., 2013).

Lesbian couples tend to engage in sex less often than gay male couples or heterosexual couples. However, it may be interesting to note that lesbian women experience orgasm more often than heterosexual women. In a large U.S. sample of adults ($N = 52,588$), 89% of gay men, 88% of bisexual men, 86% of lesbian women, and 66% of bisexual women were most likely to say they usually or always experienced orgasm when sexually intimate (Fredrick et al., 2017). This compares with 95% of heterosexual men and 65% of heterosexual women who stated that they usually or always experienced orgasm when sexually intimate. Women were more likely to orgasm if their last sexual encounter included more oral sex or was of longer duration, if they were more satisfied in their relationship, and if they asked for what they want in bed.

Love Without Sex: Celibacy and Asexuality

Celibacy may be a choice for some, such as those who have taken religious vows or are in relationships in which nonsexual affection provides adequate fulfillment. For others, celibacy is a result of life circumstances, such as the absence of a partner. Others report very low interest in sex or express concern over acquiring HIV/AIDS or other sexually transmitted infections.

Though some researchers may blur the definitions of celibacy with asexuality, or the lack of sexual attraction, differences do exist. Implicit in this discussion is consideration about what constitutes a "normal" level of sexual desire. A diverse set of understandings and theories about what constitutes asexuality has been proposed. Is it a psychiatric syndrome, sexual dysfunction, or a paraphilia? Additionally, can asexuality be considered a sexual orientation (Brotto & Yule, 2017)? Although the definition and views about asexuality vary, most researchers studying it agree that when they refer to an asexual person, they use the criteria of "self-identified asexual."

Asexual individuals have reported varying attitudes toward sex, ranging from lack of interest to being disgusted by it. Research on the sexual behaviors within the asexual community found that sexual experience varied considerably, with some studies reporting similar levels to that of the general population while others report lower levels of sexual experience or activity. Also, compared to a group of controls, asexual individuals tend to exhibit more negative attitudes toward both romance and sex (Bulmer & Izuma, 2018). Other researchers found that asexual persons were less likely to form social and emotional connections—sexual and otherwise—with others (Bogaert et al., 2018).

● How Do I Love Thee? Approaches and Attitudes Related to Love

For most people, love and sex are closely linked in the ideal intimate relationship. Love reflects the positive factors—such as caring—that draw people together and sustain them in a relationship. Sex reflects both emotional and physical elements, such as closeness and sexual excitement, and differentiates romantic love from other forms of love, such as parental love. Although love and sex are related, they are not necessarily connected. One can exist without the other; that is, it is possible to love someone without being sexually involved, and it is possible to be sexually involved without feeling love.

Because sexuality is an interdisciplinary field, it relies on a broad range of theoretical constructs that not only guide sexuality research, but also enhance our understanding of sexuality and interactions in our sexual relationships. The following are a few of the theories that are have been adopted in researching human sexuality.

"Love and you shall be loved. All love is mathematically just, as much as two sides of an algebraic equation."

—Ralph Waldo Emerson (1803–1882)

Styles of Love

Sociologist John Lee describes six basic styles of love (Borrello & Thompson, 1990; Lee, 1973, 1988). These styles of love, he cautions, reflect relationship styles, not individual styles. The style of love may change as the relationship changes or when individuals enter different relationships.

Eros was the ancient Greek god of love, the son of Aphrodite, the goddess of love and fertility. (The Romans called him Cupid.) As a style of love, **eros** is the love of beauty. Erotic lovers are passionate and delight in the tactile, the sensual, the immediate; they are attracted to beauty though beauty is in the eye of the beholder. They love the lines of the body, its feel and touch. They are fascinated by every physical detail of their beloved. Their love burns brightly and is idealized but soon flickers and dies.

"If you love somebody, let them go. If they return, they were always yours. If they don't, they never were."

—Anonymous

Mania, from the Greek word for madness, is obsessive and possessive love. For manic lovers, nights are marked by sleeplessness and days by pain and anxiety. The slightest sign of affection brings ecstasy for a short while, only to disappear. Satisfactions last for but a moment before they must be renewed. Manic love is roller-coaster love.

Ludus, from the Latin word for play, is playful love. For ludic lovers, love is a game, something to play at rather than to become deeply involved in. Love is ultimately *"ludicrous";* encounters are casual, carefree, and often careless. "Nothing serious" is the motto of ludic lovers. Those with a ludus style thrive on attention and are often willing to take risks.

Storge (STOR-gay), from the Greek word for natural affection, is the love between companions. It is, wrote Lee, "love without fever, tumult, or folly, a peaceful and enchanting affection." It usually begins as friendship and gradually deepens into love. If the love ends, that also occurs gradually, and the people often become friends once again.

Agape (AH-ga-pay), from the Greek word for brotherly love, is the traditional Christian love that is chaste, patient, undemanding, and altruistic; there is no expectation of reciprocation. It is the love of saints and martyrs. Agape is more abstract and ideal than concrete and real. It is easier to love all of humankind than an individual in this way.

Pragma, from the Greek word for business, is practical love. Pragmatic lovers are, first and foremost, businesslike in their approach to looking for someone who meets their needs. They use logic in their search for a partner, seeking background, education, personality, religion, and interests that are compatible with their own. If they meet a person who satisfies their criteria, erotic, manic, or other feelings may develop.

According to sociologist John Lee, there are six styles of love: eros, mania, ludus, storge, agape, and pragma. What style do you believe this couple illustrates? Why?

John Rowley/Digital Vision/Getty Images

"Love never dies a natural death. It dies because we don't know how to replenish its source."

—Anaïs Nin (1903–1977)

"When you are courting a nice girl an hour seems like a second. When you sit on a red-hot cinder a second seems like an hour. That's relativity."

—Albert Einstein (1879–1955)

"You know you're in love when you can't fall asleep because reality is finally better than your dreams."

—Dr. Seuss (1904–1991)

"Don't threaten me with love, baby."

—Billie Holiday (1915–1959)

In addition to these pure forms, there are mixtures of the basic types, for example: storge-eros, ludus-eros, and storge-ludus. Lee believes that to have a mutually satisfying relationship, people have to find a partner who shares the same style and definition of love. The more different two people are in their styles of love, the less likely they are to understand each other's love.

One could expect there to be some consistency between love styles and sexual attitudes, since beliefs about sexuality could help determine the choice and maintenance of a romantic relationship. But are there gender differences in the ways men and women express their love style? Research reports the presence of significant gender differences in love styles and attraction criteria among college students (Grello et al., 2006; Lacey et al., 2004). Surveying the love styles of college students, researchers have found that men were more likely than women to have a ludus style, while others who endorsed an eros style were more likely to either be virgins or engage in sexual activity with only a romantic partner (Grello et al., 2006).

The Triangular Theory of Love

The **triangular theory of love**, developed by psychologist and educator Robert Sternberg (1986), emphasizes the dynamic quality of love relationships. According to this theory, love is composed of three elements, as in the points of a triangle: intimacy, passion, and commitment (see Figure 1). Each can be enlarged or diminished in the course of a love relationship, which will affect the quality of the relationship. They can also be combined in different ways (see Table 1). Each combination produces a different type of love, such as romantic love, infatuation, empty love, and liking. Partners may combine the components differently at different times in the same love relationship.

The Components of Love Intimacy refers to the warm, close, bonding feelings we get when we love someone. According to Sternberg and Grajek (1984), there are 10 signs of intimacy:

1. Wanting to promote your partner's welfare
2. Feeling happiness with your partner
3. Holding your partner in high regard
4. Being able to count on your partner in times of need
5. Being able to understand your partner
6. Sharing yourself and your possessions with your partner
7. Receiving emotional support from your partner
8. Giving emotional support to your partner
9. Being able to communicate with your partner about intimate things
10. Valuing your partner's presence in your life

The passion component refers to the elements of romance, attraction, and sexuality in the relationship. These may be fueled by a desire to increase self-esteem, to be sexually active or fulfilled, to affiliate with others, to dominate, or to subordinate.

The commitment component consists of two separate parts—a short-term part and a long-term part. The short-term part refers to an individual's decision that he or she loves someone. People may or may not make the decision consciously. But it usually occurs before they decide to make a commitment to the other person. The long-term part refers to commitment, or the maintenance of love. But a decision to love someone does not necessarily entail a commitment to maintaining that love.

Kinds of Love The intimacy, passion, and commitment components can be combined in eight basic ways, according to Sternberg:

1. Liking (intimacy only)
2. Infatuation (passion only)

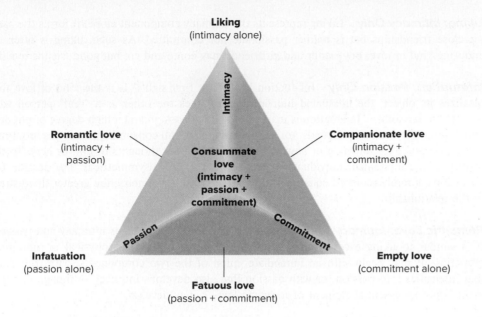

Liking
(intimacy alone)

Intimacy

Romantic love
(intimacy +
passion)

Companionate love
(intimacy +
commitment)

Consummate
love
(intimacy +
passion +
commitment)

Passion

Commitment

Infatuation
(passion alone)

Empty love
(commitment alone)

Fatuous love
(passion + commitment)

Nonlove
(absence of intimacy, passion, and
commitment; takes many forms)

● FIGURE 1

Sternberg's Triangular Theory of Love. The three elements of love are intimacy, passion, and commitment.

Source: From Sternberg, R. J. (1988). *The triangle of love: Intimacy, passion, commitment.* Basic Books. Used by permission of Robert J. Sternberg.

TABLE 1 ● Taxonomy of Kinds of Triangles of Love. When combined, the three components of love result in eight possible kinds of love.

Types of Love	Intimacy	Passion	Commitment
Nonlove	No	No	No
Friendship	Yes	No	No
Infatuated love	No	Yes	No
Empty love	No	No	Yes
Romantic love	Yes	Yes	No
Companionate love	Yes	No	Yes
Fatuous love	No	Yes	Yes
Consummate love	Yes	Yes	Yes

Source: Sternberg, R. J. (2019). When love goes awry (Part I): Applications of the duplex theory of love and its development to relationships gone bad. In R. J. Sternberg & K. Sternberg (Eds.), *The new psychology of love* (2nd ed.). Cambridge University Press.

3. Romantic love (intimacy and passion)

4. Companionate love (intimacy and commitment)

5. Fatuous love (passion and commitment)

6. Consummate love (intimacy, passion, and commitment)

7. Empty love (commitment only)

8. Nonlove (absence of intimacy, passion, and commitment)

These types represent extremes that few of us are likely to experience. Not many of us, for example, experience infatuation in its purest form, in which there is absolutely *no* intimacy. And empty love is not really love at all. These categories are nevertheless useful for examining the nature of love.

Liking: Intimacy Only Liking represents the intimacy component alone. It forms the basis for close friendships but is neither passionate nor committed. As such, liking is often an enduring kind of love. Boyfriends and girlfriends may come and go, but good friends remain.

Infatuation: Passion Only Infatuation is "love at first sight." It is the kind of love that idealizes its object; the infatuated individual rarely sees the other as a "real" person with normal human foibles. Infatuation is marked by sudden passion and a high degree of physical and emotional arousal. It tends to be obsessive and all-consuming; one has no time, energy, or desire for anything or anyone but the beloved (or thoughts of him or her). To the dismay of the infatuated individual, infatuations are usually asymmetrical: The passion (or obsession) is rarely returned equally. And the greater the asymmetry, the greater the distress in the relationship.

Romantic Love: Intimacy and Passion Romantic love combines intimacy and passion. It is similar to liking except that it is more intense as a result of physical or emotional attraction. It may begin with an immediate union of the two components, with friendship that intensifies into passion, or with passion that also develops intimacy. Although commitment is not an essential element of romantic love, it may develop.

Companionate Love: Intimacy and Commitment Companionate love is essential to a committed friendship. It often begins as romantic love, but as the passion diminishes and the intimacy increases, it is transformed into companionate love. Some couples are satisfied with such love; others are not. Those who are dissatisfied in companionate love relationships may seek extrarelational partners to maintain passion in their lives. They may also end the relationship to seek a new romantic relationship that they hope will remain romantic.

Fatuous Love: Passion and Commitment Fatuous, or deceptive, love is whirlwind love; it begins the day two people meet and quickly results in cohabitation or engagement, and possibly marriage. It develops so quickly that they hardly know what happened. Often, nothing much really did happen that will permit the relationship to endure. As Sternberg and Barnes (1989) observe, "It is fatuous in the sense that a commitment is made on the basis of passion without the stabilizing element of intimate involvement—which takes time to develop." Passion may fade soon enough, and all that remains is commitment. But commitment that has had relatively little time to deepen is a poor foundation on which to build an enduring relationship. With neither passion nor intimacy, the commitment wanes.

Consummate Love: Intimacy, Passion, and Commitment Consummate love results when intimacy, passion, and commitment combine to form their unique constellation. It is the kind of love we dream about but do not expect in all our love relationships. Many of us can achieve it, but it is difficult to sustain over time. To sustain it, we must nourish its different components, for each is subject to the stress of time.

Empty Love: Commitment Only This is love that lacks intimacy or passion. Empty love involves staying together solely for the sake of appearances or the children, for example.

Nonlove: Absence of Intimacy, Passion, and Commitment Nonlove can take many forms, such as attachment for financial reasons, fear, or the fulfillment of neurotic needs.

Though all three components of Sternberg's love triangle are important in a loving relationship, each often manifests in varying degrees over time and in different patterns. Regardless of these shifts and variations, evidence shows that when both partners experience similar levels of passion, commitment, and intimacy, there is greater compatibility (Drigotas et al., 1999).

The Geometry of Love The shape of the love triangle depends on the intensity of the love and the balance of the parts. By varying both the area and the shape of the triangles, it becomes possible to represent a wide variety of kinds of relationships. Intense love relationships lead to triangles with greater area; such triangles occupy more of one's life. Just as

"Being deeply loved by someone gives you strength; loving someone deeply gives you courage."

—Lao Tzu (sixth century BCE)

"We are never so defenseless against suffering as when we love."

—Sigmund Freud (1856–1939)

"You learn to speak by speaking, to study by studying, to run by running, to work by working; in just the same way, you learn love by loving."

—Saint Francis de Sales (1567–1622)

love relationships can be balanced or unbalanced, so can love triangles. The balance determines the shape of the triangle (see Figure 2). A relationship in which the intimacy, passion, and commitment components are equal results in an equilateral triangle. But if the components are not equal, differences in amounts of love are experienced and unbalanced triangles form. The size and shape of a person's triangle give a good pictorial sense of how that person feels about another. The greater the match between the triangles of the two partners in a relationship, the more likely each is to experience satisfaction in the relationship.

Love as Attachment

Humans desire to bond with other people. At the same time, many people fear bonding. Where do these contradictory impulses and emotions come from? Can they ever be resolved?

Attachment theory, a prominent approach to the study of love, helps us understand how adult relationships develop, what can go wrong in them, and what to do when things do go wrong. In this theory, love is seen as a form of **attachment**, a close, enduring emotional bond that finds its roots in infancy (Hazan & Shaver, 1987; Shaver, 1984; Shaver et al., 1988). Research suggests that romantic love and infant-caregiver attachment have similar emotional dynamics; that is, seeking and maintaining physical proximity, obtaining comfort when needed, experiencing distress when separated, and viewing the attachment figure as a secure base (Muise et al., 2018).

Infant-Caregiver Attachment

- The attachment bond's formation and quality depend on the attachment object's (AO) responsiveness and sensitivity.
- When the AO is present, the infant is happier.
- The infant shares toys, discoveries, and objects with the AO.
- The infant coos, talks baby talk, and "sings."
- The infant shares feelings of oneness with the AO.

Romantic Love

- Feelings of love are related to the lover's interest and reciprocation.
- When the lover is present, the person feels happier.
- Lovers share experiences and goods and give gifts.
- Lovers coo, sing, and talk baby talk.
- Lovers share feelings of oneness.

The implications of attachment theory are far-reaching. Attachment affects the way we process information, interact with others, and view the world. Basically, it influences our ability to love and to see ourselves as lovable (Fisher, 2004.8a).

The core elements of love appear to be the same for children as for adults: the need to feel emotionally safe and secure. When a partner responds to a need, for instance, adults view the world as a safe place. In this respect, we don't differ greatly from children.

The most basic concept of attachment theory is that to be whole adults we need to accept that we are also vulnerable children. In a secure, intimate adult relationship, it is not demeaning, diminishing, or pathological to share honest emotions. It is the capacity to be vulnerable and open and accepting of others' giving that makes us lovable and human.

Based on observations made by Mary Ainsworth and colleagues (1978, cited in Shaver et al., 1988), Phillip Shaver and colleagues (1988) hypothesized that the styles of attachment developed in childhood—secure, anxious/ambivalent, and avoidant—continue through adulthood. Their surveys revealed similar styles in adult relationships.

Adults with **secure attachments** found it relatively easy to get close to other people. They felt comfortable depending on others and having others depend on them. They didn't frequently worry about being abandoned or having someone get too close to them. More than anxious/ambivalent and avoidant adults, they felt that others usually liked them; they believed

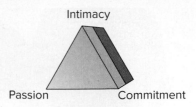

Perfectly matched relationship
(Amount of love and balance of love are matched.)

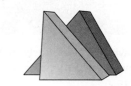

Closely matched relationship

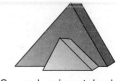

Moderately mismatched relationship

Severely mismatched relationship

 Self Other

• FIGURE 2

The Geometry of Love. According to Steinberg's triangular theory of love, the shape and size of each person's triangle indicate how well each is matched to the other.

Source: From Sternberg, R. J. (1988). *The triangle of love: Intimacy, passion, commitment.* Basic Books. Used by permission of Robert J. Sternberg.

Adults with secure attachments may find it easy to get close to others.

Asia Images Group/Getty Images

that people were generally well-intentioned and good-hearted. Their love experiences tended to be happy, friendly, and trusting. They accepted and supported their partners. About 56% of the adults in the Shaver and colleagues (1988) study were secure.

Adults with **anxious/ambivalent attachments** believed that other people did not get as close as they themselves wanted. They worried that their partners didn't really love them or would leave them. They also wanted to merge completely with another person, which sometimes caused others to withdraw. More than others, they felt that it was easy to fall in love. Their experiences in love were often obsessive and marked by desire for union, high degrees of sexual attraction, and jealousy. Approximately 19–20% of the adults were identified as anxious/ambivalent. Those high in anxious attachment, expressed as feelings of vulnerability and rejection, often have a need for high sexual frequency, possibly because they seek signs of their partner's availability, commitment, and continuing interest (Gerwirtz-Meydan & Finzi-Dottan, 2017).

Adults with **avoidant attachments** felt discomfort in being close to other people; they were distrustful and fearful of being dependent. More than others, they believed that romance seldom lasts but that at times it can be as intense as it was at the beginning. Their partners wanted more closeness than they did. Avoidant partners were not likely to focus on their partners' needs, which explains why partners were often sexually dissatisfied (Peloquin et al., 2014). Avoidant lovers feared intimacy and experienced emotional highs and lows and jealousy. Those high in avoidant attachment were found to have lower sexual frequency, perhaps because they sought to maintain distance and a sense of invulnerability in their sexual relationships (Gerwirtz-Meydan & Finzi-Dottan, 2017). Approximately 23–25% of the adults were found to be avoidant.

In applying attachment theory to our understanding of sexuality in the context of romantic relationships, researchers have found that people use sex to meet specific attachment-related needs, including proximity to and reassurance from a partner (Muise et al., 2018). Differences in attachment styles, for example having a partner with an avoidant attachment style, are associated with different motivations for engaging in sex as well as the desire for different types of sexual relationships.

In adulthood, the attachment style developed in infancy combines with sexual desire and caring behaviors to give rise to romantic love. However, it is also important to know that an individual's past does not necessarily determine the future course of his or her relationships. Rather, as individuals and couples mature and evolve, so can their capacity to foster physical proximity, to be attuned to each other's needs and distress cues, and work together to help solve problems. Not only are these qualities satisfying to the relationship, but they nurture sexual satisfaction as well. According to Peter Fonagy, professor of psychoanalysis at University College London, having secure attachment is not about being a perfect parent or partner, but about maintaining communication to sustain the relationship. If free-flowing communication is impaired, so is the relationship (Murphy, 2017).

Examining different forms of relationships can provide new insights into how attachment styles relate to sexuality. When studying consensual nonmonogamy, for example, in which all parties agree that it is acceptable to have additional romantic or sexual partners, researchers found that individuals in consensual nonmonogamy were lower in attachment avoidance relative to those in monogamous relationships (Muise et al., 2018). This dimension reflects the extent to which a person feels uncomfortable with closeness in romantic relationships and strives for independence and emotional distance from partners. Low avoidants perceive others as available or responsive and depend on them for distress regulation (Mikulincer & Shaver, 2008) or social support (Collins & Feeney, 2000). Researchers have speculated this connection might be due to the level of trust and communication required to maintain consensual non-monogamous relationships; perhaps not surprising given avoidant individuals' positive attitudes toward nonexclusive sexual relationships (Muise et al., 2018).

Unrequited Love

As most of us know from painful experience, love is not always returned. People may suffer tremendous anguish when they feel they have been rejected or ignored, even if the relationship was imagined. **Unrequited love**—love that is one-sided or not openly reciprocated or understood—is distressing for both the would-be lover and the rejecting person. Among college and high school students, unrequited love is four times more common than reciprocal love (Bringle et al., 2013). Would-be lovers may have both positive and intensely negative feelings about their failed relationship. The rejectors, however, often feel uniformly negative about the experience. Unlike the rejectors, the would-be lovers feel that the attraction is mutual, that they have been led on, and that the rejection was never clearly communicated. Rejectors, in contrast, feel that they have not led the other person on; moreover, they feel guilty about hurting him or her. Nevertheless, many find the other person's persistence intrusive and annoying; they wish the would-be lover would simply get the hint and go away. Rejectors view would-be lovers as self-deceiving and unreasonable; would-be lovers see their rejectors as inconsistent and mysterious.

To better understand unrequited love, it may be useful to explore its various forms (Bringle et al., 2013):

1. A crush on someone who is unavailable. This form of love is most often a crush on a person (i.e., movie star, famous athlete) that is not known personally by the infatuated.

2. A crush on someone nearby, without ever trying to initiate a romantic relationship. Regardless of the reasons for this type of infatuation (i.e., a classmate, co-worker), the feelings do not change the frustration that accompany it.

3. Continuing to pursue someone you've fallen in love with, in spite of their having rejected you. Being turned down by a previous lover can be very painful and prompt unwise actions and responses.

4. Longing for a past lover. Following a breakup, even if the person was not right for you, can provoke attraction and determination that can contribute to "frustration attraction" (Fisher, 2004.8b).

5. An unequal love relationship in which the partners stay together in spite of their different degrees of love. For example, loving for different reasons might involve one partner who feels infatuated, while the other seeks stability or distance.

● Jealousy

Jealousy is an aversive response that occurs because of a partner's real, imagined, or likely involvement with a third person. Jealousy sets boundaries for the behaviors that are acceptable in relationships; the boundaries cannot be crossed without evoking jealousy. Though a certain amount of jealousy can be expected in any loving relationship, it is important that partners communicate openly about their fears and boundaries. A strong connection or closeness to a significant other can create the potential for jealousy when the relationship is threatened. Jealousy can also occur when partners are not spending enough time together, creating for some suspicious thoughts about the exclusiveness of one's partner. Jealousy is a paradox; it doesn't necessarily signal difficulty between partners, nor does it have to threaten the relationship.

Many of us think that the existence of jealousy proves the existence of love. We may try to test someone's interest or affection by attempting to make him or her jealous by flirting with another person. If our date or partner becomes jealous, the jealousy is taken as a sign of love. But provoking jealousy proves only that the other person can be made jealous. Making jealousy a litmus test of love is dangerous, for jealousy and love are not necessarily companions. Jealousy may be a more accurate yardstick for measuring insecurity or immaturity than for measuring love.

"Jealousy is not a barometer by which the depth of love can be read. It merely records the depth of the lover's insecurity."

—Margaret Mead (1901–1978)

"Beware, my lord, of jealousy. It is the green-eyed monster that mocks the meat it feeds on."

—William Shakespeare (1564–1616)

think about it

The Science of Love

To love or to have loved, that is enough. Don't ask for more.
—Victor Hugo (1802–1885)

Throughout history there have been poems and stories, plays and pictures that have attempted to explain love. Each has provided some insight into the ways that passion grabs us and, almost as quickly, leaves us. More recently, science has explored the complexities involved in love by examining the parts of the brain linked to reward and pleasure, and providing us with particulars of its chemical components.

The scientific tale of love begins with the reward and pleasure part of the brain: the ventral tegmental area, the part of the midbrain that is rich in the chemicals, dopamine and serotonin, and the caudate nucleus, located deep within the brain and involved with the control of involuntary movement. Dopamine and serotonin are powerful chemical messengers that regulate numerous physical and emotional responses, including sexual arousal and response. Anthropologist Helen Fisher, senior research fellow at the Kinsey Institute and professor emeritus at Rutgers University, has studied the biochemical pathways of love with the aid of an MRI machine (Fisher, 2004.8a, 2004.8b). Fisher found that love lights up the caudate nucleus—home to a dense spread of receptors for dopamine, the chemical in the brain that stimulates feelings of attraction and accompanies passion. This is the same chemical that is produced in response to the ingestion of cocaine. Following the flooding of dopamine, the caudate then sends signals for more dopamine. "The more dopamine you get, the more high you feel," says Lucy Brown, neurologist at the Albert Einstein College of Medicine in New York. In the right proportions, dopamine creates intense energy, focused attention, exhilaration, and desire. It is why a newly-in-love person can live passionately without sleep, feel bold and bright, and take risks.

In contrast to the rewards experienced by dopamine, the neurotransmitter serotonin appears to inhibit sexual activity. Male ejaculation, for example, triggers the release of serotonin, which by inhibiting the release of dopamine, temporarily reduces the sex drive (Hull et al., 1999). There is also an interaction that occurs between oxytocin and serotonin, though the exact mechanisms are unknown (Humble & Bejerot, 2016; Marazziti et al., 2012). We do know that when individuals are prescribed a type of medication known as serotonin reuptake inhibitors (SRIs), which are widely used for the treatment of psychiatric disorders, including depression and obsessive-compulsive disorder, the release of serotonin in the brain may cause decreased libido, genital insensitivity, and delayed orgasm (Muskin et al., 2017). Together, these studies reveal the powerful impacts of dopamine which increases sexual response, and serotonin, which tends to diminish it.

Consequently, when a couple breaks up one can become afflicted by what is known as 'broken heart syndrome,' medically known as Takotsubo syndrome, whereby the brain and its control center impacts how the nervous system handles stress (Ghardi et al., 2018). This rare, yet serious condition, causes the sympathetic nervous system to rev up the body, including the heart, in response to danger. When there is a disruption in the interplay among the parasympathetic and limbic systems that help to balance or calm the nervous system, the brain overreacts to stress which can result in heart damage. The study underlines the fact that our brains and hearts are connected even more intimately than scientists have previously believed.

The simple behavior of kissing triggers and sends a flood of chemicals, including testosterone, and neural messages that transmit tactile sensations, sexual excitement, feelings of closeness, and euphoria (Brizendine, 2010; Walter, 2008). Since lips are densely populated with sensory neurons, when we kiss, these neurons, along with those in the tongue and mouth, send messages to the brain and body that intensify emotions and physical reactions. Kissing also unleashes a cocktail of chemicals that govern stress, motivation, social bonding, and sexual stimulation. While enjoyable for both, kissing has different meanings for some men and women. For men, it may be an indicator of sexual readiness, while for women, it may be a key to the significance of the relationship (Kirshenbaum, 2011). As the relationship continues, those who kiss for affection rather than as part of a sexual expression report being more sexually satisfied (Northrup et al., 2014). Regardless of when it first occurred, the first kiss is said to provide some of our strongest romantic memories.

Interestingly, the brains of love-struck men and women seem to differ. For example, more activity exists for men in the brain region that integrates visual stimuli, whereas for women the areas of the brain that govern memories are more active. Women's brain activity is different than men's, but it may be that when a woman really studies a man, she can remember things about his behavior in order to determine whether he'd make a reliable mate and father. Though differences appear in the male and female brain while they are being stimulated, there are few differences that occur during orgasm itself (Linden, 2011).

When hormones and naturally-occurring opioids in the brain get activated, individuals may start drawing emotional connections to another that may not be accurate. For example, a person may think that their lover made them feel a certain way; however it's actually the brain that initiates the responses. Romantic love appears to be a natural feeling and for some, a compulsion (Frascella et al., 2010). Brain scanning studies show that feelings of intense romantic love engage the brain's "reward system," associated with dopamine pathways responsible for learning, motivation, energy, ecstasy, craving, and addiction (Fisher et al., 2016). At the same time, problems associated with maladaptive love can cause activity in the caudate nucleus, adjacent to a brain region also associated with addiction, to prompt the rejected lover to ignore reasoning or advice in a similar way an alcoholic will avoid advice to stop drinking (Fisher, 2004.8b; Fisher et al., 2016).

An array of neurochemicals help promote orgasm. Testosterone, a sex steroid, influences both the brain and the genitals and is linked to feelings of desire and arousal. Oxytocin, often referred to as the "cuddle chemical," because it encourages people to bond, is released at the onset of orgasm by a small cluster of cells in the brain's hypothalamus. It quickly floods the brain receptors with the feel-good neurotransmitter, causing the pleasant rush that accompanies orgasm (Sukel, 2016). As mentioned, the neurotransmitter serotonin and the protein prolactin then act as breaks, resulting in feelings of satisfaction and relaxation after orgasm.

In studying romance and passion historically and globally, scientists now believe that romance is universal and has been embedded in our brains since prehistoric times. It has been observed that, in all societies, passion usually diminishes over time. From a physiological perspective, this makes sense. The dopamine-drenched state of romantic love adapts and changes into a relatively quiet one that is explained by the presence of oxytocin. For most, these changes are anticipated and welcomed. However, for some who experience the novelty of new love replaced with a more companionate love composed of deep affection and liking, the change may be both unwelcome and unacceptable.

What researchers have learned from lovers' brains is that romantic love isn't really an emotion—it's a drive that is based deep within our brains that results in a flood of hormones and helps explain why we might do crazy things for love.

Think Critically

1. How important is it that science investigates the "brain in love"? What impact might this information have on you or others?

2. How accurate do you feel the various chemical changes that the brain undergoes actually occurs in response to love? Have you experienced these variations?

3. What gender differences do you see, if any, between how men and women respond to love?

4. Do you agree with the statement that romantic love is an addiction? Why or why not?

It is important to understand jealousy for several reasons. First, jealousy is a painful emotion associated with anger, hurt, and loss. If we can understand jealousy, especially when it is irrational, then we can eliminate some of its pain. Second, jealousy can help cement or destroy a relationship. Jealousy helps maintain a relationship by guarding its exclusiveness. But in its irrational or extreme forms, it can destroy a relationship by its insistent demands and attempts at control. We need to understand when and how jealousy is functional and when it is not. Third, jealousy is often linked to violence in marriages and dating relationships (Buss, 1999; Easton & Shackelford, 2009). Furthermore, marital violence and rape are often provoked by jealousy. Rather than being directed at a rival, jealous aggression is often used against the partner.

The Psychological Dimension of Jealousy

As most of us know, jealousy is a painful emotion. It is an agonizing mixture of hurt, anger, depression, fear, and doubt. Some psychologists regard it as a scar of childhood trauma or a symptom of a psychological problem (Fisher, 2009). While it may be true that those who feel inadequate, insecure, or overly dependent are more jealous than others, jealousy can also enrich relationships and spark passion by increasing the attention individuals pay to their partner. According to David Buss (2000), professor of psychology at the University of Texas at Austin, the total absence of jealousy is a more ominous sign than its presence for romantic partners, because it signals indifference. Though both sexes may elicit jealousy intentionally as an assessment tool to gauge the strength of a partner's commitment, they seem to use it unequally. Buss (2000) found that 31% of women and 17% of men had intentionally elicited jealousy in their relationship.

Neither gender is more subject to jealousy, although women are more likely to work to win back a lover, while men are more likely to leave the relationship to protect their self-esteem (Fisher, 2009). Sex differences, however, can be noted in the context and expression of jealousy. For example, when individuals were asked to imagine if their partner became interested in someone else, what would distress them more: (a) their partner forming a deep emotional attachment to that person, or (b) their partner enjoying passionate sexual intercourse with that person? Researchers found that 60% of the men chose the partner's sexual infidelity as more upsetting, whereas 17% of women felt that way. Conversely, 83% of women indicated that emotional infidelity was more concerning, compared to 40% of men (Buss, 2018). In a different study of respondents who identified as non-heterosexual, the majority of men and women reported that they would be more distressed/upset by their partner forming an emotional tie to another person than by their partner having sex with another person (de Visser et al., 2019). Likewise, in this study, the majority of bisexual men and women reported that they would be more distressed or upset by emotional infidelity. These

"Love is like quicksilver in the hand. Leave the fingers open and it stays. Clutch it, and it darts away."

—Dorothy Parker (1893–1967)

threats to relationships appear real and can cause emotional reactions. Gender differences can partly be explained using an evolutionary model, which proposes that men, because they cannot be completely confident about the paternity of any offspring from a relationship, will be more upset by sexual nonexclusiveness. Women, in contrast, are more often upset by emotional nonexclusiveness, which might signal the man's lack of commitment to the long-term success of the relationship and any offspring.

An expectation occurs because our intimate partner is different from everyone else. With him or her, we are our most confiding, revealing, vulnerable, caring, and trusting. There is a sense of exclusiveness. Being intimate outside the relationship violates that sense of exclusiveness because intimacy (especially sexual intimacy) symbolizes specialness. Words such as "disloyalty," "cheating," and "infidelity" reflect the sense that an unspoken pledge has been broken. This unspoken pledge is the normative expectation that serious relationships will be sexually exclusive. In the worst cases, when jealousy goes awry, individuals can become violent. Worldwide, jealousy is the leading cause of spousal homicide (Fisher, 2009).

Social media can induce jealousy in romantic relationships. Even after a relationship ends, the visibility and associations made when viewing photos or discussions of an ex-lover or a partner's romantic history can cause what is known as a retroactive jealousy despite ex-partners not actively interfering in the current relationship (Frampton & Fox, 2018) (see Figure 3). This type of jealousy occurs in response to events such as individuals comparing their current romantic partners to ex-partners, saying something positive about an ex-partner to a current partner, or sharing information about sexual experiences. Social media, particularly social networking sites (SNS), provide an opportunity for some to maintain a personal profile and create visible connections or links to other users as well as to view and monitor, "friend," or privately or publicly comment on another's post. In spite of information-seeking and possibly reframing information about the ex-relationship, some research has found that the use of SNS may backfire to actually trigger jealousy in a relationship because of the way their current partner interacts with others on these sites (Frampton & Fox, 2018). Another source of struggle in a relationship can be cellphones. Given that 51% say their partner is often or sometimes distracted by their cellphone while they are trying to have a conversation with them, it may not be surprising that some persons may be tempted to look through their partner's phone for what could be disturbing texts or images (Pew Research Center, 2020.8). But social media can also be a platform for showing love and affection, as when individuals meet through dating websites or as a means to communicate with a loved one. When it begins to interfere with the quality of a relationship, however, its use needs to be addressed.

Managing Jealousy

Dealing with irrational suspicions can often be very difficult, for such feelings touch deep recesses in ourselves. As noted previously, jealousy is often related to personal feelings of insecurity and inadequacy. The source of such jealousy lies within ourselves, not within the relationship.

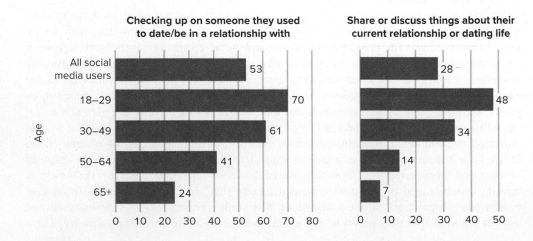

● FIGURE 3

Percentage of Social Media Users, Ages 18–65+, Who Report Checking on Their Exes.

Source: Pew Research Center. (2020). Dating and relationships in the digital age.

If we can work on the underlying causes of our insecurity, then we can deal effectively with our irrational jealousy. Excessively jealous people may need considerable reassurance, but at some point they must also confront their own irrationality and insecurity. If they do not, they emotionally imprison their partner. Their jealousy may destroy the very relationship they have been desperately trying to preserve. If this is the case, it may be time to consult a mental health professional.

But jealousy is not always irrational. Sometimes there are valid reasons, such as the relationship boundaries being violated. In this case, the cause lies not within ourselves but within the relationship. If the jealousy is well-founded, the partner may need to modify or end the relationship with the third party whose presence initiated the jealousy. Modifying the third-party relationship reduces the jealous response and, more important, symbolizes the partner's commitment to the primary relationship. If the partner is unwilling to do this, because of a lack of commitment, unsatisfied personal needs, or problems in the primary relationship, the relationship is likely to reach a crisis point. In such cases, jealousy may be the agent for profound change.

Extradyadic Sex

A fundamental assumption in our culture is that committed relationships are sexually exclusive. Each person remains the other's exclusive intimate partner in terms of both emotional and sexual intimacy. **Extradyadic sex**, also known as extramarital sex, adultery, cheating, or infidelity, refers to having a romantic or sexual relationship outside a primary or dating relationship. It violates the explicit or implicit expectation of sexual exclusivity. It is most often perceived as a transgression and is associated with feelings of betrayal.

It is difficult to accurately determine how many people experience extradyadic sex because the term may be defined differently by researchers and individuals. The definitions can be classified into three categories: extradyadic as sexual intercourse; extradyadic as other sexual activities; or extradyadic as emotional betrayal (Moller & Vossler, 2015). Defining extradyadic sex in terms of sexual intercourse may not be helpful for several reasons: It assumes that sexual terms have one universally understood meaning and that some couples may not equate couple commitment with sexual exclusivity. A broader definition may include behaviors such as oral sex, masturbation in the presence of another, sexual play, flirting, and visiting sex clubs apart from one's partner. Internet behaviors that include exchanging sexts and online dating may also be in this category. Extradyadic sex can include "falling in love with another person" or "deep emotional attachment," and involves both time and loyalty to another person other than the primary partner. This can mean sharing secrets or discussing complaints of the primary partner.

Because of these varying definitions, it is difficult to determine accurately how many people have experienced extradyadic involvement. Additionally, individuals may be reluctant to acknowledge their involvement with another because of negative terms and connotations associated with it (e.g., "affairs," "cheating," "hooking up," "sleeping around"). Compounding this are the various ways that individuals and couples regard extradyadic involvement (e.g., exclusive by agreement or not) and the nature of the nonexclusiveness (e.g., one-time sexual event, long-term relationship, or both). Depending on how extradyadic sex is defined, men are more likely than women to have sex with someone other than their spouse (20% vs. 13%, respectively). This gender gap varies by age, with older adults engaging in extradyadic sex more frequently than younger adults (Wang, 2018) (see Figure 4).

When examining the motivations for extradyadic sex, researchers found both variety and diversity among individuals, ranging from deficits in the relationship (i.e., anger, neglect, lack of love or commitment, insecurity) to momentary shifts in judgment/decision making, need for autonomy, or sexual variety (Selterman et al., 2019). Research has shown that motivations vary by gender with men more likely to be driven by sexual desire, variety, and situational forces, while women more likely to be motivated by neglect and seek an emotional connection. Additionally, social scripts, which downplay women's sexual desires and exaggerate men's, may motivate individuals to bias or exaggerate their responses.

"Love withers under constraints: its very essence is liberty: it is compatible neither with obedience, jealousy, nor fear: it is there most pure, perfect, and unlimited where its votaries live in confidence, equality and unreserve."
—Percy Bysshe Shelley (1792–1822)

"What I have seen of the love affairs of other people has not led me to regret that deficiency in my experience."
—George Bernard Shaw (1856–1950)

"There is one thing I would break up over, and that is if she caught me with another woman. I won't stand for that."
—Steve Martin (1945–)

Sensitive customer information, including names, street addresses, e-mail addresses, and credit card fragments from the married dating website Ashley Madison.com was stolen by hackers in 2015 and posted on the web.

sjscreens/Alamy Stock Photo

• **FIGURE 4**

Percentage of Persons, Ages 18–80+, Who Reported Having Extramarital Sex at Least Once in Their Life.

Source: General Social Survey 2010–2016. This is compiled information from a series of data charts.

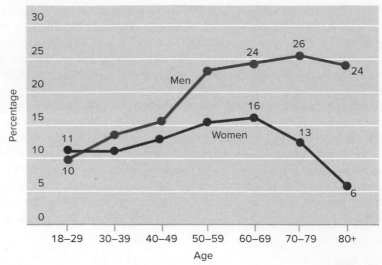

Note: Based on adults who are either currently married or have been married before.

> "To be faithful to one is to be cruel to all the others."
>
> —Wolfgang Amadeus Mozart (1756–1791)

In marriages and committed partnerships that assume emotional and sexual exclusivity, mutuality and sharing are emphasized. Extradyadic sex is assumed to be destructive of marriage and committed partnerships.

As a result of assumptions, both sexual and nonsexual extradyadic relationships take place without the knowledge or permission of the other partner. If the extradyadic sex is discovered, a crisis often ensues. Many people feel that the partner who is not exclusive has violated a basic trust. Sexual accessibility implies emotional accessibility. When a person learns that their partner is having another relationship, the emotional commitment of that spouse is brought into question. How can the person prove that he or she still has a commitment? He or she cannot—commitment is assumed; it can never be proved. Furthermore, the extradyadic sex may imply to the partner (rightly or wrongly) that he or she is sexually inadequate or uninteresting.

> "Thou shalt not commit adultery . . . unless in the mood."
>
> —W. C. Fields (1879–1946)

Consensual Nonmonogamous Relationships The umbrella term used to describe any relationship in which individuals agree to participate in sexual and/or emotional and romantic interactions with more than one person is **consensual nonmonogamy (CNM)** (Fairbrother et al., 2019). Although the specific nature of CNM relationships varies, (e.g., open relationships, swinging, polyamory) those in nonmonogamous relationships have a mutual arrangement and agreement around the openness, transparency, and parameters of the relationship. Two nationally representative surveys of the adult U.S. population indicate that couples in CNM relationships make up approximately 2.4% to 4% of those in romantic relationships (Herbenick et al., 2017; Levine et al., 2018). When examining the gender difference for CNM relationships, researchers found 18% of men and 6% of women prefer CNM, with a higher incidence among same-sex men (Fairbrother et al., 2019).

Several types of CNM relationships exist: (1) **open relationships**, in which partners may mutually agree to have sexual contact with others, (2) **swinging**, or the practice of extradyadic sex with members of another couple, and (3) **polyamory**, or the practice of engaging in multiple emotional close relationships that may or may not be sexual in nature, with the consent of everyone involved. The committed relationship is considered the primary relationship in both nonsexual extradyadic relationships and open marriages. Only the group marriage/multiple relationships model rejects the primacy of the relationship. Group marriage is the equal sharing of partners, as in polygamy. Open marriages are more common than group marriages.

While monogamous relationships remain the norm in the United States, polyamory is on the rise. Numbers and demographics are reflected in both popular media (magazines and television programs) and more significantly, in the increased numbers of online searches

(Balzarini et al., 2019; Moors, 2016). Polyamory has a pervasive stigma surrounding it and the potential for inciting jealousy in either or both partners. Who engages in polyamory? Compared to participants in monogamous relationships, those in polyamorous relationships were more likely to identify as a sexual minority, be in a civil union, be previously divorced, and earn less than $40,000 per year. When asked to identify other demographics, including gender identity, sexual orientation, or political affiliation, they chose "other" more often than those who were not in polyamorous relationships (Balzarini et al., 2019).

Rebound Sex

Sexual experiences in the aftermath of a romantic relationship breakup are sometimes referred to as **rebound sex**. Also called revenge sex, or being on the rebound, many who engage in this behavior report having been in a committed relationship followed by a loss that some otherwise regard as "being dumped" or "ghosted." Negative reactions that occur among individuals following a breakup include sadness, distress, and anger (Sprecher, 1994; Tashiro & Frazier, 2003). A longitudinal, online diary study of research among 170 undergraduate students found that having sex to cope and to get back at the ex-partner increased immediately following the split-up. Sexual activity, however, was shown to decline over time, as did the probability of having sex with a new partner (Barber & Cooper, 2014). This was particularly true for those who considered themselves "dumped" by their ex-partner. The motivations for rebound sex included a need to boost self-esteem, to ease pain and loneliness, and to get over the breakup. Anger and distress might have also played a role in the desire to get back at the ex-partner.

● Making Love Last: From Passion to Intimacy

Ultimately, passionate love is transformed or replaced by a quieter, more lasting love. Otherwise, the relationship will likely end, and each person will search for another who will once again ignite passion.

> "'Tis better to have loved and lost Than never to have loved at all."
> —Alfred, Lord Tennyson (1809–1892)

Although love is one of the most important elements of our humanity, it seems to come and go. The kind of love that lasts is what we might call **intimate love**. In intimate love, each person knows they can count on the other. The excitement comes from the achievement of other goals—from creativity, from work, from child rearing, from friendships—as well as from the relationship. The key to making love endure seems to be not maintaining love's passionate intensity but transforming it into intimate love. Intimate love is based on commitment, caring, and self-disclosure.

Commitment is an important component of intimate love. It reflects a determination to continue a relationship or marriage in the face of bad times as well as good. It is based on conscious choices rather than on feelings, which, by their very nature, are transitory. Commitment involves a promise of a shared future, a promise to be together, come what may. We seem to be as much in search of commitment as we are in search of love or marriage. We speak of making a commitment to someone or to a relationship. A committed relationship has become almost a stage of courtship, somewhere between dating and being engaged or living together.

Caring involves the making of another person's needs as important as your own. It requires what the philosopher Martin Buber (1958) called an "I-Thou" relationship. Buber described two fundamental ways of relating to people: I-Thou and I-It. In an I-Thou relationship, each person is treated as a Thou—that is, as a person whose life is valued as an end in itself. In an I-It relationship, each person is treated as an It; the person has worth only as someone who can be used. When a person is treated as a Thou, his or her humanity and uniqueness are paramount.

Self-disclosure is the revelation of personal information that others would not ordinarily know because of its riskiness. When we self-disclose, we reveal ourselves—our hopes, our fears, our everyday thoughts—to others. Self-disclosure deepens others' understanding of us. It also deepens our own understanding, for we discover unknown aspects as we open up to others. Without self-disclosure, we remain opaque and hidden. If others love us, such love can make us anxious: Are we loved for ourselves or for the image we present to the world?

> "Everyone has experienced that truth: that love, like a running brook, is disregarded, taken for granted; but when the brook freezes over, then people begin to remember how it was when it ran, and they want it to run again."
> —Kahlil Gibran (1883–1931)

think about it

Slow Love: A New Path to Romance

We all crave the excitement and chemical juices, including dopamine, norepinephrine, and serotonin, that creates what the ancient Greek poet Homer called "the pulsing rush of longing." When that initial cocktail dries up, it is replaced with another more soothing one that includes oxytocin and vasopressin, which are associated with memory, attention, and positive illusions. Should we rely on those initial exciting yet fleeting chemical cocktails to inform our opinion of a potential partner?

"It seems everyone is swept up in a very myopic understanding of sex, love, and romance," notes Dr. Helen Fisher, senior research fellow at the Kinsey Institute (cited in Parker-Pope, 2019). At the same time, Fisher sees signs of a new approach to the courtship process, with many people behaving with more caution around the ways they meet and interact with others. Coronavirus (COVID-19), technology, and financial issues are among those that seem to be shifting our views about what to expect and how to interact in a new relationship. While each of these is altering how singles meet and interact, none are necessarily changing our innate human disposition to love.

Though we still have a lot to learn about love, many in the millennial generation (those born from around 1980 to the mid-1990s) are opting for what Fisher calls "slow love," which includes dating less, having less sex, and marrying much later than previous generations. Fisher and her colleague Justin Garcia (2017) note that people who date three years or more before marrying are 39% less likely to divorce than people who rush into marriage.

Researchers have learned that many younger millennials (those born in the 1990s) are forgoing sex during young adulthood, with 15% being sexually inactive since age 18, twice as many as among those born in the 1960s (Twenge et al., 2017). (See Think About It, Chapter 6: "Are Young People Really Having Less Sexual Activity?") While it's unclear why this is occurring, Fisher and Garcia point out that this generation may be carving a more successful path to lasting love than seen in previous generations. For example, before they even enter a sexual relationship, a Match.com study (2019.8) among a representative sample of 5,000 individuals revealed that 40% of young singles feel they need to achieve self-acceptance before they seek love, 23% say they desire to reach a certain point in their career, and 20% desire to reach a particular income before committing to a serious relationship. Additionally, today's young people seek to learn as much as possible about a potential partner before they spend time, energy, and money and possibly risk their happiness and health on dating. This has resulted in a changed pathway to romance, with courtship coming later in the relationship.

Some suggest that extensive digital use has made millennials more socially isolated and restless, which could explain why they are having less sex than earlier generations. And when they have sex, it may be viewed as less meaningful, given their frequent engagement in hookups. Others argue the point, especially in light of COVID-19, that technology is allowing them to socially connect in an otherwise socially distant time.

For many millennials, financial issues take precedence over their decisions about whether to engage or nurture a new relationship. The combination of student debt coupled with a desire to find and maintain satisfying jobs and careers may influence the ways in which many approach and maintain relationships.

Perhaps the changing attitudes and behaviors as are seen in this generation may provide younger generations with a more thoughtful example of what commitment might look like. Slow love may be just one way to achieve that.

Think Critically

1. How has courtship changed from the time your parents dated to now? Do you believe these changes are impacting the way you regard commitments and relationships?

2. What is your opinion of "slow love"? Is this something you and/or a potential partner have discussed?

3. How do you regard having a "sex interview" before considering a first date?

Together, these principles help transform love. But in the final analysis, perhaps the most important means of sustaining love are our words and actions; caring words and deeds provide the setting for maintaining and expanding love.

Being able to sustain love in the day-to-day world involves commitment, compassion, and most importantly, communication. Clear communication can take the guesswork out of relationships, subdue jealousy, increase general satisfaction, and possibly put couple therapists out of business.

● The Nature of Communication

Feelings or emotions are the universal language and are to be honored. They are the authentic expression of who you are at your deepest place."

—Judith Wright (1915–2000)

Communication is a transactional process by which we use symbols, such as words, gestures, and movements, to establish human contact, exchange information, and reinforce or change our own attitudes and behaviors and those of others. Communication takes place simultaneously within cultural, social, and psychological contexts. These contexts affect our ability to communicate clearly by prescribing rules (usually unwritten or unconscious) for communicating about various subjects, including sexuality. The ability to communicate is important in developing and maintaining relationships. Partners satisfied with their sexual communication tend to be satisfied with their relationship as a whole.

The Cultural Context

The cultural context of communication consists of the language that is used and the values, beliefs, and customs associated with it. In many cultures, sexual topics have been traditionally taboo. Children and adolescents are discouraged from obtaining sexual knowledge; they learn that they are not supposed to talk about sex. Censorship abounds in the media, with the ever-present "bleep" on television, though on the Internet there appears to be virtually no filtering. Our language has a variety of words for describing sex, including scientific or impersonal ones ("sexual intercourse," "coitus," "copulation"), moralistic ones ("fornication"), euphemistic ones ("doing it," "hooking up," "sleeping with"), and taboo ones ("fucking," "screwing," "banging"). A few terms place sexual interactions in a relational category, such as "making love." But love is not always involved, and the term does not capture the erotic quality of sex. Furthermore, LGBTQ+ communities have developed their own sexual slang, because society suppresses the open discussion or expression of same-sex and gendered behavior.

"The greatest science in the world, in heaven and on earth, is love."
—Mother Teresa (1910–1997)

The Social Context

The social context of communication consists of the roles we play in society as members of different groups. For instance, we may play out masculine and feminine roles. As partners in marriage, many people act out roles of husband or wife. As members of cohabiting units, we perform what we consider to be heterosexual, gay, lesbian, or queer cohabiting roles.

Social ties play a significant role in the well-being of individuals and couples. When we compare married or partnered friends with those who are single, we may notice that single people generally have a wider social network than their married counterparts, who often withdraw into couplehood. Stephanie Coontz (2018), a family researcher and historian, suggests that socializing and communicating with family and participating in social clubs, teams, and political organizations are part of what is known as "social integration." Maintaining a large network of friends can enhance and even revitalize a marriage because people may feel better when their spouses have good friendships. Recently, however, with the introduction of COVID-19 into the global population, the lives of just about everyone have been fundamentally changed. Social connections have been disrupted, and sexual activity has been discouraged outside one's household. Moving beyond video chats into real-life encounters is complicated, to say the least, as social distancing has added a new dimension to our social and sexual lives.

One group we may overlook when discussing communication relative to sexuality is older adults. Though the sexual revolution of the 1960s brought tremendous societal changes with regard to sexuality, research has shown that many older adults are hesitant to discuss sexual issues with their children, friends, partners, or physicians (Ayalon et al., 2019). Hence their upbringing, which for many included limited and accurate information, has negatively impacted their interpersonal relations.

Roles exist in relation to other people; thus, status—a person's position or ranking in a group—is important. In traditional gender roles, men are accorded higher status than women; in traditional marital roles, husbands are superior in status to wives. And in terms of sexual orientation, society awards higher status to heterosexual people than to LGBTQ+ individuals. Because of these disparities, heterosexual couples tend to have a greater power imbalance than do gay, lesbian, or queer couples (Lips, 2007).

The Psychological Context

We are not prisoners of culture and society; we are unique individuals. We may accept some cultural or social aspects, such as language taboos, but we may reject, ignore, or modify others, such as traditional gender roles. Because we have distinct personalities, we express our uniqueness by the way we communicate: We may be assertive or submissive, rigid or flexible, and sensitive or insensitive; we may exhibit high or low self-esteem.

Our personality characteristics affect our ability to communicate, change, or manage conflict. Rigid people, for example, are less likely to change than are flexible ones, regardless of the quality of communication. People with high self-esteem may be more open to change because they do not necessarily interpret conflict as an attack on themselves. Personality characteristics such as negative or positive feelings about sexuality affect our sexual communication more directly.

"The cruelest lies are often told in silence."

—Robert Louis Stevenson (1850–1894)

Nonverbal Communication

There is no such thing as not communicating. Even when we are not talking, we are communicating by our silence: an awkward silence, a hostile silence, a tender silence. We are communicating by our body movements, our head positions, our facial expressions, our physical distance from another person, and so on. We can make sounds that aren't words to communicate nonverbally; screams, moans, grunts, sighs, and so on communicate a range of feelings and reactions. Look around you: How are the people in your presence communicating nonverbally?

Most of our communication of feeling is nonverbal. We radiate our moods: A happy mood invites companionship; a solemn mood pushes people away. Joy infects; depression distances—all without a word being said. Nonverbal expressions of love are particularly effective—a gentle touch, a loving glance, or the gift of a flower.

One of the problems with nonverbal communication, however, is the imprecision of its messages. Is a person frowning or squinting? Does the smile indicate friendliness or nervousness? Is the silence reflective, or does it express disapproval or remoteness?

Three of the most important forms of nonverbal communication are proximity, eye contact, and touching.

Proximity   Nearness in physical space and time is called **proximity**. Where we sit or stand in relation to another person signifies a level of intimacy. Many of our words that convey emotion relate to proximity, such as feeling "distant" or "close" or being "moved" by someone. We also "make the first move," "move in" on someone else's partner, or "move in together."

In a social gathering, the distances between individuals when they start a conversation are clues to how they wish to define the relationship. All cultures have an intermediate distance in face-to-face interactions that is neutral. In most cultures, decreasing the distance signifies either an invitation to greater intimacy or a threat. Moving away denotes the desire to terminate the interaction. When we stand at an intermediate distance from someone at a party, we send the message "Intimacy is not encouraged." If we move closer, however, we invite closeness but risk rejection.

From a partner's perspective, physical proximity, along with a touch or a hug when needing comfort, may set the stage for both psychological intimacy and sexual closeness and affection. It may also increase the frequency and level of satisfaction in sexual interactions by underscoring greater ease and comfort for both partners.

Proximity, eye contact, and touching are important components of nonverbal communication. What do you think this man and woman are "saying" to each other?

franckreporter/Getty Images

Eye Contact   Much can be discovered about a relationship by watching how the two people look at each other. Making eye contact with another person, if only for a split second longer than usual, is a signal of interest. When we can't take our eyes off another person, we may find ourself having a strong attraction to that person. In addition to eye contact, dilated pupils may be an indication of sexual interest. They may also indicate fear, anger, and other strong emotions.

The amount of eye contact between partners in conversation can reveal couples who have high levels of conflict and those who don't. Those with the greatest degree of agreement have the most eye contact with each other. Those in conflict tend to avoid eye contact unless it is a daggerlike stare. As with proximity, however, the level of eye contact may differ by culture.

Touching It is difficult to overestimate the significance of touch and its relevance to human development, health, and sexuality. Touch is the most basic of all senses. The skin contains receptors for pleasure and pain, heat and cold, roughness and smoothness. "Touch is the mother sense and out of it, all the other senses have been derived," writes anthropologist Ashley Montagu (1986). Touch is a life-giving force for infants. If babies are not touched, they can fail to thrive and may even die. We hold hands and cuddle with small children and with people we love. Levels of touching differ among cultures and ethnic groups. Although the value placed on nonverbal expression may vary across groups and cultures, the ability to communicate and understand nonverbally remains important in all cultures.

But touch can also be a violation. Strangers or acquaintances may touch inappropriately, presuming a level of familiarity that does not actually exist. A date or partner may touch the other person in a manner he or she doesn't like or want. And sexual harassment includes unwelcome touching.

Touch often signals intimacy, immediacy, and emotional closeness. In fact, touch may very well be the closest form of nonverbal communication. One researcher writes: "If intimacy is proximity, then nothing comes closer than touch, the most intimate knowledge of another" (Thayer, 1986). And touching seems to go hand in hand with self-disclosure. Those who touch appear to self-disclose more; in fact, touch seems to be an important factor in prompting others to talk more about themselves.

No matter the type of relationship, be prepared to accept individual differences. In spite of honest and ongoing communication, people still have unique comfort levels. Again, honest feedback will help you and your partner find a mutually acceptable level. If you are both able to understand and enjoy the rich and powerful messages that touch sends, then your relationship can be enriched by yet another dimension.

● Sexual Communication

Communication is important in developing and maintaining healthy sexual relationships. In childhood and adolescence, communication is critical for transmitting sexual knowledge and values and forming our sexual identities. As we establish our relationships, communication enables us to signal sexual interest and initiate sexual interactions. In developed relationships, communication often allows us to explore and maintain our sexuality as couples.

Our interpersonal sexual scripts provide us with "instructions" on how to behave sexually, including the initiation of potentially sexual relationships. Because as a culture we share our interpersonal sexual scripts, we know how we are supposed to act at the beginning of a relationship. These scripts are changing, however, as individuals rely more on social media to communicate and share their personal and sexual desires and needs. Using the anonymity feature that various social media platforms allow, an individual is free to become anyone they wish, without consequences, until a face-to-face meeting occurs. Still, the questions remain: How do we begin a relationship? What is it that attracts and allows us to bond with certain individuals?

Imagine yourself unattached at a party. You notice someone standing next to you as you reach for some chips. In a split second, you decide whether you are interested in them. On what basis do you make that decision? Is it looks, personality, style, sensitivity, intelligence, smell, or what?

If you're like most people, you base this decision, consciously or unconsciously, on appearance. Physical attractiveness is particularly important during the initial meeting and early stages of a relationship. If you don't know anything else about a person, you tend to judge on appearance.

Sexual minorities, just as heterosexual men and women, rely on both nonverbal and verbal communication in expressing sexual interest in others. Unlike heterosexual people, however, they cannot necessarily assume that the person in whom they are interested is of the same sexual orientation. Instead, they must rely on specific identifying factors, such as meeting at a gay/lesbian/queer bar, wearing a gay/lesbian/queer pride button, participating in gay/lesbian/queer events, being introduced by friends to others identified as LGBTQ+ or joining an LGBTQ+ dating website. In situations in which sexual orientation is not clear, some

"Touch is a language that can communicate more love in five seconds than words can in five minutes."
—Ashley Montagu (1905–1999)

"Married couples who love each other tell each other a thousand things without talking."
—Chinese proverb

"Healing touch belongs to all of us."
—Dolores Krieger (1935–)

"The most precious gift we can offer anyone is our attention."
—Thich Nhat Hanh (1926–)

"Whereas a lot of men used to ask for conversation when they really wanted sex, nowadays they often feel obliged to ask for sex even when they really want conversation."
—Katharine Whitehorn (1928–)

Nontraditional roles are changing the ways in which couples make contact and initiate conversation. What appear to be the roles of each person in this photograph?

Digital Vision/Getty Images

"When in doubt, tell the truth."

—Mark Twain (1835–1910)

"If you don't risk anything, you risk even more."

—Erica Jong (1942–)

Regardless of our sexual orientation, age, gender, or ethnicity, much of our sexual communication is nonverbal.

Rawpixel/Getty Images

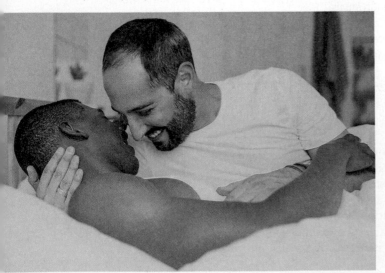

LGBTQ+ individuals use "gaydar" (gay radar), in which they look for clues as to orientation. They give ambiguous cues regarding their own orientation while looking for cues from the other person. They may include the mention of specific places for entertainment or recreation that are frequented mainly by lesbian, gay, queer, or transgender individuals, songs that can be interpreted as having "gay" meanings, or movies with LGBTQ+ themes. Once a like orientation or gender identity is established, LGBTQ+ individuals often use nonverbal communication to express interest.

Most people would deny that they are attracted to others simply because of their looks. We like to think we are deeper than that. But appearances are important, in part because we tend to infer qualities based on looks. This inference is based on what is known as the **halo effect**, the assumption that attractive or charismatic people also possess more desirable social characteristics than are actually present.

Gender Differences and Similarities in Partner Communication

How individuals regard their partnerships, the way they talk about it, and how they express themselves influence both their feelings and expectations about it (Brooks, 2016). In developing relationships, partners begin modifying their individual sexual scripts as they interact with each other. The scripts become less rigid and conventional as each partner adapts to the uniqueness of the other. Partners ultimately develop a shared sexual script. Through their sexual interactions, they learn what each other likes, dislikes, wants, and needs. Verbal communication best addresses these needs. Much of this learning takes place nonverbally: Partners in established relationships, like those also in emerging relationships, tend to be indirect and ambiguous in their sexual communication. Like partners in new relationships, they want to avoid rejection. Indirection allows them to express sexual interest and, at the same time, protect themselves from embarrassment or loss of face.

Not surprisingly, achieving desired sexual outcomes requires both coordination and communication between the partners, such as planning sexual events, enticing one another, or developing shared meaning about their sex life.

Though most people speak about the same number of words each day, gender differences lie in the topics they discuss and the terms they use. In a traditional heterosexual script, men often talk about technology, sports, and money, while women often talk about social events, fashion, and relationships. According to Deborah Tannen, author and professor of linguistics at Georgetown University, men's talk tends to focus on relative hierarchy—competition for relative power—while women's tends to focus on connection—relative closeness or distance (Tannen, 2016). For example, following the same conversation between a man and a woman, the man might wonder whether the conversation put him in a one-up or one-down position, whereas the woman may question whether it brought them closer together or pushed them apart? Although most partnered conversations reflect both hierarchy and connection along with differing conversational styles, most functioning couples communicate to reach the same or similar goals.

However, among couples with sexual problems, a lack of sexual communication is often reported (Mallory et al., 2019). It may be that sexual difficulties make communication more challenging; it might also be true that couples who are hesitant about talking openly about their sexual concerns may be more likely to develop sexual problems. In a recent meta-analysis consisting of 48 studies focused on assessing the relationship between couples' sexual communication and the various dimensions of sexual function, it was found that sexual communication was positively associated with all domains of sexual function (desire, arousal, erection, lubrication, orgasm, and less pain) (Mallory et al., 2019). Most of this research was centered on heterosexual men and women, with little to no

think about it

Let's (Not) Talk About Sex: Avoiding the Discussion About Past Lovers

Seal up your lips and give no words but mum.
—William Shakespeare *Henry IV, Part 2*, 1592

Revealing one's past sexual experiences early in a new relationship—as difficult and as threatening as it may seem—can both enhance trust in a new relationship as well as protect the other by, for example, providing information about sexually transmitted infections (STIs). Still, many refrain from honest conversations about past sexual experiences. In effect, they "seal up their lips," as Shakespeare stated. Deciding what to reveal and conceal in any close relationship is often difficult to navigate because it represents a tension between self-disclosure and privacy. Self-disclosure is a fundamental component for the development of relationship intimacy; however, too much can hinder relationship growth (Anderson et al., 2011; Dindia, 1994; Ijams & Miller, 2000).

One-hundred and two students (49 men and 53 women) from a large midwestern university who were currently in a romantic relationship and who had prior sex experience with a partner were assessed about disclosure of past romantic relationships (Anderson et al., 2011). They were asked to: (1) list all the topics they avoided discussing in their current romantic relationship (i.e., taboo topics) and (2) describe reasons for avoiding discussing one's sexual history if they or their current partner were reluctant to have that discussion. Here are the major study findings:

- Past romantic relationships, and in particular past sexual experiences, was the most frequently cited taboo topic. Men and women were similar in the frequency with which they indicated particular reasons for avoidance.

- Four reasons for avoiding discussion of prior sexual experiences were given: (1) belief that the past should be kept in the past, (2) identity issues, (3) perceived threats to their current relationship, and (4) emotionally upsetting feelings.

- Relative to "the past should be the past," participants commonly cited the lack of its relevance to the current relationship. Some stated that they did not want to know, think about, or visualize the details of a partner's prior sexual activities.

- The identity theme captured the respondents' desire to not be subjected to evaluation, especially not being compared to prior partners. Many worried about whether their level of sexual experience differed from their partner's level—that is, having had "too much" or "too little" past experiences. However, the greatest concern was being perceived as too inexperienced.

- Participants expressed concern that revealing past sexual experiences would be a threat to current relational soundness, as individuals or the relationship might be judged to be less close or special.

- The possibility of jealousy and embarrassment for oneself or by the partner was another somewhat commonly cited reason for avoiding discussion of sexual past.

The researchers stressed the importance of keeping any damage to the current relationship to a minimum by assuring one's partner that nothing from the past can make the current relationship less special. They noted that identifying how individuals become comfortable with self-disclosure "may provide further insights into why and how past sexual experience in romantic relationships may be beneficially discussed" (p. 390).

Think Critically

1. If you have had sexual experiences with another person(s), what topics about past relationships did you find to be the most taboo in a new relationship?

2. Do you believe that there are gender differences between what individuals share about past lovers? If so, why do these exist? If not, why not?

3. If you were starting a new relationship with a person who has had prior sexual relationships, what would you want to know and not want to know about the sexual relationship?

4. If you or a new partner has had prior sexual relationships, what can be done to help both of you feel secure in the new relationship?

studies on sexual communication and sexual function among same-sex or mixed-orientation partners. Nevertheless, it was found that:

- When discussing desire and orgasms, sexual communication was more significant for women than for men.

- The correlation between sexual communication and overall sexual function was stronger among those who were married as compared to those who were not in a committed relationship.

- Sexual communication was found to play a particularly strong role in facilitating women's sexual desire. The researchers speculated that women may be more likely to experience responsive desire, that is to have effective communication with a partner, rather than spontaneous desire.

- Couples' sexual communication appears to be particularly relevant for women with sexual difficulties.

Regardless of their gender, many people believe that talking about sex will cause embarrassment or discomfort, or inhibit open communication (Blunt-Vinti et al., 2018). In response to these common fears, couples may rely on more ambiguous communication (e.g., nonverbal cues or innuendos) in order to test a partner's responses or help "save face." Given that most people are highly vulnerable when engaging in sexual activity, a negative reaction may inhibit them from discussing sex, or when they do have a conversation, it may occur apart from the sexual experience. As a result, many persons rely on nonverbal communication, which is often perceived to be less awkward or threatening than verbal communication, especially as it's related to preferences, desire, or pleasure.

Researchers examined what effect verbal communication *during* sex has on sexual satisfaction. In a sample of 536 participants, researchers found that for all genders and sexual orientations, more communication during sex (both verbal and nonverbal) was: (a) associated with greater satisfaction with sexual communication and (b) sexual communication satisfaction predicts sexual satisfaction (Blunt-Vinti et al., 2018). This is important when considering traditional sexual scripts, in which communication about sexual desire, pleasure and satisfaction, particularly by women, deviates from how individuals are expected to communicate. Additionally, research suggests that young people, in particular, are uncomfortable and may lack the skills to communicate about desires, needs, or pleasure (Widman et al., 2014). While many variables are responsible for sexual satisfaction, sexual communication satisfaction is an important component of sexual satisfaction as well as relationship satisfaction.

● Developing Communication Skills

Generally, poor communication skills precede the onset of relationship problems. The material that follows will help you understand and develop your skills in communicating about sexual matters.

Talking About Sex

Good communication is central to a healthy intimate relationship. Unfortunately, it is not always easy to establish or maintain.

Obstacles to Sexual Discussions The process of articulating our feelings about sex can be very difficult, for several reasons. First, we rarely have models for talking openly and honestly about sexuality. As children and adolescents, we probably never discussed sex with our parents, let alone heard them talking about sex. Second, talking about sexual matters defines us as being interested in sex, and interest in sex is often identified with being sexually obsessive, immoral, prurient, or "bad." If the topic of sex is tabooed, we further risk being labeled "bad." Third, we may believe that talking about sex will threaten our relationships. We don't talk about tabooed sexual feelings, fantasies, or desires because we fear that our partners may be repelled or disgusted. We also are reluctant to discuss sexual difficulties or problems because doing so may bring attention to our own role in them. (See Think About It, "Let's (Not) Talk About Sex: Avoiding the Discussion About Past Lovers.")

Keys to Good Communication Being aware of communication skills and actually using them are two separate matters. Furthermore, even though we may be comfortable sharing our feelings with another, we may find it more difficult to discuss our sexual preferences and needs. Self-disclosure, trust, and feedback are three keys to good communication.

Self-Disclosure **Self-disclosure** creates the environment for mutual understanding. Most people know us only through the conventional roles we play as female or male, married or partnered, a parent or child, and so on. These roles, however, do not necessarily reflect our deepest selves. If we act as if we are nothing more than our roles, we may reach a point at which we no longer know who we are.

Through the process of self-disclosure, we not only reveal ourselves to others but also find out who we are. We discover feelings we have hidden, repressed, or ignored. We nurture forgotten aspects of ourselves by bringing them to the surface. Moreover, self-disclosure is reciprocal: In the process of our sharing, others share themselves with us. The ability to disclose or reveal private thoughts and feelings, especially positive ones, can contribute to enhancing relationships (MacNeil & Byers, 2009). Men, in general, are less likely than women to disclose intimate aspects of themselves (Lips, 2007). Because they have been taught to be "strong and silent," they are more reluctant to express feelings of tenderness or vulnerability. Women generally find it easier to disclose their feelings because they have been conditioned from childhood to express themselves (Tannen, 2016). These differences can drive wedges between people. Even when individuals are partnered, they can feel lonely because there is little or no interpersonal contact. And the worst kind of loneliness is feeling alone when we are with someone to whom we want to feel close.

Within the context of sexual activity, there are several ways in which the lack of self-disclosure and deception can occur: (1) deception regarding the authenticity of response to sexual activity, (2) deception regarding orgasm, and (3) deception regarding safer sex practices (Horan, 2015). A study of 183 university students with an average age of 22, found that 60% of participants had at some point acted deceptively with representing their number of previous partners and of those, nearly 20% never disclosed their number of previous partners (Horan, 2015). The implications for these findings suggest that individuals either do not recognize or desire to communicate the association between their number of sexual partners, their own sexual practices, and the significance of both in preventing sexually transmitted infections.

Trust When we talk about intimate relationships, the two words that most frequently pop up are "love" and "trust." Trust is the primary characteristic we associate with love. But what, exactly, is trust? **Trust** is a belief in the reliability and integrity of a person. When someone says, "Trust me," he or she is asking for something that does not easily occur.

Trust is experienced in all nearly forms of social and interpersonal and sexual relationships. In fact, trust is among the most commonly cited means of gaining knowledge and understanding in a partnership and has become synonymous with attachment, pair bonding, love, and monogamy (Brady et al., 2009; Carter, 2014). According to Dennis Fortenberry, pediatrician at Indiana University School of Medicine (2019), trust helps to guide sexual relationships and its presence or absence can impact behaviors in both positive and negative ways. On the positive side, trust contributes to feelings of safety, intimacy, satisfaction, and pleasure and is a standard for evaluation of relationship quality and stability. Contrary to this, distrust is associated with both jealousy and intimate partner violence. Fortenberry states:

> Trust appears to be both antecedent and consequence of sex, and violations of sexual trust distort the comfort and safety of many relationships. Trust, it seems has many contradictions (p. 425).

Trust is critical in close relationships for two reasons. First, self-disclosure requires trust because it makes us vulnerable. A person will not self-disclose if the person believes the information may be misused—by mocking or revealing a secret, for example. Second, the degree to which we trust a person influences how we interpret ambiguous or unexpected messages from him or her. If, for example, our partner says that they want to study alone tonight, we are likely to take the statement at face value if we have a high level of trust. But if we have a low level of trust, we may believe that they actually will be meeting someone else.

"A little sincerity is a dangerous thing, and a great deal of it is absolutely fatal."

—Oscar Wilde (1854–1900)

"The other night I said to my wife, Ruth: 'Do you feel that the sex and excitement has gone out of our marriage?' Ruth said: 'I'll discuss it with you during the next commercial.'"

—Milton Berle (1908–2002)

"Ninety-nine lies may save you, but the hundredth will give you away."

—West African proverb

practically speaking

Communication Patterns and Partner Satisfaction

Give me the gift of a listening heart.
— King Solomon (c. 970–931 BCE)

Researchers studying relationship satisfaction have found a number of communication patterns that offer clues to enhancing our intimate relationships (Byers, 2005; Caron, 2020; Gottman & Carrere, 2000; Hess & Coffelt, 2012). They found that those in satisfying heterosexual relationships tend to have the following common characteristics regarding communication:

- *Use humor to diffuse anger.* Occasionally, cracking a joke in the middle of a serious discussion or argument can sometimes diffuse the negativity and redirect each partner to a more neutral stance.

- *Stay calm and treat your partner with respect.* While the tendency may be to flee, yell or say something you may not mean, none of these are helpful in resolving issues. If you need to take a break, let your partner know when you will return to rejoin the conversation.

- *The ability to disclose or reveal private thoughts and feelings, especially positive ones.* Dissatisfied partners tend to disclose mostly negative thoughts. Satisfied partners say such things as "I love you," "You're sexy," or "I feel vulnerable; please hold me." Unhappy partners may also say that they love each other, but more often they say things like "Don't touch me; I can't stand you," "You turn me off," or "This relationship makes me miserable and frustrated."

- *The expression of more or less equal levels of affective disclosures.* Both partners in satisfied couples are likely to say things like "You make me feel happy," "I love you more than I can ever say," or "I love the way you touch me."

- *More time spent talking, discussing personal topics, and expressing feelings in positive ways.* Satisfied couples talk about their sexual feelings and the fun they have in bed together.

- *Ability to talk explicitly about sex using a variety of terms.* Talking explicitly with one's partner about desired specific behaviors or using erotic words can enhance sexual experiences and result in more satisfying sexual interactions.

- *A willingness to accept and engage in conflict in nondestructive ways.* Satisfied couples view conflict as a natural part of intimate relationships. When partners have sexual disagreements, they do not accuse or blame; instead, they exchange viewpoints, seek common ground, and, when appropriate, compromise.

- *Less frequent conflict and less time spent in conflict.* Both satisfied and unsatisfied couples, however, experience perpetual problems surrounding the same issues, especially communication, children, sex, money, and personality characteristics.

- *The ability to accurately encode (send) verbal and nonverbal messages and accurately decode (understand) such messages.* This ability to send and understand nonverbal messages is especially important for couples who seek satisfying sexual interactions.

When engaged in conflict, try and remember what brought you together and what your partner is doing right.

How good are your sexual communication skills? Take the following Dyadic Sexual Communication Scale to find out.

Instructions

The following is a list of statements people have made about discussing sex with their partner. Thinking about your current or past partner, indicate how much you agree or disagree with each statement.

1 = Strongly disagree
2 = Slightly disagree
3 = Neutral—neither agree nor disagree
4 = Slightly agree
5 = Strongly agree

1. My partner rarely responds when I want to talk about our sex life.
2. Some sexual matters are too upsetting to discuss with my sexual partner.
3. There are sexual issues or problems in our sexual relationship that we have never discussed.
4. My partner and I never seem to resolve our disagreements about sexual issues.
5. Whenever my partner and I talk about sex, I feel like he or she is lecturing me.
6. My partner often complains that I am not very clear about what I want sexually.
7. My partner and I have never had a heart-to-heart talk about our sex life together.
8. My partner has no difficulty in talking to me about his or her sexual feelings and desires.
9. Even when angry with me, my partner is able to appreciate my views on sexuality.
10. Talking about sex is a satisfying experience for both of us.
11. My partner and I can usually talk calmly about our sex life.
12. I have little difficulty in telling my partner what I do or don't do sexually.
13. I seldom feel embarrassed when talking about the details of our sex life with my partner.

Scoring

Add up the scores for each question, *reversing your scores for questions 1 through 7* (so that 5 = 1, 4 = 2, 3 = 3, and so on). A higher total score indicates better sexual communication skills.

Source: Catania, J. A. (2019). Dyadic Sexual Communication Scale. In Milhausen, et al. (Eds.), *Handbook of sexuality related measures.* (4th ed.). Routledge.

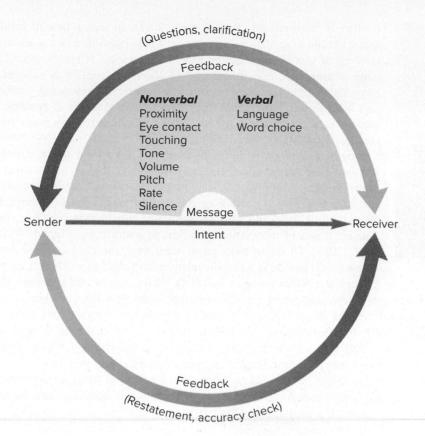

• **FIGURE 5**

Communication Loop. In successful communication, feedback between the sender and the receiver ensures that both understand or are trying to understand what is being communicated. For communication to be clear, the message and the intent behind the message must be congruent. Nonverbal and verbal components must also support the intended message. Communication includes not just language and word choice but also nonverbal characteristics such as tone, volume, pitch, rate, and silence.

Self-disclosure is reciprocal. If we self-disclose, we expect our partner to self-disclose as well. As we self-disclose, we build trust; as we withhold self-disclosure, we erode trust. To withhold ourselves is to imply that we don't trust the other person, and if we don't, that person will not trust us.

Feedback A third critical element in communication is **feedback**, the ongoing process of restating, checking the accuracy of, questioning, and clarifying messages. Feedback often begins with active listening, a technique in which the listener accurately paraphrases or restates what he or she has heard. If someone self-discloses to a partner, his or her response to that self-disclosure is feedback, and the partner's response is feedback to that feedback. It is a continuous process, or loop (see Figure 5). The most important form of feedback for improving relationships is constructive feedback. Constructive feedback focuses on self-disclosing information that will help partners understand the consequences of their actions—for each other and for the relationship. For example, if your partner discloses his or her doubts about the relationship, you can respond in a number of ways. Among these are remaining silent, venting anger, expressing indifference, and giving constructive feedback. Of these responses, constructive feedback is the most likely to encourage positive change.

• Conflict and Intimacy

Conflict is the process in which people perceive that incompatible goals and interference from others is hindering them from achieving their goals.

We expect love to unify us, but sometimes it doesn't. Two people do not become one when they love each other, although at first they may have this feeling or expectation. Their love may not be an illusion, but their sense of ultimate oneness is. In reality, we retain our individual identities, needs, wants, and pasts—even while loving each other. It is a paradox that the more intimate two people become, the more likely they are to experience conflict. The sharing of space, time, resources, and investments creates arenas for both support and

"A half-truth is a whole lie."

—Yiddish proverb

"There are three sides to every story: your side, my side, and the truth."

—Robert Evans (1930–2019)

Conflict is natural in intimate relationships because each person has his or her unique identity, values, needs, and history.

Daniel Thistlewaite/Image Source

"Years of love have been forgot in the hatred of a minute."

—Edgar Allan Poe (1809–1849)

conflict in relationships (Robles et al., 2013). In fact, a lack of arguing can signal trouble in a relationship because it may mean that issues are not being resolved or that there is indifference. Conflict itself is not dangerous to intimate relationships; it is the manner in which the conflict is handled that is more significant. The presence of conflict does not necessarily indicate that love is waning or has disappeared. It may mean that love is growing. A willingness to accept and engage in conflict in nondestructive ways can assist couples in enhancing their relationship.

How one quarrels is far more important than what one quarrels about, whether it be finances, careers, sex, communication, or a wet towel on the floor. The key to a satisfying relationship is how the couple approaches and discusses the issues. In reviewing 100 middle-income couples, married for an average of 12 years and with an average of two to three children, the most frequent source of conflict were children, by a wide margin (nearly 40%) (Papp et al., 2009). Of these, most issues were what the children were doing and why, how to respond to a certain behavior, and child care. Moderately frequent sources of conflict included annoying habits, money and spending, demands of work and jobs, leisure and recreation, communication and listening, and chores (16–25%). Least frequent sources of conflict were annoying personality styles, friends, intimacy and sex, commitment and expectations, and relatives (6–12%). It's important to note that this sample involved only couples who had been successful in negotiating 12 years of marriage, which suggests that many of these issues had been managed pretty well.

A study of 1,782 same-sex attracted participants in a variety of living arrangements found that meeting needs for connection, intimacy, and mutual understanding were the strongest predictors of relationship satisfaction. Other factors included authentic sexual expression, resolving conflicts with religion, and reducing depression and anxiety (Lefevor et al., 2019).

Resolving conflicts requires many tactics, including maintaining an open dialogue and managing the feelings each partner has about the issue, as well as embracing the knowledge that each partner may never have as much time, money, or patience as he or she desires. Partners who understand and accept the unique demands and issues that will inevitably complicate and enrich their relationship will be in a better position to address conflict when it arises.

Sexual Conflicts

Common practices such as using sex as a scapegoat for nonsexual problems and using arguments as a cover-up for other problems frequently lead to additional disagreements and misunderstandings. Clinging to these patterns can interfere with problem solving and inhibit conflict resolution.

Disagreement About Sex Conflict about sex can be intertwined in several ways. A couple may have a disagreement about sex that leads to conflict. For example, if one person wants to be sexual and the other does not, they may argue.

Sex can also be used as a scapegoat for nonsexual problems. If a person is angry because a partner has called him or her a lousy communicator, that person may take it out on the partner sexually by calling him or her a lousy lover. They argue about their lovemaking rather than about the real issue, their lack of honest communication.

Finally, an argument can be a cover-up. If a person feels sexually inadequate or disinterested and does not want to have sex as often as his or her partner, the person may argue and make the other feel so angry that the last thing the partner would want to do is to be sexual with him or her.

For couples with children, relationships tend to follow a predictable pattern of satisfaction in the early years, a decrease in satisfaction during the child-rearing years, and if both partners are healthy, a return to a higher level after the children are grown. An awareness of this

Lessons from the Love Lab

Perhaps love is the process of my leading you gently back to yourself.

—Antoine de Saint-Exupery (1900–1944)

For many people, forming a new relationship appears to be a lot easier and a lot more fun than maintaining one. If this were not the case, then couples therapy and how-to articles and books on keeping love alive would not be so prevalent. Two people who have spent a significant part of his career investigating the quandaries of partnerships are John M. Gottman, professor emeritus of psychology at the University of Washington–Seattle's Family Research Lab, better known as the "Love Lab," and his wife Julia. Over the past 40 years, they, along with colleagues, have videotaped thousands of conversations between couples, scoring words and sentences based on facial expressions such as disgust, affection, and contempt. Though most of their work has involved married couples, applications can be made to any couple interested in improving their relationship.

The Gottmans believe that in order to keep love going strong or to rescue a relationship that has deteriorated, partners, regardless of their gender identity or sexual orientation, need to follow seven principles:

1. *Enhance your love map.* Emotionally intelligent couples are intimately familiar with each other's world. They have a richly detailed love map—they learn the major events in each other's history, and they keep updating their information as their partner's world changes.

2. *Nurture fondness and admiration.* Without the belief that your partner is worthy of honor and respect, there is no basis for a rewarding relationship. By reminding yourself of your partner's positive qualities—even as you grapple with each other's flaws—and verbally expressing your fondness and admiration, you can prevent a happy partnership from deteriorating.

3. *Turn toward each other.* In long-term commitments, people periodically make "bids" for their partner's attention, affection, humor, or support. Turning toward one another is the basis of emotional connection, romance, passion, and a good sex life.

4. *Let your partner influence you.* The happiest, most stable partnerships are those in which each individual treats the other with respect and does not resist power sharing and decision making. When the couple disagree, individuals actively search for common ground rather than insisting on getting their way.

5. *Solve your solvable problems.* Start with good manners when tackling your solvable problems by: (1) using a softened startup, such as stating your feelings without blame, expressing a positive need, and using "I" statements; (2) learning to make and receive repair attempts, such as de-escalating the tension and sharing what you feel; (3) soothing yourself and each other; and (4) when appropriate, compromising.

6. *Overcome gridlock.* Many ongoing conflicts have a sustained base of unexpressed dreams behind each person's stubborn position. In happy relationships, partners incorporate each other's goals into their concept of what their partnership is about. The bottom line in getting past gridlock is not necessarily to become a part of each other's dreams but to honor these dreams.

7. *Create shared meaning.* Long-term partnerships can have an intentional sense of shared purpose, meaning, family values, and cultural legacy that forms a shared inner life. This culture incorporates both of their dreams, and it is flexible enough to change as both partners grow and develop. When a marriage or partnership has this shared sense of meaning, conflict is less intense and perpetual problems are unlikely to lead to gridlock.

Source: This article is adapted from Bainbridge Island-based *YES! Magazine's* Winter 2011 Issue, "What Happy Families Know." It was adapted from *Seven Principles for Making Marriage Work*, by John M. Gottman and Nan Silver, Three Rivers Press, 1999.

pattern can be helpful to couples whose levels of conflict are escalating. Acknowledging a relationship's changing nature and focusing on strengths that each person brings to the relationship are ways to adapt to the inevitable changes that occur over time.

Conflict Resolution

The ways in which couples deal with conflict reflect and perhaps contribute to their relationship happiness. Partners who communicate with affection and interest and who integrate humor when appropriate can use such positive affect to defuse conflict (Gottman & Carrere, 2000).

Sometimes, differences can't be resolved, but they can be lived with. If a relationship is sound, differences can be absorbed without undermining the basic ties. All too often, we regard differences as threatening rather than as the unique expression of two personalities. Coexistence focuses on the person over whom we have the most power—ourselves.

"For a marriage to be peaceful, the husband should be deaf and the wife blind."

—Spanish proverb

"Hatred does not cease by hatred at any time. Hatred ceases by love. This is an unalterable law."

—Siddhartha Gautama, the Buddha (c. 563–483 BCE)

Final Thoughts

The study of love, while still evolving, is helping us understand the various components that make up this complex emotion. Understanding how it works in the day-to-day world may help us keep our love vital and growing.

If we can't talk about what we like and what we want, there is a good chance we won't get either one. Communication is the basis for good sex and good relationships. Communication and intimacy are reciprocal: Communication creates intimacy, and intimacy, in turn, creates good communication. But communication is learned behavior. If we have learned *not* to communicate, we can learn how to communicate. Communication allows us to expand ourselves and to feel more connected to and intimate with another person.

Summary

Friendship and Love

- Close friend relationships are similar to spouse/lover relationships in many ways. But lovers/spouses have more fascination and a greater sense of exclusiveness with their partners.

Love and Sexuality

- Sexuality and love are intimately related in our culture. Sex is most highly valued in loving relationships. For many persons, a loving relationship rivals marriage as an acceptable moral standard for intercourse.

- Nonmarital sex among young adults, but not adolescents, in a relational context has become the norm. An important factor in this shift is the surge in the numbers of unmarried men and women.

- Men and women tend to have different ideas about how they view love, sex, and attraction. Love, however, is equally important for persons of all sexual orientations and gender identities.

- Some people choose celibacy as a lifestyle. These individuals may have a better appreciation of the nature of friendship and an increased respect for the bonds of long-term partnerships. Fewer people may be asexual, or not attracted to either sex. Asexual individuals report varying attitudes towards sex.

How Do I Love Thee? Approaches and Attitudes Related to Love

- According to sociologist John Lee, there are six basic styles of love: *eros, mania, ludus, storge, agape,* and *pragma.*

- The *triangular theory of love* views love as consisting of three components: intimacy, passion, and commitment.

- The *attachment* theory of love views love as being similar in nature to the attachments we form as infants. The attachment (love) styles of both infants and adults are *secure, anxious/ambivalent,* and *avoidant.*

- *Unrequited love*—love that is not returned—is distressing for both the would-be lover and the rejecting partner.

Jealousy

- *Jealousy* is an aversive response to a partner's real, imagined, or likely involvement with a third person. Jealous responses are most likely in committed or marital relationships because of the presumed "specialness" of the relationship, symbolized by sexual exclusiveness.

- As individuals become more interdependent, there is a greater fear of loss. There is some evidence that jealousy may ignite the passion in a relationship.

- *Extradyadic sex* exists in dating, cohabiting, and marital relationships. In exclusive partnerships, extrarelational involvement is assumed to be destructive and is kept secret. In nonexclusive partnerships, extrarelational involvement is permitted.

- *Consensual nonmonogamous relationships* involve nonexclusive partnerships that include *open relationships, swinging,* and *polyamory.*

- Sexual experiences in the aftermath of a romantic relationship breakup are sometimes referred to as *rebound sex.*

Making Love Last: From Passion to Intimacy

- Time affects romantic relationships, potentially transforming it, with words and actions, into something that sustains and expands. *Intimate love* is based on *commitment, caring,* and *self-disclosure,* the revelation of information not normally known by others.

The Nature of Communication

- *Communication* is a transactional process by which we use symbols, such as words, gestures, and movements, to establish human contact, exchange information, and reinforce or change the attitudes and behaviors of ourselves and others.

- The ability to communicate is important in developing and maintaining relationships. Partners satisfied with their sexual communication tend to be satisfied with their relationship as a whole.

- Communication takes place within cultural, social, and psychological contexts. The cultural/ethnic context consists of the language that is used and the values, beliefs, and customs associated with it. Different cultural and ethnic groups communicate about sex differently, depending on their language patterns and values. The social context consists of the roles we play in society that influence our communication. The most important roles affecting sexuality are those relating to gender and sexual orientation. The psychological context consists of our personality characteristics, such as having positive or negative feelings about sex.

- Communication is both verbal and nonverbal. The ability to correctly interpret nonverbal messages is important in successful relationships. *Proximity,* eye contact, and touching are important forms of nonverbal communication.

Sexual Communication

- In initial encounters, physical appearance is especially important. Because of the *halo effect,* we infer positive qualities about people based on their appearance.

- In established heterosexual relationships, many women feel more comfortable in initiating sexual interactions than in newer relationships. Sexual initiations are more likely to be accepted in established relationships; sexual disinterest is communicated verbally. Many women do not restrict sexual activities any more than do men.

Developing Communication Skills

- The keys to effective communication are self-disclosure, trust, and feedback. *Self-disclosure* is the revelation of intimate information about ourselves. *Trust* is the belief in the reliability and integrity of another person. *Feedback* is a constructive response to another's self-disclosure.

Conflict and Intimacy

- *Conflict* is typical in intimate relationships. Conflicts about sex can be specific disagreements about sex, arguments that are ostensibly about sex but that are really about nonsexual issues, or disagreements about the wrong sexual issue.

- Conflict resolution both reflects and contributes to relationship happiness.

Questions for Discussion

- Using Sternberg's triangular theory of love, identify one significant past or a current relationship and draw triangles for yourself and your partner. Compare the components of each. Have you partnered with someone who shares the same view of love as you? Why or why not is/was this person your "ideal match"? What characteristics in a relationship are important to you?

- What has been your experience when friends ask, "Are you two attracted to each other?" Can individuals be "just friends"? What are the reasons and implications of engaging in sex with a friend?

- Do you think sexual activity implies sexual exclusiveness? Do you feel that it is important for you and your partner to agree on this? If not, how might you address this?

- How comfortable are you about sharing your sexual history with your partner? Do you feel that individuals should be selective in what they share, or do you find it beneficial to discuss your likes, dislikes, and past partners? How does this type of disclosure influence the nature of a dating, cohabiting, or married relationship?

Sex and the Internet

Guide to Getting it On

Psychologist and author, Paul Joannides of *Guide to Getting it On,* an award-winning book that has been adopted in universities across the country, writes from both an educated and humorous vantage point to provide accurate and accessible sex information. Go to his website, Guide2getting.com, select the 'Sex' icon, read two articles that sound interesting, then answer these questions:

- What caught your attention about this topic? How important was the image that represented each topic?

- What was the main point?

- How was your thinking influenced by the viewpoint of the author?

Suggested Websites

Advocate
http://www.advocate.com
A comprehensive and current LGBTQ+ news and resource site.

American Association for Marriage and Family Therapy

https://aamft.org

Provides referrals to therapists, books, and articles that address family and relationship problems and issues.

Asexual Visibility and Education Network (AVEN)

asexuality.org

Houses the largest body of education and information pertaining to the experiences of asexual individuals, and serves as a hub for research on this topic.

Psychology Today Relationship Center

www.psychologytoday.com/topics/us/basics/relationships

Articles on playfulness, control, sex, moods, and behavior, to name a few.

Singles in America

https://www.singlesinamerica.com

Surveying over 5,000 singles across the nation each year, this site provides the most comprehensive study on singles in the United States to-date.

Your Tango

www.yourtango.com

A media company that is dedicated to love and relationships and helps connect people in matters of the heart.

Suggested Reading

Ackerman, D. (2004). *An alchemy of mind: The marvel and mystery of the brain.* Scribner. Reports on discoveries in neuroscience and addresses such subjects as the effects of trauma, nature versus nurture, and male versus female brains.

Buss, D. M. (2016). *Evolution of desire: Strategies of human mating.* Basic Books. A study encompassing more than 10,000 people, which resulted in a unified theory of human mating behavior.

Chen, A. (2020). *Ace: What asexuality reveals about desire, society and the meaning of sex.* Penguin Random House. Written by a self-identified asexual woman, the book reveals what it's like going through life without sexual attraction and what that means to gender roles, romance, and consent.

de Bottom, A. (2017). *The course of love.* Simon & Schuster. Though written as a novel, the author uses psychology to analyze and differentiate between romantic love and a more-enduring type of love.

Fisher, H. (2016). *Anatomy of love: A natural history of mating, marriage, and why we stray.* W.W. Norton. By examining the brain in love, love addictions, and why we are biologically drawn to specific partners, the author suggests we are returning to patterns of sex, romance, love, and attachment that echo our ancient past.

Gottman, J. M., & Silver, N. (2015). *The seven principles for making marriage work.* Harmony Books. Based on couples counseling, the author outlines the principles that guide couples on a path toward a harmonious and long-lasting relationship.

Gottman, J., Gottman, J. S., Abrams, D. & Abrams, R. C. (2019) *Eight dates: Essential conversations for a lifetime of love* and *Eight dates: To keep your relationship happy, thriving and lasting.* Workman Publishing. A guide to communicating about things that matter in a romantic relationship. Includes conversations on money, sex, and trust.

Jones, D. (2015). *Love illuminated.* HarperCollins. Drawing from 50,000 stories about love from his column in the *New York Times,* the author explores 10 aspects of love in a funny and lively book.

Lehrer, J. (2017). *A book about love.* Simon & Schuster. Using scientific research from various disciplines, the author explores the mystery of love.

Sternberg, R. J. & Sternberg, K. (Eds.) (2019). *The new psychology of love* (2nd ed.). Cambridge University Press. These readings from some of the best scientific work currently being done in the field of love are intended for any educated person with an interest in love.

Tannen, D. (2017). *You're the only one I can tell: Inside the language of women's friendships.* Ballantine. A revealing book about women's friendships—how they work or fail, how they help and hurt, and how they can be made better.

chapter

9

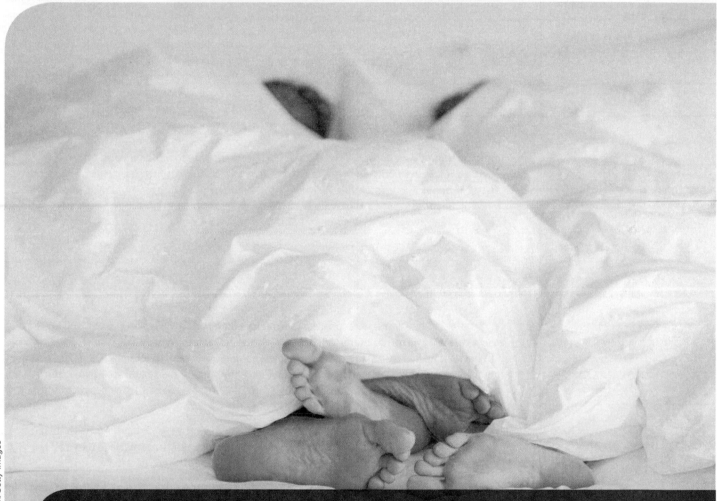

Sexual Response and Expression

Tom Merton/Getty Images

CHAPTER OUTLINE

Human Sexual Response

Female Sexual Response

Male Sexual Response

Sexual Attractiveness

Sexual Scripts

Autoeroticism

Sexual Behavior With Others

229

Student Voices

"I grew up thinking that I would wait until I got married before having sex. It was not just a religious or moral issue—it was more about being a 'good' girl. When I went away to college, some of my new friends were sexually active and had more open thoughts about having sex. I did have sex with someone during my first year in college, but afterwards I felt really embarrassed about it. When some of my friends at home found out, they were really shocked as well. Even though my first sexual relationship was one full of love and commitment, these feelings of shame and embarrassment and shock kept me from sleeping with my boyfriend for the next four months. I really struggled with the 'good girl' versus 'slut' extreme images I had grown up with."

—**29-year-old female**

"I think I am a good sexual partner and enjoy pleasing a woman. I especially love the foreplay that occurs between two people because it get the body more excited than just going at it. I can go on forever with foreplay because I get to explored my partner's body, whether it is with my hand, lips, or tongue."

—**25-year-old male**

"I remember the first time one of my girlfriends told me she went down on a guy. I was seventeen and she was eighteen. We were still in high school. I thought it was the grossest thing and couldn't imagine doing it. I'm embarrassed to admit that I kind of thought she was a slut. Then a few months later, I tried it with my boyfriend. He really liked it and to my surprise, I didn't feel like a slut. Actually it was cool giving pleasure to my boyfriend. Then I wanted him to go down on me."

—**20-year-old female**

"It's funny now how easy it is to talk about masturbation. When you get to college, some of the taboo is lifted from the subject, at least between the guys, I think. When someone brings up masturbating, we all kind of have that uncomfortable moment, but then we get into talking about when our last time was, how often, how we administer cleanup, techniques. It has become a normal subject with us. Considering how many males I have spoken to about masturbation, I think it is less taboo than they thought."

—**20-year-old male**

"Sex is as important as eating or drinking and we ought to allow one appetite to be satisfied with as little restraint or false modesty as the other."

—Marquis de Sade (1740–1814)

Sexual expression is a process through which we reveal our sexual selves. Sexual expression involves more than simply sexual behaviors; it involves our feelings as well. "Behavior can never be unemotional," one scholar observes (Blechman, 1990). As human beings, we do not separate feelings from behavior, including sexual behavior. Our sexual behaviors are rich with emotions, ranging from love to anxiety and from desire to antipathy. Sociologist Lisa Wade (2017) has stated that:

> Saying we can have sex without emotions is like saying we can have sex without bodies. There simply is no such emotion-free human state. Feelings are part of our basic biochemical operating system. We don't get to set them aside at will. (p. 135)

To fully understand our sexuality, we need to examine our sexual behaviors and the emotions we experience along with them. If we studied sexual activities apart from our emotions, we would distort the meaning of human sexuality. It would make our sexual behaviors appear mechanistic, nothing more than genitals rubbing against each other.

In this chapter, we first discuss sexual arousal and response, and then examine the role of sexual attraction in partner selection. Next, we turn to the sexual scripts that give form to our sexual drives. Finally, we examine the most common sexual behaviors, both autoerotic, such as fantasies and masturbation, and interpersonal, such as oral-genital sex, sexual intercourse, and anal eroticism. When we discuss sexual behaviors, we cite results from numerous studies to illustrate the prevalence of those behaviors in our society. These results most often represent self-reports of a certain group of people. As discussed previously, self-reporting of sexual behavior is not always exact or unbiased. The research data provide only a general idea of what behaviors actually occur and do not indicate how people should express their sexuality or what "normal" behavior is. Sexuality is one of the most individualistic aspects of life; each of us has our own sexual values, needs, and scripts.

● Human Sexual Response

A person's sexuality, though typically thought of as personal and individual, is significantly influenced by the social groups to which one belongs. Sociocultural variables include gender, religious preference, class, educational attainment, age, marital status, race, and ethnicity. For many people, the social and cultural characteristics associated with being a particular gender is probably the most influential variable in shaping their sexual desires, behaviors, and partnerships.

Research into the anatomy and physiology of sexuality has helped us increase our understanding of sexual arousal, response, and **orgasm**, the climax of sexual sensation that involves rhythmic contractions in the genital area and intensely pleasurable sensations. By looking beyond the genitals to the central nervous system, where electrical impulses travel from the brain to the spinal cord, researchers are examining nerves and pathways to better understand the biology of sexual response and orgasm. What is probably most critical to all of these functions are the ways we interpret sexual cues.

One way in which researchers investigate and describe sexual response is through the creation of models, hypothetical descriptions used to study or explain something. Although models are useful for promoting general understanding or for assisting in the treatment of specific clinical problems, we should remember that they are only models. It may be helpful to think of sexual functioning as interconnected, linking desire, arousal, orgasm, and satisfaction. Turbulence, distraction, or any other number of factors at any one point affects the functioning of the others.

Sexual Response Models

A number of sexologists have attempted to outline the various physiological changes that both men and women undergo when they are sexually stimulated and aroused (see Table 1). The sequence of changes and patterns that take place in the body during sexual arousal is referred to as the **sexual response cycle**. Three important models are described here. Probably the most classic sexual response model comes from William Masters and Virginia Johnson. **Masters and Johnson's four-phase model of sexual response** which identifies the significant stages of response as excitement, plateau, orgasm, and resolution.

"Passion, though a bad regulator, is a powerful spring."
—Ralph Waldo Emerson (1803–1882)

Since their research culminated in 1966, alternative and expanded models have been developed. Helen Singer Kaplan (1979) collapses the excitement and plateau phases into one, eliminates the resolution phase, and adds a phase to the beginning of the process. **Kaplan's tri-phasic model of sexual response** consists of desire, excitement, and orgasm phases. Though Masters and Johnson's and Kaplan's are the most widely cited models used to describe the phases of the sexual response cycle, they do little to acknowledge the affective parts of human response. A third but much less known pattern is **Loulan's sexual response model**, which incorporates both the biological and affective components into a six-stage cycle. Beyond any questions of similarities and differences in the female and male sexual response cycle is the more significant issue of variation in how individuals experience each phase. No single model has been accepted as a normative description of women's sexual response (Nowosielski et al., 2016).

In both men and women, **vasocongestion**, the swelling of the genital tissues with blood and **myotonia**, or increased muscle tension accompanying the approach of orgasm, occur during sexual arousal. Both responses depend on effective and ongoing stimulation to the genitals. In men, vasocongestion causes the penis to become erect and in women, the clitoris to swell. The increased muscle tension accompanying the approach of orgasm is released during orgasm, when the body undergoes involuntary muscle contractions, followed by relaxation. These patterns are the same for all forms of sexual behavior, whether autoerotic or sex with a partner.

TABLE 1 ● Models of the Sexual Response Cycle

Psychological/Physiological Process	Name of Phase
People make a conscious decision to have sex even if there might not be emotional or physical desire.	Willingness (Loulan)
Some form of thought, fantasy, or erotic feeling causes individuals to seek sexual gratification. (An inability to become sexually aroused may be due to a lack of desire, although some people have reported that they acquire sexual desire after being sexually aroused.)	Desire (Kaplan, Loulan)
Physical and/or psychological stimulation produces characteristic physical changes. In men, increased amounts of blood flow to the genitals produce erection of the penis; the scrotal skin begins to smooth out, and the testicles draw up toward the body. Later in this phase, the testes increase slightly in size. In women, vaginal lubrication begins, the upper vagina expands, the uterus is pulled upward, and the clitoris becomes engorged. In both women and men, the breasts enlarge slightly, and the nipples may become erect. Both men and women experience increasing muscular contractions.	Excitement (Masters/Johnson, Loulan) — Excitement (Kaplan)
Sexual tension levels off. In men, the testes swell and continue to elevate. The head of the penis swells slightly and may deepen in color. In women, the outer third of the vagina swells, lubrication may slow down, and the clitoris pulls back. Coloring and swelling of the labia increase. In both men and women, muscular tension, breathing, and heart rate increase.	Plateau (Masters/Johnson) — Engorgement (Loulan)
Increased tension peaks and discharges, affecting the whole body. Rhythmic muscular contractions affect the uterus and outer vagina in women. In men, there are contractions of the glands and tubes that produce and carry semen, the prostate gland, and the urethral bulb, resulting in the expulsion of semen (ejaculation).	Orgasm (Masters/Johnson, Kaplan, Loulan)
The body returns to its unaroused state. In some women, this does not occur until after repeated orgasms.	Resolution (Masters/Johnson) — Pleasure (Loulan)
Pleasure is one purpose of sexuality and can be defined only by the individual. One can experience pleasure during all or only some of the above stages, or one can leave out any of the stages and still have pleasure.	

To help organize our thinking about the complexities of human behavior, the **dual control model**, developed by researchers at The Kinsey Institute, provides a theoretical perspective of sexual response that is based on brain function and the interaction between sexual excitation (responding with arousal to sexual stimuli) and sexual inhibition (inhibiting sexual arousal) (Bancroft et al., 2009; Bancroft & Janssen, 2000). The authors of this model argue that though much research has been dedicated to understanding sexual excitation, little research has been conducted on the inhibitory brain mechanisms that provide an equally significant role in sexual arousal and response. They purport that the adaptive role the inhibitory mechanism produces is relevant to our understanding of "normal" sexuality, individual variability, and problematic sexuality.

Scales have been developed to measure sexual excitation and sexual inhibition (e.g., Milhausen et al., 2020; Bancroft & Janssen, 2000). Examples of both excitation and inhibition statements in which the reader indicates the level of agreement or disagreement are:

Excitation items:

When an attractive person flirts with me, I easily become sexually aroused.
When a sexually attracted person accidentally touches me, I easily become aroused.
When I start fantasizing about sex, I quickly become sexually aroused.
When I see others engaged in sexual activities, I feel like having sex myself.

Inhibition items:

I cannot get aroused unless I focus exclusively on sexual stimulation.
When I have a distracting thought, I easily lose my erection/my arousal.
If I realize there is a risk of catching a sexually transmitted disease, I am unlikely to stay sexually aroused.

If I am masturbate on my own and I realize that someone is likely to come into my room at any moment, I will lose my erection/sexual arousal.

The dual control model views sexual excitation and sexual inhibition as separate systems, as opposed to other models that view these as two ends of a single dimension. The excitation component can be viewed like pushing on an automobile gas pedal; the inhibition component is like pushing on the brake pedal. Major findings from this model include the following:

- Though most people fall in the moderate range on propensities toward sexual excitation and sexual inhibition, there is great variability from one person to the next.

- Men, on average, score higher on excitation and lower on inhibition than women.

- Gay men, on average, score higher on excitation and lower on inhibition than straight men.

- Bisexual women, on average, score higher on excitation than lesbian and straight women, who did not differ from each other in scores.

The dual control model suggests that individuals who have a low propensity for sexual excitation or a high propensity for sexual inhibition are more likely to experience difficulties related to sexual response or sexual interest. Furthermore, those who have a high propensity for sexual excitation or low propensity for sexual inhibition are more likely to engage in problematic sexuality such as high-risk sexual behaviors, for example, not using a condom. Because the focus is on sexual arousal, questions remain about if and how this model might apply to orgasm.

Desire and Arousal: Two Sides of the Same Coin?

What is sexual desire? What do women and men want? Are their desires similar? Over the past three decades, though sexual desire and sexual arousal have become widely researched and debated, our understanding of it remains somewhat elusive. If there is anything that we now know about arousal and desire is that they are intermingled, with little demarcation between the two.

"Some desire is necessary to keep life in motion."
—Samuel Johnson (1709–1784)

Desire, the psychological component of sexual arousal is, according to John Bancroft and Cynthia Graham (2011), two prominent sex researchers, "a somewhat arbitrary concept we use to describe our experiences and is socially, rather than scientifically, constructed." Desire varies within an individual and between people and exhibits by means of a wide spectrum of thoughts and behaviors, with variation being the norm (Bancroft & Graham, 2011; Hodgons et al., 2016). Its physical manifestations encompass a complex and overlapping interaction of thoughts and feelings, sensory organs, neural responses, and hormonal reactions. These involve parts of the body, including the nucleus accumbens, cerebellum, and hypothalamus of the brain, the nervous system, the circulatory system, and the endocrine glands—as well as the genitals.

Much of the science behind sexuality was designed around a linear model: first there's desire, then arousal, followed by orgasm, then resolution. For most women, however, this process is more circular, context- and situation-dependent. Sex itself can be the trigger for desire and arousal, or an orgasm might lead to the desire for another one (Nuwer, 2016). According to Lisa Diamond (2008), professor of psychology and gender studies at the University of Utah, "Often for women, genital, physical arousal precedes the psychological experience of desire, whereas in men, desire precedes arousal." At the same time, desire does not always imply partnered sex; it can include masturbation, fantasy, or a varied pattern of sexual expression that may have nothing to do with physical intimacy. Factors that elicit and suppress desire are also part of the variation that exists within and among individuals. For example, a woman who is not interested in having sex with her partner may feel this way for any number of reasons: she may be menstruating, just discovered she received a poor grade, is stressed by finances, or finds her partner's drinking to be problematic. Variations in desire also occur among men. Though societal norms suggest that men's sexual desires are higher than women's, when examining differences in desire between the sexes researchers find them to be nuanced to nonexistent, depending on how desire is defined and measured (Dawson & Chivers, 2014). The range of experiences that men and women find desirable,

"I'm not always in the mood to have sex, but afterward I'm always glad I did. It's the just-do-it model of doing it. And it works."
—Cheryl Strayed (1953–)

however, are unlimited. Thus, it's important to educate to give meaning and acceptance to what individuals find pleasurable.

Desire is also about how individuals feel about themselves. If they do not feel desirable or comfortable with their bodies, including their genitals, it's likely that they will not be able to relax and enjoy their sexuality or sexual expression (Wortman & van den Brink, 2012). For example, in a variety of sexual activities, negative genital perceptions are associated with body and/or genital self-consciousness, less sexual enjoyment, lower sexual esteem, decreased sexual function, and limited sexual experience (Fudge & Byers, 2017).

Given our understanding of individuality and variations of sexual desire and the impact of psychosocial/interpersonal and biological factors on it, recommended treatment of persistent and troublesome low sexual desire now uses a combination of psychosocial and biological strategies (Achilli et al., 2017). For the rest of us who experience ongoing variability in our sexual desires and arousal, we would be better off accepting these patterns and becoming more accepting of the diversity that exists in ourselves and in others.

The Neural System and Sexual Stimuli   The brain is crucial to sexual response and is currently a focus of research to understanding how we respond to sexual stimulation. Through the neural system, the brain receives stimuli from the five senses plus one: sight, smell, touch, hearing, taste, *and* the imagination.

The Brain   The brain, of course, plays a major role in all of our body's functions. Nowhere is its role more apparent than in our sexual functioning. The relationship between our thoughts and feelings and our actual behavior is not well understood and what is known would require a course in neurophysiology to satisfactorily explain it. Relational factors and cultural influences, as well as expectations, fantasies, hopes, and fears, combine with sensory inputs and neurotransmitters (chemicals that transmit messages in the nervous system) to bring us to where we are ready, willing, and able to be sexual. Even then, potentially erotic messages may be short-circuited by the brain itself, which can inhibit as well as incite sexual responses. It is not known how the inhibitory mechanism works, but negative conditioning and emotions will prevent the brain from sending messages to the genitals. In fact, the reason moderate amounts of alcohol and marijuana appear to enhance sexuality is that they reduce the control mechanisms of the brain that act as inhibitors. Conversely, women who feel persistent sexual arousal and no relief from orgasm reveal unusually high activation in regions of the brain that respond to genital stimulation (Komisaruk et al., 2010).

Anatomically speaking, the part of the body that appears to be involved most in sexual behaviors of both men and women is the vast highway of nerves called the vagus nerve network, which stretches to all the major organs, including the brain. Using MRI scans to map the brain, researchers have found increases in brain activity during sexual arousal (Cacioppo et al., 2012; Komisaruk et al., 2010). Since specific parts of the brain send their sensory signals via specific nerves, the different quality of orgasms that result from clitoral or anal stimulation, for example, is divided among the different genital sensory nerves.

As many of us know, the early stages of a new romantic relationship are characterized by intense feelings of euphoria, well-being, and preoccupation with the romantic partner. This was observed in one study in which college students were shown photos of their beloved intermixed with photos of an equally attractive acquaintance (Younger et al., 2010). Induced with pain during the experiment, students reported their pain was less severe when they were looking at photos of their new love. The test results suggest the chemicals the body releases in the early stages of love—otherwise referred to as endogenous opioids—work on the spinal cord to block the pain message from getting to the brain. MRI scans showed that, indeed, the areas of the brain activated by intense love are the same areas targeted by pain-relieving drugs.

The Senses   An attractive person (sight), a body fragrance or odor (smell), a lick or kiss (taste), a loving caress (touch), and erotic whispers (hearing) are all capable of sending sexual signals to the brain. Preferences for each of these sensory inputs are both biological and learned and are very individualized. Many of the connections we experience between sensory data and emotional responses are probably products of the **limbic system**, or those structures of the brain that are associated with emotions and feelings and involved in sexual arousal. Some sensory inputs may evoke sexual arousal without a lot of conscious thought or emotion. Certain areas of the skin, called **erogenous zones**, are highly sensitive to touch. These areas may include the genitals, breasts, mouth, ears, neck, inner thighs, and buttocks, or any part of the skin; erotic associations with these areas vary from culture to culture and from individual to individual. Our olfactory sense (smell) may bring us sexual messages below the level of our conscious awareness. Scientists have isolated chemical substances, called pheromones, that are secreted into the air by many kinds of animals, including humans, ants, moths, pigs, deer, dogs, and monkeys. One function of pheromones, in animals at least, appears to be to arouse the libido.

The libido in both men and women is biologically influenced by the hormone **testosterone**. In men, testosterone is produced mainly in the testes; in women, it is produced in the adrenal glands and the ovaries. Evidence suggests that testosterone may play an important role in the maintenance of women's bodies (Davis et al., 2005). Although it does not play a large part in a woman's hormonal makeup, it is present in the blood vessels, brain, skin, bone, and vagina. Testosterone is believed to contribute to bone density, blood flow, hair growth, energy and strength, and libido.

Although women produce much less testosterone than men, this does not mean that they have less sexual interest; apparently, women are much more sensitive than men to testosterone's effects. Though testosterone decreases in women as they age, the ovaries manufacture it throughout life. Symptoms produced by the decrease of testosterone can be similar to those related to estrogen loss, including fatigue, vaginal dryness, and bone loss. Signs specific to testosterone deficiency are associated with reduced sexual interest and responsiveness in men. It is believed that for some women, very low levels of testosterone may contribute to reduced libido and weaker orgasmic responses (North American Menopause Society, 2017.9). In spite of widespread media claims of testosterone's effect in treating low sex desire in women, the Food and Drug Administration is still reviewing long-term safety data. Though research has shown that testosterone delivered via a skin patch increases sexual desire and frequency of satisfying sex among some menopausal women with low desire, common side effects of supplemental testosterone range from acne and increased facial and body hair to rare but sometimes observed liver problems and declines in HDL cholesterol (sometimes called "good cholesterol") (North American Menopause Society, 2017.9).

Although sexual problems, including low libido and/or sexual dissatisfaction, may have a physiological link, they can also be caused, for example, by relationship issues, work fatigue, past experiences, or financial problems. Thus, it is necessary to look beyond medical solutions when assisting women who have the desire to confront their sexual dissatisfaction.

Estrogen also plays a role in sexual functioning, though its effects on sexual desire are not completely understood. In addition to protecting the bones and heart, in women estrogen helps maintain the vaginal lining and lubrication, which can make sex more pleasurable. Like testosterone replacement, some doctors are also promoting estrogens and bioidentical, or natural, estrogen supplements to treat conditions caused by estrogen deficiency. The most significant push is aimed at menopausal women. Because no risk-free hormone has ever been identified, claims that human estrogens will protect against cardiovascular effects and other maladies are misleading. While a number of estrogens are effective treatments for hot flashes and vaginal dryness, any health-promotion claims for these drugs are clearly misguided. Nevertheless, over-the-counter lubricants and/or long-acting vaginal moisturizers may be helpful for women who have insufficient lubrication. Men also produce small amounts of estrogen, which facilitates the maturation of sperm and maintains bone density. Too much estrogen, however, can cause erection difficulties.

DHEA (dehydroepiandrosterone) is another natural androgen hormone that is converted to testosterone and estrogen in the body. Now available as a nonprescription supplemental pill, it has been marketed to improve libido, vaginal atrophy, arousal, and orgasm in women. These claims, however, have limited and mixed evidence and are not endorsed by government regulators. Though more research is needed, there is some evidence that an intravaginal tablet form of DHEA may improve female sexual function in postmenopausal women (North American Menopause Society, 2017.9).

Sensory inputs, such as the sight, touch, or smell of someone we love or the sound of his or her voice, may evoke desire and sexual arousal.

Darren Greenwood/Design Pics

"The best tunes are played on the oldest fiddles."

—Ralph Waldo Emerson (1803–1882)

Oxytocin is a hormone more commonly associated with contractions during labor and with breastfeeding. It is also increased by nipple stimulation in women and men. This neurotransmitter has also been linked to parental behavior, social bonding, and the management of stressful experiences (Carter et al., 2007). It is released in variable amounts in women and men during orgasm and remains raised for at least 5 minutes after orgasm. This is why oxytocin is sometimes referred to as the "love hormone." It helps us feel connected and promotes touch, affection, and relaxation. Interestingly, oxytocin is important in stimulating the release of all the other sex hormones and, since it peaks during orgasm, it may be responsible for the desire to touch or cuddle after orgasm occurs.

In spite of what we do know about the importance of biological influences on sexual desire and function, when biological determinants or evolutionary accounts are given undue weight and psychosocial forces are ignored or minimized, a medical model that negates the significance of culture, relationships, and equality can emerge.

● Female Sexual Response

Sexual Excitement

One of the first signs of sexual excitement in women is the seeping of moisture through the vaginal walls through a process called vaginal transudation or **sweating**. Some women also report "tingling" in the genital area. Blood causes lymphatic fluids to push by the vaginal walls, engorging them, lubricating the vagina, and enabling it to encompass the penis or other object. The upper two thirds of the vagina expands in a process called **tenting**; the vagina expands about an inch in length and doubles its width. The labia minora begin to protrude outside the labia majora during sexual excitement, and breathing and heart rate increase (see Figure 1). These signs do not occur on a specific timetable; each woman has her own pattern of arousal, which may vary under different conditions, with different partners, and so on.

Contractions raise the uterus, but the clitoris remains virtually unchanged during this early phase. Although the clitoris responds more slowly than the penis to vasocongestion, it is still affected. The initial changes, however, are minor. Clitoral tumescence (swelling) occurs simultaneously with engorgement of the labia minora. During masturbation (see Figure 2) and oral sex, the clitoris is generally stimulated directly. During intercourse, clitoral stimulation is mostly indirect, caused by the clitoral hood being pulled over the clitoris or by pressure in the general clitoral area. At the same time that these changes are occurring in the genitals, the breasts are also responding. The nipples become erect, and the breasts may enlarge somewhat because of the engorgement of blood vessels; the areolae may also enlarge. Many women (and men) experience a **sex flush**, a darkening of the skin or rash that temporarily appears as a result of blood rushing to the skin's surface during sexual excitement.

As excitement increases, the clitoris retracts beneath the clitoral hood and virtually disappears. The labia minora become progressively larger until they double or triple in size. They deepen in color, becoming pink, bright red, or a deep wine-red color, depending on the woman's skin color. This intense coloring is sometimes referred to as the "sex skin." When it appears, orgasm is imminent. Meanwhile, the vaginal opening and lower third of the vagina decrease in size as they become more congested with blood. This thickening of the walls, which occurs in the plateau stage of the sexual response cycle, is known as the **orgasmic platform**. The upper two thirds of the vagina continues to expand, but lubrication decreases or may even stop. The uterus becomes fully elevated through muscular contractions.

Changes in the breasts continue. The areolae become larger even as the nipples decrease in relative size. If the woman has not breastfed, her breasts may increase by up to 25% of their unaroused size; women who have breastfed may have little change in size.

Orgasm

Continued stimulation brings **orgasm**, a peak sensation of intense pleasure that creates an altered state of consciousness and is accompanied by involuntary, rhythmic uterine and anal contractions, myotonia, and a state of well-being and contentment. The upper two thirds of

"Those who restrain desire do so because theirs is weak enough to be restrained."

—William Blake (1757–1827)

"What is the earth? What are the body and soul without satisfaction?"

—Walt Whitman (1819–1892)

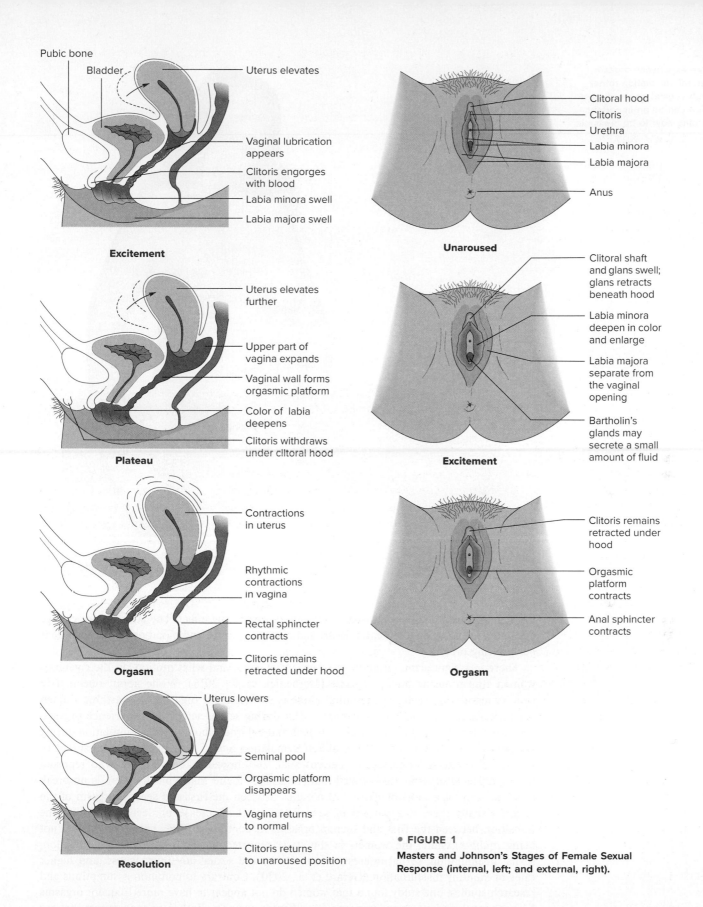

Excitement

- Pubic bone
- Bladder
- Uterus elevates
- Vaginal lubrication appears
- Clitoris engorges with blood
- Labia minora swell
- Labia majora swell

Plateau

- Uterus elevates further
- Upper part of vagina expands
- Vaginal wall forms orgasmic platform
- Color of labia deepens
- Clitoris withdraws under clitoral hood

Orgasm

- Contractions in uterus
- Rhythmic contractions in vagina
- Rectal sphincter contracts
- Clitoris remains retracted under hood

Resolution

- Uterus lowers
- Seminal pool
- Orgasmic platform disappears
- Vagina returns to normal
- Clitoris returns to unaroused position

Unaroused

- Clitoral hood
- Clitoris
- Urethra
- Labia minora
- Labia majora
- Anus

Excitement

- Clitoral shaft and glans swell; glans retracts beneath hood
- Labia minora deepen in color and enlarge
- Labia majora separate from the vaginal opening
- Bartholin's glands may secrete a small amount of fluid

Orgasm

- Clitoris remains retracted under hood
- Orgasmic platform contracts
- Anal sphincter contracts

● **FIGURE 1**

Masters and Johnson's Stages of Female Sexual Response (internal, left; and external, right).

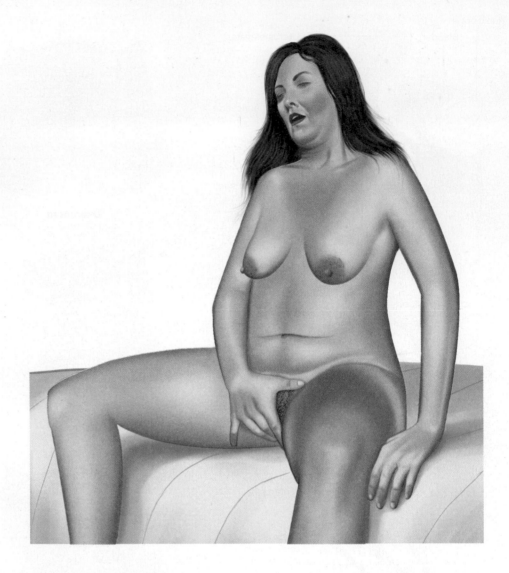

the vagina does not contract; instead, it continues its tenting effect. The labia do not change during orgasm, nor do the breasts. Heart and respiratory rates and blood pressure reach their peak during orgasm.

There is a significant variation in where, what kind, and what motion on their genitals women find arousing and preferable (Herbenick et al., 2016). While about one in five women report that vaginal penetration alone is sufficient for orgasm, one in three women say they need clitoral stimulation prior and/or during sexual activity to experience orgasm. (For women to learn more about one's beliefs and behavior about clitoral stimulation during sex, see Practically Speaking, "Clitoral Self-Stimulation Scale.") An Internet-based survey of 419 sexually diverse women (66% heterosexual; 26% bisexual), ages 18–69, who reported having repeated orgasms (also called multi-orgasmic) found that typically there is no break of stimulation or a short break of 1–3 minutes between the first and second orgasm of the series. Usually there is a pattern of sexual arousal (an increase or decrease) during the transition between the first and second orgasm. In contrast to their peers who report not being multi-orgasmic, the women in the study reported greater levels sexual motivation, sexual disinhibition, sexual interest, sexual desire, and sexual adventurousness, and higher rates of monthly masturbation (Gerard et al., 2020). Contrary to common assumptions and research studies, one study found that women do not appear to have more frequent orgasms when they masturbate or experiment with different partners. Rather, women report that the key to more frequent orgasms lies in the importance she gives it, her sexual desire and

Clitoral Self-Stimulation Scale

Self-stimulation of the clitoris may not be part of one's sensual touching when being sexual with a partner (Gagnon, 1977). Some women may not be comfortable with this behavior during partner sex nor understand its role in experiencing pleasure. Many women indicate they need clitoral stimulation prior and/or during sexual intercourse to experience an orgasm. The Clitoral Self-Stimulate Scale ". . .assesses the frequency of women's self-stimulation of the clitoris and genitals in the presence of a partner, as well as their attitudes and affective reactions to such self-stimulation" (McIntyre-Smith, 2010; McIntyre-Smith & Fisher, 2020).

DIRECTIONS:

For each question below, circle the response number that represents your thoughts and feelings and sexual experiences with a partner.

Stimulating myself (i.e., massaging my genitals/clitoris) to help me have an orgasm during intercourse would be:

Good

7	6	5	4	3	2	1
Very good	Moderately good	Slightly good	Neither good nor bad	Slightly bad	Moderately bad	Very bad

Important

7	6	5	4	3	2	1
Very important	Moderately important	Slightly important	Neither good nor unimportant	Slightly unimportant	Moderately unimportant	Very unimportant

Exciting

1	2	3	4	5	6	7
Strongly disagree	Moderately disagree	Slightly disagree	Neither agree nor disagree	Slightly agree	Moderately agree	Strongly agree

Embarrassing

7	6	5	4	3	2	1
Strongly agree	Moderately agree	Slightly agree	Neither agree nor disagree	Slightly disagree	Moderately disagree	Strongly disagree

Easy

1	2	3	4	5	6	7
Very difficult	Moderately difficult	Slightly difficult	Neither easy nor difficult	Slightly easy	Moderately easy	Very easy

When having sex with a partner, how often do you stimulate your clitoris to orgasms? (If you have not had sex with someone else, imagine how often you stimulate your clitoris to experience orgasm during partnered sex.)

0. 0% of the time
1. 1–25% of the time
2. 26–50% of the time
3. 51–75% of the time
4. 76–99% of the time
5. 100% of the time

INTERPRETATION:

Calculate the total score of all items. Higher scores indicate a greater proclivity for engaging in self-stimulation of the clitoris or genitals during sexual intercourse with a partner.

Source: McIntyre-Smith, A., & Fisher, W. A. (2020). Clitoral Self-Stimulation Scale. In R. R. Milhausen, J. K. Sakaluk, T. D. Fisher, C. M. Davis, & W. L. Yarber (Eds.), *Handbook of Sexuality-Related Measures* (4th ed., pp. 510–513). Routledge.

sexual self-esteem, and the sexual communication she shares with a partner (Kontula & Miettinen, 2016).

After orgasm, the orgasmic platform rapidly subsides. The clitoris reemerges from beneath the clitoral hood. Orgasm helps the blood flow out of the genital tissue quickly. If a woman does not have an orgasm once she is sexually aroused, the clitoris may remain engorged for up to an hour. This unresolved vasocongestion sometimes leads to a feeling of frustration, analogous to what men call "blue balls." The labia slowly return to their unaroused state, and the sex flush gradually disappears. About 30–40% of women perspire as the body begins to cool.

Prolactin levels double immediately following orgasm and remain elevated for about 1 hour (Meston & Buss, 2009). This prolactin is thought to be responsible for the refractory period in which men are unable to ejaculate again. In contrast, women are often physiologically able to be orgasmic immediately following the previous orgasm. An estimated 12–15% of women reported experiencing repeated orgasms. Women can have repeated orgasms usually in a series of two or three if they continue to be stimulated by themselves or a partner.

• Male Sexual Response

Even though their sexual anatomy is quite different, women and men follow roughly the same pattern of excitement and orgasm, with two exceptions: (1) generally, men become fully aroused and ready for sexual behavior in a shorter amount of time than women do; and (2) once men experience ejaculation, they usually cannot do so again for some time, whereas women may experience repeated orgasms.

One of the most controversial topics in sexuality theory is whether sexual desire is shaped more by nature or culture. Societal expectations, health, education, class, politics, and relational factors are thought to influence both men's and women's sexual desire and functioning. Combined, these influence sexual desire and response in profound ways.

Sexual arousal in men includes the processes of myotonia (increased muscle tension) and vasocongestion (engorgement of the tissues with blood). Vasocongestion in men is most apparent in the erection of the penis.

Erection

"An erection at will is the moral equivalent of a valid credit card."

—Alex Comfort (1920–2000)

When a male becomes sexually aroused, the blood circulation within the penis changes dramatically (see Figure 3). During the process of attaining an **erection**, the blood vessels expand, increasing the volume of blood, especially within the corpora cavernosa. At the same time, expansion of the penis compresses the veins that normally carry blood out, so the penis becomes further engorged. Secretions from the Cowper's glands appear at the tip of the penis during erection.

The length of time an erection lasts varies greatly from individual to individual and from situation to situation. Not attaining an erection when one is desired is something most men experience at one time or another. Some conditions including diabetes, stress, depression, abnormalities in blood pressure, and some medications that treat these conditions may have an adverse effect on blood flow and erectile capacity. If any of these are present, or if the failure to attain an erection is persistent, a man should see his physician. Contrary to this, when a man has unwanted erections at inappropriate times, he can distract himself or stop his thoughts or images, which in turn, may cause the erection to subside.

Ejaculation and Orgasm

What triggers the events that lead to ejaculation are undetermined, but it appears that it may be the result of a critical level of excitation in the brain or spinal cord (Komisaruk et al., 2010). Regardless, increasing stimulation of the penis generally leads to ejaculation. Orgasm occurs when the impulses that cause erection reach a critical point and a spinal reflex sends a massive discharge of nerve impulses to the ducts, glands, and muscles of the reproductive system. Ejaculation then occurs in two stages: emission and expulsion.

"When the prick stands up, the brain goes to sleep."

—Yiddish proverb

Emission   In the first stage, **emission**, contractions of the walls of the tail portion of the epididymis, send sperm into the vasa deferentia (plural for *vas deferens*). Rhythmic contractions also occur in the prostate, seminal vesicles, and vasa deferentia, which spill their contents into the urethra. The bladder's sphincter muscle closes to prevent urine from mixing

(1) Excitement

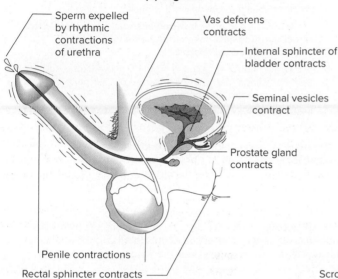

Vasocongestion of penis results in erection

Partial erection

Unstimulated state

Testes elevate toward perineum

Skin of scrotum tenses, thickens, and elevates

(2) Late Excitement or Plateau

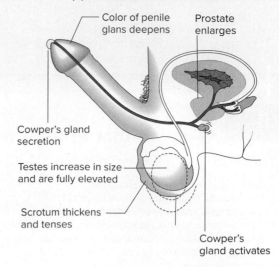

Color of penile glans deepens

Prostate enlarges

Cowper's gland secretion

Testes increase in size and are fully elevated

Scrotum thickens and tenses

Cowper's gland activates

(3) Orgasm

Sperm expelled by rhythmic contractions of urethra

Vas deferens contracts

Internal sphincter of bladder contracts

Seminal vesicles contract

Prostate gland contracts

Penile contractions

Rectal sphincter contracts

(4) Resolution

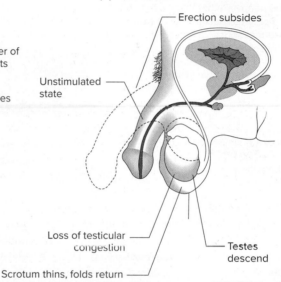

Erection subsides

Unstimulated state

Loss of testicular congestion

Testes descend

Scrotum thins, folds return

● **FIGURE 3**

Masters and Johnson's Stages in Male Sexual Response.

with the semen and semen from entering the bladder, and another sphincter below the prostate also closes, trapping the semen in the expanded urethral bulb. At this point, the man feels a distinct sensation of **ejaculatory inevitability**, the point at which ejaculation will occur even if stimulation ceases. These events are accompanied by increased heart rate and respiration, elevated blood pressure, and general muscular tension. About 25% of men experience a sex flush, a darkening of the skin that temporarily appears during sexual excitement.

Expulsion In the second stage of ejaculation, **expulsion**, there are rapid, rhythmic contractions of the urethra, the prostate, and the muscles at the base of the penis. The first few contractions are the most forceful, causing semen to spurt from the urethral opening. Gradually, the intensity of the contractions decreases and the interval between them lengthens. Breathing rate and heart rate may reach their peak at expulsion. There is a growing consensus that there are no major biological differences between men's and women's orgasms. Observed and reported in both sexes are contractions in the pelvic floor muscles, intensely pleasurable

think about it

Factors that Prompt and Inhibit Men's Sexual Desire

When we think about sexual desire in a heterosexual relationship, many of us assume that it's a woman's issue since men supposedly are always interested in and ready for sexual activity. However, neither perception is necessarily true. Though research on men's reasons for engaging in sexual activity suggests that their motivations to engage in sex are higher and their reasons for engaging in sex may be less relational than women's (Meston & Buss, 2009), for many men these sexual scripts suggest more about how men *should* behave rather than how men truly feel (Masters et al., 2013). For heterosexual relationships, not all men have higher desire than their female partners (Mark & Murray, 2011).

Women's and men's sexual desire and arousal are closely related. That is, desire and arousal are impacted by a partner's level of desire coupled with their own emotional connection to that partner (Janssen et al., 2008; Mitchell et al., 2012). One significant difference between men and women is that men's sexual desire remains high despite the duration of the relationship, at least among younger college-educated individuals, whereas women report lower levels of sexual desire the longer the length of their relationship (Murray et al., 2017).

To further understand the ways men experience sexual desire and arousal in long-term relationships, sex therapist and researcher Sarah Murray (2017) conducted semi-structured interviews of 30 heterosexual men, ages 30–65, who were in relationships for at least 2.5 years. Factors that elicited or prompted men's sexual desire included, in this order (Murray et al., 2017):

1. Feeling desired—Nearly three fourths of men, regardless of their age, wanted to be desired.
2. Visual sexual cues—Men's sensitivity to visual cues are both physically and psychologically arousing.
3. Exciting and unexpected sexual encounters—Two thirds of men preferred sexual encounters that had some variety and that occurred spontaneously.
4. Intimate communication—Over half of the men felt that communication was necessary to spark closeness. This, in turn, sometimes led to sex.
5. Cognitions and moods—Both thoughts and emotions can increase or diminish sexual interest.
6. Context of the sexual encounter—Settings and novelty, for example, can increase desire.
7. Feeling sexy, attractive, and desirable—Sometimes this is an underrated and unknown factor about men's need to feel desirable.

Factors that inhibited or decreased sexual desire included, in this order:

1. Rejection—Reported by 6 in 10 men, being turned down when they initiated sexual activity had a deeply negative and sometimes long-term impact on their desire.

2. Physical ailments and negative health characteristics—Feeling sick was cited by 6 in 10 men, and in some cases, it was the only reason some men provided for having decreased desire.
3. Life pressures and stresses—Distractions and preoccupations can negatively impact the mood of men.
4. Lack of emotional connection with partner—Slightly over half of men (57%) described emotional connection as central to their experience of desire. When lacking, such as during an argument, men's sexual desire decreased.
5. Less emphasis and effort invested in sexual encounters—Men felt deflated when they perceived their partner was not invested in the sexual relationship.
6. Partner not equally engaged in sexual activity—Expecting to "perform" without the input or response of their partner is not sexually enhancing for most men.
7. Sexual abuse—Sometimes, flashbacks or "unfinished business" can seriously dampen or stop the sexual encounter.

From her interviews, Murray also found that men face enormous pressure to prove their masculinity by demonstrating pervasive sexual interest in sex and never turning down sexual opportunities. One man said *"My wife initiated sex last night but I had a long day at work and was just too tired and stressed out. I never thought I would turn down an opportunity to have sex. Is something wrong with me?"* (quoted in Murray, 2019, p. xvii). Among the numerous traditional, Western cultural sexual scripts for men is the assumption that men always want sex and "real men" never refuse sex. This stereotype is continually reinforced through movies, TV shows, advertisements, social media, and song lyrics, for example. The study found that this assumption does not accurately represent men's true sexual experiences with women nor is it working anymore for men.

Murray, in her book, *Not Always in the Mood: The New Science of Men, Sex and Relationships* (2019), reports what the research team discovered about men who have sex with women are saying about the assumption of men always wanting sex. For example:

- In dyadic analysis (research on two persons dating each other) showed that men are not any more or less likely to be the relationship partner with more desire. That is, in any heterosexual relationship, women are just as likely to have a higher interest in sex than men. This is one example of how the "gender gap" between men and women's sexuality is narrowing.
- Some men reported never saying no to sex. The primary pressure to say yes came from the social pressures of what it mean to be a "real man." Actually, men report engaging in sexual compliance (having consensual sex without desire) as often as women do. Some men reported that they had sex to avoid a partner's negative reaction.

- Some men believe that their sexual interest is higher than their female's partner because they miss some of her cues that she is "in the mood" and that women are downplaying their sexual interest.

- While "good looks" and appearances make a difference, men indicate valuing a woman's confidence and comfort with herself as more important.

- Men consistently indicate that their most important motivation when having sex is to provide sexual pleasure to their female partner.

The research findings suggest that men's sexual desire may be more complex, nuanced and relationship focused than previous research has suggested. The researchers contend that to promote partner connection and intimacy, desire within a relationship requires deliberate effort and coordination among the partners. In this study, men's sexual desire was higher when they perceived an interaction with their partner to be mutual, connected, and intimate and that it diminished when they experienced a lack of shared connection or misunderstanding. Murray noted that "It may be that men are deviating from past traditional masculine roles, wanting instead to hold, at least at times, the traditional female role of being an object of desire" (p. 327).

Think Critically

1. What in this study surprised you? Why?

2. Do you feel that men's and women's sexual desires and arousal are more similar or different? What thoughts or experiences do you have to support your conclusion?

3. What are factors in your own life that stimulate and inhibit your sexual desire and arousal? Would you be willing to share these with an intimate partner?

sensations, release of endorphins and hormones, and a release of a small amount of fluid, though a significantly lower amount in women. In fact, because orgasm is a very individual and subjective experience with commonalities shared by both sexes, it is difficult to identify self-reported differences between the sexes ("Male and female orgasm—different?", 2013). However, where differences in orgasm are noticed, it is not between the sexes but rather among cultures, where beliefs about male and female sexuality influence people's ideas about what an orgasm should be like.

Some men experience **retrograde ejaculation**, the "backward" expulsion of semen into the bladder rather than out of the urethral opening. This unusual malfunctioning of the urethral sphincters may be temporary (e.g., induced by tranquilizers), but if it persists, the man should seek medical counsel to determine if there is an underlying problem. Retrograde ejaculation is not normally harmful; the semen is simply collected in the bladder and eliminated during urination.

Orgasm   The intensely pleasurable physical sensations and general release of tension that typically accompany ejaculation constitute the experience of orgasm. Orgasm is a series of muscular contractions of the pelvis that occurs at the height of sexual arousal. Orgasm does not always occur with ejaculation, however. It is possible to ejaculate without having an orgasm and to experience orgasm without ejaculating. Additionally, ejaculation and orgasm don't necessarily require an erection. Some men have reported having more than one orgasm without ejaculation ("dry orgasm") prior to a final, ejaculatory orgasm. Following ejaculation, men experience a **refractory period**, during which they are not capable of having an ejaculation again. This is the time in which nerves cannot respond to additional stimulation. Refractory periods vary greatly in length, ranging from a few minutes to many hours. Other changes occur immediately following ejaculation. The erection diminishes as blood flow returns to normal, the sex flush (if there was one) disappears, and fairly heavy perspiration may occur. Men who experience intense sexual arousal without ejaculation may feel some heaviness or discomfort in the testes; this is generally not as painful as the common term "blue balls" implies. If discomfort persists, however, it may be relieved by a period of rest or by ejaculation. When the seminal vesicles are full, feedback mechanisms diminish the quantity of sperm produced. Excess sperm die and are absorbed by the body. For some men, the benefits of strengthening the muscles that surround the penis by doing what are called **Kegel exercises** (see Chapter 14) can produce more intense orgasms and ejaculations.

"When the appetite arises in the liver, the heart generates a spirit which descends through the arteries, fills the hollow of the penis and makes it hard and stiff. The delightful movements of intercourse give warmth to all the members, and hence to the humor which is in the brain; this liquid is drawn through the veins which lead from behind the ears to the testicles and from them it is squirted by the penis into the vulva."

—Constantinus Africanus (c. 1070)

● Sexual Attractiveness

Sexual attractiveness is an important component in sexual expression. As we will see, however, there are few universals in what people from different cultures consider attractive.

A Cross-Cultural Analysis

In a landmark cross-cultural survey, anthropologists Clelland Ford and Frank Beach (1951) discovered that there appear to be only two characteristics that women and men universally consider important in terms of sexual attractiveness: youthfulness and good health. All other aspects may vary significantly from culture to culture. Even though this large survey was conducted nearly 75 years ago, subsequent smaller and more-local studies support the importance of youthfulness and good health in sexual attraction, as well as the significance of culture in determining sexual attractiveness. One might ask why youthfulness and health were the only universals identified by Ford and Beach. Why not other body traits, such as a certain facial feature or body type?

Although we may never find an answer, sociobiologists offer a possible, but untestable, explanation. They theorize that all animals instinctively want to reproduce their own genes. Consequently, humans and other animals adopt certain reproductive strategies. One of these strategies is choosing a mate capable of reproducing one's offspring. Men prefer women who are young because young women are the most likely to be fertile. Good health is also related to reproductive potential, because healthy women are more likely to be both fertile and capable of rearing their children. Evolutionary psychologist David Buss (1994.9, 2003.9) notes that our ancestors looked for certain physical characteristics that indicated a woman's health and youthfulness. Buss identifies certain physical features that are cross-culturally associated with beauty: good muscle tone; full lips; clear, smooth skin; lustrous hair; and clear eyes. Our ancestors also looked for behavioral cues such as animated facial expressions; a bouncy, youthful gait; and a high energy level. These observable physical cues to youthfulness and health, and hence to reproductive capacity, constitute the standards of beauty in many cultures.

Vitality and health are important to human females as well. Women prefer men who are slightly older than they are, because an older man is likely to be more stable and mature and to have greater resources to invest in children. Similarly, in the animal kingdom, females choose mates who provide resources, such as food and protection. Among American women, Buss (1994.9, 2003.9) points out, countless studies indicate that economic security and employment are much more important for women than for men. If you look in the personal ads on online dating sites for a person aiming to meet the other sex, you'll find this gender difference readily confirmed. A woman's ad typically reads: "Lively, intelligent woman seeks professional, responsible man for committed relationship." A man's ad typically reads: "Financially secure, fit man looking for attractive woman interested in having a good time. Send photo."

Women also prefer men who are strong, in good health, and physically fit so as to be good providers (Barber, 2017). If a woman chooses someone with hereditary health problems, she risks passing on his poor genes to her children. Furthermore, an unhealthy partner is more likely to die sooner, decreasing the resources available to the woman and her children. Ford and Beach (1951) found that signs of ill health are universally considered unattractive.

Aside from youthfulness and good health, however, Ford and Beach found no universal standards of physical sexual attractiveness. In fact, they noted considerable variation from culture to culture in what parts of the body are considered erotic. In some cultures, the eyes are the key to sexual attractiveness; in others, it is height and weight; and in still others, the size and shape of the genitals matter most. In our culture, female breasts, for example, are considered erotic; in other cultures, they are not.

Since the classic study by Ford and Beach (1951), researchers have continued to attempt to identify other factors that influence sexual attractiveness, such as physical characteristics, personality traits, and fertility factors. Through research involving various cultures, it has been

What constitutes physical attractiveness may vary.

(first) Andersen Ross/Blend Images LLC; (second) Distinctive Images/Alamy Stock Photo; (third) David Buffington/Blend Images LLC; (fourth) Image Source, all rights reserved.; (fifth) John Lund/Drew Kelly/Blend Images LLC; (sixth) Jordan Siemens/Getty Images; (seventh) Cultura Creative/Alamy Stock Photo; (eighth) John Lund/Sam Diephuis/Blend Images LLC

discovered that one of the most important physical traits of attractiveness is symmetry. That is, both sides of the person—the right and left sides—are the same. For example, both eyes are the same shape, the ears are similar, the hands are the same size, and the arms are the same length. Throughout the animal kingdom, which includes humans, males and females rate persons whose right and left sides are symmetrical as more attractive. One very noticeable physical feature is the face, and studies have shown that the more symmetrical a face, the more attractive persons of the other sex find it (Fisher, 2009; Jasienska et al., 2006; Little et al., 2007; Quist et al., 2012).

Another significant factor in sexual attraction is scent. The other person's smell—that is, his or her natural body scent mixed with the lingering smells of the day—plays a major role in drawing people together and finding optimal partners. Some people report that they know right away from his or her smell that a person is the one for them, and, of course, conversely some conclude that his or her body odor is a "deal-breaker." Psychologist Rachel Herz, author of the book *The Scent of Desire: Discovering Our Enigmatic Sense of Smell* (2007), states that "body odor is an external manifestation of the immune system and smells we think are attractive come from people who are most genetically compatible with us" (quoted in Svoboda, 2008). Men and women whose body odors are judged to be sexy by others are also more likely to have symmetrical faces. For partners to find out each other's true scent, they can go fragrance-free for a few days. People may worry about their own scent, and some people may indeed not like it, but there will always be persons who will be attracted to their natural body odor (Fisher, 2009; Herz, 2007; Martins et al., 2005; Moalem, 2009; Svoboda, 2008).

"Ken, my husband, just smelled like he belonged to me. I'm talking about when you hug him, he either feels like a member of your tribe or not. It's their scent."

—Erica Jong (1942–)

Cultures that agree on which body parts are erotic may still disagree on what constitutes attractiveness. In terms of female beauty, American culture considers a youthful and slim body attractive. But worldwide, Americans are in the minority, for the type of female body most desired cross-culturally is plump. Similarly, Americans prefer slim hips, but in the majority of cultures in Ford and Beach's study, wide hips were most attractive. In our culture, large breasts are ideal, but other cultures prefer small breasts or long and pendulous breasts.

Male preference for female breast size varies within any given culture. For example, a study of British white men from London, England, required participants to view rotating (360 degrees) figures of women with varied breast sizes. Findings revealed that medium breasts were rated the most attractive (33%), followed by large (24%), very large (19%), small (16%), and very small (8%) breasts (Swami & Tovée, 2013).

In recent years, well-defined pectoral, arm, and abdominal muscles have become part of the ideal male body. Interestingly, a study of college undergraduate women rated muscular men as sexier than nonmuscular and very muscular men, but men with moderate muscularity were considered most attractive and more desirable for long-term relationships. Participants thought that the more brawny men would be more domineering, volatile, and less committed to their partners, whereas the moderately muscular man would be more sexually exclusive and romantic (Frederick & Haselton, 2007; Jayson, 2007).

In other sections of this text, we discuss men's and women's views about ideal erect penis length, largely relative to sexual satisfaction of the female partner, and whether they are satisfied with their own or their partner's penis. In an Australian study, heterosexual women were shown digitally projected life-size, computer-generated images of men with their penises in the flaccid state (Mautz et al., 2013). The women rated the males with a large flaccid penis as being relatively more attractive; however, the attractiveness rating stopped increasing past the length of about 3 inches. The women also rated men who were taller and more broad-shouldered as more attractive, although being "well-endowed" mattered almost as much as height. Even though we seemed to be obsessed about penis length in judging a male's attractiveness and ability to provide sexual satisfaction for female partners, research has shown that women appear to be more interested in penis girth than penis length; that is, width is rated more important to their sexual satisfaction (Shaeer et al., 2012; Stulhofer, 2006). Given these results, researchers contend that female pre-intercourse sexual selection of males ("mate choice") can play an important role in the evolution of penis size and predict that in time the human penis will exhibit less variation in girth than in length (Apostolou, 2015; Vergano, 2013).

Another aspect of mate preference is the age limits in mate selection. Psychologist Jan Antfolk (2017) investigated the age limits (youngest and oldest) of considered and actual sex partners among a population-based sample of 2,655 Finnish adults, aged 18–50 years. Findings revealed that men's and women's sexual age preferences develop differently. That is, over the life span women reported a narrower age range than reported by men and the women tended to prefer slightly older men. However, men's age range increases as they get older. Men continue to consider sex with young women but also consider sex with women of their own age or older. Thus, men's sexual activity reflects their own age range, although their potential interest in younger women does not likely result in sexual activity. Also, unlike homosexual men, both bisexual and heterosexual men were not likely to convert their preferences for young partners into actual behavior.

The above discussion is largely focused on sexual attraction among mixed-sex couples, As mentioned prior, less research has dealt with varied aspects of same-sex sexuality, including sexual attraction. Here are the findings of two studies. A Harvard University study found that gay men, who in general are attracted to masculine traits, prefer more masculine faces, and straight men are attracted to more feminized faces (Tankard, 2009). In this same study, straight women were not necessarily attracted to the most masculinized male faces, and lesbian women were not always attracted to the most feminized faces. Sex researcher Michael Bailey and colleagues (1994) found that gay men had strong preference for younger men.

Lesbian women showed greater attraction in visual sexual stimuli than heterosexual women. What a person considers important attractions can vary from person to person. Nevertheless, all persons, no matter their sexual orientation or gender identity, are attracted to personal attributes beyond physical appearance, such as maturity, similarity, kindness, personality traits, and other characteristics as described in Chapter 8, Love and Communication in Intimate Relationships.

Evolutionary Mating Perspectives

One prominent theoretical explanation for human mating is the **sexual strategies theory** (Buss, 2003.9b; Buss & Schmitt, 1993). An important component of this theory addresses gender differences in short-term and long-term heterosexual relationships from an evolutionary mating perspective. This theory posits that males and females face different adaptive problems in "casual," or short-term, mating and long-term, reproductive mating, leading to different strategies or behaviors for solving these problems. A woman may select a partner who offers immediate resources, such as food or money, for short-term mating, whereas for long-term mating, more substantial resources are important. For males, a sexually available female may be chosen for a short-term relationship, but this type of woman would be avoided when selecting a long-term mate (Hyde & DeLamater, 2008).

David Geary and colleagues (Geary et al., 2004) reviewed the evolutionary theory and empirical research on mating and identified the potential costs and benefits of short-term and long-term sexual relationships in both men and women. The most fundamental difference is that women are predicted to be most selective in mate choices for both short-term and long-term relationships, given the costs of reproduction. Even in selecting a short-term mate, a woman may be more choosy than a man because she is evaluating him as a potential long-term mate. But in general, women are predicted to avoid short-term relationships, given that the possible costs outweigh the possible benefits. In contrast, the opposite is evident for men, given that the potential benefits outweigh the potential costs. In choosing a short-term partner, the man may want to minimize commitment. Once a man commits to a long-term relationship, the costs increase and the level of choosiness is predicted to increase. In their research on short-term sexual relationships, Todd Shackelford and colleagues (2004) found that women preferred short-term partners who are not involved in other relationships to present a greater potential as a long-term partner and that men were more likely than women to pursue short-term, or casual, sexual relationships.

Evolutionary biologists have hypothesized that men's short-term mating strategy is rooted in the desire for sexual variety, and a massive cross-cultural study of 16,288 people across 10 major world regions seems to demonstrate this (Schmitt, 2003). This study on whether the sexes differ in the desire for sexual variety found strong and conclusive differences that appear to be universal across the world regions: Men possess more desire than women for a variety of sexual partners and are more likely than women to seek short-term relationships. This was true regardless of the participant's relationship status or sexual orientation. The researchers concluded that these findings confirm that men's short-term sexual strategy is based on the desire for numerous partners. This behavior, from an evolutionary perspective, would maximize reproductive success. The study also found that men required less time to elapse than women before consenting to intercourse.

Continuing through the lens of an evolutionary perspective, a study of 561 college students examined which 23 partner characteristics were preferred in a short-term sexual relationship versus a long-term romantic relationship (Regan et al., 2000). For both types of relationships, participants preferred the more internal traits (e.g., personality, intelligence) to a greater degree than external qualities (e.g., wealth, physical attractiveness, high social status). However, for both short-term and long-term relationships, men valued characteristics related to sexual desirability more than women and women valued social status more than men. When evaluating a short-term partner, both men and women focused upon sexual desirability (e.g., attractiveness, health, sex drive, athleticism); for a long-term romantic relationship, both

"A promiscuous person is someone who is getting more sex than you are."
—Victor Lownes (1928–2017)

"The degree and kind of a person's sexuality reaches up into the ultimate pinnacle of his spirit."
—Friedrich Nietzsche (1844–1900)

men and women placed greater importance on appealing personality traits (e.g., intelligence, honesty, and warmth).

Various preferences and behaviors that occur both immediately before and after sexual intercourse that may reflect adaptive reproductive strategies from an evolutionary perspective were examined among 170 undergraduate females and male students (Hughes & Kruger, 2011). Behaviors related to pair-bonding with long-term mates and short- and long-term mating contexts were assessed. The study's hypothesis that females would be more likely than males to value and initiate post-coital activities that reflect pair-bonding with a long-term partner was strongly supported. Females expressed greater importance than did males of five pre- and post-coital behaviors: intimate talking, kissing, cuddling and caressing, professing their love for their partner, and talking about their relationship. Females were also more likely to engage in post-intercourse behaviors with both short-term and long-term partners. The researchers stated that these findings "further support the idea that females tend to have a greater need than males to pair-bond in order to secure provisioning and care for themselves and their offspring from their mate." The study also found that males were more likely to participate in behaviors that were extrinsically rewarding or that increased the likelihood of further sexual behavior. For example, males were more likely to initiate kissing prior to sex, possibly to increase the likelihood of their partner being sexually aroused, and females were more likely to initiate kissing after sex, possibly to help secure a bond with their long-term partner. Lastly, intimate talk and kissing were rated by both females and males as more important than intercourse with a long-term partner, and cuddling and professing one's love was rated more important after having intercourse than before.

In another investigation of post-coital affection, sex researcher Amy Muise and colleagues (2014) conducted a study of persons in romantic relationships. The results found that longer and higher quality post-sex affection was associated with both persons' sexual and relationship satisfaction, although these associations were stronger for women. The authors concluded that ". . . one way for couples to promote sexual and relationship satisfaction is to make time for shared intimacy, such as cuddling, kissing, and intimate talk, following their next sexual encounter" (p. 1401).

One mating strategy is **mate poaching**, the behavior designed to lure a person who is already in a romantic relationship into either a temporary, brief sexual liaison or a long-term relationship. Buss (2006) states that mate poaching evolved as a mating strategy because desirable mates attract many suitors and usually end up in relationships. Hence, to find a desirable mate, it is often necessary to attempt to seek (mate poach) persons already in relationships. Table 2 presents the frequency of romantic attraction and mate-poaching experiences of 173 college undergraduates (45 men and 128 women) (Schmitt & Buss, 2001). As shown, mate poaching is a common practice, with nearly equal frequencies for men and women undergraduates but occurs less often than just trying to attract someone. The vast majority had experienced someone trying to poach them or their partner, but many attempts were not successful. Mate-poaching tactics were also assessed, and these included trying to drive a wedge in the relationship, enhancing one's physical appearance, providing easy sexual access, developing an emotional connection, and demonstrating that one has resources. Like mate poaching, sexual nonexclusiveness in relationships poses significant adaptive threats (Buss, 2006).

Numerous investigations have been conducted to assess factors associated with mate poaching. For example, a study of 184 undergraduates found that single women were significantly more interested in poaching a male when he was already attached to a women (Parker & Burkley, 2009). The researchers speculated the reason for that was ". . . because an attached man has demonstrated his ability to commit and in some ways his qualities have already been 'pre-screened' by another woman." Little is known about what happens to the relationship when one of the partners was poached. Psychologist Joshua Foster and

"Sex is one of the nine reasons for reincarnation. . . . The other eight don't count."

—Henry Miller (1892–1980)

TABLE 2 ● Frequency of Romantic Attraction and Mate-Poaching Experiences of Undergraduates

	Have You Ever?	
Mate Attraction Experience	**% of Men**	**% of Women**
Attempted to attract someone		
as a long-term mate	87	86
as a short-term mate	91	74
Attempted to poach someone		
as a long-term mate	52	63
as a short-term mate	64	49
Experienced someone try to poach you		
as a long-term mate	83	81
as a short-term mate	95	91
Been successfully poached away from a past partner		
as a long-term mate	43	49
as a short-term mate	50	35
Experienced someone try to poach your partner		
as a long-term mate	70	79
as a short-term mate	86	85
Had a past partner successfully poached from you		
as a long-term mate	35	30
as a short-term mate	27	25

Source: Adapted from Schmitt, D. P., & Buss, D. M. (2001).

colleagues (2014) found that persons (96 heterosexual individuals) who were poached by their current romantic partners were less committed, less satisfied, and less invested in their relationships than nonpoached research participants. They also paid more attention to romantic alternatives, believed that their alternatives would be higher quality, and engaged in higher rates of extra-dyad sexual behavior. In another study, heterosexual undergraduate students ($N = 215$) were asked to report the amount of wealth and physical attractiveness that would be required to lure them to another person: The mean wealth and physical attractiveness required to attract them was greater if they were dating, living with a partner, and married than if they were not in an exclusive relationship (Davies & Shackelford, 2015).

Scientists have been critical of the perspective that gender differences in human sexual behavior are rooted in evolutionary grounds. These scientists question whether there is adequate empirical evidence to justify the claimed differences. Some contend that gender differences are more the effect of cultural norms than biology (Slater, 2013). Evolutionary biologists David Buss and David Schmitt, developers of the sexual strategies theory, acknowledge that the research support for the theory model was limited in scope when it was developed in the early 1990s (Buss & Schmitt, 1993) but that a large body of research worldwide has been and continues to be generated in support of the theory, as shown in Table 3 (Buss & Schmitt, 2011). This list shows consistent differences in sexual behaviors between men and women. However, we need to remind ourselves that there are individual differences within each sex and group variation among populations and cultures for all of the behaviors that may not reflect these findings. Even with the research showing these behaviors, the debate will continue on whether they are the effects of evolution or culture, or a combination of both.

TABLE 3 ● Results of Research Studies Related to the Sexual Strategies Theory
Men are more likely than women to engage in extradyadic sex (sex outside of a committed relationship).
Men are more likely than women to be sexually nonexclusive multiple times with different sexual partners.
Men are more likely than women to seek short-term partners who are already married.
Men are more likely than women to have fantasies involving short-term sex and multiple other-sex partners.
Men are more likely than women to pay for short-term sex with male or female sex workers.
Men are more likely than women to enjoy sexual magazines and videos containing themes of short-term sex and sex with multiple partners.
Men are more likely than women to desire, have, and reproductively benefit from multiple mates and spouses.
Men desire larger numbers of sex partners than women do over brief periods of time.
Men are more likely than women to seek "one-night stands."
Men are quicker than women to consent to having sex after a brief period of time.
Men are more likely than women to consent to sex with a stranger.
Men are more likely than women to want, initiate, and enjoy a variety of sex behaviors.
Men have more positive attitudes than women toward casual sex and short-term mating.
Men are less likely than women to regret short-term sex or hookups.
Men have more unrestricted sociosexual attitudes and behaviors than women.
Men are less selective of mates in short-term contexts whereas women increase selectivity for physical attractiveness.
Men perceive more sexual interest from strangers than women do.

Source: Adapted from Buss & Schmitt. (2011).

Sexual Desire

Desire can exist separately from overtly physical sexual expression. Recall that desire is the psychobiological component that motivates sexual behavior. Even though desire is difficult to define and quantify, research on sexual desire exists and is increasing, and several studies will be discussed throughout this book. For example, here is a summary of a study of sexual desire by sexual orientation. An online survey of 423 adults (mean age = 30 years) assessed the subjective reports of four groups—men and women in same-sex relationships, and men and women in mixed-sex relationships—relative to their sexual desire for both solitary (e.g., masturbation) and couple sexual behavior (Holmberg & Blair, 2009). This research showed that heterosexual men clearly report desiring sex more than heterosexual women, but whether these differences were also reflected in same-sex relationships was not clear. As anticipated, men in both same-sex and mixed-sex relationships expressed higher, but only moderately higher, levels of sexual desire than women in same-sex and mixed-sex relationships. Men and women in same-sex relationships reported greater sexual desire than men and women in mixed-sex relationships. Persons in same-sex relationships expressed slightly stronger sexual desire for solitary sexual behaviors and for attractive dating partners than individuals in mixed-sex relationships, and individuals in same-sex relationships tended to place greater value on the more sensual or erotic aspects of sexuality. In interpreting these findings, the researchers (Holmberg & Blair, 2009) stated:

> Possibly, those in same-sex relationships, having already broken one major sexual taboo, also tend to be slightly more permissive regarding other sexual matters than heterosexuals, viewing masturbation or harmless fantasizing about attractive others as natural outlets for sexual desire. (p. 64)

Sexual desire is affected by physical, emotional, and sexual relationship issues, as discussed throughout this book. Life events can have both positive and negative impacts on sexual desire.

Two factors affecting sexual desire are erotophilia and erotophobia. **Erotophilia** is a positive emotional response to sexuality, and **erotophobia** is a negative emotional response to sexuality. Researchers have hypothesized that where someone falls on the erotophilic/erotophobic continuum strongly influences his or her overt sexual behavior (Fisher, 1986, 1998; Fisher et al., 1988). In contrast to erotophobic individuals, for example, erotophilic men and women accept and enjoy their sexuality, experience less guilt about engaging in sex, seek out sexual situations, engage in more autoerotic and interpersonal sexual activities, enjoy talking about sex, and are more likely to engage in certain sexual health practices, such as obtaining and using contraception. Furthermore, erotophilic people are more likely to have positive sexual attitudes, to engage in more involved sexual fantasies, to be less homophobic, and to have seen more erotica than erotophobic people. A person's emotional response to sex is also linked to how he or she evaluates other aspects of sex. Erotophilic individuals, for example, tend to evaluate sexually explicit material more positively.

Erotophilic and erotophobic traits are not fixed. Positive experiences can alter erotophobic responses over time. In fact, some therapy programs work on the assumption that consistent positive behaviors, such as loving, affirming, caring, touching, and communicating, can do much to diminish sexual fears and anxieties. Positive sexual experiences can help dissolve much of the anxiety that underlies erotophobia.

"To be desired is perhaps the closest anybody in this life can reach to feeling immortal."

—John Berger (1962–2017)

"I am never troubled by sexual desires. In fact I rather enjoy them."

—Tommy Cooper (1921–1984)

● Sexual Scripts

As discussed previously, gender roles have a significant impact on how we behave sexually, for sexual behaviors and feelings depend more on learning than on biological drives. Our sexual drives can be molded into almost any form. What is "natural" is what society says is natural; there is very little spontaneous, unlearned behavior. Sexual behavior, like all other forms of social behavior, such as courtship, classroom behavior, and sports, relies on scripts.

As you will also recall from Chapter 5, sexual scripts are rules and expectations associated with a particular role that organize and give direction to our sexual behavior. Sex researcher Emily Nagoski (2015) states that sexual scripts are written into our brains early in life by one's family and the culture, but that they are not always what we intellectually believe is true. Nagoski notes that "You can disagree with a script and still find yourself behaving according to it and interpreting experiences in terms of it" (p. 300). The **sexual scripts** in our culture are highly gendered, meaning that they strongly influence our sexuality as men and women (Mahay et al., 2001; Murray, 2019; Wiederman, 2005). Our sexual scripts have several distinct components (Simon & Gagnon, 1987):

- *Cultural.* The cultural component provides the general pattern that sexual behaviors are expected to take. Our cultural script, for example, emphasizes heterosexuality, gives primacy to sexual intercourse, does not validate masturbating, and states that men's sexual desire is constant.

- *Intrapersonal.* The intrapersonal component deals with the internal and physiological states that lead to, accompany, or identify sexual arousal, such as a pounding heart and an erection or vaginal lubrication.

- *Interpersonal.* The interpersonal component involves the shared conventions and signals that enable two people to engage in sexual behaviors, such as body language, words, and erotic touching.

Cultural Scripting

Our culture sets the general contours of our sexual scripts. It tells us which behaviors are acceptable ("moral" or "normal") and which are unacceptable ("immoral" or "abnormal"). For example, a norm may have a sequence of sexual events consisting of kissing, genital caressing, and sexual intercourse. Imagine a scenario in which two people from different cultures try to initiate a sexual encounter. One person follows the script of kissing, genital caressing, and sexual intercourse, while the one from a different culture follows a sequence

"Many are saved from sin by being inept at it."

—Mignon McLaughlin (1913–1983)

beginning with sexual intercourse, moving to genital caressing, and ending with passionate kissing. At least initially, such a couple might experience frustration and confusion as one partner tries to initiate the sexual encounter with kissing and the other with sexual intercourse.

However, this kind of confusion occurs fairly often because there is not necessarily a direct correlation between what our culture calls erotic and what any particular individual calls erotic. This confusion was shown in a recent interview study of 44 men and women ages 18 to 25. The study sought to determine how young, heterosexually active men and women dealt with the cultural traditional gender scripts relative to the intrapersonal and interpersonal scripts (discussed below) of their own relationships. The researchers found that many of the young people interviewed seemed to desire or to enact very different scripts from those they mentioned as cultural norms and that some of their gender scripts changed over time (Masters et al., 2013). Culture sets the general pattern, but there is too much diversity in terms of individual personality, socioeconomic status, and ethnicity for everyone to have exactly the same erotic script. Thus, sexual scripts can be highly ambiguous and varied.

We may believe that everyone shares our own particular script, projecting our experiences onto others and assuming that they share our erotic definitions of objects, gestures, and situations. But often, they initially do not. Our partner may have come from a different socioeconomic or ethnic group or religious background and may have had different learning experiences regarding sexuality. Each of us has to learn the other's sexual script and be able to complement and adjust to it, which may take patience and time. If our scripts are to be integrated, we must make our needs known through open and honest communication involving words, gestures, and movements. This is the reason many people view their first sexual episode as something of a comedy or tragedy—or perhaps a little of both.

Intrapersonal Scripting

On the intrapersonal level, sexual scripts enable people to give meaning to their physiological responses. The meaning depends largely on the situation. An erection, for example, does not always mean sexual excitement. Young boys sometimes have erections when they are frightened, anxious, or worried. Upon awakening in the morning, adolescent boys and men may experience erections that are unaccompanied by arousal. Adolescent girls sometimes experience sexual arousal without knowing what these sensations mean. They report them as funny, weird kinds of feelings or as anxiety, fear, or an upset stomach. The sensations are not linked to a sexual script until the girl becomes older and her physiological states acquire a definite erotic meaning.

Intrapersonal scripts provide a sequence of body movements by acting as mechanisms that activate biological events and release tension. We learn, for example, that we may create an orgasm by manipulating the penis or clitoris and other body parts, such as nipples, during masturbation.

Interpersonal Scripting

The interpersonal level is the area of shared conventions, which make sexual activities possible. Very little of our public life is sexual, yet there are signs and gestures—verbal and nonverbal—that define encounters as sexual. We make our sexual motives clear by the looks we exchange, the tone of our voices, the movements of our bodies, and other culturally shared phenomena. A bedroom or a hotel room, for example, is a potentially erotic location; a classroom or an office is not. The movements we use in arousing ourselves or others are erotic activators. Within a culture, there are normative scripts leading to intimate sexual behavior.

People with little sexual experience, especially young adolescents, are often unfamiliar with sexual scripts. What do they do after kissing? Do they embrace? Caress above the waist? Below? Eventually, they learn a comfortable sequence based on cultural inputs and personal and partner preferences. For gay men, lesbian women, and other sexual minorities, learning the sexual script is more difficult because it is socially stigmatized. The sexual script is also related to age. Older children and young adolescents often limit their scripts to kissing, holding hands, and embracing, and they may feel completely satisfied. Kissing for them may be as exciting as intercourse for more experienced people. When the range of their scripts increases, they lose some of the sexual intensity of the earlier stages.

● Autoeroticism

Autoeroticism consists of sexual activities that involve only the self. Autoeroticism, sometimes called solo or solitary sex, is an *intrapersonal* activity rather than an *interpersonal* one. It includes sexual fantasies, erotic dreams, viewing sexually explicit material by oneself, using vibrators and other sex toys by oneself, and **masturbation**, stimulating one's genitals for pleasure. A universal phenomenon in one form or another (Ford & Beach, 1951), autoeroticism is one of our earliest and most common expressions of sexual stirrings. It is also one that traditionally has been condemned in our society. Figure 4 shows devices created to curb masturbation. By condemning it, however, our culture set the stage for the development of deeply negative and inhibitory attitudes toward sexuality.

Do people participate in autoerotic activities because they do not have a sex partner? The National Health and Social Life Survey (Laumann et al., 1994) found the opposite to be true:

> Those who engage in relatively little autoerotic activity are less likely to prefer a wider range of sexual techniques, are less likely to have a partner, and if they have a partner, are less likely to have sex frequently or engage in oral or anal sex. Similarly, individuals who engage in different kinds of autoerotic activity more often find a wider range of practices appealing and are more likely to have had at least one partner with whom they have sex frequently. Individuals who frequently think about sex, masturbate, and have used some type of pornography/erotica within the last year are much more likely to report enacting more elaborate interpersonal sexual scripts. (p. 139)

Sexual Fantasies and Dreams

Men and women think about sex often and experience numerous different fantasies. According to sex researchers Harold Leitenberg and Kris Henning (1995), about 95% of men and women say that they have had sexual fantasies in one context or another. And a *Details* magazine study of more than 1,700 college students reported that 94% of men and 76% of women think about sex at least once a day (Elliott & Brantley, 1997). A study of 1,516 adults from Quebec, Canada, who completed an interview questionnaire revealed that the most common sexual fantasies of both men and women included having romantic feelings during sex with a partner, experiencing cunnilingus/fellatio, and imagining sex in a particular setting (see Table 4). Significant differences were found in about half of the fantasies between men and women (Joyal et al., 2015). Relative to types of fantasies based on sexual orientation, Leitenberg and Henning (1995) found that the content of sexual fantasies for gay men and lesbian women tends to be the same as for their heterosexual counterparts, except that homosexuals imagine same-sex partners and heterosexuals imagine other-sex partners.

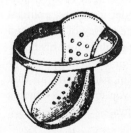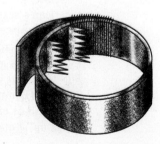

● **FIGURE 4**

Devices Designed to Curb Masturbation. Because of the widespread belief in the nineteenth century that masturbation was harmful, various devices were introduced to prevent the behavior.

Source: Rathus, S. A., et al. (2020).

Sexual Fantasy	%women	%men
I have fantasized about taking part in fellatio/cunnilingus	79	88*
I have fantasized about having sex in an unusual place (e.g., office, public toilets)	82	82
I have fantasized about masturbating my partner	68	76
I have fantasized about being masturbated by my partner	71	72
I have fantasied about having sex with two women	37	85
I have fantasied about watching two women make love	42	82
I have fantasied about making love openly in a public place	57	66
I have fantasied about being dominated sexually	65	53
I have fantasied about being masturbated by an acquaintance	37	65
I have fantasied about masturbating an acquaintance	33	66
I have fantasied about being tied up by someone in order to obtain sexual pleasure	52	46
I have fantasied about tying someone up in order to obtain sexual pleasure	42	48
I have fantasied about having anal sex	33	64
I have fantasied about having interracial sex	28	61
I have fantasied about having sex with two men	57	16
Atmosphere and location are important in my sexual fantasies	86	82
I have fantasied about having sex with a star or a well-known person	52	62
I have fantasied about forcing someone to have sex	11	22
I have fantasized about being photographed or filmed during a sexual relationship	32	44
I have fantasized about spanking or whipping someone else to obtain sexual pleasure	24	44
I have fantasized about being spanked or whipped to obtain sexual pleasure	36	29
I have fantasized about indulging in sexual swinging with a couple that I know	18	42
I have fantasized about being forced to have sex	29	31
I have fantasized about having sex with a fetish or non-sexual object	26	28
I have fantasized about having sex with a prostitute or a stripper	13	40
I have fantasized about showing myself naked or partially naked in a public place	17	23
I have fantasized about watching two men make love	19	16
I have fantasized about dominating someone sexually	48	60
I have fantasized about having sex with an unknown person	49	73
I have fantasized about having sex with someone I know who is not my spouse/partner	66	83

*Numbers rounded to the nearest whole number.

Source: Adapted from Joyal, C.C., Cossette, A., & Lapieree, V. (2015).

Lehmiller (2018) conducted the largest, most recent and comprehensive survey of American's sexual fantasies. A non-representative sample of 4,175 adults, ages 18–87, representing all states, a widely diverse population of varied sexual and gender identities, political and religious affiliations, and relationship types responded to an online survey of more than 350 questions about their favorite fantasies. The specific findings were published in his book, *Tell Me What I Want: The Science of Sexual Desire and How It Can Help Improve Your Sex Life* (Lehmiller, 2018). Lehmiller stated ". . .most Americans' fantasies aren't all that outlandish or elaborate; rather, most Americans fantasize about what you might call 'spicing things up'" (quoted in Fetters, 2018). He highlighted the major findings:

- The number one fantasy was a threesome.
- Almost every study participant had fantasized about group sex and BDSM (bondage, discipline, sadism, and masochism) at some point.
- Women were more likely than men to report same-sex fantasies.

- Men were more likely to fantasize about cross-dressing with someone who is a transgender person.

- Extroverts had more nonexclusive fantasies than introverts.

- Men often fantasized about romantic and emotional fulfillment.

Erotic fantasy is probably the most universal of all sexual activities. Fantasies help create an equilibrium between our environment and our inner selves, as we seek a balance between the two. We use them to enhance our masturbatory experiences, as well as oral-genital sex, sexual intercourse, and other interpersonal experiences. Nearly everyone has experienced such fantasies, but because they touch on feelings or desires considered personally or socially unacceptable, they are not widely discussed. Furthermore, many people have "forbidden" sexual fantasies that they never act on.

Whether occurring spontaneously or resulting from outside stimuli, fantasies are part of the body's regular, healthy functioning and align closely with our sexual interests (Noorishad et al., 2019). Research indicates that sexual fantasies are related to sexual drives: the higher the sexual drive, the higher the frequency of sexual fantasies and level of satisfaction in one's sex life (Leitenberg & Henning, 1995). Studies have also found that fantasizing about one's partner increases desire for that partner, leading to the display of more love, affection, and support even if one is not satisfied with the relationship. Further, sexual fantasizes about another person will not help nor harm one's relationship with his or her partner (Bernstein, 2016).

Hicks and Leitenberg (2001) found that fantasies about another person did not necessarily harm the current relationship and the men's fantasies of having sex with another person did not result in them having sex with someone else. In response to these findings, Kinsey Institute sex researcher Justin Lehmiller stated that "If fantasizing about another person was harmful, not many relationships would survive because almost all of us do it" (quoted in Bernstein, 2016).

The Function of Sexual Fantasies Sexual fantasies are common and represent a broad range of behaviors, as shown in Table 4, and have a number of important functions. First, they help direct and define our erotic goals. They take our generalized sexual drives and give them concrete images and specific content. We fantasize about certain types of men or women and reinforce our attraction through fantasy involvement. Unfortunately, our fantasy model may be unreasonable or unattainable, which is one of the pitfalls of fantasy; we can imagine perfection, but we rarely find it in real life.

Second, sexual fantasies allow us to plan for or anticipate situations that may arise. They provide a form of rehearsal, allowing us to practice in our minds how to act in various situations. Our fantasies of what might take place on a date, after a party, or in bed with our partner serve as a form of preparation.

Third, sexual fantasies provide escape from a dull or oppressive environment. Routine or repetitive behavior often gives rise to fantasies as a way of coping with boredom.

Fourth, even if our sex lives are satisfactory, we may indulge in sexual fantasies to bring novelty and excitement into the relationship. Fantasy offers a safe outlet for sexual curiosity. One study found that some women are capable of experiencing orgasm solely through fantasy (Whipple et al., 1992).

Lastly, sexual fantasies have an expressive function in somewhat the same manner that dreams do. Our sexual fantasies may offer a clue to our current interests, pleasures, anxieties, fears, or problems. Repeated fantasies of extradyadic relationships, for example, may signify deep dissatisfaction with a marriage or steady relationship, whereas mental images centering around erectile difficulties may represent fears about sexuality or a particular relationship.

Fantasies During Sexual Expression A sizable number of people fantasize during sex. The fantasies are usually a continuation of daydreams or masturbatory fantasies, transforming one's partner into a famous, attractive Hollywood star, for example. Couples often believe that they should be totally focused on each other during sex and not have any thoughts about

"Grant yourself and your lover freedom of fantasy. Sexual fantasies are normal, healthy and sex enhancing."
—Michael Castleman (1950–)

"The only way to get rid of temptation is to yield to it."
—Oscar Wilde (1854–1900)

"When two people make love, there are at least four people present—the two who are actually there and the two they are thinking about."
—Sigmund Freud (1856–1939)

others, particularly sexual thoughts. However, during the passion of sex, many people have thoughts not only about their partner but also about others such as past lovers, acquaintances, and movie stars. In another study, Thomas Hicks and Harold Leitenberg (2001) found gender differences in the proportion of sexual fantasies that involved someone other than a current partner (extradyadic fantasies). In a sample of 349 university students and employees in heterosexual relationships, 98% of men and 80% of women reported having extradyadic fantasies in the past 2 months. Many people feel guilty about such thoughts, feeling that they are being "mentally unfaithful" to their partner. However, sex therapists consider fantasies of other lovers to be quite normal and certainly typical.

Women who fantasize about being forced into sexual activity or about being victimized do not necessarily want this to actually occur. Rather, these women tend to be more interested in a variety of sexual activities and to be more sexually experienced than women who don't have these fantasies.

Erotic Dreams Almost all of the men and two thirds of the women in Alfred Kinsey's studies reported having had overtly erotic or sexual dreams (Kinsey et al., 1948, 1953). Sexual images in dreams are frequently very intense. Although people tend to feel responsible for their fantasies, which occur when they are awake, they are usually less troubled by sexual dreams.

Overtly sexual dreams are not necessarily exciting, although dreams that are apparently nonsexual may cause arousal. It is not unusual for individuals to awaken in the middle of the night and notice an erection or vaginal lubrication or to find their bodies moving as if they were having sex. They may also experience nocturnal orgasm or emission. About 2–3% of women's total orgasms may be nocturnal, whereas for men the number may be around 8% (Kinsey et al., 1948, 1953).

Dreams sometimes accompany nocturnal orgasm. The dreamer may awaken, and men usually ejaculate. Although the dream content may not be overtly sexual, it is always accompanied by sensual sensations. Erotic dreams run the gamut of sexual possibilities: Women seem to feel less guilty or fearful about nocturnal orgasms than men do, accepting them more easily as pleasurable experiences.

Masturbation

"Masturbation is an intrinsically and seriously disordered act."

—Vatican Declaration on Sexual Ethics, 1976

People report that they masturbate for many reasons, including for relaxation, for relief of sexual tension, because a partner is not available or does not want sex, for physical pleasure, as an aid to falling asleep, and as a means to avoid STIs and unintended pregnancy. They may masturbate during particular periods or throughout their entire lives. For older adults, often after the loss of their partners, masturbation regains much of the primacy of their earlier years and is often the most common sexual activity. Sex researchers Allison Kirschbaum and Zoe Peterson (2018) note that while the term masturbation is a common word in our society, and used in sexuality education, sex research, and clinical settings, it is not clearly defined. Hence, they conducted what is, to their knowledge, the first study of what behaviors individuals typically consider to be masturbation. Participants were 309 men and 254 women, ages 18 to 74, who completed an online survey. The study found that a wide variety of behaviors were considered to be masturbation by a majority of participants (see Table 5). No difference was found between men and women participants in the total number of behaviors labeled as masturbation. Findings revealed that both men and women were more likely to consider a behavior as masturbation: (1) if there was no sex partner present when the behavior occurred than if there was, and (2) if an orgasm was experienced than if it did not. Women were more likely than men to consider a behavior as masturbation if the person was alone and if no orgasm occurred. The researchers note that findings suggest the need for behavioral specificity (e.g., uses a vibrator on genitals for pleasure) when discussing masturbation with students, clients, and in sex research.

"MASTURBATION, n. An extremely disgusting act performed on a regular basis by everyone else."

—Robert Tefton

Masturbation is an important means of learning about our bodies. Through masturbation, individuals learn what is sexually pleasing, how to move their bodies, and what their

TABLE 5 ● Percentages of Participants Labeling Each Behavior as "Masturbation"

Behavior	Orgasm		No Orgasm	
	With partner	No partner	With partner	No partner
Touched/stroked genitals with hand for pleasure	Men = 79%	Men = 96%	Men = 65%	Men = 81%
	Women = 77%	Women = 98%	Women = 63%	Women = 89%
Used a Vibrator on genitals for pleasure	Men = 76%	Men = 96%	Men = 62%	Men = 85%
	Women = 77%	Women = 97%	Women = 68%	Women = 97%
Put pressure on genitals for pleasure	Men = 71%	Men = 95%	Men = 47%	Men = 67%
	Women = 67%	Women = 94%	Women = 56%	Women = 80%
Used the shower jet water on genitals for pleasure	Men = 71%	Men = 95%	Men = 57%	Men = 79%
	Women = 73%	Women = 95%	Women = 67%	Women = 85%
Rubbed genitals against on object or surface for pleasure	Men = 70%	Men = 95%	Men = 56%	Men = 76%
	Women = 70%	Women = 95%	Women = 57%	Women = 84%
Stimulated your anus	Men = 67%	Men = 88%	Men = 53%	Men = 69%
	Women = 70%	Women = 94%	Women = 58%	Women = 81%
Inserted a vibrator or some other object into your vagina or anus for pleasure	Men = 72%	Men = 94%	Men = 60%	Men = 82%
	Women = 76%	Women = 98%	Women = 69%	Women = 97%
Touched/stimulated/stroked your breast or chest for pleasure	Men = 92%	Men = 72%	Men = 33%	Men = 43%
	Women = 50%	Women = 71%	Women = 34%	Women = 48%
Had fantasy (without touching yourself) for pleasure	Men = 28%	Men = 42%	Men = 13%	Men = 16%
	Women = 27%	Women = 35%	Women = 13%	Women = 15%
Touched/stimulated partners genitals with your hand to give him or her pleasure	Men = 498%		Men = 43%	
	Women = 38%		Women = 34%	

Note: Percentages rounded to the nearest whole number.

Source: Kischbavm, A. L., & Peterson, Z. D. (2018).

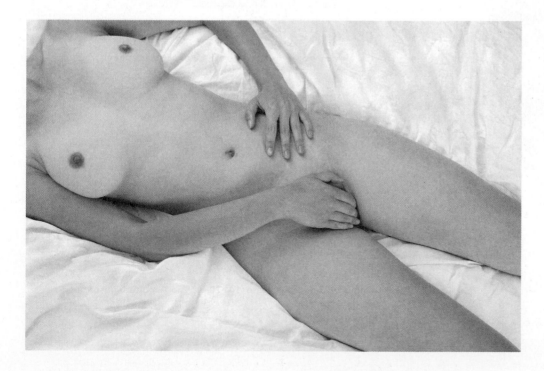

Female masturbation: Many people "discover" their sexual potential through masturbation. Sometimes, women learn to be orgasmic through masturbation and then bring this ability to their relationships.

Jochen Schoenfeld/AGE Fotostock

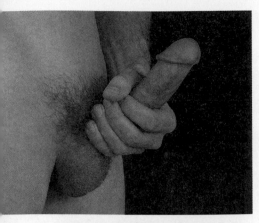

Male masturbation: Masturbation is an important form of sexual behavior in which individuals explore their erotic capacities and bring pleasure to themselves.

H. S. Photos/Science Source

natural rhythms are. The activity has no harmful physical effects. Although masturbation often decreases when individuals are regularly sexual with another person, it is not necessarily a temporary substitute for sexual intercourse but rather is a legitimate form of sexual activity in its own right. Sex therapists may encourage clients to masturbate as a means of overcoming specific sexual problems and discovering their personal sexual potential. Masturbation, whether practiced alone or mutually with a partner (see Figure 5), is also a form of safer sex.

Most young people report that they received very little positive information about masturbation from parents or school sexuality education programs and that most information came from media, peers, and partners. They learned and internalized the social contradiction of the taboo and stigma of masturbation as opposed to the pleasure it provides. As part of healthy sexual development, many have to come to terms with the dual stigma and pleasure cultural message that they internalized about masturbation (Kaestle & Allen, 2011; Watson & McKee, 2013).

Prevalence of Masturbation As shown in Figure 6, all 10 of the age groups (14–70+) of the National Survey of Sexual Health and Behavior (NSSHB) (see Chapter 2) reported solo masturbation last year. In general, the vast majority of males in all age groups except 70+ reported masturbation alone in the last year and at a frequency higher than women. More than 7 in 10 men, ages 14–59, reported solo masturbation in the past year.

• **FIGURE 5**

Mutual Masturbation. Many couples enjoy mutual masturbation, one form of safer sex.

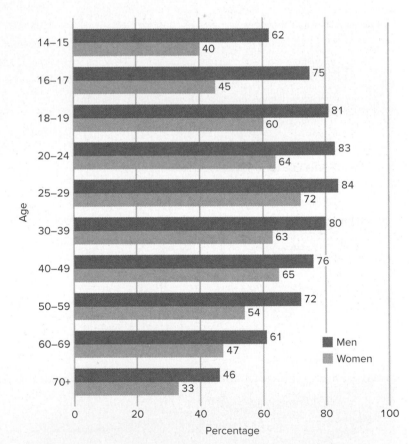

Note: Data based on 5,865 Americans.

• **FIGURE 6**

Percentages of Americans, Ages 14–70+, Who Reported Masturbating Alone in the Past Year.

Note: Data based on 5,865 Americans.

Source: Herbenick, D., et al. (2010.2a, 2010.9a).

Assessing Your Attitude Toward Masturbation

Masturbation guilt is a learned script in which the negative effects of guilt, disgust, shame, and fear are related to masturbation (Abramson & Mosher, 1975). As discussed in this chapter, feelings of shame and guilt have long been associated with masturbation, and a positive attitude has emerged only recently. Still, many people continue to feel guilty about their own masturbatory activity. Take this inventory to determine how much you have been affected by negative messages about masturbation.

Directions

Indicate how true each of the following statements is for you, on a scale from "Not at all true" to "Very true," by circling the appropriate number.

	Not at all true				Very true
1. People masturbate to escape feelings of tension and anxiety.	1	2	3	4	5
2. People who masturbate will not enjoy sexual intercourse as much as those who refrain from masturbation.	1	2	3	4	5
3. Masturbation is a private matter that neither harms nor concerns anyone else.	1	2	3	4	5
4. Masturbation is a sin against yourself.	1	2	3	4	5
5. Masturbation in childhood can help a person develop a natural, healthy attitude toward sex.	1	2	3	4	5
6. Masturbation in an adult is juvenile and immature.	1	2	3	4	5
7. Masturbation can lead to deviant sexual behavior.	1	2	3	4	5
8. Excessive masturbation is physically impossible, so it is needless to worry.	1	2	3	4	5
9. If you enjoy masturbating too much, you may never learn to relate to a sex partner.	1	2	3	4	5
10. After masturbating, a person feels degraded.	1	2	3	4	5
11. Experience with masturbation can potentially help a woman become orgasmic for sexual intercourse.	1	2	3	4	5
12. I feel guilt about masturbating.	1	2	3	4	5
13. Masturbation can be a "friend in need" when there is no "friend indeed."	1	2	3	4	5
14. Masturbation can provide an outlet for sex fantasies without harming anyone else or endangering oneself.	1	2	3	4	5
15. Excessive masturbation can lead to problems with erections in men and women not being able to have an orgasm.	1	2	3	4	5
16. Masturbation is an escape mechanism that prevents a person from developing a mature sexual outlook.	1	2	3	4	5
17. Masturbation can provide harmless relief from sexual tension.	1	2	3	4	5
18. Playing with your own genitals is disgusting.	1	2	3	4	5
19. Excessive masturbation is associated with neurosis, depression, and behavioral problems.	1	2	3	4	5
20. Any masturbation is too much.	1	2	3	4	5
21. Masturbation is a compulsive, addictive habit that once begun is almost impossible to stop.	1	2	3	4	5
22. Masturbation is fun.	1	2	3	4	5
23. When I masturbate, I am disgusted with myself.	1	2	3	4	5
24. A pattern of frequent masturbation is associated with introversion and withdrawal from social contacts.	1	2	3	4	5
25. I would be ashamed to admit publicly that I have masturbated.	1	2	3	4	5
26. Excessive masturbation leads to mental dullness and fatigue.	1	2	3	4	5
27. Masturbation is a normal sexual outlet.	1	2	3	4	5
28. Masturbation is caused by an excessive preoccupation with thoughts about sex.	1	2	3	4	5
29. Masturbation can teach you to enjoy the sensuousness of your own body.	1	2	3	4	5
30. After I masturbate, I am disgusted with myself for losing control of my body.	1	2	3	4	5

Scoring

To obtain an index of masturbation guilt, sum the circled numbers to yield a score from 30 to 150. Before summing, reverse the scoring for these 10 items: 3, 5, 8, 11, 13, 14, 17, 22, 27. That is, a 1 would be converted to a 5, a 2 to a 4, a 4 to a 2, and 5 to a 1. The lower your score, the lower your guilt about and negative attitude toward masturbation.

TABLE 6 ● Percentage of United States Adults Ages 18–70+ Who Participated in Selected Partnered Sexual Behavior in the Past Year by Gender and Age

Past year partnered sexual behaviors	AGE GROUP														Total Men	Total Women
	18–24		25–29		30–39		40–49		50–59		60–69		70+			
	%M*	%W*	%M	%W	%M	%W	%M	%W	%M	%W	%M	%W	%M	%W		
Vaginal intercourse	53	62	74	84	75	85	79	74	66	65	58	39	51	24	66	62
Gave partner oral sex	50	57	69	76	71	78	68	63	58	54	42	28	34	15	57	53
Received oral sex	62	60	77	70	71	69	75	55	60	49	46	28	30	16	61	49
Intersitive anal sex	12		21		26		22		13		8		3		15	
Received anal sex	9	17	7	26	11	18	7	15	3	10	1	1	1	1	5	12
Wore sexy underwear or lingerie for a partner	8	46	18	63	10	55	10	36	9	38	6	15	2	7	9	36
Had sex with someone in a public place	11	7	13	13	3	6	8	5	5	4	4	0	2	0	6	5
Tied up your partner or been tied up part of sex	8	7	15	15	4	9	3	2	3	4	1	0	0	0	4	5
Sucked/licked partner feet/toes	6	2	14	9	8	4	10	2	12	2	2	2	4	2	8	3
Masturbated with someone else	15	5	29	12	26	14	29	12	33	13	27	9	16	7	26	11
Masturbated in front of partner	17	18	29	40	26	32	31	27	20	16	13	6	12	1	21	20
Role played with partner	13	8	17	13	6	14	10	5	9	6	2	4	1	1	8	7
Playfully whipped or been whipped by partner as part of sex	7	7	13	16	6	14	6	7	6	3	3	1	1	0	6	6
Spanked or been spanked as part of sex	13	40	39	51	28	37	14	16	9	10	4	11	0	0	14	20

Note: Percentage rounded to the nearest whole number.

* M = Men; W = Women

Source: Herbenick, D.,, et al. (2017).

More than 6 in 10 of women, ages 14–49, reported solo masturbation in the past year. Table 6 also presents the prevalence in the past year of 14 partnered sexual behaviors, including masturbation with someone else and masturbation in front of someone else, among persons aged 18–70+, as reported in the 2015 Sexual Exploration in America Study (SEAS) (see Chapter 2). Partnered masturbation in the last year was reported by both men and women to occur much less often than solo masturbation (Herbenick et al., 2017). Both studies indicate that masturbation alone or in a partnered relationship occurs among all age groups and can be considered a typical and pleasurable part of an individual's and a couple's sexuality.

Masturbatory behavior is influenced by education, ethnicity, religion, and age, with education a particularly strong factor. The more educated one becomes, the more frequently one masturbates. A nationally representative British study of masturbation among the general population (aged 16–44) found that masturbation frequency was greater for both men and women with higher levels of education, in higher social classes, and at younger ages (Gerressu et al., 2008).

A large probability sample of American adults, ages 18–60 (7,648 men and 8,090 women), examined the association between partnered sex frequency and masturbation. The study found that women who felt content with their sex lives appeared to more likely supplement recent sex with masturbation while men who were not content with their sex lives were mildly less likely to masturbate as recent sexual encounters increased (Regnerus et al., 2017).

Masturbation in Adulthood Masturbation is common among youth, peaks in young adulthood, and tends to decrease in later years (see Figure 6).

"Masturbation! The amazing availability of it!"

—James Joyce (1882–1941)

Women and Masturbation One way in which women become familiar with their own sexual responsiveness is through masturbation.

One study of 765 American women (79% under 30; 75% white; 85% with at least a bachelor's degree; 67% heterosexual) revealed several reasons for masturbation: sexual pleasure, to learn about or achieve greater understanding of their bodies, to experience sexual release, to experience sexual pleasures as a substitute for partner sex, and for general sexual satisfaction. Some of the women reported conflicting feelings about masturbation such as difficulties in accepting the normalcy of masturbation, shame, sexual empowerment, and fear that one is actually selfish. However, most of the women did not feel shame but felt sexually empowered. These women reported being more sexually efficacious, had higher genital self-image, and masturbated to experience sexual pleasure and to learn more about their bodies (Bowman, 2014).

Though no two women masturbate in exactly the same manner, a number of common methods are used to experience orgasm. Most involve some type of clitoral stimulation, by using the fingers, rubbing against an object, or using a vibrator (see Figure 7). The rubbing or stimulation tends to increase just prior to orgasm and continues during orgasm.

Because the glans clitoris is often too sensitive for prolonged direct stimulation, women tend to stroke gently on the shaft of the clitoris. Another common method, which exerts less direct pressure on the clitoris, is to stroke the mons pubis area or the labia minora (inner lips). Individual preferences play a key role in what method is chosen, how rigorous the stimulation is, how often masturbation occurs, and whether it is accompanied by erotic aids such as a vibrator or sensual oils. One study found that water- and silicon-based lubricants were associated with significantly higher reports of sexual pleasure and satisfaction and rarely associated with genital symptoms (Herbenick et al., 2011). Some women find that running a stream of warm water over the vulva or sitting near the jet stream in a hot tub is sexually arousing. Stimulation of the breasts and nipples is also very common, as is stroking the anal region. Some women enjoy inserting a finger or other object into their vagina; however, this is less common than clitoral stimulation. Some women apply deep pressure in the region of the G-spot to give themselves a different type of orgasm. Using common sense in relation to cleanliness, such as not inserting an object or a finger from the anus into the vagina and keeping vibrators and other objects used for insertion clean, helps prevent infection.

Men and Masturbation Like women, men have individual preferences and patterns in masturbating. Nearly all methods involve some type of direct stimulation of the penis with the hand. Typically, the penis is grasped and stroked at the shaft, with up-and-down or circular movements of the hand, so that the edge of the corona around the glans and the frenulum on the underside are stimulated. How much pressure is applied, how rapid the strokes are, how many fingers are used, where the fingers are placed, and how far up and down the hands move vary from one man to another. Whether the breasts, testicles, anus, or other parts of the body are stimulated also depends on the individual, but it appears to be the up-and-down stroking or rubbing of the penis that triggers orgasm. The stroking tends to increase just prior to ejaculation and then to slow or stop during ejaculation.

To add variety or stimulation, some men may elect to use lubricants, visual or written erotic materials, artificial vaginas, inflatable dolls, or rubber pouches in which to insert their penis (see Figure 8). Regardless of the aid or technique, it is important to pay attention to cleanliness to prevent bacterial infections.

Masturbation in Sexual Relationships Most people continue to masturbate after they marry or are in a steady relationship, although the rate is lower. Actually, the National Health and Social Life Survey (NHSLS) found that married people are less likely to have masturbated during the preceding 12 months than those never married or formerly married (Laumann et al., 1994).

There are many reasons for continuing the activity during marriage or other sexual relationships; for example, masturbation is pleasurable, a partner is away or unwilling, sexual intercourse or other intimate sexual behavior is not satisfying, the partner(s) fear(s)

"What I like about masturbation is that you don't have to talk afterwards."
—Milos Forman (1932–2018)

● FIGURE 7

The rabbit vibrator is used by many women to provide quick sexual arousal.

Hugh Threlfall/Alamy Stock Photo

"Masturbation is the primary sexual activity of [human] kind. In the nineteenth century it was a disease; in the twentieth, it's a cure."
—Thomas Szasz (1920–2012)

● FIGURE 8

The masturbatory sleeve, a commonly used sex toy by men.

Eillen/Shutterstock

sexual inadequacy, the individual acts out fantasies, or he or she seeks to release tension. During times of relationship conflict, masturbation may act as a distancing device, with the masturbating partner choosing masturbation over sexual interaction as a means of emotional protection.

• Sexual Behavior With Others

We often think that sex is sexual intercourse, but sex is not limited to sexual intercourse. Partners engage in a wide variety of sexual activities, which may include erotic touching, kissing, and oral and anal sex. A study of four groups—men and women (mean age = 30) in both same-sex and mixed-sex relationships—found that they were strikingly identical in their sexual repertoires. The study measured solitary behaviors such as masturbation, orgasm alone and with partner, and couple behavior such as kissing your partner, watching your partner undress, and oral sex (Holmberg & Blair, 2009). Which of these "sexual" activities actually constitute sex? This topic has been publicly debated, largely fueled by former president Bill Clinton's declaration that he did not have sex with Monica Lewinsky despite the fact that she performed oral sex on him. (To find out what a representative sample of young adults believed constituted having "had sex," see Think About It, "You Would Say You 'Had Sex' If You . . .") In this section we focus on selected partnered sexual behaviors, such as kissing, oral sex, sexual intercourse, and anal eroticism. Certainly couples participate in other activities, such as tied up partner or been tied up; see Table 6 to learn the percentage of adults whom participated last year in such sexual behaviors as well as oral sex, intercourse and anal sex.

Most Recent Partnered Sex

Like many national sex surveys, the National Survey of Sexual Health and Behavior (NSSHB) assessed the contextual factors during the last, single event of couple or partnered sex (Herbenick et al., 2010.9a). The contextual findings from this nationally representative sample of 3,990 adults, aged 18–59, provide greater understanding of the circumstances and experiences of couple sex. Some of the more intriguing findings give us a brief "snapshot" of the sexual repertoire of Americans' reported last-partnered sexual event:

- Most participants reported that their most recent sexual event occurred in their or their partner's home.

- The majority of the most recent sexual events occurred within a relationship or with a dating partner, although a sizable minority reported their most recent sexual event occurred with a friend. However, most of the participants aged 18–24 reported that their partner was a casual or dating partner.

- The vast majority, but not all, reported that their most recent sexual event was with an other-sex partner.

- An enormous variability in the sexual repertoire of the participants was found, with a diverse range of sexual behaviors in a given sexual episode.

- Penile-vaginal intercourse was the most commonly reported sexual behavior of both men and women during the most recent sexual event, although oral sex (given and received) occurred frequently.

- The largest proportion of men and women reported engaging solely in penile-vaginal intercourse during their most recent sexual event, although some indicated participating solely in noncoital behaviors such as partnered oral sex and masturbation.

- Most men and women reported that neither they nor their partner used alcohol or marijuana around the time of their most recent sexual event.

The authors concluded that the findings not only illustrate that sexual interactions include numerous sexual behaviors that may have occurred in varied sequences but also provide insight into possible pathways for STI transmission from one anatomical site to another.

You Would Say You "Had Sex" If You . . .

When people say they "had sex," "hooked up," or "did some things" but did not have sex, what do they mean? Many people have different ideas about what it means to have sex; it all depends on the behavioral criteria they use. Some definitions may be used by couples or individuals to justify a wide range of intimate behaviors other than penile-vaginal intercourse or penile-anal intercourse in order to, for example, preserve or lose their virginity, not to "have cheated" on another person, or to believe they had sex. Without a universal definition of "having sex," confusion or false assumptions can result (Sanders & Reinisch, 1999).

Researchers at The Kinsey Institute and the Rural Center for AIDS/STD Prevention at Indiana University conducted a public opinion study of a representative sample of adults to determine if certain sexual behaviors, as well as whether male ejaculation, female orgasm, condom use, or brevity during penile-vaginal intercourse or penile-anal intercourse, are considered "having sex." The opinions of 486 adult Indiana residents of varying ages were obtained by telephone, using random digital dialing. Results of the participants, aged 18–29, are shown in the accompanying table (Sanders et al., 2010; Yarber et al., 2007).

Not surprisingly, nearly all of the participants considered penile-vaginal intercourse—even under the specific circumstances listed—as having "had sex." This was basically true for penile-anal intercourse, although the percentage indicating "yes" was not quite as high. In general, these findings were replicated in subsequent studies (Sewell & Strassberg, 2015; Peck et al., 2016). As expected, the percentage indicating "yes" to oral sex and manual stimulation of the genitals was less than intercourse; interestingly, the responses varied considerably by gender, with a much greater percentage of women than men indicating "yes" to these two behaviors.

In a unique assessment of what behaviors constitute having sex, researchers documented the types of sexual behavior included in the definitions of "having sex with a man" and "having sex with a woman" among a sample of women who have sex with women and who have sex with men (Schick et al., 2016). The women participants in the study included more behaviors in their definition of having sex with a woman than their definition of having sex with a man. This finding indicates the need for health care providers and researchers to be aware of possible different criteria for using the term "having sex" when women discuss female versus male partners. Further, asking a health care patient a limited number of questions about her sexual behavior history may result in an inaccurate assessment of the sexual risk of the patient and sex partner. For example, this study found that 90% of the women would include vaginal fingering as having sex with a woman, yet fewer than 60% included genital-to-genital rubbing (i.e., vulvar stimulation with unclothed genitals) as having sex with a woman.

A study of 164 heterosexual Canadian university students not only asked their views of what constitutes "having sex" but also examined what constitutes a sexual partner and what they consider to be "unfaithful" in a sexual partner. The results showed discrepancies in the students' opinions on these three issues. For example, although 25% of the students considered oral-genital behaviors as having sex, more than 60% thought that the giver or receiver of oral sex was a sex partner, and more than 97% considered a sex partner who had oral sex with someone else to have been unfaithful (Randall & Byers, 2003). Further, while masturbating to orgasm in the presence of another person was considered as having sex by less than 4% of the students, 34% reported that this behavior would make that person a sexual partner, and 95% considered it to be unfaithful if done with someone else.

Percentages of 18- to 29-year-old Indiana residents (31 females, 31 males) answering "yes" to the question "Would you say you 'had sex' with someone if the most intimate behavior you engaged in was . . . ?" (Sanders, et al., 2010; Yarber, et al., 2007)

Behavior	% of Women Yes	% of Men Yes
You touched, fondled, or manually stimulated a partner's genitals	29	10
A partner touched, fondled, or manually stimulated your genitals	32	17
You had oral (mouth) contact with a partner's genitals	61	33
A partner had oral (mouth) contact with your genitals	67	40
Penile-vaginal intercourse	94	97
Penile-vaginal intercourse with no ejaculation; that is, the man did not "come"	94	90
Penile-vaginal intercourse with no female orgasm; that is, the woman did not "come"	90	97
Penile-vaginal intercourse, but very brief	97	97
Penile-vaginal intercourse with a condom	94	100
Penile-anal intercourse	84	77
Penile-anal intercourse with no male ejaculation	84	77
Penile-anal intercourse with no female orgasm	84	77
Penile-anal intercourse, but very brief	84	76
Penile-anal intercourse with a condom	84	83

A study of 594 undergraduates also assessed perceptions of "being unfaithful." Both men and women were found to be significantly more certain that a sexual behavior would be considered as "having sex" when evaluating their partner's behavior outside of the relationship than when they considered their own behavior (Sewell & Strassberg, 2015).

Think Critically

1. Do any of the results of the research studies on the definition of "having sex" surprise you? Do you agree or disagree with the findings?
2. Does it make any difference how "having sex" is defined?
3. How do you define "having sex"? Has your definition changed over time?

Frequency and Duration of Sex

"Whatever kind of sex works for two (or more) individuals will be more enticing with the partners are alive, embodied and integrated within themselves and absorbed in and engaged with one another in the moment."

—Peggy Kleinplatz

In many ways, American culture has become more sexualized and open to sex than ever before. For example, there is greater acceptance of nonmarital sex, increased availability to sexual messages and information online, development of online dating and hookup apps, more accessible and effective contraception, and increased acceptance and use of sexually explicit videos. From all of this, one might expect that there would be a similar increase in sexual frequency among Americans. However, an analysis of national data found the opposite (Twenge et al., 2015; Sherman & Wells, 2015, 2017).

Sex researcher Jean Twenge and colleagues (2017) analyzed data from the nationally representative General Social Survey, 1989–2017, involving 26,620 Americans over the age of 18. They found that people were actually having sex less often than in recent years. Here is what they reported:

- American adults had, on the average, sex 53 times a year in 2014 as compared to 62 times a year a quarter-century ago.

- Sexual frequency decreased among the partnered (married or living together) but stayed constant among those not partnered.

- Declines in sexual frequency was similar across gender, race, religion, educational level, and work status and were the largest among those in their 50s, those with school-age children, and those who did not watch sexually explicit videos.

- Those born in the 1930s (Silent Generation) had sex the most often, and those born in the 1990s (millennials and iGen) had sex the least often. The decline was not linked to greater number of working hours or increased viewing of sexually explicit videos.

- The millennials had fewer lifetime sexual partners than any group since the 1990s: an average of 8 compared to 11 for the baby boomers (those born between mid-1940s and mid-1960s).

In sum, the declines found in this study suggest that Americans are having sex less frequently due to two primary factors: an increasing number of persons not having a steady or marital partner and a decrease in sexual frequency in those having partners. The researchers speculate the causes of the decline: greater accessibility of entertainment and social media, a decline in happiness in persons over 30 years of age, and the use of antidepressants that can cause sexual function difficulties.

A study of 822 adults aged 18–79 years (mean = 30 years old) assessed both the frequency of sex and the duration of individual sexual encounters among both men and women in mixed-sex and same-sex relationships (Blair & Pukall, 2014). Similar to past research, the women in same-sex relationships reported lower levels of sexual frequency—but only slightly lower—than both men in same-sex relationships and men and women in mixed-sex relationships (see Figure 9). However, women in same-sex relationships reported significantly longer durations of sexual encounters than both men in same-sex relationships and

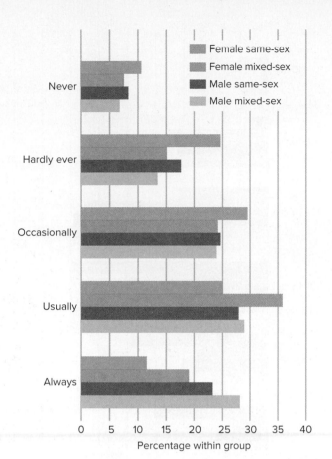

• FIGURE 9

Frequency of Engaging in Sex More Than Two Times per Week by Relationship Type of 822 Adults, Aged 18–79.

Source: Blair, K. L., & Pukall, C. F. (2014).

men and women in mixed-sex relationships (see Figure 10). The study also found that the more frequently a person engaged in sex and the longer the duration of their last encounter, the greater their reported sexual satisfaction. (To learn more about the frequency of sex and satisfaction see "Think About It, "The Frequency of Sex: The More, the Better?")

The frequency of sex has become a concern for several countries worldwide, but not specifically for relationship reasons. Many regions of the world have undergone a downward trend in the birth rate during the past half-century. In many countries, a large number of women have limited their family size to some desired size or have chosen not to have children (Timaeus & Moultrie, 2020). According to a report in *Business Insider*, 11 countries desperately want people to have more sex because of low fertility rates. Demographers suggest that to fill the spaces left behind by death, a country needs a fertility rate of just over two children per woman to hit "replacement fertility." Only about half of the world's countries currently achieve this rate. The strategies used to encourage people to have more sex vary from highly explicit to unconventional (Weller, 2017). A small-town politician in northern Sweden, for example, proposed that municipal employees be given a paid, one-hour break from work each week to go home and have sex as a way to help combat the dwindling local population, add spice to long-term marriages, and improve morale. People in the local community and even around the world reacted with astonishment. The town's council overwhelmingly rejected the proposal because members felt that if sexual intercourse is subsidized, so should personal activities such as gardening and cleaning (Belifsky & Anderson, 2017a, 2017b).

Couple Sexual Styles

Barry McCarthy, a psychologist and renowned sex therapist, and his wife, Emily McCarthy, in their book *Discovering Your Couple Sexual Style* (2009), challenge couples, married or not, to develop a mature sexuality rather than adhering to unrealistic expectations of sexuality. The McCarthys contend that each couple develops their own sexual style. The challenge is for each partner to maintain individuality as well as experience being part of an intimate,

• FIGURE 10

Duration of Average Sexual Encounter by Relationship Type of 822 Adults, Aged 18–79.

Source: Blair, K. L., & Pukall, C. F. (2014).

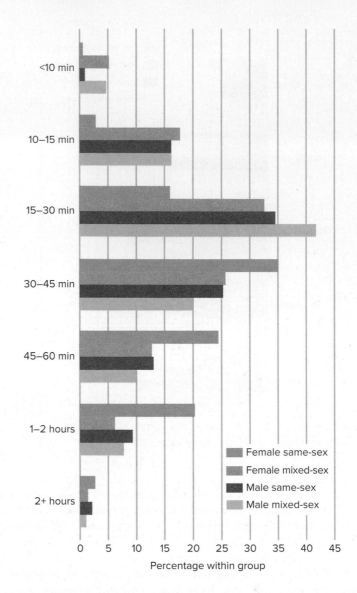

erotic sexual couple. They state, in talking to couples, that "it takes most couples six months or longer to transition from the romantic love/passionate sex/idealized phase to develop a mature, intimate couple sexual style" (p. 33). They continue by telling couples that they can develop a mutually comfortable level of intimacy that promotes sexual desire and eroticism and provides energy for their relationship.

The McCarthys identify four couple sexual styles and state that there is no "right" style that is best for all couples. They state that most couples maintain their core sexual style because it is comfortable and satisfying, but the McCarthys also encourage couples to make adjustments and modifications as the relationship continues. These styles are applicable to all couples regardless of their sexual identity or orientation.

Complementary Style   This is the most common sexual style, and it allows each partner to have a positive sexual voice while sharing an intimate relationship. The couples who choose this style realize that the best aphrodisiac is an involved, aroused partner. Each partner is responsible for his or her sexual desire and response and feels free to initiate sex, say no to sex, and request a different sexual scenario. In this style, it is not the partner's role to give the partner an orgasm but rather to be an intimate friend receptive and responsive to the partner's sexual feelings and preferences. The strength of this style is its variability, its flexibility, and the value each person places on intimacy and eroticism. A possible vulnerability is that sex can become routine and, if the couple takes sex and each other for granted, they may become disappointed and frustrated in their sexual relationship.

think
about it

The Frequency of Sex: The More, the Better?

Sex is like money, only too much is enough.
                                    —John Updike (1932–2009)

Regularly having sex is important to both an individual and a couple's well-being and satisfaction, but how much is enough? The media often tout that having more sex makes one happier and improves a couple's relationship. The more, the better. Some research also supports this (e.g., Byers, 2005; Call, Sprecher, & Schwartz, 1995; Twenge et al., 2017). However, researchers have wondered if there is a point where the frequency of sex is enough or even too much. Psychologist and sex researcher Amy Muise and colleagues conducted three studies to determine if having more sex stops translating into more happiness (Muise et al., 2015; Shute, 2015).

- In the first study, the researchers examined data of 25,510 Americans, married or in relationships and aged 18–89 from 1989–2012. More sex was associated with more happiness but for the married couples only. However, the happiness maxed out at having sex about once a week.

- A second study, an online survey of 335 people, most whom identified as heterosexual, found that these individuals tended to be happier as the frequency increased, but the happiness leveled off with sex occurring more than once a week. The "once-a-week" finding held true regardless of people's gender, age, or relationship length.

- The third study confirmed that sex and relationship satisfaction was not significantly related when the frequency of sex occurred more than once a week. A novel analysis examined which is more important: sex or money? Regularly having sex was found to be even more important to having a happy relationship than money was.

Muise stated that the study findings reveal that it is not necessary, on the average, for couples to try to have as much sex as possible. Having sex more than once a week was not bad, but it was not associated with greater well-being on the average (Shute, 2015; Dotinga, 2015). Why did the happiness flatten out at once a week? Muise conjectured that one possibility is that people are satisfied when they are having sex as much as they think they should be based on the standard established by their peers: on the average, couples have sex once a week (Hutson, 2016).

But is having lots of sex actually good? Researchers from Carnegie Mellon University (Loewenstein et al., 2015) tested this by encouraging couples to have more sex and then determined if that made them happier. The researchers recruited 64 heterosexual and married couples: Half were randomly assigned to continue their current frequency of sex and the other half were asked to double their frequency of sex. Some of the couples in the experiment group did double their frequency of sex, but the average increase was only 40%. Couples completed a short daily online questionnaire for 90 days. Here is what the data showed: The increase in sex did not make the couples happier; both men and women reported that the additional intercourse wasn't much fun. The quality of sex and well-being related to energy and enthusiasm declined as did the quality of sex (Reynolds, 2015). The researchers conjecture that the directive to have more sex may have affected the couple's motivation to have sex; that it changed from a voluntary activity for pleasure to one that was a research duty. In applying the findings to couples, George Loewenstein, the study's lead author, stated that:

> Concentrate on quality rather than quantity if you wish to be happy. Studies associating sexual frequency and happiness may have missed the underlying link between the two, which is the pleasurability of the sex. People who like their couplings probably have more of them, and it is the pleasure of the act that raises mood, not how often it happens (quoted in Reynolds, 2015, p. 18).

Think Critically

1. Have you heard from friends or other sources about how often couples should have sex? If so, what was the frequency?
2. If you have been in a sexual relationship did you and your partner try to adhere to a certain frequency of sex based on what you thought was expected?
3. Did any of the findings from the above studies surprise you? If so, what did?
4. How often do you think you would want to have sex if you were in a sexual relationship?

Traditional Style This is the most predictable and stable style and is often called "acceptance and security," as it places high value on keeping the peace, commitment, and stability. In this conflict-minimizing relationship, traditional gender scripts of sex being the man's domain and affection and intimacy being the woman's domain are paramount. Since emotional and erotic expression is discouraged, this is the least intimate and erotic couple sexual style, with sex being a lower priority than it is in the other couple sexual styles. The male initiates sex and the female is less erotically active but is open to the male's preferences.

The strength of this style is predictability, security, and clearly defined roles, with sex rarely becoming an explosive issue. The vulnerability is that this style does not have enough mutual and sexual intimacy and, of all the couple sexual styles, it is most resistant to change.

Soulmate Style Being soulmates means experiencing the highest level of intimacy and closeness, a sexual couple style that has been considered the "perfect" style. These couples share feelings, spend a lot of time together, enjoy shared experiences, and place a high priority on meeting each other's needs. The fundamental tenet of this style is that the greater the intimacy, the better the couple sex. The advantages of this style are a feeling of being accepted for who one truly is; feeling loved, desired, and desirable; and not having a fear of judgment or rejection. When working well, this style really meets the partners' needs for intimacy and security. A major danger of this style is that too much closeness and predictability can subvert sexuality and partners can "de-eroticize" each other as described in Esther Perel's book *Mating in Captivity* (2006). That is, people can become so close to their partner that they lose erotic feelings for him or her. In this style, the couple is hesitant to face the problems that come up in their relationship. Persons in this style need to be autonomous enough to maintain their own sexual voice, and partners should be committed to integrating intimacy and eroticism.

Emotionally Expressive Style This is the most erotic style and is dominated with strong emotion and drama. Each partner is free to share positive and negative passions in word and deed. Of the four couple sexual styles, this one is the most engaging, exciting, fun, and unpredictable. It focuses on external stimuli to enhance eroticism while downplaying intimacy. The openness to emotional and sexual expression and spontaneity are major strengths of this style. This style is the most resilient and engaging of the four styles, and couples often use sex to reconnect after a conflict. The major drawback of this style is that it is the highest in relational instability. These couples "wear each other out" with all of their emotional upheavals. Partners in this sexual style should honor personal boundaries and not be hurtful when the issue involves sexuality.

Touching

Whether sex begins with the heart or the genitals, touch is the fire that melds the two into one. Touching is both a sign of caring and a signal for arousal.

Touching does not need to be directed solely toward the genitals or erogenous zones. The entire body is responsive to a touch or a caress. Even hand-holding can be sensual for two people sexually attracted to each other. Most women appear to be especially responsive to touch, but traditional male gender roles give little significance to touching. Some men regard touching as simply a prelude to intercourse. When this occurs, touch is transformed into a demand for intercourse rather than an expression of intimacy or erotic play. The man's partner, if a female, may become reluctant to touch or show affection for fear her gestures will be misinterpreted as a sexual invitation.

William Masters and Virginia Johnson (1970) suggest a form of touching they call "pleasuring." **Pleasuring** is nongenital touching and caressing. Neither partner tries to sexually stimulate the other; they simply explore, discovering how their bodies respond to touching. One partner guides the other partner's hand over his or her body, telling the partner what feels good; the roles are then reversed. Such sharing gives each a sense of his or her own responses; it also allows each to discover what the other likes and dislikes. We can't assume we know what a particular person likes, for there is too much variation among people: Watching a partner masturbate can provide clues on how he or she likes to be stimulated. Pleasuring opens the door to communication; couples discover that the entire body, not just the genitals, is erogenous. Actually, Masters and Johnson (1970) noted that women tend to prefer genital touching after general body contact, whereas many men prefer stroking of their genitals early.

Some forms of touching are directly sexual, such as caressing, fondling, or rubbing our own or our partner's genitals or breasts. Sucking or licking earlobes, the neck, toes, or the insides of thighs, palms, or arms can be highly stimulating. Oral stimulation of a woman's or man's breasts or nipples is often exciting. Moving one's genitals or breasts over a partner's face, chest, breasts, or genitals is very erotic for some people. The pressing together of bodies with genital thrusting is called **tribidism**, "dry humping," or "scissoring." Many lesbian women enjoy the overall body contact and eroticism of this form of genital stimulation; sometimes, the partners place their pelvic areas together to provide mutual clitoral stimulation (see Figure 11). Rubbing the penis between the thighs of a partner (female or male) is a type of touching called **interfemoral intercourse**. Heterosexual couples who do not use contraception must be sure the man does not ejaculate near the vaginal opening so as to avoid conception, however unlikely it may seem.

• **FIGURE 11**
Tribidism.

"The essence of sexuality is giving and receiving pleasure-oriented touch."

—Barry McCarthy (1943–) and Emily McCarthy (1945–)

Stimulating a partner's clitoris or penis with the hand or fingers can increase excitement and lead to orgasm. A word of caution: Direct stimulation of the clitoral glans may be painful for some women at specific stages of arousal, so stimulation of either side of the clitoris may work better. Certainly, the clitoris and surrounding areas should be moist before much touching is done. Inserting a finger or fingers into a partner's wet vagina and rhythmically moving it at the pace she likes can also be pleasing. Some women like to have their clitoris licked or stimulated with one hand while their vagina is being penetrated with the other. Men like having their penises lubricated so that their partner's hand glides smoothly over the shaft and glans penis. Be sure to use a water-based lubricant if you plan to use a condom later, because oil-based lubricants may cause the condom to deteriorate. Masturbating while one partner is holding the other can be highly erotic for both people. Mutual masturbation can also be intensely sexual. Some people use sex toys such as dildos, vibrators, or ben-wah balls to enhance sexual touching.

Touching can increase relaxation and enhance intimacy.

Tom & Dee Ann McCarthy/Corbis/Getty Images

Kissing

Kissing is usually our earliest interpersonal sexual experience, and its primal intensity may be traced back to our suckling as infants. The kiss is magic: Fairy tales keep alive the ancient belief that a kiss can undo spells and bring a prince or princess back to life. Parental kisses show love and often remedy the small hurts and injuries of childhood.

Kissing is probably the most acceptable of all sexual activities. The tender lover's kiss symbolizes love, and the erotic lover's kiss, of course, simultaneously represents and *is* passion. Both men and women regard kissing as a romantic expression, a symbol of affection as well as desire. A study of both men and women, aged 18–63, found that kissing frequency was related to relationship quality: For couples in an exclusive relationship, the couples who reported the most frequent kissing also reported the greater relationship satisfaction. Actually, the higher frequency of kissing was more strongly related to greater relationship quality than higher occurrence of sexual intercourse, although both predicted relationship quality to greater relationship quality. Interestingly, the study also found that although kissing did cause sexual arousal, it was not the primary driver for kissing (Wlodarski & Dunbar, 2013).

"The kiss originated when the first male reptile licked the first female reptile, implying in a subtle, complimentary way that she was as succulent as the small reptile he had for dinner the night before."

—F. Scott Fitzgerald (1896–1940)

"If it's uplift you're after, if it's that thrust, stop talking, put lips and tongue to other use."

—Horace (65–8 BCE)

The lips and mouth are highly sensitive to touch and are exquisitely erotic parts of our bodies. Kisses discover, explore, and excite the body. They also involve the senses of taste and smell, which are especially important because they activate unconscious memories and associations. Often, we are aroused by familiar smells associated with particular sexual

think
about it

The First Kiss: A Deal-Breaker?

The decision to kiss for the first time is the most critical in any love story. It changes the relationship of two people more strongly than even the final surrender, because this kiss already has in it that surrender.

—Emil Ludwin (1881–1948)

The first kiss is a memorable, once-in-a-lifetime experience. Is there more to kissing than just lips touching? Surprisingly, there has been little scientific research on this topic, although philosophers have written about "the kiss" for centuries.

A seminal study on college students and kissing published in the scientific journal *Evolutionary Psychology* revealed that a lot of information is exchanged during kissing (Hughes et al., 2007). The study, involving in-depth interviews, provided a descriptive account of kissing behavior in a sample of 1,041 undergraduate students (limited to those indicating kissing preference only or mostly with the other sex) at a large university in the eastern United States. About 70% of the students reported kissing 6 or more people, and 20% estimated to have kissed more than 20 people; no differences were found between men and women in the number of kissing partners or the age of first romantic kiss.

An intriguing finding of the study was that the majority of both men and women noted that a bad kiss is a "deal-breaker," often leading to the ending of a potential new relationship. Slightly more women than men—66% versus 59%—said they were attracted to someone until they kissed the person, then they were no longer interested. One of the study's researchers, Gordon Gallup, stated that while a kiss may not make a relationship, it can kill one and that "there may be unconscious mechanisms that would make people make an assessment of genetic compatibility through a kiss" (Gallup, quoted in Best, 2007). Another study of 904 men and women, aged 18–63 years (mean = 25 years), showed similar results: Women were more likely than men to restate that a first kiss would affect their attraction to a potential mate (Wlodarski & Dunbar, 2013).

The research by Hughes and colleagues (2007) suggests that the meanings associated with kissing vary considerably between men and women. In this study, women placed more significance on kissing as a way of assessing the person as a potential mating partner and as a means of initiating, bonding, maintaining, and monitoring the current status of a long-term relationship. Men, on the other hand, placed less emphasis on kissing, especially with short-term partners, and appeared to use kissing as a means to an end—that is, to gain sexual access. About one half of the men, in contrast to one third of the women, assumed that kissing would lead to sex whether they were in a short-term or long-term relationship. Gallup notes that kissing for males is one way of keeping their partners physically interested, stating that "as a consequence of male saliva exchange extending over a long period of time, it's conceivable that the testosterone in male saliva can stimulate female sex hormones and make females more receptive to sex" (Gallup, quoted in Best, 2007).

Other notable gender differences found in the study were the following:

- Taste and smell of the person were more important to women.
- Women were more likely to rebuff sex with a partner unless they kissed first.
- More women indicated that they would refuse to have sex with a bad kisser.
- Men were more likely to desire exchanging saliva during a kiss, showing greater preference for tongue contact and open-mouth kissing.
- Men were more likely to believe that kissing could stop a fight.
- More men felt that it was OK to kiss on the first date and it was OK for the female partner to make the move for the first kiss.

A study of 356 heterosexual students at a large university in the western United States examined the emotional responses that commonly accompany the first kiss (Regan et al., 2007). The researchers found that most reported an array of emotions—dread, nervousness, fright, awkwardness, and confusion—as they approached their first kiss. They found that emotions shifted during the kiss. For men, their anxiety and fear were replaced with elation, happiness, sexual arousal, enjoyment, and other positive feelings. Women experienced a mixed reaction: disgust, uncertainty, boredom, enjoyment, tenderness, and excitement. Following the first kiss, most men continued to feel positive responses, but some experienced embarrassment and other negative feelings. For women, although many reported positive feelings, negative responses such as disappointment, regret, and distress were more commonly experienced.

Kissing is one of the primal ways we express affection with other persons, as well as being one of our earliest evolutionary mechanisms for social bonding. Further, beyond the pleasure experienced, kissing has shown scientific health benefits, such as releasing of feel-good hormones such as oxytocin, making a personal more alert, reducing stress levels, improving relationship satisfaction, and reducing the psychological aspects of stress (Rosenfeld, 2019).

Think Critically

1. Do you agree that a bad first kiss can be a potentially new relationship "deal-breaker"? Has this happened to you?
2. How important is kissing to you in a relationship?
3. What is a good kiss? Should a kiss lead to sexual intercourse?
4. What were your experiences with your first kiss?

memories, such as a person's body scent or a perfume or fragrance. In some languages—among the Borneans, for example—the word *kiss* literally translates as "smell." In fact, among the Eskimos and the Maoris of New Zealand, there is no mouth kissing, only the touching of noses to facilitate smelling.

Although kissing may appear innocent, it is in many ways the height of intimacy. The adolescent's first kiss is often regarded as a milestone, a rite of passage, the beginning of adult sexuality. It is an important developmental step, marking the beginning of a young person's sexuality. (To find out the meanings of kissing, including their first kiss, among a sample of college students, see Think About It, "The First Kiss: A Deal-Breaker?")

Ordinary kissing is considered safer sex. French kissing is probably safe, unless the kiss is hard and draws blood or either partner has open sores or cuts in or around the mouth.

Given the above descriptions of the erotic nature of kissing, one might think that the romantic-sexual kiss is universal throughout the world. The romantic-sexual kiss is defined as lip-to-lip contact, which may or may not be prolonged. Research, however, has shown that not to be true: Romantic kissing is not the norm in half of the world cultures and some consider it uncomfortable or even repulsive (Haseltine, 2017). An assessment of 168 cultures found that the romantic-sexual kiss occurred in only 77 cultures (46%). Romantic kissing was found to be the most common in the Middle East where all 10 of the cultures engaged in it. Next was Asia (73%), followed by Europe (70%), and North America (55%). There was no evidence of romantic-sexual kissing in Central America. The study also revealed that the more socially complex and stratified a society is, the higher the frequency of romantic-sexual kissing (Jankowiak et al., 2015).

Oral-Genital Sex

In recent years, oral sex has become a part of many people's sexual scripts. The two types of **oral-genital sex** are cunnilingus and fellatio, which may be performed singly or simultaneously. Recall that cunnilingus is the erotic stimulation of a woman's vulva and/or clitoris by her partner's mouth and tongue. Recall, too, that fellatio is the oral stimulation of a man's penis by his partner's sucking and licking. When two people orally stimulate each other simultaneously, their activity is sometimes called "sixty-nine" (see Figure 12). The term comes from the configuration "69," which visually suggests the activity.

For high school and college students of every sexual orientation, oral sex is an increasingly important aspect of their sexual lives. The percentages of American men and women who received oral sex in the past year and gave oral sex, by the 10 SEAS age groups, are shown in Table 6.

"As for the topsy turvy tangle known as soixante-neuf, personally I have always felt it to be madly confusing, like trying to pat your head and rub your stomach at the same time."

—Helen Lawrenson (1904–1982)

● **FIGURE 12**

Simultaneous mouth-genital stimulation in the sixty-nine position.

Source: Hyde, J. & DeLamater, J. (2020).

Although oral sex has become the norm among young persons, little is known about the level of pleasure both men and women experience in giving and receiving oral sex and the extent to which relationship context is related to levels of pleasure. Sex researcher Jessica Wood and colleagues surveyed online 899 heterosexual students at a Canadian university to investigate those gaps in research (Wood et al., 2016). Here is what they found:

- More than two thirds of participants reported that their last sexual encounter included giving and/or receiving oral sex.

- More women (59%) than men (52%) reported giving oral sex to their partner.

- More men (63%) than women (44%) reported receiving oral sex.

- Most men (73%) and women (69%) reported that receiving oral sex was at least "somewhat pleasurable." Men were significantly more likely than women to indicate that giving oral sex was very pleasurable (52% vs. 28%).

- Regardless of gender, higher pleasure ratings were reported when giving and receiving oral sex with more committed partners compared to more casual ones.

• **FIGURE 13**
Cunnilingus.

Is oral sex considered more intimate than intercourse? A study at another Canadian university involving 50 female and 35 male undergraduates (95% heterosexual, aged 17–24) found that 91% perceived intercourse as more intimate than oral sex (Vannier & Byers, 2013).

Cunnilingus   In **cunnilingus**, a woman's genitals are stimulated by her partner's tongue and mouth, which gently and rhythmically caress and lick her clitoris and the surrounding area (see Figure 13). During arousal, the mouth and lips can nibble, lick, and kiss the inner thighs, stomach, and mons pubis and then move to the sensitive labia minora clitoral area. Orgasm may be brought on by rhythmically stimulating the clitoris. During cunnilingus, some women also enjoy insertion of a finger into the vagina or anus for extra stimulation. Many women find cunnilingus to be the easiest way to experience orgasm because it provides such intense stimulation.

Some women, however, have concerns regarding cunnilingus. The most common worries revolve around whether the other person is enjoying it and, especially, whether the vulva has an unpleasant odor. Concerns about vaginal odors may be eased by washing. Undeodorized white soap will wash away unpleasant smells without disturbing the vagina's natural, erotic scent. If an unpleasant odor arises from the genitals, it may be because the woman has a vaginal infection.

A woman may also worry that her partner is not enjoying the experience because he or she is giving pleasure rather than receiving it. What she may not recognize is that such sexual excitement is often mutual. Because our mouths and tongues are erotically sensitive, the giver finds erotic excitement in arousing his or her partner.

An interview study of 43 college women explored women's attitudes toward and experiences with cunnilingus (Backstrom et al., 2012). The authors note that contemporary sexual scripts of college students assume cunnilingus will occur in relationships but not as often in hookups, where this behavior is more frequently contested. The interviews found that tension occurred when the desire for cunnilingus contradicted the relationship's sexual script.

Fellatio   In **fellatio**, a man's penis is taken into his partner's mouth. The partner licks the glans penis and gently stimulates the shaft (see Figure 14). Also, the scrotum may be gently licked. If the

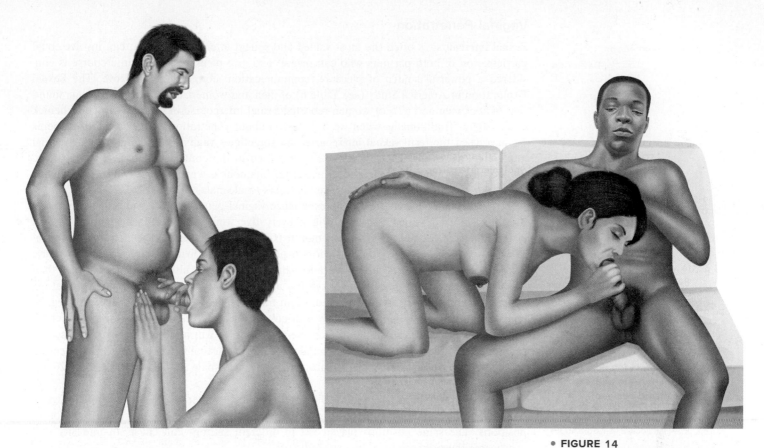

• FIGURE 14

Fellatio involves stimulation of the penis and surrounding genital area with the mouth, lips, and tongue.

penis is not erect, it usually will become erect within a short time. The partner sucks more vigorously as excitement increases, down toward the base of the penis and then back up, in a rhythmical motion, being careful not to bite hard or scrape the penis with the teeth. While the man is being stimulated by mouth, his partner can also stroke the shaft of the penis by hand. Gently playing with the testicles is also arousing as long as they are not held too tightly. As in cunnilingus, the couple should experiment to discover what is most stimulating and exciting. The man should be careful not to thrust his penis too deeply into his partner's throat, for that may cause a gag reflex. He should let his partner control how deeply the penis goes into the mouth. The partner can do this by grasping the penis below his or her lips so that the depth of insertion can be controlled. Furthermore, gagging is less likely when the one performing fellatio is on top. The gag reflex can also be reconditioned by slowly inserting the penis into the mouth at increasing depth over time. Most men find fellatio to be highly arousing.

For men who have sex with men, fellatio is an important component of their sexuality. As with sexual intercourse for heterosexual men, however, fellatio is only one activity in their sexual repertoire. Generally, the more often gay couples engage in giving and receiving oral sex, the more satisfied they are. Because oral sex often involves power symbolism, reciprocity is important. If one partner always performs oral sex, he may feel he is subordinate to the other. The most satisfied gay couples alternate between giving and receiving oral sex.

A common concern about fellatio centers around ejaculation. Should a man ejaculate into his partner's mouth? Some people find semen to be slightly bitter, but others like it. Some find it exciting to suck even harder on the penis during or following ejaculation; others do not like the idea of semen in the mouth. For many, a key issue is whether to swallow the semen. Some swallow it; others spit it out. It is simply a matter of personal preference, and the man who is receiving fellatio should accept his partner's feelings about it and avoid equating a dislike for swallowing semen with a personal rejection.

Some men try to provide oral stimulation to their own penis, a practice called **autofellatio**. Kinsey and his colleagues (1948) found that many males try this behavior, but less than 1% of their sample were actually able to achieve it.

Vaginal Penetration

Sexual intercourse is often the most valued and sought after behavior that can involve equal participation of both partners who can receive and give pleasure. Sexual intercourse is considered a powerful source of pleasure, communication, connection, and love. The Sexual Exploration in America Study (see Table 6) of men and women, ages 18 to 70+ years, found that 66% of men and 62% of women reported sexual intercourse in the past year (Herbenick et al., 2017). Traditionally, when we have talked about penetration of the vagina by a penis we have used the term **sexual intercourse** and sometimes vaginal intercourse, penile-vaginal intercourse, or **coitus**. These terms are largely used in the context of female-male partners. Sometimes penile-anal sex is labeled as sexual intercourse whether or not the participants are mixed-sex (female-male) or same-sex partners (male-male).

Female-female partners frequently experience vaginal penetration. A study of lesbian and bisexual women revealed that four out of every five women reported engaging in vaginal penetration at least once in the past month (Cohen and Bowers, 2014). Through years of research on the various sexual behaviors experienced by individuals and couples we have learned—no matter their sexual orientation—that many people also use methods other than the penis to erotically penetrate the vagina and anus. Sex toys such as dildos, vibrators, strapped on artificial penis can be used. From this perspective, we will be discussing vaginal penetration in this section, followed by a discussion of anal penetration in the next section. Also, in our discussion of sexual intercourse positions, we will often use the terms "insertive partner" and "receptive partner" to remind us that many sexual behaviors that bring pleasure can be performed by female-male, female-female, and male-male couples (Rathus et al., 2020).

The Positions   The playfulness of the couple, their movement from one bodily configuration to another, and their ingenuity can provide an infinite variety of sexual intercourse positions. The same positions played out in different settings can cause an intensity that transforms the ordinary into the extraordinary.

The most common position is face-to-face with the insertive partner on top and the receptive partner on bottom (see Figure 15). Many people prefer this position, for several reasons. First, for mixed-sex partners, it is the traditional, correct, or "official" position in our culture, which many people find reassuring and validating in terms of their sexuality. This position is commonly known as the missionary position because it was the position missionaries traditionally encouraged people to use. Second, it can allow the insertive partner maximum activity, movement, and control. Third, it allows a woman freedom to stimulate her clitoris to assist in her orgasm. The primary disadvantages are that it makes it difficult for the insertive partner to caress the receptive partner or to stimulate the receptive partner's genitals (e.g., clitorial stimulation) while supporting himself with his hands and for the receptive partner to control the angle, rate, and depth of penetration. Furthermore, some men have difficulty controlling ejaculation in this position, because the

• **FIGURE 15**

Face-to-Face, Insertive Partner on Top, Receptive Partner with Physical Disability.

• FIGURE 16
Face-to-Face, Receptive Partner Sitting Astride.

"When I said I had sex for seven hours, that included dinner and a movie."
—Phil Collins (1951–)

• FIGURE 17
Face-to-Face, Receptive Partner Squatting.

[Credit placeholder]

penis is highly stimulated. A dildo or vibrator, for example, may also be inserted by either the receptive or insertive partner.

Another common position is face-to-face with the receptive partner on top. The receptive partner either lies on top of the partner, sits astride (see Figure 16), or squats (see Figure 17). This position allows the receptive partner maximum activity, movement, and control. The depth to which the penis penetrates can be controlled. Additionally, when the woman sits astride her partner, either of them can caress or stimulate her labia and clitoris, thus facilitating orgasm in the woman. As with the face-to-face position, kissing is easy. Further, the receptive partner can stimulate the insertive partners breasts, chest, or scrotum. This position tends to be less stimulating for the man, thus making it easier for him to control ejaculation.

Intercourse can also be performed with the insertive partner positioned behind the receptive partner. There are several variations on the rear-entry position. The receptive partner may kneel and receive the penis or a sex toy from behind. The couple may lie on their sides, with the receptive partner's back to her partner (see Figure 18). This position offers variety and may be particularly suitable during pregnancy because it minimizes

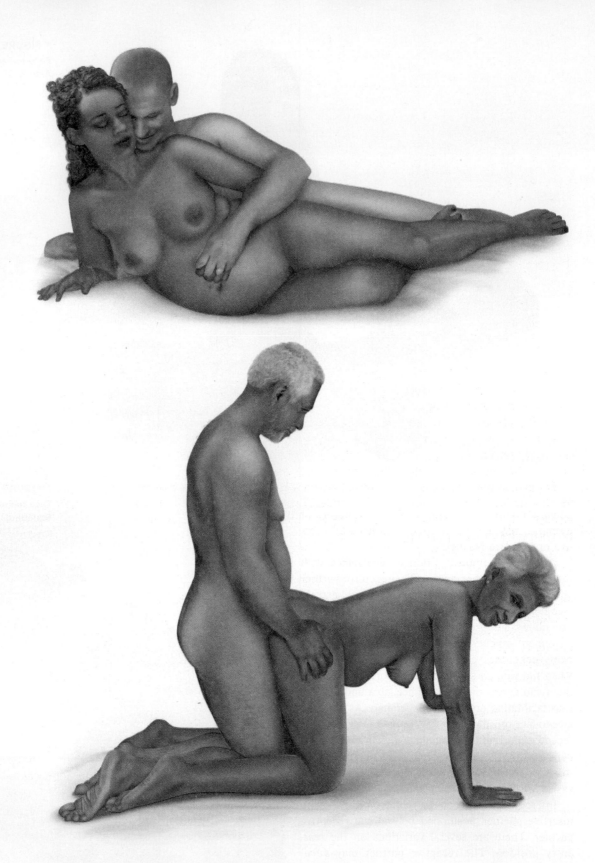

• FIGURE 18

Back Side-to-Side Entry and Rear-Entry Positions.

• FIGURE 19

Face-to-Face on Side.

pressure on the woman's abdomen. This position facilitates clitoral stimulation. Generally, it is also possible for the man to stimulate her during intercourse.

In the face-to-face side position, both partners lie on their sides, facing each other (see Figure 19). Each partner has greater freedom to caress and stimulate the other. As with the rear-entry position, a major drawback is that keeping the penis in the vagina may be difficult.

For people who use a wheelchair, sexual intimacy is important, although it may be challenging. Persons, no matter the gender, can have wheelchair sex. Being creative helps. A wheelchair can serve as a stable platform for varied sexual positions (see Figure 20). Sometimes men who use a wheelchair cannot get an erection, but they can ejaculate. Also, if a person in the wheelchair has trouble moving while having sex, their partner can help out.

Tantric sex is a type of sexual intimacy based on eastern religious beliefs beginning in India around 5000 BCE. The tantric sex technique involves the couple sharing their "energies" by initially thrusting minimally, generating energy via subtle, inner sexual movements. They visualize the energy of the genitals moving upward in their bodies (see Figure 21). The couple may harmonize their breathing and achieve intimacy (often looking into each other's eyes), ecstasy, and abandon. Many books have been written on tantric sex, and numerous websites are devoted to it.

• FIGURE 20

Persons with physical disabilities can still experience sexual intimacy.

Anal Penetration

Anal penetration and eroticism refers to sexual activities involving the anus, whose delicate membranes, as well as taboo nature, make it erotically arousing for many people. Besides the insertion of the penis into the rectum, anal penetration can involve sex toys such as dildos, vibrators, and strapped on artificial penises. During anal sex, the partners may face each other and one partner may be behind and above or below (see Figures 18 and 22). Many mixed-sex couples engage in anal penetration along with fellatio or vaginal penetration among mixed-sex partners. Anal eroticism can also include **analingus**, the licking of the anal region colloquially known as "rimming" or "tossing salad." Anal-manual contact consists of stimulating the anal region with the fingers; sometimes an entire fist may be inserted (known as "fisting"). Some people enjoy a finger in their own rectum (latex glove is suggested) during increased sexual arousal and orgasm as the rectal sphincter muscles contract during orgasm. Though little is known about the prevalence of this activity, many report it to be highly arousing because of the sensitivity of the skin around the anus.

Keeping the anal area clean is extremely important because the intestinal tract, which extends to the anus, carries a variety of organisms. Besides washing the anal region, partners should use a condom over the penis to prevent transmission of sexually transmitted infections (STIs). Further, as the rectum does not lubricate, the application of adequate water-based lubrication is important to minimize any tears of the rectum that would increase odds of acquiring an STI.

Anal penetration and eroticism is practiced by all sexual orientations, genders, and couple arrangements. The Sexual Exploration in America Study of 18-70+ ages found that 15% of the men had been the insertive sex anal partner during the past year and 5% of men and 12% of women had been the anal sex receptive partner. Anal penetration sex was more common in the 25-50 age range. For example, for the 25-29 age group, 21% of the men had been the insertive sex partner and 7% of men and 26% of the women had been the recipient partner (Herbenick et al., 2017). While penetrative anal sex is prevalent among gay men, not all gay couples practice anal sex. For example, a study of men visiting gay venues in Vancouver, British Columbia found that 30% reported not practicing anal sex in the prior 6 months (Trussler et al., 2010). A study of lesbian and bisexual women revealed that about 3 out of every 10 had practiced anal stimulation or penetration in the past month (Cohen & Byers, 2014).

Not all persons are comfortable with anal sex as may consider it as unnatural or disgusting and risky behavior that could lead to acquisition and transmission of an STI. Further, some may find it painful (Reynolds et al., 2015). However, other persons enjoy anal penetration and eroticism as one part of a broad range of sexual behaviors that at times they share with their partner.

• FIGURE 21

Tantric Sex.

Cleaning up After Sex

Even though many people do not think about cleaning up after sex, there are some things that one should do to protect themselves, and their partners, from urinary tract infections and STIs. One does not need to get out of bed immediately and shower, but here are some suggestions on what to do. Women should wash around their genitals (but not inside the vagina) with plain warm water or mild soap. Most doctors recommend that women do not douche, because douching upsets the natural balance of bacteria that protect the vagina. A mild vaginal smell is normal and may not indicate a medical problem. Men should pull the foreskin back and wash underneath, particularly if they are not circumcised. Because bacteria can enter into the urethra during sex which increases the chance of getting an infection, partners should urinate after sex. This helps flush out the pathogens. Stay hydrated after sex by drinking a glass of water which will also can lead to urination that can flush out bacteria out of the body. Washing one's hands is a good way to get rid of bacteria that might be picked from touching your or your partner's genitals. Also, sex toys should be washed after sex and not be shared between partners unless a condom is used on the toy ("Things You Should (and Shouldn't) Do After Sex", 2017). After this, it's "cuddle time," knowing that you and your partner just made each other safer.

Health Benefits of Sexual Activity

Throughout this chapter and others in this textbook, we have emphasized ways to enhance sexual pleasure. And, certainly, experiencing sexual pleasure is a powerful motive itself to participate in sexual activity. When sex is fun, it brings a unique joy and satisfaction. But beyond the pleasure reward of sexual expression, does sex have health benefits? Physician Eric Braverman, author of the book *Younger (Sexier) You* (2011), states that "sex is like an electric charge, and an orgasm is like rebooting your entire computer, powering up your health in multiple ways." Braverman contends that being sexually active can help keep one

• **FIGURE** 22
Anal Intercourse.

younger by decreasing stress, enhancing intimacy in relationships, and keeping hormone levels up, including testosterone, estrogen, and oxytocin, the "love hormone."

Persons who frequently engage in sexual activity are reported to experience numerous benefits, such as a longer life, a healthier heart, a better defense against illnesses, enhanced sleeping, pain relief, lower blood pressure, a healthier body weight, a lower risk of prostate cancer, better cognitive skills, better hormone levels, a lower risk of breast cancer, and more satisfying relationships (Braverman, 2011; Brody, 2010; Cohen, 2010; Jannini et al., 2009; Whipple et al., 2007). But does good sex enhance health or does good health make sex more frequent and pleasurable? Sex researcher Beverly Whipple states that "it is not entirely clear whether sex makes people healthier, or whether healthy people tend to have more sex" (Whipple et al., 2007). Nearly all of the studies on the health benefits of sex are correlational; that is, they show a relationship but not cause and effect (Jannini et al., 2009). Nevertheless, what we can say with some certainly is that good sex and good health reinforce each other (Braverman, 2011).

Final Thoughts

As we have seen, sexual behaviors cannot be separated from attraction and desire. Our autoerotic activities are as important to our sexuality as are our interpersonal ones. Although the sexual behaviors we have examined in this chapter are the most common ones in our society, many people engage in other, less typical activities. We discuss these atypical behaviors subsequently.

Tom Merton/Getty Images

Summary

Human Sexual Response

- *Masters and Johnson's four-phase model of sexual response* includes four stages: excitement, plateau, *orgasm,* and resolution. *Kaplan's tri-phasic model of sexual response* has three phases: desire, excitement, and orgasm. *Loulan' sexual response model* includes biological and affective components in a six-stage cycle. The *dual control model* helps explain the interaction between sexual excitation and sexual inhibition.

- The physical manifestations of sexual arousal involve an interaction of thoughts and feelings, sensory organs, neural responses, and hormonal reactions occurring in many parts of the body. For both females and males, physiological changes during sexual excitement depend on two processes: *vasocongestion,* the concentration of blood in body tissues, and myotonia muscle tension with approaching orgasm.

- For women, one early sign of sexual excitement is the moistening, or vaginal transudation or *sweating,* of the vaginal walls. The upper two thirds of the vagina expands in a process called *tenting;* the labia may enlarge or flatten and separate; the clitoris swells. Breathing and heart rate increase. The nipples become erect, and the breasts may enlarge somewhat. The uterus elevates. As excitement increases, the clitoris retracts beneath the clitoral hood. The vaginal opening decreases by about one third, and its outer third becomes more congested, forming the *orgasmic platform.*

- Continued stimulation brings *orgasm* in both men and women, a peak sensation of intense pleasure that creates an altered state of consciousness and is accompanied by contractions, myotonia, and a state of well-being and contentment. Women are often able to experience orgasm following a previous one if they continue to receive sexual stimulation.

- Male sexual response, like that of females, involves the process of vasocongestion and myotonia. *Erection* of the penis occurs when sexual or tactile stimuli cause its chambers to become engorged with blood. Continuing stimulation leads to ejaculation, which occurs in two stages. In the first stage, *emission,* semen mixes with sperm in the urethral bulb. In the second stage, *expulsion,* semen is forcibly expelled from the penis. Ejaculation and orgasm, a series of contractions of the pelvis muscles occurring at the height of sexual arousal, typically happens simultaneously. However, they can occur separately. Following ejaculation is a *refractory period,* during which ejaculation is not possible.

Sexual Attractiveness

- The characteristics that constitute sexual attractiveness vary across cultures. Youthfulness and good health appear to be the only universals. Body symmetry and smell are important to sexual attraction. A study on the importance of attractiveness and status found that heterosexual men valued attractiveness the most, followed by homosexual men, heterosexual women, and homosexual women.

- Sexual desire is affected by *erotophilia,* a positive emotional response to sex, and by *erotophobia,* a negative response to sex.

Sexual Scripts

- *Sexual scripts* organize our sexual expression. The cultural script provides the general forms sexual behaviors are expected to take in a particular society. The intrapersonal script interprets our physiological responses as sexual or not. The interpersonal script is the shared conventions and signals that make sexual activities between two people possible.

Autoeroticism

- *Autoeroticism* refers to sexual activities that involve only oneself. These activities include sexual fantasies, erotic dreams and *nocturnal orgasm,* and *masturbation,* or stimulation of the genitals for pleasure. Persons practicing various types of autoerotic activity are also more likely to report enacting more elaborate interpersonal sexual scripts.

- Sexual fantasies and dreams are probably the most universal of all sexual behaviors; they are normal aspects of our sexuality. Erotic fantasies take our generalized sexual drives and help define and direct them, they allow us to plan or anticipate erotic situations, they provide pleasurable escape from routine, they introduce novelty, and they offer clues to our unconscious.

- Most men and women masturbate. Masturbation may begin as early as infancy and continue throughout old age and can be practiced alone or in a partnered relationship.

Sexual Behavior With Others

- Each couple develops their own sexual style, although it may take several months for that to occur. Four common couple styles are complementary, traditional, soulmate, and emotionally expressive.

- The erotic potential of touching has been undervalued, especially among males, because our culture tends to be orgasm-oriented.

- Erotic kissing is usually our earliest interpersonal sexual experience and is regarded as a rite of passage into adult sexuality. Higher frequency of kissing is related to greater relationship quality.

- *Oral-genital sex* is becoming increasingly accepted, especially among young adults. *Cunnilingus* is the stimulation of the vulva with the tongue and mouth. *Fellatio* is the stimulation of the penis with the mouth.

- *Sexual intercourse,* which refers to sexual activities involving either the vagina and anus, can be an intimate and rewarding interaction between two people.
- Good health and good sex are highly associated with each other. By cleaning up after sex, individuals can protect themselves and their partners from urinary tract infections and STIs.

Questions for Discussion

- What is your sexual script relative to initiating sexual behavior with another person? Do you always want to take the lead, or are you comfortable with the other person doing that or sharing in initiating the sexual behavior?

- How often do you fantasize about sex? Are you comfortable about your fantasies? Have you ever shared them with anyone?

- What can be done to help persons become more accepting of pleasure-oriented touching that does not include intercourse?

Sex and the Internet

WebMD Sexual Health Center

A comprehensive website, the WebMD Sexual Health Center offers the latest information on several topics such as the health benefits of sex, how to clean up after sex, relationships, digital aspects of sex, what happens when one stops having sex, safer sex, and sex-drive killers. Specific sections of the Sexual Health Center include Latest News & Features, Latest Videos, WebMD Blogs, Related WebMD Comments (message boards), Top Search Terms for Sexual Health, and Tools and Resources.

Visit this website (www.webmd.com/sex/default.htm) and find out the following:

- What are the stories included in the Latest News & Features section?

- What are some of the topics of the videos?

- What blogs and message boards interest you the most?

- What terms for sexual health were most valuable to you?

Suggested Websites

American Sexual Health Association

www.ashasexualhealth.org/

Provides information on several aspects of sexual health related to sexual expression, such as sexual pleasure, talking about sex, sex and relationships, and men's and women's health.

JackinWorld

www.jackinworld.com

Provides articles, forums, questions and answers, and surveys related to masturbation.

Online Tantra.com

www.online-tantra.com/tantric-relationships

Describes the varied aspects of a tantric relationship such as tantric relationship and tantric sex, what is tantric love, and 10 tantric practices.

Suggested Reading

Cook, M., & McHenry, R. (2013). *Sexual attraction.* Pergamon Press. This monograph includes eight chapters that explore sexual attraction and why individuals are attracted to some people and not others.

Corwin, G. (2010). *Sexual intimacy for women: A guide for same-sex couples.* Seal. Written by a clinical psychologist, this book includes exercises and client-based anecdotes to help women in same-sex relationships increase intimacy.

Giles, J. (2008). *The nature of sexual desire.* University Press of America. Sexual desire is explored from a psychological, philosophical, and anthropological perspective and in relation to sexual interaction, erotic pleasure, the experience of gender, and romantic love.

Groy, P. B., & Garcia, J. R. (2013). *Evolution and human sexual behavior.* Harvard University Press. Provides an interdisciplinary synthesis of the latest discoveries in evolutionary theory, genetics, neuroscience, comparative primate research, and cross-cultural sexuality studies.

Joannides, P. (2017). *Guide to getting it on* (9th ed.). Goofy Foot Press. A very popular and thorough sex manual that has been translated into over 10 languages; has superb anatomical and sexual behavior drawings.

Kirshenbaum, S. (2011). *The science of kissing: What our lips are telling us.* Grand Central. A noted science journalist presents a wonderful, witty, and fascinating exploration of how and why we kiss.

Kleinplatz, P. J., & Menard, A. D. (2020). *Magnificent sex: Lessons from extraordinary lovers.* Routledge. This book discusses findings from in-depth study of actual couples who are say they have magnificent sex after years of marriage. The couples disclose the personal and relationship qualities and attitudes that make sex magnificent.

McCarthy, B. W., & McCarthy, E. (2009). *Discovering your couple sexual style.* Routledge. The goal of this book is to assist persons to discover and enjoy their couple sexual style.

Murray, S. H. (2019). *Not always in the mood: The new science of men, sex, and relationships.* Rowman & Littlefield Publishers. This book debunks long-held myths and stereotypes about male sexuality as always high, ready, and desiring sex with sole focus on the physical but emotional aspects of sex. A valuable book that can enlighten couples and enhance their sex.

Northrup, C., Schwartz, P., & Witte, J. (2012). *The normal bar: The surprising secrets of happy couples and what they reveal about creating a new normal in your relationship.* Harmony. This book answers what constitutes "normal" behavior among happy couples. Based on data from nearly 100,000 respondents, the book offers readers an array of perspective tools that will help them establish a "new normal."

10

Variations in Sexual Behavior

Mark Wragg/Getty Images

CHAPTER OUTLINE

Sexual Variations and Paraphilic Behavior

Types of Paraphilias

Origins and Treatment of Paraphilias

S EXUALITY CAN BE EXPRESSED in a variety of ways, some more common than others. Many of the less common behaviors have been negatively labeled by the public, often implying that the behavior is unnatural, pathological, or "perverted." In this chapter, we examine variations in sexual behavior that are not within the range of sexual expression in which most people typically engage, including fetishism, exhibitionism, sexual masochism, and sexual sadism. We then turn to issues such as college students and voyeurism, sexual addiction, and BDSM (bondage, discipline, sadism, and masochism), to name a few. We discuss these and other topics through a variety of perspectives with the intent of distinguishing between the clinical, judgmental, or causal connotations of terms.

> *"There is hardly anyone whose sexual life, if it were broadcast, would not fill the world at large with surprise and horror."*
>
> **—Somerset Maugham (1874–1965)**

● Sexual Variations and Paraphilic Behavior

The range of human sexual behavior is almost infinite. Yet most of our activities and fantasies, such as intercourse, oral-genital sex, and masturbation, cluster within the general range of our predominant cultural and social sexual norms. Those behaviors and fantasies that do not fall within this general range are considered variations. In this chapter and throughout the textbook, we use the term **sexual variations** to refer to those behaviors that are not *statistically* typical of American sexual behaviors or that occur in addition to the "mainstream" expression of sexuality.

What Are Sexual Variations?

Sexual variation is the most common term used, although terms like **atypical sexual behavior** or *kinky sex* are used. It is important to note, however, that atypical does not necessarily mean abnormal; it simply means that the majority of people do not engage in that behavior or that it occurs outside of the culturally sanctioned sexual behaviors. Even though today's society is less judgmental about sex, resulting in people who engage in sexual variations feeling less shame and guilt, some sexual variations are considered to be so extreme by the American Psychiatric Association (APA) that they are classified as mental disorders. Classifying out-of-the-ordinary sexual behavior as deviant is not new. Psychiatry has long classified some sexual behaviors as mental disorders (De Block & Adriaens, 2013), and there continues to be debate among psychiatry and scientific communities about which sexual behaviors are and are not pathological (Belluck & Carey, 2013; Bradford & Ahmed, 2014; Drescher, 2014; Voosen, 2013).

> *"It is very disturbing indeed when you can't think of any new perversions that you would like to practice."*
>
> **—James Dickey (1923–1997)**

What Is Paraphilia?

The *Diagnostic and Statistical Manual of Mental Disorders, Fifth Edition (DSM-5)*, published by the American Psychiatric Association (APA, 2013), defines **paraphilia** as "any intense and

think
about it

Classifying Variant Sexual Behaviors as Paraphilia: The Changing Views of Psychology

Over the past 150 years, American and European psychologists and psychiatrists have conceptualized and categorized what they consider to be sexual deviance. Numerous sexual preferences, desires, and behaviors were pathologized and depathologized during that time, revealing psychiatry's constant and continuing challenge to distinguish out-of-the-ordinary sexual behavior from immoral, unethical, or illegal sexual behavior. This struggle is revealed in the works of nineteenth- and early-twentieth-century psychiatrists and sexologists, as well as in more recent psychiatric textbooks and diagnostic manuals such as the *Diagnostic and Statistical Manual of Mental Disorders, Fifth Edition* (*DSM-5*) published by the American Psychiatric Association (De Block & Adriaens, 2013).

Certain sexual behaviors were labeled mental disorders in earlier *DSM* editions but deleted in later editions (Byne, 2014; De Block & Adriaens, 2013; Drescher, 2014). A prime example of this involves the *DSM*'s views on homosexuality. It was included in the *DSM* from the first edition until 1973, when it was removed as a mental disorder. A major change reflected in *DSM-5* is that the distinction between paraphilias and paraphilic disorders represents a greater acceptance of some unconventional sexual behaviors. For example, sexual masochism, sexual sadism, and fetishes are considered mental disorders only if they result in emotional distress and involve nonconsensual behaviors (Boskey, 2013).

Even though there has been increasing acceptance of certain sexual variant behaviors by the American Medical Association, the controversy over which behaviors represent mental disorders continues. Philosophy professors Andreas De Block and Pieter R. Adriaens (2013) state:

> The fact that the problem of distinguishing between sexual deviance and mental disorder keeps on haunting the literature has little to do with the scientific status of sexology, psychology, or psychiatry but rather with the hard-to-crack philosophical problem with defining (mental) disease and (mental) health (p. 294).

Think Critically

1. Do you believe that the *DSM*'s classification of certain variant sexual behaviors as paraphilic disorders is "an attempt to pathologize sexual behaviors not approved by society" or a necessary way to address sexual behaviors that indeed represent mental illness and need medical or psychological/psychiatric treatment?

2. Where would you draw the line between out-of-the-ordinary sexual variation and sexual variation that is a mental disorder?

---

persistent sexual interest other than sexual interest in genital stimulation or preparatory fondling with phenotypically normal, physically mature consenting human partners." The paraphilia is thus an out-of-the-ordinary sexual behavior that does not necessarily need psychiatric treatment. The *DSM-5* maintains the basic types of paraphilias from the prior edition but alters how they are diagnosed. *DSM-5* distinguishes between paraphilias, which are considered to be relatively harmless, and paraphilic disorders, which are considered harmful sexual behaviors. A **paraphilic disorder** is defined as "a paraphilia that is currently causing distress or impairment to the individual or a paraphilia whose satisfaction has entailed personal harm, or risk of harm, to others." Furthermore, in order to be considered paraphilic, the disorder needs to be recurrent, that is, occurring over a period of at least 6 months. The *DSM-5* notes that when an individual with a particular paraphilic impulse does not declare personal distress, has no impairment in functioning, and has no history of acting on the paraphilic urge, the person would be considered to have **paraphilic interest** (e.g., fetishism sexual interest) but not a paraphilic disorder. For further discussion of the change of the views toward sexual variation and paraphilias, see Think About It, "Classifying Variant Sexual Behaviors as Paraphilia: The Changing Views of Psychology."

The distinction between a sexual interest, variation, or behavior that might be classified as a paraphilia as opposed to a paraphilic disorder is sometimes vague and often more a difference of degree than kind. For example, many men find that certain objects, such as

TABLE 1 ● Paraphilias	
Most Common Paraphilias	**Sexual Arousal Activity**
Exhibitionism	Exposing one's genitals to an unsuspecting person
Fetishism	Using an inanimate object or focus on nongenital body parts
Frotteurism	Touching or rubbing sexually against a nonconsenting person in public places
Pedophilia	Having a sexual focus on a prepubescent child or children
Sexual masochism	Being humiliated, beaten, bound, or otherwise made to suffer
Sexual sadism	Inflicting psychological or physical suffering upon another person
Transvestism	Cross-dressing in clothing of the other sex
Voyeurism	Observing an unsuspecting person who is naked, disrobing, or having sex
Less Common Paraphilias	**Sexual Arousal Activity**
Coprophilia	Being sexually aroused from use of feces
Klismaphilia	Being sexually aroused from having enemas
Necrophilia	Having sexual activity with dead bodies
Telephone scatologia	Making sexual and obscene phone calls
Urophilia	Being sexually aroused from sight or thought of urine
Zoophilia	Having sexual activity with nonhuman animals (bestiality)

black lingerie, intensify their sexual arousal; for other men, these objects are necessary for sexual arousal. In the first case, nothing is particularly unusual or harmful. But if the fetishistic fantasies, urges, or behaviors cause significant distress, last at least 6 months, and are recurrent, the behavior would be considered a fetishistic disorder in the *DMS-5* (APA, 2013).

Table 1 lists eight of the most common, as well as six less common, paraphilias. To minimize the negative message of labeling and to recognize individuals' many components, we believe it is more appropriate to use the term "person with paraphilia" than "paraphiliac." This is the term we will use in this textbook.

One important aspect of paraphilias is whether they involve coercion. **Noncoercive paraphilias** are regarded as relatively benign or harmless because they are victimless; that is, they involve only oneself or another consenting adult. Few noncoercive paraphilias are brought to public attention because of their private, victimless nature. Typically, domination and submission, fetishism, and transvestism are considered noncoercive paraphilias. Victimizing or **coercive paraphilias** represent nonconsensual sexual activity, such as voyeurism, exhibitionism, sexual masochism, sexual sadism, zoophilia, telephone scatologia, frotteurism, necrophilia, and pedophilia. These behaviors are a source of concern for society because of the harm they cause others.

It is also important to recognize that seemingly scientific or clinical terms may not be scientific at all. Instead, they may be pseudoscientific terms hiding moral judgments, as in the case of *nymphomania* and *satyriasis*. **Nymphomania** is a pejorative term referring to "abnormal or excessive" sexual desire in a woman and is usually applied to sexually active single women. But what is "abnormal" or "excessive" is often defined moralistically rather than scientifically. Nymphomania is not recognized as a clinical condition by the APA (2013), as the term is based on prejudice, double standards, and male chauvinism (Kaplan & Krueger, 2010). Although the term *nymphomania* dates back to the seventeenth century, it was popularized in the nineteenth century by Richard von Krafft-Ebing and others. Physicians and psychiatrists used the term to pathologize women's sexual behavior if it deviated from nineteenth-century moral standards.

"Of all the sexual aberrations, the most peculiar is chastity."

—Remy de Gourmont (1858–1915)

"Sexual Addiction": Repressive Morality in a New Guise?

Are you a sex addict? As you read descriptions of sexual addiction, you may begin to think that you are. But don't believe everything you read. Consider the following: "The moment comes for every addict," writes psychologist Patrick Carnes (1983, 1991), who developed and marketed the idea of sexual addiction, "when the consequences are so great or the pain so bad that the addict admits life is out of control because of his or her sexual behavior." Money is spent on sexually explicit videos, affairs threaten a marriage, masturbation replaces jogging, and fantasies interrupt studying. Sex, sex, sex is on the addict's mind. And he or she has no choice but to engage in these activities. Even though the term sex addiction is not new, it has recently become more familiar to the public. The media has used it frequently to describe the misbehavior of celebrities such as Hollywood mogul Harvey Weinstein, actors Kevin Spacey, Michael Douglas, and Jada Pinkett Smith, and golfer Tiger Woods (Simon, 2018).

According to Carnes, sex addicts cannot make a commitment; instead, they move from one hookup to another. Their addiction is rooted in deep-seated feelings of worthlessness, despair, anxiety, and loneliness. These feelings are temporarily allayed by the "high" obtained from sexual arousal and orgasm. According to Carnes, sexual addiction is viewed in the same light as alcoholism and drug addiction; it is an activity over which the addict has no control. And, as for alcoholism, a 12-step treatment program for sex addiction has been established by the National Council on Sexual Addiction/Compulsivity.

Are you wondering, "Am I a sex addict?" Don't worry; you're probably not. The reason you might think you're suffering from sexual addiction is that its definition taps into many of the underlying anxieties and uncertainties we feel about sexuality in our culture. The problem lies not in you but in the concept of sexual addiction.

One problematic issue with the term *sex addiction* is that it does not fit the definition of addiction that alludes to physical and psychological dependence. Many behaviors associated with sex addiction are considered within the realm of sexual variation, although some may be extreme (Coleman, 1986; Levine & Troiden, 1988). A study of brain responses to visual images, including sexual ones, suggests that self-professed addicts may simply have a high sexual drive (Preidt, 2013; Steele et al., 2013).

Attempts to describe certain sexual behaviors by labeling them as sexual addictions continue to be problematic for the professional sexuality community. Different terms have been used in attempts to describe certain behavioral patterns. For example, Eli Coleman (1991, 1996; cited in Tepper & Owens, 2007), director of the Program in Human Sexuality at the University of Minnesota Medical School, favors *sexual compulsivity* over *sexual addiction* and goes further by distinguishing between compulsive and problematic sexual behavior:

> There has been a long tradition of pathologizing behavior which is not mainstream and which some might find distasteful. Behaviors which are in conflict with someone's value system may be problematic but not obsessive-compulsive. Having sexual problems is common. Problems are caused by a number of nonpathological factors. . . . Some people will use sex as a coping mechanism similar to the use of alcohol, drugs, or eating. This pattern of sexual behavior is problematic. Problematic sexual behavior is often remedied by time, experience, education, or brief counseling (Coleman, 1991, p. 1).

Coleman and colleagues (1987; Coleman et al., 2003; Miner et al., 2007) consider compulsive sexual behavior as a clinical syndrome in which the person experiences sexual urges, fantasies, and behaviors that are recurrent and intense and interfere with daily functioning. A new definition of "too frequent sexual behavior" was published by the World Health Organization (WHO) in 2018 with hope of shifting the perception of "moral failing" and "mental disorder" of being a "sex addict" to a medical issue (Simon, 2018). WHO, in its *International Classification of Diseases* (2018), lists "compulsive sexual behavior disorder" as a "persistent pattern of failure to control intense, repetitive sexual impulses or urges resulting in repetitive sexual behavior." Numerous studies, conducted prior to the WHO definition of compulsive sexual behavior and hence may have used different definitions, reported that the prevalence of the behavior ranged from between 1% and 6% of the population in the United States (Kraus et al., 2018) and about one half of persons having compulsive sexual behavior developed it prior to age 18 (Reid et al., 2012).

The term *hypersexuality* has sometimes been used as a less pejorative term for sexual addiction, but it has not been accepted by the APA (Walters et al., 2011). Further, there is little in the literature about the frequency of sexual activity among "hypersexual" persons, particularly compared to nonhypersexual persons (Walton et al., 2016). John Bancroft, senior research fellow and former director of The Kinsey Institute, and colleague Zoran Vukadinovic (2004) add even another perspective. After reviewing the concepts and theoretical bases of sexual addiction, sexual compulsivity, and sexual impulsivity (another labeling term), they concluded that it is premature to attempt an overriding definition. They continue by noting that until there is better understanding of this type of sexual expression, they prefer the general descriptive term "out-of-control sexual behavior" (Bancroft, 2009).

All of this discussion has challenged us to consider what is "excessive sexual behavior" and how culture shapes norms and our reactions and thoughts surrounding it. Certainly, it has caused mental health professionals to consider ways to address highly sexual persons.

If your sexual fantasies and activities are distressing to you, or your behaviors are emotionally or physically harmful to yourself or others, you should consult a therapist. The chances are, however, that your sexuality and your unique expression of it are healthy. Having a strong sex drive or frequent sex likely does not mean that you have any of the conditions described here.

Think Critically

1. What are your thoughts about the term *sexual addiction*? Do you prefer the term *sexual compulsivity* or *out-of-control sexual behavior*? If neither, what term, if any, would you prefer to describe a person who has a lot of sex? Is a term necessary?

2. Do you agree or disagree that the idea of sexual addiction is really repressive morality in a new guise?

3. Which term would you prefer: excessive sexual behavior or highly sexual person? What is the difference in their meanings?

4. Have you ever wondered if you are a sex addict or that your sexual behavior is out of control? On what did you base this label?

Satyriasis, referring to "abnormal" or "uncontrollable" sexual desire in men, is less commonly used than *nymphomania* because society has come to believe and expect men to be more sexual than women, resulting in less research interest in men's hypersexual behaviors and needs (Kelly, 2013). For this reason, definitions of satyriasis infrequently include the adjective *excessive*. Instead, reflecting ideas of male sexuality as a powerful drive, *uncontrollable* becomes the significant adjective. Satyriasis is not recognized as a clinical condition by the APA (2013). Note that an alternative term more currently used than *nymphomania* or *satyriasis* is **hypersexuality**, meaning a very high desire for or frequency of sexual activity. In recent years, some have labeled very highly sexual persons as being "sex addicts." To read a discussion about sex addiction, see Think About It, "'Sexual Addiction': Repressive Morality in a New Guise?"

As you read this chapter, remember to distinguish clearly between the clinical, judgmental, or casual connotations of the various terms. It can be tempting to define a behavior you don't like or approve of as paraphilic. But unless you are clinically trained, you cannot diagnose someone, including yourself, as having a mental disorder.

As touched on previously, the line between a harmless sexual variation and a paraphilic disorder may not be exact and the "labeling" of specific behaviors as either may be open to debate and void of adequate scientific justification. Some mental health professionals believe that classifying some sexual behaviors as paraphilias is flawed and reflects a pseudoscientific attempt to judge, control and medicalize sexuality. As authors of this text, we recognize that paraphilia is a historical medical label and that under most circumstances paraphilic behavior is simply out-of-the-ordinary sexual expression that does not need mental health treatment nor harms oneself or others. However, for the sake of discussion, the presentation of sexual variation in this chapter is based on the paraphilias described in the *DSM-5*.

The Frequency of Paraphilia Behaviors and Desire

Many of the early reports of paraphilic behaviors came from studies of clinic patients, making it difficult to know the prevalence of paraphilia within a population. We do know that paraphilia behaviors occur more often in males, in all ethnic and socioeconomic groups, and among all sexual orientations and identities. Sex researchers Christian Joyal and Julie Carpentier (2017) found from their review of prior studies that the prevalence of paraphilic behaviors among nonclinic samples varied considerably in the few existing studies, which were conducted in different eras prior to the publication of the *DSM-5*, used different definitions that may not have corresponded with those used in psychiatric manuals, and had diverse data collection methods. These limitations may underestimate the real prevalence of paraphilic behavior. The overall rates of paraphilic experience have increased steadily from, for example, the increased use of the Internet and the publication of novels such as *Fifty Shades of Grey*, which are associated with increased interest in varied sexual behaviors (Peter & Valkenburg, 2006).

Joyal and Carpentier (2017) concluded that the actual occurrence of paraphilic behaviors and interests in non-clinic samples remains unknown. Hence, they conducted interviews to determine the paraphilic behaviors and desires among a non-clinic sample of 1,040 men and women, aged 18–64 years old, who matched as closely as possible to the corresponding populations of the province of Quebec, Canada. The paraphilias from the *DSM-5* (APA, 2013) (see Table 1) were assessed, plus an additional item "extended exhibition" (sex with a partner in front of other people or where you are at risk of being seen) was added. To assess behaviors, each question began with "Have you ever been sexually aroused by or while . . . [definition of paraphilia given]?" For example: "Have you ever been sexually aroused while watching a stranger, who was unaware of your presence, while they were nude, were undressing, or were having sexual relations?" For pedophilia, the question assessed if the person had ever engaged in sexual activity with a child aged 13 years or less after you were an adult. Note that these questions did not assess if the behavior, for example, caused distress or impairment to the individual or occurred over a period of at least 6 months, all components of the *DSM-5* definition of a paraphilic disorder that needs treatment. For the desire questions, the items began with "Would you like to . . . [definition of paraphilia given]?" (Ahlers et al.,

2001). Finally, the researchers assessed the level of intense and persistent paraphilic desires and experiences of the participants. Overall, more men than women had experienced a paraphilic behavior at least once in their lifetime (see Figure 1) and had a greater desire (see Figure 2) to experience a paraphilic behavior than women. The researchers note that the distinction between a paraphilia, paraphilic disorder, and paraphilic interest should be clear. The prevalence of intense and persistent paraphilic experiences or desires was less than 10% of the participants for all of the paraphilic behaviors. They caution that "these data should not be interpreted as evidence of a high prevalence of paraphilic disorders or paraphilias among the general population" (Joyal & Carpentier, 2017).

The 2015 Sexual Exploitation in America Study (SEAS), an Internet-based survey of 2,021 adults in the United States (975 men, 1,046 women) assessed the frequency and appeal of a broad range of sexual behaviors, including those historically considered "variant" (Herbenick et al., 2017). The frequency and appeal of the "variant" behaviors most relevant to this chapter—BSDM, playful whipping, public sex, spanking, tying/being tied up, and experiencing pain during sex—will be presented in the specific paraphilia section. To learn about sexual novelty in committed relationships, see Practically Speaking, "Sexual Novelty Scale."

• FIGURE 1

Percent of Men and Women Reporting at Least One Lifetime Episode of a Paraphilic Behavior.

Source: Joyal, C. C., & Carpentier, J. (2017).

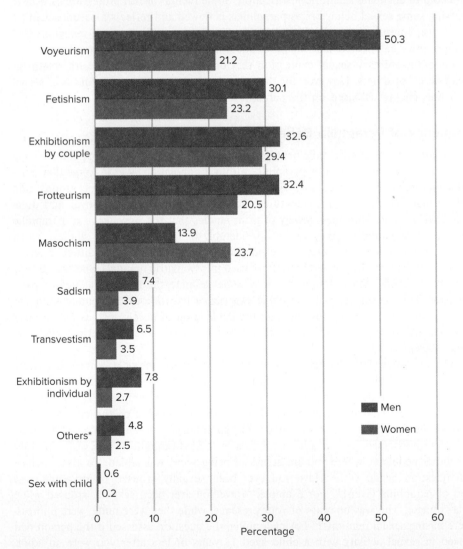

*Have you ever been aroused by an animal, fecal matter, enema, urine, cadavers, or other unusual things?

Note: Each paraphilia question began with, "Have you ever been sexually aroused by . . . [definition of paraphilia given]?" except for sex with child, which asked, "Have you ever engaged in sexual activity with a child aged 13 years old or less after you were an adult?" For example, "Have you ever been sexually aroused while watching a stranger who was unaware of your presence while they were nude, were undressing, or were having sexual relations?" Note that these questions do not assess if the behavior, for example, caused distress or impairment to the individual or occurred over a period of at least 6 months, all components of the *DSM-5* definition of a paraphilia disorder that needs treatment.

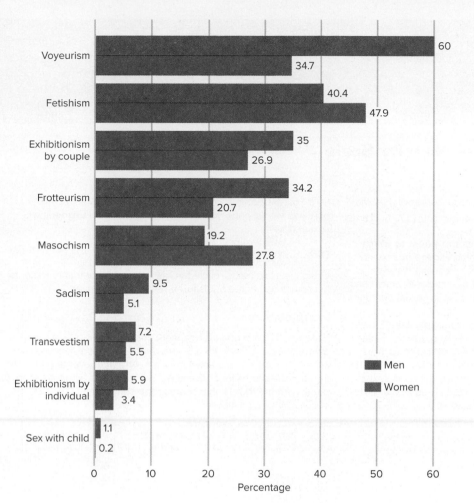

● **FIGURE 2**

Percent of Men and Women Reporting Desire (Wish to Experience) Paraphilic Behaviors.

Source: Joyal, C. C., & Carpentier, J. (2017).

Note: Each paraphilia question began with, "Would you like to . . . [definition of paraphilia given]?" For example, for exhibitionism: "Would you like to engage in sex acts knowing that someone is watching you or could be watching you?" The percentage listed for each paraphilic behavior is the total percentage of participants who indicated desire by choosing the alternatives, "I have thought about it," "maybe," and "absolutely."

● Types of Paraphilias

Fetishism

We attribute special or magical powers to many things: a lucky number, a saint's relic, an heirloom, a lock of hair, or an automobile. These objects possess a kind of symbolic magic. We will carry our boyfriend's or girlfriend's photograph, and sometimes talk to it or kiss it, ask for a keepsake if we part, and become nostalgic for a former love when we hear a particular song. All these behaviors are common, but they point to the symbolic power of objects, or fetishes.

Fetishism is sexual attraction to objects that become, for the person with the fetish, sexual symbols. The fetish is usually required or strongly preferred for sexual arousal because the person enjoys the way the object looks, tastes, smells, and/or feels (Kafka, 2010). Instead of relating to another individual, a person with fetishism gains sexual gratification from kissing a shoe, caressing a glove, drawing a lock of hair against his or her cheek, or masturbating with a piece of underwear. But the focus of a person with fetishism is not necessarily an inanimate object; the individual may be attracted to a specific body part and an inanimate object. Commonly used fetish objects include rubber articles, leather clothing, and other wearing apparel. Exclusive attraction to body parts is known as **partialism**. However, using objects for sexual stimulation, such as vibrators, or using articles of clothing for cross-dressing is not a sign of fetishism (APA, 2013).

Some people sexualize inanimate objects or parts of the body, such as the foot.

Fuse/Getty Images

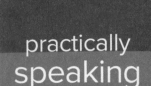

Sexual Novelty Scale

"One half of the world cannot understand the pleasures of the other."
—Jane Austin (1775–1816)

The Sexual Novelty Scale (SNS) measures the extent to which partners in committed romantic relationships engage in sexually novel behavior. The SNS was created to help researchers learn whether sexual novelty plays a role in relationship development and maintenance, sexual satisfaction, and a decrease in sexual boredom.

Research using the SNS found that persons who reported greater levels of sexual novelty in their relationships scored lower on sexual boredom and higher in novelty seeking, sensation seeking, openness to experience, and sex-positive attitudes such as erotophilia, sexual sensation seeking, sexual assertiveness, sexual self-esteem, and sex drive. Further, SNS predicted overall sexual satisfaction and relationship satisfaction, including egalitarianism and commitment to the relationship (Mathews et al., 2020, 2018).

If you are not in a committed romantic relationship, imagine how you would hope you and your partner would experience sexual novelty.

Directions:

Using the scale below, circle the response number that represents how much you agree or disagree with each statement.

Interpretation:

For Item #1, the scoring is reversed; that is, give answer #1 a 7, answer #2 a 6, answer #3 a 5, answer #4 stays as a 4, answer #5 a 3, answer #6 a 2, and answer #7 a 1. After the reverse scoring for Item #1, the scores for all five items are averaged, with total scores ranging from 1 to 7. Higher scores represent greater levels of novelty within a relationship.

MOTIVE	Strongly Disagree	Disagree	Somewhat Disagree	Neutral	Somewhat agree	Agree	Strongly Agree
1. Sex between my partner and me tends to follow a predictable routine.	1	2	3	4	5	6	7
2. Sexual experimentation is an important part of our relationship.	1	2	3	4	5	6	7
3. My partner and I often try new things.	1	2	3	4	5	6	7
4. It is common for my partner and me to try new sex positions.	1	2	3	4	5	6	7
5. My partner and I like to "mix things up" to keep our sex life exciting.	1	2	3	4	5	6	7

A study of the prevalence of fetishes involving Internet discussion groups representing at least 5,000 individuals found that the most common fetishes were for body parts or features (33%) and objects associated with the body (30%), such as panties and diapers. Feet and objects associated with feet, such as rubber, were the most frequently listed fetish targets (Scorolli et al., 2007).

Fetishistic behavior may be viewed as existing on a continuum, or existing in degrees, moving from a slight preference for an object, to a strong preference for it, to the necessity of the object for arousal, and finally to the object as a substitute for a sexual partner. Sex researchers Giselle Rees and Justin Garcia (2017) examined whether persons reporting sexual object fetishism require the presence of the fetish object for sexual activity. From two studies of persons with an inanimate object fetish (not body parts), the researchers found that for the majority of participants the fetish object was not obligatory for sexual arousal to occur, nor was it required for sexual activities to be considered enjoyable and sexually satisfying. Rather, the sexual fetishism appeared to be an erotic preference in which fetish sexual activities were preferred and perceived to be more sexually satisfying than nonfetish sexual behavior.

Most fetish behavior does not cause harm. However, a fetishistic disorder causes significant personal distress or impairment in social, occupational, or other important areas. Mental health clinicians report that it occurs nearly exclusively in males. However, as mentioned earlier, Joyal and Carpentier (2017) found no significant difference between males and females in fetishism experience and desire among a nonclinical population sample (see Figures 1 and 2). As shown in Figure 1, the population study of Joyal and Carpentier (2017) found that about 30% and 23% of the men and women, respectively, reported experiencing a fetish behavior at least once in their lifetime. About 40% of the men and 48% of the women desired to experience fetish behavior (Figure 2). Many persons who self-identify as fetish practitioners do not report clinical impairment and thus would not be diagnosed with a fetishistic disorder (APA, 2013). Actually, there has been debate about whether fetishism should be considered a clinical disorder. An argument has been made that the reason fetishism has been considered pathological is because it is considered to be unusual (Moser & Kleinplatz, 2006; Reiersøl & Skeid, 2006) although the Joyal and Carpentier (2017) research challenges that belief.

Transvestism

Transvestism (*trans* means "cross," *vest* means "dress") is the wearing of clothing of the other sex for sexual arousal (Wheele et al., 2008). Note that this paraphilia differs from transgender in which a transgender person is an individual whose gender expression or identity is not congruent with the sex assigned at birth. Many individuals with transvestism prefer to be labeled as "**cross-dressers**" instead of the more clinical label "transvestite," a term that some believe pathologizes cross-dressing behavior (Lehmiller, 2014). Joyal and Carpentier (2017) found that about 7% and 4% of men and women, respectively, reported at least one lifetime transvestism behavior (Figure 1) and about 7% of the men and 6% of the women expressed the desire to experience a transvestism behavior (Figure 2). The lower prevalence of transvestism among women may have several reasons. One may be that our society is more accepting of women wearing "men's" clothing, such as pants and ties, than men wearing "women's" clothes. So, women are not perceived as cross-dressing.

Female and male impersonation and dressing in drag are not considered to be transvestism. **Female impersonators** are men who dress as women and **male impersonators** are women who dress

"Those hot pants of hers were so damned tight, I could hardly breathe."

—Benny Hill (1924–1992)

Cross-dressing may be a source of humor and parody, as the traditional boundarles of gender are explored and challenged.

Mark Ralston/AFP/Getty Images

as men, often in a playful way as part of their job in entertainment. Hollywood movies such as Robin Williams in *Mrs. Doubtfire* and Dustin Hoffman in *Tootsie* feature male characters who are female impersonators. Gay men who cross-dress to entertain are often referred to as **drag queens**. The television series *RuPaul's Drag Race* is a media example of drag in our society.

Transvestism covers a broad range of behaviors. Some persons with transvestism prefer to wear only one article of clothing (usually a brassiere or panties) of the other sex in the privacy of their home; others choose to don an entire outfit in public. The frequency of cross-dressing ranges from a momentary activity that produces sexual excitement, usually through masturbation, to more frequent and long-lasting behavior, depending on the individual, available opportunities, and mood or stressors.

Men with transvestism are usually quite conventional in their masculine dress and attitudes. Dressed as women or wearing only one women's garment, they may become sexually aroused and masturbate or have sex with a woman. As time passes, however, the erotic element of the female garment may decrease and the comfort level increase. The majority of people with transvestism have no desire to live full-time as the other gender or to undergo gender-confirming surgery. If they do, there may be an accompanying diagnosis of gender dysphoria. *TV* is the acronym for *transvestism* and often appears in personal ads in underground newspapers and in Internet dating services.

Participating in cross-dressing can interfere with relationships and be a major source of personal stress. Many people with transvestism marry or establish other committed relationships in hopes of "curing" their desire to cross-dress. Some people with transvestism and their spouses and families are able to adjust to the cross-dressing. Data suggest, however, that women merely tolerate rather than support their partner's cross-dressing, and many feel betrayed, angry, and scared that outsiders will find out about their partner's behavior (Reynolds & Caron, 2000). Sometimes, however, the stress is too great, and separation follows soon after the transvestism is discovered. Cross-dressing that is done on occasion is a harmless and victimless sexual variation, especially if it happens in private. It would only become a problem, like other atypical behavior, when it is the only sexual outlet and if it is so compulsive that it cannot be controlled and interferes with other aspects of life (Hyde & DeLamater, 2020).

"I don't mind drag—women have been female impersonators for some time."

—Gloria Steinem (1934–)

The television series *RuPaul's Drag Race* is a media example of drag in our society.

Mediapunch/Shutterstock

Zoophilia

Zoophilia, sometimes referred to as "bestiality," involves deriving sexual pleasure from animals. True zoophilia occurs only when animals are the preferred sexual contact regardless of what other sexual outlets are available. Zoophilia is considered a coercive paraphilia based on the assumption that the animal is an unwilling participant. Few studies on the prevalence of zoophilia have been conducted. As of 2014, 46 states criminalize engaging in sexual contact with an animal (Wisch, 2019). The percentage of persons in the United States who have had sex with animals is not known, but reported prevalence rates range from 4.9% to 8.3% for men and 1.9% to 3.6% for women (Singg, 2017).

Among those who derive sexual pleasure from animals, the behavior usually begins and occurs in males during adolescence as a transitory phenomenon (Earls & Lalumière, 2009). Males are likely to have penetration with the animal such as a calf, lamb, or goat, or to have their genitals licked by the animal. Females are more likely to have contact with a household pet, having penetration, having the animal lick their genitals, or masturbating the animal. Some women have reported that they trained their dogs to engage in intercourse with them (Singg, 2017). Despite earlier beliefs to the contrary, studies found that very few persons who had sex with animals considered the sex as a substitute for human sex; rather, for them it was just their preferred behavior (Beetz, 2004; Miletski, 2000, 2002). One study found that half were in a committed relationship with a human partner (Sendler & Lew-Starowicz, 2017).

A research study of 114 self-identified men with zoophilia examined sexual interest in animals (Williams & Weinberg, 2003). The participants were primarily acquired through the use of an online questionnaire, and those who volunteered were asked to refer others who had similar interests. More than 9 of every 10 men who self-identified as "zoophiles" indicated that they were concerned with the welfare of the animals. Actually, research of the clinic patients with zoophilia found that the prevalence of sexual sadism upon the animal was less than 1% (Sendler & Lew-Starowicz, 2017). They emphasized the importance of consensual sexual activity with animals in contrast to persons they labeled as "**bestialists**," those who have sex with animals but are not concerned with the animals' welfare. The men listed desire for affection and pleasurable sex as the most important reasons for sexual interest in animals.

Three study participants made these comments (Williams & Weinberg, 2003):

My relationship with animals is a loving one in which sex is an extension of that as it is with humans, and I do not have sex with a horse unless it consents (p. 526).

Although I do get an erection when interacting sexually with a stallion, my first priority is always the animal's pleasure, erection, and personal affection to me (p. 526).

Humans use sex to manipulate and control. Humans have trouble accepting who you are. They want to change you. Animals do not judge you. They just love and enjoy the pleasures of sex without all the politics (p. 527).

The most commonly reported animal for sex were dogs (63%) and horses (29%); others were sheep, cats, cows, and chickens. Many of the men had not had sex with a human partner of either sex in the past year. The researchers suggest that sexual activity with animals is usually immediate, easy, and intense, thus reinforcing the behavior (Williams & Weinberg, 2003). Medical experts have noted that various organisms such as bacteria, parasitic worms, and viruses like rabies can be transmitted from animals to humans. Sex with animals is also a risk factor for urological diseases and penile cancer in humans (Singg, 2017; Zequi et al., 2012)

Voyeurism

Viewing sexual activities is a commonplace activity. Voyeuristic behaviors are the most frequently occurring of potentially law-breaking sexual behaviors (APA, 2013). Many individuals have used mirrors to view themselves during sexual behavior, watched their partners masturbate, video-recorded themselves and their partner having sex for later viewing, or watched others having intercourse. Americans' interest in viewing sexual activities has spawned a multibillion-dollar sex industry devoted to fulfilling those desires. Sexually explicit magazines, books, and Internet sites are widely available. Topless bars, live sex clubs, strip and peep shows, reality TV, sexting, and erotic dancing attest to the attraction of visual erotica. These

"I have a mirrored ceiling over my bed because I like to know what I am doing."

—Mae West (1893–1980)

activities are not considered **voyeurism** because the observed person is willing and these activities typically do not replace interpersonal sexuality. Hence, some degree of voyeurism appears to be socially acceptable (Lehmiller, 2014).

Joyal and Carpentier (2017) found that about 50% and 21% of men and women, respectively, reported at least one lifetime voyeurism behavior (Figure 1) and about 60% of the men and 35% of the women expressed desire to experience a voyeurism behavior (Figure 2). To learn what percentage of college students would watch a person undress or a couple have sex, see Think About It, "Would You Watch? College Students and Voyeurism."

think about it

Would You Watch? College Students and Voyeurism

Most research on voyeurism has focused on males in clinical and criminal settings. To investigate aspects of voyeurism in a relatively "normal" group of individuals, a sample of Canadian university students (232 women and 82 men) enrolled in a human sexuality class were asked to indicate whether they would watch an attractive person undressing or two attractive persons having sex in a hypothetical situation (Rye & Meaney, 2007). Students responded to the following scenario using a 0–100% scale, with 0% meaning "extremely unlikely to watch" to 100% being "extremely likely to watch." They were also asked if their responses would be different if there were a possibility of being caught and punished for their behavior.

Students were presented with the following scenario:

You see someone whom you find *very* attractive. The person does not suspect that you can see him or her. He/she begins undressing.

Two questions were then posed:

1. If there were no chance of getting caught, how likely would it be that you would watch the person undressing?

2. He or she begins to have sex with another attractive person. How likely is it that you would watch the two people having sex?

Here is what the study found:

- With both men and women combined, the self-reported likelihood of watching an attractive person undress was significantly higher (67% on the 0 to 100% scale) than watching two attractive people having sex (45%).

- Men and women were not significantly different in their reported likelihood of watching an attractive person undress (73% men, 65% women).

- Men were significantly more likely than women (64% men, 39% women) to be willing to watch two attractive people having sex.

- When there was no possibility of being caught, men and women were much more likely to be willing to watch an attractive person undress.

- When there was no possibility of being caught, men and women were only slightly more likely to be willing to watch two attractive people having sex.

In discussing the results, the researchers noted that the students may have considered watching a couple having sex as more invasive than watching a person undress. They note that there are many more opportunities to observe others, covertly, in the different stages of undress (e.g., at the gym, at the beach) than seeing people having sex (usually limited to sex clubs or accidentally walking in on a roommate or exhibitionistic or thrill-seeking couples in the college library stacks). The researchers also state that voyeuristic behavior may be acquired in several ways, such as evolutionary adaptations and social learning, then modified by social constraints, and that this perspective "fits well with Buss's (1998) sexual strategies theory. . . . Similarly, women may have less desire for sexual viewing, but may still engage in such behavior when social constraints are relaxed." The researchers also conclude that the study results support contentions that social constraints are a regulator of voyeurism.

Think Critically

1. How would you have answered the questions presented in this research study? Were there any responses that surprised you? Would the possibility of being caught alter your responses?

2. How would you feel if you found out you had been watched while undressing or having sex with someone?

3. If you have had sex, did you enjoy watching your partner undress? If so, what impact did this have on your sexual interaction?

Persons having this paraphilic behavior but declare no personal distress, have no impairment in functioning, and have no history of acting on these urges could be considered as having voyeuristic sexual interest rather than voyeuristic disorder (APA, 2013).

In order to become aroused, people with voyeuristic behavior must hide and remain unseen, and the person or couple being watched must be unaware of their presence. The excitement is intensified by the possibility of being discovered. Sometimes, the person with voyeurism will masturbate or imagine having sex with the observed person. People with voyeurism are sometimes called "peepers" or "peeping Toms." Watching others who know they are being observed, such as a sex partner, a stripper, or an actor in a sexually explicit film, is not classified as voyeurism. Voyeurism appeals primarily to heterosexual men (Seligman & Hardenburg, 2000), most of whom are content to keep their distance from their victim. Many lack social and sexual skills and may fear rejection.

Exhibitionism

Also known as "indecent exposure," **exhibitionism** is the revealing of one's genitals to an unsuspecting and nonconsenting person. The individual, almost always male and sometimes called a "flasher," may derive sexual gratification from the exposure of the genitals. The experiencing of someone exposing their genitals is commonly known as being "flashed." The Joyal and Carpentier (2017) research found low prevalence for exhibitionism: about 8% and 3% for men and women, respectively, reporting at least one lifetime exhibitionism behavior. About 6% of men and 3% of women indicated a desire to experience exhibitionism. Recall that Joyal and Carpentier also assessed couple exhibition; that is, having sex with a partner in front of other people or where one is at risk for being seen. About 33% of men and 29% of women, respectively, reported experiencing couple exhibitionism at least once in their lifetime and about 35% of men and 27% of women wish to experience it. To read about a novel form of exhibitionism that would not be considered an actual paraphilia, see Think About It, "College Students Making Out: Sometimes an Audience is Required."

The 2015 national U.S. study (SEAS) cited earlier found that 45% and 43% of men and women, respectively, reported having had sex with someone in a public place in their lifetime (Herbenick et al., 2017). Thirty-two percent of men and 23% of women, respectively, found having sex where someone might see them as appealing (very appealing and somewhat appealing combined).

What is considered exhibitionism varies cross-culturally, but throughout most of the United States it is illegal to expose one's genitals or for a woman to expose her nipples unless for a good reason such as breastfeeding. Exhibitionism is more often considered a problem and legally punishable when committed by a man, in contrast to such behavior by a woman. An online study of 459 undergraduates (mean age = 20 years) at an urban university in New York City accessed the lifetime prevalence of exhibitionism. Forty percent of women and 12% of men reported having been a victim of exhibitionism at least once in their lifetime. Most exhibitionism occurred on a subway station or platform, in crowded areas, or on the street. Among women, more than half of all exhibitionists were masturbating at the time of the incident. Victims of exhibitionism reported being more cautious where they go and began avoiding being alone, as well as feeling disgusted, and shocked (Clark et al., 2017).

The nonconsenting person is considered a victim, as the experience can be very traumatizing. Persons who have this paraphilic impulse but declare no personal distress, have no impairment in functioning, and have no history of acting on these urges could be considered having exhibitionism sexual interest but not exhibitionism disorder (APA, 2013). A person with exhibitionism often also has voyeuristic behaviors.

Genital exposure by a man is not a prelude or an invitation to intercourse. Instead, it is an escape from intercourse, for the man never exposes himself to a willing person—only to strangers or near-strangers. Typically, he obtains sexual gratification after exposing himself as he fantasizes about the shock and horror he caused his victim. Other people with exhibitionism experience orgasm as they expose themselves; still others may masturbate during or after the exhibitionism. In those few instances in which an individual shows interest, the person with exhibitionism immediately flees. Usually, there is no physical contact and rarely

"If modesty disappeared, so would exhibitionism."

—Mason Cooley (1927–2002)

Some people like to exhibit their bodies within public settings that are "legitimized," such as Mardi Gras. Such displays may be exhibitionistic, but they are not considered exhibitionism in the clinical sense.

David McNew/Getty Images

think about it

College Students Making Out: Sometimes an Audience is Required

As we learned in this text, people have sex for numerous reasons such as romance, emotional connection, and experience. Actually, a study of 444 men and women, ages 17–52, identified 237 reasons why people have sex (see Think About It, "Why College Students Have Sex" in Chapter 7) (Meston & Buss, 2007). These studies presumably assessed reasons for sex that occurred in private. However, not all sexual behaviors occur in private; for example, making out, sexual touching, and sexualized dancing are conducted in public settings that allow viewing and communication to other persons beyond the couple. Maybe the reasons for the sexual behavior are different if the sex is done "in front of others." A novel study examined why college students had a type of sex known as performance making out or PMO, that is, making out with someone and wanting a specific audience to view the behavior (Esterline & Muehlenhard, 2017).

As defined by the American Psychiatric Association (2013), performance making out would not be considered as paraphilia exhibitionism, which is being sexually aroused by the revealing of one's genitals to an unsuspecting person. But PMO does represent individual acceptance and deliberate utilization of "exhibiting" a specific type of sexual expression to others, whatever the motive. PMO, like persons revealing their body to a lover during sex, is typically a harmless, mild form of exhibitionism but not in the true sense of paraphilia.

An online questionnaire study involving 194 men and 155 women students at a large, public university in the Midwestern United States was conducted to investigate the prevalence, motivations, and outcomes of college student's experiences of performance making out (Esterline & Muehlenhard, 2017). The researchers chose to ask about "making out" rather than "kissing" or "sexual behavior." Making out is an American euphemism that is sometimes used synonymously with terms like petting, kissing, necking, and non-penetrative behaviors such as heavy petting. Making out is seemly understood to be sexual but without requiring any specific sexual behaviors. Here are the study's major findings:

Who Engaged in PMO

- Thirty-two percent of the women and 37% of the men reported having participated in PMO of which often began in either middle school/junior or high school.

- Most participants reported engaging in PMO with a person of the other sex although more women (8%) than men (2%) reported same-sex PMO.

- For more than one-third incidents of PMO, participants mentioned alcohol, being intoxicated or being in a bar or club.

Motivations for PMO

- When men described their motivations for experiencing PMO, their language was more positive than negative. They expressed that they wanted to look better among their peers, feel "happy" and "proud" having someone to make out with, and anticipated greater closeness with their male friends as a result of PMO.

- Men, in particular, and some women, reported engaging in PMO to enhance their image or status by proving that they are capable of making out with a particular person, usually someone they perceived as attractive. Several men reported that they wanted to show off to their fraternity brothers that they can attract a "hot" woman and women indicated that they wanted to be perceived as attractive and desirable.

- The most common PMO reason women mentioned for participating in PMO was to make their peers feel envious or jealous. Some wanted to send a message to an ex-partner that they had "moved on" from that partner and that they are still desirable, and a few wanted to rekindle romantic feelings with an ex-partner. Few men mentioned indicated these reasons.

- Both men and women reported using PMO to show others that they were in a relationship with their make-out partner, expecting that their image to be enhanced.

- Several women mentioned that they expected male onlookers to experience sexual arousal from watching the PMO.

- Some participants described that during participation in PMO they felt carefree, spontaneous, adventurous, and just having fun.

Outcomes of Engaging in PMO

- Women, more than men, were more balanced in their language used to describe PMO. They used many positive descriptors like the men did, but also used more negative descriptors such as desiring to induce jealousy in others, feeling "insecure" and concerned about their reputation being damaged.

- Men experienced more positive outcomes than negative ones from PMO but women experienced the opposite: more negative than positive outcomes.

- Men reported that PMO enhanced their reputations more often than damaged it; the opposite were found for the women participants.

The college students of this study were exhibiting making out that requires an audience. In doing so, the performance making out was a form of communication that fulfilled several functions such as enhancing image, demonstrating availability and desire to be sexually adventurous. However, gender differences of the impact of PMO on one's reputation reflects the sexual double standard in which women are judged more negatively than men when performing the same behaviors.

Think Critically

1. Have you ever observed PMO? If so, what were your impressions?

2. Have you ever participated in PMO? If so, what was your experience? If not, are you more or less likely to do so after reading this Think About It?

3. Do you consider PMO a harmless, mild form of exhibitionism or an actual paraphilic disorder?

is there violence. Exotic dancers and nude sunbathers are not considered people with exhibitionism because they typically do not derive sexual arousal from the behavior, nor do they expose themselves to unwilling people. Furthermore, stripping for a sex partner to arouse him or her involves willing participants.

Sometimes, the term *exhibitionist* is used in a pejorative way to describe a woman who dresses provocatively. These women, however, do not fit the American Psychiatric Association (2013) definition of exhibitionism. For example, they do not expose their genitals, nor does the provocative dressing cause marked distress or involve interpersonal behavior. Labeling women who dress provocatively as "exhibitionists" is more a case of a moral judgment than a scientific assessment. Actually, women in our culture have more socially acceptable ways of exposing their bodies than men. Showing breast cleavage, for example, is widely accepted in our culture (Carroll, 2010).

If a person with exhibitionism confronts you, it is best to remain calm and ignore and distance yourself from the person and then report the incident to the police. Reacting strongly, though a natural response, only reinforces the behavior.

Telephone Scatologia

Telephone scatologia—the making of obscene phone calls to unsuspecting people—is considered a paraphilia because the behaviors are compulsive and repetitive or because the associated fantasies cause distress to the individual.

Those who engage in this behavior typically get sexually aroused when their victim reacts in a shocked or horrified manner. Obscene phone calls are generally made randomly, by chance dialing. Some people with this paraphilia repeatedly make these calls.

The overwhelming majority of callers are male, but there are female obscene callers as well (Price et al., 2002). Some make their female victims feel annoyed, frightened, anxious, upset, or angry, while the callers themselves often suffer from feelings of inadequacy and insecurity. They may use obscenities, breathe heavily into the phone, or say they are conducting sex research. Also, they usually masturbate during the call or immediately afterward. The victims of male callers often feel violated, but female callers have a different effect on male recipients, who generally do not feel violated or may find the call titillating (Matek, 1988). Women callers are usually motivated by anger resulting from actual or fantasized rejection rather than from a desire to be sexually aroused.

If you receive a harassing or obscene phone call, the best thing to do is not to overreact and end the call. Don't engage in a conversation with the caller, such as trying to determine why the person is calling or why the person won't stop calling. Remember, the caller wants an audience. You should not give out personal information such as your name, e-mail address, or phone number to anyone who is a stranger or respond to any questions if you do not know the caller.

If the phone immediately rings again, don't answer it. If obscene calls are repeated, the telephone company or service provider suggests changing your number (many companies will do this at no charge), keeping a log of the calls, or, in more serious cases, working with law enforcement officials to trace the calls. Other solutions include screening calls with a phone message and obtaining caller ID, in which the caller's telephone number is displayed on the receiving person's phone. By the way, don't include your name, phone number, or other personal information, such as when you will be away and returning, in the outgoing message on your phone, social media account, or e-mail. One final suggestion—be cautious in placing ads in newspapers or on electronic media or allowing strangers access to personal information on social networking sites. Use a post office number or e-mail address. If you feel you must give your phone number, don't give the address of your residence.

Frotteurism

Frotteurism (also known as "mashing," "groping," or "frottage") refers to the obtaining of sexual gratification by sexual pressing, rubbing, or touching against a nonconsenting person in a public location. As shown in Figure 1, the population study of Joyal and Carpentier (2017) found that about 32% and 21% of men and women, respectively, reported experiencing

Frotteurism, the rubbing or touching against a nonconsensual person, can occur in crowded public places such as buses or subways.

Matej Kastelic/Shutterstock

"The dead person who loves will love forever and will never be weary of giving and receiving caresses."

—Ernest Jones (1879–1958)

a frotteurism behavior at least once in their lifetime. About 34% of the men and 21% of the women desired to experience frotteurism behavior (Figure 2). The online questionnaire study of 459 undergraduate students in New York City cited in the discussion of exhibitionism found that about 24% of women and 7% of men had experienced frotteurism. Most incidents occurred in a subway train or platform and in crowded areas. Victims of frotteurism reported feelings of being violated, disgust, and shock. Many women but none of the men reported that they changed their behavior (e.g., being more cautious) following the incident. Among male victims, about half of the perpetrators were female (Clark et al., 2017).

The *DSM-5* describes a person with frotteuristic disorder as a person who experiences, for at least 6 months, significant personal distress or social impairment from recurrent and intense sexual arousal from rubbing or touching against a nonconsenting person. If this paraphilic impulse does not cause personal distress or impairment of other important areas of functioning and there is no acting on the urges, individuals are considered to have frotteuristic sexual interest, but not frotteuristic disorder (APA, 2013).

The person with frotteurism usually carries out the touching or rubbing in crowded public places like subways or buses or at large sporting events or rock concerts. The initial rubbing can be disguised by the crush of people. For example, a male usually rubs his clothed erect penis against the fully clothed female's buttocks or thighs. Less commonly, he may use his hands to rub a woman's buttocks, pubic region, thighs, or breasts. The type of contact may appear unintended, and a woman may not even notice the touch or pay heed to it, given the crowded situation. However, some women may feel victimized. If the woman discovers it, the man will usually run away. Hence, nearly all men with frotteurism are able to escape being caught. While mashing, the male may fantasize about having consensual sex with the woman, and he may recall the episode when masturbating in the future.

Necrophilia

Necrophilia is sexual activity with a corpse. It is regarded as nonconsensual because a corpse is obviously unable to give consent. There are relatively few instances of necrophilia, largely because few people have access to cadavers, yet it retains a fascination in horror literature, especially vampire stories and legends, and in gothic novels. It is also associated with ritual cannibalism in other cultures. Within our own culture, *Sleeping Beauty* features a necrophilic theme, as does the crypt scene in Shakespeare's *Romeo and Juliet.* Most likely, necrophilia sexual behaviors are committed largely by those who work with corpses in mortuaries and morgues and who have become desensitized by them. Such behavior is illegal under laws regarding the handling of dead bodies (Kelly, 2013). However, the vast majority of persons working with corpses do not have urges to be sexual with a corpse.

There are three types of necrophilia: regular necrophilia in which the person is sexual with a dead person; necrophilic homicide in which the person kills a person to obtain a corpse for sex; and, necrophilic fantasy, during which the person fantasizes about sex with a dead person but does not, in reality, carry out the behavior (Holmes & Holmes, 2002). In a review of 122 cases of supposed necrophilia or necrophilic fantasies, researchers found only 54 instances of true necrophilia (Rosman & Resnick, 1989). The study found that neither sadism, psychosis, nor mental impairment was inherent in necrophilia. Instead, the most common motive for necrophilia was the possession of a partner who neither resisted nor rejected.

Pedophilia

Pedophilia is characterized by a sexual interest in or actual sexual behavior with prepubescent children. A person with a sexual focus on prepubescent children who does not report feelings of shame, guilt, or anxiety about these impulses, is not functionally limited by these impulses, and never acted on these impulses is considered to have pedophilia sexual interest but not pedophilic disorder (APA, 2013). According to the APA, the children are aged 13 or younger and a person with pedophilic disorder must be at least 16 and at least 5 years older than the child. A late adolescent is not considered to have pedophilic disorder if he or she is involved in an ongoing sexual relationship with a 12-year-old or older child. The diagnostic criteria for this paraphilia did not change with the update to *DSM-5;* the only change was in renaming the diagnosis from pedophilia to pedophilic disorder. Almost all people with pedophilic disorder are males, although on rare occasions females with this paraphilia have been reported (Hamby et al., 2017). Their sexual contacts with children are relatively rare, occurring probably in 3–5% of the male population (APA, 2013). Girls are about twice as likely as boys to be the sexual objects of pedophilic behavior. The occurrence and desire for sex with children was very low in the Joyal and Carpentier population study (2017): less than 1% (0.6% for men, 0.2% for women) reported having experienced sex with a child once in their lifetime, and 1.1% of men and 0.2% of women indicate a desire to experience sex with a child.

In this section, we discuss only pedophilic disorder. Pedophilic disorder is different from "child sexual abuse," "child molestation," and "incest," although all denote sex with minors, which is a criminal action. Pedophilic disorder, as defined by the APA, is a psychiatric disorder. Not all of those who sexually abuse minors would be considered people with pedophilic disorder unless the APA criteria are met. Sexual contact with a minor is not, in itself, a determination of pedophilic disorder (Fagan et al., 2002). It is, however, illegal. Nonpedophilic child sexual abuse and incest, their impact on the victims, and prevention of child sexual abuse are discussed in Chapter 17. Child sexual abuse is illegal in every state.

Some individuals with pedophilic disorder prefer only one sex, whereas others are aroused by both male and female children. Those attracted to females usually seek 8- to 10-year-olds, and those attracted to males usually seek slightly older children. Some people with pedophilic disorder are sexually attracted to children only, and some are aroused by both children and adults (APA, 2013).

Research has shown that many persons with pedophilic disorder have personality disorders, but why pedophilic disorder exists remains a puzzle (Madsen et al., 2006; Seto, 2008). Pedophilic disorder seems to be a lifelong condition. Although it may fluctuate, increase or decrease with age, the use of sexually explicit videos depicting prepubescent children is a helpful diagnostic indicator of pedophilic disorder. Many are fearful that their sexual abilities are decreasing or that they are unable to perform sexually with their partners (APA, 2013). Often they are deficient in interpersonal skills to successfully be in adult relationships (Dreznick, 2003). Some adult males report that they were sexually abused as a child, although whether this correlation represents a causal influence of childhood sexual abuse on adult pedophilia remains unclear.

People with pedophilic disorder often use seduction and enticement to manipulate children—their own children, relatives, or children outside the family. The Internet provides a way for a person with pedophilic disorder to make contact with unsuspecting children. For example, a man sometimes cruises chat rooms designed for children, and he may convince a girl to agree to e-mail, text, social media network, or telephone contact. He may befriend the girl, talking to her and giving her gifts.

Pedophilic behaviors rarely involve sexual intercourse. The person with pedophilic disorder usually seeks to fondle or touch the child, usually on the genitals, legs, and buttocks. Sometimes, the genitals are exposed and the individual has the child touch his penis. The person may masturbate in the presence of the child. Occasionally, oral or anal stimulation is involved.

BDSM, Sexual Masochism, and Sexual Sadism

One of the more widespread forms of sexual variation is **BDSM**—a term often used in popular culture for **b**ondage, **d**iscipline, **s**adism, and **m**asochism. BDSM represents a broad possibility of experiences in which sexual gratification is derived from being dominated, dominating another person, giving pain (sadism), or receiving pain (masochism) (Carroll, 2010; Kleinplatz & Moser, 2004; Krueger, 2010a, 2010b). Often, there is no clear dividing line

"I had to give up masochism—I was enjoying it too much."
—Mel Calman (1931–1994)

between domination and submission and sexual sadism and sexual masochism. Persons practicing BSDM are often stigmatized by the public largely because of unfamiliarity of this practice and because it is marginalized (Coppens et al., 2020).

Numerous studies to determine the prevalence of BSDM-related behaviors have been conducted: We highlight a sample of the more important ones. A general population study revealed that 2.2% of men and 1.3% of women reported participating in BSDM behavior in the past year (Richters et al., 2008). An online study of 62 "BSDM-related" behaviors of women recruited from "kink" community was conducted to broaden understanding of the sensual, erotic, and sexual behavior of women as most prior studies focused on men. Results revealed that the vast majority (75% to 85%) reported participating in behaviors that caused pain, such as breast play (slap, clothespins), flogging, padding, genital play (slap, kick, clothespins), and whipping and caning. Eighty-five percent reported use of bondage toys for erotic and sensual pleasure (Rehor, 2015). A Belgian study of 770 persons participating in BSDM either within community groups or in private revealed that common BSDM-related activities included movement restriction, blindfolding, use of ice cubes, hitting/scratching/biting, fantasy/role play, kneeling/role play, spanking, clamps, and use of pain (Coppens et al., 2020).

The Joyal and Carpentier population study (2017) found that about 14% and 24% of men and women, respectively, reported participating in masochism at least once in their lifetimes and about 7% of the men and about 4% of women reported participating in sadism at least once in their lifetime. These numbers may seem high using the APA (2013) definition for paraphilic disorder, which involves psychological stress, for example. As stated earlier, the researchers indicated that the overall prevalence of intense and persistent paraphilic experiences was reported as being frequent by no more than 10% of the research sample. Hence, the findings should not be considered as evidence of high prevalence of paraphilic behavior or paraphilic disorder among the general population. In this sample, about 19% and 28% of men and women, respectively, reported a desire to experience masochism and about 10% of men and 5% of women reported desire to experience sadism.

The writings of self-identifying BDSM practitioners suggested that their participation in unconventional activities contributed to them experiencing optimal sexual experiences. The writers noted that exceptional levels of communication and trust are needed in their BDSM behaviors, both of which enhance the probability of great sexual episodes (Kleinplatz & Menard, 2020; Ortmann & Sprott, 2013; Shahbaz & Chirinos, 2017; Sprott & Hadcock, 2017).

The 2015 SEAS survey of sexual behaviors (Herbenick et al., 2017) found that:

- Twenty-two percent and 21% of men and women, respectively, reported they had tied up their partner or been tied up as part of sex in their lifetime. Twenty-nine percent of both men and women indicated that tying up their partner or being tied up as part of sex appealed to them (very appealing and somewhat appealing combined).

- Sixteen percent and 14% of men and women, respectively, reported they had playfully whipped or been whipped by a partner as part of sex. Twenty percent and 21% of men and women, respectively, indicated that playfully whipping or being whipped by a partner as part of sex appealed to them.

- Thirty percent and 34% of men and women, respectively, reported having spanked a partner or been spanked as part of sex in their lifetime. Twenty-six percent and 30% of men and women, respectively, indicated that spanking or being spanked as part of sex appealed to them.

- Nine percent of the men and 14% of the women indicated that experiencing pain as part of sex appealed to them.

- Forty-five percent of the men and 43% of the women indicated that playfully biting, or being bitten, as part of sex appealed to them.

- Four percent of the men and 3% of the women reported having gone to a BDSM party or dungeon in their lifetime. Seven percent of the men and 6% of the women indicated that going to a BDSM club, party, or dungeon appealed to them.

Beyond any possible harmful effects of extreme BSDM many couples incorporate light, physically gentle, playful forms of BDSM into their sexual life on an occasion. As shown in the SEAS study, it is not uncommon for couples to have tied each other up, to have been playfully whipped or whipped their partner, to have been spanked or spanked their partner, and to state that pain and biting during sex appealed to them (Herbenick et al., 2017). Domination and submission is not considered a mental disorder, as it is considered consensual and does not result in psychological distress, but sexual sadism and sexual masochism, which can cause significant distress and involve a nonconsenting partner for sexual sadism, are listed as paraphilic disorders. Coercion separates sexual sadism from domination. But for consensual behaviors, there is no clear distinction. A rule of thumb for separating consensual sexual sadism and sexual masochism from domination and submission may be that sadism and masochism behaviors can be extreme, compulsive, and dangerous and are not commonly practiced. Sexual partners practicing sadism and masochism often make specific agreements ahead of time concerning the amount of pain and punishment that will occur during sexual activity. Nevertheless, the acting out of fantasies involves risk such as physical injury; thus, it is important that individuals communicate their preferences and limits before they engage in any new activity. The term *sadomasochism* (*S&M*) is also used by the general public to describe domination and submission, but it is no longer used as a clinical term in psychology and psychiatry to describe consensual domination and submission.

Bondage and discipline, or B&D, often involves leather straps, handcuffs, and other restraints as part of its scripting.

Francis Hanna/Alamy Stock Photo

Research involving 68 self-identifying, nonexclusive persons who participated in BDSM revealed that they became interested in BDSM in their early twenties but did not act on their interest until the late twenties and that most BDSM activities occurred at home with a partner. Further, the participants reported that both BDSM and non-BDSM sexual activities were similarly satisfying (Pascoal et al., 2015).

One misconception about BDSM is the stereotype that individuals who associate pain with sexual arousal are victims of childhood abuse who have developed psychological problems in adulthood (Lehmiller, 2014). However, persons who practice BDSM are no more likely to have psychological disorders than anyone else. A research study showed that BDSM is not linked to having experienced childhood sexual abuse, nor is it associated with greater levels of psychological distress in adulthood (Richters et al., 2008).

Domination and submission (D-S) are forms of fantasy sex, and the D-S behaviors are carefully controlled by elaborate shared scripts, thus not being violent. The critical element is not pain but power. The dominant partner is perceived as all-powerful and the submissive partner as powerless. Significantly, the amount or degree of "pain," which is usually feigned or slight, is controlled by the submissive partner, typically by subtle nonverbal signals. As such, fantasy plays a central role, especially for the submissive person. As two people enact the agreed-upon master-slave script, the control is not complete. Rather, it is the *illusion* of total control that is fundamental to D-S (Hyde & DeLamater, 2020).

Domination and submission take many forms. The participants generally assume both dominant and submissive roles at different times; with men and women changing position from time to time. Probably the most widely known form is **bondage and discipline (B&D)**. B&D is a fairly common practice in which a person is bound with scarves, leather straps, underwear, handcuffs, chains, or other such devices while another simulates or engages in light-to-moderate discipline activities such as spanking or light flagellation (e.g., whipping or flogging). The bound person may be blindfolded or gagged. A woman specializing in disciplining a person is known as a **dominatrix**, and her submissive partner is called a slave. Bondage and discipline may take place in specialized settings called "dungeons" furnished with restraints, body suspension devices, racks, whips, and chains, which are often depicted in adult videos. A large-scale study of a nonclinical population revealed that the majority of people who engage in domination and submission do so as a form of sexual enhancement which they voluntarily and mutually choose to explore (Weinberg et al., 1984).

*"Ah beautiful, passionate body
That never has ached with a heart!
On the mouth though the kisses are
 bloody,
Though they sting till it shudder and
 smart,
More kind than the love we adore is,
They hurt not the heart or the brain,
Oh bitter and tender Dolores,
Our Lady of Pain."*

—Algernon Swinburne (1837–1909)

Bettie Page, who has become a cult figure among those interested in domination and submission, was one of the most photographed women in the 1950s.

Michael Ochs Archives/Getty Images

Janus and Janus (1993) reported that 11% of both men and women had experience with bondage. Another investigation of four "kinky" sexual behaviors—bondage or domination, sadomasochism, photo or video exhibitionism, and asphyxiation or breath play—among 347 lesbian and 58 bisexual women found that 32% and 41%, respectively, had ever participated in bondage/domination. The study also found that 40% reported ever engaging in at least one of the four behaviors and 25% reported engaging in multiple behaviors (Tomassilli et al., 2009).

Another common form of domination and submission is humiliation, in which the person is debased or degraded. Examples of humiliation include being verbally humiliated, receiving an enema ("water treatment"), being urinated on ("golden showers"), and being defecated on ("scat"). Sexual pleasure derived from receiving enemas is known as **klismaphilia** (klis-muh-FIL-ee-uh), that derived from contact with urine is called **urophilia** (yore-oh-FIL-ee-uh), and that derived from contact with feces is called **coprophilia** (cop-ro-FIL-ee-uh). Humiliation activities may also include servilism, infantilism (also known as babyism, or adult baby diaper lover—ABDL), kennelism, and tongue-lashing. In servilism, the person desires to be treated as a servant or slave. In ABDL, the person acts in a babyish manner—using baby talk, wearing diapers, and being pampered, scolded, or spanked by his or her "mommy" or "daddy."

A study of 2012 persons who practice ABDL found that a clear contingent of the sample participated in ABDL for sexual reasons, whereas others believed it violates the boundaries of baby play. Nonsexual motivations included a desire to relax, be carefree, and a desire to be nurtured. The researchers concluded that "ABDL practices may be a diverse as seemingly typical sexual behaviors" (Zamboni, 2019, p. 191). "Kennelism" refers to being treated like a dog (wearing a studded dog collar and being tied to a leash) or ridden like a horse while the dominant partner applies whips or spurs. Tongue-lashing is verbal abuse by a dominant partner who uses language that humiliates and degrades the other person.

People engage in domination and submission in private or as part of an organized subculture complete with clubs and businesses catering to the acting out of D-S fantasies. This subculture is sometimes known as "the velvet underground." There are scores of noncommercial D-S clubs throughout the United States. The clubs are often specialized: lesbian S&M, dominant men/submissive women, submissive men/dominant women, gay men's S&M, and transvestite S&M. Leather sex bars are meeting places for gay men who are interested in domination and submission. The D-S subculture includes videos, websites, books, social media networks, newspapers, and magazines.

A questionnaire study of 184 Finnish men and women who were members of two sado-masochistic-oriented clubs identified 29 sexual behaviors that were grouped in four different sexual scripts: hypermasculinity (e.g., using a dildo, an enema), administration and receipt of pain (e.g., hot wax, clothespins attached to nipples), physical restriction (e.g., using handcuffs), and psychological humiliation (e.g., face slapping and using knives to make surface wounds) (Alison et al., 2001; Santtila et al., 2002). Research has shown that sadomasochistic behavior occurs among gay men, lesbian women, and heterosexual individuals (Sandnabba et al., 2002). Nineteen percent and 26% of lesbian and bisexual women, respectively, reported ever participating in sadomasochism (Tomassilli et al., 2009).

Sexual Sadism Disorder The term "sexual sadism" is named after the eighteenth-century French writer Marquis de Sade (1740–1814), who wrote about inflicting pain or humiliation during sex with others. According to the *DSM-5,* a person may be diagnosed with **sexual sadism** if, over a period of at least 6 months, she or he experiences intense, recurring sexual urges or fantasies involving real (not simulated) behaviors in which physical or psychological harm, including humiliation, is inflicted upon a victim for purposes of intense sexual arousal. The individual either has acted on these urges with a nonconsenting person or finds them extremely distressful (APA, 2013). Characteristic symptoms include violent sexual thoughts and fantasies involving a desire for power and control centering on a victim's physical suffering, which is sexually arousing (Kingston & Yates, 2008). The victim may be a consenting person with masochism or someone abducted by a person with sadism. The victim may be tortured, raped, mutilated, or killed; often, the victim is physically restrained and blindfolded or gagged. However, most rapes are not committed by sexual sadists.

Persons acknowledging sexual interest in physical and psychological suffering of others but declare no personal distress, have no impairment in functioning, and have no history of acting on these urges could be considered having sadistic sexual interest but would not meet the criteria for sadistic sexual disorder (APA, 2013). How often sexual sadism disorder occurs is unknown and is largely based on persons from forensic settings, nearly all males. *DSM-5* states that the prevalence varies widely, from 2% to 30%, depending on the criteria used. Among individuals who have committed sexually motivated homicides, rates of sexual sadism disorder range from 37% to 75% (APA, 2013).

Sexual Masochism Disorder   According to the *DSM-5,* for a diagnosis of **sexual masochism disorder** to be made, a person must experience for a period of at least 6 months intense, recurring sexual urges or fantasies involving real (not simulated) behaviors of being "humiliated, beaten, bound, or otherwise made to suffer." These fantasies, sexual urges, or behaviors must result in significant distress or social impairment. A person who indicates no stress and the sexual masochism impulses do not impede personal goals is considered having masochistic sexual interest but not sexual masochistic disorder. Some individuals express the sexual urges by themselves (e.g., through self-mutilation or by binding themselves); others act with partners. Masochistic behaviors expressed with a partner may include being restrained, blindfolded, face-slapped, paddled, spanked, whipped, beaten, shocked, cut, "pinned and pierced," and humiliated (e.g., being urinated or defecated on or forced to crawl and bark like a dog). The individual may desire to be treated as an infant and be forced to wear diapers (ABDL). The degree of pain one must experience to achieve sexual arousal varies from symbolic gestures to severe mutilations. As noted previously, sexual masochism is the only paraphilia that occurs with some frequency in women (Hucker, 2008).

Autoerotic Asphyxia   A form of sexual masochism called **autoerotic asphyxia** (also called AEA, hypoxphilia, breath play, sexual asphyxia, or asphyxiphilia) links strangulation with masturbation. Autoerotic asphyxia is an increasing phenomenon, with more than 1,000 fatalities in the United States per year, and the ratio of male to female accidental deaths being more than 50 to 1 (Gosink & Jumbelic, 2000). Interest in AEA often begins in adolescence. One study found that many persons practicing AEA discovered it via the Internet (Baxendale et al., 2019). Because of the secrecy and shame that accompany this and other masturbatory activities, it is difficult to know the exact number of individuals who find this practice arousing. Reports by participants are extremely rare or are masked by another cause of death.

Self-hanging is the most common method of AEA, although some type of suffocation is frequently used (Hucker, 2011). Individuals often use ropes, cords, or chains along with padding around the neck to prevent telltale signs. Others may place plastic bags or blankets

Masochistic behaviors expressed with a partner may include being restrained, blindfolded, and humiliated, as seen here.

Eddie Gerald/Alamy Stock Photo

over their heads. Still others inhale asphyxiating gases such as aerosol sprays or amyl nitrate ("poppers"), a drug used to treat heart pain. Those who are participants in this activity temporarily cut off the oxygen supply to the brain in the belief that this will heighten their masturbatory arousal and orgasm, although there is no scientific proof that it results in increased arousal and stronger orgasms. Possibly, the heightened arousal is an outcome of experiencing risk instead of a lower brain oxygen level. Their plan is to discontinue oxygen deprivation prior losing consciousness, but sometimes individuals miscalculate, which can result in death by suffocation or strangulation. A study of 165 persons who were classified as having AEA by mild to strong sexual arousal during found that 19% of participants reported that they did not use safety precautions to prevent accidental death. Most were not distressed by their AEA interests (Baxendale et al., 2019). Studies of survivors found that many of these individuals fantasized about masochistic scenarios during the autoerotic behavior (Hucker, 2011). The possibility of suicide should always be considered even in cases that initially appear to be accidental (Byard & Botterill, 1998).

Although researchers have some understanding of why people participate in this practice, it is more important that medical personnel, parents, and other adults recognize signs of it and respond with strategies commensurate with its seriousness. Those who engage in such sexual practices rarely realize the potential consequences of their behavior; therefore, parents and others must be alert to physical and other telltale signs. An unusual neck bruise; bloodshot eyes; disoriented behavior, especially after the person has been alone for a while; and unexplained possession of or fascination with ropes or chains are the key signs.

● Origins and Treatment of Paraphilic Disorders

Recall that the latest edition of the American Psychiatric Association's *Diagnostic and Statistical Manual of Mental Disorders, Fifth Edition (DSM-5)* distinguishes between paraphilias, which are considered to be relatively harmless sexual activities not needing mental health treatment, and paraphilic disorders, which are considered harmful sexual activities needing medical attention. Another category created by APA was paraphilic sexual interest, in which the individual has interest in a paraphilic activity but has no personal distress and has not acted on the interest. We presented data for both Canadian (Joyal & Carpenter, 2017) and U.S. (Herbenick et al., 2015) studies revealing that many persons have participated in a consensual playful way, and/or had interest in paraphilias such as voyeurism, couple exhibition, and whipping a partner or being whipped, none which would require medical intervention. Thus in this discussion, we largely focus on paraphilic disorders.

How do people develop paraphilic disorders? Research on the causes of paraphilias has been limited and difficult to conduct; hence, findings, though informative, are largely speculative. As with many other behaviors, paraphilic disorders probably result from some type of interaction among biology, sociocultural norms, and life experiences. Because most people with paraphilic disorders are male, biological factors may be particularly significant. Some researchers have postulated that males with paraphilia may have higher testosterone levels than those without paraphilias, that they have had brain damage, or that the paraphilia may be inherited. Because the data are inconclusive, however, it has not been possible to identify a specific biological cause of paraphilic disorder. People with paraphilic disorder seem to have grown up in dysfunctional environments and to have had early experiences that limited their ability to be sexually stimulated by consensual sexual activity; as a result, they obtain arousal through varied means. They may have low self-esteem, poor social skills, and feelings of anger and loneliness; be self-critical; and lack a clear sense of self (Fisher & Howells, 1993; Goodman, 1993; Marshall, 1993; Ward & Beech, 2008). Another factor may be a limited ability to empathize with the victims of their behavior. The psychological outcomes of these behaviors direct sexual attraction and response away from intimate relationships in later life (Schwartz, 2000).

Therapists have found paraphilic disorders to be difficult to treat (Laws & O'Donohue, 2008; McConaghy, 1998). Most people who are treated are convicted sex offenders, who have the most severe paraphilic disorders, while those with milder paraphilias go undiagnosed and untreated. Multifaceted treatments, such as psychodynamic therapy, aversive conditioning, cognitive-behavioral programs, relapse prevention, and medical intervention including the use of certain medication, have been tried to reduce or eliminate the symptoms of the paraphilic disorder. Enhancing social and sexual skills, developing self-management plans, modifying sexual interests, and providing sexuality and relationship education may help people with paraphilic disorder engage in more appropriate behavior (Baez-Sierra et al., 2016; Marshall, et al., 2006). However, even when the client desires to change, treatments may not be effective, and relapses often occur. A review of 80 studies found a 37% reduction in the re-offense rate among persons with paraphilic disorder in contrast to those not receiving any treatment (Schmucker & Losel, 2008). Hence, some experts believe that prevention is the best approach, although prevention programs are currently very limited.

Final Thoughts

Studying variations in sexual behaviors reveals the variety and complexity of sexual behavior. It also underlines the limits of acceptance of sexual behavior outside of the predominant culture and social sexual norms. Mental health professionals and many others believe unconventional sexual behaviors, undertaken in private between consenting adults as the source of erotic pleasure, should be of concern only to the people involved. As long as physical or psychological harm is not done to oneself or others and the behavior is consensual, paraphillic behaviors can be a healthy part of partnered sexual behavior. Paraphilic disorders, particularly those that are coercive, may be injurious and should be treated.

Mark Wragg/Getty Images

Summary

Sexual Variations and Paraphilic Behavior

- *Sexual variation* is behavior in which less than the majority of individuals engage or that is outside of the "mainstream" of sexual behavior. Variant sexual behavior is not "abnormal" or "deviant" behavior, the definition of which varies from culture to culture and from one historical period to another.

- The American Psychiatric Association (APA) defines *paraphilia* as an intense and recurring sexual interest and impulse other than sexual interest in genital stimulation or preparatory fondling with a normal, physically mature adult.

- In *The Diagnostic and Statistical Manual of Mental Disorders, Fifth Edition (DSM-5),* a distinction was made between relatively harmless and relatively harmful sexual behaviors. *Paraphilia* is considered an out-of-the-ordinary sexual behavior that does not necessarily require psychiatric treatment; a *paraphilic disorder* is a persistent and recurring (for at least 6 months) sexual behavior that causes distress or social impairment and whose satisfaction entails personal harm, or risk of harm, to others. This distinction is a major change in the *DSM-5,* reflecting greater acceptance of some unconventional sexual behaviors.

- The distinction between sexual interests, variations, and behavior that might be classified as *paraphilic* or *paraphilic disorder* is often vague and often more a difference of degree than kind.

- *Paraphilic interest* describes a particular paraphilic impulse that does not cause personal distress nor impaired function and there is no history of the person acting on the impulse.

- Paraphilic behaviors may be noncoercive or coercive. *Noncoercive paraphilias,* such as *domination and submission, fetishism,* and *transvestism,* are considered relatively benign or harmless because they are victimless. *Coercive paraphilias* represent nonconsensual sexual activity with children and adults; examples include *voyeurism, sexual masochism, sexual sadism, frotteurism,* and *pedophilia.*

Types of Paraphilias

- *Fetishism* is sexual attraction to inanimate objects or nongenital body parts. The fetishism is usually required or strongly preferred for sexual arousal.

- *Transvestism* is the wearing of clothes of a member of the other sex, usually for sexual arousal, and is also called cross-dressing.

- *Zoophilia* involves animals as the preferred sexual outlet even when other outlets are available. It is also called bestiality.

- *Voyeurism* is the nonconsensual and secret observation of others who are naked, disrobing, or having sex for the purpose of sexual arousal.

- *Exhibitionism* is the exposure of the genitals to a nonconsenting stranger.

- *Telephone scatologia* is the nonconsensual telephoning of strangers and often involves the use of obscene language.

- *Frotteurism* involves touching or rubbing against a nonconsenting person for the purpose of sexual arousal.

- *Necrophilia* is sexual activity with a corpse.

- *Pedophilia* refers to sexual arousal and contact with children aged 13 or younger by adults. A person with pedophilia must be at least 16 and at least 5 years older than the child. Child sexual abuse is illegal in every state.

- *BDSM* is an acronym used to describe the combination of bondage, discipline, sadism, and masochism.

- *Domination and submission (D-S)* is a form of consensual fantasy sex involving no pain with perceived power as the central element.

- *Sexual sadism disorder* refers to sexual urges or fantasies of intentionally inflicting real physical or psychological pain or suffering on a person.

- *Sexual masochism disorder* is the recurring sexual urge or fantasy of being humiliated or made to suffer through real behaviors, not simulated ones.

- *Autoerotic asphyxia* is a form of sexual masochism linking strangulation with masturbatory activities.

Origins and Treatment of Paraphilias

- Paraphilias are likely the result of social/environmental, psychological, and biological factors.

- Paraphilic disorders are difficult to treat, and relapses often occur.

- Prevention programs may be the most effective way to address paraphilic disorders.

Questions for Discussion

- Are you comfortable with the term *sexual variations*? If yes, why is it a good term for you? If no, which term do you like to describe "unusual" sexual behavior? Explain.

- Do you consider certain sexual behaviors to be "deviant," "abnormal," or "perverted?" If so, how did you come to believe this?

- From the types of paraphilias discussed in this chapter, do you find any of them to be repulsive or even "pathological?"

- Do you agree with the new *DSM-5* distinction between paraphilias, which are considered to be relatively harmless, and paraphilic disorders, which are considered harmful sexual behaviors? In your opinion, is this distinction a progression of the APA toward a greater acceptance of sexual variation? Explain.

- Should any sexual behaviors, such as pedophilia, be controlled? If no, why do you think certain sexual behaviors are labeled paraphilias?

Sex and the Internet

Paraphilias

The web is one resource for locating information about paraphilias. Go to the Google website (http://www.google.com) and type "paraphilias" in the Google Search box. As you can see, there are a wide range of sites posted. Look over the posted sites and answer the following questions:

- What types of websites are listed?

- Are the sites primarily from medical and academic organizations, individuals, or commercial groups?

- Are there sites for specific paraphilias?

- Which sites provide the most valuable information to you? Why?

- Did you learn anything new about paraphilias from the websites? If so, what?

- Do you believe that any of the sites contain inaccurate or harmful information? Explain.

Suggested Websites

AllPsych Online
http://allpsych.com/disorders/paraphilias
Offers information on numerous psychiatric disorders, including symptoms, etiology, treatment, and prognosis for paraphilias and sexual disorders.

Psychology Today
https://www.psychologytoday.com/us/conditions/paraphilias
Provides information on the APA's classification of paraphilias and paraphilic disorders.

WebMD
https://www.webmd.com/sexual_conditions/paraphilias
Describes common paraphilias and provides a search for paraphilia information.

Suggested Reading

Fedonoff, J. P. (2019). *The paraphilias: Changing suits in the evolution of sexual internet paradigms.* Oxford University Press. Examines current and past perspectives of current unconventional sexual interests with new ways to understand and provide assistance to people with paraphilias.

Frances, A. (2013). *Saving normal: An insider's revolt against out-of-control psychiatric diagnosis, DSM-5, big pharma and the medicalization of ordinary life.* William Morrow. The author presents a history of medical illness and an account of an explosion of psychiatric disorder in the

United States. He cautions the mislabeling and diagnosis of normal daily issues as mental illness.

Galon, R. (Ed.). (2016). *Practical guide to paraphilia and paraphilic behaviors*. Springer International. Written by experts, the chapters of the book discuss the ethical, legal, and cultural issues of paraphilic behaviors as defined by the *DSM-5*.

Greenberg, G. (2013). *The book of woe: The* DSM *and the unmaking of psychiatry*. Penguin Books. Psychotherapist Gary Greenberg details a critical historical analysis of the APA's *Diagnostic and Statistical Manual of Mental Disorders* with interviews of persons on both sides of the treacheries and valuable strengths of the *DSM*.

Kleinplatz, P. J., & Moser, C. (2006). *Sadomasochism: Powerful pleasures*. Harrington Park Press. Articles from leading experts discuss the results of research into practitioners' behaviors and perspectives and stresses greater tolerance and understanding of S&M.

Thorne, M. (2014). *Exploring BDSM: A workbook for couples (or more!) discovering kink*. Morgan Thorne. A workbook for couples describing different categories of kink with emphasis on effective communication in BDSM.

Valdez, N. (2010). *A little bit kinky: A couple's guide to rediscovering the thrill of sex*. Broadway Books. This book, for both men and women, provides ideas for the "kinky" side of sex, from the little bit kinky to the kinkiest behaviors.

chapter

11

Contraception and Abortion

Rafe Swan/Cultura/Getty Images

CHAPTER OUTLINE

TODAY, MORE THAN EVER BEFORE, we are aware of the impact of fertility on our own lives, as well as on the world. Reproduction, once considered strictly a personal matter, is now a subject of open debate and political action. Yet, regardless of our public views, we must each confront fertility on a personal level. In taking charge of our reproductive potential, we need to be informed about the availability and effectiveness of contraception, as well as ways to protect ourselves against sexually transmitted infections (STIs). But information is only part of the picture. We also need to understand our own personal needs, values, and habits, so that we can choose methods we will use consistently and effectively, thereby minimizing our risks.

In this chapter, we begin by examining the psychology of risk-taking and the role of individual responsibility in contraception. We then describe in detail the numerous contraceptive devices and techniques that are used today: methods of use, effectiveness rates, advantages, and possible problems. Finally, we look at abortion, its effect on individuals and society, and research issues.

● Risk and Responsibility

A typical American woman who wants to have two children spends about 3 years pregnant, postpartum, or attempting to become pregnant and about 30 years trying to avoid an **unintended pregnancy**, one that was either mistimed or unplanned (Guttmacher Institute, 2020.11a). This includes about 43 million women (70%) who are at risk of unintended pregnancy. During her lifetime, a woman's contraceptive needs will change; however the most important factor in her choice of a method of contraception will often be its effectiveness.

In the United States, nearly half (45% or 2.8 million) of the 6.1 million pregnancies each year are unintended. When rates include only those who are sexually active, women aged 15–19 have the highest unintended pregnancy rate of any age group (Guttmacher Institute, 2019.11a). Unintended pregnancy rates are also highest among low-income women, women aged 18–24, cohabiting women, and women of color. Forty-two percent of those who experience an unintended pregnancy choose to end their pregnancies with an abortion (Ireland, 2019).

The question often arises about the difference between contraception and birth control. Though often used interchangeably, birth control or family planning refers to the regulation of the number of children born through the deliberate control or prevention of conception, whereas **contraception** is the deliberate prevention of conception or impregnation by any of various drugs, techniques, or devices. This chapter will primarily use the term contraception to describe those methods of preventing conception that are currently available to men and women.

• FIGURE 1

Percentage of Women Aged 15–49 by Contraceptive Status: United States, 2015–2017.

Source: Daniels, K., & Abma, J. C. (2020). *Current contraceptive status among women aged 15–49: United States, 2017–2019.* NCHS Data Brief, 388.

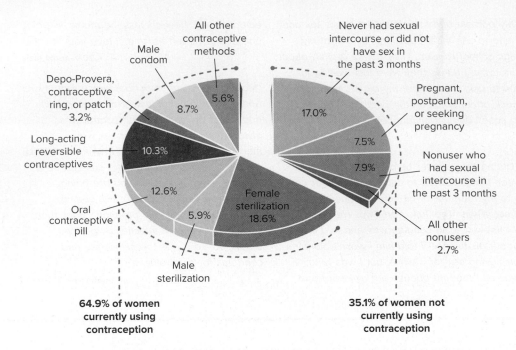

All other contraceptive methods 5.6%

Male condom 8.7%

Depo-Provera, contraceptive ring, or patch 3.2%

Long-acting reversible contraceptives 10.3%

Oral contraceptive pill 12.6%

Male sterilization 5.9%

Female sterilization 18.6%

Never had sexual intercourse or did not have sex in the past 3 months 17.0%

Pregnant, postpartum, or seeking pregnancy 7.5%

Nonuser who had sexual intercourse in the past 3 months 7.9%

All other nonusers 2.7%

64.9% of women currently using contraception

35.1% of women not currently using contraception

Notes: Percentages may not add to 100 due to rounding. Women currently using more than one method are classified according to the most effective method they are using. Long-acting reversible contraceptives include contraceptive implants and intrauterine devices.

Because the gap between first sexual intercourse and first birth is nearly 10 years and the potential for getting pregnant is so high for a sexually active, childbearing-age couple, it would seem reasonable that sexually active couples would use contraception to avoid unintended pregnancy. Unfortunately, all too often, this is not the case. In 2015–2017, approximately 65% of sexually active women aged 15–44 were using some type of contraceptive method, while 35% were sterile, pregnant, postpartum and breastfeeding, trying to become pregnant, or abstinent (Daniels & Abma, 2020) (see Figure 1). Not surprisingly, the nonusers of contraception accounted for about half of unintended pregnancies; those who used contraception reported that the method either failed or was not used correctly or consistently (see Figure 2).

Numerous studies have indicated that the most consistent users of contraception are those who explicitly communicate about the subject. People at greatest risk for not using contraceptives are under age 20, in casual dating relationships, and infrequently discuss contraception with their partners or others.

Women, Men, and Contraception: Who Is Responsible?

If oral contraceptives for men became available, how many women would trust their partner to use them? Because women bear children and have most of the responsibility for raising them, women often have a greater interest than their partners in controlling their fertility.

Also, it is generally easier to keep one egg from being fertilized once a month than to stop millions of sperm during each episode of intercourse. For these and other reasons, contraception has traditionally been seen as the woman's responsibility. The responsibility for preventing pregnancy, sometimes referred to as "fertility work," falls almost exclusively upon women. It involves not only the use of contraception, including experiencing its side effects, but also the time, attention, expense, and stress that this task involves. Some suggest this may be part of a broader pattern of women assuming responsibility for health decisions within heterosexual couples (Kimport, 2018). Shifts in behaviors and practices (e.g., when appropriate, including men in contraceptive counseling, considering long-acting contraception, etc.) can reduce the amount of time, attention, and stress that women often undertake to prevent an unintended pregnancy. Because decisions related to contraceptive use are often made by individuals in the

• FIGURE 2

Pregnancies, by Intention Status.

Nearly half of the 6.1 million pregnancies in the United States each year are unwanted or wanted later. Most unintended pregnancies are attributable to nonuse, ambivalence, fear of side effects, or inconsistent or incorrect use of contraceptives.

Source: Guttmacher Institute. (2019.11a). Unintended pregnancies in the United States.

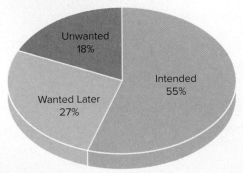

Unwanted 18%

Wanted Later 27%

Intended 55%

think about it

Factors that Influence College Students' Contraceptive Use

There's no doubt that college students have a strong desire to prevent an unintended pregnancy in order to achieve their academic and professional goals. With the average age at first vaginal intercourse being 17 and the average age at first marriage between 27 and 29, the college years are when most individuals are sexually active and unmarried. It's also a time when individuals establish romantic and sexual relationships that will influence and shape their later sexual experiences.

Across colleges, kissing, touching, performing and receiving oral sex and penetrative sex has increased, while contraceptive use and condom use in particular have decreased (Lefkowitz et al., 2019). (See Figure 3 below for methods of contraceptives used by college students.) In a sample of 730 racially and ethnically diverse college students, researchers found that students were more likely to engage in a variety of sexual behaviors and were less likely to use condoms in semesters when they were in serious relationships. In fact, relationship factors tend to guide students' decisions around contraceptive use. At the same time, it may be surprising to learn that many students do not consider themselves to be at risk of pregnancy, despite reporting high rates of unprotected sex. Regarding contraceptive use, rates of use were lower when students reported that they were in a serious romantic relationship. This was particularly true for men. Condom use also decreased for both men and women in semesters they were in serious relationships. Consistent use of any form of contraception did not increase with age, as might be expected with growing maturity and experience. Instead, about 85% of first-semester students used a form of contraception when engaging in penetrative sex as compared to about 77% of students in their senior year (Lefkowitz et al., 2019). While it is common, appropriate, and healthy to express interest in and explore sexuality during young adulthood (Tolman & McClelland, 2011), it's important that students be aware that they may also be potentially at risk for life-altering health risks if they do not take precautions.

Lack of information coupled with a sense of invulnerability often prevents students from using effective and consistent contraception (Cabral et al., 2018). When 57 community college students in California were asked specific questions about their contraceptive experiences, pregnancy intentions, and risks, and how these factors related to their educational goals, they reported that contraceptive knowledge, particularly around the effectiveness of a method and fears about contraception, were the most significant barriers to preventing pregnancy. Few students in this study were aware of methods other than condoms or the pill, and when discussing IUDs or implants, many held negative views and incorrect beliefs about them. Students also overestimated the effectiveness of their birth control method, even when they were using it inconsistently or believed that having unprotected sex would not lead to pregnancy. The researchers concluded that in order to help support college students make informed decisions about their reproductive health, they need medically accurate information and resources as well as affordable and available access to contraception (Cabral et al., 2018).

Think Critically

1. What, if anything, surprised you about contraceptive use among college students?

2. Do you agree with the findings that contraceptive use is not affected by the age of the student? Do you see any differences in contraceptive use by gender?

3. How might an unintended pregnancy affect your future plans? If you are sexually active and do not wish to have a child now, what measures are you taking to prevent that from happening?

context of a relationship, partners and relationship factors usually influence the use of specific methods (Harvey et al., 2018). Perceived vulnerability, including that related to HIV/STIs and pregnancy, along with confidence in their ability to use a method was found to increase the use of a method of contraception. (See Think About It: "Factors that Influence Students' Contraceptive Use.")

Additionally, the more education couples have, the more likely they are to talk about and utilize family planning. Education appears to instill confidence in both partners to discuss intended family size and contraception methods. Regardless of the motive or level of education, society no longer views the responsibility for contraception to lie solely with women. Rather, the majority of men as well as women perceive that there is gender equality in sexual decision making and equal responsibility for decisions about contraception. Overall, 60% of men need family planning services, the greatest percent being among those who are young

• FIGURE 3

Percentage of U.S. College Students That Used Select Methods of Contraception, 2019*.

Source: Statistica. (2020). Birth control methods used by U.S. college students as of Fall 2019.

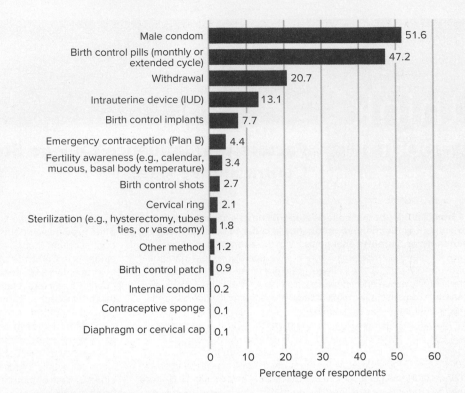

*Results included 17,549 college students, ages 18+, who responded to the question: "Please indicate which of the following method(s) you or your partner used to prevent pregnancy the last time you had vaginal intercourse. (Please select ALL that apply) (Only includes students who used a method of pregnancy prevention the last time hey had vaginal intercourse)."

and unmarried (Marcell et al., 2016). Though most of these men in need of family planning had access to care, few reported receiving family planning services (<19%), consistently used condoms (26%), or had partners who consistently used contraception (41%). Though we know that condoms can help prevent pregnancy and the spread of sexually transmitted infections (STIs), only about one third of Americans use them (Reinberg, 2017). Male methods account for approximately 20% of all reversible contraceptive use (Guttmacher Institute, 2020.11a). These methods, the most common of which are the male condom and withdrawal, may be effective when used correctly and consistently. As opposed to an irreversible method, such as a vasectomy, reversible methods of contraception can be changed or stopped at any time.

In addition to using a condom, a man can take contraceptive responsibility by: (1) being sexual without intercourse; (2) helping pay doctor or clinic bills and sharing the cost of pills, injections, or other contraception methods; (3) when appropriate, checking on supplies, helping keep track of his partner's menstrual cycle, and helping her with her part in the birth control routine; and (4) in certain circumstances like a long-term relationship, if no or no more children are planned, having a vasectomy.

Access to Contraception

"When the history of our civilization is written, it will be a biological history, and Margaret Sanger will be its heroine."

—H. G. Wells (1866–1946)

Reproductive health care reflects a deep commitment to supporting the family and makes a significant and necessary contribution to humankind. Margaret Sanger, widely regarded as the founder of the modern birth control movement, first acknowledged this when, in 1915, she opened an illegal clinic where women could obtain and learn to use the diaphragms she had shipped from Europe. Sanger believed that in order for women to lead healthier lives, they needed to be able to determine when to have children. Her advocacy also took the form of published birth control information, for which she was soon arraigned for violating the

Comstock Laws, which made it a crime to sell or distribute materials that could be used for contraception or abortion. Later, in 1921, she founded the American Birth Control League, which we now know as Planned Parenthood Federation of America. It wasn't, however, until 1960 that the first birth control pills entered the U.S. marketplace. Fertility control, rather than abstinence, proved to be a major shift in the way women and some men regarded their sexuality and sexual expression.

Disparities in unintended pregnancy rates and access to health services are among the factors that are influenced by the **social determinants of health**, the social and economic conditions that impact an individual's and a group's health status. Barriers to use of family planning services include cost of services, limited access to publicly funded services and insurance coverage, inconvenient family planning clinic locations and hours, lack of awareness of services among hard-to-reach populations, no or limited transportation, inadequate services for men, and lack of youth-friendly services. Because of these barriers, women with low levels of education and income, uninsured women, Latinx women, and non-Hispanic Black women are less likely than others to access family planning and related health care services (National Family Planning & Reproductive Health Association, 2020). Originally promoted in the United States over a decade ago by women of color, **reproductive justice** is a concept that links reproductive rights with social justice and describes the complete physical, mental, spiritual, political, social, and economic well-being of a person. It also takes into consideration a broad array of factors that affect a person's ability to have or not have and/or raise children and goes to the fundamental question of whether we believe that all people deserve equal access and opportunity.

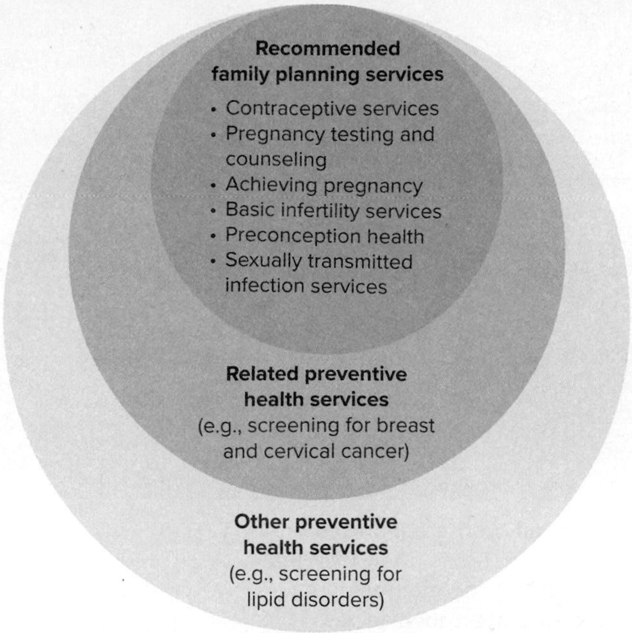

Currently, the backbone of the nation's publicly funded family planning efforts is the Title X Family Planning Program, the only federal grant program devoted solely to providing individuals with comprehensive family planning and related preventive health services. Title X offers and subsidizes services, supplies, and information, maintains the national network of family planning centers, and sets the standards for the provision of family planning services. For every $1.00 invested in helping women avoid unintended pregnancies, $7.09 is saved in Medicaid expenditures (Guttmacher Institute, 2016). By law, priority is given to low-income and uninsured individuals. Although safety-net health centers, such as those supported by Title X, typically focus on serving women, most also offer services to men, including STI diagnosis and treatment as well as exams and condoms. (See Figure 4 for recommended services.)

The Title X package of care overlaps with services provided by the Affordable Care Act's (ACA) preventive services by expanding eligibility for private and public programs and guaranteeing contraceptive coverage without co-pays. More than 4 million people each year, 40% of whom are served by Planned Parenthood, rely on federal Title X funding for contraception and other essential health care (Planned Parenthood, 2020.11a). However, in 2019, Planned Parenthood withdrew from the federal family planning program rather than comply with a new rule that forbids referrals to doctors who perform abortions (Belluck, 2019). The rule states that while clinics accepting Title X funds may continue to talk to patients about abortion, they may not refer women to an abortion provider or suggest where to obtain an abortion. They may, however, provide a referral for abortion in the event of an emergency medical situation. A current proposal to reinstate the prior regulations will, if passed, ensure access to all family planning services.

Until 2020, under the Affordable Care Act, employers were required to provide their employees with birth control coverage with only a few permitted exemptions. However, a U.S. Supreme Court ruling in July 2020 allows any employer to drop contraceptive coverage without penalty if they have a religious or moral objection (Liptak, 2020).

Recommended family planning services

- Contraceptive services
- Pregnancy testing and counseling
- Achieving pregnancy
- Basic infertility services
- Preconception health
- Sexually transmitted infection services

Related preventive health services
(e.g., screening for breast and cervical cancer)

Other preventive health services
(e.g., screening for lipid disorders)

• **FIGURE 4**

Recommended Family Planning and Related Preventive Health Services.

Source: Gavin, L., et al. (2014). Providing quality family planning services: Recommendations of CDC and the U.S. Office of Population Affairs. *Morbidity and Mortality Weekly Report, 63*(RR-4), 1–54.

Nearly all teen pregnancies are unplanned. Teens often lack the information and methods they need to protect themselves.

Katarzyna Bialasiewicz/Getty Images

Planning contraception requires us to acknowledge our sexuality. One way a person or couple can reduce their risk of unintended pregnancy is by visiting a family planning clinic.

B. Boissonnet/BSIP/AGE Fotostock

Adolescents and Contraception On average, young people in the United States have sexual intercourse for the first time at about age 18 but typically do not marry until their late-20s. During this decade or longer, they may be at increased risk for unintended pregnancy and STIs. In 2018, just under 180,000 infants were born to teens ages 15–19 years old (WebMD, 2020.11a). However, since peaking in the early 1990s, the teen birth rate has fallen 70% overall and 7% in 2019. This decline occurred among all racial/ethnic groups. Despite significant reductions, the teen birth rate is still roughly twice as high among Latinx teens (29 births per 1,000) and African American teens (28 births per 1,000) as compared with non-Hispanic white teens (13 births per 1,000). Rates are even higher among young people living in poverty, living in foster care, or facing persistent racism and discrimination (Child Trends, 2019).

Declines in the majority of unintended pregnancy rates have, to a great extent, been attributed to improvements in contraceptive use (Guttmacher Institute, 2016.11). Access to and use of contraceptive services by teens are buoyed by the availability of publicly supported family planning centers. While school-based health centers are an important source of sexual and reproductive health services for students, only a minority of these centers dispense contraceptives. Despite the gains made in the reduction of unplanned pregnancies among teens, the U.S. teen pregnancy rate continues to be one of the highest in the developed world and substantially higher than other western industrialized nations.

● Methods of Contraception

The methods we use to prevent pregnancy or its progress vary widely. Thus, the best method of contraception is one that will be used consistently and correctly. Hopefully, this method is also one that is safe, available, and in harmony with one's preferences, fears, and expectations.

As stated earlier, contraception is the deliberate prevention of conception or impregnation by any drug, technique, or device. This is done in a variety of ways, including: (1) barrier methods, such as condoms and diaphragms, which place a physical barrier between the sperm and the egg; (2) spermicides, which kill the sperm before they can get to the egg; (3) hormonal methods, such as the pill, the shot, the patch, the implant, and the ring, which inhibit the release of the oocyte from the ovary; and (4) intrauterine devices, which prevent the sperm from fertilizing the egg.

Choosing a Method

To be fully responsible in using a contraceptive, individuals must know what options they have, how reliable these methods are, and what advantages and disadvantages including possible side effects each has. Thus, it is important to be aware of both personal health issues and the specifics of the methods themselves. (Table 1 shows the failure rates of contraceptives by perfect and typical use.)

Most women who are not currently using contraception go to a clinic or doctor's office knowing exactly what method they want, others may purchase a product over the counter. However, many are not aware of other options available to them. In some instances, the method they think they want may not be medically appropriate or may not be one they will use correctly and consistently. Knowing the facts about the methods gives you a solid basis from which to make decisions, as well as more security once you reach a decision.

TABLE 1 ● Percent of Women Who Will Become Pregnant Over One Year of Use of Contraceptives

Method	Typical use*	Perfect use*
Implant	0.1	0.1
Vasectomy (male sterilization)	0.15	0.1
Intrauterine device (IUD)		
Hormone-releasing	0.1–0.4	0.1–0.3
Copper-T	0.8	0.6
Tubal (female) sterilization	0.5	0.5
Injectable	4	0.2
Pill (combined & progestin-only)	7	0.3
Vaginal ring	7	0.3
Patch	7	0.3
Male condom	13	2
Sponge (for women who have not given birth)	14	9
Fertility awareness methods***	2–34	<1–12
Internal (female) condom	21	5
Withdrawal	20	4
Diaphragm (with spermicide)	17	16
Spermicides	21	16
Sponge (for women who have given birth)	27	20
No method	85	85

*"Perfect use" denotes effectiveness among couples who use the method both consistently and correctly; "Typical use" refers to effectiveness experienced among all couples who use the method (including inconsistent and incorrect use).

***Includes cervical mucus methods, body temperature methods, and periodic abstinence.

Source: Guttmacher Institute. (2020.11b). Contraceptive effectiveness in the United States.

To help you make an informed decision about which method of birth control is medically appropriate and will be used every time, consider these questions (Hatcher et al., 2011):

- Do you have any particular preferences or biases related to birth control?
- Do you know the advantages and disadvantages of each of the contraceptive methods?
- How convenient and easy is it to use this method?
- If you or your partner is at risk, does this method protect against STIs, including HIV?
- What are the effects of this method on menses?
- Is it important that you negotiate with your partner to help determine the method?
- What other influences such as religion, privacy, past experience, friends' advice, access, cost, and frequency of intercourse might affect your decision?
- Have you discussed potential methods with your health care practitioner?

Knowledge and familiarity about contraceptive methods are strong determinants of use. Other factors that increase the usage of a contraceptive method include having a higher income, being married, being religious, and cohabiting. The proportion of at-risk women who are not using a method is highest among 15- to 19-year-olds and lowest among women ages 40–44. The pill remains one of the most popular methods of birth control for women, along with female sterilization and male condoms (Guttmacher Institute, 2020.11c).

Technology has expanded the ways in which women can track their periods, locate and assess contraceptives, and accept reminders about when to utilize a device all in a manner that is personal and easy-to-use. Though apps can be helpful in navigating the various topics and decisions related to contraception and safer sex, they should not replace a discussion with a doctor or professional medical advisor.

In the following discussion of method effectiveness, the term **contraceptive failure** is a measure of a woman's probability of becoming pregnant during typical and perfect use of a method within a given period, usually the first 12 months of use. It is important to distinguish between typical use and perfect use of a contraceptive method, and the failure rates associated with each. Typical use refers to the way a method is actually used by women and their partners, including inconsistent or incorrect use, or nonuse among individuals who report using it. Perfect use of a method refers to women and their partners following the exact directions for use and are rates estimated during clinical trials. Typical use is the more significant number to use when considering a method of contraception. Of those who use contraceptives consistently and correctly throughout the course of a year, only 5% become pregnant. This is in contrast to couples who do not use any method of contraception who have an approximately 85% chance of experiencing a pregnancy over the course of a year (Guttmacher Institute, 2020.11a). (For why some take risks with contraception, see Think About It: "Risky Business: Why Couples Fail to Use Contraception.")

Sexual Abstinence

Before we begin our discussion of devices and techniques for preventing conception, we must acknowledge the oldest and most reliable birth control method of all: abstinence. There is a wide variety of opinions about what constitutes sexual activity. However, from a family planning perspective, **abstinence** is the absence of genital contact that could lead to a pregnancy. The term "celibacy" is sometimes used interchangeably with "abstinence." We prefer "abstinence" because "celibacy" often implies the avoidance of *all* forms of sexual activity and, often, a commitment to maintain a nonsexual life.

Individuals who choose not to have intercourse are still free to express affection and to give and receive sexual pleasure if they so desire, including talking, hugging, massaging, kissing, petting, and manually and orally stimulating the genitals. Those who choose abstinence from sexual intercourse as their method of birth control need to communicate this clearly to their partners. They should also be informed about other forms of contraception. And in the event that either partner experiences a spontaneous change of mind, it would be wise to have a condom handy if both persons consent.

Withdrawal (Coitus Interruptus)

Often dismissed from lists of contraceptive methods, **withdrawal**, otherwise called coitus interruptus, is a traditional family planning method in which the man completely removes his penis from the vagina and away from the external genitalia of the female partner before he ejaculates. This prevents sperm from entering the woman's vagina and impregnating an egg. Withdrawal is practiced the world over, both as a sole or additional method of birth control. The percentage of contraceptive users who use withdrawal as a contraceptive method is 12% (Fu et al., 2019).

Who relies on withdrawal as a method of birth control? The use of withdrawal is related to situational and relational contexts, such as when it is used during transitions between contraceptive methods and when other methods are not desired (Arteaga & Gomez, 2016). Additionally, many rely on the withdrawal method to increase intimacy with their partners because they feel condoms are no longer in the context of their monogamous relationship or to fulfill their partner's preference to increase sexual pleasure.

Given the relatively high failure rate (20% with typical use), the withdrawal method might be appropriate for couples who are highly motivated to avoid pregnancy and able to use the method effectively. In fact, among those women and couples who reported using withdrawal in combination or in rotation with condoms may be more vigilant about pregnancy prevention than those using other methods of contraception (Jones et al., 2014). Those with religious or philosophical reasons for not using other methods of contraception, those who need contraception immediately or temporarily until the start of another method, or are having sexual intercourse infrequently seemed to be inclined to use it. If practiced correctly, withdrawal does not affect breastfeeding, is always available, involves no economic cost or use of chemicals or hormones, and has no known health risks. It does not protect against STIs.

think
about it

Risky Business: Why Couples Fail to Use Contraception

Most persons having sexual intercourse know they are taking a chance of getting pregnant when they don't use contraception. But the more frequently a person takes chances with unprotected intercourse without resultant pregnancy, the more likely they are to do so again. Eventually, the woman or couple will feel almost magically invulnerable to pregnancy. Each time they are lucky, their risk taking is reinforced.

The consequences of an unintended pregnancy—economic hardships, adoption, or abortion—may be overwhelming. So why do people take chances in the first place? Lack of knowledge, misperceptions, and exaggerated concerns about the safety of contraceptive methods are among the barriers to contraceptive use (ACOG, 2017.11a). Thus, people often underestimate how easy it is to get pregnant, or they may not know how to use a contraceptive method correctly. Additionally, talking about or using some types of contraception can be uncomfortable and can interrupt spontaneity.

Perceived Costs of Contraceptive Planning

One reason people avoid taking steps to prevent pregnancy is that they don't want to acknowledge their own sexuality. Acknowledging our sexuality is not necessarily easy, for it may be accompanied by feelings of guilt, conflict, and shame.

Planning contraception requires us to acknowledge not only that we are sexual but also that we plan to be sexually active. Without such planning, individuals can pretend that their sexual intercourse "just happens"—when a moment of passion occurs, when they have been drinking, or when there is a full moon—even though it may happen frequently.

Another reason people don't use contraception is difficulty in obtaining it (ACOG, 2017.11a). It is often embarrassing for sexually inexperienced people to be seen in contexts that identify them as sexual beings. The cost of contraceptives is also a problem for some. Although free or low-cost contraceptives may still be obtained through family planning clinics or other agencies, people may have transportation or work considerations that keep them away. Since the start of the COVID-19 pandemic, social support systems and financial security for those seeking contraceptive services have been rapidly upended. Barriers including access to contraception, travel restrictions, quarantine measures, caregiving responsibilities, fear of exposure to the virus, and fewer appointments due to limited provider and staff availability reduce access to contraception and people's ability to obtain a first-trimester abortion (Ruggiero et al., 2020). Additionally, since the start of the pandemic, a number of states have attempted to halt abortion services by deeming them "non-essential" or "elective" procedures. Accessing health care has become a particular challenge for the underserved population, including individuals with disabilities, minors, undocumented people, those experiencing intimate partner violence, and rural populations.

Because it is the woman who gets pregnant, men may be unaware of their responsibility or downplay of their role in conception (WebMD, 1999). However, with the popularity of the condom, responsibility has become more balanced especially if women insist on it. Nevertheless some males, especially adolescents, often lack the awareness that supports contraceptive planning.

Many people, especially women using the pill, practice birth control consistently and effectively within an ongoing relationship but may give up their contraceptive practices if the relationship breaks up. When individuals begin a new relationship, they may not use contraception, because the relationship has not yet become established. They do not expect to have sexual intercourse or to have it often, so they are willing to take chances.

How methods influence the user's sexual experiences and family planning preferences, otherwise referred to as sexual acceptability, can have a significant impact on whether and how contraception is used (Higgins & Smith, 2016). For example, using a condom may destroy sexual spontaneity, leading to what some refer to as a pleasure deficit. For those who justify their sexual behavior by romantic impulsiveness, using these devices seems cold and mechanical.

Anticipated Benefits of Pregnancy

Ambivalence about pregnancy is a powerful incentive *not* to use contraception (Cutler et al., 2018). For many people, being pregnant proves that a woman is indeed feminine on the most fundamental biological level. Getting a woman pregnant provides similar proof of masculinity for some men.

Pregnancy also proves beyond any doubt that a person is fertile. Many have lingering doubts about whether they can have children. This is especially true for partners who have used contraception for a long time, but it is also true for those who take chances.

Another anticipated benefit of pregnancy is that it requires the partners to define their relationship and level of commitment to each other. It is a form of testing, albeit often an unconscious one. Many men and women unconsciously expect their partners to be pleased, but this is not always the reaction they get.

Think Critically

1. If sexually active, do you take risks relative to not adequately protecting yourself or your partner from conception? If so, what kinds? Why?
2. When do you believe a person is more inclined to take sexual risks?
3. Are there other reasons why couples fail to use contraception that are not listed here? If so, what are they?
4. What is a good way to initiate a discussion about contraception with a partner?

Hormonal Methods

In addition to the tried-and-true birth control pill, several varieties of hormonal contraception are available. These include a pill that causes menstrual suppression, a birth control shot, a patch, a vaginal ring, and an implant.

The Pill Oral contraceptives (OCs), popularly called "the pill," are the most widely used form of reversible contraception in the United States, accounting for 14% of all contraceptives used (Daniels & Abma, 2020). The pill is actually a series of pills (various numbers to a package) containing synthetic estrogen and/or progesterone that regulate egg production and the menstrual cycle. When taken for birth control, oral contraceptives accomplish some or all of the following:

- Suppresses ovulation 90–95% of the time
- Thickens cervical mucus thereby preventing sperm penetration into the woman's upper genital tract
- Thins the lining of the uterus to inhibit implantation of the fertilized ovum
- Slows the rate of ovum transport
- Disrupts transport of the fertilized egg
- Inhibits capacitation of the sperm, which limits the sperm's ability to fertilize the egg

The pill produces basically the same chemical conditions that would exist in a woman's body if she were pregnant.

Types and Usage In most states, oral contraceptives must still be prescribed by a physician or family planning clinic. However, in a few states, hormonal birth control can be purchased from a pharmacist without a doctor's prescription. Several other states have proposed similar legislation. The American College of Obstetrics and Gynecology (2019.11) supports over-the-counter access to oral contraceptives as a potential way to improve access to and use of contraceptives and decrease unintended pregnancy rates.

The most commonly prescribed birth control pills are the combination pills, which contain a fairly standard amount of estrogen (usually about 35 micrograms) and different amounts of progestin, a synthetic form of progesterone, according to the pill type. In the triphasic pill, the amount of progestin is altered during the cycle, purportedly to approximate the normal hormonal pattern. Progestin-only pills (POPs), sometimes called "minipills," contain the hormone progestin. The minipill is considered slightly less effective than the combination pill, and it must be taken with precise, unfailing regularity to be effective. Taken at the same time each day, with no hormone-free days, the minipill provides an alternative to those who cannot safely take estrogen. These include women who are breastfeeding, have had weight-loss (bariatric) surgery, have liver disease, or have had breast cancer.

A woman can begin taking oral contraceptives on the same day as she obtains her pills, provided she is not pregnant and not in need of emergency contraception. Women may prefer this "quick start" practice because other approaches generally leave a time gap between the time the pills are prescribed and the time one starts taking them. If a woman starts taking the pill within 7 days after starting her period, she is protected against pregnancy immediately.

The pill is considered among the most effective birth control methods available when used correctly. But the pill is *not* effective when taken inconsistently. It must be taken every day, as close as possible to the same time each day. If one pill is missed (i.e., taken after an interval of more than 24 hours or not at all), it should be taken as soon as the woman remembers, and the next one taken on schedule. If two pills are missed, the method cannot be relied on, and an additional form of contraception should be used for the rest of the cycle.

A shift to continuous use of oral contraceptives acknowledges a little-known fact: Women don't need to have monthly periods. Continuous use of oral contraceptives provides women with a safe, acceptable, and effective form of contraception (Mayo Clinic, 2020.11a). The use of these regimens provides women with more options and almost certainly improves the acceptability and efficacy of hormonal contraception, including the option of not having a period.

Although oral contraceptives are effective in preventing pregnancy, they do not provide protection against STIs, including HIV infection.

Don Farrall/Getty Images

Since none of the hormonal methods of birth control offer protection against STIs, women on the pill should consider the additional use of a condom, if she is not in an exclusive relationship or is unsure of her partner's STI status.

Effectiveness   Oral contraceptives are more than 99.7% effective if used correctly. The typical-use rate is 91%.

Advantages   The benefits of hormonal methods generally far outweigh any significant negative effects. Pills are easy to take. They are dependable. No applications or interruptions are necessary before or during intercourse. In fact, millions of women use the pill with moderate to high degrees of satisfaction. For many women, if personal health or family history does not contraindicate it, the pill is both effective and safe. Some women experience benefits such as more regular or reduced menstrual flow, less menstrual cramping, and relief from premenstrual syndrome (Planned Parenthood, 2020.11b). The pill may offer some protection against bone thinning and ovarian and endometrial cancer, may reduce or help prevent acne, and may decrease the risk of benign breast conditions and iron deficiency anemia. In addition, research has shown that women on the birth control pill are protected from ovarian cancer, even decades after they stop taking it. In fact, 14% of women use oral contraceptives for non-contraceptive reasons (Kaiser Family Foundation, 2019.11a).

Disadvantages   Similar to other medications, the birth control pill can have side effects. Most of these go away after 2 or 3 months. If the side effects are still bothersome after 3 months, changing the brand of pill or starting a new method of contraception may be recommended. It's important, however, to continue to take the pill until another method is used or a woman will be at risk of pregnancy.

"Literature is mostly about sex and not much about having children; life is the other way round."

—David Lodge (1921–2003)

The hormones in the pill can cause spotting, breast tenderness, nausea or vomiting, or bleeding between periods (most often with progestin-only or minipills). They can also change a woman's level of sexual desire. Certain women react unfavorably to the pill because of existing health factors or extra sensitivity to female hormones. Women who are over 35 and smoke shouldn't use any kind of contraception that contains the hormone estrogen because it can increase the risk of stroke. If she smokes, however, she can use progestin-only or minipills. While there is no age limit on any contraceptive option, it's clear that some kinds are more appropriate than others based on a woman's health profile and individual circumstances. Women who should avoid using combination pills include those with a history of high cholesterol, certain inherited blood clotting disorders or vein inflammation, uncontrolled high blood pressure, breast cancer, heart attack, stroke, angina, or other serious heart problems, migraine headaches with aura, or liver disease.

The pill also creates certain health risks, but to what extent is a matter of controversy. Though the pill has been studied extensively and is very safe, in rare instances hormonal methods can lead to serious problems. Women who take the pill may have a rare but dangerous risk of blood clots.

Certain medications may react differently or unfavorably with the pill, either diminishing in their therapeutic effect or interfering with oral contraceptive effectiveness. Thus, it is important to check with a doctor before starting any new prescriptions if a woman is taking the pill.

A woman should see a doctor or nurse immediately if she has any of the following symptoms: sudden back/jaw pain along with nausea, sweating, or trouble breathing; chest pain or discomfort; achy soreness in the leg; trouble breathing; severe pain in the stomach; sudden, very bad headache or aura (flashing light); or yellowing of the skin or eyes. Since the introduction of the pill 60 years ago, questions about its effects on women's sexual functioning remain unanswered. It is widely recognized that the mechanisms involving sexual difficulties are complex and involve psychosocial, relational, and cultural factors as well as hormonal influences (Graham, 2019). One of the most consistent findings regarding the link between sexual functioning and oral contraceptives has been the variability in women's experiences, with some showing improved sexual functioning while others indicating adverse or no changes. A comprehensive review of the literature found that a minority of women experience a change in sexual functioning related to general sexual response, desire, lubrication, orgasm, and relationship satisfaction (Both et al., 2019). Women who experience side effects should be aware that there are various formulations available and discuss this option and any other concerns she may have with her health care provider.

Certain other factors may need to be considered in determining if oral contraceptives are appropriate for a woman. Since it is possible to get pregnant again shortly after a pregnancy or delivery, birth control needs to be considered. Since combination pills can reduce the amount and quality of breast milk in the first 3 weeks of breastfeeding, a woman should wait at least 3 weeks after giving birth to start using combination pills. The breast milk will contain traces of the pill's hormones that are unlikely to have any effect on the baby. Progestin-only pills, or minipills, however, are safe to use while breastfeeding, typically don't have any effect on how much milk a woman produces, and won't harm a baby (Planned Parenthood, 2020.11b).

Once a woman stops taking the pill, her menstrual cycle will usually resume within 2 months, though it may take several more months before it becomes regular.

Birth Control Shot (Depo-Provera) The **birth control shot**, known by the brand name Depo-Provera (DMPA), is an injection of the hormone progestin that is used to prevent pregnancy for 13 weeks. Thus, a woman needs to get a shot every 12–13 weeks. Some women may be able to get a supply of shots from a health center and give it to herself. The progestin works by stopping ovulation and thickening the cervical mucus, which keeps sperm from reaching the eggs (Planned Parenthood, 2020.11c). When DMPA is given within 7 days of the start of a woman's menstrual period, the drug is effective immediately. Otherwise, she needs to use another form of contraception (e.g., the condom) for the first week after getting the shot. If the shot is given within 5 days after a miscarriage or an abortion, or within 3 weeks after giving birth, a woman is protected from pregnancy immediately. Most women can use the birth control shot safely; however, risks and side effects are similar to those of the pill. Irregular bleeding is the most common side effect, especially in the first 6–12 months of use. Additionally, half of those using the shot will stop having periods completely. This side effect is very common and may cause some women who are not having periods to worry that they are pregnant. When the shot is used correctly, it is very effective. There is no way to stop the side effects of DMPA; they may continue for 12–14 weeks after the shot. Because it can take 6 to 10 months to become pregnant following the last shot, DMPA is not a good birth control method for those desiring an immediate pregnancy. It is safe to use DMPA while breastfeeding.

Effectiveness The perfect-use effectiveness rate is 99.8%, while the typical-use rate is slightly less at 94%.

Advantages Because DMPA injections contain no estrogen, they do not appear to cause the rare but potentially serious problems associated with estrogen. Additionally, DMPA is highly effective for 3 months and causes women to have very light or missed periods (women vary in their reactions to this). DMPA can also be a good choice for women who are breastfeeding. The shot may also ease cramps and premenstrual syndrome, and protect a woman from certain health conditions, including cancer of the uterus and anemia.

Disadvantages Menstrual cycle disturbances may occur, including unpredictable or prolonged episodes of bleeding or spotting, temporary weight gain, and reversible decrease in bone density. As a result of these, the injectable has the highest discontinuation rate among contraceptives used in the United States (Kaiser Family Foundation, 2020.11).

Women who have had breast cancer should not use the shot. Serious health problems are rarely associated with DMPA use; however, if a woman develops very painful headaches, heavy bleeding, serious depression, severe lower abdominal pain (may be a sign of pregnancy), or pus or pain at the site of the injection, she should see her physician. Additionally, the shot may cause hair loss, nausea, weight gain, and breast tenderness. Because DMPA lowers estrogen levels, it may cause women to lose calcium stored in their bones, causing temporary bone thinning, which will abate once a woman stops taking the shot. A woman can protect her bones by exercising regularly and getting extra calcium and vitamin D through diet or supplements.

Birth Control Patch   The **birth control patch**, known as Xulane in the United States, is a thin, beige, plastic transdermal reversible method of contraception that releases synthetic estrogen and progestin to protect against pregnancy for 1 month (Planned Parenthood, 2020.11d). Each week for three consecutive weeks, one patch is removed and a new one is placed on the stomach, buttocks, upper arm, or back. This is followed by a patch-free week, when menstruation occurs. The combination of hormones works the same way that oral contraceptives do. The patch is most effective when it is changed on the same day of the week for three consecutive weeks. Pregnancy can happen if an error is made in using the patch, especially if it becomes loose for longer than 24 hours, falls off, or if the same patch is left on for more than 1 week.

If the patch has partially or completely detached for less than 3 days, the woman should try to reapply it; however, if it does not stick well, a replacement should be applied. If a woman applies the patch late during week 1, she should apply a new patch as soon as she remembers. This becomes her new patch "change day." A backup method, such as a condom, should be used for 7 days after the patch is applied. If vaginal intercourse occurs without a backup method, emergency contraception may be used up to 5 days after unprotected intercourse.

Some medications or supplements can make the patch less effective, including specific antibiotics (ask your doctor about this), the antifungal griseofulvin, certain HIV medications, some anti-seizure medicines, and the herb St. John's Wort.

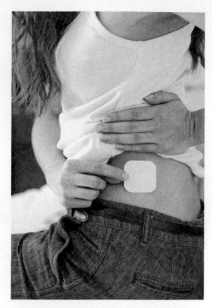

The birth control patch, prescribed by a physician, protects against pregnancy for 1 month.

Image Point Fr/Shutterstock

Effectiveness   Overall, contraceptive efficacy of the patch is similar to that of oral contraceptives; if used perfectly, the patch is more than 99% effective. Typical use results in a success rate of 91%.

Advantages   Like those who take oral contraceptives, many women who use the patch report the same benefits, including more-regular, lighter, and shorter periods. It may also help reduce or help prevent acne, bone thinning, cysts on the breasts and ovaries, ectopic pregnancy, endometrial and ovarian cancers, serious infections of the reproductive tract, iron deficiency, pelvic inflammatory disease, and PMS. Furthermore, a woman's ability to become pregnant returns quickly when the patch is discontinued. The patch is safe, simple, and convenient, and it does not interfere with sex. Additionally, a woman does not have to remember to take a pill each day.

Disadvantages   The most common side effects reported by users of the patch include spotting or bleeding between periods, mild skin reactions, breast tenderness usually in the first one or two menstrual cycles following its first application, headaches, bloating between periods, tender breasts, headaches, and nausea. The risk of stroke or heart attack is similar to that of combined oral contraceptives.

The Vaginal Ring   A **vaginal ring**, commonly referred to as the birth control ring, is a form of reversible, hormonal birth control (Planned Parenthood, 2020.11e). It is a small, flexible ring inserted high into the vagina once every 28 days (see Figure 5). The ring is kept in place for 21 days and removed for a 7-day break to allow a withdrawal bleed. The ring releases synthetic estrogen and progestin, preventing ovulation in a manner similar to that of other combined hormonal contraceptives. It also thickens the cervical mucus, making it difficult for the sperm to penetrate the cervical canal. The vaginal ring is prescribed by a doctor and provides protection against pregnancy if implanted during the first 5 days of a woman's period. Note that the same medications or supplements that can make the birth control patch less effective can also interfere with the effectiveness of the vaginal ring.

Until recently, only one vaginal ring was on the market: NuvaRing. In 2018, the FDA approved a second vaginal ring, Annovera, which like the NuvaRing also contains the

"My best birth control now is to leave the lights on."

—Joan Rivers (1933–2014)

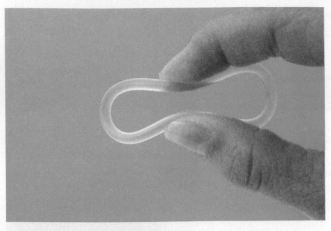

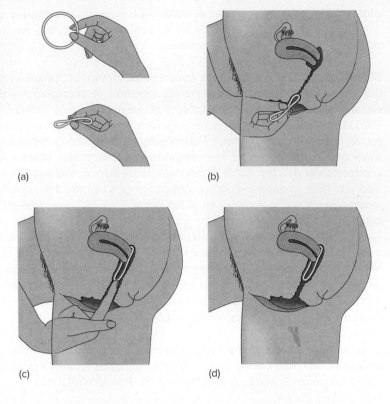

● **FIGURE 5**

The Vaginal Ring. Like a tampon, the ring can be placed anywhere in the vagina that is comfortable. There is no specific fit or need to check the position of the ring. If it causes pressure, the user may just push it farther into the vagina.

(first) imageBROKER/Alamy Stock Photo

combination of progestin and estrogen (WebMD, 2020.11b). The devices are used similarly, in that both are inserted for 3 weeks and removed for 1 week during which a period occurs. However, unlike the NuvaRing, which must be replaced every 3 weeks, Annovera is reusable for up to 1 year; in other words, you clean and re-use the same ring each month. The efficacy, safety, and side effects are similar for both devices; however, oil-based and silicon-based lubricants should not be used with Annovera. In 2020, a generic version of NuvaRing, EluRyng, received FDA approval, allowing a lower cost but equally effective vaginal ring for women who wish to avoid pregnancy.

Sometimes the vaginal ring might slip out of the vagina; in that event, there are still ways to prevent pregnancy. If the ring has been out of the vagina for less than 2 days, there is no loss of effectiveness if it is placed back in the vagina within 48 hours. If it has been out of the vagina for more than 2 days and the woman is not on her ring-free week, it should be washed in cool water and put back into the vagina right away. If vaginal sex occurs over the next 7 days, a condom should also be used. In some instances, emergency contraception might be considered.

Since the vaginal ring is designed to be worn all the time, including during sex, it's best to leave the ring in the vagina as much as possible. If it bothers the woman or her partner, it can be moved around until it feels comfortable. If a woman does take out the ring during sex, it should be rinsed in cool water and inserted soon after sexual intercourse. For those women who choose to skip their periods, the ring should be kept in place every day throughout the month and not removed for a 7-day break. This would mean replacing the ring with a new one on the same day each month. Annovera cannot be used continuously to skip a period.

Effectiveness   Like the other methods of hormonal contraception, if used perfectly, the vaginal ring is more than 99% effective. Typical use results in a success rate of 91%.

Advantages   The ring protects against pregnancy for 1 month and is easy to use. Many women who use the ring have more regular, lighter, and shorter periods. A woman can stop using the vaginal ring at any time, offering her more control over contraception than with some other hormonal methods of birth control. The ring provides a consistent release of hormones, does not usually cause weight gain, and can be removed for up to 3 hours without compromising effectiveness.

Disadvantages The side effects of the ring are similar to those associated with oral contraceptives. Additionally, there may be an increased risk of blood clots possibly due to the hormone desogesterel. Vaginal discharge, irritation, or infection; sensation of a foreign body; expulsion; and headaches may also occur. The ring should not be used by women who have weak pelvic floor muscles. Regularly using oil-based medicines in the vagina for yeast infections while the ring is in place may increase the level of hormones released into the blood. This, however, will not reduce the effectiveness of the ring. The effect of using these types of yeast infection medications with long-term use of the vaginal ring is unknown.

Implants The contraceptive **implant**, also known as Nexplanon, is a thin, flexible, plastic rod about the size of a cardboard matchstick that is inserted under the skin of the upper arm and protects against pregnancy for up to 5 years (Planned Parenthood, 2020.11f). The implant is available under older version, Implanon, or the newer one, Nexplanon. Like several other progestin-containing methods of contraception, implants prevent ovulation and fertilization and thicken the cervical mucus to block sperm.

Implants are among the most effective of the available contraceptives, similar in effectiveness to intrauterine devices (IUDs) and sterilization (see Table 1). Currently, there is no distinction between the implant and other progestin-only methods with respect to increased risk of blood clots. An implant requires a doctor to insert and remove it, along with the use of local anesthesia. If a woman desires to become pregnant within the 5 years following insertion, the device can be removed. If the implant is inserted during the first 5 days of a woman's period, she is protected right away from pregnancy (but not STIs). If it is inserted after that time, she should use some other type of birth control (e.g., condoms) for the first week after getting her implant.

Advantages The device is highly effective, easy to insert, and discrete; does not interrupt sex or require maintenance; makes periods lighter or stops them completely; has no estrogen-related side effects; is easily reversible; and may provide relief from menstrual cramps. It can also be used while breastfeeding.

Disadvantages Implants may cause arm pain that lasts for longer than a few days, an infection in the arm, or scarring. A doctor or nurse should be notified if there is ongoing bleeding, pus, or redness or pain in the arm, yellowing of the eyes and skin, heavier or longer than normal menstrual bleeding, or the implant seems to have moved. Because the implant, like the minipill and the shot, contains only progestin, the possible side effects are similar to those methods. The implant is also clinician-dependent, so once it is inserted, women have little control over its side effects or outcomes.

Barrier Methods

Barrier methods are designed to keep sperm and egg from uniting. The barrier device used by men is the condom. Barrier methods available to women include the diaphragm, the internal condom (also known as the female condom), the contraceptive sponge, and the cervical cap. These methods of birth control have become increasingly popular because, in addition to preventing conception, they can reduce the risk of STIs. The effectiveness of some barrier methods is increased by use with spermicides.

The Male Condom A **condom (male condom)** is a thin, soft, flexible sheath of latex, plastic (polyurethane, nitrile, or polyisoprene), or lambskin that fits over the erect penis to help prevent semen from being transmitted. Latex and plastic condoms protect against infections by covering the genitals and protecting them from many STI organisms, including HIV

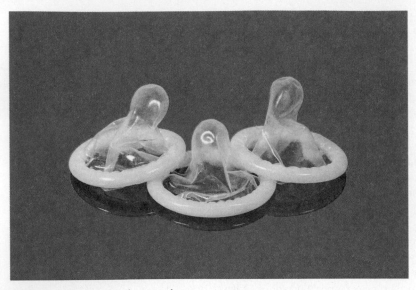

Male condoms come in a variety of sizes, colors, and textures; some are lubricated, and nearly all have a reservoir tip designed to collect semen.

Shutterstock/Looka

(Planned Parenthood, 2020.11g). Condoms are available in a wide variety of shapes, sizes, and colors. Some are dry, while others are lubricated. Since a condom is designed to be used on their own, doubling up (using two male condoms or a male and an internal condom) won't give extra protection.

A small proportion of condoms are made of polyurethane or other synthetic materials. These condoms are more resistant to deterioration than latex condoms, have a longer shelf life, and can provide an alternative if a person is allergic to latex. Unlike latex condoms, oil-based lubricants can be used with condoms made from synthetic materials.

Most condoms are very thin, but also strong, conduct heat well, and allow quite a bit of sensation to be experienced. While picking out condoms can be a fun experience, if a person needs them for protection, be sure to read the label to see if they are FDA-approved for use against unplanned pregnancy and STIs. Latex condoms should be used with water-based lubricants, like K-Y Jelly or glycerine only, because oil-based lubricants such as Vaseline can weaken the rubber. If a condom breaks, slips, or leaks, there are some things a person can do to avoid an unintended pregnancy (see the section "Emergency Contraception" later in the chapter).

Women and Condom Use

Today, a vast number of male condoms are purchased by women, and condom advertising and packaging increasingly reflect this trend. Several key points are relevant to the issue of women and condom use:

- Women experience more health consequences than men from STIs, including permanent infertility, for example. When used consistently and correctly condoms are an effective means of reducing the risk of STI transmission and acquisition.

- Since women are far more likely to contract an STI from intercourse with a male partner than vice versa, it is in the woman's best interest to use or have her partner use a condom.

- Condoms help protect women against unplanned pregnancy, ectopic pregnancy, bacterial infections such as vaginitis and pelvic inflammatory disease (PID), viral infections such as herpes and HIV, cervical cancer, and infections that may harm a fetus or an infant during delivery.

- A woman can protect herself by insisting on condom use. Even if a woman regularly uses another form of birth control, such as the pill or an intrauterine device (IUD), she may want to have the added protection provided by a condom.

Condoms, dental dams, sanitary pads & tampons, pregnancy tests, lubrication, and emergency contraception are often available in vending machines on university campuses as well bathrooms and subway stations. They act as a public health measure to promote safer sex and provide access to sexual wellness products.

James Copeland/Shutterstock

Effectiveness   With perfect use, condoms are 98% effective in preventing conception, but user effectiveness is about 87%. Failures sometimes occur from using the condom incorrectly, but they are usually the result of not putting it on until after some semen has leaked into the vagina, simply not putting it on at all, or taking it off prior to ejaculation. When used in anal sex, a male condom is more likely to break and slip than when used for vaginal sex if adequate lubrication is not used.

Advantages   Condoms are easy to obtain and do not cause harmful side effects. They are simple to carry and are inexpensive or even free. Latex condoms help protect against STIs, including HIV infection, and lower the risk of unplanned pregnancy. Some men appreciate the slightly reduced sensitivity they experience when using a condom because it may help delay ejaculation.

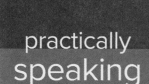

Tips for Effective Male Condom Use

Condoms can be very effective contraceptive devices when used consistently and correctly. They also can reduce the risk of STIs, including HIV. Here are some tips for their use:

1. Use condoms every time you have vaginal, anal, or oral sex. (Note: An unlubricated condom is best for use during oral sex.)

2. Check the expiration date on the package and press the container to make sure there is an air pocket.

3. Carefully open the condom package—teeth or fingernails can tear the condom.

4. If the penis is uncircumcised, pull back the foreskin before putting on the condom.

5. Put on the condom before it touches any part of a partner's body.

6. If you accidentally put the condom on wrong-side up, discard the condom and use another.

7. Leave about a half inch of space at the condom tip, and roll the condom all the way down the erect penis to the base. Push out any air bubbles.

8. Withdraw the penis soon after ejaculation. Make sure the male or his partner holds the base of the condom firmly against the penis as it is withdrawn.

9. After use, check the condom for possible tears. If you find a tear or hole, consider the use of emergency contraception. If torn condoms are a persistent problem, use a water-based lubricant such as K-Y Jelly.

10. Do not reuse a condom.

11. Keep condoms in a cool, dry, and convenient place.

12. To help protect against HIV and other STIs, always use a latex rubber or polyurethane condom, *not* one made of animal tissue.

13. Don't forget to incorporate sensual ways of placing the condom on the penis.

When using a condom, here are some things to avoid:

1. DON'T reuse a condom.

2. DON'T use nonoxynol-9 (a spermicide), as this can cause irritation.

3. DON'T use oil-based products such as baby oil, lotion, petroleum jelly, or cooking oil because they will cause the condom to break.

4. DON'T use more than one condom at a time.

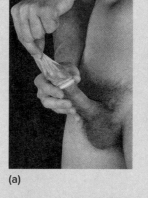
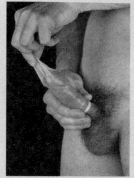

(a) (b)

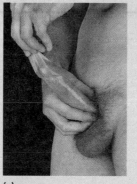
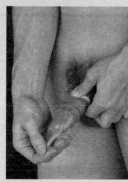

(c) (d)

(a) Place the rolled condom on the erect penis, leaving about a half inch of space at the tip (first, squeeze any air out of the condom tip). (b) Roll the condom down, smoothing out any air bubbles. (c) Roll the condom to the base of the penis. (d) After ejaculation, hold the condom base while withdrawing the penis.

(all) H.S. Photos/Science Source

Possible Problems Condoms can reduce but cannot eliminate the risks of STIs or unplanned pregnancy. The chief drawback of a condom is that it should be put on after the penis has become erect but before penetration. This interruption is a major reason users neglect to put condoms on. Some men and women complain that sensation is dulled, and very rarely cases of allergy to rubber are reported. Couples should try different types of condoms to see which one(s) they prefer.

A disturbing, nonconsensual trend that is documented in the online community is **stealthing**, or when a man secretly removes his condom during sex despite agreeing to wear

"It is now vitally important that we find a way of making the condom a cult object of youth."
—Germaine Greer (1939–)

practically speaking

Correct Condom Use Self-Efficacy Scale

Correct and consistent condom use is one of the most effective methods for preventing the transmission of HIV, reducing the risk of other STIs, and lowering the risk of unplanned pregnancy. It is also known that young people aged 15–24 account for half of all STIs, and that 25% of all sexually active females have an STI (CDC, 2018.11). Just what prevents individuals from making a decision to use condoms? The Condom Use Self-Efficacy Scale (CUSES) is designed to measure an individual's perception of the ease or difficulty with which he or she can correctly apply and use a male condom. It measures an individual's perception of his or her ability to purchase condoms, apply and remove them, and negotiate their use with partners.

Directions

Circle the number that represents how easy or difficult it would be to do what each question asks.

1. How easy or difficult would it be for you to find condoms that fit you properly?

   Very difficult   Very easy

      1   2   3   4   5

2. How easy or difficult would it be for you to apply condoms correctly?

   Very difficult   Very easy

      1   2   3   4   5

3. How easy or difficult would it be for you to keep a condom from drying out during sex?

   Very difficult   Very easy

      1   2   3   4   5

4. How easy or difficult would it be for you to keep a condom from breaking during sex?

   Very difficult   Very easy

      1   2   3   4   5

5. How easy or difficult would it be for you to keep an erection while using a condom?

   Very difficult   Very easy

      1   2   3   4   5

6. How easy or difficult would it be for you to keep a condom on when withdrawing after sex?

   Very difficult   Very easy

      1   2   3   4   5

7. How easy or difficult would it be for you to wear a condom from start to finish of sex with your partner?

   Very difficult   Very easy

      1   2   3   4   5

Interpretation

A higher score indicates greater self-efficacy for correct use of male condoms.

source: Crosby, R. A., et al. (2019). In R. R. Milhausen et al. (Eds.) *Handbook of sexuality-related measures* (4th ed.). Routledge.

---

one. Such a practice can transform consensual sex into nonconsensual sex by outright dishonesty, exposing a person to pregnancy and STIs, and potentially causing emotional, physical, and financial harm. Though laws don't necessarily cover stealthing, some people still consider it a form of sexual assault (Brodsky, 2017).

The Internal Condom The **internal condom**, previously called the female condom, is a disposable, thin, loose-fitting sheath with a diaphragm-like ring at each end (Planned Parenthood, 2020.11h). Currently, the FC2 is the only brand of internal condom that is FDA approved and available in the United States. The device is designed such that one of the two rings is sealed shut inside the sheath and is used to insert and anchor the condom against the cervix. The open outer ring remains outside the vagina and acts as a barrier, protecting the vulva and the base of the penis (see Figure 6). When inserted, the device lines the entire inner wall of the vagina and protects women against sperm. The pouch is lubricated both inside and outside with a non-spermicidal lubricant and is meant for one-time use in either

contraceptive methods. The insertion and removal of the sponge are similar to that of the diaphragm and, with a little practice, are easy to do. Several advantages of the sponge are that it can be inserted up to 24 hours before sex and can be left in place for up to 24 hours without reinsertion or the application of more spermicide. It must, however, be left in place 6 hours after having sex. The sponge should not be left in place longer than 30 hours because it can increase the risk of toxic shock syndrome. The perfect-use effectiveness rate varies, depending on whether a woman has had a baby, but averages 80% for typical use. The lowered effectiveness rate may be because the one size in which the sponge is available may not adequately cover a cervix that has been stretched during childbirth. The shelf life of the sponge is limited.

The Cervical Cap   A **cervical cap** is a silicone, cup-shaped device that is inserted into the vagina to prevent pregnancy (Planned Parenthood, 2020.11k). Shaped like a sailor's cap, the cervical cap (brand name FemCap) comes in three sizes and must stay in place 6 hours after the last intercourse. It can also be worn for up to 48 hours, double the time recommended for similar birth control devices. If intercourse is desired a second time, a woman can leave her cervical cap in place, but a second application of spermicide should be inserted into the vagina. The device is held in place by suction, must be used with a spermicide, and needs to be obtained through a health care provider. Adding spermicide to the cervical cap before insertion increases its effectiveness. The perfect-use and typical-use effectiveness rates are similar to those of the diaphragm. It is more effective for women who have never given birth.

Advantages   The cervical cap may be more comfortable and convenient than the diaphragm for some women. Much less spermicide is used than with the diaphragm. The cap can be inserted 15 minutes to several hours before intercourse and can be worn for as long as 48 hours. It does not interfere with the body physically or hormonally.

Possible Problems   Some women find the cap slightly difficult to insert. It can also move out of place during sex. There is some concern that the cap may contribute to erosion of the cervix if left in too long or if it is ill-fitting. If a partner's penis touches the rim of the cap, it can become displaced during intercourse. Theoretically, the same risk of toxic shock syndrome exists for the cervical cap as for the diaphragm. And, unless it is used in combination with a condom, it does not protect against STIs or HIV infection.

Spermicides   A **spermicide** is a substance that is toxic to sperm. The most commonly used spermicide in products sold in the United States is the chemical **nonoxynol-9 (N-9)**. Though most women can use it safely, with repeated use for vaginal and anal intercourse, N-9 may irritate genital or rectal tissues and if used several times a day, can increase the risk of HIV, other STIs, or urinary tract infection (Planned Parenthood, 2020.11l). Spermicidal preparations are available in a variety of forms—foam, film, cream, jelly, and suppository—and are considered most effective when used in combination with a barrier method of contraception such as the diaphragm, sponge, or cervical cap. Spermicides are sold in tubes, packets, or other containers that hold 12–20 applications. The perfect-use effectiveness is 84%, while the typical-use effectiveness is 79%.

Some people have allergic reactions to spermicides. Some women dislike the messiness or odor involved. Others experience irritation or inflammation, especially if they use any of the chemicals frequently.

Nonhormonal Contraceptive Gel   New to the market is Phexxi, a non-hormonal, prescription contraceptive gel (U.S. Food and Drug Administration, 2020.11a). Unique to this product is that it keeps the vaginal pH in a normal range, between 3.5 and 4.5. Usually, when sperm enter the vagina, they raise the pH level to around 7 or 8, which allows the sperm to move through the vagina and enter the uterus. By keeping the pH in a normal range, Phexxi immobilizes and kills the sperm. The gel comes in pre-filled applicator similar to a tampon and should be inserted somewhere between an hour and immediately before

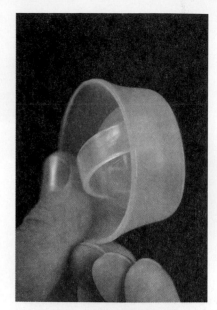

The cervical cap is smaller than a diaphragm and covers only the cervix.

Jill Braaten/McGraw-Hill Education

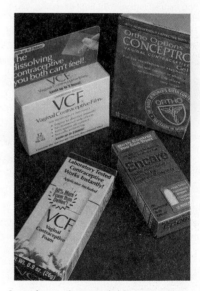

A variety of spermicides are among the contraceptive options available without a prescription.

Christopher Kerrigan/McGraw-Hill Education

"Wherefore, since if the parts be smooth conception is prevented, some anoint that part of the womb on which the seed falls with oil of cedar, or with ointment of lead or with frankincense, commingled with olive oil."

—Aristotle (384–322 BCE)

intercourse. Unlike the spermicide nonoxynol-9, which can increases the risk of HIV and other STIs if used frequently, Phexxi's ingredients are claimed to be safe and "naturally occurring" (Hohman, 2020). They include lactic acid, citric acid, and potassium bitartrate. Like other spermicides, its typical use effectiveness is similar to that of condoms: about 86% for typical use or 93% with ideal use.

Intrauterine Devices (IUDs)

An **intrauterine device (IUD)** is a long-acting, reversible contraceptive method that is inserted by a doctor into the uterus where it emits either copper or the hormone progestin, both of which are hostile to sperm (Planned Parenthood, 2020.11m). There are five brands of IUDs available in the United States—one of which is copper based (Paragard) and four of which are hormone (progestin) based (Mirena, Kyleena, Liletta, and Skyla). Both types prevent pregnancy by damaging or killing sperm. The IUD also affects the uterine lining, where a fertilized egg would implant and grow. Paragard, the most commonly used IUD, releases copper ions that trigger a sterile inflammatory response, which in turn disables sperm and thereby makes it difficult for sperm to meet and fertilize the egg. Paragard protects against pregnancy for up to 10 years. The hormonal IUDs contain the hormone progestin, which prevents fertilization by thickening the cervical mucus and thinning out the uterine lining. This creates a hostile environment where the sperm cannot reach the egg. The hormonal IUDs also help reduce menstrual bleeding and cramping. Hormonal IUDs can remain in-place for 3 to 6 years, depending on which device is chosen (see Figure 7).

• **FIGURE 7**

Once the IUD is inserted, the threads attached to the IUD will extend into the vagina through the cervical opening. After each period, it's important to check for the string of the IUD to help make sure that it is in place.

(top middle) Image Point Fr/Shutterstock; (top right) EdnaM/Getty Images; (bottom left) Image Point Fr/Shutterstock; (bottom right) JPC-PROD/Shutterstock

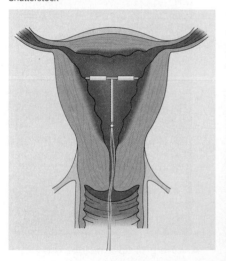
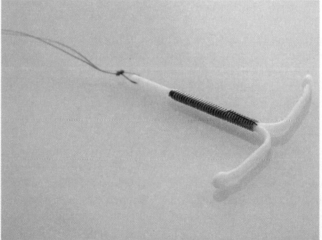
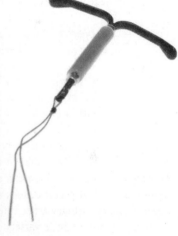
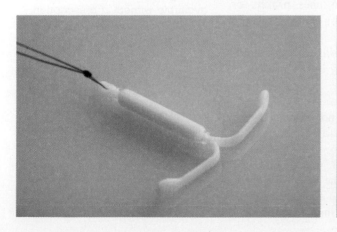
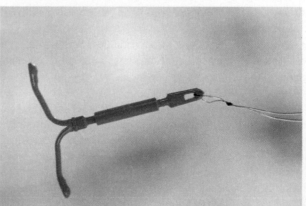

Current evidence does not support the belief that the IUD is an **abortifacient**, a device or substance that causes an abortion (International Planned Parenthood Federation, 2019). Rather, it prevents fertilization.

Effectiveness   All IUDs are extremely effective. Once inserted, IUDs are 99% effective with perfect use; the typical-use effectiveness rate is 98%.

Advantages   Few methods of birth control are as long-acting, convenient, effective, and economical as the IUD. Additionally, fertility rebounds quickly upon discontinuation. Once inserted, IUDs require little care and don't interfere with spontaneity during intercourse. The copper IUD, if inserted within 5 days (120 hours) after having unprotected sex, can be used as emergency contraception. That is, the IUD will prevent the sperm from reaching the egg. However, if a pregnancy has already occurred, insertion of an IUD will not cause an abortion.

Disadvantages   Insertion may be uncomfortable and cramping or backache may persist for a few days. Spotting between and irregular periods may also occur in the first 3–6 months. Heavier periods and increased menstrual cramps may be experienced with Paragard. Though serious problems with the IUD are rare, it can slip out of the uterus. This is more likely to occur to those who are younger and who have never had a baby. In rare situations, a woman could develop an infection when using the IUD or in very rare circumstances when the IUD is inserted, it can push through the wall of the uterus. The IUD does not protect against STIs, including HIV.

Long-Acting Reversible Contraception (LARC)

Long-acting reversible contraceptives (LARC), which include the IUD and the birth control implant, provide highly effective protection against pregnancy, last for several years, and are easy to use (American College of Obstetricians and Gynecologists, 2017.11b). Over the long term, LARC methods are 20 times more effective than birth control pills, the patch, or the ring. Because of their efficacy, continuation, and satisfaction rates, leading medical groups including the American College of Obstetricians and Gynecologists and the American Academy of Pediatrics have recommended the use of LARCs for a woman who may not wish to become pregnant in the future as well as for those who desire long-term, highly effective pregnancy prevention (Kaiser Family Foundation, 2019.11b).

Fertility Awareness–Based Methods

Fertility awareness–based methods (FAMs) and natural family planning are ways to track ovulation in order to prevent pregnancy (Planned Parenthood, 2020.11n). Requiring a high degree of motivation and self-control, these methods are not for everyone. Natural family planning does not include the use of any contraceptive device or medication.

FAMs include the calendar (rhythm) method, the basal body temperature (BBT) method, and the cervical mucus method to track signs of fertility. When used together, they're called the **symptothermal method**. These methods are free and pose no health risks. If a woman wishes to become pregnant, awareness of her own fertility cycles is useful. But these methods are not suitable for women with irregular menstrual cycles or for couples not highly motivated to use them. Certain conditions or circumstances, such as recent menarche, approaching menopause, recent childbirth, breastfeeding, and recent discontinuation of hormonal contraceptives, make FAMs more difficult to use and require more extensive monitoring. Among typical users of fertility awareness, about 34% of women experience unintended pregnancy during the first year of use if they don't use the method correctly or consistently. The first FDA-approved birth control app, *Natural Cycles*, is a fertility awareness app that charts a woman's fertility cycle so that she can plan or avoid a pregnancy. Women track their menstrual cycles and enter their body temperature into the app each morning. (See below for more about the calendar method.)

The Calendar (Rhythm) Method The **calendar (rhythm *or* standard days) method** is based on calculating "safer" days, which depends on knowing the range of a woman's longest and shortest menstrual cycles and abstaining from unprotected penile-vaginal intercourse during her peak fertile times. Because sperm can live 6 days and an egg lives about 1 day after ovulation, the period of time in which fertilization could be expected to occur is about 7 days. To prevent pregnancy, a woman should not rely on this method alone. This method may not be practical or safe for women with irregular cycles.

Ovulation generally occurs 14 days (plus or minus 2 days) before a woman's menstrual period. However, ovulation can occur anytime during the cycle, including the menstrual period. Taking this into account, and charting her menstrual cycles for a minimum of 8 months to determine the longest and shortest cycles, a woman can determine her expected fertile period. (Figure 8 shows the interval of fertility calculated in this way.)

The Basal Body Temperature (BBT) Method A woman's temperature tends to be slightly lower during the first part of her menstrual cycle and usually rises slightly during and after ovulation. It stays high until just before the next menstrual period. Changes will be in fractions of a degree from one tenth to one half of a degree.

A woman practicing the **basal body temperature (BBT) method** must record her temperature every morning upon waking for 6–12 months to gain an accurate idea of her temperature pattern. This change can best be noted using a BBT thermometer before getting out of bed. Some BBT thermometers are meant to be used in the mouth, while others are designed for use in the rectum. When a woman can recognize the rise in her temperature and predict when in her cycle ovulation will occur, she can begin using the method. She should abstain from intercourse or use an alternative contraceptive method for 3–4 days before the expected rise in temperature and for 4 days after it has taken place.

> "Women who miscalculate are called mothers."
>
> —Abigail Van Buren (1918–2013)

Cervical Mucus Method Women who use the **cervical mucus method**, also called the ovulation method or the Billings method, determine their stage in the menstrual cycle by examining the mucus secretions of the cervix. In many women, there is a noticeable change in the appearance and character of cervical mucus prior to ovulation. After menstruation, most women experience a moderate discharge of cloudy, yellowish or white mucus. Then, for a day or two, a clear, stretchy mucus is secreted. Ovulation occurs immediately after the clear, stretchy mucus secretions appear. The preovulatory mucus is elastic in consistency, rather like raw egg white, and a drop can be stretched into a thin strand. Following ovulation, the amount of discharge decreases markedly. The 4 days before and 4 days after these secretions are considered the unsafe days. Fewer pregnancies

• **FIGURE 8**

Fertility Awareness Calendar. To use the calendar method or other fertility awareness methods, a woman must keep track of her menstrual cycles. (a) This chart shows probable safe and unsafe days for a woman with a regular 28-day cycle. (b) This chart shows safe and unsafe days for a woman whose cycles range from 25 to 31 days. Note that the woman with an irregular cycle has significantly more unsafe days. The calendar method is most effective when combined with the basal body temperature (BBT) and cervical mucus methods.

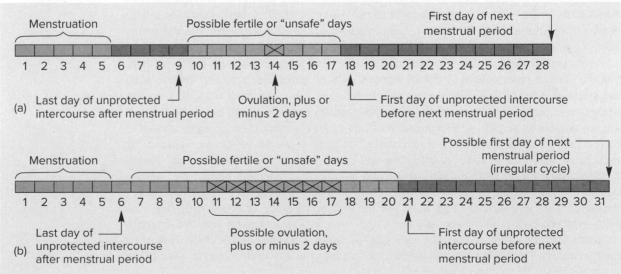

occur when intercourse takes place only on the "dry days" following ovulation. However, certain activities or conditions (e.g., douching, breastfeeding) can make this method less effective and difficult to use.

The Symptothermal Method   When all three fertility indicators are used together, the approach is called the **symptothermal method**. The signs of one method can help confirm those of the others, which helps predict safer days. Additional signs that may be useful in determining ovulation are midcycle pain in the lower abdomen on either side, a slight discharge of blood from the cervix ("spotting"), breast tenderness, feelings of heaviness, and/or abdominal swelling.

Lactational Amenorrhea Method (LAM)

A highly effective, albeit temporary, method of contraception used by exclusively breastfeeding mothers is called the **lactational amenorrhea method**, or **LAM** (Planned Parenthood, 2020.11o). LAM relies on lactational infertility for protection from pregnancy. This method is more than 98% effective the first 6 months following a birth if the woman breastfeeds about every 4 hours during the day and 6 hours at night and has not experienced her first postpartum menses.

Breastfeeding women may start progestin-only methods at any time after delivery. Should a woman choose to use contraception, the minipill, the implant, the shot, and the IUDs containing only the hormone progestin are the methods of choice because they do not typically suppress milk production, which may result in the discontinuation of breastfeeding or poor infant growth. Other nonhormonal options include condoms, the diaphragm, and cervical cap.

Sterilization

Sterilization involves surgical intervention that makes the reproductive organs incapable of producing or delivering viable gametes (sperm and eggs). Female sterilization and the IUD are the most widely used methods of contraception by married or partnered women worldwide (United Nations, 2019). In the United States, female sterilization is the most common method of contraception used (18%), followed by oral contraceptives (14%), LARCs (10%), and the male condom (8%) (Daniels & Abma, 2020). Couples and individuals choose sterilization because they want to limit or end childbearing. All sterilization procedures are meant to be permanent (Planned Parenthood, 2020.11p).

Sterilization for Women   Female sterilization is now a relatively safe, simple, and common procedure. Most female sterilizations are **tubal ligations**, familiarly known as "tying the tubes" (Planned Parenthood, 2020.11p) (see Figure 9). The fallopian tubes can also be sealed or closed with clips, clamps, or rings. Sometimes a small piece of the fallopian tube is also removed. The three most common methods of tubal ligations are mini-laparotomy, laparotomy, and laparoscopy. A mini-laparotomy is a procedure that is done within 48 hours of childbirth. It differs from a laparotomy, which requires a larger incision and can be performed anytime. The third option, laparoscopy, is a sophisticated surgical procedure in which a fiber-optic device is inserted through the abdominal wall. Since none of these procedures are considered reversible, only women who are absolutely certain that they want no or no more children should choose this method.

Laparoscopy   Sterilization by **laparoscopy** is performed on an outpatient basis and takes 20–30 minutes. The woman's abdomen is inflated with gas to make the organs more visible. The surgeon inserts a rodlike instrument with a viewing lens (the laparoscope) through a small incision at the edge of the navel and locates the fallopian tubes. Through this incision or a second one, the surgeon inserts another instrument that closes the tubes, usually by electrocauterization (burning). Small forceps that carry an electric current clamp the tubes and cauterize them. The tubes may also be closed off or blocked with tiny rings or clips; no

• **FIGURE 9**

Female Sterilization. A variety of
techniques are used to render a
woman sterile.

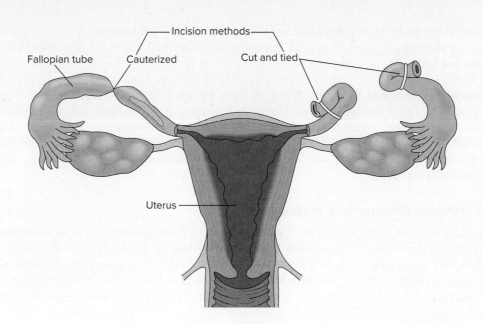

stitches are required. There is a recovery period of up to a week. During this time, the woman will experience some tenderness, cramping, and vaginal bleeding. Rest is important.

Essure   An implantable sterilization device, known as Essure, is a nonincisional, permanent birth control system that uses small devices to block the fallopian tubes. During the first 3 months following insertion, the device forms a tissue barrier that prevents sperm from reaching the egg. In December, 2018, Bayer, the producer of the device, stopped selling and distributing the Essure device in the United States, and as of the end of 2019, the company informed their customers that all Essure units that had not been implanted should be returned to the company because of serious health problems associated with their use. The U.S. Food and Drug Administration (2020.11b) advises women who have been successfully using Essure to prevent pregnancy can and should continue to use it.

Evaluating the Sterilization Methods for Women   Once sterilization has been done, no other method of birth control will ever be necessary. A woman who risks exposure to STIs, however, should protect herself with a condom.

Sterilization does not reduce or change a woman's hormone levels. It is not the same as menopause, nor does it hasten the onset of menopause. A woman still has her menstrual periods until whatever age menopause naturally occurs for her. The regularity of menstrual cycles is also not affected. A woman's ovaries, uterus (except in the case of hysterectomy), and hormonal system have not been changed. The only difference is that sperm cannot now reach her eggs. The eggs, which are released every month as before, are reabsorbed by the body. Sexual enjoyment is not diminished. In fact, a high percentage of women report that they feel more relaxed during intercourse because anxiety about pregnancy has been eliminated. There appear to be no harmful side effects associated with female sterilization.

Sterilization for Men   A **vasectomy** is a permanent method of birth control in which each vas deferens is severed, thereby preventing sperm from entering the vas deferens and mixing with seminal fluids to form semen (Planned Parenthood, 2020.11q). Instead of being ejaculated with the semen, the sperm are absorbed by the body. A vasectomy takes approximately half an hour and can be done in a doctor's office or clinic. In this procedure, the physician makes a small incision (or two incisions) in the skin of the scrotum. Through the incision, each vas deferens is lifted, cut, tied, and often cauterized with electricity (see Figure 10). With the "no-incision method," the skin of the scrotum is not cut. Rather, one puncture is made to reach both tubes, which are then tied off, cauterized, or blocked. After a brief rest, the man is able to walk out of the office; complete recuperation takes only a few days. Because the vas deferens is so close to the skin's surface,

it is easier, safer, and less expensive to perform a vasectomy on a man than it is to sterilize a woman.

A man may retain some viable sperm in his system for days or weeks following a vasectomy. Because it takes about 3 months to use up these sperm, a couple should use other birth control until a semen analysis reveals no sperm are present in the semen.

Vasectomies are 99.9% effective. Regardless, a man who may be at risk for an STI should still use a condom. Sexual enjoyment will not be diminished; the man will still have erections and orgasms and ejaculate semen. A vasectomy is relatively inexpensive compared with female sterilization. The problems associated with a vasectomy, such as excessive pain, swelling, or infection are very low.

Men who equate fertility with virility and potency may experience psychological problems following a vasectomy. However, most men experience no adverse psychological reactions if they understand what to expect and have the opportunity to express their concerns and ask questions. In fact, some men may experience more pleasure from sex knowing that they no longer have to fear impregnating a partner. Vasectomy should be considered permanent.

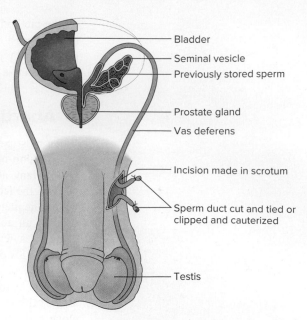

• FIGURE 10

Male Sterilization, or Vasectomy. This is a relatively simple procedure that involves local anesthesia and results in permanent sterilization.

Emergency Contraception (EC)

No contraceptive device is 100% effective, and sexual intercourse sometimes occurs unexpectedly. **Emergency contraception (EC)** is the use of hormones or a copper IUD to prevent pregnancy in the event of unprotected sex or sexual assault. There are two options available: the Paragard IUD and an emergency contraceptive pill, otherwise known as the "morning-after pill" (Planned Parenthood, 2020.11r).

The Paragard IUD can be used as EC when inserted by a health care practitioner within 120 hours (5 days) after unprotected sex and then left in place to provide ongoing contraception for up to 10 years. The mechanism interferes with implantation, may act as a contraceptive if inserted prior to ovulation, and is 99% effective. It does not contain hormones.

There are two types of morning-after pills: one containing an ingredient called ulipristal acetate, with the brand name ella, or a pill with levonorgestrel (progestin), with the brand names Plan B One-Step, Take Action, My Way, and AfterPill. While a prescription for ella is necessary, the other brands can be purchased over-the-counter, without a prescription, regardless of a person's age or gender. Ella is the most effective type of morning-after pill and works best when taken within 5 days (120 hours) of unprotected sex. Pills containing progestin work best if they are taken within 3 days (72 hours) after unprotected sex. Though some research has suggested that efficacy of progestin-based pills is lower among women with a body mass index (BMI) greater than 25, the FDA found that the current scientific data regarding the effectiveness of the pills in overweight and obese women are inconclusive (Kaiser Family Foundation, 2018.11).

The sooner the pill is taken after unprotected intercourse, the more effective it is. A morning-after pill is a form of birth control and is not the same as medication abortion (RU-486). It will not terminate an established pregnancy, in which the fertilized egg has already attached itself to the wall of the uterus. Rather, EC inhibits ovulation and thickens the cervical mucus, which prevents the sperm from fertilizing the egg.

Progestin-only pills like Plan B One-Step and Next Choice One Dose are specially packaged as emergency contraception. They do not, however, have the same risks as taking hormonal contraceptives because the hormones do not stay in a woman's body as long as they do with ongoing birth control. Emergency contraception should not be used as a form of regular birth control, because it is less effective. Though many women use EC with few or no problems, nausea and vomiting are among the most common side effects. Other side effects may include breast tenderness, irregular bleeding, dizziness, and headaches. The exact effectiveness of emergency contraception pills is difficult to measure and varies depending

on the method that is used and when it is taken (Kaiser Family Foundation, 2018.11). Tablet labels suggest that Plan B and other levonorgestrel morning-after pills can reduce the risk of pregnancy by up to 87% if taken within 3 days (72 hours) after unprotected sex but is even more effective if taken within 24 hours after unprotected sex.

● Abortion

When most people hear the word abortion, they think of a medical procedure. But **abortion**, or expulsion of the fetus, can happen naturally or can be made to happen in one of several ways. Many abortions occur spontaneously—because a woman suffers a physical trauma, because the fetus is not properly developed, or, more commonly, because physical conditions within the uterus break down and end the development of the conceptus. Approximately one third of all abortions reported annually in the United States are **spontaneous abortions** or death of a fetus before it can survive on its own, otherwise referred to as **miscarriage**. In 2017, 18% of pregnancies, excluding miscarriages, ended in abortion, resulting in 862,320 abortions, or 13.5 abortions per 1,000 women aged 15–44. This is the lowest rate ever observed in the United States (Guttmacher Institute, 2019.11b). Reasons for the decrease include the growing use of long-term contraceptive methods, including the IUD and implants, along with a decline in pregnancies, as evidenced by fewer births.

Methods of Abortion

The vast majority (over two thirds) of abortions are performed within the first 8 weeks of pregnancy (see Figure 11). There are two main types of abortion procedures: medication abortion and surgical abortion, which includes vacuum aspiration and dilation and evacuation. Methods for early abortions (those performed in the first 3 months of pregnancy) differ from those for late abortions (those performed after the third month).

Medication Abortion   **Medication abortion**, also known as RU-486 or the brand name, Mifeprex, is a two-drug regimen used to terminate an early pregnancy. Having become available in the United States in 2000, the pills contain mifepristone and misoprostol and are used to end an early pregnancy, that being 77 days or 11 weeks since a woman's last menstrual period began. The medication works by blocking the activity of progesterone, a substance in the body that helps sustain a pregnancy. Medication abortions accounted for 39% of all nonhospital abortions in 2017 (Guttmacher Institute, 2019.11b).

A medication abortion requires a doctor's visit, where a dose of mifepristone is administered, while the second drug, misoprostol, can be taken up to 48 hours later and at home (Planned Parenthood, 2020.11s). The first tablet, mifepristone, causes the placenta to separate from the endometrium, softens the cervix, and starts uterine contractions. The second tablet, misoprostol, can be taken by mouth or inserted into the vagina and causes additional uterine contractions so that the body passes the uterine contents. Depending on when a woman takes this regime, the effectiveness varies from 87% to 98%. A follow-up visit to get an ultrasound or blood test will assess whether the abortion is complete and the patient is well. In the unlikely case the abortion does not work, a woman may need to take another round of the medication or have an in-clinic abortion to end the pregnancy.

In very rare cases, such as a medical problem or illness in the pregnant woman or fetus, abortion in the second trimester can be induced by administering medications that cause the uterus to contract and eventually expel the fetus and placenta. Only 1.3% of abortions are performed at 21 weeks of gestation or later (Guttmacher Institute (2019.11b)).

Surgical Abortion   Surgical abortion, also referred to as in-clinic abortion, is a medical procedure that ends a pregnancy. There are primarily two procedures that are done, vacuum aspiration and dilation and evacuation (D&E) (Planned Parenthood, 2020.11t).

● **FIGURE 11**

Weeks of Pregnancy When Women in the United States Have Abortions, 2017. Two thirds of abortions occurred at 8 weeks of pregnancy or earlier while 88% occurred in the first 12 weeks.

Source: Guttmacher Institute. (2019.11b). Induced abortion in the United States.

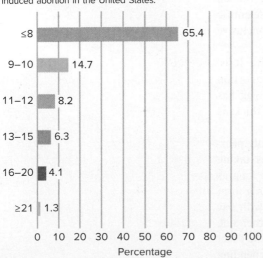

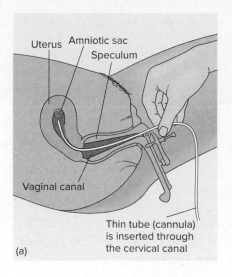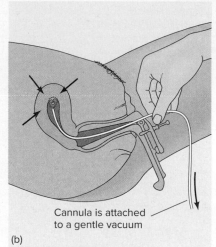

• FIGURE 12

Vacuum Aspiration. (a) A speculum is inserted into the vagina, local anesthesia is given for pain or sedation, the cervical canal is dilated, and a thin, hollow tube (cannula) is passed into the cervical canal. (b) The cannula is attached to a gentle vacuum, which draws out the tissue from the uterus. Following the procedure, the empty uterus will collapse.

Vacuum Aspiration (First-Trimester Method) **Vacuum aspiration**, or suction abortion, is the method used for nearly all first-trimester (up to 16 weeks) abortions. This safe and simple method is performed under local anesthesia. The first step involves the rinsing of the vagina with an antiseptic solution. Next, the cervix is dilated with a series of graduated rods. Then, a small tube attached to a vacuum is inserted through the cervix. The uterus is gently vacuumed, removing the fetus, placenta, and endometrial tissue (see Figure 12).

Dilation and Evacuation (D&E) (Second-Trimester Method) Dilation and evacuation **(D&E)** is a second-trimester method of abortion (beyond 16 weeks of pregnancy and up to 24 weeks) in which the cervix is slowly dilated and the fetus removed by alternating the curettage with other instruments and suction. It is usually performed to end an unhealthy or unviable pregnancy or after a miscarriage. Local or general anesthesia is used. Because it is a second-trimester procedure, a D&E is far less commonly performed than the other procedures and somewhat more risky than a first-trimester abortion.

Safety of Abortion

The single greatest factor influencing the safety of abortion is gestational age, with those performed in early pregnancy being the safest. Abortions performed in the first trimester pose virtually no long-term physical or psychological complications (Planned Parenthood, 2020.11t). Regardless of the method performed, however, almost all women who have an abortion have some bleeding after the procedure that lasts from several days to several weeks. For most women, transient feelings of loss, sadness, or stress that accompany the decision to have an abortion are often replaced with relief and satisfaction with their decision.

Women and Abortion

Many women are reluctant to talk openly about their abortion experiences, but accurate information about women who have abortions may help dispel their possible feelings of isolation or rejection.

Women in the United States who have had abortions come from a broad cross section of society (Guttmacher Institute, 2019.11c):

- More than half of women obtaining abortions were in their 20s, and 12% were adolescents
- 75% were economically disadvantaged
- 39% were non-Hispanic white women, 28% were non-Hispanic Black women, 25% were Hispanic women, and 9% were women of other races
- 54% reported being Protestant or Catholic
- 59% had at least one child

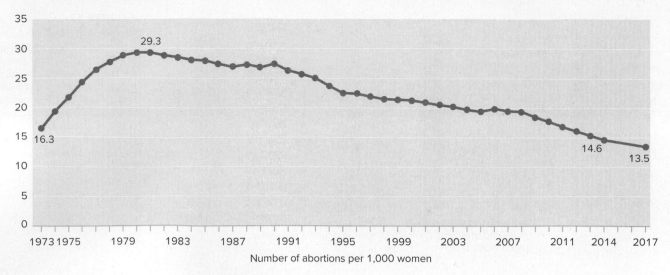

Number of abortions per 1,000 women

● FIGURE 13

Number of Abortions per 1,000 Women Aged 15–44 by Year. In 2017, the U.S. abortion rate reached its lowest level since 1973, and since that time, the rate has continued to drop.

Source: Guttmacher Institute. (2019.11c). Induced abortion in the United States.

With an estimated 862,320 million procedures performed in 2017, abortion is a common experience among women in the United States (Guttmacher Institute, 2019) (see Figure 13). In spite of this, abortion rates in the United States are at their lowest in nearly 50 years. It is important to remember that women who have abortions are as diverse as their reasons for doing so. The motives women have given for why they had an abortion underscore their understanding of the responsibilities of parenthood and family life. The following motives for getting an abortion were cited by the majority of women: (1) inability to afford a child; (2) concerns or responsibility for others; (3) having a child would interfere with work, school, or the ability to care for dependents; (4) they did not want to be a single parent; or (5) they were having problems with their husband or partner (Guttmacher Institute, 2019.11c).

Making a decision about abortion, regardless of the ultimate outcome, raises many emotional issues for women. There are few painless ways of dealing with an unintended pregnancy. For many women, such a decision requires a reevaluation of their relationships, an examination of their childbearing plans, a clarification of their moral perspectives related to abortion, a search to understand the role of sexuality in their lives, and an attempt to clarify their life goals. Clearly, women *and* men need accurate information about fertility cycles and the risk of pregnancy when a contraceptive is not used consistently or correctly, as well as access to contraceptive and abortion services.

There has been a significant amount of research about women's emotions following an abortion. While some women experience sadness, guilt, and anger, others feel relief. For many, it's a mix of these feelings and more. In a recent analysis known as the Turnaway study, researchers from the University of California, San Francisco recruited a racially and ethnically diverse sample of 667 women from 30 sites across the country about how abortion affected them physically, socially, emotionally, and economically (Steinberg, 2020). The study revealed that over a course of 5 years, all emotions, good and bad, tended to fade away. Immediately after their abortions, 95% who agreed to interviews said they had made the right decision. At 5 years, that percentage increased to 99%. Relief was the most common emotion felt by women, while negative emotions or regret did not emerge or remain over time.

Men and Abortion

In the abortion decision-making process, it's important for many women to have the support of their partner. For others, there may be little reason to inform the biological father. It's probably not surprising to know that the ability to rely on their partner for support vastly improves a woman's postabortion well-being and adjustment.

Still, there is the lure of fatherhood. A pregnancy forces a man to confront his own feelings about parenting. Parenthood for males, as for females, can be perceived as a

"If men could get pregnant, abortion would be a sacrament."

—Florynce Kennedy (attributed) (1916–2000)

profound right. For young men, there is a mixture of pride and fear about potential father-hood and adulthood.

After an abortion, many men feel residual guilt, sadness, and remorse. It is also somewhat common for couples to end their relationship after an abortion; the stress, conflict, and guilt can be overwhelming. Many clinics now provide counseling for men, as well as women, involved in an abortion.

The Abortion Debate

For decades, the debate about abortion was between the rights of women and the rights of fetuses. Planned Parenthood is among those organizations that has moved in the direction of abandoning use of the traditional "pro-life versus pro-choice" labels in favor of a more nuanced approach that takes into account the complexity of women's individual situations while at the same time avoiding such "binary" expressions of their outlook. To be more clear, the organization now uses the terms "pro-reproductive rights" and "anti-abortion" to describe people's beliefs about abortion access (Planned Parenthood, 2020.11u).

Constitutional Issues   In 1969 in Texas, 21-year-old Norma McCorvey, a single mother, discovered she was pregnant. In the hope of obtaining a legal abortion, she lied to her doctor, saying that she had been raped. Her physician informed her, however, that Texas prohibited all abortions except those to save the life of the mother. He suggested that she travel to California, where she could obtain a legal abortion, but she had no money. Two lawyers heard of her situation and took her case in order to challenge abortion restrictions as an unconstitutional invasion of the individual's right to privacy. For the case, McCorvey was given "Roe" as a pseudonym. Dallas County District Attorney Henry Wade was the defendant representing the State of Texas. In 1970, a court in Texas declared the law unconstitutional, but the state appealed the decision. Meanwhile, McCorvey had her baby and gave it up for adoption. Ultimately, the case reached the U.S. Supreme Court, which issued its famous *Roe v. Wade* decision in 1973. Under the 1973 *Roe* decision, a woman's right to abortion is guaranteed as a fundamental right, part of the constitutional right to privacy. At the time, only four states permitted abortion at the woman's discretion.

Since the 1973 Supreme Court decision in *Roe V. Wade,* states have been undergoing rigor-ous debate about abortion law, regulating, and limiting whether, when, and under what circum-stances a woman may obtain an abortion (Guttmacher Institute, 2020.11d). In fact, states are currently issuing more abortion bans than previously seen at any time since *Roe v. Wade* was first passed (Kaiser Health News, 2019). While some of these bans prohibit abortions after a specific point in pregnancy, others forbid a specific method of abortion, while still others target specific pregnancy conditions (e.g., a fetus that has or may have Down syndrome or a diagnosis of a genetic anomaly). In some states, the courts have prohibited or limited doctors from performing abortions. For example, in 2020, the Supreme Court struck down a Louisiana abortion law that could have left the state with a single abortion clinic by requiring doctors who perform abortions to have admitting privileges at nearby hospitals. It is anticipated that the Supreme Court will continue to take up challenges to the legality of abortion, including the possibility of complete bans on the procedure.

The Hyde Amendment, passed in 1977, bans federal dollars from being used for abortion coverage for women insured by Medicaid. While the Affordable Care Act (ACA) has made sexual and reproductive health care accessible to millions of people, the ACA enforces the Hyde Amendment restrictions and limits federal funds to pay for abortions only in cases of life endangerment, rape, or incest. Still, states may use their own, nonfederal funds to provide Medicaid coverage of abortion.

The objective shared by both sides in the abortion debate is reducing the number of abortions performed each year in this country. Research has demonstrated that education about effective and safe sexual choices and access to contraceptive services can decrease abortion rates (Guttmacher Institute, 2019.11a). While each state will continue to define and enforce laws according to the ideological standpoints of its elected officials and voters, the protection of legal abortion ultimately is in the hands of the Supreme Court.

"I have noticed that all the people who favor abortion have already been born."

—Ronald Reagan (1911–2004)

"There are few absolutes left in the age after Einstein, and the case of abortion, like almost everything else, is a case of relative goods and ills to be evaluated one against the other."

—Germaine Greer (1939–)

● Research Issues

Most users of contraception find some drawbacks to whatever method they choose. Hormonal methods may be costly or have undesirable side effects. Putting on a condom or inserting a sponge may seem to interrupt sexual expression. The inconveniences, the side effects, the lack of 100% effectiveness—all point to the need for more effective and more diverse forms of contraception than we have now.

High developmental costs, government regulations, social issues, political constraints, and marketing priorities all play a role in restricting contraceptive research. The biggest barrier to developing new contraceptive techniques may be the fear of lawsuits. Pharmaceutical manufacturers will not easily forget that the IUD market was virtually destroyed in the 1970s and 1980s by numerous costly lawsuits.

Another reason for limited contraceptive research is extensive government regulation, which requires exhaustive product testing. Although no one wants to be poisoned by medicines, perhaps it wouldn't hurt to take a closer look at the process by which new drugs become available to the public. Approval by the FDA takes an average of 12 years. Drug patents are in effect for only 20 years, so the pharmaceutical companies have less than 10 years to recover their developmental costs once a medication is approved for sale. Furthermore, pharmaceutical companies are not willing to expend millions in research only to have the FDA refuse to approve the marketing of new products. According to chemist Carl Djerassi (1981), the "father" of the birth control pill, safety is a relative, not an absolute, concept. We may need to reexamine the question "How safe is safe?" and weigh potential benefits along with possible problems.

Though research has investigated a number of contraceptives for men, none have been found to adequately eliminate sperm production while maintaining both the libido and physical health.

Final Thoughts

Contraception helps us plan our lives. It also helps us to prosper and in some parts of the world survive. The topic of contraception provokes much emotional and political controversy. As each of us tries to find their own path through the quagmire of controversy, we can be guided by what we learn. We need to acquire knowledge—not only about the methods and mechanics of contraception but also about our own motivations, needs, weaknesses, and strengths.

Summary

Risk and Responsibility

- Over the period of 1 year, sexually active couples who do not use *contraception,* or birth control that works specifically by preventing the union of the sperm and the egg, have an 85% chance of getting pregnant. Not surprising, the nonusers of contraception account for about half of unintended pregnancies.

- The foundation of the nation's publicly funded family planning efforts is Title X, which now overlaps with services provided by the Affordable Care Act (ACA).

Methods of Contraception

- The most reliable method of contraception is *abstinence—* refraining from sexual intercourse.

- *Contraceptive failure* is a measure of a woman's probably of becoming pregnant during typical and perfect use of a method of contraception within a given period, usually the first 12 months of use.

- *Withdrawal,* otherwise called *coitus interruptus,* is a traditional family planning method in which the man completely removes his penis from the vagina, and away from the external genitalia of the female partner before he ejaculates.

- *Oral contraceptives* are the most widely used form of reversible contraception in the United States. The majority of birth control pills contain synthetic hormones: progestin and usually estrogen. The pill is highly effective if taken regularly. There are side effects and possible problems for some users. The greatest risks are to smokers and women with certain health disorders, such as cardiovascular problems. Other methods of hormonal contraception include the *birth control shot,* the *birth control patch,* the *vaginal ring,* and the *implant.*

- A *condom* (*male condom*) is a thin sheath of latex, rubber, plastic, or processed animal tissue that fits over the erect penis and prevents semen from being transmitted. It is the third most widely used contraceptive method in the United States. Condoms are very effective for contraception when used consistently and correctly. Latex and plastic condoms also help provide protection against STIs.

- The *internal condom, diaphragm, birth control sponge,* and *cervical cap* are barrier methods used by women. Each covers the cervical opening and is used with spermicidal jelly or cream. Internal condoms, in addition to lining the vagina, cover much of the vulva (or anus, when used for anal sex), providing protection against disease organisms.

- *Spermicides* are chemicals that are toxic to sperm. Though *nonoxynol-9 (N-9)* is the most common ingredient in spermicides, it is no longer recommended for use on condoms. Spermicidal products include film, cream, jelly, vaginal suppositories, and a nonhormonal contraceptive gel.

- An *intrauterine device (IUD)* is a small, flexible, plastic device that is inserted through the cervical opening into the uterus. It disrupts the fertilization and implantation processes.

- *Long-acting, reversible contraceptive methods (LARCs),* which include the IUD and birth control implant, are recommended as first-line contraceptive choices for adolescents and adult women.

- *Fertility awareness–based methods (FAMs)* involve a woman's awareness of her body's reproductive cycles. These include the *calendar (rhythm), basal body temperature (BBT),* and *cervical mucus methods,* which when used together constitute the *symptothermal method.* These methods are suitable only for women with regular menstrual cycles and for couples with high motivation.

- The *lactational amenorrhea method (LAM)* is an effective, temporary method of contraception used by mothers who are exclusively breastfeeding their children.

- *Sterilization* is the most widely used method of contraception in the world. The most common form for women is *tubal ligation,* closing off the fallopian tubes. The surgical procedure that sterilizes men is a *vasectomy,* in which each vas deferens (sperm-carrying tube) is closed off. These methods of contraception are very effective.

- The use of *emergency contraception* prevents pregnancy by keeping a fertilized egg from implanting into the uterus. Depending on the brand, when used within 3–5 days of unprotected intercourse, the emergency contraceptive pill, known as the "morning-after pill," can be quite effective. The ParaGard IUD can also be used as a form of emergency contraception.

Abortion

- *Abortion,* the expulsion of the conceptus from the uterus, can be spontaneous or induced. *Medication abortion* is available in the United States to terminate early pregnancy. Surgical methods of abortion are *vacuum aspiration* and *dilation and evacuation (D&E).* Abortion is generally safe if done in the first trimester. Second-trimester abortions are riskier. The abortion rate in the United States in recent years has declined to the lowest rate ever observed in the United States.

- For women and society, the abortion debate is complex and raises many emotional and political issues. The majority of women report feeling relief following the procedure.

- The current constitutional doctrine on abortion is evolving and dependent upon decisions of the U.S. Supreme Court and interpretations of state governments.

Research Issues

- High developmental costs, government regulations, political agendas, and marketing priorities all play a part in restricting contraceptive research. The biggest barrier, however, may be the fear of lawsuits.

Questions for Discussion

- Who, in your opinion, should have access to contraception? Should the parent(s) of individuals younger than age 18 be informed that the minor has obtained contraception? Why or why not?

- What considerations do you have before you would use a contraceptive? With whom would you discuss these? What sources of information might you use to verify your concerns or issues?

■ If you or your partner experienced an unplanned pregnancy, what would you do? What resources do you have that would support your decision?

Sex and the Internet

Planned Parenthood

Most of us have heard about Planned Parenthood and the services it offers related to family planning. What we might not be aware of is the scope of the organization and the information it provides to aid us in our decisions. To learn more about Planned Parenthood or a specific topic related to its work, go to the group's website: https://www.plannedparenthood.org. Go to the "Learn" icon, select a content area and answer the following:

■ What topic did you choose? Why?

■ What are five key points related to this topic?

■ As a result of what you have learned, what opinions do you have or action would you take concerning this issue?

■ Would you recommend this site to a person interested in learning more about family planning? Why or why not?

Suggested Websites

Contraception Atlas

https://www.contraceptioninfo.eu/node/89
The Atlas tracks government policies on access to contraceptive, counseling, and online information in 46 European countries.

Centers for Disease Control and Prevention Reproductive Health Information Source

www.cdc.gov/reproductivehealth/contraception/index.htm
Provides information, research, data, and scientific reports on men's and women's contraceptive needs.

The Emergency Contraception Website

ec.princeton.edu
Operated by the Office of Population Research at Princeton University, this project is designed to provide accurate information about emergency contraception and where to obtain it.

MedlinePlus

https://medlineplus.gov/birthcontrol.html
Run by the U.S. National Library of Medicine (NLM), this site provides the basics, research, and resources for individuals seeking birth control.

NARAL Pro-Choice America

www.prochoiceamerica.org
A pro-choice group that advocates for comprehensive reproductive health policies to secure reproductive rights for all Americans.

National Right to Life

http://www.nrlc.org
The mission of National Right to Life is to provide legal protection to human life, whether born or unborn.

Plan C

https://plancpills.org
Providing physician oversight, this website offers information about and access to medication abortion pills in order that women might have both self-managed and effective abortions.

Population Council

http://www.popcouncil.org
An international, nonprofit, nongovernmental organization that conducts biomedical, social science, and public health research on such topics as family planning, contraceptive development, and abortion.

Power to Decide

https://powertodecide.org
A campaign to prevent unplanned pregnancy by providing trusted, high-quality, accurate information on sexual health and contraceptive methods, with the belief that all young people should have the opportunity to pursue the future they want.

United Nations Population Fund

http://www.unfpa.org
An international development agency that advocates for the rights of young people, including accurate information and services related to sexuality and reproductive health.

Suggested Reading

Eig, J. (2015). *The birth of the pill.* W. W. Norton. A fascinating look into the evolution of medical practices, funding, and ethics as well as a portrait of how women's reproductive lives are woven into our cultural history.

Guillebaud, J. (2019). *Contraception today* (9th ed.). Taylor & Francis. A thorough resource of contraceptives and birth control written by individuals and health professionals.

Hatcher, R. A., Zieman, M., Allen, A. Z., Lathrop, E., & Haddad, L. (2019). *Managing contraception 2019-2020: For your pocket* (15th ed.). Bridging the Gap Communications. Information on all methods of contraception, reproductive needs, and abortion.

Hill, S. (2019). *This is your brain on birth control: The surprising science of women, hormones, and the law of unintended consequences.* Avery. Reveals crucial information about hormonal birth control and what every woman should know about it and how it affects them.

Ussher, J. M., Chrisler, J. C., & Perz, J. (Eds). (2020). *Routledge international handbook of women's sexual and reproductive health.* Routledge. A reference work on leading developments in women's sexual and reproductive health.

Conception, Pregnancy, and Childbirth

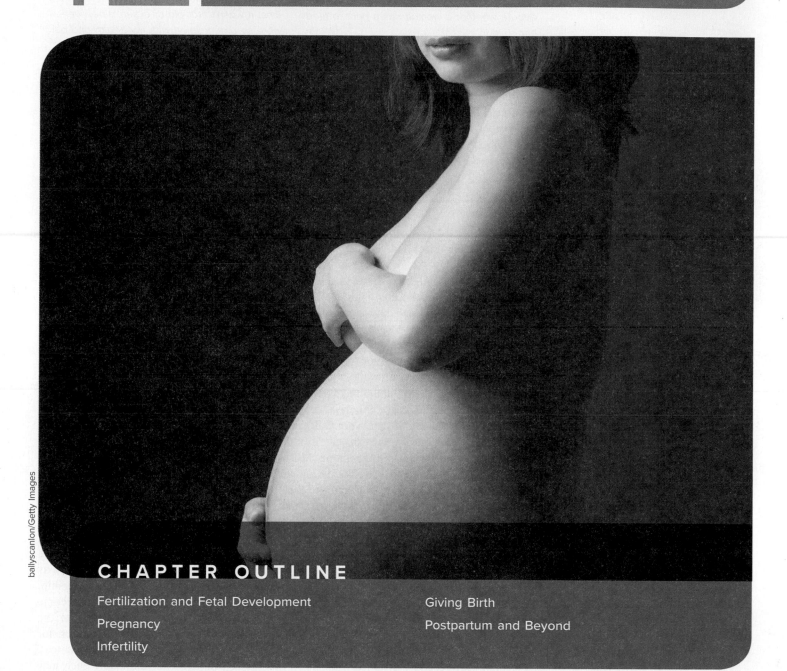

ballyscanlon/Getty Images

CHAPTER OUTLINE

Student Voices

"When I was in my teens, I moved from my home [Guatemala] to the states and found things turned upside [down] from my traditional background. Take, for example, breastfeeding. In my country, it is a normal thing to breastfeed; you would not think twice about seeing a nurturing mother breastfeeding her child in public. Here, it seems to upset people's sensibilities when a nursing mother feeds her child in public. I wonder, that which is so natural and necessary, how can we debate whether a woman has a right to feed her child in public?"

—20-year-old female

"Pregnancy and childbirth have changed my life. As the mother of three young children, I look back at my pregnancies as probably three of the best periods of my life. Oh, sure, there were the days of exhaustion and nausea, pelvic heaviness, the large cumbersome breasts, and lost sleep, but in retrospect, they were overshadowed by the life growing inside of me. In giving life, I celebrate my womanhood."

—43-year-old female

"After getting married and having a daughter, things changed. While I was pregnant we, maybe, had sex 10 times. I was really sick during the first trimester and on bed rest during the second and third trimesters. At the time, it wasn't that big of a deal since we were so preoccupied with my health and our daughter. After she was born, it seemed that we were just out of practice and had a hard time initiating sex. When we did have sex, we would both say, 'WOW, we should do this more often,' but then life would get in the way and 2 weeks would go by before we had sex again."

—28-year-old female

MANY PARENTS CONSIDER THE BIRTH of a child to be one of the happiest events of their lives. For most individuals, pregnancy is relatively comfortable and the outcome predictably joyful. Yet for increasing numbers of others, especially among the poor, the prospect of having children raises the specters of drugs, disease, malnutrition, and familial chaos. And there are those couples who have dreamed of and planned for families for years, only to find that they are unable to conceive.

In this chapter, we view pregnancy and childbirth from biological, social, and psychological perspectives. We consider pregnancy loss, infertility, and reproductive technology. And we look at the challenges of the transition to becoming a family.

Parenthood is now a matter of choice, thanks to the widespread use of contraception and changing perceptions of child-free couples. In the past, individuals or couples without children were referred to as "childless," implying they desired children but were not able to have any. This term is different from **child-free**, to reflect the cultural shift and demographic trend in the direction of increasing numbers of individuals and couples who choose not to take on the responsibility of parenthood. Most people cite the desire for freedom as a factor for a decision not to enter parenthood; however, women, more than men, may be especially concerned that childbearing will hamper their careers (Khazan, 2017). Additional factors that contribute to this decision include timing, divorce, ambivalence on the part of one partner, lack of desire to conceive or adopt a child when single, and the desire to preserve a happy relationship.

Those who become pregnant enter a new phase of their lives. The pregnancy affects people's feelings about themselves and their relationships with their partners, as well as the interrelationships of other family members. Even more than marriage or partnership, parenthood signifies adulthood—the final, irreversible end of childhood. A person can become an ex-spouse but never an ex-parent. The irrevocable nature of parenthood may make the first-time parent doubtful and apprehensive, especially during the pregnancy. However, for the most part, parenthood is learned experientially, although ideas can modify practices. A person may receive assistance from more experienced parents, but ultimately each new parent must learn on their own.

● Fertilization and Fetal Development

Once the **oocyte** (ovum, or unfertilized egg) has been released from the ovary, it drifts into the fallopian tube, where it may be fertilized if live sperm are present (see Figure 1). If the pregnancy proceeds without interruption, the birth will occur in approximately 266 days. Traditionally, health care professionals count the first day of the pregnancy as the day on which the woman began her last menstrual period; they calculate the due date to be 280 days, which is also 10 lunar months, from that day.

The Fertilization Process

The oocyte remains viable for 12–24 hours after ovulation; most sperm are viable in the female reproductive tract for 12–48 hours, although some may be viable for up to 5 days. Therefore, for fertilization to occur, intercourse must take place within 5 days before and 1 day after ovulation.

Of the 200–400 million sperm ejaculated into the vagina, only a few thousand or even a few hundred actually reach the fallopian tubes. The others leak from the vagina or are destroyed within its acidic environment. Those that make it into the cervix, which is easier during ovulation when the cervical mucus becomes more fluid, may still be destroyed by white blood cells within the uterus. Furthermore, the sperm that actually reach the oocyte within a few minutes of ejaculation are not yet capable of getting through its outer layers. They must first undergo **capacitation**, the process by which their membranes become fragile enough to release the enzymes from their acrosomes, the helmetlike coverings of the sperm's nuclei. It takes 6–8 hours for this reaction to occur. It has been observed that sperm have receptor molecules that are attracted to a chemical released by the ovum. Furthermore, the membrane of the sperm cell contains a chemical that helps the sperm adhere to, and eventually penetrate, the outer layer of the egg.

Once a single sperm is inside the oocyte cytoplasm, a chemical reaction occurs that prevents any other sperm from entering the oocyte. Immediately, the oocyte begins to swell, detaching the sperm that still cling to its outer layer. Next, it completes the final stage of

> *"If your parents didn't have any children, there's a good chance that you won't have any."*
>
> —Clarence Day (1874–1935)

> *"Expectant parents who want a boy will get a girl, and vice versa; those who practice birth control will get twins."*
>
> —John Rush

● **FIGURE 1**

Ovulation, Fertilization, and Development of the Blastocyst. This drawing charts the progress of the released oocyte (unfertilized egg) through fertilization and pre-embryonic development. Note that the fertilization takes place in the fallopian tube.

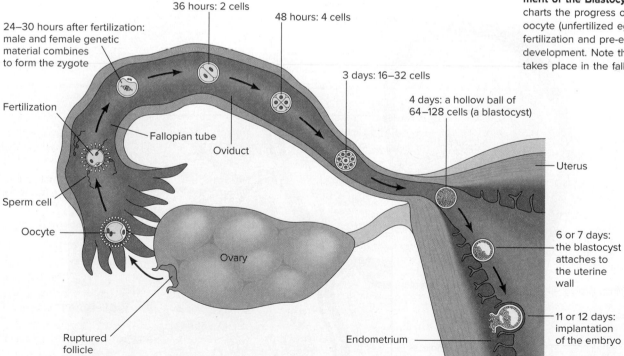

24–30 hours after fertilization: male and female genetic material combines to form the zygote

36 hours: 2 cells

48 hours: 4 cells

3 days: 16–32 cells

4 days: a hollow ball of 64–128 cells (a blastocyst)

Fertilization

Fallopian tube

Oviduct

Uterus

Sperm cell

Oocyte

Ovary

6 or 7 days: the blastocyst attaches to the uterine wall

Ruptured follicle

Endometrium

11 or 12 days: implantation of the embryo

cell division and becomes a mature ovum by forming the ovum nucleus. The nuclei of sperm and ovum then release their chromosomes, which combine to form the diploid zygote, containing 23 pairs of chromosomes. Each parent contributes one chromosome to each of the pairs. Fertilization is now complete, and pre-embryonic development begins. Within 9 months, this single cell, the zygote, may become the 600 trillion cells that constitute a human being.

Development of the Fetus

Following fertilization, the zygote undergoes a series of divisions, during which the cells replicate. After 4 or 5 days, there are about 100 cells, now called a **blastocyst**. On about the 5th day, the blastocyst arrives in the uterine cavity, where it floats for a day or two before implanting in the soft, blood-rich uterine lining (endometrium), which has spent the past 3 weeks preparing for its arrival. The process of **implantation** takes about 1 week. Human chorionic gonadotropin (hCG) secreted by the blastocyst maintains the uterine environment in an "embryo-friendly" condition and prevents the shedding of the endometrium, which would normally occur during menstruation.

The blastocyst, or pre-embryo, rapidly grows into an **embryo**, which will, in turn, be referred to as a **fetus** after the 8th week of **gestation**, or the time between conception and birth; better known as pregnancy. During the first 2 or 3 weeks of development, the **embryonic membranes** are formed. These include the **amniotic sac** (also called the bag of water), a sac that holds the embryo and later fetus. It consists of two membranes: The inner membrane, the **amnion**, contains the **amniotic fluid** and the fetus, while the outer membrane, the **chorion**, encloses the embryo and contributes to the development of the placenta (see Figure 2).

During the 3rd week, extensive cell migration occurs and the stage is set for the development of the organs. The first body segments and the brain begin to form. The digestive and circulatory systems begin to develop in the 4th week, and the heart begins to pump blood. By the end of the 4th week, the spinal cord and nervous system have also begun to develop. The 5th week sees the formation of arms and legs. In the 6th week, the eyes and ears form. At 7 weeks, the reproductive organs begin to differentiate in males; female reproductive organs continue to develop. At 8 weeks, the fetus is about the size of a thumb although the

"What was your original face before you were born?"

—Zen koan (riddle)

● **FIGURE 2**

The Fetus in the Uterus and a Cross Section of the Placenta. The placenta is the organ of exchange between mother and fetus. Nutrients and oxygen pass from the mother to the fetus, and waste products pass from the fetus to the mother via blood vessels within the umbilical cord.

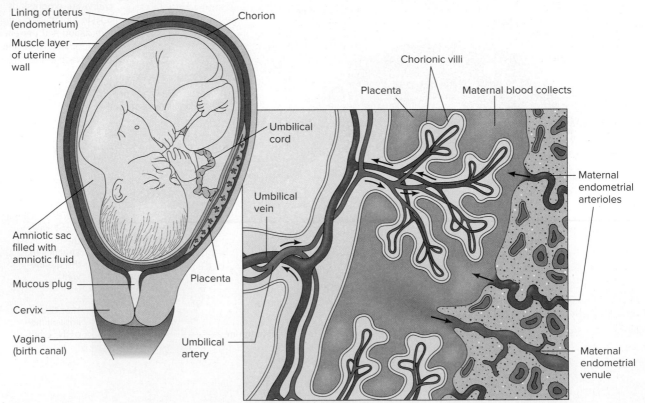

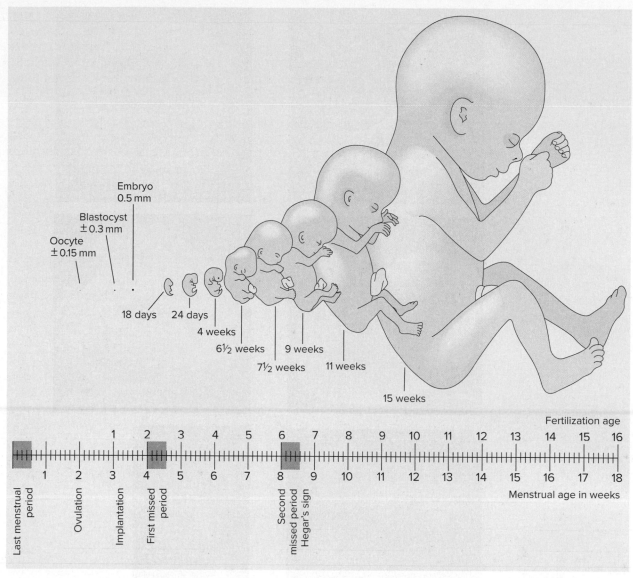

Oocyte
±0.15 mm

Blastocyst
±0.3 mm

Embryo
0.5 mm

18 days

24 days

4 weeks

6½ weeks

7½ weeks

9 weeks

11 weeks

15 weeks

Fertilization age

1 2 3 4 5 6 7 8 9 10 11 12 13 14 15 16

1 2 3 4 5 6 7 8 9 10 11 12 13 14 15 16 17 18

Menstrual age in weeks

Last menstrual period

Ovulation

Implantation

First missed period

Second missed period Hegar's sign

● **FIGURE 3**

Growth of the Embryo and Fetus. In this drawing, the actual sizes of the developing embryo and fetus are shown, from conception through the first 15 weeks.

head is nearly as large as the body. The brain begins to function to coordinate the development of the internal organs. Facial features begin to form and bones begin to develop. Arms, hands, fingers, legs, feet, toes, and eyes are almost fully developed at 12 weeks. At 15 weeks, the fetus has a strong heartbeat, some digestive functioning, and active muscles (see Figure 3). Most bones are developed by then and the eyebrows appear. At this stage, the fetus is covered with a fine, downy hair called **lanugo** and it is the size of a naval orange.

The **placenta**, an organ that connects the developing fetus to the uterine wall to provide nutrients and oxygen via the mother's bloodstream to the fetus while also removing waste products from the fetus's blood, grows larger as the fetus does. Fetal blood and maternal blood do not normally intermingle. Rather, exchanges between the fetal and maternal circulatory systems occur through the walls of the blood vessels. The placenta attaches to the wall of the uterus and the fetus's **umbilical cord**, which connects the placenta and fetus and through which nutrients pass. The placenta serves as a biochemical barrier, allowing dissolved substances to pass to the fetus but blocking some kinds of viruses and bacteria from passing into the fetal circulatory system. At the same time, certain prescriptions and other drugs, tobacco (including secondhand smoke), alcohol, and some viruses do cross the placenta and can harm the fetus (Stanford Children's Health, 2020.12a). This can occur as early as 10 to 14 days after conception.

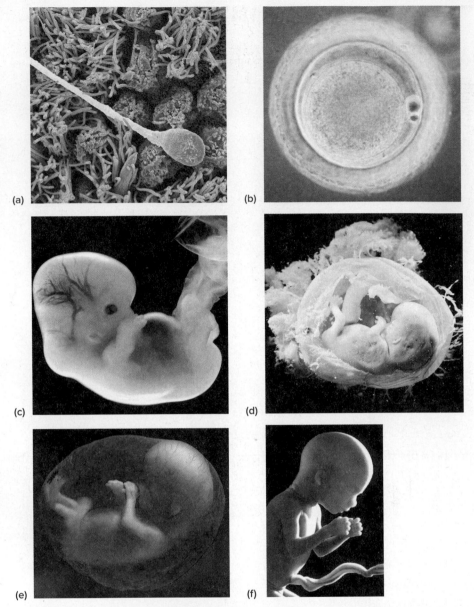

Developmental Stages of a Fetus. (a) After ejaculation, several million sperm move through the cervical mucus toward the fallopian tubes; an oocyte has moved into one of the tubes. On their way to the oocyte, millions of sperm are destroyed in the vagina, uterus, or fallopian tubes. Some go the wrong direction in the vagina, and others swim into the wrong tube. **(b)** The woman's and man's chromosomes have united, and the fertilized ovum has divided for the first time. After about 1 week, the blastocyst will implant itself in the uterine lining. **(c)** The embryo is 5 weeks old and is two fifth of an inch long. It floats in the embryonic sac. The major divisions of the brain can be seen, as well as an eye, hands, arms, and a long tail. **(d)** The embryo is now 7 weeks old, is almost 1 inch long, and is connected to its umbilical cord. Its external and internal organs are developing. It has eyes, nose, mouth, lips, and tongue. **(e)** At 12 weeks, the fetus is over 3 inches long and weighs almost 1 ounce. **(f)** At 16 weeks, the fetus is more than 6 inches long and weighs about 7 ounces. All its organs have been formed. The time that follows is now one of simple growth.

By 5 months, the fetus is 10-12 inches long and weighs between ½ and 1 pound. The internal organs are well developed, although the lungs cannot function well outside the uterus. At 6 months, the fetus is 11-14 inches long and weighs more than 1 pound. At 7 months, it is 13-17 inches long and weighs about 3 pounds. At this point, most healthy fetuses are viable, that is, capable of surviving outside the womb. Although some fetuses are viable at 5 or 6 months, they require specialized care to survive. The fetus spends the final 2 months of gestation growing rapidly. At term (9 months), it will be about 20 inches long and will weigh about 7 pounds. A full-term pregnancy lasts 40 weeks. Even though 37 weeks is also considered full term, studies show that babies born even a few weeks early are at greater risk for health problems than those who are born later (Dekker, 2020).

● Pregnancy

Preconception Health

The health of both parents before conception and for women in early pregnancy affect the health of the fetus. **Preconception health** refers to the health of women and men during their reproductive years and focuses on the steps necessary to protect the health of a baby they might have sometime in the future (CDC, 2020.12a). This focus differs from **prenatal care**, which is recommended after a woman becomes pregnant and involves the monitoring of the baby's development and mother's health. In 2018, 77.5% of women began prenatal care in the first trimester, while 6.2% had late (beginning in the third trimester) or no prenatal care (March of Dimes, 2020.12).

There are a number of ways that lifestyle choices can influence the outcomes of a pregnancy. One example of this is physical activity, which in all stages of life improves cardiorespiratory fitness, enhances psychological well-being, reduces the risk of obesity and associated health problems, and results in greater longevity in both men and women. Physical activity, particularly aerobic and strength-conditioning exercises, has been shown to benefit most women, before, during, and after pregnancy (American College of Obstetricians and Gynecologists [ACOG], 2020.12a). While physical activity can prevent excessive weight gain, which can complicate the pregnancy and contribute to obesity, it may also lower the likelihood of cesarean section, breathing problems in newborns, maternal hypertension, and a baby that is significantly larger than average at birth. Thus, a goal of moderate-intensity exercise for at least 150 minutes per week should be maintained both during pregnancy and the postpartum period (6 weeks after childbirth) (ACOG, 2020.12a). For example, increasing one's intake of folic acid, getting up-to-date on vaccines, discussing preexisting medical conditions, maintaining a healthy weight, and avoiding smoking, drinking, and taking drugs are among those behaviors that can reduce the risk of complications and improve the chances of a healthy pregnancy. It is extremely important that women and men who are sexually active and not consistently or effectively using contraception be mindful of the lifestyle choices they are making and seek medical attention before the woman attempts to become pregnant.

Pregnancy Detection

Chemical tests designed to detect the presence of **human chorionic gonadotropin (hCG)**, a hormone produced by the placenta after implantation, can usually determine pregnancy approximately 1 week following a missed or spotty menstrual period. Pregnancy testing may be done in a doctor's office or family planning clinic, or at home with a test purchased from a drugstore or online. Such tests diagnose pregnancy within 7 days after conception with 97-99% accuracy.

There are two types of pregnancy tests: urine and blood. Both tests detect the presence of hCG. Urine tests, which can be used at home, can be taken after the first day of a missed period, or about 2 weeks after conception. When performed correctly, these tests are around 99% accurate. Blood tests, which are taken at a doctor's office or lab, can detect pregnancy at about 6-8 days

An at-home pregnancy test taken close to or on the day of a missed period is highly accurate regardless of the brand or cost of the test.

Shutterstock/Ioannis Pantzi

after ovulation and are 99% accurate. False negatives, meaning that a woman is pregnant despite the test indicating she is not, could mean that the test was taken too early or was used incorrectly (WebMD, 2020.12).

The first reliable physical sign of pregnancy can be observed about 4 weeks after a woman misses her period. By this point, changes in her cervix and pelvis are apparent during a pelvic examination. At this stage, the woman is considered to be 8 weeks pregnant. Clinicians calculate pregnancy as beginning at the time of the woman's last menstrual period rather than at the time of actual fertilization because that date is often difficult to determine. Another signal of pregnancy, called **Hegar's sign**, is a softening of the uterus just above the cervix, which can be felt during a vaginal examination. In addition, a slight purple hue colors the labia minora; the vagina and cervix also take on a purplish color rather than being the usual pink. Pregnancy is frequently confirmed through the use of **ultrasound**, a test that uses high-frequency sound waves to capture a live image inside the uterus. The test is also used during pregnancy to check the baby's development, the presence of a multiple pregnancy, and to help identify certain abnormalities.

Adjustments and Psychological Changes in Women During Pregnancy

A woman's early response to pregnancy will vary dramatically according to who she is, how she feels about pregnancy and parenthood, whether the pregnancy was planned, whether she has a secure home situation, and many other factors. Her feelings may be ambivalent and they will probably change over the course of the pregnancy.

A couple's relationship is likely to undergo changes during pregnancy. (The principal developmental tasks for the expectant parents are summarized in Table 1). It can be a stressful time, especially if the pregnancy was unanticipated. On the other hand, women with supportive partners often have fewer health problems in pregnancy and more positive feelings about their changing bodies than those whose partners are not supportive (Albuja et al., 2019). Communication is especially important during this period for many reasons, including the possibility that each partner may have preconceived ideas about what the other is feeling. Both partners may have fears about the baby's well-being, the approaching birth, their ability to parent, and the ways in which the baby will interfere with their own relationship. All of these concerns are typical. Sharing them, perhaps in the setting of a prenatal group, can strengthen the relationship. If the pregnant woman's partner is not supportive or if she does not have a partner, it is important that she find other sources of support—family, friends, women's groups—and that she not be reluctant to ask for help.

A pregnant woman's relationship with her own mother may also undergo changes. In a certain sense, becoming a mother makes a woman the equal of her own mother. She can now lay claim to co-equal status as an adult. Women

"Only through sexual union are new beings capable of existing. This union, therefore, represents a place between two worlds, a point of contact between being and nonbeing, where life manifests itself and incarnates the divine spirit."

—Alain Daniélou (1907–1994)

The physical and psychological changes that accompany pregnancy can have a ripple effect on a woman's relationship with her partner and family.

RuslanDashinsky/Getty Images

TABLE 1 ● Principal Tasks of Expectant Parents	
Mothers	**Fathers/Partners**
Development of an emotional attachment to the fetus	Acceptance of the pregnancy and attachment to the fetus
Differentiation of the self from the fetus	Acceptance and resolution of the relationship with his own father
Acceptance and resolution of the relationship with her own mother	Resolution of dependency issues involving parents or wife/partner
Resolution of dependency issues involving parents or husband/partner	Evaluation of practical and financial responsibilities
Evaluation of practical and financial responsibilities	

who have depended on their mother tend to become more independent and assertive as their pregnancy progresses. Women who have been distant from, hostile to, or alienated from their mother may begin to identify with their mother's experience of pregnancy. Even women who have delayed childbearing until their thirties may be surprised to find their relationships with their mother changing and becoming more "adult." Working through these changing relationships is a kind of "psychological gestation" that accompanies the physiological gestation of the fetus.

The first trimester (3 months) of pregnancy may be physically difficult for the expectant woman. Approximately 70–80% of pregnant women experience **morning sickness**, the nauseous feeling that often occurs during the first trimester of pregnancy (Bustos et al., 2018). These symptoms, which can begin 2–4 weeks after fertilization, and peak between 6 and 9 weeks of gestation, can be one of the first signs of pregnancy, can occur at any time of the day, and usually subside by the end of the first trimester. Others may have these symptoms for the duration of their pregnancies. Researchers from the National Institutes of Health (2016) have found that nausea and vomiting during pregnancy are associated with a lower risk of miscarriage in pregnant women, proposing that morning sickness may protect the fetus against toxins and disease-causing organisms in food and beverages.

The pregnant woman may also have fears that she will miscarry or that the child will not be normal. Her sexuality may undergo changes, resulting in unfamiliar needs for more, less, or differently expressed sexual behaviors, which may, in turn, cause anxiety. (Sexuality during pregnancy is discussed further in Think About It: "Sexual Behavior During Pregnancy.") Education about the birth process and her own body's functioning and support from a partner, friends, relatives, and health care professionals are the best antidotes to fear.

During the second trimester, most of the nausea and fatigue disappear, and the pregnant woman can feel the fetus move. Worries about miscarriage will probably begin to diminish, too, for the riskiest part of fetal development has passed. The pregnant woman may look and feel radiant. She will very likely be proud of her accomplishment and be delighted as her pregnancy begins to show. She may feel in harmony with life's natural rhythms. Some women, however, may be concerned about their increasing size, fearing that they are becoming unattractive. A partner's attention and reassurance may help ease these fears.

The third trimester may be the time of the greatest challenges in daily living. The uterus, originally about the size of the woman's fist, enlarges to fill the pelvic cavity and pushes up into the abdominal cavity, exerting increasing pressure on the other internal organs (see Figure 4). Water retention (edema) is a fairly common problem during late pregnancy. It also tends to be worse at the end of the day and in warm temperatures. Edema may cause swelling in the face, hands, ankles, and feet, but it can often be controlled by cutting down on the intake of salt, elevating the feet, eating healthy, and exercising. A woman should call her physician if she notices swelling in her face, puffiness around her eyes, more than slight swelling in her hands, or excessive swelling of her feet or ankles. Her physical abilities also are limited by her size, and she may need to cut back her work hours or stop working.

The woman and her partner may become increasingly concerned about the upcoming birth. Some women experience periods of antepartum depression, a mood disorder, preceding delivery. Untreated, it can lead to problems in both the woman and baby. Others feel a sense of exhilaration and anticipation marked by bursts of industriousness. For some the fetus already is a member of the family. Both parents may begin talking to the fetus and "playing" with it by patting and rubbing the mother's belly.

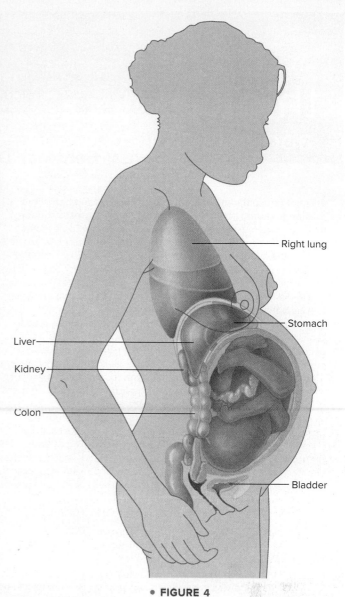

Right lung

Stomach

Liver

Kidney

Colon

Bladder

● **FIGURE 4**

Mother and Fetus in Third Trimester of Pregnancy. The expanding uterus affects the mother's internal organs, causing feelings of pressure and possible discomfort.

think
about it

Sexual Behavior During Pregnancy

It is not unusual for a woman's sexual desires and behaviors **to change during pregnancy, although there is great variation among women in these expressions of sexuality.** Some women feel beautiful, energetic, and sensual and are very much interested in sex; others feel awkward and decidedly unsexy. Exhaustion, tender breasts, hormonal fluctuations, and self-consciousness may diminish sexual desire. It is also quite possible for a woman's sexual desires to fluctuate during this time. The mother's partner may also feel confusion or conflicts about sexual activity.

Though sexual intercourse or other activities that may lead to orgasm during pregnancy is thought by some to trigger the onset of contractions and therefore labor, in low-risk pregnancies, orgasms do not significantly increase the likelihood of early labor (Carbone et al., 2019). When couples are educated and have positive attitudes about having sex during pregnancy, higher sexual satisfaction for both partners can occur (Jawed-Wessel et al., 2019).

Changes in sexual patterns are not necessarily a problem; however, significant variations or long pauses in sexual activity have the potential to impact relationships. To learn more about how pregnancy and the postpartum period (to be discussed later in the chapter) impact pregnant couples, a review of 56 studies published between 1996 and 2015 was conducted to assess what is known about sexual behaviors during this period (Jawed-Wessel & Sevick, 2017). Focusing on pregnancy, the articles revealed:

1. A gradual decline in vaginal intercourse in early pregnancy and again between second and third trimesters occurred among most couples.

2. Little to no change in noncoital sexual behaviors took place, though there was considerable variation of rates depending on the study. This included the percent who engaged in anal sex (0–20%), oral sex (30–59%), masturbation (6–64% of women), and use of sex toys (about 13%).

3. Rear-entry position increased, but missionary position remained popular for most.

4. Concerns about having sex during pregnancy were common.

The authors highlighted the sociological and cultural influences that impact sexuality. Because of this, they focused more on the nature of the pregnant woman and her partner rather than on precautions against practices that might harm the pregnancy, citing that communication about sexuality was extremely important during this time.

Although there are no "rules" governing sexual behavior during pregnancy, a few basic precautions should be observed:

- If the woman has had a prior miscarriage, she should check with her health care practitioner before having intercourse, masturbating, or engaging in other activities that might lead to orgasm. Powerful uterine contractions could induce a spontaneous abortion in some women, especially during the first trimester.

- If the woman has vaginal bleeding, she should refrain from all sexual activity and consult her health care provider or midwife at once.

- If the insertion of the penis or other object into the vagina causes pain that is not easily remedied by a change of position, the couple should refrain from penetration.

- Pressure on the woman's abdomen should be avoided, especially during the final months of pregnancy.

- Late in pregnancy, an orgasm may induce uterine contractions. Generally, this is not considered harmful, but the pregnant woman may want to discuss it with her practitioner.

A couple may be uncertain as to how to express their sexual feelings, especially if it is their first pregnancy. The following guidelines may be helpful:

- Even during a normal pregnancy, sexual intercourse may be uncomfortable. The couple may want to try such positions as side by side or rear entry to avoid pressure on the woman's abdomen and to facilitate shallow penetration.

- If sexual activity is not comfortable for the woman, orgasm may still be intensely pleasurable. She may wish to consider masturbating alone or with her partner or engaging in cunnilingus. It is important to note that air should *not* be blown into the vagina during cunnilingus.

Once the baby has been born, a couple can resume intercourse after the bleeding has stopped and the vaginal walls have healed. This may take anywhere from 4 to 8 weeks. At the same time, it's important to remember that communication about sexual preferences can build intimacy and mutual understanding necessary to withstand the invariable shifts and changes that will occur in sexual relationships (Jawed-Wessel et al., 2019).

Think Critically

1. What are your views about having sex during pregnancy?

2. How comfortable would you be in discussing with your doctor the topic of sexuality during pregnancy?

3. What new information did you learn as a result of reading this box?

Complications of Pregnancy and Dangers to the Fetus

Usually, pregnancy proceeds without major complications. Good nutrition, a moderate amount of exercise, and manageable levels of stress are among the most significant factors in a complication-free pregnancy. In addition, early and ongoing prenatal care is important.

Maternal mortality is a significant indicator of the quality of both national and international health care. Unfortunately, not all expectant parents have access to health care or live in a safe environment. This can be witnessed in the United States, which in 2018 reported 17.4 maternal deaths (a death that occurs during pregnancy or within 1 year postpartum) per 100,000 live births (CDC, 2020.12b). Though this rate is higher than the last-published national rate (12.7 in 2007), the current rate reflects changes in the way the data was collected and reported. When reporting maternal mortality rates, it's important to call attention to the wide racial/ethnic gaps that exist between non-Hispanic Black women (37.1 per 100,000 live births), non-Hispanic white women (14.7), and Hispanic women (11.8) (CDC, 2020.12b). When examining national versus global rates, among 183 countries reporting maternal mortality data, with 183 indicating the highest rate, the United States ranked 129th, just above Russia and Saudi Arabia (CIA World Factbook, 2019). As the number of childbirth-related deaths has risen, the United States now has the dubious reputation of being the most dangerous place in the developed world to give birth (Rettner, 2018). Although a host of factors, including being overweight and having a pre-existing health condition, have been among the factors blamed for the high maternal mortality rates, a *USA Today* investigation reviewed more than 500,000 pages of records from dozens of hospitals and found that many hospitals weren't following recommendations that could save women's lives (Young, 2019). "Experts say that about 50% of the deaths of women from childbirth-related causes could be prevented if they were given better medical care," noted Alison Young, lead author of the investigation.

Effects of Teratogens Substances other than nutrients may reach the developing embryo or fetus through the placenta. Although few extensive studies have been done on this, toxic substances in the environment can also affect the health of the fetus. Whatever a woman breathes, eats, or drinks is eventually received by the conceptus in some proportion. A fetus's blood-alcohol level, for example, is equal to that of the mother. **Teratogens** are substances or other factors that cause defects (e.g., brain damage or physical deformities) in developing embryos or fetuses.

The most critical periods of vulnerability, when exposure to particular teratogens can cause the greatest harm to the embryo or fetus, are during the embryonic stage (weeks 1–7) and early fetal development (first trimester of pregnancy). The embryo is most vulnerable to the effects of teratogens during the embryonic stage, when the major organ systems differentiate. Unfortunately, this is also a time when many women are not aware that they are pregnant.

Birth defects affect 1 in every 33 babies born in the United States each year (CDC, 2020.12c). **Birth defects** are structural changes that are present at birth and can affect almost any part or parts of the baby's body. They are common, costly, and can be critical. Depending on the severity of the defect and what body part is affected, the expected lifespan of a person with a birth defect may or may not be affected.

It is important to note that any screening done during routine prenatal care visits is to identify potential risks and, if appropriate, encourage treatment. Such interventions are not intended to punish a woman. However, patients should also be informed of the ramifications of a positive drug screening result, including any mandatory reporting requirements (ACOG, 2017).

Environmental Concerns Chemicals, environmental pollutants, and climate change are potentially threatening to both mothers and their unborn children. For example, a systematic review of 68 U.S. studies dating back to 2007, which included over 32 million births, found that 84% of the births showed a statistically significant association between increased air pollution and heat exposure and serious risks for pregnancy (Bekkar et al., 2020).

Adverse pregnancy outcomes include preterm birth, low birthweight, and stillbirth, with the populations at highest risk being those with asthma and people of color, especially Black mothers. Living near an airport, for example, can expose pregnant women to fine particles emitted from aircraft and increase her risk for having a preterm birth (Wing et al., 2020). Exposure to pesticides can also increase a woman's chance of having a miscarriage, cause developmental disabilities in children, and may pass into breast milk (National Institute for Occupational Safety and Health, 2020). Many doctors are also warning about exposure to phthalates, a group of chemicals used to make plastics more flexible, which belong to a category of endocrine-disrupting chemicals (Rutkowska & Diamanti-Kandarakis, 2016). Found in a wide array of plastics, household goods, drugs, cleansers, and personal care products, toxins can escape from these products as vapors or particles, which in turn have been detected in a wide variety of bodily fluids, including breast milk, urine, and semen. Whether phthalates are causing fertility problems is uncertain, however, a growing body of research is linking higher levels of the chemicals to a greater risk of miscarriage, lower fertility, and difficulty conceiving (ACOG, 2013).

Alcohol   Fetal alcohol exposure is one of the leading preventable causes of physical, behavioral, and intellectual disability among children. Risks associated with alcohol to the central nervous system exist throughout the pregnancy. The Centers for Disease Control & Prevention (2020.12d) warn that there is no known safe time or amount of alcohol consumption for a woman during pregnancy or when trying to get pregnant and highlight the risk of miscarriage, stillbirth, low birth weight, premature labor, and fetal alcohol spectrum disorders that are associated with drinking. **Fetal alcohol spectrum disorder (FASD)** is an umbrella term used for a group of conditions that can cause various kinds of disabilities in a child. Often the symptoms, including hyperactivity, poor language skills, concentration, and poor math skills are not obvious at birth, and hence are often difficult to diagnose before childhood. Depending on the symptoms, one type of FASD is **fetal alcohol syndrome (FAS)** and is the most extreme outcome from drinking alcohol during pregnancy. FAS can include abnormal facial features, growth problems, and central nervous system problems. Children born with FAS can have problems with learning, memory, attention, communication, vision, and/or hearing. Its visible characteristics include three common facial features: a thin upper lip, a smooth philtrum, or

The problems caused by fetal alcohol syndrome vary from child to child, but defects caused by fetal alcohol syndrome are not reversible.

Rick's Photography/Shutterstock.com

groove between the nose and upper lips, and a reduced distance between an eye's inner and outer corner. Another type of FASD is **alcohol-related neurodevelopmental disorder (ARND)** in which children might have intellectual, behavioral, and learning problems. They might, for example, have difficulties with math, memory, attention, and judgment, and poor impulse control. Those with **alcohol-related birth defects (ARBD)** may have physical problems, including a mixture of those related to the heart, kidneys, bones, or with hearing.

Tobacco   Cigarette smoking reduces a woman's chances of becoming pregnant. If she becomes pregnant and smokes, her risk for pregnancy complications increases (CDC, 2020.12e). These complications include tissue damage in a developing child, particularly in the lung, brain, and lip (cleft lip is a birth defect that occurs when a baby's lip or mouth does not form properly during pregnancy). Studies also suggest a relationship between tobacco use and miscarriage because the carbon monoxide in tobacco smoke can prevent the developing fetus from receiving sufficient oxygen. Smoking during pregnancy has also been linked to sudden infant death syndrome (SIDS), which is discussed later in this chapter. One in five babies born to mothers who smoke during pregnancy has low birth weight, and mothers who are exposed to secondhand smoke while pregnant are more likely to have lower birth weight babies (CDC, 2020.12e).

Although the aerosol of electronic cigarettes (also called e-cigarettes) has fewer harmful substances than cigarette smoke, other products in e-cigarettes contain nicotine and are not safe during pregnancy because they can damage a developing baby's brain and lungs (CDC, 2019.12a). Additionally, some of the flavorings used in e-cigarettes may be harmful to the developing baby.

Marijuana   Because marijuana has been legalized for medicinal and/or recreational purposes in many states, its use by adults, including pregnant women, is increasing. About 1 in 20 women in the U.S. reports using marijuana while pregnant (CDC, 2018.12).

The chemicals in marijuana, in particular TCH, pass through the woman's system to the baby and can negatively affect its development (CDC, 2018.12). Though more research is needed to better understand how marijuana use during pregnancy affects the developing fetus, some research suggests that using marijuana while pregnant can result in a baby having low birth weight and developmental problems, including learning disabilities. Data on the effects of marijuana exposure to the infant through breastfeeding are limited and conflicting. Because of concerns regarding impaired neurodevelopment during pregnancy and beyond, the Committee Opinion by the American Congress of Obstetricians and Gynecologists (2017) states that women who are pregnant or contemplating pregnancy should discontinue marijuana use prior to and during pregnancy and while she is breastfeeding.

Other Drugs   Mothers who regularly use opioids (e.g., morphine, codeine, fentanyl, oxycodone, and opium) are at greater risk for spontaneous abortion and preterm labor and are likely to have infants who are addicted to opioids at birth. In addition, these infants are at risk for neonatal intoxication, respiratory depression, low birth weight, heart defects, and learning and behavioral problems (March of Dimes, 2017).

Prescription drugs should be used during pregnancy only under careful medical supervision. Additionally, over-the-counter drugs, including vitamins, aspirin, and acetaminophen, as well as large quantities of caffeine-containing food and beverages, should be avoided or used only under medical supervision.

Infectious Diseases   Infectious diseases can also damage the fetus. For example, if a woman contracts rubella (also called German measles or three-day measles) during the first 3 months of pregnancy, her child may be born with physical or mental disabilities. Concerns about risks from inactivated virus or bacterial vaccinations during pregnancy are theoretical or uncertain. The benefits of vaccinating generally outweigh potential risks when the likelihood of disease exposure is high (CDC, 2019.12b). However, immunization against some diseases, including those for varicella zoster virus (chickenpox), measles, mumps, and rubella should be done at least a month before the woman becomes pregnant; otherwise, the vaccine can pose a risk to the fetus. [For a list of general recommendations for use in pregnant women, see CDC's "Vaccinating Pregnant Women" (2019.12b).]

Since the start of the COVID-19 pandemic, doctors and researchers have wondered whether the disease can be transmitted from an infected mother to the fetus. HIV and Zika (see below) can infect a fetus this way. While data on pregnancy and COVID-19 are incomplete, the research is evolving. Fetal infections later in pregnancy appear to be rare, and experts are beginning to suggest that COVID-19 won't impact early fetal development (ACOG, 2020.12a; CDC, 2020.12f). However, studies indicate that pregnant women with COVID-19 are more likely to be hospitalized and are at an increased need for severe illness (CDC, 2020.12f,h; 2021.12). This is particularly true for racial minorities, especially non-Hispanic Black adults, who are disproportionately impacted by the virus. Social and economic inequity, not biological differences, are thought to contribute to the risk factors associated with the virus. The rapidly evolving research provides explanations and guidance for vaccinations, pregnancy and breastfeeding, (ACOG, 2020.12a,b,c; CDC, 2020.12f,g; 2021.12a,b,c; Khalil et al., 2020; Waldman, 2020):

- Women who are pregnant or who are breastfeeding may choose to receive the COVID-19 vaccine, however at the time of this book's publication, data have not identified any safety concerns for pregnant women who were vaccinated or for their babies.

- Viral infections, including COVID-19, can be more severe in pregnant women in part because the mother's immune system, which is normally compromised in order to preserve the baby's health, is further compromised because of the virus.

- About half of hospitalized pregnant women with COVID-19 had symptoms. Among those who were symptomatic and hospitalized with the virus, pregnant women were three times more likely than nonpregnant women to be admitted to an intensive care unit, need mechanical ventilation and face a 70% increased risk of death, when compared to nonpregnant women who were symptomatic.

- Ninety-eight percent of women who were hospitalized experienced a live birth.

- Preterm deliveries appear to be linked to coronavirus infections. In fact, they were three times more common in symptomatic patients than those who asymptomatic.

- Because of the stress that COVID-19 places on the cardiovascular system, coupled with a pregnant woman's ongoing need for extra oxygen and blood, the workload on the heart is increased. With so much blood circulating and the organs more active, the extra fluid caused by the virus can fill the lungs, thereby further impacting the toll the virus takes on the lungs.

- Because a pregnant woman's blood has an increased tendency to clot, COVID-19 may increase the risk of blood clots in women who are pregnant.

- Once she has a baby, COVID-19 vaccines are thought to not be a risk to the breastfeeding infant. Breastmilk is the baby's best source of nutrition and its antibodies help to protect the infant from infections.

Zika is a virus that is spread mostly by the bite of an infected mosquito (CDC, 2019.12c). The virus can be passed from a pregnant woman to her fetus through a mosquito bite; vaginal, anal, and oral sex; sharing sex toys; and possibly through blood transfusions. Symptoms in the mother, which can be nonexistent or mild, may include fever, rash, headache, and muscle or joint pain. However, infection of the fetus with Zika virus during pregnancy can cause serious birth defects, including microcephaly (a smaller than expected head size and brain) and other brain defects, miscarriage, and stillbirth. The best way to prevent Zika is for the mother to protect herself from mosquito bites.

Sexually Transmitted Infections STIs can complicate a pregnancy, be transmitted, and have serious effects on both a woman and her developing baby. The Centers for Disease Control and Prevention (CDC) (2017.12g) recommends that all pregnant women be screened for chlamydia, gonorrhea, hepatitis B, hepatitis C, HIV, and syphilis. If a pregnant woman has contracted any of these or other STIs, she should discuss with her doctor potential effects on the baby, delivery procedures, treatment, and breastfeeding. The sooner a woman begins receiving medical care during pregnancy, the better the outcomes will be for both her and her unborn child.

Women who are pregnant can acquire an STI from an infected partner. Because avoidance of STIs is critical throughout a woman's pregnancy, she may want to consider consistent and correct use of latex condoms for each episode of sexual intercourse.

Maternal Obesity   Obesity is a major public health and economic concern in the United States. Using data collected from 2017 to 2018, the prevalence of obesity in adults was 42.4% (Hales et al., 2020). Maternal obesity, often defined as pre-pregnancy body mass index (BMI) of greater than 30, increases the risk of infertility, miscarriage, and adverse pregnancy outcomes, including a higher risk of preterm birth, neural tube defects (including spina bifida), and stillbirth (ACOG, 2016). In the mother, obesity increases the risk of gestational hypertension, preeclampsia, strokes, gestational diabetes, stillbirths, and cesarean section. Seeking early and regular prenatal care, maintaining a healthy diet, and engaging in regular exercise are imperative measures to take to help ensure having a healthy baby.

Pregnancy After Age 35   Delaying pregnancy until after age 35, sometimes referred to as **advanced maternal age**, has become a common reality for many women, and most healthy women who get pregnant after age 35 and even into their 40s have healthy babies. In fact, as teen birth rates have dropped, births to older mothers have risen. An analysis of four decades of births demonstrated that the age that women become mothers varies by geography and education, with first-time mothers being older and found primarily in big cities and on the coasts, whereas younger mothers are more likely found in rural areas, the Great Plains, and the South (Bui & Miller, 2018). Women with college degrees have children an average of 7 years later than those without college degrees (32 years vs. 21 years) and tend to use the years after high school to focus on education and a career. While men can father children late in life, the quality and quantity of a woman's eggs begin to decline in her late 20s and fall off rapidly after age 35, so that by age 40 her odds of conceiving have decreased and her risk of pregnancy-related complications and having a live baby with a chromosomal abnormality have increased. While the chromosomal abnormality Down syndrome affects 1 in 940 births at maternal age 30, the rate gradually increases to 1 in 30 births at maternal age 45 (ACOG, 2018.12b) (see Table 2 for the risk by age). Paternal age also increases the likelihood of gene mutation; however, current testing methods do not take this into account. As women age, chronic illnesses such as high blood pressure and diabetes may also present pregnancy- and birth-related complications. Genetic counseling may help a woman and her partner assess their risks, make an informed choice about pregnancy, and decide whether or not to have testing for chromosomal abnormalities. The American College of Obstetricians and Gynecologists (2016.12b) recommends that all pregnant women be offered a screening test for genetic disorders. Screening may include a blood test along with an ultrasound. If the screening test result shows increased risk of a birth defect or if a couple has risk factors for having a baby with certain birth defects, diagnostic tests are available. (These tests are discussed later in the chapter.)

Many assume that advancing age in pregnancy is only a concern for women. However, a study of more than 40 million births in the United States revealed potentially harmful effects of advanced paternal age on a baby's risk of prematurity and low birth weight, with more than 12% of births involving fathers aged 45 or older having adverse outcomes (Khandwala et al., 2018).

Ectopic Pregnancy   In **ectopic pregnancy** (tubal pregnancy), the fertilized egg grows outside the uterus, usually in a fallopian tube (ACOG, 2018.12b). Any sexually active woman of childbearing age is at risk for ectopic pregnancy. Women who have abnormal fallopian

TABLE 2   ●   Risk of Having a Baby with Down Syndrome, by Mother's Age

- 1 in 1,480 at age 20 years
- 1 in 940 at age 30 years
- 1 in 353 at age 35 years
- 1 in 85 at age 40 years
- 1 in 30 at age 45 years

Source: American College of Obstetricians and Gynecologists (ACOG). (2018.12a). Having a baby after age 35: How aging affects fertility and pregnancy.

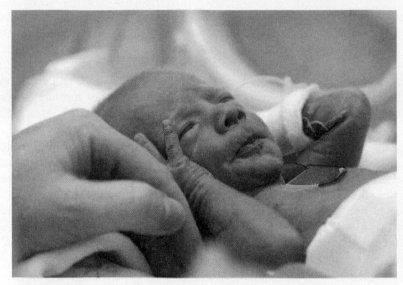

Preterm births affect about 10% of newborns in the United States. Adequate prenatal care significantly reduces the risk of low birth weight.

Peter Banos/Alamy

tubes are at higher risk for ectopic pregnancy. Generally, this occurs because the tube is obstructed, often as a result of pelvic inflammatory disease due to STIs, including chlamydia and gonorrhea infections. Factors such as a previous ectopic pregnancy, treatment with assisted reproductive technology (discussed later in the chapter), and **endometriosis**, a growth of tissue outside the uterus, can also increase the risk. The pregnancy will never come to term. The embryo may spontaneously abort, or the embryo and placenta will continue to expand until they rupture the fallopian tube. If the pregnancy is early and has not ruptured, drugs may be used instead of surgery to remove the conceptus. A ruptured ectopic pregnancy, however, is a medical emergency that can endanger the mother's life.

Gestational Hypertension   **Gestational hypertension**, also referred to as **pregnancy-induced hypertension**, is characterized by high blood pressure and edema, along with protein in the urine. It can occur after 20 weeks of pregnancy or shortly after delivery and occurs in 1 in every 12 to 17 pregnancies among women ages 20 to 44 (CDC, 2020.12h) in the United States. It can usually be treated by diet, bed rest, and medication. If untreated, it can progress to maternal convulsions and stroke, which pose a threat to mother and child. It is important for a pregnant woman to have her blood pressure checked regularly.

Preterm Births   Births that take place prior to 37 weeks of gestation are considered to be **preterm births**. About 10% of all pregnancies in the United States result in preterm births (CDC, 2019.12d). A consequence of this is **low-birth-weight infants**, those who weigh less than 2,500 grams, or 5.5 pounds, at birth. About 35% of infant deaths in the United States are associated with preterm birth–related causes, more than any other single cause. The fundamental problem of prematurity is that many of the infant's vital organs are insufficiently developed. Most premature infants will grow normally, but many will experience long-term neurological disabilities, including breathing problems, feeding difficulties, cerebral palsy, and developmental delays. As premature infants get older, problems such as low intelligence, learning difficulties, poor hearing and vision, and physical awkwardness may become apparent. Nevertheless, the majority of preterm babies eventually catch up with their peers and thrive.

Preterm births are one of the greatest problems confronting obstetrics today; though we don't know what causes a woman to deliver early, several known factors include low or high maternal age, smoking, poor nutrition, and high blood pressure. Prenatal care is extremely important as a means of preventing prematurity.

Genetic Carrier Screening

Both the desire to bear children and the wish to ensure that those children are healthy have encouraged the use of screening and diagnostic technologies. Because of the number of screening tests available, guidelines discuss the advantages and disadvantages of each test and some of the factors that determine which screening test should be offered and when. The following prenatal tests are available to address concerns about birth defects (University of California, San Francisco Health, 2019):

- Screening tests, including ultrasounds, are non-invasive ways to identify women who are at increased risk of having a baby with a birth defect such as a neural tube defect. These tests have no risks of miscarriage but cannot determine with certainty whether a fetus is affected.

- **Prenatal cell-free DNA**, also known as noninvasive prenatal screening because it utilizes some of the mother's blood to test for DNA, is a blood test conducted as early as 10 weeks that can detect a baby's risk of Down syndrome as well as other chromosomal abnormalities (Mayo Clinic, 2020.12a). The test poses no risks for the mother or baby. If the test results indicate that the fetus has an increased risk of a chromosomal abnormality, the mother may need amniocentesis or CVS to confirm the diagnosis. The test can also be used to screen for fetal sex.

- Diagnostic tests are extremely accurate at identifying certain abnormalities in the fetus. **Chorionic villus sampling (CVS)** involves the removal of a small sample of cells taken from the placenta sometime between 10 and 14 weeks of pregnancy. **Amniocentesis** involves the withdrawal of a small amount of amniotic fluid from the uterus usually 15–20 weeks' pregnancy (see Figure 5). Although CVS and amniocentesis are considered to be safe procedures, they each carry a small risk of miscarriage. The risk of pregnancy loss from amniocentesis is 0.3%, while that for CVS is 1.4% (Salomon et al., 2019).

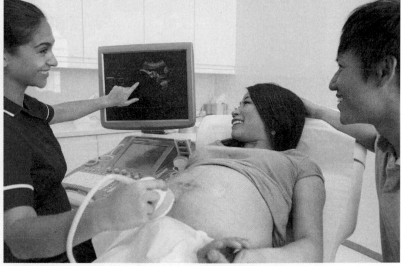

The pictures produced by ultrasound are called sonograms. They are used to determine fetal age, position of the fetus and placenta, and possible developmental problems.

Monkey Business Images/Shutterstock

● **FIGURE 5**

Diagnosing fetal abnormalities via (a) amniocentesis and (b) chorionic villus sampling (CVS).

Amniocentesis

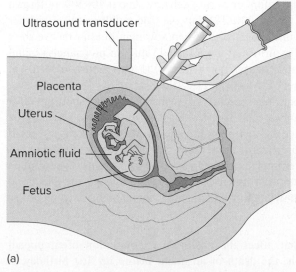

Ultrasound transducer

Placenta

Uterus

Amniotic fluid

Fetus

(a)

Chorionic villus sampling

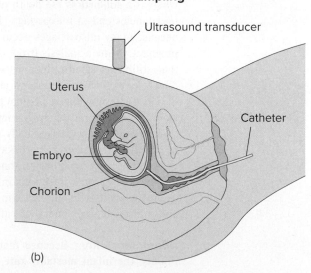

Ultrasound transducer

Uterus

Catheter

Embryo

Chorion

(b)

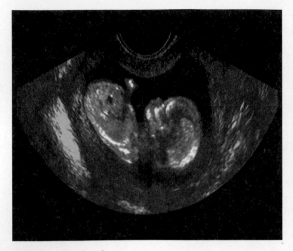 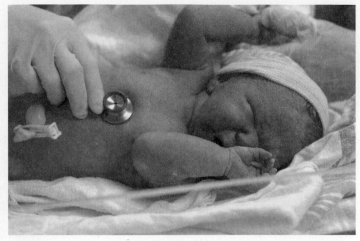

For parents interested in viewing their child's face before birth, a 3D ultrasound provides an image of the fetus before birth. The image on the left was taken at approximately 37 weeks while the image on the right was taken at birth.

(left) Zephyr/Science Photo Library/Getty Images; (right) 1joe/Getty Images

- **Neural tube defect screening**, performed on the mother's blood to measure the level of alpha-fetoprotein, reveals possible defects of the spine, spinal cord, skull, and brain. This test should be offered during the second trimester to women who elect only first-trimester screening (CVS) for Down syndrome.
- Other tests can be performed to provide further information.

Regardless of the kind of prenatal diagnostic procedure done, there may be complications or risks for pregnancy loss associated with the tests, so the cost-benefit ratio of the procedure should be discussed with one's doctor.

Pregnancy Loss

A normal pregnancy lasts about 40 weeks. The death of a fetus before 20 weeks is called early pregnancy loss. Often, the death is a miscarriage (spontaneous loss of a fetus before it can survive on its own), stillbirth, or death during early infancy—a devastating experience that has been largely ignored in our society. The death of a baby at any stage in the pregnancy is as emotional as it is physical. The statement, "You can always have another one," may be meant as consolation, but it can be particularly chilling to a grieving mother or father.

Miscarriage Whether called early pregnancy loss, spontaneous abortion, or miscarriage, the death of a baby represents a significant loss. While both miscarriage and stillbirth describe pregnancy loss, they differ according to when the loss occurs. A **miscarriage** is usually defined as the spontaneous expulsion of the fetus before the 20th week of pregnancy, whereas a **stillbirth** is the death of a baby before or during delivery. About 10–20% of known pregnancies end in miscarriage (Mayo Clinic, 2019.12), but the true number is likely higher because many miscarriages occur early in the pregnancy when a woman doesn't realize she's pregnant. A meta-analysis from 13 studies involving more than 15 million pregnancies found that stillbirths steadily rose with gestational age, rising from 0.11 per thousand births at 37 weeks to 3.18 per thousand at 42 weeks (Muglu et al., 2019).

The first sign that a pregnant woman may miscarry is vaginal bleeding (spotting). If a woman's symptoms of pregnancy disappear and she develops pelvic cramps, she may be miscarrying; the fetus is usually expelled by uterine contractions. Most miscarriages occur in the first trimester (13 weeks) of pregnancy. Sometimes the embryos are healthy, but women miscarry for other reasons: for example, a misshapen or scarred uterus, uncontrolled diabetes, or chronic infections in the uterus. Women can take steps to lessen the likelihood of pregnancy loss, including taking a multivitamin with folic acid, not smoking or using drugs, and minimizing her intake of caffeine.

Infant Mortality Because factors that affect the health of a population often impact infants, the **infant mortality rate**, that is, the death of an infant before its first birthday, is often used as a barometer to measure the health and well-being of a nation. The U.S. infant mortality rate, although at its lowest point in many decades, remains far higher than most of the developed world: an estimated 5.8 deaths for every 1,000 live births (CDC, 2019.12e).

Although many infants die of poverty-related conditions, including lack of prenatal care, others die from congenital problems (conditions appearing at birth) or from infectious diseases, accidents, or other causes. Sometimes the causes of death are not apparent; approximately 3,700 infant deaths per year are attributed to sudden unexpected infant death (SUID). The majority of these occur while the infant is sleeping in an unsafe environment (American Association of Pediatrics, 2017). **Sudden infant death syndrome (SIDS)** is one type of SUID whereby an infant of less than 1 year of age dies of an unexplained cause. Unsafe sleep practices that can lead to accidental suffocation include soft bedding, rolling on top or against the infant while sleeping, wedging or entrapping an infant in a mattress, and strangulation by, for example, a crib railing. The American Academy of Pediatrics (2017) recommends that infants be breastfed and placed on their backs to sleep, and that parents not cover the heads of babies or over-bundle them in clothing and blankets, not let them get too hot, not use soft bedding, including fluffy blankets, stuffed animals, and bumper rails, use a firm mattress, and keep the baby away from smoke.

Coping With Loss   The feelings of shock and grief felt by individuals whose child dies before, during, or after birth can be difficult to understand for those who have not had a similar experience. What they may not realize is that most parents form a deep attachment to their children even before birth. At first, the attachment may be to a fantasy image of the unborn child. During the course of the pregnancy, the mother forms an acquaintance with her infant through the physical sensations she feels within her. Thus, the death of the fetus can also represent the loss of a dream and hope for the future. For both parents, this loss must be acknowledged and felt before psychological healing can take place.

"Dear Auntie will come with presents and will ask, 'Where is our baby, sister?' And, Mother, you will tell her softly, 'He is in the pupils of my eyes. He is in my bones and in my soul.'"

—Rabindranath Tagore (1864–1941)

● Infertility

Infertility, also referred to as impaired fecundity, is characterized by the failure to establish a pregnancy after 12 months of regular, unprotected sexual intercourse or 6 months if a woman is 35 or older. (See Table 3 for percentages of infertility, by age.)

Fertility problems are equally likely to occur in both men and women. About one third of infertility cases are caused by women's problems, about one third are due to the man, and the rest are caused by a mixture of problems or are of an unknown source (Womenshealth. gov, 2019). Combined, the most common risk factors for infertility are advancing age, overweight or obesity, excessive alcohol use, smoking, and excessive stress.

Women who do not have a regular menstrual cycle or are older than 35 years and have not conceived during a 6-month period of trying should consider seeing an infertility specialist. The good news is that many infertile couples can now be successfully treated using conventional fertility treatments to correct problems with the reproductive tract. For the remaining couples, assisted reproductive technologies offer the greatest possibility of pregnancy.

TABLE 3 ● Percentage of Women, Aged 15–49, Who Are Infertile by Current Age, 2015–2017*		
	0 births	**1 or more births**
Total 15–49 years	14.2%	12.3%
15–29 years	9.4%	11.7%
30–39 years	24.1%	11.5%
40–49 years	33.9%	13.3%

*Percentage of women 15–49 years of age (of all marital statuses) who have impaired fecundity (i.e., who are not surgically sterile, and for whom it is difficult or impossible to get pregnant or carry a pregnancy to term), by parity and age.

Source: Centers for Disease Control & Prevention (2019.12f). Key statistics from the National Survey of Family Growth – I listing. National Center for Health Statistics.

Female Infertility

About 10% of women aged 15–44 in the United States have some difficulty getting pregnant or carrying a pregnancy to term (Womenshealth.gov, 2019).

Physical Causes   While age is the best predictor of a woman's reproductive potential, physical problems that are associated with smoking, excess alcohol use, poor diet, excessive athletic training, stress, being overweight or underweight, STIs, and health problems that cause hormonal changes also influence the ability to become pregnant (Office on Women's Health, 2017). More specifically, ovarian problems often caused by polycystic ovarian syndrome, blocked fallopian tubes due to pelvic inflammatory disease, endometriosis, surgery for an ectopic pregnancy, and problems with the uterus and uterine fibroids can interfere with a woman's ability to conceive.

Given that the number of women having children after age 35 is continuing to grow, many who postpone their pregnancy fear that they may not be able to become pregnant. We know that women are born with a finite number of oocytes, or eggs, that die over time so that as women age the chance of pregnancy decreases and the risk of miscarriage increases. Women should schedule a pre-conception consultation with her primary care physician or gynecologist to discuss and answer any concerns she has about fertility.

Male Infertility

Among men, fertility is not only important for conception, it also is related to a man's general health and life expectancy (Nassan et al., 2020). As stated previously, in approximately a third of infertility cases, the man is not fertile. This is most often due to a man's sperm production or delivery, which can be the result of heredity or lifestyle choices including smoking, consuming alcohol, taking certain medications, long-term illness (e.g., kidney failure), childhood infection (e.g., mumps), or chromosome or hormone problems (e.g., low testosterone). Additionally, age, obesity, being diagnosed with an STI, having a **varicocele,** or varicose vein on the testicle, experiencing retrograde ejaculation (semen that travels backward into the bladder), having antibodies that attack a man's own sperm, or obstructions in any part of a man's reproductive track can interfere with fertility (Urology Care Foundation, 2019).

In a recent cross-sectional study of nearly 3,000 young Danish men, a higher adherence to the Western diet pattern (e.g., processed foods, French fries, sweets) was associated with lower sperm quality; conversely, a higher adherence to a healthier diet pattern (e.g., fish, chicken, whole grains, vegetables, and fruits) was associated with higher sperm quality (Nassan et al., 2020). The authors concluded that changing diet patterns to a healthy diet may be a simple and inexpensive way to protect a man's testicular function.

Emotional Responses to Infertility

By the time partners seek medical advice about their fertility problems, they may have already experienced a crisis in confronting the possibility of not being able to become biological parents. Many such couples feel they have lost control over a major area of their lives. Coming to a joint decision with one's partner about goals, acceptable and affordable therapies, and an endpoint for therapy is important and advisable.

Infertility Treatment

Almost without exception, fertility problems are physical, not emotional, despite myths to the contrary. The two most popular myths are that anxiety over becoming pregnant leads to infertility and that if an infertile couple adopts a child, the couple will then be able to conceive on their own. Neither has any basis in medical fact, although some presumably infertile couples have conceived following an adoption. This does not mean, however, that one should adopt a child to remedy infertility. In some cases, fertility is restored for no discernible reason; in others, the infertility remains a mystery. Treatment for a successful outcome, defined as delivering a child or achieving an ongoing pregnancy within 18 months, can be both emotionally and financially costly.

Enhancing Fertility There are many ways that fertility can be enhanced, the most important of which involves the timing of coitus with respect to the woman's menstrual cycle. Because an ovum is viable for about 24 hours after ovulation, a pregnancy is most likely to occur when intercourse takes place at the same time as ovulation. If a man wears tight underwear, he might switch to boxer-type shorts to allow his testicles to descend from his body. However, for many couples, these techniques are not enough; they may seek medical intervention to diagnose and treat infertility.

Medical Intervention Medical technology now offers more treatment options to those who are trying to conceive a child. Prior to investing in any one of these, preventive steps such as avoiding alcohol, tobacco, and drugs; exercising; maintaining a healthy weight; and eating a healthy diet should be taken to maximize the odds of becoming pregnant. The techniques and technologies developed to promote conception include the following:

CBS™ High Security sperm straws are made of clear flexible resin and are used for the storage and preservation of sperm.
Alain Jocard/AFP/Getty Images

- *Fertility medications.* A variety of drugs can cause the body to release hormones that trigger or regulate ovulation.

- *Egg freezing.* Egg freezing is a method used to harvest a woman's eggs from the ovaries and then freeze and store in liquid nitrogen for up to 10 years. Once thawed, an egg must be fertilized with sperm in the lab using a process called intracytoplasmic sperm injection, or ICSI (discussed below), and implanted in the uterus.

- *Surgery.* This is a treatment option for both male and female infertility. Used to correct a structural problem, surgery can often return normal fertility.

- *Artificial insemination.* Used if sperm numbers are too low, **artificial insemination (AI)**, also called intrauterine insemination (IUI), involves introducing sperm into the woman's uterus. This procedure may be performed in conjunction with ovulation-stimulating medications.

- *Assisted reproductive technology.* All fertility treatments in which both eggs and sperm are handled are known as **assisted reproductive technology (ART)**. In general, ART procedures involve surgically removing eggs from a woman's ovaries, combining them with sperm in the laboratory, and returning them to the woman's body or donating them to another woman. Approximately 1.7% of all infants born in the United States each year are conceived using ART (CDC, 2020.12j). The types of ART include (Society for Reproductive Technology [SART], 2020):

  - **IVF (in vitro fertilization).** This involves extracting a woman's eggs, fertilizing the eggs in the laboratory, and then transferring the resulting embryos into the woman's uterus through the cervix.

The most common and effective form of ART, in vitro fertilization of an egg, takes place by manually combining an egg and sperm in a laboratory dish and physically placing the embryo in the uterus.
MedicalRF.com

  - **Intracytoplasmic sperm injection (ICSI).** A single sperm is injected directly into a mature egg. The embryo is then transferred to the uterus or fallopian tube. This procedure is most often used by couples in which the male is infertile.

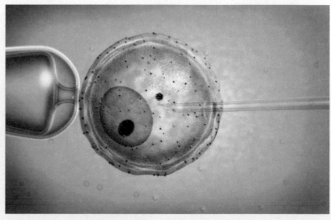

ART is often categorized according to whether the procedure uses a woman's own eggs (nondonor) or eggs from another woman (donor) and according to whether the embryos used were newly fertilized (fresh) or previously fertilized, frozen, and then thawed. The success rates of ART vary and depend on many factors, including the age of the partners, the cause of infertility, the skill of the practitioner, the type of ART used, and whether the egg or the embryo is fresh or frozen.

While ART can alleviate the burden of infertility on individuals and families, it can also present challenges, including high rates of

When assisted reproductive technology is used to treat infertility, multiple births can result. This can be minimized by limiting the number of embryos that are transferred back to the uterus.

Big Cheese Photo/Getty Images

Increasingly, LGBTQ+ couples are creating families that are diverse along dimensions of gender, race, and social class.

Bruce Rogovin/Getty Images

multiple pregnancies (SART, 2020). Although most births resulting from assisted technologies are free of birth defects, ART has been associated with an increased risk of birth defects. This increased risk, however, may also be due in part to a woman's advancing age and other health factors.

Options for childless couple also include:

- **Surrogate motherhood**. In this case, one woman, a surrogate mother, agrees to become pregnant using the man's sperm and her own egg.

- **Gestational carrier**. A woman with ovaries but no uterus may use a gestational carrier whereby she uses her own egg, which is fertilized by the man's sperm. The embryo is then placed inside the carrier's uterus. In this case, the carrier will not be related to the baby.

The most important factor for success of these procedures is the age of the woman. When a woman is using her own egg, success rates decline as she ages and decrease even more dramatically after about age 37. Other factors to consider are whether the woman is using her own eggs and the number of embryos transferred. Still, thorny questions also plague the procedures: How much will a surrogate be paid? Are there additional costs for a cesarean section, multiple births, or loss of a surrogate's uterus? What if the intended parents change their mind or die during the pregnancy? If the surrogate needs bed rest, how much will the intended parents pay to replace her lost wages, child care, and housekeeping? What happens if the child has serious health problems? In spite of significant costs, risks, and uncertainty, it appears that patients are accepting these because the alternative is even more daunting to them: not having a child.

Gender selection, also known as sex selection, is a technology that allows couples to choose whether to have a boy or a girl. It can be accomplished via both pre- and post-implantation of an embryo. By creating embryos outside the womb, then testing them for gender, pre-implantation genetic diagnosis can guarantee the sex of a baby. Controversy arises, however, over potential sex imbalances in our population and cases in which the gender selection results do not match the parents' expectations.

Each of these techniques can create new opportunities for individuals and partnerships. For example, some lesbian women, especially those in committed relationships, are choosing to create families through artificial insemination. At the same time, some questions may arise when a same-sex couple contemplates having a baby in this way: Who will be the birth mother or sperm donor? What will be the role of each parent? Will the donor be known or unknown? If known, will the child have a relationship with that person? Will the child have a relationship with the donor's parents? Who gets custody if the couple breaks up? Will there be a legal contract between the parenting parties? Another issue such couples face is that the non-biological parent may have no legal tie to the child. In fact, in some states, the nonbiological parent may adopt the child as a "second parent." (For more about same-sex couples and families, see Think About It: "Are Same-Sex Couples and Families Any Different from Heterosexual Ones?")

think
about it

Are Same-Sex Couples and Families Any Different from Heterosexual Ones?

What impact does sexual orientation have on the longevity of relationships and families? Are those qualities that sustain heterosexual couples and families any different for same-sex partners? What researchers have found may have implications for all of us who desire healthy relationships and longevity with those we love.

Though the legality of and public support for same-sex marriage is increasing both in the United States and globally, the notion that committed same-sex relationships are atypical or psychologically immature remains. Research, however, does not support this nor the idea that gay or lesbian individuals are less satisfied with their relationships (Gottman & Levenson, 2012). Rather, it is the level and type of communication that partners share that underscores much of the success or lack of success in any relationship.

Accompanying a rise in the prevalence of same-sex marriage has been an increase in same-sex parenting. LGBTQ+ individuals and couples come to be parents in many ways including adoption, fostering, artificial insemination, and surrogate parenting. Approximately half of all same-sex households in the United States are married couples, but among all same-sex couples, married and unmarried, 114,000 or roughly 16% are raising children. Similar to mixed-sex couples with children, the majority (68%) of same-sex couples with children were raising biological children (Williams Institute, 2018.12).

The literature reveals that same-sex couples are as good at parenting as their mixed-sex counterparts (Gates, 2015). Any differences in the well-being of children raised in either same- or mixed-sex households are explained not by their parents' sexual orientation, but by the possibility that children being raised by a same sex-couple may have experienced more family instability. This is often the result of being born to mixed-sex parents, one of whom is now in a same-sex relationship. However, we've learned that as more same-sex couples marry, their children are more likely to be raised in stable relationships.

The American Academy of Pediatrics recognizes the value of affirming same-gender couples to marry and have families. In their policy statement, titled "Promoting the Well-Being of Children Whose Parents Are Gay or Lesbian" (2013), the organization states:

> Scientific evidence affirms that children have similar developmental and emotional needs and receive similar parenting whether they are raised by parents of the same or different genders. If a child has two living and capable parents who choose to create a permanent bond by way of civil marriage, it is in the best interests of their child(ren) that legal and social institutions allow and support them to do so, irrespective of their sexual orientation.

Though controversy about this issue remains (see Allen, 2015), most research studies conclude that children raised by same-sex parents perform as well as children with mixed-sex parents. This is true across a wide spectrum of child-well-being measures, including academic performance, cognitive development, social development, psychological health, early sexual activity, and substance abuse (American Association for Marriage and Family Therapy, 2017).

A longitudinal study of adult offspring conceived through donor insemination and raised by 84 lesbian couples found the children to have the same mental well-being as those who grew up with mixed-sex parents (Gottman & Levinson, 2012). To date, there are no long-term studies involving children exclusively raised by gay male couples.

A relatively understudied subject is parenting among transgender families. Like other couples, trans parents form their families in a range of ways, including biological parenthood, step-parenthood, adoption, fostering, and assisted reproduction. Concerns about the potential challenges of children with trans parents have tended to focus on a child's psychological adjustment, especially related to a child's ability to negotiate a relationship with a parent with a different gender identity than that which they had originally known or assumed. However, findings from an exploratory study consisting of 35 families have found good quality relationships between trans parents and their children and good psychological adjustment among school-aged children (Imrie et al., 2020). When looking at the quality of family relationships, a review of 26 studies published between 1990 and 2017 found that people who identify as trans are as invested and committed to their loved ones as anyone else, however at the same time have concerns that knowledge about their authentic selves may alienate and destroy some family ties. When the nature of trans family relationships was analyzed, it was found that the more stable the relationship between the parents before and during the transition, the more stable the family would be after the transition (Hafford-Letchfield et al., 2019).

While society has become more accepting in its views about LGBTQ+ individuals and their families, it has also changed its attitudes about gender norms around how people organize their relationships and families. Though we have learned a great deal about these changes and their implications over the past decade, research is still needed that explores parenting and family formation and longevity, including among those who identify as sexual minorities.

Think Critically

1. What characteristics are important for you in maintaining a committed relationship?
2. Why does society perpetuate concerns about same-sex parents?
3. How might the presence or absence of children influence the longevity of a same-sex relationship?

● Giving Birth

Throughout pregnancy, numerous physiological changes occur to prepare the woman's body for childbirth. Hormones secreted by the placenta regulate the growth of the fetus, stimulate maturation of the breasts for lactation, and ready the uterus and other parts of the body for labor. During the later months of pregnancy, the placenta produces the hormone **relaxin**, which increases flexibility in the ligaments and joints of the pelvic area. In the last trimester, most women occasionally feel uterine contractions that are strong but generally not painful. These **Braxton-Hicks contractions** exercise the uterus, preparing it for labor.

Labor and Delivery

Childbirth is typically divided into three stages: labor, delivery of the baby, and delivery of the placenta. During labor, contractions begin the **effacement** (thinning) and **dilation** (gradual opening) of the cervix. It is difficult to say exactly when labor starts, which helps explain the great differences reported in lengths of labor for different women. True labor begins when the uterine contractions are regularly spaced, effacement and dilation of the cervix occur, and the fetus presents a part of itself into the vagina.

"If men had to have babies, they would only ever have one each."
—Princess Diana (1961–1997)

Labor has three phases. In the early *first phase* of labor, the expulsion of a plug of slightly bloody mucus that has blocked the opening of the cervix during pregnancy may appear. At the same time or later, there is a second fluid discharge from the vagina, consisting of amniotic fluid, which comes from the ruptured amnion. In this phase, contractions are spaced far apart (15–20 minutes) and last approximately 45 seconds, during which time the lengthwise muscles of the uterus involuntarily pull open the circular muscles around the cervix, which typically dilates to 4 centimeters. This early phase of labor is relatively easy. During the *second phase,* also known as active labor, the cervix dilates from 4 to 7 centimeters, with contractions occurring every 3 to 4 minutes and lasting about 60 seconds. As the labor progresses, the amniotic sac may break, which in turn can speed up contractions. The *third phase* is marked by **transition**, whereby the contractions come more quickly, are much more intense, and the cervix opens to its fullest (7 to 10 centimeters). This is typically the shortest and most difficult part of labor. This last phase marks the shift from dilation of the cervix to the expulsion of the infant. The first stage of labor can last from 2 to 24 hours or longer. Its duration depends on the size of the baby, the baby's position in the uterus, the size of the mother's pelvis, and the condition of the uterus.

The second stage of labor begins when the baby's head moves into the birth canal and ends when the baby is born. During this time, many women experience a great force in their bodies. Some women find this the most difficult part of labor; others find that the contractions and bearing down bring a sense of euphoria.

The baby is usually born gradually. When the baby's head emerges and does not slip back in as a woman is pushing during birth, is known as crowning. With each of the final few contractions, a new part of the infant emerges (see Figure 6). The baby may even cry before it is completely born, especially if the mother did not have medication.

The baby will still be attached to the umbilical cord connected to the mother, which is not cut until it stops pulsating. The newborn will appear wet and often be covered by a waxy substance called **vernix**. The head may look oddly shaped at first, from the molding of the soft plates of bone during birth. This shape is temporary; the baby's head usually achieves a normal appearance within 24 hours.

After the baby has been delivered, the uterus continues to contract, expelling the placenta, the remaining section of the umbilical cord, and the fetal membranes. Completing the third, and final, stage of labor, these tissues are collectively referred to as the **afterbirth**. The doctor or midwife examines the placenta to make sure it is whole. If the practitioner has any doubt that the entire placenta has been expelled, they may examine the uterus to make sure no parts of the placenta remain to cause adhesions or hemorrhaging. Immediately following birth, the attendants assess the physical condition of the **neonate**, or

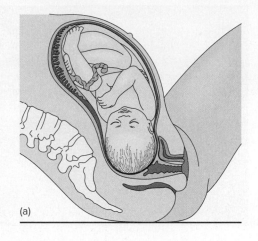

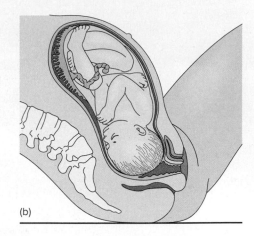

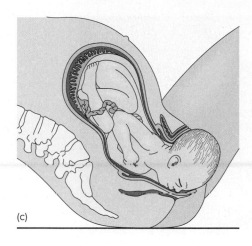

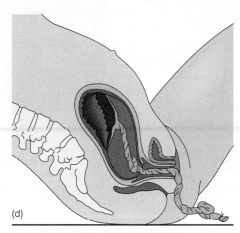

● **FIGURE 6**

The Birth Process: Labor and Delivery.
(a) In the first stage, the cervix begins to efface (thin out) and dilate. (b) During transition, the cervix dilates from 8 to 10 centimeters. (c) In the second stage, the infant is delivered. (d) In the third stage, the afterbirth (placenta) is delivered.

newborn. Heart rate, respiration, skin color, reflexes, and muscle tone are individually rated with a score of 0–2. The total, called an **Apgar score**, will range between 7 and 10 if the baby is healthy. For a few days following labor, especially if it is a second or subsequent birth, the mother will probably feel strong contractions as the uterus begins to return to its prebirth size and shape. This process takes about 6 weeks. She will also have a vaginal discharge containing blood, mucus, and uterine tissue, called **lochia**, which continues for several weeks.

Following birth, the baby will probably be alert and ready to nurse. Breastfeeding (discussed later) provides benefits for both mother and child. Some refer to these later decisions and feelings as the fourth stage of delivery, or recovery.

Choices in Childbirth

Women and couples planning the birth of a child have decisions to make in a variety of areas: place of birth, birth attendant(s), medications, preparedness classes, circumcision, breastfeeding, to name just a few. The "childbirth market" has responded to consumer concerns, so it's important for prospective parents to fully understand their options.

Hospital Birth Because of the traditional and sometimes impersonal care provided in hospitals, many people have recognized the need for family-centered childbirth. Partners and

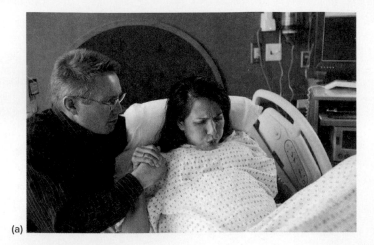

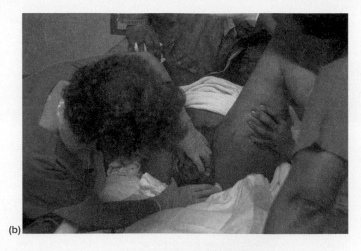

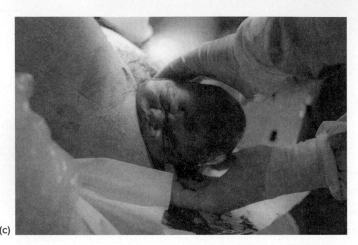

Labor and Delivery. (a) During labor, uterine contractions cause the opening and thinning of the cervix. The length of labor varies from woman to woman and birth to birth. Encouragement from her partner can help the mother relax. (b) During transition, the mother is coached to push as the baby's head begins to crown. (c) The baby's head emerges from the womb. The placenta will soon follow.

(a) RubberBall Productions/Getty Images; (b) Angela Hampton/Alamy; (c) Janine Wiedel Photolibrary/Alamy Stock Photo

other relatives or close friends often participate today. Most hospitals permit while others require rooming-in, in which the baby stays with the mother rather than in the nursery, or a modified form of rooming-in.

Some form of pain relief is often administered during hospital deliveries, as are various hormones to intensify the contractions and to shrink the uterus after delivery. There are two types of pain-relieving drugs: analgesics, which provide pain relief without loss of feeling or muscle movement, and anesthetics, which block all feelings, including pain. The most common form of analgesic administration is the **epidural**, a regional anesthesia that is administered through a tiny catheter placed in the woman's lower back. When administered properly, an epidural diminishes the sensations of labor in the lower areas of the body. Each year in the United States, approximately 60–70% of laboring women get epidurals (Johns Hopkins Medicine, 2019). A study of 400 patients found that giving epidural anesthesia during the late stage of delivery does not lengthen the duration of labor (Shen et al., 2017). According to Philip E. Hess, associate professor of anesthesia at Harvard University and one of the authors of the study, "If you decide you want an epidural for pain relief, you should not be concerned that it's going to prevent a vaginal delivery or cause any effect on labor." Though epidurals have been used successfully and safely during the vast majority of labors, there is still a small chance that they may cause a woman's blood pressure to drop, a severe headache (rare), and other side effects.

Epidurals are a combination of anesthetics and opioid analgesics. Epidurals do not increase the risk of cesarean section nor do they have an immediate effect on neonatal status as determined by Apgar scores or in admissions to neonatal intensive care (Anim-Somuah et al., 2018). Because pain relief is important for women in labor, whatever method is used to ameliorate maternal discomfort, it is important that it be both effective and safe for the mother and baby.

Once a routine part of childbirth, an **episiotomy** is an incision that enlarges the vaginal opening by cutting through the perineum toward the anus to assist in the delivery of a baby. The procedure is sometimes used for emergencies, such as when a baby's shoulders get stuck, the baby does not have enough oxygen, or the mother needs a forceps or vacuum delivery (Stanford Children's Health, 2020.12b). The American College of Obstetricians and Gynecologists (ACOG) (2016.12c) recommends that doctors take steps to mitigate the risk of lacerations such as perineal massage or warm compresses during vaginal delivery rather than using a routine episiotomy. Although there is no national consensus on how frequently the procedure should be used, a leading hospital safety group recommends that the cuts should occur in no more than 5% of vaginal deliveries, compared to 8% which is the national average (Leapfrog, 2018).

Labor Induction   A normal pregnancy lasts about 40 weeks. By the time a woman reaches her due date and does not begin labor, the current practice in the United States is to induce labor at 41 weeks. **Labor induction** is the use of medications or other methods to bring on (induce) labor. It may be recommended if the health of the mother or fetus is at-risk. When used for non-medical reasons, such as living far away from a hospital, it is referred to as elective induction.

Cesarean Section   **Cesarean section**, or **C-section** involves the delivery of a baby through an incision in the mother's abdominal wall and uterus. In 1970, 5.5% of American births were performed by C-section. Today, about 32% of all births in the United States are done by C-section (Cesareanrates.org, 2020). In a medical emergency, the procedure can save the lives of the mother and the baby.

Often the need for a C-section does not become obvious until labor is underway. Reasons for a C-section can include abnormalities of the placenta and umbilical cord and prolonged or ineffective labor. Cesarean births have been linked to an increased risk of various short- and long-term health issues for both women and children. Immediate risks to the baby can involve breathing problems and surgical injury while risks to the mother can include infection, hemorrhage, reactions to anesthesia, and blood clots (Mayo Clinic, 2020.12b). After a C-section, a woman faces a higher risk of potentially serious complications in a subsequent pregnancy. While a C-section can save the life of a baby, mother, or both, a recent meta-analysis looked at data from 61 studies, including more than 20 million deliveries, and found that birth by C-section was associated with a 33% higher risk of autism and a 17% higher risk of attention deficit disorder in the child (Zhang et al., 2019). It should be noted that the study was an observational one, which does not prove causation. Previous studies have also reported negative health outcomes in offspring born C-section including obesity, allergy, asthma, type 1 diabetes, and leukemia (Zhang et al., 2019).

The fact that a woman has had a previous cesarean delivery does not mean that subsequent deliveries must be C-sections. In fact, more than 87% of women who attempt a vaginal delivery after cesarean (VBAC) have successful vaginal deliveries (Cesareanrates.org, 2020). Many times the condition that made a C-section necessary in one birth will not exist in the next; thus, a VBAC is safer than a scheduled repeat C-section.

Prepared Childbirth   Increasingly, Americans are choosing from among such childbirth alternatives as prepared childbirth, rooming-in birthing centers, home birth, and midwifery.

Prepared childbirth or natural childbirth was popularized by English gynecologist Grantly Dick-Read (1972) who observed that fear causes muscles to tense, which in turn increases pain and stress during childbirth. He taught both partners about childbirth and gave them physical exercises to ease muscle tension. Prepared childbirth is not so much a matter of controlling the birth process as of understanding it and having confidence in

"All is beautiful
All is beautiful
All is beautiful, yes!
Now Mother Earth
And Father Sky
Join one another and meet forever
helpmates
All is beautiful
All is beautiful
All is beautiful, yes!
Now the night of darkness
And the dawn of light
Join one another and meet forever
helpmates
All is beautiful
All is beautiful
All is beautiful, yes!
Now the white corn
And the yellow corn
And the yellow corn
Join one another and meet forever
helpmates
All is beautiful
All is beautiful
All is beautiful, yes!
Life that never ends
Happiness of all things
Join one another and meet forever
helpmates
All is beautiful
All is beautiful
All is beautiful, yes!"

—Navajo night chant

Childbirth classes enable both partners to understand and share the birth process.

Shutterstock

Making a Birth Plan

A good beginning makes a good ending.

—Anonymous (English proverb)

Prospective parents must make many important decisions. The more informed they are, the better able they will be to decide what is right for them. Often the choices they make are part of a collaborative process that occurs between the couple and their health care provider. If you were planning a birth, how would you answer the following questions?

■ Who will be the birth attendant—a physician or a nurse-midwife? Do you already have someone in mind? If not, what criteria are important to you in choosing a birth attendant? Have you considered hiring a labor assistant, sometimes called a *doula,* a professional childbirth companion employed to guide the mother during labor?

■ In light of the restrictions that may be in place as a result of COVID-19, who will be allowed to be present at the birth—the spouse or partner? Other relatives or friends? Children? If they are allowed, how will these people participate?

■ Where will the birth take place—in a hospital, in a birthing center, or at home? If you're considering a birth center, ask about its licensing and accreditation, knowing that both involve scrutiny and oversight for its practices. Inquire about the center's criteria for accepting patients, as well as the plan for transfer if you go to a hospital.

■ What kind of environment will you create in terms of lighting, room furnishings, and sounds? Is there special music you would like to hear? Do you wish the birth to be recorded?

■ What kinds of medication, if any, would you feel comfortable being given? Do you know what the options are for pain-reducing drugs? What about medications to speed up or slow down labor?

■ What about fetal monitoring? Will it be continuous or intermittent?

■ What is your attendant's policy regarding food and drink during labor?

■ What about freedom of movement during labor? Will you or your partner want the option of walking around during labor? Will there be a shower or bath available? Will the baby be delivered with the mother lying on her back with her feet in stirrups, or will she be free to choose her position, such as squatting or lying on her side?

■ Who will cut the umbilical cord, and at what point will it be cut?

■ What will be done with the baby immediately after birth? What kinds of tests will be performed on the baby, and when? What other kinds of procedures, such as shots and medicated eyedrops, will be given, and when?

■ Will the baby stay in the nursery, or is rooming-in available? Is there a visiting schedule?

■ How will the baby be fed—by breast, bottle, or a combination of both? Will feeding be on a schedule or "on demand"? Is there someone with breastfeeding experience available to answer questions if necessary? Will the baby have a pacifier between feedings?

■ If the baby is a boy, will he be circumcised? If so, when?

nature's plan. Prepared mothers, who usually attend classes with their partner, handle pain better, use fewer pain-relieving drugs, express greater satisfaction with the childbirth process, and experience less postpartum depression than women who undergo routine hospital births.

Birthing Rooms and Centers Birthing (maternity) centers, institutions of long-standing in England and other European countries, are now integrated into many hospitals in the United States. Although they vary in size, organization, and orientation, birthing centers share the view that childbirth is a normal, healthy process that can be assisted by skilled practitioners (midwives or physicians) in a homelike setting. Some centers provide emergency care; all have procedures for transfer to a hospital if necessary.

Home Birth Home births have increased during the past three decades, although they still constitute a small fraction of total births. Careful medical screening and planning that eliminate all but the lowest-risk pregnancies can make this a viable alternative for some couples.

Midwifery and Doulas In most countries, midwives attend the majority of births. The United States has an increasing number of certified nurse-midwives who are registered nurses trained in obstetrical techniques. They are qualified for routine deliveries and minor medical emergencies. They also often operate as part of a medical team that includes a backup physician. A woman should investigate the midwife's or doula's training and experience, the backup services available in the event of complications or emergencies, and the procedures for a transfer to a hospital if necessary.

Unlike midwives, who are medical professionals, *doulas* do not make clinical decisions. Rather, they offer emotional support and help to manage pain using massage, acupressure, and birthing positions.

Breastfeeding

Breast milk is the ideal food for babies. It contains the right amount of nutrients for the baby, boosts the baby's immune system, and is the best way to keep a baby healthy. About 2–5 days after childbirth, increased production of milk occurs. Sometimes as early as the second trimester, a thick liquid called **colostrum** is secreted by the nipples. Colostrum is high in protein and contains antibodies that help protect the baby from infectious diseases. Hormonal changes during labor trigger the changeover from colostrum to milk, but unless a mother nurses her child, her breasts will soon stop producing milk. If a woman chooses not to breastfeed, there are several things she can do to gradually diminish her supply of milk. Because the excess milk stored in her breasts will signal the body to produce less, leaving the breasts full will stop them from making milk. (For more information about breastfeeding, see Practically Speaking, "Breast Versus Bottle: Which is Better for You and Your Child?")

Breastfeeding provides the best nutrition for infants. It also helps protect against many infectious diseases, can lower breast and ovarian cancer risk, especially if a woman breastfeeds longer than 1 year, and gives both mother and child a sense of well-being.

Compassionate Eye Foundation/Three Images/ DigitalVision/Getty Images

● Postpartum and Beyond

The time immediately following birth is a critical period for family adjustment. No amount of reading, classes, and expert advice can prepare expectant parents for the "real thing." The 3 months or so following childbirth (the "fourth trimester") constitute the **postpartum period**. This time is one of physical stabilization and emotional adjustment. The abrupt transition from being a nonparent to being a parent may create considerable stress. Parents take on parental roles literally overnight, and the job goes on without relief around the clock. Many parents express concern about their ability to meet all the responsibilities of child rearing.

To support couples in the adjustment and care of their newborn child, the federal **Family and Medical Leave Act (FMLA)** assures eligible employees up to 12 weeks in a 12-month period of unpaid, job-protected leave for specified family and medical reasons along with continuation of group health insurance (U.S. Department of Labor, 2020). If the employee has to use some of that leave for another reason, including a difficult pregnancy, it may be counted as part of the 12-week FMLA leave entitlement. In 2015, the U.S. Department of Labor (2015) announced a Final Rule that revised the definition of spouse so that eligible employees in legal same-sex marriages are able to take FMLA leave to care for their spouse or family member, regardless of where they live. Additionally, as of October 2020, legislation provides federal workers up to 12 weeks of paid leave to mothers and fathers of newborns, newly adopted children, or foster children (American Bar Association, 2020). Note though, that among 41 nations, the United States is the only country without federally mandated paid maternity leave (Pew Research Center, 2019.12).

The postpartum period may be a time of significant emotional upheaval. Even women who had easy and uneventful pregnancies may experience the "baby blues." New mothers often have irregular sleep patterns because of the needs of their newborn, the discomfort of childbirth, or the strangeness of the hospital environment. Some mothers may feel isolated from their familiar world. These are considered normal, self-limiting postpartum symptoms and generally go away within a week or two.

"Before I got married, I had six theories about bringing up children. Now I have six children and no theories."

—John Wilmot, Earl of Rochester (1647–1680)

Breast Versus Bottle: Which Is Better for You and Your Child?

If you are a woman who plans to have children, you will have to decide whether to breastfeed or bottle-feed your infant. Perhaps you already have an idea that breastfeeding is healthier for the baby but are not sure why.

The American Academy of Pediatrics (AAP) and the World Health Organization recommend exclusive breastfeeding for about 6 months, followed by continued breastfeeding as solid foods are introduced, with continuation for 1 year or longer as mother and baby desire (AAP, 2014.12a). The World Health Organization (2017.12) recommends some breastfeeding along with solid food until age 2 or beyond. While fewer than 16% of mothers in the United States are still nursing at 18 months, longer nursing is more common in certain pockets of the country where being educated and having strong social support encourage it (CDC, 2020.12k). Adequate space, equipment, and time to breastfeed or express milk in workplaces and childcare centers can be beneficial to both mother and child.

Breastfeeding is best for the baby because (ACOG, 2020.12d):

- Breast milk has the right amount of fat, sugar, water, protein, and minerals needed for a baby's growth and development. As the baby grows, the breast milk changes to adapt to the baby's changing nutritional needs.
- Breast milk is easier to digest than formula.
- Breast milk contains antibodies that protect infants from certain illnesses, such as ear infections, diarrhea, respiratory illnesses, and allergies. The longer a baby breastfeeds, the greater the health benefits.
- Breastfed infants have a lower risk of sudden infant death syndrome (SIDS).
- Breast milk can help reduce the risk of many of the short-term and long-term health problems that preterm babies face.

Breastfeeding is best for the mother because:

- Breastfeeding triggers the release of oxytocin, a hormone that causes the uterus to contract. This helps the uterus return to its normal size more quickly and may decrease the amount of bleeding a woman has after giving birth.
- Breastfeeding may make it easier to lose the weight gained during pregnancy.
- Breastfeeding may reduce the risk of breast cancer and ovarian cancer.
- Breastfeeding can decrease the risk of early natural menopause (before age 45), which in turn can lower the risk of osteoporosis, depression, dementia, cardiovascular disease, and premature death among women (Langston et al., 2020).

Breastfeeding is best for psychological health because:

- The close physical contact provides a sense of emotional well-being for mother and baby.
- Breastfeeding may help lower the risk of postpartum depression.

Breastfeeding has logistical advantages:

- Breastfeeding requires no buying, mixing, or preparing of formulas. It is always available.
- Breast milk is not subject to incorrect mixing or spoilage; it is clean and not easily contaminated.
- Breastfeeding provides some protection against pregnancy if the woman is breastfeeding exclusively.
- Better infant health means fewer health insurance claims and less time off work to care for a sick child.

Bottle-feeding

For those women whose work schedules, health problems, or other demands prohibit them from breastfeeding, holding and cuddling the baby while bottle-feeding can contribute to the sense of emotional well-being that comes from a close parent-baby relationship. Bottle-feeding also affords a greater opportunity for partners to become involved in the feeding of the baby.

"We learn from experience. A man never wakes up his second baby just to see it smile."

—Grace Williams

A father's involvement in their children's lives has been shown to have a positive effect on their well-being, including their academic success and reducing the chances of delinquency and substance abuse (Jones & Mosher, 2013). Though fewer fathers now live with their children because of increases in nonmarital childbearing, most children are still being born into cohabiting unions. Critical to a child's well-being are engagement or direct interaction, accessibility or availability, responsibility for the child's care, and economic support. Though many men can take unpaid time off to care for a baby or family member through the FMLA, many do not take the leave for financial reasons (Picchi, 2020).

Postpartum depression, or moderate to severe depression in a woman after she has given birth, occurs in approximately 10–20% of new mothers (Postpartumdepression.org, 2020).

Postpartum depression is thought to be related to hormonal changes brought on by sleep deprivation, weaning, and the resumption of the menstrual cycle. A prior history of depression also increases a woman's risk. It is common as well for anxiety disorders to arise or recur in the postpartum period, when some women feel hypervigilant about possible harm to their baby. The most serious and rarest postpartum mental illness is **postpartum psychosis**. Unlike the other disorders, postpartum psychosis is thought to be exclusively biologically based and related to hormonal changes. Affected women tend to have difficulty sleeping, be prone to agitation or hyperactivity, and intermittently experience delusions, hallucinations, and paranoia. This behavior represents a medical emergency and usually requires hospitalization. Depression rates, in comparison, vary from industrialized cultures (more) to nonindustrialized ones (less), suggesting that psychological, cultural, and social factors have a significant effect on whether a woman experiences postpartum depression. The U.S. Food and Drug Administration (2019.12) has recently approved an intravenous drug infusion specifically indicated for the treatment of postpartum depression. In spite of its high cost ($20,000 to $35,000 per treatment), the drug, sold as Zulresso, has been shown to be effective regardless of when postpartum depression symptoms begin, is effective immediately, and is shown to have a meaningful reduction in depression scores.

In rare instances, when, for example, a parent feels overwhelmed or experiences severe depression, they may abandon or leave their child to die. As a result, every state has enacted a provision to provide a safe and confidential means of relinquishing an unwanted infant (Guttmacher Institute, 2018).

Though there is great variability among pregnant women, a woman's sexual desire generally decreases during her pregnancy and following delivery. For some couples, vaginal intercourse or other expressions of sexuality resume 6 to 8 weeks postpartum, while for most, sexual activity resumes within 6 months of giving birth (Gutzeit et al., 2020). It is not uncommon that some women experience dyspareunia, or genital pain, in early postpartum. Occasionally, the pubococcygeal muscle may be damaged, especially if a woman has had an episiotomy. Doing Kegel exercises can be helpful in strengthening this muscle in order to help improve the intensity of orgasm.

"Cleaning and scrubbing can wait till tomorrow.
For babies grow up we've learned to our sorrow.
So quiet down cobwebs, dust go to sleep.
I'm rocking my baby and babies don't keep."

—Anonymous

Final Thoughts

For many people, the arrival of a child is one of life's most significant events. It signifies adulthood and conveys social status for those who are now parents. It creates the lifelong bonds of family. And it can fill the new parents with a deep sense of accomplishment and well-being.

ballyscanlon/Getty Images

Summary

Fertilization and Fetal Development

- Fertilization of the *oocyte* by a sperm usually takes place in the fallopian tube. The chromosomes of the oocyte combine with those of the sperm to form the diploid zygote; it divides many times to form a *blastocyst,* which *implants* itself in the uterine wall.

- The blastocyst becomes an *embryo* and then a *fetus,* which is nourished through the *placenta* via the *umbilical cord.*

- Pregnancy is now a matter of choice. Increasing numbers of individuals and couples are choosing to remain *child-free.*

Pregnancy

- *Preconception health care* refers to the health of women and men during their reproductive years and focuses on the steps necessary to protect the health of a baby they might have some time in the future.

- Tests designed to measure *human chorionic gonadotropin (hCG)* can determine pregnancy approximately 7–12 days from conception. *Hegar's sign* can be detected by a trained examiner. Pregnancy is confirmed by the detection of the fetal heartbeat and movements and thorough examination by ultrasound.

- A woman's feelings vary greatly during pregnancy. It is important for her to share her concerns and to have support from her partner, friends, relatives, and health care practitioners. Her feelings about sexuality are likely to change during pregnancy. Partners may also have conflicting feelings. Sexual activity is generally safe unless there is pain, bleeding, or a history of miscarriage.

- Harmful substances may be passed to the embryo or fetus through the placenta. Substances or other factors that cause birth defects are called *teratogens;* these include alcohol, tobacco, certain drugs, and environmental pollutants. Infectious diseases such as COVID-19, rubella, and the Zika virus may damage the fetus. Sexually transmitted infections may be passed from the mother to the infant and have serious effects on both.

- *Ectopic pregnancy, gestational hypertension,* and *preterm birth* are the most common complications of pregnancy.

- Abnormalities of the fetus may be diagnosed using *ultrasound, prenatal cell-free DNA, amniocentesis, chorionic villus sampling (CVS),* or *neural tube defect screening.*

- Some pregnancies end in *miscarriage.* About 10–20% of recognized pregnancies end before 20 weeks' gestation. Loss of a pregnancy or death of a young infant is a serious life event.

Infertility

- *Infertility* is characterized by the failure to establish a pregnancy after 12 months of regular, unprotected sexual intercourse or due to an impairment of a person's capacity to reproduce either as an individual or with his or her partner. This is also referred to as impaired fecundity.

- Techniques for combating infertility include fertility medications, egg freezing, surgery, artificial insemination, and *assisted reproductive technology. Surrogate motherhood* or relying on a *gestational carrier* may be options for childless couples.

Giving Birth

- In the last trimester of pregnancy, a woman feels *Braxton-Hicks contractions.* These contractions help with the *effacement* and *dilation* of the cervix to permit delivery.

- Labor can be divided into three stages. First-stage labor begins when uterine contractions become regular. When the cervix has dilated approximately 10 centimeters, the baby's head enters the birth canal; this is called *transition.* In second-stage labor, the baby emerges from the birth canal. In third-stage labor, the *afterbirth* is expelled.

- *Labor induction* refers to the use of medications or other methods to bring on (induce) labor.

- *Cesarean section,* or *C-section,* is the delivery of a baby through an incision in the mother's abdominal wall and uterus.

- *Prepared childbirth* encompasses a variety of methods that stress the importance of understanding the birth process, teaching the mother to relax, and giving her emotional support during childbirth.

- Birthing centers and birthing rooms in hospitals provide viable alternatives to traditional hospital birth settings for normal births. Instead of medical doctors, many women now choose trained nurse-midwives, while others have doulas as labor assistants.

- Mother's milk is more nutritious than formula or cow's milk and provides immunity to many diseases and conditions. Breastfeeding also offers benefits to mother, family, society, and the environment.

Postpartum and Beyond

- A critical adjustment period—the *postpartum period*—follows the birth of a child. The mother may experience feelings of depression (sometimes called "baby blues") that are a result of biological, psychological, and social factors. Though transient, the majority of women experience a decrease in sexual desire.

- Depending on a couple's ability to adjust to the physical and psychological changes that occur during this time, most new parents experience a fulfilling sexual relationship.

Questions for Discussion

- Most likely you have a strong opinion about pregnancy and how one would affect your life. If you or your partner became pregnant today, what would you do? Where would you go in order to receive support for your decision?

- If you or your partner were to have a child, where and how would you prefer to deliver the baby? Whom would you want present? What steps would you be willing to take in order to ensure that your wishes were granted?

- After trying but not being able to conceive for 1 year, you now realize that you or your partner may have a fertility problem. What measures would you consider in order to have a child? How much would you be willing to pay?

- Like many issues related to sexual orientation, adoption by same-sex couples is a controversial issue. What are your views on this, and do you feel that enacting laws is the best way to support your point of view?

Sex and the Internet

Pregnancy and Childbirth

Even though pregnancy is a natural and normal process, there are still myriad issues, questions, and concerns surrounding it. This is especially true when couples are considering pregnancy, are trying to become pregnant, or find out that the woman is pregnant. Fortunately, there is help and support on the Internet. One website aimed specifically at educating individuals about pregnancy is run by the Centers for Disease Control and Prevention (CDC): www.cdc.gov/pregnancy. Go to this site and select two topics you wish to learn more about. You might choose "Before Pregnancy" or "After the Baby Arrives." Once you have investigated the topics and perhaps linked them to another resource, answer these questions:

- What topics did you choose? Why?

- What three new facts did you learn about each topic?

- How might you integrate this information into your own choices and decisions around pregnancy or parenthood?

- What additional link did you follow, and what did you learn as a result?

Suggested Websites

American College of Obstetricians and Gynecologists (ACOG)

www.acog.org/
Founded in 1951, the site is dedicated to the improvement of women's health and provides a wealth of information and resources for reproductive health and well-being.

American Pregnancy Association

americanpregnancy.org
Committed to promoting reproductive and pregnancy wellness through education, support, advocacy, and community awareness.

Fatherhood.gov (National Responsible Fatherhood Clearinghouse)

https://www.fatherhood.gov
Provides tips and hints for dads and a library for laypeople and professionals.

La Leche League International

www.llli.org
Provides advice and support for nursing mothers.

Resolve: The National Infertility Association

resolve.org
Dedicated to providing education, advocacy, and support for men and women facing infertility.

Share: Pregnancy & Infant Loss Support

nationalshare.org
Serves those whose lives are touched by the death of a baby.

Society for Assisted Reproductive Technology (SART)

www.sart.org
Promotes and advances the standards for the practice of assisted reproductive technology.

Suggested Reading

For the most current research findings in obstetrics, see *Obstetrics and Gynecology,* the *New England Journal of Medicine,* and *JAMA: Journal of the American Medical Association.*

Allers, K. S. (2017). *The big letdown: How medicine, big business, and feminism undermine breastfeeding.* St. Martin's Press. A combination of research and personal stories to support breastfeeding and its importance to mothers and their children.

Brott, A. A., & Ash, J. (2015). *The expectant father* (4th ed.). Abbeville Press. A guide to the emotional, physical, and financial changes the father-to-be may experience during the course of his partner's pregnancy.

Gardner, D. K., & Simon, C. (Eds.) (2017). *Handbook of in vitro fertilization* (4th ed.). CRC Press. A primer on the central topics involved in human in vitro fertilization (IVF).

Jana, L. A., & Shu, J. (2020). *Heading home with your newborn* (4th ed.). American Academy of Pediatrics. Offers parent-tested, pediatrician-approved advice.

Murkoff, H., & Mazel, S. (2016). *What to expect when you're expecting* (5th ed.). Workman. Covers preconception care through postpartum.

Nilsson, L., & Hamburger, L. (2020). *A child is born* (5th ed.). Random House. The study of birth, beginning with fertilization, told in stunning photographs with text.

Oster, E. (2019). *Cribsheet: A data-driven guide to better, more relaxed parenting, from birth to preschool.* Penguin Press. Helps parents feel less confused and more confident in their choices by arming them with data and a healthy understanding of the principles of economics-driven decision-making.

Richardson, S. S. (2021). *The maternal imprint.* University of Chicago Press. A history of the idea that a pregnant woman's health, behavior, and milieu can have intergenerational effects on her descendants and an analysis of issues provoked by the rise of epigenetics, or how behaviors and environments can affect the way that genes work.

13

The Sexual Body in Health and Illness

Goodshoot/Getty Images

CHAPTER OUTLINE

"I have learned not to take the media or anyone else's opinion as the gospel. Now when I look in the mirror, I see the strong, beautiful, Black woman that I am. I no longer see the woman who wanted breast implants and other superficial aspects of beauty. My beauty now flows from within, and all I had to acquire was love for myself and knowledge of myself, and it did not cost me anything."

—21-year-old female

"It was never about food; it was always about the way I felt inside. The day that changed my life forever was January 29, 2016. It was the mortifying reflection of myself off the porcelain toilet I hovered over that made me see the truth. At that moment, I knew I could no longer go on living or dying like a parched skeleton. I had to hit rock bottom before I realized that what I was doing was wrong. I feel that, even if twenty people had sat me down at that time and told me I had an eating disorder, I would have laughed. I was blind."

—20-year-old male

"Interestingly, I am writing this paper with a bald head. I used to have long, beautiful blonde hair. Chemotherapy took care of that little social/sexual status symbol. I was not at all prepared for losing my looks along with that much of my sexual identity. It has taken me by surprise to realize how much the way you look influences how people react to you, especially the opposite sex. The real lesson comes from the betrayal I feel from my body. I was healthy before, and now that I am sick, I feel as if my identity has changed. I always saw my body as sexual. Now after surgery, which left a large scar where my cleavage used to be, and with chemotherapy, which left me bald, I feel like my body is a medical experiment. My sexual desire has been very low, and I think it is all related to not feeling good about the way I look. Amazing how much of our identities are wrapped around the way we feel about the way we look. The good news for me is that my foundation is strong: I am not just what is on the outside."

—26-year-old female

"On the weekend, I like to go out with my friend. When I drink alcohol in excessive amounts, I never have any problems performing sexually. But when I smoke marijuana, I have a major problem performing up to my standards."

—19-year-old male

THE INTERRELATEDNESS OF OUR PHYSICAL HEALTH, our psychological well-being, and our sexuality is complex. It's not something that most of us even think about, especially as long as we remain in good health. On the other hand, we may encounter physical and emotional problems and limitations, many of which may profoundly influence our sexual lives. We need to inform ourselves about these problems so that we can help prevent or deal with them effectively.

In this chapter, we examine our attitudes and feelings about our bodies and look at specific health issues. We begin with a discussion of body image and its impact on sexuality. Next we look at the relationship between alcohol, marijuana, and other drugs and our sexuality. Then we turn to issues of sexuality and disability. We also discuss the physical and emotional effects of specific diseases such as diabetes, heart disease, arthritis, and cancer as they influence our sexual functioning. Finally, we address other topics specific to women and men and look at the impact that sexual orientation has on health and well-being.

As we grow emotionally and physically, we may also develop new perceptions of what it means to be healthy. We may discover new dimensions in ourselves to lead us to a more fulfilled and healthier sex life.

"The essence of beauty is the unity of variety."

—William Somerset Maugham (1874–1965)

● Living in Our Bodies: The Quest for Physical Perfection

Two broad elements that have taken root in various organizations' definitions of **sexual health** include: (1) sexuality or relationships with a sexual or romantic component have intrinsic value as part of health and (2) healthy sexual relationships require positive experiences for individuals and their partners (Becasen et al., 2015).

Contrary to popular stereotypes, people of all shapes, sizes, and ages can lead healthy and happy sexual lives.

Image Source/Getty Images

"Don't let your mind bully your body."

—June Tomaso Wood (1953–)

"Muscles I don't care about—my husband likes me to be squishy when he hugs me."

—Dixie Carter (1939–2010)

O, that this too, too solid flesh would melt; Thaw, and resolve itself into a dew!

—William Shakespeare, *Hamlet* (1564–1616)

Good health requires us to know and understand our bodies, to feel comfortable with them. It requires a woman to feel at ease with the sight, feel, and smell of her vulva, and to be comfortable with and aware of her breasts—their shape, size, and contours. Sexual health requires a man to accept his body, including his penis, and to be aware of physical sensations such as lower back pain or a feeling of congestion in his bladder. A sexually healthy man abandons the idea that masculinity means he should ignore his body's pains, endure stress, and suffer in silence. It requires all genders to be knowledgeable, honest, and responsible about themselves and their sexuality.

Our general health affects our sexual functioning. Fatigue, stress, and minor ailments all affect our sexual interactions. If we ignore these aspects of our health, we are likely to experience a decline in our sexual desires, as well as suffer physical and psychological distress. A person who always feels tired or stressed or who is constantly ill or debilitated is likely to feel less sexual than a healthy, rested person. Health and sexuality are gifts we must nurture and respect, not use and abuse.

Body Image and Sexuality

Many of us are willing to pay high costs—physical, emotional, and financial—to meet the expectations of our culture and to feel worthy, lovable, and sexually attractive. Although having these desires is clearly a normal human characteristic, the means by which we try to fulfill them can be extreme and even self-destructive. Many Americans try to control their weight by dieting and exercising excessively, but some people's fear and loathing of fat often combined with anxiety or disgust regarding sexual functions impels them to extreme eating behaviors. There is a common belief that eating disorders are a lifestyle choice. Actually, **eating disorders** are serious and often fatal illnesses that cause disturbances to a person's eating behaviors (National Institute of Mental Health, 2016). Obsessions with food, body weight, and shape; compulsive overeating (binge eating); compulsive overdieting, which may include self-starvation and binge eating and purging; and combinations thereof all may signal an eating disorder.

Most people with eating disorders have certain traits, such as low self-esteem, perfectionism, difficulty dealing with emotions, unreasonable demands for self-control, negative perceptions of self in relation to others, and, of course, a fear of becoming fat. Often, the person lacks adequate skills for dealing with stress. The American Psychiatric Association (2017) states that a primary goal for those experiencing eating disorders is to have an accurate diagnosis, which can help define a treatment plan. Eating disorders are frequently present with other psychiatric disorders, such as depression, substance abuse, and anxiety disorders.

Although many studies of eating disorders have singled out white middle-class and upperclass women, these problems transcend ethnic, socioeconomic, gender, and age boundaries. Positive body image is important because people who appreciate their bodies experience a wide variety of benefits, including positive feelings about their sexuality (Grower & Ward, 2018). In the United States (National Association of Anorexia Nervosa and Associated Disorders {ANAD], 2021.):

- Eating disorders affect approximately 9% of the population, suggesting that nearly 29 million Americans will have one in their lifetime.
- Eating disorders are among the deadliest mental illnesses, second only to opioid overdose. Each year, over 10,000 deaths are the direct result of an eating disorder.
- Approximately one fifth of men (18%) and one fourth of women (27%) reported being very-to-extremely dissatisfied with one aspect of their body (Frederick et al., 2020).
- Gay men are 7 times more likely to report binge-eating and 12 times more likely to report purging than heterosexual men.
- Non-binary people may restrict their eating to appear thin, consistent with the common stereotype of androgynous people in popular culture.

think
about it

Body Modification: You're Doing What, Where?

Have you ever wondered whether your genitals were normal? Desired to modify a part your body? Had a procedure done that somewhat altered your appearance? Though the majority who seek cosmetic surgery do so to increase their attractiveness or improve their body image, we still might wonder about the motivations and/or psychological state of those who seek these changes, especially if the modifications are to otherwise healthy parts of their body.

Our culture, more than most, places a newfound emphasis on face and fat. In this case, it appears that more Americans than ever are using their own fat to sculpt their face and body; from body fat reduction to harvesting fat to enhance other parts of the body, most commonly, the breast and the buttocks. According to the American Society of Plastic Surgeons (ASPS), there were 17.1 million surgical and cosmetic procedures performed in the United States in 2016, costing Americans approximately $8 billion (Gould & Mosher, 2017). Because of the pressure to achieve the ideal body image coupled with the instant improvements that surgery can offer; millions of individuals are now having ongoing discussions with their plastic surgeons about all areas of their body that they seek to "rejuvenate" (ASPS, 2017).

One growing trend is fat grafting, whereby surgeons use liposuction to harvest a patient's unwanted fat from their abdomen and then inject it to lift and "rejuvenate" other areas of the body, including the face (13% of procedures), buttocks (26%), and breasts (72%) (ASPS, 2017).

If someone is unhappy with the size of their breasts, a breast lift, breast implant, or fat transfer breast augmentation can be performed. Less often, a breast reduction can provide relief for some women whose breast size compromises posture and/or causes physiological or physical discomfort. For most procedures, however, including for those related to breast volume lost after weight reduction or pregnancy or simply a desire for one's breasts to be larger, breast augmentation can be used by some to improve body image and/or self-esteem. In the case of breast reconstruction after mastectomy or injury, breast implants can be inserted.

The U.S. Food and Drug Administration (FDA) has approved two types of breast implants for sale in the United States: saline breast implants, filled with salt water solution, and silicone gel-filled ones (FDA, 2017a). For those women who choose to increase the shape and volume of the breast but prefer to avoid implants, fat grafting can be done.

Though breast implants undergo extensive testing to establish their safety and effectiveness, there are risks associated with each type including additional surgeries, scar tissue, breast pain, rupture, capsular contracture, or internal scar tissue that causes a tight or constricting capsule around the implant, and silent ruptures. The FDA has a breast implant web page that can be helpful to current or prospective patients (http://www.fda.gov/breastimplants). According to the FDA (2017b), "Breast implants are not lifetime devices. The longer a woman has implants, the more likely it is that she will need to have surgery to remove or replace them."

Of concern among physicians and others is the increasing number of young girls who, during their ob–gyn appointment, express an interest in cosmetic surgery to improve the appearance of their breasts and vulva (Parry, 2016). Julie Strickland, Chair of Adolescent Health Care Committee at the American College of Obstetricians and Gynecologists (ACOG), identifies unrealistic expectations as one of the primary reasons why young girls are worried about the appearance of their breasts and genitals. Additionally, lack of knowledge about the wide variation in appearance of normal anatomy along with a misunderstanding about healthy growth and development may be fueling young women's concerns about their bodies. While some procedures may be necessary for the patient's health and well-being, for example, the need for breast reduction surgery in some girls with excessively heavy breasts, in many cases the teenagers' appeal for surgery is not. It's important to examine the person's motivations, including self-esteem, that may be the contributing factors of the request for body modifications as well as be extremely cautious about supporting adolescents who desire breast or genital surgery.

Though women's experiences of their genital self-perceptions are subjective, research suggests that these perceptions are connected to their sexual well-being (Fudge & Byers, 2017). For example, concerns about their genital odor, the amount or texture of their pubic hair, and their overall genital appearance are commonly experienced by many women. Recent evidence tells us that women have mixed genital self-perceptions that fluctuate across situations and people and evolve over time, and that negative genital self-perceptions have consequences for women. Perhaps as a result of these and other factors, including more information about and images of the genitals and related grooming practices on social media, there has been an increase in the number of surgeries that "rejuvenate" the labia, otherwise known as **labiaplasty**. This procedure reduces the labia minora so they don't hang below the labia majora. The usual goal is to alter the labia's appearance and/or to reduce their length so that the labia appear differently and, for some, no longer chaff or pull against clothing. There are several groups of women who seek this cosmetic genital surgery: those with congenital conditions, otherwise known as disorders of sexual development (i.e., intersex), those with physical discomfort, or those who wish to alter the appearance because they do not feel they fall with a "normal" range (Lloyd et al., 2005). ASPS statistics now included data on labiaplasty, which has been reported to have increased 39% in 2016, with more than 12,000 procedures performed in the United States (ASPS, 2017). Though labiaplasty is occurring more often, the procedure constitutes a small portion of overall cosmetic surgeries.

A variety of cosmetic procedures are requested by men, one of which is penis augmentation. However, only rarely is a man's penis too small; a more common problem is a partner's complaint that it is too large. Nevertheless, a variety of procedures and techniques promise penis enlargements, including vacuum pumps, exercises, pills, and surgical practices such as fat injections, fat flaps, and silicone injections. The long- and short-term side effects of these lengthening surgeries are numerous and include infections and scarring, which can result in a shorter penis, nerve damage, reduced sensitivity, and difficulty in getting erections. The short- and long-term effectiveness and safety of these methods have not been well established, and the degree of patient satisfaction varies. Given that size has been found to play a role in some women's preferences and men's confidence and self-esteem (Prause et al., 2015), it is important that we learn more about the potential consequences of this and other body modification procedures.

If you are unhappy with your breast, vulva, or penis size or other part of your anatomy, talk to a professional health care provider. If you are in a relationship, talk to your partner. In most cases, you will learn that size is usually not an important issue. However, intimacy, communication, mutual respect, and acceptance of your body and sexuality are.

Think Critically

1. How do you feel about the appearance of your penis, breasts, and genitals? If you are uncomfortable, what might help you to feel satisfied?

2. Have you ever been rejected by a sexual partner because he or she was dissatisfied with your breast, genital, or penis size? Have you ever rejected a sexual partner for the same reason?

3. What could you do to help a sexual partner feel more comfortable about accepting their body?

Lammily dolls are made according to the proportions of the average 19-year-old American woman. They received praise for being the first dolls made with realistic body proportions.

CB2/ZOB/Supplied by WENN.com/Newscom

- Black and Latinex teenagers have a higher prevalence of bulimic behavior, such as binge eating and purging, compared to white teenagers.

- Latinex people are significantly more likely to suffer from bulimia nervosa than their non-Latinex peers.

When examining the origins of body image, we know that body image is an important aspect of adolescent social, sexual, and emotional development. In a study which followed 2,586 Norwegian adolescents, researchers found that an adolescent's body satisfaction predicted components of sexual satisfaction 13 years later (Kvalem et al., 2019). A positive body image was strongly associated with a positive self-concept, and this close association remained stable from adolescence to adulthood. The study found that adolescent's body satisfaction predicted adult sexual satisfaction, signifying adolescence as the most significant period for establishing a body image. The study also revealed that body image was a gendered phenomenon, with men reporting both higher body and sexual satisfaction than women, implying that the social meaning of body satisfaction within a sexual context differed from women and men.

● Alcohol, Marijuana, Other Drugs, and Sexuality

In the minds of many Americans, sex and alcohol or sex and "recreational" drugs go together. Although experience shows us that sexual functioning and enjoyment generally decrease as alcohol or drug consumption levels increase, many people cling to the age-old myths.

Alcohol Use and Sexuality

The belief that alcohol and sex go together, although not new, is certainly reinforced by popular culture. Alcohol advertising often features attractive, scantily clad women. Beer drinkers are portrayed as young, healthy, and fun-loving. Wine drinkers are romantics, surrounded by candlelight and roses. Those who choose scotch are the epitome of sophistication, while tequila invites images of interesting men. These portraits reinforce long-held cultural myths associating alcohol with social prestige and sexual enhancement.

Alcohol use and sexual behavior are significant risk behaviors in adolescent development (Bleakley et al., 2017). The two are positively associated with acquiring STIs, the risk factors of which include numerous partners, and unprotected sexual intercourse. These relationships tend to be stronger among female adolescents compared to males, and among white adolescents compared to African American, Hispanic, or Asian adolescents (Ritchwood et al., 2015). Exposure to media portrayals of alcohol and sex among both white and Black adolescent teens also impacts their attitudes and beliefs. When adolescents view media content

Alcohol is associated with risky sexual behavior and may also be part of a risky health behavior problem.

PNC/Getty Images

that features on-screen combinations of alcohol and sex, they often acquire favorable evaluations of performing that behavior, believe that people like them are combining sex and alcohol, and feel that their peers approve of them engaging in the alcohol/sex combination (Bleakley et al., 2017). Whether these specific attitudes carry into adulthood is unknown; however, more adverse forms of risk behaviors initiated during adolescence may result in adverse long-term outcomes (Kann et al., 2014).

Alcohol use among college students is very common. Nearly 55% of college students ages 18–22 reported drinking in the last month, and more than 33% engaged in binge drinking (4+ drinks for women and 5+ drinks for men) during that same time frame (National Institute on Alcohol Abuse and Alcoholism, 2020). Drinking is associated with sexual risks. In fact, most risky first-time sexual encounters involve being inebriated (Livingston et al., 2015). In highly charged sexual situations, intoxication has been reported to increase drinkers' willingness to engage in unprotected intercourse by fostering their belief that they are aroused (George et al., 2009).

Because of the ambivalence we often have about sex—"It's good but it's bad"—many people feel more comfortable about initiating or participating in sexual activities if they have had a drink or two. This phenomenon of activating behaviors that would normally be suppressed is known as **disinhibition**. Although a small amount of alcohol may have a small disinhibiting, or relaxing, effect, greater quantities can result in aggression, loss of judgment, poor coordination, and loss of consciousness.

Alcohol affects the ability of individuals to become sexually aroused. Men may have difficulty getting or maintaining an erection as well as hypoactive sexual desire and either premature or delayed ejaculation (George, 2019). Women may not experience vaginal lubrication and may have difficulty experiencing orgasm ("What happens when people mix alcohol and sex?", 2020). Physical sensations are likely to be dulled. Drinking a six-pack of beer in less than 2 hours can affect testosterone and sperm production for up to 12 hours. This does not mean, however, that no sperm are present; production is slowed, but most men will remain fertile when drinking alcohol. However, ingestion of large amounts of alcohol by anyone can contribute to infertility and birth defects.

Heavy drinking is a significant predictor of sexual violence on college campuses. Approximately 97,000 students between the ages of 18 and 24 report experiencing alcohol-related sexual assault or date rape (National Institute on Drug Abuse [NIDA], 2020). Other consequences include diminished academic performance, suicide attempts, health problems, injuries, unsafe sex, and DUIs. Though some students arrive on campus with some experience with alcohol, the environment can intensify drinking, including unstructured time, loneliness, inconsistent enforcement of underage drinking laws, and social pressures.

The disinhibiting effect of alcohol allows some men to justify various types of sexual violence they would not otherwise commit. Men may expect that alcohol will make them sexually uninhibited and act accordingly. In drinking situations, women are viewed as more sexually available when impaired. Thus, some males may participate in drinking situations expecting to find a sexual partner. Additionally, a woman who has been drinking may have difficulty in sending and receiving cues about desired behavior and in resisting assault. Research also shows that the higher the amount of alcohol consumption by either person up to a point when alcohol impairs performance in men, the more likely the sexual victimization to the woman will be severe. This is particularly true for intoxicated men who have hostile attitudes toward women (Abbey, 2012).

Marijuana Use and Sexuality

With the increasing legalization of marijuana, medically and recreationally, marijuana use has increased in the United States (Lynn et al., 2019). In fact, annual marijuana use is at historic highs among college and non-college peers. In 2018, 6% of college students reported daily use of marijuana, while 11% of non-college respondents reported daily or near daily use of marijuana (NIDA, 2019).

How marijuana affects the body depends on the plants used to prepare the mixture, the dose and frequency of use, and the individual who is using it. Regarding its impact on sexuality, it is postulated that marijuana works through a variety of mechanisms to lead to changes in sexual functioning. While many may tout the sexual benefits of marijuana, including increased libido, arousal, and orgasm, scientific research on its effects on sexual functioning is both limited and mixed. Though some find that cannabis helps them to relax, heighten their sensitivity to touch, and increase their intensity of feelings, others report that cannabis interferes with their perceptions by making them sleepy and less focused or has no effect on their sexual experience (Wiebe & Just, 2019). Among men, marijuana has been shown to affect testosterone levels, which play a role in sex drive. Some men report that their sexual performance increases when they use marijuana, particularly if they are feeling anxious while others report sexual problems including low desire, erectile dysfunction, difficulty in experiencing orgasms, and early ejaculation ("Can marijuana affect a man's sexual function?", 2020). Among women, dopamine, a key ingredient in female sexual function, may be activated by cannabinoid receptors in the brain, which control sexual function. One study of 373 women in a medical practice found that 69% of those who used marijuana before having sex stated that their overall sexual experience was more pleasurable, while 61% noted an increase in sex drive and 53% reported an increase in satisfying orgasms (Lynn et al., 2019). While cannabis may improve the sexual experience, it may also influence a person's judgment, leading to risky or unsafe sex.

To determine whether there is a relationship between marijuana use and sexual frequency, data from a nationally representative sample of 50,000 reproductive-age heterosexual men and women (average age of 30) were analyzed. The study found the following results to be similar for individuals, regardless of marital status or race (Sun & Eisenberg, 2017):

- Marijuana users were found to have significantly higher sexual frequency compared with never users.
- Women who didn't use marijuana reported having sex 6 times on average during the past 4 weeks, compared to 7.1 times for women who used marijuana daily.
- Men who abstained from marijuana said they had sex on average 5.6 times in the 4 weeks before the survey, compared with the daily marijuana users who reported on average have sex 6.9 times.
- Marijuana use did not appear to impair sexual function.

"Lechery, sir, it provokes and unprovokes. It provokes the desire, but it takes away the performance. Therefore, much drink may be said to be an equivocator with lechery. It makes him, and it mars him; it sets him on, and it takes him off; it persuades him, and disheartens him; makes him stand to and not stand."

—William Shakespeare, *Macbeth*
(1564–1616)

Other Drug Use and Sexuality

Substances that purport to increase sexual desire or improve sexual function are called **aphrodisiacs**. In addition to drugs, aphrodisiacs can include perfumes and certain foods, particularly those that resemble genitals, such as bananas and oysters. Ground rhinoceros horn has been considered an aphrodisiac in Asia, possibly giving rise to the term "horny" (Taberner, 1985). Research, both personal and professional, inevitably leads to the same conclusion: One's inner fantasy life and a positive image of the sexual self, coupled with an interested and involved responsive partner, are the most powerful aphrodisiacs. Nevertheless, the search continues for this elusive magic potion.

Most recreational drugs, although perceived as increasing sexual enjoyment, actually have the opposite effect. Many prescribed medications have negative effects on sexual desire and functioning as well, and users should read the information accompanying the prescription or ask the pharmacist about any sexual side effects. Although some recreational drugs may reduce inhibitions and appear to enhance the sexual experience, many also cause problems with sexual desire and functioning. They can also interfere with fertility and have a serious impact on overall health and well-being.

The substance amyl nitrate, also known as "poppers," is a fast-acting muscle relaxant and coronary vasodilator, meaning it expands the blood vessels around the heart. Medically, it is used to relieve attacks of angina. Some people attempt to intensify their orgasms by "popping" an amyl nitrate vial and inhaling the vapor. The drug causes engorgement of the blood vessels in the penis, vagina, and anus. It also causes a drop in blood pressure, which may result in feelings of dizziness and giddiness. The most common side effects are severe headaches and fainting, and if allowed to touch the skin, the drug can cause burns.

LSD and other psychedelic drugs (including mescaline and psilocybin) have no positive effects on sexual response. They may actually cause constant and painful erections, a condition called priapism.

Cocaine, a central nervous system stimulant, reduces inhibitions and enhances feelings of well-being. But regular use nearly always leads to sexual function difficulties in both men and women, as well as an inability to have an erection or orgasm. Male cocaine users also have a lower sperm count, less active sperm, and more abnormal sperm than nonusers. The same levels of sexual impairment occur among those who snort the drug and those who smoke or "freebase" it. Those who inject cocaine experience the greatest sexual function difficulties. Approximately 11% of college-age individuals report using cocaine in their lifetime (NIDA, 2020).

MDMA (Ecstasy or Molly) is a hallucinogenic amphetamine that produces heightened arousal, a mellowing effect, and an enhanced sense of self, as well as distortions in sensory and time perception. It is an illegal drug with no legitimate use. Many of these tablets also contain a number of other drugs or drug combinations that can be harmful. The drug has been associated with dehydration due to physical exertion without breaks for water; heavy use has been linked to paranoia, liver damage, and heart attacks. Because MDMA can promote trust and closeness, when combined with sildenfil (Viagra), it can lead to unsafe sexual behavior.

The use of methamphetamine, often referred to as "crystal," "Christina," "crank," or "Tina," is increasingly becoming associated with casual sex. Prized as an aphrodisiac and stimulant used to prolong sexual arousal without orgasm, methamphetamine can be snorted, inhaled, swallowed, or injected. The sharp increase in sexual interest caused by crystal use can lead to dangerous behavior. And methamphetamine

The use of recreational drugs has become an all too common part of the party scene.

Brand X Pictures/SuperStock

use may increase the user's susceptibility to HIV infection and progression through the use of contaminated needles, increased risky sexual behaviors, and poor medication adherence. Some men, in an attempt to enhance sexual functioning, mix recreational drugs such as methamphetamine, amyl nitrate, and ecstasy with Viagra or other prescription erection-enhancing drugs. The combination of methamphetamine or amyl nitrate and erection-enhancing prescription drugs has sometimes resulted in a phenomenon known as a "sexual marathon," during which sexual activity can be prolonged over hours or even days and cause erectile dysfunction.

Aside from the adverse physical and psychological effects of recreational drugs themselves, their use is associated with greater risk for acquiring STIs, including HIV infection. Addiction to cocaine, especially crack cocaine, has led to the widespread bartering of sex for cocaine. This practice, as well as the injection of cocaine or heroin, combined with the low rate of condom use, has led to epidemics of STIs, including HIV, in many urban areas.

Current interest in nutrition, natural healing, and nutritional supplements, coupled with the accessibility of the Internet, has helped fuel an industry that is selling products to stimulate or improve sexuality. This phenomenon has led to the concern about the outcomes of using such products, the most common of which include yohimbine, maca, fenugreek, red ginseng, and l-arginine (Medscape, 2019.13). Each of these substances has been reported to have adverse outcomes, including psychological symptoms such as mood changes, anxiety, and hallucinations. The impact of these substances, particularly among those with psychiatric disorders who are also at risk for sexual dysfunction, may be significant. Additionally, lotions such as Zestra, a blend of botanical oils and extracts that promise to enhance sexual arousal for women, are available. There is no current evidence to support any of these medicinal aids as effective at improving sexual functioning. However, if some individuals do benefit, it may be because they believe that the products work. It is important to be aware that many of the herbs mentioned previously can have side effects ranging from mild to severe.

● Sexuality and Disability

A wide range of disabilities and physically limiting conditions affect human sexuality, yet the sexual needs and desires of those with disabilities have generally been overlooked and ignored. The percentage of people with disabilities in the U.S. population in 2018 was 13.1% (Disability Statistics Annual Report, 2020). Certainly, a disability or chronic condition does not inevitably mean the end of a person's sexual life. In 1987, Ellen Stohl, a young woman who uses a wheelchair, created a controversy by posing seminude in an eight-page layout in *Playboy.* Some people, including some editors at *Playboy,* felt that the feature could be construed as exploitive of people with disabilities. Others, Stohl among them, believed that it would help normalize society's perception of individuals who have disabilities. She said, "I realized I was still a woman. But the world didn't accept me as that. Here I am a senior in college [with] a 3.5 average, and people treat me like I'm a 3-year-old" (quoted in Cummings, 1987). Though Stohl's layout in *Playboy* occurred over three decades ago, even today we rarely see media depictions of people living with disabilities or chronic illness as having sex lives.

Among the most significant issues facing those with disabilities as well as those who care for them is the belief that people with disabilities are less sexual than those without disabilities. In fact, sexual expression is a component of personality, which is separate from erectile function, orgasm, or fertility status. Other common myths about disability and sexuality include:

- Sex means sexual intercourse.
- Among those who have disabilities, talking about sex is not natural, proper, or necessary.
- Sex is for younger people who are able-bodied.
- Sex should be spontaneous.
- A firm penis and an orgasm are requirements for satisfying sex.

Though media may be portraying more disabilities in movies, such as *The Theory of Everything,* people with disabilities remain neglected and, if they are seen, misrepresented.

Pictorial Press Ltd/Alamy Stock Photo

Because of the complexity of physical, psychological, and emotional changes that may occur as a result of a disability, it's important to educate the person with a disability about sexuality, as well as to involve and communicate with those who support them. Issues related to desires, needs, and sexual function should be explored and addressed in a comfortable and nonjudgmental setting.

Physical Limitations and Changing Expectations

Many people are subject to sexually limiting conditions for some or all of their lives. These conditions may be congenital, appearing at birth, such as cerebral palsy (a neuromuscular disorder) and Down syndrome (a developmentally disabling condition). They may be caused by a disease such as diabetes, arthritis, or cancer or be the result of an accident, as in the case of spinal cord injuries.

"I get the feeling people think that because I am in a chair there is just a blank space down there."

—Anonymous quote in the book *The Ultimate Guide to Sex and Disability*

In cases in which the spinal cord is completely severed, for example, there is no feeling in the genitals, but that does not eliminate sexual desire or exclude other possible sexual behaviors. Many men with spinal cord damage are able to have full or partial erections; some may ejaculate.

However, the effects on sexual response are generally associated with the degree and location of the injury. Though the ability to have an erection is a primary concern of men who have spinal cord injuries, ejaculation difficulties is the second most common issue for men who have paralysis. Researchers have found that ejaculation occurs in 17–70% of men, depending on the location of injury, but almost never in men with complete upper-level injuries (Christopher & Dana Reeve Foundation, 2017a). Fertility is another primary concern of men who have spinal cord injuries. Because of some men's inability to ejaculate, it becomes more difficult for them to biologically father a child. However, intracytoplasmic sperm injection, which involves direct injection of a single mature sperm into an oocyte (egg), can often solve the problem of conception for some men.

Paralysis often impacts a woman's sexuality, including her self-image, physical functioning, sensations, and response (Christopher & Dana Reeve Foundation, 2017b). While a woman's level of sexual desire may be the same after she is paralyzed, her level of sexual activity may be impacted or changed, including positioning during sex, loss of vaginal muscle control, minimal vaginal lubrication, or other factors. Orgasm can be experienced if there are still

All individuals, including those with physical and mental limitations, have a need for touch and intimacy.

P. Broze/Getty Images

in-tact pelvic nerves. Individuals with spinal cord injuries (and anyone else) may engage in oral or manual sex—anything, in fact, they and their partners find pleasurable and acceptable. They may discover a wide variety of erogenous areas, such as their breasts, thighs, necks, ears, or underarms. Many women with spinal cord damage injuries can have painless child-birth, although forceps delivery, vacuum extraction, or cesarean section may be necessary.

To establish sexual health, people with disabilities must overcome previous sexual function expectations and realign them with their actual sexual capacities. A major problem for many people with disabilities is overcoming the anger or disappointment they feel because their bodies don't meet the cultural "ideal." They often live in dread of rejection, which may or may not be realistic, depending on whom they seek as partners. Many people with disabilities have rich fantasy lives. This is fortuitous because imagination is a key ingredient in developing a full sex life. Robert Lenz, a consultant in the field of sexuality and disability, received a quadriplegic (paralyzed from the neck down) spinal cord injury when he was 16 (Lenz & Chaves, 1981). In the film *Active Partners,* he says:

> One thing I do know is that I'm a much better lover now than I ever was before.
> There are a lot of reasons for that, but one of the biggest is that I'm more relaxed.
> I don't have a list of do's and don'ts, a timetable or a proper sequence of moves to follow, or the need to "give" my partner an orgasm every time we make love. Sex isn't just orgasm for me; it's pleasuring, playing, laughing, and sharing.

Educating people with physical limitations about their sexuality and using a holistic approach that includes counseling to build self-esteem and combat negative stereotypes are increasingly being recognized as crucial issues by the medical community. Important tasks of therapists working with people who have disabilities are to give their clients "permission" to engage in sexual activities that are appropriate to their capacities and to suggest new activities or techniques. Nonpenetrative sexual behaviors should be affirmed as valid and healthy expressions of the individual's or couple's sexuality. Clients should also be advised about the use of vibrators, artificial penises or dildos and vaginas, and other aids to sexual enhancement. Certainly, with proper and adequate support, people with disabilities can have full and satisfying sex lives.

Vision and Hearing Impairment

Loss of sight or hearing, especially if it is total and has existed from infancy, presents many difficulties in both the theoretical and the practical understanding of sexuality. A young person who has been blind from birth is unlikely to know what a person actually "looks" or feels like. Children who are deaf often do not have parents who communicate well in sign language; as a result, they may not receive much instruction about sexuality at home, nor are they likely to understand abstract concepts such as "intimacy." Older individuals who experience significant loss of sight or hearing may become depressed, develop low self-esteem, and withdraw from contact with others. Because they don't receive the visual or auditory cues that most of us take for granted, people with hearing or vision impairments may have communication difficulties within their sexual relationships. These difficulties often can be overcome with education or counseling, depending on the circumstances. Schools and programs for children who are sight- and hearing-impaired offer specially designed curricula for teaching about sexuality.

Sexuality and Chronic Illness

Cardiovascular disease, cancer, and chronic lung disease are three of the most common chronic diseases in America, while diabetes ranks six. (Because it is so common and the various types affect individuals differently, cancer is discussed in the next section of the chapter.) Although these conditions are not always described as disabilities, they may require considerable adjustments in a person's sexuality because they, or the medications or treat-ments given to control them, can affect libido, sexual capability or responsiveness, and body image. It is important to acknowledge that the partner's sexuality may also be affected by chronic illness. Additionally, many older partners find themselves dealing with issues of disease and disability as well as those of aging.

There may be other disabling conditions, too numerous to discuss here, that affect our lives or those of people we know. Some of the information presented here may be applicable to conditions not specifically dealt with, such as multiple sclerosis or post-polio syndrome. We encourage readers with specific questions regarding sexuality and chronic diseases to seek out networks, organizations, and self-help groups that specialize in those issues.

Diabetes **Diabetes mellitus**, commonly referred to simply as diabetes, is a chronic disease characterized by an excess of sugar in the blood and urine, due to a deficiency of insulin, a protein hormone. About 34 million people in the United States, or 10.5% of the population, have diabetes (CDC, 2020.13a). Nerve damage or circulatory problems caused by diabetes can cause sexual function difficulties. Men with diabetes are often more affected sexually by the disease than are women. Erectile difficulties are common in men with diabetes, affecting more than half of men with the disease (Kouldrat et al., 2017). Some men with diabetes experience problems with sexual desire, difficulty getting an erection, and not experiencing orgasm. Heavy alcohol use, obesity, age, smoking, and poor blood-sugar control also increase the risk of erectile problems.

Diabetes can affect a woman's sexuality as well. Female sexual function difficulties have been found to occur in 68% of sexually active women with type-2 diabetes (Rahmanian et al., 2019). Some women with diabetes report being less sexual because of vaginal dryness or vaginal infections. High blood-sugar levels can make some women feel tired or irritable, resulting in reduced sexual interest. Also, intercourse may be painful because of vaginal dryness.

Problems with sexual functioning in men and women with diabetes are also associated with fear of failure, reduced self-esteem, and problems with acceptance of the disease. While it may be difficult to discuss these feelings with a partner, it's important not to give up. Finding someone on your health care team to talk with may also be helpful.

Cardiovascular Disease Obviously, a heart attack or stroke is a major event in a person's life, affecting important aspects of daily living. Following an attack, a person often enters a period of depression in which the appetite declines, sleep habits change, and there may be fatigue and a loss of libido. There is often an overwhelming fear of sex based on the belief that sexual activity might provoke another heart attack or stroke. Sexual function difficulties are common in cardiac patients and, in men, may precede cardiac symptoms; 50–60% of men with coronary artery disease have erectile problems (Cleveland Clinic, 2019). The partners of male heart attack patients also express great concern about sexuality. They are fearful of the risks, concerned over sexual function difficulties, and apprehensive about the possibility of another attack during intercourse. If a heart attack does occur during sexual activity, the partner should not hesitate to perform CPR. Most people can start sexual activity again 3 to 6 weeks after their condition becomes stable following an attack if the physician agrees. In general, the chance of a person with a prior heart attack having another one during sex is no greater than that of anyone else.

Chronic Lung Disease Bacterial and viral infections are a major cause of chronic obstructive pulmonary disease (COPD), a progressive respiratory disorder that can not only affect a person's breathing but also their sex life. Over time, exposure to irritants, the primary of which is smoking, can damage a person's lungs and airways and cause shortness of breath, coughing, and wheezing. Mucus and fatigue can accompany these symptoms, severely limit daily activities, and dampen all aspects of a person's life, including their sex life (Connell, 2019). Difficulty in maintaining an erection or having an orgasm, both of which are impeded by the restriction of air to the lungs, can also occur. While there are complications related to having COPD, many couples still find new ways to enjoy intimacy, while moving beyond the frustrations that can put pressure on their sex life.

"LAMENT OF A CORONARY My doctor has made a prognosis that intercourse fosters thrombosis, but I'd rather expire fulfilling desire than abstain, and suffer neurosis."

—Anonymous

Developmental Disabilities

"I choose not to place 'DIS' in my ability."

—Robert M. Hensel (1969–)

Developmental disabilities are a diverse group of lifelong, chronic conditions attributable to mental and/or physical impairments that begin during the developmental period and result in major lifestyle limitations. People with developmental disabilities most often have problems with major life activities such as language, mobility, learning, self-help, and independent living. The sexuality of those who have developmental disabilities has been widely acknowledged by those who work with them. The capabilities of individuals with developmental disabilities vary widely. People with mild or moderate disabilities may be able to learn to behave appropriately, protect themselves from abuse, and understand the basics of reproduction. This is especially important since it has been shown that those with intellectual disabilities have a three times greater risk of being sexually abused than their nondisabled peers. The perpetrators may be people with whom those with disabilities share an environment, including peers, staff members, or family members (Schaafsma et al., 2015). Depending on the severity of the disability, some individuals have romantic relationships, marry, work, and raise families with little assistance.

Sexuality education is extremely important for adolescents who have developmental disabilities. Some parents may fear that this will "put ideas into their heads," but it is more likely given the combination of explicit media and Internet images and the effects of increased hormonal output, that the ideas are already there. It may be difficult or impossible to teach more severely affected people how to engage in safer sexual behaviors. There is ongoing debate about the ethics of mandatory birth control or sterilization for those who have developmental disabilities. These issues are especially salient in cases in which there is a chance of passing the disability to a child.

The Sexual Rights of People With Disabilities

Although many of the concerns of people with disabilities are becoming more visible through the courageous efforts of certain groups and individuals, much of their lives still remains hidden. By refusing to recognize the existence and concerns of those with physical and developmental limitations, the rest of us do a profound disservice to those who have a disability and, ultimately, to ourselves. The United Nations General Assembly (1993) noted that states "should promote their [persons' with disabilities] rights to personal integrity and ensure that laws do not discriminate against persons with disabilities with respect to sexual

Though most people support the right of consenting adults to have access to sexuality education and a sexual life, few acknowledge the needs and rights of those with disabilities to have the same.

Realistic Reflections

relationships, marriage, and parenthood." The federal Developmental Disabilities Assistance and Bill of Rights Act of 2000 explicitly states that individuals with intellectual disability have the fundamental right to engage in meaningful relationships with others (U.S. Department of Health and Human Services, 2000).

The disability rights movement is a global social effort aimed to provide equal opportunities and rights for all people with disabilities. Working to break barriers that prevent people with disabilities from living their lives like other citizens, these rights include the following:

- The right to sexual expression
- The right to privacy
- The right to be informed about and have access to needed services, such as contraceptive counseling, medical care, genetic counseling, and sex counseling
- The right to choose one's marital status
- The right to have or not have children
- The right to make one's own decisions and develop to one's full potential

"A hero is an ordinary individual who finds the strength to persevere and endure in spite of overwhelming obstacles."
—Christopher Reeve (1952–2004)

● Sexuality and Cancer

Cancer is not a single disease; rather, it is the name given to a collection of related diseases. In all types, some of the body's cells continually divide and spread into surrounding tissues. Cancer can start anywhere in the body. Many cancers form solid tumors, or masses of cells, while others such as leukemia generally do not form tumors. Cancer and its treatments can have a devastating effect on a person's sense of self, including their sexuality, because they can impact the hormonal, neurological, and vascular functions related to sexual arousal and response. Additionally, exhaustion, pain, and the medications' side effects can impair the quality of life associated with sexuality and arousal. Education, support, and compassion are part of the tools that cancer survivors and their loved ones can use to address the diagnosis and treatment of cancer.

All cancers have one thing in common: they are the result of the aberrant behavior of cells. Cancer-causing agents (carcinogens) are believed to scramble the messages of the DNA within cells, causing the cell to abandon its normal functions. Tumors are either benign or malignant. **Benign tumors** usually are slow growing and remain localized. **Malignant tumors**, however, are cancerous. Instead of remaining localized, they invade nearby tissues and disrupt the normal functioning of vital organs. The process by which the disease spreads from one part of the body to another unrelated part is called **metastasis**. This metastatic process, not the original tumor, accounts for the vast majority of cancer deaths.

Women and Cancer

Because of their fear of cancer, coupled with lack of education or access to medical care, some women avoid having regular cancer screenings, including breast examinations or Pap tests. If a woman feels a lump in her breast or her doctor tells her she has a growth in her uterus, she may plunge into despair or panic. These reactions are understandable, but they are also counterproductive. Most lumps and bumps are benign conditions, including uterine fibroids, ovarian cysts, and fibroadenomas of the breast.

"Life is not the way it's supposed to be, it's the way it is. The way you cope with it is what makes the difference."
—Virginia Satir (1916–1988)

Breast Cancer Excluding cancer of the skin, breast cancer is the most common cancer in women and the second leading cause of cancer deaths (only lung cancer kills more women each year). It was predicted that in 2020, about 276,000 new cases of invasive breast cancer will be diagnosed in the United States, with about 49,000 women dying from the disease (American Cancer Society [ACS], 2020.13a). Experts estimate that about one of every eight American women born today will be diagnosed with breast cancer at some time during their life. Despite these staggering numbers, death rates from breast cancer have been steady in women younger than 50, but have decreased in older women (ACS, 2020.13b).

This decrease is believed to be the result of earlier screening, increased awareness, and improved treatments.

The most significant risk factors for breast cancer is being a woman and age. Other risk factors include (CDC, 2020.13b):

- Inherited changes in certain genes, such as BRCA1 and BRCA2
- Personal or family history of breast cancer
- Having dense breasts
- Beginning to menstruate before age 12 or starting menopause after age 55
- Not being physically active
- Being overweight or obese after menopause
- Taking hormones
- Personal history of breast cancer or certain noncancerous breast diseases
- Having taken the drug DES (diethylstilbestrol)
- Drinking alcohol

Research suggests that other factors, including smoking, having a high fat diet, being exposed to chemicals that can cause cancer, and night shift work may also increase the risk of breast cancer. Because some types of breast cancer need estrogen and progesterone to grow, the female hormone estrogen may promote the growth of breast cancer cells in some women.

Compared to other women, lesbian and bisexual women tend to get less routine health care, including colon, breast, and cervical cancer screening tests. Postponing any of these tests can result in diagnosing cancer at a later stage, when it is less treatable (ACS, 2020.13b). Some reasons for this include lower rates of health insurance, fear of discrimination, and negative experiences with health care providers. It is especially important for sexual minorities to find providers who are accepting and medically competent.

Detection   Breast cancer screening means checking a woman's breasts for cancer before there are signs or symptoms of the disease. Research has not shown a benefit of regular physical breast exams done by a health professional, referred to as a clinical breast exam, or by a woman herself, called a self-breast exam (ACS, 2020.13b). Nevertheless, a woman should be familiar with how her breasts normally look and feel and report any changes to a health care provider. Women should decide for themselves along with guidance from their health care provider whether to get screened.

Recommendations from several leading organizations provide guidelines for women by age and risk; however, all women need to be informed about the benefits and risks of the screening options and decide with their health care provider which, if any, is right for them (CDC, 2020.13b). Some women judged to be at higher risk of breast cancer are offered more frequent screenings, including those with a strong family history of breast cancer. (See Practically Speaking, "Screening Guidelines for Early Detection of Prostate Cancer" for guidelines recommended by leading health organizations.)

A **mammogram** is an X-ray of the breast. It is the best way to find breast cancer early, especially for women have nondense breast tissue, and when it is easier to treat and before it is large enough to feel or cause symptoms. This procedure can lower the risk of dying from breast cancer. **Breast magnetic resonance imaging (MRI)** uses magnets and radio waves to produce detailed 3D images of breast tissue after a contrast dye is injected into a vein. Though breast MRI is not limited by breast density, it is only slightly more sensitive than mammography at locating breast cancer, finding about one extra breast tumor for every 1,000 American women screened (Marinovich et al., 2018). This newer technology isn't necessarily better and can carry risks including over-diagnosis, over-treatment, and exposure to unnecessary radiation.

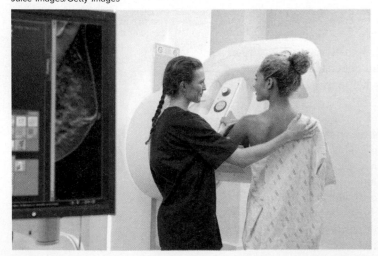

Regular mammograms are the best tests doctors have to find breast cancer early, especially if a woman is over age 50.

Juice Images/Getty Images

Screening Guidelines for the Early Detection of Breast Cancer

	U.S. Preventive Services Task Force	American Cancer Society	American College of Obstetricians and Gynecologists
Clinical breast exam (all ages)	Insufficient evidence to recommend for or against	Does not recommend	May be offered every 1–3 years for women aged 25–39 and annually for women 40 and older
Mammogram: Women aged 40–54 with average risk	Individual decision before age 50	Individual decision between ages 40 and 45. Yearly after age 45 to 54	Recommends screening every 1–2 years beginning at age 40 but no later than age 50 and clinical breast exam every year for women 40 years or older
Mammogram: Women aged 55–74 with average risk	Every other year	Every 1–2 years and continued as long as a woman is in good health and expected to live 10 more years or longer	Every 1–2 years until age 75
Women 75+ with average risk	Insufficient evidence for any detection methods	Screenings should stop when life expectancy is less than 10 years	Decision to discontinue screening mammography should be based on shared decision-making informed by a woman's health status and longevity
Women with higher than average risk	Women may benefit from beginning screenings in their 40s	Yearly screening with MRI and a mammogram should begin by age 30	Twice yearly clinical breast exams, annual mammography, annual MRI, and self-breast exams

Sources: American Cancer Society. (2020.13b). *American Cancer Society recommendations for the early detection of breast cancer;* American College of Obstetricians and Gynecologists. (2017). *Mammography and other screening tests for breast problems;* and U.S. Preventive Services Task Force. (2016). *Screening for breast cancer: U.S. Preventive Services Task Force Recommendation Statement.*

Early detection is an important part of preventive care. The earlier breast cancer is found, the better the chances that treatment will be effective and the breast can be saved. The goal is to discover cancer prior to symptoms appearing. The majority of physicians believe that early detection of breast cancer saves thousands of lives each year.

Most breast lumps—75-80%—are *not* cancerous. Many disappear on their own. Of lumps that are surgically removed for diagnostic purposes (biopsied), 80% prove to be benign. Most are related to **fibrocystic disease**, a common and generally harmless breast condition, or they are fibroadenomas, which have round movable growths that occur in young women.

Treatment The stage or extent of breast cancer is the guiding factor in making decisions about treatment options. The more cancer has metastasized or spread, the more treatment will be needed. Most women with breast cancer undergo some type of surgery to remove the primary tumor. These include **breast conserving surgery**, also called lumpectomy, which is a procedure that involves the removal of only the breast lump and some normal tissue around it, or **mastectomy**, which involves the removal of all the breast tissue and sometimes other nearby tissue. Surgery may also be combined with other treatments such as chemotherapy, hormone therapy, targeted therapy, and/or radiation therapy.

Following a mastectomy, many plastic surgeons and oncologists suggest breast reconstruction for women to "feel whole again." Reconstruction surgery, however, is not a simple

"Scars are tattoos with better stories."

—Anonymous

Robin Roberts, co-host of Good Morning America, received a breast cancer diagnosis in 2007, followed by a rare blood disorder five years later. She has shared her breast cancer journey with viewers by describing the challenges and inspiration she has faced though a memoir, *From the Heart: Seven Rules to Live By.*

MediaPunch/Shutterstock

procedure. Up to 40% of women who undergo reconstruction following a double mastectomy experience complications and when examining the outcomes of mastectomy, quality of life, body image, and sexuality were not found to be different between mastectomy with reconstruction and mastectomy only (Verner, 2017). An emerging movement to defy medical advice and social convention and remain breastless after breast cancer, also referred to as "going flat," gives women a perspective about whether and how they wish to live as a woman without breasts.

Sexual Well-Being and Adjustment After Treatment   Sexuality is one aspect of life that may be profoundly altered by cancer. In fact, it is widely recognized that changes to sexual well-being following diagnosis and treatment of breast cancer can be one of the most problematic aspects of life with the impact lasting for many years following successful treatment.

Treatment for breast cancer often results in dramatic changes to a patient's self-image and as a result to their sexual function. Though the frequency of and pain during intercourse are often indicators of responses to treatment, female sexual satisfaction or quality of life may not be addressed during follow-up doctor visits. When concerns are raised with their physicians, the focus often becomes vaginal lubricants, which do not address the entirety of women's issues. Women with metastatic breast cancer need information and additional resources from their health care provider about specialized vaginal lubricants, nonpenetrative and nongenitally focused sex, and sexual positions that do not compromise their physical health yet still provide pleasure. While many women with breast cancer have adjusted well, there is still a need for a woman and her partner to decide what is satisfying and pleasurable. Being comfortable with her own sexuality along with partner support can enhance a woman's self-esteem and make coping with cancer somewhat easier.

Surviving cancer can deepen one's appreciation of life. Notice the tattoo along this woman's mastectomy scars.

Steve Wisbauer/Photographer's Choice/Getty Images

Cervical Dysplasia and Cervical Cancer **Cervical dysplasia**, also called cervical intraepithelial neoplasia (CIN), is the abnormal growth of cells on the surface of the cervix. It is usually caused by certain types of the human papillomavirus (HPV) and is detected during a Pap smear or cervical biopsy. Cervical dysplasia is not cancer, but it is considered precancerous and can become cancer and spread to nearby healthy tissue. There are several factors that may increase a woman's risk of cervical dysplasia, including having had sexual intercourse before age 18, giving birth at a very young age, having had numerous sexual partners, having another illness such as diabetes or HIV, using medications that suppress the immune system, and smoking. Early diagnosis and prompt treatment cure nearly all cases of cervical dysplasia (MedlinePlus, 2020.13a).

It may take 10 or more years for cervical dysplasia to develop into cancer. The most advanced and dangerous malignancy is invasive cancer of the cervix, or **cervical cancer**. The American Cancer Society (2020.13c) estimates about 14,000 new cases of cervical cancer will occur in 2020 and that 4,000 deaths in the United States will result. Despite these numbers, the cervical cancer death rate has gone down significantly, most likely the result of increased use of the Pap test and the HPV vaccine. (For more about the HPV vaccine, see Chapter 15.) More Black and Hispanic women get HPV-associated cervical cancer than women of other races, most likely because of decreased access to screening or follow-up treatment. Approximately 9 Hispanic women, 8 Black women, 7 white women, 6 American Indian/Alaska Native women, and 6 Asian/Pacific Islander women per 100,000 are diagnosed each year with HPV-associated cervical cancer (CDC, 2020.13c).

What makes this finding particularly disturbing is that, with the use of condoms, vaccination, and early diagnosis, cervical cancer is largely preventable. As previously stated, the most significant risk factor for cervical cancer is infection by the sexually transmitted human papillomavirus (HPV), a group of more than 100 different viruses. It's important to note that most women with HPV do not get cervical cancer because the infection usually goes away on its own without treatment. If, however, the infection does not go away, becomes chronic, and is caused by certain high-risk HPV types, it can cause certain cancers, the most common of which is cervical cancer (ACS, 2020.13c). Risk factors for cervical cancer are similar to those associated with cervical dysplasia, the most significant of which is exposure to HPV.

Detection Screening for cervical cancer for women ages 21 to 65 can prevent cervical cancer. The most reliable means of early detection of cervical cancer is the **Pap test** (or Pap smear). This simple procedure aims to detect potentially precancerous changes in the cells of the cervix. A Pap test can warn against cancer even before it begins, and the use of the Pap test has resulted in dramatic decreases in cervical cancer deaths in the United States.

The Pap test is usually done during a pelvic exam (see Figure 1). Cell samples and mucus are lightly scraped from the cervix and examined under a microscope. If anything unusual is found, the physician will do further tests.

"Some days there won't be a song in your heart. Sing anyway."
—Emory Austin (1931–2013)

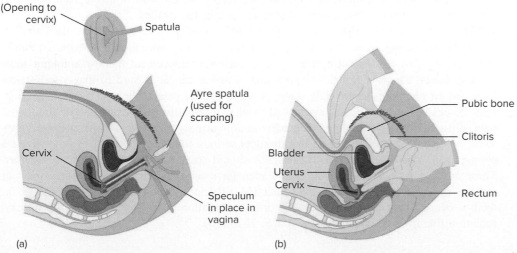

• **FIGURE 1**

Pap Test and Pelvic Exam. A Pap test and pelvic exam are used to diagnose cervical cancer or other reproductive problems. The Pap test (a) involves inserting a speculum into the vagina to obtain a sample of cells. The pelvic exam (b) is conducted to evaluate the reproductive organs.

The following guidelines for early detection of precancerous changes of the cervix include (ACS, 2020.13c; Mayo Clinic, 2020.13a):

- *Women aged 21-65* should get a Pap test every 3-5 years.

- *Women aged 21 to 65* should have an HPV test with their Pap test every 3–5 years to test for cervical cancer (also referred to as co-testing).

- *Women older than 65* can stop having cervical cancer screening if they do not have a history of cervical dysplasia or cervical cancer and if they have had either three negative Pap test results in a row or two negative co-test results in a row within the past 10 years, with the most recent test performed within the last 5 years.

- *A woman who has had a total **hysterectomy*** (removal of the uterus and cervix) should stop Pap tests if the procedure was for a noncancerous condition. Women who have had a hysterectomy without removal of the cervix should continue cervical cancer screening according to the preceding guidelines.

Some women—because of their history—may need to have a different screening schedule for cervical cancer.

To make the Pap test more accurate, women should not schedule the appointment during their menstrual period. Additionally, for 48 hours prior to the test, they should not have intercourse, douche, or use birth control foams, jellies, or other vaginal creams or vaginal medications.

Diagnosis and Treatment If a woman has certain symptoms that suggest cancer or if the Pap test shows abnormal cells, she will have a test called a colposcopy. This test itself causes no more discomfort than any other speculum exam, has no side effects, and can be done safely even if a woman is pregnant. If an abnormal area is seen on the cervix, a **biopsy**, or a surgical removal of the tissue for diagnosis, will be done. A biopsy is the only way to tell for certain if abnormal cells are precancer, true cancer, or neither. Several types of biopsies are used.

Treating women with abnormal test results can prevent cervical cancer from developing. Thus, if a doctor sees an abnormal area during the procedure (called a colposcopy), they will be able to remove it with any one of a variety of procedures.

Ovarian Cancer Most, if not all, ovarian cancers start in the fallopian tubes. Ovarian cancer is a type of cancer that is more aggressive than many others because it is difficult to diagnose in its earliest and most treatable stages. The American Cancer Society (2020.13d) estimates that there will be about 22,400 new cases of ovarian cancer in the United States in 2020, and about 14,000 women will die from the disease. The odds of a woman getting ovarian cancer during her lifetime are about 1 in 78. Evidence links pregnancy, breastfeeding, tubal ligation or hysterectomy, and use of oral contraceptives or the birth control shot with a lower risk of ovarian cancer, perhaps because each gives the woman a rest from ovulation and eases the hormonal fluctuations that occur within the ovaries.

Factors that increase risk include age (about half of all ovarian cancers are found in women over 63), use of the fertility drug clomiphene citrate, more monthly periods, a family history of ovarian cancer, not having children, estrogen replacement therapy, smoking, alcohol use, breast cancer, obesity, and poor diet. Ovarian cancer is hard to diagnose because there are no symptoms in the early stages; it is not usually detectable by a Pap test. If symptoms do occur, they can include abdominal swelling or bloating, pelvic pressure or abdominal pain, difficulty eating or feeling full quickly and/or urinary symptoms. Most of these symptoms, however, can also be caused by other less serious conditions. If these symptoms are a change from how a woman usually feels, she should consult with her health care provider. There are two tests used most often to screen for ovarian cancer; however, for women at average risk, these tests do not lower their risk of death. Depending on several individual factors, ovarian cancer is treated by one or a combination of treatments, including surgery, radiation therapy, and chemotherapy (ACS, 2020.13d).

"The patient must combat the disease along with the physician."

—Hippocrates, *Aphorisms* (460–370 BCE)

Endometrial Cancer   Endometrial cancer, sometimes also referred to as uterine cancer, starts when the inner lining of the uterus (endometrium) begins to grow out of control. Though uterine body cancer does occur, it represents only 10% of cancers of the uterus; the remaining 90% are located in the endometrial tissue. About 66,000 new cases of cancer of the uterus will be diagnosed in the United States in 2020, with nearly 13,000 women dying from the disease (ACS, 2020.13e). Factors that increase risk include being of older age; having taken medications that affect hormone levels, including estrogen therapy; poor diet; lack of exercise; being obese; being diabetic; having a family history of uterine cancer; and treatment with radiation therapy. Unfortunately, the Pap test is not as effective in detecting cancer in the body of the uterus, which occurs in women most frequently during or after menopause.

Hysterectomy   Surgery to remove a woman's uterus is called a hysterectomy. Several reasons can prompt this procedure, including uterine fibroids, uterine prolapse (sliding of the uterus from its normal position into the vaginal cavity), cancer of the uterus, cervix, or ovaries, uncontrolled heavy bleeding, or endometriosis (WebMD, 2020.13). Depending on the diagnosis, all or parts of the uterus may be removed. Because various terms are used to describe a hysterectomy, it's important for a woman to clarify with her health care provider what type of hysterectomy will be performed and whether the cervix and/or ovaries will also be removed during this procedure. If the ovaries are removed, a woman will enter menopause; if they are not removed, a woman may enter menopause at an earlier age than she would have otherwise. If the cervix is removed, a woman will no longer need to get a Pap test. Because a hysterectomy is considered a major surgery, it is not without risks, all of which should be discussed with a woman's health care provider.

The effects of a hysterectomy on a woman's sexuality can vary, depending on which procedure is performed, her degree of satisfaction with the sexual relationship prior to surgery, and the extent of damage to the nerves in the pelvis. If the uterus was entirely removed, then sensations she previously experienced from uterine vasocongestion and elevation during sexual arousal as well as uterine contractions during orgasm can disappear. Additionally, scar tissue or alterations to the vagina as well as some damage to the nerves of the pelvis can affect her sexual response. A hysterectomy, however, does not affect the sensitivity of the clitoris, so if a woman's preferred stimulation is clitoral, her sexual arousal should not be interrupted. A review of published reports on post-hysterectomy changes in sexual functioning found that the majority of women demonstrated either unchanged or improved sexual function after a hysterectomy, while only a minority of women reported sexual function difficulties following the same procedure (Thakar, 2015). The review concluded: "Women can be positively reassured that hysterectomy does not negatively affect sexuality."

Men and Cancer

Generally, men are less likely than women to get regular checkups and to seek help at the onset of symptoms. This tendency can have unfortunate consequences because early detection can often mean the difference between life and death. Men should be alert for any changes in their genital and urinary organs, as well as in the rest of their bodies.

Prostate Cancer   Prostate cancer is the most common form of cancer among American men, excluding skin cancer, and it causes the second highest number of deaths among men diagnosed with cancer (lung cancer is first). The American Cancer Society (2020.13f) estimates that there will be about 192,000 new cases of prostate cancer in the United States in 2020, with about 33,000 deaths. One man in nine will get prostate cancer during his lifetime, but most men diagnosed with prostate cancer will not die from it.

Risk factors for prostate cancer include aging, a family history, being African American or Caribbean of African ancestry, and gene changes. Prostate cancer is more common in

North America and northwestern Europe than in Asia, Africa, Central America, and South America. For reasons still unknown, African American men are more likely to have prostate cancer, to have a more advanced disease when it is diagnosed, and to die from it than men of other races. Prostate cancer occurs less frequently in Asian American and Latinx men than in non-Hispanic white men. About 60% of prostate cancers are found in men over age 65.

Researchers have sought to determine if there is an association between risk for prostate cancer and ejaculation frequency. One study found that ejaculating frequently did not prevent cancer but that it was associated with a reduction in risk. It might be that a range of factors such as lifestyle, reduced stress, genetics, nature of sexual activity, and education may influence its rate (Rider et al., 2016).

Detection   Various symptoms may point to prostate cancer, a slow-growing disease, but often there are no symptoms or symptoms may not appear for many years. Although the symptoms in the following list are more likely to indicate prostatic enlargement or benign tumors than cancer, they should never be ignored. By the time signs do occur, the cancer may have spread beyond the prostate and may include:

- Urine flow that is not easily stopped, weak urinary stream, or the need to urinate more frequently
- Difficulty in getting an erection
- Blood in urine or semen
- Pain in the lower back, pelvis, hips, or other areas from cancer that has spread to bones
- Weakness or numbness in the legs or feet, or loss of bladder control from cancer pressing on the spinal cord

One should be aware that other diseases or problems can also cause these symptoms.

Prostate cancer can often be found early using a simple blood test called a **prostate-specific antigen (PSA) test**; however, it's not clear if the benefits of testing outweigh the risks. This is especially true because though this test may show changes in blood levels that indicate prostate cancer, there is also a high likelihood that false positives can lead to unnecessary treatment of a type of cancer that probably would have not caused problems (ACS, 2019.13; U.S. Preventive Services Task Force, 2018.3). (See Practically Speaking, "Screening Guidelines for Early Detection of Prostate Cancer.") Research also shows that the PSA test poses dilemmas, particularly because levels of PSA can be elevated in men with a benign condition called **prostatic hyperplasia**, during which the prostate gland enlarges and blocks the flow of urine. Additionally, the test cannot distinguish between aggressive and mild forms of the disease.

When a person is diagnosed with cancer, there is a strong desire to treat or remove it. This may be true, despite potential harms of the treatment. Because many, and probably most, prostate tumors discovered are so small and slow growing they are unlikely to do any harm to a man, active treatment has no potential benefits (U.S. Preventive Services Task Force [USPSTF], 2018.13). Instead, more men along with the support of their doctors are choosing active surveillance, which can reduce harm by allowing men to delay or avoid treatment. The USPSTF also did not find enough evidence to make a separate recommendation for screening in high-risk men.

"Oh, to be seventy again [at the age of 90, upon seeing a young woman]."

—Oliver Wendell Holmes Jr. (1841–1935)

Treatment   When a man is diagnosed with prostate cancer, there is often a strong desire to treat or remove the gland, despite potential harms of the treatment. Because many or most prostate tumors discovered are small and slow-growing they are unlikely to do any harm, some authorities suggest that active treatment has no potential benefits (USPSTF, 2018.13). The USPSTF suggests that observation might be a more appealing option to some men, such as those who are older and in whom the PSA level is rising slowly. If, however, the PSA is

Screening Guidelines for the Early Detection of Prostate Cancer

Screening for prostate cancer remains controversial because of the high rate of over-diagnosis and potential harm that may follow in men who might otherwise not have symptoms (Hugosson, 2018). Permanent side-effects from unnecessary treatments and their impact on a man's quality of life need to be weighed, particularly among older men when the disease is neither aggressive nor likely to kill them before something else does. There are exceptions that favor screening beginning at age 40 or 45: those with a strong family history of prostate cancer; men who carry a BRCA1 or BRCA2 mutation; and African American men, who are more likely to develop an aggressive prostate cancer.

The goal of prostate cancer screening is to find the cancer in its earliest stage in order to prevent cancer death. Currently, 90% of prostate cancers are found while the disease is still encapsulated in the gland and nearly 100% of men with the disease will survive 5 or more years when it's diagnosed at this early stage (Brody, 2020).

Updated guidelines from the American Cancer Society (2020.13f) recommend a more individual approach, suggesting that men make an informed decision with their health care provider. The ACS also recommends that doctors stop giving the digital rectal exam (DRE) because it has not clearly shown a benefit, though it can remain an option.

TABLE 1 ● **Screening Guidelines for the Early Detection of Prostate Cancer**

	American Cancer Society	U.S. Preventive Services Task Force	American Urological Association
Age 40	Only for men at high risk	Not recommended	Not recommended
Age 50	For average-risk men expected to live 10+ years	Not recommended	Not recommended for men aged 40–54. Individual decision for men younger than 55 and at higher risk
Aged 55–69	For men who wish to be screened. Digital rectal exam may be done with PSA test. Future screenings depend on PSA results	Benefits and harms are balanced. Decision for testing is an individual one	Shared decision making between doctor and patient with screening intervals every 2+ years
Aged 70+	Not recommended	Not recommended	Not recommended

Sources: American Cancer Society (2020.13f). Early detection, diagnosis, and staging. Screening tests for prostate cancer; American Urological Association. (2018). Patient access to PSA testing; and U.S. Preventive Services Task Force. (2018.13). *Prostate cancer: Screening.*

rising quickly enough to warrant treatment, the 5-year survival rates with treatment are 84–92% (Ussher et al., 2019).

It's important that clinicians discuss with patients the potential long-term effects of treatment on sexual functioning, quality of life, and psychological well-being. These include erectile difficulties, nonejaculatory orgasms, decreases in sexual satisfaction, and bowel and urinary incontinence. Some side effects of treatment may also be associated with anxiety and depression and concerns about sexual relationships. Sexual rehabilitation after prostate cancer treatment has primarily focused on regaining erectile function to improve sexual satisfaction. Common interventions include prescription enhancing erection medications (e.g., Cialis and Viagra), penile injection therapy, penile implants, and vacuum pump erection devices as well as information about sexual rehabilitation. At the same time, problematic sexual recovery after prostate cancer treatment along with a high discontinuation rate of assistive aids has led clinicians to conclude that the specific needs and concerns of all men must be addressed by clinicians (Rosser et al., 2019; Ussher et al., 2019).

Testicular Cancer   According to the American Cancer Society (2020.13g), about 9,600 new cases of testicular cancer will be diagnosed in 2020, with an estimated 440 deaths. The chance of a man developing testicular cancer in his lifetime is 1 in about 250. The exact cause of most cases of testicular cancer is unknown, but risk factors include age (the average age at the time of diagnosis is 33), undescended testicle(s), a family history of testicular cancer, HIV infection, cancer of the other testicle, race, and ethnicity. A man who has had cancer in one testicle has about a 4% chance of developing cancer in the other testicle. The risk of developing testicular cancer for white men in the United States is about 4 to 5 times greater than that of Black men and Asian-American men (ACS, 2020.13g).

Detection   Most cases of testicular cancer can be found at an early stage. The first sign of testicular cancer is usually a painless lump or slight enlargement or swelling of the testicle. Some types of testicular cancers, however, have no symptoms until the advanced stage.

The examination of a man's testicles is a valuable part of a general physical examination. Whether or not a man should conduct a regular testicular self-examination is debated. The American Cancer Society (2020.13g) states that it is important to make men aware of testicular cancer and to remind them that any testicular mass should be evaluated right away by a physician. If a man has certain risk factors that increase his chance of developing testicular cancer, such as an undescended testicle, abnormal testicular development, or family history of testicular cancer, he should consider monthly self-exams and talk about these issues with his doctor.

Treatment   Testicular cancer is a highly treatable form of cancer. Depending on its type and stage, the treatment options can include surgery, radiation, chemotherapy, and chemotherapy along with stem cell transplants.

The loss of a testicle can have an impact on the sexual and overall quality of life for testicular cancer survivors because, for many, the loss of a testicle may be felt as a threat to masculinity. In particular, feelings of uneasiness or shame about impaired body image is quite common. Depending on the extent of the cancer, fertility may also be impaired. Although surgical removal of the affected testicle usually keeps the scrotal sac intact and looking about the same on the outside, a testicular implant could improve some men's body image. This is particularly true if men are younger (Dieckmann et al., 2015).

Since boys and men usually develop cancer in only one testicle, the remaining testicle usually can make enough testosterone to keep a man healthy and able to reproduce. If the other testicle needs to be removed because the cancer is in both testicles or if it has spread, the man will need to take some form of testosterone therapy for the rest of his life. However, testicular cancer or its treatment can make a man infertile. Thus, before treatment starts, a man who might wish to become a father may choose to store sperm in a sperm bank for later use. Advances in assisted reproductive methods such as in vitro fertilization have also made fatherhood possible, even if a man's sperm counts are extremely low. In some cases, if one testicle is left, fertility returns after the testicular cancer has been treated.

Breast Cancer in Men   Breast cancer is about 100 times less common among men than among women. The lifetime risk of a man getting breast cancer is 1 in 1,000. Approximately 2,600 new cases of breast cancer are estimated to occur in 2020 in men in the United States, with about 520 deaths (ACS, 2020.13h). As is the case for women, most breast disorders in men are benign. Known risk factors include aging (the average age is about 72 at diagnosis), family history of breast cancer for both male and female blood relatives, heavy alcohol use, inherited gene mutation, especially the BRCA 1 and 2 genes, Klinefelter syndrome, radiation exposure, testicular conditions, obesity, and estrogen treatment (for prostate cancer, for example). Symptoms of possible breast cancer include a lump or swelling of the breast, skin dimpling or puckering, nipple retraction (turning inward), redness or scaling of the nipple or breast skin, and discharge from the nipple. Diagnosis involves clinical breast examination, mammography, ultrasound, MRI, nipple discharge examination, and biopsy. Male breast cancer is treated with surgery, radiation therapy, and chemotherapy. The survival rate is very high following early-stage detection and is about the same for both men and women for each stage of breast cancer (ACS, 2020.13h).

Anal Cancer

Anal cancer is fairly uncommon, although the number of cases has been increasing for many years. The American Cancer Society (2020.13i) estimated that about 8,600 new cases (5,900 in women and 2,700 in men) of anal cancer will be diagnosed in 2020, with about 1,350 deaths. Most cases of anal cancer are linked to infection with HPV. Women with a history of cervical or precervical cancer have an increased risk of anal cancer. Additionally, risk factors include having multiple lifetime sex partners, history of receptive anal intercourse, HIV infection, lowered immunity, and smoking. Pain in the anal area, change in the diameter of the feces, abnormal discharge from the anus, and swollen lymph glands in the anal or groin areas are the major symptoms of anal cancer. Rectal bleeding is usually the first sign of the disease. The digital rectal examination for prostate cancer will find some cases of rectal cancer. Like many other cancers, surgery, radiation therapy, and chemotherapy are the major treatments for anal cancer. Because the majority of anal cancers are linked to HPV and HIV, condoms will provide some protection against the virus. The HPV vaccine, discussed more fully in Chapter 15, is effective in preventing anal cancer and precancers in all genders.

● Other Sexual Health Issues

In this section, we discuss several disorders of the female reproductive system—toxic shock syndrome, vulvodynia, and endometriosis—as well as some other sexual health issues.

Toxic Shock Syndrome

Toxic shock syndrome (TSS) is a rare, life-threatening outcome of certain types of bacteria, most commonly the toxins produced by *Staphylococcus aureus*. This organism is normally present in the body and usually does not pose a threat. Although the earliest cases of TSS involved women who were using tampons, the United States no longer uses the materials or designs in tampons that were associated with this syndrome. Toxic shock syndrome can affect anyone; however, about half of the cases occur in women of menstruating age; the rest can occur among all ages of individuals with burn wounds (Mayo Clinic, 2020.13b). TSS has been associated with having had recent surgery; using contraceptive sponges, diaphragms, menstrual cups, or tampons; or having a viral infection, such as the flu or chickenpox. The symptoms associated with TSS, including sudden and high fever, diarrhea, low blood pressure, severe rash, shock or renal failure, can progress rapidly. One should seek immediate medical attention if any of these symptoms appear.

It is recommended that all women who use tampons reduce the already low risk by carefully following the directions for insertion, choosing the lowest-absorbing one for their blood flow, changing tampons more frequently, and using tampons less regularly (Mayo Clinic, 2020.13b).

Vulvodynia

Vulvodynia is the experience of chronic pain, discomfort, or throbbing of or around the vulva (opening of the vagina) for which there is no definable cause and which lasts at least 3 months (Shallcross et al., 2019). The pain or burning can be so intense that sitting for long periods or sexual penetration is impossible. The pain tends to be diagnosed when other causes of vulvar pain, such as infections or skin diseases, are ruled out. Additionally, the condition may be associated with any number of factors, including injury or irritation of the nerves in the pelvic region, elevated levels of inflammatory substances in the vulvar tissue, or pelvic floor muscle weakness or spasm. Vulvodynia is estimated to be experienced by 4–16% of women, yet only half of them seek medical attention (Shallcross et al., 2019). Because of this, individuals may become abstinent. However, once diagnosed, a variety of treatment options are available, including topical medications; drug treatments, including pain relievers, antidepressants, or anticonvulsants; biofeedback therapy; physical therapy to strengthen pelvic floor muscles; and surgery to remove the affected skin and tissue in localized vulvodynia (Mayo Clinic, 2020.13c).

Endometriosis

Endometriosis is a disorder in which the endometrium (lining of the uterus) grows outside the uterus (MedlinePlus, 2020.13b). It is one of the most common gynecological disorders, with its primary symptoms including pain, spotting, and bleeding. As many as 30% to 50% of women with endometriosis may experience infertility (American Society for Reproductive Medicine, 2016). Most lesions or patches of endometriosis occur in the pelvic cavity, either on or under the ovaries, the fallopian tubes, behind the uterus, or on the bowels or bladder. Additionally, it may alter immune functioning, change the hormonal environment of the eggs, and impair implantation of a fertilized egg. Some women have endometriosis but may not have symptoms or have it diagnosed only when they have trouble getting pregnant. Factors that may increase the risk of endometriosis include problems with the menstrual flow, most notably retrograde menstrual flow, where some of the tissue shed during the period flows backwards through the fallopian tube into other areas of the body, including the pelvis. Other risk factors include genes, immune system problems, hormones, and previous surgery.

Endometriosis is usually diagnosed during a pelvic exam, followed by an ultrasound or MRI, and laparoscopy, which can both diagnose and treat the disorder. Though there is no cure for endometriosis, there are ways to minimize the symptoms caused by the condition, including hormonal birth control or surgery. For women who wish to become pregnant, surgical treatment and medical therapy may be beneficial through in vitro fertilization. For some women, the painful symptoms of endometriosis improve after menopause.

Polycystic Ovary Syndrome (PCOS)

Polycystic ovary syndrome (PCOS) is a hormonal problem that is common among women of reproductive age (Mayo Clinic, 2020.13d). In fact, it is the most common endocrine problem in reproductive age women (Klass, 2020). The underlying cause is a higher level of androgens, commonly thought of as male sex hormones, than is usual for adolescent girls. The disorder can also cause acne and body hair growth along with infrequent or prolonged menstrual periods.

The precise cause of PCOS is unknown. A diagnosis should not be made until at least 2 years after menarche. Though there is no test to definitively diagnose PCOS, signs can include an irregular menstrual period and weight changes. A physical exam will include checking for signs of excess hair growth, insulin resistance, and acne. An ultrasound may be used to check the appearance of the ovaries and the thickness of the lining of the uterus. Treatment for the condition often includes oral contraceptives, which stimulate the shedding of the endometrium. If a woman is overweight, losing weight can help with the symptoms. If the metabolic issues are not addressed with lifestyle changes and medication, there is an increased risk for Type 2 diabetes and cardiovascular problems, along with reproductive and fertility problems. In addition to these, depression, anxiety, and body image problems may accompany the diagnosis.

Prostatitis

Prostatitis is a painful condition that involves swelling and inflammation of the prostate gland. Other symptoms, though varied depending on the cause, can include difficult urination, pain in the groin, pelvic area, or genitals, and sometimes flulike symptoms (Mayo Clinic, 2020.13e). There are four types of prostatitis: one is chronic, two are bacterial, and one is asymptomatic and inflammatory. The factors that affect a man's chance of developing prostatitis differ depending on the type; however, men with nerve damage in the lower urinary tract due to surgery or trauma and men with a history of lower urinary tract infections are more vulnerable to this problem.

Prostatitis can be difficult to diagnose because the symptoms often are similar to those of other medical conditions such as bladder infections, bladder cancer, or prostate enlargement. Urine and blood tests are used to diagnose prostatitis. A CT scan may also be taken. Treatment depends on the type of prostatitis and can include anti-inflammatory agents, antibiotics, and/or alpha blockers.

A man does not necessarily need to avoid sexual intercourse if he has prostatitis. Prostatitis is usually not made worse by sexual activity, although sometimes men with prostatitis will experience pain with sexual intercourse or ejaculation. If sex is too painful, a man may consider abstaining from sexual activity until the prostatitis symptoms improve.

COVID-19 and Sexuality

COVID-19, also called coronavirus or SARS-CoV-2, is an acute respiratory illness caused by a new virus that is having profound effects on how people are living their lives, including their sexual lives. Though young people are, in general, at lower risk for hospitalization and death from COVID-19, they are still at risk for the disease and its negative effects on their sexual health and social behaviors. Symptoms for the virus vary widely and range from mild to severe. They appear 2–14 days after exposure to the virus and may include fever or chills, cough, shortness of breath or difficulty breathing, fatigue, muscle or body aches, and loss of taste or smell. Getting vaccinated is the best way to prevent the virus from occuring.

One's risk for the coronavirus starts as soon as a person gets within approximately 6 feet of someone who is infected because the virus is transmitted by drop nuclei or tiny specks of infectious material that are sprayed from the nose and mouth by breathing, talking, coughing, and sneezing. Because of this, they can also be infected by sharing the same airspace. We do not know if COVID-19 can be spread through vaginal or anal sex; however, traces of the virus have been found in the semen and feces of people with COVID-19 (New York Health Department, 2020). Thus, at this time and until a partner is vaccinated against COVID-19, it is recommended that you have sex only with people close to you. If you do have sex with others outside of your household, have as few partners as possible and pick partners you trust. In the meantime, COVID-19 probably means less partnered sex overall, whether that's because the lack of a safe sex partner or a drop in desire, or both. (For more about ways to express your sexuality and how to protect yourself against COVID-19, see Practically Speaking, "COVID-19 and Sexuality: It's Complicated.")

An online survey of 1,559 adults, ages 18 to 81, inquired about the pandemic's impact on their sexual lives. Nearly half of the sample, 70% of whom were living with a partner, reported a decline in their sex life, while one in five reported expanding their sexual life by incorporating new activities (Lehmiller et al., 2020). The authors suggested that even in the face of

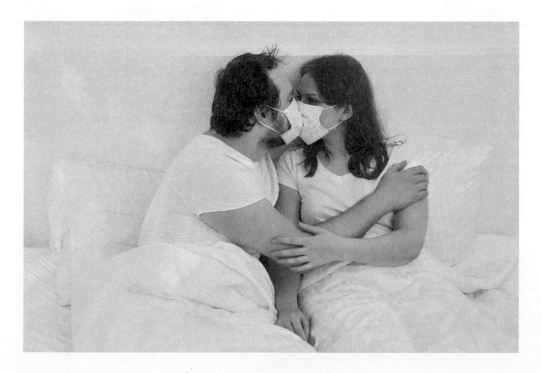

The COVID-19 pandemic has interrupted many of the usual aspects of intimacy and sexuality, however it may also offer an opportunity for new ways of interacting.

Andrey Zhuravlev/Getty Images

COVID-19 and Sexuality: It's Complicated

It's obvious that the COVID-19 pandemic is impacting people's lives. The social restrictions put in place have disrupted the ability to interact with others, enjoy sexual routines and for many, has inhibited or interfered with the expression of their sexuality. How are individuals and couples adjusting and what can they do to both keep themselves and their partners safe?

We now recognize that COVID-19 is a serious and life-threatening illness that requires restrictions on our movement and social contact. These include physical distancing, wearing a mask, washing hands regularly, assessing your own and your partner's risk of having COVID-19, practicing safer sex, limiting your number of partners, and getting vaccinated.

Given the different levels of risk that individuals experience coupled with what we currently know about COVID-19 and how it's transmitted, the safest sexual activity is solo (e.g., masturbation) and, for sexual activity with a non-household partner, remote (e.g., video chats, sexting). The New York Health Department (2020) along with the National Coalition for Sexual Health (2020) and Avert (2021) offer the following strategies to help reduce the risk of spreading COVID-19 during sex:

- **Understand how COVID-19 spreads.** COVID-19 is not an STI, though it can be spread through close contact during sex or when intimate with another person. As previously stated, though scientists do not yet know if COVID-19 can be spread through vaginal or anal sex, the virus has been found in the semen and feces of people with COVID-19. More studies are needed about the sexual transmission of the virus.

- **Have sex only with people who you trust and are close to you.** Limited close contact, including sex, with anyone outside your household and having as few partners as possible is recommended. Large gatherings are not safe, and close contact with multiple people should be avoided unless everyone has been vaccinated. If you or others have not been vaccinated, you may consider. During this time, you may consider taking a break from in-person dates and, if comfortable, use sextech, such as sexual wellness sites or online sex toy shops, instead.

- **Use test results with caution in helping you to make decisions about sex.** Having antibodies against the virus that causes COVID-19 or a prior positive test does not mean you are protected against reinfection with COVID-19. It is estimated that people who recover from COVID-19 produce antibodies for at least 5 to 7 months or longer. Confirmed and suspected cases of reinfection, while rare, have been reported.

- **Slow the pace in a new relationship.** Most singles are spending more time getting to know another by using the phone, video chat or having socially distant dates before removing masks. Taking that next step into the relationship involves detailed discussions about whom each is seeing to help determine the right time to share a hug or kiss.

- **Take precautions during sex.** Kissing can easily spread the virus. Rimming (mouth on the anus) may spread the virus and lead to infection. Wearing a face cover or mask during sex may help avoid passing the virus as heavy breathing and panting can spread it. This practice, along with being creative with sexual positions, can help make sex feel a little kinky. Masturbating together, using condoms and dental dams, and washing up before and after sexual activity is advised.

- **Skip sex if you or your partner are not feeling well.** If you feel unwell, or have been exposed to someone with COVID-19, or if you or your partner has a medical condition that put you at risk for severe COVID-19 illness, consider quarantining.

- **Prevent HIV, other STIs, and unintended pregnancy.** Because it is important that public health resources not be pulled away from combating COVID, individuals are urged to continue to use condoms, contraception, and/or medications to prevent HIV and other STIs. If appropriate, a health care provider can prescribe short-acting contraception, such as pills, patches, or rings, along with condoms and a prescription for emergency contraception as backup measures. Increased use of telemedicine may expand access to health care; however, for some, barriers such as privacy or lack of access to the Internet may make this option difficult.

- **If you are in an abusive relationship, try to minimize your risk.** As COVID continues and people are required to stay at home, many may not be safe. Economic disaster, disconnect from family and friends, and widespread uncertainty may create or worsen situations in homes where violence and abuse has been a problem. If possible and safe to do so, try and put some space between you and your abuser by, for example, taking walks, sitting on a park bench, or going for a drive. Prepare a safety plan, have an emergency bag hidden, including cash and prepaid credit cards, keepsakes, toys and books for your children, photos and other evidence proving abuse, and stay connected with family and friends. For immediate help, call 911.

If you and your partner are living apart under stay-at-home orders, it's still important to keep in touch and connected. Even with extra time on your hands, it's ok if your sex life isn't all you want it to be during the pandemic. Communicate with one another and share your frustrations as well as your desires and fantasies. If you're with a trusted partner, consider trying new sexual positions, watching sexually explicit videos together, and searching for sex-related information online. You might try something new with a remote partner such as texting or sexting, online video date nights, watching movies or TV together, or playing games online. Getting vaccinated and taking care of your sexual relationships and health is important, even during a pandemic!

drastic changes in daily life, many adults are reporting improvements in their sex life as they adapt to lifestyle changes in creative ways and get vaccinated. As a result of the disruptions and barriers that COVID-19 is presenting in peoples' lives, there are some fundamental adjustments that many are making to fulfill their sexual desires and needs, especially when opportunities for in-person, partnered sex are limited. For many, **sextech**, or online activities designed to enhance human sexual experiences and understanding, can be used to fill the void in sexual expression (Lehmiller et al., 2020).

Final Thoughts

In this chapter, we've explored issues of self-image and body image as they interact with our society's ideas about beauty, body image, and sexuality. We've considered the effects of alcohol, marijuana, and other drugs on our sexuality. We've looked at the impact of physical limitations and disabilities, as well as cancer and other health issues, including COVID-19. Our intent is to provide you with information in order to help assist you in identifying potential problems and making responsible decisions around your own health and well-being as well as to stimulate your thinking about how society deals with certain aspects of sexual health. We encourage you to learn more about your own body and your own sexual functioning. If things don't seem to work right, if you don't feel well, or if you have questions, consult your physician or other health care practitioner. Read about health issues that apply to you. By taking care of ourselves physically and mentally, we can maximize our pleasures in sexuality and in life.

Summary

Living in Our Bodies: The Quest for Physical Perfection

- *Sexual health* is a state of physical, emotional, mental, and social well-being related to sexuality. As such, it requires us to know, understand, and feel comfortable with our bodies.

- Our society is preoccupied with bodily perfection. As a result, *eating disorders* have become common, especially among young women. Eating disorders reduce a person's health and vigor; are carried out in secrecy; are accompanied by obsessions, depression, anxiety, and guilt; lead to self-absorption and emotional instability; and are characterized by a lack of control.

Alcohol, Marijuana, Other Drugs, and Sexuality

- Alcohol, marijuana, and other drugs are commonly perceived as enhancers of sexuality, although in reality this is rarely the case.

- Researchers are beginning to conclude that alcohol use among young people is just one component of an overall risky health behavior pattern—not the cause of sexual risk behavior—and that other factors are powerful contributors of risk.

- Some people use alcohol or marijuana to give themselves permission to be sexual. People under the influence of alcohol or drugs tend to place themselves in risky sexual situations, such as exposing themselves to sexually transmitted infections.

- Substances that purport to increase sexual desire or improve sexual performance are called *aphrodisiacs*. Most recreational drugs, though perceived as increasing sexual desire, have the opposite effect.

Sexuality and Disability

- A wide range of disabilities and physical limitations can affect sexuality. People with these limitations need support and education so that they can enjoy their full sexual potential. Society as a whole needs to be aware of the concerns of people with disabilities and to provide them the same sexual rights as others have.

- Chronic illnesses such as diabetes, cardiovascular disease, chronic lung disease, and cancer pose special problems with regard to sexuality. People with these diseases and their partners can learn what to expect of themselves sexually and how to best cope with their particular conditions.

Sexuality and Cancer

- Cancer in its many forms occurs when cells begin to grow aberrantly. Most cancers form tumors. *Benign tumors* grow slowly and remain localized. *Malignant tumors* can spread throughout the body. When malignant cells are released into the blood or lymph system, they begin to grow away from the original tumor; this process is called *metastasis.*

- Other than cancers of the skin, breast cancer is the most common cancer among women. Although the survival rate is improving, those who survive it may still suffer psychologically. *Mammograms* (low-dose X-ray screenings) are the principal method of detection, though some are challenging its risks versus benefits. Surgical removal of the breast tissue and sometimes nearby tissue is called *mastectomy;* surgery that removes only the tumor and surrounding lymph nodes is called *lumpectomy.* Radiation and chemotherapy are among the treatments available used to fight breast cancer.

- *Cervical dysplasia,* or cervical intraepithelial neoplasia (CIN), the growth of abnormal cells on the surface of the cervix, can be diagnosed by a *Pap test.* It may then be further diagnosed by *biopsy.* If untreated, cervical dysplasia may lead to cervical cancer.

- Nearly all cancers of the uterus involve the endometrium, the lining of the uterus. Uterine cancer is treated with surgery (hysterectomy), radiation, or both.

- A *hysterectomy* is the surgical removal of the uterus in order to treat some cancers or severe gynecological problems.

- Prostate cancer is the most common form of cancer among men, excluding skin cancer. If detected early, it has a high cure rate. It is recommended that men discuss with their doctor the risks and benefits of prostate cancer screening. Surgery, radiation, hormone therapy, and chemotherapy are possible treatments.

- Testicular cancer affects relatively young men. If caught early, it is curable.

- Anal cancer is uncommon, although it has been increasing in both men and women in recent years.

Other Sexual Health Issues

- *Toxic shock syndrome (TSS)* is a life-threatening complication of certain types of bacteria, most commonly by *Staphylococcus aureus* bacterium. The disease is easily cured with antibiotics if caught early.

- *Vulvodynia* is a chronic vulvar pain or discomfort of the vulva that lasts at least 3 months. A variety of options are available to treat vulvodynia.

- *Endometriosis* is a disorder in which the endometrium grows outside the uterus. It is a major cause of infertility. Symptoms include intense pelvic pain and abnormal spotting or bleeding. Treatment can include hormonal therapy and surgery.

- *Prostatitis* is a painful condition that involves swelling and inflammation of the prostate gland. Urine and blood tests are used to diagnose prostatitis and a CT scan may be taken.

Treatment depends on the type of prostatitis and can include anti-inflammatory agents, antibiotics, and/or alpha blockers.

- *Polycystic ovary syndrome (PCOS)* is a hormonal problem that is common among women of reproductive age.

- *COVID-19,* also referred to as coronavirus, is an illness caused by a virus that is having profound effects on people's lives. It is transmitted by infectious material sprayed from the nose and mouth or sharing the same airspace. Getting vaccinated helps to eliminate the spread of COVID-19.

Questions for Discussion

- **Is there too much emphasis on body perfection in our society? Have you had friends who took extreme measures to make their body fit the cultural ideal? How have you dealt with pressure to have a certain body?**

- **How comfortable are you in discussing your sexual and reproductive health with your health care practitioner? If you feel uncomfortable, why do you think you feel that way?**

- **Do many of your peers use alcohol, marijuana, or other drugs as a "sexual lubricant," hoping that its use will lead to sexual activity? Do you know of individuals who regret being sexual while under the influence of alcohol or other drugs? What, in your opinion, is the role of alcohol or other drugs in dating?**

Sex and the Internet

Cancer and Sexuality

The American Cancer Society (ACS) has an extensive website that provides detailed information on the prevention, risk factors, detection, symptoms, treatment, and impact of the various cancers, including those of the reproductive system. Go to the ACS website (www.cancer.org) to research this issue. After getting on the website, select a specific type of cancer that was discussed in this chapter, and answer the following questions:

- What are the risk factors for the cancer?

- How can that type of cancer be prevented?

- What are some of the methods used to treat this form of cancer?

- What are the sexuality-related outcomes of the cancer and its treatment?

Suggested Websites

Centers for Disease Control & Prevention

https://www.cdc.gov/coronavirus/2019-nCoV/index.html
Provides up-to-date information about COVID-19.

Center of Excellence for Transgender Health

https://prevention.ucsf.edu/transhealth
The mission of the Center is to increase access to comprehensive, effective, and affirming health care services for transgender and gender diverse communities.

Kaiser Family Foundation (Publisher of *Kaiser Health News*)

https://www.kff.org
Provides facts, analysis and journalism that focuses on national health issues, including reproductive health, HIV/AIDS, and the United States role in global health. It is not associated with Kaiser Permanente.

National Breast Cancer Foundation

www.nationalbreastcancer.org/
Aims to help and inspire hope to those affected by breast cancer through early detection, education, and support.

National Cancer Institute

www.cancer.gov/
Supports and disseminates research and information that help expand our understanding of cancer: its screening, causes, treatments, and prevention.

National Coalition for Sexual Health

https://nationalcoalitionforsexualhealth.org
Aims to improve sexual health and well-being by encouraging conversations and promoting high-quality sexual health information and services.

National Eating Disorders Association

www.nationaleatingdisorders.org/
Dedicated to providing education, resources, and support to those affected by eating disorders.

National Institute on Drug Abuse

www.drugabuse.gov
Supports scientific research on drug use and its consequences.

Sexuality and Disability

https://sexualityanddisability.org/
Though primarily directed at women with disabilities, the information is also helpful to those of all genders. Believes that people with disabilities are sexual beings, just like anyone else.

Services and Advocacy for Gay, Lesbian, Bisexual, and Transgender Elders (SAGE)

www.sageusa.org/
The country's largest and oldest organization dedicated to improving the lives of lesbian, gay, bisexual, and transgender (LGBT) older adults, including quality-of-life issues related to health and wellness.

Testicular Cancer Foundation (TCF)

https://testicularcancer.org/
Provides education and support to young males, ages 15–34, about testicular cancer.

Suggested Reading

Grogan, S. (2017). *Body image: Understanding body dissatisfaction in men, women and children* (3rd ed.). Routledge. Drawing from psychology, sociology, and gender studies, this book offers a comprehensive summary of research on body image.

Kaufman, M., Silverberg, C., & Odette, F. (2016). *The ultimate guide to sex and disability.* Cleis Press. A complete sexual guide for those who live with disabilities, including pain, illness and chronic conditions and education and support those who love them.

Langford, J. (2018). *The pride guide: A guide to sexual and social health for LGBTQ youth.* Rowman & Littlefield. Written for teens and young adults who identify as LGBTQ+, the book explores sex, dating, relationships and puberty and safety. Helpful for adults who can teach queer youth to find resources, explore who they are and encourage them to be true to themselves.

Meyer, I. H., & Northridge, M. E. (Eds.) (2010). *The health of sexual minorities. Public health perspectives on lesbian, gay, bisexual and transgender populations.* Springer. Challenges assumptions about how people manage their identities at various stages of their lives.

Rothblum, E. D. (Ed.) (2020). *The Oxford handbook of sexual and gender minority mental health.* Oxford University Press. A comprehensive review of research on the mental health of sexual minorities, identifying gaps in research to motivate scientist to expand their knowledge about this issue.

14 Sexual Function Difficulties, Dissatisfaction, Enhancement, and Therapy

Radius Images/Alamy Stock Photo

CHAPTER OUTLINE

Student Voices

Rawpixel.com/Shutterstock

THE QUALITY OF OUR SEXUALITY is intimately connected to the quality of our lives and relationships. Because our sexuality is an integral part of ourselves, it reflects our excitement and boredom, intimacy and distance, emotional well-being and distress, and health and illness. As a consequence, our sexual desires and activities ebb and flow. Sometimes, they are highly erotic; other times, they may be boring. Furthermore, many of us who are sexually active may sometimes experience sexual function difficulties or problems, often resulting in disappointment in ourselves, our partners, or both. Studies indicate that many men and women report occasional or frequent lack of desire, problems in arousal or orgasm, and pain during intercourse or noncoital sex. Here are the "real-life" facts that illustrate that not all couple sex matches media portrayals of couples always having great sex (McCarthy & McCarthy, 2003, 2009):

- Less than 50% of happy, sexually satisfied couples described having similar desire, arousal, orgasm, and pleasure during a particular sexual episode.

- For about 25% of the sexual experiences, one partner described the sex as positive, whereas the other considered it as "OK." However, these experiences were good for nourishing the intimacy of the relationship. Sometimes one partner "went along for the ride."

- 15% of sexual experiences were considered unremarkable even though there were no sexual function problems. If the couple had to do it over again, they probably would have chosen something else to do.

- 5–15% of the sexual experiences were dissatisfying or represented a sexual function problem.

Later in this chapter, we discuss the prevalence and predictions of sexual function difficulties found in two nationally representative studies to illustrate the commonality of sexual problems. The widespread variability in our sexual functioning suggests how "normal" at least occasional sexual difficulties are. Sex therapist Bernie Zilbergeld (1999) writes:

Sex problems are normal and typical. I know, I know, all of your buddies are functioning perfectly and never have a problem. If you really believe that, I have a nice piece of oceanfront property in Kansas I'd like to talk to you about.

In this chapter, we look at several common sexual function difficulties, their causes, and ways to enhance your sexuality to bring greater pleasure and intimacy.

"When sex is good, it's 10% of the relationship. When it is bad, it's 90%."

—Charles Muir

"When our innermost desires are revealed and are met by our own loved one with acceptance and validation, the shame dissolves."

—Esther Perel (1958–)

● Sexual Function Difficulties: Definitions, Types, and Prevalence

Most of the literature concerning sexual difficulties or problems with sexual functioning deals with heterosexual couples; thus much of the discussion in this chapter reflects that bias. Unfortunately, too little research has been done on the sexual function difficulties of gay, lesbian, bisexual, transgender or queer individuals, and couples. In general, persons of all sexual orientations and identities seemingly experience similar kinds of sexual function problems, yet further research is needed on sexual function difficulties among varied populations.

Defining Sexual Function Difficulties: Different Perspectives

The line between "normal" sexual functioning and a sexual difficulty or problem is not always clear. Enormous variation exists in levels of sexual desire and forms of expression, and these differences do not necessarily indicate any sexual function difficulty. It can be challenging to determine exactly when something is a sexual function problem, so we must be careful in defining a particular sexual function difficulty as a problem. Some people have rigid and possibly unrealistic expectations for their own or their partner's sexual expression and may perceive something wrong with their behavior that need not be considered a "sexual function problem." Still, people sometimes experience difficulties in sexual function that are so persistent that they would benefit from sex therapy (Strassberg & Mackaronis, 2014).

Health care providers, including sex therapists, need to be aware of different types of sexual function difficulties that can interfere with sexual satisfaction and intimacy. Therefore, a structure to diagnose and address difficulties can be valuable. However, there has been some debate among sexuality and mental health professionals about which terms accurately describe sexual function problems and how to classify these difficulties (West et al., 2004). Though categories such as "dysfunction," "disorder," "difficulty," and "problems" have been used, this chapter presents alternate classification models.

The standard medical diagnostic classification of sexual function difficulties is found in the American Psychiatric Association's *Diagnostic and Statistical Manual of Mental Disorders, Fifth Edition* (APA, 2013), which uses the terms *dysfunction* and *disorders.* Because the *DSM*'s is the most widely used classification system, the discussion of various sexual function difficulties in the professional literature is largely based on the *DSM* and uses the terms *sexual dysfunction* and *sexual disorders.* Thus the *DSM* terminology is quoted often in this chapter, particularly in the context of the *DSM* categories of sexual dysfunction.

"Most of sex is psychological—most of it is between our ears and not between our legs."

—Joy Browne (1944–)

Couples can experience sexual function difficulties that may lead to dissatisfaction, as well as frustration, with their sex lives.

Shutterstock/Pormezz

An alternative term to *sexual dysfunction* is **sexual function dissatisfaction**. Sexual dissatisfaction is a common outcome of a difficulty in sexual functioning. In contrast to the broad medical focus of the *DSM* term, this term reflects an individual perception. That is, a person or couple can experience some of the *DSM* dysfunctions yet be satisfied with their sex lives. The difficulty in functioning might be considered a "dysfunction" only when the individual or two people of a couple are dissatisfied and decide they may have a problem. The "dissatisfaction" concept is a fundamental tenet of the classification system for women's sexual problems of the Working Group for a New View of Women's Sexual Problems (2001). The system begins with a woman-centered definition of sexual function problems as "discontent or dissatisfaction with any emotional, physical, or relational aspects of sexual experience"—a definition that could also be applied to men. Furthermore, according to the World Health Organization's (2018) *International Classification of Diseases for Mortality and Morbidity Statistics, Eleventh Revision (ICD-11),* "sexual dysfunctions are syndromes that comprise the various ways in which adult people may have difficulty experiencing satisfying, non-coercive sexual activities."

An advantage of the term *sexual function dissatisfaction* is that it acknowledges sexual scripts as individual and avoids an overarching definition of what is "normal" versus what is dysfunctional (i.e., pathological). Adopting this subjective and personal view might help people be more comfortable with their own sexuality and less likely to feel "sexually flawed." We favor the terms *sexual function difficulties* and *sexual function dissatisfaction* and use them in this chapter whenever possible. However, in citing reports or research related to sexual difficulties, we often utilize the terms used therein.

Two alternate classifications of sexual function difficulties and dissatisfaction, based on medical and feminist models, illustrate different perspectives on the origins and causes of sexual problems: the *DSM-5* and the Working Group for a New View of Women's Sexual Problems.

The *Diagnostic and Statistical Manual of Mental Disorders* The fifth edition of the APA's *Diagnostic and Statistical Manual of Mental Disorders* (*DSM-5*) (2013) labels sexual function difficulties as disorders and characterizes them according to the four phases of Masters and Johnson's sexual response cycle. The *DSM-5* defines **sexual dysfunction** as "a clinically significant disturbance in a person's ability to respond sexually or to experience sexual pleasure." The *DSM-5* sexual dysfunctions/disorders are presented in Table 1. All dysfunctions, except for dysfunctions caused by substance or medication use, require the symptoms to be present for at least 6 months and cause significant distress to the individual. The disorders could occur at any time during sexual activity, meaning that the person could have more than one disorder, as often occurs.

The *DSM-5* states that "sexual response has a requisite biological underpinning, yet it is usually experienced in an intrapersonal, interpersonal, and cultural context." That is, sexual response and function occur as an interaction of biological, sociocultural, and psychological factors, including those related to the sexual partner; the relationship; individual vulnerability, psychological problems, or stressors; culture or religion; and medical issues.

For each sexual dysfunction, the *DSM-5* has subtypes based on the onset of the dysfunction and the context in which it occurs. Lifelong dysfunctions are those sexual problems present from the first sexual experience; acquired patterns develop only after a period of relatively normal functioning. A generalized pattern of dysfunction refers to sexual problems that are not limited to certain types of situations, stimulation, or partners. A situational sexual dysfunction is one that occurs only with certain types of situations, stimulation, or partners. In most instances, the dysfunction, whether generalized or situational, occurs during sexual activity with a partner. Acquired and situational dysfunctions typically are more successfully addressed in sex therapy (APA, 2013).

Although the *DSM-5* is the most widely used categorization of sexual function difficulties, it largely reflects a psychiatric medical model and has been criticized. It generally presents problems only in the heterosexual context, and it focuses on genital events in a linear sequence of desire, arousal, orgasm, and so on (Basson et al., 2010).

TABLE 1 ● *DSM-5* Sexual Dysfunctions/Disorders	
Female sexual interest/arousal disorder	Absent/reduced sexual thoughts, fantasies, initiation, and receptivity, and absent/reduced arousal and pleasure during sexual activity
Male hypoactive sexual desire disorder	Persistence or absence of sexual thoughts, fantasies, and desire for sexual activity
Erectile disorders	Difficulty with erections during partnered sexual activity
Female orgasmic disorders	Difficulty in experiencing orgasms or reduced intensity of orgasms during sexual activity
Premature (early) ejaculation	Experiencing "early" ejaculation following vaginal penetration
Delayed ejaculation	Marked delay in or inability to ejaculate, usually during partnered sexual activity
Genito-pelvic pain/penetration disorder	Difficulties related to genital and pelvic pain and vaginal penetration during intercourse
Substance/medication-induced sexual dysfunction	A specific substance presumed to cause the sexual dysfunction

Source: American Psychiatric Association (APA). 2013.

A New View of Women's Sexual Problems In recent years, more attention has been directed to increasing our understanding of female sexual desire and function difficulties (Basson et al., 2010; Burghardt et al., 2020; Katz-Wise & Hyde, 2014). The Working Group for a New View of Women's Sexual Problems (2001), a group of clinicians and social scientists, offers a classification system called A New View of Women's Sexual Problems. This system classifies women's sexual function difficulties based on women's needs and sexual realities. The Working Group contends that the widely used *DSM* framework for sexual dysfunctions does not adequately address the totality of factors impacting female sexuality—specifically, situational factors. This contention was based on the fourth edition of the *DSM* (APA, 2000). The more recently published *DSM-5* (APA, 2013) stresses that five factors—sexual partner factors; relationship factors; individual vulnerability factors, psychological problems, or stresses; culture and religion factors; and medical factors—must be considered in the assessment and diagnosis of sexual function problems in that they may be relevant to the cause of the problem and/or the treatment of the dysfunction. These factors are nearly similar to the four categories of possible underlying factors of female sexual dissatisfaction identified by the Working Group. Even though the *DSM-5* now addresses nonphysiological aspects of female sexuality and this "new" Working Group perspective was published two decades ago, the Working Group's contribution remains an important addition to our understanding of female sexual response and pleasure.

The Working Group (2001) claims that a physiological framework for sexual dysfunction has shortcomings as applied to women:

- *A false notion of sexual equivalency between men and women.* Early researchers emphasized similarities in men's and women's physiological responses during sexual activities and concluded that their sexual problems must also be similar. The few studies that asked women to describe their own experiences found significant differences.

- *The unacknowledged role of relationships in sexuality.* The Working Group states that the relational aspects of women's sexuality, which are often fundamental to sexual function satisfaction and problems, have not been adequately addressed. It contends that the reduction of "normal sexual functioning" to physiology implies, incorrectly, that sexual dissatisfaction can be treated without considering the relationship in which sex occurs.

- *The leveling of differences among women.* The Working Group contends that women are dissimilar and the varied components of their sexuality do not fit neatly into the categories of desire, arousal, orgasm, and pain.

The Working Group suggests a woman-centered definition of sexual function problems "as discontent or dissatisfaction with any emotional, physical, or relational aspect of sexual experience," which may arise in one or more of four categories underlying the dissatisfaction:

- *Sociocultural, political, or economic factors.* These include inadequate sexuality education, lack of access to health services, a perceived inability to meet cultural norms regarding correct or ideal sexuality, inhibitions due to conflict between the sexual norms of the subculture or culture of origin and those of the dominant culture, and a lack of interest, time, or energy due to family and work obligations.

- *Partner and relationship problems.* These include discrepancies in desire for sexual activity or in preferences for various sexual activities, inhibitions about communicating preferences, loss of interest due to conflicts over commonplace issues, and inhibitions due to a partner's health status or sexual problems.

- *Psychological problems.* These include past abuse; problems with attachment, rejection, cooperation, or entitlement; fear of pregnancy and sexually transmitted infections (STIs); and loss of partner or good sexual reputation.

- *Medical factors.* These include numerous local or systemic medical conditions, pregnancy, STIs, and side effects of drugs, medications, and medical treatments, including surgery.

Prevalence and Cofactors of Sexual Function Difficulties

A review of the epidemiological literature on the incidence and prevalence of sexual dysfunction among men and women found that the most frequent sexual function difficulties for women were low desire and arousal problems and that many women experience multiple sexual function problems. For men, early ejaculation and erection difficulties were the most common problems (McCabe et al., 2016).

Several national studies provide data on the prevalence of sexual function difficulties and factors related to them. We will briefly describe the major findings of two such studies conducted in Britain and the United States. Looking at the results of these studies will provide an overview of how common and universal certain sexual function difficulties are and the factors related to the problems. The prevalence of sexual function difficulties and their cofactors are generally in the same range from study to study. Differences in prevalence may reflect varied study methodologies, such as how sexual function problems are defined or perceived by the respondent, how the presence of sexual dysfunction is determined, method of data collection, and variations in the period of time assessed (e.g., the problem may have occurred in the past year, in the past month, or at the last sexual event), which may make it difficult to compare the data from one study to the other (McCabe et al., 2016). Note that the following studies are cross sectional, which means it is not possible to determine causality—some of the factors identified in the studies (e.g., sociodemographic factors, relationship difficulties) may have caused the sexual function problems and dissatisfaction, whereas other factors may be a consequence of sexual function problems.

National Survey of Sexual Attitudes and Lifestyle From a nationally representative study, called the third National Survey of Sexual Attitudes and Lifestyle (Natsal-3), 4,913 men and 6,777 women aged 16–74 years who lived in Britain (England, Scotland, and Wales) and who were sexually active in the past year were interviewed concerning their sexual functioning (Mitchell et al., 2013). "Sexually active" was defined as vaginal, oral, or anal intercourse with an other-sex or same-sex partner or partners. A major strength of this study was that it defined partners as either other-sex or same-sex and its assessment of factors related to sexual problems. Figure 1 presents the percentage of individual sexual function problems and dissatisfaction lasting 3 months or more in the past year by gender and age group. Sexual response problems persisting at least 3 months in the preceding year were common, even among the younger study participants. More than 40% of men and 50% of women reported one or more problems. For men, the most frequently reported problems were lack of interest in sex (15%), reaching climax more quickly than desired (15%), and difficulty in getting or keeping an erection (13%). For women, the most commonly reported problems were lack of interest in sex (34%), difficulty in reaching climax (16%), an uncomfortably dry vagina (13%), and lack of enjoyment (12%). As shown in Figure 1, for the youngest participants (16–24 years) the most commonly reported problem for men was reaching climax too soon (17%) and for women it was lacking sex interest (25%) and difficulty reaching climax (21%). Despite these difficulties, only 10% of both men and women reported distress about their sex lives (defined as sexual thoughts, sexual feelings, sexual activity, and sexual relationships). The most frequently reported issue within relationships was an imbalance in the level of sexual interest between partners. The study found that for both men and women, low sexual function was associated with several factors, such as:

- Increased age
- Depression
- Self-reported poor health status
- Experiencing the end of a relationship
- Inability to talk easily about sex with a partner
- Not being happy in the relationship
- Negative sexual health outcomes such as experience of nonvoluntary sex

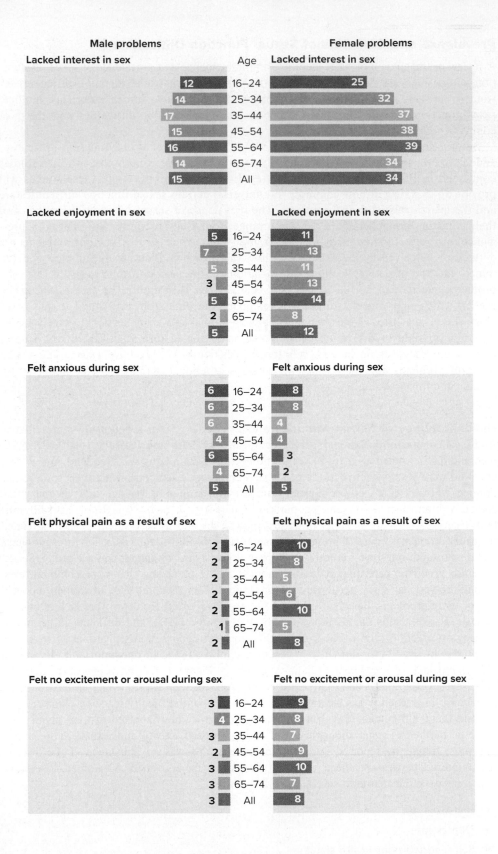

● FIGURE 1

Percentage of Sexually Active Men and Women in Britain, Aged 16–74, Reporting Selected Sexual Problems Lasting 3 Months or More in the Past Year

Source: Adapted from Mitchell et al., 2013.

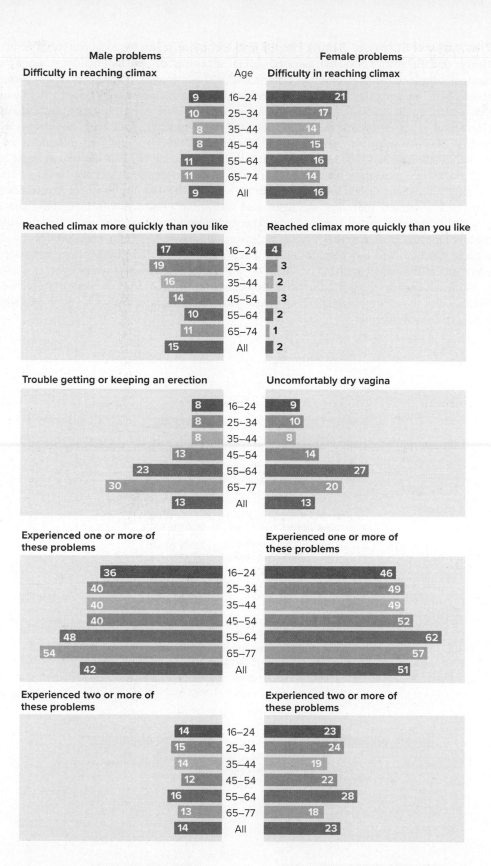

Male problems

Difficulty in reaching climax

Age	
9	16–24
10	25–34
8	35–44
8	45–54
11	55–64
11	65–74
9	All

Female problems

Difficulty in reaching climax

	Age
21	16–24
17	25–34
14	35–44
15	45–54
16	55–64
14	65–74
16	All

Reached climax more quickly than you like

	Age
17	16–24
19	25–34
16	35–44
14	45–54
10	55–64
11	65–74
15	All

Reached climax more quickly than you like

	Age
4	16–24
3	25–34
2	35–44
3	45–54
2	55–64
1	65–74
2	All

Trouble getting or keeping an erection

	Age
8	16–24
8	25–34
8	35–44
13	45–54
23	55–64
30	65–77
13	All

Uncomfortably dry vagina

	Age
9	16–24
10	25–34
8	35–44
14	45–54
27	55–64
20	65–77
13	All

Experienced one or more of these problems

	Age
36	16–24
40	25–34
40	35–44
40	45–54
48	55–64
54	65–77
42	All

Experienced one or more of these problems

	Age
46	16–24
49	25–34
49	35–44
52	45–54
62	55–64
57	65–77
51	All

Experienced two or more of these problems

	Age
14	16–24
15	25–34
14	35–44
12	45–54
16	55–64
13	65–77
14	All

Experienced two or more of these problems

	Age
23	16–24
24	25–34
19	35–44
22	45–54
28	55–64
18	65–77
23	All

The National Survey of Sexual Health and Behavior The National Survey of Sexual Health and Behavior (NSSHB) assessed several measures of sexual functioning among a random sample in the United States. Data from 3,900 adults aged 18–59 years who reported about their last partnered sexual event were analyzed. Participants were asked to evaluate that sexual event relative to pleasure, arousal, erection/lubrication difficulty, and orgasm (Herbenick et al., 2010). The degree to which the participants reported their experiences for each of the five measures is shown in Figure 2. The NSSHB found that most men and women, including those in their 50s, evaluated the experience of their last sexual event as high on a scale measuring pleasure and arousal. For men, age was associated with greater erection difficulties, greater pain during sexual activity, and less likelihood of experiencing orgasm. For women, older age was associated with more problems with lubrication and a greater likelihood of experiencing orgasm. The study also found that men with a relationship partner reported greater arousal, greater pleasure, more frequent orgasm, fewer problems with erectile function, and less pain during their last sexual event than those whose last sexual event was with a nonrelationship partner. For women, those whose last sexual event was with a relationship partner reported greater problems with arousal and lubrication yet greater likelihood of their partner experiencing orgasm than women whose last sexual event was with a nonrelationship partner.

● FIGURE 2

Percentage of Self-Reported Sexual Functioning at Most Recent Partnered Sexual Event Among U.S. Adults Aged 18–59, 2009

Source: Adapted from Herbenick et al. 2010.

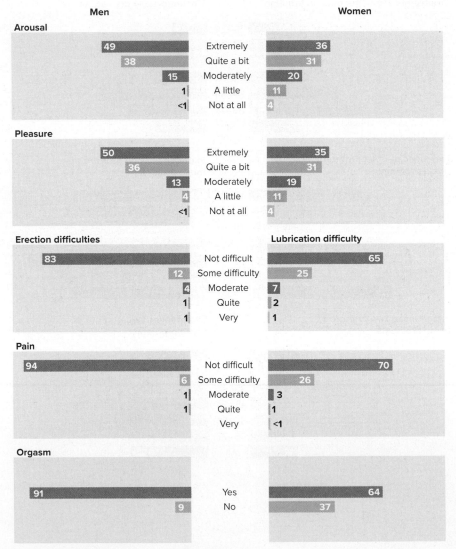

Note: Percents are rounded; hence, the total may exceed 100%.

Sexual Desire: When Appetites Differ

Sexual desire is a fragile mysterious appetite.

—Michael Castleman (1950–)

How much sexual desire is "normal" and what can romantic couples do when one partner has more—or less—desire than the other? Sex therapist and clinical psychologist David Schnarch (2002) observes:

Couples frequently argue about low desire, but their real issue is *difference* in desires. Neither partner's desire need be particularly low or high. Disparity in sexual desire is couples' most common sexual complaint.

For most long-term relationships, sexual passion subsides, but not always at the same rate for each partner. Differences in sexual desire are normal and expected, and may impact the couple relationship. One study of 1,054 married couples found that higher individual sexual desire discrepancies among married persons may erode the well-being of the relationship. Yet studies involving 82 couples and 191 individuals in committed long-term relationships suggested that variation in sexual desire levels between partners was not necessarily a problem in the relationship. Most couples found ways to deal with desire discrepancies without them negatively impacting their sexual satisfaction (Sutherland et al., 2015).

Most sex therapists believe that differences arise because, for example, one or both partners may be fatigued, ill, under the influence of alcohol or other drugs, or consumed with the tasks of daily living. Additionally, there may be problems with the sexual relationship of the couple, such as anger or imbalance of power between the partners.

Michael Castleman (2004), an award-winning medical writer, notes in his book *Great Sex: A Man's Guide to the Secret Principles of Total-Body Sex* that there is no magic formula for resolving sexual desire differences, but here are some suggestions for dealing with libido differences in couples:

- *Count your blessings.* Typically the lower-desire person wants sex sometimes. Isn't some sex better than none? Adapting to the change is the key.

- *Don't try to change your partner's libido.* In a couple with desire differences, each partner may hope that the other person will change and acquire a compatible level of desire. Sexual desire can change, but this must come from within the person.

- *Consider your choices and negotiate.* A couple having chronic difficulties with sexual desire has three choices: (1) break up, (2) do nothing and live in misery, or (3) negotiate a mutually agreed compromise.

- *Schedule sex dates.* Scheduling has an advantage of eliminating sexual uncertainty for couples facing major desire differences. Both partners know when sex will occur.

- *Cultivate nonsexual affection.* Once sex dates are scheduled, nonsexual affection has less chance of being misconstrued as having sexual expectations.

- *Savor your solution.* Once a couple negotiates a mutual compromise, the relationship often improves and resentments slowly fade. There may still be some desire differences; the ability to compromise means that the couple has found a workable solution for their relationship.

A recent study identified the strategies individuals and couples in long-term relationships use to deal with sexual desire differences and whether these specific strategies influenced sexual and relationship satisfaction and sexual desire (Vowels & Mark, 2020). Data were collected from 229 participants: average age 35 years; 32% men, 63% women, 3% genderqueer or genderfluid participants; 56% heterosexual, 30% bisexual, 5% lesbian or gay, and had been in a relationship with their partner for an average 8 years. Most defined having sex as vaginal penetration. Major findings included:

- Seventeen strategies used to deal with sexual desire differences were identified with resulting in five main groups: (1) masturbation alone or with partner (69%), (2) engaging in a different sexual activity such as oral sex as a trigger to enhance desire (33%), (3) communication about why desire level is different (35%), (4) having "maintenance sex" to "preserve the relationship" regardless of the lower level of desire (33%), and (5) doing nothing (39%).

- Half of the participants reported that the strategies were very helpful. The strategies used by these couples were communication (57%), engaging in a different sexual activity (54%), or having maintenance sex (58%). These individuals had higher sexual and relationship satisfaction than those indicating that the activities were somewhat or not at all helpful.

- People who did nothing to address desire discrepancy and disengaged from their partner had lower sexual and relationship satisfaction than those who dealt with desire discrepancy.

- Strategies involving the couple were associated with higher levels of sexual and relationship satisfaction than activities that were individual focused.

- Participants who communicated about the discrepancy or participated in an alternative activity with their partner compared to disengaging from their partner reported higher relationship satisfaction, and those who engaged in any sexual activity reported higher sexual satisfaction.

The researchers concluded that the study shows "that addressing and dealing with desire discrepancy is important for relationships and some strategies are more successful than others" (p. 1026).

Disorders of Sexual Desire

The number-one sexual function problem of American couples is inhibited sexual desire. Discrepancies in sexual desire, discussed in Practically Speaking, "Sexual Desire: When Appetites Differ", is the most common complaint that leads couples to sex therapy. More than one half of married couples experience inhibited sexual desire or desire discrepancy at some time in their marriage. Inhibited sexual desire causes more stress in a marriage and long-term relationships than any other sexual function problem (McCarthy & McCarthy, 2003; Northrup et al., 2012).

Defining low desire is tricky, often subjective, as there is no norm level of sexual desire; further, any such definition is often based on an assumption that there is an optimal level of sexual desire (Hall, 2004; van Lankveld, 2013). Certainly, sexually "normal" people vary considerably in their sexual interests, fantasies, and desires and occasionally experience a lack of desire (see Figure 1). Research has found that men reported more sexual desire than women (Buss & Schmitt, 2011). Persons in a same-sex relationship reported a slightly higher sexual desire than those in other-sex relationships (Holmberg & Blair, 2009; Laumann et al., 1999; Michell et al., 2013). Low sexual desire is most often acquired; that is, the person felt sexual desire previously but no longer experiences desire. The good news: It is often transitory. People with lower sexual desire often reluctantly participate in sex when it is initiated by a partner. A study of 63 persons aged 18–24 in a committed heterosexual relationship found that 17% of all sexual activity was rated as compliant/obliging with no difference between men and women being compliant (Vannier & O'Sullivan, 2010). A study of 299 persons in long-term relationships found that one third who had a lower level of sexual desire than their partner reported having "maintenance sex" to protect their partner's feelings or for the well-being of the relationship, for example (Vowels & Mark, 2020). Most often, lower sexual desire develops in adulthood in association with psychological distress resulting from depression, stressful life events, or interpersonal difficulties. The loss of desire, whether ongoing or situational, can negatively affect a relationship (APA, 2013; Brotto & Smith, 2014).

One should note that beyond any individual, situational, or relationship factors that can result in low sexual desire, sexual desire declines for most people through time. For example, a Finnish study of 2,650 adults found that feelings of sexual desire decreased as the individual aged (Figure 3) and as a relationship continued through the years (Figure 4) (Kontula, 2009; Kontula & Haavio-Mannila, 2009). A caution in interpreting these findings: the decreases do not necessarily indicate loss of sexual satisfaction when having sex; numerous studies have found that many long-term couples report increasing in sexual satisfaction as the relationship continues (e.g., Kleinplatz & Menard, 2020; Traen et al., 2018).

• **FIGURE 3**

Percentage of Finnish Adults Who Indicated That They Feel Sexual Desire at Least a Few Times a Week

Source: Kontula, 2009.

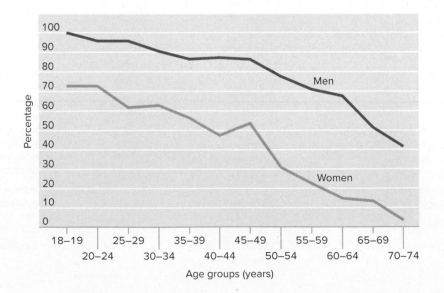

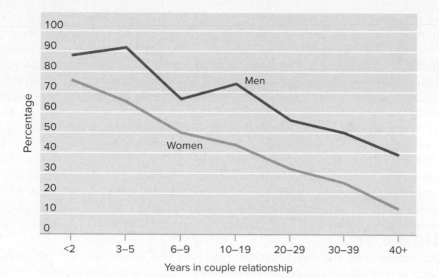

• FIGURE 4

Percentage of Finnish Adults Who Indicated That If They Could Choose Freely They Would Like to Have Intercourse at Least Twice a Week

Source: Kontula, 2009.

The lack of sexual pleasure is a common complaint of women with low sexual desire and is frequently associated with problems experiencing orgasm, pain during sexual activity, low frequency of sexual activity, and couple discrepancies in desire. Unrealistic expectations and norms regarding the "normal or appropriate" level of sexual interest or arousal, poor sexual techniques, relationship problems, lack of accurate information, and mood disorders are also associated with this dissatisfaction (APA, 2013). A study of 741 women of mean age 48 years verified many of these associations. This study found that sexual desire was lower among older, postmenopausal women; those being in the current relationship for a long time; and those whose partner experienced a sexual dysfunction, suggesting that a sexual difficulty in one partner is likely associated with sexual difficulties in the other partner (McCabe & Goldhammer, 2012). A representative study of 1,345 women (ages 18–91) in 2005 and 1314 women (ages 18–91) in 2016 residing in Germany found that the absence of sexual desire increased from 24% in 2005 to 26% in 2016 and partnered sexual activity declined from 67% to 62%. The declines in sexual desire and activity affected mostly young and middle-aged women. Women living without a partner indicated considerably less sexual desire and activity (Burghardt et al., 2020).

The term "frigid" was once used to describe low sexual desire in women, but this pejorative and value-laden term is no longer used by professionals. Sex researchers Lucia O'Sullivan and Saran Vannier (2016) examined the literature to explore what is known about female sexual desire. Many studies found that sexual desire is lower for older women than for women who are younger and that this decline begins in early adulthood; however, other studies showed conflicting findings. Hence, the researchers concluded that women's sexual desire does not necessarily decline over time. Further, some research suggests that rates of low desire among a substantial minority of women might be fairly consistent over time. A major methodological problem is the dearth of longitudinal research on sexual desire that tracks sexual desire of an individual over time. O'Sullivan and Vannier (2016) note that traditional socialization expects women to be "sexual gatekeepers"; that is, being responsible for controlling men's sexual advances and keeping their own sexual desires in check. They continue by declaring that:

> Some are concerned that this socialization ultimately has suppressed girls' and women's ability to recognize and verbalize, truly to experience, sexual desire in full, but also has served to ensure that girls and women are not free to express their desire through a wide range of activities and partners. (p. 53)

Many sex therapists believe that sexual arousal is much more of a psychological process in women than in men (Keesling, 2006). Some women report that their clitoris engorged and their vagina lubricated, but they did not feel psychologically arousal. Female sexual arousal problems are often accompanied by sexual desire and orgasm difficulties, as well as sexual avoidance and stress in couple relationships. A study by Dewitte and Mayer found that "women's desire for emotional closeness predisposes them to participate in sexual activity which in itself contributes to future intimacy and closeness." While they acknowledge that this finding did not uniformly apply to all women, it illustrates that women's sexual responses may depend more on the relationship context than men's do (Dewitte & Mayer, 2019).

The *DSM-5* states that there is a normative decline in sexual desire as men age and that mental health, alcohol use, self-directed homophobia in gay men, interpersonal and relational problems, lack of healthy attitudes and lack of accurate knowledge, and trauma from early life experiences may account for low desire (APA, 2013). Another factor that may account for low libido in men is strenuous exercise. A study of over 1,077 physically active adult men found strenuous exercise to be associated with lower sexual desire. Men who exercised moderately or light in intensity or duration were much more likely to indicate moderate or high libidos than those whose workouts were especially prolonged or intense (Hackney et al., 2017).

Men experiencing erection difficulties may have low self-esteem, low self-confidence, decreased sexual satisfaction, reduced sexual desire, and a decreased sense of masculinity. According to the *DSM-5,* about 20% of men fear erection difficulties on their first sexual episode, with about 8% reporting problems that hindered penetration during their first sexual episode. These erection difficulties are likely to continue in most men (APA, 2013).

At one time, this problem was called "impotence," but like "frigid," this value-laden and pejorative term is no longer used. This very common male sexual difficulty was treated primarily by therapists before the introduction of Viagra and other prescription erection-enhancing drugs. Sexual anxiety, fear of failure, high performance standards, concerns about sexual performance, and low sexual desire and excitement, as well as specific medical conditions and medications, are often associated with erectile disorder (APA, 2000, 2013; Hall et al., 2010).

Eighteen percent of the men in the NSSHB reported at least some difficulty with erections during their most recent partnered sexual event (see Figure 2). The prevalence of erectile difficulties increases with age. Nearly four times as many men aged 65–77 reporting problems with erection as men aged 16–44 in the Natsal-3 (see Figure 1). However, it is important to note that, like female arousal problems, male erectile difficulties are not an inevitable consequence of aging. But the health problems that often accompany aging increase the problem's prevalence. The prevalence of erectile difficulty has been directly correlated with certain diseases, such as hypertension, diabetes mellitus, and heart disease; certain medications, such as cardiac drugs and antihypertensives; cigarette smoking in association with treated heart disease and treated hypertension; excessive alcohol consumption; suppression and expression of anger; obesity; and depression (Bancroft, 2009; Nusbaum, 2002; Wu et al., 2012). Erection problems could also be a symptom of profound psychological disturbances developed over a lifetime (Nicolini et al., 2019).

Erection problems are usually psychologically based. Men who have erections while sleeping or masturbating obviously are physically able to have erections, meaning that an erectile disorder during two-person sexual activity has a psychological origin. As with the other sexual difficulties, erectile disorder is a diagnosable problem in the *DSM-5* only when the man or his partner is dissatisfied and distressed by the occurrence (Schwartz, 2000).

Sex therapist and author Barbara Keesling (2006) gives some cautions relative to expectations of erections. She notes that men's concept of an adequate erection varies considerably from person to person, and that a man does not necessarily have an erection problem if he doesn't have reflex or spontaneous erections from viewing a partner's body, for example. Many men, even young men, almost always need direct stimulation to have an erection. Also, she says that "it's probably also unrealistic to expect that your erection will maintain the same level of rigidity throughout the course of a sexual encounter." During any particular sexual encounter, a man's erection can vacillate between several levels of rigidity depending on the amount of stimulation.

Interestingly, the *DSM-5* does not include a "hyperactive sexual desire disorder," implying that its authors, mental health professionals, do not believe that high sexual desire, a relative label, is a mental disorder. This is contrary to the view of the general public and some professionals who espouse the concept of sexual addiction. Sexual desire exists on a continuum, with some people having very low desire and others having very high desire. Most people seem to be somewhere in the middle, however.

Orgasmic Difficulties

Orgasmic difficulties are the second most common sexual function difficulty (after low sexual desire) treated by therapists (Keesling, 2006). The most common sexual functioning problems of women in the Natsal-3 study (see Figure 1) were lacking interest in sex (34%) and difficulty experiencing orgasm (16%) (Mitchell et al., 2013). Women not experiencing orgasm has also been called anorgasmia, inorgasmia, pre-orgasmia, inhibited female orgasm, and the pejorative "frigidity." Most female orgasmic difficulties are lifelong rather than acquired; once a woman learns how to have an orgasm, it is uncommon for her to lose that capacity (APA, 2000).

Female orgasm is not universal; a slight minority of women rarely or never have them. The NSSHB found that 37% of women reported not having an orgasm at their most recent partnered sexual event (see Figure 2). About 10% of women do not experience orgasm throughout their lifetime (APA, 2013). An interview study examined how women described the absence of orgasm during their sexual episodes with a male partner. From a sample of 17 cisgender, college women ages 18–28, 20% reported never or hardly ever having an orgasm with their current partner (Bell & McClelland, 2018). Three themes illustrated the strategies the women used to contend with orgasmic absence: (1) what's the big deal?, (2) it's just biology, and (3) not now, but someday. The women were clearly interested in being sexual with men and hoped to have orgasms in the future but also noted that they can have pleasure without orgasm such as experiencing emotional intimacy. Research suggests that many women define sexual pleasure in multiple ways without orgasm being essential (Goldey et al., 2016). The researchers concluded that the women's explanations allowed them to decrease their feelings of abnormality and enabled them to distance themselves from cultural expectations regarding perceived significance of orgasms during partnered sex.

Women have reported a wide variability in the type and intensity of stimulation that results in orgasm. A method in which the women moves her pelvic area and trunk of her body during intercourse is described in Practically Speaking, "The 'Pelvic Swing' During Penile-Vaginal Intercourse Facilitates Sexual Arousal and Orgasm Among Women." Clitoral stimulation is required by many to experience orgasm, and among women who have sex with men a relatively small proportion indicate that they always experience orgasm during penile-vaginal intercourse. The age of first orgasm for women is more variable than for men—it may occur anytime from the prepubertal period to well into adulthood. Women's reports of having experienced orgasm increase with age, as shown in the Natsal-3 data (see Figure 1). Many women learn to experience orgasm as they try a wide array of stimulation and become more knowledgeable about their bodies. Orgasm consistency (i.e., usually or always) among women is higher during masturbation than during partnered sexual behavior (APA, 2013).

Some women who enjoy sexual activity with partners have difficulty experiencing orgasm with them, thereby sometimes causing dissatisfaction or distress within the relationship. Many women with orgasm problems have negative or guilty attitudes about their sexuality, relationship difficulties, and physical and mental health problems and are influenced by sociocultural factors such as gender role expectations and religion. Inadequate sexual stimulation is also a factor (APA, 2000, 2013).

Studies have found that women were more likely to experience orgasm during partnered sex that included a wider variety of sexual behaviors than penetrative sex. A large U.S. sample of adults ($N = 52,588$) found that compared to women who orgasmed less frequently, women who orgasmed more frequently were likely to: receive more oral sex, have longer duration of sex, be more satisfied with their relationship, ask for what they want during sex, praise their partner for something they did, call/e-mail to tease about doing something sexual, wear sexy lingerie, try new sexual positions, engage in anal stimulation, act out fantasies, incorporate

The "Pelvic Swing" During Penile-Vaginal Intercourse Facilitates Sexual Arousal and Orgasm Among Women

Many women who have sex with men are not able to experience an orgasm during penile-vaginal intercourse. Studies have found that up to 4 in 10 women (38%) report rarely or never experiencing an orgasm during vaginal intercourse (Dunn et al., 2005; Kontula & Miettinen, 2016). Having an orgasm without simultaneous clitoral stimulation during intercourse has been found to range from 8% to 55% in women (Fugl-Meyer et al., 2006; Kontula & Miettinen, 2016). Further, the inability to have an orgasm during vaginal intercourse is related to less pleasurable perceptions about vaginal intercourse (Kontula, 2009). Several factors, such as personal conflict with one's sexuality, relationship issues, mental health problems, and physical limitations, can impact a women's ability to have orgasms. Numerous studies have investigated the association of these factors in having penile-vaginal intercourse orgasms, but little research has examined the role of physical stimulation.

Annette Bischof-Campbell at the Zurich Institute for Clinical Sexology and Sexual Therapy and colleagues have learned from their experience as sex therapists that swinging movements of the pelvis ("pelvic swing") plays an important role in enhancing a woman's likelihood of experiencing an orgasm during penile-vaginal intercourse (Bischof-Campbell, 2019). The "pelvic swing" has been described as the circling, undulating, and back-and-forth swinging movements of the pelvis and trunk against a partner's pelvis and penis that may include pelvic floor muscle contractions. This technique may facilitate stimulation of the external part of the clitoris and vaginal walls, the pelvic muscles surrounding the vagina, and internal clitoral structures (Biscof-Campbell, 2012; Buisson & Jannini, 2013; Plaus et al., 2016).

Noting the sparse research to determine the effectiveness of the "pelvic swing" arousal technique, the researchers examined the impact of two stimulation techniques on the frequency of women's orgasms: (1) body movement, particularly the slow, rock-ing rhythmic movements of the pelvis and trunk, and (2) precise rubbing of the clitoris with an immobilized body. The researchers acknowledge that not all women are interested in having an orgasm during vaginal intercourse but those who desire to might benefit from learning the study results and practicing a new sexual technique during solo masturbation

This study was limited to 1,239 women aged 18–75 who reported penile-vaginal intercourse in the past year and had vaginal intercourse at least 30 times in their life. Seventy-four percent were in a committed relationship with an average duration of 7 years. Forty-eight percent had a bachelor's or master's degree. Here is what the study found:

- Women reporting more body movement during penile-vaginal intercourse reported more orgasms.
- More orgasms were not found for women reporting body immobilization or precise clitoral stimulation during penile-vaginal intercourse although clitoral stimulation can provide added sexual arousal.

The researchers concluded that "body movement is conducive to orgasms during vaginal intercourse in women regardless of their reliance on simultaneous external stimulation of the clitoris" (p. 364). They further noted that women who do the "pelvic swing" are more likely to increase their arousal during penile-vaginal intercourse, but self-stimulation of the clitoris during intercourse will not necessarily result in experiencing more orgasms if it is done with an immobilized body. As this study is limited to women having penile-vagina sex, no studies have explored the "pelvic swing" during vaginal penetration, for example, with a partner using a strapped-on dildo. Further research could determine if pelvic movement happens during dildo-vaginal sex, and if so, in what form.

Another study involving 2,371 women asked them to respond to the sentence "In addition to getting specific physical

Most Frequent Activities Reported by Women to Facilitate Orgasm During Penile-Vaginal Intercourse

Activity	Percent Reporting
Positioned my body to get the stimulation I needed	90
Paid attention to my physical sensations	83
Tightened and released my pelvic muscles	75
Synchronized the rhythm of my movements to my partner's	75
Asked or encouraged my partner to do what I needed	74
Got myself in a sexy mood beforehand	71
Focused on my partner's pleasure	68
Felt/thought about how much I love my partner	65
Engaged in a fantasy of my own	56

stimulation, I often have done the following to help me reach orgasm during sex with my partner" (Ellison, 2000). From a list of 14 possible answers, the answers that were chosen by at least one half of the women are presented in the below table. As shown, the vast majority of women did certain activities to enhance experiencing orgasm: physical activities, such as positioning their body to get the stimulation needed and synchronizing their movements to their partner's (i.e., "pelvis swing"); and psychological activities like getting themselves in a sexy mood and having erotic fantasies.

sexy talk, and express love during sex. Further, women were more likely to orgasm if their last sexual encounter included deep kissing, manual stimulation, and/or oral sex in addition to vaginal intercourse (Frederick et al., 2017).

The study also found that 86% of lesbian women, 66% bisexual women, and 65% of heterosexual women indicated that they usually always orgasm when sexually intimate. Despite these high frequencies of orgasm during sex, many women report high levels of satisfaction during sexual activity despite never or rarely experiencing orgasm (APA, 2013).

Many of us measure whether or not we are "good lovers" by whether or not we and our partner experience orgasm. Orgasm has become an indicator of a healthy and satisfying relationship, but it can be filled with distress and difficulty. Actually, orgasm is often not simple, as discussed in Think About It, "Orgasm, That Simple? Young Adults' Experiences of Orgasm and Sexual Pleasure."

One of the most common sexual function difficulties in the male general population is premature ejaculation, also called **early ejaculation**, the preferred term. Early ejaculation is used to describe an issue within the context of penile penetrative sex, notably vaginally. Men in the Natsal-3 study reported between 10% and 17% reached climax more quickly than desired (see Figure 1). As with many sexual function difficulties, there is a problem with definitions: What is early ejaculation? The definition may vary among individuals, populations, and cultures. Some sex therapists have defined it according to how long intercourse lasts, how many pelvic thrusts there are, and how often the partner experiences orgasm. Therapist Helen Singer Kaplan (1974) suggested that the absence of voluntary control at orgasm is the key to defining early ejaculation. Actually, many males with early ejaculation report a lack of control over the moment of ejaculation (APA, 2013). Some sex therapists suggest that the term *involuntary ejaculation* is the more accurate term, given that the treatment focuses on acquiring voluntary control over something that has been involuntary (Castleman, 2004). Early ejaculation is a problem when the man or his partner is dissatisfied by the amount of time it takes him to ejaculate. Some couples want intercourse or other intimate sexual behavior to last a long time, but others are not concerned about that.

Couples often are confused, bewildered, and unhappy when the man consistently ejaculates too early. The man may feel considerable guilt and anxiety. The couple may begin to avoid sexual contact with each other. The man may experience erectile problems because of his anxieties over premature ejaculation, and he may withdraw from sexual activity completely. Other factors may contribute to early or involuntary ejaculation in men, such as inexperience in negotiating with a sexual partner, inadequate understanding of sexual response, unwittingly training themselves to ejaculate quickly during masturbation, inability to relax deeply during sexual intercourse, nonsensual lovemaking, and a narrow focus on the penis and a partner's genitals during sex (Castleman, 2004; Rowland, 2012b).

Most men with early or involuntary ejaculation can delay ejaculation during self-masturbation for a longer period of time than during intercourse. With sexual experience and aging, many males learn to delay ejaculation, but others continue to ejaculate early and ultimately may seek professional help (APA, 2000, 2013). This problem more often occurs in young and sexually inexperienced males, especially those who have primarily been in situations in which speed of ejaculation was important so as, for example, to avoid being discovered. It is the number-one sexual function complaint of young men.

What about premature, or early, orgasm among women? This phenomenon is not typically considered a sexual function difficulty by women or their partners and is not listed as a sexual dysfunction disorder in the *DSM-5*. The prevalence of early orgasm is rarely reported

think
about it

Orgasm, That Simple? Young Adults' Experiences of Orgasm and Sexual Pleasure

la petite mort (French) "The little death"—the human orgasm

Many of us measure both our sexuality and ourselves in terms of orgasm. Did we have one during sex? Did our partner have one? If so, was it good? If not, did I or the partner fake it? Did we have simultaneous or repeated orgasms? Did orgasm occur through oral sex, vaginal or anal sex, or a combination of these or other means? To have pleasurable sex, is orgasm necessary? The questions go on and lead to the conclusion: Orgasm is not simple.

As we look at our sexuality, we can see some pressure to be "good lovers," and experiencing orgasm is often considered a barometer of that expectation. Our bodies are designed to have orgasms; they are a source of potentially intense and fulfilling pleasure. Cultural, personal, and interpersonal emphasis has been placed on orgasm such that it is now considered an indicator of a healthy sexuality and satisfying relationship. Yet, orgasm can be filled with difficulty and distress, particularly for women, and the meaning of orgasm can be contradictory and complex for both men and women (Fahs, 2011; Jackson & Scott, 2007; Opperman et al., 2014; Tiefer, 2004).

To further understand orgasm, a qualitative study was conducted among 199 sexually experienced British largely self-identified heterosexual young adults to explore the meanings associated with orgasm and sexual pleasure during sex with a partner (Opperman et al., 2014). Sex was explicitly defined to include any type of sexual activity with any partner. The data revealed five main themes:

■ **Orgasm: The Purpose and End of Sex**

Experiencing an orgasm was stated as the overriding goal of "sex" and other sexual activities for nearly all study participants. The majority reported that they "aimed" to have an orgasm or that having an orgasm was the primary reason they engaged in sexual activities. Orgasm was frequently characterized in terms of a trajectory in which each sexual behavior "step" was en route to an orgasm. Orgasm was usually the finishing point of sex, however, it was largely men's and not women's orgasm that signaled the end of (heterosexual) sex regardless of whether the female partner had an orgasm. The "typical" pattern of sex and orgasm reported was for the woman to orgasm first followed by the man. Sex would then be over.

■ **It's More About My Partner's Orgasm**

Even though many participants reported experiencing an orgasm was important to them, nearly all reported that it was more important that their partner experience orgasm than that they did themselves. Many felt responsible for their partner's orgasm, and orgasm or pleasure was often described as something they "gave" their partner. Most participants felt happy when their partner orgasmed, but when they did not, they felt negative feelings like "not being good in bed."

Participants needed confirmation from their partners that the sexual episode was pleasurable and enjoyable.

■ **Orgasm: The Ultimate Pleasure**

Orgasm was experienced as the "ultimate pleasure," described, for example, as the most extraordinary feeling ever experienced not comparable to anything else, a form of extreme and/or unusual pleasure, and that "it feels so good that it almost hurts." Most participants still indicated experiencing physical pleasure and enjoyment from the sex even when they did not experience an orgasm. Participants commonly reported feeling happy after orgasm, feelings of love and intimacy for their partner, and a reinforcement of pre-existing love. Those in a relationship were more likely to report feelings of intimacy and love regardless of whether they experience an orgasm.

■ **Orgasm Is Not a Simple Physiological Response**

The context, such as relational, psychological, and physical factors, had an important role of whether orgasm was experienced. Some reported that an orgasm depended on their partner and the relationship status: They were less likely to orgasm in casual sex and more likely in a long-term relationship. Participants identified psychological or emotional states, such as being relaxed and unstressed, as necessary conditions for orgasm. Some women reported that intercourse did not provide adequate stimulation for them to orgasm and that other forms of stimulation (oral or manual) were necessary either alone or in combination with intercourse to experience an orgasm.

■ **Faking Orgasm Is Not Uncommon**

More than one half (predominantly women) indicated that they had faked an orgasm during sex with a partner. Among those faking orgasm, the most common justification was for the partner: Their partner's pleasure was related to their own orgasm, they wanted to avoid upsetting their partner, or they did not want their partner to think they were not able to pleasure them. The second most common reason for faking orgasms was so that sex would be over, followed by that they knew they could not have an orgasm. Some participants who had not faked orgasm had faked their level or arousal so the partner would continue to pleasure them. For participants who did not fake orgasms, three main reasons were given: faking an orgasm would reduce the chances of future orgasms; they did not want to offend or upset their partner; and belief that faking is dishonest. Some participants stated that faking an orgasm would not help their partner learn how to "give" them an orgasm and once they started to fake orgasms, they might have to continue to fake them.

The researchers concluded that the meaning and experience of orgasm was highly context-, situation-, and partner-dependent and included an expectation of reciprocity and an imperative to have intercourse and orgasm. The study results suggested that even though having an orgasm was a strong expectation for young women, as was for men, this is not necessarily good. The researchers state that:

> The social, relational, and personal meanings of having and "giving" orgasms mean that orgasm is not necessarily easy to experience or the *simple* pleasure it might appear to be. For young women and young men, heterosexual or otherwise, it appears that orgasm is not always a desirable expectation of sex, and it carries potential shifting and *stable* meanings associated with both its presence and absence. (p. 513)

Think Critically

1. What did you learn about experiencing orgasm during partnered sex?
2. Can a person experience physical and emotional satisfaction and not experience orgasm during sex? Do all people feel the same about this?
3. If you are or have been sexually active with a partner, have you or your partner faked an orgasm? Why or why not?
4. If a sexually inexperienced person of your age group asked you about the importance and role of orgasm with a sexual partner, what would you tell them?

by women: Between 1% and 4% of women in the Natsal-3 study (see Figure 1) indicated that they reached climax more quickly than they liked (Mitchell et al., 2013). Some women who have orgasms very quickly may not be interested in continuing sexual activity; others, however, are open to continued stimulation and may have repeated orgasms.

Delayed ejaculation refers to the inability or difficulty of a man to ejaculate despite adequate sexual stimulation and the desire to experience ejaculation. The complaint from the man or his partner usually comes from this problem occurring during partnered sexual activity. Prolonged thrusting to experience orgasm to the point of exhaustion or genital discomfort often occurs, resulting in the couple ceasing attempts. Some men report that they began to avoid partnered sexual activity because of repeated difficulties in ejaculating. Ejaculation and orgasm are two separate events that usually occur at the same time, but not always. Given this, a man experiencing delayed ejaculation may have an orgasm (full-body experience) but is unable to ejaculate at all or have delayed ejaculation. In the most common form of delayed ejaculation, the man cannot ejaculate during intercourse but can from a partner's manual or oral stimulation.

How often delayed ejaculation occurs is difficult to ascertain because there is no consensus as to what constitutes a reasonable time to experience ejaculation or what is unreasonably long for most men and their partners. Clinicians report that it is the least commonly reported sexual function complaint. Only 75% of men report always ejaculating during sexual activity; of the remainder, less than 1% complain of difficulty in ejaculating that lasts more than 3 months. Around 1 in 10 men of the Natsal-3 study reported difficulties with experiencing orgasm (see Figure 1). Men in their 80s report twice as much difficulty in ejaculating than men younger than 50 years. Age-related decreases in fast-conducting peripheral sensory nerves and in sex steroid secretion may be related to increased occurrence of delayed ejaculation in men older than 50 years (APA, 2013).

As with other sexual function difficulties, delayed ejaculation may occur as an interaction of biological, sociocultural, and psychological factors, including those related to the sexual partner; the relationship; individual vulnerability, psychological problems, or stressors; culture or religion; and medical issues. Anxiety-provoking sexual situations can interfere with a man experiencing an orgasm, or a man may not be able to have an ejaculation in situations in which he feels guilty or conflicted. Often, the individual can overcome this disorder when he and his partner are able to comfortably discuss the issue, when the situation or partner changes, or when he engages in a fantasy or receives additional stimulation (APA, 2013).

Sexual Pain Disorders

The *DSM-5* combined the conditions **vaginismus** (muscle spasms around the vagina) and **dyspareunia** (painful intercourse) from the *DSM-IV-TR* into one category, **genital-pelvic pain/penetration disorder**, with four diagnostic categories: (1) marked difficulty having vaginal intercourse/penetration, (2) marked vaginal or pelvic pain during a vaginal intercourse or penetration attempt, (3) marked fear or anxiety about vaginal or pelvic pain in anticipation of, during, or as a result of vaginal penetration, and (4) marked tensing or tightening of the pelvic floor muscles during attempted vaginal penetration. These issues may occur in conjunction with other sexual function difficulties, such as low sexual desire, and partner difficulties, such as problems with erections and ejaculation. Like most sexual function difficulties, factors related to the partner, the relationship, individual vulnerability, religion/culture, and medical issues may be relevant to experiencing genital-pelvic pain/penetration disorder.

The diagnostic vaginal intercourse/penetration category of the genital-pelvic pain/penetration disorder represents a range from a total inability to experience vaginal penetration in any circumstance (e.g., intercourse, gynecological examinations, tampon insertion) to an ability to easily experience penetration in one situation but not another. Women experiencing the marked vaginal or pelvic pain report mild to severe pain associated with intercourse that can be characterized as burning, cutting, shooting, or throbbing, for example. The pain may continue after intercourse and may occur during urination. Many women experience pain occasionally during intercourse, but much fewer men report pain (see Figures 1 and 2). A population study of 6,669 sexually active British women found that 7.5% of the sample reported painful partnered sex of which one quarter experienced pain symptoms very often or always lasting 6 months or longer and causing stress (Mitchel, et al., 2017). Findings revealed that painful sex was associated with other sexual function difficulties, particularly vaginal dryness and lacking pleasure during sex, and poor mental and physical health. Young women reported the highest proportion of painful sex. Genital or vaginal pain may create anxiety about having intercourse, often resulting in avoidance of intercourse and vaginal penetration. The researchers noted that health professionals should be alert about possible pain during sex among women and provide appropriate support and treatment. Persistent pain among women may indicate difficulties that need to be addressed (Bergeron et al., 2015).

The tensing or tightening of pelvic muscles represents an involuntary spasm of the outer third of the vagina (the pubococcygeus muscle); that is, the muscles around the vaginal opening go into involuntary spasmodic contractions, preventing the insertion of a penis, finger, tampon, or speculum, for example. The most frequent clinical issue is when a woman is not able to experience intercourse or vaginal penetration with a partner, although this problem may also occur during gynecological examinations. This difficulty is found more often in younger women than older women (APA, 2000, 2013).

Another type of pain associated with sex that is not included in the *DSM-5* is **anodyspareunia**, pain experienced by the recipient during anal intercourse. Men and women sometimes experience this, often due to lack of adequate lubrication. The depth of penile penetration into the anus, the rate of thrusting, and anxiety or embarrassment about the situation often are associated with anodyspareunia (Rosser et al., 1998). One study of gay men found that anodyspareunia, along with lack of sexual desire, was the most frequently reported sexual problem (Peixoto & Nobre, 2015). A study of 404 men who have sex with men found that 55 (14%) experienced anodyspareunia; these men reported their pain as lifelong, experienced psychological distress as a result, and avoided anal sex for periods of time (Damon & Rosser, 2005). Among women who have sex with men, a substantial proportion experience pain at initial and subsequent anal intercourse. A study of 1,265 women, aged 18–30, who reported two or more episodes of anal intercourse, found that nearly one half (49%) had discontinued their first episode because of pain or discomfort, although a majority of women subsequently continued anal sex (Stulhofer & Ajdukovic, 2011). Of the 505 women who reported two or more anal intercourse episodes in the past year, nearly 1 in 10 reported severe pain. More than two thirds

Discussing sexuality and becoming educated about one's sexual functioning with a qualified health care professional can sometimes help resolve questions, issues, or problems.

of these women reported that their pain level remained unchanged from their first anal intercourse experience. The researchers hypothesized that the inability to relax was the major cause of the pain.

Substance/Medication-Induced Sexual Dysfunction

The *DSM-5* added a category of sexual disorder, called **substance/medication-induced sexual dysfunction**. Sexual function difficulties can occur with intoxication use of numerous drugs such as alcohol, opioids, sedatives, antidepressants, hypnotics, antipsychotics, stimulants, illicit/recreational drugs, and other unknown substances. The prevalence of substance/medication-induced sexual dysfunction is not known, although some research has been conducted. For example, studies have shown that 25–80% of persons taking certain antidepressants report sexual side effects. About one half of persons taking antipsychotic medications report experiencing sexual side effects, including difficulties with sexual desire, erection, lubrication, ejaculation, and orgasm. Difficulties with sexual functioning appear greater in persons abusing heroin or other opioids (about 60–70%) than in individuals who abuse amphetamines and ecstasy (APA, 2013). Many persons using prescription medications do not realize that the drug may impair sexual functioning. One should inquire about this possibility from a health care provider or pharmacist.

Other Disorders

Two other disorders not mentioned in the *DSM-5* because they are based on physical conditions are Peyronie's disease and priapism. These conditions can also cause other difficulties in sexual functioning.

Peyronie's Disease   A condition in which calcium deposits and tough fibrous tissue develop in the corpora cavernosa within the penis is known as **Peyronie's disease**. This problem occurs primarily in older men—usually for no apparent reason—and can be quite painful. The disease results in a curvature of the penis, which, in severe cases, interferes with erection and intercourse and the penis might become shorter. Medical treatments can alleviate the source of discomfort, and sometimes the condition disappears without treatment (Mayo Clinic, 2020). A study involving 4,432 men in Germany found the prevalence of Peyronie's disease was 3.2% (Schwarzer et al., 2001). For the record, rarely are penises perfectly straight; most curve to one side.

Priapism   Prolonged and painful erection, occurring when blood is unable to drain from the penis, is called **priapism**. Lasting from several hours to a few days, this problem is not associated with sexual thoughts or activities. Rather, it results from certain medications, including some antidepressants, erectile-enhancing medications, and excessive doses of penile injections for producing an erection. Medical conditions such as sickle-cell disease and leukemia may also cause priapism.

● Physical Causes of Sexual Function Difficulties and Dissatisfaction

Until recently, researchers believed that most sexual function difficulties and dissatisfaction were almost exclusively psychological in origin. Current research challenges this view as more is learned about the intricacies of sexual physiology, such as the subtle influences of hormones. Our vascular, neurological, and endocrine systems are sensitive to changes and disruptions. As a result, various illnesses and disturbances to these systems may have an adverse effect on our sexual functioning. Some prescription drugs, such as medication for hypertension or for depression, may affect sexual responsiveness. Chemotherapy and radiation treatment for cancer, and pain from cancer, can affect sexual desire and responsiveness (American Cancer Society, 2017.14).

Men who smoke are more likely to experience erection problems ("impotence") than men who do not smoke.

Jerzy Dabrowski/picture-alliance/dpa/AP Images

Physical Causes in Men

Diabetes and alcoholism are leading causes of male erectile difficulties; together, they account for several million cases. Diabetes damages blood vessels and nerves, including those within the penis. Other causes of sexual function difficulties include lumbar disc disease and multiple sclerosis, which interfere with the nerve impulses regulating erection. In addition, atherosclerosis causes blockage of the arteries, including the blood flow necessary for erection. Spinal cord injuries and prostate cancer treatment may affect erectile abilities as well. Alcoholism and drug use are widely associated with sexual difficulties. Smoking may also contribute to erection difficulties. An analysis of eight research studies involving a total of 28,842 men suggested that the risk of erectile problems was increased by 51% for current smokers and 20% for ex-smokers as compared with never smokers (Cao et al., 2013). Research has also shown that having smoked more than 23 years is a significant risk for erection problems and those who smoked 20 or more cigarettes daily had a higher risk for erectile problems (Wu et al., 2012). Bicycle-induced sexual difficulties can occur as a result of a flattening of the main penile artery, thereby temporarily blocking the blood flow required for erections. Diseases of the heart and circulatory system may be associated with erectile difficulty.

Physical Causes in Women

Organic causes of female orgasmic problems include medical conditions such as diabetes and heart disease, hormone deficiencies, and neurological disorders, as well as general poor health, extreme fatigue, drug use, and alcoholism. Spinal cord injuries may affect sexual responsiveness. Multiple sclerosis can decrease vaginal lubrication and sexual response.

Genital pain during intercourse may result from an obstructed or thickened hymen, clitoral adhesions, infections, painful scars, a constrictive clitoral hood, vulvodynia, or a weak **pubococcygeus** (pew-bo-kawk-SEE-gee-us) (PC) muscle, the pelvic floor muscle surrounding the urethra and the vagina. Antihistamines used to treat colds and allergies can reduce vaginal lubrication, as can marijuana. Endometriosis and ovarian and uterine tumors and cysts may affect a woman's sexual response.

The skin covering the clitoris can become infected. Women who masturbate too vigorously can irritate their clitoris, making sexual interactions painful. A partner can also stimulate a woman too roughly, causing soreness in the vagina, urethra, or clitoral area. And unclean hands may cause a vaginal or urinary tract infection.

● Psychological Causes of Sexual Function Difficulties and Dissatisfaction

Sexual function difficulties and dissatisfaction may have their origin in any number of psychological causes. Some difficulties and dissatisfaction originate from immediate causes, others from conflict within the self, and still others from a particular sexual relationship.

Immediate Causes

The immediate causes of sexual function difficulties and dissatisfaction include fatigue, stress, ineffective sexual behavior, and sexual anxieties.

Fatigue and Stress   Many sexual function difficulties and dissatisfaction have fairly simple causes. Individuals may find themselves physically exhausted from the demands of daily life. They may bring their fatigue into the bedroom in the form of sexual apathy or disinterest. "I'm too tired to be sexual tonight" can be a truthful description of a person's feelings. What these couples may need is not therapy or counseling but temporary relief from their daily routines.

Stress can also contribute to lowered sexual drive and reduced responsiveness. A person preoccupied with making financial ends meet, dealing with a demanding job, raising children, or coping with prolonged illness, for example, can temporarily lose sexual desire.

On rare occasions, there may be dramatic events, such as a public health event or a war, that can heighten individual and couple stress. This is the case for the global COVID-19 pandemic. The factors cited above can be an outcome of the pandemic, as well other aspects such as social isolation, fear of losing one's job, having one's education interrupted, demands of home schooling, and fear of inquiring the virus. All of these factors can impact sexual desire, pleasure, and function, which has been shown in numerous studies (e.g., Lehmiller et al., 2020; Milhausen et al., 2020).

The demands of work and child rearing may create fatigue and stress which can create sexual apathy for one or both partners.

digitalskillet/Getty Images

Ineffective Sexual Behavior   Ignorance, ineffective sexual communication, and misinformation prevent partners from being effectively sexual with each other. Some individuals have not learned effective sexual stimulation behaviors, because they are inexperienced. They may have grown up without easily accessible sexual information or positive role models.

Sexual Anxieties   A number of anxieties, such as performance anxiety, can lead to sexual function difficulties or dissatisfaction (Bancroft, 2009). If a man fails to experience an erection or a woman is not orgasmic, he or she may feel anxious and fearful. And the anxiety may block the very response desired.

Performance anxieties may give rise to **spectatoring**, in which a person becomes a spectator of her or his own sexual behaviors (Masters & Johnson, 1970). When people become spectators of their sexual activities, they critically evaluate and judge whether they are "performing" well or whether they are doing everything "right." Some sex therapists suggest that spectatoring is involved in most orgasmic difficulties.

Excessive Need to Please a Partner   Another source of anxiety is an excessive need to please a partner. A man who feels this need, sometimes labeled as trying to be the "delivery boy," may want a speedy erection to please or impress his partner. If his partner is a woman, he may feel that he must "give her orgasms" through his expert lovemaking or always delay his orgasm until after his partner's orgasm. A woman who experiences this anxiety may want to have an orgasm quickly to please her partner (Castleman, 2004; Salisbury & Fisher, 2013; Harris ct al., 2019). She may worry that she is not sufficiently attractive to her partner or that she is sexually inadequate.

One result of the need to please is that men and women may pretend to have orgasms, also called "faking" or feigning orgasms. (Meg Ryan famously demonstrated faking an orgasm in a deli in the film *When Harry Met Sally.*) A study at one U.S. university found that 69% of college women and 28% of college men reported faking orgasms, saying they weren't just doing it—they were performing it (Caron, 2013). Research involving Canadian and American men aged 18–29 years revealed that, on average, participants reported pretending orgasm in about one fourth of sexual encounters in their current relationship, most often during vaginal sex (Seguin & Milhausen, 2016). Frequently reported reasons for pretending orgasm reported by both sexes were that orgasm was unlikely, they wanted sexual activity to end, the partner was not desired, they wanted to avoid negative consequences (e.g., hurting their partner's feelings) and to obtain outcomes like pleasing their partners (Muehlenhard & Shippee, 2009; Seguin & Milhausen, 2016). A study of 462 self-identify heterosexual women (mean age, 38 years) from the United Kingdom assessed why women pretend orgasms and factors associated with the behavior (Harris et al., 2019). The women who espoused anti-feminist value (i.e., high in hostile sexism) pretended more orgasms over their lifetime in contrast to those high in benevolent sexism. Those who thought that orgasm was necessary for men's sexual pleasure were more likely to have faked an orgasm at least once in their lives compared to women who had never faked an orgasm. Further, the study revealed that women who pretended orgasms rated their partners as less sexually skilled. Unfortunately, faking orgasm miscommunicates to the partner that a person is equally satisfied. Because the orgasmic problem is not addressed, negative emotions may simmer. The wisest decision is never to pretend to experience feelings, interests, or pleasures that do not happen (Hall, 2004). To take a questionnaire that assesses motives for pretending orgasms, see Practically Speaking, Chapter 2, "Answering a Sex Research Questionnaire: Motives for Feigning Orgasm Scale."

"In the 1990s a feminist joke asked, "Why do women fake orgasm?" and answered "Because men fake fore-play." In the masculinist version, the question was "Why do women fake orgasm?" and the answer, "Because they think men care."

—Angus McLaren

Conflict Within the Self

Negative parental attitudes toward sex are frequently associated with subsequent sexual function difficulties and dissatisfaction. Much of the process of growing up is a casting off of the sexual guilt and negativity instilled in childhood. Some people fear becoming emotionally intimate with another person. They may enjoy the sex but fear the accompanying feelings of vulnerability and so withdraw from the sexual relationship before they become emotionally close to their partner (Hyde & DeLamater, 2014). And among gay men, lesbian women, and bisexual and queer individuals, internalized homophobia—self-hatred because of one's homosexuality—is a major source of conflict that can be traced to a number of factors, including conservative religious upbringing (Frost & Meyer, 2009).

Sources of severe sexual function difficulties include childhood sexual abuse, adult sexual assault, and rape. Guilt and conflict do not usually eliminate a person's sex drive; rather, they inhibit the drive and alienate the individual from his or her sexuality. He or she may come to see sexuality as something bad or "dirty," rather than something to happily affirm.

Therapists Robert Firestone, Lisa Firestone, and Joyce Catlett (2006) provide an alternative perspective on the decline of sexual passion in long-term relationships and marriage. They believe that the decline cannot be attributed to the reasons usually given, such as familiarity, gender differences, economic hardships, and other stressors, but rather to changes in the relationship dynamics, the emergence of painful feelings from childhood, and fears of rejection that cause partners to retreat to a more defended posture. Many people have difficulty in maintaining sexually satisfying relationships "because in their earlier relationships, hurt and frustration caused them to turn away from love and closeness and to become suspicious and self-protective." In advising couples in longer-term relationships, the therapists note:

> To sustain a loving sexual relationship, individuals must be willing to face the threats to the defense system that loving another person and being loved for oneself evoke. To be able to accept genuine affection, tenderness, love, and fulfilling sexual experiences as part of an ongoing relationship, they must be willing to challenge their negative voices, modify the image of themselves formed in the family, and give up well-entrenched defenses, which would cause them a great deal of anxiety.

Relationship Causes

Sexual function difficulties do not exist in a vacuum, but usually within the context of a relationship. All couples at some point experience difficulties in their sexual relationship. Sex therapist David Schnarch (2002) writes that "sexual problems are common among healthy couples who are normal in every other way—so common, in fact, that they are arguably a sign of normality." Most frequently, married couples go into therapy because they have a greater investment in the relationship than couples who are dating or cohabiting. Sexual function difficulties in a dating or cohabiting relationship often do not surface; it is sometimes easier for couples to break up than to change the behaviors that contribute to their sexual function problems.

Sex therapist Esther Perel, in her book *Mating in Captivity* (2006), presents a provocative view of desire difficulties in marriage, one that is counter to often-held perspectives among sex therapists. She contends that eroticism thrives on the unpredictable and that increased intimacy often leads to a decrease in sexual desire. Perel states that love is fed by knowing everything about one's partner, while desire needs mystery, and that love wants to shrink the distance between the two people, while desire is energized by it. She continues by declaring that "as an expression of longing, desire requires elusiveness." Perel contends that couples may be more successful in maintaining and cultivating sexual desire by enriching their separate lives instead of always striving for closeness. The challenge for many couples is balancing separateness with togetherness, as both are important components of a loving relationship.

If sexual function problems are left unresolved, disappointment, rage, anger, resentment, power conflicts, and hostility often become a permanent part of couple interaction.

"Pleasure is the object, duty, and the goal of all rational creatures."

—Voltaire (1694–1770)

"As with singers in a harmony, a harmonious sex life is not necessarily one in which you are both wanting and doing exactly the same things in the same way, but one that is characterized by blending the strengths that you each have to create an agreeable and pleasant sex life."

—Sandra Pertot (1950–)

● Sexual Function Enhancement

Improving the quality of a sexual relationship is referred to as **sexual function enhancement**. There are several sexual function–enhancement programs for people who function well sexually but who nevertheless want to improve the quality of their sexual interactions and relationships. The programs generally seek to provide accurate information about sexuality, develop communication skills, foster positive attitudes, provide sexual homework for practicing techniques discussed in therapy, and increase self-awareness.

Developing Self-Awareness

Being aware of our own sexual needs is often critical to enhancing our sexual functioning.

What Is Good Sex?   Sexual stereotypes present us with images of how we are supposed to behave sexually. Images of the "sexually in charge" man and the "sexual but not too sexual" woman may interfere with our ability to express our own sexual feelings, needs, and desires. We follow the scripts and stereotypes we have been socialized to accept, rather than our own unique responses. Following these cultural images may impede our ability to have what therapist Carol Ellison calls "good sex." In an essay about intimacy-based sex therapy, Ellison (1985) writes that we will know we are having good sex if we feel good about ourselves, our partners, our relationships, and our sexual behaviors. Further, we will feel good about sex before, during, and after being sexual with our partners. Good sex does not necessarily include orgasm or intercourse. It can be kissing, cuddling, masturbating, performing oral or anal sex, and so on. Sex therapist and clinical psychologist Marty Klein (2012) states that culture dictates a hierarchy of sexual behaviors, with some activities being superior to others. In Western culture the pinnacle of heterosexual sexual behavior is intercourse; it is considered to be the most enjoyable, natural, and intimate sexual behavior. Below intercourse in the hierarchy are other forms of genital sex (touching of the genitals) with a partner, such as oral sex, anal sex, and manual manipulation, then followed by solo masturbation and intimate behaviors not involving touching the genitals, such as touching of the breasts. Kissing is the ultimate expression of intimacy for some people; for others, it is considered boring or a turn-off. One limitation of the concept of sexual hierarchy is that it can minimize the intimacy and pleasure of behaviors "lower" on the hierarchy, and it implies that intercourse must occur in order to have successful sex.

Discovering Your Conditions for Good Sex   Zilbergeld (1999) has suggested that to fully enjoy our sexuality we need to explore our "conditions for good sex." There is nothing unusual about requiring conditions for any activity. Of conditions for good sex, Zilbergeld (1999) writes:

> In a sexual situation, a condition is anything that makes you more relaxed, more comfortable, more confident, more excited, more open to your experience. Put differently, a condition is something that clears your nervous system of unnecessary clutter, leaving it open to receive and transmit sexual messages in ways that will result in a good time for you.

Each individual has his or her own unique conditions for good sex. This might include factors such as feeling intimate and emotionally close with one's partner, feeling trust toward one's partner, being physically and mentally alert, and embracing one's own sexual desire and eroticism. If you are or have been sexually active, to discover your conditions for good sex, think about the last few times you were sexual and were highly aroused. Then compare those times with other times when you were much less aroused. Identify the needs that underlie these factors and communicate these needs to your partner. To learn what one study found were the components of "magnificent sex" as reported by those who experience great sex, see Think About It, "Those Who Experience 'Magnificent Sex': What they Say That Makes it Happen."

Good sex involves the ability to communicate well nonverbally—through laughter and positive body language and facial expressions—as well as verbally.
Dmytro Zinkevych/Shutterstock

"Sexuality is with us from the moment of birth to the moment of death. We can deny it or deflect it, we can pretend it's something other than what it is, we can do all sorts of things regarding our sexuality. The only thing we can't do is get rid of it."

—Bernie Zilbergeld (1939–2002)

"When adults experience passion, it's usually not in response to incredible sex or the perfect body—it's in response to giving themselves permission to let go emotionally."

—Marty Klein (1950–)

think about it

Those Who Experience "Magnificent Sex": What They Say That Makes It Happen

Sex is not just some bonus activity in life. It can define who we are, where we're going and what we're capable of being.

—Peggy Kleinplatz and A. Dana Menard

What makes sex magnificent? Sex researchers and therapists Peggy Kleinplatz and A. Dana Menard (2020) state that they have found that many people and couples in new relationships say that their sex life is "satisfactory" or "functional" yet they suspect that it could be better. Kleinplatz and Menard believe that great sex is desired and available, but many people do not know how to get it. So they conducted a study to identify the components of what can be called "great," "remarkable," "wonderful," and/or "memorable" partnered sex. The goal of their study was to learn what makes some sex magnificent in hope that the information can be valuable to individuals and couples who desire more pleasurable, intimate, and rewarding sex. The results of their study were presented in their book *Magnificent Sex: Lessons from Extraordinary Lovers* (2020).

Participants recruited for the study were (1) persons over the age of 60 who had been in a relationship more than 25 years, (2) self-identified members of a sexual minority group, and (3) sex therapists. The researchers chose older individuals who were able to maintain a relationship for 25 or more years based on the contention that they may possess valuable knowledge about what makes for a lasting and fulfilling sexual relationship. Research has shown that sex often improves with an increasing age and the length of the relationship (e.g., Forbes et al., 2017; Traeen et al., 2018). Thirty men and women aged 62 to 89 years (mean age 66 years) were interviewed.

Individuals were asked open-ended questions about how they defined magnificent partnered sex. Eight major components of magnificent sex were found. The researchers stated that a surprising finding was the commonality of the components across different population groups: men and women, healthy and disabled or chronically ill, LGBTQ+ and straight, exclusive and consensually nonmonogamous, kinky and vanilla (non-kinky).

Being Completely Present in the Moment, Embodied, Focused, Absorbed

The first major component of magnificent sex cited by the participants was the feeling of being totally present, immersed, and absorbed in the sexual experience as it unfolds. Being utterly engrossed in the moment was often stated as the major difference between great sex and very good sex and average sex. Being present meant being focused at all levels—mentally, physically, emotionally, and spiritually—and not allowing oneself to be distracted.

Connection, Alignment, Being in Synch, Merger

The second major element of magnificent sex cited was feeling absolutely connected to one's sexual partner, and having deep respect for and trust in their partner. Words often used were "synchronicity," "merger," "bridging the gap," "electricity," and "energy." One woman stated, "At that moment, there was no one else in the world" (p. 24).

Deep Sexual and Erotic Intimacy

A major component of magnificent sex declared by nearly everyone was the intensity and depth of the intimacy shared with their partner and mutual respect. Some noted that optimal sex cannot be separated from the relationship in which it occurs.

Extraordinary Communication and Deep Empathy

Having extraordinary communication with one's partner was a recurring theme. Being able to share oneself completely with another person—that is, revealing parts of themselves not usually shared—was often stated as a major aspect of magnificent sex. Verbal and "hands-on" demonstrations were also mentioned as important. The participants seemingly excelled in giving and receiving touch.

Being Genuine, Authentic, Transparent

Being able to be completely, genuinely, and honestly themselves—that is, freedom to be uninhibited and unselfconscious—was, for many, the trademark of having magnificent sex. Giving themselves to revel in pleasure, being available to their lover, feeling joy of receiving such revelations for the partner, and getting comfortable with the uncomfortable were mentioned.

Vulnerability and Surrender

Being able to be vulnerable and to surrender, both to the sex itself and one's partner, were mentioned as critical components of magnificent sex. Some compared being vulnerable and surrendering during optimal sex to jumping off a cliff. Several indicated loss of conscious thought. One women said that "If you're not going to give yourself up to it, then what's the point?" (p. 29)

Exploration, Interpersonal Risk-Taking and Fun

Many participants stated that having magnificent sex involves taking risks and exploring. That is, sexual encounters in which lovers can play, push or expand their own personal boundaries, and have a sense of human and unadulterated fun without worrying about making mistakes. Experiencing sex as an avenue for personal growth was cited.

Transcendence and Transformation

Magnificent sex was described as heightened states, and such terms as "soulful," "ecstatic," "other-worldly," and "out-of-body" were used to describe the sex. Many indicated that magnificent sex was inherently growth-enhancing, life-affirming, and life-altering. One man said in describing a sexual episode that "The truly great ones really take me and the persons I'm with. . . to another realm. And it really takes me almost out of my body even though I am in it." (p. 32).

Great sex is not found in adhering to advice from pop culture; on the contrary, we must look within ourselves to find optimal sexual experiences. Persons need to unlearn much that they were taught about sex when growing so they can overcome shame, guilt, and normative expectations of performance and sexual scripts. The researchers stated that the participants taught them that rather than worrying about establishing new bars for magnificent sex that are unattainably high, persons need to refine "sex" (Kleinplatz & Menard, 2020). Kleinplatz and Menard concluded that "Improving one's sex life takes notable time, devotion, intentionality and cannot begin without acknowledging and discarding the restrictive sexual and heteronormative values and beliefs endemic in our society" (p. 44).

Think Critically

1. What surprised you about the findings?
2. Do the results apply to young adults even though the study participants were older individuals?
3. If you are in a sexual relationship, or hope to be, which major finding(s) do you feel you will/would try to make the sex more pleasurable and intimate?

Doing Homework Exercises Sexual function–enhancement programs often specify exercises for couples to undertake in private. Such "homework" exercises require individuals to make a time commitment to themselves or their partner. Typical assignments include the following exercises:

- *Mirror examination.* Use a full-length mirror to examine your nude body. Use a hand mirror to view your genitals. Look at all your features in an uncritical manner; view yourself with acceptance.

- *Body relaxation and exploration.* Take 30–60 minutes to fully relax. Begin with a leisurely shower or bath; then, remaining nude, find a comfortable place to touch and explore your body and genitals.

- *Masturbation.* In a relaxed situation, with body oils or lotions to enhance your sensations, explore ways of touching your body and genitals that bring you pleasure. Do this exercise for several sessions without having an orgasm; experiencing erotic pleasure without orgasm is the goal. If you are about to have an orgasm, decrease stimulation. After several sessions without having an orgasm, continue pleasuring yourself until you have an orgasm.

- *Sexual voice.* Each person has his or her own erotic "sexual voice," which is enhanced by discovering, nurturing, and integrating into the couple's sexual style. For example, many women traditionally have been dependent on the male partner's eroticism and his sexual lead; the woman was not supposed to have her own erotic voice (McCarthy & McCarthy, 2009). Individuals who develop their own sexual voice open themselves up to a more satisfying and rewarding sexual experience with a partner.

A vibrator can be a valuable aid in increasing sexual arousal and experiencing an orgasm.

H. S. Photos/Science Source

- *Kegel exercises for women and men.* Originally developed to help women with controlling urination, Kegel exercises involve exercising a muscle in the pelvic floor called the pubococcygeus (P.C.) muscle. The Kegel exercises basically involve tightening the P.C. muscle as one does to stop the flow of urine. These exercises can aid in increasing one's sexual awareness and functioning. (See Practically Speaking, "Kegel Exercises for All Genders" to learn about why and how to do these exercises.)

- *Erotic aids.* Products designed to enhance erotic responsiveness, such as vibrators, dildos, G-spot stimulators, artificial vaginas and mouths, clitoral stimulators, vibrating nipple clips, explicit videos, oils, lubricants, and lotions, are referred to as **erotic aids**. They are also called **sex toys**, emphasizing their playful quality. Vibrators and dildos seem to be the most common sex toys and are usually considered "women's toys." But, of course, they can be for any gender and can be used alone or with a partner.

Kegel Exercises for All Genders

Kegel exercises were originally developed by gynecologist
Arnold Kegel (KAY-gul) to help women with problems controlling
urination. They were designed to strengthen and give women
voluntary control of a muscle called the pubococcygeus, or P.C.
for short. Strengthening this muscle during pregnancy can help a
woman develop her ability to control her muscles during labor
and delivery. The P.C. muscle is part of the sling of muscle
stretching from the pubic bone in front to the tailbone in back,
also called the pelvic floor. Because the muscle encircles not only
the urinary opening but also the outside of the vagina, some of
Kegel's patients discovered a pleasant side effect—increased sexual awareness. Many report that the sensations are similar for
men and women. If you are a man, the exercises can be valuable
to you for improving erectile function and learning ejaculatory
control. In fact, a British study found that erection function
improved significantly in men after 3 months of Kegel exercises
(Dorey et al., 2005). So men, when reading the directions, just
substitute your genitals in places where the directions talk about
"vagina" and so on.

Why Do Kegel Exercises?

- They can help you be more aware of feelings in your genital
  area.
- They can increase circulation in the genital area.
- They may help increase sexual arousal started by other kinds
  of stimulation.
- They can be useful during childbirth to help control the
  strength and duration of pushing.
- They can be helpful after childbirth to restore muscle tone in
  the vagina.
- They can help men improve erection function and control the
  timing of ejaculation.
- If urinary incontinence is a problem, strengthening these muscles may improve urinary control.

Identifying Your P.C. Muscle

Sit on the toilet. Spread your legs apart. See if you can stop and start
the flow of urine without moving your legs. That's your P.C. muscle,
the one that turns the flow on and off. If you don't find it the first time,
don't give up; try again the next time you have to urinate. From the

British study cited previously, the researchers instructed the men to
tighten their pelvic floor as if they were trying to prevent intestinal
gas from escaping or to try retracting the penis and lifting the
scrotum and testicles.

How to Do the Exercises

- *Slow Kegels:* Tighten the P.C. muscle as you did to stop the
  urine. Hold it for a slow count of three. Relax it.
- *Quick Kegels:* Tighten and relax the P.C. muscle as rapidly as
  you can.
- *Pull in–push out:* Pull up the entire pelvic floor as though
  trying to suck water into your vagina. Then push or bear down
  as if trying to push the imaginary water out. This exercise will
  use a number of stomach or abdominal muscles as well as
  the P.C. muscle.

At first, do 10 of each of these three exercises (one set)
five times every day. Each week, increase the number of times
you do each exercise by 5 (15, 20, 25, etc.). Keep doing five
"sets" each day.

Exercise Guidelines

- You can do these exercises anytime during daily activities that
  don't require a lot of moving around—for example, while
  driving your car, watching television, sitting in school or at
  your computer, using a smartphone, or lying in bed.
- When you start, you will probably notice that the muscle
  doesn't want to stay "contracted" during "slow Kegels" and that
  you can't do "quick Kegels" very rapidly or evenly. Keep at it.
  In a week or two, you will probably notice that you can control
  the muscle quite well.
- Sometimes, the muscle will start to feel a little tired. This is not
  surprising—you probably haven't used it very much before.
  Take a few seconds' rest and start again.
- A good way to check on how you are doing is to insert one or
  two lubricated fingers into your vagina. Men can place a
  lubricated, latex-gloved finger into their rectum to feel the
  anus contract. Because it may be a month or so before you
  notice results, be patient.

Finally, always remember to keep breathing naturally and
evenly while doing your Kegels.

A nationally representative study of 2,021 adults (975 men, 1,046 women) found
that 50% of women and 33% of men had used a vibrator or dildo in their lifetime
(Herbenick et al., 2017). You may wish to try using a sex toy or shower massage as
you masturbate with your partner or by yourself. You may also want to view erotic
films, go online to find sexually explicit images, or read erotic poetry or stories to
yourself or your partner.

Intensifying Erotic Pleasure

One of the most significant elements of enhancing our physical experience of sex is intensifying arousal. In intensifying arousal, the focus is on erotic pleasure rather than on sexual functioning. This can be done in a number of ways.

Developing Bridges to Desire Sex therapist Barry McCarthy and author Emily McCarthy (2009) state that sexual desire is the core element of a healthy sexuality and that developing and maintaining sexual desire is important to a satisfying couple sexual style. Couples prefer to experience the fun and energizing effect of spontaneous sex that is common in the romantic/passionate sex/idealization phase of a new sexual relationship in which sex occurs nearly every time the couple gets together. But for couples past the 6-month to 2-year passionate sex phase, especially those with demanding jobs, kids, mortgages, and so on, most sexual encounters are planned and many couples begin to experience lower sexual desire.

Sex researcher Emily Nagoski (2015) states that the standard belief about sexual desire is that it just appears, spontaneously. Spontaneous sexual desire occurs for about three quarters of men, but only for about one in seven women. However, a minority of individuals say they want to have sex only after erotic things begin to happen. Nagoski calls this responsive normal and healthy. She continues by saying, "It turns out everyone's sexual desire is responsive and context dependent" (p. 225). Because couples are not able to transfer from the passionate sex stage to an enduring intimate and erotic couple sexual style, the key is to integrate intimacy and eroticism by "building bridges to desire."

The McCarthys state that "bridges to desire require ways of thinking, anticipating, and experiencing a sexual encounter that makes sex inviting." The most important bridge to desire involves couples anticipating a sexual encounter in which the partner is involved, giving, and aroused. Each partner and the couple should be creative in developing and maintaining bridges to desire. Even though individual bridges are important, discovering unique, mutual bridges can be a valuable couple resource. The more varied the bridges, the easier it is to maintain desire. Further, the more bridges to desire, the more ways to connect and reconnect through touch. One way to develop a bridge to desire is for each partner to inform the other partner what his or her two favorite ways to initiate a sexual encounter are and two favorite ways to be invited for a sexual encounter. Revealing your thoughts on how your partner can be a better lover may enhance sexual pleasure for both of you. An Internet study of over 77,000 individuals around the world asked respondents to select from a long list of choices the top two things they feel are missing from their sexual relationship (Northrop et al., 2014). The top three preferences of what men want from their partners were: sexual diversity (30%), less passivity (22%), and sexual noises (16%). The top three preferences of what women want from their partners were: foreplay (25%), romance (20%), and less predictability (19%). The researchers stated that even couples who have been together long-term may be hesitant and embarrassed to ask for and explain what they want. Unfortunately, our culture has taught many of us that "wild abandon sex" is shameful and even wrong. If you keep your intimate sexual thoughts a secret, your sexual relationship has no chance to improve. So be brave and tell your partner what you are thinking, and welcome your partner declaring their desires.

Sexual Arousal Sexual arousal refers to the physiological responses, fantasies, and desires associated with sexual anticipation and activity. We have different levels of arousal, and they are not necessarily associated with particular types of sexual activities. Sometimes, we feel more sexually aroused when we kiss or masturbate than when we have sexual intercourse or oral sex.

The first element in increasing sexual arousal is having your conditions for good sex met. If you need privacy, find a place to be alone; if you need a romantic setting, go for a relaxing walk or listen to music by candlelight; if you want limits on your sexual activities, tell your partner; if you need a certain kind of physical stimulation, show or tell your partner what you like. To learn sexual arousal specifically among young adults, read what turns on (and off) college men and women in Think About It, "Sexual Turn-ons and Turn-offs: What College Students Report."

Some individuals and couples use erotic aids such as vibrators, dildos, videos, oils, lubricants, and lotions to enhance their sexual pleasure and responsiveness.

Adam Bronkhorst/Alamy Stock Photo

"The best aphrodisiac is an involved, aroused partner."

—McCarthy and McCarthy (2009)

"License my roving hands, and let them go,
Before, behind, between, above, below."

—John Donne (1572–1631)

A second element in increasing arousal is focusing on the sensations you are experiencing. Once you begin an erotic activity such as massaging or kissing, do not let yourself be distracted. When you're kissing, don't think about what you're going to do next or about an upcoming test. Instead, focus on the sensual experience of your lips and heart.

Maintaining Sexual Passion   Sexual passion and satisfaction typically decline over a long-term relationship; however, this decline need not be inevitable. Keeping sexual passion alive and fresh over a long-term relationship is challenging for many couples as they find that passion is difficult to sustain. To maintain the passion of the early days of their relationship, couples may try numerous strategies such as experimenting with new sexual activities, increasing communication about their desires, trying new ways to increase the mood for sex, and accessing self-help books and websites. In spite of these strategies, little is known about whether these strategies are effective in promoting increased sexual passion and sexual satisfaction in long-term relationships.

To determine what differentiated sexually satisfied men and women from those not satisfied, researchers identified sexual attitudes and behaviors of cohabiting and married men and women ($N = 38,747$) who had been together at least 3 years (Frederick et al., 2017). Here is what the researchers found:

- The vast majority of participants reported being satisfied with their sex lives during their first 6 months together.

- Most participants felt that their sexual satisfaction and passion declined over time.

- Nearly two thirds of sexually satisfied participants reported that their sex lives now were as passionate as in their early days together.

- One in three women and one in four men said they felt more emotional closeness during sex now than at the start of their relationship.

- There was not one sexuality-related item where men reported aspects of their sex lives as better "now" versus "then," whereas women chose four items: lower inhibition, more single orgasms, more multiple orgasms, and feeling emotionally closer during sex now than at the beginning of the relationship.

- Overall, sexual satisfaction and maintenance of passion were higher among people who had sex most frequently, received more oral sex, had more consistent orgasms, and incorporated more variety of sexual behaviors (see Table 2), mood setting, and sexual communication (see Table 3).

The researchers concluded that:

Our results indicate some ways that may improve a sagging sex life. Taking the time to set the mood, sexual variety, and communication were important predictors of sexual satisfaction for both men and women. If properly nurtured, passion can last for decades. (pp. 198–199)

"Most desire is unspoken."

—Northrop, Schwartz, and Witte (2012)

In his book, *Resurrecting Sex* (2002), David Schnarch, a prominent sex therapist and clinical psychologist, discusses common sexual function problems, including decreasing sexual desire in long-term relationships, and presents a provocative suggestion for addressing them. Schnarch says that every couple has sexual function problems at some point, although most couples do not anticipate that they will end up experiencing sexual dissatisfaction. In a statement that might seem surprising, he notes, "If your sexual relationship stays the same, you are more likely to have sexual dysfunctions (and be bored to death)."

"Sex is more about imagination than friction."

—Erica Jong (1942–)

Schnarch guarantees one thing: To resurrect or improve an intimate relationship, you have to change the current relationship. He notes that this is no small task. Rather, it involves, for example, raising your level of stimulation, accepting new truths about you and your partner, becoming closer, and changing yourself in the process. Resurrecting sex requires being able to make positive changes without taking out frustrations on your partner, even if you think he or she deserves it.

TABLE 2 ● Percentage of Sexually Satisfied Men and Women Versus Those Dissatisfied Who Indicated They Had Done Different Activities in the Past Year to Improve Their Sex Life.

	Men		Women	
	Sat.%	Dis.%	Sat.%	Dis.%
Activities of Sexual Variety Past Year (% Yes)				
At least one of us got a mini-massage or backrub	72	48	68	40
One of us wore sexy lingerie/underwear	67	33	71	45
Took a shower or bath together	64	35	66	37
Made a "date night" to be sure we had sex	63	41	55	37
Tried a new sexual position	59	22	63	25
Went on a romantic getaway	53	30	47	28
Used a vibrator or sex toy together	48	28	47	30
Tried anal stimulation	42	19	37	19
Viewed pornography together	40	19	45	28
Talked about or acted out our fantasies	40	14	37	16
Had anal intercourse	25	10	26	14
Had sexual contact in a public place	23	6	19	6
Integrated food into sex (e.g., chocolate/whipped cream)	22	8	22	9
Tried light S&M (e.g., restraints, spanking)	18	6	21	9
One of us took Viagra or a similar drug	17	12	9	10
Videotaped our sex or posed for pictures in the nude	15	5	13	5
Invited another person into bed with us	6	2	3	2

Note: Participants were asked, "Have you done any of the following *in the past year* to improve your sex life? If so, select all that apply."

Participants provided their answers on a 7-point Likert scale: 1 = very dissatisfied, 7 = very satisfied. For this table, dissatisfied represent answers 1–3 combined and satisfied as 5–7 answers combined.

Source: Adapted from Frederick, et al. 2017.

TABLE 3 ● Percentage of Sexually Satisfied Men and Women Versus Those Dissatisfied Who Indicated They and Their Partner Had Talked In the Past Month About Sex in Any of These Ways

	Men		Women	
	Sat.%	Dis.%	Sat.%	Dis.%
Communication Past Month (% Yes)				
I asked for something I wanted in bed	51	28	42	15
One of us praised the other about something they did in bed	50	12	56	14
My partner asked for something they wanted in bed	37	8	50	21
One of us asked for feedback on how something felt	34	13	33	12
One of us called/emailed to tease about doing something sexual	33	11	40	14
One of us gently criticized how the other did something in bed	7	7	7	7

Note: Participants were asked, "In the *past month,* have you and your partner talked about sex in any of these ways? Please select all that apply."

Participants provided their answers on a 7-point Likert scale: 1 = very dissatisfied, 7 = very satisfied. For this table, dissatisfied represent answers 1–3 combined and satisfied as 5–7 answers combined.

Source: Adapted from Frederick, et al. 2017.

think
about it

Sexual Turn-ons and Turn-offs: What College Students Report

What turns college men and women on and off sexually? Are there gender differences and similarities? Sex researcher Robin R. Milhausen conducted an online study of 822 heterosexual students (440 women and 382 men) aged 18–37 from Indiana University who were randomly selected to participate. She contends that a greater understanding of factors that turn on and turn off men and women can be valuable in increasing sexual well-being and improving sexual relationships. Here are the study's major findings (Milhausen, 2004; Milhausen et al., 2004).

Some Important Factors Men and Women Agreed On

Factors that *enhance sexual arousal* for both men and women were:

- A good sense of humor, self-confidence, and intelligence
- Feeling desired as a partner
- Spontaneous and varied sex (e.g., not the same activities every time, having sex in a different setting)
- Fantasizing about and anticipating a sexual encounter
- Doing something fun together

Turn-offs for both men and women were:

- A lack of balance in giving and receiving during sex
- A partner who is self-conscious about his or her body
- Worrying about getting a bad sexual reputation
- Worrying about STIs
- Using condoms

Some Important Factors Men and Women Disagreed On

- Women were more concerned about their sexual functioning (e.g., being a good lover, worrying about taking too long to become aroused, feeling shy, or self-conscious).

- Being in a relationship characterized by trust and emotional safety was considered more important to sexual arousal for women than for men.
- More women than men indicated that "feeling used" was a big turn-off.
- Men more often considered a variety of sexual stimuli (e.g., thinking about someone they find sexually attractive, "talking dirty," thinking and talking about sex, being physically close to a partner) as enhancers to sexual arousal.
- Women more often considered partner characteristics and behaviors (e.g., partner showing talent, interacting well with others, doing chores) as enhancers to sexual arousal.
- Women more often considered elements of the sexual setting (e.g., a setting where they might be seen or heard while having sex) as inhibitors to sexual arousal.
- Women were more aware of the role of their own hormones in sexual arousal.
- Women more often considered elements of the sexual interaction (e.g., partner not sensitive to the signals being given and received during sex, being uncertain how her partner feels) as inhibitors of sexual arousal.
- More men than women *agreed* that "going right to the genitals" during sex would be a turn-on during sex.

Think Critically

1. Were you surprised by any of the findings? Which one and why?
2. Are some of the results similar to what you would consider sexual turn-ons and turn-offs?
3. Have you learned anything from this study that you might use in your future sexual encounters?
4. Do you think the results would be similar for gay, lesbian, and other sexual minority couples?

● Treating Sexual Function Difficulties

There are several psychologically-based approaches to sex therapy, the most important ones being behavior modification and psychosexual therapy. A systematic and meta-analysis review of available studies of psychological interventions for sexual dysfunctions from 1980 to 2009 found that they are effective options for treating sexual dysfunctions. Evidence varies across the different sexual function difficulties, but good efficacy exists for female sexual interest/arousal disorder (Fruhauf et al., 2013). William Masters and Virginia Johnson were the pioneers in the cognitive-behavioral approach; one of the most influential psychosexual therapists is Helen Singer Kaplan. Medical approaches may also be effective with some sexual function problems.

Masters and Johnson: A Cognitive-Behavioral Approach

The program developed by Masters and Johnson for the treatment of sexual function difficulties was the starting point for contemporary sex therapy. They not only rejected the Freudian approach of tracing sexual function problems to childhood; they also relabeled sexual function problems as sexual dysfunctions rather than aspects of neuroses. Masters and Johnson (1970) argue that the majority of sexual function problems are the result of sexual ignorance, faulty techniques, or relationship problems. They treated difficulties using a combination of cognitive and behavioral techniques, and they treated couples rather than individuals.

Couples With Difficulties   Cognitive-behavioral therapists approach the problems of erectile and orgasmic difficulties by counseling the couple rather than the individual. They regard sexuality as an interpersonal phenomenon rather than an individual one. In fact, they tell their clients that there are no individuals with sexual function difficulties, only couples who experience these issues. Sex therapist Sandra Pertot (2007) states that "even people with secure, happy personal histories can end up with unsatisfying sexual relationships, because it is how your individual sexuality interacts with your partner's that defines what is a problem and what isn't." In this model, neither individual is to blame for any sexual dissatisfaction; rather, it is their mutual interaction that sustains a difficulty or resolves a problem. Masters and Johnson (1974) called this principle "neutrality and mutuality."

Sensate Focus   A common therapeutic method is **sensate focus**, the focusing on touch and the giving and receiving of pleasure (see Figure 5). The other senses—smell, sight, hearing, and taste—are worked on indirectly as a means of reinforcing the touch experience. To increase their sensate focus, the couple is given "homework" assignments. In the privacy of their own home, the partners are to take off their clothes so that nothing will restrict their sensations. One partner must give pleasurable touch with no expectations, and the other receives it. The giver touches, caresses, massages, and strokes his or her partner's body everywhere except the genitals and breasts. The purpose is not sexual arousal but simply the recipient being present to sensations in the moment (Weiner & Avery-Clark, 2014).

Specific Treatment Techniques   Sex therapy utilizes different techniques for treating specific problems. Treatment techniques for four major problems are briefly described in this section.

Female Orgasmic Difficulties   After doing sensate focus, the woman's partner begins to touch and caress her vulva; she guides the partner's hand to show what she likes. The partner is told, however, not to stimulate the clitoris directly because it may be extremely sensitive and stimulation may cause pain rather than pleasure. Instead, the partner caresses and stimulates the area around the clitoris, the labia, and the upper thighs. During this time, the partners are told not to attempt to have an orgasm, because it would place undue performance pressure on the woman. They are simply to explore the woman's erotic potential and discover what brings her the greatest pleasure.

Here is a special message to partners of women who have difficulty experiencing orgasm during sex: Support her to have an orgasm any way it happens for her. Sexual partners do not give each other orgasms—lovers are traveling companions experiencing their own erotic journey (Castleman, 2004). Sex therapist and author Marty Klein, speaking to partners of women with orgasmic difficulties, states that "you can create the environment in which your lover feels relaxed enough and turned on enough to have one [orgasm]. But, she creates her own orgasm. You don't *give* it to her" (quoted in Castleman, 2004).

Erection Difficulties   When the problem is erection difficulties, the couple is taught that fears and anxieties are largely responsible and that the removal of these fears is the first step in therapy. Once these are removed, the man is less likely to be an observer of his sexuality; he can become a participant rather than a spectator or judge.

After integrating sensate focus into the couple's behavior, the partners are told to play with each other's genitals, but not to attempt an erection. Often, erections may occur

"Surprising how the most common sexual problem is not low libido, rapid ejaculation, or difficulty with orgasm. It is that people are not prepared for the extent of individual differences in human sexuality."

—Sandra Pertot (1950–)

"Full nakedness! All joys are due to thee,
As souls unbodied, bodies unclothed must be,
To taste whole joys."

—John Donne (1572–1631)

"The penis, far from being an impenetrable knight in armor, in fact bears its heart on its sleeve."

—Susan Bordo (1947–)

• **FIGURE 5**
Sensate Focus

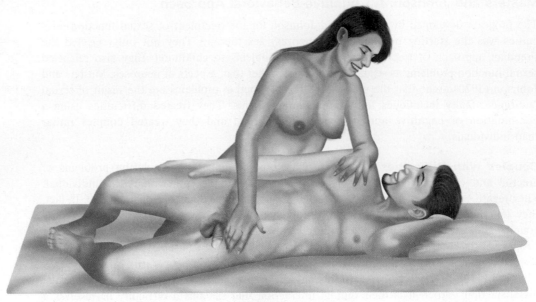

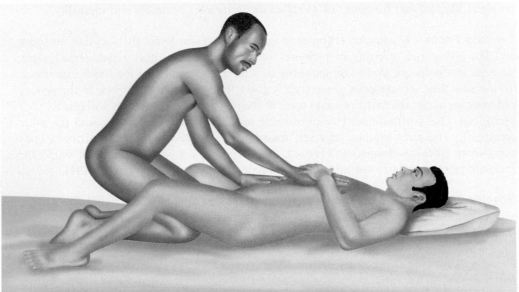

because there is no demand on the man; however, he is encouraged to let his penis become flaccid again, then erect, then flaccid, as reassurance that he can successfully have erections. This builds his confidence, as well as his partner's, by letting him know that the partner can excite him.

Therapists also try to dispel many of the erection myths. Although the majority of difficulties with erections are caused by a combination of factors, such as relationship difficulties, cardiovascular problems, and depression, becoming more knowledgeable and realistic about erections is an important step to overcoming difficulties (Rosen et al., 2014). Common erection myths include the following (Castleman, 2004):

- *Erection is something that is achieved.* Penises don't become erect through work, but from just the opposite. The more sensual the lovemaking, the more likely an erection will occur.

- *Men are sex machines, always ready, always hard.* A man can really enjoy sex, but if certain conditions are not met, his penis might not become aroused. Instead of thinking of sex as performance, think about it as play that occurs best when both partners are able to relax.

• FIGURE 6
Squeeze Technique
Two methods of helping a man delay
ejaculation that can be done by the
man's partner or himself are squeeze
technique and start-stop technique

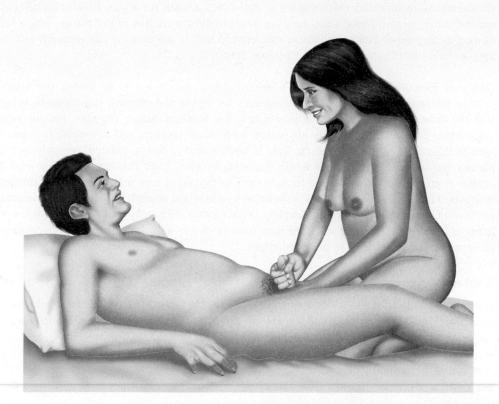

- *During a sexual encounter, you get only one shot at an erection.* Erection changes during a sexual encounter are very common. If an erection subsides during sex, the man shouldn't tense up and decide it is over but instead breathe deeply, keep the faith, and ask the partner to provide stimulation that is sensual.

- *I blew it last time; I will never get it up again.* It's a mistake to overgeneralize from a single sexual episode to a lifetime of erection difficulties. Overgeneralizing can cause stress, sometimes resulting in a self-fulfilling prophecy.

- *If I can't have an erection, my partner can't be sexually satisfied.* Certainly, there are numerous ways of providing sexual stimulation to a partner without an erection. How many people who care about their partners would leave him if he has erection problems? Most would want to help him resolve them.

Early Ejaculation Cognitive-behavioral therapists treat early ejaculation by using initially the same pattern as in treating erection difficulties. They concentrate especially on reducing fears and anxieties and increasing sensate focus and communication. Then they use a simple exercise called the **squeeze technique** (see Figure 6). The penis is brought manually to a full erection and stimulation continues. Just before he is about to ejaculate, his partner squeezes his penis with thumb and forefinger just below the corona. After 30 seconds of inactivity, the partner arouses him again and, just prior to ejaculation, squeezes again. Using this technique, the couple can continue for 15–20 minutes before the man ejaculates.

Some sex therapists suggest that a man can learn ejaculatory control by increasing his ability to extend the plateau phase of his sexual response cycle, largely through learning to delay ejaculation during masturbation. They encourage men to learn their plateau phase well, and when the "point of no return" is reached during masturbation, the man should stop stroking his penis but not cease caressing completely. This "start-stop" technique can be done by the man himself or by a sexual partner. He should also strengthen his P.C. muscle, so that he can squeeze it to delay ejaculation at the point of no return. Then he returns to masturbation and repeats the cycle several times. For a man to learn ejaculatory control, sex therapists recommend masturbation several times a week for about 30–60 minutes per session. After several weeks, many men are able to hold themselves in the plateau phase for as long as they want. Further, if a man can learn to last 15 minutes, he can probably last as long as he'd like (Castleman, 2004; Keesling, 2006).

Delayed Ejaculation One way of treating delayed ejaculation is by having the man's partner manipulate his penis. The partner asks for verbal and physical directions to bring him the most pleasure possible. It may take a few sessions before the man has his first ejaculation. The idea is to identify his partner with sexual pleasure and desire. He is encouraged to relax to keep the P.C. muscle from tightening and to feel stimulated, not only by his partner but also by the partner's erotic responses to him. After the man has experienced orgasm from manual touch, he can then proceed to vaginal or anal intercourse. With further instruction and feedback, the man should be able to function sexually without fear of delayed ejaculation. Sex therapist Barbara Keesling (2006) states, "Ejaculation will happen when it happens," and it will happen when the man focuses on the sensations that allow ejaculation to occur rather than trying to make it happen.

Kaplan: Psychosexual Therapy

Helen Singer Kaplan (1974, 1979; Kaplan & Horwith, 1983) modified Masters and Johnson's behavioral treatment program to include psychosexual therapy. The cognitive-behavioral approach works well for arousal and orgasmic difficulties resulting from mild to midlevel sexual anxieties. But if the person has severe anxieties from intense relationship or psychic conflicts or from childhood sexual abuse, a behavioral approach alone often does not work. Such severe anxieties may manifest themselves in female sexual interest/arousal disorder, male hypoactive sexual desire disorder, and sexual aversion disorder.

Other Nonmedical Approaches

Both cognitive-behavioral and psychosexual therapy are expensive and take a considerable time. Hence, "brief" sex therapy and self-help and group therapy have developed.

PLISSIT Model of Therapy One of the most common approaches used by sex therapists is based on the **PLISSIT model** (Annon, 1974, 1976). PLISSIT is an acronym for the four progressive levels of sex therapy: **p**ermission, **l**imited **i**nformation, **s**pecific **s**uggestions, and **i**ntensive **t**herapy. Most sexual function difficulties can be successfully addressed in the first three levels; only about 10% of patients require extensive therapy.

The first level in the PLISSIT model involves giving permission. At one time or another, most sexual behaviors were prohibited by important figures in our lives. Because desires and activities such as fantasies or masturbation were not validated, we often question their "normality" or "morality." We shroud them in secrecy or drape them with shame. Without permission to be sexual, we may experience sexual difficulties and dissatisfaction. Sex therapists act as "permission givers" for us to be sexual.

The second level involves giving limited information. This information is restricted to the specific area of sexual function difficulties. If a woman has orgasmic difficulties, for example, the therapist might explain that not all women are orgasmic in coitus without additional manual stimulation before, during, or after penetration.

The third level involves making specific suggestions. If permission giving and limited information are not sufficient, the therapist next suggests specific "homework" exercises. For example, if a man experiences early or involuntary ejaculation, the therapist may suggest that he and his partner try the squeeze technique. A woman with orgasm difficulties might be instructed to masturbate with or without her partner to discover the best way for her partner to assist her in experiencing orgasm.

The fourth level involves undergoing intensive therapy. If the individual continues to experience a sexual function problem, he or she will need to enter intensive therapy, such as psychosexual therapy.

Self-Help and Group Therapy The PLISSIT model provides a sound basis for understanding how partners, friends, books, sexuality education films, self-help exercises, and group therapy can be useful in helping us deal with the first three levels of therapy: permission, limited information, and specific suggestions. Partners, friends, books, the Internet, sexuality education films, and group therapy sessions under a therapist's guidance, for example, may provide "permission" for us to engage in sexual exploration and discovery. From these sources, we may learn that many of our sexual fantasies and behaviors are very common.

The first step in dealing with a sexual function difficulty can be to tap your own immediate resources. Begin by discussing the problem with your partner; find out what he or she thinks. Discuss specific strategies that might be useful. Sometimes, simply communicating your feelings and thoughts will resolve the dissatisfaction. Seek out friends with whom you can share your feelings and anxieties. Find out what they think; ask them whether they have had similar experiences and, if so, how they handled them. Try to keep your perspective—and your sense of humor.

Medical Approaches

Sexual function difficulties are often a combination of physical and psychological problems. Even people whose difficulties are physical may develop psychological or relationship problems as they try to cope with their difficulties. Thus treatment for organically based problems may need to include psychological counseling. The combined medical and psychological intervention has several advantages, such as greater treatment efficacy and patient satisfaction (Althof, 2010).

Vaginal pain caused by inadequate lubrication and thinning vaginal walls often occurs as a result of the decreased estrogen associated with menopause. The lack of vaginal lubrication may be misleading, as some women reporting dryness indicate the presence of sexual excitement and arousal. These women often use supplemental lubricants. A lubricating jelly or estrogen cream may help. Vaginitis, endometriosis, and pelvic inflammatory disease may also make intercourse painful. Lubricants or short-term menopausal hormone therapy often resolves difficulties. Loss of sex drive and function, low energy and strength, depressed mood, and low self-esteem may sometimes occur from testosterone deficiency. The sex lives of people with significant testosterone deficiencies, though quite rare, may be helped by testosterone supplements prescribed by physicians.

Most medical and surgical treatments for men have centered on erection difficulties. Such approaches include microsurgery to improve a blood flow problem, suction devices to induce and maintain an erection, a prosthesis implanted in the penis and abdomen, and drugs injected into the penis. Because these methods are not practical or pleasant, they became virtually obsolete with the introduction of an erection-enhancing drug, Viagra, in 1998 by Pfizer. Viagra, the trade name for sildenafil citrate, was the first effective and safe oral drug for the treatment of male erection difficulty, whether caused by psychological or medical conditions. Viagra was originally developed to treat cardiovascular disease. Men using the drug experienced an unplanned side effect: an erection.

In 2003, two other drugs were approved by the FDA for the treatment of erection problems: GlaxoSmithKline and Bayer's Levitra (vardenafil HCl) and Eli Lilly's Cialis (tadalafil). These three drugs are one of the most popular groups of drugs in pharmaceutical industry history. In April 2012, the U.S. Food and Drug Administration approved another erection-enhancing drug, Metuchen Pharmaceuticals' Stendra (avanafil). Among the several benefits of the erection-enhancing drugs is that they are often effective in treating erection difficulties that occur as a result of prostate-cancer treatment and surgery, including complete removal of the prostate (American Cancer Society, 2017.14).

Erection-enhancing drugs allow the muscles in the penis to relax and penile arteries to dilate, thus increasing blood flow and expanding the erectile tissues that squeeze shut the veins in the penis. They are taken before sex; the amount of time the effects last varies depending on the drug. The medications do not increase

"The penis used to have a mind of its own. Not anymore. The erection industry has reconfigured the organ, replacing the finicky original with a more reliable model."

—David Friedman (1949–)

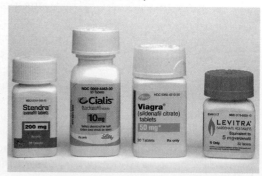

Four prescription drugs—Viagra, Cialis, Stendra, Levitra—have revolutionized the treatment of male erection difficulties.

Studio Works/Alamy

sexual desire, nor do they produce an erection itself; there still must be sexual stimulation. After sex is over, the erection goes away. The primary psychological role of the erection drugs is to eliminate the anticipatory and performance anxiety surrounding intercourse, which will usually, in itself, result in erections and increased confidence. Some men take the drugs as a "quick fix" for a temporary problem or as "insurance," even though they may not really need them. Sometimes the woman's sexual desire, orgasm, and enjoyment decrease when her male partner is having erection problems, but improved for many women when the man begins to uses erection-enhancing drugs. The importance to an erection in relationship satisfaction was examined in an international study of relationships: Among men in stable, long-term relationships and in their 50's, erection difficulties did not necessarily affect overall relationship happiness (Rosen et al., 2016).

The U.S. Food and Drug Administration (FDA) notes that these drugs are safe for most men if used according to the directions, except for men taking nitrates (often prescribed for chest pain) and those having poor cardiovascular health. Headaches, visual disturbances, and flushing sometimes occur, and in rare cases extended and painful erections occur (Ashton, 2007; Reitman, 2004). Some men, including college men who do not need to, are using the erection drugs casually as party drugs or as insurance against the effects of alcohol and for a desired increase in "prowess" (Harte & Meston, 2011). The mixing of street drugs and an erection-enhancing drug is dangerous. And people should never use someone else's erection-enhancing drug; they should always get their own prescription from a doctor.

After rejecting the drug twice for failing to show significant benefits, in 2015 the FDA approved the first prescription drug—flibanserin—designed to boost women's sexual desire (Ungar, 2015). The pill, sold under the brand name Addyi and dubbed as "pink Viagra" or the "little pink pill" was considered to be the biggest breakthrough prescription drug for women's sexual fulfillment since the oral contraceptive. Unlike Viagra and the other male erection-enhancing prescription drugs that increase blood flow to the penis, Addyi alters the woman's brain chemistry by changing the balance of certain brain transmitters like dopamine and serotonin. Addyi is taken daily in contrast to the male erection-enhancing drugs being taken prior to sexual activity. Women must abstain from alcohol. Some of the side effects include low blood pressure, dizziness, drowsiness, and fainting. Alcohol can make these symptoms worse. Addyi must be taken for 4 weeks to be effective, if it works at all. Studies of Addyi involving nearly 6,000 women found that the average benefit from taking the drug was just one half of one satisfying sexual event a month and that it worked for only 8–13% of women who take it. Despite the initial excitement about the drug, the number of prescriptions written for Addyi has been few. The possible side effects, having to take the drug every day, and the need to abstain from alcohol may account for the low sales. Or perhaps women feel like the benefit of Addyi does not make any meaningful difference in their level of desire (Romm, 2015; Thomas & Morgenson, 2016). In 2019, the FDA approved Vyleesi, another prescription drug developed for women low sex drive. This drug was tested on a narrow subset of women and, like Addyi, was minimally effective, with only 8% report improved sexual desire. One difference between Vyleesi and Addyi is that having a few drinks may be safe with Vyleesi. Neither drug makes experiencing having orgasms easier, nor do they necessarily make sex more enjoyable for both partners (National Women's Health Network, 2019).

Some experts caution people not to overrely on medical approaches to solve sexual function difficulties. The erection-enhancing drugs—Viagra, Levitra, Cialis, and Stendra—enable some men suffering from hypertension, diabetes, and prostate problems to get an erection by increasing the flow of blood to the penis, provided there is sexual stimulation. However, the pills do not cure fractured relationships, make people more sensual lovers, enlarge penises, end age-related sexual limits, or address the complexity of all sexual problems (Marshall, 2012; Moynihan & Mintzes, 2010; Reitman, 2004; Slowinski, 2007). One problem with the erection-enhancing drugs is that they reinforce the widespread, but mistaken, belief that an erection equals a satisfying sexual experience for both men and women. It perpetuates the notion, fed by many erotic videos and websites, that sticking an erection into an erotic opening is the only thing sex is about (Castleman, 2004). Sex therapist Marty Klein says that "it's possible to have a rock-hard erection and still have lousy sex" (quoted in

Castleman, 2004). The pills often help individuals postpone or avoid self and couple analysis. Some experts contend that the erection-enhancing pills, and now Addyi, have medicalized sexual problems, resulting in the prevailing medical model that promotes a specific norm of sexual functioning: correct genital performance (Bancroft, 2009; Tiefer, 2001, 2004). Most sexual function difficulties can be resolved through individual and couple therapy. See Practically Speaking "Seeking Professional Assistance." The optimal approach in the use of drugs is in concert with psychotherapy. For example, research has shown that the combined use of erectile medication and couple sex therapy is more effective in treating erection difficulties than the sole use of the medication (Aubin et al., 2009).

Numerous homeopathic products, often known as "natural sexual enhancers," are being sold on the Internet and at health-food stores, convenience stores, and drugstores, promising to "spice up your sex life," "rekindle desire," and "improve sexual performance." Supported by unsubstantiated claims and personal testimonials, these capsules, herbal erection creams, sprays, lubricants, gels, and tonics promise greater sexual arousal and rock-hard erections. These products are not regulated by the U.S. Food and Drug Administration, may or may not contain ingredients listed on the label, and instead may contain ingredients that could be harmful to people, especially those with medical conditions. Conclusive evidence of the effectiveness of the natural sexual enhancers treating male and female sexual function problems has not been established. In short, there aren't any natural "magic bullets" that turn you into an instant, perfect love machine. As suggested throughout this book, enhancing your emotional and physical health, as well as your relationship with your partner, is usually the best path to sexual fulfillment.

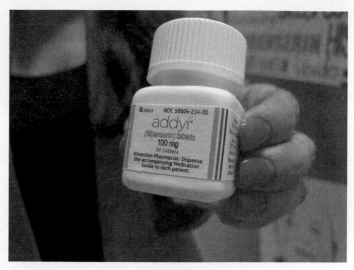

Addyi, the first female drug to enhance women's sexual desire, has been a disappointment to many women, and prescription sales have been low.

Allen G. Breed/AP Images

Lesbian, Gay, Bisexual, Transgender, and Queer+ Sex Therapy

Until recently, sex therapists treated sexual function difficulties as implicitly heterosexual. The model for sexual functioning, in fact, was generally orgasmic heterosexual intercourse. There was little mention of gay, lesbian, bisexual, transgender, or queer sexual concerns.

For LGBTQ+ individuals, sexual issues differ from those of heterosexual people in several ways. First, sexual minority individuals may have arousal, desire, erectile, or

It is important for sexual minority individuals with sexual difficulties to choose a therapist who affirms their orientation and understands the special issues confronting them.

wavebreakmediamicro/123RF

Seeking Professional Assistance

Just because something is not "functioning" according to a therapist's model does not necessarily mean that something is wrong. You need to evaluate your sexuality in terms of your own and your partner's satisfaction and the meanings you give to your sexuality. If, after doing this, you are unable to resolve your sexual function difficulties yourself, seek professional assistance. It is important to realize that seeking such assistance is not a sign of personal weakness or failure. Rather, it is a sign of strength, for it demonstrates an ability to reach out and a willingness to change. It is a sign that you care for your partner, your relationship, and yourself. As you think about therapy, consider the following:

- What are your goals in therapy? Are you willing to make changes in your relationship or personal behavior to achieve your goals?

- Do you want individual, couple, or group therapy? If you are in a relationship, is your partner willing to participate in therapy?

- What characteristics are important for you in a therapist? What gender of therapist do you prefer? Is the therapist's age, religion, sexual orientation, gender identity, or ethnic background important to you?

- What are the therapist's professional qualifications? There are few certified sex therapy programs; most therapists who treat sexual function difficulties come from various professional backgrounds, such as psychiatry, clinical psychology, psychoanalysis, marriage and family counseling, and social work. The American Association of Sexuality Educators, Counselors, and Therapists certifies sex therapists and has a list of licensed certified

persons with contact information, by state and country, on its website (http://www.aasect.org). Because there is no licensing in the field of sex therapy, it is important to seek out those trained therapists who have licenses in their generalized field.

- What is the therapist's approach? Is it behavioral, psychosexual, psychoanalytic, medical, religious, spiritual, feminist, or something else? Do you feel comfortable with the approach?

- If necessary, does the therapist offer a sliding-scale fee, based on your level of income?

- If you are a lesbian, gay, bisexual, transgender, or queer individual, does the therapist affirm your sexual orientation and gender identity? Does the therapist understand the special problems that sexual minorities face?

- After a session or two with the therapist, do you have confidence in that person? If not, discuss your feelings with the therapist. If you believe your dissatisfaction is not a defense mechanism, change therapists.

Most sex therapists believe that their work results in considerable success. Not all problems can be resolved completely, but some—and often great—improvement usually occurs. Short-term therapy of 10 or fewer sessions helps some people, although most require therapy for 4 months or longer (McCarthy & McCarthy, 2009). Much of therapy's success depends on a person's willingness to confront painful feelings and to change. This entails time, effort, and often considerable amounts of money. But ultimately, the difficult work may reward partners with greater satisfaction and a deeper relationship.

---

orgasmic difficulties, the context in which they occur may differ significantly from that of heterosexual individuals (Institute of Medicine, 2011). Problems among heterosexual individuals most often focus on penile-vaginal intercourse, whereas the sexual dissatisfaction among LGBTQ+ persons may focus on other behaviors. Gay men in sex therapy, for example, most often experience aversion toward anal eroticism (Reece, 1988; Sandfort & de Keizer, 2001). Lesbian women in sex therapy frequently complain about aversive feelings toward cunnilingus. Female orgasmic difficulty, however, is not frequently viewed as a problem (Margolies et al., 1988). Heterosexual women, in contrast, frequently complain about lack of sexual desire and orgasm.

Second, lesbian, gay, bisexual, and transgender individuals must deal with both societal homophobia, internalized homophobia and questioning as well as lack of social acceptance. Fear of violence may make it difficult for LGBTQ+ individuals to openly express their affection in the same manner as those who are heterosexual. As a consequence, these individuals learn to repress their expressions of feelings in public; this repression may carry over into the private realm as well. Internalized homophobia may result in diminished sexual desire, creating sexual aversion and fostering guilt and negative feelings about sexual activity.

These unique concerns along with those who identify as gender nonconforming or a sexual minority person require that sex therapists expand their understanding and treatment of

"Impulse arrested spills over, and the flood is feeling, the flood is passion, the flood is even madness: It depends on the force of the current, the height and strength of the barrier. . . . Feeling lurks in that interval of time between desire and its consummation."

—Aldous Huxley (1894–1963)

TABLE 4 ● Strategies to Cope With Sexual Function Difficulties
Explore ways to change the situation
■ One could end the current relationship and seek to begin another, or look for ways to resolve the problem psychologically or medically (e.g., erection-enhancing drugs).
Amend your goals to fit the circumstances
■ One could take a flexible perspective toward the importance of sex by focusing more on other relationship aspects and other priorities.
■ One could lower expectations by accepting a trade-off between having a relationship with a person one loves and experiencing the perfect physical sexual experience. A person could expect to have "good sex" less often.
■ One could adapt flexible definitions of "good-enough" sex by shifting from perceiving excitement as most important to considering intimacy as the most important.
Live with a gap between one's sexual goals and the circumstances
■ One could perceive one's experience as normal and favorably compare one's experience with other persons.
■ One could avoid thinking about the problem, initiating sexual relationships, and experiencing sexual activity.

Source: Adapted from Mitchell, et al. 2001.

sexual function problems. For example, if the therapist is heterosexual, he or she needs to have a thorough knowledge of sexual orientation issues and the special needs of LGBTQ+, and gender nonconforming individuals. Therapists further need to be aware of their own assumptions and internalized feelings about varied sexual orientations and gender identities (Schwartz, 2016).

When Treatment Fails

Biomedical and behavioral interventions are effective for treating some individuals experiencing sexual function difficulties. However, sometimes treatment fails, resulting in individuals having to find ways to cope with and adjust to the difficulties. Little research has been conducted on how to do this. An interview study of 32 individuals living in Portugal and who experienced varied sexual function difficulties was conducted to identify the range of coping responses to their sexual problems (Mitchell et al., 2001). Three broad coping approaches, along with strategies, were identified (see Table 4): changing circumstances to fit goals, changing goals to fit circumstances, and living with a gap between goal and circumstances either by normalizing one's experience or by avoiding the problem.

Final Thoughts

As we consider our sexuality, it is important to realize that sexual function difficulties and dissatisfaction are commonplace. But sex is more than orgasms or certain kinds of activities. Even if we have function difficulties in some areas, there are other areas in which we may be fully sexual. If we have erection or orgasmic problems, we can use our imagination to expand our repertoire of erotic activities. We can touch each other sensually, masturbate alone or with our partner, and caress, kiss, eroticize, and explore our bodies with fingers and tongues. We can enhance our sexuality if we look at sex as the mutual giving and receiving of erotic pleasure, rather than a command performance. By paying attention to our conditions for good sex, maintaining intimacy, being realistic about our expectations, and focusing on our own erotic sensations and those of our partner, we can transform our sexual relationships.

Radius Images/Alamy Stock Photo

Summary

Sexual Function Difficulties: Definitions, Types, and Prevalence

- The line between "normal" sexual functioning and a sexual function difficulty is often not definitive.

- Difficulties in sexual functioning are often called sexual problems, sexual disorders, or *sexual function dissatisfaction.*

- The *Diagnostic and Statistical Manual of Mental Disorders, Fifth Edition (DSM-5)* classifies four types of sexual dysfunctions: sexual desire problems, orgasmic disorders, sexual pain disorders, and substance/medication-induced sexual dysfunction. According to a woman-centered classification system, sexual function difficulties arise from cultural and relational factors, as well as psychological and medical problems.

- A sexual function difficulty can be defined as a disappointment on the part of one or both partners.

- National studies show that many men and women experience, on occasion, sexual function difficulties. Numerous factors, such as personal and relationship problems, aging, personal health, socioeconomic issues, unrealistic expectations, and attitudes toward sexuality, impact sexual functioning.

- *Female sexual interest/arousal problem* is the absence or reduction of sexual thoughts, fantasies, initiation, and receptivity, and absent/reduced arousal and pleasure during sexual activity. This difficulty is frequently associated with problems of experiencing orgasm, pain during sexual activity, low frequency of sexual activity, poor sexual techniques, and relationship problems. Lack of sexual interest is the most common female sexual function difficulty.

- *Male hypoactive sexual desire problem* is the persistence or absence of sexual thoughts, fantasies, and desire for sexual activity. This difficulty may be associated with erectile and/or ejaculatory difficulties.

- *Erectile problem* is the difficulty with erections during partnered sexual activity. Many men experiencing erection difficulties may have low self-esteem, low self-confidence, decreased sexual satisfaction, reduced sexual desire, and a decreased sense of masculinity.

- *Sexual aversion problem* is a consistently phobic response to sexual activities or the idea of such activities.

- *Female orgasmic problem* is the difficulty in experiencing orgasms or reduced intensity of orgasms during sexual activity. Orgasmic difficulties are the second most common female problem treated by therapists.

- *Delayed ejaculation* is inability or difficulty in ejaculating despite adequate sexual stimulation or desire to experience ejaculation.

- *Premature (early) ejaculation* is, according to the *DSM-5,* a pattern of early ejaculation during partnered sexual activity within one minute following vaginal penetration and before the individual desires. Some debate exists on how long intercourse should take place to be classified as having premature/early ejaculation. Early ejaculation is fairly common in the general population.

- *Genito-pelvic/penetration problem* is difficulty related to genital and pelvic pain and vaginal penetration during intercourse. The category represents a total inability to experience vaginal penetration in any circumstance (e.g., intercourse, dildo, gynecological examination, tampon insertion) to being able to easily experience penetration in one situation but not another.

- *Substance/medication-induced sexual problem* is the difficulty in sexual functioning that can occur with intoxication or soon after or during withdrawal of numerous drugs including prescription and illicit/recreational drugs.

Physical Causes of Sexual Function Difficulties and Dissatisfaction

- Health problems such as diabetes and alcoholism can cause erectile difficulties. Some prescription drugs affect sexual responsiveness.

- Coital pain caused by inadequate lubrication and thinning vaginal walls often occurs as a result of decreased estrogen associated with menopause. Lubricants can resolve the difficulties.

Psychological Causes of Sexual Function Difficulties and Dissatisfaction

- Sexual function difficulties may have their origin in any number of psychological causes. The immediate causes of these difficulties lie in the current situation, including fatigue and stress, ineffective sexual behavior, sexual anxieties, and an excessive need to please a partner. Internal conflict caused by religious teachings, guilt, negative learning, and internalized homophobia can contribute to dissatisfaction, as can relationship conflicts.

Sexual Function Enhancement

- Many people and all couples experience sexual function problems and dissatisfaction at one time or another. Differences in sexual desire are the most common complaint among couples. The widespread variability of sexual functioning suggests the "normality" of at least occasional sexual function difficulties.

- *Sexual function enhancement* refers to improving the quality of one's sexual relationship. Sexual function-enhancement programs generally provide accurate information about sexuality, develop communication skills, foster positive attitudes, and increase self-awareness.

Awareness of your own sexual needs is often critical to enhancing your sexuality. Enhancement of sex includes the intensification of arousal.

- There has been a dramatic increase in over-the-counter, natural sexual enhancers, but none have been scientifically shown to be effective.

Treating Sexual Function Difficulties

- Masters and Johnson developed a cognitive-behavioral approach to sexual function difficulties. They relabeled sexual problems as dysfunctions rather than neuroses or diseases, used direct behavior modification practices, and treated couples rather than individuals. Treatment includes *sensate focus* without intercourse, "homework" activities, and finally, "permission" to engage in sexual intercourse. Kaplan's psychosexual therapy program combines behavioral activities with insight therapy.

- The *PLISSIT model* of sex therapy refers to four progressive levels: *p*ermission, *l*imited *i*nformation, *s*pecific *s*uggestions, and *i*ntensive *t*herapy. Individuals and couples can often resolve their sexual function difficulties by talking them over with their partners or friends, reading self-help books, and attending sex therapy groups. If they are unable to resolve their difficulties in these ways, they should consider intensive sex therapy.

- Viagra was introduced in the United States in 1998 and was the first effective and safe oral drug for treatment of male erection difficulty. Subsequently, three other prescription drugs, Levitra, Cialis, and Stendra, have been approved by the U.S. Food and Drug Administration. These drugs do not increase sexual excitement but rather facilitate blood engorgement in the penis.

- In 2015, the FDA approved the first prescription drug designed to boost a woman's sexual desire. The pill, Addyi (the "pink Viagra"), alters a woman's brain chemistry but has been effective for only a minority of women. In 2019, another prescription drug, Vylessi, was approved by FDA to increase sex desire among women but it also has shown mininal effectiveness.

- Some sexuality professionals claim that drug companies have exaggerated and "medicalized" sexual function difficulties to promote sales.

- There are significant concerns for lesbian, gay, bisexual, transgender, and queer persons in sex therapy. For example, the context in which problems occur may differ significantly from that of a heterosexual person; there may be issues revolving around anal eroticism and cunnilingus. Further, they must deal with both societal homophobia, internalized homophobia, and lack of social acceptance.

- In seeking professional assistance for a sexual problem, it is important to realize that seeking help is not a sign of personal weakness or failure but rather a sign of strength.

Questions for Discussion

- Do you think that sexual function difficulties should be determined by a medical group such as the American Psychiatric Association or by what the individual and/or couple decides is dissatisfying?

- If you have been sexual with another person, have you ever experienced sexual function dissatisfaction or difficulty? After reading this chapter, do you think that this experience is actually a "sexual dysfunction" or possibly a dissatisfaction based on an unrealistic expectation of what sex should be like? Did you talk to your partner about the disappointment?

- What do you consider to be a satisfying sexual experience with a partner? Did the information in this chapter cause you to reevaluate what you consider "good sex" for you and a partner?

- If you had a sexual function difficulty, how comfortable would you be in seeking help from a sex therapist?

- If you or your male partner were having difficulties with erections, would you seek prescription drugs—Viagra, Levitra, Cialis, or Stendra—to deal with the problem? Is it possible for a man and his partner to have good sex without an erection?

- If you or your female partner were having difficulties with low sexual desire, would you seek prescription drugs—Addyi or Vyleesi—to deal with the problem.

Sex and the Internet

Sexual Difficulties

The website WebMD provides information on various health issues, including those related to sexual health and sexual functioning difficulties. Go to this site (www.webmd.com) and at the top open the "Living Healthy" box. Then, in the Search box type in various sexual function difficulty terms, like "sexual dysfunction," "erectile dysfunction," and "orgasm problems." Also on that page click the highlighted "Sex and Relationships" and answer the following questions:

- Is the information provided helpful for non-medical people?

- Were you able to find new information about sexual function difficulties?

- What videos or blogs did you find most informative?

Suggested Websites

American Family Physician

http://www.aafp.org

Provides information about both female and male sexual function difficulties.

Cleveland Clinic

http://my.clevelandclinic.org/disorders/sexual_dysfunction/
hic_sexual_dysfunction_in_males.aspx

Provides an overview of sexual dysfunction and a discussion of diseases and medications that affect sexual function.

New View Campaign

http://www.newviewcampaign.org

Promotes an alternative view of female sexual function difficulties, challenges the pharmaceutical industry, and calls for further research on these difficulties.

Women's Sexual Health

http://www.womenssexualhealth.com

Addresses the questions and concerns of women and their partners concerning female sexual function difficulties and includes a "Physician Locator" to help them find local physicians who treat these difficulties.

Suggested Reading

Binik, Y. M., & Hall, K. S. K. (2014). *Principles and practice of sex therapy* (5th ed.). Guilford Press. A multidisciplinary perspective on the causes and treatment of sexual dysfunctions that integrates current research with clinical practice. All chapters are authored by internationally recognized experts.

Brotto, L. (2018). *Better sex through mindfulness: How women can cultivate desire.* Description of research studies and suggested specific exercises focusing on improving desire, arousal, and sexual satisfaction through mindfulness.

Castleman, M. (2004). *Great sex: A man's guide to the secret principles of total-body sex.* Rodale. An exceptionally easy-to-read and practical book for men in which the author quotes well-respected sex therapists throughout the book to show therapists' suggestions for various sexual function problems.

Karp. J. R. (2020). *Sexercise: Exercising Your Way to Better Sex.* Bookbaby Publishers. The text discussed the importance and value of physical fitness and well-being toward fulfilling sexual behavior. Suggestions for specific exercise activities are described and depicted.

Keesling, B. (2006). *Sexual healing: The complete guide to overcoming common sexual problems* (3rd ed.). Hunter House. A greatly expanded edition of the classic book on the healing power of sex that offers more than 125 exercises that help with a wide range of sexual function difficulties.

Klein, M. (2012). *Sexual intelligence: What we really want from sex—and how to get it.* HarperOne. Presents a very sex-positive, realistic, and healthy perspective on enhancing sexual pleasure for individuals and couples.

Kleinplatz, P. J., & Menard, A D. (2020). *Magnificent sex: Lessons from extraordinary lovers.* Routledge. The text describes the components of great sex as identified during interviews of individuals who say that have magnificent sex. These "sexperts" provide insight on how person who are experiencing "oK" or "functional" sex can make more pleasurable and intimate.

McHugh, M. C., & Christian, J. C. (Eds). (2015). *The wrong prescription for women: How medicine and media create a "need" for treatments, drugs, and surgery.* Phaeger. The book addresses aspects of women's lives that have been targeted as "deficient" in order to support the billion-dollar medical-pharmacological industry.

Metz, M. E., & McCarthy, B. W. (2011). *Enduring desire: Your guide to lifelong intimacy.* Routledge. A superb guide on creating and maintaining a satisfying sex life across ages of a long-term relationship.

Nagoski, E. (2015). *Come as you are.* Simon & Schuster Paperbacks. An exploration of why and how women's sexuality works based on research and brain science.

Ogden, G. (2008). *The return of desire: A guide to discovering your sexual passions.* Trumpeter. Written by an experienced sex therapist, this book is a wise guide that focuses on women and enhancing their sexual desire and passion.

Perel, E. (2006). *Mating in captivity.* Harper. Presents a provocative perspective on intimacy and sex in exploring the paradoxical union of domesticity and sexual desire.

Pertot, S. (2007). *When sex drives don't match.* Marlow & Company. Presents 10 libido types and how they affect a couple, along with rational ways for couples to work through differing sex drives.

chapter

15

Sexually Transmitted Infections

Peter Dazeley/Getty Images

CHAPTER OUTLINE

Student Voices

"Up to this date, I have slept with about 13 men. My most recent 'wake-up call' was from a threat from a prospective partner and from a human sexuality course. I took a test for HIV; the result was negative. However, I did get infected and passed on genital warts to my ex-boyfriend. I simply pretended that I had never slept with anyone else and that if anyone had cheated it was him. It never fazed me that I was at such a risk for contracting HIV. My new resolutions are to educate my family, friends, and peers about sex; take a proactive approach toward sex with prospective partners; and discuss sex openly and honestly with my mother."

—23-year-old female

"My partner and I want to use a condom to protect ourselves from STIs. But I feel inadequate when we are intimate and he cannot keep an erection to put a condom on. I feel too embarrassed for him to discuss the situation. So we both walk away a bit disappointed—him because he could not stay erect and me because I did not take the time or have the courage to help him. I think if he masturbated with a condom on it would help him with his performance anxiety problem."

—22-year-old female

"STIs and HIV are precisely the reason I exercise caution when engaging in sexual activity. I don't want to ever get an STI, and I'd rather never have sex again than have HIV."

—24-year-old male

"Why do males often convince women to have sex without proper protection? I don't understand this because there is always a risk of getting an STI. I know that women think about this just as often as men do, but why is it that men do not seem to care?"

—21-year-old female

"I am usually very careful when it comes to my sexual relations and protecting myself from STIs, but there have been a couple of times when I've drunk a lot and have not practiced safe sex. It scares me that I have done things like that and have tried to make sure it doesn't happen again. STIs are just a very uncomfortable subject."

—27-year-old male

"O rose, thou art sick!
The invisible worm
That flies in the night,
In the howling storm,
Has found thy bed
Of crimson joy,
And his dark secret love
Does thy life destroy."

—William Blake (1757–1827)

THE TERM *SEXUALLY TRANSMITTED INFECTIONS* (STIs) refers to more than 30 different bacteria, viruses, and parasites known to be passed from person to person primarily through sexual contact (World Health Organization, 2019). STIs were once called venereal diseases (VDs), a term derived from Venus, the Roman goddess of love. More recently, the term *sexually transmitted diseases* (STDs) replaced *venereal diseases*. Actually, many health professionals continue to use *STD*. However, some believe that *STI* is a more accurate and less judgmental term. That is, a person can be infected with an STI organism but not have developed the illness or disease associated with the organism. So in this book, we use *STI*, although *STD* may appear when other sources are cited.

There are two general types of STIs: (1) those that are bacterial and curable, such as chlamydia and gonorrhea and (2) those that are viral and incurable—but treatable—such as HIV infection and genital herpes. STIs are a serious health problem in our country, resulting in considerable human suffering.

In this chapter and the next, we discuss the **incidence** (number of new cases) and **prevalence** (total number of cases) of STIs in our country, particularly among youth, the disparate impact of STIs on certain population groups, the factors that contribute to the STI epidemic, and the consequences of STIs. We also discuss the incidence, transmission, symptoms, and treatment of the principal STIs that affect Americans, with the exception of HIV/AIDS, which we discuss in a separate chapter. The prevention of STIs, including protective health behaviors, safer sex practices, and communication skills, is also addressed in this chapter.

● The STI Epidemic

The World Health Organization (2019) states that the "STIs have a profound impact on sexual and reproductive health worldwide" and that more than 1 million new STI cases are acquired each day. As you will read in this chapter, the United States faces major challenges in controlling the rate of new STI infections. Actually, the scope, impact, and outcomes of the STIs have long been underestimated. A 1997 Institute of Medicine report characterizes STD [STIs] as "hidden epidemics of tremendous health and economic consequences in the United States" (Eng & Butler, 1997). In 2019, the Centers for Disease and Prevention stated that "since well before this report was published, and two decades later, those facts remain remain unchanged" (CDC, 2019.15a).

STIs: The Most Common Reportable Infectious Diseases

STIs are a substantial health threat facing the United States. Three STIs—chlamydia, gonorrhea, and syphilis—accounted for 2,457,118 cases in 2019, a record high and 100,000 more than in 2017. This increase was attributed to several factors, including a decline in condom use among young persons and men who have sex with men, increased testing among certain groups, and a decrease in funding for sexual health programs and public health clinics (CDC, 2019.15a; Stack, 2019). In the beginning of 2020, the CDC reported that the reported cases of STIs were higher than during the same time period in 2019 and on track to hit a continued record high in the United States. However, the CDC reported in the fall of 2020 that the number of new cases abruptly decreased. Public health officials attributed this downturn on the COVID-19 pandemic. Although some studies have reported that sexual behavior decreased during the pandemic (e.g., Schiavi et al., 2020; Luetke et al., 2020), the CDC believes that STIs are largely being undetected because health care service resources are being directed toward the COVID-19 pandemic, resulting in cutbacks for STI detection, treatment, and prevention services. Furthermore, physicians believe that many persons with STIs may be avoiding clinics for fear of being exposed to COVID-19. When sexual behavior rebounds and if interrupted service resulting from the pandemic continues, the number of new STI and HIV cases could increase (Hoffman, 2020). Jonathan Mermin, former director of the CDC's National Center for HIV/AIDS, Viral Hepatitis, STD, and TB Prevention, has stated that "STDs are a persistent enemy, growing in number, and outpacing our ability to respond" (CDC, 2017.15a). Even with this increase, identifying exactly how many cases there are is impossible, and even estimating the total number is difficult. National CDC surveillance data only captures a fraction of America's STI epidemic.

Often, an STI is "silent"—that is, it goes undiagnosed because it has no early symptoms or the symptoms are ignored and untreated, especially among people with limited access to health care. Asymptomatic infections can be diagnosed through testing, but routine screening programs are not widespread, and social stigmas and the lack of public awareness about STIs may result in no testing during visits to health care professionals. And even when STIs are diagnosed, reporting regulations vary. Only a few STIs—gonorrhea, syphilis, chlamydia, hepatitis A and B, HIV/AIDS, and chancroid—must be reported by health care providers to local or state health departments and to the federal CDC. But no such reporting requirement exists for other common STIs, such as genital herpes, human papillomavirus (HPV), and trichomoniasis. In addition, the reporting of STI diagnoses is inconsistent. For example, some private physicians do not report STI cases to their state health departments. In spite of the underreporting and undiagnosed cases, several significant indicators illustrate the STI problem in the United States:

- STIs are the most commonly reported infectious diseases in the United States. In 2018, STIs represented four of the six most frequently reported infectious diseases (CDC, 2017.15b , 2019.15b) (see Figure 1).

- An estimated 20 million new STI cases occur each year (CDC, 2019.15a).

- STIs impact the lives of more than 110 million men and women across the United States, costing the American health care system nearly $16 billion yearly in direct medical costs alone (CDC, 2017.15d; Owusu-Edusei et al., 2013; CDC, 2019.15a).

- By age 25, one in two young persons will acquire an STI (CDC, 2019.15a).

- More than one half of sexually active men and women will become infected with an STI at some point in their lives (CDC, 2011).

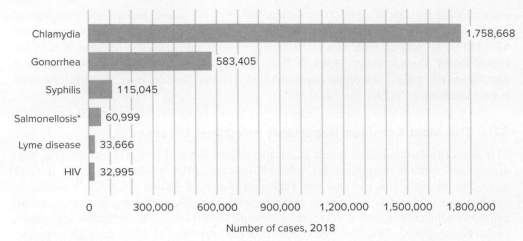

Number of cases, 2018

*Infection with the *Salmonella* bacterium that causes diarrheal illness.

- One in four sexually active adolescent females has an STI, such as chlamydia and human papillomavirus (HPV) (Forhan et al., 2009).
- Nearly every sexually active person will get human papillomavirus some time in their life if they do not get the HPV vaccine (CDC, 2019.15a).

Who Is Affected: Disparities Among Groups

Anyone, regardless of gender, race/ethnicity, social status, sexual orientation, or gender identity, can get an STI. What people do—not who they are—exposes them to the organisms that cause STIs. Nevertheless, some population groups are disproportionately affected by STIs; this disparity reflects gender, age, and racial and ethnic differences.

Gender Disparities   Overall, the consequences of STIs for women often are more serious than those for men. Generally, women contract STIs more easily than men and suffer greater damage to their health and reproductive functioning. STIs often are transmitted more easily from a man to a woman than vice versa. Women's increased likelihood of having an asymptomatic infection results in a delay in diagnosis and treatment (CDC, 2019.15a).

A type of "biological sexism" means that women are biologically more susceptible to infection than men when exposed to an STI organism (Hatcher et al., 2007). A woman's anatomy may increase her susceptibility to STIs. The warm, moist interior of the vagina and uterus is an ideal environment for many organisms. The thin, sensitive skin inside the labia and the mucous membranes lining the vagina may also be more receptive to infectious organisms than the skin covering a man's genitals. The symptoms of STIs in women are often very mild or absent, and STIs are more difficult to diagnose in women due to the physiology of the female reproductive system. The long-term effects of STIs for women may include pelvic inflammatory disease (PID), ectopic pregnancy, infertility, cervical cancer, and chronic pelvic pain, as well as possible severe damage to a fetus or newborn, including spontaneous abortion, stillbirth, low birth weight, neurological damage, and death (CDC, 2017.15d).

Women who have sex with other women and who have sex with both women and men can acquire and transmit STIs. Women can acquire STIs such as herpes, genital warts, and chlamydia when exchanging bodily fluids. Any one-on-one contact, such as oral sex, touching by fingers, mutual vulva rubbing, or using the same hand when touching yourself and then your partner, can put a woman at risk. If two women are both menstruating they are at a higher risk, too. Also, STIs can be transmitted by using contaminated sex toys (National Health Service, 2019). A nationally representative study found the rates of self-reported genital herpes and genital warts to be 15–17% among self-identified bisexual women and 2–7% among self-identified lesbian women, both groups aged 15–44 (Tao, 2008). A nationally representative study of 7,296 women, aged 24–32, found that more than 9 in 10 women reporting having had one or more female partners also reported having had penile-vaginal sex with a man (Lindley et al., 2013). A study of 35 lesbian and bisexual women aged 16–35 found that bacterial vaginosis (BV) was associated with reporting a partner with BV, vaginal lubricant use, and the sharing of sex toys (Marrazzo et al., 2010). Studies have found that women who had sex with both men and women had greater odds of having acquired a bacterial STI and had more HIV/STI behavioral risk factors than women who had sex only with men or women (Bauer et al., 2010; Kaestle & Waller, 2011; Lindley et al., 2013). A case study found that female-to-female transmission of syphilis occurred through oral sex (Campos-Outcalt & Hurwitz, 2002).

Surveillance data on several STIs suggest that an increasing number of men who have sex with men (MSM) are acquiring STIs. For example, in recent years, MSM have accounted for an alarming number of estimated syphilis cases in the United States. In 2014, MSM accounted for 78% of the male primary and secondary syphilis cases (CDC, 2019.15a).

Age Disparities   Compared to older adults, sexually active young adolescents aged 15–19 and young adults aged 20–24 are at higher risk for acquiring an STI. About one half of new STI cases are among individuals aged 15–24, although they comprise only about one quarter of the sexually active population (CDC, 2019.15a; Satterwhite et al., 2013). Young people are at greater risk because they are, for example, more likely to have multiple sexual partners, to engage in risky behavior, to select higher-risk partners, and to face barriers to accessing quality STI prevention products and health services (CDC, 2014.15b; 2017.15d).

Racial and Ethnic Disparities   Race and ethnicity in the United States are STI risk markers that correlate with other basic determinants of health status, such as poverty, access to quality health care, health care–seeking behavior, illegal drug use, and communities with high prevalence of STIs. STI rates are higher among racial and ethnic minorities. (See Figures 2, 3, and 4 for rates of three STIs—chlamydia, gonorrhea, and syphilis —by race/ethnicity, 2018.) Social factors, such as poverty and lack of access to health care, in contrast to inherent factors, account for this discrepancy.

Factors Contributing to the Spread of STIs

According to the National Academy of Medicine, "STDs are behavioral-linked diseases that result from unprotected sex," and behavioral, social, and biological factors contribute to their spread (Eng & Butler, 1997). These factors are obstacles to the control of STIs in the United States.

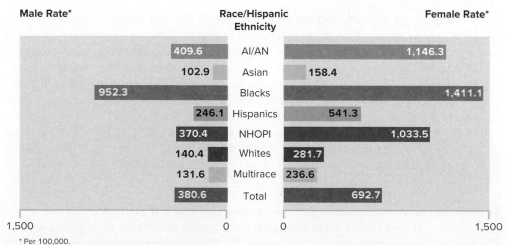

Male Rate*	Race/Hispanic Ethnicity	Female Rate*
409.6	AI/AN	1,146.3
102.9	Asian	158.4
952.3	Blacks	1,411.1
246.1	Hispanics	541.3
370.4	NHOPI	1,033.5
140.4	Whites	281.7
131.6	Multirace	236.6
380.6	Total	692.7

1,500   0   0   1,500

* Per 100,000.
ACRONYMS: AI/AN = American Indians/Alaska Natives;
NHOPI = Native Hawaiians/Other Pacific Islanders.

● FIGURE 2

Rates of Chlamydia by Race/Hispanic Ethnicity and Sex, United States, 2018

Source: CDC, 2019.15a.

• FIGURE 3

**Rates of Gonorrhea by Race/Hispanic
Ethnicity and Sex, United States, 2018**

Source: CDC, 2019.15a.

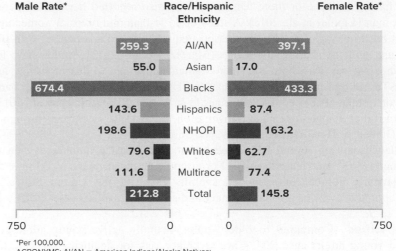

• FIGURE 4

**Rates of Primary and Secondary
Syphilis, United States, 2018**

Source: CDC 2019.15a.

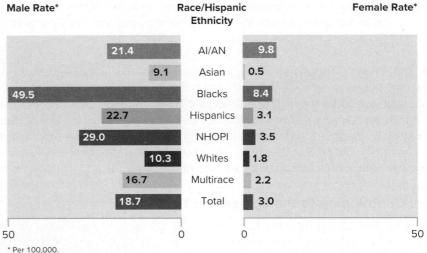

Behavioral Factors

Early Initiation of Intimate Sexual Activity   People who are sexually active at an early
age are at greater risk for STIs because this early initiation increases the total time they are
sexually active and because they are more likely to have nonvoluntary intercourse, to have a
greater number of sexual partners, and to use condoms less consistently (Manlove et al.,
2003). For example, a nationally representative sample of 9,844 respondents found that the
odds of contracting an STI for an 18-year-old who first had intercourse at age 13 were more
than twice those of an 18-year-old who first had intercourse at age 17 (Kaestle et al.,
2005). Another study found nearly the same results: A longitudinal study of students from
public schools in Seattle and a nearby school district found that the rate of diagnosed
STIs for early initiators (less than age 15) was 33% compared to 17% for later initiators
(age 15 or greater) (Epstein et al., 2014).

Sequential Sexual Relationships   The more exclusive sexual partners an individual has
over a period of time (called **serial monogamy**), the greater the chance of acquiring an STI.
For example, according to one national study, 1% of respondents with one sexual partner
within the past year, 4.5% of those with two to four partners, and 5.9% of those with five or

more partners reported that they had become infected with an STI. In addition, the more sexual partners respondents had, the more likely it was that each of those partners was unfamiliar and nonexclusive. Being unfamiliar with partners, especially knowing the person for less than 1 month before first having sex, and having nonexclusive partners were both strongly associated with higher STI incidence (Laumann et al., 1994). Data from the National Survey of Men and the National Survey of Women discovered that the likelihood of contracting an STI increased with an increase in the number of lifetime sexual partners: Compared to persons with 1 partner, those reporting 2 or 3 partners have 5 times the likelihood of having an STI, and the odds are as high as 31 to 1 for those reporting 16 or more lifetime partners (Tanfer et al., 1995). A nationally representative study of women of varied sexual orientations found that women who had 1-5 sexual partners were less likely to report being diagnosed with an STI than those who had 10 or more sexual partners (Lindley et al., 2013).

Short Gap Between Partners The amount of time between partnerships, called the **gap length**, may affect the rate at which STIs spread through populations. The gap length, along with the timeliness of diagnosis and treatment, may impact the chance of STI exposure between infected and uninfected individuals. The duration of infectivity varies among STIs, and symptoms may not always be present. For example, the mean duration of infectivity has been estimated to be as long as about 15 months for chlamydia and as short as 2 months for gonorrhea. Hence, persons having gaps shorter than 15 months may, if infected with chlamydia from an earlier relationship, infect their later partner with chlamydia if there was no diagnosis and treatment (Brunham & Plummer, 1990; Kraut-Becher & Aral, 2003). Research has shown this occurs. A Danish study of individuals aged 15-29 years with diagnosed chlamydia and a random sample of Danes from the general population found a strong association between a short gap length between serially exclusive partners and having a diagnosed chlamydia infection. Half of the participants who engaged in serially exclusive partnerships had a gap length of less than 64 days, which is much shorter than the infectious period of chlamydia (Jorgensen et al., 2015).

Concurrent Sexual Relationships Having **concurrent sexual relationships**—overlapping sexual partnerships—facilitates the spread of STIs. Research has shown that sexual concurrency, along with short gaps between partners, is associated with individual STI risk (Manhart et al., 2002). This risk is especially true during acute HIV infection when transmission is greatest. A nationally representative study of men found that 11% reported concurrent sexual relationships in the past year, mostly involving women. These men were less likely to use a condom during their last sexual encounter; were less likely than those not reporting concurrent sexual partners to be married; and were more likely to report several risk factors, including drug or alcohol intoxication during sexual intercourse, nonmonogamous female and male partners, and sexual intercourse with men (Adimora et al., 2007; Doherty et al., 2009). Among women in a nationally representative study, the prevalence of reported concurrent sexual relationships was 12%, with lowest concurrency being among those currently married (Adimora et al., 2002). The same Danish study reported above not only found a short gap length between partnerships but also revealed concurrent partnerships, showing the importance of these two risk factors: gap length and concurrent relationships. Further, about half of the individuals with two or more partners in the last year (36% of young adults) reported concurrency (Jorgensen et al., 2015).

High-Risk Sexual Partners Having sexual intercourse with a person who has had many partners increases the risk of acquiring an STI. One example of this is a female who has a bisexual male partner. Often, the female does not know that her male partner also has sex with men. Another example is when an older, sexually experienced person has sex with a younger and less experienced partner (Boyer et al., 2000; Thurman et al., 2009). Also, a survey of 1,515 men aged 18-35 attending health centers found that those who had purchased sex were twice as likely to be infected with an STI than those who had not purchased sex (Decker et al., 2008). People often select new sexual partners from their social network. If a person acquires an STI, then the social network could be considered a high-prevalence group, thus increasing a person's chance of future STI infections (Adimora & Shoenbach, 2013). Research has shown that selecting new partners from outside one's social network is associated with reduced risk for repeat STIs (Ellen et al., 2006).

High-Risk Sexual Behavior   Certain sexual behaviors such as having numerous and high-risk partners, anal sex, and condomless sex put individuals at higher risk for acquiring an STI than other behaviors. For example, a study of 1,084 heterosexual men and women patients at an STI clinic found that individuals who had ever engaged in anal intercourse were more likely to report a history of having had an STI (Gorbach et al., 2009). A comprehensive review of data of the HIV epidemic in men who have sex with men showed that the high probability of HIV transmission per each episode of receptive anal intercourse has a central role in explaining the disproportionate disease burden among MSM (Beyer et al., 2012). A study of women in the rural southern United States found that those who reported engaging in more high-risk behaviors in the past 12 months were more likely to report having an STI during the same time (Yarber et al., 2000).

Inconsistent and Incorrect Condom Use   Correctly using a latex male condom during each sexual encounter and at any time the penis comes into contact with the partner significantly reduces the risk of STIs. Several studies have shown that both correct and consistent condom use are associated with lower STI rates in both men and women and lower rates of pelvic inflammatory disease (PID) outcomes in women (Crosby & Bounse, 2012; Hutchinson et al., 2007; Nielson et al., 2010; Wald et al., 2005). See Think about It "Preventing STIs: The Role of Male Condoms, Female Condoms, and Dental Dams."

Substance Abuse   The abuse of alcohol and drugs is associated with high-risk sexual behavior, although researchers are not certain if there is a cause-and-effect relationship between alcohol/drug use and risky sexual behavior. Substances may affect cognitive and negotiating skills before and during sex, lowering the likelihood that partners will protect themselves from STIs and pregnancy (U.S. Department of Health and Human Services, 2011.15a). A review of 11 studies of problem drinking and STIs showed an overall association between problematic alcohol use and STI infection (Cook & Clark, 2005).

Another review of 29 studies found that alcohol use was significantly associated with casual sexual relationships and experiences (Claxton, DeLuca, & Manfred, 2015) and a study of young Croatian adults reported associations between condom-use errors and problems and alcohol or drug use (Bacak & Stulhofer, 2012). A strong, positive relationship was found among 7,414 undergraduates at 14 public California universities between frequency of attendance at fraternity or sorority parties, residence-hall parties, and off-campus parties and the occurrence of alcohol-related sexual behavior with a stranger (Bersamin et al., 2012).

Sexual Coercion   Not all persons enter sexual relationships as willing partners, particularly women. The 2019 Youth Risk Behavior Survey of students grades 9–12 revealed that among the 66% of students nationwide who dated or went out with someone, 14% of females and 4% of males had been forced to kiss, and had been touched or physically forced to have sexual intercourse that they did not want one or more times during the 12 months before the survey. Seventeen percent of females and 5% of males reported sexual violence by anyone of which 50% were a dating partner (Basile et al., 2020). Individuals experiencing sexual violence are less able to protect themselves from STIs.

Lack of Knowledge of and Concern About STIs   With increased STI information on the Internet and in school health classes, most persons have some fundamental knowledge of STIs and the potential for acquiring an STI through risk behavior. However, there are gaps in knowledge among some persons. A study of 300 sexually active adolescent females, some of whom had received an STI diagnosis and were recruited from health care sites, concluded that they knew more about their previous STI than about other STIs, including ones they had unknowingly contracted. That is, they appeared to learn about STIs mainly after an STI diagnosis, too late for effective prevention behavior, early medical detection, or prompt

Preventing STIs: The Role of Male Condoms, Female Condoms, and Dental Dams

For decades, the male condom has been promoted by public health officials as an important STI prevention device for sexually active individuals. However, there has been much discussion about how effective condoms really are in preventing HIV and other STIs. Some skeptics argue that condoms fail too often and that claims of condom effectiveness are misleading and exaggerated. Public opinion surveys show otherwise. For example, despite these claims and denunciations by skeptics, a random telephone survey of 517 Indiana residents found that nearly 92% considered condoms at least somewhat effective in preventing HIV and STIs (Yarber et al., 2005).

The Centers for Disease Control and Prevention (CDC) has issued statements and recommendations on male condoms, female condoms, and STI prevention for public health personnel.

Male Condoms

The CDC (2013) recommendations about male latex condoms and the prevention of STIs, including HIV, are based on information about the ways the various STIs are transmitted, the physical nature of condoms, the coverage or protection that condoms provide, and epidemiological studies of condom use and individual STIs. Laboratory studies have shown that latex condoms provide an effective barrier against the STIs; they are essentially impermeable barriers to particles the size of HIV and other STI pathogens. And epidemiologic studies that compare rates of HIV infection between condom users and nonusers who have HIV-infected sex partners demonstrate that consistent condom use is highly effective in preventing transmission of HIV. Further, epidemiologic research has shown that condom use reduces the risk of many other STIs. CDC states that "Overall, the preponderance of available epidemiological studies have found that when used consistently and correctly, condoms are highly effective in preventing the sexual transmission of HIV infection and reduce the risk of other STDs."

Inconsistent use can lead to STI acquisition because transmission can occur with a single episode of sexual intercourse with an infected partner. Similarly, if condoms are not used correctly, the protective effect may be diminished even when they are used consistently.

Condoms can be expected to provide different levels of protection for various STIs depending on how the diseases are transmitted. In addressing specific STIs, the CDC has stated that latex condoms, when used consistently and correctly, are highly effective in preventing the sexual transmission of HIV and reducing the risk of transmission of gonorrhea, chlamydia, and trichomoniasis. Correct and consistent use of latex condoms reduces the risk of genital herpes, syphilis, and chancroid only when the infected area or site of potential exposure is protected. Genital ulcer diseases and human papillomavirus (HPV) infections can occur in all gender genital areas that are covered or protected by a latex condom, as well as areas that are not covered. Condom use may reduce the risk for HPV infection and HPV-associated diseases such as genital warts and cervical cancer. Three other nonlatex condoms are available. Polyurethane (plastic) or polyisoprene (synthetic rubber) condoms provide protection against STIs and are good options for people with latex allergies. The other type is natural membrane condoms, which are not recommended for protection against STIs (CDC, 2013).

Internal Condoms

Internal condoms, also called female condoms, are thin pouches made of a synthetic latex product called nitrile. When worn in the vagina, female condoms are just as effective as male condoms at preventing STIs, HIV, and pregnancy. Internal condoms can also be used for anal sex. Research has shown that HIV cannot travel through the nitrile barrier. It is safe to use any kind of lubricant with nitrile female condoms. Some men who have sex with men use the internal condom for anal sex; however, there is very little research on the efficacy of the internal condom for STD prevention among MSM (National Health Service, 2018).

Dental Dams

Dental dams are latex or polyurethane sheets used between the mouth and the vagina or anus during oral sex and can reduce the risk of STI and HIV transmission. Ready-to-use dental dams can be purchased online. A latex condom can also be cut length-wise and used like a dental dam (CDC, 2016).

disease treatment (Downs et al., 2006). Further, a review of 55 research articles focusing on barriers to HPV vaccination initiation and completion among U.S. adolescents found that some underserved and disadvantaged youth had limited knowledge about HPV and HPV vaccination. The researchers concluded that their limited knowledge is an impediment to more adolescents taking advantage of the HPV vaccination (Holman et al., 2014). To learn about the results of a national study of selected STI knowledge and attitudes, see Think About It, "Are Persons Knowledgeable about STIs and Worried They Might Become Infected? Results of a National Study."

Are Persons Knowledgeable about STIs and Worried They Might Become Infected? Results of a National Study

"And he died in the year fourteen-twenty. Of the syphilis, which he had a-plenty."

—Francois Rabelais (1490–1553)

To protect themselves and their partners, persons who are sexually active need to have knowledge about the wide range of sexually transmitted infections, their prevalence, and the ways they are transmitted and prevented. Recall from the beginning of this chapter we stated that the sexually transmitted infections are a serious health problem in the United States with the rates of three STIs—chlamydia, gonorrhea, and syphilis—continuing to increase each year reaching record rates in 2018. Half of all persons in the United States will become infected with an STI in their lifetime. Correct knowledge about the STIs is a key component in avoiding STIs.

The Kaiser Family Foundation conducted a poll of selected STI knowledge and attitudes from a nationally representative probability-based sample of 1,215 adults ages 18 and over, living in the United States (Kirzinger et al., 2020). Interviews were administered online and by telephone from December 20th to December 30th, 2019, in English and Spanish. The margin of sampling error for the full sample is plus or minus three percentage points. Here are key findings:

Know of the Severity of STIs. About two thirds of the public did not know how common STIs are among adults in the United States. Only 36% know that STIs had become more prevalent in the past 10 years; 26% said that the STIs had stayed about the same or become less common among adults in the United States. Only 13% were aware that half of the population will acquire an STI other than HIV or AIDS at some point in their lives. Thirty-seven percent and 21% believed that 1 out of every 10 and 1 out of every 100, respectively, would get an HIV infection in their lifetime. Just one half were aware that being infected with an STI increases one's chance of becoming infected with HIV.

Know Someone Who Had an STI. Slightly over one half (54%) of the respondents indicated that they personally know someone, including themselves, who has been diagnosed with an STI. Fifty-eight percent and one half of women and men, respectively, said they know someone who ever had an STI. Younger age groups were more likely to know someone compared to older adults: 18–29-year-olds, 54%; 30–49-year-olds, 63%; 50–64-year-olds, 57%; 65 and older, 36%.

Worried They Will Contract an STI New During the Next Year. Only 8% are worried that they personally will acquire a new STI sometime in the next year. Larger proportions (20%) of young adults (ages 18–29) indicated being worried which is consistent with CDC data that this age group has the highest STI risk. Rates of STIs are higher among Black adults and Hispanic adults than in white adults. Thirteen percent of both Black and Hispanic adults indicated that they were worried about contracting an STI compared to 5% of white adults.

Felt Comfortable Talking About STIs and Sexual Health. The vast majority of adults said they are very comfortable or somewhat comfortable talking about STIs with their doctor or health care provider (84%) or sexual partner(s) (75%). Sixty-seven percent and 61% were comfortable talking about STIs with their close friends or family, respectively. A greater proportion of women than men indicated that they were comfortable talking about STIs with their close friends (71% vs. 61%, respectively) and about their sexual health (62% vs. 52%).

Are Aware STIs Are Often Asymptomatic Yet Transmissible. Ninety-six percent knew that STIs are transmissible to a partner even if there are no symptoms and that some people have an STI but do not know it. Nearly 9 of 10 (87%) knew that an STI can be transmitted from a mother to her unborn child during pregnancy or childbirth. Nine of 10 knew that some people with an STI may not display symptoms for years after being infected.

Know Whether Certain Common STIs are Curable or Not. Many of the participants were unsure about whether many STIs can be cured with medication or not. Slightly over half knew that gonorrhea and chlamydia are curable with medication (56% and 54%, respectively) but that genital herpes is not curable with medication (54%). Forty-five percent were aware that syphilis is curable with medication but about half (51%) were unsure if HPV is curable or not with medication.

In summary, the findings found that most of the participants were unaware of how prevalent STIs are and what proportions of people would get an STI in their lifetime. This helps explain why only about 1 in 10 indicated that they were worried about getting an STI. The vast majority knew that STIs can be transmitted even if symptoms are present, yet the lack of complete knowledge was revealed in that about half did not know if certain STIs were curable or not. The nearly total sample indicated that they felt comfortable about talking about STIs and sexual health with a partner and health care provider, which is a valuable skill toward preventing STI transmission and acquisition.

Think Critically

1. Were any of the findings surprising to you? If so, in what way?
2. How would you have answered the questions?
3. If you were an STI prevention educator, what would you emphasize based on this study's findings?

think
about it

Accurately Judging If a Potential Sexual Partner Is Infected with an STI: Easily Done?

Knowing whether a possible sexual partner might be infected with an STI can be tricky. Thus, this strategy of avoiding sexually transmitted infections is often unreliable. Certainly you would want to avoid sexual contact with someone at high risk for having an STI, such as an individual who has had numerous or concurrent partners and/or who uses high-risk drugs, including alcohol. Of course, the surest way to discover if a partner has an STI is to visit a health care provider and get medical tests together. However, some people don't do that because they believe they can, for example, accurately judge if a partner is infected by looking at the person, by assessing his or her reputation, or from what the person disclosed about his/her sexual past. Let's see what research shows about how accurate that approach is:

- A study of STI clinic patients found that many used partner attributes and relationship characteristics, such as family, trust, or knowledge of partner's sexual history, as an index of evaluating partner safety. In this case, their assessments were inaccurate when compared to their partner's self-reported risk (Masaro et al., 2008).

- College students' evaluation of different vignettes found that vignette partners who were described as being familiar were judged to be at lower risk for STI transmission, as well as more trustworthy and appealing sexually and romantically. The researchers concluded that partner familiarity can be established relatively quickly and that it impacts perceptions of new partners despite knowing little about their sexual history (Sparling & Cramer, 2015).

- A study of college students found that about 60% had, at some point, acted deceptively in their reported number of prior sexual partners, and of those, nearly one fifth never disclosed their number of previous sexual partners. Students who reported omitting their number of prior sexual partners from all sexual partners reported being the least comfortable with safer sex communication (Horan, 2015). Of those who did disclose the number of past sexual partners, about one in six of both men and women stated a lower number of past partners to their significant one. Interestingly, the Match.com *Singles in America* study of 5,675 singles aged 18 to over 70 found that 57% of participants did not want to know how many sexual partners their significant other has had (Bernstein, 2015).

- A study of heterosexual couples attending outpatient clinics found that 10% of women and 12% of men were unaware that their partner had recently received an STI diagnosis. Two percent were unaware that their partner was HIV-positive (Witte et al., 2010).

- Sexual delay discounting (i.e., disregarding the value of post-poning sexual behavior and/or risk prevention) as an STI risk factor was assessed among college students using vignettes. The students indicated that they were less likely to use an immediately available condom and less likely to wait to engage in condom-protected sex when partners are perceived as more desirable and less likely to have an STI. Males were less likely to use an immediately available condom and less likely to wait to engage in condom-protected sex relative to females under these same circumstances. Additionally, risky sexual behavior is particularly likely when the partner is viewed as very sexually attractive (Collado et al., 2017).

- A study of the effects of probability of contracting HIV/AIDS and other STIs, and partner desirability on likelihood of hypothetical condom-protected sex vignettes among undergraduate college students found that as odds against contracting an STI increased (i.e., risk of contracting an STI decreased), the reported likelihood of condom-protected sex generally decreased. Greater discounting of the need for condom-protected sex was indicated for less severe STIs (chlamydia, genital herpes) relative to a more severe STI (HIV/AIDS) or an unspecified STI. Condom-protected sex was discounted more when the potential partner was more rather than less desirable based on appearance and especially so when the STI type was less severe. Lastly, women reported a higher likelihood of condom-protected sex within the chlamydia and genital herpes hypothetical conditions (Berry et al., 2019).

Ideally, the decision of whether a potential sexual partner may have an STI infection should be based on accurate information such as STI test results. As illustrated here, some persons use strategies for assessing a sexual partner's STI status that lead to faulty judgment and, hence, place them at increased risk for acquiring an STI. As mentioned above, the surest strategy is for both persons to seek and share medical assessments.

Think Critically

1. Did any of the research findings cited here surprise you? Explain.

2. If you have ever been sexual with another person, did you try to judge if he/she was infected with an STI by any of the partner traits described above? If so, what were the traits you relied on and was your judgment accurate?

3. If you have been sexual with another person, were you deceptive in representing the number of any past sexual partners? If so, why were you deceptive? And why do you think some persons underreport the number of past sexual partners?

4. If you have sexual partners in the future, do you believe that the results of the studies presented here will impact how you will assess if a potential partner is infected with an STI? Explain.

It is important for persons who are sexually active to have knowledge about the wide range of STIs and the ways they are transmitted and prevented.

Image Source/Getty Images

Erroneous Perception of Partner's STI Status People also often do not have an adequate perception of whether or not their sexual partner has been diagnosed with an STI. Many rely on unreliable strategies, such as judging if a partner is disease-free by their appearance, character, how familiar the person is, and sexual history, for example (Bird et al., 2017). These methods are not reliable. See Think About It, "Accurately Judging If a Potential Partner Is Infected with an STI: Easily Done?" to learn what research has found about these nonmedical assumptions.

Social Factors

Poverty and Marginalization Individuals in lower socio-economic groups and those in social networks in which high-risk behavior is common and access to health care is limited are disproportionately affected by STIs. These groups include sex workers (people who exchange sex for money, drugs, or other goods), adolescents, persons living in poverty, migrant workers, incarcerated individuals, and some racial minorities. STIs, substance abuse, and sex work are closely connected (Adimora & Shoenbach, 2013; Eng & Butler, 1997). Analysis of nationally representative data of adults aged 18–27 found that contextual conditions were associated with prevalence and recent contraction of STIs. As the number of contextual conditions increased, STI prevalence similarly increased. Conditions associated with STIs included housing insecurity, exposure to crime, having been arrested, gang participation, childhood sexual abuse, frequent alcohol use, and depression (Buffardi, 2008). Other factors that result in STI disparities among certain population groups are limitations related to income, employment, insurance coverage, and educational attainment, many of which lead to poverty. Persons who cannot afford basic necessities often have difficulty accessing and affording quality health care, including sexual health services (CDC, 2019.15a; Kirkcaldy et al., 2016).

Access to Health Care and Condoms Access to high-quality and culturally sensitive health care is imperative for early detection, treatment, and prevention counseling for STIs. Unfortunately, health services for STIs are limited in many low-income areas where STIs are common, and funds for public health programs are scarce. Without such programs, many people in high-risk social networks have no access to STI care. Even when health care is available to racial and ethnic minority populations, fear and distrust of health care institutions can negatively affect the health care seeking experience. Social and cultural discrimination, language barriers, provide bias, or the perception that these may exist, likely discourage some persons from seeking care. Further, the quality of health care can substantially differ for minority groups (CDC, 2019.15a). Many young persons do not have access to condoms for numerous reasons. For example, many adults and organizations do not support condom availability or work to make them available to teenagers fearing that would encourage teen sexual behavior; hence, for teens getting condoms is often difficult or impossible. In a revolutionary decision, on October 5, 2020, the Vermont state legislature became the first state to pass a law, effective July 1, 2021, to make free condoms available in all public middle and high schools (Best, 2020.)

Secrecy and Moral Conflict About Sexuality One factor that separates the United States from other countries with lower rates of STIs is the cultural stigma associated with STIs and our general discomfort with sexuality issues. Historically, a moralistic, judgmental stance on STIs has hindered public health efforts to control STIs. For example, significant funding for AIDS research did not begin until it was clear that heterosexual individuals as well as gay men were threatened (Altman, 1985; Shilts, 1987).

Biological Factors

Asymptomatic Nature of STIs   Most STIs either do not produce any symptoms or cause symptoms so mild that they go unnoticed or disregarded. A longtime lag—sometimes years—often exists between the contracting of an STI and the onset of significant health problems. During the time in which the STI is asymptomatic, a person can unknowingly infect others. The individual may not seek treatment, allowing the STI to damage the reproductive system.

Resistance to Treatment or Lack of a Cure   Because resistant strains of viruses, bacteria, and other pathogens are continually developing, antibiotics that have worked in the past may no longer be effective in treating STIs. Infected people may continue to transmit the STI, either because they believe they have been cured or because they currently show no symptoms. And some STIs, such as genital herpes, genital warts, and HIV, cannot be cured but can be treated. The individual who has any of these viruses is always theoretically able to transmit them to others.

Susceptibility in Women   Adolescent women are highly susceptible to acquiring chlamydia and gonorrhea because of an immature cervix (ASHA, 1998b). Women who practice vaginal douching are also at greater risk for pelvic inflammatory disease (PID) and STIs. The vagina is a self-contained environment that is designed to clean itself (CDC, 2014; Steward, 2014).

Circumcision   In recent years, an increasing research attention has been given to determine whether or not male penile circumcision could protect against HIV infection and other STIs. From a biological perspective, protection is plausible since the foreskin of the penis can be a portal for entry of pathogens. Circumcision of foreskin decreases the number of target cells for pathogens to infect, eliminates an environment that favors pathogen survival and replication, and reduces the possibility for micro-abrasions occurring during sexual intercourse that allow for the entry of pathogens into the body. However, the protective value of circumcision against other STIs may be less than the circumcision impact on HIV infection as STIs other than HIV are transmitted more effectively through sexual behaviors besides anal intercourse (e. g., syphilis transmission can occur via intimate skin-to-skin contact), thereby reducing the protective effect of circumcision (Yuan et al., 2019).

Much of the research related to HIV and STI prevention and circumcision are from randomized clinical trials conducted among men in sub-Saharan Africa in regions with high rates of heterosexually acquired HIV infection. In the United States, the prevalence of HIV and lifetime risk of HIV infection are generally much lower than that in sub-Saharan Africa. Also, most new HIV infections in the United States are attributed to male-male sexual contact.

The CDC (2017.15d, 2018) has examined the available scientific evidence on the benefits and health risks associated with medically performed male circumcision and has made summary statements whether circumcision reduces the risk of HIV and STI acquisition or transmission applicable for men and women in the United States:

- Male circumcision reduces, but not eliminates, the risk of men acquiring HIV and other STIs during penile-vaginal sex. Particularly, uncircumcised heterosexual men living in areas with high HIV prevalence are likely to experience the most risk-reduction benefit from elective male circumcision.

- Results from observational studies indicate that among MSM who practice mainly or exclusively insertive anal sex, circumcision was associated with a decreased risk of acquiring a new HIV infection and other STIs for the insertive partner; however, clinical trials have not included sufficient sample sizes of MSM necessary to make a definitive conclusion.

- Male circumcision has not been shown to reduce the risk of HIV during receptive anal sex.

STI Attitude Scale

What one believes about STIs, how one feels about STIs, and one's intention to behave in a particular way influence STI risk-related behavior. The STI Attitude Scale was developed to measure the attitudes of young adults to determine whether they may be predisposed to high or low risk for contracting a sexually transmitted infection. The scale presented here is an updated version of the originally published scale. Follow the directions, and mark your responses to the statements below. Then calculate your risk as indicated.

Directions

Read each statement carefully. Indicate your first reaction by writing the abbreviation that corresponds to your answer.

Key

SA = Strongly agree
A = Agree
U = Undecided
D = Disagree
SD = Strongly disagree

1. How I express my sexuality has nothing to do with STIs.
2. It is easy to use the prevention methods that reduce my chances of getting an STI.
3. Responsible sex is one of the best ways of reducing the risk of STIs.
4. Getting early medical care is the main key to preventing the harmful effects of STIs.
5. Choosing the right sexual partner is important in reducing my risk of getting an STI.
6. A high prevalence of STIs should be a concern for all people.
7. If I have an STI, I have a duty to get my sexual partners to seek medical treatment.
8. The best way to get my sexual partner to STI treatment is to take him or her to the doctor with me.
9. Changing my sexual behaviors is necessary once the presence of an STI is known.
10. I would dislike having to follow the medical steps for treating an STI.
11. If I were sexually active, I would feel uneasy doing things before and after sex to prevent getting an STI.
12. If I were sexually active, it would be insulting if a sexual partner suggested we use a condom to avoid getting an STI.

13. I dislike talking about STIs with my peers.
14. I would be uncertain about going to the doctor unless I was sure I really had an STI.
15. I would feel that I should take my sexual partner with me to a clinic if I thought I had an STI.
16. It would be embarrassing to discuss STIs with my sexual partner if I were sexually active.
17. If I were to have sex, the chance of getting an STI makes me uneasy about having sex with more than one partner.
18. I like the idea of sexual abstinence (not having sex) as the best way of avoiding STIs.
19. If I had an STI, I would cooperate with public health workers to find the source of my infection.
20. If I had an STI, I would avoid exposing others while I was being treated.
21. I would have regular STI checkups if I were having sex with more than one partner.
22. I intend to look for STI signs before deciding to have sex with anyone.
23. I will limit my sexual activity to just one partner because of the chances of getting an STI.
24. I will avoid sexual contact anytime I think there is even a slight chance of getting an STI.
25. The chance of getting an STI will not stop me from having sex.
26. If I had a chance, I would support community efforts to control STIs.
27. I would be willing to work with others to make people aware of STI problems in my town.

Scoring

Calculate points as follows:

Items 1, 10–14, 16, and 25: Strongly agree = 5, Agree = 4, Undecided = 3, Disagree = 2, Strongly disagree = 1
Items 2–9, 15, 17–24, 26, and 27: Strongly Agree = 1, Agree = 2, Undecided = 3, Disagree = 4, Strongly disagree = 5

The higher the score, the stronger the attitude that may predispose a person toward risky sexual behaviors. You may also calculate your points within three subscales: Items 1–9 represent the "belief subscale," items 10–18 the "feeling subscale," and items 19–27 the "intention to act" subscale.

Source: Adapted from Yarber, W. L., et al. 1989.

- The effect of male circumcision on reducing the risk of HIV and STI transmission during oral sex has not been evaluated.

- Male circumcision has not been shown to reduce the risk of HIV transmission to female partners. However, research has shown that medically performed male circumcision reduced the prevalence of STIs such as genital herpes, vaginitis, syphilis, and bacterial vaginosis among female partners. Male circumcision has been shown to reduce the risk of genital herpes, syphilis, HPV in adult males, and urinary tract infections in children and adult males.

- Evidence benefits of circumcision among bisexual men are inconclusive.

- During adulthood, uncircumcised males are more likely than circumcised males to experience invasive penile cancer.

CDC (2017.15d, 2019.15a) states that the benefits and risk of elective neonatal, adolescent, or adult medically performed male circumcision should be considered in consultation with medical providers while taking into account factors, including religion, societal norms and social customs, hygiene, aesthetic preference, and ethical considerations. Health care providers should provide information to sexually active adolescent and adult males regardless of circumcision status. Further, all sexually active adolescent and adult males should consider using other proven HIV and STI risk-reduction strategies such as reducing the number of partners, correct and consistent use of male latex condoms, and HIV pre-exposure or post-exposure prophylaxis.

The American Academy of Pediatrics (AAP) (2012) states that the preventive benefits of elective male circumcision of male newborns, including prevention of penile cancers, urinary tract infections, genital ulcer disease, and HIV, outweigh the risks of the procedure. The AAP recommends that newborn male circumcision should be made available to families that desire it. Male circumcision of newborn male children has considerably lower complications than when performed later in life.

Consequences of STIs

The list of problems caused by STIs seems almost endless. Women and infants suffer more serious health damage than men from all STIs. Without medical attention, some STIs can lead to blindness, cancer, heart disease, infertility, ectopic pregnancy, miscarriage, and even death (CDC, 2014.15b).

People who have STIs are more likely to get HIV, when compared to people who do not have STIs. In the United States, people who get syphilis, gonorrhea, and herpes often also have HIV or are more likely to get HIV in the future. This is because the same behaviors and circumstances that may put you at risk for getting an STI can also put you at greater risk for getting HIV. Further, having a sore or break in the skin from an STI may allow HIV to more easily enter your body (CDC, 2019.15a).

Besides having human costs, the estimated cost of STI treatment within the U.S. health care system is almost $16 billion every year. This cost does not include indirect, nonmedical costs such as lost wages and productivity due to illness, out-of-pocket expenses, and costs related to STI transmission to infants (CDC, 2017.15d; Owusu-Edusei et al., 2013).

● Principal Bacterial STIs

In this section, we discuss chlamydia, gonorrhea, urethritis, and syphilis, the major bacterial STIs. As indicated earlier, bacterial STIs are curable. Table 1 summarizes information about all of the principal STIs, including bacterial STIs, viral STIs, vaginal infections, other STIs, and **ectoparasitic infestations** (parasites that live on the outer skin surfaces).

TABLE 1 ● Principal Sexually Transmitted Infections

STI and Infecting Organism	Symptoms	Time from Exposure to Occurrence	Medical Treatment	Comments
Bacterial STIs				
Chlamydia (*Chlamydia trachomatis*)	*Women:* Usually are asymptomatic; others may have abnormal vaginal discharge or pain with urination. *Men:* About one half asymptomatic; others may have discharge from penis, burning or itching around urethral opening, or persistent low fever.	7–21 days, but symptoms may not develop for several weeks.	Antibiotics	If untreated, may lead to pelvic inflammatory disease (PID) and subsequent infertility in women. Sexually active females younger than 25 and older women with risk factors need testing every year.
Gonorrhea (*Neisseria gonorrhoeae*)	*Women:* Most are asymptomatic; others may have symptoms similar to bladder or vaginal infection. *Men:* Many asymptomatic; others may have itching, burning or pain with urination discharge from penis ("drip").	*Women:* Often no noticeable symptoms. *Men:* Usually 2–5 days, but possibly 30 days or more.	Antibiotics	If untreated, may lead to pelvic inflammatory disease (PID) and subsequent infertility mainly in women. People with gonorrhea can more easily contract HIV.
Urethritis (various organisms)	Painful and/or frequent urination; discharge from penis; women may be asymptomatic. Can have discharge from vagina and penis, and painful urination. Many have no symptoms.	1–3 weeks.	Antibiotics	Laboratory testing is important to determine appropriate treatment. Untreated urethritis can lead to infertility in all genders.
Syphilis (*Treponema pallidum*)	*Stage 1:* Red, painless sore (chancre) at bacterium's point of entry. *Stage 2:* Skin rash over body, including palms of hands and soles of feet. *Stage 3:* No visible signs or symptoms.	*Stage 1:* 10–90 days (average 21 days). *Stage 2:* 6 weeks after chancre appears. *Stage 3:* Within past 12 months or later.	Antibiotics	Easily cured, but untreated syphilis can lead to damage of internal organs. There is a two- to fivefold increase of acquiring HIV when already infected with syphilis.
Viral STIs				
Human immunodeficiency virus (HIV) infection and AIDS	Possible flulike symptoms but often no symptoms during early phase. Variety of later symptoms, including weight loss, persistent fever, night sweats, diarrhea, swollen lymph nodes, bruise-like rash, persistent cough.	Several months to several years.	No cure available, although new treatment drugs have improved the health and lengthened the lives of many HIV-infected individuals.	HIV infection is usually diagnosed by tests for antibodies against HIV. A person who takes HIV medicine as prescribed and becomes virally suppressed, or undetectable, has no risk of transmitting HIV to others.
Genital herpes (herpes simplex virus)	Small sore or itchy bumps on genitals or rectum, becoming blisters that may rupture, forming painful sores; flulike symptoms with first outbreak. Symptoms may go unnoticed or mistaken for another skin condition.	Between 2 and 12 days after exposure.	No cure, although antiviral medications can relieve pain, shorten and prevent outbreaks, and reduce transmission to partners when medication is taken.	Virus remains in body, and outbreaks of contagious sores may recur. Symptoms of recurrent outbreaks are most noticeable in first year and decrease in frequency over time.
Genital human papillomavirus infection (HPV) (group of viruses)	Over 40 HPV sexually transmitted types, including genital warts, infect the genitals, rectum, mouth, and throat.	Most people with genital HPV infection do not know they are infected; some get visible genital warts. In 90% of cases, the body clears HPV naturally within 2 years.	Visible genital warts can be removed by patient or health care provider with prescribed medication.	Some HPV types can cause cervical cancer. HPV usually disappears on its own without causing health problems. Most people who have sex acquire HPV at some time in their lifetime. Vaccines protect girls and women against genital warts and cervical, anal, vaginal, and vulvar cancers and boys and men against genital warts and certain cancers.

STI and Infecting Organism	Symptoms	Time from Exposure to Occurrence	Medical Treatment	Comments
Viral hepatitis (hepatitis A or B virus)	Fatigue, diarrhea, nausea, abdominal pain, jaundice, darkened urine due to impaired liver function.	1–3 months.	No medical treatment available; rest and fluids are prescribed until disease runs its course.	Hepatitis B is more commonly spread through sexual contact. Both A and B can be prevented by vaccinations.
Vaginal Infections				
Vaginitis (*Candidiasis, Trichomonas vaginalis,* or *bacterial vaginosis*)	Intense itching of vagina and/or vulva, unusual discharge with foul or fishy odor, painful intercourse. Men who carry organisms may be asymptomatic.	Within a few days up to 4 weeks.	Depends on organism; oral, topical, and vaginal medications are available. Self-diagnosis not recommended.	Not always acquired sexually. Other causes include stress, birth control pills, pregnancy, tight pants or underwear, antibiotics, douching, vaginal products, and poor diet.
Ectoparasitic Infestations				
Pubic lice, crabs (*Pediculosis pubis*)	Itching, blue and gray spots, and insects or nits (eggs) in pubic area; some people may have no symptoms.	Hatching of eggs in 6–10 days.	Creams, lotions, or shampoos—both over-the-counter and prescription.	Avoid sexual contact with people having unusual spots or insects or nits in the genital area. Also avoid contaminated clothing, sheets, and towels.

Chlamydia

The most common bacterial STI and most commonly reported infectious disease (see Figure 5)) in the United States are caused by an organism call *Chlamydia trachomatis,* commonly called chlamydia. In 2018, 1,758,668 cases of chlamydia were reported to CDC from 50 states and the District of Columbia to the rate of 540 per 100,000 people, more likely an estimated 2.86 million infections occur annually. A large number of cases are not reported because most people with chlamydia are asymptomatic and do not seek testing, or because many may not recognize the symptoms associated with the infection. The rate of per 100,000 population from 2000 to 2018 has dramatically increased (see Figure 5). Substantial racial/ethnic disparities in chlamydial infection exist, with prevalence among non-Hispanic Blacks being 5.6 times the prevalence among non-Hispanic whites (CDC, 2019.15a).

Chlamydia is so common in young women that, by age 30, 50% of sexually experienced women show evidence that they had chlamydia sometime during their lives, and an estimated 1 in 20 sexually active women aged 14–29 has chlamydia (Torrone et al., 2014) (see Figure 6). Women who develop the infection three or more times have as great as a 75% chance of becoming infertile. Pelvic inflammatory disease (PID) occurs in 10–15% of

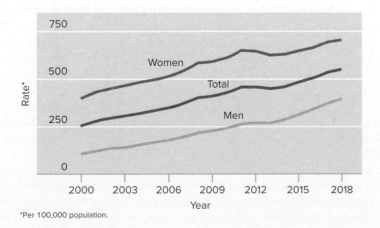

• FIGURE 5

Chlamydia—Rates of Reported Cases by Sex, United States, 2000–2018

Source: CDC, 2019.15a.

Chlamydia—Rates of Reported Cases by Age Group and Sex, United States, 2018

Source: CDC 2019.15a.

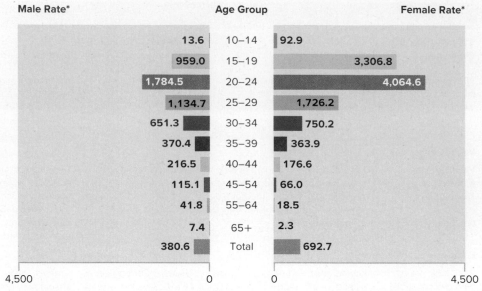

Male Rate*	Age Group	Female Rate*
13.6	10–14	92.9
959.0	15–19	3,306.8
1,784.5	20–24	4,064.6
1,134.7	25–29	1,726.2
651.3	30–34	750.2
370.4	35–39	363.9
216.5	40–44	176.6
115.1	45–54	66.0
41.8	55–64	18.5
7.4	65+	2.3
380.6	Total	692.7

4,500   0   0   4,500

* Per 100,000 population.

women with untreated chlamydia. Actually, chlamydia infection is the strongest risk factor for PID (Hay et al., 2016). Also, research shows that women infected with chlamydia have a five times greater chance of acquiring HIV if exposed (CDC, 2017.15i). Untreated chlamydia can be quite painful and can lead to conditions requiring hospitalization, including reactive arthritis. Infants of mothers infected with chlamydia may develop dangerous eye, ear, and lung infections.

Any sexually active person can become infected with chlamydia. This is particularly true for adolescent girls and young women since their cervix is not fully matured and is probably more susceptible to infection. Chlamydia can be transmitted during unprotected vaginal, anal, or oral sex from someone who has chlamydia and from an infected mother to her baby during vaginal childbirth. Men who have sex with men are at risk for chlamydial infections, since chlamydia can be transmitted during oral or anal sex. If the sex partner is male, one can still get chlamydia even if he does not ejaculate. Chlamydia is known as the "silent disease." Surveys estimate that only about 10% of men and 5–30% of women with laboratory confirmed chlamydia infection develop symptoms. In those persons who develop symptoms, they may not appear until several weeks after exposure (CDC, 2017.15i).

When early symptoms occur in women, they are likely to include unusual vaginal discharge, a burning sensation when urinating, frequent urination, and unexplained vaginal bleeding between menstrual periods. Later symptoms, when the infection spreads from the cervix to the fallopian tubes, are low abdominal pain, low back pain, bleeding between menstrual periods, a low-grade fever, and pain during intercourse. One third to one half of men are asymptomatic when first infected. Men's symptoms may include unusual discharge from the penis, a burning sensation when urinating, itching and burning around the urethral opening (urethritis), pain and swelling of the testicles, and a low-grade fever. The last two symptoms may indicate the presence of chlamydia-related **epididymitis**, inflammation of the epididymis. Untreated epididymitis can lead to infertility. Rectal pain, discharge, or bleeding may occur in men or women who acquired chlamydia during receptive anal intercourse. Chlamydia can be cured with antibiotics. A study of 3,076 men who have sex with men that was conducted in London HIV clinics found that the prevalence of chlamydia in the rectum was 8% and in the urethra 5%. HIV and rectal chlamydia coinfection was 38% (Annan et al., 2009). Chlamydia can also be found in the throats of men and women engaging in oral sex with an infected person (CDC, 2019).

Little is known about whether chlamydia can be transmitted between women or how often it occurs in women who have sex with women (WSW). A sample of African American WSW who reported a lifetime history of sex only with women was matched with a group of women reporting having sex with both men and women (WSWM). One third of the women (33%) who exclusively had sex with women in their lifetime were positive with chlamydia, a significant lower percentage than 69% for WSWM. The researchers speculated that chlamydia may be less transmissible via sexual behaviors of exclusive WSW (i.e., receptive oral sex, digital vaginal sex, use of sex toys) versus women having penile-vaginal sex with men (Muzny et al., 2015).

The CDC recommends yearly chlamydia testing for all sexually active women aged 25 and younger, older women with risk factors (new sex partner, multiple sex partners, or sex partner who has an STI), and all pregnant women. Sexually active men who have sex with men who had insertive intercourse should be screened for urethral chlamydia infection and MSM who had receptive intercourse should be screened for rectal infection at least annually. Screening for pharyngeal infection is not recommended. Repeat infection with chlamydia is common. One should be tested 3 months after treatment, even if the sexual partner was treated. Two types of laboratory tests can be used to detect chlamydia. One kind tests a urine sample; another tests fluid from a man's penis or a woman's cervix. A Pap smear does not test for chlamydia (CDC, 2017.15i). Chlamydia can easily be cured by antibiotics (CDC, 2017, 2019).

Gonorrhea infection in men is often characterized by a discharge from the penis. The discharge is gathered for medical examination by a cotton swab.

Dr P. Marazzi/Science Source

Gonorrhea

In 2018, a total of 583,405 cases of gonorrhea were reported to the CDC, making it the second most common notifiable condition in the United States. Rates of reported gonorrhea have increased 82.6% since the historic low in 2009 (see Figure 7). During 2014-2018, the rate among males increased 78.7% (from 119.1 to 212.8 cases per 100,000 males) and the rate among females increased 45.2% (from 100.4 to 145.8 cases per 100,000 females). The higher case rate among men and women and the magnitude of recent increases suggest either increased transmission or increased screening, or both. In 2018, rates of reported gonorrhea cases continued to be highest among adolescents and young adults: for females, the highest rates were among those aged 20-24 followed by those 15-19 years, and for males, the highest rates were those ages 20-24 years followed by those ages 25-29 years (see Figure 8). Data suggests that men who have sex with men are disproportionately affected by gonorrhea (CDC, 2019.15a).

Popularly referred to as "the clap" or "the drip," gonorrhea is caused by the *Neisseria gonorrhoeae* bacterium. The organism thrives in the warm, moist environment provided by the mucous membranes lining the mouth, throat, vagina, cervix, urethra, and rectum. Gonorrhea is transmitted through sexual contact with the penis, mouth, or anus of an infected person. Ejaculation does not have to occur for gonorrhea to be transmitted or acquired.

Men tend to experience the symptoms of gonorrhea more readily than women, notably as a watery discharge ("drip") from the penis, the first sign of urethritis. (*Gonorrhea* is from the Greek, meaning "flow of seed.") Some men infected with gonorrhea may have no symptoms at all. Other men have signs and symptoms that appear 1-14 days after infection. But symptoms can take as long as 30 days to appear (CDC, 2011.15c). Besides a watery discharge, symptoms in men may include itching or burning at the urethral opening and pain when urinating.

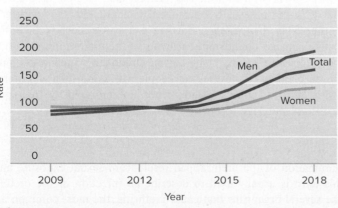

*Per 100,000 population.

• FIGURE 7

Gonorrhea—Rates of Reported Cases by Sex, United States, 2009–2018

Source: CDC 2019.15a.

• FIGURE 8

Gonorrhea—Rates of Reported Cases by Age Group and Sex, United States, 2018

Source: CDC 2019.15a.

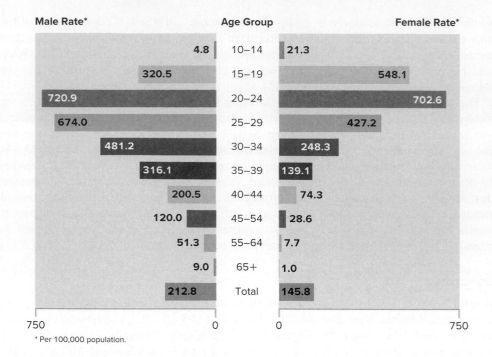

Male Rate*	Age Group	Female Rate*
4.8	10–14	21.3
320.5	15–19	548.1
720.9	20–24	702.6
674.0	25–29	427.2
481.2	30–34	248.3
316.1	35–39	139.1
200.5	40–44	74.3
120.0	45–54	28.6
51.3	55–64	7.7
9.0	65+	1.0
212.8	Total	145.8

750   0   0   750

* Per 100,000 population.

If untreated, the disease soon produces other symptoms, such as thick yellow or greenish discharge, increasing discomfort or pain with urination, and painful or swollen testicles.

Up to 80% of women with gonorrhea show no symptoms or very mild symptoms, which they tend to ignore or are mistaken for a bladder or vaginal infection. Because untreated gonorrhea, like untreated chlamydia, can lead to PID, it is important for sexually active women to be on guard for symptoms and to be treated if they think they may have been exposed to gonorrhea (e.g., if they have had numerous sexual partners). Symptoms a woman may experience include thick yellow or white vaginal discharge that might be bloody, a burning sensation when urinating, unusual pain during menstruation, and severe lower abdominal pain. Both females and males may have mucous discharge from the anus, blood and pus in feces, irritation of the anus, and mild sore throat.

Gonorrhea is curable with several antibiotics. However, drug-resistant strains of gonorrhea are increasing in many parts of the United States and the world, making successful treatment more difficult. In 2018, more than half of all infections were estimated to be resistant to at least one antibiotic. Drug resistance occurs when a strain of bacteria evolves to resist medical treatment until none of the treatments are effective, leaving this so-called "superbug" untreatable. For some strains of gonorrhea, there are no alternative treatments. Continued efforts to discover new drugs against "superbugs" are ongoing (CDC, 2017.15d, 2019.15a).

The CDC recommends yearly gonorrhea screening for all sexually active women younger than 25, as well as older women with risk factors such as new or multiple sex partners, or a sex partner who has a sexually transmitted infection. Persons with gonorrhea should be tested for other STIs. Untreated gonorrhea can cause sterility in both sexes, ectopic pregnancy, prostate damage, epididymitis, scarring of the urethra in men, and testicular pain. Gonorrhea may be passed to an infant during childbirth, causing conjunctivitis (an eye infection) and even blindness if not treated. People with gonorrhea can more easily contract HIV. People with HIV infection and gonorrhea are more likely than people with HIV infection alone to transmit HIV to others (CDC, 2017.15j, 2019.15a).

Urethritis

Urethritis, inflammation of the urethra, can result from sexual exposure and noninfectious conditions. This term is usually used to describe an infection of the urethra caused by an STI. Among the several organisms that cause urethritis, the most common and most serious is chlamydia. Infections of the urethra that are not caused by gonorrhea are sometimes

I had the honor
To receive, worse luck!
From a certain empress
A boiling hot piss."

—Frederick the Great (1712–1786)

referred to as **nongonococcal urethritis (NGU)** which is the focus here (Terris, 2018). Gonorrhea is discussed in the prior section. The diagnosis of NGU occurs more frequently in men, largely due to their anatomy. In men, urethritis may produce a burning sensation when urinating, burning or itching around the opening of the penis, white or yellowish discharge from the penis, and underwear stain. Women are likely to be asymptomatic. They may not realize they are infected until a male partner is diagnosed. If a woman does have symptoms, they are likely to include itching or burning while urinating and unusual vaginal discharge.

It is important to have a laboratory test for an unusual discharge from the penis or vagina so that the appropriate antibiotic can be prescribed. Antibiotics are usually effective against NGU. Untreated NGU may result in permanent damage to the reproductive organs of both men and women and problems in pregnancy. The organisms that cause NGU in men may cause other infections in women, such as cervicitis, which is discussed later in this chapter (CDC, 2014.15i).

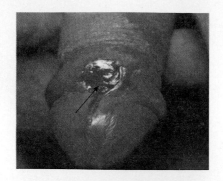

Syphilis

Syphilis, a genital ulcerated disease, is caused by the bacterium *Treponema pallidum*. In 2018, 115,045 cases of syphilis were reported in the United States, including 35,063 cases of primary and secondary (P&S) syphilis, the most infectious stages of the disease. Since reaching a historic low in 2000 and 2001, the rate of P&S syphilis has increased almost every year, increasing 14.9% during 2017–2018. Rates increased among both males and females, in all regions of the United States, and among all racial/ Hispanic ethnicity groups.

Since 2000, rates of P&S syphilis have increased among men, primarily attributable to increases in cases among MSM. Similar to past years, in 2018, MSM accounted for the majority (53.5%) of all reported cases of P&S syphilis (see Figure 9) and, of these, 41.6% were known to be living with diagnosed HIV. There is an estimated two- to five-fold increased risk of acquiring HIV if exposed to that infection when syphilis is present. Although rates of P&S syphilis are lower among women, rates have increased substantially in recent years, increasing 30% during 2017–2018 and 172.7% during 2014–2018, suggesting a rapidly growing heterosexual epidemic. Figure 10 shows rates of reported primary and secondary syphilis cases by age group and sex in the United States in 2018.

Treponema pallidum is a spiral-shaped bacterium (a spirochete) that requires a warm, moist environment such as the genitals or the mucous membranes inside the mouth to survive. It is spread by direct contact with a syphilis sore during vaginal, anal, and oral sexual behavior. Syphilis cannot be spread through contact with toilet seats, doorknobs, swimming pools, hot

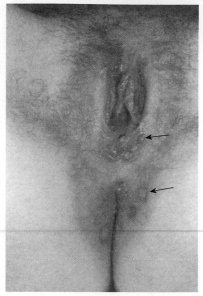

The first symptom of syphilis is a red, pea-sized bump called a chancre at the site where the bacterium originally entered the body as shown by the arrows above.

(first) SPL/Science Source; (second) Centers for Disease Control

● **FIGURE 9**

Primary and Secondary Syphilis— Distribution of Cases by Sex and Sex of Sex Partners, United States, 2018

Source: CDC, 2019.15a.

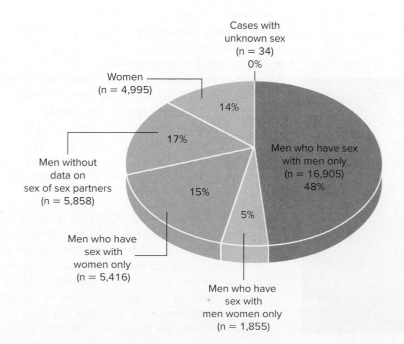

Cases with unknown sex (n = 34) 0%

Women (n = 4,995) 14%

Men without data on sex of sex partners (n = 5,858) 17%

Men who have sex with women only (n = 5,416) 15%

Men who have sex with men women only (n = 1,855) 5%

Men who have sex with men only (n = 16,905) 48%

• FIGURE 10

Primary and Secondary Syphilis—Rates of Reported Cases by Age Group and Sex, United States, 2018

Source: CDC, 2019.15a.

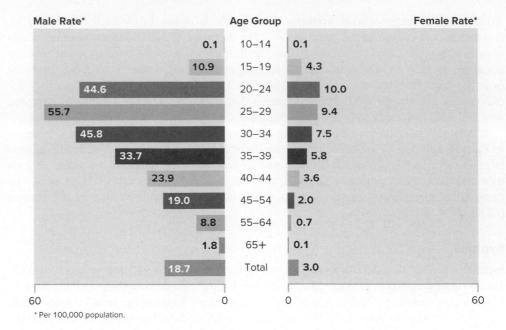

Male Rate*	Age Group	Female Rate*
0.1	10–14	0.1
10.9	15–19	4.3
44.6	20–24	10.0
55.7	25–29	9.4
45.8	30–34	7.5
33.7	35–39	5.8
23.9	40–44	3.6
19.0	45–54	2.0
8.8	55–64	0.7
1.8	65+	0.1
18.7	Total	3.0

* Per 100,000 population.

tubs, bathtubs, shared clothing, or eating utensils. The syphilis bacterium of an infected mother can infect the baby during the pregnancy. Depending on how long the woman has been infected, she may have a high risk of having a stillborn baby or giving birth to a baby who dies soon after birth. An infected baby may be born and not have any signs or symptoms, but if not treated immediately the baby may develop serious health problems within a few weeks. Untreated infants may become developmentally delayed, have seizures, or die. Untreated syphilis in adults may lead to brain damage, heart disease, blindness, and death.

The 2013 rate of congenital syphilis (9.2 cases per 100,000 live births) marked the first increase in congenital syphilis since 2008. Congenital syphilis means that syphilis was acquired by the fetus in the uterus before birth. Since 2013, the rate of congenital syphilis has increased each year. In 2018, 1,306 cases of congenital syphilis were reported. The national rate of 33.1 cases per 100,000 live births in 2018 represents a 39.7% increase relative to 2017 and a 185.3% increase relative to 2014. During 2017–2018 the number of syphilitic stillbirths increased (from 64 to 78 stillbirths), as did the number of congenital syphilis-related infant deaths (from 13 to 16 deaths) (CDC, 2019.15a).

Syphilis has often been called "the great pretender," since many of its signs and symptoms are indistinguishable from those of other diseases. However, many people infected with syphilis do not have any symptoms for years but remain at risk for complications if they are not treated. Although transmission can more easily occur from individuals with sores who are in the primary and secondary stages, many of these sores are unrecognized or hidden. Thus, transmission may occur from people who are unaware of their infection. Syphilis typically progresses through three discrete stages that can last weeks, months, or even years. Syphilis is most often treated during the first two:

Skin rash is a common symptom of untreated syphilis that appears about 6 weeks once the chancre has disappeared.

CDC/Susan Lindsley

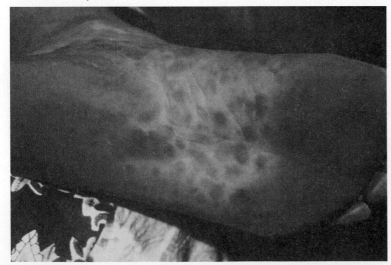

- *Stage 1: Primary syphilis.* The first symptom of syphilis appears from 10 to 90 days (average 21 days) after contact with an infected partner. It is a small, red, pea-sized bump that soon develops into a round, painless sore called a **chancre** (SHANK-er). The person's lymph nodes may also be swollen. The chancre may appear on the labia, the shaft of the penis, the testicles, or the rectum; within the vagina;

think
about it

The Tuskegee Syphilis Study: A Tragedy of Race and Medicine

"The Tuskegee study is perhaps the most enduring wound in American health science."

—Vann R. Newkirk, II (1990–)

In 1932 in Macon County, Alabama, the U.S. Public Health Service, with the assistance of the Tuskegee Institute, a prestigious Black college, recruited 600 African American men to participate in an experiment involving the effects of untreated syphilis on Blacks. Of this group, 399 men had been diagnosed with syphilis and 201 were controls. The study was originally meant to last 6–9 months, but "the drive to satisfy scientific curiosity resulted in a 40-year experiment that followed the men to 'end point' (autopsy)" (Thomas & Quinn, 1991). The history of this experiment—the racial biases that created it, the cynicism that fueled it, and the callousness that allowed it to continue—is chillingly chronicled by James Jones (1993) in *Bad Blood: The Tuskegee Syphilis Experiment* and

Susan Reverby (2009) in *Examining Tuskegee: The Infamous Syphilis Study and Its Legacy.*

The purpose of the study was to determine if there were racial differences in the developmental course of syphilis. The racial prejudice behind this motivation may seem hard to fathom today, yet, as we shall see, the repercussions still reverberate strongly through African American communities (Ross et al., 2006).

Much of the original funding for the study came from the Julius Rosenwald Foundation (a philanthropic organization dedicated to improving conditions within African American communities), with the understanding that treatment was to be a part of the study. Although Alabama law required prompt treatment of diagnosed venereal diseases, the state Public Health Service managed to ensure that treatment was withheld from the participants. Even after 1951, when penicillin became the standard treatment for syphilis, the Public Health Service refused to treat

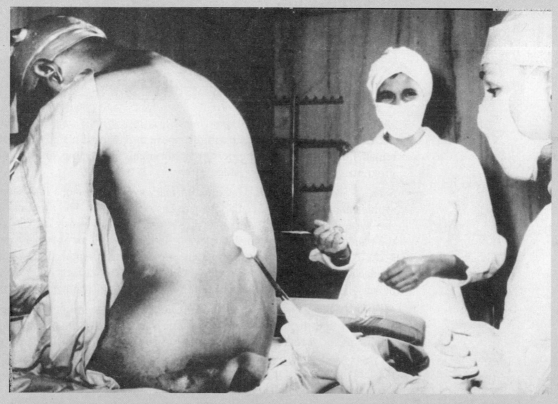

Blood being drawn from an African American man, one of the participants of the Tuskegee Syphilis Study. All participants were told they were being treated for "bad blood."

The National Archives

the Tuskegee "subjects" on the grounds that the experiment was a "never-again-to-be-repeated opportunity" (Jones, 1993).

The Tuskegee participants were never informed that they had syphilis. The Public Health Service, assuming they would not understand medical terminology, referred to it as "bad blood," a term used to describe a variety of ailments in the rural South. The participants were not told their disease was sexually transmitted, nor were they told it could be passed from mother to fetus.

It was not until 1966 that anyone within the public health system expressed any moral concern over the study. A congressional subcommittee headed by Senator Edward Kennedy began hearings in 1973. The results included the rewriting of the Department of Health, Education, and Welfare's regulations on the use of human subjects in scientific experiments. A $1.8-billion class-action suit was filed on behalf of the Tuskegee participants and their heirs. A settlement of $10 million was reached out of court. Each survivor received $37,500 in damages, and the heirs of the deceased each received $15,000. Also, a congressionally mandated program, the Tuskegee Health Benefit Program, provides comprehensive lifetime medical benefits to the affected widows and offspring of participants in the Tuskegee syphilis study (Reverby, 2009).

Current public health efforts to control the spread of HIV infection, AIDS, and other STIs raise the specter of genocide and beliefs of conspiracy among many members of the African American community. Research on African American people living in the United States has found that a significant proportion of respondents endorsed HIV/AIDS conspiracy beliefs; that is, HIV/AIDS was created by the federal government to kill and wipe out African Americans. Black medical patients consistently indicate they have less trust in their physicians and the medical system and are less likely to report positive experiences in health care settings (Newkirk II, 2016). Among African American men, stronger conspiracy beliefs were significantly associated with negative attitudes about condoms and lower likelihood of condom use (Bogart et al., 2011; Hutchinson et al., 2007).

The distrust of medicine has continued into the present during COVID-19 pandemic. While COVID-19 has disproportionately affected Black communities, research shows that Black individuals are the least likely to desire to use a vaccine. Researchers have had difficulty getting Black persons to volunteer for vaccine development trials. One tenant of a predominately Black public housing complex said "I won't be used as a guinea pig for white people" (quoted in Hoffman, 2020, p. A1). A Pew Research Group poll conducted in Fall 2020 found that just 32% of Black adults say they would definitely or probably get a COVID-19 vaccine, compared with 52% of white adults (Hoffman, 2020). The stance reflects present mistrust and a long history of medical abuse that includes the Tuskegee study. Jamil Bey, head of the UrbanKind Institute, a Pittsburgh nonprofit organization, stated that "It's not the science we distrust; it's the scientists" (quoted in Hoffman, 2020, p. A6). On both physiological and psychological levels, there is much healing to be done. Even though it is unthinkable that such a study would be done today, efforts must still be made to ensure that all people are protected against such tragedies.

For reflections on the legacy of the Tuskegee study, see Caplan (1992), Jones (1993), King (1992), and Reverby (2009). Several Internet sites provide further information about this terrible experiment, including the transcript of President Clinton's 1997 formal apology to study participants.

Think Critically

1. Is it possible for another medical experiment like the Tuskegee syphilis study to happen in America today? Explain your view.
2. What can be done to prevent another Tuskegee syphilis study?
3. What can the medical and scientific community do to gain the trust of all Americans?

within the mouth; or on the lips. Unless it is in a visible area, it may not be noticed. Without treatment, it will disappear in 3–6 weeks, but the bacterium remains in the body and the person is still highly contagious and the disease progresses to the secondary stage.

- *Stage 2: Secondary syphilis.* Untreated primary syphilis develops into secondary syphilis about 6 weeks after the chancre has disappeared. The principal symptom at this stage is a skin rash that neither itches nor hurts. The rash is likely to occur on the palms of the hands and the soles of the feet, as well as on other areas of the body. The individual may also experience fever, swollen lymph nodes, patchy hair loss, headaches, weight loss, muscle aches, and fatigue. The rash or other symptoms may be very mild or may pass unnoticed. The person is still contagious.

- *Stage 3: Latency.* If secondary syphilis is not treated, the symptoms disappear within 2–6 weeks and the latent stage begins. The infected person may experience no further symptoms for years or perhaps never. After about a year, the bacterium can no longer be spread to sex partners, although a pregnant woman can still transmit the disease to her fetus. The late stages of syphilis can develop in about 15% of people who have not been treated for syphilis and can appear 10–30 years after infection was acquired. In the late stages, damage may occur many years later in internal organs, such as the brain, nerves, eyes, heart, blood vessels, liver, bones, and joints. Damage could also include difficulty coordinating muscle movements, paralysis, numbness, gradual blindness, dementia, and even death.

In the primary, secondary, and early latent stages, syphilis can be successfully treated with antibiotics. There is an estimated two- to fivefold increase in the chances of acquiring HIV if exposed to that infection when syphilis is present (CDC, 2017.15k).

● Principal Viral STIs

There are four principal viral STIs—HIV and AIDS, genital herpes, human papillomavirus infection, and hepatitis. Recall that diseases caused by viruses are treatable but not curable.

HIV and AIDS

On June 5, 1981, the U.S. government published a report warning about a rare disease, eventually named acquired immunodeficiency syndrome, or AIDS (CDC, 1981.15a). Since that time, this disease has become an enormous public health challenge nationally and globally. Human immunodeficiency virus (HIV)—the virus that causes AIDS—and AIDS have claimed millions of lives worldwide, becoming one of the deadliest epidemics in human history. Despite advances in medical testing and treatment and prevention efforts, HIV/AIDS remains a significant public health problem. Because of its major global impact and continued medical and prevention challenge, we devote a separate chapter to HIV and AIDS.

Genital Herpes

Genital herpes is a common STI in the United States caused by **herpes simplex virus (HSV)** type 1 (HSV-1) and type 2 (HSV-2). In the past, it was thought that any herpes infection affecting the mouth or lips was HSV-1, while HSV-2 occurred largely below the waist primarily in the genital area. No longer is that believed; either type of HSV can cause cold sores or genital herpes as noted below (Grimes, 2014). The CDC (2019.15a) estimates that 776,000 people in the United States get new genital herpes infections annually. Most genital HSV infections in the United States are caused by HSV 2 type; nationwide, about 12% of persons aged 14–49 years have HSV-2 infection. However, the prevalence of genital herpes infection is higher than that because an increasing number of genital herpes infections are caused by HSV-1, which is typically acquired in childhood, and because oral sex is an increasingly common behavior among adolescents and young adults. Most infected persons may be unaware of their infection; in the United States, an estimated 87.4% of those ages 14 to 49 years infected with HSV-2 have never received a clinical diagnosis. HSV-2 infection is more common among women than among men; 14- to 49-year-olds the percentages of those infected during 2015–2016 were 15.9% versus 8.2%, respectively. This is possibly because genital infection is more easily transmitted from men to women than from women to men during penile-vaginal sex. HSV-2 infection is more common among non-Hispanic Blacks (34.6%) than among non-Hispanic whites (8.1%). A previous analysis found that these disparities exist even among persons with similar numbers of lifetime sexual partners.

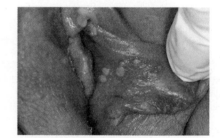

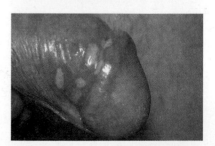

Herpes lesions may develop on the penis, perineum, anus, or vulva or within the vagina.

(first) Dr P. Marazzi/Science Source; (second) Clinical Photography, Central Manchester University Hospitals NHS Foundation Trust, UK/ Science Source

HSV-1 and HSV-2 can be found and released from the sores that the viruses cause, but it also can be released between outbreaks from skin that does not appear to be broken or have a sore (Tronstein, 2011). Generally, a person can get HSV-2 infection only during sexual contact with someone who has a genital HSV-2 infection. Transmission commonly occurs from an infected partner who does not have a visible sore and may not know that he or she is infected. HSV-1 can cause genital herpes, but it more often causes infections of the mouth and lips, so-called fever blisters. HSV-1 infection of the genitals can be caused by oral-genital or genital-genital contact with a person infected with HSV-1. Genital HSV-1 outbreaks recur less regularly than genital HSV-2 outbreaks.

Most people with the herpes virus don't have symptoms yet herpes can still be transmitted to another person even without signs of the disease. When signs appear, they appear between 2 and 12 days after the virus is transmitted and appear as one or more blisters on or around the genitals or rectum. These symptoms are sometimes called "having an outbreak." The blister breaks, leaving tender ulcers (sores) that may take 2–4 weeks to heal the first time they occur. Most people diagnosed with a first episode of genital herpes can expect to have several (typically four or five) outbreaks within a year, but they are almost always less severe and shorter than the first outbreak. Even though the infection can stay in the body indefinitely, the number of outbreaks tends to decrease over a period of years (CDC, 2017.15aa).

Managing HSV   There is no cure for herpes, but there are medications that can help keep the virus in check. Antiviral medications can relieve pain, shorten the duration of sores, prevent bacterial infections at the open sores, and prevent outbreaks while the person is taking the medications. To avoid spreading herpes to another part of the body, such as the eyes, infected persons should not touch the sores or fluids. Other actions that may be useful in preventing, shortening the duration of, or lessening the severity of recurrent outbreaks include getting plenty of rest, maintaining a balanced diet, avoiding tight clothes, keeping the area cool and dry, taking aspirin or other painkillers, and reducing stress.

Individuals with herpes should inform their partners and together decide what precautions are right for them. Because having sex during a recognized outbreak or when other symptoms are present (e.g., flulike symptoms, swollen glands, fever) puts an uninfected partner at risk, people should abstain from sex when signs and symptoms of either oral or genital herpes are present. Recall that even if an infected person has no symptoms, he or she can still infect his or her partners. The male latex condom or the nitrile internal condom can help prevent infections, but only when the condom covers the ulcer. However, outbreaks can also occur in areas that are not covered by a condom, so condoms may not fully protect someone from getting herpes. Condoms should be used between outbreaks of the ulcers because even if someone does not have symptoms, that person can still infect sexual partners. Also, daily suppressive therapy for symptomatic herpes can reduce transmission to partners. Pregnant women or their partners who have HSV should be sure to discuss precautionary procedures with their medical practitioners.

Human Papillomavirus (HPV)

Human papillomavirus (HPV) refers to more than 100 different viruses, over 40 are sexually transmitted and can infect the genitals, rectum, mouth, and throat. Currently, about 79 million people in the United States are infected with HPV, with 14 million new infections reported each year, accounting for one third of all new STIs. According to the CDC, nearly one half (43%) of all Americans, aged 18–59, have some strain of HPV. HPV is the most common STI among young, sexually active people, particularly women. HPV is so common that nearly all sexually active individuals get it at some point in their lives if they don't get the HPV vaccine. By age 50, at least 80% of women will have acquired genital HPV infection and national data revealed that nearly one half (45%) of men are currently infected with genital HPV infections (CDC, 2017.15c, 2017.15d; Han et al., 2017).

You can get HPV by having oral, vaginal, or anal sex with someone who has the virus. It is most commonly spread during vaginal or anal sex. HPV can be passed even when an infected person has no signs or symptoms. In rare instances, a pregnant woman can pass HPV to her baby during vaginal delivery. The incubation period—the period between the time a person is first exposed to a disease and the time the symptoms appear—is usually 6 weeks to 8 months. You cannot see HPV. Most people who have a genital HPV infection do not know they are infected. Also, you can develop symptoms years after you have sex with someone who is infected, making it difficult to know when you first became infected.

Sometimes, certain types of HPV can cause **genital warts** in men and women. Other HPV types can cause cervical cancer and less common cancers of the vulva, vagina, anus, penis, back of the throat, the base of the tongue, and the tongue. The types of HPV that can cause genital warts are not the same as the types that can cause cancer. HPV types are referred to as "low risk" (wart causing) or "high risk" (cancer causing). In 90% of the cases, the body's immune system clears the HPV—both high-risk and low-risk types—naturally within 2 years. If a high-risk HPV infection is not cleared by the immune system, it can linger for many years and turn abnormal cells into cancer over time. CDC researchers found that one quarter and one fifth of men and women, respectively, have a high-risk strain that can cause cancer of the cervix, vulva, vagina, penis, anus, or throat (CDC, 2017.15m; "HPV Infections

Rampant," 2017). There is no way to know which people who have HPV will develop cancer or other health problems. Those with weak immune systems may be less able to fight off HPV.

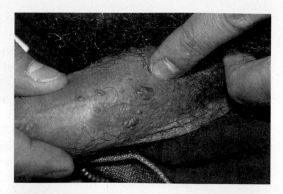

The Pap test can identify abnormal or precancerous tissue in the cervix so that it can be removed before cancer develops. Abnormal changes on the cervix are likely caused by HPV. An HPV DNA test, which can find high-risk HPV on a women's cervix, may also be used with a Pap test in certain cases. If a woman is 30 years old or older, she may choose to have an HPV DNA test along with the Pap test. There is no general test to check one's overall "HPV status," nor is there an approved HPV test to find HPV on the genitals or in the mouth or throat. HPV usually goes away on its own, without causing health problems. So an HPV infection that is found today will most likely not be there a year or two from now. Hence, there is no reason to be tested just to find out if you have HPV now. But you should get tested for signs of diseases that HPV can cause, such as cervical cancer (CDC, 2017.15m, 2019.15a).

Before HPV vaccines were introduced (discussed below), about 340,000–360,000 women and men were affected by genital warts caused by HPV every year. Also, about 1 in 100 sexually active adults in the United States has genital warts at one time (CDC, 2017.15m, 2019.15a). One study found that having a lifetime history of STIs and having five or more lifetime partners was associated with greater odds of having a medical diagnosis of genital warts (Uuskula et al., 2015). Research has shown that being infected with genital warts can be a psychological burden, with adverse effects resulting in decreased quality of life (Senecal et al., 2011; Tan et al., 2014). Since the introduction of the HPV vaccine, the rates of diagnosed genital warts have decreased.

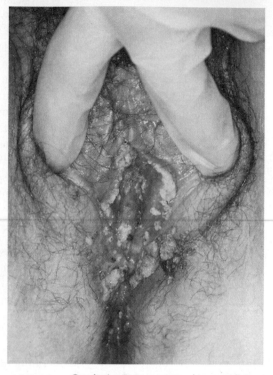

Some people find out they have HPV when they get genital warts. They usually appear as soft, moist, pink or flesh-colored swellings, usually in the genital area. They can also be flat, single or multiple, small or large, and sometimes cauliflower shaped. They can appear on the penis or scrotum, in or around the vagina or anus, on the cervix, or on the groin or thigh. Visible genital warts can be removed by the patient him- or herself with prescribed medications or treated by a health care provider. Some people choose not to treat warts but see if they disappear on their own. No one treatment is better than another. If the warts cause discomfort or problems such as interfering with urination, they can be removed by cryosurgery (freezing) or laser surgery. Removal of the warts does not eliminate HPV from the person's system. Because the virus can lie dormant in the cells, in some cases warts can return months or even years after treatment. The extent to which a person can still transmit HPV after the visible warts have been removed is unknown.

Genital warts appear in a variety of forms.

(first) Dr Harout Tanielian/Science Source; (second) Joe Miller/Centers for Disease Control and Prevention

In recent years, a major medical breakthrough occurred in protecting thousands of females and males against the health-impairing outcomes of HPV infection. HPV vaccines were developed and then approved by the federal Food and Drug Administration, first for females in 2009 and then for males in 2014. The vaccinations are routinely given at 11 and 12 years of age, but may be given beginning at 9 years through 26 years. However, some adults aged 27–45 years who are not vaccinated may decide to get the HPV vaccination after speaking with their health care provider about their risk of new HPV infections and the possible benefits of vaccination. The HPV vaccines prevent infection with HPV types that cause genital herpes in both females and males (CDC, 2015.15aa, 2016.15d, 2017.15aa, 2017.15m, 2017.15n). A recent meta-analysis that included data from over 60 million individuals from 14 high-income countries, including the United States, showed a substantial impact of HPV vaccination on HPV infections after 5–8 years of vaccination. Genital wart diagnoses decreased significantly by 48% and among men aged 20–24 years they decreased significantly by 32% (CDC, 2019.15a; Drolet et al., 2019). A study conducted in 27 clinics participating in the STD Surveillance Network observed significant declines in prevalence of genital warts during 2010–2016 among women and men who have sex with women only (MSW) aged less than 40 years, and among MSM of all ages (CDC, 2019.15a; Mann et al., 2019)

For maximum protection, two doses of the HPV vaccine are recommended for persons under 15 years of age and three doses for those 15 years and above. Studies have shown that some girls taking the HPV vaccine did not complete the vaccine series on schedule (Widdice et al., 2011) or would not take the vaccine even if it was free (Crosby et al., 2011). In addition, parental acceptance of the HPV vaccine has been mixed (Dempsey et al., 2011; Milhausen et al., 2008). At the beginning of the availability of the HPV vaccination, some parents believed that vaccinating girls against HPV condones premarital/teen sex (Darden et al., 2013; Holman et al., 2014). However, more recent research found that only a minority of parents choose not to have their children take the vaccine because of concerns that the vaccine would encourage or support sexual behavior. The study found, instead, that safety concerns, lack of belief in the necessity, lack of knowledge about HPV, and absence of physician recommendation were major parental concerns (Krakow et al., 2017). Research has shown that HPV vaccination does not increase sexual behavior among teens. For example, in a Canadian study, 128,712 girls in grades 8 and 9 who received the HPV vaccination were followed to grades 10–12; results found that the vaccination did not have any significant effect on increased risk of pregnancy or non-HPV-related STIs (Smith et al., 2014).

If you have HPV, don't blame your current sexual partner or assume that your partner is not sexually exclusive with you. Remember, most people who have sex will have HPV at some time in their lives, and they may have HPV for a very long time before it is detected. Most people do not realize they are infected or that they are passing on the virus to a sexual partner. Remember, there is no medical test to determine if someone is infected with HPV. Sexual partners usually share HPV, particularly those who are together for a long time. There should be no shame or blame involved with having genital HPV; the virus is very common.

Viral Hepatitis

Hepatitis means inflammation of the liver. When the liver is inflamed or damaged, its function can be affected. Hepatitis is often caused by a virus. The most common types of the virus than can be transmitted are hepatitis A and hepatitis B. A third type, hepatitis C, is a common virus passed on primarily through contact with infected blood. Hepatitis A is usually a short-term infection and does not become chronic. Hepatitis B and hepatitis C can also begin as short-term, acute infections, but in some people, the virus remains in the body, resulting in chronic disease and long-term liver problems. Both hepatitis A and hepatitis B can be prevented by a vaccine which can be taken as a child, adolescent, or adult; however, there is no vaccine for hepatitis C.

People who get hepatitis A may feel sick for a few weeks to several months but usually recover completely and do not have lasting liver damage. In 2018, a total of 12,474 hepatitis A cases were reported in the United States. Because some people don't ever get diagnosed, the actual number of cases reported in that year is probably closer to 24,900. The hepatitis A virus is found in the stool and blood of people who are infected and can be spread from close, personal contact with an infected person, such as through certain types of sexual contact (like oral-anal sex), caring for someone who is ill, or using drugs with others or through contaminated food. Symptoms include yellow eyes, no appetite, upset stomach, throwing up, stomach pain, dark urine or light-colored feces, and diarrhea. A single shot of the hepatitis A vaccine can help prevent hepatitis A if given within 2 weeks of exposure. Once you recover from hepatitis A, you develop antibodies, protecting you for life. Some people with severe symptoms will need medical care in a hospital (CDC, 2020.15a)

In 2018, a total of 3,322 cases of acute (short-term) hepatitis B were reported to CDC. Since many people may not have symptoms or don't know they are infected, their illness is often not diagnosed so it can't be reported or counted. CDC estimates the actual number of acute hepatitis B cases was closer to 21,600 in 2018. Many more people (about 862,000) are estimated to be living with chronic, long-term hepatitis B. Hepatitis B is spread when blood, semen, or other body fluid infected with the hepatitis B virus enters the body of someone who is not infected. People can also become infected with the virus from birth (spread from an infected mother to her baby during birth), sex with an infected partner, sharing needles, syringes, or drug preparation equipment, sharing items such as toothbrushes, razors, or medical equipment (like a glucose monitor) with an infected person, direct contact with the blood or open sores of an infected person, and exposure to an infected person's blood through needle sticks or other sharp instruments. Many people with hepatitis B don't know they are infected with the virus (CDC, 2020.15b).

Hepatitis C can range from a mild illness lasting a few weeks to a serious, long-term illness resulting in long-term health problems, including liver damage, liver failure, cirrhosis, liver cancer, and even death. It is the most common reason for liver transplantation in the United States. There were 15,713 deaths related to hepatitis C virus reported to CDC in 2018, but this is believed to be an underestimate. More than half of people who become infected with hepatitis C virus will develop a chronic infection. In 2018, a total of 3,621 cases of acute hepatitis C were reported to CDC, however, the CDC believes the actual number of acute hepatitis C cases in 2018 was probably closer to 50,300. In 2016, an estimated 2.4 million people were living with HCV. The hepatitis C virus is usually spread when someone comes into contact with blood from an infected person. This can happen most commonly by people becoming infected with hepatitis C by sharing needles, syringes, or any other equipment used to prepare and inject drugs. While uncommon, hepatitis C can spread during sex, though it has been reported more often among men who have sex with men (CDC, 2020.15c).

● Vaginal Infections

Vaginal infections, or **vaginitis**, affect most women at least once in their lives. **Vaginitis** is often the result of an infection with yeast, bacteria, or Trichomonas, but it may also occur due to physical or chemical irritation of the vaginal area. Not all infections that cause vaginitis are considered sexually transmitted infections, but some STIs cause vaginitis (Mayo Clinic, 2017). They may also be induced by an upset in the normal balance of vaginal organisms by such things as stress, birth control pills, antibiotics, tight pants, wet underwear, and douching. The three principal types of vaginitis are bacterial vaginosis, candidiasis, and trichomoniasis.

Bacterial Vaginosis

Bacterial vaginal infections, referred to as **bacterial vaginosis (BV)**, may be caused by a number of different organisms, most commonly *Gardnerella vaginalis,* often a normal inhabitant of the healthy vagina. An overabundance of *Gardnerella,* however, can result in vaginal discharge, odor, pain, itching, or burning. Bacterial vaginosis is the most common vaginal infection in women aged 15–44, and in the United States, it is common among pregnant women. The prevalence of bacterial vaginosis in the United States is estimated to be over 21 million or about 3 of every 10 women. Most women having bacterial vaginosis report no symptoms (CDC, 2020.15d).

Not much is known about how women get bacterial vaginosis, and there are many unanswered questions about the role that harmful bacteria play in causing it and what role sexual activity plays in its development. BV is not considered an STI, per se, as doctors and scientists do not completely understand how BV is transmitted although BV increases as woman's chances of getting STIs as described below. Any woman can get BV, although some activities can upset the normal balance of bacteria in the vagina and put women at risk, including having a new sexual partner or numerous partners and douching. BV rarely affects women who have never had sex (CDC, 2020.15d). Research has shown that douching at least once a month is associated with BV but that most female hygienic behaviors, such as type of underwear, menstrual protection, or hygienic spray or towelettes, were found not to be related to BV (Hutchinson et al., 2007; Klebanoff et al., 2010). Bacterial vaginosis may also be spread between female sex partners (Bailey et al., 2004). BV is not acquired from toilet seats, bedding, or swimming pools. Most often this infection causes no complications, although having it can increase a woman's susceptibility to HIV infection and other STIs, such as chlamydia and gonorrhea, and can increase the chances that an HIV-infected woman can pass HIV to her sexual partner (Cohen et al., 2012). BV may also put a woman at increased risk for some complications during pregnancy.

Even though bacterial vaginosis sometimes clears up without treatment, all women with symptoms of BV should be treated with antibiotics, so that the bacteria that cause BV do not infect the uterus and fallopian tubes. BV may return even after treatment. Treatment may also reduce the risk for some STIs. Male partners generally do not need to be treated (CDC, 2017.15, 2020.15d). A study of women at high risk for STIs found that consistent condom users had a 45% decreased risk for BV than women not using condoms consistently (Hutchinson et al., 2007).

Genital Candidiasis

Genital candidiasis, also known as a "yeast infection" is a common fungal infection that occurs when there is an overgrowth of the fungus *Candida albicans*. It is not considered an STI. *Candida* is always present in the body (e.g., vagina, mouth, throat, gastrointestinal tract, and skin) in small amounts without causing problems. Scientists estimate that about 20% of women normally have *Candida* in the vagina without having any symptoms. When an imbalance occurs, such as when the normal acidity of the vagina changes or when hormonal balance changes, *Candida* can multiply. Women with a vaginal yeast infection usually experience itching or burning, painful intercourse, and pain or discomfort when urinating with or without a "cottage cheese–like" vaginal discharge. Males with genital candidiasis, which occurs on rare occasions, may have an itchy rash on the penis. Nearly 75% of all adult women have had at least one vaginal yeast infection in their lifetime. While most cases are caused by the person's own *Candida* organisms, the use of birth control pills or antibiotics, frequent douching, pregnancy, and diabetes can promote yeast infections. Less commonly, *Candida* infections are transmitted from person to person through sexual intercourse. Genital candidiasis occurs more often and with more severe symptoms in people with weakened immune systems. Wearing cotton underwear might help reduce the chances of getting a yeast infection (CDC, 2019.15c).

Antifungal drugs, taken orally, applied directly to the affected area, or used vaginally, are the drug of choice for vaginal yeast infections and are effective 80–90% of the time. Because over-the-counter (OTC) treatments are becoming more available, more women are diagnosing themselves with vaginal yeast infections. However, personal misdiagnosis is common, and studies show that as many as two thirds of OTC drugs sold to treat vaginal yeast infections are used by women *without* the disease, which may lead to resistant infections. Resistant infections are very difficult to treat with currently available medications. Therefore, it is important to be sure of the diagnosis before treating with OTC or other antifungal medications (CDC, 2017.15v; 2019.15c). Because taking antibiotics can lead to genital candidiasis, they should be taken only when prescribed and exactly as the health care provider directs.

Trichomoniasis

Trichomoniasis is an STI caused by a single-celled protozoan parasite, *Trichomonas vaginalis*. Trichomoniasis is the most common curable STI. In the United States, an estimated 3.7 million people have the infection, but only 30% develop any symptoms of trichomoniasis. Infection is more common in women than in men. In one study of 1,209 women attending three STI clinics, trichomoniasis, unlike other STIs, was found more often in older compared to younger women (Helms et al., 2008). In women, the vagina, vulva, cervix, or urethra are the most common sites of infection; in men, it is the urethra. The parasite is sexually transmitted during penile-vaginal intercourse or vulva-to-vulva contact with an infected person. Women can acquire the disease from infected men or women, but men usually contract it only from infected women. Trichomoniasis can increase the risk of getting or spreading other STIs, such as HIV. Symptoms are more common in women than men. It is unclear why some people with the infection get symptoms, while others do not. About 70% of infected people do not have any signs or symptoms. Some women have signs and symptoms within 5–28 days after exposure, which include frothy, yellow-green vaginal discharge with a strong odor. The infection may also cause discomfort during intercourse and urination, as well as itching and irritation of the female genital area and, rarely, lower abdominal pain. Some men may temporarily have an irritation of the urethra, mild discharge, or slight burning after urination or ejaculation. For both women and men, a physical examination and a laboratory test are used to diagnose trichomoniasis, although it is harder to detect in men (CDC, 2020.15e).

Prescription drugs are effective in treating trichomoniasis. About one in five people get reinfected again within 3 months after receiving treatment. To prevent reinfection, both partners must be treated at the same time, even if the partner is asymptomatic.

● Other STIs

A number of other STIs appear in the United States, but with less frequency than they do in some developing countries. Among these other STIs are the following:

- Chancroid is a painful sore or group of sores on the penis, caused by the bacterium *Haemophilus ducreyi*. Women may carry the bacterium but are generally asymptomatic for chancroid.

- Cytomegalovirus (CMV) is a virus of the herpes group that affects people with depressed immune systems. A fetus may be infected with CMV in the uterus.

- Enteric infections are intestinal infections caused by bacteria, viruses, protozoans, or other organisms that are normally carried in the intestinal tract. Amebiasis, giardiasis, and shigellosis are typical enteric infections. They often result from anal sex or oral-anal contact.

- Granuloma inguinale appears as single or multiple nodules, usually on the genitals, that become lumpy but painless ulcers that bleed on contact.

- Lymphogranuloma venereum (LGV) begins as a small, painless lesion at the site of infection and then develops into a painful abscess, accompanied by pain and swelling in the groin.

- Molluscum contagiosum, caused by a virus, is characterized by smooth, round, shiny lesions that appear on the trunk, on the genitals, or around the anus.

● Ectoparasitic Infestations

Although they are not infections per se, parasites such as scabies and pubic lice can be spread by sexual contact. Scabies and pubic lice are considered ectoparasitic parasites or infestations, since they live on the outer surfaces of the skin.

Scabies

Scabies is a red, intensely itchy, pimple-like skin rash caused by the barely visible mite *Sarcoptes scabiei*. It usually appears on the genitals, nipples, buttocks, feet, wrists, elbows, knuckles, abdomen, armpits, shoulder blades, or scalp as a result of the mites' tunneling beneath the skin to lay their eggs and the baby mites making their way back to the surface. Typically, fewer than 15 mites can be present on the entire body of an infested person. On a person, scabies mites can live as long as 1-2 months, but off a person they usually do not survive more than 48-72 hours. When a person is infected with scabies mites for the first time, it usually takes 2-6 weeks for symptoms to appear after being infected; an infected person still can spread scabies during this time, even though he or she does not have symptoms. If a person has had scabies before, symptoms appear 1-4 days after exposure. It is highly contagious and spreads quickly among people who have close contact, both sexual and nonsexual. An infected person can transmit scabies, even if they do not have symptoms. The mites can also be transferred during prolonged contact with infested linens, furniture, or clothing. Scabies is usually treated with a prescribed lotion, applied at bedtime and washed off in the morning. Clothing, towels, and bedding of people who have scabies should be disinfected by washing in hot water and drying in high heat or by dry cleaning (CDC, 2010.15c, 2017.15x).

Pubic Lice

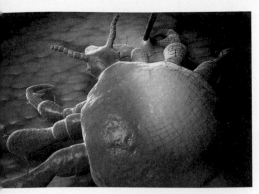

Pubic lice, or "crabs," are easily spread during intimate contact; they can also be transmitted via bedding, towels, or underwear.

MedicalRF.com

The tiny *Phthirus pubis,* commonly known as a "crab," moves easily from the hair of one person to that of another (probably along with several of its relatives). **Pubic lice** usually are found in the genital area on pubic hair, although less commonly they can be found on other body hair such as hair on the legs, armpits, mustache, beard, eyebrows, and even eyelashes. Lice found on the head generally are head lice, not pubic lice. To live, lice must feed on blood. When pubic lice mate, the male and female grasp adjacent hairs; the female soon begins producing eggs (nits), which she attaches to the hairs at the rate of about three eggs a day for 7–10 days. The nits hatch within 6–10 days and begin reproducing in about 2–3 weeks, creating a very ticklish (or itchy) situation. Although pubic lice and nits can be large enough to be seen with the naked eye, a magnifying lens may be necessary to find lice or eggs.

Pubic lice can be transmitted during sexual contact with a person who has crabs, moving from the pubic hair of one person to the pubic hair of another. Contact generally must be prolonged; a quick handshake or hug, for example, will usually not spread pubic lice. They may fall into underwear, sheets, or towels, where they can survive up to a day and lay eggs, which hatch in about a week. Thus it is possible to get crabs simply by sleeping in an infected person's bed, wearing his or her clothes, or sharing a towel. A common misconception is that pubic lice can be spread easily by sitting on a toilet seat. This would be extremely rare because lice cannot live long away from a warm body and they do not have feet designed to hold on to or walk on smooth surfaces such as toilet seats. Also, animals do not spread pubic lice.

People can usually tell when they have pubic lice. There is intense itching, and upon inspection, they discover a tiny, pale, crablike louse or its minuscule, pearly nits attached near the base of a pubic hair. There are both prescription and over-the-counter treatments for pubic lice. An infested person does not have to shave off his or her pubic hair to get rid of crabs. In addition to killing all the lice and nits on the body, infested individuals must wash all linen and clothing in hot water and dry it in high heat, or the crabs may survive (CDC, 2020.15f).

● Infections Caused by STIs

In addition to the direct effects that STIs have on the body, women are vulnerable to complications from STIs that threaten their fertility. These are related to the biological factors, discussed earlier, that make women more susceptible to STIs and make STIs more difficult to detect in women.

Pelvic Inflammatory Disease (PID)

Pelvic inflammatory disease (PID), also known as salpingitis, is one of the leading causes of female infertility. One in eight women with a history of PID experiences difficulties getting pregnant. Despite declining trends, PID is a frequent and important infection that occurs among women of reproductive age, especially among those at increased risk such as a history of STIs. An estimated 4.4% of sexually experienced women of reproductive age (18–44 years) self-reported lifetime PID, which equates to an estimated 2.5 million women in the United States (CDC, 2017.15y; Kreisel et al., 2017).

PID occurs when bacteria move upward from a woman's vagina or cervix into her uterus, fallopian tubes, and other reproductive organs. Several organisms can cause PID, but one third to one half of cases are associated with gonorrhea and chlamydia. About 15% of untreated chlamydial infections progress to diagnosed PID and the risk with untreated gonococcal infection may be even higher (CDC, 2017.15d). A prior episode of PID increases the risk of another episode because the reproductive organs may have been damaged during the initial episode. A Scandinavian study found that women with PID were more likely to have ectopic pregnancy (6 times increased rate), infertility from fallopian tube damage (ranging from 8% after first episode of PID to as high as 40% after three episodes), and chronic pelvic pain (18% following one episode) (Westrom et al., 1992). Sexually active women in their childbearing years are at most risk, and those under age 25 are more likely to develop PID than those older than 25. Because the cervix of teenage girls and young women is not fully mature, their susceptibility to the STIs that are linked to PID is increased. Women with repeated episodes of PID are more likely to suffer infertility, ectopic pregnancy, or chronic pelvic pain than those who have had just one episode. Risk behaviors for PID include having numerous sex partners, having a partner who has more than one sex partner, and douching.

Symptoms of PID vary from none, to subtle and mild, to severe. PID is difficult to diagnose because of the absent or mild symptoms, and many episodes go undetected. PID goes unrecognized by women and their health care providers about two thirds of the time. Because there is no precise test for PID, a diagnosis is usually based on clinical findings. Symptoms of PID include lower abdominal pain, fever, unusual vaginal discharge that may have a foul odor, painful intercourse, painful urination, irregular menstrual bleeding, and, rarely, pain in the upper right abdomen. If diagnosed early, PID can be cured with antibiotics. However, treatment won't undo any damage that has already been done to the reproductive system. The longer a person waits for diagnosis and treatment, the more likely there will be complications from PID. Additionally, a woman's sex partner(s) should be treated to decrease the risk of reinfection, even if the partner(s) has no symptoms (CDC, 2017.15y, 2019.15a).

Cervicitis

Cervicitis is an inflammation of the cervix, the lower narrow end of the uterus. Cervicitis might be a sign of a genital tract infection, most often caused by an STI such as gonorrhea, chlamydia, genital herpes, and trichomoniasis. Frequently there are no signs of cervicitis, but some women complain of abnormal vaginal discharge, painful urination, and vaginal bleeding between menstrual periods, such as after sexual intercourse. A woman is at greater risk for cervicitis associated with STIs if she engages in high-risk sexual behavior, such as not using condoms or having sex with numerous partners, and if she began having sex at an early age. Having a history of STIs is also a risk factor. An allergic reaction to contraceptive spermicides, latex condoms, and feminine hygiene productions such as douches or feminine deodorants may also result in cervicitis. Since the signs of cervicitis are not often noticed, the infection may be discovered only in the course of a medical test. This is one important reason to have regular pelvic exams. A woman may not need treatment for cervicitis if it is not caused by an STI. If it is caused by an STI, both the woman and her partner are likely to need treatment. Antibiotics often are effective in clearing up the inflammation of cervicitis (Mayo Clinic, 2017.15a, 2020). The use of condoms can reduce the risk of cervicitis.

Cystitis

A bladder infection that affects mainly women, **cystitis** is often related to sexual activity, although it is not transmitted from one partner to another. Cystitis, also called urinary tract infection (UTI), is an infection of the bladder characterized by painful, burning urination and a nearly constant need to urinate.

Cystitis occurs when a bacterium such as *Escherichia coli,* normally present in the lower intestine and in fecal material, is introduced into the urinary tract. This can occur when continuous friction (from intercourse or manual stimulation) in the area of the urethra traumatizes the tissue and allows nearby bacteria to enter the urinary tract. It often occurs at the beginning of a sexual relationship, when sexual activity is high (hence the nickname "honeymoon cystitis"). However, sexually active girls and women can get cystitis as the genital area often harbors bacteria that can cause urinary tract infections. Physicians often recommend several behaviors for preventing repeated bladder infections: drink plenty of liquids, urinate frequently, wipe from front to back after a bowel movement, take showers rather than hot baths, gently wash the skin around the vagina and anus, empty the bladder as soon as possible after intercourse, and avoid using deodorant sprays and feminine products in the genital area. Cystitis resulting from a bacterial infection is generally treated by antibiotics (Mayo Clinic, 2020). If cystitis is not treated promptly with antibiotics, more serious symptoms such as lower abdominal pain, fever, and kidney pain will occur. Damage to the kidneys may occur if treatment is delayed.

● Preventing and Treating STIs

It seems that STIs should be easy to prevent, at least in theory. But in reality, STI prevention involves a subtle interplay of knowledge, psychological factors, couple dynamics, and behaviors.

Avoiding STIs

As noted in this chapter, STIs can be transmitted by sexual contact with an infected partner, by infected blood in injection-drug equipment, and from an infected mother to her child. Because we know that STIs are transmitted by certain behaviors, we know exactly how to keep from getting them. Those behaviors are particularly important because research has shown, for example, that many people underestimate their risk of becoming infected with an STI and the risk behavior of potential sexual partners, and in one study most heterosexual dating couples with a sexual relationship had not done anything in the past 4 weeks to avoid STIs (Billy et al., 2009; Masaro et al., 2008). In a survey of 1,497 women and men at 75 clinics and physician offices across California, a considerable proportion of study participants said that they would have unprotected sex, even when they were recently counseled about birth control and had access to subsidized contraceptive services. In response to whether they would have sex without contraception, 30% said a definite "yes," and 20% indicated "sometimes" or "maybe" (CDC, 2017.15z; Foster et al., 2012). Further, as mentioned in Think About It, "Are Persons Knowledgeable about STIs and Worried They Might Become Infected? Results of a National Study" only 20% of the adults ages 18–29 indicated that they were worried that they will get an STI over the next year despite being the age group of the highest risk of acquiring an STI. The type of attitudes and decision-making cited in these studies can contribute significantly to the rise in incidence and outcomes associated with STIs. Here is how to avoid STIs:

1. *Practice sexual abstinence.* The closest thing to a foolproof method of STI prevention is abstaining from intimate sexual contact, especially penile-vaginal intercourse, anal intercourse, and oral sex. Hugging, kissing, caressing, and mutual masturbation are all ways of sharing intimacy that are extremely unlikely to transmit STIs. Freely adopted, abstinence is a legitimate personal choice regarding sexuality. If you wish to remain abstinent, you need to communicate your preferences clearly to your dates or partners.

2. *Practice sexual exclusivity.* **Sexual exclusivity** means that you agree to be sexually active with only one person, who has agreed to be sexually active only with you. Partners who practice sexual exclusivity will not contract an STI through sexual contact unless one partner had an STI when he or she started having sexual contact. Being in a long-term, mutually exclusive relationship with an uninfected partner is one of the most reliable ways to avoid STIs. Certainly, it is not always possible to know if someone is infected or if he or she is exclusive. This is one reason it is wise to refrain from sexual activity until you can form a trusting relationship with a partner.

3. *Reduce risk during sexual intimacy.* Unless you are certain that your partner is not infected, you should not allow his or her blood, semen, or vaginal fluids to touch your genitals, mouth, or anus. One of the best ways to prevent these fluids from entering your body is to properly use the male latex condom (or polyurethane or polyisoprene condom if allergic to latex) or internal condom. You will learn in Chapter 16 that college students make numerous errors in using male condoms and often complain that using condoms interferes with sexual arousal and pleasure (see Think About It, "Do You Know What You Are Doing?" Common Condom-Use Mistakes Among College Students"). Some mistakes may increase exposure to STIs and interfere with sexual pleasure, which may result in less motivation to use condoms. To get some ideas about ways to increase correct condom use and sexual pleasure, see Chapter 16, Practically Speaking, "Learn to Use Condoms Correctly and Experience Sexual Pleasure: Try Self-guided Practice at Home."

practically speaking

Safer and Unsafe Sex Behaviors

Safer sex behaviors are an integral part of good health behaviors. Many people prefer the term *safer sex* to *safe sex* because all sexual contact carries at least a slight risk—a condom breaking, perhaps—no matter how careful we try to be.

Safer Behaviors

- Hugging
- Kissing (but possibly not deep, French kissing)
- Massaging
- Petting
- Masturbation (solo or mutual, unless there are sores or abrasions on the genitals or hands)
- Erotic videos, books, and so on

Possibly Safe Behaviors

- Deep, French kissing, unless there are sores in the mouth
- Vaginal intercourse with a latex condom (or polyurethane or polyisoprene condom if allergic to latex)

- Fellatio with a latex condom
- Cunnilingus, if the woman is not menstruating or does not have a vaginal infection (a latex dental dam provides extra protection)
- Anal intercourse with a latex condom (experts disagree about whether this should be considered "possibly safe" even with a condom because it is the riskiest sexual behavior without one)

Unsafe Behaviors

- Vaginal or anal intercourse without a latex condom
- Fellatio without a latex condom
- Cunnilingus, if the woman is menstruating or has a vaginal infection and a dental dam is not used
- Oral-anal contact without a dental dam
- Contact with blood, including menstrual blood
- Semen in the mouth
- Use of vibrators, dildos, and other "toys" without washing them between uses

4. Studies have shown that some couples who use male condoms at the beginning of their sexual relationship often stop using them and turn to hormonal contraception, which does not provide protection against STIs. For example, a study of 115 men and women, aged 18–29 years, found that in a new sexual relationship during a 3-month period, men started at an average condom use of 56% that declined to 26% during the first 17 coital events then stabilized at 25%. Women started at an average condom use of 43% that declined to 6% during the first 17 coital events and remained at that percentage. Higher levels of couple relationship and sexual satisfaction were related to more rapid declines in condom use, even after very few coital events, and particularly for women (He, 2016). The lack of condom use for these couples makes them vulnerable to STI transmission if one of the partners is not sexually exclusive or has an undiagnosed STI. Douching, washing, and urinating after sex have been suggested as possible ways of reducing STI risk, but their effectiveness has not been proved.

5. *Select partners carefully.* Beyond abstinence, the surest way to avoid the acquisition and transmission of STIs is to have sex with those who are not infected. This means being very selective of partners. If you decide to have sex with another person, you and your partner should get tested for STIs and use condoms. Unfortunately, not all persons and their partners get tested. As noted previously in Think About It, "Accurately Judging If a Potential Sexual Partner is Infected with an STI: Easily Done?" many rely on nonmedical strategies such as judging if a partner is disease-free by their appearance, character, familiarity, and sexual history. These methods are not reliable.

6. *Avoid numerous partners.* As noted in this chapter, having numerous sexual partners (concurrent or sequential sexual relationships with a short time period between relationships) increases the risk for STIs.

An important part of controlling the spread of STIs is having free access to condoms and relevant information.

Kmlaw/Stockimo/Alamy Stock Photo

7. *Avoid injection and other drugs.* Another way to avoid HIV and hepatitis B is to not inject drugs and to not share needles and syringes if drugs are injected. Certainly, the drug equipment should be cleaned if sharing occurs. Drugs can not only harm your health, they can also alter your judgment.

8. *Get tested.* Since many STIs don't have early symptoms in most infected persons, getting tested for STIs before having sex with someone is a critical step in stopping the transmission and acquisition of STIs. To learn about recommended STI testing and what to do if tested positive, see Practically Speaking, "Which STI Tests Should I Get and What Do I Do If I Test Positive?" If you are infected, then you can take steps to protect yourself and your partner. When seeing a health care provider, ask specifically for STI tests. It is important that one's sexual partner be tested also. Many couples go for STI testing together prior to beginning a sexual relationship. If either you or your partner is infected, both of you need to receive treatment at the same time to avoid getting reinfected.

9. *Get vaccinated.* Vaccines are a safe, effective, and recommended method to prevent hepatitis A, hepatitis B, and HPV.

10. *Protect babies.* Most STIs can be transmitted from mother to child during pregnancy or childbirth. Most often, proper medical treatment can protect the baby from permanent damage. HIV-infected mothers should not breast-feed their babies. A woman who has an STI and becomes pregnant should inform her doctor, and all pregnant women should be checked for STIs.

11. *Be a good communicator.* Acquiring an STI requires that you have been sexually intimate with another person. Avoiding an STI demands even more intimacy because it frequently means having to talk. You need to learn how best to discuss prevention with potential sexual partners and to communicate your thoughts, feelings, values, needs, and sexual boundaries. Ideally, discussing one's past sexual experiences can be helpful in revealing vital health-related information, such as possible risk of STI infection. Good communicators are less likely to do things against their values or beliefs. And you should never have sex with someone who will not talk about STI prevention.

Treating STIs

"We kill our selves, to propagate our kinde."

—John Donne (1572–1631)

If you contract an STI, you can infect others. Practicing health-promoting behaviors will prevent others from acquiring an STI.

1. *Recognize STI symptoms.* People who practice risky sexual behaviors or inject drugs should be alert to possible STI symptoms, especially if they have sex with partners at risk for STIs. To help avoid STIs, you should know what symptoms to look for, in yourself and others. Changes in the genitals may indicate an infection, although symptoms of some STIs can appear anywhere, and some changes may indicate a health problem other than an STI. If you suspect an infection, you should not try to diagnose the condition yourself but should consult a physician or health care provider. In general, the symptoms of STIs are genital or rectal discharge, abdominal pain, painful urination, skin changes, genital itching, and flulike conditions. However, some STIs do not have any symptoms until the disease is well advanced, symptoms often disappear and then come back, and most STIs can still be passed on to someone even when the symptoms are not visible, are absent, or disappear. Actually, most people who are infected with an STI have no noticeable symptoms. Males are likely to notice symptoms earlier and more frequently than females. If you suspect an infection, you should stop having sex, stop injecting drugs, promptly see a health care provider, and have sexual partners go to a doctor or clinic.

2. *Seek testing and treatment.* If you suspect that you have an STI, you should seek testing and medical care immediately. Knowing your STI status is a critical step in

Which STI Tests Should I Get and What Should I Do If I Test Positive?

If you are sexually active, getting tested for STIs including HIV is one of the most important things you can do to protect your health. Make sure you have an open and honest conversation about your sexual history with your doctor and ask whether you should be tested for STIs. If you are not comfortable talking with your regular health care provider about STIs, there are many clinics that provide confidential and free or low-cost testing. You can get tested and treated at your local health department's STI clinic, a family planning clinic, a student health center, or an urgent care clinic.

Brief overview of STD/HIV testing recommendations from the Centers for Disease Control and Prevention (CDC, 2014).

- **All adults and adolescents from ages 13 to 64** should be tested at least once for HIV.

- **All sexually active women** younger than 25 years should be tested for gonorrhea and chlamydia every year. Women 25 years and older with risk factors such as new or multiple sex partners or a sex partner who has an STI should also be tested for gonorrhea and chlamydia every year.

- **All pregnant women** should be tested for syphilis, HIV, and hepatitis B starting early in pregnancy. At-risk pregnant women should also be tested for chlamydia and gonorrhea at that time. Testing should be repeated as needed to protect the health of mothers and their infants.

- **All sexually active gay, queer, and bisexual men** should be tested at least once a year for syphilis, chlamydia, and gonorrhea. Those who have multiple or anonymous partners should be tested more frequently for STIs such as at 3- to 6-month intervals.

- **Sexually active gay, queer and bisexual men** may benefit from more frequent HIV testing such as every 3 to 6 months.

- **Anyone who has unsafe sex or shares injection drug equipment** should get tested for HIV at least once a year.

What you should do if you find out that you have an STI? (CDC, 2020.15g)

- **Immediately seek medical treatment.** Left untreated, some STIs can cause serious health problems like PID, infertility, potential deadly ectopic pregnancy, cervical cancer, blindness, heart disease, and damage to internal organs. Without treatment you may pass on the STI to a partner.

- **Tell your partner about your STI infection.** Your partner may also be infected and not know it; hence, they also need to get tested and treated. Informing your partner allows them to protect their health. Being diagnosed with an STI can cause many strong emotions. You may begin to question your trust in your partner or be worried that they will question their trust in you. Before you blame anyone, know that STIs are common and don't always cause symptoms. It is possible that you or your partner got the STI in a previous relationship without even knowing it. Keeping that in mind, talk to your partner as soon as possible. Be honest and straightforward. Also, without treatment, your partner might pass the STI back to you.

- **Listen to your partner's concerns and fears and offer information about the STI and its symptoms and treatment.** During and after your talk, your partner may also have many strong emotions. Give your partner time to absorb this information. Help your partner understand that they may also have the STI. Sometimes, no one knows for sure who had the infection first.

- **Inform your partner about how to get medical care.** Just like you, your partner needs to receive medical attention as soon as possible, and there are a number of ways and places that your partner can get that care: (1) You can bring your partner to the health care provider you went to; (2) You can tell your partner to go to the health care provider you went to. Your partner should tell clinic staff which infection you were diagnosed with. Sharing this information will help your partner get the correct tests and treatment; (3) You may be able to get a prescription or medicine for both you and your partner from the clinic or from your doctor; this is called expedited partner therapy; and (4) Your partner can go to their own doctor or clinic such as the local health department's STI clinic, a family planning clinic, a student health center, or an urgent care clinic.

stopping STI transmission. Public STI and HIV/AIDS clinics, private doctors, family planning clinics, and hospitals are all places to get treatment. Do not use home remedies, products bought in the mail or online, or drugs obtained from friends.

3. *Get partners to treatment.* People who get treatment for an STI are doing the right thing, but they also need to encourage sexual partners and injection-drug-use partners to seek professional care immediately. This helps prevent serious illness in the partner, prevents reinfection, and helps control the STI epidemic. Because the first sign that a woman has an STI is often when her male partner shows symptoms, female partners especially should be advised. And even if a partner has no symptoms of an STI, he or she should still see a health care provider.

A national panel of public health officials and youth, in its 2004 report addressing the STI problem among youth aged 15–24, *Our Voices, Our Lives, Our Futures: Youth and Sexually Transmitted Diseases* (Cates, Herndon, Schulz, & Darroch, 2004), emphasized in the conclusion the importance and role of youth in stemming the STI problem in America. Still pertinent today, the report stated:

> In conclusion, young people need to participate in protecting their health, talking with their partners and others about sexual issues, pursuing how and when to get medical testing, and making wise choices as they grow up. It is the responsibility of the larger community to support young people with adequate and easy access to STD information and services. Young people are not mere statistical victims of this country's STD epidemic, and they are not unique in acquiring sexually transmitted infections. They have a crucial role to play in designing, running, and evaluating programs aimed at protecting youth from STDs. In partnership with parents, policy makers, health-care providers, religious leaders, educators, and others, youth hold the key to conquering this epidemic in American society. When youth are able to prevent STDs and make healthy choices for themselves, the results benefit not only youth, but society at large and potentially future generations.

Summary

The STI Epidemic

- STIs are a "hidden" epidemic in the United States, representing four of the six most frequently reported infectious diseases. An estimated 20 million new STI cases occur annually in the United States. Women, teens and young adults, and minority racial and ethnic groups are disproportionately affected by STIs. By age 25, one in two young persons will acquire an STI.

- STIs are behavior-linked diseases resulting largely from unprotected sexual contact. Behavioral, social, and biological factors contribute to the spread of STIs. The behavioral risk factors include early initiation of intimate sexual activity, sequential sexual relationships, concurrent sexual relation-ships, short gaps between partners, high-risk sexual partners, high-risk sexual behavior, inconsistent and incorrect condom use, substance abuse, sexual coercion, lack of personal knowledge and concern about STIs, and erroneous percep-tion of partner's risk. Social risk factors include poverty and marginalization, lack of access to health care, and secrecy and moral conflict about sexuality. Biological factors include the asymptomatic nature of STIs, resistance to treatment, and lack of cures.

- Without medical attention, STIs can lead to serious health problems, including sterility, cancer, heart disease, blindness, ectopic pregnancy, miscarriage, and death. The presence of an STI increases the risk of acquiring an HIV infection if exposed.

Principal Bacterial STIs

- Bacterial STIs are curable and include chlamydia, gonorrhea, urinary tract infections (NGU), and syphilis.

- *Chlamydia* is the most common bacterial STI in the United States and very common in young women, in whom repeated chlamydial infections can lead to infertility.

- *Gonorrhea* is the second most commonly notifiable disease in the United States. Men tend to experience the symptoms of gonorrhea more readily than women. Untreated gonorrhea can lead to pelvic inflammatory disease.

- *Urinary tract infections* can occur in both men and women and are sometimes referred to as nongonococcal urethritis (NGU). Untreated NGU can lead to damage of the repro-ductive organs of both men and women.

- *Syphilis,* a genital ulcerative disease, increases by two- to fivefold the chances of an infected person acquiring HIV if exposed to an HIV-infected person.

Principal Viral STIs

- Viral STIs are incurable, but treatable, and include HIV and AIDS, genital human papillomavirus infection, genital herpes, and hepatitis.

- *HIV/AIDS* has become one of the deadliest epidemics in human history.

- *Genital human papillomavirus* infection, or HPV, is the most common STI among sexually active young people,

Peter Dazeley/Getty Images

particularly women. Some people infected with HPV get genital warts. Persistent HPV infection is a key risk factor for cervical cancer. Vaccines have been approved for both males and females that protect against HPV strains that can result in cervical and anal cancer and genital warts.

- An estimated 776,000 persons in the United States get a new genital herpes infection annually. Genital herpes can make people more susceptible to HIV infection, and it can make HIV-infected individuals more infectious.

- *Hepatitis* is a viral disease affecting the liver. The most common types that can be sexually transmitted are hepatitis A and hepatitis B.

Vaginal Infections

- Vaginal infections, or *vaginitis,* are often, though not always, sexually transmitted and include bacterial vaginosis, candidiasis, and trichomoniasis.

- *Bacterial vaginosis (BV)* is the most common vaginal infection in women of childbearing age. Any woman can get BV, even women who never have had sexual intercourse.

- *Candidiasis,* also known as a "yeast infection," is an overgrowth of a normally present fungus in the body. Nearly 75% of all adult women have at least one vaginal yeast infection in their lifetime.

- *Trichomoniasis* is the most common curable STI in young, sexually active women. An estimated 3.7 million people in the United States have the infection, yet only 30% develop any symptoms of trichomoniasis.

Other STIs

- Several STIs that do not appear in the United States as often as in developing countries are chancroid, cytomegalovirus, enteric infections, granuloma inguinale, lymphogranuloma, and molluscum contagiosum.

Ectoparasitic Infestations

- Ectoparasitic infestations are parasites that live on the outer surface of the skin and can be spread sexually. They include scabies and pubic lice.

- *Scabies* is caused by a barely visible mite and is highly contagious. It spreads quickly among people who have close contact, sexually or nonsexually (e.g., prolonged contact with infested bedding).

- *Pubic lice,* commonly known as "crabs," can move easily from the pubic hair of one person to that of another.

Infections Caused by STIs

- Women tend to be more susceptible than men to STIs and to experience graver consequences, such as *pelvic inflammatory disease* (PID), an infection of the fallopian tubes that can lead to infertility, and ectopic pregnancy. *Cervicitis* is the

inflammation of the cervix, most commonly caused by an STI. Intense stimulation of the vulva can irritate the urethra, leading to *cystitis* (bladder infection).

Preventing and Treating STIs

- STI prevention involves the interaction of knowledge, psychological factors, couple dynamics, and risk-avoiding behaviors. Ways to avoid STIs include abstinence, sexual exclusivity, careful partner selection, condom use, avoidance of numerous partners and injection drugs. People practicing risky behavior should be alert to possible STI symptoms, seek treatment promptly if an STI is suspected, and inform partners of a known or suspected STI.

Questions for Discussion

- Given that condoms are one of the most important measures for reducing the risk of STI transmission and that many young people do not like condoms, what can be done to make condom use more appealing?

- What would be your most important concern if you just learned you had an STI? Who would you tell? What resources would you need? And where could you go to get help?

- Would it be difficult for you to inform a past sexual partner that you have an STI and that he or she might have it too? What would be your "opening line" to get the discussion started?

Sex and the Internet

The American Sexual Health Association

The American Sexual Health Association (ASHA), founded in 1914, is a nonprofit organization focusing on STI prevention. ASHA publishes a variety of educational materials, provides direct patient support through a national STI hotline and resource centers, and advocates increased funding for STI programs and sound public policies on STI control. ASHA also operates a website: http://www.ashasexualhealth.org. Go to it and then answer the following questions:

- What programs does ASHA offer?

- What services are provided on its website?

- What are the current ASHA headlines?

- What links are available at the ASHA website?

If you were diagnosed with an STI, would you seek more information from this site? Why or why not?

Suggested Websites

Centers for Disease Control and Prevention
http://www.cdc.gov/std
Provides information on STIs.

Joint United Nations Programme on HIV/AIDS
http://www.unaids.org
Contains epidemiological information on HIV/AIDS worldwide, as well as perspectives on HIV/AIDS-related issues.

Kaiser Family Foundation
http://www.kff.org
Offers fact sheets and news releases on STIs and HIV/AIDS.

Rural Center for AIDS/STD Prevention
http:rcap.indiana.edu
Provides information about issues related to HIV/STI prevention in rural communities

World Health Organization
http://www.who.int/reproductivehealth/topics/rtis/en/
Provides STI fact sheets and publications as well as information on related topics.

Suggested Reading

Brandt, A. M. (1987). *No magic bullet: A social history of venereal disease in the United States since 1880.* Oxford University Press. An informative and highly readable history of the social and political aspects of STIs.

Dizon, D. S., & Krychman, M. L. (2011). *Questions and answers about human papillomavirus (HPV).* Jones & Bartlett. Written by two medical doctors, this book provides authoritative answers to the most commonly asked questions about HPV.

Hayden, D. (2003). *Pox: Genius, madness, and the mysteries of syphilis.* Basic Books. From Beethoven to Oscar Wilde, from Van Gogh to Hitler, this book describes the effects of syphilis on the lives and works of seminal figures from the fifteenth to twentieth centuries.

Lowry, T. P. (2005). *Venereal disease and the Lewis and Clark expedition.* University of Nebraska Press. Describes how sex and venereal disease affected the men and mission of the Lewis and Clark expedition.

Newton, D.E. (2018). *STDs in the United States: A reference handbook.* ABC-CLIO. Provides information on the diagnosis and treatment of STIs and their impact of individuals and society. Helps reader make informed decisions related to their sexual health.

Park, I. (2021). *Strange bedfellows: Adventures in the science, history, and surprising secrets of STDs.* Flatiron Books. Not only does Dr. Park discuss the transmission of STDs, she presents a sex-positive style to talk about the history, mystery and fascination of the STDs and uses narratives to distigmatize STDs.

Reverby, S. M. (2009). *Examining Tuskegee: The infamous syphilis study and its legacy.* University of North Carolina Press. An analysis of the 40-year syphilis experiment by the U.S. Public Health Service involving hundreds of African American men.

Wilton, L., Palmer, R. T., & Maramba, D. C. (Eds.). (2014). *Understanding HIV and STI prevention for college students.* Routledge. This edited volume explores HIV/STI-related topics of interest to college students such as the hooking-up culture, sexual violence, LGBTQ, and students of color, as well as HIV/STIs in community colleges, rural colleges, and minority-serving institutes.

chapter

16

HIV and AIDS

MANDEL NGAN/Getty Images

Student Voices

"I am aware of HIV and STIs, and they are not something I take lightly. In my relationship, trust and honesty are key points, and we discussed our histories ahead of time. We then made educated decisions."

—20-year-old female

"I no longer hate you or feel angry with you [AIDS]. I realize now that you have become a positive force in my life. You are a messenger who has brought me a new understanding of my life and myself. So for that I thank you, forgive you, and release you. Because of you I have learned to love myself."

—21-year-old male

"My father had AIDS. When he found out, I was only 4 years old. My parents chose to keep it a secret from me and my brothers. I lived with my dad then. Though he felt sick sometimes, we did the normal things that a family would do throughout the rest of my childhood. When I turned 12 Dad became very sick and was hospitalized. I went to live with my mother. When Dad came out of the

hospital, he went to live with my grandparents. Still, no one told me what was wrong with him. Two years later, my mom finally told me that Dad had AIDS and was going to die soon. I was shocked and mad at both of my parents for not telling me earlier. My mom wouldn't let me go see Dad because he looked really bad and was in a lot of pain. I didn't get to see him or talk to him before he died. If I had known he was going to die so soon, I would have found a way to see him."*

—19-year-old female

"You have to deal not only with the illness [AIDS] but with the prejudices that you encounter every day."

—26-year-old male

"I think HIV and STIs are the biggest reasons why I'm not promiscuous. I'd love to have sex with multiple partners and experiment, but even if I used a condom every time, I would still feel very much at risk. That is why I am monogamous in my relationship."

—20-year-old female

"AIDS has changed us forever. It has brought out the best of us, and the worst."

—Michael Gottlieb, MD (1948–)

FEW PHENOMENA HAVE CHANGED the face of sexuality as dramatically as the appearance four decades ago of the microscopic virus known as **human immunodeficiency virus**, or **HIV**. In the early 1980s, physicians in San Francisco, New York, and Los Angeles began noticing repeated occurrences of formerly rare diseases among young and relatively healthy men. Kaposi's sarcoma, a cancer of the blood vessels, and *Pneumocystis carinii* pneumonia, a lung infection that is usually not dangerous, had become killer diseases because of the breakdown of the immune system of the men in whom these diseases were being seen (Centers for Disease Control and Prevention [CDC], 1981.15a). Even before the virus responsible for the immune system breakdown was discovered, the disease was given a name: **acquired immunodeficiency syndrome**, or **AIDS**. In the mid-1980s, the causative agent of AIDS, HIV, was discovered.

At first, AIDS within the United States seemed to be confined principally to three groups: gay men, Haitians, and people with hemophilia. Soon, however, it became apparent that AIDS was not confined to just a few groups; the disease spread into communities with high rates of injection drug use and into the general population, including heterosexual men and women (and their children) at all socioeconomic levels. The far-reaching consequences of the AIDS epidemic, in addition to the pain and loss directly caused by the illness, have included widespread fear, superstition, stigmatization, prejudice, and hatred. Ignorance of its modes of transmission has fueled the flames of homophobia among some people. Among others, it has kindled a general fear of sexual expression.

Great progress has been made in the prevention of HIV and the treatment for AIDS, yet HIV/AIDS remains a persistent problem in the United States and countries around the world. By now, most of us know how HIV is spread. And yet, for a variety of reasons, people continue to engage in behaviors that put them at risk. We hope that the material in this chapter will help you make healthy, informed choices for yourself and become an advocate for education and positive change in the community.

Because of the tremendous amount of AIDS research being conducted, some of the information presented here, particularly HIV/AIDS incidence and prevalence, could be outdated by the time this book appears in print. For updates on HIV/AIDS research findings and news, check the U.S. Centers for Disease Control and Prevention (CDC) website (the address is given in the "Sex and the Internet" section) or one of the websites listed at the end of this chapter. We begin the chapter by describing the biology of the disease and the immune system. We next discuss the epidemiology and transmission of HIV and the demographic aspects of the epidemic—that is, the effect of HIV/AIDS on various groups and communities. Then we address HIV prevention, testing, and current treatment. Finally, we discuss living with HIV or AIDS.

● What Is AIDS?

AIDS is an acronym for acquired immunodeficiency syndrome. This medical condition was so named because HIV is acquired (not inherited) and subsequently affects the body's immune system to the point where it often becomes deficient in combating disease-causing organisms, resulting in a group of symptoms that collectively indicate or characterize a disease or syndrome.

To monitor the spread of AIDS through a national surveillance system, the CDC has established a definition of AIDS. To receive an AIDS diagnosis under the CDC's classification system, a person must, in most cases, have a positive blood test indicating the presence of HIV antibodies and a CD4 (also called T lymphocyte or T cell) count (discussed later) below 200. AIDS can still be diagnosed if the person has one or more of the diseases or conditions associated with AIDS (discussed shortly) regardless of the CD4 count. If a person has HIV antibodies, as measured by a blood test, but does not meet the other criteria, they are said to "have HIV," "be HIV-positive," "be HIV-infected," or "be living with HIV." Infection with HIV produces a spectrum of diseases that progress from an asymptomatic state to AIDS, the final stage of HIV infection. The rate of this progression varies (CDC, 1992, 2014.16a, 2017.16a).

In 1993, the CD4 count, along with cervical cancer/cervical intraepithelial neoplasia (CIN), pulmonary tuberculosis, and recurrent bacterial pneumonia, was added to the CDC definition of AIDS (CDC, 1992). These additions led to a dramatic increase in the number of people who "officially" have AIDS.

Conditions Associated With AIDS

The CDC lists over 20 clinical conditions to be used in diagnosing AIDS along with HIV-positive status (CDC, 1996, 2014.16b). These conditions fall into several categories: **opportunistic infections (OIs)** such as **pneumocystis carinii pneumonia**, cancers such as **Kaposi's sarcoma**, conditions associated specifically with AIDS, and conditions that may be diagnosed as AIDS under certain circumstances. A person cannot rely on symptoms to establish that he or she has AIDS. Each symptom can be related to other illnesses. Remember, AIDS is a medical diagnosis made by a physician using the specific CDC criteria. OIs are less common now than they were in the early days of HIV and AIDS because early detection and better treatments reduce the amount of HIV in a person's body and keep a person's immune system stronger. Once someone has a dangerous opportunistic illness, life expectancy without treatment falls to about 1 year (CDC, 2014.16a, 2017.16b).

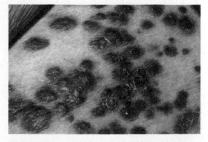

Kaposi's sarcoma is a cancer of the blood vessels commonly associated with AIDS. It causes red or purple blotches to appear under the skin.

National Cancer Institute (NCI)

The Immune System and HIV

The principal components of blood are plasma (the fluid base), red blood cells, white blood cells, and platelets.

think about it

The Stigmatization of HIV and Other STIs

The fear of stigma leads to silence, and when it comes to fighting AIDS, silence is death.

—Kofi Annan, former secretary general, United Nations (1938–2018)

The deep ambivalence our society feels about sexuality is clearly revealed by the way in which we deal with HIV and other STIs. If we think we have strep throat, we waste no time getting ourselves to a health center or doctor to obtain the appropriate medication. But let's say we're experiencing some discomfort when we urinate, and there's an unusual discharge. We may disregard the symptoms at first. Soon, we're feeling some pain, and we know something is definitely not right. With fear and trepidation, we slink into the clinic or doctor's office, hoping we don't see anyone we know so we won't have to explain why we're there. And then there's the whole problem of telling our partner—or, worse yet, partners—about our predicament.

Why all this emotion over an STI but not over strep throat? Where does all the fear, denial, embarrassment, guilt, shame, and humiliation come from? Why are STIs the only class of illnesses we categorize by their *mode of transmission* rather than by the type of organism that causes them? All these questions stem from a common source: the stigmatization of persons who contract HIV or another STI. HIV/STI stigma consists of negative beliefs, feelings, and attitudes toward people having an STI or living with HIV and persons of groups that have been heavily impacted by HIV/STI. The stigma can lead to unfair and unjust treatment of someone based on their real or perceived HIV/STI status, and resultant discrimination is often fueled by HIV/STI-related myths and pre-existing biases against certain groups, certain sexual behaviors, and drug use (CDC, 2019.16a). The Joint United Nations Programme on HIV/AIDS (UNAIDS) (2005) describes the origin of HIV stigmatization and some of its negative outcomes:

> HIV stigma stems from fear as well as associations of AIDS with sex, disease and death, and with behaviors that may be illegal, forbidden, or taboo, such as pre- and extramarital sex, sex work, sex between men, and injecting drug use. Stigma also stems from lack of awareness and knowledge about HIV. Such stigma can fuel the urge to make scapegoats of, and blame and punish, certain people or groups. Stigma taps into existing prejudices and patterns of exclusion and further marginalizes people who might already be more vulnerable to HIV infection.

Fear of stigmatization and feelings of shame are among the principal factors contributing to the spread of HIV and other STIs (Conley et al., 2013). For example, in a sample of clinic patients and others at high risk for gonorrhea and HIV in seven cities, both shame and stigma were related to seeking STI-related care, but stigma may have been a more powerful barrier to obtaining such care (Fortenberry et al., 2002). A telephone survey in Alabama found that STIs are shrouded in secrecy and shame and that infected women are more stigmatized than infected men, although men are held responsible for spreading STIs (Lichtenstein et al., 2005). A study of 40 African American men who have sex with men (MSM) found that 88%

experienced HIV stigma, 90% experienced sexual minority stigma, and 78% experienced both. Men with high HIV stigma were significantly more likely to engage in unprotected sex while high or intoxicated. Those endorsing more HIV stigma reported more receptive anal intercourse (Radcliffe et al., 2010). HIV-infected patients in the Netherlands were assessed to determine if HIV stigma was related to their taking of HIV medications: Those with the higher HIV stigma had greater nonadherence to the daily taking of all of the HIV medications (Sumari-de Boer et al., 2012).

A nationally representative survey of 1,794 18- to 30-year-olds conducted between January 25 and February 16, 2017, by the Kaiser Family Foundation found that most young people indicated that they would be comfortable having someone with HIV as friends (65%) or work colleagues (66%). However, for other situations, stigma was more evident. Half or more said they would be uncomfortable having a roommate infected with HIV (51%) or food prepared by someone living with HIV (58%). Seventy-three percent responded that they are "very uncomfortable" having a sexual partner with HIV, and 18% indicated they would be "somewhat uncomfortable" (Kaiser Family Foundation, 2017).

Obstetrician and gynecologist Jen Gunter (2019) in an article in the *New York Times* wonders if STIs are one of the last taboos and states that the sexual revolution apparently stopped short of liberating people from stigma and shame surrounding STIs. Somehow, having an STI makes women feel like "damaged goods." Gunter also questions why it should be any more shameful to acquire an infection from sexual behavior than from shaking hands, a kissing another person or being coughed upon. She concludes that "I suspect it is because shame and stigma are effective weapons of control that have been used throughout history to marginalize women, people of color, and the LGBTQ+ community."

The UNAIDS (2008, 2010) says that stigma and other societal causes of HIV risk and vulnerability are roadblocks to HIV prevention worldwide and need to be addressed as a "rights-based" response to the epidemic. The organization states that "long-term success in responding to the epidemic will require sustained progress in reducing human rights violations associated with it, including gender inequality, stigma, and discrimination."

Think Critically

1. How have you observed HIV/STI stigma among your friends or others in our society? How were these stigmas demonstrated?

2. In your view, what can be done to eliminate the cultural stigma of HIV/STIs?

3. If you became infected with HIV or another STI, would stigma and shame be an issue for you? If so, how would you deal with it? From what resources would you seek help and support?

Leukocytes There are several kinds of **leukocytes**, or white blood cells, all of which play major roles in defending the body against invading organisms and mutant (cancerous) cells. Because HIV invades and eventually kills some kinds of leukocytes, it impairs the body's ability to ward off infections and other harmful conditions that ordinarily would not be threatening. The principal type of leukocyte we discuss is the lymphocyte.

Macrophages, Antigens, and Antibodies White blood cells called **macrophages** engulf foreign particles and display the invader's antigen (*anti*body *gen*erator) like a signal flag on their own surfaces. **Antigens** are large molecules that are capable of stimulating the immune system and then reacting with the antibodies that are released to fight them. **Antibodies** bind to antigens, inactivate them, and mark them for destruction by killer cells. If the body has been previously exposed to the organism (by fighting it off or being vaccinated), the response is much quicker because memory cells are already biochemically programmed to respond.

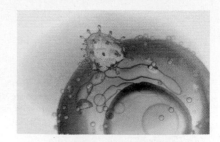

A T cell infected with HIV begins to replicate the virus, which buds from the cell wall, eventually killing the host cell.

MedicalRF.com

B Cells and T Cells The **lymphocytes** (a type of leukocyte) crucial to the immune system's functioning are **B cells** and several types of **T cells**. Like macrophages, **helper T cells** (also called CD4T or CD4 cells) are programmed to "read" the antigens and then begin directing the immune system's response. They send chemical signals to B cells, which begin making antibodies specific to the presented antigen. Helper T cells also stimulate the proliferation of B cells and T cells (which are genetically programmed to replicate, or make copies of themselves) and activate both macrophages and **killer T cells**, transforming them into agents of destruction whose only purpose is to attack and obliterate the enemy. Helper T cells display CD4, a type of protein receptor. The number of helper T cells (CD4 cells) in an individual's body is an important indicator of how well the immune system is functioning, as we discuss later.

The Virus

A **virus** is a protein-coated package of genes that invades a cell and alters the way in which the cell reproduces itself. Viruses can't propel themselves independently, and they can't reproduce unless they are inside a host cell. It would take 16,000 human immunodeficiency viruses to cover the head of a pin in a single layer. Under strong magnification, HIV resembles a spherical pin cushion, bristling with tiny, pinhead-like knobs (see Figure 1). These knobs are the antigens, which contain a protein called GP 120; the CD4 receptors on a helper T cell are attracted (fatally, as it turns out) to GP 120. Within the virus's protein core is the genetic material (RNA) that carries the information the virus needs to replicate itself. Also in the core is an enzyme called **reverse transcriptase**, which enables the virus to "write" its RNA (the genetic software or program) into a cell's DNA. In the normal genetic writing process, RNA is transcribed from DNA. Viruses with the ability to reverse the normal genetic writing process are known as **retroviruses**. There are numerous variant strains of HIV as a result of mutations. The virus begins undergoing genetic variation as soon as it has infected a person, even before antibodies develop. This tendency to mutate is one factor that makes HIV difficult to destroy.

Effect on T Cells When HIV enters the bloodstream, helper T cells rush to the invading viruses, as if they were specifically designed for them. Normally at this stage, a T cell reads the antigen, stimulating antibody production in the B cells and beginning the process of eliminating the invading organism. In the case of HIV, however, although antibody production does begin, the immune process starts to break down almost at once. HIV injects its contents into the host T cell and copies its own genetic code into the cell's genetic material (DNA). As a result, when the immune system is activated, the T cell begins producing HIV instead of replicating itself. The T cell is killed in the process. HIV also targets other types of cells, including macrophages, dendritic cells (leukocytes found in the skin, lymph nodes, and intestinal mucous membranes), and brain cells.

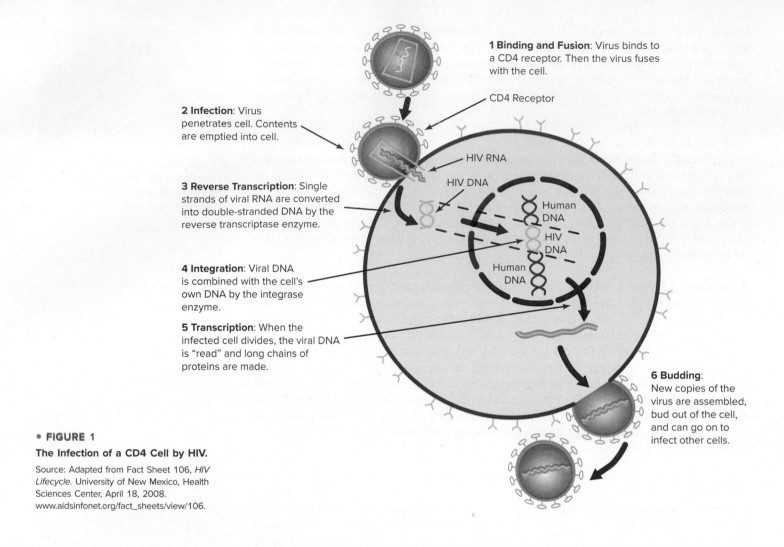

1 **Binding and Fusion**: Virus binds to a CD4 receptor. Then the virus fuses with the cell.

CD4 Receptor

2 **Infection**: Virus penetrates cell. Contents are emptied into cell.

HIV RNA

HIV DNA

Human DNA

HIV DNA

Human DNA

3 **Reverse Transcription**: Single strands of viral RNA are converted into double-stranded DNA by the reverse transcriptase enzyme.

4 **Integration**: Viral DNA is combined with the cell's own DNA by the integrase enzyme.

5 **Transcription**: When the infected cell divides, the viral DNA is "read" and long chains of proteins are made.

6 **Budding**: New copies of the virus are assembled, bud out of the cell, and can go on to infect other cells.

● **FIGURE 1**

The Infection of a CD4 Cell by HIV.

Source: Adapted from Fact Sheet 106, *HIV Lifecycle*. University of New Mexico, Health Sciences Center, April 18, 2008. www.aidsinfonet.org/fact_sheets/view/106.

HIV-1 and HIV-2   Almost all cases of HIV in the United States involve the type of the virus known as HIV-1. Another type, HIV-2, has been found to exist mainly in West Africa. Both HIV-1 and HIV-2 have the same mode of transmission and are associated with similar OIs and AIDS, although HIV-2 is less infectious than HIV-1.

How the Disease Progresses

As discussed earlier, when viruses are introduced into the body, they are immediately taken up by helper T cells and quickly moved to the lymph nodes. HIV begins replication right away within the host cells. Most people will develop detectable antibodies to HIV within 3–8 weeks after exposure. The process by which a person develops antibodies is called **seroconversion**. A person's **serostatus** is HIV-negative if antibodies to HIV are not detected and HIV-positive if antibodies are detected.

T-Cell (CD4) Count   T-cell count—also called CD4 count—refers to the number of helper T cells that are present in a cubic millimeter of blood. A healthy person's CD4 count averages about 1,000, but it can range from 500–1,600, depending on a person's general health and whether he or she is fighting off an illness.

Phases of Infection   When people with HIV do not get treatment, they typically progress through three stages. But, HIV medicine can slow or prevent progression of the disease. With the advancements in treatment, progression to Stage 3 is much less common today than in the early days of HIV (CDC, 2017.16a, 2020.16a, 2020.16b; Scaccia, 2020). (See Figure 2 for a schematic representation of the general pattern of untreated HIV infection.)

Stage 1: Acute HIV Infection

- People have a large amount of HIV in their blood and are very contagious.
- Some people experience flu-like symptoms within 2 to 4 weeks. These symptoms usually disappear within a week to a month and are often mistaken for those of another viral infection.
- Some people may not feel sick right away or at all.
- If one has flu-like symptoms and thinks they may have been exposed to HIV, the person should seek medical care and ask for a test to diagnose acute infection.
- Only antigen/antibody tests or nucleic acid tests (NATs) can diagnose acute infection.

Stage 2: Chronic HIV Infection

- This stage is also called asymptomatic HIV infection.
- HIV is still active but reproduces at very low levels.
- People may not have symptoms or get sick during this phase.
- Without taking HIV medicine, this period may last a decade or longer, but some may progress faster.
- People can transmit HIV in this phase.
- By the end of this phase, the amount of HIV in the blood (called viral load) has increased and the CD4 cell count had gone down. The person may have symptoms as the virus levels increase in the body, and the person moves into stage 3.

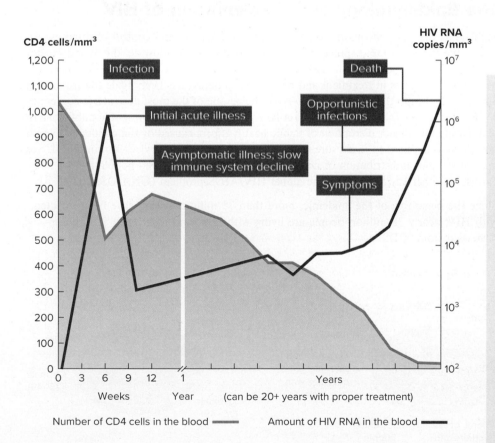

Number of CD4 cells in the blood ——— Amount of HIV RNA in the blood ▬▬▬

• FIGURE 2

The General Pattern of Untreated HIV Infection.

Source: Adapted from Fauci, A.S., et al., 1996.

During the initial acute illness, CD4 levels (green line) fall sharply and HIV RNA levels (red line) increase; many infected people experience flulike symptoms during this period. Antibodies to HIV usually appear 3–8 weeks after the initial infection. During the asymptomatic phase that follows, CD4 levels (a marker for the status of the immune system) gradually decline, and HIV RNA levels again increase. Due to declines in immunity, infected individuals eventually begin to experience symptoms; when CD4 levels drop very low, people become vulnerable to serious opportunistic infections characteristic of AIDS. Modern treatment delays or slows the decline of the CD4 level. Without treatment, chronic or recurrent illnesses continue until the immune system fails and death results.

Stage 3: Acquired Immunodeficiency Syndrome (AIDS)

- In the absence of treatment, AIDS usually develops 8 to 10 years after initial HIV infection.

- People with AIDS have such badly damaged immune systems that can lead to an increasing number of certain opportunistic infections.

- People with AIDS can have a high viral load and be very infectious.

- Life expectancy is different for every person living with Stage 3 HIV. Some people may die within months after being diagnosed with AIDS, but the majority can live fairly healthy lives with regular **antiretroviral therapy** (**ART**), the drugs used to treat the HIV retrovirus.

- Without treatment, people with AIDS typically survive about 3 years.

As time goes by without treatment, the T cells gradually diminish in number, destroyed by newly created HIV. HIV is still active but reproduces at very low levels. People may not have any symptoms or get sick during this time. For people who aren't taking medicine to treat HIV, this period can last a decade or longer, but some progress through this stage faster. People who correctly take medicine to treat HIV may stay in this stage for several decades. At the end of this phase, a person's viral load starts to go up and the CD4 cell count begins to go down, moving them in to the advanced phase (CDC, 2017.16a).

When AIDS is in the advanced phase, the T cells and other fighter cells of the immune system are no longer able to trap foreign invaders. Infected cells continue to increase, and the CD4 count drops to under 200. The virus is detectable in the blood. At this point, the person may be fairly ill to very ill, although some may not have symptoms. The CD4 count may continue to plummet to zero. The person with AIDS dies from one or more of the opportunistic infections.

● The Epidemiology and Transmission of HIV

Epidemiology is the study of the incidence, process, distribution, and control of diseases. An **epidemic** is the wide and rapid spread of a contagious disease. Worldwide, the World Health Organization (WHO) and the Joint United Nations Programme on HIV/AIDS have declared that because of successes in treatment and prevention, progress has been made toward ending AIDS as a public health threat despite HIV/AIDS being one of the most destructive epidemics in recorded history (UNAIDS, 2020.16a). Yet HIV/AIDS remains a major global public health problem. Despite the major disruption of public health efforts caused by the pandemic, health officials are working hard to make sure that the disruption of HIV services is minimized. See Figure 3 for the global distribution of new HIV infections by gender and population for 2019. Here are some other key facts about the global HIV/AIDS problem (UNAIDS, 2020.16b):

- Since the beginning of the epidemic, more than 75 million people have been infected with HIV, nearly 38 million people are living with HIV, and more than 32 million have died from AIDS.

● **FIGURE 3**

Distribution of New HIV Infections by Gender and Population, Global, 2019

Source: Adapted from UNAIDS, 2020.16b.

- In 2019, around 1.7 million people were newly infected with HIV, a reduction in 40% since the peak in 1998. The annual number of new infections has been falling more rapidly among women and girls (27% decrease since 2010) than among men and boys (18% decrease).

- The majority of new adult HIV infections in 2019 were among key populations and their partners, including sex workers, people who inject drugs, prisoners, transgender persons, and men who have sex with men.

- The global decrease of new infections largely occurred in South Africa, Caribbean, western and central Africa, western and central Europe and North America, Asia, and the Pacific. The epidemic continued to expand in Eastern Europe, Central Asia, Middle East, North Africa, and Latin America. Over two thirds of all people living with HIV live in the WHO African Region.

- In 2019, AIDS-related deaths have been reduced by 60% since the peak in 2004.

- By end of 2019, an estimated 81% of persons living with HIV knew their status, 67% were receiving ART and 59% had achieved suppression of the HIV with no risk of infecting others.

The Epidemiology of HIV/AIDS in the United States

In the United States, since the diagnosis of the first AIDS case four decades ago, the number of persons living with HIV has grown from a few dozen to an estimated 1.2 million people at the end of 2018. Annual infections have been reduced by more than two thirds since the height of the epidemic in the mid-1980s. However, CDC data indicate that the progress has stalled in recent years and great disparities occur in some population groups (HIV.gov, 2020; CDC, 2019.16b). Below is a broad overview of the HIV epidemic in the United States; more information about many of these statistics are provided later in this chapter.

Nearly 38,000 persons were diagnosed with HIV infection in 2018, a 7% decrease from 2014. The proportion of HIV cases differs by sex: In 2018, males accounted for 81% of diagnosed HIV cases. Most men contract HIV through male-to-male sexual contact and most women acquire HIV through heterosexual contact (see Figure 4). Also, from 2014 to 2018, HIV diagnoses were:

- Down 8% among all women
- Up 6% for 25- to 34-year-olds
- Up 5% for transgender women
- Up 51% among people who inject drugs

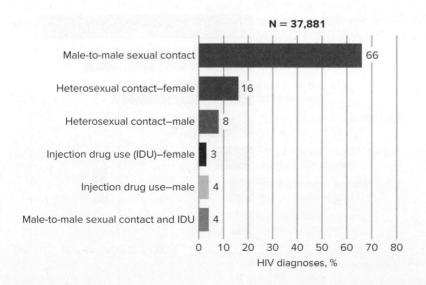

N = 37,881

Transmission Category	HIV diagnoses, %
Male-to-male sexual contact	66
Heterosexual contact—female	16
Heterosexual contact—male	8
Injection drug use (IDU)—female	3
Injection drug use—male	4
Male-to-male sexual contact and IDU	4

• **FIGURE 4**

Percentages of Diagnoses of HIV Infection among Adults and Adolescents, by Transmission Category, 2018—United States and Six Dependent Areas

Source: CDC, 2020.16c.

Sixty-six percent of the adult and adolescent HIV/AIDS cases were attributed to male-to-male sexual contact, and 29% of the adult and adolescent HIV/AIDS cases were attributed to high-risk heterosexual contact (CDC, 2020.16a).

The proportional distribution of AIDS cases by transmission category has shifted since the beginning of the epidemic (see Figure 5), with the percentage of cases for male-to-male sexual contact decreasing from 65% in 1985, then rising to 52% of all AIDS diagnoses in 2018 and the percentage for high-risk heterosexual contact increasing and then leveling off. New HIV diagnoses among most-affected populations are presented in Figure 6. Ninety-eight percent were from male-to-male sexual contact.

The Centers for Disease Control and Prevention researchers used HIV diagnoses and AIDS death rates from 2009 to 2013 to project the lifetime risk of HIV diagnosis in the United States by sex, ethnicity, HIV risk group, and states, assuming diagnoses rates remain constant (CDC, 2016.16b). Overall, the lifetime risk of HIV diagnosis in the United States is now 1 in 99, an improvement from a previous analysis using 2004–2005 data that reported overall risk at 1 in 78. However, this overall progress masks large disparities, as shown in Figure 7:

- Gay and bisexual men continue to be the most affected by the HIV epidemic in the United States. At the current rates, 1 in 6 MSM will be diagnosed in their lifetime, including 1 in 2 Black MSM, 1 in 4 Latino MSM, and 1 in 11 white MSM.

FIGURE 5

Percentages of Stage 3 AIDS Among Adults and Adolescents with Diagnosed HIV Infection, by Transmission Category and Year of Classification, 1985–2017, United States and Six Dependent Areas.

Source: CDC, 2020.16c.

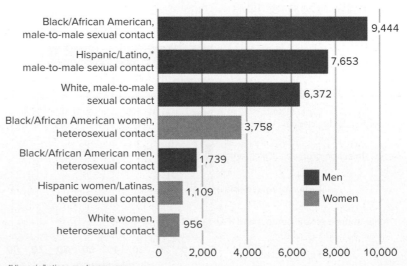

[a]Heterosexual contact with a person known to have, or to be at high risk for, HIV infection.
[b]Includes hemophilia, blood transfusion, perinatal exposure, and risk factor not reported or not identified.

FIGURE 6

New HIV Diagnoses in the United States and Dependent Areas for the Most-Affected Subpopulations, 2018

Source: CDC, 2020.16d.

*Hispanic/Latinos can be any race.

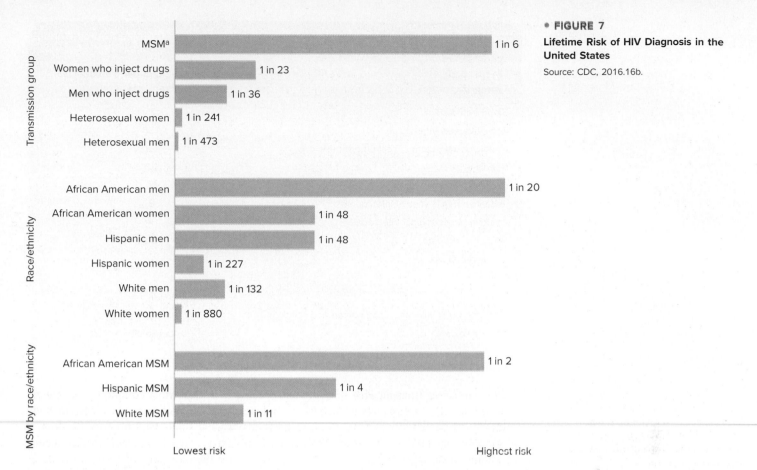

• FIGURE 7

Lifetime Risk of HIV Diagnosis in the United States

Source: CDC, 2016.16b.

[a]**MSM** = Men who have sex with men.

Sources: Adapted from Patel, P., et al., 2014; Anderson, G. S., et al., 1999; CDC, 2016.16c.

- African Americans are by far the most affected racial and ethnic group with a lifetime HIV risk of 1 in 20 for men compared to 1 in 132 for whites and 1 in 48 for women compared to 1 in 880 for whites.

- People who inject drugs are at much higher lifetime risk than the general population, and women who inject drugs have a higher risk than men (1 in 23 compared with 1 in 36).

Modes and Myths of Transmission

Research has revealed a great deal of valuable medical, scientific, and public health information about HIV transmission, and the ways HIV is transmitted have been clearly identified. However, false information not supported by scientific findings still persists. Because of this, the CDC has described the ways HIV is transmitted and has corrected misconceptions about HIV.

The risk of getting HIV varies widely depending on the type of exposure or behavior such as sharing needles or having sex without a condom. Some exposures to HIV carry a much higher risk of transmission than other exposures. For some exposures, such as spitting or sharing sex toys, while the transmission is biologically possible, the risk is so low that it is not possible to put a precise number on it. However, even relatively small risks can add up over time and lead to a high lifetime risk of getting HIV. In other words, there may be a relatively small chance of acquiring HIV when engaging in a risky behavior with an infected partner only once; but if repeated many times, the overall likelihood of becoming infected after repeated exposures is actually much higher (CDC, 2020.16a). Table 1 lists the risk of transmission per 100,000 exposures for various types of exposures. A detailed discussion of the various HIV transmission behaviors is presented later.

TABLE 1 ● Estimated Probability of Acquiring HIV from an Infected Source During One Episode of a Specific Behavior

Type of Exposure	Risk of Exposure per 100,000 Exposures
Blood transfusion	9,250
Receptive anal intercourse	138
Needle-sharing during injection drug use	63
Needle-stick	23
Insertive anal intercourse	11
Receptive penile-vaginal intercourse	8
Insertive penile-vaginal intercourse	4
Receptive oral sex	low
Insertive oral sex	low
Biting	low
Spitting	negligible
Throwing body fluids including semen and saliva	negligible
Sharing sex toys	negligible

Sources: Adapted from Patel, P., et al., 2014; Pretty, L. A., et al., 1999.

You can get or transmit HIV only through specific activities. Most commonly, people get or transmit HIV through sexual behaviors and needle or syringe use. Only certain body fluids—blood, semen, pre-seminal fluid, rectal fluids, vaginal fluids, and breast milk—from a person who has HIV can transmit HIV. These fluids must come in contact with a mucous membrane or damaged tissue or be directly injected into the bloodstream (from a needle or syringe) for transmission to occur. Mucous membranes are found inside the rectum, vagina, penis, and mouth. The CDC has described how common varied behaviors are in HIV transmission (CDC, 2020.16a):

- **Primary Ways HIV Is Spread** In the United States, having anal or vaginal sex with someone who has HIV without using a condom or not taking medicines to prevent or treat HIV (discussed later) is a major mechanism for HIV transmission. For the HIV-negative partner, receptive anal sex (bottoming) is the highest-risk sexual behavior, but you can also get HIV from insertive anal sex (topping). Either partner can get HIV through vaginal sex, though it is less risky for getting HIV than receptive anal sex. HIV can also be transmitted by sharing needles or syringes, rinse water, or other equipment used to prepare drugs for injection with someone who has HIV. HIV can live in a used needle up to 42 days, depending on temperature and other factors.

- **Less Common Ways HIV Is Spread** A less frequent way of HIV transmission is from mother to child during pregnancy, birth, or breastfeeding. Although the risk can be high if a mother is living with HIV and not taking medicine, recommendations to test all pregnant women for HIV and to start HIV treatment immediately for those who are positive have lowered the number of babies born with HIV. Being stuck with an HIV-contaminated needle or other sharp object is a risk mainly for health care workers.

- **Extremely Rare Ways HIV Is Spread** On rare occasions, HIV has been transmitted by:
  - Oral sex—putting the mouth on the penis (fellatio), vagina (cunnilingus), or anus (rimming). In general, there's little to no risk of getting HIV from oral sex. But transmission of HIV, though extremely low, is theoretically possible if an HIV-positive man ejaculates in his partner's mouth during oral sex. Factors that may increase the risk of transmitting HIV through oral sex are ejaculation into a mouth with oral ulcers and/or bleeding gum and a partner with penile sores and the presence of other STIs that may or may not be visible.
  - Receiving blood transfusions, blood products, or organ/tissue transplants that are contaminated with HIV. This was more common in the early years of HIV, but

now the risk is extremely small because of rigorous testing of the U.S. blood supply and donated organs and tissues.

- Eating food that has been pre-chewed by an HIV-infected person. The contamination occurs when infected blood from a caregiver's mouth mixes with food while chewing. The only known cases of this mode of transmission are among infants.

- Being bitten by a person with HIV. Each of the very small number of documented cases has involved severe trauma with extensive tissue damage and the presence of blood. There is no risk of transmission if the skin is not broken.

- Contact between broken skin, wounds, or mucous membranes and HIV-infected blood or blood-contaminated body fluids.

- Deep, open-mouth kissing if both partners have sores or bleeding gums and blood from the HIV-positive partner gets into the bloodstream of the HIV-negative partner. HIV is not spread through saliva.

Given that AIDS has been a major health problem for four decades, one could assume that nearly all people have an accurate understanding of HIV/AIDS and know the difference between actual transmission routes and transmission myths. However, the Kaiser Family Foundation national representative study of 1,794 18–30-year-olds cited earlier found that more than a third of the participants incorrectly believe that HIV can be spread through everyday items such as plates and glasses (38%) or toilets (38%). The majority are misinformed in believing that HIV can be transmitted by spitting (54%) or kissing (58%) (Kaiser Family Foundation, 2017). So just to briefly review: Scientific and epidemiological evidence shows that the chances are essentially zero of acquiring HIV from an environmental surface (e.g., toilet seat), from nonsexual contact with an HIV-infected person at home or work, from typical social contact (e.g., hugging, shaking hands), from food serving establishments, from closed-mouth or social kissing, from insect (e.g., mosquito) bites, from sport-participation accidents involving blood, or from donating blood. Contact with the saliva (e.g., being spit on by an HIV-infected person), tears, or sweat from an HIV-infected person has never been shown to result in the transmission of the virus. The CDC knows of no instances of HIV being transmitted through tattooing or body piercing, although hepatitis B virus has been transmitted during some of these procedures. Also, being bitten by an HIV-infected person is not a common method of transmitting HIV. There is no risk of transmission if the skin is not broken. Also, reports are extremely rare of HIV transmission from contact between broken skin, wounds, or mucus and HIV-infected blood or blood-contaminated body fluids. Further, HIV is not transmitted through the air.

Some people have been concerned about the possibility of acquiring HIV from a blood transfusion and organ donations. Contaminated donated blood, plasma, body organs, and semen are all capable of sustaining HIV. Because of this, medical procedures in the United States involving these materials now include screening for HIV or destroying the virus, and the chance of acquiring HIV from these procedures is extremely low. To be absolutely safe, some people who know they will have surgery donate their own blood a few weeks before the operation so that it will be available during surgery if needed. Donated organs are screened for HIV, and there are guidelines regarding semen donation for artificial insemination. One controversial aspect of blood donation is the Food and Drug Administration (FDA) guidance for blood donation by men who have sex with men. In 1983, at the start of the AIDS crisis, the FDA enacted a lifetime ban on any man who had sex with men (even just one sexual intercourse episode) donating blood. In December 2015, the ban was reduced to 12 months. Then, in April 2020, because of a shortage of blood donations during the COVID-19 pandemic, the FDA relaxed its restriction to 3 months. Advocates still contend that the restriction is archaic, demeaning, and not based on science (Shaw, 2020).

Sexual Transmission

Recall that HIV can be found in the semen, pre-seminal fluid, vaginal fluid, or blood of a person infected with the virus. Latex barriers, condoms, dental dams, and surgical gloves, if used properly, can provide good protection against the transmission of HIV.

Anal Intercourse Unprotected anal sex (no condom use) is considered to be the most risky sexual behavior for getting or transmitting HIV, and either sexual partner can become infected during anal sex. In general, the partner receiving the semen is at greater risk of getting HIV because the lining of the rectum is thin and may allow the virus to enter the body. Actually, the receptive partner is 13 times more likely to get infected than the insertive partner. However, the insertive partner is also at risk, since HIV can enter through the urethra or through small cuts, abrasions, or open sores on the penis (CDC, 2019.16f). Exposure to certain body fluids—blood, semen, pre-seminal fluid, or rectal fluids—can place an individual at risk for acquiring HIV. The vast majority of men who get HIV get it through anal sex. However, anal sex is also one of the ways women can get HIV. The 2015 Sexual Exploration in America Study found that 43% of men during their lifetime had been the insertive partner during anal sex and 9% the receptive partner. Thirty-seven percent of women had during their life had received anal sex (Herbenick et al., 2017). Further, the National College Health assessment found that during spring semester in 2019, 7% and 5% of college men and women reported anal intercourse in the past 30 days, with only 35% and 21% of men and women, respectively, using a condom (American College Health Association, 2019).

Vaginal Intercourse Both male and female partners can get HIV from vaginal sex. Vaginal-penile sex is the second highest sexual risk behavior. When a woman has vaginal sex with a partner who is HIV-positive, she can get HIV because the lining of the vagina and cervix can allow HIV to enter her body if her partner's bodily fluids carry HIV, including blood, semen, and pre-seminal fluid. Most women who get HIV get it from having vaginal sex, especially if they have vaginal sex with men more likely to be infected, such as men who inject drugs or have sex with other men. Even if a woman's male partner withdraws or pulls out before ejaculating, she can still get infected because pre-seminal fluid can carry HIV.

Men can also get HIV from having vaginal sex with a woman who is HIV-positive. This is because vaginal fluid and blood can carry HIV. Men get HIV through the opening at the tip of the penis (urethra); the foreskin if they're not circumcised; or small cuts, scratches, or open sores anywhere on the penis. There is evidence that male circumcision may decrease the risk of the man getting HIV during vaginal sex. There is no evidence that circumcision benefits the woman, though more studies are underway. (See Chapter 15 to learn more about male circumcision and HIV.) Withdrawal before ejaculating may, in theory, reduce the risk of getting HIV for the woman. But, it does not change the risk of getting HIV for the man. Many things can increase someone's risk of getting HIV from vaginal sex. For example, both women and men are more likely to get HIV from vaginal sex if an HIV-positive partner is not on HIV treatment and virally suppressed. It is also more likely for the HIV-negative partner to get HIV if either partner has a sexually transmitted infection (STI). In addition to HIV, a person can get STIs like chlamydia and gonorrhea from vaginal sex (CDC, 2020.16a).

Adolescent females are biologically more susceptible to HIV than older women because their immature cervixes may be more easily infected (Braverman & Strasburger, 1994). However, the virus can enter the bloodstream through the urethra or through small cuts or open sores on the penis. Menstrual blood containing HIV can also facilitate the transmission of the virus to a sexual partner.

Oral Sex HIV may be transmitted during fellatio, cunnilingus, or analingus (oral-anal contact), although evidence suggests that the risk is much less than that from unprotected anal or vaginal sex. Receiving fellatio, giving or receiving cunnilingus, and giving or receiving analingus carries an extremely low chance that an HIV-negative person will get HIV from an HIV-positive person. The highest oral sex risk is to individuals (male or female) to whom an HIV-infected man ejaculates in his or her mouth. The risk of HIV transmission increases if the person performing oral sex has cuts or sores around or in the mouth or throat or if the person receiving oral sex has another STI. If the person performing oral sex has HIV, blood from the mouth may enter the body of the person receiving oral sex through the lining of the urethra, vagina, cervix, or anus or directly into the body through small cuts or open sores. If the person receiving oral sex has HIV, the blood, semen, pre-seminal fluid, or vaginal

think about it

"Do You Know What You Are Doing?" Common Condom-Use Mistakes Among College Students

For those wanting to prevent STIs and pregnancy, condom use is necessary for all sexual episodes. But consistent use is only part of the answer—the condom must be used correctly if it is to be effective.

Very little research has been conducted on correct condom use, but the first comprehensive study of college male students produced some startling and alarming results. Researchers at The Kinsey Institute Condom Use Research Team (KI-CURT) and the Rural Center for HIV/STD Prevention at Indiana University determined the prevalence of male condom-use errors and problems among samples of undergraduate, single, self-identified heterosexual men ($N = 158$) who applied the condom to themselves and single, self-identified heterosexual women ($N = 102$) who applied a condom to their male partner. These studies were conducted at a large, Midwestern University. Participants were asked to indicate if the error or problem occurred at least once during the past 3 months during sex, defined as when the male put his penis in a partner's mouth, vagina, or rectum. The percentage of the errors and problems that occurred at least once in the past 3 months were remarkably similar, whether or not the male applied the condom to himself or whether his female partner applied the condom to him. The table indicates some of the most important errors and problems (Crosby et al., 2002; Sanders et al., 2003).

Error/Problem	Male Appliers	Female Appliers
Put condom on after starting sex	43%*	51%*
Did not hold tip and leave space	40%	46%
Put condom on the wrong side up (had to flip it over)	30%	30%
Used condom without lubricant	19%	26%
Took condom off before sex was over	15%	15%
Did not change to new condoms when switching between vaginal, oral, and anal sex (for those switching)	81%	75%
Condom broke	29%	19%
Condom slipped off during sex	13%	19%

Error/Problem	Male Appliers	Female Appliers
Lost erection before condom was put on	22%	14%
Lost erection after condom was on and sex had begun	20%	20%

* Percentage reporting that the error or problem occured at least once in the past three months.

A subsequent focus group study of undergraduates who reported male condom use for other-sex behavior in the previous month found that they had concerns about male condoms, including mistrust of each gender in supplying and properly using condoms, inadequate lubrication during condom use, condoms partially or fully slipping off during sex, "losing" part or all of the condom in the vagina, delayed applications, and irritation and reduced sensation (Yarber et al., 2007). An Internet study of men examined another aspect of condom-use problems: ill-fitting condoms. Men reporting ill-fitting condoms were more likely to report breakage and slippage as well as incomplete condom use (late application and/or early removal of the condom). Interestingly, the study also found that ill-fitting condoms diminished sexual functioning and pleasure during penile-vaginal intercourse for both men and women (Crosby et al., 2010).

The researchers concluded that the condom-use errors and problems reported in these studies indicate a possible high risk of exposure of the participants to HIV/STIs and unintended pregnancy. They also stated that the effectiveness of condom use against HIV/STIs and unintended pregnancy is contingent upon correct condom use.

Think Critically

1. Did the types and frequency of condom-use errors and problems found in these studies surprise you? Explain.
2. Why do you think these errors and problems occurred?
3. Is it really that difficult to use condoms correctly? Why or why not?
4. What can be done to promote correct condom use?

fluid may contain the virus. Cells lining the mouth of the person performing oral sex may allow HIV to enter the body. The exact risk of HIV transmission is difficult to measure because people who participate in oral sex may also participate in other sexual behaviors. When HIV transmission occurs, it may be the result of oral sex or other, riskier sexual activities such as unprotected anal or vaginal sex (CDC, 2020.16a).

Kissing Kissing, because it involves saliva, is frequently a concern among those who are unsure how HIV is transmitted. HIV is not transmitted casually, so kissing on the cheek is very safe. Transmission through kissing alone is extremely rare. Although HIV can be detected in saliva, it cannot be passed to other people through kissing because a combination of antibodies and enzymes found naturally in saliva prevent HIV from infecting new cells (National Health Service, 2018). There are extremely rare cases of HIV being transmitted via deep "French" kissing, but in each case, infected blood was exchanged due to bleeding gums or sores in the mouth. Prolonged open-mouth kissing could damage the mouth or lips and allow HIV to pass from an infected person to a partner and then enter the body through cuts or sores in the mouth (CDC, 2014.16g). Because of this possible risk, the CDC (2010.16b) recommends against open-mouth kissing with an HIV-infected partner.

Sex Toys Although unlikely, HIV can be transmitted in vaginal secretions on such objects as dildos and vibrators; therefore, it is very important that (1) these objects not be shared, (2) they be washed thoroughly before use, (3) each partner has a different set of toys, and (4) penetrative toys, such as vibrators, be covered with a condom each time they are used.

Substance and Injection Drug Use

Substance use disorders, which are problematic patterns of using alcohol or another substance, such as crack cocaine, methamphetamine ("meth"), amyl nitrite ("poppers"), prescription opioids, heroin, and fentanyl are closely associated with HIV and other sexually transmitted infections. Injection drug use (IDU) can be a direct route of HIV transmission if people share needles, syringes, or other injection materials that are contaminated with HIV. The risk for getting or transmitting HIV is very high if an HIV-negative person uses injection equipment that someone with HIV has used. This high risk is because the drug materials may have blood in them, and blood can carry HIV. Drinking alcohol and/or ingesting, smoking, or inhaling drugs are also associated with increased risk for HIV. These substances alter judgment, which can lead to risky sexual behaviors (e.g., having sex without a condom, having numerous partners) that can make people more likely to get and transmit HIV. In people living with HIV, substance use can hasten disease progression, affect adherence to antiretroviral therapy (HIV medicine), and worsen the overall consequences of HIV. Commonly used substances and HIV risk are:

- *Alcohol.* Excessive alcohol consumption, notably binge drinking, can be an important risk factor for HIV because it is linked to risky sexual behaviors and, among people living with HIV, can hurt treatment outcomes.

- *Opioids.* Opioids, a class of drugs that reduce pain, include both prescription drugs, heroin and fentanyl. They are associated with HIV risk behaviors such as needle sharing when infected and risky sex, and have been linked to severe recent HIV outbreaks in the United States.

- *Methamphetamine.* "Meth" is linked to risky sexual behavior that places people at greater HIV risk. It can be injected, which also increases HIV risk if people share needles and other injection equipment.

- *Crack cocaine.* Crack cocaine is a stimulant that can create a cycle in which people quickly exhaust their resources and turn to other ways to get the drug, including trading sex for drugs or money, which increases HIV risk.

- *Inhalants.* Use of amyl nitrite ("poppers") has long been linked to risky sexual behaviors, illegal drug use, and sexually transmitted infections among gay, bisexual, and queer men.

A number of behavioral, structural, and environmental factors make it difficult to control the spread of HIV among people who use or misuse substances. People who are alcohol dependent or use drugs often have other complex health and social needs. Those who use substances are more likely to be homeless, face unemployment, live in poverty, and experience multiple forms of violence, creating challenges for HIV prevention efforts. Often, illicit drug use is viewed as a criminal activity rather than a medical issue that requires counseling and rehabilitation. Fear of arrest, immigration status, poverty, stigma, feelings of guilt, and low self-esteem may prevent people who use illicit drugs from seeking treatment services, which places them at greater risk for HIV. Since HIV testing often involves questioning about substance use histories, those who use substances may feel uncomfortable getting tested. As a result, it may be harder to reach people who use substances with HIV prevention services. People living with HIV who use substances are less likely to take antiretroviral therapy (ART) as prescribed due to side effects from drug interaction or the substance may impair judgment. Not taking medical treatment as prescribed can worsen the effects of HIV and increase the likelihood of spreading HIV to sex and drug-sharing partners. IDU in nonurban areas has created prevention challenges and has placed new populations at risk for HIV.

Several challenges impeded efforts to prevent substance and injection drug use, such as:

- **The high-risk practices of sharing needles, syringes, and other injection equipment are common among persons who inject drugs (PWID).** In a study of cities with high levels of HIV, 40% of new PWID (those who have been injecting for 5 years or less) shared syringes. From 2005 to 2015, syringe sharing declined 34% among Black PWID and 12% among Hispanic/Latino PWID, but did not decline among white PWID.

- **Risk estimates** show that the average chance that an HIV-negative person will get HIV each time that person shares needles to inject drugs with an HIV-positive person is about 1 in 160.

- **Injecting drugs can reduce inhibitions and increase sexual risk behaviors,** such as having sex without a condom or without medicines to prevent HIV, having sex with multiple partners, or trading sex for money or drugs.

- Studies have found that young PWID (aged < 30 years) are at higher risk for HIV than older users because young persons are more likely to share needles and engage in risky sexual behaviors such as sex without a condom or without medicines to prevent HIV.

- **The epidemic of prescription opioid misuse and abuse has led to increased numbers of PWID,** placing new populations at increased risk for HIV. Nonurban areas with limited HIV prevention and treatment services and substance use disorder treatment services, traditionally areas at low risk for HIV, have been disproportionately affected. For example, an HIV epidemic in rural Scott County, Indiana, in 2015 was attributed to syringe-sharing partners injecting the prescription opioid oxymorphone. CDC declared the outbreak as one of the worst documented outbreaks of HIV among injection drug users in the past two decades (Conrad et al., 2015; Rudavsky, 2015).

- **Social and economic factors limit access to HIV prevention and treatment services among PWID.** In a study of cities with high levels of HIV, more than half (51%) of HIV-positive PWID reported being homeless, 30% reported being incarcerated, and 20% reported having no health insurance in the last 12 months.

- **Stigma and discrimination are associated with illicit substance use.** Often, IDU is viewed as a criminal activity rather than a medical issue that requires counseling and rehabilitation. Stigma and mistrust of the health care system may prevent PWID from seeking HIV testing, care, and treatment.

- **IDU can cause other diseases and complications.** In addition to being at risk for HIV and other bloodborne and sexually transmitted infections such as viral hepatitis, PWID can get other serious health problems, like skin infections, abscesses, or even infections of the heart. People can overdose and get very sick or even die from IDU (CDC, 2014.16f, 2017.16g).

Mother-to-Child Transmission

Perinatal HIV transmission, also known as mother-to-child transmission, can happen at any time during pregnancy, labor, delivery, and breastfeeding. CDC recommends that all women who are pregnant or planning to get pregnant take an HIV test as early as possible before and during every pregnancy. This is because the earlier HIV is diagnosed and treated, the more effective HIV medicines, called antiretroviral treatment (ART), will be at preventing transmission and improving the health outcomes of both mother and child. Advances in HIV research, prevention, and treatment have made it possible for many women living with HIV to give birth without transmitting the virus to their babies. The annual number of HIV infections through perinatal transmission has declined by more than 95% since the early 1990s, from 141 in 2014 to 65 in 2018 (CDC, 2020.16c). Today, if a woman takes HIV medicines as prescribed throughout pregnancy, labor and delivery, and provides HIV medicines to her baby for 4–6 weeks, the risk of transmitting HIV to her baby can be 1% or less. In some cases, a cesarean delivery can also prevent HIV transmission. After delivery, a mother can prevent transmitting HIV to her baby by not breastfeeding and not pre-chewing her baby's food. For babies living with HIV, starting treatment early is important because the disease can progress more rapidly in children than adults. Providing ART early can help children with perinatal HIV live longer, healthier lives. It is important that all women who are pregnant or trying to get pregnant encourage their partners to also get tested for HIV. Women who are HIV-negative but have an HIV-positive partner should talk to their doctor about taking pre-exposure prophylaxis (PrEP) medicines to protect themselves from becoming infected with HIV while trying to get pregnant, and to protect themselves and their baby during pregnancy and while breastfeeding.

Unfortunately, some pregnant women with HIV may not know they are infected. The CDC recommends HIV testing for all women as part of routine prenatal care. According to the CDC research, more women take the prenatal HIV test if the opt-out approach is used. Opt-out prenatal HIV testing means that a pregnant woman is told she will be given an HIV test as part of routine prenatal care unless she opts out, that is, chooses not to have the test. In some parts of the country where HIV among women is more common, the CDC recommends a second test during the third trimester of pregnancy. Women living with HIV may not know they are pregnant, how to prevent or safely plan a pregnancy, or what they can do to reduce the risk of transmitting HIV to their baby. These women need to be advised to:

- Visit their health care provider regularly and take HIV medicines (ART) as directed for their own health if they think they might want to become pregnant.
- When pregnant, take HIV medicines the right way every day throughout the pregnancy, labor, and delivery. Taking HIV medicines reduces the amount of HIV in the body (viral load) to a very low level, which is called viral suppression, or an undetectable viral load. Getting and keeping an undetectable viral load is the best thing you can do to stay healthy and help prevent transmission to your baby.
- After delivery, ensure their infants take HIV medicines.
- Avoid breastfeeding.
- Avoid pre-chewing food for an infant, toddler, or anyone else.

Social and economic factors, especially poverty, affect access to all health care and disproportionately affect people living with HIV. Pregnant women living with HIV may face more barriers to accessing medical care if they also use injection drugs, abuse other substances, or are homeless, incarcerated, mentally ill, or uninsured.

● AIDS Demographics

The statistical characteristics of populations are called **demographics**. Public health researchers often look at groups of people in terms of age, socioeconomic status, living area, ethnicity, sex, and so on in order to understand the dynamics of disease transmission and prevention. When STIs are involved, they naturally look at sexual behaviors as well. No one is exempt from HIV exposure by virtue of belonging or not belonging to a specific group. But certain groups appear to be at greater risk than others because they have unique challenges in the prevention, diagnosis, and treatment of HIV/AIDS. Many individuals within these groups may not be at risk, however, because they do not engage in risky behaviors.

Minority Races/Ethnicities and HIV

In the early 1980s in the United States, HIV/AIDS was primarily considered a gay, white disease. Today, however, the epidemic has expanded, and the proportional distribution of AIDS cases among minority racial and ethnic groups has shifted and, as mentioned earlier, Blacks and Hispanics are disproportionately affected (see Figure 8). Being of a minority race/ethnic group is not, in itself, a risk factor for HIV infection and other STIs. However, race/ethnicity in the United States is a risk marker that correlates with other, more fundamental determinants of health status, such as poverty, homelessness, lack of access to quality health care and HIV prevention education, avoiding seeking health care, substance abuse, stigma and discrimination, and residence in communities with a high prevalence of HIV and other STIs (CDC, 2017.16i).

Although poverty itself is not a risk factor, studies have found a direct relationship between higher AIDS incidence and lower income. A study of a diverse sample of women from urban health clinics found that socioeconomic status, not race/ethnicity, had both direct and indirect associations with HIV risk behaviors; the women with lower income had riskier sexual behaviors (Ickovics et al., 2002). Several socioeconomic problems associated with poverty (e.g., housing insecurity and limited access to health care) directly or indirectly raise HIV risk (Buffardi et al., 2008; Dean & Myles, 2013). Some minority race/ethnic communities are reluctant to acknowledge sensitive issues such as homosexuality and substance use.

African Americans   Of all racial and ethnic groups in the United States, Blacks and African Americans have been impacted most severely by HIV and AIDS (see Figure 7). In the United States, HIV/AIDS is a health crisis for African Americans. At all stages of HIV/AIDS—from infection with HIV to death from AIDS—Blacks are disproportionately affected compared to other racial/ethnic groups. The reasons for this are not directly related to race or ethnicity but rather to the barriers faced by many African Americans, including poverty, high incidence of another STI, limited HIV prevention education, and the stigma of HIV/AIDS. Another barrier to HIV prevention is homophobia and concealment of male-to-male sexual behavior. Homophobia and stigmatization can cause some African American men who have sex with men to identify themselves as heterosexual or not to disclose their same-sex behaviors. Black men are more likely than other MSM not to identify themselves as men who are gay. This absence of disclosure of self-identification may make it more difficult to present appropriate HIV prevention education. Other factors that contribute to higher risk among African Americans include higher rates of STIs than other racial/ethnic groups in the United States, lack of awareness of HIV status, and the tendency to have sex with partners of the same race/ethnicity, resulting in their facing a greater risk of HIV infection with each new sexual encounter (CDC, 2020.16e; Dean & Myles, 2013).

Blacks account for a higher proportion of new HIV diagnoses and people with HIV, compared to other races/ethnicities. In 2018, African Americans accounted for 13% of the U.S. population but had 42% of the 37,832 new HIV diagnoses in the United States and dependent areas (Puerto Rico, the U.S. Virgin Islands, America Samoa, Guam, the Northern Mariana Islands, and the Republic of Palau). Yet only one in seven African Americans with HIV are unaware they have it. Blacks account for a higher proportion of those living with HIV and those ever diagnosed with AIDS. Nearly one-half of those diagnosed with AIDS in the United States are African American. Blacks living with HIV/AIDS often do not live as long and die more frequently. In 2017, there were 7,053 deaths among adult and adolescent Blacks/African Americans with diagnosed HIV in the United States. Also, Blacks have a much greater lifetime estimate risk of being diagnosed with HIV than whites: 1 in 20 for Black males; 1 in

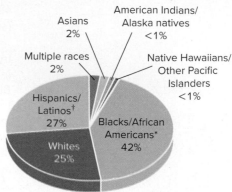

• **FIGURE 8**

New HIV Diagnoses in the United States by Race/Ethnicity, 2018

Black refers to people having origins in any of the black racial groups of Africa. *African American* is a term often used for Americans of African descent with ancestry in North America.

†Hispanics/Latinos can be of any race.

Source: CDC, 2020.16c.

The HIV epidemic has dramatically and disproportionately affected African Americans. The disease poses a serious threat to the future health and well-being of many African American communities.

Jake Lyell/Alamy Stock Photo

48 for Black females, compared to 1 in 132 for white males and 1 in 880 for white females (see Figure 7) (CDC, 2020.16b).

Eighty percent of new HIV diagnoses in the United States in 2018 among Blacks were from male-to-male sexual contact. As shown in Figure 6, the leading mode of transmission in 2018 was African American male-to-male sexual contact with 9,444 new cases. Young Black gay and bisexual men are especially impacted by HIV/AIDS. HIV diagnoses decreased from 2007 to 2017 in all demographic groups of Black Americans except gay and bisexual men ages 25 to 34% whom had an increased (CDC, 2020.16e).

The HIV problem among gay, bisexual, and queer men in Southern states of the United States is considered "America's Hidden H.I.V. Epidemic" (Villarosa, 2017). Whereas in many areas of the United States, such as cities like New York and San Francisco, the rates of HIV infection and AIDS-related deaths have plummeted, the HIV/AIDS problem—unknown to most Americans—is still ravaging communities in the Deep South. The poverty rate among Blacks is high. The socioeconomic issues associated with poverty—including limited access to high-quality health care, housing, and HIV prevention education—directly and indirectly increase the risk for HIV infection and affect the health of people living with and at risk for HIV. These factors may explain why Blacks have worse outcomes on the HIV continuum of care, including lower access to medical care and lower viral suppression. Stigma, fear, discrimination, and homophobia may prevent African Americans from accessing HIV prevention and care services (CDC, 2020.16e).

Hispanic/Latino   The Hispanic/Latino community, which includes a diverse mixture of ethnic groups and cultures, continues to be impacted by HIV. In 2018, adult and adolescent Latinxs made up 27% (10,246) of the 37,881 new diagnoses in the United States yet comprise 18% of the U.S. population (CDC, 2020.16c, 2017.16d). As shown in Figure 6, the second leading category of the most-affected groups of new HIV infections in 2018 in all populations was Hispanic/Latino male-to-male sexual contact, with 7,653 new HIV cases. Nearly 9 out of every 10 new HIV infections in men were from male-to-male sexual contact, and for women almost 9 of 10 new HIV infections were from heterosexual contact. The estimated lifetime risk of an HIV diagnosis for Hispanic men is 1 in 48 and for Hispanic women, 1 in 227 (see Figure 7). Poverty, migration patterns, lower educational level, language barriers, mistrust of the health care system and fear of disclosing their immigration status are barriers for some Latinx to get HIV testing and care. Given the growth of the Latinx community in the United States, the prevalence of HIV/AIDS among this group will increasingly affect the health status of the nation. Prevention programs must give special attention to the cultural diversity that exists with this and other diverse communities. (CDC, 2020.16a, 2020.l6f)

Asian Americans   Between 2014 and 2018, the Asian population in the United States grew around 10%, which is more than 3 times as fast as the total U.S. population. During the same period, the number of Asians receiving an HIV diagnosis remained stable, driven primarily by HIV diagnoses among Asian gay, bisexual, and other men who have sex with men remaining stable. Asians, who make up 6% of the population, accounted for about 2% of HIV diagnoses in 2018 in the United States and dependent areas. Of the 37,881 new HIV infections in 2018, 875, or 2%, occurred among Asians. Most new HIV diagnoses among Asian persons were from male-to-male sexual contact (685, or 89%). Among new HIV diagnoses among women, 94% (98) of were from heterosexual contact. During 2018, there were 79 deaths among Asians with diagnosed HIV in the United States and territories. Compared to other people with HIV, Asians were less likely to have received some HIV care. Some Asians may avoid seeking testing, counseling, or treatment because of language barriers or fear of discrimination, the stigma of homosexuality, immigration issues, or fear of bringing shame to their families.

Limited research about Asian health and HIV infection means there are few targeted prevention programs and behavioral interventions for this population. The reported number of HIV cases may not reflect the true HIV diagnoses among Asians because their race/ethnicity is sometimes misidentified. This could lead to the underestimation of HIV infection in this population (CDC, 2020.16g).

How to Negotiate Condom Use and What to Say When Your Partner Refuses

To be able to negotiate condom use with a partner is an **important skill sexually active men and women should have to avoid STI/HIV and unintended pregnancy.** Often, a person may be able to convince a partner to use a condom simply by having a conversation about safe sex or by simply taking out a condom and using it without discussion. However, this approach does not always work as some partners will want to avoid using condoms. Sometimes, a person needs to persuade or influence a partner to use condom (Noar et al., 2002; Tschann et al., 2010). Given this, understanding the specific ways individuals negotiate condom use would be valuable.

Researchers surveyed primarily heterosexual college men and women to determine their strategies for negotiating condom use (Debro et al., 1994; Edgar, 1988; McCormick, 1979; Holland & French, 2012), and a subsequent study using the results of the studies lead to the development of a validated questionnaire called the Condom Influence Strategy Questionnaire (CISQ) (Noar et al., 2002). The CISQ resulted in six subscales: withholding sex, direct requests, seduction, relationship conceptualizing, risk information, and deception. The questionnaire development found that the CISQ was positively related to sexual assertiveness, condom self-efficacy, negotiation self-efficacy (beliefs about one's capability to negotiate condom use), partner communication, intentions to use condoms consistently, and condom use.

Here are the definitions of the six CISQ negotiation strategies and examples of questionnaire statements to persuade a partner to use a condom:

Withholding Sex Person states/threatens that sexual activity will be withheld if partner does not use condoms

- *Let my partner know that no condoms means no sex.*
- *Tell my partner that I have made the decision to use condoms, and so we are going to use them.*

Direct Request Person requests the use of condoms in a direct, straightforward manner.

- *Tell my partner that I would be more comfortable if we use condoms.*
- *Say that since we are going to have sex, I'd like to use condoms.*

Seduction Person uses (non-verbal) sexual arousal to distract or direct partner in order to persuade partner to use a condom.

- *Get the partner very sexually excited and then take out a condom.*
- *Begin putting a condom on at the appropriate moment.*

Relationship Conceptualizing Person uses caring or concern for the partner or relationship in order to get partner to use a condom.

- *Tell my partner that it would really means a lot to our relationship if he/she would use a condom.*
- *Let my partner know that using a condom would show respect for my feelings.*

Risk Information Person presents information about the risks of STIs and AIDS to persuade partner to use a condom.

- *Tell my partner that if we don't use condoms, then one of us could end up with an STI.*
- *Tell my partner that we need to use condoms to protect ourselves from AIDS.*

Deception Person uses false information or deception to get partner to use a condom

- *Tell my partner that I only have sex with condoms even though sometimes I don't.*
- *Make up a reason why I want my partner to use a condom even though my real reason is to protect myself against diseases.*

Despite using the methods above, sometimes a partner refuses to use a condom (Tschann et al., 2010). Then, one might decide to counter the refusal statement. Here are some refusals and responses to the statements contributed by college students (Yarber et al., 2019). A space is provided to you to contribute another possible response to a refusal.

Partner	*I know where I've been. You can trust me.*
Response	*I need to be relaxed to enjoy sex. Protecting both of us helps me feel more relaxed. We need to use a condom.*
	Create another response_____
Partner	*Condoms are awkward to put on.*
Response	*I think it's hot if you help me put a condom on. Let's do it together.*
	Create another response_____
Partner	*I don't need a condom to show you I care about you.*
Response	*Using a condom would show respect for my feeling about it.*
	Create another response_____
Partner	*The chances are super low that we'll get HIV.*
Response	*There are lot of other diseases out there that we can catch besides HIV.*
	Create another response_____
Partner	*You probably have sex without condoms sometimes.*
Response	*No way. I've only ever had intercourse with a condom (even though sometimes I haven't used one).*
	Create another response_____

Partner	Let's just do it without a condom this time.		Partner	We already did it without a condom once.
Response	It only takes one time to get an STI. I just can't have sex unless I know I'm as safe as I can be.		Response	And that was a mistake. I have been worried about STIs since.
	Create another response_____			Create another response_____
Partner	I always pull out in time. Don't worry.		Partner	It just isn't as sensitive.
Response	I know, but when we use a condom you don't have to pull out. It can feel even better.		Response	With a condom you might last even longer, and that will make up for it. I will enjoy sex more when it is not over for you so quickly.
	Create another response_____			Create another response_____
Partner	No one else makes me use a condom!			
Response	This is for both of us. . .and I won't have sex without protection. Sex can be good even with a condom.			
	Create another response_____			

Native Hawaiians and Other Pacific Islanders   Although Native Hawaiians and other Pacific Islanders (NHOPI) account for a very small percentage of new HIV diagnoses, HIV affects NHOPI in ways that are not always apparent because of their small population size (NHOPI make up 0.2% of the U.S population). In 2018, 68 NHOPI were diagnosed with HIV, representing less than 1% of new HIV diagnoses in the United States. Male-to-male sexual contact accounted for 84% of HIV diagnoses among NHOPI in 2015. Between 2014 and 2018, the annual number of HIV diagnoses among NHOPI increased 51% (from 45 to 68). Socioeconomic factors such as poverty, inadequate or no health coverage, language barriers, and lower educational attainment among NHOPI may contribute to lack of awareness about HIV risk and high-risk behaviors. Further, NHOPI customs, such as those that prioritize obligations to family and taboos on intergenerational sexual topics and sexual health discussion, may stigmatize sexuality in general and homosexuality specifically, as well as interfere with HIV risk-reduction strategies such as condom use (CDC, 2017.16m, 2020.16h).

American Indians and Alaska Natives   HIV is a public health issue among American Indians and Alaska Natives (AIs/ANs), who represent about 1.3% of the U.S. population. HIV affects AIs/ANs in ways that are not always obvious because of their small population sizes. Of the 37,881 HIV diagnoses in the United States, 0.5% (157) were among AIs/ANs. Of the 157 HIV diagnoses among AI/AN men in 2018, 77% (121) were among gay and bisexual men. Most of the 55 HIV diagnoses among AI/AN women in 2015 were attributed to heterosexual contact (73%; 40). From 2014 to 2018, the annual number of HIV diagnoses increased 39% (from 172 to 205) among AIs/ANs. Poverty, lower levels of education and higher levels of unemployment, and less access to health care coexist as risk factors for HIV infection among AIs/ANs. Alcohol and illicit drug use are higher among AIs/ANs than among people of other races or ethnicities. AI/AN gay and bisexual men may face culturally based stigma and confidentiality concerns that limit opportunities for education and HIV testing, especially among those living in rural communities or on reservations. These indicators increase the vulnerability of AIs/ANs to additional health stress, including HIV infection (CDC, 2020.16i). To be effective, HIV/AIDS prevention education must account for the numerous populations of American Indians and Alaska Natives by tailoring programs to individual tribal cultures and beliefs.

The Gay Community

"AIDS has given a human face to an invisible minority," says Robert Bray of the National LGBTQ Task Force. From the beginning of the HIV/AIDS epidemic in the United States, the most disproportionate impact has been among men who have sex with men (MSM). Although epidemiologists do not know for certain how HIV first arrived in the gay community, they do know that it spread like wildfire, mainly because anal sex is such an efficient

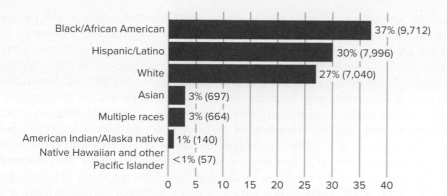

● **FIGURE 9**

New Diagnoses Among Gay and Bisexual Men in the United States by Race/Ethnicity, 2018

Source: CDC, 2020.16j.

Chart data (Figure 9):
- Black/African American: 37% (9,712)
- Hispanic/Latino: 30% (7,996)
- White: 27% (7,040)
- Asian: 3% (697)
- Multiple races: 3% (664)
- American Indian/Alaska native: 1% (140)
- Native Hawaiian and other Pacific Islander: <1% (57)

mode of transmission. Furthermore, initial research, education, and prevention efforts were severely hampered by a lack of government and public interest in what was perceived to be a "gay disease" (Shilts, 1987). Now 40 years after the virus first appeared, the gay community continues to reel from the repeated blows dealt by AIDS and to represent the largest HIV transmission category.

Male-to-male sexual contact is a behavioral description of a diverse population, many of whom identify themselves either privately or publicly as gay, bisexual, or queer men. Others may engage in sex with men but not think of themselves as a gay, bisexual, or queer person. Gay, bisexual, queer, and other men who reported male-to-male sexual contact are the population most affected by HIV in the United States. Approximately 492,000 sexually active gay and bisexual men are at high risk for HIV. Below are further data that illustrate the major and disproportionate impact of HIV/AIDS on the gay and bisexual men community (CDC, 2020.16j):

- In 2018, male-to-male sexual contact accounted for 62% (23,469) of the total new HIV diagnoses in the United States (see Figure 6). For the entire new HIV diagnoses in 2018 in the United States, 66% of the new diagnoses were gay and bisexual men (see Figure 4).

- Black/African American gay and bisexual men had the highest total of new HIV diagnoses with 37% (9,712) (see Figure 9).

- In 2018, gay and bisexual men aged 13 to 34 made up the most new HIV diagnoses (64%, 16,958) among gay and bisexual men.

- An estimated one in six MSM are projected to get HIV in their lifetime; for African American men, the estimate is one in two; and for Hispanic men, one in four. These are the top three highest lifetime risks for HIV infection for any population group (see Figure 7).

- In 2018, there were 8,049 deaths among gay and bisexual men with diagnosed HIV in the United States.

- Anal sex is the riskiest type of sex for getting or transmitting HIV; receptive sex is 13 times as risky for getting HIV as insertive anal sex (see Table 1).

- One in six gay and bisexual men with HIV are unaware they have it.

Homophobia, stigma, and discrimination may place gay, bisexual, and queer men at risk for multiple physical and mental health problems and affect whether they take protective actions with their partners or seek and are able to obtain high-quality health services (CDC, 2017.16o). Other than sexual risk behavior, factors that increase HIV risk among MSM are high rates of STIs, social discrimination, poverty, lack of access to health care, stigmatization, concurrent psychological problems, lack of risk assessment, alcohol and illicit drug use, homophobia, complacency about HIV, and partner violence.

Activism continues to focus public attention on the need for greater resources to control the HIV/AIDS epidemic.

JES AZNAR/Getty Images

Anal sex without a condom continues to be a major health threat to MSM, particularly having unprotected anal sex ("barebacking") with casual partners. The reasons for unprotected sex are not completely understood, but research points to several factors, including optimism about improved HIV treatment, substance use, being unsure of their HIV serostatus, complex sexual decision making, and seeking partners on the Internet. The success of newer medical treatments may have had the unintended consequence of increasing risk behaviors among MSM because some men seem to have abandoned safer sex practices. Some of these men may be **serosorting**, or having sex or unprotected sex with a partner whose HIV serostatus, they believe, is the same as their own. For men with casual partners, serosorting alone is likely to be less effective than always and correctly using condoms, in part because some men do not know or disclose their HIV serostatus (Golden, Stekler, Hughes, & Wood, 2008; Golden, Dombrowski, Kerani, & Stekler, 2012). Actually, a study using a mathematical modeling found that serosorting is unlikely to be beneficial to many MSM populations and could more than double the risk of acquiring HIV in settings with low HIV testing (Wilson et al., 2010).

Women and HIV/AIDS

Early in the epidemic, HIV infection and AIDS were diagnosed for relatively few women and female adolescents. Now we know that many women were infected with HIV resulting from injection drug use but their infections were not diagnosed. Though HIV diagnoses among women have declined in recent years, more than 7,000 women (16% of total U.S. cases) received an HIV diagnosis in the United States in 2018. At the end of 2018 in the United States and dependent areas, 245,154 female adults and adolescents were living with diagnosed HIV infection. In 2018 in the United States, Blacks/African Americans made up 13% of the female population but accounted for 58% of diagnoses of HIV infection among females. Whites made up 62% of the female population and accounted for 21% of diagnoses of HIV infection among females. Hispanics/Latinos made up 16% of the female population and accounted for 17% of diagnoses of HIV infection among females. Black/African American female adults and adolescents had the largest percentage (92%) of diagnoses of HIV infection attributed to heterosexual contact, followed by Hispanic/Latino (87%) and white (64%) females (see Figure 10). The lifetime risk of acquiring HIV varied dramatically, with the risk being 1 in 48 among African women, 1 in 227 among Hispanic women, and 1 in 880 among white women (see Figure 7). In 2017, there were 4,006 deaths among women diagnosed with HIV in the United States. (CDC, 2020.16a).

Because some women may be unaware of their male partner's risk factors for HIV, such as injection drug use or having sex with men, they may not use condoms. Assuming no prevention methods, such as condoms or medicines to prevent HIV are used, women have

● FIGURE 10

Percentages of Diagnoses of HIV Infection Among Adult and Adolescent Females, by Race/Ethnicity of Transmission Category, 2018, United States

Source: CDC, 2020.16d.

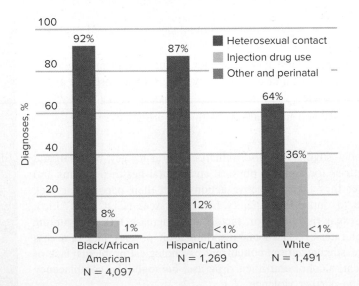

a higher risk for getting HIV during vaginal sex than men do. The riskiest behavior for getting HIV is receptive anal sex. In a behavioral survey of heterosexual women at increased risk for HIV, 92% of HIV-negative women reported having vaginal sex without a condom in the previous year, and 26% reported having anal sex without a condom. Some sexually transmitted infections, such as gonorrhea and syphilis, greatly increase the likelihood of getting or transmitting HIV. Women who have been sexually abused may be more likely to engage in sexual risk behaviors like exchanging sex for drugs, having multiple sex partners, or having sex without a condom (CDC, 2020.16b).

Female-to-female transmission of HIV appears to be a rare occurrence, but there are case reports of it. The well-documented risk of female-to-female transmission of HIV shows that vaginal secretions and menstrual blood may contain the virus and that mucous membrane (e.g., oral, vaginal) exposure to these secretions has the potential to lead to HIV infection. To reduce the risk of HIV transmission, women who have sex with women should avoid exposure of a mucous membrane, such as the mouth, to vaginal secretions and menstrual blood. Condoms should be used correctly and consistently for each sexual contact or when using sex toys, and sex toys should not be shared. Also, natural rubber latex sheets, dental dams, cut open condoms, latex gloves, or plastic wrap may provide some protection from contact with body fluids during oral sex and possibly reduce the risk of HIV transmission (CDC, 2010.16b).

Transgender People and HIV

Transgender communities in the United States are among the groups at highest risk for HIV infection. Recall that transgender is a term that can be used to describe people whose gender identity or expression is different from their sex assigned at birth. Transgender women describe individuals who were assigned the male sex at birth but identify as women. Transgender men describe individuals who were assigned the female sex at birth but identify as men.

Nearly 1 million people in the United States identify as transgender. Transgender individuals, particularly transgender women, are at high risk for HIV infection. In fact, evidence suggests that in relation to their population size, transgender women are among the groups most affected by HIV in the United States. To estimate the percentage of transgender people living with HIV in the United States, or HIV prevalence, CDC scientists recently conducted a meta-analysis of 88 studies published from 2006 to 2017. This analysis is important because there are limited HIV surveillance data for transgender populations. The analysis confirmed that transgender women and men are disproportionately affected by HIV. HIV prevalence was 14.1% for transgender women, 3.2% for transgender men, and 9.2% for transgender people overall. By comparison, the estimated HIV prevalence for U.S. adults overall is less than 0.5%. The analysis also showed that transgender women of color are at particularly high risk. Mean HIV prevalence was 44.2% among African American transgender women and 25.8% among Hispanic/Latina transgender women, compared to 6.7% among white transgender women. Not enough data were available to examine HIV prevalence by race/ethnicity for transgender men.

While the results of the above-cited analysis are useful, they should be interpreted with caution, in part because transgender people at high risk of HIV may have been overrepresented in the studies that comprised the review. Since the beginning of the epidemic, there has been limited national information on the impact of the HIV infection among transgender infections. In large part, this is because there has been no reliable system for collecting and sharing both sex and gender identity information in health records. Transgender men's sexual health has not been well studied. Additional research is needed to understand HIV risk behavior among transgender men, especially those who have sex with men.

Several behavioral factors, which often serve as a way for transgender people to cope with stigma and discrimination, put transgender persons at risk for HIV. These include elevated rates of injecting hormones or drugs, anal sex without condoms or medicines to prevent HIV, and commercial sex work. Insensitivity to transgender issues by health care providers can be a barrier for transgender people with HIV who are seeking quality treatment and care services. Few health care providers receive proper training or are knowledgeable about transgender health issues and their unique needs. This can lead to limited health care access and negative health care encounters. Transgender women and men might not be sufficiently reached by current HIV testing measures. Tailoring HIV testing activities to overcome the unique barriers faced by transgender women and men might increase rates of testing among these populations (CDC, 2019.16b).

Children and HIV/AIDS

As noted previously, perinatal transmission (HIV transmission from mother to child during pregnancy, labor and delivery, or breastfeeding) is the most common route of HIV infection in children. In 2018, an estimated 65 children aged less than 13 years were diagnosed with HIV infection: 42 were Black/African American, 9 white, 3 Asian, 6 Hispanic/Latino, and 5 multiple races. From 2014 to 2018, HIV testing and preventive interventions have resulted in more than a 90% decline in the number of children perinatally infected with HIV in the United States (CDC, 2020.16a).

The incidence of AIDS among children has been dramatically reduced by CDC recommendations for routine counseling and voluntary prenatal HIV testing for women and the use of medical treatment to prevent perinatal transmission.

HIV/AIDS Among Youth

"I have never shared needles. And obviously I'm not a gay man. The only thing I did was something every single one of you has already done or will do."

—Krista Blake, infected with HIV as a teenager

In 2018, youth aged 13 to 24 made up 21% of the 37,881 new HIV diagnoses in the United States although the number of new cases decreased by 10% since 2010 (see Figure 11). As shown in Figure 12, among young men, the transmission category male-to-male accounted for 92% of the new HIV diagnoses in 2018; for young women, heterosexual contact accounted for 85% of the new HIV diagnoses. Black/African American (51%), Hispanic/Latino (27%), and white (17%) youth had the highest incidence of new HIV diagnoses in 2018. In 2017, there were 149 deaths among youth diagnosed with HIV. Youth with HIV are the least likely of any age group to be aware of their infection, to be retained in care, and to have a suppressed viral load (CDC, 2020.16b).

Several factors contribute to the HIV/AIDS problem among youth. The status of sexual health education varies throughout the United States and is insufficient in many areas according to the CDC. Sexuality education is not starting early enough: in no state did more than half of middle and high schools teach all 20 recommended sexual health topics. Sexuality education has been declining over time. The percentage of U.S. middle schools in which students are required to receive instruction on HIV prevention has decreased (CDC, 2020.16a). The 2019 data from the Youth Risk Behavior Survey (CDC, 2020.16), which monitors health risk behaviors that contribute to the leading causes of death and disability

● FIGURE 11

Estimated HIV Incidence among Persons Aged >13 Years, by Age, 2010–2018—United States

Source: CDC, 2020.16b.

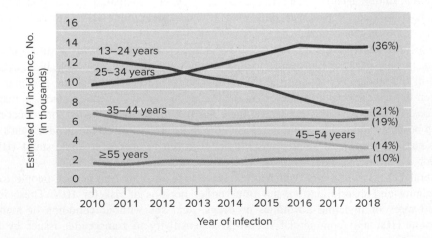

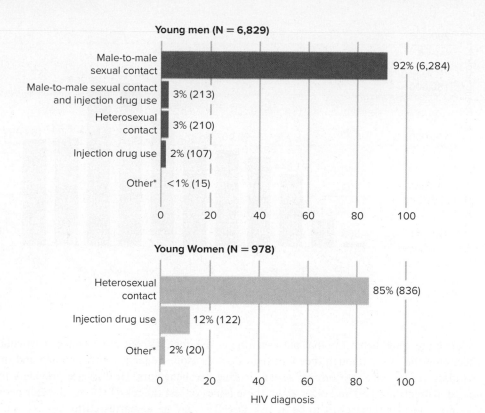

Young men (N = 6,829)

Male-to-male sexual contact	92% (6,284)
Male-to-male sexual contact and injection drug use	3% (213)
Heterosexual contact	3% (210)
Injection drug use	2% (107)
Other*	<1% (15)

0 20 40 60 80 100

Young Women (N = 978)

Heterosexual contact	85% (836)
Injection drug use	12% (122)
Other*	2% (20)

0 20 40 60 80 100

HIV diagnosis

• FIGURE 12

New HIV Diagnoses Among Youth Ages 13 to 24 by Transmission Category and Sex in the United States and Dependent Areas, 2018

Source: CDC, 2020.16b.

among high school students grades 9–12, revealed that some youth participate in risk behavior; for example, only 54% of all sexually active high school students reported that they had used a condom the last time they had sexual intercourse. Further details of sexual behavior, condom use, and HIV testing among youth are provided in Chapter 2. Other factors that place many youth at risk for HIV/AIDS include substance use, socioeconomic challenges, feelings of isolation, older sexual partners, and stigma and misperceptions about HIV (CDC, 2020.16a; Szucs et al., 2020).

Some of the highest STI rates are among youth aged 20–24, especially youth of color. The presence of another STI greatly increases the likelihood that a person exposed to HIV will become infected. In a 2012 Kaiser Family Foundation survey, 84% of youth aged 15–24 said there is stigma surrounding HIV in the United States (Kaiser Family Foundation, 2012). This could mean that they are not comfortable discussing their status with others and talking with their partners about ways to protect themselves from HIV and other STIs. For gay, bisexual, and queer youth who are just beginning to explore their sexuality, homophobia can pose obstacles to utilizing HIV prevention services, testing, and treatment. Gay, bisexual, and queer high school students may engage in risky sexual behaviors and substance abuse because they feel isolated and lack support. They are more likely than heterosexual youth to experience bullying and other forms of violence, which also can lead to mental distress and engagement in risk behaviors that are associated with getting HIV (CDC, 2017.16r, 2020.16b).

Older Adults and HIV/AIDS

In 2018, over half (51%) of people in the United States (U.S.) and dependent areas with diagnosed HIV were aged 50 and older. One in six new HIV diagnoses were among people aged 50 and older (see Figure 13). Among people aged 50 and older, most new HIV diagnoses were among men: male-to-male sexual contact (66%), heterosexual contact (21%), injection drug use (9%), and male-to-male contact and injection drug use (3%). For women, heterosexual contact was the primary transmission mode (86%), followed by injection drug use (15%).

• FIGURE 13

New HIV Diagnoses among Adults and
Adolescents in the United States and
Dependent Areas by Age, 2018

Source: CDC, 2020.16c.

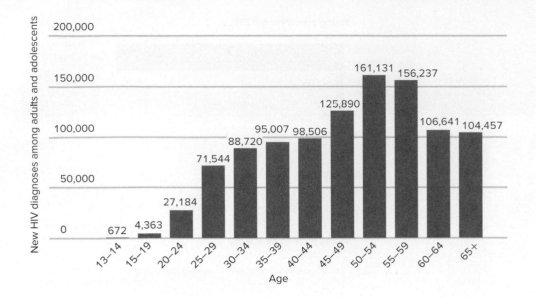

There are some behaviors that put everyone at risk for HIV, but other factors particularly affect older people. Although they visit their doctors more frequently, older people and their providers are less likely to discuss sexual or drug use behaviors. Health care providers may not ask patients aged 50 and older about these issues or test them for HIV. Also, older people may not consider themselves to be at risk for HIV, may be embarrassed to discuss sex, or may mistake HIV symptoms for those of normal aging.

Older people may have many of the same HIV risk factors as younger people, including a lack of knowledge about HIV prevention and sexual risk, such as having multiple sex partners, and may be less likely to use a condom or other prevention options. Older people in the United States are more likely than younger people to have late-stage HIV infection at the time of diagnosis. People aged 50 and older may start treatment late, which may put this population at risk of more immune system damage. Among people aged 55 and older who received an HIV diagnosis in 2015, 50% had HIV for 4.5 years before they were diagnosed—the longest diagnosis delay for any age group. Stigma is common among adults with HIV and negatively affects people's quality of life, self-image, and behaviors. People aged 50 and older may avoid getting the care they need or disclosing their HIV status because they may already face isolation due to illness or loss of family, friends, or community support.

Aging with HIV presents special challenges for preventing other diseases. Both age and HIV increase the risk for cardiovascular disease, lung disease (specifically chronic obstructive pulmonary disease), bone loss, and certain cancers. People aged 50 and older also need to be careful about interactions between medications used to treat HIV and those used to treat common age-related conditions such as hypertension, diabetes, elevated cholesterol, and obesity (CDC, 2020.16l).

Geographic Region and HIV

In the United States and dependent areas, HIV diagnoses are not evenly distributed across states and regions. Of the 37,881 new HIV diagnoses in the United States and dependent areas in 2018 about one half (19,369) were in the South (see Figure 14). The Midwest had 4,904 new HIV diagnoses cases in 2018, the West, 7,229 cases; and the Northeast, 5,496. Overall, most people who receive an HIV diagnosis live in urban areas. Blacks in the Southern region had the highest percentage of new HIV cases at 52% compared to Blacks residing in other regions. In 2018, there were 15,820 deaths among adults and adolescents with diagnosed HIV in the United States. Nearly half (47%) of these deaths were in the South; 22% were in the Northeast; 17% were in the West; 12% were in the Midwest; and 2% were in the U.S. dependent areas. (CDC, 2020.16b).

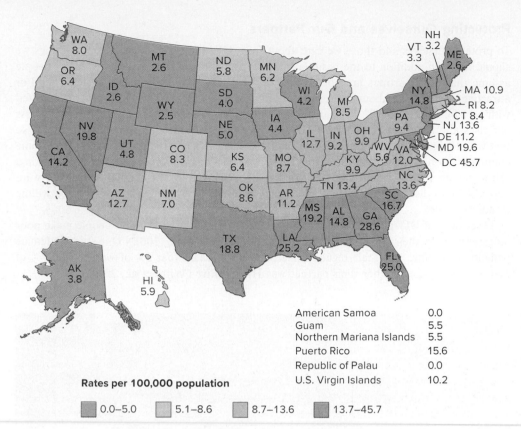

● FIGURE 14

Rates of HIV Infection Among Adults
and Adolescents in the United States
by State, 2018

Source: CDC, 2020.16c.

State	Rate
WA	8.0
OR	6.4
MT	2.6
ID	2.6
ND	5.8
MN	6.2
NH	3.2
VT	3.3
ME	2.6
WI	4.2
SD	4.0
WY	2.5
NY	14.8
MA	10.9
MI	8.5
NV	19.8
IA	4.4
RI	8.2
CA	14.2
UT	4.8
NE	5.0
PA	9.4
CT	8.4
CO	8.3
IL	12.7
IN	9.2
OH	9.9
NJ	13.6
KS	6.4
DE	11.2
MO	8.7
WV	5.6
VA	12.0
MD	19.6
AZ	12.7
NM	7.0
KY	9.9
DC	45.7
OK	8.6
AR	11.2
TN	13.4
NC	13.6
MS	19.2
AL	14.8
SC	16.7
TX	18.8
LA	25.2
GA	28.6
FL	25.0
AK	3.8
HI	5.9

Territory	Rate
American Samoa	0.0
Guam	5.5
Northern Mariana Islands	5.5
Puerto Rico	15.6
Republic of Palau	0.0
U.S. Virgin Islands	10.2

Rates per 100,000 population

0.0–5.0   5.1–8.6   8.7–13.6   13.7–45.7

In 2017, 82% of all new HIV diagnoses in the South were among Black/African American MSM (31%), Black/African American heterosexuals (19%), Hispanic/Latino MSM (16%), and white MSM (16%). An estimated 82,000 people in the South have HIV and do not know they are infected. Twenty-four percent new HIV diagnoses in the South are in suburban and rural areas—more than any other region. This poses unique challenges: The nation's opioid crisis is putting people at risk for HIV and hepatitis C (HCV) predominately in non-urban areas. Sixty-eight counties vulnerable to an HIV or HCV outbreak among people who inject drugs are found in the South (CDC, 2019.16c).

● Prevention and Treatment

Despite dramatic medical advances in HIV prevention and treatment, HIV/AIDS remains a serious problem in the United States. A 2019 Kaiser Family Foundation national poll found that most Americans (80%) indicated that the impact of HIV/AIDS in the country is a "serious issue," and large portions of the public, especially Black/African Americans and Hispanic Americans, say that HIV/AIDS is a "serious concern" for people they know. Four of 10 of Black adults (41%) and half of Hispanic adults (51%) are concerned about acquiring HIV, with more than 3 in 10 (32% Black, 36% Hispanic) saying they are "very concerned" (Kirzinger et al., 2019). In 2019, the CDC noted that progress in preventing new infections has stalled; that is, the prior dramatic decline in the number of HIV infection has stopped and new infections have stabilized in recent years. With tens of thousands of persons becoming infected with HIV each year and the number not decreasing, major efforts to address the HIV/AIDS problems remain. (CDC, 2019.16c). The CDC (2017.16u) states that research clearly indicates that HIV prevention works and saves lives. Today, an increasing number of ways to prevent HIV transmission and acquisition are available. For specific prevention behaviors, see Think About It, "Which Would Strategies Would You Use to Reduce Risk of STI/HIV? What One Group of Women Did."

Protecting Ourselves and Our Partners

To protect ourselves and those we care about from HIV infection, there are some things we should know in addition to the basic facts about transmission and prevention. Many people assume that their partners are not HIV-infected because they look healthy, "clean," and/or attractive. (See Think About It, "Accurately Judging If a Potential Sexual Partner is Infected with an STI: Easily Done?" in Chapter 15.) To protect ourselves, we need to honestly assess our risks and act to avoid acquiring HIV. We need to develop our communication skills so that we can discuss risks and prevention with our partner or potential partner. To learn some communication statements to a partner refusing to use a condom, see Practically Speaking, "How to Negotiate Condom Use and What to Say When Your Partner Refuses." If we want our partner to disclose information about past high-risk behavior, we also have to be willing to do the same.

Disclosure of HIV-positive status is critical, as research has shown that people make poor judgments about their sexual partner's HIV status (Niccolai et al., 2002). One study of female patients at a clinic and their regular male partners revealed that 2% of women and 4% of men were unaware whether their partner was HIV-positive (Witte et al., 2010).

think about it

Which Strategies Would You Use to Reduce Your Risk of STI/HIV? What One Group of Women Did

Varied health-promoting strategies can reduce a person's vulnerability of contracting a sexually transmitted infection (STI). Research has shown that many sexually active young people purposely assess their risk for STIs and make plans to reduce such risk, but most studies on prevention strategies have focused only on abstinence and condom-use prevention behaviors; other behaviors are often neglected (Gielen et al., 1994; Hensel & Fortenberry, 2013; Hock-long et al., 2013). Limited research has been conducted on what STI risk-reduction methods are used by women but none have explored any variation of strategies by race/ethnicity.

From 2015 to 2016, 790 women aged 13–24 years who were patients at five Northern California family planning clinics were surveyed about their STI prevention strategies (Cipres et al., 2017). One third had been diagnosed with an STI in the past, although few perceived themselves as at least somewhat likely to acquire an STI. Over half (54%) were worried about STIs. The incidence of the varied prevention behaviors assessed by race/ethnicity is presented below:

- 69% had an STI prevention plan that varied by race/ethnicity.
- Most (91%) reported using at least one strategy to reduce their vulnerability to STIs, with over half (56%) using more than one strategy.
- The most commonly used strategies included using condoms (67%), asking partners about STIs (47%), limiting sexual partners (35%), testing themselves for STIs (35%), and asking their partner about other sexual partners (33%).
- Black, Hispanic, and Asian women had decreased odds of utilizing strategies prior to intercourse compared to White women.

- Black women had decreased odds of using strategies requiring partner involvement.
- White women were more likely to report having talked to their partners about STIs than non-white women.
- The women reported many features were very important to them when choosing an STI prevention strategy: efficacy (84%), safety (83%), having few or no side effects (72%), preventing pregnancy in addition to STIs (65%), convenience (65%), and being able to control the method without relying on their sexual partner for use (61%).

The researchers noted that the study revealed that many women use diverse methods to reduce their vulnerability to STI acquisition and concluded that racial/ethnic difference in method choice helps explain disparities in STI rates among varied groups. They suggest that further research should examine why some methods are chosen over others and the methods used by men.

Think Critically

1. Did the study results surprise you? Explain.
2. Why do you think some STI prevention methods were chosen over others?
3. Would the study results be similar for men? Explain.
4. Do you have an STI prevention plan? If so, are your most favorite strategies similar to those in this study? If not, why do you not have a plan?

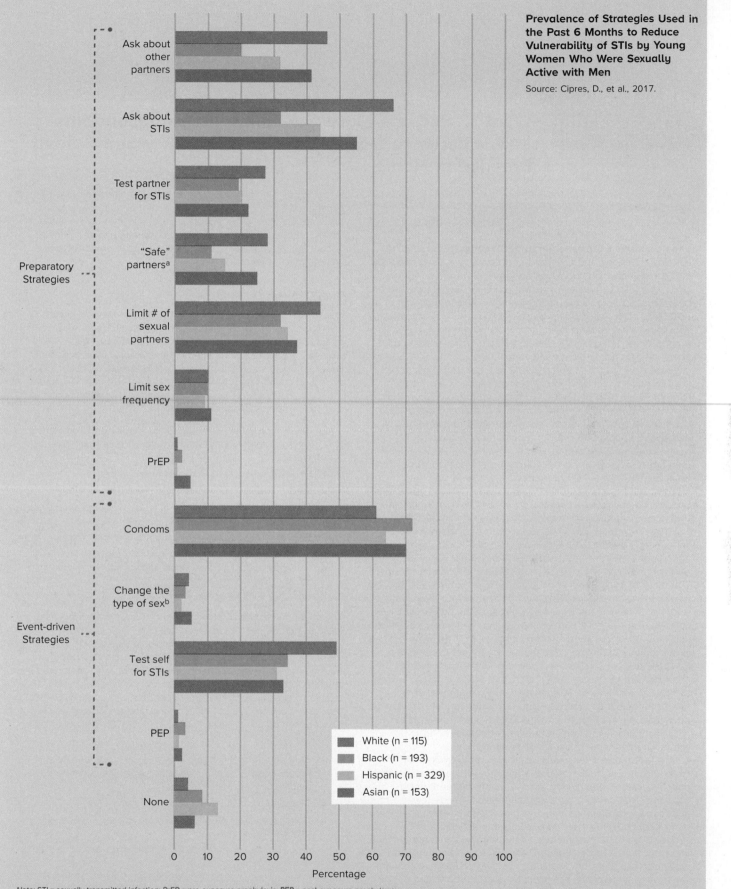

Prevalence of Strategies Used in the Past 6 Months to Reduce Vulnerability of STIs by Young Women Who Were Sexually Active with Men

Source: Cipres, D., et al., 2017.

Preparatory Strategies

- Ask about other partners
- Ask about STIs
- Test partner for STIs
- "Safe" partners[a]
- Limit # of sexual partners
- Limit sex frequency
- PrEP

Event-driven Strategies

- Condoms
- Change the type of sex[b]
- Test self for STIs
- PEP
- None

Percentage
0 10 20 30 40 50 60 70 80 90 100

White (n = 115)
Black (n = 193)
Hispanic (n = 329)
Asian (n = 153)

Note: STI = sexually transmitted infection; PrEP = pre-exposure prophylaxis; PEP = post-exposure prophylaxis;

[a]"Safe" partners refer to those whom subjects believed would not have HIV or other STIs.

[b]Changing type of sex refers to engaging in less risky behaviors (e.g., having oral sex instead of vaginal or anal sex).

Want to Become More Confident in Using Condoms and Experience More Sexual Pleasure? Try Self-Guided Practice at Home

For the things we have to learn before we can do them, we learn by doing them.

—Aristotle (384 BCE–322 BCE)

Male condoms remain a very effective means of reducing HIV/STI infections and unintended pregnancy if used correctly and consistently. Unfortunately, condom-use errors and problems, which can lead to greater exposure to HIV/STIs and increase odds of unintended pregnancy, are common worldwide (Sanders et al., 2012) and occur among college students. (See Think About It, "Do You Know What You are Doing? Common Condom Use Mistakes Among College Students.") Condom failure typically stems from personal use errors as opposed to manufacturer defects. Use of condoms that do not fit correctly nor feel good may increase the likelihood of condom breakage and slippage and condom-associated erection problems. Condoms come in different widths, lengths, textures, colors, thicknesses, and shapes. One study of condom "turnoffs" found that about one third of men and women indicated that condoms interfered with their own and their partner's sexual pleasure and orgasm (Crosby et al., 2008). Recall that the correct steps in using the condom are detailed in Chapter 11, Practically Speaking, "Tips for Effective Condom Use."

Research has shown that behavioral interventions can improve correct and consistent condom use as well as sexual pleasure during condom use. For example, the Kinsey Institute Condom Use Research Team (KI-CURT) developed and tested home-based, self-guided condom-use behavioral programs for men, women, and couples that are designed to address some of the primary barriers and user errors and problems related to condom use. The focus of these interventions is to aid individuals and couples find condoms and lubricants that they like best, to learn ways to enhance sexual enjoyment and pleasure during sex with condoms, and to build condom-use skills, confidence, self-efficacy, and motivation. The fundamental component of the interventions is the repeated practice, or rehearsal, of correct condom use. Participants were provided a small bag of diverse types of condoms and lubricants (use optional) to practice condom use at home in a safe and "no pressure" environment. After an orientation about condom use and the program, the participants completed questionnaires and then did home-work practice activities using several different types of condoms, followed with taking the same questionnaires again.

KI-CURT found good results with this approach in their interventions with both gay and straight individuals and mixed-sex couples. Many of the study participants got better at using condoms, experienced more sexual pleasure, made fewer errors, and found a condom that fits and feels good in which they used more frequently in subsequent sexual interactions.

Below are brief descriptions of the homework components. If you want to feel more confident and have good condom-use skills while also experiencing sexual arousal and pleasure, you might want to try some of the activities. Of course, you would not be practicing as part of a formal research study and you may not experience all the positive outcomes of the study participants, but you may learn more about condom use that can result in increased correct and pleasurable condom-use with a partner. Remember, the programs are based on repeated condom-use activities; that is, practice.

Condom-Use Program for Males

The condom-use behavioral intervention for males, the *Kinsey Institute Homework Intervention Strategy* (KI-HIS), can be used by both men who have sex with men and men who have sex with women. Two studies of men found, for example, fewer problems with condom fit and feel and fewer problems with erections, increased confidence in ability to use condoms during sex, and a reduction in unprotected sex (Emetu et al., 2014; Milhausen et al., 2011). The home-based activities include:

- Choosing a variety of condoms, such as those of different widths, lengths, shapes, and textures, for the home-based practice.
- Choosing a variety of lubricants (use optional).
- Practicing putting on the condom correctly.
- Masturbating with each of the different condoms to find which one(s) fits and feels the best.
- Focusing on pleasurable sensations while masturbating with the condoms.
- Rating the sexual pleasure experienced with each condom.

Condom-Use Program for Females

The condom-use behavioral intervention for females, the *Kinsey Institute Home-based Exercises for Increasing Responsible Sex* (KI-HERS), focused on increasing women's attention on pleasure while using condoms, thus decreasing the possibility of women having unprotected sexual intercourse. Women who completed the study reported, for example, increased sexual desire, orgasm, and emotional closeness the last time a condom was used, as well as increased condom-use self-efficacy and less embarrassment about condom negotiation and use (Yarber et al., 2018). The home-based activities include:

- Choosing a variety of condoms, such as those of different widths, lengths, shapes, and textures, for the home-based practice.
- Choosing a variety of lubricants (use optional).
- Opening condom package and removing the condom and observe how it feels.
- Touching the condom to your genitals and observe how does that feel?
- Opening the lubrication package and rub between fingers.

- Putting condom on your fingers or sex toy and insert, then commence self-pleasuring.
- Rating the sexual pleasure experienced with each condom.

Condom-Use Program for Couples

The condom-use behavioral intervention for couples, *The Home-based Exercises for Increasing Responsible Sex* (KI-THEIRS), is an adaptation of KI-HIS and KI-HERS to couple use of condoms. Involving each person of a couple dyad adds another dynamic in condom use. This study was for mixed-sex couples (Gesselman et al., 2020). The study found that after the the homework activities both men and women reported less unprotected vaginal inter-course, women reported increased sexual pleasure and self-efficacy, and men reported a decrease in embarrassment in condom use. Several couples reported that their discussion about condoms led them to increased communication about how they make their sexual life more pleasurable. Beyond several home-based activities utilized in KI-HIS and KI-HERs, the couple activities for KI-THEIRS include:

- The couple jointly selects the condoms and lubricants they want to try.
- The couple chooses which condom to use on each day they decide to have sex.
- The couple discusses which condoms and lubricants (if used) and the ones they liked best.
- The couple discusses how their conversations about the condom-use activities may have influenced their sexual behavior and sexual pleasure.
- Each person of the couple completes questionnaire at the beginning and end of the study, which included rating the level of sexual pleasure experienced with each condom used.

If you did some of the practice activities, you could take questionnaire in Chapter 11, Practically Speaking, "Correct Condom Use Self-Efficacy Scale." Completing the questionnaire before and after doing the homework practice indicates if there were positive changes in your condom self-efficacy. Also, after the activities you could reflect on what you learned about condom use, such as which type of condoms you like, whether you become more confident and skillful in using condoms, and whether you learned how to experience more pleasure when using a condom.

We may need to have information on HIV testing. If we have engaged in high-risk behavior, we may want to be tested for our own peace of mind and that of our partner. If we test positive for HIV, we need to make important decisions regarding our health, sexual behavior, and lifestyle. Actually, research has shown that people living with HIV who know of their infection, in contrast to those living with HIV who don't know they are infected, are more likely to take precautions to prevent HIV transmission (Pinkerton et al., 2008).

If we are sexually active with more than one long-term, exclusive partner, we need to use condoms correctly and consistently. Many people remain unconvinced regarding either their own vulnerability to HIV or the usefulness of condoms in preventing its transmission. Male latex, polyurethane, polyisoprene, and internal (female) condoms, when used consistently and correctly, can greatly reduce the risk of HIV and other STIs. Beyond problems with correct condom use, some individuals face issues such as lack of self-assurance and pleasure when using condoms. See Want to Become More Confident in Using Condoms and Experience More Sexual Pleasure? Try Self-Guided Practice at Home."

Representing a major breakthrough in HIV prevention, the U.S. Food and Drug Administration approved in July 2012 the first drug shown to reduce the risk of acquiring HIV infection. This HIV prevention method is called **pre-exposure prophylaxis**, or **PrEP**. The word *prophylaxis* means to prevent the spread or control the spread of an infection or a disease.

PrEP is used when people at risk for HIV take daily medicine to prevent HIV from sex or injection drug use. PrEP can stop HIV from taking hold and spreading throughout your body. When taken daily, PrEP is highly effective for preventing HIV from sex or injection drug use. Studies have shown that PrEP reduces the risk of getting HIV from sex by about 99% when taken daily. Among people who inject drugs and have unprotected intercourse, PrEP reduces the risk of getting HIV by at least 74% when taken daily. Since PrEP does not protect against other STDs, condoms should be used correctly every time you have sex. PrEP is much less effective when it is not taken consistently.

Two medications sold under the brand names Truvada and Descovy® are approved for daily use as PrEP to help prevent a person without HIV from getting the virus from sex or injection drug use. Studies have shown that PrEP is highly effective for preventing HIV if it is used as prescribed. Truvada for PrEP is recommended to prevent HIV for all people at risk through sex or injection drug use. Descovy for PrEP is recommended to prevent HIV for people at risk through sex, *excluding people at risk through receptive vaginal sex.*

Descovy has not yet been studied for HIV prevention for receptive vaginal sex, so it may not be appropriate for some people.

Federal guidelines recommend that PrEP be considered for people who are HIV-negative and who:

- Have a sexual partner with HIV (especially if the partner has an unknown or detectable viral load), or
- Have not consistently used a condom, or
- Have been diagnosed with an STD in the past 6 months

PrEP is also recommended for people who inject drugs and have an injection partner with HIV, or:

- share needles, syringes, or other equipment to inject drugs (e.g., cookers).

PrEP should also be considered for people who have been prescribed post-exposure prophylaxis (PEP) for people who did not have medical occupation exposure and:

- report continued risk behavior, or
- have used multiple courses of PEP.

If you have a partner with HIV and are considering getting pregnant, talk to your doctor about PrEP if you're not already taking it. PrEP may be an option to help protect you and your baby from getting HIV while you try to get pregnant, during pregnancy, or while breastfeeding.

There are no known drug conflicts or interactions between the medicines used in PrEP and hormone therapy such as medication used by a transgender person. There is no known scientific reason why the drugs cannot be taken at the same time. If you are worried that PrEP will affect your hormone therapy, ask your health care provider to check your hormone levels. People who use PrEP should see their health care provider every 3 months for follow-up, for HIV tests, and to have their prescriptions refilled. This visit could be combined with your hormone therapy appointments (CDC, 2020.16m).

PEP (post-exposure prophylaxis) means taking antiretroviral medicines (ART) after being potentially exposed to HIV to prevent becoming infected. PEP should be used only in emergency situations and must be started within 72 hours after a recent possible exposure to HIV. If you think you've recently been exposed to HIV during sex or through sharing needles and works to prepare drugs or if you've been sexually assaulted, talk to your health care provider. PEP must be started within 72 hours after a recent possible exposure to HIV, but the sooner you start PEP, the better. Every hour counts. If you're prescribed PEP, you'll need to take it once or twice daily for 28 days. PEP is effective in preventing HIV when administered correctly, but not 100%. Research has shown that PEP has little or no effect in preventing HIV infection if it is started later than 72 hours after HIV exposure.

PEP is not a substitute for regular use of other proven HIV prevention methods, such as PrEP, PEP is not the right choice for people who may be exposed to HIV frequently; for example, if you often have sex without a condom with a partner who is HIV-positive. Because PEP is given after a potential exposure to HIV, more drugs and higher doses are needed to block infection than with PrEP. PrEP is when people at high risk for HIV take HIV medicines daily to lower their chances of getting HIV. If you are at ongoing risk for HIV, speak to your doctor about prescribing PrEP (CDC, 2019.16e).

HIV Testing

HIV testing and other HIV-related services are available in many areas, including health departments, clinics, substance abuse programs, offices of private physicians, hospitals, and sites especially set up for that purpose. One could use the CDC HIV Service Locator (https://www.cdc.gov/hiv/library/hiv-service-locators.html) for services on HIV testing, PrEP, PEP, and condoms, visit gettested.cdc.gov, or call 1-800-CDC-INFO (232-4636).

"Ignorance breeds passivity, pessimism, resignation, or a sense that AIDS is someone else's problem."

—Paul Farmer, MD (1959–)

Who Should Get Tested for HIV? The CDC recommends that everyone between the ages of 13 and 64 gets tested for HIV at least once as part of routine health care. Even if you are in an exclusive relationship, you should find out for sure whether you or your partner has HIV. About one in seven people in the United States who have HIV don't know they have it. People at higher risk should get tested more often. If you were HIV-negative the last time you were tested, and that test was more than 1 year ago, and you answer yes to any of the following questions, you should get an HIV test as soon as possible because these factors increase your chances of getting the virus:

Many national drug store chains provide free HIV testing.
John Konstantaras/AP Images for Walgreens

- Are you a man who has had sex with another man?

- Have you had sex—anal or vaginal—with an HIV-positive partner?

- Have you had more than one sex partner since your last HIV test?

- Have you injected drugs and shared needles or injection drug equipment (e.g., water or cotton) with others?

- Have you exchanged sex for drugs or money?

- Have you been diagnosed with or sought treatment for another sexually transmitted infection?

- Have you been diagnosed with or treated for hepatitis or tuberculosis (TB)?

- Have you had sex with someone who could answer yes to any of the preceding questions or someone whose sexual history you don't know?

If you continue these behaviors, you should be tested at least once a year. Sexually active gay, bisexual, and queer men may benefit from more frequent testing (e.g., every 3–6 months). Before having sex for the first time with a new partner, you and your partner should talk about your sexual and drug-use history, disclose your HIV and STI status, and consider getting tested for HIV and learning the results. But keep in mind that partners may not know or be wrong about their HIV status, and some may not tell you if they have HIV even if they are aware of their status. Consider getting tested together so you both can know your HIV status and take steps to keep yourself healthy.

Knowing your HIV status gives you powerful information to help you take steps to keep you and your partner healthy. If you test positive, you can take medicine to treat HIV to stay healthy for many years and greatly reduce the chance of transmitting HIV to your sex partner. If you test negative, you have more prevention tools available today to prevent HIV than ever before.

When Should One Get Tested? No test can detect HIV immediately after infection. If you think you've been exposed to HIV in the last 72 hours, talk to your health provider right away about PEP. The immune system usually takes 3–8 weeks to produce antibodies to fight HIV, but tests differ in how soon they are able to detect antibodies. Nearly all the HIV tests look for the antibodies, but some look for the virus itself. The time period following infection but prior to a positive result is called the **window period**. Hence, deciding when to get tested depends on when you may have been exposed and which test is used. People should ask their health care provider about the window period for the HIV test they are taking. If a home HIV test is used, that information can be found in the materials included in the test packaging. A few people will have a longer window period, so if a person gets a negative antibody test result in the first 3 months after possible exposure, a repeat test should be taken after 3 months. Ninety-seven percent of people will develop antibodies in the first 3 months after they are infected. In rare instances, however, it can take up to 6 months to develop antibodies to HIV.

What Kinds of Tests Are Available and How Soon Do they Detect HIV? There are three types of tests available: nucleic acid tests (NAT), antigen/antibody tests, and antibody tests. HIV tests are typically performed on blood or saliva. They may also be performed on urine.

- A NAT looks for the actual virus in the blood and involves drawing blood from a vein. The test can either tell if a person has HIV or tell how much virus is present in the blood (known as an HIV viral load test). While a NAT can detect HIV sooner than other types of tests, this test is very expensive and not routinely used for screening individuals unless they recently had a high-risk exposure or a possible exposure and have early symptoms of HIV infection. The results may take several days to be available and can usually tell you if have HIV infection 10 to 33 days after exposure.

- An antigen/antibody test looks for both HIV antibodies and antigens. Antigen/antibody tests are recommended for testing and done in labs and are now common in the United States. The test results take 30 minutes or less and can tell you if you have HIV infection in 18 to 45 days after exposure for the blood from view test and 18 to 90 days for the finger prick test.

- HIV antibody tests only look for antibodies to HIV in your blood or saliva. In general, antibody tests that use blood from a vein can detect HIV sooner after infection than tests done with blood from a finger prick or with saliva. Most rapid tests and the only currently approved HIV self-test are antibody tests. The saliva antibody self-test provides results within 20 minutes. Antibody tests can take 23 to 90 days.

If you get an HIV test after a potential HIV exposure and the result is negative, get tested again after the window period. Remember, you can only be sure you are HIV-negative if your most recent test is after the window period, and you haven't had a potential HIV exposure during the window period. If you do have a potential exposure, then you will need to be retested.

A person can get an HIV test to use at home or in a private location. These are known as HIV self-tests. There are two kinds:

- A Rapid Self-Test is done entirely at home or in a private location and can produce results within 20 minutes. You can buy a rapid self-test kit at a pharmacy or online. The only rapid self-test currently available in the United States is a saliva test.

- A Mail-In Self-Test includes a specimen collection kit that contains supplies to collect dried blood from a fingerstick at home. The sample is then sent to a lab for testing and the results are provided by a health care provider. Mail-in self-tests can be ordered through various online merchant sites. Your health care provider can also order a mail-in self-test for you.

There is currently one FDA-approved rapid self-test (OraQuick). For this test, you must swab your gums to collect a saliva sample and use the materials in the kit to test your sample. You will be able to get a result within 20 minutes. It is important to follow the directions as described in the instructions or the test will not work. There is a phone number included with the HIV self-test for anyone to call to get help with conducting the test.

Some people have difficulty in conducting a rapid self-test and the test does not perform as it should. If a rapid HIV self-test is invalid as described in the instructions, then the test has not worked. In this case, you will need to use another rapid self-test or a mail-in self-test, or to get tested at a health care provider or testing center. There are many mail-in self-testing services available through online merchants. The kit you receive provides the tools you will need to safely prick your finger and collect a very small sample of blood on a card. The sample is then mailed to a laboratory for testing. When the testing is completed, a health care provider will contact you with the results. If the test result is negative, and you haven't had a possible exposure during the previous 3 months, you can be confident you don't have HIV. If your test result is positive, go to a health care provider for follow-up testing (CDC, 2020.16a).

What Does a Negative or Positive HIV Test Mean? A negative result doesn't necessarily mean that you don't have HIV. This is due to the window period. If you test again after the window period, have no possible HIV exposure during the window period, and the result comes back negative, you do not have HIV. If you're sexually active or use needles to inject drugs, continue to take actions to prevent HIV, like taking medicines to prevent HIV if you're at high risk. If you have certain risk factors, you should continue getting tested at least once a year. HIV is not necessarily transmitted every time you have sex or share needles, syringes, or other drug injection equipment. And the risk of getting HIV varies depending on the type of exposure or behavior. It is important to remember that taking an HIV test is not a way to find out if your partner has HIV. It's important to be open with your partner and ask them to tell you their HIV status. But keep in mind that your partner may not know or may be wrong about their status, and some may not tell you if they have HIV even if they are aware of their status. Consider getting tested together so you can both know your HIV status and take steps to keep yourselves healthy.

If you use any type of antibody test and have a positive result, you will need another (follow-up) test to confirm your results. If you test in a community testing program or take a self-test and it's positive, you should go to a health care provider to get follow-up testing. If your test is done in a health care setting or a lab and it's positive, the lab will conduct the follow-up testing, usually on the same blood sample as the first test. If the follow-up test is also positive, it means you have HIV (or are HIV-positive).

It is important that you start medical care and begin HIV treatment as soon as you are diagnosed with HIV. Being HIV-positive does not mean you have AIDS. AIDS is the most advanced stage of HIV infection. HIV can lead to AIDS if a person does not get treatment or take care of their health. But if a person with HIV takes their HIV medicine as prescribed, they may stay healthy for many years and may never be diagnosed with AIDS (CDC, 2020.16a; Scaccia, 2020).

Treatments

When AIDS first surfaced in the United States in the early 1980s, there were no drugs to combat the underlying immune deficiency and few treatments for the opportunistic diseases that resulted. People with AIDS were not likely to live longer than a few years. Researchers, however, have developed drugs to fight both HIV infection and its associated infections and cancers. HIV treatment is the use of anti-HIV medications to keep an HIV-infected person healthy. Treatment can help people at all stages of HIV disease. Although anti-HIV medications can treat HIV infection, they cannot cure it.

People with HIV should take medicine to treat HIV as soon as possible. HIV medicine is called **antiretroviral therapy (ART)**. If taken as prescribed, HIV medicine reduces the amount of HIV in the body (**viral load**) to a very low level, which keeps the immune system working and prevents illness. This is called **viral suppression**—defined as having less than 200 copies of HIV per milliliter of blood. HIV medicine can even make the viral load so low that a test can't detect it. This is called an **undetectable viral load**. A person with an undetectable viral load cannot transmit HIV through unprotected sex (see Table 2).

TABLE 2 ● Risk of HIV Transmission with Undetectable Virus Load by Transmission Category	
Transmission Category	**Risk for People Who Keep An Undetectable Viral Load**
Sex (oral, anal, or vaginal)	Effectively no risk
Pregnancy, labor, and delivery	1% or less*
Sharing syringes or other drug injection equipment	Unknown, but likely reduced risk
Breastfeeding	Substantially reduces but does not eliminate risk. Current recommendation in the United States is that mothers with HIV should not breastfeed their infants.

*The risk of transmitting HIV to the baby can be 1% or less if the mother takes HIV medicine daily as prescribed throughout pregnancy, labor, and delivery and gives HIV medicine to her baby for 4–6 weeks after giving birth.

Source: CDC, 2020.16a.

● Living With HIV or AIDS

People infected with HIV or diagnosed with AIDS have the same needs as everyone else—and a few more. If you are HIV-positive, in addition to dealing with psychological and social issues, you need to pay special attention to maintaining good health. If you are caring for someone with HIV or AIDS, you also have special needs.

If You Are HIV-Positive

A positive antibody test is scary to just about anyone. However, a positive test result is a valuable news: It is news that may make it possible to save your life. If you don't learn about your status in this way, you probably will not know until a serious opportunistic infection announces the presence of HIV. At that point, many of your best medical options have been lost, and you might have spread the virus to others who would not otherwise have been exposed. But remember, although HIV infection is serious, people with HIV are living longer, healthier lives than ever before, thanks to new and effective treatments.

Staying Healthy Longer   It is important to find a physician who has experience working with HIV and AIDS, and—even more important, perhaps—who is sensitive to the issues confronted by individuals infected with HIV. Begin treatment promptly once your doctor tells you to. Keep your appointments and follow the doctor's instructions. If your doctor prescribes medicine for you, take the medicine exactly the way they tell you, since taking only some of your medicine gives your HIV infection more chance to fight back. Taking ART medications on schedule increases their effectiveness and greatly reduces the chance of transmitting HIV to sex partners if taken the right way, every day. If you get sick from your medicine, call your doctor for advice; don't make changes to what your doctor has prescribed on your own or because of advice from friends. In addition to appropriate medical treatment, factors that can help promote your continuing good health include good nutrition, plenty of rest, exercise, limited (or no) alcohol use, and stress reduction. You should also stop smoking tobacco because it increases susceptibility to pneumonia. And you should get immunizations to prevent infections such as pneumonia and flu.

In addition, if you decide to have sexual contact with another person, it means practicing safer sex, even if your partner is also HIV-positive. Researchers caution that one can become reinfected with different HIV strains. Moreover, STIs of all kinds can be much

The Names Project Foundation created the AIDS Memorial Quilt as a poignant and powerful tool in preventing HIV infection. Each square has been lovingly created by friends and families of people who have died of AIDS. The quilt now contains more than 48,000 panels.

Hisham Ibrahim/PhotoV/Alamy Stock Photo

worse for people with an impaired immune system. HIV doesn't mean an end to being sexual, but it does suggest that different ways of expressing love and sexual desire may need to be explored. If you are living with HIV or AIDS, you may need many kinds of support: medical, emotional, psychological, and financial. Your doctor, local health department and social services departments, local AIDS service organizations, and the Internet can help you find all kinds of help.

Addressing Your Other Needs   The stigma and fear surrounding HIV and AIDS often make it difficult to get on with the business of living. Among gay, bisexual, and queer men, social support is generally better for whites than for Blacks/African Americans; in Black communities, there tends to be less affirmation from primary social support networks and less openness about sexual orientation. Women, who often concern themselves with caring for others, may not be inclined to seek out support groups and networks. But people who live with HIV and AIDS say that it's important not to feel isolated. If you are HIV-positive, we encourage you to seek support from AIDS organizations in your area.

Partner Notification   Both current and past partners should be notified so that they can be tested and receive counseling. In many states, HIV-infected people are required by law to notify current and recent sexual and needle-sharing partners. AIDS counselors and health care practitioners encourage those with HIV to make all possible efforts to contact past and current partners. In some cases, counselors try to make such contacts, with their clients' permission.

Final Thoughts

MANDEL NGAN/Getty Images

As we have seen, HIV/AIDS remains a major public health challenge. HIV continues to take a severe toll on many communities in the United States, with gay and bisexual men of all races and Black/African American and Latino individuals bearing the heaviest burden. Not only is HIV/AIDS a medical problem, but barriers such as stigmatization, discrimination, limited health care and prevention education messages, and gender inequity impede progress in controlling the epidemic. We must do more—as individuals, in our communities, and as a nation—to expand our prevention efforts to people at risk and stop the spread of HIV. As we know, HIV can be avoided.

Summary

What Is AIDS?

- *AIDS* is an acronym for *acquired immunodeficiency syndrome.* For a person to receive an AIDS diagnosis, he or she must have a positive blood test indicating the presence of *HIV (human immunodeficiency virus)* antibodies and have a T-cell count below 200; if the T-cell count is higher, the person must have 1 or more of over 20 diseases or conditions associated with AIDS to be diagnosed with the disease.

- A host of symptoms are associated with HIV/AIDS. Because these symptoms may indicate many other diseases and conditions, HIV and AIDS cannot be self-diagnosed; diagnosis by a clinician or physician is necessary.

- *Leukocytes,* or white blood cells, play a major role in defending the body against invading organisms and cancerous cells. One type, the *macrophage,* engulfs foreign particles and displays the invader's *antigen* on its own surface. *Antibodies* bind to antigens, inactivate them, and mark them for destruction by *killer T cells.* Other white blood cells called *lymphocytes* include *helper T cells* (also called CD4T or CD4 cells), which are programmed to "read" the antigens and then begin directing the immune system's response. The number of helper T cells in an individual's body is an important indicator of how well the immune system is functioning.

- *Viruses* are primitive entities; they can't propel themselves independently, and they can't reproduce unless they are inside a host cell. Within the HIV's protein core is the genetic material (RNA) that carries the information the virus needs to replicate itself. A *retrovirus* such as HIV can "write" its RNA (the genetic program) into a host cell's DNA.

- Although HIV begins replication right away within the host cells, it is not detectable in the blood for some time—often years. HIV antibodies, however, are generally detectable in the blood within 3–8 weeks. A person's *serostatus* is HIV-negative if antibodies are not present and HIV-positive if antibodies are detected. "T-cell count," or "CD4 count," refers to the number of helper T cells that are present in a cubic millimeter of blood.

- When a person is first infected with HIV, he or she may experience severe flu-like symptoms. During this period, the virus is dispersed throughout the lymph nodes and other tissues. The virus may stay localized in these areas for years, but it continues to replicate and destroy T cells. As the number of infected cells goes up, the number of T cells goes down. In advanced AIDS, the T-cell count drops to under 200, and the virus itself is detectable in the blood.

The Epidemiology and Transmission of HIV

- The number of adults and adolescents living with HIV in the United States has grown to over 1.2 million. Worldwide, about 38 million people are now living with HIV. Rates of new infections are the highest in sub-Saharan Africa.

- Rates of new HIV infection are decreasing all over the globe—the annual diagnosis of HIV in the United States has decreased 79% between 2014 and 2018.

- HIV is not transmitted by casual contact.

- Activities or situations that may promote HIV transmission include sexual transmission through vaginal or anal intercourse without a condom; fellatio without a condom; cunnilingus without a latex or other barrier; the sharing of needles and syringes contaminated with infected blood; in-utero infection from mother to fetus, from blood during delivery, from pre-chewed baby food, or in breast milk; the sharing of sex toys without disinfecting them; accidental contamination when infected blood enters the body through mucous membranes (eyes or mouth) or cuts, abrasions, or punctures in the skin (relatively rare); and blood transfusions (very rare).

- Certain physiological or behavioral factors increase the risk of contracting HIV. In addition to anal intercourse, numerous sexual partners, and injection drug use, these factors include having an STI (especially if genital lesions are present) and multiple exposures to HIV.

AIDS Demographics

- HIV/AIDS is often linked with poverty, which has roots in racism and discrimination. In the United States,

Blacks/African Americans and Latinx have been disproportionately affected by HIV and STIs in comparison to other racial/ethnic groups.

- Certain groups have been particularly impacted by the AIDS epidemic in the United States: racial/ethnic minorities (particularly Blacks/African Americans in the Deep South) and gay, bisexual, and queer men, women, and young adults.

- Because young people often have a sense of invulnerability, they may put themselves at great risk without understanding the consequences of their sexual behavior.

Prevention and Treatment

- To protect ourselves and those we care about from HIV, we need to be fully knowledgeable of what constitutes risky behaviors and how to avoid them, develop communication skills so that we can talk with our partners, and get information on HIV testing. If we are sexually active with more than one long-term, exclusive partner, we need to use condoms correctly and consistently.

- Pre-exposure prophylaxis (or PrEP) is when people at high risk for HIV take HIV medicines to lower their chance of getting infected. PrEP is highly effective if taken as prescribed.

- Post-exposure prophylaxis (PEP) is given after a potential exposure to HIV. PEP is not the correct choice for people who may be exposed to HIV frequently such as a person who has sex often without a condom with a partner who is HIV-positive.

- Free or low-cost HIV testing is available in many areas.

- Antiretroviral medications—the combination of drugs is called antiretroviral therapy (ART)—are available for the treatment of HIV/AIDS. Many people on the ART regimen have an increase in quality of life and longevity.

- Getting and keeping an undetectable viral load is the best thing a person living with HIV can do to stay healthy.

- A person with an undetectable viral load effectively has no risk of transmitting HIV to an uninfected person.

Living With HIV or AIDS

- An HIV or AIDS diagnosis may be a cause for sadness and grief, but it also can be a time for reevaluation and growth. Those whose friends or family members are living with HIV, or who are themselves HIV-positive, need information and practical and emotional support.

- Early detection and treatment of HIV can greatly enhance both the quality and the longevity of life. Appropriate medical treatment and a healthy lifestyle are important. People with HIV or AIDS also need to practice safer sex and consider seeking support from AIDS organizations.

Questions for Discussion

- What behaviors or measures have you taken or will you take to prevent yourself from contracting HIV?

- Despite the seriousness of the HIV/AIDS epidemic, some people continue to practice risky sexual behaviors and injection drug use; many of them are not receptive to HIV prevention messages. What do you suggest as strategies to reach these individuals?

- Individuals who are diagnosed with an HIV infection react in many ways. How do you think you would react?

- What would be your most important concern if you just learned that you had been infected with HIV?

Sex and the Internet

CDC HIV Risk Reduction Tool

The Centers for Disease Control and Prevention (CDC) provides a web tool called CDC HIV Risk Reduction Tool. This tool can help a person find fast, free, and confidential testing. It can also help a person locate housing, local health centers, substance abuse assistance, access to HIV medication, and much more. Go to https://hivrisk.cdc.gov and answer these questions:

- What are the varied topics the site discusses?

- Do the topics address issues you are curious about?

- Choose and explore one topic. Was this topic helpful to you?

- What other topics were of interest to you?

- As a result of this exploration, what did you learn about HIV/AIDS prevention and issues?

Suggested Websites

Centers for Disease Control and Prevention
www.cdc.gov/hiv/
Provides information on HIV/AIDS.
http://www.cdc.gov/std/
Provides information on STIs.

Joint United Nations Programme on HIV/AIDS
www.unaids.org
Contains epidemiological information on HIV/AIDS worldwide, as well as perspectives on HIV/AIDS–related issues.

Kaiser Family Foundation
www.kff.org
Offers fact sheets and new releases on STIs and HIV/AIDS.

National Institutes of Health
www.nih.gov
Provides current information about HIV/AIDS.

Rural Center for AIDS/STD Prevention
rcap.indiana.edu
Provides information about issues related to HIV/STI prevention in rural communities in the United States.

U.S. Government
www.hiv.gov/
The federal government's Internet source for HIV prevention and treatment.

Suggested Reading

Halkitis, P. (2014). *The AIDS generation: Stories of survival and resilience.* University of Oxford Press. Stories of pain, suffering, hope, survival, and resilience of a generation of gay men in the midst of the AIDS epidemic.

Harden, V. A., & Fauci, A. S. (2012). *AIDS at 30: A history.* Potomac Books. A history of HIV/AIDS written for a general audience that emphasizes the medical response to the epidemic.

Pepin, J. (2011). *The origins of AIDS.* Cambridge University Press. The author looks back to the early-twentieth-century events in Africa that triggered the emergence of HIV/AIDS and traces its subsequent development into the most dramatic and destructive epidemic of modern times.

Pozorski, A. et al. (2019). *Literary and visual representations of HIV/AIDS: Forty years later.* Lexington Press. By focusing on literature and the visual arts, this book helps us understand the HIV/AIDS epidemic and how it impacts people.

Royles, D. (2020). *To make the wounded whole: The African struggle against HIV/AIDS.* The University of North Carolina Press. Recounts one of the greatest health challenges to African Americans in the twentieth and twenty-first centuries.

Quammen, D. (2015). *The chimp and the river: How AIDS emerged from an African forest.* W. W. Norton. The real story of how AIDS originated from a virus in a chimpanzee, jumped to one human, and then infected 60 million people.

Shilts, R. (1987). *And the band played on: People, politics, and the AIDS epidemic.* Martin's Press. The fascinating story behind the "discovery" of AIDS, complete with real heroes and, unfortunately, real villains.

Whitside, A. (2017). *HIV & AIDS: A very short introduction.* University of Oxford Press. Provides an introduction to AIDS and discusses the science, international and local politics, and the devastating consequences of the disease.

chapter 17

Sexual Assault and Sexual Misconduct

©Mario Mitsis/Alamy Stock Photo

CHAPTER OUTLINE

Sexual Harassment

Harassment and Discrimination Against Lesbian, Gay, Bisexual, Transgender, and Queer People

Sexual Assault

Child Sexual Abuse

530

Student Voices

"I was sexually harassed at work, but I stood my ground. I told the guy to knock it off or I'd sue him. It worked—he quit 3 weeks later."

—20-year-old female

"At a very young age, I remember being sexually molested by two neighbors who were a couple years older than I. They did not insert anything in me. I was not physically hurt, but I remember losing my voice and the will to defend myself. I remember my father calling my name from the back porch and I could not answer him. I felt I had lost all power to speak or move. The regret of allowing this to happen to me still lingers in my feelings toward others and myself. I believe this event has contributed to shaping some deep paranoia and mistrust toward my peers, and I have carried this for a long time."

—22-year-old female

"When I reached the first grade, my mother's boyfriend moved in with us. Living with him was the biggest nightmare of my life. One night I was asleep and was awakened by something. It was my mother's boyfriend, and what woke me up was his hand. He was touching me in my sleep while he watched television. He did not touch me under my clothes and he did not caress me, but he would place his hand on my private parts and that made me feel very uncomfortable. I used to move and roll around a lot so he would move his hand. I became afraid to sleep at night because I thought he would be there. These events affected me emotionally and psychologically."

—20-year-old male

"I was sexually abused when I was about eight years old. My cousin and uncle molested me several times. They abused me for as long as 3 years. After this time, I decided to run away because I did not have a father, and I knew that my mother would not believe what happened to me. I tried to tell people what had happened to me, but everyone would call me a liar or crazy. In my town, people believed that if a woman was sexually abused it was her fault because she provoked the men. This includes child abuse. In my home, my family never talked about sex or sexuality, and I think that is one of the reasons I did not know that what happened to me wasn't my fault."

—21-year-old female

ALTHOUGH SEXUALITY PERMITS US to form and sustain deep bonds and intimate relationships, it has a darker side. For some people, sex is linked with coercion, degradation, aggression, and abuse. In these cases, sex becomes a weapon—a means to exploit, humiliate, or harm others. In this chapter, we first examine the various aspects of sexual harassment, including the distinction between flirting and harassment, stalking, and the sexual harassment that occurs in schools, colleges, and the workplace. Next, we look at harassment, prejudice, and discrimination directed against lesbian women, gay men, and bisexual, transgender, and queer (LGBTQ+) people. Then we examine sexual assault/rape and issues related to sexual consent, particularly on college campuses. Finally, we discuss child sexual abuse, examining factors contributing to abuse, the types of abuse and their consequences, and programs for preventing it.

Before we begin, a note about terminology. In recent years, we have increasingly expanded our knowledge of sexually aggressive behavior and its consequences. Earlier, researchers had focused primarily on **rape**, usually defined as penile-vaginal penetration performed against a *woman's* will through the use of force or threat of force. Contemporary research now focuses on a broader range of sexual-related behaviors against another person and also utilizes varied terms like *sexual assault, sexual violence,* and *sexual coercion.* These terms are often used interchangeably and without clear definition, leading to possible confusion by the reader; further, legal definitions of rape, sexual battery, and sexual assault vary across jurisdiction (Cantor et al., 2020; Eileraas, 2011; Muehlenhard et al., 2011). Both *survivor* and *victim* are used to describe persons who have experienced sexual assault/violence. Many agencies and individuals prefer the term *survivor,* believing that term is more empowering. The term *victim* is still used in some research studies and reports, and in the criminal justice context (The White House Council on Women and Girls, 2014). In this book, our preference was to use the term *survivor;* however, we also use terms utilized in the cited research and reports.

"Being forced is poison for the soul."
—Ludwig Borne (1786–1837)

As you can see, we choose to title this chapter "Sexual Assault and Sexual Misconduct," the vocabulary used in a report prepared for the Association of American Universities, *Report on the AAU Campus Climate Survey on Sexual Assault and Misconduct* (Cantor et al., 2020). We prefer these terms as they represent a broader range of behaviors: nonconsensual sexual contact involving sexual penetration, sexual touching, sexual harassment, and stalking, all of which are discussed in this chapter. Again, other terms are used in our discussion to follow those used in a particular research study. Because of the varied terms, one should attempt to ascertain exactly what behaviors are studied in reports when interpreting the findings.

● Sexual Harassment

Sexual harassment refers to two distinct types of behavior: (1) the abuse of power for sexual ends and (2) the creation of a hostile environment. In terms of abuse of power, sexual harassment consists of unwelcomed sexual advances, requests for sexual favors, or other verbal or physical conduct of a sexual nature as a condition of instruction or employment. Refusal to comply may result in reprisals. Only a person with power over another can commit the first kind of harassment. When someone acts in sexual ways that interfere with another person's performance at school or in the workplace, he or she is creating a **hostile environment**. Such harassment is illegal.

What Is Sexual Harassment?

Title VII of the Civil Rights Act of 1964 first made various kinds of discrimination, including sexual harassment, illegal in the workplace. Title VII applies to employers with 15 or more employees, including local, state, and federal employees, employment agencies, and labor organizations. In 1980, the U.S. Office of Equal Employment Opportunity Commission (EEOC) issued guidelines regarding both verbal and physical harassment in the work and education environments. The EEOC defined sexual harassment as unwelcome sexual advances, requests for sexual favors, and other verbal or physical conduct of a sexual nature when this conduct: (1) explicitly or implicitly affects an individual's employment, (2) unreasonably interferes with an individual's work performance, or (3) creates an intimidating, hostile, or offensive work environment. A major component of the EEOC guidelines is that the behavior is unwanted and unwelcome and might affect employment conditions. The sexual aggression does not have to be explicit, and even the creation of a hostile environment that can affect work performance constitutes sexual harassment. The victim as well as the harasser may be anyone. Also, it is unlawful for an employer to retaliate against an individual for filing a discrimination charge or opposing employment practices that discriminate based on sex (U.S. Equal Employment Opportunity Commission, 2009; U.S. Merit Systems Protection Board, 1995). Further, the victim does not have to be the person harassed but could be anyone affected by the conduct.

Sexual harassment is a mixture of sex and power; however, power is often the dominant element. In school and the workplace, individuals are devalued by calling attention to their sexuality. For women especially, sexual harassment may be a way to keep them "in their place" and make them feel vulnerable.

There are other forms of behavior that, although not illegal, are considered by many to be sexual harassment. These include unwanted sexual jokes and innuendos and unwelcome whistles, taunts, and obscenities directed, for example, from a man or group of men to a woman walking past them. As with all forms of harassment, these apply to all genders, including male-female, male-male, and female-female interactions. They also include a man "talking to" a woman's breasts or body during conversation or persistently giving her the "once-over" as she walks past him, sits down, or enters or leaves a room. It may also be a suggestive comment or unsolicited photograph sent via e-mail or social media. Examples of sexual harassment include (Powell, 1996; Cantor et al., 2020):

- Making sexual remarks or told jokes or stories that were insulting or offensive
- Making inappropriate or offensive comments about a person's or someone else's body, appearance, or sexual activities

- Saying crude or gross sexual things to a person or tried to get a person to talk about sexual matters when they did not want to

- Using social or online media to send offensive unwanted sexual remarks, jokes, stories, pictures, or videos to a person

- Continuing to ask a person to go out, get dinner, have drinks, or have sex even though they said no

- Brushing against a person's body or engaged in unwelcomed touching, patting, or pinching

- Making demands for sexual favors, accompanied by implied or overt threats

Masturbating in front of an unsuspecting person can also be considered sexual harassment. Such incidents may make a person feel uncomfortable and vulnerable. They have been described, in fact, as "little rapes." The cumulative effect of these behaviors is to lead women and some men to limit their activities, to avoid walking past groups of men, and to stay away from beaches, concerts, parties, and sports events unless they are accompanied by others. Sometimes, charges of sexual harassment are ignored or trivialized, and blame often falls on the victim. Sexual harassment more commonly occurs in school or the workplace, as well as in other settings, such as between patients and doctors or mental health and sex therapists.

Sexual harassment, particularly in the workplace, creates a stressful and hostile environment for the victim.

©Dmytro Zinkevych/Shutterstock

One type of harassment that may not be explicit sexually, per se, is **stalking**. The Centers for Disease and Prevention's National Intimate Partner and Sexual Violence Survey (NISVS) is an ongoing, nationally representative survey of the prevalence and characteristics of stalking as well as sexual violence and intimate partner violence among adult men and women (18 years or older) in the United States (Smith et al., 2018). A number of stalking tactics were assessed that included being watched or followed; being repeatedly contacted by phone, electronically, and through social media; and being threatened by physical harm. The 2015 NISVS survey found that about 1 in 6 women (16% or 19.1 million) and 1 in 17 men (5.8% or 6.4 million) in the United States have experienced stalking victimization at some point during their lifetime in which they felt very fearful or believed that they or someone close to them would be harmed or killed. The 2010–2012 NISVS survey found that 68% and 70% of female and male stalking victims, respectively, reported that their perpetrators made threats of physical harm. About 6 in 10 (61.5%) female victims and 4 in 10 (42.8%) male victims were stalked by a current or former intimate partner. A variety of tactics were used to stalk persons as reported in the 2015 NISVS survey (Figure 1). Overall the tactics were similar between women and men.

During the 2019 spring semester, 181,752 undergraduate and graduate/professional students at 33 universities participated in the Association of American Universities national study AAU Campus Climate Survey on Sexual Assault and Sexual Misconduct (AAU Survey), one of the largest student surveys on sexual assault and misconduct (Cantor et al., 2020). The AAU Survey provided estimates on the incidence, prevalence, and characteristics of incidents involving sexual assault and tactics used to acquire nonconsensual sex, as well as behaviors such as sexual harassment, stalking, and intimate partner violence. From a survey question to measure gender identity, students were classified into four groups: (1) female, (2) male, (3) transgender, genderqueer, or nonconforming, questioning, or identity not listed (TGQN), and (4) decline to state. The 2019 AAU Survey found that:

- 5.8% of all students indicated that they had been victims of stalking since they enrolled at the college or university.

- Similar to almost all the different measures of assault and sexual misconduct, persons identified as TGQN reported the highest stalking rates: 15.2% undergraduates and 8.5% for graduate/professional students. Rates for female students were 10% for

• FIGURE 1

Stalking Tactics Used Against American Men and Women Who Reported Being Stalked in Their Lifetime.

Source: Smith et al. (2017).

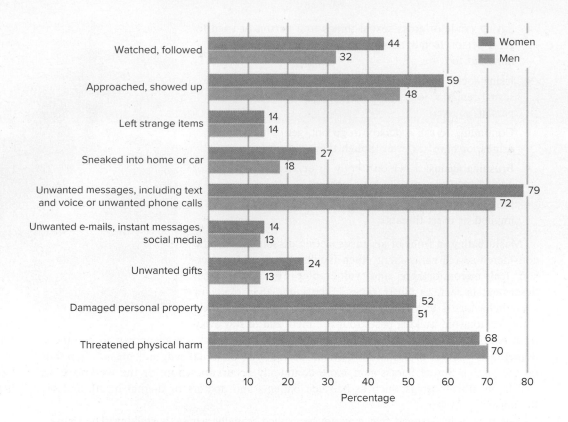

undergraduates and 5.9% for graduate/professional students; for males, 3.1% for undergraduates and 1.8% for graduate/professional students. The 2015 AAU study (Cantor et al., 2020) revealed the type of relationship to the victim who experienced stalking since enrolling in school. Figure 2 shows that, for undergraduate students, the two most frequent types of relationships were "Someone I previously had been involved with or intimate with" and "Someone I know and recognize but was not a friend."

Persons who are stalked sometimes fear that the behavior will never stop and that they will be physically harmed. They may wonder what will happen next and experience negative psychological outcomes, such as anxiety, depression, and insomnia. Most college campuses provide educational and support services for persons who experience being stalked. Stalking is a crime in all 50 states, the District of Columbia, and the U.S. Territories, which allows the police to arrest a person who continually stalks.

Flirtation Versus Harassment

Flirting is an ambiguous, goal-oriented behavior with potential sexual or romantic overtones. That is, we flirt with a purpose, but since we are "testing the waters," we try not to reveal what the purpose might be. Scientists believe, from an evolutionary mating perspective, that flirting was developed to advance the human race as a way to help males find a mate and for females to judge a potential partner and his level of commitment prior to any continued social contact (Bernstein, 2012).

There is nothing wrong with flirtation, per se. A smile, look, or compliment can give pleasure to both people. But persistent and unwelcome flirtation can be sexual harassment if the flirtatious person holds power over the other or if the flirtation creates a hostile school, work, or social environment. Whether flirtation is sexual harassment depends on three factors:

- *Whether you have equal power.* Flirting may lead to trouble when there is a power difference between the two people. A person having power over you limits your ability to refuse, for fear of reprisal. For example, if a professor or teaching assistant in your class asks you for a date, you are placed in an awkward position. If you say no, will your grade suffer? Will you be ignored in class? What other consequences might

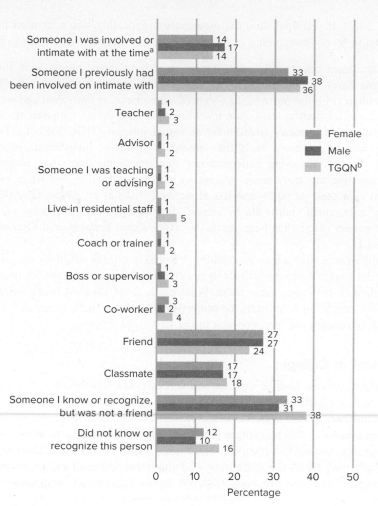

● **FIGURE 2**

Relationship to Victim among Female, Male, and TGQN Students Who Experienced Stalking Since Enrolling in College.

Source: Adapted from Cantor et al. (2020).

Note: Students were directed to mark all that apply; hence, percentages add up to more than 100%.

[a]Percentages rounded to the nearest whole number.

[b]TGQN: Transgender women, transgender men, genderqueer, gender non-conforming, questioning and identity not listed on questionnaire.

occur? Or if your supervisor asks for a date, you may be similarly concerned about losing your job, being demoted, or having your work environment become hostile if you refuse.

- *Whether you are approached appropriately.* "Hi babe, nice tits, wanna get it on?" and "Hey stud, love your buns, wanna do it?" are obviously offensive. But approaches that are complimentary ("You look really nice today"), indirect ("What do you think of the class?"), or direct ("Would you like to have some coffee?") are acceptable because they do not pressure you. You have the opportunity to let the overture pass, respond positively, or politely decline. Sometimes, it is difficult to determine the intent of the person doing the approaching. One way to ascertain the intent is to give a direct "I" message and ask that the behavior cease. If the person stops the behavior, and especially if an apology follows, the intent was friendly; if the behavior continues, it is the beginning of sexual harassment. If he or she does not stop, you should contact a trusted supervisor, an academic advisor/counselor, or a resident assistant.

- *Whether you wish to continue contact.* If you find the other person appealing, you may want to continue the flirtation. You can express interest or flirt back. But be very cautious about touching the person you are flirting with. Placing your hand on the arm of a date may be OK, but doing that with a colleague is probably unwise (Bernstein, 2012). One problem with touching while flirting is that it may be based on a false assumption that the person is flirting with someone who is interested but they are not

(Hall, 2013). If you don't find the other person appealing, you may want to stop the interaction by not responding or by responding in a neutral or discouraging manner.

Three significant gender differences may contribute to sexual harassment. First, men are generally less likely to perceive activities as harassing than are women. The difference in perception often is for the more subtle forms of harassment, as both men and women believe that overt activities such as deliberate touching constitute sexual harassment. Second, men tend to misperceive women's friendliness as sexual interest (Hall, 2013; La France et al., 2009). Third, men are more likely than women to perceive male-female relationships as adversarial. A study involving undergraduate students found that when women flirt in a sexually suggestive way men perceive them to be more attractive, but when men flirt this way women view them as pushy and less attractive (Frisby et al., 2011). Given this, the vast majority of harassment claims are by women. Interestingly, the percentage of males filing sexual harassment claims has been increasing (U.S. Equal Employment Opportunity Commission, n.d.).

Power differences also affect perception. Personal questions asked by an instructor or a supervisor, for example, are more likely to be perceived as sexual harassment than they would be if a student or co-worker asked them. What needs to be clarified is the basis of the relationship: Is it educational, business, or professional? Is it romantic or sexual? Flirtatious or sexual ways of relating are inappropriate in the first three contexts.

Harassment in College

Sexual harassment on college and university campuses has become a major concern. The AAU Survey (2020) reported that 41.8% of students had indicated that they had experienced sexual harassment since being enrolled in college. The methodology report of the AAU survey noted that this percentage is relatively higher than other campus climate surveys possibly because the AAU definition varied from other surveys and that some students may not have read all of the definitions of harassment included in the introductory text when answering questions. To be considered sexual harassment, respondents must have experienced at least one of the behaviors listed in Figure 3 and reported that the behavior interfered with their academic or professional performance, limited their ability to participate in an academic program, or created an intimidating, hostile, or offensive environment (Cantor et al., 2016, 2020). Major findings include:

- Among all students, 18.9% reported having experienced sexual harassment.
- Undergraduate TGQN students (transgender women, transgender men, genderqueer, gender nonconforming, questioning, or identity not listed) and women reported the highest levels of harassment (46.3% TGQN students; 31.3% women).
- Undergraduate students had a higher rate of harassment than graduate/professional students. For example, among undergraduate women, 31.3% reported on the survey that they were sexually harassed compared to 19.9% of graduate/professional students. A similar pattern occurred for men and TGQN students.
- Graduate and professional students were more likely to have experienced sexual harassment by a faculty member or instructor. Twenty-four percent of graduate/professional women were harassed by a faculty member or instructor compared to 5.5% of undergraduate women. For men, 18.2% of graduate/professional men were harassed by a faculty member or instructor compared to 4.3% of undergraduate men.

Two major problems in dealing with issues of sexual harassment in college are gender differences in levels of tolerance and attribution of blame. Women are often blamed for not taking a "compliment" and for provoking unwanted sexual attention by what they wear or how they look. These attitudes are widely held, especially among men.

Because of sexual harassment, many students, especially women students, find it difficult to study; others worry about their grades. If the harasser is an instructor controlling grades or a coach providing team leadership, students fear reporting the harassment. They may use strategies such as avoiding courses or sports taught by the harasser or choosing another

• FIGURE 3

Types of Sexual Harassment Tactics Experienced by Female, Male, and TGQN* Students Enrolling in College.

*TGQN: Transgender woman, transgender man, genderqueer, gender non-conforming, questioning, and identity not listed in questionnaire.

Source: Cantor et al. (2020).

Since you have been a student at [University], has a student, or someone employed by or otherwise, associated with [University]:

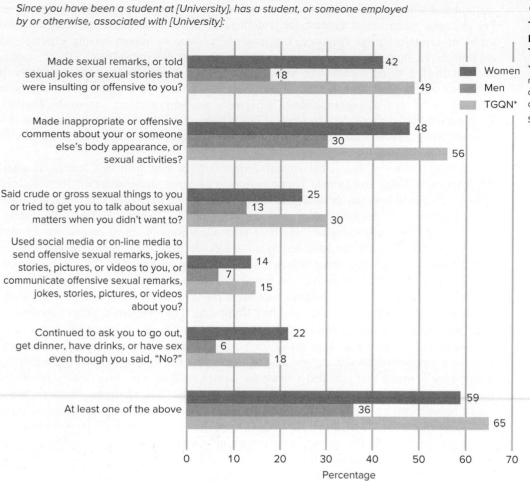

Note: Students were directed to mark all that apply; hence, percentages add up to more than 100%. Numbers are rounded to the nearest whole number.

*TGQN: Transgender woman, transgender man, genderqueer, gender non-conforming, questioning, and identity not listed on questionnaire.

advisor. In extreme cases, the emotional consequences may be as severe as for rape survivors. However, many students, particularly women, view the dating of students by professors as unethical behavior rather than harassment.

Most universities and colleges have developed sexual harassment policies, most of which prohibit romantic/sexual relationships between students and professors. A fundamental principle of these policies is that the student-professor relationship cannot be truly consensual, given the professor's considerable power over the student's academic standing and career plans.

Harassment in the Workplace

Issues of sexual harassment are complicated in the workplace because the work setting, like college, is one of the most important places where adults meet potential partners. As a consequence, sexual undercurrents or interactions often take place. Flirtations, romances, and "affairs" are common in the work environment. The line between flirtation and harassment can be problematic—especially for men (Bowles, 2017). Many women do not realize they are being harassed until much later. When they identify the behavior, they report feeling naïve or gullible, as well as guilty and ashamed. As they learn more about sexual harassment, they are able to identify their experiences for what they are: harassment.

Sexual harassment in the workplace is a serious problem affecting tens of thousands of individuals. A U.S. Equal Employment Opportunity Commission (2016) review of studies on workplace harassment found anywhere from 25% to 85% of women report having experienced sexual harassment in the workplace. The difference is attributed to the sampling method and whether sexual harassment is defined or not and if so, what the definition is. For example, when sexual harassment is defined as both unwanted sexual attention and sexist or crude/offensive behavior, the majority of women report having experienced harassment in surveys. In a large-scale survey of transgender individuals, 50% of respondents indicated being harassed at work, 41% reported having been asked unwelcomed questions about their transgender or surgical status, and 45% reported having been referred to by the wrong pronouns "repeatedly and on purpose" at work. Further, 7% reported being physically assaulted at work because of their gender identity and 6% reported being sexually assaulted. These rates are greater for transgender individuals of color (Human Rights Commission, 2011).

While allegations of sexual harassment against famous men such as Clarence Thomas, Bill Clinton, R. Kelly, and Donald Trump have long gathered media attention, there seemed to be no change in how culture addressed the issue. However, in October 2017, sexual harassment became a major American social concern when Harvey Weinstein, a Hollywood movie industry giant, was fired after allegations of sexual harassment by over 30 actresses including Ashley Judd and Salma Hayek. In May 2018, Weinstein was arrested and charged with rape and other offenses, and eventually sentenced to 23 years in prison. The Weinstein case led to a landslide of sexual harassment accusations and admissions that resulted in either the firing or resignation of many powerful figures in entertainment, media, and politics. The ramifications reverberated worldwide. The "Weinstein effect" resulted in many women feeling safe in coming forward with their story of being sexually harassed at work—a story that they had kept secret for years and decades with damaging outcomes. Further, a groundswell of sharing and healing began with the #MeToo movement, a hashtag used on social media that provided a venue for women to share their experiences, learn that they were not alone, and be validated. Industries and the U.S. Congress began to tackle sexual harassment, an issue that they had long buried. Some believe that the firing of Weinstein and other powerful men in industry and in politics is a "watershed" moment that has awakened the world to the widespread existence of workplace sexual harassment, and that women and men are demanding that they no longer will remain silent and that they deserve to be safe in the place they choose to work (Hampson, 2017; Jayson, 2017; Kelly & Jensen, 2017). Since the beginning of the #MeToo movement in 2017, stigma and awareness surrounding sexual harassment have increased, and more women have come forward to with their history of being harassed. Men have been likewise impacted, although possibly not as much as desired. For example, in 2019 The Kinsey Institute published a national study of 5,000 single Americans and found that only 40% and 34% of men indicated that they are more reserved to some extent at work and on a date, respectively (Wisely, 2019). Some advocates and survivors wonder how much progress has been made. Kristen Houser, chief public affairs officer at the National Sexual Violence Resource Center stated that "People are paying attention, but I'm not convinced that we're able or ready to behave differently about it as a nation" (Dastagir, 2019, p. 1A).

Two polls taken after the Weinstein case examined the prevalence of sexual harassment in the workplace. An NBC/WSJ poll found that 48% of currently employed women in the United States say that they have personally experienced an unwelcome sexual advance or verbal or physical harassment at work. Sixty-two percent of men and 71% of women said that workplace sexual harassment is widespread (Dann, 2017). A Quinnipiac University poll found that 41% of women and 23% of men indicated that they had been sexually assaulted at work (Quinnipiac Poll, 2017).

Sexual harassment tends to be most pervasive in male-dominated occupations, in which it is a means of exerting control over women and asserting dominance. Women experience high levels of harassment in male-dominated industries such as technology, building trades, trucking, law enforcement, and the military, which have traditionally been resistant to the presence of women. For example, the Pentagon bi-annual survey of sexual assault in the military found a 44% increase in the percentage of females reporting sexual assault, from 4.3% in 2016 to 6.2% in 2018. No change in percentage was found for male members. Two thirds (64%) of service members who reported sexual assaults perceived negative experiences or retaliation associated with their reporting (Martinez, 2019).

Although most sexual harassment situations involve men harassing women, men can be the victims of harassment, from either a woman or a man. The U.S. Supreme Court has ruled that any woman or man can file legal action against an individual for sexual harassment (Solomon, 1998). Sexual harassment can have a variety of consequences for the victim, including depression, anxiety, shame, humiliation, and anger, as will be discussed later in the chapter (Cantor et al., 2016).

Gender-Based Harassment in Public Spaces

Sexual harassment in public places, also called **street harassment**, is a common occurrence experienced by many people, often with profound consequences. The organization Stop Street Harassment (2017) states that "gender-based street harassment is unwanted comments, gestures, and actions forced on a stranger in a public place without their consent and is directed at them because of their actual or perceived sex, gender, gender expression, or sexual orientation." Persons who experience street harassment can feel not only annoyed, angry, and humiliated but also scared. Some people are harassed because of risk factors such as their race, perceived gender expression, sexual orientation, nationality, religion, disability, or social class. Street harassment can occur in all public places, including in stores, on public transportation, in parks, and at beaches, and includes the following unwanted behaviors (Rape Abuse & Incest National Network, 2021.17a):

- Calling out offensive comments
- Honking, whistling, and making vulgar gestures
- Requests that persist for someone's name, phone number, or destination after they have said no
- Making sexually explicit comments or demands and sexist comments
- Stating homophobic or transphobic slurs
- Following someone
- Leering and stalking
- Flashing or masturbating in public
- Grabbing or rubbing against someone
- Sexually assaulting someone
- Showing sexually explicit images without someone's consent
- Taking a photo of someone without their consent
- Up-skirting, which is taking a photo up a skirt or dress without their permission
- Using a mirror to look up someone's skirt or dress without their permission

The fear and intimidation resulting from stranger intrusion are real and harmful (Baptist & Coburn, 2019). Most women in the United States across all ages, races, income levels, sexual orientations, gender identities, and geographical areas experience street harassment, which can be a daily occurrence. Some men, especially those who self-identify as gay, bisexual, queer, or transgender, also experience street harassment. Persons of color and those who identify as LGBTQ+ are disproportionately impacted by street harassment. Street harassment is unique from sexual harassment in school and the workplace or dating or domestic violence because it occurs between strangers in public places, making any legal recourse very difficult.

Stop Street Harassment commissioned a national study of street harassment of 2,000 people in the United States in early 2014 (see Figure 4) (Kearl, 2014). Major findings included:

- Sixty-five percent of women reported that they have experienced street harassment in their lifetime, 57% experienced verbal harassment, 41% physical aggression, including sexual touching (23%), being followed (20%), flashing (14%), and being forced to do something sexual (9%).

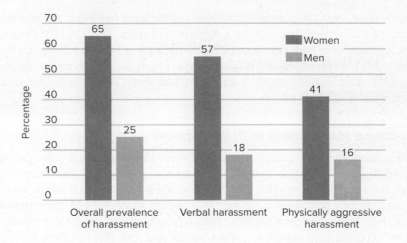

- One quarter of men reported experiencing street harassment, including 18% experiencing verbal harassment and 16% experiencing physically aggressive forms (see Figure 4).

- Gay, bisexual, queer, or transgender men were 20% and 19% more likely to report street harassment and physical aggression, respectively, than men who were not gay, bisexual, queer, or transgender.

- Eighty-six percent of women and 79% of men reported experiencing street harassment more than once. Women more often than men indicated that the harassment happened often or daily.

- Men were overwhelmingly the harassers of both men and women, although 20% of men said their harasser was a lone woman.

- As a result of street harassment, most harassed persons changed their lives in some way, such as constantly assessing their surroundings, going places with others, and to a more extreme end, quitting a job or moving to a different neighborhood.

- About one half said they did something proactive about the harassment, such as telling the harasser to stop or back off.

The Stop Street Harassment website (http://www.stopstreetharassment.org/) provides valuable tips on what to do before or after being harassed, educating boys and men on how to interact with women, and what bystanders can do. The organization also has a toll-free National Street Harassment Hotline: 855-897-5910. Stop Street Harassment declares that harassment in public places is a human rights violation and a form of gender violence, resulting in many harassed persons, especially women, feeling unsafe in public places and thus limiting their time there. Stop Street Harassment states that "everyone deserves to be safe and free from harassment as they go about their day."

● Harassment and Discrimination Against Lesbian, Gay, Bisexual, Transgender, and Queer People

Researchers have identified two forms of discrimination, or bias, based on sexual orientation: heterosexual bias and anti-gay prejudice.

Heterosexual Bias

Heterosexual bias, also known as **heterosexism** or **heterocentric behavior**, and widely (and silently) accepted in society, media, and the family, involves the tendency to see the world in heterosexual terms and to ignore or devalue persons who do not identify as heterosexual (Griffin, 1998; Walls, 2008). Heterosexual bias may take many forms. Examples of this type of bias include the following:

- *Ignoring the existence of lesbian, gay, bisexual, transgender, and queer people.* Discussions of various aspects of human sexuality may ignore LGBTQ+ people, assuming that such individuals do not exist, are not significant, or are not worthy of inclusion. Without such inclusion, discussions of human sexuality are really discussions of *heterosexual* sexuality.

- *Segregating LGBTQ+ people from heterosexual people.* When gender identity is irrelevant, separating certain groups from others is a form of segregation, as in efforts to not permit sexual minorities to openly date or bring a same-sex partner to a social work event or a school event such as a prom.

- *Subsuming LGBTQ+ people into a larger category.* Sometimes, it is appropriate to make sexual orientation and sexual identity category in data analysis, as in studies of adolescent suicide rates. If orientation is not included, findings may be distorted.

Prejudice, Discrimination, and Violence

Anti-gay prejudice is a strong dislike, fear, or hatred of lesbian, gay, bisexual, transgender, and queer people because of their sexual orientation. Homophobia is an irrational or phobic fear of LGBTQ+ people. Not all anti-gay feelings are phobic in the clinical sense of being excessive and irrational, but they may be unreasonable or biased. The feelings may, however, be within the norms of a biased culture.

Outcomes of Anti-Gay Prejudice and Discrimination As a belief system, anti-gay prejudice justifies discrimination based on sexual orientation and gender identity. This discrimination can take varied forms: LGBTQ+ people are often discriminated against in access to housing, employment opportunities, adoption of children, and parental rights. Even though the climate for LGBTQ+ persons has improved in recent years, these individuals still face obstacles to personal rights. For example, 53% of LGBTQ+ individuals reside in a state that does not prohibit employment discrimination based on sexual orientation or gender identity, and 67% live in states that are silent on child fostering by LGBTQ+ parents (Movement Advancement Project, 2017a, 2017b; Schulze et al., 2019).

Persons experiencing anti-gay prejudice may be harassed and bullied and become victims of physical violence. Anti-gay prejudice influences parents' reactions to their lesbian, gay, bisexual, transgender, and queer children, often leading to estrangement. As a result, many sexual minority persons suffer various negative outcomes, including these:

- The 2019 Youth Risk Behaviors Survey reported that high schools students aged 14–18 who reported having seriously considered suicide was highest for students who reported having sex with persons of the same sex or with both sexes (54.2%) and students who identified as lesbian, gay, or bisexual (46.8%). The prevalence of students reporting having attempted suicide were highest among students who reported having sex with persons of the same sex or with both sexes (30.0%) and students who identified as lesbian, gay, or bisexual (23.4%) (Ivey-Stephenson et al., 2020).

- The 2019 National School Climate Survey of middle and high school students found that 59.1% of LGBTQ+ students felt unsafe at school because of their sexual orientation, 42.5% because of their gender expression, and 37.4% because of their gender. Sixty-eight percent of LGBTQ+ students experienced verbal harassment at school, 25.7% were physically harassed, 11% were physically assaulted, and 44.9% experienced electronic harassment in the past year. Ninety-five percent heard homophonic remarks, such as "dyke" or "faggot." Compared to LGBTQ+ students who did not experience LGBTQ+ related discrimination at school, those who did were nearly 3 times as likely to have missed school in the past year, had a lower GPA (3.14 vs. 3.39), and were more likely to have been disciplined at school (40.2% vs. 22.6%) (Kosciw et al., 2020).

- The 2018 National Health Interview Survey data revealed that for persons aged 18 and over, 7.6% of gay/lesbian persons and 10.4% of bisexual persons indicated that they had experienced serious psychological distress in the past 30 days, compared to 3.7% of straight adults (National Center for Health Statistics, 2019).

- More LGBTQ+ individuals live in poverty compared to non-LGBTQ+ individuals. Women in same-sex couples and African American LGBTQ+ people are at greatest risk for poverty (Badgett et al., 2013; Badgett & Schneebaum, 2016; Mushovic, 2011).

- More than one in four LGBTQ+ adults (27%) experienced a time last year when they did not have sufficient money to purchase food for themselves or their family, compared to 17% non-LGBTQ+ adults. Among LGBTQ+ persons, 42% of African Americans, 33% of Hispanics, 32% of American Indians and Alaska Natives, and 21% of whites indicated that they did not have an adequate amount of money in the past year to purchase food (Brown et al., 2016).

- In a national online poll of 1,197 LGBTQ+ individuals, 39% indicated that at some point in their lives a family member or close friend rejected them because of their sexual orientation or gender identity. Thirty percent said that they had been physically

During the Middle Ages, gay men (called sodomites) were burned at the stake as heretics (above left). In Germany in 1933, the Nazis burned the library of sex reformer Magnus Hirschfeld and forced him to flee the country (above right). (See Chapter 2 to learn of Hirschfeld's sexual reform efforts.) Gay men and lesbian women were among the first Germans the Nazis forced into concentration camps, where over 50,000 of them were killed. Today, violence against LGBTQ+ individuals continues (bottom right). The pink triangle recalls the symbol the Nazis required lesbian women and gay men to wear, just as they required Jews to wear the Star of David.

attacked, 29% indicated that they had been made to feel unwelcome in a place of worship, and 21% indicated that they had been treated unfairly by an employer. Fifty-eight percent said they had been a target of slurs or jokes (Pew Research Center's Social and Demographic Trends, 2013).

Violence Against Sexual Minorities Violence against sexual minorities has a long history. At times, such violence has been sanctioned by religious institutions. During the Middle Ages, leaders of the religious court called the Inquisition condemned "sodomites" to death by burning. In the sixteenth century, England's King Henry VIII made sodomy punishable by death. In more recent times, homosexual individuals were among the first victims of the Nazis, who killed 50,000 in concentration camps. Because of worldwide violence and persecution against lesbian women and gay men, in 1992 the Netherlands, Germany, and Canada granted asylum to men and women based on their homosexuality (Farnsworth, 1992; Parker, 2020).

Today, gay men, lesbian women, and other sexual minorities are frequent targets of violence. Hate violence is a pervasive and persistent issue for all LGBTQ+ people. A 2020 report of the FBI showed that hate crimes based on sexual orientation represented 16.7% of all hate crimes, following only race and religion. Gender-based hate crimes rose from 2.2% in 2018 to 2.7% in 2019 (Ronan, 2020). Shooting at Pulse, a gay nightclub in Orlando, Florida, on June 12, 2016, resulted in 49 deaths. It was reported that the majority of the victims were LGBTQ+ and Latinx.

The brutal murder of Matthew Shepard, a gay University of Wyoming student, in 1998 and the dragging death of a 34-year-old African American man, James Byrd, Jr., in 1998 received national media attention. After more than a decade of advocacy, the Matthew Shepard and James Byrd, Jr., Hate Crimes Prevention Act was signed into law by President Obama on October 28, 2009. This law gives the Department of Justice the power to investigate and prosecute, as a federal crime, bias-motivated violence against an individual because of the person's actual or perceived sexual orientation, gender identity, color, religion, national origin, or disability. More recent violence against LGBTQ+ individuals illustrates the continuing problem faced by sexual minorities. For example, during the George Floyd protests in late May and early June 2020, an LGBTQ+ bar was vandalized with a white power symbol; in May 2002, a Black transgender male was shot and killed by Tallahassee police; in 2019, an arsonist burned the drop-in office of SisTers PGH, a transgender resource center

Members and allies of the gay community show their support of the gay community at the scene of Pulse, a gay nightclub in Orlando, Florida, following a mass shooting that killed 49 people in 2016.

©Joe Burbank/TNS/Newscom

led by black and transgender people; and in March 2018, a gay man was fatally shot as he left the Aura nightclub in Kansas City, Missouri.

An analysis of the 2017 National Crime Victimization Survey found that sexual and gender minorities (SGMs) had disproportionate rates of victimization when compared to cisgender, heterosexual counterparts. The findings provide the first nationally representative assessment of violent victimization of SGMs (Flores et al., 2020):

- The odds of violent victimization among SGMs were nearly 4 times (rate of 71.1 per 1,000 persons per year) compared to that of non-SGMs (19.2 per 1,000 per year).

- SGM persons had higher rates of victimization for nearly all violent crime subtypes.

- Compared to non-SGMs, SGMs were more likely to experience violence both by someone known well by the victim and by a stranger.

- Only about half of violent episodes were reported to the police, a rate like non-SGMs.

A study by the National Center for Transgender Equality found that nearly one half of all transgender people experience being sexually assaulted in their lifetime with persons of color experiencing the greatest sexual assault: American Indian (65%), multiracial (59%), Middle Eastern (58%), and Black (53%). The lifetime prevalence of rape is greater among bisexual women (46%) in contrast to heterosexual women (17%) (Hauck, 2019).

A 2018 FBI study examined victims' perceptions of whether the violence was motivated by biases, finding that LGBT individuals, per capita, are the group most likely to be victims of bias-motivated crimes in the United States (Fitzsimons, 2019).

Ending Anti-Gay Prejudice and Enactment of Antidiscrimination Laws

As mentioned, LGBTQ+ people are discriminated against in many ways that harm their self-esteem and mental health. Education and positive social advocacy and interactions are important ways to combat anti-gay prejudice. Another way is to create legislation to guarantee sexual minority individuals equal protection under the law.

The Movement Advancement Project (MAP) is an independent think tank focusing on expediting equality for LGBTQ+ people (Movement Advancement Project, 2020.17a). MAP has created equality maps that summarize nearly 40 laws and policies that affect LGBTQ+ Americans on a state-by-state and issue-by-issue basis.

For each of these laws and policies (as of January 1, 2020), a score or point value was assigned and then the scores were summed to create a "policy tally" for each state. Seven major categories were covered by the policy tally: relationship and parental recognition, nondiscrimination, religious exemptions, LGBTQ+ youth, health care, criminal justice, and identity documents. The policy tally was divided into simple categories—high, medium, fair, low, or negative equality—which allows comparison of the LGBTQ+ climate across states. The tallies examined only exiting laws but did not measure social climate or whether the laws were implemented.

The 2020 report (MAP, 2020.17a) also compared the current laws to the same laws as of January 2, 2010. MAP found remarkable advancement in policy accomplishments facing LGBTQ+ individuals over the past 10 years. For example:

- From 2010 to 2020, the average overall policy tally scores across all states increased by more than 10 points.

- The number of LGBTQ+ people living within "negative" equality states fell by more than half.

- Nearly all aspects of LGBTQ+ law saw remarkable changes over the past 10 years. So-called **conversion therapy** (also called reparative therapy) is an attempt to change a person's sexual orientation or gender identity. In 2010, no state had banned conversion therapy, while as of January 1, 2021, 20 states plus Washington, D.C., and Puerto Rico have banned it. This type of therapy is not endorsed by the licensed mental health and medical communities, and laws prohibit mental health practitioners from subjecting LGBTQ+ minors to this harmful practice. These laws do not restrict the practice among religious providers.

MAP notes that even though changes over the past decade show impressive progress toward LGBTQ+ equality, significant challenges remain. For example, the progress has not been equally experienced across the country or across varied LGBTQ+ communities, and pro-LGBTQ+ policy changes in one state or region may spur similar action in other states, in both positive and negative ways.

In 2020, 43% of the LGBTQ+ population live in states that have an overall high policy tallies combining the seven major categories, and 3% live in states with medium overall policy tallies, yet a similar percentage (45%) live in states with low or negative policy tallies. This pattern illustrates that different legal protections are available to LGBTQ+ persons depending on where they live, as well as the need for more progress in legalizing equality for all LGBTQ+ individuals (MAP, 2020.17a, 2020.17b).

Among several legal and policy areas representing LGBTQ+ equality, we have selected sexual orientation and gender identity for more detailed review. Figure 5 shows which states provide law and policy protection from discrimination and harm based on sexual orientation, defined by MAP as "person's pattern of emotional, romantic, or sexual attraction (or lack thereof) to people." Relative to the total LGBTQ+ population, 4 out of every 10 (41%) individuals live in states with high sexual orientation policy tallies. Only 2% live in states with negative sexual orientation policy tallies. Figure 6 shows which states provide law and policy protection from discrimination and harm based on gender identity, defined by MAP as a "person's deeply-felt inner sense of being male, female, or something else or in-between." Relative to the total LGBTQ+ population, slightly more than 4 out of 10 (43%) individuals live in states with high gender policy tallies. Sixteen percent live in states with negative gender identity policy tallies (MAP, 2020.17a, 2020.17b).

In a landmark ruling for the LGBTQ+ community, in June 2020, the U.S. Supreme Court ruled that the Civil Rights Act of 1964 protects gay, lesbian, and transgender employees from workplace discrimination. The Court stated that the language of the law prohibits

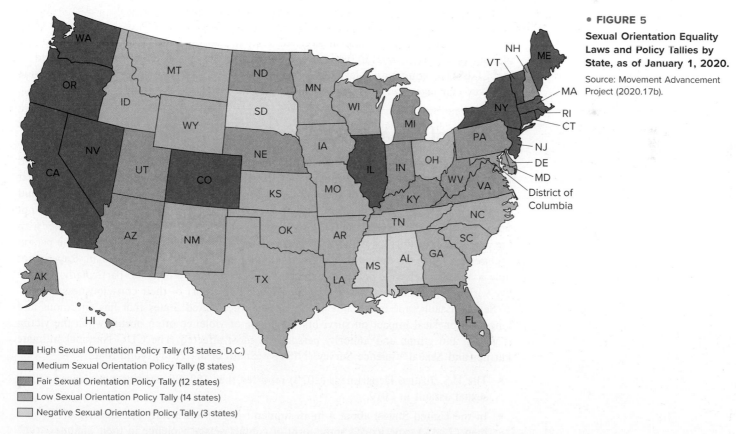

• **FIGURE 5**

Sexual Orientation Equality Laws and Policy Tallies by State, as of January 1, 2020.

Source: Movement Advancement Project (2020.17b).

■ High Sexual Orientation Policy Tally (13 states, D.C.)
■ Medium Sexual Orientation Policy Tally (8 states)
■ Fair Sexual Orientation Policy Tally (12 states)
■ Low Sexual Orientation Policy Tally (14 states)
■ Negative Sexual Orientation Policy Tally (3 states)

Note: A state's "policy tally" represents the number of laws and policies within the state that helps protect persons from discrimination and harm based on sexual orientation. Each state has a tally score. For example, a "high policy tally" represents states with the highest number of equality laws and policies.

• FIGURE 6

Gender Identity Equality
Laws and Policies Tallies by
State, as of January 1, 2020.

Source: Movement Advancement
Project (2020.17b).

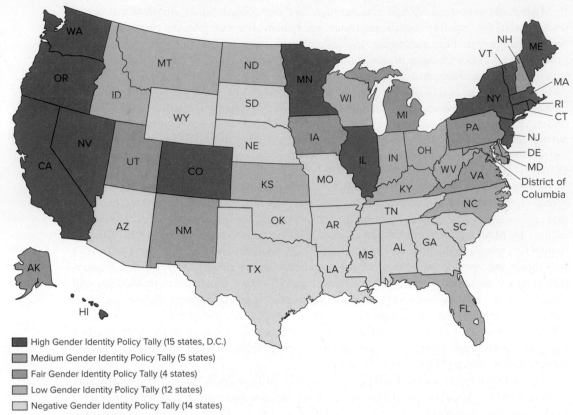

High Gender Identity Policy Tally (15 states, D.C.)
Medium Gender Identity Policy Tally (5 states)
Fair Gender Identity Policy Tally (4 states)
Low Gender Identity Policy Tally (12 states)
Negative Gender Identity Policy Tally (14 states)

Note: A state's "policy tally" represents the number of laws and policies within the state that helps protect persons from discrimination and harm based on gender identity. Each state has a tally score. For example, a "high policy tally" represents states with the highest number of equality laws and policies.

discrimination not only based on assigned sex but also on sexual orientation and gender identity (Edmonson, 2021). Two other landmark rulings by the Supreme Court related to the LGBTQ+ community—legalizing private, consensual sexual behavior, and legalizing same-sex marriage—are discussed in Chapter 18.

• Sexual Assault

In recent years, we have increasingly expanded our knowledge about sexually aggressive and violent behavior and its consequences. In the 1970s, feminists challenged the belief that sexual assault/rape is a form of a harmful sexual disorder. Instead, they argued, **sexual assault** is an act of violence and aggression against women, and the principle motive is power, not sexual gratification. Sexual assault forces its survivor into an intimate physical encounter with the perpetrator against his or her will. The survivor does not experience pleasure; the person experiences terror. In most cases, but certainly not all, the survivor is a woman. Rape is not only a specific behavior but also a threat. As a result, many persons, particularly, women live with the possibility of being sexually assaulted as a part of their consciousness.

Sexual assault/rape is a major public issue in the United States that has enormous and long-term physical impact on survivors. This type of violence often occurs when the victim is young, and ethnic and minority persons are most affected. The CDC National Intimate Partner and Sexual Violence Survey (NISVS) (Smith et al., 2018) found that:

- The U.S. Justice Department (2020) reported that 459,310 persons experienced rape/sexual assault in 2019.
- In the United States, about 4 in 10 women (43.6%) and nearly one quarter of men (24.8%) experienced some form of contact sexual violence in their lifetime (see Figure 7).

- Every 73 seconds an American is sexually assaulted (Rape, Abuse, & Incest National Network, 2017). The violence includes rape, being made to penetrate someone else, sexual coercion (e.g., nonphysically pressured unwanted penetration), unwanted sexual contact (e.g., fondling, kissing), and noncontact unwanted sexual experiences (e.g., harassed in a public place).

- About 26 million women (21.3%) and 2.8 million men (2.6%) have been the victims of completed or attempted rape at some point in their life.

- Of all female victims of completed rape, 43% reported that it first occurred prior to age 18.

- An estimated 6.8 million men (1 in 14) were made to penetrate another person in their lifetime; 26% reported that it occurred prior to age 18.

Perpetrators of sexual violence against female and male victims were typically intimate partners or acquaintances. The NISVS report states that "Survey findings underscore the heavy toll of this violence, the young age at which people often experience violence, and the negative health conditions associated with these forms of violence."

National data also show that many experience sexual assault as adolescents. The Centers for Disease Control and Prevention (CDC) found that 11% of female students and 3% of male students in grades 9–12 had been forced to have sexual intercourse when they did not want to (CDC, 2020.2a).

Sexual assault of males Sexual assault/rape against males may be perpetrated by other men or by women. Most sexual assaults are by other men. In some states, the word *rape* is used only to define forced vaginal sexual intercourse, whereas forced anal intercourse is termed *sodomy.* More recently, states have started using gender-neutral terms such as *sexual assault* or *criminal sexual conduct,* regardless of whether the survivor is a man or woman.

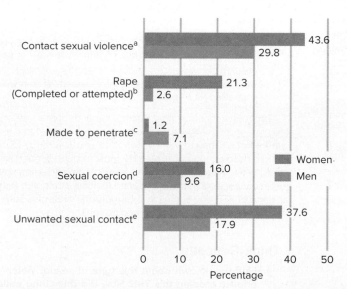

● FIGURE 7

Lifetime Prevalence of Sexual Violence Victimization, U.S. Women and Men, 2015.

Source: Smith et al. (2018).

[a]Contact sexual violence is a combined measure that includes rape, being made to penetrate someone else, sexual coercion, and/or unwanted sexual contact.

[b]Among women, rape includes vaginal, oral, or anal penetration by a male using his penis. It also includes vaginal or anal penetration by a male using their fingers or an object. Among men, rape includes oral or anal penetration by male using his penis. It also includes anal penetration by a male or female using their fingers or an object.

[c]Victim made or an attempt to make them penetrate someone without the victim's consent.

[d]Unwanted vaginal, oral, or anal sex after being pressured.

[e]Unwanted sexual experiences not involving touching or penetration, such as someone exposing their sexual body parts, masturbating in front of a victim, flashing, and making a victim look at or participate in sexual photos or movies.

think about it

An Unexplored Form of Sexual Violence: Women Forcing Penile Penetration

Female sexual aggression toward men, particularly compelled penile penetration, has received limited research attention. The few studies have largely focused on the prevalence of men being "forced-to-penetrate" (FTP) such as the National Intimate Partner and Sexual Violence Survey (2015), which found that 7.9 million (1 in 14) men in the United States were forced into penile penetration in their lifetime. Of these men, about 1.6% were made to penetrate through completed forced penetration and 1.4% experienced situations involving attempts to make them penetrate another person through force. Further, 5.5% were made to penetrate another individual through completed alcohol/drug facilitation (Smith et al., 2018). However, research on women's tactics used to force penile penetration is often lacking.

A study conducted by researcher Siobhan Weare at Lancaster University in the United Kingdom explored aggressive strategies used by women, as reported by 154 men in the United Kingdom who had experienced FTP by women (Weare, 2018). FTP was defined as a man being forced to penetrate, with his penis and without his consent, a women's vagina, anus, or mouth. For this study, "sexual aggression" connotes sexual behavior that is unwanted and performed against the man's will, but not limited only to the use of force.

Some persons wonder if a man can experience an erection without his consent. Research has shown that is biologically possible; that is, a man can have an erection and maintain it without being emotionally sexually aroused and/or while experiencing anxiety, fear, or terror (e.g., Sarrel & Masters, 1982). Hence, a male experiencing an erection in response to another person's advances or touch does not automatically indicate arousal nor consent by the man.

From the study findings, strategies used by women were grouped into four major categories. Specific strategies reported by the men who had experienced FTP for each category are listed below.

Blackmail, Threats, Coercion, and Continued Verbal Pressures

The most frequent aggressive strategy used by women: 51 (33.3%) men indicated this strategy used on them.
Strategies include:

- threatening to end the relationship
- threatening to spread rumors about you
- continuing to pressure you after you indicated you did not want penetration
- criticizing your sexuality or attractiveness
- getting angry after you said no but not being forceful

Taking Advantage of Men's Intoxication via Drugs or Alcohol

The second most frequent aggressive strategy used by women: 41 (26.8%) men indicated this strategy used on them.
Strategies included:

- forcing penetration when you are asleep or unconscious from consensually consuming alcohol but after regaining consciousness did not give consent or request what was happening to stop
- forcing penetration when you are asleep or unconscious from using drugs consensually but when regaining consciousness was not able to stop what happened
- forcing penetration after you have been drinking alcohol and was conscious but too drunk to give consent or stop what was happening

Use Force and Threats of Physical Harm

The third most frequently aggressive strategy used by women: 30 (19.6%) men indicated this strategy used on them.
Strategies included:

- using force such as holding you down with their body weight
- pinning your arms
- having a weapon
- threatening to harm you or a person close to you

Actively Involved in Encouraging Intoxication via Alcohol or Drugs

The least frequently aggressive strategy used by women: five (3.3%) men indicated this strategy used on them.
Strategies included:

- giving you a drug without your knowledge to make you too intoxicated (drunk) to consent or stop what was happening
- encouraging you or pressuring you to consume alcohol until you were too intoxicated (drunk) to give consent or stop what was happening

The researcher indicated that the study debunks the "myth of the nonaggressive women" and the traditional belief that a woman cannot force a man to have penetration sex. This study found that women used a range of strategies, most frequently coercive strategies, taking advantage of men's intoxication, and using force and threats of physical harm. Some used multiple strategies within one episode of FTP, and some used "gendered" strategies such as threatening to make false rape accusations.

Think Critically

1. Had you known about this type of sexual violence prior to reading this TAI? How did this study enlighten or support what you know about female sexual aggression?
2. Had you believed that "a woman cannot force a man to have penetrative sex" prior to reading this study? If so, what did you hear about it?
3. What specific findings did you find to be particularly noteworthy?
4. If you were educating a group of college men about "forced-to-penetrate" sexual aggression, what would you emphasize?

Surveys reveal that men experience sexual victimization, although not at the same levels as women (Stemple & Meyer, 2014). As stated earlier, in the NISVS 24.8% of men reported experiencing some form of sexual violence in their lifetime and 3.6% reported being victims of completed or attempted rape in their life (Smith et al., 2018). Experts, however, believe that the statistics vastly underrepresent the actual number of males who are raped. For example, research conducted at John Hopkins University found that boys experienced higher levels of sexual abuse, physical violence, and neglect by adults than girls, and that the more frequently a boy was victimized the more likely he was to do violence to others (Brown, 2021). Though society is becoming increasingly aware of sexual assault, the lack of complete tracking of sexual crimes against males and the lack of research about the effects on survivors are indicative of the attitude held by society at large that although male rape and sexual assault occur, the topic is not taken seriously. While many people believe that the majority of male rape occurs in prison, research suggests that the conditions for male rape are not unique to prison. Rather, all men and boys, regardless of who or where they are, should be regarded as potential victims of sexual assault.

In the aftermath of an assault, many men blame themselves, believing that they in some way granted permission to the perpetrator. Male rape survivors suffer from fears similar to those felt by female rape survivors, including the belief that they actually enjoyed or somehow contributed or consented to the assault. Heterosexual male survivors sometimes worry that they may have given off "gay vibes" that the perpetrator picked up and then acted on. Some men may suffer additional guilt because they became sexually aroused and ejaculated during the rape. These men, and our culture, may assume that if a man had an erection he must have wanted the sexual contact (Rosin, 2014). However, these are normal, involuntary, physiological reactions to the parasympathetic fear response and do not imply consent or enjoyment. Another concern for male rape survivors is society's belief that men should be able to protect themselves and that rape is somewhat their own fault.

Although they are uncommon, there are some instances of women sexually assaulting a man. As shown in Figure 7, about 1 in 14 men (7.1% or nearly 7.9 million) in the United States have been made to penetrate someone else (attempted or completed) within their lifetime. Despite being threatened with knives and guns, some men are able to have erections. No matter whether the male was sexually assaulted by a female or male, many of these survivors may believe that the rape threatens the very essence of their masculinity and manhood. To learn more about men being compelled to penetrate, see the Think About It box, "An Unexplored Form of Sexual Violence: Forced Penile Penetration by Women."

Statutory rape Consensual sexual contact with a person younger than a state's age of consent—the age at which a person is legally deemed capable of giving informed consent—is termed **statutory rape**. The laws rarely are limited to sexual intercourse but instead include any type of sexual contact. The age of consent varies from 16 to 18 in most states. This means that individuals below the age of consent cannot legally consent to sex, and anyone having sex with them is, by definition, in violation of the law. In some states, factors such as age differences between partners, the age of the survivor, and the age of the defendant are considered (Office of the Assistant Secretary for Planning and Evaluation, 2014). To address situations in which both individuals are below the age of consent or the offender is near the age of the minor, some states have created "Romeo and Juliet laws." In some states, a defense for no criminal charges is allowed. Other states have reduced punishment for statutory rape, such as imposing only a fine or probation, eliminating the requirement to register as a sex offender (Findlaw, 2019). The enforcement of statutory rape laws, however, is generally sporadic or arbitrary.

Marital rape **Marital rape** is defined as unwanted sexual behaviors by a spouse or ex-spouse committed without consent, against a person's will, and done by force, intimidation, or when a person is not able to consent. This form of sexual violence is not common but occurs often among married women: men undoubtedly experience marital rape but rarely. The women's movement in the 1970s resulted in the criminalization of marital rape. In 1976, Nebraska become the first state to eliminate its marital rape exception law. By 1989, all 50 states had revoked their marital rape exceptions. Currently in 20 states, a husband is exempt when he

"The husband cannot be guilty of rape committed by himself upon his lawful wife, for by their mutual matrimonial consent and contract, the wife gives herself in kind unto the husband which she cannot retract."

—Sir Matthew Hale (1609–1676)

does not have to use force because his wife is legally unable to give consent; that is, she is mentally or physically impaired, unconscious, or asleep, for example. Also, because of the marital contract, the wife's consent is assumed (England, 2020; Stritof, 2017).

Many people discount rape in marriage as a "marital tiff" that has little relation to "real" rape. Women are more likely than men to believe that a husband would use force to have sexual intercourse with his wife. When college students were asked to describe marital rape, they created "sanitize" images: "He wants to and she doesn't, so he does anyway," or "They are separated, but he really loves her, so when he comes back to visit, he forces her because he misses her." The realities to these myths are very different.

Marital rape survivors experience feelings of betrayal, anger, humiliation, and guilt. Following their rape, many wives feel intense anger toward their husbands; others experience constant terror because they are living with their assailant. Others develop negative self-images and view their lack of sexual desire as a reflection of their own inadequacies rather than as a consequence of being assaulted. Many do not report rape, thinking that no one will believe them. Some do not even recognize that they have been legally raped. Most of these responses to rape are experienced by both heterosexual and same-sex couples.

Campus Sexual Assault

Sexual assault on college campuses is a serious problem. One in five women report being assaulted/raped while in college, most often during their freshman or sophomore year (Cantor et al., 2015; Krebs et al., 2009; Muehlenhard et al., 2017). Reported rapes are very low; that is, many more rapes occur than are reported. As you recall, the 2019 AAU Campus Climate Survey on Sexual Assault and Sexual Misconduct (Cantor et al., 2020) assessed sexual assault and sexual misconduct of 181,752 students from 32 colleges and universities nationwide. Data for the prevalence of two types of sexual misconduct—stalking and harassment—was presented earlier. This section will present other data of the AAU campus report, including that of the most serious form of sexual victimization: sexual assault, or nonconsensual sexual contact.

Nonconsensual Sexual Contact

The AAU campus report (2020) defines **nonconsensual sexual contact** (NCSC) as incidents resulting from either physical force, the inability to consent, or stop what was occurring (i.e., inability to consent). This form of victimization meets the legal definition of rape or sexual assault in many jurisdictions. To be considered a victim of this type of incident, the

● **FIGURE 8**

Percent of College Students Experiencing Nonconsensual Sexual Contact Involving Physical Force or Inability to Consent by Gender and Sexual Orientation.

Source: Cantor et al. (2020).

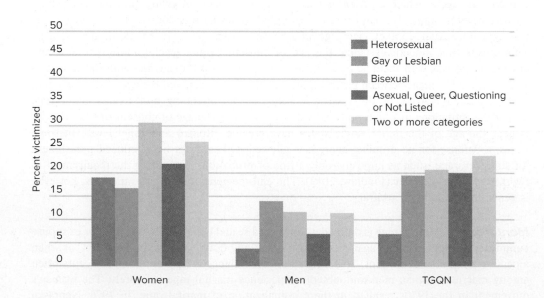

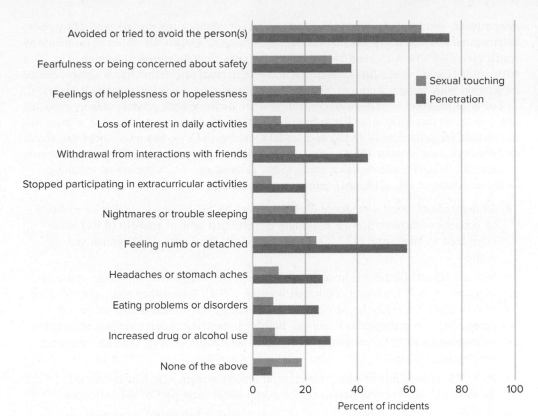

• **FIGURE 9**

Behavioral and Emotional Consequences of Nonconsensual Sexual Contact by Physical Force or Inability to Consent for College Women by Type of Sexual Contact.

Source: Cantor et al. (2020).

student had to respond as "yes" to at least one of five different questions about two types of sexual contact—penetration and sexual touching—as described below:

- *Penetration:* putting a penis, finger, or object inside someone else's vagina or anus, when someone's mouth or tongue contacts someone else's genitals.

- *Sexual touching:* kissing; touching someone's breast, chest, crotch, groin, or buttocks; grabbing, groping, or rubbing against the other in a sexual way, even if the touching is over the other's clothes.

Physical force was defined as ". . .the use of force or threats of physical force against an individual. Physical force could include someone using their body weight to you hold the person down, pinning their arms, hitting, or kicking them, or using or threatening to use a weapon against them." The inability to consent or stop what was happening was defined as ". . . when the student was unable to consent or stop what was happening because they were passed out, asleep, or incapacitated due to alcohol or drugs" (Cantor et al., 2020).

Overall, 13% of students from 33 colleges and schools reported having experienced nonconsensual penetration, attempted penetration, sexual touching by force, or inability to consent since enrolling in their respective schools. Undergraduates reported higher rates than graduate/professional students. For example, the estimated prevalence among women undergraduates was 2 to 3 times higher at 25.9% than women who were graduate and professional students (9%). Men undergraduates were twice more likely to report NCSC than men graduate/professional students (6.8% vs. 2.5%). Similar patterns were found for students identifying as TGQN and those who declined to indicate their gender.

As shown in Figure 8, large differences of experiencing NCSC were found relative to self-identified sexual orientation and gender identity. All categories representing non-heterosexual orientations were higher than heterosexual identity. Bisexual students had the highest rate (25.6%), followed by those selecting more than one category (22.2%), asexual, queer, questioning or not listed (18.5%), gay or lesbian (15.1%), and heterosexual (11.5%). This pattern also holds for women. TGQN students (transgender women, transgender men, genderqueer, gender nonconforming, questioning, or identity not listed) who chose non-heterosexual as their sexual orientation had rates that are statistically different from heterosexual men (6.9% vs. 4.1%) and have much lower rates than heterosexual women. The 2015 AAU study (Cantor et al., 2017) found that non-heterosexual orientation had a higher positive correlation with being a victim of NCSC than identifying in a gender minority category.

For both penetration and sexual contact, most students of each gender category reported one person as responsible for the behavior. Virtually all women reported that a man was responsible for penetration (99.1%) and sexual touching (97.8%). For men, about two thirds of offenders were women (66.4%) and one third (38.6%) were men. The most common offender for TGQN students was a man (85.6% penetration, 72.2% for sexual touching).

Other results of the 2019 AAU campus survey include:

- Undergraduate women are more likely to report NCSC by physical force or inability to consent occurred since the beginning of their first year of school (16.1%) when compared to later years (13.3% second year, 11.5% third year, 11.3% fourth year or higher).

- Women reported incidents involving penetration occurred in the university residence hall/dorm (26.1%), another residential housing (30.2), some other place not specified (19.3), and a fraternity house (10.7%). This pattern was similar across all gender categories. For undergraduate women, incidents involving sexual touching occurred in fraternities (20.1%), restaurants/bars, other residential housing (17.2%), and other residential housing.

- In 35.3% of incidents involving penetration among women who had consumed alcohol, the survivor was passed out or asleep for at least part of the incidence.

- A high proportion of victims of NCSC experienced a behavioral, emotional, or physical consequence. Almost all victims reported either behavioral or emotional consequences (see Figure 9 for women). On average, women reported 4.6 behavioral or emotional consequences, TGQN students reported 6.1, and men reported 3.0. Fewer students reported consequences related to sexual touching. (See Figure 9 for more details on the outcomes of the NSCS and sexual touching.)

- When asked for more information on why the survivors of penetration did not think the incident was "serious enough" to report, most reported because they had not been injured (69.8% of women, 59.4% of TGQN students, and 67.9% of men).

As you can see, the college culture fuels sexual assault. Perpetrators often prey on those they perceive to be vulnerable, and sometimes surreptitiously provide their victims with alcohol and so-called date rape drugs (see Think About It, "Drug-Facilitated Sexual Assault: An Increasing Threat"). The majority of college sexual assault survivors are assaulted at parties by someone they know, such as perpetrators who drink prior to an assault who are more likely to believe that alcohol increases their sex drive and that a woman's drinking itself signals that she is interested in sex. A study of college men ($N = 238$) surveyed at the end of their 4 years in college found that of those who reported at least one incident of sexual coercion and assault (SCA) (unwanted sexual contact against a woman, sexual coercion, attempted rape, and completed incapacitated or forcible rape), 68% engaged in repeated SCA, with repeat offenders engaging in more aggressive behaviors at higher severity (Zinzow & Thompson, 2015). Further, repeat offenders scored higher than single offenders on risky behaviors, sexually aggressive beliefs, and antisocial traits. As studies have shown (e.g., Cantor et al., 2020) that although sexual assault among college men occurs far less often than among women, men also experience sexual assault. Unfortunately, many survivors are left feeling isolated, ashamed, or to blame.

Men who believe in rape myths (see below) are more likely to see alcohol consumption in women as a sign that they are sexually available. Other factors associated with campus sexual assault are the availability of a private room in a fraternity or off-campus house, loud noise that can drown out a person's call for help, and a cover-up by the house's residents. Rape by a stranger, which is much less common than rape by a date or an acquaintance on

think about it

Drug-Facilitated Sexual Assault: An Increasing Threat

Drug-facilitated sexual assault refers to the use of alcohol or drugs to compromise a person's ability to consent to sexual activity. The substances or drugs are typically placed in beverages so that the person consuming the drink will be incapacitated, which interferes with her or his consent to sexual contact, thus increasing the person's vulnerability to sexual assault. They can also minimize resistance and memory of the victim. Both men and women can be drugged with the substances. Traditionally, the phrase "date rape drugs" has been used, but the person who commits the crime might not be in a relationship, or on a date, with the victim. Someone who commits the crime can be someone you know well, someone you know through friends, or someone you just met (RAINN, 2021b).

Drugging an unwilling or unknowing person is a crime. In 1996, the Drug-Induced Rape Prevention and Punishment Act was passed, making it a felony to distribute controlled substances, such as those then classified as date rape drugs, to someone without that person's knowledge and with the intent to commit violence, including rape, against that person (Congressional Research Service, n.d.).

Briefly, here are some of the major date rape drugs (WebMD, 2020; Womenshealth.gov, 2019):

- *Alcohol.* Alcohol is the most frequently used substance in drug-facilitated sexual assault. In most cases, the person consumes the alcohol voluntarily. Often he or she is encouraged to drink enough to lose inhibition or consciousness. People who use alcohol or other drugs and substances to commit sexual assault most often use alcohol alone or in combination with other drugs.

- *Rohypnol.* Also known as "roofies," "roach," "forget pill," "Mexican valium," and "mind erasers," Rohypnol is not approved for medical use in the United States and is not available legally but is becoming an increasingly popular street drug. This small, white tablet quickly dissolves in liquid. Alcohol increases the effects of Rohypnol.

- *GHB.* Also known as "grievous bodily harm," "easy lay," "liquid ecstasy," and "bedtime scoop," GHB has not been approved for sale by the FDA since 1990. GHB is sold on the street as a clear, odorless liquid or a white, crystalline powder, but since it is made in home labs, its effects can be unpredictable. Alcohol increases the effects of GHB.

- *Benzodiazepines.* These drugs are legal forms of Rohypnol that are prescribed as anti-anxiety and sleep medications in the United States. Put into a drink in powder or liquid form, they markedly impair or eliminate functions that typically allow a person to resist an assault. Alcohol increases the effects of benzodiazepines, possibly resulting in death.

- *Ketamine.* Also known as "Special K," "Vitamin K," and "K," ketamine is an anesthetic typically used by veterinarians. A fast-acting liquid, ketamine causes individuals to feel detached from their bodies and unable to fight back or remember what happened.

- *Ecstasy.* Also known as "X-TC," "X," and "E," ecstasy is the most common club drug. Illegal in the United States, ecstasy is a hallucinogenic and stimulant with psychedelic effects. Available in powder or liquid form, ecstasy causes people to feel extreme relaxation, sensitivity to touch, and a lowered ability to perceive danger.

- *Prescription drugs.* Drugs like sleeping aids, medication for anxiety, muscle relaxers, and tranquilizers may be used by perpetrators.

To protect yourself from date rape drugs, it is essential that you watch what you drink at parties or on dates. Date rape drugs often have no color, smell, or taste and you cannot tell if you are drugged. Do not take any drinks (soda, coffee, or alcohol) from someone you do not know well and trust, and refuse open-container beverages. Don't share drinks or drink from punch bowls or other common containers. If someone offers to get you a drink from a bar or at a party, go with that person to order your drink and carry it yourself. Never leave your drink unattended, and go to parties with a friend and also leave with a friend. Don't drink anything that smells or tastes strange.

If you think you've been drugged, call 911 or get to an emergency room quickly, as many of these substances leave a person's body within 12 to 72 hours. If possible, keep a sample of the beverage. Call the police from the hospital. Ask the hospital to take a urine sample that can test for date rape drugs. If you are a victim of drug-facilitated assault, do not blame yourself. The sexual assault was not your fault; the offender is solely to blame and is the one who took advantage of your diminished capacity. If necessary, get counseling and treatment (RAINN, 2021b).

Think Critically

1. How common is the use of drugs to facilitate sexual assault on your campus? In what type of situations does it occur?

2. What can a person do to avoid being vulnerable to date or acquaintance rape?

Just because a woman is dressed provocatively does not mean she is inviting nonconsensual sexual contact.

©Ryan McVay/Getty Images

college campuses, usually occurs in isolated parts of campus, such as campus garages or wooded areas; in these cases, the victim may not have consumed any alcohol and have no prior relationship (or even acquaintance) between the survivor and the rapist.

An increasing acknowledgment of the college student sexual assault problem has fueled demands that colleges and universities make their campuses safer. Students and activists across the country have formed national movements challenging campuses to improve how they handle rape. Lawsuits have been filed by rape survivors, contending that their campuses have a "sexually hostile environment" and did not or inadequately respond to rape cases. Dozens of colleges have faced federal complaints and investigations under Title IX on how they handled alleged sexual assaults on campus. Many schools struggle with their legal responsibility in responding to students' allegations of being sexually assaulted. Some believe that a university-led review of sexual assault accusations encourages survivors to report sexual assault. However, others have criticized the standard, claiming it made it easier to rule against an alleged perpetrator. Numerous cases of convicted students have been overturned by courts. In 2013, Congress passed the Campus Sexual Violence Elimination Act, which mandates that colleges offer prevention programs, and the U.S. Department of Education has issued rules designed to make colleges safer from sexual violence. However, dealing with alleged sexual assault on college campuses remains challenging.

Myths About Rape

Our society has a number of myths about rape, which may justify the behavior for the perpetrator and increase the survivor's feelings of shame, guilt, and self-blame. According to one myth, women, for example, are to blame for their own rapes, as if they somehow "deserved" them or were responsible for them. Often, women who were raped worried that they may be blamed for their assaults.

Rape myths, such as "If I only wore different clothes," or "I must have led the person on," can influence sexual scripts that, in turn, impact one's attitudes about sexuality and sexual behavior. Recall that sexual scripts are culturally determined patterns of sexual expression that inform desire and actual behavior. Research shows that many individuals still have rape myths. This may be a barrier preventing persons who have been raped from acknowledging the assault as well as allowing persons who rape to engage in sexual violence while denying it is rape (Edwards et al., 2011; Ryan, 2011). Belief in rape myths is also part of a larger belief structure that includes gender-role stereotypes, sexual conservatism, acceptance of interpersonal violence, and the belief that men are different from women. Men are more likely than women to believe rape myths. The following list of 13 common rape myths can clarify misunderstandings about rape. As you can see, the majority of rape myths present men as perpetrators and women as survivors. This is largely resulting from women being raped much more often than men; hence, the research and literature are typically addressed toward women. As we learned in this chapter, men can also be raped, and many of the myths below can be relevant to all genders.

- *Myth 1: Rape is a crime of passion.* Rape is an act of violence and aggression and is often a life-threatening experience. While sexual attraction may be one component, power, anger, and control are the dominant factors resulting in gratification. Actually, most persons who rape have access to other, willing sexual partners but choose to rape.

- *Myth 2: Women want to be raped.* It is popularly believed that women have an unconscious wish to be raped. Also, some people believe that many women mean "yes" when they say "no." This myth supports the misconception that a woman enjoys being raped because she sexually "surrenders," and it perpetuates the belief that rape is a sexual behavior rather than a violent one.

- *Myth 3: "But she wanted sex."* This myth contends that some rape survivors wanted to have sex. That is, they had desire and so the forced sex cannot be rape. Of course, it is possible to want to have sex but decide not to consent to sex. It is rape if the victim did not consent to sex even if the survivor wanted sex. Sex researchers Zoë Peterson and Charlene Muehlenhard (2007) stated that "rape is about the absence of consent, not the absence of desire."

- *Myth 4: Women ask for it.* Many people believe that women "ask for it" by their behavior. Many people also believe that provocative dress on the part of the survivor of a date rape resulted in a greater perception that the survivor was responsible and that the rape was justified. Despite some attempts to reform rape laws, women continue to bear the burden of proof in these cases. No one ever deserves to be raped, and regardless of what a person says, does (such as flirting), or wears, they do not cause the rape. Actually, most rapes are premeditated and planned by the perpetrator. Opportunity is the critical factor in determining when a person will rape.

- *Myth 5: The woman did not fight back or scream, so it wasn't rape.* Women may be scared of being hurt or losing their lives; they are paralyzed with fear even if there is no weapon or obvious physical force used. Rape is rape whether or not there is a struggle.

- *Myth 6: Women are raped only by strangers.* Women are warned to avoid or distrust strangers as a way to avoid rape; such advice, however, isolates them from normal social interactions. Furthermore, studies indicate that most rapes/sexual assaults of women are committed by nonstrangers such as current or past intimate partners or friends (Smith et al., 2017; U.S. Department of Justice, 2010).

- *Myth 7: Women could avoid rape if they really wanted to.* This myth reinforces the stereotype that women "really" want to be raped or that they should curtail their activities. Women are often warned not to be out after dark alone. Approximately two thirds of rapes/sexual assaults occur between 6 p.m. and 6 a.m., but nearly 6 in 10 occur at the victim's home or the home of a friend, relative, or neighbor (McCabe & Wauchope, 2005a). Women are also approached at work, on their way to or from work, or are kidnapped from shopping centers or parking lots at midday. Restricting women's activities does not seem to have an appreciable impact on rape. Men are often physically larger and stronger than women, making it difficult for women to resist. Sometimes, weapons are used and physical violence occurs or is threatened. And assailants catch their victims "off guard" because they choose the time and place of attack.

- *Myth 8: Women cry rape for revenge.* This myth suggests that women who are "dumped" by men accuse them of rape as a means of revenge. Actually, the prevalence of false rape accusations is very low. False reporting is unlikely because of the many obstacles women face before an assailant is brought to trial and convicted.

- *Myth 9: Persons who rape are crazy or psychotic.* Very few men who rape are clinically psychotic; they are usually "ordinary" men. The vast majority are psychologically indistinguishable from other men, except that rapists appear to have more difficulty handling feelings of hostility and are more likely to express their anger through violence. Studies on date rape find that rapists differ from nonrapists primarily in a greater hostility toward women, acceptance of traditional gender roles, and greater willingness to use force.

- *Myth 10: Most persons who rape are a different race/ethnicity than their victims.* Most rapists and their victims are members of the same racial/ethnic group.

- *Myth 11: Men cannot control their sexual urges.* This myth is based on the belief that men, when subjected to sexual stimuli, cannot control their sexual feelings. This also implies that women have some responsibility for rape by provoking this "uncontrollable" sexuality of men through their attire or appearance. Men, like women, can learn to appropriately and responsibly express their sexuality.

- *Myth 12: Rape is "no big deal."* About one in three women who are injured during rape or physical assault require medical care. Rape survivors can also experience negative mental health outcomes and are more likely to engage in harmful behaviors to cope with the trauma, such as drinking, smoking, or using drugs.

- *Myth 13: Men cannot be raped.* Men can be victims of sexual assault from either men or women.

practically speaking

What Can You Do to Prevent Sexual Assault? Be a "Bystander"

"**B**ystanders" are individuals who witness a situation that they are not directly involved in that may lead to sexual assault and then intervene to change the situation. The 2019 AAU Campus Climate Survey on Sexual Assault and Misconduct (Cantor et al., 2020) found that the most common situation that college students from 33 colleges and universities observed was someone making others feel uncomfortable or offended (25.7%), followed by witnessing a situation that could lead to sexual assault (14.5%), witnessing someone behaving in a controlling or abusive manner (12.6%), and witnessing harassing behavior (6.8%). The bystander approach is based on the premise that all of us have a role and the ability to look out for each other's safety. Bystanders also speak out against social norms that support sexual assault, motivate others to promote protective norms, help others recognize behaviors that put persons at risk, and teach others how to safely and effectively intervene.

The Rape, Abuse & Incest National Network (RAINN) (2021c, 2021d) says that the key to keeping one's friends safe is knowing how to intervene in a fashion that fits the specific situation. The knowledge will give you the confidence to step in when it is needed. Here is what RAINN states as your role in preventing sexual assault when the situation does not seem right:

- *Create a distraction.* A distraction can provide the person facing the possible assault a chance to get to a safe place. You could end a scary conversation with a diversion like, "Let's get a bite to eat; I am really hungry." Bring out food or drink at a party and offer them to all the people, particularly to those you are concerned about.

- *Ask directly.* Start a conversation with the person you think might be in trouble and ask questions like, "Who did you come here with?" or "Would you like for me to stay with you?"

- *Refer to an authority.* One safe way to interrupt a possible bad situation is to refer to a neutral person with authority, such as a resident hall advisor or manager. At a bar, you could talk with a security guard, bartender, or another employee about your concerns. These individuals want to ensure that their patrons are safe and are usually most willing to step in. You can also call 911.

- *Enlist others:* Approaching a situation can be intimidating, so enlisting another person to support you can be very helpful. Ask someone to come with you when you approach the person at risk. Sometimes there is power in numbers. You could ask someone to intervene on your behalf, such as someone who

knows the person. That person could escort the individual to the bathroom, for example. You could say to a friend of the person at risk, "Your friend looks like she had too much to drink. Can you check on her?"

- *Offer a ride home.* One way to get a friend at risk out of the possible dangerous situation is to offer a ride to his or her home. The person may have had too much to drink, thus making him/her more vulnerable to sexual assault. Further, that person should not be driving home himself or herself but instead calling for a taxi if someone is not taking them home.

Some persons are hesitant to be a bystander. They may think that it is not any of their business or that they don't want to cause a scene or know what to say. They may also be concerned about their own physical safety. They may believe that someone else will step in. However, your actions can make a big difference. In many situations, bystanders can prevent sexual assault before it happens. Further, whether you change the situation or not, your actions can be a valuable model for others in helping change the way they think about their roles in preventing sexual assault. The 2019 AAU Campus study cited earlier found that 45.1% of students witnessing a situation that might lead to sexual assault directly intervened; that is, interrupted the situation or confronted or expressed concern to the person engaging in the behavior (Cantor et al., 2020).

An important bystander role is combating social norms that promote and accept sexual violence. Given that the vast majority of sexual assaults are against women, many universities and businesses have bystander training programs that are directed at men, although some have also focused on empowering women. These programs are based on the acknowledgment that most men often do not intervene when they are with abusive peers or when confronted with attitudes that dehumanize women and girls. Traditional unhealthy masculinity places social pressure on men to play typecast roles of aggression, toughness, and being hostile toward women, as well as believing that male superiority, sexual entitlement, and sexual violence is acceptable. Most men are uncomfortable when women are belittled or mistreated, yet they do not know how they can intervene in helping stop sexual abuse of women. The goal of the programs is to move men toward being a social change agent in helping their peers to achieve a healthy, positive, and nonviolent form of masculinity. The programs foster men's participation as women's allies in preventing sexual assault (Campus Technical Assistance and Resource Project, 2016; Men Can Stop Rape, 2011a; National Center for Injury Prevention and Control, 2016a, 2016b).

 ## practically
speaking

Being Safe: Strategies for Avoiding Being Sexually Assaulted

There are no guaranteed ways to prevent sexual assault. Each situation, assailant, and targeted woman or man is different. Specific strategies can be effective in reducing one's vulnerability to being sexually assaulted (Rape, Abuse & Incest National Network, 2016a, 2016b, 2021.17e, 2021.17f).

To reduce the risk of sexual assault, consider these guidelines if you are on a date or you just know someone or someone just met you:

1. When dating someone for the first time, even if you have established a relationship over the Internet, go to a public place such as a restaurant, movie, or sports event.

2. Share expenses. A common scenario is a date expecting you to exchange sex for his or her paying for dinner, the movie, drinks, and so on.

3. Avoid using drugs or alcohol if you do not want to be sexual with your date. Such use is associated with sexual assault.

4. Know your limits and keep track of how many drinks you have consumed.

5. Make a plan. If you are going to a party, go with friends you trust. Make an agreement to watch out for each other and plan to leave together. Don't leave someone stranded alone in an unfamiliar or unsafe situation.

6. Avoid ambiguous verbal or nonverbal behavior, particularly any behavior that might be interpreted as "teasing." Make sure your verbal and nonverbal messages are identical. If you want to only cuddle or kiss, for example, tell your date that those are your limits. Tell him or her that if you say no you mean no.

7. Trust your gut feeling. No one should feel obligated to do anything they don't want to do, no matter what the reason is. Not being interested is reason enough. One should do only what feels right and what one is comfortable with. If one senses pressure that feels scary, they can contact friends or family by using a code word that means, "I'm uncomfortable and scared," or "I need help." On a phone call to a friend, a person can use an agreed-upon phrase like, "I look forward to reading the book you recommended." Using these strategies can communicate your concern and need for help without alerting the person who is pressuring you.

8. If the person becomes sexually aggressive despite your direct communication, consider physical denials such as pushing, slapping, and kicking. Make up a reason to leave even if it's a lie, such as you're not feeling well.

To reduce the risk of sexual assault from a stranger, consider the following guidelines. But try to avoid becoming overly vigilant; use reasonable judgment. Do not let fear control your life.

1. Do not identify yourself as a person living alone, especially if you are a woman. Use initials on the mailbox and in the telephone directory.

2. Don't open your door to strangers; keep your house and car doors locked. Have your keys ready when you approach your car or house. Look in the back seat before getting into your car. Don't isolate yourself with someone you don't trust or know.

3. Avoid dark and isolated areas such as public restrooms. Be aware of your surroundings and walk with a purpose. Don't put music headphones in both ears that lessen your awareness of the surroundings. Carry a whistle or air horn, and take a cell phone when you are out by yourself. Let people know where you are going and what time you expect to get home. Consider using the Companion app (or similar one) on your cell phone, which allows friends to keep track of your whereabouts.

4. If someone approaches you threateningly, turn and run. If you can't run, resist. Studies indicate that resisting an attack by shouting, causing a scene, or fighting back can deter the assailant. Fighting and screaming may reduce the level of the abuse without increasing the level of physical injury. Many who are injured during a rape appear to have been injured *before* resisting. Trust your intuitions, whatever approach you take.

5. Be sure your cell phone is with you and you have taxi money or bus fare. Use tips for a cell phone code word described in these date rape guidelines.

6. Be alert to possible ways to escape. Talking with an assailant may give you time to find an escape route.

7. Take self-defense training. It will raise your level of confidence and your fighting abilities. You may be able to scare off the assailant, or you may create an opportunity to escape. Many people take self-defense training following an incidence of sexual aggression to reaffirm their sense of control.

8. Do not post personal data or contact information on social networking sites.

If you are sexually assaulted (or the survivor of an attempted assault), report the assault as soon as possible. As much as you might want to, do not change your clothes or shower. Semen and hair or other materials on your body or clothing may be very important in arresting and convicting a rapist. You may also want to contact a rape crisis center; its staff members are knowledgeable about dealing with the police and the traumatic aftermath of rape. But most important, remember that you are not at fault. The person who sexually assaulted is the only one to blame.

To learn more about sexual assault, visit the Rape, Abuse & Incest National Network at https://rainn.org. This organization also has the 24/7, confidential, and free National Sexual Assault Hotline (1-800-656-4673).

Confusion Over Sexual Consent

What does it mean to give consent to a possible sex partner? There are varied opinions about how sexual consent should be conceptualized. Four meanings of consent have been suggested and described as follows: consent as an internal state of willingness, as an act of explicitly agreeing to something, as behavior that someone else interprets as willingness, and as distinct from wanting (Muehlenhard et al., 2016; Orenstein, 2019; RAINN, 2021.17g):

- *Consent as an internal state of willingness.* Consent is sometimes conceptualized as an internal state of willingness that is not directly observable and that observers make inferences based on behavior. Ultimately, a person's internal states are private and unknowable; hence, consent based on words and behavior is the surest way to reveal agreement, or disagreement, to be sexual with another person.

- *Consent is an act of explicitly agreeing to do something.* Consent can be conceptualized as agreeing to do something such as agreeing to participate in a sex research study. This explicit agreeing contrasts to implied consent and is exemplified by a statement such as, "I consent to have sexual intercourse with you." Most persons do not give consent this directly, but usually rely on more indirect cues and signals that might be misinterpreted as willingness to have sex.

- *Consent as behavior that someone else interprets as willingness.* Consent can be conceptualized as behaviors that others use to infer a person's willingness. This requires that another person observes and interprets the individual's behavior and speculates about how willing the individual feels. This also depends on assumptions about how behavior should be interpreted and what should be considered consent. Many of these assumptions are contentious and may vary from person to person.

- *Consent as distinct from wanting.* Wanting and consenting to sex are different concepts that often correspond to each other, but at other times they do not. Discrepancies between wanting to be sexual with another person and consenting to sex are common. A person may want to have sex but is not willing (e.g., because they or their partner does not have a condom); conversely, someone may not want to have sex but nevertheless are willing (e.g., they may want their partner to experience sexual satisfaction). Wanting does not indicate consent, although behaviors indicative of desire are sometimes wrongly interpreted as consent (e.g., "she wanted it" has been used to dismiss a claim of rape).

In efforts to end confusion about consent for sex, an **affirmative consent** standard has been created. This standard requires individuals trying to initiate sexual activity to get the other person's consent before preceding to sex. Silence or lack of resistance from the other person cannot be interpreted as consent, and nonconsent must be assumed until consent is actively communicated. This standard is in contrast to the sexual script of many persons in which consent is assumed until nonconsent is actively communicated. Some affirmative consent standards mandate verbal consent in efforts to ensure that verbal consent occurs (Muehlenhard et al., 2016). (To learn about issues of verbal consent, see Think About It, "Verbally Consenting to Sex: As Simple as One Might Think?"). For example, Canada switched to affirmative consent in 1992, and Antioch College was one of the earliest colleges in the United States to establish a policy that all sexual interactions on campus must be consensual and have verbal request and verbal giving or refusing for all levels of sexual behavior (Antioch College, 2014–2015).

The California legislature in September 2014 passed a bill that would require California colleges receiving state-financed student aid to change their definition of consent in their state's sexual assault policies. The traditional "no means no" standard has been replaced with "yes means yes." The bill defined consent as "affirmative, conscious, and voluntary agreement to engage in sexual activity." The affirmative consent needs not be spoken, although the underlying message of the new definition is that silence does not necessarily mean consent. Sex researcher Charlene Muehlenard and colleagues (2016) note that this

think
about it

Verbally Consenting to Sex: As Simple as One Might Think?

When someone is sexually interested in another person, verbal communication of consent is considered ideal. However, individuals give verbal consent less often than nonverbal cues to show their own sexual consent and to infer their partner's sexual consent. Many young people consider verbal consent as unnecessary. Actually, most sex is initiated nonverbally. Hence, adoption of required verbal consent as part of a student code of behavior by universities is likely counter to student norms and met with resistance.

Studies have shown that verbal consent is used more often in some situations than others. For example, it is more likely to be used for penile-vaginal intercourse and anal intercourse, and perhaps for oral sex, than for kissing, hugging, and other forms of intimate touching. Verbal communication for sex seems to be used for behaviors that are novel or not part of the couple's sexual script. Verbal consent has been found to occur more frequently for same-sex encounters than for heterosexual encounters, possibly because same-sex couples cannot rely on the more common heterosexual script to guide their behavior. Most persons in the bondage, discipline, sadism, and masochism (BDSM) community use detailed communication to indicate what they do and do not consent to. Further, students have reported that they consider consent more important for first-time sexual encounters than subsequent encounters (Muehlenhard et al., 2016).

What Counts as Verbal Consent

A common example of verbal consent is saying yes. This is considered affirmative consent that is commonly promoted in sexual assault prevention programs. However, just saying yes can be unclear without knowing the question. What if one asked, "Will you come with me to my apartment?" If the response is yes, does that count as verbal consent to sex? Suppose the question is, "Will you give me a massage?" Does that indicate consent for sex? A statement like, "I consent to have sexual intercourse with you," is clear consent but a statement like, "I want to sleep with you," does not specifically mention sexual desire. If these statements would be considered verbal consent, then consent for what? Even if a person consents to sex, there are situations in which a "yes" should not be interpreted as consent, such as when a person is under duress, not making the consent willingly nor voluntarily, is under the influence of drugs and/or alcohol, and does not have sufficient information to know what one is consenting to, for example (Doherty, 2020).

Level of Specificity: Consenting to What?

The lack of specificity in requesting and consenting to sex can be problematic. So how specific does a request for sex need to be? What if a partner says during sex, "Is this OK?" Does that refer to sexual behavior the couple is already doing? If so, is it too late, as the activity is already occurring? If the question refers to sexual activity the individual intends to do, the question is unclear and the other person would not know the asker's intentions. On the contrary, some people might feel offended when an individual describes what sexual behaviors he or she wanted to do with the other person. Further, a code of behavior that states each new level of sexual behavior requires consent can be unclear and cumbersome. For example, is touching under the clothes a different level than above the clothes and, hence, requires another yes?

Continuously Asking for or Giving Consent Seems Unrealistic

Communicating consent (or refusal) to have sex with another person is often sequential. That is, a person might try subtle cues; if not effective, they might try a more direct verbal approach. It seems that consent as a continuous process must rely on nonverbal cues by necessity and that to continuously ask for or give verbal consent is unrealistic (e.g., to ask for consent to move one's hands a few inches). Possibly a more realistic model would be a hybrid communication approach of verbal and nonverbal consent. The authors (Muehlenhard et al., 2016) state:

> Even if someone has obtained a partner's verbal consent before a sexual activity, it seems important to attend to the partner's nonverbal cues during the activity to make sure that the partner continues to feel comfortable. Nonverbal and metacommunication can serve as guides for whether verbal "check-ins" are needed. This hybrid model, however, would still involve subjectivity as to when these verbal check-ins would be appropriate and would still require interpreting the other person's nonverbal cues. (p. 476)

Complicating these issues is that verbal consent is predicated on an assumption that individuals know in advance about whether they would be sexual with the other person and about what behaviors they would be willing to do during a sexual encounter. Uncertainty is common in sexual situations. Sometimes persons tentatively begin a sexual activity and at that point evaluate their reactions and make decisions about further sexual behavior as the encounter unfolds.

Many individuals engage in multiple behaviors beyond verbal communication in conveying consent or refusal. For example, consent is conveyed by not resisting, especially when it occurs with other behaviors such as hugging and kissing. Refusal is conveyed by being passive or nonresponsive (Jozkowski & Humphreys, 2014; Marcantonio et al., 2018). Behaviors used most frequently to show consent are not necessarily the behaviors most indicative of consent. For example, behaviors such as kissing, smiling, and not resisting a partner's advance do not clearly indicate consent. These behaviors can be used to convey consent (probably along with other behaviors), but they could also be used in other situations. Case in point: Not resisting a partner's advance is one of the most frequently used methods of conveying consent. However, this behavior is not sufficient to infer consent. Also, consent cues are indicators but not agreement to be sexual. For example, research has shown that a person willing to go home with someone they meet at a bar is probably more likely to consent to sex than someone who is unwilling to go home with that person. Hence, going home with the person represents a likelihood, but not an agreement, to have sex. Muehlenhard and colleagues (2016) state that:

> If going home with someone is treated as an agreement to have sex, this is problematic. Someone who interprets this behavior as an agreement might conclude that unless the other person retracts consent, they can have sex with that person, with the rationale that the other person has agreed. Worse still would be treating the willingness to go home with someone as an irrevocable agreement—as an *obligation*—so that even if the other person refuses sex, it doesn't matter because they are now obligated. (p. 481)

These issues represent the challenges of sexual consent. Consent is a behavior that another person interprets as willingness that requires inference and speculation. It is also open to misrepresentation and claims of misrepresentation that can lead to allegations of sexual assault. Colleges and universities are striving to find the most accurate and fair way to resolve claims of sexual assault. In the meantime, it becomes increasingly clear that honest and direct communication of sexual consent and refusal needs to be specific and verbal.

Think Critically

1. What do you believe counts as sexual consent?
2. How specific does one need to be in asking for consent?
3. Is continuously asking for or giving consent realistic? Explain.

Confusion over whether consent for sex has been given may lead to a strong disagreement between partners.

©Stockbyte/Getty Images

California university policy and Canada's criminal code do not require that consent be given verbally and state that:

> When affirmative action consent policies allow for consent to be communicated nonverbally, which nonverbal behaviors should count as consent? There are numerous behaviors that some people interpret as indicative of sexual consent: dressing in revealing clothing, drinking alcohol, going home with someone, flirting, and so on. If nonverbal behaviors can count as expressions of affirmative consent, the affirmation consent standard becomes less distinguishable from the traditional script. (p. 465)

Further, lack of protest or resistance does not mean consent. The affirmative consent must be ongoing throughout the sexual activity and can be withdrawn at any time. Intoxication cannot be used as an alibi for thinking that there was consent (Doherty, 2020). The burden for obtaining consent would rest on the student initiating sex to obtain a "yes" instead of the intended partner to state a "no" (Marcantonio et al., 2018; Muehlenhard et al., 2016). Proponents understand that the policy has limitations but also believe that it is worth trying. Opponents including college students feel that it is vague, impractical, difficult to prove legally (e.g., who would corroborate that the person said "yes"?), represents an effort to micromanage sex, and does not eliminate the "he said, she said" quandary. Some question what happens if a "yes" is not obtained.

Sex researchers Kristen Jozkowski and Zoë Peterson (2013) state:

> An important question to consider is this: If a man goes ahead with a sexual encounter without affording his female partner the opportunity to provide an affirmation agreement or a refusal, does this fit a legal or perhaps an ethical definition of sexual assault or rape? Such sexual activity seems to fall into a gray space between consensual and nonconsensual sex. (p. 522)

Some opponents to the "yes" consent standard point out that nonverbal cues can accurately indicate consent (Vendituoli, 2014; "When yes means yes," 2014). The results of studies by New Zealand sex researcher Melanie Beres and colleagues (2010, 2014) suggest that men and women are easily able to identify a casual partner's willingness to have sex and that there is little miscommunication between them. In 2003, Illinois became the first state to pass a law explicitly stating that people have a right to withdraw their consent to sexual activity at any time. The law specified that, no matter how far the sexual interaction has progressed, a "no" means no when someone wants to stop (Parsons, 2003). (To learn about whether and how sexual consent is expressed and verified by college students, see Think About It box, "Are College Students Verbally and Unambiguously Affirming Sexual Consent? Research Shows That Rarely Happens.")

Our sexual scripts often assume "yes" unless a "no" is directly stated (Muehlenhard et al., 1992). This makes individuals "fair game" unless they explicitly say "no." But the assumption

think
about it

Are College Students Verbally and Unambiguously Affirming Sexual Consent? Research Shows That Rarely Happens

Affirmative sexual consent is an individual explicitly indicating "yes" to participating in any sexual behavior with another person. This standard is being promoted as a major method of decreasing sexual assault, yet it is not certain whether if it is being incorporated into individual sexual scripts during sexual interactions.

Sex researchers Erin Shumlich and William Fisher (2018) at Western University in Canada examined how sexual consent is expressed and verified as part of individuals' sexual encounters. Undergraduate students (58 males, 34 females) from an Ontario university completed open-ended questions that sought their description of sexual interactions, from beginning to end, with a new or long-term partner. Analysis of the descriptions revealed the following six themes:

Indirect Verbal Communication of Interest in Sex

Verbal communication about being interested in having sex was most often indirect and implied, and not directly communicated. Many students used questions about "going home" or "going back to someone's place" as an indirect question about a new partner's willingness to have sex. "Going home" with someone was specifically mentioned as the same as consenting to have sex. Some indirectly communicated their interest in having sex by alluding to their desire for sex. Indirect indications of willingness to have sex related to contraception use and safer sex, in that consent was implied based on a partner's questions about contraception. Several students explicitly stated that sexual activity should occur only without verbal behaviors or the absence of verbal communication leading to sex.

Passive Behaviors Did Not Indicate Lack of Willingness to Have Sex

Students reported a range of passive behaviors that did not indicate an unwillingness or resistance to have sex. Female students described passive behaviors more often than male students in both new and long-term partners. Male students were less likely to describe passive behaviors with a new partner than with a long-term partner. Situations in which passive behaviors did not indicate unwillingness to have sex appeared to reflect everything from acquiescence (if not "enthusiastic willingness") to coercion and victimization by sexual assault. Some students described taking their partner to a private or semi-private area and closing or locking the door.

Indications That Sex "Just Happened"

Students described sexual interactions that suggested that the progression to intercourse was "obvious" or that "sex just happened" without any discussion of consent or positive or negative partner response. "Both of us knew" and "tension got too strong" were the basis for proceeding to sexual interaction. Some participants noted that they had an intuitive sense of their partner's "internal willingness" in having sexual activity with a new or long-term partner, although it is unclear how this understanding is known or if this is actually representative of willingness to be sexual.

Sex Proceeding with Escalating Intensity of Nonverbal Sexual Behavior

Students reported use of escalating intensity of behaviors, including physical contact, engaging in foreplay, and removing a partner's clothing with both new and long-term partners. However, their accounts did not include use or interpretation of these nonverbal behaviors to infer sexual consent. A slow pace of nonverbal behaviors was generally for sexual activity with a long-term partner; a fast pace was generally, but not always referenced in sexual activity with a new partner.

Descriptions of the Context in Which Sex Occurred

Different aspects of "setting the mood" as a way of establishing a favorable context for interactions were described. Setting the mood themes was more common in female descriptions of sexual activities than male descriptions for both new and long-term partners and included situations such as "perhaps after a date" or "we were at a party." Most of the sexual encounters with new partners began in bars and then moved to a private location, such as a residence or hotel room. Students' descriptions of the context of the sexual activity revealed emphasis on things other than consent and only indirect interpretation of whether consent was present.

Direct Discussions Relevant to Sexual Consent

Direct discussions about sexual activity and consent were rare overall but appeared to be more common for long-term partners than for new partners. For sexual activity among long-term partners, some mentioned that conversations about sex occurred well in advance of sexual activity. Mostly men described expressing their interest in sex verbally and directly, whereas women rarely communicated willingness or interest in sex, although some males indicated their female partners directly expressed willingness. In some instances, sexual consent was considered unimportant or unnecessary. In other times, clarification of sexual interest occurred after sexual activity had began or something was awry.

The researchers noted that, overall, the students' accounts of sexual interactions lacked descriptions of explicit discussion about sexual consent and behavioral indications regarding consent. They concluded that verbal, direct, and unambiguous behaviors seeking sexual consent were not in the normative sexual scripts of the participants; hence, they were rarely a part of individual sexual interactions in "real life" situations. The results fail to show adherence with the suggested normative requirements of affirmative sexual consent.

Another study of sexual consent supports the above findings and provides other insights. Sex researcher Kristen Jozkowski and colleagues (2012, 2014) examined how men and women at a midwestern U.S. university (*N* = 185) define, communicate, and interpret consent and non-consent. Here are some of the major findings:

- Men, more than women, were more likely to use nonverbal cues to interpret their partner's consent. However, women were more likely to rely on verbal cues or a combination of verbal and nonverbal cues for the partner's consent.

- There was no difference by gender regarding how consent was defined; most said an agreement of two people to have sex with each other.

- Relative to verbal cues, men (27%) often reported telling their partner that they were "going to engage in sexual activity with them," and women frequently reported just allowing the sexual activity to happen or not saying no to the sexual activity. About

one in five men (22%) said they ask a woman if she wants to have sex.

- Verbal communication or combination of verbal and nonverbal cues was often reported for more intimate sexual behaviors such as penile-vaginal and penile-anal sex. Nonverbal communication was frequently reported for less intimate behaviors such as "fooling around/intimate touching."

Think Critically

1. Do the findings of the two studies surprise you? If so, in what way? If not, why do you feel this way?
2. Is the affirmative sexual consent standard realistic?
3. From the study's results would you likely change your method of getting sexual consent from a partner? If so, in what way?
4. Which of the cues—verbal or non-verbal—would you find most easy or difficult to do?

of consent puts women at a disadvantage. Because men traditionally initiate sex, a man can initiate sex whenever he desires without the woman explicitly consenting. Actually, some men feel that the best way to have sex with a women, whether she is willing or not, is to simply engage in the desired behavior and then pretend that the behavior was unintentional or occurred because of a misunderstanding. A woman's refusal of sex can be considered "insincere" because consent is always assumed, and some men feel a sense of entitlement for sex which can prioritize their own pleasure over the other person's values and feelings (Orenstein, 2019). Such thinking reinforces a common sexual script in which men initiate and women refuse so as not to appear "promiscuous." A research study of 185 college men suggested that men are conceptualized as the gender that initiates sex and that women are the gatekeepers whose sexual pleasure is secondary to that of the male partner. These scripts may contribute to an environment in which women may be reluctant to initiate sex or to say yes to sex too quickly out of fear of being labeled negatively (Jozkowski & Peterson, 2013). In this script, the man continues, believing that the woman's refusal is "token." Some common reasons for offering "token" refusals include a desire not to appear "loose," not being sure how the partner feels, inappropriate surroundings, and game playing, which few women (and men) actually engage in. Because some women sometimes say "no" when they mean "coax me," male-female communication may be especially unclear regarding consent. Studies of college students found that more women than men reported sexual teasing, a form of provocation implying a promise of sexual contact but followed with refusal, and that they were more likely to agree that various forms of sexual violence are justified in situations in which the woman is perceived as "leading a man on" or "giving mixed signals" (Locke & Mahalik, 2005; Meston & O'Sullivan, 2007). However, contemporary beliefs of most people and the law say that if a rape survivor did not explicitly consent to sex, it is rape, even though the survivor flirted with the perpetrator, had been drinking, or experienced sexual arousal or orgasm during the incident (Peterson & Muehlenhard, 2007).

Postrefusal Sexual Persistence Researcher Cindy Struckman-Johnson and her colleagues (2003) investigated college students' pursuit of sexual contact with a person after he or she has refused an initial advance, a behavior they call **postrefusal sexual persistence**. They believe that all postrefusal behaviors are sexually coercive, in that the other person has already communicated that he or she does not consent to the sexual behavior. The researchers examined tactics in four areas: (1) sexual arousal (e.g., kissing and touching, taking off clothes), (2) emotional manipulation and deception (e.g., repeatedly asking, telling lies),

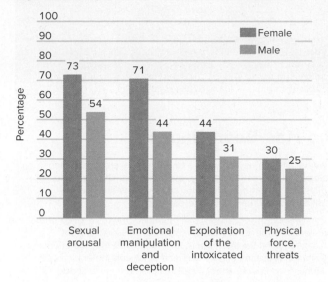

Experienced the tactic

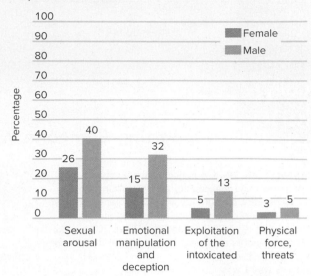

Perpetrated the tactic

• **FIGURE 10**

Percentage of College Men and Women Experiencing Postrefusal Sexual Persistence Tactics Since Age 16.

Source: Adapted from Struckman-Johnson et al. (2003).

(3) exploitation of the intoxicated (e.g., taking advantage of and purposely getting a target drunk), and (4) physical force (e.g., blocking a target's retreat, using physical restraint) (see Figure 10). The researchers found that postrefusal sexual persistence was fairly common: Nearly 70% of the students had been subjected to at least one tactic of postrefusal sexual persistence since the age of 16, and one third indicated that they had used a tactic. More women (78%) than men (58%) reported having been subjected to such tactics since age 16, and more men (40%) than women (26%) reported having used such tactics.

The Aftermath of Rape

Sexual assault and other sexual misconduct can be a traumatic event to which the survivor may have a number of responses, any of which will vary depending upon the situation. The effects of sexual assault/rape can include physical, mental, sexual, and/or social problems. The rape often results in a crisis in a person's life and relationships.

Physical and Psychological Outcomes Most rape survivors report being roughed up by the assailant; about 90% report some physical injury (Rape Network, 2000), although the vast majority do not sustain serious physical harm. Rape survivors are likely to experience depression, anxiety, restlessness, and guilt, all responses consistent with posttraumatic stress disorder (PTSD), an official diagnostic category of the American Psychiatric Association (2013) (Senn et al., 2015). Anyone who has been raped can develop PTSD. The National Intimate Partner and Sexual Violence Survey (NISVS) found numerous negative impacts and health conditions associated with sexual assault and sexual misconduct in their national survey (Smith et al., 2018):

Rape crisis centers help sexual assault survivors cope with the effects of rape trauma.

©SCPhotos/Alamy Stock Photo

- Of the about the one in three women (36.3%) and nearly one in six men (17.1%) who experienced sexual contact violence, physical violence, and/or stalking by an intimate partner, and experienced an intimate partner violence impact during their lifetime, 62% of women and 18% of men were feeling fearful, and 57% of women and 17% of men were concerned about their physical safety. Fifty-two percent of women and 17% of men had symptoms of PTSD.

- Significantly more women and men with a history of sexual violence or stalking by any perpetrator, or physical violence by an intimate partner, reported asthma, irritable bowel syndrome, frequent headaches, chronic pain, difficulty sleeping, and limitations of their activities compared to women and men without a history of these forms of violence.

practically speaking

Supporting Someone Who Has Been Raped

Men Can Stop Rape (MCSR) is a major national organization focusing on redefining male masculinity and mobilizing boys and young men to prevent sexual and physical violence against women. MCSR has provided suggestions for helping individuals who say they have been raped (Men Can Stop Rape, 2011b, n.d.). The suggestions are valuable no matter the gender of the sexual assault survivor or the perpetrator

When someone says, "I was raped," you should:

1. *Accept what the person said.* One should not question if the rape actually occurred but be present to help ease the pain.

2. *Assist the person in identifying options.* One may feel an urge to tell a rape survivor what to do, but rather, one should provide the freedom of the survivor to choose the best path of recovery even if you would do something different. There is no one correct path for the survivor in responding to being sexually assaulted.

3. *Listen to the person.* One should let the survivor know that you are available to talk about the experience when the person is ready. Some survivors may not want to immediately talk, but at some time in the healing process, the person may accept your offer. When that happens, be a good listener by not interrupting, yelling, or injecting your feelings, for example.

4. *Not touch before asking.* One should not assume that any physical contact, even a gentle touch, would be comforting to the survivor. Many survivors, especially in the early days and

weeks after an assault, desire to neither have sex nor even simple touch from those they love and trust. One can offer physical comfort by sitting with an open posture, arms uncrossed, and hand with the palm up.

5. *Recognize that you, as a family member, friend, or loved one, have also experienced the effects of the assault.* Do not blame yourself for the numerous feelings you may experience. Common reactions of survivors and significant others include sadness, confusion, anger, helplessness, fear, guilt, shock, anxiety, desperation, and compassion.

6. *Not blame the survivor for being assaulted.* No one deserves to be raped, no matter the situation. This includes being drunk, what clothing they wore, if they were out alone at night, married, if they went to the perpetrator's room or apartment, or already had sex with the person. Even if the survivor feels responsible for the rape, clearly tell the person that being raped was not their fault.

7. *Get support for yourself.* No one should go through the experience alone. The impact of a sexual assault extends farther than the survivor. Reach out to others, be it a friend, family member, mental health professional, a religious official, or whoever who will help you. Most rape crises centers offer counseling support. Keeping your feelings inside will hinder you from being able to be there for the survivors.

Source: Adapted from Men Can Stop Rape, http://www.mencanstoprape.org.

Lara Logan, a South African journalist and CBS correspondent, broke a months-long silence when she revealed that she was sexually assaulted by a mob of men in Cairo's Tahrir Square in February 2011, as the dictatorship of Hosni Mubarak was falling.

©Chris Hondros/Getty Images

In a nationally representative sample of 4,451 Australian women, aged 16–85 years, those who had been the survivor of rape, sexual assault, stalking, or intimate partner violence (27%) were drastically more likely to develop a mental disorder at some point in their lives. Fifty-seven percent reporting a history of sexual abuse also experienced depression, bipolar disorder, PTSD, substance abuse, or anxiety versus 28% of the women who had not experienced sexual violence. Nearly 9 out of 10 (89%) women who had been exposed to at least three different types of violence experienced mental illness or substance abuse. Episodes of violence often occur early in life but the mental disorders may not emerge until years later. Given that the rates of sexual violence are nearly comparable in the United States and Australia, it has been hypothesized that a similar study conducted in the United States would reveal comparable findings (Rees et al., 2011).

RAINN (2021.17h) provides suggestions for self-care following a trauma like sexual assault whether it occurred recently or years ago. RAINN states that it is important to keep oneself healthy; that is, good physical health can provide support through injuries or emotional challenges. A counselor may want to ask questions, such as do you have a sleep pattern or nap ritual that makes you feel more restful, what means make you feel more healthy, are there exercises that make you feel more energized, and what activities do you do to start the day or wind down at the day's end? Emotional self-care helps a person be in tune with oneself. RAINN asks the person to recall a time which they felt balanced and grounded, then to consider questions like, were there events and outings that you looked forward to, did you write down your thoughts in a journal, were meditation or relaxation activities part

practically speaking

Having Sex Again After Being Sexually Assaulted: Reclaiming One's Sexuality

Being sexually assaulted can alter not only the way a person experiences sex but also their mental and physical well-being. Among the negative outcomes of being sexually assaulted are the challenges of being intimate with a partner whether that is just hugging or kissing, or more intimate behaviors like intercourse. There can be serious emotional and physical outcomes of sexual assault on sexual functioning, such as a disconnect between the mind and the body, fear or avoidance of sexual contact, lack of sexual desire, engaging in sex work, feeling safer with women as intimate partners, diminished sexual pleasure, sexual pain, lack of orgasm, perception of feeling less desirable, and for some increased sexual desire and behavior (O'Callaghan, 2019). A social stereotype is that sex is impossible after sexual assault. Often sexual assault survivors feel like they will never be able to have sexually intimate contact again. Author and sexual assault survivor Sarah Trotta (2015) says:

> Sometimes it feels hard to exist in a body after being assaulted, and sometimes it feels even harder to experience physical pleasure. Survivors find themselves wondering if they deserve to feel pleasure, if it's safe to feel pleasure, how in the world they will ever be able to survive physical intimacy with another person.

- *The most highly recommended suggestion is counseling.* Many sexually assaulted survivors discover that talking about their experience to be very difficult because it brings up painful memories and feelings. However, counseling is considered the most effective and safest way to reclaiming a person's ability to be sexually intimate. Beyond therapy, family and friends can be helpful. Having a supportive, significant partner also can be valuable for recovery.

- *Keep the body healthy.* After being sexually abused, it is important to keep one's body strong and healthy. Good health can be the foundation during recovery. Continuing one's sleeping, food, exercise, and certain routines that made you healthy are valuable.

- *A partner needs to "reclaim" his or her own body after the assault.* The survivor should have total control over how his/her body is shared with another individual. Aspects of sexual sharing such as needs, wants, boundaries, individual, and shared decision making are all components of reclaiming one's sexuality. Once a person starts having sex again, he or she may find that certain behaviors may trigger a negative response that should be avoided until the survivor is comfortable with it.

- *Choose a partner who respects you and your needs, and with whom you like and want to have sex with.* Many persons who have been sexually assaulted are fearful and hesitant to tell a new dating partner about the sexual assault, yet this experience should be discussed before any romantic relationship gets too serious. There are persons who will listen and be supportive. If you are not ready for physical affection, be sure your partner knows and respects your decision, and embraces your need to become physical only when it is the right time for you. Trust your gut and engage in the conversation when you feel safe and ready.

- *Get acquainted again with your body.* Taking a bath, masturbating, or looking at one's body in a mirror are ways of becoming safe and comfortable with one's naked body. These activities are steps in appreciating and reclaiming one's body.

- *Masturbate.* Masturbation is a great way to increase comfort with one's body and a tool for declaring ownership of your sexual self. So practice touching your body. Reclaiming one's body through self-pleasure is important before one feels truly safe in sharing it with someone else.

- *Treat yourself kindly and appreciate your victories.* There will be good days and bad days in the recovery from sexual assault. Reminders will feel intense at times and manageable at other times. Be kind and gentle with yourself as you embark on your journey of reclaiming your sexuality and remind yourself that you were not responsible for the sexual assault. Recall the times when you felt balanced and grounded, and try to do as many of those things as you can. Having sex again may not go well once you resume it, but the first time you experience enjoyable sex, it will be empowering, freeing, and overwhelming and perhaps give joy that you thought would never happen again.

Hale (2013), who indicated having experienced being raped, listed 12 things that nobody had said about rape. Here is a particularly important one that all persons who have been sexually assaulted should know:

> Nobody tells you that people are capable loving you after you've been raped, and that you are capable of loving. You are allowed to give yourself to somebody completely. Likewise, you are allowed to hold back. You are allowed to be fearful but you are also allowed to trust again. Your healing process is your own and regardless of how you get there, know that as long as you are taking care of yourself, nobody has any right to tell you different.

Recovering from sexual assault is not always easy to do by oneself. If you need support, information, advice or referral, or just want to talk to someone, contact the National Assault Hotline, free, confidential, 24/7: 800-656-HOPE (4673). Trained specialists are ready to assist you.

of your regular schedule, what inspiration works were you reading, was there someone or a group of people that made you felt safe and supported, and was there a special place where you felt comfortable and grounded? As noted previously, help is available 24/7 through the National Sexual Assault Hotline: 800-656-HOPE (4673).

• Child Sexual Abuse

Child sexual abuse is any sexual-related activity between an adult and a child or any minor. Child sexual abuse is not limited to penetration, force and pain, or touching, but involves an adult engaging in any sexual behavior (e.g., looking, showing, or touching) with a child to meet the adult's interest or sexual needs. Abusive physical contact or touching includes: (1) an adult touching the child's genitals; (2) forcing a child to touch someone else's genitals or play sexual games; (3) putting a foreign object inside a child's vagina or anus; (4) oral sex and vaginal or anal penetration by any body part of the adult; and (5) masturbation in the presence of a minor or forcing the minor to masturbate. Noncontact sexual abuse includes: (1) showing sexually explicit images to a child; (2) deliberately exposing an adult's genitals to a child; (3) photographing a child in sexual poses; (4) encouraging a child to witness sexual behaviors; (5) inappropriately viewing a child undress or use the bathroom; and (6) communicating in a sexual manner by phone or the Internet. A growing and serious type of child sexual abuse is the making and posting of sexual images of children on the Internet. A person who views sexually abusive images of children on the Internet is also considered to be participating in the abuse. In a broad sense, sexual touching between children can be considered child sexual abuse. This type of abuse is usually defined as when there is a significant age gap between the children (usually 3 or more years) or if the children are very different in terms of their development or size (Rape, Abuse, and Incest National Network, 2016d; "What is considered child sexual abuse?", 2014).

It does not matter whether the adult perceives the child to be engaging in the sexual activity voluntarily. Because of the child's age, he or she cannot give informed consent; the activity can only be considered as self-serving to the adult. The topic of child sexual abuse has received increased national attention due to the widespread allegations and verifications of child molestation by the clergy in the Catholic Church. The number of allegations (4,434 during July 2018 through June 2019) of Catholic clergy sex abuse of minors more than quadrupled in 2019 compared to the average in the previous 5 years (Boorstein, 2020). The revelation of widespread child sexual abuse by priests, bishops, and cardinals has rocked the nation and the world, resulting in resignations, lawsuits, imprisonments, and suicide.

There are no reliable annual surveys of sexual assaults on children. It is also difficult to know how many children are sexually abused because many cases are not reported. Further, because of the stigma of sexual abuse and the enormous emotional distress caused by abuse, many survivors keep the abuse a secret. The prevalence is much greater than most people believe. The U.S. Department of Health & Human Services (2017) reported that for the fiscal year 2015 there were nearly 60,000 reported cases of child sexual abuse. The Centers for Disease Control and Prevention 2015 Intimate Partner and Sexual Violence Survey (IPSVS) (Smith et al., 2018) found that 25.8% of females reported that the age of their first victimization of sexual violence (rape, being made to penetrate someone else, sexual coercion, and/or unwanted sex contact), physical violence, and/or stalking occurred under age 18; for males, 14.6% reported the first victimization below the age 18. The IPSVS also revealed that 43.2% of females reported that their first completed or attempted rape victimization was under age 18; for males, the percentage of first rape or made to penetration victimization under age 18 was 51.3%. (Figure 11 shows the type of relationship between the child survivor and the perpetrator in one study.) As shown, nonparent relatives were the most common offenders (30%) and parents were the least common (3%) (Snyder & Sickmund, 2006). About 90% of children who are sexually abused know their abuser as someone they trust, which makes it even harder to notice.

Men who have sex with men are no more likely to sexually abuse children than persons who are sexual with persons of the other sex. Most sexual abuse of children occurs at the residence of either the victim or the perpetrator. Abusers typically manipulate victims to stay quiet about the sexual abuse; actually, about 60% of children sexually abused never tell anyone and only about one third of sexual abuse incidents are identified. The perpetrator will exert the position of power over the victim to intimidate and coerce the child, and may threaten

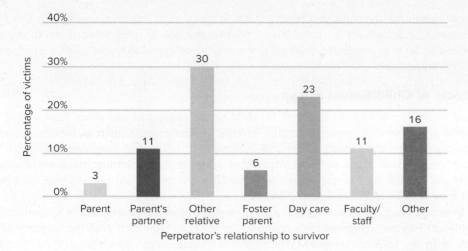

● FIGURE 11

Relationship Between the Child Survivor and the Perpetrator of Sexual Abuse.

Source: Snyder, H. N., & Sickmund, M. (2006). *Juvenile Offenders and Victims: 2006 National Report.* U.S. Department of Justice.

the child if the child refuses to participate or plans to tell an adult (Darkness to Light, 2015; Rape, Abuse, and Incest National Network, 2016d).

Pedophilic disorder is classified by the American Psychiatric Association (2013) as recurrent (for at least 6 months), intense sexual urges with a prepubescent child or children that the individual has acted upon or finds distressing or that results in interpersonal difficulty. Sometimes the terms *child sexual abuse* and *pedophilia* are used interchangeably, and the line between them may be muddled, but the APA definition of pedophilic disorder is a more stringent definition than child sexual abuse. Most occurrences of child sexual abuse are attributed to pedophilic disorder (Murray, 2000). A more thorough discussion of the differences between pedophilic disorder and child sexual abuse is found in Chapter 10.

Suspecting a Child Is Harmed and Protecting One's Child From Sexual Assault The Rape, Abuse & Incest National Network (RAINN) (2021.17i, 2021.17j) has excellent guidelines for detecting a child who might be experiencing sexual abuse and what parents can do to protect their child from sexual abuse. For more information, go to their website (http://www.rainn.org). Persons who suspect a child has been sexually abused may not know what to do. The offender may be a parent, family member, teacher, coach, religious leader, babysitter, or friend. The signs of being sexually abused are not always obvious, but learning some of the behavioral or physical changes can make a big difference in protecting a child from further abuse. Here are some warning signs:

- *Behavioral changes.* Shrinking away or seemingly being threatened by physical contact, regressive behaviors like thumb sucking, changing personal hygiene routines like refusing to bathe, sexual behavior inappropriate for the child's age, sleep disturbances, or nightmares.

- *Physical signs.* Bruising or swelling near genital area, blood on bedlinen or the child's undergarments, or broken bones.

- *Verbal cues.* Using words or phrases that are "too adult" or out of character for the child's age, unexplained silence, or being suddenly less talkative.

- *Emotional signs.* Changing eating habits, mood or personality, having nightmares or fear of being alone at night, experiencing a decrease in confidence or self-image, excessive worry or fearfulness, self-harming behaviors, suicide ideation, or loss or decrease in interest in school, activities, and friends.

If you are concerned about sexual abuse, talk to the child and keep in mind some guidelines to create a nonthreatening environment that may help the child open up to you. Steps can include picking a time and place where there is privacy, trying to make the conversation more casual, talking to the child directly, listening and following up, avoiding judgment and blame, reassuring the child, and being patient. If you do not feel comfortable with this type of conversation, then ask a trusted friend, relative, teacher, or other professional to inquire. Depending on your role in the child's life, you may be obligated to report suspicions of abuse to legal authorities.

Effects of Child Sexual Abuse

Until recently, much of the literature on child sexual abuse was anecdotal, case studies, or small-scale surveys of nonrepresentative groups. Nevertheless, numerous well-documented consequences of child sexual abuse that include both initial and long-term consequences. Many child sexual abuse survivors experience symptoms of posttraumatic stress disorder. Girls and women tend to experience more negative effects of child sexual abuse than boys and men (Cooke & Weathington, 2014).

In recent years, some women and men have stated that they were sexually abused during childhood but had repressed their memories of it. They later recovered the memory of it, often with the help of therapists. When these recovered memories surfaced, those accused often expressed shock and denied the abuse ever happened. Instead, they insisted that those memories were figments of the imagination. The question of whom to believe has given rise to a vitriolic "memory war": recovered memories versus false memories. Each side has its proponents, and the fierce controversy about the nature of recovered memories of child sexual abuse continues today.

Initial Effects   The initial consequences of sexual abuse occur within the first couple of years or so and appear in many of the children survivors. Typical effects include the following (Darkness to Light, 2015):

- *Emotional disturbances,* including fear, sadness, self-hatred, anger, temper tantrums, depression, hostility, guilt, and shame.
- *Physical consequences,* including difficulty in sleeping, changes in eating patterns, and headaches.
- *Substance abuse,* including alcohol abuse and increased rates of substance abuse/ dependence.
- *Sexual disturbances,* including significantly higher rates of open masturbation, sexual preoccupation, exposure of the genitals, and indiscriminate and frequent sexual behaviors that might lead to unintended pregnancy and STIs.
- *Social disturbances,* including difficulties at school, truancy, running away from home, and early romantic relationships and marriages by abused adolescents. In fact, a large proportion of homeless youths are fleeing parental sexual abuse.

Long-Term Effects   Although there can be some healing of the initial effects, child sexual abuse may leave lasting scars on the adult survivor. These adults often have significantly higher incidences of psychological, physical, and sexual problems than the general population. Abuse may, for example, predispose some women to sexually abusive dating relationships.
Long-term effects of child sexual abuse include the following:

- *Depression,* the symptom most frequently reported by adults sexually abused as children.
- *Self-destructive tendencies,* including suicide attempts and thoughts of suicide.
- *Somatic disturbances and dissociation,* including anxiety and nervousness, insomnia, chronic pain, eating disorders (anorexia and bulimia), irritable bowel syndrome, feelings of "spaciness," out-of-body experiences, and feelings that things are "unreal."
- *Health risk behaviors,* including tobacco use, alcoholism or drug abuse, obesity, and unsafe sexual behaviors that may result in STIs and unintended pregnancy.
- *Negative self-concept,* including feelings of low self-esteem, isolation, and alienation.
- *Interpersonal relationship difficulties,* including problems in relating to both sexes and to parents, in responding to their own children, and in trusting others.

- *Revictimization,* in which women abused as children are more vulnerable to rape and marital violence.
- *Sexual function difficulties,* in which survivors find it difficult to relax and enjoy sexual activities or in which they avoid sex and experience hypoactive (inhibited) sexual desire and lack of orgasm.

Many survivors of child sexual abuse do not suffer these consequences. Child sexual abuse does not necessarily sentence the survivors to an impaired life (Darkness to Light, 2015).

Treatment Programs

As stated earlier in this section, survivors of childhood sexual abuse often suffer both immediate and long-term negative outcomes. It is vital that they receive adequate support and therapy involving both cognitive and behavioral approaches. It is common now to deal with child sexual abuse by offering therapy programs that function in conjunction with the judicial system, particularly when the offender is an immediate family member, such as a father. Sex abusers also need treatment. This is important not only to assist these individuals in developing healthier child and adult relationships but also to avoid any future abuse episodes.

Preventing Child Sexual Abuse

Although there are no sure ways of protecting children from sexual abuse, both parents and organized programs can reduce the risk. One of the most important things parents can do is to talk to their children about sexual assault. Instead of being stressed about a big "sexual assault conversation," a parent can bring up the topic as part of the safety conversations that already occur. RAINN (2021.17k, 2021.17l) makes these suggestions:

- *Show interest in their day-to-day life.* Inquire what they did during the day and who they did it with. Who did they eat lunch with and what games did they play after school?
- *Get to know the people in your child's life.* Learn who your child is spending time with, including other children and adults. Ask your child about the kids they go to school with and their parents and others like teammates or coaches. Talk about these people openly so your child will feel comfortable doing the same.
- *Choose caregivers carefully.* Whether it is a babysitter, a new school, or an afterschool activity, be diligent in screening caregivers of your child.
- *Teach children the names of their body parts.* Children may find it easier to ask questions and express concern when they know the names of body parts.
- *Some parts of the body are private.* Children need to know that other people should not look or touch private body parts. A parent should be present when a health care professional has to examine parts of the body.
- *It's OK to say "no."* Children need to know that they are allowed to say "no" to any touch they find uncomfortable even if it is hugs from grandparents or tickling from a parent. Support your child who says "no" even if it makes you feel uncomfortable. Also, let them know that they do not have the right to touch another if that person does not want to be touched.
- *Talk about secrets.* Perpetrators often try to force secret-keeping. Let your children know that they can always talk to you, especially if someone has told them to keep a secret.
- *Reassure them that they will not get in trouble.* Young children may fear that they will get in trouble or upset their parents if they talk about their experience. A parent should be a safe place for a child to share information or ask questions about an experience that made them uncomfortable. Let the child know that they will not be punished for sharing information with you.
- *Show them what it looks like to do the right thing.* When a parent models helping behavior, such as helping a person with directions to get somewhere or helping someone carry groceries, the parent signals normal, positive ways to behave.

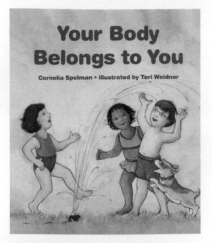

One objective of child sexual abuse prevention programs is to teach children the difference between "good" touching and "bad" touching.

Courtesy of "Your Body Belongs to You" by Cornelia Spelman and illustrated by Teri Weigner/Albert Whitman & Company

- *When they come to you, make time for them.* Parents should give their child undivided attention when the child comes to them with something they feel is important. If parents take the time to listen and let the child know that their concerns are taken seriously, they will more likely come to them again in the future.

Programs focusing on preventing child sexual abuse have been developed. Most programs include group instruction in schools, either as a component of regular classroom instruction or as an after-school program. These programs typically address three audiences: children, parents, and professionals. CAP programs aimed at children use plays, puppet shows, films, visual media, books, and comic books to teach children that they have rights: to control their own bodies (including their genitals), to feel "safe," and to not be touched in ways that feel confusing or wrong (Holtzhausen et al., 2016).

CAP programs also seek to educate professionals, especially teachers, physicians, mental health workers, and police officers. Because of their close contact with children and their role in teaching children about the world, teachers are especially important. Professionals are encouraged to watch for signs of sexual abuse and are mandated to report abuse if they suspect a child has been abused.

In 1997, the U.S. Supreme Court ruled in favor of what is now referred to as Megan's Law. Enacted in 1995, the law requires law enforcement authorities to make information about registered sex offenders available to the public. That is, the law calls for schools, day-care centers, and youth groups to be notified about moderate-risk sex offenders in the community. For high-risk offenders, the law requires that the police go door-to-door, notifying neighborhood residents. It also requires sex offenders who have been paroled or recently released from prison to register with local authorities when moving to a community. The law is named for Megan Kanka, a 7-year-old who was raped and murdered by a twice-convicted sex offender who lived across the street from her.

In efforts to further prevent child sexual abuse, most states and many communities have enacted laws directed toward sex offenders to, for example, extend prison sentences, require offenders to register with the police, restrict where they can live (not near schools or playgrounds), improve public notification of their whereabouts, and order electronic monitoring. All states have Internet registries of sex offenders. For many of the legal attempts to make identity of sex offenders easily accessible to the public, constitutional and safety issues relative to the rights of the offender have been raised.

Final Thoughts

Sexual harassment, anti-sexual minorities harassment and discrimination, sexual violence, and sexual abuse represent the darker side of human sexuality. Their common thread is the control, humiliation, subordination, or victimization of others. But we need not to experience sexual assault, and misconduct. We can educate ourselves and others about these activities, and we can work toward changing attitudes and institutions that support these destructive and dehumanizing behaviors.

Summary

Sexual Harassment

- *Sexual harassment* includes two distinct types of illegal harassment: the abuse of power for sexual ends and the creation of a *hostile environment.* Sexual harassment may begin as early as middle childhood. In college, about 40% of all students have experienced some form of sexual harassment (verbal or physical) since they had enrolled in college.

- About 6% of men and women have experienced being stalked since enrolling in college.

- In the workplace, both fellow employees and supervisors may engage in sexual harassment. In many instances, harassment does not represent sexual attraction as much as an exercise of power.

Harassment and Discrimination Against Lesbian, Gay, Bisexual, Transgender, and Queer People

- Researchers have identified two forms of discrimination or bias against lesbian, gay, bisexual, transgender, and queer people: heterosexual bias and anti-gay prejudice.

- *Heterosexual bias* includes ignoring, segregating, and submerging LGBTQ+ people into larger categories that make them invisible.

- *Anti-gay prejudice* is a strong dislike, fear, or hatred of LGBTQ+ people. It is acted out through offensive language, discrimination, and violence. Anti-gay prejudice is derived from a deeply rooted insecurity concerning a person's own sexuality and gender identity, a strong fundamentalist religious orientation, or simple ignorance.

Sexual Assault

- Sexual assault/rape is a major public health issue in the United States that has enormous and long-term impact on survivors. This type of sexual violence often occurs early in the life span of survivors with ethnic and minority persons being most affected. It includes rape, being made to penetrate someone else, sexual coercion (e.g., nonphysically pressured, unwanted sexual penetration), unwanted sexual contact (e.g., fondling and kissing), and noncontact unwanted sexual experiences (e.g., harassed in a public place).

- Myths about rape encourage rape by blaming women. Men are more likely than women to believe rape myths.

- In the United States, about 4 in 10 women and 1 in 4 men have experienced some form of contact sexual violence in their lifetime.

- Sexual assault on many college campuses is a serious problem, with one in five women reporting being sexually assaulted while in college. An increasing acknowledgment of the extent of student sexual assault has fueled demands that colleges and universities make their campuses safer.

- The college culture appears to fuel the sexual assault problem with many survivors being assaulted while drunk, under the influence of drugs, passed out, or incapacitated in some way.

- Overall, 13% of students from 33 colleges and universities reported experiencing nonconsensual penetration, attempted penetration, sexual touching be force, or inability to consent since enrolling in their schools.

- Sexual consent is often difficult to determine, given that we usually don't give verbal consent to sexual activity.

- Most male rape survivors have been raped by other men. Because the motive in sexual assaults is power and domination, sexual orientation is often irrelevant.

- Survivors of rape may experience depression, anxiety, restlessness, and guilt. The symptoms following rape are consistent with *posttraumatic stress disorder (PTSD)*. Rape trauma syndrome consists of an acute phase and a long-term reorganization phase. Women find their sexuality severely affected for at least a short time after being raped.

Child Sexual Abuse

- *Child sexual abuse* is any sexual interaction between an adult and a child. The definition of child sexual abuse is different than that of pedophilic disorder, which is more stringent. However, most occurrences of child sexual abuse are attributed to pedophilic disorder.

- The initial effects of abuse include physical consequences and emotional, social, and sexual disturbances. Child sexual abuse may leave lasting scars on the adult survivor.

- *Sexual abuse trauma* includes traumatic sexualization, betrayal, powerlessness, and stigmatization. Treatment programs use both cognitive and behavioral psychotherapy to assist the survivor.

- Child abuse prevention (CAP) programs aimed at children use plays to teach them that they have the right to control their bodies (including their genitals), to feel "safe," and to not be touched in ways that feel confusing or wrong.

Questions for Discussion

- Do you know how common sexual harassment is on your campus? What makes it sometimes difficult to determine the difference between flirting and sexual harassment?

- Does your campus post statistics on sexual assault?

- What are your reactions to the Antioch College and California affirmative consent (i.e., say "yes") policies for partnered sex?

- Why do you think people sexually assault another person? Are they mainly motivated by need for sexual gratification, by need for power and control, or by other reasons?

- What do you think you could do to help someone who has been sexually assaulted? What resources or organizations would you recommend?

- Have you observed anti-gay prejudice? If so, what could have been done to prevent it, if anything?

- What do you think can be done to prevent child sexual abuse?

Sex and the Internet

Sex and the Internet

The Rape, Abuse & Incest National Network (RAINN) is the nation's largest anti-sexual violence organization. RAINN (rainn.org) operates the National Sexual Assault Hotline (800-656-HOPE) in partnership with 1,000 local sexual assault services providers across the country and the Department of Defense (DoD) Safe Helpline for the DoD community. RAINN also conducts programs to prevent sexual violence, helps survivors, and ensures that perpetrators are brought to justice. College and high school students can help RAINN educate other students about sexual assault prevention and recovery. RAINN has a free app (RAINN.app) that offers survivors of sexual violence and their loved one's support, self-care tools, and information about managing the effects of trauma.

Click on the various RAINN resources and answer the following questions:

- What is the mission of RAINN?

- What are the programs offered by RAINN?

- In what ways can students volunteer for RAINN?

- What type of support does RAINN offer for persons who have been sexually assaulted?

- What is the focus of #ActWithRAINN?

Suggested Websites

Darkness to Light
https://www.d2l.org
An organization focused on empowering adults to prevent child sexual abuse.

Feminist Majority Foundation
http://www.feminist.org
Discusses its latest projects and gives information about feminist issues.

Human Rights Campaign
http://www.hrc.org
Offers the latest information on political issues affecting lesbian, gay, bisexual, transgender, and queer Americans.

Movement Advancement Project
http://www.lgbtmap.org
An independent think tank that provides research, insight, and analyses that help expedite equality for lesbian, gay, bisexual, transgender, and queer people.

National Coalition of Anti-Violence Programs
http://www.avp.org
The only national coalition dedicated to reducing violence among lesbian, gay, bisexual, transgender, and queer individuals.

National Sexual Violence Resource Center
http://www.nsvrc.org
A project of the Pennsylvania Coalition Against Rape; a resource for information about rape and links to other sites.

Stop It Now
http://www.stopitnow.org
Provides support, information, and resources to help keep children safe.

Stop Street Harassment
http://www.stopstreetharassment.org
A nonprofit organization dedicated to documenting and ending gender-based street harassment worldwide.

Stop Violence Against Women
http://www.stopvaw.org
A forum for information, advocacy, and change in promoting women's human rights worldwide.

U.S. Equal Employment Opportunity Commission
http://www.eeoc.gov
Provides information on federal laws prohibiting job discrimination and gives directions for filing a charge.

Suggested Reading

Abdulali, S. (2018). *What we talk about when we talk about rape.* The New Press. A straightforward and insightful account of sexual assault and the rape culture all in the context of the American #MeToo movement.

Bass, E., & Davis, L. (2008). *The courage to heal* (4th ed.). Harper Collins. A comprehensive guide that weaves together personal experience and professional knowledge to assist survivors of sexual abuse.

Clark, A. E., & Pino, A. L. (2016). *We believe you: Survivors of campus sexual assault speak out.* Holt Paperbacks. Students from every type of college and university share their experiences of being sexually assaulted. The stories are prominently featured in the award-winning documentary *The Hunting Ground.*

Cook, P. W., & Hodo, T. L. (2013). *When women sexually abuse men: The hidden side of rape, stalking, harassment, and sexual assault.* Praeger. Addresses an overlooked aspect of sexual violence: male rape by females. Beyond rape, the text also examines sexual harassment, stalking, and sexual assault of men by women.

Dick, K., & Ziering, A. (2016). *The hunting ground: The inside story of sexual assault on American college campuses.* Hot Books. An excellent insight into the epidemic of college sexual assault.

Fetner, T. (2008). *How the religious right shaped lesbian and gay activism.* University of Minnesota Press. Descriptions of the two movements are significantly shaped by their rivals.

Hirsch, J. S. (2020). *Sexual citizens: A landmark study of sex, power, and assault on campus.* W. W. Norton. A timely and thought-provoking assessment of campus sexual assault. Important reading for the general audience, students, and campus policy makers.

O'Donohue, W. T., & Schewe, P. A. (eds.). (2019). *Handbook of sexual assault and sexual assault prevention.* Springer. This timely handbook presents in-depth descriptions of the multi-faceted issues of sexual assault. Seven sections address such topics as risk factors, theoretical frameworks, prevention models, and special populations.

Real, A. K., & Evans, P. (2014). *Living through this: Listening to the stories of sexual violence survivors.* Beacon Press. Rape and sexual violence survivors describing how their lives have been shaped, but not redefined, by their sexual violence.

Richards, T. N., & Marcum, C. D. (2014). *Sexual victimization: Then and now.* Sage. Examines the continuum of sex crimes and the perception of survivors and society.

©David Angel/Alamy Stock Photo

chapter

18

Sexually Explicit Materials, Sex Workers, and Sex Laws

CHAPTER OUTLINE

Sexually Explicit Material in Contemporary Society

Sex Work and Sex Trafficking

Sexuality and the Law

"My boyfriend and I sometimes look at pornographic movies while we have sex. We have learned some new techniques from them, and they really help us get turned on. Some of our friends had recommended that we look at them. At first, we were a little hesitant to use them, but now watching the movies has become a regular part of our sex. But I wonder if something is wrong with us having to use the movies. And, at times, I still feel uncomfortable using them."

—21-year-old female

"I was only sixteen when I traveled to Peru with Carlos, who was twenty-nine. We were in Lima for two days, and while we were there, Carlos took me to a hotel so we could both have sex with prostitutes. At the time, I did not really understand what was happening until after it occurred. Carlos knew that I was a virgin and thought this would be a fantastic way for me to become a 'man.' I felt embarrassed, dirty, and ashamed of myself."

—24-year-old male

"I seriously began dating women when I came to college. I often fantasized what it would be like to be married to another woman but I knew that could never happen. Then, amazingly one day in 2015 all of that changed when the U.S. Supreme Court made gay marriage legal. That decision not only gave me the opportunity to marry whomever I want but also validated my love of women."

—23-year-old female

"The difference between pornography and erotica is lightning."

—Gloria Leonard (1940–2014)

M ONEY AND SEX are bound together in the production and sale of sexually explicit material and in the commercial sex industry. Money is exchanged for sexual images or descriptions contained in films, electronic media, magazines, books, music, and photographs that depict people in explicit or suggestive sexual activities. Money is also exchanged for sexual services provided by street-based sex workers, escorts, massage parlor workers, and other sex workers. The sex industry is a multibillion-dollar enterprise with countless millions of consumers and customers. As a nation, however, we feel ambivalent about sexually explicit material and sex for sale. Many people condemn it as harmful, immoral, and exploitative and wish to censor or eliminate it. Others see it as a harmless and even beneficial activity, an erotic diversion, or an aspect of society that cannot or should not be regulated; they believe censorship and police action do greater harm than good.

In this chapter, we examine sexually explicit material, including depictions of sex in popular culture, the role of technology in the distribution of sexually explicit material, the effects of sexually explicit videos and films, and censorship issues. We then examine prostitution, focusing on female and male workers in the commercial sex industry, the legal issues involved, and the impact of HIV and other STIs. We then discuss current laws dealing with private, consensual sexual behavior among adults and end the chapter with legal issues related to gay marriage.

• Sexually Explicit Material in Contemporary Society

Studying sexually explicit material objectively is difficult because such material often triggers deep and conflicting feelings we have about sexuality. Many people enjoy sexually explicit material, others find it degrading, and still others may simultaneously feel aroused and guilty.

Pornography or Erotica: Which Is It?

"Obscenity is best left to the minds of man. What's obscene to one may not offend another."

—William O. Douglas (1898–1980)

"How can you accuse me of liking pornography when I don't even have a pornograph?"

—Groucho Marx (1890–1977)

As sexual themes, ideas, images, and music increasingly appear in art, literature, and popular culture, the boundaries blur between what is socially acceptable and what is considered erotic or obscene. Much of the discussion about sexually explicit material concerns the question of whether such material is, in fact, erotic or pornographic—that is, whether viewing it causes positive or harmful outcomes. Unfortunately, there is a lack of agreement about what constitutes erotica or pornography. Part of the problem is that *erotica* and *pornography* are subjective terms, and the line separating them can be blurred. **Erotica** describes sexually explicit material that can be evaluated positively. (The word *erotica* is derived from the Greek *erotikos,* meaning "a love poem.") It often involves mutuality, respect, affection, and a balance of power and may even be considered to have artistic value. **Pornography** represents sexually explicit material that may be evaluated negatively and might include anything that depicts sexuality and causes sexual arousal in the viewer. (*Pornography* is a nineteenth-century word derived from the Greek *porne,* meaning "prostitute," and *graphos,* meaning "depicting.") *Dictionary.com* defines pornography as "sexually explicit videos, photographs, writings, or the like whose purpose is to elicit sexual arousal."

Sexually explicit materials are legal in the United States; however, materials that are considered to be obscene are not. Although the legal definition of **obscenity** varies, the term generally implies a personal or societal judgment that something is offensive; it comes from the Latin word for "filth." Often, material depicting the use of violence and aggression or degrading and dehumanizing situations is deemed obscene. Because such a determination involves a judgment, critics often point to the subjective nature of this definition. (Obscenity and the law are discussed in detail later in the section.)

The same sexually explicit material may evoke a variety of responses in different people. "What I like is erotica, but what you like is pornography," may be a facetious statement, but it's not entirely untrue. It has been found that people view others as more adversely affected than themselves by sexually explicit material. Judgments about sexually explicit material tend to be relative.

Because of the tendency to use *erotica* as a positive term and *pornography* as a negative term, we will use the neutral term *sexually explicit material* whenever possible. **Sexually explicit material (SEM)** is material such as photographs, videos, films, magazines, and books whose primary themes, topics, or depictions involve sexuality that may cause sexual arousal. A widely consumed type of SEM is sexually explicit videos or films, commonly called pornography (Kohut et al., 2020). We have chosen to use *sexually explicit videos* (SEV) instead of *pornography,* as it is more specific than the broader definition of pornography given above and because it, like SEM, is more neutral. However, in the discussion of sexually explicit videos that follows, we will use the term utilized by the authors and researchers. As you will see, numerous terms beyond pornography have seen used, such as *visual sexual stimuli, sexually explicit media, cyberporn,* and *Internet pornography.* The lack of a uniform term can be problematic, as will be discussed later.

> "Obscenity is whatever happens to shock some elderly and ignorant magistrate."
>
> —Bertrand Russell (1872–1970)

Sexually Explicit Material and Popular Culture

In the nineteenth century, technology transformed the production of sexually explicit material. Cheap paper and large-scale printing, combined with mass literacy, created an enormous market for books and drawings, including sexually explicit material. Today, technology is once again extending the forms, largely through the Internet, in which this material is conveyed.

In recent decades, sexually explicit material has become an integral part of popular culture. Until the advent and expansion of the Internet, *Playboy, Penthouse,* and *Hustler* were among the most widely circulated magazines in America. The depiction of sexual activities is not restricted to online and print material, however. Various establishments offer live entertainment. Some clubs or adult entertainment establishments employ erotic dancers who expose themselves and simulate sexual behaviors before their audience, and some even have "live sex shows."

In contrast to the 1980s, when one would have to go to a store to ask for "porn" magazines (often located behind the counter) or visit an adult theatre (located in a "seedy" part of town), because of dramatic increases in technology people can easily access sexually explicit images, especially videos. The Internet, cable, and television on-demand programming, and DVD revolutions have been so great that homes have largely supplanted adult theaters or "porno" movie houses as sites for viewing sexually explicit films. The availability of in-home media such as sexually explicit videos and downloadable films on the Internet has had a profound effect on *who* views erotic films. For example, in the past adult movie houses were the domain of men; relatively few women entered them. Most SEV or films, as well as books and magazines, had been marketed to heterosexual men. However, in part because of the success of shows like *Sex and the City* and books and films like *Fifty Shades of Grey,* women are increasingly becoming consumers of adult entertainment and erotica, including sexually explicit materials and sex toys. But with SEV available for viewing in the

The touching of one's genitals by music performers such as Rihanna sends a strong sexually explicit message.

©Kevin Mazur/WireImage/Getty Images

The *Fifty Shades of Grey* novels and the movies have been polarizing: Some believe they depict a romantic and erotic story that encourages women to explore their sexuality, whereas others think that they glorify abusive intimate relationships.

©Guy Corbishley/Alamy Stock Photo

"Perversity is the muse of modern literature."

—Susan Sontag (1933–2004)

privacy of the home and on one's computer, tablet, or smartphone, women and couples have now become consumers of sexually explicit videos. As we know, the increased Internet availability of sexually explicit videos has made it very easy for all groups of individuals, no matter their gender identity or sexual orientation, to access these types of materials.

The Consumption of Sexually Explicit Materials

Studies have been conducted to assess public consumption of sexually explicit materials, why people use online erotic videos, and their preferences for visual sexual stimuli. Many people use SEM. (See Practically Speaking "Pornography Usage Measure" to indicate your viewing or use of sexual content.) For example, a nationally representative, Internet-based survey of U.S. adults (975 men, 1,046 women, aged 18–70+) examined how often participants utilized varied SEM (Herbenick et al., 2017). Here is what the survey found for lifetime use for all men and women and for ages 18–24, the age range of most undergraduate college students:

- *Read erotic stories.* Fifty-seven percent of all men and 44% of those aged 18–24 had read erotic stories in their lifetime. Fifty-seven percent of all women and 54% of those aged 18–24 had read erotic stories in their lifetime.

- *Used phone app.* Twelve percent of all men and 17% of those aged 18–24 had used a phone app related to sex in their lifetime. Six percent of all women and 15% of those aged 18–24 had used a phone app related to sex in their lifetime.

- *Looked at a sexually explicit magazine.* Seventy-nine percent of all men and 52% of those aged 18–24 looked through a sexually explicit magazine in their lifetime. Fifty-four percent of all women and 23% of those aged 18–24 had looked through a sexually explicit magazine in their lifetime.

- *Sent nude or semi-nude photo.* Twenty-four percent of all men and 29% of those aged 18–24 had sent a nude or semi-nude photo of self to someone else in their lifetime. Twenty-seven percent of all women and 50% of those aged 18–24 had sent a nude or semi-nude photo of self to someone else in their lifetime.

- *Received nude or semi-nude photo.* Forty-one percent of all men and 47% of those aged 18–24 had received a nude or semi-nude photo of someone in their lifetime. Twenty-seven percent of all women and 48% of those aged 18–24 had received a nude or semi-nude photo of someone in their lifetime.

- *Watched sexually explicit videos.* Seventy-one percent of all men and 73% of those aged 18–24 watched sexually explicit videos or DVDs (porn) in their lifetime. Sixty percent of all women and 48% of those aged 18–24 watched sexually explicit videos or DVDs (porn) in their lifetime. (See Table 1 for the percentages of persons who indicated they consumed sexually explicit videos or DVDs.)

TABLE 1 ● Percentage of U.S. Men (*n* = 975) and Women (*n* = 1,046), by Age, Who Indicated That They Had Watched Sexually Explicit Videos or DVDs (porn) in the Post Month, the Past Year, and in Their Lifetime

		Men %								Women %							
	Total %	Total Men	18–24	25–29	30–39	40–49	50–59	60–69	70+	Total Women	18–24	25–29	30–39	40–49	50–59	60–69	70+
Past month	23.9	35.3	39.5	40.5	49.2	37.9	31.0	26.8	22.7	13.4	22.1	34.1	21.6	13.8	5.0	5.3	1.0
Past year	38.8	53.4	59.6	69.0	59.8	56.1	51.1	45.2	35.9	25.3	33.6	51.6	38.3	32.0	15.6	10.9	3.5
Lifetime	70.9	82.3	73.3	83.5	84.0	89.7	84.9	83.2	72.0	60.4	47.6	61.1	69.6	69.2	66.8	57.7	37.1

Source: Adapted from Herbenick et al. (2017).

Pornography Usage Measure

"I may not be able to define pornography but I know it when I see it."

—Supreme Court Justice Potter Stewart

(1915–1985)

With the greater availability and usage of sexually explicit materials (SEM), research on sexually explicit videos (SEV) use has likewise increased. To assess the outcomes of SEV, researchers have developed standardized measures (questionnaires) that assess varied psychological, interpersonal, and behavioral outcomes of SEV use. However, the definition of "pornography" is not always defined in the measure, and definitions vary among varied SEV questionnaires (Busby et al., 2017, 2020; Kohut et al., 2020). This dilemma can result in difficulty comparing results across studies and not having confidence that the respondent's definition of SEV is the same as the researcher's, thus limiting the validity of the measure.

Researchers at Brigham Young University developed the Pornography Usage Measure (PUM) (Busby et al., 2017, 2020), a set of statements that evaluate how often a person uses "common types" of sexually explicit material. The measure items describe varied types of sexual media (texts, videos, photographs) with different levels of explicitness. Many of the participants from the United States and numerous countries around the world considered the items as describing "pornography." Hence, the PUM provides a measure for researchers that include items determined to be depicting pornography by a large international sample of adults.

Directions

The completion of the measure has two components:

Component One:

Using the below 6-point scale, indicate for each statement how often in the last 12 months you have viewed or used the following sexual content mentioned in the statement.

1 = Never
2 = Once a month or less
3 = 2 or 3 days a month
4 = 1 or 2 days a week
5 = 3 to 5 days a week
6 = Every day or almost every day

Component Two:

Using the choices below, indicate for each statement whether you believe it represents "pornography."

Y = yes, it describes pornography
N = no, it does no describe pornography

1. A detailed description in writing of a couple passionately kissing and touching each other's clothed bodies and describing their arousal.

2. A detailed description in writing of a couple engaging in foreplay and sex that includes a mention of specific sexual body parts that are touched and aroused as sexual acts are performed.

3. A video of two men having sexual intercourse with each other.

4. A swimsuit issue of a magazine showing models in skimpy swimsuits or strategically covered topless views in a variety of provocative poses.

5. A television program showing the filming of a swimsuit edition of a magazine that shows models being filmed in a variety of provocative poses but no full nudity of breasts or genitalia.

6. An image of a woman alone posing in a suggestive way with underwear on.

7. An image of a woman alone posing in a suggestive way with exposed breasts and panties on.

8. An image of a woman alone posing in a suggestive way without any clothes on.

9. An image of a man alone posing is a suggestive way with only underwear on.

10. An image of a man alone posing in a suggestive way without any clothing on.

11. A short video depicting a couple having consensual sex. The women's breasts are shown but neither partner's genitalia are shown.

12. A picture of a couple having sex, the women's breasts are shown but neither partner's genitals are shown.

13. An image of a heterosexual couple having sex which shows the man's penis penetrating the woman.

14. A video showing two naked women or men kissing each other.

15. A video showing two naked women or men manually stimulating each other.

16. A video of a woman or man alone masturbating.

17. A novel that includes one graphic depiction of sexual intercourse.

18. A television show focused on strippers that includes multiple instances of blurred nudity.

19. A video that graphically depicts a three-way sexual encounter.

20. A major Hollywood film or movie that includes one graphic sexual encounter.

Source: Adapted from Busby, D. M., et al. (2020). Measuring the multidimensional construct of pornography: A long and short version of the pornography usage measure. *Archives of Sexual Behavior, 49,* 3027–3030.

Specific to college students, a study of 969 students in the United States found that 33% reported viewing SEV in the past 30 days: Among these students, 35% reported viewing the videos once, 31% a few times a month, 10% about weekly, 14% a few times a week, 6% daily, 2% a few times a day, and 2% several times a day (Braithwaite et al., 2015).

The reason people utilize online SEV has not been thoroughly studied. A study of 321 undergraduate male and female students assessed specific motivations for Internet pornography use and how gender and erotophilia/erotophobia are associated with motivations (Paul & Shim, 2008). Four motivations for online viewing of erotic material were found: (1) to build or maintain a relationship; (2) for mood management, such as to increase arousal, or for entertainment; (3) out of habit; and (4) for the purpose of sexual fantasy—to feel as if they themselves were interacting with the actors in the sexual scenes. Males showed stronger motivations for viewing the pornography than females for all four of the motivations. Lastly, the more erotophilic students (those who had more positive sexual attitudes) were more likely than the more erotophobic students to be motivated to use Internet pornography for all four motivations.

Researchers have investigated whether the COVID-19 has impacted SEM use, given the social distancing, quarantine, and national lockdowns that have occurred as the pandemic spread globally. These measures have resulted in increased social isolation, loneliness, and stress that might be altering the use of SEM. Several porn websites (e.g., Pornhub) offered free access during the pandemic (Doring, 2020). One of the most extensive studies was a global assessment of the trend of online pornography and coronavirus-themed porn interest from January 9, 2020, to May 25, 2020 (Zattoni, 2020). The study was conducted using a worldwide trend search-engine (Google Trends) involving the five most popular porn websites (Porn, XNXX, PornHub, xVideos, and xHamster) and six nations worldwide. The findings revealed that there was an increasing search trend for online pre-pandemic type of porn and coronavirus-themed porn (shows sex with masks, surgical gloves, and hazmat suits) in nations with a strict "stay at home orders." The researchers contended that the increased in pornography use may contributed to boredom, novelty-seeking, using sex as a surviving mechanism, as well as a method to avoid intimate body contact that possibly could expose one to COVID-19. Further, some studies have found that the pandemic has had a negative sexual satisfaction and frequency (e.g., Lehmiller et al., 2020; Milhausen et al., 2020; Hensel, 2020). Psychologist Joshua Grubbs (2020) stated that:

> For most users, pornography is probably just another distraction—one that might actually help "flatten the curve" by keeping people safely occupied and socially distanced. Combined with the fact that many people are isolating alone, pornography may provide a low-risk sexual outlet that does not cause people to risk their own safety or the safety of others.

The findings of follow-up and subsequent studies may be different at the publication of this text as the result of COVID-19 vaccinations and decreasing of social distancing; people will increase social interaction and SEV use may return to pre-epidemic levels.

Themes, Content, and Actors of SEV

Many "mainstream" SEV target a male, heterosexual audience and are typically oriented toward men's needs, fantasies, and preferences (Blais-Lecours et al., 2016). They portray stereotypes of male sexuality: dominant men with huge, erect penises, able to "last long" and satisfy eager and acquiescent women who are driven mad by their sexual prowess. The major theme of the films is "cookbook" sex; they show fellatio, cunnilingus, vaginal and anal sex, orgasm with the man ejaculating on the woman's body or face (called "the cum shot"), and the woman often faking an orgasm. The focus is typically on the physical beauty of the woman "star," with threesomes (two women and one man) or group sex sometimes featured. The male actors may not even be "good-looking" (Cassell, 2008; Paul, 2006).

Studies assessing the impact of viewing Internet SEV have been increasing, but little research on the content of the videos has been conducted. One major contentious issue of these videos is whether or not they depict gender equality (e.g., women are generally objectified). Researchers from the University of Amsterdam conducted a content analysis of 400 sexually mainstream explicit Internet videos (both professional and amateur produced) from four of the most visited "porn" websites (Pornhub, RedTube, YouPorn, and xHamster) (Klaassen & Peter, 2014). These websites are mainly aimed for the heterosexual audience. The analysis focused on three main dimensions of gender equality: objectification, power, and violence. The objectification dimension was defined as instrumentality (a female or male body used for another person's sexual gratification and an emphasis of the body or body parts of one actor while the other actor gained sexual pleasure) and dehumanization (whether the actor was depicted as having feelings and thoughts and as making his or her own choices). Power was defined as depicted dominance/submission power differences independent of sexual activity (e.g., boss, doctor, secretary, student, social roles) and power differences in the context of sex. Violence was defined as physically violent acts and responses and coerced sex. The researchers concluded from the study findings that "the vast majority of sexual activities in these videos were depicted as consensual" (p. 10). Here are detailed findings of the study that lead to the researchers' conclusions:

- *Objectification.* The women actors, in contrast to the men actors, were more likely to be instrumentalized. Close-ups of women's body parts (61% of sex scenes) included close-ups of their genitals, buttocks, and/or breasts; close-ups of men's genitals, buttocks, and/or chest (19%) occurred less frequently. Men actors (69%) were more often manually stimulated than women (59%). Oral stimulation of men (81%) was more often depicted than women (48%) being stimulated orally. Men (76%) were more likely to experience orgasm than were women (17%). Relative to dehumanization, no evidence was found of a general dehumanization of women. But men were more likely dehumanized than women. About an equal proportion of the sex scenes showed men (36%) initiating sex and women (32%) initiating sex. Men actors (94%) were slightly more likely to be depicted as having sex for their own enjoyment and pleasure than were women actors (85%). However, more scenes showed women's faces in close-ups (59%) than the faces of men (12%).

- *Power.* The depiction of power independent of sexual activity between the men actors and women actors was nearly equal. However, power differences in the sexual activities more likely depicted men as dominant and women as submissive, although over 4 of 10 scenes (46%) showed equal dominance/submission.

- *Violence.* When violent behaviors were shown, women (37%) were more likely than men (3%) to be the recipients. The violent behaviors toward women were typically spanking (in 27% of scenes) and inserting penis very far into a woman's mouth (19%). More violent behaviors were rarely depicted. In response to these violent behaviors, women responded neutrally (61%), positively (12%), or first appearing to be in displeasure then switching to expressing pleasure (20%). Relative to depiction of coerced sex, 6% of both men and women were depicted as not initially wanting to engage in sexual activity. Less than 1% of the scenes depicted both men and women actors as intoxicated. Although scenes of being manipulated were rare, women (5%) were depicted as being manipulated more frequently than men (1%).

One criticism of most heterosexual-oriented sexually explicit films is that they do not represent the unique individuality of sexual expression or how women experience erotic fulfillment. Very little focus is on relationships, emotional intimacy, nonsexual aspects of life, or the woman's sexual satisfaction. Rarely are lovers shown massaging each other's shoulders or whispering, "I love you." Nor do lovers ask each other questions such as "Is this OK?" or "What can I do to help you feel more pleasure?" (Castleman, 2004). Some criticize these films as reinforcing an unhealthy and unrealistic image of sexuality: that men are all-powerful and that women are submissive objects, deriving all sexual satisfaction from male domination. Further, the films can also give a false impression of how sex should be experienced and how bodies should look. They can give an impression that all men have large penises and that women derive more pleasure from large penises despite that research shows that most women indicate that a larger penis does not increase their ability to experience an orgasm (Costa et al., 2012).

The Representation of Female and Male Orgasms in Mainstream Sexually Explicit Videos: Realistic or Fantasy?

Experiencing orgasm is a highly valued sexual expression that is a physiological reflex yet also has symbolic, personal, interpersonal, and sociocultural components and meanings. Orgasm can provide pleasure but also cause distress and difficulty, particularly among women. Given that research has shown that exposure to media can influence one's sexual scripts such as sexuality-related attitudes, beliefs, and behavior, it may be possible that media representations can shape an individual's understandings and expectations of orgasm (Brown, 2002; Bryant & Oliver, 2009; Simon & Gagnon, 1984, 1986). Pornography, being explicit, widely used, and easily accessible, is an important medium for examining the representation of female and male orgasms, yet the depictions of orgasms in pornography have not generally been investigated.

This study examined the ways in which female and male orgasms are represented in mainstream pornography. Researchers at Universite du Quebec a Montreal (Seguin et al., 2018) reviewed *PornHub's* 50 most viewed videos of all time (mean views = 29,843,812) and coded them for frequency of female and male orgasms (overt or ambiguous), orgasm-inducing sexual behaviors including clitoral stimulation, and auditory (verbal, vocal) and visual (bodily) indicators of orgasm. The mean time of the videos was 16 minutes and 29 seconds. Forty-five videos depicted sexual activity between a man and a woman; the remaining five showed group sex. The major findings include:

Female Orgasm

■ One fifth of the women were shown experiencing an orgasm: 20 overt orgasms and 8 ambiguous orgasms. Of the 20 overt orgasms, 45% were induced through vaginal intercourse, 35% through anal intercourse, 5% through oral sex, and the remaining 15% from a combination of sexual behaviors.

■ Only one fourth of female orgasms involved direct or indirect clitoral or vulva stimulation.

■ Most commonly depicted orgasm indicators were moaning (in 100% of orgasms), followed by facial contortions (90%), and hyperventilation (85%). The least represented indicator was squirting (5%) and absence of breathing during the pre-orgasmic phase (55%).

■ Female orgasm was the final event of sex in only 1 of 39 sexual encounters in which at least one partner experienced orgasm.

Male Orgasm

■ Four fifths of the men were shown experiencing an orgasm. Of the 39 male orgasms, 51% were ultimately induced (i.e., the "final" sexual behavior accompanying orgasm) by self-stimulation of the penis, 26% were induced by vaginal intercourse, 8% by manual stimulation of the penis by the partner, 5% by oral sex, 5% by anal intercourse, and 5% through other means (e.g., penis between breasts).

■ The most frequent indicators of orgasm were the presence of semen (external ejaculation = 72%; internal ejaculation = 18%), followed by moaning (87.2%) and hyperventilation (74%). Facial indicators or orgasm (eyes closed, facial contortions) was the least frequent indicator of orgasms at 10%.

■ Male orgasm was the final event of sex in 94.9% of encounters during which at least one partner experienced orgasm.

The researchers concluded that the finding that the women experienced orgasm most commonly through penile or anal penetration without additional clitoral stimulation supports the cultural "coital imperative discourse" (McPhillips et al., 2001) in which penile-vaginal intercourse is considered the most desired, typical, and "normal" behavior, and that most female orgasms are induced solely by penetration. Hence, non-coital behaviors are not considered as a valuable and effective component of sexual interactions for women. Such depiction also supports a false fantasy of how women experience orgasm during partnered sex and is contrary to research on women's experiences with coital orgasm. An analysis of 33 studies conducted over 80 years has revealed that only about one quarter of women reliably experience orgasm through intercourse (Lloyd, 2006). The depictions found in this study also support the connection of male masculinity and sexual prowess, in that the sexual scripts says that women's orgasms are result of men's sexual techniques.

Think Critically

1. Did any of the findings surprise you? Explain if they did or not.
2. Do you believe that watching this type of pornography actually will influence how both individuals behave sexually?
3. Given what the study found, what types of sexual scripts for sexually explicit videos would you create if given the chance?

Other myths portrayed by the videos are that all women remove their hair in the genital and anal areas and that women can experience orgasm easily and from almost any intercourse position. (See Think About It "The Representation of Female and Male Orgasms in Mainstream Sexually Explicit Videos: Realistic or Fantasy?")

As women have become increasing consumers of SEV, the desire for videos that reflect a feminist perspective and emphasize female pleasure and mutual respect has also increased. SEV that reflect feminist values "are about showing an authentic representation of human sexuality" (Lust, quoted in Ryan, 2017) instead of an emphasis on female genitals and body parts. Called **femme porn**, these feminist-values videos typically involve women in their production, have a female lead or dominant character, and have story lines that depict clear verbal consent, emotional intimacy, and equality between the sexes. The videos are less male-centered, void of aggression or violence, and more reflective of women's erotic fantasies. Further, they cast women that represent different ages, body types, races, and ethnicities, and produce SEV focused on straight and LGBTQ+ couples (Ryan, 2017).

Gay and lesbian sexually explicit films differ somewhat from heterosexual-focused films. Gay porn typically features attractive, young, muscular, "well-hung" men and focuses on the eroticism of the male body. Lesbian-explicit films usually depict realistic sexual interactions with a range of body types and both butch (notably masculine in manner or appearance) and femme styles (traditional expressions of femininity). Sex between men is rarely shown in heterosexual films, presumably because it would make heterosexual men uncomfortable. But heterosexual-focused films may sometimes portray sex between women because many heterosexual men find such depictions sexually arousing.

Beyond any negative or positive attitudes toward sexually explicit videos, many people wonder what type of a person chooses to be a "porn star." In general, actresses in the adult video entertainment industry are viewed more negatively than typical women. This stereotyped perception of adult video performers and sex workers, in general, is called the "damaged goods" hypothesis. This hypothesis has not been based on scientific studies but comes from public perception. It contends, for example, that actresses in the sexually explicit video industry have come from extremely bad backgrounds, are less psychologically healthy than nonperformer women, are drug abusers, and were abused as children. However, these perceptions lack scientific support. To address this void, a study was conducted to compare the self-reports of 177 "porn actresses" to a matched sample of women based on age, ethnicity, and marital status (Griffith et al., 2013). The study found that the actresses were more likely to consider themselves bisexual, had first sex at an earlier age, had more sexual partners, were more concerned about contracting an STI, and enjoyed sex more than the matched sample. However, there was no difference in child sexual abuse. Porn actresses had higher levels of self-esteem, positive feelings, social support, sexual satisfaction, and spirituality than nonporn actresses. However, women performers were more likely to have ever used 10 different types of drugs than the comparison group. The researchers concluded by declaring that the findings did not support the "damaged goods" hypothesis. They state that "the majority of indicators of recent functioning suggested that porn actresses are not impaired compared to the matched sample with regard to CSA [child sexual abuse] rates, quality of life, self-esteem, and recent drug use, and that they appear more similar to women not employed as porn actresses than previously thought" (Griffith et al., 2012).

Little is known about the characteristics of men adult film performers. A study was conducted to compare the self-reports of 105 men porn actors to a sample of matched men based on age, ethnicity, and marital status (Griffith et al., 2012). The findings indicated that the actor's first sex was at an earlier age, they had more sexual partners and a higher enjoyment of sex, they were more concerned about contracting an STI, and they were less likely to use a condom during a first-time sexual encounter in comparison to the matched sample of men. The actors also had higher levels of self-esteem and quality-of-life indicators, were more likely to have used five different types of drugs, and were more likely to have used marijuana in the past 6 months than the matched group. There was no difference in the self-report of childhood sexual abuse between the two groups. The researchers concluded that the findings indicate a mixed support for negative stereotypes of men adult film performers.

The Effects of SEV

There are a number of concerns about the effects of sexually explicit material. Beyond what was discussed in the prior section on the Internet and SEV, researchers have

"Western man, especially the Western critic, still finds it very hard to go into print and say: 'I recommend you go and see this because it gave me an erection.'"

—Kenneth Tynan (1927–1980)

questions such as: Does SEV cause people to engage in "deviant" behavior? Is it a form of sex discrimination against women? And finally, does it cause violence against women (Mikkola, 2019)?

Sexual Expression   People who view SEV usually recognize it as fantasy; they use it as a release from their everyday lives. Exposure to such material temporarily encourages sexual expression and may activate a person's *typical* sexual behavior pattern or enhance experimentation.

For example, a study of 280 men examined whether time spent in a laboratory viewing films of one man and one woman engaging in consensual intercourse, called visual sexual stimuli (VSS) in this study, was related to sexual responsiveness felt in a laboratory versus responses with a sexual partner (Prause & Pfaus, 2015). The men who reported viewing more VSS in their own life indicated higher sexual arousal to films in the laboratory and self-reported erectile functioning with a partner was not related to the number of hours weekly viewing VSS. And the men who viewed VSS more reported stronger desire for sex with a partner and solo sexual behaviors. The researchers concluded that men's sexual arousal may not be impaired by watching VSS at one's home and that the data "suggests that those who view more VSS likely have a higher sexual drive and experience a stronger response to standardized VSS than those who view less VSS" (p. 95).

A study of 4,600 young people, aged 15–25, living in the Netherlands found that there was a direct association between watching sexually explicit media and a variety of sexual behaviors—in particular, adventurous behaviors—but the association was small (Hald et al., 2013). Given this, the researchers concluded that the "data suggest that other factors such as personal disposition—especially sexual sensation seeking—rather than consumption of sexually explicit material may play a more important role in a range of sexual behaviors of adolescents and young adults" (quoted in Molnar, 2013).

SEV deal with fantasy sex, not sex as we know it in the context of human relationships. This sex usually takes place in a world in which people and situations are defined in exclusively sexual terms. People are stripped of their nonsexual connections. They are interested in SEV for a number of reasons. First, they enjoy the sexual sensations erotica arouses; it can be a source of intense pleasure. For example, research has shown that in a laboratory study, both heterosexual men and women demonstrated significant increases, but no differences between both sexes, in sexual arousal during viewing female-oriented and male-oriented sexually explicit videos (Landry et al., 2016). Masturbation or other sexual activities, pleasurable in themselves, may accompany the use of SEV or follow it. Second, since the nineteenth century, SEM has been a source of sexual information and knowledge. Eroticism generally is hidden from view and discussion. Because the erotic aspects of sexuality are rarely talked about, SEM can fill the void. Third, sexually explicit material, like fantasy, may provide an opportunity for people to rehearse sexual activities. Fourth, reading or viewing SEM to obtain pleasure or to enhance one's fantasies or masturbatory experiences may be regarded as safer sex.

Sex therapist Barbara Keesling (2006) states that she often recommends the use of SEV to women who experience low sexual desire and sexual arousal problems. She notes that "women can sometimes learn to become more aroused by retraining themselves in the ability to feel physical arousal at the sight of sexually explicit images." Keesling also states that since some women may "shut down" because of their belief that some SEV may be disgusting, they should try to find material that is both acceptable and arousing to them. Men are cautioned that SEV are typically all-genital and that such focus can cause problems in sexual expression with others; they should not buy into the idea that sex should occur as it does in most adult films. Medical writer Michael Castleman (2004) suggests the following for men, although his advice could also apply to women:

> Stop trying to imitate what you see in pornography—the rushed, mechanical sex that's entirely focused on the genitals. Instead, cultivate the opposite of porn: leisurely, playful, creative, whole-body, massage-based lovemaking that includes the genitals, but is not obsessed with them.

"The only thing pornography has been known to cause is solitary masturbation."

—Gore Vidal (1925–2012)

"Whatever you choose, however many roads you travel, I hope that you choose not to be a lady. I hope you will find some way to break the rules and make a little trouble out there. And I also hope that you will choose to make some of that trouble on behalf of women."

—Nora Ephron (1941–2012)

think
about it

Sexually Explicit Video Use in Romantic Couples: Beneficial or Harmful?

The impact of watching sexually explicit videos (SEV) by individuals has been widely studied. However, what about couples? Is SEV use related to couple sexual and relationship quality?

This box highlights the major findings of studies of SEV and couples, followed with a brief summary of a sample of other reports. As varied terms are used in these studies, we use the terms used in the specific study. An association between two study variables, such as SEV use and relationship commitment, does not show cause and effect. For example, the use of SEV may contribute to less relationship commitment or a weaker relationship commitment may lead to more SEV use. As you will see, the studies show mixed results.

Four hundred and four primarily heterosexual students from a large U.S. university were assessed to determine their expectations for pornography use while in a committed relationship or while married (Olmstead et al., 2013). Here are the major findings, followed by a few of the student comments:

- Seventy percent of men and 46% of women reported circumstances (alone or with a partner) in which pornography use is acceptable.

- About one quarter of men and women viewed pornography use unacceptable because they were in a committed relationship.

- Five percent and 13% of men and women, respectively, reported that pornography use is unacceptable in any situation.

- The acceptance was more conditional for women than men. Women were less accepting if pornography use became habitual and "addictive" and wanted to protect the quality of their partner's continued love, respect, and commitment.

- Many believed watching pornography alone or together would enhance the relationship.

- Among those accepting pornography, many comments focused on viewing pornography to improve the quality of their sexual relationship and add "spice" to the sexual and couple relationship.

- Among those not accepting pornography, comments largely focused on a belief that pornography was not necessary since they had a partner to fulfill their sexual needs and that their partner used pornography because of deficits in the partner or the relationship.

"My expectation is for each of us to use proper discretion. Yes, I think it is okay for each of us to view them while we are alone or together. I think it is completely normal for someone to be turned on or sexually attracted to the way someone else looks. I admit that I am at times. But at the same time there is a bold line of discretion when a harmless couple minutes turns into a couple hours habit."

—18-year-old woman (p. 631)

"Viewing these materials could help the relationship. A circumstance in which you can view these alone is if you want to surprise your loved one with a new move that you couldn't think of. To watch it together can help you think of another way to have sex, like coming up with different positions."

—18-year-old man (p. 630)

"Viewing porn can be potentially dangerous to a relationship. If viewed alone, without a partner knowing, it can create secrets in the relationship and could be their first step to cheating. It could, however, be used as a way to spice up things in the bedroom if viewed together."

—22-year-old man (p. 628)

"Personally, I don't believe it's bad or it's good. Sexually explicit material simply shows human sexuality put into action. One partner or the other can view it as long as both consent to the sexually explicit material. However, it should not take away from the overall passion of the relationship, and if it does then it has become excessive."

—20-year-old woman (p. 630)

"Sexually explicit material should not be in a marriage or a relationship. That adds additional stress to be perfect or compare yourself to the people that your partner is fantasizing about. You shouldn't view them even together, because sometime down the road it will cause problems whether it be addiction, jealousy, or infidelity."

—18-year-old man (p. 631)

Higher frequencies of SEM use were related to less sexual and relationship satisfaction among a sample of 782 college students (Morgan, 2011). A Canadian study of 340 women found that those women who believed that their partners were honest about their pornography use reported higher levels of relationship satisfaction. Mutual pornography use was not associated with higher levels of relationship satisfaction (Resch & Alderson, 2013).

A sample (N = 430) of Canadian and American men and women in heterosexual relationships in which SEV use was used by a least one partner was recruited though online and offline sources to assess their perceived outcomes of SEV use for each couple member and for their relationship (Kohut et al., 2017). For this sample, "no negative effects" was the most commonly reported consequence of reported SEV use. Perceived positive effects of SEV use included: improved communication, more sexual experimentation, enhanced sexual comfort. Perceived negative effects—which were reported much less frequently than positive impacts—included: unrealistic expectations, decreased sexual interest in partner, and increased insecurity. The researchers noted that "while we have emphasized the predominant positive . . . effects reported in this sample, we have also revealed considerable information that suggests different ways that pornography may be harmful in some relationships." (p. 600)

Lastly, a large study of 3,313 heterosexual, mixed-sex couples examined selected factors associated with pornography use and relationship satisfaction (Mass et al., 2018). Findings revealed that associations between pornography use and relationship satisfaction differed by one's level of pornography satisfaction and anxious attachment (amount of anxious feeling toward the relationship). From the study findings, the researchers suggested that it would be helpful for practitioners who work with heterosexual couples to address how women are portrayed in pornography so that both partners agree with the types of sexual behaviors they find acceptable to view. The researchers also state that:

> Further, in a couple, the partners should be encouraged to discuss pornography use with each other to establish ground rules for whether such behavior would constitute a betrayal to the relationship in order to mitigate issues that may rise from pornography use. (p. 780)

Think Critically

1. Did any of the study findings concur with or dispute your beliefs about SEV? Explain.
2. If you are in relationship (or imagine you are), how would you feel about using SEV alone, or with your partner? If your partner used SEV?
3. In your view, does the use of SEV among couples have more positive or negative outcomes? Explain.

Some contemporary video games, such as Grand Theft Auto, have strong, suggestive sexual messages.

©Paul Sakuma/AP Images

Among some romantic couples, the use of SEV occurs by individual partners or with both partners jointly. Studies have been conducted on the relationship of video use in couples and components of the romantic relationship such as sexual and relationship satisfaction. To find out what the studies found, see Think About It "Sexually Explicit Video Use in Romantic Couples: Beneficial or Harmful?"

With the increasing availability of sexual videos, a new label for high-frequency use has emerged in the popular media and clinical practice: porn addiction. Related to the term *sex addiction,* proponents who espouse this label believe that "excessive use" of porn leads directly to individual breakdown such as job loss and divorce. This label is rarely used by scientists who study high-frequency sexual behavior, and many actually reject the label. The latest edition of the American Psychiatric Association's manual on mental disorders, the *Diagnostic and Statistical Manual of Mental Disorders, Fifth Edition* (*DSM-5*) does not include porn addiction, illustrating the contention that it may not even exist. Clinical psychologist David Ley and colleagues (Ley et al., 2014) examined the scientific literature dealing with SEV use, concluding that there is insufficient scientific evidence to support this model. Simply because someone frequently repeats a behavior does not mean it is a problem and certainly not an addiction. Whenever negative outcomes follow such behaviors, the impact of other factors such as relationship status and culture must first be examined. Persons using visual sexual stimuli (VSS) report being more aroused by VSS as well as reporting greater sexual desire. Ley and colleagues state that:

> the ability to label VSS use as addictive appears to serve sociocultural functions. The label supports moralistic judgments, the stigmatization of sexual minorities, and suppression of certain sexual expressions and behaviors. The concept of porn addiction is one mechanism to exert social control over sexuality as expressed or experienced through modern technological means. (p. 101)

Sexual Aggression In 1970, the President's Commission on Pornography and Obscenity concluded that pornography did not cause harm or violence. It recommended that all legislation restricting adult access to it be repealed as inconsistent with the First Amendment.

In the 1980s, President Ronald Reagan established a new pornography commission under Attorney General Edwin Meese. In 1986, the Attorney General's Commission on Pornography stated that "the most prevalent forms of pornography" were violent; it offered no evidence, however, to substantiate its assertion (U.S. Attorney General's Commission on

Pornography [AGCOP], 1986). There is, in fact, no evidence that the majority of sexually explicit material is violent; actually, very little contains aggression, physical violence, or rape, as shown in the Klaassen and Peter (2014) study cited earlier.

In the 1970s, feminists and others working to increase rape awareness began to call attention to the violence against women portrayed in the media. They found rape themes in sexually explicit material especially disturbing, arguing that those images reinforced rape myths. Again, however, there is no evidence that nonviolent sexually explicit material is associated with actual sexual aggression against women. Even the conservative commission on pornography agreed that nonviolent sexually explicit material had no such effect (AGCOP, 1986). It did assert that "some forms of sexually explicit materials bear a causal relationship . . . to sexual violence," but it presented no scientific proof.

A review of research studies and violent crime data was conducted to determine any influence of pornography on sexual aggression (Ferguson & Hartley, 2009). The review found that evidence for a causal relationship between exposure to pornography and sexual aggression was slim and inconsistent. Further, at the time of the study, the U.S. rate for rape was decreasing and the availability and consumption of pornography were increasing, as also occurred in most industrial countries. From the review, the researchers concluded that "Considered altogether, the available data about pornography consumption and rape rates in the United States seem to rule out a causal relationship, at least with respect to pornography availability causing an increase in the incidence of rape." The researchers suggested that the available research and official statistics might actually provide evidence of a catharsis effect of pornography; that is, the use of pornography might actually be a way of alleviating sexual aggression. However, they point out that the data cannot scientifically be used to determine that pornography has a cathartic effect on rape behavior. As we have previously noted in this book, a correlation between two variables does not show cause and effect.

Contact with sexually explicit material is a self-regulated choice, and research on factors related to such self-directed behavior is very limited: "Existing findings by and large fail to confirm fears of strong antisocial effects of self-directed exposure to sexually explicit media" (Fisher & Barak, 2001). Despite some of these more recent findings, whether violent sexually explicit material causes sexual aggression toward women remains a fractious issue.

Feminist Views of Pornography Since the 1980s, feminists have been divided over the issue of SEV. One segment of the feminist movement, which identifies itself as antipornography, views SEV as inherently degrading and dehumanizing to women. Many in this group believe that SEV provides the basis for women's subordination by turning them into sex objects. They argue that SEV inhibits women's attainment of equal rights by encouraging the exploitation and subordination of women.

To help further understand any possible harmful effects of SEV use among men, an experimental study examined the relationship between viewing two different types of nonviolent pornography and attitudes toward the porn actress and women in general (Skorska et al., 2018). Eighty-two undergraduate college men were randomly assigned to watch video clips of erotic pornography (non-degrading, nonviolent, consensual), degrading pornography (debasing, dehumanizing, nonviolent), and a news clip (control). The study found that exposure to degrading pornography generated the strongest hostile sexist beliefs and the greatest amount of objectification of the women. The researchers concluded that ". . . pornography use may not be generally harmful or harmless, but the effect of pornography exposure may depend on the type of pornography and the specific outcome" (p. 261).

Feminist and other critics of this approach point out that it has an antisexual bias that associates sex with exploitation. Sexually explicit images, rather than specifically sexist images, are singled out. Furthermore, discrimination against and the subordination of women in Western culture have existed since ancient times, long before the rise of sexually explicit material. The roots of subordination lie far deeper. The elimination of sexual depictions of women would not alter discrimination against women significantly, if at all. Sex researchers William Fisher and Clive Davis, in their review of research on the impact of SEV, state that sexual scientists are against any anti-woman attitudes and aggression that some people fear would result from experience with SEV. They suggest that remedies for such attitudes and

"My reaction to porno films is as follows: After the first ten minutes, I want to go home and screw. After the first twenty minutes, I never want to screw anything as long as I live."

—Erica Jong (1942–)

"What's wrong with appealing to prurient interests? We appeal to killing interest."

—Lenny Bruce (1925–1966)

behavior linked to SEV could be achieved through education, policies and laws, and social change, for example (Fisher & Davis, 2007). However, they also state:

> The inconsistent evidence connecting pornography with harm would indicate that efforts to fight pornography as a way of combating anti-woman attitudes and anti-woman aggression would not effectively bring about the sought-after result.

Some feminist theory contends that SEV further the subordination of women by training men, and women also, to view women as sex objects over which men should have control. Researchers at Western University in Canada tested the view that SEV are associated with nonegalitarian attitudes within a large American sample by using data from the General Social Survey (GSS), a personal interview survey that has been conducted in the United States every 1 or 2 years since 1973 (Kohut et al., 2016). The study sample was 10,946 American males and 14,101 American females from all of the GSS surveys. The findings did not support the nonegalitarian attitude hypotheses: In fact, pornography users had more egalitarian attitudes toward women in positions of power, toward women working outside the home, and toward abortion than those who did not view pornography. The researchers stated that although other variables may also help explain the correlational findings, "the attitudinal differences [between users and nonusers] suggest that many pornography users may be useful allies in the struggles that women face in obtaining public office, economic independence (and perhaps equal pay), and reproductive autonomy and bodily integrity" (p. 7).

Leonore Tiefer (2004), sex researcher and therapist who is a primary spokesperson for newer views of women's sexuality, states that sexually explicit materials can contribute to women's sexual power. She notes that empowerment, not protection, is the path to sexual growth in women. Tiefer states that:

> if we accept that women's sexuality has been shaped by ignorance and shame and is just beginning to find new opportunities and voices for expression, then now is exactly the wrong time to even think about campaigns of suppression. Suppressing pornography will harm women struggling to develop their own sexualities.

Child Pornography   Child pornography is a form of child sexual exploitation. Children used for the production of sexually explicit materials, who are usually between the ages of 6 and 16, are typically motivated by friendship, interest in sexuality, offers of money, or threats. Younger children may be unaware that their photographs are being used sexually. A number of these children are related to the photographer. Many children who have been exploited in this way exhibit distress and poor adjustment; they may suffer from depression, anxiety, and guilt. Others engage in destructive and antisocial behavior.

Digital cameras and smartphones, plus the ability to download photographs onto computers, have made this into what some call the "golden age of child pornography." Children and teenagers have been reported taking pictures of each other and posting them on the Internet or sending them to each other, a practice called "sexting." The fact that the possession of such images is a crime does not deter people from placing or viewing them on the Internet. Laws governing obscenity and child pornography already exist and, for the most part, can be applied to cases involving the Internet to adequately protect minors. Unlike some SEV, child pornography has been found to be patently offensive and therefore not within the zone of protected free speech.

Censorship, Sexually Explicit Material, and the Law

To censor means to examine in order to suppress or delete anything considered objectionable. **Censorship** occurs when the government, private groups, or individuals impose their moral or political values on others by suppressing words, ideas, or images they deem offensive. Obscenity, as noted previously, is the state of being contrary to generally accepted standards of decency or morality. During the first half of the twentieth century, under American obscenity laws, James Joyce's *Ulysses* and the works of D. H. Lawrence were prohibited, Havelock Ellis's *Studies in the Psychology of Sex* was banned, nude paintings were removed from gallery and museum walls, and everything but chaste kisses was banned from the movies for years.

The U.S. Supreme Court decisions in the 1950s and 1960s eliminated much of the legal framework supporting literary censorship on the national level. But censorship continues to flourish on the state and local levels, especially among schools and libraries. The women's health book *The New Our Bodies, Ourselves* has been a frequent object of attack because of its feminist perspective and descriptions of lesbian sexuality. The American Library Association Office for Intellectual Freedom yearly compiles a list of the Top 10 Most Challenged Books (The Association, n.d.) states that they tracked 377 challenges of books in 2019; the vast majority of challenges requested that the books be removed from libraries and schools. Among the most challenged books include *George* which features a transgender woman, *A Day in the Life of Marlon Brando,* which deals with same-sex marriage, and *Sex is a Funny Word,* which discusses gender identity. Judy Blume's books for teenagers, J. K. Rowling's *Harry Potter* series, and the *Sports Illustrated* swimsuit issue are also regular items on banned-publications lists. And exhibits of the photographs taken by the late Robert Mapplethorpe have been strenuously attacked by the more conservative groups for "promoting" homoeroticism.

A Day in the Life of Marlon Bundo, a children's picture book that has been challenged and banned in libraries for LGBTQ+ content, presents a story about a boy bunny who falls in love with another boy bunny.
Chronicle Books

Obscenity Laws Sexually explicit material itself is not illegal, but materials defined as legally obscene are. It is difficult to arrive at a legal definition of obscenity for determining whether a specific illustration, photograph, novel, or video is obscene. Traditionally, U.S. courts have considered material obscene if it tended to corrupt or deprave its user. Over the years, the law has been debated in a number of court cases. This process has resulted in a set of criteria for determining what is obscene:

- The dominant theme of the work must appeal to prurient sexual interests and portray sexual conduct in a patently offensive way.

- Taken as a whole, the work must be without serious literary, artistic, political, or scientific value.

- A "reasonable" person must find the work, when taken as a whole, to possess no social value.

> *"I would like to see an end to all obscenity laws in my lifetime. I don't know that it will happen, but it's my goal. If I can leave any kind of legacy at all, it will be that I helped expand the parameters of free speech."*
> —Larry Flynt (1942–2021)

The problem with these criteria, as well as the earlier standards, is that they are highly subjective. For example, who is a reasonable person? Most of us would probably find that a reasonable person has opinions regarding obscenity that closely resemble our own. Otherwise, we would think that he or she was unreasonable. However, there are many instances in which "reasonable people" disagree about whether material has social value. In 1969, the U.S. Supreme Court ruled, in *Stanley v. Georgia,* that private possession of obscene material in one's home is not illegal (Sears, 1989). This does not, however, apply to child pornography.

As we saw earlier, our evaluation of SEV is closely related to how we feel about such material. Our judgments are based not on reason but on emotion.

Challenges of Research on Sexually Explicit Materials As noted in this chapter and others, most studies related to sexual behavior are correlational, not experimental. That is, they show the association of one variable to another, but do not indicate cause and effect. This limitation is true for the vast majority of studies of SEV and is cited several times in the review of the studies in this chapter. For the most part, the findings of SEV studies are inconsistent and their generalizability is limited, although popular media misrepresents research findings. (See Think About It "What Popular Media Says About Sexually Explicit Videos and Relationships: Supported by Research?") Most often there is lack of sufficient evidence to conclude that watching SEV causes, for example, sexual aggression against women or damage to romantic relationships (Campbell & Kohut, 2017; Kohut et al., 2020;

think about it

What Popular Media Says About Sexually Explicit Videos and Relationships: Supported by Research?

"Since the human body is perfect in all forms, we cannot see it often enough."

—Kenneth Clark (1903–1983)

The public has long been concerned about pornography. A degree of "moral panic" has occurred from fears that sexually explicit material has damaging effects on individuals and romantic couples. The dominant belief, but not exclusively, is that sexually explicit videos (SEV) are harmful and the list of asserted harms is long, including claimed associations of SEV with communism, organized crime, aggression against women, and sexual addiction. Media discussion about the impact of SEV has been a major source of information for the public. This discourse comes from two broad types of media: empirically grounded research on the impact of SEV and the popular media. Each type of media presents evidence, arguments, and assertions that address consequences of SEV viewing on individuals and their relationship, and society in general. However, is there congruence on what the popular media reports and what is found in scientific research (Montgomery-Graham et al., 2015)?

Researchers at Western University, Canada, systematically analyzed popular media messages concerning the impact of pornography on the couple relationship to assess whether these assertions matched conclusions reported in research (Montgomery-Graham et al., 2015). One hundred and one popular media items (30 blogs, 39 magazines, 32 news articles) were analyzed and 138 peer-reviewed research articles from the academic literature were reviewed. The focus was limited to the impact of pornography on heterosexual couples, as the popular media discussion on the impact of pornography on same-sex was relatively scarce.

Fourteen themes emerged from the review of popular media sources examined. The research report presented five of the themes in order of greatest to lesser frequency; each theme appeared in at least 20% of the popular media sources examined. Here is what the study found for each of the themes:

Pornography Addiction

Popular media. Pornography addiction was the most common theme, appearing in 53% of all items. Pornography addiction is presented with considerable certainty and statements like "porn is addictive" and addiction terms like "cravings," "increased tolerance," "needs for more hits," and "withdrawal" experiences. Discussions focused on perceived negative outcomes resulting from "pornography addiction" such as detachment from their partner, changing their interest in the couple's typical sexual routine, or offending or horrifying the "nonaddicted" partner. Most depictions were that men will have pornography addiction and that the women will bear the burden of the addiction.

Scientific literature. Because of a lack of peer-reviewed, scientific evidence to establish "pornography addiction" as a mental disorder, no recognized diagnostic category of "pornography addiction" is found in the medical, psychological, or scientific literature.

The researchers conclude that while some persons may become compulsively and intrusively involved with viewing pornography, popular media use of the term *pornography addiction* to describe such involvement seems to be unjustified.

Pornography Is Good for Sexual Relationships

Popular media. Thirty-five percent of the data items analyzed stated that pornography use enhanced heterosexual sexual relationships such as pornography's ability to add interest in a couple's sex life. Some popular media mentioned that women in particular may watch pornography alone as a source of empowerment and sexual exploration to add to the couple's sexual relationship. Some media sources note that coupled viewing of pornography improves relationships but solitary use harms them.

Scientific literature. In general, media's assertion that pornography's sexual arousal and interest increases information, reduces sexual anxiety, and has the potential to empower its viewers is consistent with research literature. Pornography users and their partners are more likely to report more positive perceptions of pornography use on their relationships than negative effects. However, these conclusions are not always consistent with studies that suggest that pornography may lower relationship satisfaction or there are no positive or negative effects on individual's ratings of their partner's sexual skills.

Pornography Use as a Form of Adultery

Popular media. The theme that pornography use is a form of adultery was in 26% of the items; 41% of these were from clearly religiously affiliated sources. Popular media discussions seemed to be directed toward women who perceive their male partner's pornography use as adultery; none of the items mentioned men lamenting their female partner's use of pornography as cheating. Some items discussed the significance of secretive use of pornography as a form of deception.

Research literature. The contention that "viewing pornography is a form of adultery" is frequency declared in popular media as self-evident without a need for research support. In general, some studies suggest that neither men nor women believe that viewing pornography represents adultery. Research has shown that heterosexual women report higher relationship satisfaction when their male partners are honest with them about their pornography use.

Male Partner's Pornography Use Makes Women Feel Inadequate

Popular media. Twenty-three percent of the items conveyed the theme "male partner's pornography use makes women feel inadequate." Only 3% discussed the effect of pornography on men's feelings of adequacy. Popular media's discussion centers on women's feelings of being physically inadequate in comparison to the women appearing in pornography.

Research literature. Research findings generally concur with the belief that a partner's viewing of pornography can have a negative impact on one's self-perception of attractiveness, although that appears to be true for only a sizable minority. There is less clarity on whether pornography use influences perceptions of a sexual partner, though the available evidence does not appear to indicate this as an inevitable impact of viewing pornography.

Pornography Use Changes Partner's Expectations About Sexual Behavior

Popular media. The theme that pornography changes a partner's expectations about sexual behavior appeared in 22% of the items. A noticeable theme is that men wish to replicate the sexual behaviors shown in pornography (e.g., ejaculation on the woman's face or anal sex) or an expectation that behaviors seen in the pornography are typical and desired by women. For example, a few items mentioned men wanting anal sex and women not wanting anal sex.

Research literature. Few research studies have convincingly shown that viewing pornography induces changes in sexual behavior. Further, experimental evidence has suggested that pornography use does not lead to the enactment of novel sexual behaviors by most persons, although recent experimental research has found that occurs under certain circumstances. A study found that female coital clitoral stimulation was more likely to occur after viewing a video demonstrating this behavior. No research was found indicating how often facial ejaculation is sought by those watching pornography or how women feel about it. Research is beginning to find that some people acquire an interest in, or initiate some sexual behaviors depicted in popular media, likely within what the individual and couple perceive to be acceptable.

Think Critically

1. Have you noticed the themes described in this study in any reading about SEV in popular media? If so, did you believe them?
2. If you had read the SEV themes, did what they say impact your attitudes or sexual behaviors?
3. Were you surprised about the conflict of the popular media depiction of the research findings relative to SEV viewing and relationship impact? Explain.

Ferguson & Hartely, 2009; Montgomery-Graham et al., 2015; AGCOP, 1986). Recall from the discussion of sexual aggression, Fisher and Barak (2001) stated that "Existing findings by and large fail to confirm fears of strong antisocial effects of self-directed exposure to sexually explicit media." Sex researchers (Campbell & Kohut, 2017; Montgomery-Graham et al., 2015) have made recommendations for strengthening future research on the effects of SEV, such as creating a standard definition of pornography, valid and reliable measures of pornography use, longitudinal studies, and experimental research designs that can test hypotheses and draw inferences of the findings. Inadequate measurement of research designs has impeded progress toward legitimizing the findings of research on pornography use. Campbell and Kohut (2017) state that research on sexually explicit videos "need to move beyond a simple 'cause-effect' view of pornography use and relationship outcomes" (p. 9). They contend that pornography use is driven by a variety of possible antecedents (e.g., individual differences, culture, life experiences, gender) and specific contexts (e.g., solitary use, couple use, hidden use, frequency of use), which all may result in varied outcomes and need to be assessed in future research on SEV.

The Issue of Child Protection   In 1988, the United States passed the Child Protection and Obscenity Enforcement Act, which supports stiff penalties for individuals involved in the production, distribution, and possession of child pornography. Since then, the development and distribution of child pornography, as well as minors' access to online pornography, have been the focus of the U.S. Congress, resulting in the passing of numerous legislative acts.

The Communications and Decency Act of 1996 tried to address the problem of sexual exploitation of children and teens over the Internet by making it a crime to send obscene or indecent messages to minors via e-mail, chat rooms, and websites (Biskupic, 2004). In 1997, the U.S. Supreme Court ruled that the statute was not constitutional because it violated the First Amendment's guarantee of free speech. However, in 2008, the U.S. Supreme Court upheld the Child Obscenity and Pornography Prevention Act of 2003, a law that made it a crime to produce or possess sexually explicit images of children as well as to "pander" to willing audiences through advertising, presenting, distributing, or soliciting such material. Free-speech proponents question whether mainstream movies or innocent photographs of babies and young children, for example, might now be subject to prosecution.

"Congress shall make no law . . . abridging the freedom of speech, or of the press . . ."

—First Amendment to the Constitution of the United States

Another law intended to keep adult material away from Net-surfing children is the Child Online Protection Act (COPA). Passed in 1998, it sought to require Internet users to give an adult ID before accessing a commercial site containing "adult" materials (Miller, 2000). The law has been blocked twice by the U.S. Supreme Court. In January 2009, COPA ended more than a decade after Congress had approved it. The U.S. Supreme Court rejected the government's final effort to revive the law by turning away the appeal without comment ("Internet pornography law dies quietly in Supreme Court," 2009).

With millions of children accessing the Internet from home, serious questions must be asked about their access to certain kinds of information, pictures, graphics, videos, animation, and interactive experiences. Government censorship, academic freedom, constitutionally protected speech, child safety concerns, public health dilemmas—these and other troublesome issues are at the core of the Internet-free-speech debate.

Our inability to find criteria for objectively defining obscenity makes it potentially dangerous to censor such material. We may end up using our own personal standards to restrict speech otherwise guaranteed by the First Amendment. By enforcing our own biases, we could endanger the freedom of others.

● Sex Work and Sex Trafficking

The exchange of sexual behaviors for money and/or goods has been historically called **prostitution**. More recently, instead of the term *prostitute,* the terms *sex worker* and *commercial sex worker* have often been used, particularly by prostitutes, to identify themselves and other work in the "sex industry," such as telephone sex, exotic dancing, Internet sex, live sex shows, erotic webcam performances, and acting in sexually explicit films. Many individuals who enter prostitution do so for monetary gains; hence, prostitution can represent a form of work (Cobbina & Oselin, 2011; Weitzer, 2012). In 2014, the Urban Institute investigated the underground commercial sex economy of eight cities in the United States and estimated that this activity generated between $39.9 million and $290 million, depending on the city. In one city, pimps, men upon whom sex workers are financially and often emotionally dependent, were earning an average of $32,833 per week (Dank et al., 2014). The total amount of money earned from sex work is not possible to accurately determine because most income is not reported as taxable income. One estimate is that $186 billion is earned each year globally and $14.6 billion in the United States ("Prostitution Statistics," 2021).

Further, *prostitution* is a pejorative or moral term that is basically negative and typically refers to women only (Herdt & Polen-Petit, 2014). *Sex work* is a term preferred by many prostitutes that is more frequently being used by health and sexuality-related professionals. We prefer and use *sex work* and *sex workers* to describe prostitution and prostitutes, as these terms are more objective and represent both women and men. *Prostitution* will on occasion be used, particularly if it is the term used in cited reports and research. Among the varied types of sex work, the following discussion will focus on "prostitution" given its historical and current societal concern and controversy. And nearly all of the prior research and writings about sex work have focused on female sex workers; hence, the majority of our discussion reflects this gender bias.

Boys and girls as well as men and women, including cross-dressers and transgender persons, are sex workers. By far the most common form of sex work is women selling sex to men. The second most common is male sex workers making themselves available to men. A less common form is males selling sex to females. Selling sex between two women is rare. A growing international market of human sex slaves has fueled the economies of developing countries and spawned a multibillion-dollar industry commonly referred to as "sex trafficking" (see Think About It "Sex Trafficking: A Modern-Day Slavery").

Male customers of female sex workers, called "johns," represent a wide range of occupations, ethnicities, ages, and marital statuses. Although the seeking of paid sex is often considered a natural part of the masculine sexual experience, research has shown that most men do not seek sex workers and very few are regular customers. Men go to sex workers for many reasons. Some want to experience a certain sexual behavior that their partner is unwilling to try, or they may not have or desire a regular partner. Others are seeking a "safe space" where

think
about it

Sex Trafficking: A Modern-Day Slavery

An estimated 4.8 million persons globally are trapped in forced sexual exploitation. Sex trafficking, a form of human trafficking, is being called a "modern-day slavery" that exists throughout the world, including the United States. Mostly women, but also men and children, are being forced to perform commercial sex against their will. Trafficking of women and children for commercial sex is considered to be the fastest growing global criminal activity despite the fact that international law and laws of over 100 countries criminalize sex trafficking. In 2016, about 1 million children and 3.8 million adults worldwide were forced into sexual exploitation; 99% of them were girls and women (United Nations International Labor Organization, 2017; 2021). In 2019, the Polaris Project's National Human Tracking Hotline (2020) received 8,248 contacts of situations of sex trafficking and 14,597 contacts from individual victims and survivors of sex trafficking, which included escort services, illicit massage, health and beauty, and forced participation in sexually explicit videos. The Polaris Project notes these contacts likely represent only a small number of actual sex trafficking in the United States.

Many types of persons can be forced into sex work: U.S. citizens, foreign nationals, children, teens, adult men and women, and LGBTQ+ individuals. Traffickers often target homeless and runaway youth who are survivors of parental and domestic abuse or sexual abuse. Sex trafficking exists in various venues, such as fake massage businesses, online escort services, and residential brothels, and at truck stops, hotels, motels, and strip clubs. To lure persons into sex work, traffickers use many methods, such as violence, lies, coercion, debt bondage, and a promise of a high-paying job. Some may promise a romantic relationship, during which they may initially establish a false love. During this period, they promise a better life, give gifts, and share sexual and physical intimacy. However, eventually, to keep the person in commercial sex work, the trafficker often resorts to various control tactics, including physical and emotional abuse, confiscation of identification and money, and isolation. The victims may be involved in sex work for a few days or weeks, or may remain in the same sex trafficking situation for years (Polaris Project, 2020).

Survivors of sex trafficking face numerous medium- to long-term physical, sexual, and mental health problems, such as drug and alcohol addiction, physical injuries (broken bones, burns, vaginal/rectal tearing), traumatic brain injury, depression, posttraumatic stress disorder, sexually transmitted infections, sterility, miscarriages, and forced abortions. Some victims may also suffer from traumatic bonding, a form of coercive control in which the perpetrator instills in the victim not only fear but also gratitude for being allowed to live (Oram et al., 2016; U.S. Department of Health & Human Services, 2012).

In the United States, the Trafficking Victims Protection Act (TVPA) of 2000 made human trafficking within the United States a federal crime. The TVPA defines sex trafficking as "the recruitment, harboring, transportation, provision, or obtaining a person for the purposes of a commercial sex act, in which the commercial sex act is induced by force, fraud, or coercion, or which the person induced to perform such an act has not attained 18 years of age." The term *commercial sex act* is defined as any sexual behavior from which anything of value is given or received by any persons (National Human Trafficking Resource Center, 2015). Further, the law allows women trafficked into the United States to receive permanent residence status after 3 years from the issuance of a temporary visa (Victims of Trafficking and Violence Protection Act of 2000). Also, according to U.S. law, Americans caught paying children for sex while in foreign countries can be prosecuted in the United States (National Center for Missing & Exploited Children, 2011). Education, social mobilization and awareness, legal support, social services, psychological counseling, and prosecution of perpetrators are but a few of the strategies that have been used to address sex trafficking. Much more needs to be done to protect the endangered lives of persons who are sexually exploited.

Think Critically

1. In your opinion, what contributes to the demand for child sex workers?

2. What more do you think could be done to address sex trafficking worldwide?

3. What, if any, additional laws should the United States enact to prevent the trafficking of children and women?

they could feel exempt from expectations to display sexual experience, skill, and stamina (Huysamen, 2020). Some desire to have sex with someone having a certain image, such as sexy or very athletic looking, and some customers find that the illicit nature of being with a sex worker is attractive. Some like the anonymity of being sexual with a sex worker: No courting is required, there are no postsex expectations, and it is less entangling than having extrarelational/extramarital sex. Some men with very active sex lives simply want more sexual partners. Nonsexual reasons, such as conversation, companionship, sympathy, and friendship, all which may challenge dominant masculine ideals, can also be motives for seeking sex workers. Finally, some young men go to a sex worker as their first sexual experience (Bernstein, 2001; Brents et al., 2010). A study of 35 male clients of female sex workers in the United Kingdom (Hammond & van Hoff, 2020) explored men's motivations for beginning and continuing to pay for sex with women, most of which were discussed here. From the study findings, the researchers concluded that "The pathologization of men who engage with paid sexual services fails to account for participant's complex, diverse motivations, which be understood in the context of other relationships and gender interactions rather than as a distinct type of interaction" (p. 651). Certainly the reasons mentioned above can also be applicable to men who seek paid sex with men and women who seek paid sex with men or women.

The Prevalence of Sex Work

Determining the number of persons who are sex workers is difficult for many reasons, including different definitions of sex work as well as the secrecy often involved with the accepting of money for sex. A study in the Netherlands found that 3% of women (and 3% of men) in the adult population aged 19–69 reported ever having received money for sex. In other countries, the prevalence is around 1% (Bakker & Vanwesenbeeck, 2006; Vanwesenbeeck, 2013). Some studies can also give us an idea of the prevalence of men purchasing sex from female sex workers, although the numbers may not reflect the true prevalence, because the stigma associated with sex work may result in underreporting. A study of a representative sample of men from around the world found that, on average, about 9–10% of the men had purchased sex from a female sex worker in the past 12 months (Carael et al., 2006). A national probability sample of 6,293 men aged 16–74 years residing in Britain found that 11% had reported ever paying for sex (Jones et al., 2015). And the National Survey of Sexual Health and Behavior (NSSHB) found that 4.3% of men and 0.8% of women reported paying or being paid for their most recent sexual event (Herbenick et al., 2010). The highest paying group was the 50–59 age group, for both men (6.2%) and women (1.6%). For the age group 18–24 years, the percentage of whoever paid for sex was 3.4% for men and 0.9% for women.

COVID-19 The COVID-19 pandemic, with its social distancing efforts, has dramatically impacted sex work nationally and internationally. Many sex workers have had a sharp decrease in either customers or frequency of visits or both, and many are barely able to meet their financial needs (Barry, 2020; Peyser, 2020; Amendral, 2021). In the summer of 2020, 21 people who engaged in sex work in the United States were interviewed about their experiences and health needs (Singer et al., 2020). Because of the pandemic, most reported a decrease in their earnings, although they continued to do in-person sex work even though most had not been tested for COVID-19. Some reported wearing personal protective equipment (PPE) on the way to sex work, but no one acknowledged wearing PPE while doing sex work. Participants were concerned about the risk of having clients and indicated that they would isolate if they contracted COVID. The study researchers note that the British Columbia Ministry of Health (2020) issued safety guidelines for sex workers in July 2020. They recommended that all sexually active persons, including sex workers, should use masks during intercourse, limit face-to-face contact, avoid heavy breathing, and utilize a "glory hole" (a hole in the wall through which oral, anal, or vaginal penetration can occur without face-to-face contact). The researchers concluded that "The U.S. must follow suit and adapt these guidelines to meet COVID-19 prevention needs of sex workers and others who are engaging in sex with people who they are not practicing social distancing with (i.e., someone they live with or someone with whom they have had conversations about reducing COVID-19 exposure)" (p. 2740).

Sex as Work Many women who accept money or drugs for sexual activities do not consider themselves prostitutes. Prostitutes often identify themselves as "working girls" or "sex workers," probably an accurate description of how they perceive themselves in relation to sex. Common but more pejorative terms are *whore* and *hooker*. They are usually sex workers, not because they like anonymous sex and different partners, per se, but because they perceive it as good-paying work. Many sex workers, particularly younger ones, can earn more money from their sex work than other types of work. The financial draw is greater for women, as the demand for them by men is much greater than the demand for male sex workers. Large groups of female sex workers, and to a much lesser degree male sex workers, often "follow the money" and travel or migrate to where large groups of men with money are located. That is, where there is money, there is sex work (Vanwesenbeeck, 2013). They generally do not expect to enjoy sex with their customers and avoid emotional intimacy by drawing boundaries around their emotional selves, thereby dissociating their physical sexuality from their inner selves. Many separate sex as a physical expression for which they are paid from sex as an expression of intimacy and pleasure (Brents et al., 2010). Two sex workers who work in Nevada's legal brothels (see discussion of Nevada's brothels in a following section) talk about the difference between sex at work and sex at home (quoted in Brents et al., 2010). Many sex workers don't kiss their clients; one said, "You don't get personal. Kissing is personal and romantic." In contrast to clients, sex with husbands or boyfriends is where, "I really put my feelings into it, and I give him all my love, you know, I'm giving him me."

Entrance into Sex Work   Many women begin doing sex work in their younger years, even in their early teens. Childhood victimization—sexual molestations, incest, and physical abuse—is often discussed as a background factor in both adolescent girls' and boys' entrance into sex work (Cobbina & Oselin, 2011; Widom & Kuhns, 1996). Sexual abuse increases the likelihood that a preadolescent or an adolescent will become involved in deviant street culture. Physically and sexually abused youths are more likely to be rejected by their conventional peers and to become involved in unhealthy and risky activities. One major reason young people flee home is parental abuse—generally sexual abuse for girls and physical abuse for boys.

Girls usually are introduced into sex work by pimps. Sex workers give their pimps the money they earn; in turn, pimps provide housing, buy them clothes and jewelry, and offer them protection on the streets. Many girls and young women are "sweet-talked" into sex work by promises of money, protection, and companionship. Adolescent sex workers are more likely than adults to have pimps.

Once involved with pimps, women are frequently abused by them. The women also run the risk of abuse and violence from their customers. Sex workers who solicit customers on the streets, called street-based sex workers, are especially vulnerable.

Personal Background and Motivation   Many adult sex workers are women who were targets of early male sexual aggression, had extensive sexual experience in adolescence, were rejected by peers because of sexual activities, and were not given adequate emotional support by their parents. There are high rates of physical and sexual abuse (including intrafamilial abuse) and neglect in their childhoods (Widom & Kuhns, 1996). Often, their parents failed to provide them with a model of affectionate interaction. As a result, as the girls grew up, they tended to be anxious, to feel lonely and isolated, and to be unsure of their own identity. Another common thread running through the lives of most sex workers is an economically disadvantaged background. However, there is a wide range of motivations and backgrounds among those who enter this "oldest profession." As one ex-sex worker notes (quoted in Queen, 2000):

> When I began sex work, I did not expect the range of education and life experience I found in my colleagues. Like many people, I believed prostitution was mainly engaged in by women who have no options. But I ended up working with women who were saving to buy houses, put kids through school, put themselves through school, and start businesses. (p. 4)

Research has shown that adolescent sex workers describe their general psychological state of mind as very negative, depressed, unhappy, or insecure at the time they first entered sex work. Many had run away from home and engaged in sexual risk behaviors. There were high levels of drug use, including alcohol, methamphetamines, marijuana,

"Identifying women as sexual beings whose responsibility is the sexual service of men is the social base for gender specific slavery."

—Kathleen Berry

cocaine, opioids, and heroin, and many of those who became drug addicts later turned to sex work to support their drug habit. Their emotional state made them particularly vulnerable to pimps.

No single motive seems to explain why someone becomes a sex worker. It is probably a combination of environmental, social, financial, and personal factors that leads a woman to this profession. When sex workers describe the most attractive things about life in the sex worker subculture, they describe them in monetary and material terms. One woman sex worker notes, "I said to myself how can I do these horrible things and I said money, money, money" (quoted in Weisberg, 1990). Compared with a minimum-wage job, which may be the only alternative, sex work appears to be an economically rational decision.

Sex workers are aware of the psychological and physical costs. A 15-year longitudinal study of 130 sex workers found that sex work was associated with higher incidences of illness—including STIs, mental health problems, and substance abuse—and death (Ward & Day, 2006). However, a study of 218 sex workers found that the participants reported both positive and negative effects of sex work on their sense of self. The researchers reported that the relationship of sex work and sense of self-worth was complex and that social background factors, work location, and life events and experiences had effects on self-esteem (Benoit et al., 2017). Sex workers fear physical and sexual abuse, HIV and other STIs, harassment, jail, and legal expenses. They are aware as well of the damage done to their self-esteem from stigmatization and rejection by family and society, negative feelings toward men and sex, bad working conditions, lack of a future, and control by pimps. Many do not enjoy being a sex worker, and one international study found that nearly 90% wanted out of sex work (Farley et al., 2003).

In many countries, the availability of sex workers has become part of the tourist economy, with the money paid to sex workers an important part of the national income. In developing countries where social and economic conditions combine with a dominant male hierarchy and acceptance of a sexual double standard, many people in those countries see sex work as a necessary and accepted occupation.

"Prostitutes are degraded and punished by society; it is their humiliation through their bodies—as much as their bodies—which is being purchased."

—Phyllis Chester (1940–)

Because of their inability to screen clients or control their working conditions, street-based sex workers are the most likely of sex workers to be victimized.

©Ingram Publishing/SuperStock

Forms of Female Sex Work   Females sell sex as streetworkers, in brothels and massage parlors, and for escort services that advertise in newspapers and the web. Some academics believe that the great majority of sex workers in the United States live indoor and, for the most part, unnoticed lives.

Street-Based Sex Workers   Estimates vary, but approximately 10% of American sex workers are **street-based sex workers** (Queen, 2000). This type of sex work is usually the first sex work in which adolescents become involved; it is also the type they prefer, despite its being at the bottom of the hierarchy of sex work and having the greatest cultural stigma. Many advertise by dressing provocatively and hanging out at locales noted for sex work. Women working as street-based sex workers are often high school dropouts or runaways who fled abusive homes and went into sex work simply to survive. An interview study of 40 female street sex workers from five U.S. cities showed that adolescent and adult women had different pathways into sex work (Cobbina & Oselin, 2011). For adolescents, many ran away from home to escape childhood victimization, including physical abuse, sexual molestation, and incest. They subsequently became a street sex worker to reclaim control over their sexuality. Ironically, those adolescents who were encouraged to become sex workers by male figures began early to feel disempowered because their work was "managed" by others. Adolescent women who had regular contact with sex workers viewed this type of work as acceptable and glamorous, and they embraced the lifestyle at an early age. The first pathway for the adult-onset street-based sex workers was to support a drug addiction. These women claimed they were morally opposed to becoming a sex worker and reluctant to do so, yet their drug addiction was so powerful that it overrode these beliefs, as they needed money to support their habit. The last pathway among the adult-onset sex workers was fueled by financial instability.

Not all street-based sex workers come out of desperate situations, however; some are married and have satisfactory sexual relationships in their private lives. Because they make their contacts through public solicitation, they are more visible and more likely to be arrested. Without the ability to easily screen their customers, street-based sex workers are more likely to be beaten, robbed, or raped. One study found that more than 95% of street sex workers had been sexually assaulted and 75% had been raped (Farley et al., 2003). The study also found that people often consider sex workers to be "unrapable" or even deserving of being raped. Street-based sex workers are also susceptible to severe mental health problems. A qualitative study of 29 street youths engaged in the sex trade found that they had a high rate of attempted suicide (Kidd & Kral, 2002). Further, most women interviewed in a study of street-bases sex workers in Scotland indicated that their work had a profoundly negative impact on their self-esteem and their life with family, friends, and partners (McKeganey, 2006).

Street-based sex workers suffer more occupational hazards such as assault, kidnapping, threats by a weapon, robbery, and rape than the so-called indoor sex workers of the brothels, massage parlors, and escort services or independent call girls, or Internet purveyors. They have less control over working conditions such as freedom to refuse clients and particular sexual behaviors, are more likely to have been coercively trafficked into sex work, have less access to protective services, and depend more on pimps than indoor workers do (Weitzer, 2005).

In contrast to other types of sex workers, street-based sex workers' sexual activity with clients typically is less varied and shorter (Hock, 2007). Fellatio is their most common activity; less than one quarter of their contacts involve sexual intercourse. In a study of men arrested for soliciting female sex workers in three western U.S. cities, fellatio was the most common behavior experienced in prior contact with a sex worker (Monto, 2001).

Brothels Brothels, traditionally called "houses of prostitution," "whorehouses," and "houses of ill repute," can be found in most large cities but in the United States are legal only in counties with a population below 700,000 in Nevada. A study of women working as sex workers at the Nevada brothels found that, prior to entering the brothels, they had worked as illegal sex workers and wanted relief from the stress of such work, had been working in other legal sex work such as stripping or in adult movies, and had worked in low-paying, service-industry jobs and needed a better-paying job to survive (Brents et al., 2010). Sex work in brothels has higher status than street-based sex work, and it is safer. Indeed, protection from violence is a major advantage of Nevada's legal brothels; they are the safest of all environments in which women sell consensual sex for money (Brents & Hausbeck, 2005). Several safety precautions, such as panic buttons, listening devices, and management surveillance, are used in Nevada brothels (Weitzer, 2005). Further, the Nevada State Board of Health requires the sex workers to be tested for sexually transmitted infections, including monthly testing for HIV and syphilis. Brothels cannot employ a sex worker until medical tests show that the sex worker does not have infectious syphilis, gonorrhea, or chlamydia, nor is infected with HIV. By law, the sex worker must require the patron to use condoms. The prices for sex are negotiated between the sex worker and the client within the sex worker's room. The sex worker can refuse clients, typically by setting the price too high (Martinez, 2016). A major attraction of brothels is their comfortable and friendly atmosphere. In brothels, men can have a cup of coffee or a drink, watch television, or casually converse with the women. Many customers are regulars. Sometimes, they go to the brothel simply to talk or relax rather than to engage in sex. In 2018 there were 20 brothels in Nevada, down from the 36 that operated during the peak years of mid-1980s; many have been replaced by massage parlors that, for some, serve the same purpose as a brothel: sexual pleasure (Montero, 2018).

Researchers from the University of Nevada, Las Vegas, conducted an in-depth study of the women who are sex workers in the Nevada brothels. The findings on the nearly 40 women who were interviewed were published in the book *The State of Sex* (Brents et al., 2010). From

Prostitution is legal and subject to government regulation in several rural counties in Nevada.
©K.M. Cannon/AP Images

the findings, the researchers concluded that "we do not believe that selling sex itself is inherently harmful to women." And they found no evidence of trafficking or women working against their will. They concluded that Nevada's legal brothels are preferable to criminalization of sex workers and that they prevent violence, STIs, and severe exploitation but that improved labor practices are needed. The findings fueled the debate on sex work among those who were critical of the study and believed that sex work exploits women and should be ended (Schmidt, 2011).

Male brothels, often called "stables," are common in Southeast Asia and in some large cities in the United States. These stables are where male sex workers are available for sex with male customers, although there are also some male brothels for female customers, called "stud farms."

Masseuses There are relatively few brothels today; most have been replaced by massage parlors. The major difference between brothels and massage parlors is that brothels present themselves as places specifically dedicated to provide sexual services, whereas some massage parlors try to disguise their intent. Most massage parlors provide only massages. However, some massage parlors are fronts to selling sex and offer customers any type of sexual service they wish for a fee, which is negotiated with the masseuses. But most are "massage and masturbation only" parlors. These so-called M-and-M parlors are probably the most widespread; their primary service is the "local," "hand finishing," or "relief" massage in which there is only masturbation. By limiting sex to masturbation, these parlors are able to avoid legal difficulties, because most criminal sex statutes require genital penetration, oral sex, discussion of fees, and explicit solicitation for criminal prosecution. Women who work in M-and-M parlors are frequently referred to as "hand whores"; these women, however, often do not consider themselves sex workers, although they may go into sex work later. Many masseuses run newspaper and website ads for their services and work on an out-call basis, meeting customers at their hotel rooms or homes.

Call Girls Call girls have the highest status among sex workers, experience less social stigma than other sex workers, and have among the safest working environments, as they can experience more control over their working conditions and whom they have as customers than streetwalkers. They are usually better educated than other sex workers, often come from a middle-class background, and dress fashionably. A call girl's fee is high—much higher than those of a street-based sex worker or masseuse. She operates through contacts and referrals; instead of the street, she takes to the telephone or computer and arranges to meet her customers at the customer's residence or at his hotel room or hers. The call girl is the one, not the agency, who arranges for the sex, thus providing the agency some protection from prosecution. Another major difference between call girls and street-based sex workers is that sex workers usually have fleeting interactions with customers, whereas call girls are much more likely to provide "emotional work," such as counseling and befriending their customers. Further, call girls often have interactions that resemble a dating experience involving conversation and receiving gifts, hugs, kisses, massages, and oral sex from the clients (Weitzer, 2005).

Call girls often work for escort services that advertise through newspapers and the web. Escort agencies supply attractive escorts for social occasions and never advertise that they provide sexual services, although most do. Agencies usually specialize in one type of sex, that is, female-for-male, male-for-male, female-for-female, or male-for-female. Some offer transgender sex workers. Not all escorts work through an agency; some are independent and communicate with clients themselves.

Male Sex Workers

Although there has been extensive research into sex work, most of it concerns females selling sex. Most research on male sex work focuses on street hustlers, the male equivalent of street-bases sex workers. There are other kinds of male sex workers, such as call boys, rent boys, masseurs, and sex workers who work out of gay bars, who have not been extensively investigated. Male sex workers represent varied backgrounds ranging from those with few literacy skills to middle-class and wealthy men working in varied conditions such as the street, clubs, and escort agencies. Increasingly, they are utilizing escort agencies and making their availability known through the Internet (Minichiello et al., 2000). A minority of males who work as sex workers are gigolos—heterosexual men providing sexual services for women in exchange for money. Their customers are usually wealthy, middle-aged women who seek sex, a social "companion," or a young man. (See Think About It "Tourist Women as Buyers of Sex from Men: Inequalities of Power and Socioeconomics.") The gigolo phenomenon illustrates that women, like men, will pay for sex. Another type of male sex worker is "kept boys"—young men financially supported for sexual services by an older "sugar daddy." The overwhelming majority of male sex workers sell their sexual services to other males and one study of 38 male sex workers from a single escort service found that most identified as gay or bisexual (Smith et al., 2013). Young male sex workers are called "chickens," and the customers who are attracted to them are known as "chickenhawks."

Historical beliefs that male sex work is clandestine and violent have not been shown in empirical studies conducted since the 1990s. A broad overview of the literature on male sex workers (MSWs) found that "MSWs should not be necessarily thought of as psychologically unstable, desperate, or destitute, with many making an occupational choice to engage in sex work as the outcome of a rational economic decision" (Minichiello et al., 2013). (The same could be said about many female sex workers.) The study of 38 MSWs from a single escort service cited earlier found that even though earning an income was the primary incentive for the sex work, there were also downsides (Smith et al., 2013). Many of the male sex workers stated that selling sex was personally offensive and inconsistent with their personal moral beliefs and they would not want others to know about their work. The researchers suggested that male sex workers must overcome social stigma, issues dealing with self-concept, and attraction to customers to become male sex workers. Renowned sex researcher Ian Vanwesenbeeck of Utrecht University in the Netherlands states that the stigma of male sex work is less than for female sex work (Vanwesenbeeck, 2013). That is, women in sex work are more frequently the object of political concerns and interventions. Male sex workers appear to have better options to be left alone to do their work. Vanwesenbeeck states that male sex workers "may be somewhat more likely to experience self-determination, autonomy, and control over their work and thus be somewhat less likely to have their health and well-being seriously threatened, but they too experience stigma and its vast social consequences." The most common types of sexual behaviors male sex workers engage in are fellatio and anal sex. Male sex workers are usually expected to ejaculate during the sexual encounters. Because of the refractory period, the number of clients seen by male sex workers in a short period of time is limited, in contrast to female sex workers. Women usually do not have orgasms during sex with a client; further, women do not have a refractory period.

Gay male sex workers engage in prostitution as a means of expressing their sexuality *and* making money. They identify themselves as gay and work primarily in gay neighborhoods or gay bars. Many are "pushed-away" children who fled their homes when their parents and peers rejected them because of their sexual orientation. The three most important reasons they give for engaging in sex work are money, sex, and fun/adventure. Sex work appears to be accepted more in the gay community, as well as less stigmatized (Koken et al., 2004).

Few studies have been published that examine clients who pay for sex with male escorts. In 2012, an online survey was conducted about male clients' most recent hire for sexual purposes (Grov et al., 2014). The survey found that:

- Ninety percent of the clients were HIV negative.
- Three quarters of the clients identified as gay, 18% bisexual, and 4% heterosexual.
- Oral sex behavior was common (80% gave, 69% received), 30% reported anal insertive sex, and 34% reported anal receptive sex.
- Only 12% reported unprotected anal sex.
- The clients reported high satisfaction with the encounters.
- Clients having receptive anal intercourse (whether protected or not) reported greater satisfaction.

Street hustlers, like female sex workers, are often young adults with drug, alcohol, and health issues.
©track5/Vetta/Getty Images

think about it

Tourist Women as Buyers of Sex from Men: Inequalities of Power and Socioeconomics

Nearly all research on transactional sex between men and women has focused on men as the buyers and women as the sellers. Yet women purchasing sexual services from men have likely always existed, but have not been adequately studied (Berg et al, 2020).

To address this research gap, a systematic review of 19 studies about sexual-economic exchanges between tourist women from the global north and local men from the Caribbean, Kenya, Gambia, Ghana, India, Indonesia, and Tunisia was conducted (Berg et al, 2020). The studies, utilizing an ethnographic or qualitative approach, covered a 40-year time span and reported mostly men's perspectives, although women's viewpoints were occasionally presented. The review synthesized the empirical research; major findings include:

- For all the studies, the setting was a coastal town or beach resort where the sexual exchanges were between white tourist women from developed countries (North American or Europe), and dark-skinned local men who lived in underdeveloped countries.

- The tourist women were mostly age 40 or above, highly educated, middle-class, and frequent travelers, whereas the local men were younger (late teens to early 30s), poorly educated, and from low socioeconomic backgrounds. The men preferred "old white women" because they spend more money than younger women (Meiu, 2015).

- The initial motivations for sexual involvement of the tourist women varied from mainly romance to largely sex. A common motivational theme of nearly all studies (all set in Caribbean and African countries) was the women's racialized fantasy of Black men's hypersexuality and the stereotypes of Black male bodies.

- All studies found that the men's main motivation for the sexual connections with the women were largely financial, with experiencing sexual pleasure and peer status as secondary reasons. In most of the studies the men resisted labeling the connections as prostitution or sex work, but characterized themselves as "players" and the activity as beach bumming, hustling, or "showing female tourists a good time" (Martis, 1999). However, all but one of the studies noted that men's broader community criticized their hustling as unmanly, subject to ridicule and gossip, and resulting in loss of respect.

- The men were exceptionally good at sweet-talking, using rehearsal flattery, and traditional gendered mating roles. Some

men indicated that their sexual work was like any other job and involved constantly securing attention, romancing, and keeping the woman's trust (Bergan, 2011).

- Most sexual exchanges occurred within a short period of time after having met with men who initiated the contact and the exchanges were brief. Sometimes the connection lasted longer, with the woman continuing to provide financial support from her home country (Frohlick, 2013). Some men noted that they hoped the connection would increase their chances of escaping poverty and long-term economic mobility through marriage and visa sponsorships, for example.

- As part of the efforts to stage affectionate involvement, the men would minimize the commercial aspect of the arrangement and not directly ask for payment. At the right moment they would insinuate an expectation for gifts and their lack of adequate money, and state that they had financial responsibilities for relatives. The women would often provide cash or bought items such as clothes, electronics, or cars. Payment for sexual services was thus generally couched as a gift, donation, or generosity, although on occasion women made outright cash payments to the men for their sexual services.

- Several of the studies found that condoms were not consistently used, as the men indicated that it reduced their pleasure. However, they would use condoms if their tourist partner insisted on their use.

The researchers concluded that the studies appear to reveal some basic characteristics of transactional sex when women buy sex and men provide sex: "the current body of evidence seems sufficient to say that commence and inequalities of power and socioeconomics are strongly influential in transaction sex where women form the demand and men the supply" (p. 115).

Think Critically

1. Do the findings of this study alter your perspectives about prostitution?

2. What does the study say about the nature of female sexuality?

3. Should transactional sex where women buy and men sell be illegal?

A major finding of the study is that the male clients and male sex workers engaged in relatively high rates of protected anal sex. Hence, the clients appear to be keenly aware of the need for protection from HIV/STIs during anal sex and the male sex workers are insisting on condom use.

Very little is known about transgender sex workers. They are a diverse group, distinct from other male and female sex workers, and they can be found in most major cities. Their clients are heterosexual, bisexual, and gay men.

Sex Work and the Law

Arrests for sex work and calls for "cleanups" seem to be a communal ritual practiced by influential segments of the population to reassert their moral, political, and economic dominance. The arrests are symbolic of community disapproval, but they are often selective and ineffective at ending prostitution.

Female sex work is the only sexual offense for which women are extensively prosecuted; the male patron is seldom arrested. Sex workers are subject to arrest for various activities, including vagrancy and loitering, but the most common charge is for solicitation. **Solicitation**—a word, a gesture, or an action that implies an offer of sex for sale—is defined vaguely enough that women, and men, who are not sex workers occasionally are arrested on the charge because they act "suspiciously." It is usually difficult to witness a direct transaction in which money passes hands, and such arrests are also complicated by involving the patron.

Whether sex work should be regulated by government and legal policy has long been debated in the United States and other countries. Those who currently favor or oppose the decriminalization and/or legalization of sex work offer numerous reasons supporting their stance. See Think About It "Should Sex Work Be Decriminalized and Legalized?" to learn more about what proponents and opponents say.

Whatever one's opinion about decriminalizing adult sex work, the criminalization of adolescent sex work needs to be reevaluated. Treating juvenile prostitutes as delinquents overlooks the fact that in many ways adolescent sex workers are more victims than criminals. As researchers and concerned persons examine such social problems as the sexual and physical abuse of children, running away, and adolescent sex work, they are discovering a disturbing interrelationship. The law, nevertheless, does not view adolescent sex work as a response to victimization and an attempt to survive on the streets. Instead, it treats it as a criminal behavior and applies legal sanctions. A more appropriate response might be to offer counseling, halfway houses, alternative schooling, and job training.

The Impact of HIV/AIDS and Other STIs on Sex Work

Sex work has received increased attention as a result of the HIV/AIDS epidemic. Numerous studies have documented a high frequency of many STIs, including HIV, among female, male, and transgender sex workers (e.g., Jin et al., 2010; McGrath-Lone et al., 2015; van Veen et al., 2010).

The Joint United Nations Program on AIDS (UNAIDS) (2017) reports that sex workers globally are at increased risk for HIV infection. UNAIDS states that:

> Sex workers—female, male and transgender adults who have consensual sex in exchange for money or goods, either regularly or occasionally—are among the populations that are being left behind in the HIV response. HIV prevalence among sex workers is 10 times higher than among the general population, and sex workers are poorly served by HIV services.

There are several reasons female and male sex workers are at higher risk for HIV and STIs than the general population. First, many sex workers are injection drug users, and injection drug use is one of the primary ways of transmitting HIV infection. Sex workers exchanging sex for crack in crack houses are also at high risk for HIV infection as well as other STIs. Second, sex workers are at higher risk for STI/HIV infection because they have numerous partners. Third, sex workers do not always require their customers to use condoms. Male sex workers are at even greater risk than female sex workers because of their high-risk sexual practices, especially anal intercourse, and their high-risk gay/bisexual clientele (CDC, 2021.18a).

The UNAIDS (2017) notes that the barriers sex workers face in accessing HIV services are due to the criminalization of sex work and the restrictive laws, regulations, and practices

"Driven underground, prostitution became integrated into the underworld of crime. Like the prohibition of liquor, the criminalization of prostitution became a self-fulfilling prophecy."
—Ruth Rosen (1945–)

"Upon these women we have no right to turn our backs. Their wrongs are our wrongs. Their existence is part of our problem. They have been created by the very injustice against which we protest."
—Carrie Chapman Catt (1859–1947)

think
about it

Should Sex Work Be Decriminalized and Legalized?

In recent years, there has been a shift throughout the world from prohibition of sex work (prostitution) to legalization, reflecting new sexual norms and a new economic climate. As of 2018, 53 of 100 countries had legalized sex work; 12% had limited legality, and 35% prohibited sex work (ProCon.org, 2018). Germany and the Netherlands are well-known for the legalization of sex work. However, the United States still lags behind in changing prohibitionist policies, except for the state of Nevada, which has limited legalization of brothels. For many people, the thought of buying and selling of sex is degrading, despicable, and dishonorable, yet others believe that sex work is just another form of sexual expression between consenting adults and that criminalization of sex workers undermines human rights (North, 2019). Certainly, there is an enduring stigma about sex work, which shapes laws and policies and marginalizes sex workers.

One cannot think about sex work without considering the legal efforts to prohibit, contain, and regulate it (Wagenaar et al., 2017; Platt et al., 2018). Whether sex work should be decriminalized and/or legalized has long been debated. Although there are no official definitions, decriminalization typically means the elimination of all laws against prostitution, whereas legalization would be the regulation of sex work regarding where, when, and how sex work could occur and that sex workers are licensed, such as in Nevada. Below are some of the stances about sex work.

Some Views in Support for Sex Work

Many reformers propose that sex work should be either legalized or decriminalized. Those who support legalizing sex work want to subject it to taxation, and to licensing and registration by police and health departments, as in Nevada and parts of Europe. Some believe that sex workers should be accorded the same political and legal protection and rights of all citizens, such as the "right" to control what one does with one's body when the sexual exchange does not harm others and is not a public nuisance (Shrage, 2015; Weitzer, 2012). Some believe that legalizing it would allow adults to pay for sex they want and for sex workers to earn a living in a way they desire to do or not to do. Legalizing sex work would help prevent underage persons from being lured into sex work. Others want to decriminalize sex work because they believe that legalization will help decrease social stigma directed toward sex workers (Valera et al., 2001; Weitzer, 2010). Sex researchers Hendrick Wagenaar and colleagues (2017) state that ". . . prostitution policy is morality politics" (p. 258). Sexual and reproductive rights advocate Jasmine Sankofa (n.d.) declared that:

> Similar to the way the United States treats and criminalizes drug use, the policing of sex work exacerbates stigma, compromises access to resources, justifies violence, and is steeped in racial disparities. Women of color, especially Black cisgender and transgender women, girls, and femmes, are particularly vulnerable.

A review of 130 research studies on 33 countries published in scientific journals between 1990 and 2018 found extensive harm associated with criminalization of sex work including laws and enforcement that targeted the sale and purchase of sex and activities related to sex work organization (Platt et al., 2018). Major findings were:

- Sex workers who had been exposed to policing such as being arrested or placed in a prison were three times more likely to experience sexual or physical violence by clients, partners, and other individuals.

- Sex workers who had experienced repressive policing practices were at increased risk of HIV/STI infection compared to those who had not.

- Repressive policing of sex workers, their clients and sex work venues disrupted sex workers' work environments, networks providing support, safety and risk reduction strategies, and access to health care services and justice.

The researchers concluded that "The removal of criminal and administrative sanctions for sex work is needed to improve sex worker's health and access to service and justice."

Some Views in Opposition to Sex Work

Many opponents to sex work contend that sex work is an expression of patriarchal gender relations and male dominance, and that it erodes marriages and relationships, as well as the family and a society's moral fiber. Sex work objectifies and commodifies women's bodies, resulting in men believing they have a right to purchase sex from women. Women who are sex workers are exposed to physical violence such as rape, exploitation, subjugation, racism, and degradation that destroys their personality and spirit. Some opponents claim that legalizing sex work is not the answer to its harms nor the gender inequality that is a fundamental component to sex work. They cite studies that indicate countries that legalized or decriminalized sex work often experience increased human trafficking, pimping, and other crimes (Demand Abolition, n.d.; Weitzer, 2012). Researcher and clinical psychologist Melissa Farley (2015) contends that sex work needs to be completely abolished although she did state that the "Nordic Model Now" (n.d.) (see below) is a solution to sex work. Farley states:

> The existence of prostitution anywhere is society's betrayal of women, especially those who are marginalized and vulnerable because of their sex, their ethnicity, their poverty, and their history of abuse and neglect. Prostitution is sexual harassment, sexual exploitation, often torture. Banks, airlines, Internet providers, hotels, travel agencies, and all media that are integral in the exploitation and abuse of women in prostitution tourism, make huge profits as part of the economy. (p. 20)

Possible Solutions

In 1999, Sweden made it illegal to buy sex but not to sell one's own body for sexual services. Called the Nordic Model or the Sex Buyer

Law, this law decriminalizes sex workers, provides support services to help them exit sex work, makes buying people for sex a criminal offense, and criminalizes pimps. The intent of the Nordic Model was to make it clear that buying people for sex services is wrong and to create sanctions that discourage people from doing it ("Nordic Model Now," n.d.). Since the creation of the Nordic Model, Norway and Iceland have adopted similar laws in 2009, followed by Canada in 2014, Northern Ireland in 2015, and France in 2016.

However, Amnesty International has a different solution. This organization states that it does not support or condemn sex work; its stance focuses on protecting sex workers rather than the rights of those who buy sex. It does not support the Nordic Model laws that forbid buying sex and does not concur with its stance that their laws lesson stigma and discrimination of sex workers. Under the Nordic Model, sex workers can still be penalized for working together and organizing in order to keep themselves safe (Kingston & Thomas, 2019). Amnesty International calls for decriminalization of sex work based on research that shows criminalization makes sex workers less safe by preventing them from securing police protection, for example. Decriminalization would give sex workers rights to access health care, report crimes to authorities, and organize and work together to increase safety (Amnesty International, 2016; Grant, 2016).

faced by sex workers. Selling and/or buying sex from sex workers is fully illegal in 39 countries and partially illegal in 12 countries. This threat of arrest and detention are major barriers to the availability and utilization of HIV prevention programs and services. In some areas, the possession of condoms is used by the police as evidence of sex work, resulting in less condom use thus increasing HIV/STI risk behavior. Further, even when sex work is not criminalized, sex workers are rarely protected by law.

● Sexuality and the Law

A basic tenet of our society is that all Americans are equal under the law. But state laws relating to sexuality vary from one state to another, with people having widely differing rights and privileges. Though most Americans don't give much thought to the government's decision making concerning their sexual lives, they generally agree that sexual behavior is private and that what occurs in their bedrooms is their own business. They may even think that sexuality-related laws are for other people, not themselves. As a result, most Americans don't think about how their lives can be impacted by the law depending on where they live or visit.

Laws related to various aspects of human sexuality, such as HIV/AIDS, child sexual abuse, sex work, and hate crimes based on sexual orientation and gender identity, have been discussed throughout the book. In this section, we discuss laws related to two specific sexuality-related areas: private, consensual sexual behavior between adults and same-sex marriage.

Legalizing Private, Consensual Sexual Behavior

Historically, the United States has enacted laws that criminalize certain sex-related behaviors, such as sexual harassment, rape, incest, sexual assault, exhibitionism, and sex work. For the most part, there has been a strong consensus among Americans as to the need for and value of such laws. However, one area of sexual behavior, referred to as **sodomy**, has provoked considerable debate. Sodomy is a disparaging and nonscientific term that has had several definitions, including any sexual behaviors between members of the other or the same sex that cannot result in procreation some of which were considered "crimes against nature" and sexual behaviors considered to be "homosexual acts." Oral and anal sex are the behaviors typically considered to be sodomy. Rooted in sixteenth-century English laws prohibiting nonprocreative sex, the first American antisodomy law was passed in 1610 in colonial Virginia; the penalty was death. In 1873, South Carolina became the last state to repeal capital punishment for sodomy. Sodomy laws were used to target individuals participating in same-sex behaviors.

Every state had laws banning sodomy until 1961, when Illinois repealed its sodomy ban. By mid-2003, only 13 states had sodomy laws, of which 9 states had laws prohibiting sodomy

"I would rather be exposed to the inconveniences attending too much liberty than to those attending too small a degree of it."

—Thomas Jefferson (1743–1826)

between both same-sex and other-sex partners, and 4 states outlawed sodomy between same-sex partners only. Civil rights activists and the gay community protested that the laws violated individual rights, were rarely enforced, and provided grounds for other types of discrimination based on sexual orientation. Other groups, particularly those that believe homosexuality is immoral, fought to retain the laws.

On June 26, 2003, in *Lawrence et al. v. Texas,* the U.S. Supreme Court struck down, by a decisive 6–3 vote, the Texas law that banned sex between people of the same gender. Considered by many as a "watershed moment" in advancing sexual rights in America, the verdict reversed the Supreme Court's 1986 ruling in *Bowers v. Hardwick* that upheld a state's right (Georgia) to criminalize sodomy. The Court said that the *Bowers* ruling was incorrect then and is incorrect today. This landmark ruling also invalidated the antisodomy laws in the 13 remaining states that had them. Thereafter, the sexual behaviors of consenting adults in private—no matter the gender of the partners—were legal in every state.

The Texas case originated in 1998 when John Geddes Lawrence and Tyron Garner were discovered having sex by a Harris County sheriff's officer who had entered Lawrence's residence while responding to a false report about an armed intruder. They were fined $200 each (Biskupic, 2003b) for violating state law prohibiting oral and anal sex between same-sex partners. In writing for the majority, Justice Anthony Kennedy (Supreme Court of the United States, 2003) stated that:

> The case does involve two adults who, with full and mutual consent from each other, engaged in sexual practices common to a homosexual lifestyle. The petitioners [Lawrence and Garner] are entitled to respect for their private lives. The State cannot demean their existence or control their destiny by making their private sexual conduct a crime. The right to liberty under the Due Process Clause gives them the full right to engage in their conduct without intervention of the government.

The *Lawrence et al. v. Texas* ruling by the U.S. Supreme Court is considered a milestone ruling for gay rights advocates. For gay men in particular, not only did the decriminalization of same-sex behavior bring relief but it also helped validate them as human beings and reduced some of the stigma they face. In recent years, there have been several court rulings significant to gay rights issues. Gay men and lesbian women can be fired from their jobs, denied the opportunity to adopt children, denied custody of their own children, and denied housing because of their sexual orientation. To keep current on legal issues related to gay men, lesbian women, bisexual, queer, and transgender persons, go to the Human Rights Campaign website: http://www.hrc.org.

Same-Sex Marriage

The right for same-sex couples to legally marry has been a major social and political issue in the United States. Concerned that some states might legalize gay marriages, Congress in 1996 passed the Defense of Marriage Act (DOMA), which defined marriage as a union between one man and one woman and that states do not have to recognize same-sex marriages from other states. By mid-2011, 12 states had created their own version.

On June 26, 2013, the U.S. Supreme Court struck down the federal Defense of Marriage Act, prompting federal judges throughout the country to eliminate states' bans on same-sex marriage. The 5–4 ruling of *United States v. Edith Windsor* forced the federal government to legally recognize married gay and lesbian couples by lifting the ban on over 1,000 federal benefits such as family medical leave, tax benefits, Social Security benefits, and veterans' benefits. At the time of the ruling, 13 states permitted same-sex marriage; the total rapidly increased to 37 states in early 2015. Further, in 2011 for the first time the majority (53%) of Americans supported gay marriage to be legal, and in 2014 56% of all Americans (and 78% of 18- to 29-year-olds) supported same-sex marriage (Gallup, 2014). Only 27% supported gay marriage in 1997. This rapid acceptance and legal rulings for a major social issue had little precedence. Richard Wolf, writer for *USA Today,* captured the essence of this swift change by stating that since the DOMA ruling, gay marriage "moved from seemingly incredible to inevitable" (Wolf, 2014b). Inevitable it was and on June 26, 2015, in a

"In considering deviant behavior, it is wise to remember that it is not the prevalence of deviance that triggers social reforms, but rather what deviance symbolizes."

—Ruth Rosen (1945–)

"The day after [we got married], we felt differently. I query everybody who has a long-ranging relationship and then gets married, and I ask, 'Is it different the next morning?' and they all say yes. There's some legitimacy that we didn't know we were lacking. . . . I think that the truth is that if you really care about the quality of somebody's life as much as you do your own, you have it made."

—Edith Windsor (1926–2017)

"Today's ruling from the Supreme Court affirms what millions across this country already know to be true in our hearts—our love is equal, that the four words etched onto the front of the Supreme Court—equal justice under law—apply to us, too."

—James Obergefell (1966–)

On the night of June 26, 2015, the date the U.S. Supreme Court legalized same-sex marriage, the White House was lit with the iconic rainbow of the gay pride flag in celebration of the landmark victory.

©Drew Angerer/Bloomberg/Getty Images

5–4 decision of *Obergefell v. Hodges,* the U.S. Supreme Court legalized same-sex marriage in all 50 states, ruling that states cannot withhold from gay and lesbian couples the same marital rights as those enjoyed by heterosexual couples for thousands of years. This milestone decision resolves one of the most significant civil rights issues of the twenty-first century by declaring that the 14th Amendment of the U.S. Constitution provides a fundamental right, regardless of sex, for individuals to marry (Wolf & Heath, 2015a, 2015b). In writing for the majority, Justice Anthony Kennedy stated that "Same-sex couples seek in marriage the same legal treatments as opposite-sex couples, and it would disparage their choices and diminish their personhood to deny them this right" (Wolf & Heath, 2015b).

As of mid-2020, 29 countries had legally approved the freedom to marry for same-sex couples nationwide (year of approval in parenthesis): the Netherlands (2000), Belgium (2003), Spain (2005), Canada (2005), South Africa (2006), Norway (2008), Sweden (2009), Portugal (2010), Iceland (2010), Argentina (2010), Denmark (2012), France (2013), Brazil (2013), Uruguay (2013), New Zealand (2013), England/Wales (2013), Luxembourg (2014), Scotland (2014), Finland (2015), Ireland (2015), Greenland (2015), United States (2015), Colombia (2016), Malta (2017), Germany (2017), Australia (2017), Taiwan (2019), Ecuador (2019), Northern Ireland (2019), and Costa Rica (2020). Regional and court-ordered provisions for gay marriage have occurred in Mexico (Perper, 2020). Many other countries worldwide offer some protections for same-sex couples.

Advocating Sexual Rights

Policymakers and advocates of free speech continue to scrutinize states' sexuality laws and enforcement practices and to monitor and report on them. One such advocacy group is the Sexuality Information and Education Council of the United States (SIECUS), which states:

> Sexual rights are human rights, and they are based on the inherent freedom, dignity, and equality of all human beings. Sexual rights include the right to bodily integrity, sexual safety, sexual privacy, sexual pleasure, and sexual healthcare; the right to make free and informed sexual and reproductive choices; and the right to have access to sexual information based on sound scientific evidence.

In many ways, sexuality-related laws reflect an ambivalence about sexuality in America's culture. For some sexuality-related issues, there is not a consensus, although laws have been enacted. This is particularly evident with issues relating to sexuality education and abortion. Although some laws seem to be based on sexuality as something from which we must be protected, in other cases, the absence of laws speaks loudly. For example, many states have yet to protect against sexual harassment and discrimination based on sexual orientation and gender identity. Every state also has work to do in developing laws that support sexual rights and sexual health. Recall the World Association for Sexual Health's Declaration of Sexual Rights (presented in Chapter 1), which identifies 16 sexual rights. The expression of many of these rights has been hampered by laws and social restriction. Further legal protection of fundamental sexual rights is needed for people to fully attain individual sexual health.

Edith Windsor (top photo) was the lead plaintiff in the Supreme Court case that struck down the Defense of Marriage Act in 2013; James Obergefell (bottom photo) was the lead plaintiff in the Supreme Court case that legalized same-sex marriage in the United States in 2015.

(top): ©ZUMA Press, Inc./Alamy Stock Photo; (bottom): ©Karl Mondon/TNS/Newscom

Final Thoughts

The world of commercial sex is one our society approaches with ambivalence. Society simultaneously condemns sexually explicit material and sex work yet provides both to customers. Because of conflicting attitudes and behaviors, our society rarely approaches the issues surrounding sexually explicit material and sex work with disinterested objectivity. Now, in every state, adults can legally participate in private consensual sexual behavior with other adults and get married, no matter what their sexual orientation is, but other fundamental sexual rights remain hampered by laws or social restriction.

©David Angel/Alamy Stock Photo

Summary

Sexually Explicit Material in Contemporary America

- There is a lack of agreement about what constitutes *erotica, pornography,* and *obscenity* because they are subjective terms. The term *sexually explicit material* is a more neutral term.

- The viewing of sexually explicit media is becoming more common. One study of college students revealed that 33% reported viewing sexually explicit videos in the past 30 days.

- The increasing availability of erotic films in the privacy of the home via the Internet, DVDs, and pay-for-view television has led to an increase in viewers. The inclusion of women in the audience has led to *femme porn,* pornography specifically designed for women.

- The legal guidelines for determining whether a work is obscene are that the dominant theme of the work must appeal to prurient sexual interests and portray sexual conduct in a patently offensive way; taken as a whole, the work must be without serious literary, artistic, political, or scientific value; and a reasonable person must find the work, when taken as a whole, to possess no social value. Obscene material is not protected by law.

- People who read or view sexually explicit material usually recognize it as fantasy. They use it as a release from their everyday lives. Sexually explicit videos temporarily encourage sexual expression, activating a person's typical sexual behavior pattern. People are interested in sexually explicit material because they enjoy sexual sensations. It is a source of sexual information and knowledge, it enables people to rehearse sexual activities, and it is safer sex.

- Child sexually explicit videos are a form of sexual exploitation that, because of the Internet, has become a worldwide problem. U.S. courts have prohibited its production, sale, and possession.

- Some feminists believe that sexually explicit videos represent a form of sex discrimination against women because it places them in what they believe to be a degrading and dehumanizing context. Other feminists believe that opponents of sexually explicit videos have an antisex bias.

- In 1970, the President's Commission on Pornography and Obscenity concluded that pornography does not cause harm or violence. Over the years, there has been a heated debate over the effects of sexually explicit videos. There is no definitive evidence, however, that nonviolent sexually explicit material is associated with sexual aggression against women, nor is there evidence that sexually violent material produces lasting changes in attitudes or behaviors.

Sex Work and Sex Trafficking

- Prostitution, also called *sex work,* is the exchange of sexual behaviors for money and/or goods. Both men and women work as sex workers. Women are generally introduced into this type of sex work by pimps.

- Adolescent sex workers describe their psychological state as negative when they first enter sex work. Street-based sex workers run the risk of abuse and violence from their customers. Sex workers report various motives for entering sex work, including quick and easy money, the sex workers' subculture, and the excitement of "the life." Fellatio is the most common sexual behavior of street-based sex workers.

- Sex workers solicit on streets and work in brothels and massage parlors. Some masseuses have intercourse with clients, but most provide only masturbation. Call girls (escorts) have the highest status among prostitutes.

- Most research on male sex work focuses on street hustlers. Male sex work is shaped by numerous factors including the gay male subcultures.

- Sex work is legal in the United States only in certain counties in the state of Nevada. A study of these brothels concluded that they are a good alternative to criminalization of sex work.

- Arrests for sex work are symbols of community disapproval; they are not effective in curbing sex work. Female sex work is the only sexual offense for which women are extensively prosecuted; the male patron is seldom arrested. Decriminalization of sex work is often urged because it is a victimless crime or because sex workers are victimized by their pimps, customers, police, and the legal system. Some people advocate regulation by police and health departments.

- Sex workers are at higher risk for HIV/AIDS and other STIs than the general population because some are injection drug users, have multiple partners, and do not always require their customers to use condoms. Female and male sex workers and their customers may provide a pathway for HIV and other STIs to spread into the general heterosexual community.

Sexuality and the Law

- In 2003, the U.S. Supreme Court overturned state *antisodomy* laws in the 13 remaining states that had them, making it legal for consenting adult gay and lesbian individuals, as well as heterosexual individuals, to have sex in private in all states.

- In June 2013, the U.S. Supreme Court struck down the federal Defense of Marriage Act (DOMA), which defined marriage as a union between one man and one woman.

Subsequently, the number of states legalizing same-sex marriage rapidly increased to 37 states in early 2015. On June 26, 2015, the U.S. Supreme Court by a 5-4 ruling legalized gay marriage in all 50 states.

- By mid-2020, 29 countries worldwide legally permitted same-sex marriage.

Questions for Discussion

- Imagine that you were assigned to argue that the federal government should regulate sexually explicit videos. What would you say? Imagine the converse: that sexually explicit videos should be available freely to adults in the marketplace. How would you advocate that position?

- Do you think that sexually explicit videos are helpful, harmful, or neutral? What place, if any, do they have in a society? Explain your position on this issue.

- Do you think that prostitution should be legalized/regulated (i.e., licensed and/or registered by health and police departments) or decriminalized (i.e., no criminal penalties and no licensing or registration) or neither? Defend your stance.

- Do you agree or disagree with the U.S. Supreme Court ruling legalizing same-sex marriage in all 50 states? Why or why not?

Sex and the Internet

American Civil Liberties Union

Protection of our First Amendment rights is part of the mission of the American Civil Liberties Union (ACLU). But what exactly is this organization, what does it do, and how can it help you? To find out, click to the ACLU's home page (http://www.aclu.org) and find one topic related to this chapter or text that interests you. This could include Internet issues, free speech, HIV/AIDS, LGBTQ+ rights, privacy, reproductive rights, or women's rights. After reading information related to this topic, answer the following:

- What new information or news release did you find related to this topic?

- What is the history or background of laws related to it?

- What is the ACLU's stance?

- What is your position, and why?

Suggested Websites

Children of the Night
Childrenofthenight.org
It is the only organization in the United States that focuses on rescuing children from sex work and sex trafficking and in which a child can call 24 hours a day to immediately reach a qualified social worker who can arrange free transportation and airfare within a day to the organization's home facility in Los Angeles.

Global Network of Sex Work Projects
nswp.org/who-we-are
The NSWP exists to uphold the voices of sex workers globally and connect regional networks advocating for the rights of female, male, and transgender sex workers.

Human Rights Campaign
hrc.org
The HRC advocates for equal rights for LGBT individuals.

National Center for Missing & Exploited Children
missingkids.com
Serves as a resource on the issues of missing and sexually exploited children.

Polaris Project
polarisproject.org
Named after the North Star, which guided slaves toward freedom along the Underground Railroad, Polaris Project provides a comprehensive approach to combating human trafficking and modern-day slavery.

Shared Hope International
sharedhope.org
The mission of Shared Hope International is to prevent sex trafficking and advocate for survivors of it.

U.S. Supreme Court
http://www.supremecourtus.gov
Lists U.S. Supreme Court decisions by year and volume. Type in "sodomy" in the search box to locate the Court's ruling on the *Lawrence et al. v. Texas* case.

Suggested Reading

Brents, B. G., Jackson, C. A., & Hausbeck, K. (2010). *The state of sex: Tourism, sex, and sin in the New American heartland.* Routledge. A decade-long multimethod study of Nevada's legal brothels that captures the voices of the brothels' sex workers.

Mercer, J. (2017). *Gay pornography.* I.B.Tarius. The author argues that gay pornography is a controversial and under-researched area of cultural production. How the Internet has generated an exponential growth in the volume and variety of gay porn has facilitated greater access is examined.

Mikkola, M. (2019). *Pornography: A philosophical introduction.* Oxford University Press.

Rosen, R. (2012). *Beaver street: A history of modern pornography.* Headpress. An electrifying account of porn's golden age by an author who worked behind the X-rated scenes of porn magazines.

Sanger, W. (2014). *The history of prostitution—Illustrated edition.* Heritage Illustrated Publishing. A detailed, objective study of prostitution in New York City illustrated with paintings by renowned artists.

Smith, T. (2012). *Whore stories: A revealing history of the world's oldest profession.* Adams Media. Sheds light on one of our more stigmatized icons—prostitution—by a wistful review of the cultural history of prostitution.

Smith, M. (2018). *Revolting prostitutes: The fight for sex workers' rights.* Verso. Two sex workers speak to issues that long have been contentious related to the emotional, social, stigma, financial and legal aspects of prostitution.

Stone, G. R. (2017). *Sex and the constitution.* Liveright Publishing. A one-volume history of how human sexuality became legalized in the United States.

Weitzer, R. (2012). *Legalizing prostitution: From illicit vice to lawful business.* New York University. The extensive field research in the Netherlands, Belgium, and Germany is used to illustrate alternatives to American-style criminalization of sex workers.

Glossary

5-alpha reductase deficiency A condition whereby a genetic male (XY) does not produce enough of a hormone called dihydrotestosterone (DHT), a shortage of which will disrupt the formation of the external sex organs, causing individuals to be born with external genitalia that appear.

abortifacient A device or substance that causes an abortion.

abortion The expulsion of the fetus, either spontaneously or by induction.

abstinence Refraining from sexual behavior with another person.

abstinence-only sexuality education A form of sexuality education that teaches not having sex outside of marriage.

acculturation The process of adaptation by an ethnic group to the attitudes, behaviors, and values of the dominant culture.

acquired immunodeficiency syndrome (AIDS) A chronic disease caused by the human immunodeficiency virus (HIV) in which the immune system is weakened and unable to fight opportunistic infections such as *Pneumocystis carinii* pneumonia (PCP) and Kaposi's sarcoma.

adolescence The social and psychological state that occurs between the beginning of puberty and full adulthood.

advanced maternal age Delaying pregnancy until after age 35.

affirmative consent Explicitly saying yes to any sexual behavior with another person.

afterbirth The placenta, the remaining section of the umbilical cord, and the fetal membranes.

agape In John Lee's typology of love, altruistic love.

agender Those who do not identify with any gender.

AIDS See acquired immunodeficiency syndrome

alcohol-related birth defects (ARBD) As a result of a mother's consumption of alcohol during pregnancy, individuals born with ARBD may have physical problems including a mixture of those related to the heart, kidneys, bones, or with hearing.

alcohol-related neurodevelopmental disorder (ARND) As a result of a mother's consumption of alcohol during pregnancy, individuals born with ARND might have intellectual, behavioral and learning problems.

alveoli (singular, *alveolus*) Small glands within the female breast that begin producing milk following childbirth.

amenorrhea The absence of menstruation, unrelated to aging.

amniocentesis A process in which amniotic fluid is withdrawn by needle from the uterus and then examined for evidence of possible birth defects.

amnion The embryo's innermost membrane.

amniotic fluid The fluid within the amniotic sac that surrounds the embryo or fetus.

amniotic sac A sac that holds the embryo (and later fetus). Also called the bag of water.

anal eroticism Sexual activities involving the anus.

anal intercourse The insertion of the erect penis into the partner's anus.

anal stage In Freudian theory, the period from age 1 to 3, during which the child's erotic activities center on the anus.

analingus The licking of the anal region.

Anatomical sex Refers to physical sex: gonads, uterus, vulva, vagina, penis, etc.

androgen Any of the male hormones, including testosterone.

androgen insensitivity syndrome (AIS) A condition whereby a genetic male (XY) is unable to respond to male hormones or androgens. As a result, the person has some or all of the physical characteristics of a woman.

androgyny A combination of masculine and feminine traits or nontraditional gender expression. May be referred to as *genderqueer* or *genderfluid*.

androphilia Refers to sexual attraction to and arousal by adult males.

anodyspareunia Pain occurring during anal intercourse.

anti-gay prejudice A strong dislike, fear, or hatred of gay men and lesbian women because of their same-sex behavior. *See also*, homophobia.

antibody A cell that binds to the antigen of an invading cell, inactivating it and marking it for destruction by killer cells.

antigen A molecular structure on the wall of a cell capable of stimulating the immune system and then reacting with the antibodies that are released to fight it.

antiretroviral therapy (ART) The use of combinations of antiretroviral drugs to combat HIV.

anus The opening of the rectum, consisting of two sphincters, circular muscles that open and close like valves.

anxious/ambivalent attachment A style of infant attachment characterized by separation anxiety and insecurity in relation to the primary caregiver.

Apgar score The cumulative rating of the newborn's heart rate, respiration, color, reflexes, and muscle tone.

aphrodisiac A substance that supposedly increases sexual desire or improves sexual function.

areola A ring of darkened skin around the nipple of the breast.

artificial insemination (AI) Involves introducing sperm into the woman's vagina, cervix, or uterus (the latter is called intrauterine insemination). This procedure may be performed in conjunction with ovulation-stimulating medications.

asexuality Lack of sexual attraction to another person.

assigned gender Based on anatomical appearance at birth. Assigned gender tells others how to respond to us.

assigned sex An assignment that is made at birth, usually male or female, typically on the basis of external genital anatomy but sometimes on the basis of internal gonads, chromosomes, or hormone levels.

assisted reproductive technology (ART) A procedure in which a woman's ovaries are stimulated and her eggs surgically removed, combined with sperm, and returned to her body. Commonly referred to as artificial insemination.

attachment The emotional tie between an infant and their primary caregiver.

atypical sexual behavior Sexual activity that is not statistically typical of usual sexual behavior.

autoerotic asphyxia A form of sexual masochism linking strangulation with masturbation.

autoeroticism Sexual self-stimulation or behavior involving only the self; includes masturbation, sexual fantasies, and erotic dreams.

autofellatio Oral stimulation of the penis by oneself.

avoidant attachment Feeling discomfort in being close to other people, and distrustful and fearful of being dependent.

B cell A type of lymphocyte involved in antibody production.

bacterial vaginosis (BV) A vaginal infection commonly caused by the bacterium *Gardnerella vaginalis.*

Bartholin's gland One of two small ducts on either side of the vaginal opening that secrete a small amount of moisture during sexual arousal.

basal body temperature (BBT) method A contraceptive method based on a woman's temperature in the morning upon waking; when her temperature rises, she is fertile.

BDSM An acronym used to describe the variant sexual behaviors that combine bondage, discipline, sadism, and masochism.

benign prostatic hyperplasia (BPH) Enlargement of the prostate gland, affecting many men over age 50.

benign tumor A nonmalignant (noncancerous) tumor that grows slowly and remains localized.

bestialists People who have sexual contact with animals but are not concerned with the animals' welfare.

bias A personal leaning or inclination.

biased sample A nonrepresentative sample.

biopsy Surgical removal of tissue for diagnosis.

birth canal The passageway through which an infant is born; the vagina.

birth control patch A transdermal reversible method of birth control that releases synthetic estrogen and progestin to protect against pregnancy for 1 month.

birth control shot An injectable, hormonal method of birth control that is used to prevent pregnancy for 12 weeks.

birth control sponge A round, plastic, foam shield that contains the spermicide N-9 and helps to prevent pregnancy. Also known as *Today Sponge.*

birth defects Structural changes that are present at birth and can affect almost any part or parts of the baby's body.

Bisexuality An emotional and sexual attraction to two or more genders or someone who is attracted to people, regardless of their gender.

blastocyst A collection of about 100 human cells that develops from the zygote.

bondage and discipline (B&D) Sexual activities in which one person is bound while another simulates or engages in light or moderate "disciplinary" activities such as spanking and whipping.

Braxton-Hicks contractions Uterine contractions during the last trimester of pregnancy that exercise the uterus, preparing it for labor.

breast conserving surgery Removal of a breast lump and some normal tissue around it. Also referred to as *lumpectomy.*

breast magnetic resonance imaging (MRI) Uses magnets and radio waves to take pictures of the breast.

calendar (rhythm or standard days) methods Methods based on calculating "safer" days, which depend on the range of a woman's longest and shortest menstrual cycles and abstinence from unprotected vaginal intercourse during her peak fertile times.

capacitation The process by which a sperm's membranes become fragile enough to release the enzymes from its acrosomes.

caring Making another's needs as important as one's own.

castration anxiety In Freudian theory, the belief that the father will cut off the child's penis because of competition for the mother/wife.

censorship The suppression of words, ideas, or images by governments, private groups, or individuals based on their political or moral values.

cervical cancer Invasive cancer of the cervix (ICC).

cervical cap A silicon, cup-shaped device that is inserted into the vagina to prevent pregnancy.

cervical dysplasia or cervical intraepithelial neoplasia (CIN) the abnormal growth of cells on the surface of the cervix.

cervical mucus method A contraceptive method using a woman's cervical mucus to determine ovulation.

cervicitis The swelling (inflammation) of the cervix, usually the result of an infection.

cervix The end of the uterus, opening toward the vagina.

Cesarean section Cesarean section, or C-section, involves the delivery of a baby through an incision in the mother's abdominal wall and uterus.

chancre A round, pea-sized, painless sore symptomatic of the first stage of syphilis.

child sexual abuse Any sexual interaction (including fondling, erotic kissing, oral sex, and genital penetration) between an adult and a child.

child-free Individuals or couples who choose not to have children.

chorion The embryo's outermost membrane.

chorionic villus sampling (CVS) A procedure in which tiny pieces of the membrane that encases the embryo are removed and examined for evidence of possible birth defects.

cilia Tiny, hairlike tissues on the fimbriae that become active during ovulation, moving the oocyte into the fallopian tube.

circumcision The surgical removal of the foreskin that covers the glans penis.

cisgender Someone whose gender identity aligns with the gender assigned at birth.

clinical research The in-depth examination of an individual or a group by a clinician who assists with psychological or medical problems.

clitoral hood A fold of skin covering the glans of the clitoris.

clitoris An external sexual structure that is the center of arousal in the female; located above the vagina at the meeting of the labia minora.

coercive paraphilia Sexual behavior involving victimization and causing harm to others.

cognitive development theory A child development theory that views growth as the mastery of specific ways of perceiving, thinking, and doing that occurs at discrete stages.

cognitive social learning theory A child development theory that emphasizes the learning of behavior from others, based on the belief that consequences control behavior.

cohabitation The practice of living together and having a sexual relationship without being married.

coitus Penile-vaginal sex.

colostrum A yellowish substance containing nutrients and antibodies that is secreted by the breasts 2–3 days prior to actual milk production.

come out To publicly acknowledge one's sexual orientation, such as gay, lesbian, bisexual, or queer.

commitment A determination, based on conscious choice, to continue a relationship or a marriage.

communication A transactional process in which symbols, such as words, gestures, and movements, are used to establish human contact, exchange information, and reinforce or change attitudes and behaviors.

Comprehensive sexuality education A method of teaching that aims to give students the knowledge, attitudes, skills, and values to make appropriate and healthy choices in their sexual lives.

concurrent sexual relationships Overlapping sexual relationships with more than one partner.

condom or male condom A thick, soft, flexible sheath of latex, plastic (polyurethane, nitrile, or polyisoprene), or lambskin, that fits over the erect penis to help prevent semen from being transmitted.

conflict A communication process in which people perceive incompatible goals and interference from others in achieving their goals.

congenital adrenal hyperplasia A group of inherited disorders of the adrenal gland whereby individuals born with this condition lack an enzyme needed by the adrenal gland to make the hormones cortisol and aldosterone.

consensual nonmonogamy (CNM) Relationships in which individuals agree to participate in sexual and/or emotional and romantic interactions with more than one partner.

contraception The deliberate prevention of conception or impregnation by any of various drugs, techniques, or devices. Other terms used to describe contraceptives are *birth control* and *family planning*.

contraceptive failure A measure of a woman's probability of becoming pregnant during her use of a method within a given period, usually the first 12 months of use.

control group A group that is not being treated in an experiment.

conversion therapy Treatments designed to change one's sexual orientation and/or gender identity, particularly among LGBTQ+ minors. Also call *reparative therapy*.

coprophilia A paraphilia in which a person gets sexual pleasure from contact with feces.

corona The rim of tissue between the glans and the penile shaft.

corpora cavernosa The hollow chambers in the shaft of the clitoris or penis that fill with blood and swell during arousal.

corpus luteum The tissue formed from a ruptured ovarian follicle that produces important hormones after the oocyte emerges.

corpus spongiosum A column of erectile tissue within the penis enclosing the urethra.

correlational study The measurement of two or more naturally occurring variables to determine their relationship to each other.

COVID-19 An acute respiratory illness in humans caused by a coronavirus and capable of producing severe symptoms and in some cases death. Also called *coronavirus* or *SARS-COV-2*.

Cowper's gland or bulbourethral gland One of two small structures below the prostate gland that secrete a clear mucus into the urethra prior to ejaculation.

cross-dresser A person who wears clothing of the other sex for sexual arousal.

crura (singular, *crus*) The internal branches of the clitoral or penile shaft.

cryptorchidism A condition that occurs in a minority of infants whereby one or both of the testes fail to descend. Also known as undescended testis.

cultural equivalency perspective The view that attitudes, behaviors, and values of diverse ethnic groups are basically similar, with differences resulting from adaptation to historical and social forces such as slavery, discrimination, or poverty.

cunnilingus Oral stimulation of the female genitals.

cyberbullying The use of electronic communication to bully, intimidate, or threaten a person.

cystitis A bladder infection, affecting mainly women, that is often related to sexual activity, although it is not transmitted from one partner to another.

demographics The statistical characteristics of human populations.

dependent variable In an experiment, a factor that is likely to be affected by changes in the independent variable.

diabetes mellitus A chronic disease characterized by excess sugar in the blood and urine due to a deficiency of insulin.

Diagnostic and Statistical Manual of Mental Disorder, Fifth Edition, (DSM-5) The 2013 update of the mental disorders classification and diagnostic tool published by the American Psychiatric Association. The *DSM-5* addresses sexual function difficulties and paraphilias.

diaphragm A cup with a flexible rim that is placed deep inside the vagina, blocking the cervix, to prevent sperm from entering the uterus.

dilation Gradual opening of the cervix.

dilation and evacuation (D&E) A second-trimester abortion method in which the cervix is slowly dilated and the fetus removed by alternating curettage with other instruments and suction.

disinhibition The phenomenon of activating behaviors that would normally be suppressed.

Disorders of sex development (DSD) A diagnosis used to describe congenital conditions in which the external appearance of the individual does not coincide with their chromosomal constitution or gonadal sex. Also referred to as *differences of sex development* or *intersex*.

domestic partnership A legal category granting some rights ordinarily reserved to married couples to committed, cohabiting heterosexual, gay men, and lesbian women couples.

dominatrix In bondage and discipline, a woman who specializes in "disciplining" a submissive partner.

drag queens Gay men who cross-dress to entertain.

dual control model A theoretical perspective of sexual response based on brain function and the interaction between sexual excitation and sexual inhibition.

dysmenorrhea Pelvic cramping and pain experienced by some women during menstruation.

dyspareunia A female sexual functioning difficulty characterized by painful intercourse.

early ejaculation Experiencing ejaculation earlier than desired. Also called involuntary ejaculation. Both are preferred terms than premature ejaculation.

eating disorder Serious and often fatal illness that causes disturbances to a person's eating behaviors.

ectoparasitic infestation Parasitic organisms that live on the outer skin surfaces, not inside the body.

ectopic pregnancy A pregnancy in which the fertilized ovum is implanted in any tissue other than the uterine wall. Most ectopic pregnancies occur in the fallopian tubes. Also known as a *tubal pregnancy*.

effacement Thinning of the cervix during labor.

egocentric fallacy An erroneous belief that one's own personal experiences and values are held by others in general.

ejaculation The process by which semen is forcefully expelled from the penis.

ejaculatory duct One of two structures within the prostate gland connecting with the vasa deferentia.

ejaculatory inevitability The point at which ejaculation is imminent in the male.

Electra complex In Freudian theory, the female child's erotic desire for the father and simultaneous fear of the mother.

embryonic membranes The embryo's membranes include the amnion, amniotic fluid, yolk sac, chorion, and allantois.

embryo The early form of life in the uterus between the stages of blastocyst and fetus.

emergency contraception (EC) The use of hormones or a copper IUD to prevent a pregnancy from occurring.

emission The first stage of ejaculation, in which sperm and semen are propelled into the urethral bulb.

endometriosis A disorder in which the endometrium (lining of the uterus) grows outside the uterus.

endometrium The inner lining of the uterine wall.

epidemic A wide and rapid spread of a contagious disease.

epidemiology The study of the causes and control of diseases.

epididymis The coiled tube, formed by the merging of the seminiferous tubules, where sperm mature.

epididymitis Inflammation of the epididymis.

epidural A method of anesthetic delivery during childbirth in which a painkilling drug is continuously administered through a catheter in the woman's lower back.

episiotomy An episiotomy is an incision that enlarges the vaginal opening by cutting through the perineum toward the anus to assist in the delivery of a baby.

erection The process of the penis becoming rigid through vasocongestion; an erect penis.

erogenous zone Any area of the body that is highly sensitive to touch and associated with sexual arousal.

eros In John Lee's typology of love, the love of beauty.

erotic aid or sex toy A device, such as a vibrator or dildo, or a product, such as oils or lotions, designed to enhance erotic responsiveness.

erotica Sexually explicit material that is evaluated positively.

erotophilia A positive emotional response to sexuality.

erotophobia A negative emotional response to sexuality.

estrogen The principal female hormone, regulating reproductive functions and the development of secondary sex characteristics.

ethnocentric fallacy or ethnocentrism The belief that one's own ethnic group, nation, or culture is innately superior to others.

exhibitionism Exposing one's genitals to an unsuspecting person.

experimental research The systematic manipulation of an individual or the environment to learn the effect of such manipulation on behavior.

expressiveness Revealing or demonstrating one's emotions.

expulsion The second stage of ejaculation, characterized by rapid, rhythmic contraction of the urethra, prostate, and muscles at the base of the penis, causing semen to spurt from the urethral opening.

extradyadic sex Refers to having a romantic and/or sexual relationship outside a primary or dating relationship. Also known as *extramarital sex, adultery, cheating,* or *infidelity.*

fallacy An error in reasoning that affects one's understanding of a subject.

fallopian tube One of two uterine tubes extending toward an ovary.

familismo Emphasis on family among Hispanics/Latinex.

Family and Medical Leave Act (FMLA) A law that allows an employee to take unpaid leave for the birth and care of a newborn child, during his or her own illness, or to care for a sick family member.

feedback The ongoing process in which participants and their messages create a given result and are subsequently modified by that result.

fellatio Oral stimulation of the penis.

female genital mutilation/cutting (FGM/C) A procedure that intentionally alters or causes injury to the female genital organs for nonmedical reasons.

female impersonators Men who dress as women.

feminism Efforts by both men and women to achieve greater equality for women.

femme porn Sexually explicit videos catering to women and heterosexual couples.

fertility awareness-based methods (FAMS) Sometimes referred to as "natural family planning"; ways to track ovulation in order to prevent pregnancy.

fetal alcohol spectrum disorder (FASD) An umbrella term used for a group of conditions that can cause physical, behavioral, and learning problems in a child.

fetal alcohol syndrome (FAS) The most extreme outcome from drinking alcohol during pregnancy; can cause abnormal facial features, growth problems, and central nervous system problems in the child.

fetishism Sexual attraction to objects that become sexual symbols.

fetus The stage of life from 8 weeks of gestation to birth.

fibrocystic disease A common and generally harmless breast condition in which fibrous tissue and benign cysts develop in the breast.

fimbriae Fingerlike tissues that drape over the ovaries, but without necessarily touching them.

flirting Coy behaviors used to indicate romantic or sexual interest in another person.

follicle-stimulating hormone (FSH) A hormone that regulates ovulation.

foreskin The portion of the sleevelike skin covering the shaft of the penis that extends over the glans penis. Also known as *prepuce.*

frenulum The triangular area of sensitive skin on the underside of the penis, attaching the glans to the foreskin.

friends with benefits An uncommitted, non-long-term casual sexual relationship between acquaintances.

frotteurism Touching or rubbing sexually against a nonconsenting person in public places.

gamete A sex cell containing the genetic material necessary for reproduction; an oocyte (ovum) or sperm.

gap length The amount of time between partnerships

gay Emotional and sexual attraction between persons of the same sex. *See also* homosexuality.

gender The socially constructed roles, behaviors, activities, and attributes that a society assigns to individuals.

gender The socially constructed roles, behaviors, activities, and attributes that a society considers appropriate for a sex.

gender binary The view that humans comprise only two types of persons: women and men.

gender confirming treatment A means for those who find it essential and medically necessary to establish congruence with their gender identity. Also referred to as *gender affirming treatment* or *gender reassignment surgery.*

gender dysphoria A medical diagnosis reflecting an individual's distress that stems from the incongruence between their expressed or experienced gender and the gender assigned at birth. Those who find it essential and medically necessary to establish congruence with their gender identity may seek gender-confirming treatment.

gender fluid People whose gender expressions and/or identity is not static; that is, it is not the same all the time.

gender identity Attitudes, behaviors, rights and responsibilities that particular cultural groups associate with our assumed or assigned sex.

gender non-binary A spectrum of gender identities that are not exclusively masculine or feminine.

gender roles Attitudes, behaviors, rights and responsibilities that particular cultural groups associate with our assumed or assigned sex.

gender schema A set of interrelated ideas used to organize information about the world on the basis of gender.

gender variant Anyone who deviates from the historical norms of masculinity and femininity. Also known as *transgender, gender diverse, gender non-binary, gender diverse,* or *genderqueer*

gender-role stereotype A rigidly held, oversimplified, and overgeneralized belief about how each gender should behave.

genderqueer A spectrum of identities that are not exclusively masculine or feminine. Rather, a person identifies with neither, both, or a combination of male or female genders.

genetic sex Chromosomal and hormonal sex characteristics.

genital candidiasis A yeast infection caused by an overgrowth of *Candida albicans,* which is always present in the body.

genital stage In Freudian theory, the period in which adolescents become interested in genital sexual activities, especially sexual intercourse.

genital warts A sexually transmitted infection caused by the human papillomavirus (HPV).

genitals The reproductive and sexual organs of males and females. Also known as *genitalia.*

genito-pelvic pain/penetration disorder Difficulties related to genital and pelvic pain and vaginal penetration during intercourse.

genitourinary syndrome Consists of various menopausal symptoms and signs that include genital (dryness, burning, and irritation), sexual (lack of irritation, discomfort or pain, and impaired function), and urinary (urgency, painful, leaking, or incontinence) symptoms.

gestation The time between conception and birth; pregnancy.

gestational carrier A carrier who is not related to the fetus. In this case, a woman with ovaries but no uterus uses her own egg and the man's sperm to create the embryo, which is then placed within the carrier's uterus.

gestational hypertension A condition characterized by high blood pressure, edema, and protein in the urine, also referred to as *pregnancy-induced hypertension.*

ghosting When an individual withdraws from a person's life without notice and ignores their attempts at communication following a date or relationship.

glans clitoris The erotically sensitive tip of the clitoris.

glans penis The head of the penile shaft.

gonad An organ (ovary or testis) that produces gametes.

gonadotropin A hormone that acts directly on the gonads.

gonadotropin-releasing hormone (GnRH) A hormone that stimulates the pituitary gland to release follicle-stimulating hormone (FSH) and luteinizing hormone (LH), initiating the follicular phase of the ovarian cycle.

gonorrhea An STI caused by the *Neisseria gonorrhoeae* bacterium.

Grafenberg spot (G-spot) An erotically sensitive area on the upper front wall of the vagina midway between the introitus and the cervix.

gynecomastia Swelling or enlargement of the male breast.

gynephilia Refers to sexual attraction to and arousal by adult females.

halo effect The assumption that attractive or charismatic people possess more desirable social characteristics than are actually present.

Hegar's sign The softening of the uterus above the cervix, indicating pregnancy.

helper T cell A lymphocyte that "reads" antigens and directs the immune system's response.

hepatitis A viral disease affecting the liver; several types of the virus can be sexually transmitted.

herpes simplex virus (HSV) The virus that causes genital herpes.

heteroflexible Individuals who identify as heterosexual or mostly heterosexual but report moderate same-sex behavior and attraction.

heteronormativity The belief that heterosexuality is normal, natural, and superior to all other expressions of sexuality.

heterosexual bias The tendency to see the world in heterosexual terms and to ignore or devalue homosexuality. Also referred to as *heterosexism* or *heterocentric behavior.*

HIV *See* human immunodeficiency virus.

homologous structure A similarity in structures that perform the same function.

homophobia An irrational or phobic fear of gay men and lesbian women. *See also* anti-gay prejudice; heterosexual bias.

homosexuality Emotional and sexual attraction between persons of the same sex. *See also* straight.

hooking up Sexual encounters with a nonromantic partner, often a friend.

hormone A chemical substance that acts as a messenger within the body, regulating various functions.

hostile environment As related to sexuality, a work or educational setting that interferes with a person's performance because of sexual harassment.

human chorionic gonadotropin (hCG) A hormone produced right after a fertilized egg attaches to the uterus; its function is to promote the maintenance of the corpus luteum.

human immunodeficiency virus (HIV) The virus that causes AIDS.

human papillomavirus (HPV) Refers to more than 100 different viruses, many of which are sexually transmitted, that infect the genital and rectal areas of both females and males. Certain types of human papillomavirus (HPV) infection can cause genital warts in men and women.

hymen A thin membrane partially covering the introitus prior to first intercourse or other breakage.

hypersexuality A very high desire for or frequency of sexual activity.

hysterectomy A surgery used to remove a woman's uterus.

implant A contraceptive device inserted under the skin that protects against pregnancy for up to 4 years. Also referred to as *Nexplanon.*

implantation The process by which a blastocyst becomes embedded in the uterine wall.

in vitro fertilization (IVF) An ART procedure that combines sperm and oocyte in a laboratory dish and transfers the blastocyst to the mother's uterus.

incidence The number of new cases of a disease within a specified time, usually 1 year.

independent variable In an experiment, a factor that can be manipulated or changed.

induction A type of reasoning in which arguments are formed from a premise to provide support for its conclusion.

infant mortality rate The death of an infant before his or first birthday.

infertility The failure to establish a pregnancy after 12 months of regular, unprotected sexual intercourse. Also referred to as *impaired fecundity.*

informed consent Assent given by a mentally competent individual at least 18 years old with full knowledge of the purpose and potential risks and benefits of participation.

infundibulum The tube-shaped end of each fallopian tube.

instrumentality Being oriented toward tasks and problem solving.

interfemoral intercourse Movement of the penis between the partner's thighs.

internal condom A disposable, thin, loose-fitting sheath with a diaphragm-like ring at each end that covers the cervix, vaginal walls, and part of the external genitals to prevent conception and help protect against STIs. Also called *semale condom*.

internalized homophobia Negative attitudes and affects toward homosexuality in other persons and toward same-sex attraction in oneself.

intersex A variety of conditions during fetal development that lead to atypical development of physical sex characteristics. These conditions can involve the external genitals, internal reproductive organs, sex and sex-related hormones. May also be known as *disorders of sex development (DSD)*.

interview A formal meeting in which one or more persons ask a person questions about a specific topic.

intimate love Love based on commitment, caring, and self-disclosure.

intracytoplasmic sperm injection (ICSI) An ART procedure that involves injecting a single sperm directly into a mature egg; the embryo is then transferred to the uterus or fallopian tube.

intrauterine device (IUD) A long-acting, reversible contraceptive method that involves the placement of a small, flexible, plastic device into the uterus to prevent sperm from fertilizing the egg.

introitus The opening of the vagina.

jealousy An aversive response that occurs because of a partner's real, imagined, or likely involvement with a third person.

Kaplan's tri-phasic model of sexual response A model that divides sexual response into three phases: desire, excitement, and orgasm.

Kaposi's sarcoma A rare cancer of the blood vessels that sometimes occurs among people with AIDS.

Kegel exercises exercises for women designed to strengthen and give voluntary control over the pubococcygeus and to increase sexual pleasure and awareness. For males, the exercises can be valuable in improving erectile function and learning ejaculatory control.

killer T cell A lymphocyte that attacks foreign cells.

kisspeptin A hormone made by the hypothalamus that initiates secretion of other hormones, in particular GnRH at puberty.

Klinefelter syndrome (XXY) A condition in which a male has one or more extra X chromosomes, causing the development of female secondary sex characteristics.

klismaphilia A paraphilia in which a person gets sexual pleasure from receiving enemas.

labia majora Two folds of spongy flesh extending from the mons pubis and enclosing the labia minora, clitoris, urethral opening, and vaginal entrance. Also known as *outer lips*.

labia minora Two small folds of skin within the labia majora that meet above the clitoris to form the clitoral hood. Also known as *inner lips*.

labiaplasty A procedure that changes the size and shape of either or both the labia majora or labia minora.

labor induction The use of medications or other methods to bring on (induce) labor.

lactation The production of milk in the breasts (mammary glands).

lactational amenorrhea method (LAM) A highly effective, temporary method of contraception used by exclusively breastfeeding mothers.

lanugo The fine, downy hair covering the fetus.

laparoscopy A form of tubal ligation using a viewing lens (the laparoscope) to locate the fallopian tubes and another instrument to cut or block and close them.

latency stage In Freudian theory, the period from age 6 to puberty, in which sexual impulses are no longer active.

leukocyte White blood cell.

Leydig cell Cell within the testes that secretes androgens. Also known as an interstitial cell.

libido The sex drive.

limbic system A group of structures in the brain associated with emotions and feelings; involved with producing sexual arousal.

lochia A vaginal discharge containing blood, mucus, and uterine tissue following childbirth.

long-acting reversible contraceptive (LARC) methods Birth control methods, including the IUD and the birth control implant, that provide highly effective protection against pregnancy, last for several years, and are easy to use.

Loulan's sexual response model A model that incorporates both the biological and the affective components into a six-stage cycle.

low-birth-weight infants Those born weighing less than 2,500 grams, or 5.5 pounds.

ludus In John Lee's typology of love, playful love.

luteinizing hormone (LH) A hormone involved in ovulation.

lymphocyte A type of leukocyte active in the immune response.

machismo In Latino culture, highly prized masculine traits.

macrophage A type of white blood cell that destroys foreign cells.

male impersonators Women who dress as men.

malignant tumor A cancerous tumor that invades nearby tissues and disrupts the normal functioning of vital organs.

mammary gland A mature female breast.

mammogram An X-ray of the breast.

mania In John Lee's typology of love, obsessive love.

marital rape Unwanted sexual behaviors by a spouse committed without consent, against a person's will, and done by force, intimidation, or when a person is not able to consent.

mastectomy A surgery that involves the removal of all of the breast tissue and sometimes other nearby tissue.

Masters and Johnson's four-phase model of sexual response A model that divides sexual response into four phases: excitement, plateau, orgasm, and resolution.

masturbation Stimulation of the genitals for pleasure.

mate poaching A deliberate effort to lure a person who is already in a relationship to a brief or long-term relationship with oneself.

MeToo movement (#MeToo) A global social media movement in which women and men speak out against their experiences of sexual harassment and sexual assault.

medication abortion A two-drug regimen used to terminate early pregnancy. Previously known as RU-486.

menarche The onset of menstruation.

menopausal hormone therapy (MHT) The administration of estrogen (often along with progestin) to relieve the symptoms of menopause. Also known as *hormone replacement therapy (HRT)*.

menopause A point in time 12 months after a woman's last menstrual period.

menorrhagia Heavy or prolonged bleeding that may occur during a woman's menstrual cycle.

menses The menstrual flow, in which the endometrium is discharged.

menstrual cycle The more-or-less monthly process during which the uterus is readied for implantation of a fertilized ovum. Also known as *uterine cycle*.

menstrual synchrony Simultaneous menstrual cycles that may occur among women who work or live together.

metastasis The process by which cancer spreads from one part of the body to an unrelated part via the bloodstream or lymphatic system.

miscarriage The spontaneous expulsion of the fetus from the uterus before 20 weeks of pregnancy. Also referred to as pregnancy loss or spontaneous abortion.

misogyny The hatred of or disdain for women.

mons pubis In the female, the mound of fatty tissue covering the pubic bone; the pubic mound. Also known as mons veneris.

mons veneris The pubic mound; literally, "mountain of Venus." Also known as mons pubis.

morning sickness The nauseous feeling a woman may have during her first trimester of pregnancy; the result of increased hormones in the body.

myotonia Increased muscle tension accompanying the approach of orgasm.

necrophilia A paraphilia involving recurrent, intense urges to engage in sexual activities with a corpse.

neonate A newborn.

neural tube defect screening A test on a pregnant woman's blood during the second trimester to measure the level of alpha-fetoprotein; test results reveal possible defects of the spine, spinal cord, skull, and brain.

neurosis A psychological disorder characterized by anxiety or tension.

nocturnal orgasm or emission Orgasm and, in males, ejaculation while sleeping; usually accompanied by erotic dreams. Also known as *wet dream*.

noncoercive paraphilia Harmless and victimless paraphilia sexual behavior.

nonconsensual sexual contact Incidents resulting from either physical force, the inability to consent, or stop what was occurring (i.e., inability to consent).

nongonococcal urethritis (NGU) Urethral inflammation caused by something other than the gonococcus bacterium.

nonoxynol-9 (N-9) The sperm-killing chemical in spermicide.

normal sexual behavior Behavior that conforms to a group's typical patterns of behavior.

nymphomania A pseudoscientific term referring to "abnormally high" or "excessive" sexual desire in a woman.

objectivity The observation of things as they exist in reality as opposed to one's feelings or beliefs about them.

obscenity That which is deemed offensive to "accepted" standards of decency or morality.

observational research Studies in which the researcher unobtrusively observes people's behavior and records the findings.

Oedipal complex In Freudian theory, the male child's erotic desire for his mother and simultaneous fear of his father.

oocyte The female gamete, referred to as an egg or ovum.

oogenesis The production of oocytes; the ovarian cycle.

open relationships Partners mutually agree to have sexual contact with others.

opinion An unsubstantiated belief in or conclusion about what seems to be true according to an individual's personal thoughts.

opportunistic infection (OI) An infection that normally does not occur or is not life-threatening but that takes advantage of a weakened immune system.

oral contraceptive (OC) A series of pills containing synthetic estrogen and/or progestin that regulate egg production and the menstrual cycle. Commonly known as "the pill."

oral stage In Freudian theory, the period lasting from birth to age 1, in which infant eroticism is focused on the mouth.

oral-genital sex The touching of a partner's genitals with the mouth.

orgasm The climax of sexual excitement, including rhythmic contractions of muscles in the genital area and intensely pleasurable sensations; usually accompanied by ejaculation in males beginning in puberty.

orgasmic platform A portion of the vagina that undergoes vasocongestion during sexual arousal.

os The cervical opening.

ovarian cycle The more-or-less monthly process during which oocytes are produced.

ovarian follicle A saclike structure in which an oocyte develops.

ovary One of a pair of organs that produce oocytes.

ovulation The release of an oocyte from the ovary during the ovarian cycle.

ovum (plural, *ova*) An egg; an oocyte; the female gamete.

oxytocin A hormone that stimulates uterine contractions during birth and possibly orgasm. Known as the "love hormone," oxytocin has a major role in pair bonding.

Pap test A method of testing for cervical cancer by scraping cell samples from the cervix and examining them under a microscope.

paraphilia Any intense and persistent sexual interest other than sexual interest in genital stimulation or preparatory fondling with phenotypically normal, physically mature, consenting human partners.

paraphilic disorder A paraphilia that is currently causing distress or impairment to the individual or a paraphilia whose satisfaction has entailed personal harm, or risk of harm, to others.

paraphilic interest A person with paraphilic interest but who are not impaired by the interest and who do not declare distress about the paraphilic impulses.

partialism A paraphilia in which a person is sexually attracted to a specific body part.

participant observation A method of observational research in which the researcher participates in the behaviors being studied.

pathological behavior Behavior deemed unhealthy or diseased by current medical standards.

pedophilia Having a sexual focus on a prepubescent child or children.

pelvic floor The underside of the pelvic area, extending from the top of the pubic bone to the anus.

pelvic inflammatory disease (PID) An infection of the fallopian tube (or tubes), caused by an organism such as *C. trachomatis* or *N. gonorrhoeae,* in which scar tissue may form within the tubes and block the passage of eggs or cause an ectopic pregnancy; a leading cause of female infertility. Also called salpingitis.

penis The male organ through which semen and urine pass.

penis envy In Freudian theory, a female desire to have a penis.

perineum An area of soft tissue between the genitals and the anus that covers the muscles and ligaments of the pelvic floor.

Peyronie's disease A painful male sexual disorder, resulting in curvature of the penis, that is caused by fibrous tissue and calcium deposits developing in the corpora cavernosa of the penis.

phallic stage In Freudian theory, the period from age 3 through 5, during which both male and female children exhibit interest in the genitals.

pheromone Chemicals that the body produces that can be sexually stimulating or impact the behavior of others.

placenta An organ that connects the developing fetus to the uterine wall to provide nutrients and oxygen via the mother's bloodstream to the fetus while also removing waste products from the fetus' blood.

pleasuring Erotic touching.

plethysmograph A device attached to the genitals to measure physiological response.

PLISSIT model A model for sex therapy consisting of four progressive levels: permission, limited information, specific suggestions, and intensive therapy.

polyamory The belief in, practice of, and/or willingness to engage in multiple close relationships that may or may not be sexual in nature, with the consent of everyone involved.

polycystic ovary syndrome (PCOS) A hormonal problem, common among women of reproductive age, that can cause infrequent or prolonged menstrual periods as well as acne and body hair growth.

pornography Sexually explicit materials such as, art, literature, photos, or videos.

post-exposure prophylaxis (PEP) Taking antiretroviral (ART) medicines after being potentially exposed to HIV to prevent becoming infected. Should be used only in emergency situations.

postpartum depression A form of depression thought to be related to hormonal changes following the delivery of a child.

postpartum period The period (about 3 months) following childbirth, characterized by physical stabilization and emotional adjustment.

postpartum psychosis A serious and rare postpartum mental illness thought to be biologically based and related to hormonal changes.

postrefusal sexual persistence Continued requests for sexual contact after being refused.

pragma In John Lee's typology of love, practical love.

pre-exposure prophylaxis (PrEP) HIV-negative persons at substantial risk for HIV taking antiretroviral medicine every day to help prevent becoming infected with HIV.

precocious puberty The appearance of physical and hormonal signs of pubertal development at an earlier age than is considered normal.

preconception health Refers to the health of individuals during their reproductive years and focuses on the steps necessary to protect the health of a baby they might have sometime in the future.

pregnancy-induced hypertension Condition characterized by high blood pressure, edema, and protein in the urine.

premenstrual dysphoric disorder A diagnosis that includes severe, distinct, and persistent symptoms associated with menstruation.

premenstrual syndrome (PMS) A set of severe symptoms associated with menstruation.

prenatal care Recommended health care after a woman becomes pregnant and involves the monitoring of the baby's development as well as the mother's health.

prenatal cell-free DNA A blood test that can detect a baby's risk of Down syndrome and some chromosomal abnormalities as early as 10 weeks. Also known as *noninvasive prenatal screening*.

prepared childbirth Based on knowledge of conditioned reflexes, women learn to mentally separate the physical stimulus of uterine contractions from the conditioned response of pain.

preterm birth Birth that takes place prior to 37 weeks of gestation.

prevalence Overall occurrence; the total number of cases of a disease, for example.

priapism Prolonged and painful erection due to the inability of blood to drain from the penis.

progesterone A female hormone that helps regulate the menstrual cycle and sustain pregnancy.

proliferative phase The buildup of the endometrium in response to increased estrogen during the menstrual cycle.

prostaglandins Natural substances made by the cells in the endometrium and other parts of the body. High levels in women can cause dysmenorrhea.

prostate gland A muscular gland encircling the urethra that produces about one third of the seminal fluid.

prostate-specific antigen (PSA) test A blood test used to help diagnose prostate cancer.

prostatic hyperplasia A benign condition in which the prostate gland enlarges and blocks the flow of urine.

prostatitis A painful condition that involves swelling and inflammation of the prostate gland.

prostitution The exchange of sex for money and/or goods.

proximity Nearness in physical space and time.

psychoanalysis A psychological system developed by Sigmund Freud that traces behavior to unconscious motivations.

psychosexual development Development of the psychological components of sexuality.

puberty The stage of human development when the body becomes capable of reproduction.

pubic lice *Phthirus pubis*, colloquially known as crabs; tiny lice that infest the pubic hair.

pubococcygeus A part of the muscular sling stretching from the pubic bone in front to the tailbone in back.

queer Those whose identified gender and sex is nonconforming, that is, not heterosexual or cisgender.

queer theory Identifies sexuality as a system that cannot be understood as gender neutral or by the actions of heterosexual males and females. It proposes that one's sexual identity and one's gender identity are partly or wholly socially constructed.

queerbating A marketing technique used to describe media where the creators integrate homoeroticism between two characters to lure in same-sex and liberal audiences, yet never include actual representations for fear of alienating a wider audience.

random sample A portion of a larger group collected in an unbiased way.

rape Sexual penetration against a person's will through the use or threat of force.

rebound sex Sexual experiences in the aftermath of a romantic relationship breakup.

refractory period For men, a period following ejaculation during which they are not capable of having ejaculation again.

relaxin A hormone produced by the placenta in the later months of pregnancy that increases flexibility in the ligaments and joints of the pelvic area. In men, relaxin is contained in semen, where it assists in sperm motility.

representative sample A small group representing a larger group in terms of age, sex, ethnicity, socioeconomic status, orientation, for example.

repression A psychological mechanism that keeps people from becoming aware of hidden memories and motives because they arouse guilt or pain.

reproduction The biological process by which individuals are produced.

reproductive justice A concept that links reproductive rights with social justice and describes the complete physical, mental, spiritual, political, social, and economic well-being of a person.

retrograde ejaculation The backward expulsion of semen into the bladder rather than out of the urethral opening.

retrovirus A virus capable of reversing the normal genetic writing process, causing the host cell to replicate the virus instead of itself.

reverse transcriptase An enzyme in the core of a retrovirus, enabling it to write its own genetic program into a host cell's DNA.

root The portion of the penis attached to the pelvic cavity.

same-sex marriage The marriage between two people of the same sex or gender through a civil or religious ceremony. Also known as *gay marriage*.

satyriasis An excessive, uncontrollable sexual desire in a man.

scabies A red, intensely itchy rash appearing on the genitals, buttocks, feet, wrists, knuckles, abdomen, armpits, or scalp, caused by the barely visible mite *Sarcoptes scabiei*.

schema A set of interrelated ideas that helps individuals process information by organizing it in useful ways.

scientific method A systematic approach to acquiring knowledge by collecting data, forming a hypothesis, testing it empirically, and observing the results.

script In sociology, the specific behaviors, rules, and expectations associated with a particular role.

scrotum A pouch of skin that holds the two testes.

secondary sex characteristics The physical changes that occur as a result of increased amounts of hormones targeting other areas of the body.

secretory phase The phase of the menstrual cycle during which the endometrium begins to prepare for the arrival of a fertilized ovum; without fertilization, the corpus luteum begins to degenerate.

secure attachment A style of infant attachment characterized by feelings of security and confidence in relation to the primary caregiver.

self-disclosure The revelation of personal information that others would not ordinarily know because of its riskiness.

self-objectification Evaluating ourselves based on appearance.

semen or seminal fluid The ejaculated fluid containing sperm.

seminal vesicle One of two glands at the back of the bladder that secrete about 60% of the seminal fluid.

seminiferous tubules Tiny, tightly compressed tubes in which spermatogenesis takes place.

sensate focus The focusing on touch and the giving and receiving of pleasure as part of the treatment of sexual difficulties.

serial monogamy A succession of monogamous (exclusive) relationships.

seroconversion The process by which a person develops antibodies.

serosorting Having sex with a partner one believes has the same HIV status (negative or positive) as one's own HIV status.

serostatus The absence or presence of antibodies for a particular antigen.

sex Consists either of the two main categories (male and female) into which humans and most other living things are divided on the basis of their reproductive functions.

sex flush A darkening of the skin or a rash that temporarily appears as a result of blood rushing to the skin's surface during sexual excitation.

sex information/advice genre A media genre that transmits information and norms about sexuality to a mass audience.

sex selection Pre- and post-implantation methods that allow couples to choose whether to have a boy or a girl. (Also marketed as "family balancing.")

sexism Discrimination against people based on their sex rather than their individual merits.

sexologist A specialist in the study of human sexuality. Also called sex researcher.

sextech Online activities designed to enhance human sexual experiences and understanding.

sexting The sending or receiving of suggestive or explicit texts, photos, or video messages via computers or mobile devices.

sextortion To trick children into sharing sexually explicit photos and videos of themselves, which they use as blackmail for more imagery or to humiliate or exact revenge.

sexual assault A legal term for forced sexual contact that does not necessarily include penile-vaginal intercourse.

sexual debut Penile-vaginal or anal intercourse that occurs for the first time in a person's life; it is often considered a milestone for many adolescents.

sexual diary The personal notes a study participant makes of his or her sexual activity and then reports to a researcher.

sexual dysfunction A clinically significant disturbance in a person's ability to respond sexually or to experience sexual pleasure.

sexual exclusivity Sexual partners who have sex only with each other.

sexual function dissatisfaction A condition in which an individual or a couple, not based on a medical diagnosis, decide they are unhappy with their sexual relationship and that they have a problem. Also known as *sexual function difficulties* or *sexual dysfunction*.

sexual function enhancement Improvement in the quality of one's sexual function.

sexual harassment The abuse of power for sexual ends; the creation of a hostile work or educational environment because of unwelcomed conduct or conditions of a sexual nature.

sexual health A state of well-being in relation to sexuality across the life span that involves physical, emotional, mental, and social dimensions.

sexual intercourse The movement of bodies while the penis is in the vagina. Sometimes also called vaginal intercourse or penile-vaginal intercourse. Sometimes penile-anus behavior is considered sexual intercourse.

sexual interest An inclination to behave sexually.

sexual masochism Being humiliated, beaten, bound, or otherwise made to suffer.

sexual response cycle A sequence of changes and patterns that take place in the genitals and body during sexual arousal.

sexual sadism A paraphilia characterized by recurrent, intense urges to engage in real (not fantasy) sexual behaviors in which the person inflicts physical or psychological harm on a victim.

sexual scripts Sexual behaviors and interactions learned from one's culture.

sexual strategies theory The theory that men and women have different short-term and long-term mating strategies.

sexual variation Sexual variety and diversity in terms of sexual orientation, attitudes, behaviors, desires, fantasies, and so on; sexual activity not statistically typical of usual sexual behavior.

sexualize (sexualization) A form of sexism that narrows a frame of a person's worth and value.

sexually explicit material (SEM) Material such as photographs, films, magazines, books, or Internet sites, whose primary themes, topics, or depictions involve sexuality or cause sexual arousal.

shaft The body of the penis.

smegma A cheesy substance produced by several small glands beneath the foreskin of the penis and hood of the clitoris.

social construction The development by society of social categories, such as masculinity, femininity, heterosexuality, and homosexuality.

social construction theory Views gender as a set of practices and performances that occur through language and a political system.

social determinants of health The social and economic conditions that impact an individual's and a group's health status.

socioeconomic status Ranking in society based on a combination of occupational, educational, and income levels.

sodomy Term used in the law to define sexual behaviors other than penile-vaginal intercourse, such as anal sex and oral sex.

solicitation In terms of prostitution, a word, gesture, or action that implies an offer of sex for sale.

spectatoring The process in which a person becomes a spectator of his or her sexual activities, thereby often causing sexual function difficulties.

sperm The male gametes.

spermarche In boys, the development of sperm in the testicles.

spermatic cord A tube suspending the testis within the scrotal sac, containing nerves, blood vessels, and a vas deferens.

spermatogenesis The process by which a sperm develops from a spermatid.

spermicide A substance that is toxic to sperm.

spontaneous abortion The natural expulsion of the conceptus, commonly referred to as *miscarriage.*

squeeze technique A technique for the treatment of early or involuntary ejaculation in which the partner squeezes the erect penis below the glans immediately prior to ejaculation.

stalking A course of action that would cause a reasonable person to feel fear.

statutory rape Consensual sexual intercourse with a person under the age of consent.

stealthing When a man secretly removes his condom during sex despite agreeing to wear one. It is a form of sexual assault.

stereotype A set of simplistic, rigidly held, overgeneralized beliefs about a particular type of individual or group of people, an idea, and so on.

sterilization A surgical procedure that makes the reproductive organs incapable of producing or "delivering" viable gametes (sperm and eggs).

stillbirth The death of a baby before or during delivery.

storge In John Lee's typology of love, companionate love.

strain gauge A device resembling a rubber band that is placed over the penis to measure physiological response.

street harassment Unwelcomed sexual advances.

street-based sex workers Sex workers who solicit customers from the street.

substance/medication-induced sexual dysfunction A specific substance presumed to cause the sexual dysfunction.

sudden infant death syndrome (SIDS) One type of sudden unexplained infant death whereby an infant of less than 1 year of age dies of an unexplained cause.

surrogate motherhood An approach to infertility in which one woman bears a child for another.

survey research A method of gathering information from a small group to make inferences about a larger group.

sweating The moistening of the vagina by secretions from its walls. Also called *vaginal transudation.*

swinging Refers to the practice of extradyadic sex with members of another couple.

symptothermal method A fertility awareness method of birth control that combines three fertility indicators: calendar (rhythm) method, basal body temperature method, and cervical mucus method.

syphilis An STI caused by the *Treponema pallidum* bacterium.

T cell Any of several types of lymphocytes involved in the immune response.

tantric sex A sexual technique based on Eastern religions in which a couple shares "energy" during sexual intercourse.

telephone scatologia A paraphilia involving recurrent, intense urges to make obscene telephone calls.

tenting The expansion of the inner two thirds of the vagina during sexual arousal.

teratogens Substances or other factors that cause defects in developing embryos or fetuses.

testicles or testes (singular, testis) The paired male gonads inside the scrotum.

testosterone A steroid hormone associated with sperm production, the development of secondary sex characteristics in males, and the sex drive in both males and females.

testosterone replacement therapy Treatment that is indicated when both clinical symptoms and signs suggestive of androgen deficiency and decreased testosterone levels are present.

Title IX An education amendment that protects people from discrimination based on sex in education programs or activities that receive federal financial assistance.

toxic shock syndrome (TSS) A rare, life-threatening complication of certain types of bacteria, most commonly the *Staphylococcus aureus* bacterium.

transgender An umbrella term for those whose gender expression or identity is not congruent with the sex assigned at birth. This includes those who identify as genderqueer or gender fluid, gender nonconforming, intersex, and trans.

transition The end of the first stage of labor, when the infant's head enters the birth canal.

triangular theory of love A theory developed by Robert Sternberg emphasizing the dynamic quality of love as expressed by the interrelationship of three elements: intimacy, passion, and commitment.

tribidism A behavior in which one partner lies on top of the other and moves rhythmically for genital stimulation.

trichomoniasis A vaginal infection caused by *Trichomonas vaginalis.* Also known as trich.

trust Belief in the reliability and integrity of another person, process, thing, or institution.

tubal ligation The cutting and tying off or other method of closure of the fallopian tubes so that ova cannot be fertilized.

Turner syndrome (45, XO) A chromosomal condition in which a female does not have the usual pair of X chromosomes.

two-spirit In many cultures, a male who assumes female dress, gender role, and status.

ultrasound A test that uses high-frequency sound waves to capture live images of the growing fetus, to check the baby's development, the presence of a multiple pregnancy, and to help identify certain abnormalities.

umbilical cord The cord connecting the placenta and fetus, through which nutrients pass.

undetectable viral load A viral load so low that it is undetectable in the blood.

unintended pregnancy A pregnancy that is either mistimed or unwanted.

unrequited love Love that is one-sided or not openly reciprocated or understood.

urethra The tube through which urine (and, in men, semen) passes.

urethral opening In females, the opening in the urethra, through which urine is expelled. In males, the opening in the urethra, through which semen is ejaculated and urine is excreted.

urethritis Inflammation of the urethra.

urophilia A paraphilia in which a person gets sexual pleasure from contact with urine.

uterus A hollow, thick-walled, muscular organ held in the pelvic cavity by flexible ligaments and supported by several muscles. Also known as *womb*.

vacuum aspiration A first-trimester form of abortion using vacuum suction to remove the conceptus and other tissue from the uterus.

vagina In females, a flexible, muscular organ that begins between the legs and extends diagonally toward the small of the back. It encompasses the penis during sexual intercourse and is the pathway (birth canal) through which an infant is born.

vaginal ring A vaginal form of reversible, hormonal birth control. Commonly referred to as NuvaRing.

vaginismus A sexual function difficulty characterized by muscle spasms around the vaginal entrance, preventing the insertion of a penis.

vaginitis Any of several kinds of vaginal infection.

value judgment An evaluation as "good" or "bad" based on moral or ethical standards rather than objective ones.

variable An aspect or factor that can be manipulated in an experiment.

vas deferens One of two tubes that transport sperm from the epididymis to the ejaculatory duct within the prostate gland.

vasectomy A permanent method of birth control in which each vas deferens is severed or blocked off, thereby preventing sperm from entering the vas deferens and mixing with seminal fluids to form semen.

vasocongestion The swelling of the genital tissues with blood.

vernix The waxy substance that sometimes covers an infant at birth.

vestibule The area enclosed by the labia minora.

viral load The amount of HIV measured in a volume of blood.

viral suppression A reduction in the amount of HIV in the blood to less than 200 copies per milliliter of blood

virus A protein-coated package of genes that invades a cell and alters the way in which the cell reproduces itself.

voyeurism Observing an unsuspecting person who is naked, disrobing, or having sex.

vulva The collective term for the external female genitals.

vulvodynia Chronic pain or discomfort around the vulva (opening of the vagina) for which there is no definable cause and which lasts at least 3 months.

window period The variable amount of time it takes for the immune system to produce enough antibodies to be detected by an antibody test.

withdrawal A traditional family planning method in which the man completely removes his penis from the vagina, and away from the external genitalia of the female partner before he ejaculates. Also known as *coitus interruptus*.

zoophilia A paraphilia involving recurrent, intense urges to engage in sexual activities with animals. Also referred to as bestiality.

zygote The fertilized egg cell that is produced by the union of egg and sperm.

References

Abbey, A. (2012). Alcohol's role in sexual violence perpetration: Theoretical explanations, existing evidence, and future directions. *Alcohol and Drug Review,* 30(5), 481–489. Available: http://www.ncbi.nlm.nih.gov/pmc/articles/PMC3177166/ (Last visited 1/2/15).

Abramson, P. R., & Mosher, D. L. (1975). Development of a measure of negative attitudes toward masturbation. *Journal of Consulting and Clinical Psychology,* 43, 485–490.

Achilli, C., Pundir, J., Ramanathan, P., et al. (2017). Efficacy and safety of transdermal testosterone in postmenopausal women with hypoactive sexual desire disorder: A systematic review and meta-analysis. *Fertility and Sterility,* 107(2), 475–482.

Adimora, A. A., & Shoenbach, V. J. (2013). Social determinants of social networks, partnership foundations, and sexually transmitted infections. In S. O. Aral, K. A. Fenton, & J. A. Lipschutz (Eds.), *The new public health and STD/HIV prevention: Personal, public and health systems approaches* (pp. 13–31). Springer.

Adimora, A. A., Schoenbach, V. J., & Doherty, I. A. (2007). Concurrent sexual partnerships among men in the United States. *American Journal of Public Health,* 97, 2230–2237.

Adimora, A. A., Schoenbach, V. J., Bonas, M., Martinson, F. E. A., Donaldson, R. H., & Stancil, T. R. (2002). Concurrent sexual partnerships among women in the United States. *Epidemiology,* 13, 320–327.

Ahlers, C. J., Schaefer, G. A., Mundt, I. A., Rolle, S., Englert, H., Willich, S. N., & Beier, K. M. (2001). How unusual are the contents of paraphilias? Paraphilia-associated sexual arousal patterns in a community-bases sample of men. *Journal of Sexual Medicine,* 8, 1362–1370.

Ahrold, T. K., & Meston, C. M. (2010). Ethnic differences in sexual attitudes of U.S. college students: Gender, acculturation, and religiosity factors. *Archives of Sexual Behavior,* 39, 190–202.

Ahrons, C. (2004). *We're still family.* HarperCollins.

Ainsworth, M., et al. (1978). *Patterns of attachment: A psychological study of the strange situation.* Erlbaum.

Albuja, A. F., Sanchez, D. T., Lee, S. J., Lee, J. Y., & Yadava, S. (2019). The effect of paternal cues in prenatal care settings on men's involvement intentions. *PLoS ONE,* 14(5). Available: https://journals.plos.org/plosone/article?id=10.1371/journal.pone.0216454 (Last visited 8/15/20).

Alcott, W. (1868). *The physiology of marriage.* Jewett.

Alexander, M. G., & Fisher, T. D. (2013). Truth and consequences: Using the bogus pipeline to examine sex differences in self-reported sexuality. *Journal of Sex Research,* 40, 27–35.

Alison, L., Santtila, P., Sandnabba, N. K., & Nordling, N. (2001). Sadomasochistically oriented behavior: Diversity in practice and meaning. *Archives of Sexual Behavior,* 30, 1–12.

Allen, D. (2015). More heat than light: A critical assessment of the same-sex parenting literature, 1995–2013. *Marriage & Family Review,* 51, 154–182.

Allen, J. A., Allison, A. E., Clark-Huckstep, A., Hill, B. J., Sanders, S. A., & Zhou, L. (2017). *The Kinsey Institute: The first seventy years.* Indiana University Press.

Althof, S. E. (2010). What's new in sex therapy. *Journal of Sexual Medicine,* 7, 5–13.

Altman, D. (1985). *AIDS in the mind of America.* Doubleday.

Amaro, H., Raj, A., & Reed, E. (2001). Women's sexual health: The need for feminist analyses in public health in the decade of behavior. *Psychology of Women Quarterly,* 25, 324–334.

Amato, P. R. (2003). Reconciling divergent perspectives: Judith Wallerstein, quantitative family research & children of divorce. *Family Relations,* 52(4), 332–339.

Amato, P. R. (2010). Research on divorce: Continuing trends and new developments. *Journal of Marriage and Family,* 72, 650–666.

Amendral, A. (February 2, 2021). How the pandemic has upended the lives of Thailand's sex workers. *NPOR.* Available: https://www.npr.org/sections/goatsandsoda/2021/02/03/960848011/how-the-pandemic-has-upended-the-lives-of-thailands-sex-workers (Last visited: 2/11/2021).

American Academy of Pediatrics. (2012). Circumcision policy statement. *Pediatrics,* 130, 385–386.

American Academy of Pediatrics. (2013). Promoting the well-being of children whose parents are gay or lesbian. *Pediatrics,* 131(4), 827–830.

American Academy of Pediatrics. (2014.12a). Policy statement: Breastfeeding and the use of human milk. *Pediatrics,* 129(3), 827–841.

American Academy of Pediatrics. (2015.4a). Circumcision. Available: https://www.healthychildren.org/English/ages-stages/prenatal/decisions-to-make/Pages/Circumcision.aspx (Last visited 5/15/17).

American Academy of Pediatrics. (2016). American Academy of Pediatrics announces new recommendations for children's media use. Available: https://www.aap.org/en-us/about-the-aap/aap-press-room/pages/american-academy-of-pediatrics-announces-new-recommendations-for-childrens-media-use.aspx (Last visited 4/15/17).

American Academy of Pediatrics. (2017). How to keep your sleeping baby safe: AAP policy explained. Available: https://www.healthychildren.org/English/ages-stages/baby/sleep/Pages/A-Parents-Guide-to-Safe-Sleep.aspx (Last visited 10/7/17).

American Academy of Pediatrics. (2018). Gender-diverse & transgender children. *Healthychildren.org.* Available: https://www.healthychildren.org/English/ages-stages/gradeschool/Pages/Gender-Diverse-Transgender-Children.aspx (Last viewed 2/20/20).

American Association for Marriage and Family Therapy. (2017). Same-sex parents and their children. Available: https://www.aamft.org/imis15/aamft/Content/Consumer_Updates/Same-sex_Parents_and_Their_Children.aspx (Last visited 7/20/17).

American Bar Association. (2020). Paid parental leave for federal employees. Available: https://www.americanbar.org/advocacy/governmental_legislative_work/publications/washingtonletter/january_2020/paid-family-leave/ (Last visited 11/9/20).

American Cancer Society [ACS]. (2017.14). Cancer can affect a man's desire and sexual response. Available from: https://www.cancer.org/treatment/treatments-and-side-effects/physical-side-effects/fertility-and-sexual-side-effects/sexuality-for-men-with-cancer/treatment-and-desire-and-response. html (Last visited 2/9/2018).

American Cancer Society. (2019.13). Screening tests for prostate cancer. Available: https://www.cancer.org/cancer/prostate-cancer/detection-diagnosis-staging/tests.html (Last visited 10/2/20).

American Cancer Society. (2020.13a). About breast cancer. Available: https://www.cancer.org/content/dam/CRC/PDF/Public/8577.00.pdf (Last visited 9/24/20).

American Cancer Society. (2020.13b). American Cancer Society recommendations for the early detection of breast cancer. Available: https://www.cancer.org/cancer/breast-cancer/screening-tests-and-early-detection/american-cancer-society-recommendations-for-the-early-detection-of-breast-cancer.html (Last visited 9/24/20).

American Cancer Society. (2020.13c). Cervical cancer. Available: https://www.cancer.org/cancer/cervical-cancer/about.html (Last visited 9/25/20).

American Cancer Society. (2020.13d). Ovarian cancer. Available: https://www.cancer.org/cancer/ovarian-cancer.html (Last visited 9/28/20).

American Cancer Society. (2020.13e). Endometrial cancer. Available: https://www.cancer.org/cancer/endometrial-cancer.html (Last visited 9/28/20).

American Cancer Society. (2020.13f). About prostate cancer. Available: https://www.cancer.org/cancer/prostate-cancer/about.html (Last visited 10/2/20).

American Cancer Society. (2020.13g). Testicular cancer. Available: https://www.cancer.org/cancer/testicular-cancer.html (Last visited 10/3/20).

American Cancer Society. (2020.13h). Breast cancer in men. Available: https://www.cancer.org/cancer/breast-cancer-in-men.html (Last visited 10/3/20).

American Cancer Society. (2020.13i). Signs and symptoms of anal cancer. Available: https://www.cancer.org/cancer/anal-cancer/detection-diagnosis-staging/signs-and-symptoms.html (Last visited 12/9/20).

American Civil Liberties Union (ACLU). (2020). Trans rights under attack in 2020. Available: https://www.aclu.org/issues/lgbt-rights/transgender-rights/trans-rights-under-attack-2020 (Last visited 5/11/20).

American College Health Association. (2019). *American College Health Association–National College Health Assessment. Undergraduate Student Reference Group. Executive Summary 2019.* American College Health Association.

American College of Obstetricians and Gynecologists (ACOG). (2012). College statement of policy: The role of obstetrician-gynecologist in cosmetic procedures. Available: https://www.acog.org/Clinical-Guidance-and-Publications/Statements-of-Policy/The-Role-of-the-Obstetrician-Gynecologist-in-Cosmetic-Procedures (Last visited 8/1/18).

American College of Obstetricians and Gynecologists. (2013). Exposure to toxic environmental agents: Committee opinion, 575. Available: https://www.acog.org/clinical/clinical-guidance/committee-opinion/articles/2013/10/exposure-to-toxic-environmental-agents (Last visited 8/31/20).

American College of Obstetricians and Gynecologists. (2013.11). *Second-trimester abortion* (p. 313). Available: https://www.acog.org/clinical/clinical-guidance/practice-bulletin/articles/2013/06/second-trimester-abortion (Last visited 7/30/20).

American College of Obstetricians and Gynecologists. (2016a). Obesity and pregnancy. Available: https://www.acog.org/Patients/FAQs/Obesity-and-Pregnancy (Last visited 10/4/17).

American College of Obstetricians and Gynecologists. (2016.12b). ACOG issues new prenatal testing guidelines. Available: https://prenatalinformation.org/2016/04/29/acog-issues-new-prenatal-testing-guidelines/ (Last visited 10/6/17).

American College of Obstetricians and Gynecologists. (2016.12c). Ob-gyns can prevent and manage obstetric lacerations during vaginal delivery, says new ACOG practice bulletin. Available: https://www.acog.org/news/news-releases/2016/06/obgyns-can-prevent-and-manage-obstetric-lacerations-during-vaginal-delivery-says-new-acog-practice-bulletin (Last visited 12/28/20).

American College of Obstetricians and Gynecologists. (2017). ACOG committee opinion. Number 706. Available: https://www.acog.org/clinical/clinical-guidance/committee-opinion/articles/2017/07/sexual-health (Last visited 4/21/20).

American College of Obstetricians and Gynecologists. (2017). Marijuana use during pregnancy and lactation: ACOG Committee Opinion. Author, No. 722. Available: https://www.acog.org/Resources-And-Publications/Committee-Opinions/Committee-on-Obstetric-Practice/Marijuana-Use-During-Pregnancy-and-Lactation (Last visited 10/5/17).

American College of Obstetricians and Gynecologists. (2017.11a). Access to contraception. Committee Opinion, No. 615. Available: https://www.acog.org/clinical/clinical-guidance/committee-opinion/articles/2015/01/access-to-contraception (Last visited 9/21/20).

American College of Obstetrics and Gynecology. (2017.11b). Long-acting reversible contraception: Implants and intrauterine devices. *Bulletin Number 186.* Available: https://www.acog.org/clinical/clinical-guidance/practice-bulletin/articles/2017/11/long-acting-reversible-contraception-implants-and-intrauterine-devices (Last visited 7/28/20).

American College of Obstetricians and Gynecologists. (2018.12b). Tubal ectopic pregnancy. No. 193. Available: https://www.acog.org/clinical/clinical-guidance/practice-bulletin/articles/2018/03/tubal-ectopic-pregnancy (Last visited 8/18/20).

American College of Obstetrics and Gynecology. (2019.11). Over-the-counter access to hormonal contraception. Committee Opinion, No. 788. Available: https://www.acog.org/clinical/clinical-guidance/committee-opinion/articles/2019/10/over-the-counter-access-to-hormonal-contraception (Last visited 7/21/20).

American College of Obstetricians and Gynecologists. (2020). ACOG committee opinion: Elective female genial cosmetic surgery. Available: https://www.acog.org/-/media/Committee-Opinions/Committee-on-Gynecologic-Practice/co795.pdf?dmc=1&ts=20200129T2316238596 (Last visited 1/29/20).

American College of Obstetricians and Gynecologists. (2020.12a). Physical activity and exercise during pregnancy and the postpartum period. Author: No. 804. Available: https://www.acog.org/clinical/clinical-guidance/committee-opinion/articles/2020/04/physical-activity-and-exercise-during-pregnancy-and-the-postpartum-period (Last visited 8/15/20).

American College of Obstetricians and Gynecologists. (2020.12a,b,c). Physical activity and exercise during pregnancy and the postpartum period. Author: No. 804. Available: https://www.acog.org/clinical/clinical-guidance/committee-opinion/articles/2020/04/physical-activity-and-exercise-during-pregnancy-and-the-postpartum-period (Last visited 8/15/20).

American College of Obstetricians and Gynecologists. (2020.12b). ACOG statement on COVID-19 and pregnancy. Available: https://www.acog.org/news/news-releases/2020/06/acog-statement-on-covid-19-and-pregnancy (Last visited 8/18/20).

American College of Obstetricians and Gynecologists. (2020.12c). Coronavirus (COVID-19), pregnancy, and breastfeeding: A message for patients. Available: https://www.acog.org/patient-resources/faqs/pregnancy/coronavirus-pregnancy-and-breastfeeding (Last visited 8/18/20).

American College of Obstetricians and Gynecologists. (2020.12d). Breastfeeding your baby. Available: https://www.acog.org/patient-resources/faqs/labor-delivery-and-postpartum-care/breastfeeding-your-baby (Last visited 9/1/20).

American College of Physicians [ACP]. (2020). Testosterone treatment in adult men with age-related low testosterone: A clinical guideline from the American College of Physicians. *Annals of Internal Medicine, 172*(2), 126–133. Available: https://annals.org/aim/fullarticle/2758507/testosterone-treatment-adult-men-age-related-low-testosterone-clinical-guideline?_ga=2.49244206.960275529.1581556861-1701250237.1581556861 (Last visited 2/12/20).

American Library Association Office of Intellectual Freedom. (n.d.). Top 10 Most Challenged Books Lists. Available: http://www.ala.org/advocacy/bbooks/frequentlychallengedbooks/top10 (Last visited: 3/10/2021).

American Psychiatric Association (APA). (2000). *Diagnostic and statistical manual of mental disorders* (4th ed., text revision). Author.

American Psychological Association. (2011). Hormones and desire. Available: https://www.apa.org/monitor/2011/03/hormones.aspx (Last visited 6/13/14).

American Psychiatric Association. (2013). *Diagnostic and statistical manual for mental disorders* (5th ed.). Author.

American Psychiatric Association. (2017). What are eating disorders? Available: https://www.psychiatry.org/patients-families/eating-disorders/what-are-eating-disorders (Last visited 11/19/17).

American Psychological Association. (2018). Report of the Division 46 Task Force on the sexualization of popular music. Society for Media Psychology & Technology. Available: https://www.apadivisions.org/division-46/publications/popular-music-sexualization.pdf (Last visited 1/19/20).

American Psychological Association. (2018). *APA guidelines for psychological practice with boys and men*. https://www.apa.org/about/policy/boys-men-practice-guidelines.pdf (Last visited 2/21/20).

American Psychological Association. (2020). Marriage & Divorce. Available: https://www.apa.org/topics/divorce/ (Last visited 4/27/20).

American Social Health Association (ASHA). (1998b). Chlamydia: What you should know. Available: http://sunsite.unc.edu/ASHA/std/chlam.html#intro (Last visited 2/14/98).

American Society for Reproductive Medicine. (2016). Endometriosis: Does it cause infertility? Available: https://www.reproductivefacts.org/news-and-publications/patient-fact-sheets-and-booklets/documents/fact-sheets-and-info-booklets/endometriosis-does-it-cause-infertility/ (Last visited 12/16/20).

American Society of Plastic Surgeons (ASPS). (2017). New plastic surgery statistics reveal focus on face and fat. Available: https://www.plasticsurgery.org/news/press-releases/new-plastic-surgery-statistics-reveal-focus-on-face-and-fat (Last visited 12/11/17).

American Society of Plastic Surgeons. (2019). 2018 Plastic surgery statistics report. Available: https://www.plasticsurgery.org/documents/News/Statistics/2018/plastic-surgery-statistics-full-report-2018.pdf (Last visited 2/7/20).

American Society of Reproductive Medicine. (2020). Menopause. Available: https://www.asrm.org/topics/topics-index/menopause/ (Last visited 12/18/20).

Amnesty International. (2016, May 2016). Q&A: Policy to protect the human rights of sex workers. Available from: https://www.amnestyusa.org/reports/qa-policy-to-protect-the-human-rights-of-sex-workers/ (Last visited 9/6/2017).

Anders, K. M., Goodcase, E., Yazadjian, A., & Toews, M. L. (2020). "Sex is easier to get and love is harder to find: Costs and rewards of hooking up among first-year college students. *Journal of Sex Research, 57*(2), 247–259.

Anderson, M., Kunkel, A., & Dennis, M. R. (2011). "Let's (not) talk about that": Bridging the past sexual experiences taboo to build healthy romantic relationships. *Journal of Sex Research, 48*, 381–391.

Anim-Somuah, M., Smyth, R., Cyna, A. M., & Cuthbert, A. (2018). Epidural verses non-epidural or no analgesia for pain management in labor. *Cochrane Systematic Review.* Available: https://www.cochranelibrary.com/cdsr/doi/10.1002/14651858.CD000331.pub4/full (Last visited 8/31/20).

Annan, N. T., et al. (2009). Rectal chlamydia—A reservoir of undiagnosed infection in men who have sex with men. *Sexually Transmitted Infections, 85*, 176–179.

Annon, J. (1974). *The behavioral treatment of sexual problems.* Enabling Systems.

Annon, J. (1976). *Behavioral treatment of sexual problems: Brief therapy.* Harper & Row.

Antfolk, J., Salo, B., Alanka, A., Bergen, E., Corander, J., et al. (2017). Women's and men's sexual preferences and activities with respect to the partner's age: Evidence for female choice. *Evolution and Human Behavior, 36*, 73–79.

Antioch College. (2014–2015). Student handbook 2014–2015. Available: https://www.antiochcollege.edu/sites/default/files/media/staff/2014-2015-Student-Handbook.pdf (Last visited: 10/31/2017).

Apostolou, M. (2015). Female choice and the evolution of penis size. *Archives of Sexual Behavior, 44*, 1749–1750.

Armstrong, H. L., & Reissing, E. D. (2015). Women's motivations to have sex in casual and committed relationships with male and female partners. *Archives of Sexual Behavior, 44*, 921–934.

Arteaga, S., & Gomez, A. M. (2016). "Is that a method of birth control?" A qualitative exploration of young women's use of withdrawal. *Journal of Sex Research, 53*(4–5), 626–632.

Ashton, A. K. (2007). The new sexual pharmacology: A guide for the clinician. In S. Leiblum (Ed.), *Principles and practice of sex therapy* (4th ed., pp. 509–542). Guilford Press.

Aubin, S., Heiman, J., Berger, R., Murally, V., & Yung-Wen, I. (2009). Comparing sildenafil alone vs. sildenafil plus brief couple sex therapy on erectile dysfunction and couples' sexual and marital quality of life: A pilot study. *Journal of Sexual and Marital Therapy, 35*, 122–143.

Austin, S. B., Conron, K. L., Patel, A., & Freedner. N. (2007). Making sense or sexual orientation measures: Findings from a cognitive processing study with adolescents on health survey questions. *Journal of LGBT Health Research, 3*, 55–65.

Ayalon, L., Levkovich, I., Gerwirtz-Meydan, A., & Karkabi, K. (2019). A life course perspective on the ways older men and women discuss sexual issues. *Archives of Sexual Behavior, 48*, 911–919.

Bacak, V., & Stulhofer, A. (2012). Condom use errors and problems in a national sample of young Croatian adults. *Archives of Sexual Behavior, 41*, 995–1003.

Backstrom, L., Armstrong, E. A., & Puentes, J. (2012). Women's negotiation of cunnilingus in college hookups and relationships. *Journal of Sex Research, 49*, 1–2.

Badgett, M. V. L. (2009). *When gay people get married: What happens when societies legalize same-sex marriage.* New York University Press.

Badgett, M. V. L. (2009.7a). Best practices for asking questions about sexual orientations on surveys. *Williams Institute.* Available: http://escholarship.org/uc/item/706057d5#page-1 (Last visited 9/23/17).

Badgett, M. V. L., & Schneebaum, A. (2016). The impact of a $15 minimum wage on poverty among same-sex couples. Available: https://williamsinstitute.law.ucla.edu/research/the-impact-of-a-15-minimum-wage-among-same-sex-couples/ (Last visited: 10/8/2017).

Badgett, M. V. L., Durso, L., & Schneedbaum, A. (2013). New patterns of poverty in the lesbian, gay, and bisexual community. *Williams Institute.* Available from: https://williamsinstitute.law.ucla.edu/research/census-lgbt-demographics-studies/lgbt-poverty-update-june-2013/ (Last visited 10/9/2017).

Baez-Sierra, D., Balgobin, C., & Wise, T. N. (2016). Treatment of paraphilic disorders. In R. Bellon (Ed.), *Practical guide to paraphilia and paraphilic disorders* (pp. 43–62). Springer International.

Bailey, J. M., Gaulin, S., Agyei, Y., & Gladue, B. A. (1994). Effects of gender and sexual orientation on evolutionary relevant aspects of human mating psychology. *Journal of Personality and Social Psychology, 66,* 1081–1903.

Bailey, J. M., Vasey, P. L., Diamond, L. M., Breedlove, S. M., Vilain, E., & Epprecht, M. (2016). Sexual orientation, controversy, and science. *Psychological Science in the Public Interest, 17*(2), 45–101.

Bailey, J. V., Farquhar, C., & Owen, C. (2004). Bacterial vaginosis in lesbians and bisexual women. *Sexually Transmitted Diseases, 31*(11), 691–694.

Bakker, F. & Vanwesenbeeck, I. (Eds.). (2006). *Seksuele gezondheid in Nederland 2006* [Sexual health in the Netherlands 2006]. [RNG-studies nr.9]. Eburon.

Balzarini, R. N., Dharma, C., Kohut, T., Holmes, B. M., Campbell, L., Lehmiller, J. J., & Harmon, J. J. (2019). Demographic comparison of American individuals in polyamorous and monogamous relationships. *Journal of Sex Research, 56*(6), 681–694.

Bancroft, J. (2009). *Human sexuality and its problems* (3rd ed.). Elsevier.

Bancroft, J., & Graham, C. A. (2011). The varied nature of women's sexuality: Unresolved issues and a theoretical approach. *Hormones and Behavior, 59,* 717–729.

Bancroft, J., & Janssen, E. (2000). The dual control model of male sexual response: A theoretical approach to centrally mediated erectile dysfunction. *Neuroscience and Biobehavioral Reviews, 24,* 571–579.

Bancroft, J., & Vukadinovic, Z. (2004). Sexual addiction, sexual compulsivity, sexual impulsivity, or what? *Journal of Sex Research, 41,* 225–234.

Bancroft, J., Graham, C. A., Janssen, E., & Sanders, S. A. (2009). The dual control model: Current status and future directions. *Journal of Sex Research, 46*(2–3), 121–142.

Bandura, A. (1977). *Social learning theory.* Prentice Hall.

Baptist, J., & Coburn, K. (2019). Harassment in public spaces: The intrusion on personal space. *Journal of Feminist Family Therapy, 31,* 114–128.

Barbach, L. (2001). *For each other: Sharing sexual intimacy* (Rev. ed.). Doubleday.

Barber, L. L., & Cooper, M. L. (2014). Rebound sex: Sexual motives and behaviors following a relationship breakup. *Archives of Sexual Behavior, 43*(2), 251–265.

Barber, N. (2017). How men attract women. *Psychology Today.* Available: https://www.psychologytoday.com/blog/the-human-beast/201704/how-men-attract-women (Last visited 1/6/18).

Barry, O. (2020, July 11). Sex workers in Europe struggle to survive as clubs slowly reopen. *The Week.* Available: https://www.pri.org/stories/2020-07-06/sex-workers-europe-struggle-survive-clubs-slowly-reopen. (Last visited: 2/11/2021).

Bartky, S. L. (1990). *Femininity and domination: Studies in the phenomenology of oppression.* Routledge.

Basile, K. C., Clayton, H. B., DeGue, S., Gilford, J. W., Vagi, K. J., Suarez, N. A., Zwald, M. L., & Lowry, R. (2020). Interpersonal violence Victimization among high school students—Youth Risk Behavior Survey, United States, 2019. *Mortality and Morbidity Weekly Report, 69,* 28–37.

Basson, R., Wierman, M. E., van Lankveld, J., & Brotto, L. (2010). Summary of the recommendations on sexual dysfunctions for women. *Journal of Sexual Medicine, 7,* 314–326.

Bauer, G. R., Braimoh, J., Scheim, A. L., & Dharam, C. (2017). Transgender-inclusive measures of sex/gender for population surveys: Mixed-methods evaluation and recommendations. *PLOS ONE, 12*(5). E.0178043. https://doc.org/10.1371/journal.pone0178043.

Bauer, G. R., Jairam, J. A., & Baidoobonso, S. M. (2010). Sexual health, risk behaviors, and substance use in heterosexual-identified women with female sex partners: 2002 U.S. National Survey of Family Growth. *Sexually Transmitted Diseases, 37,* 531–537.

Baumeister, R. (2011). *Sexual economics: A research-based theory of sexual interactions, or why the man buys dinner.* Paper presented at the annual meeting of the American Psychological Association, District of Columbia.

Baxendale, E., Roche, K., & Stephens, S. (2019). An examination of auto-erotic asphyxiation in a community sample. *Canadian Journal of Human Sexuality, 28,* 292–303.

Becasen, J. S., Ford, J., & Hogben, M. (2015). Sexual health interventions: A meta-analysis. *Journal of Sex Research, 52*(4), 433–443.

Beemyn, G. (2015). Best practices to support trans and non-binary gender students. *Campus Pride.* Available: http://www.campuspride.org/tools/best-practices-to-support-transgender-and-other-gender-nonconforming-students/ (Last visited 6/2/15).

Beetz, A. M. (2004). Bestiality/zoophilia: A scarcely investigated phenomenon between crime, paraphilia and love. *Journal of Forensic Psychology Practice, 4,* 1–36.

Bejan, T. M. (2019, November 16). What Quakers teach us about the politics of pronouns. *NY Times.* Available: https://www.nytimes.com/2019/11/16/opinion/sunday/pronouns-quakers.html (Last visited 2/20/20).

Bekkar, B., Pacheco, S., Basu, R., & DeNicola, N. (2020). Association of air pollution and heat exposure with preterm birth, low birth weight, and stillbirth in the US: A systematic review. JAMA *Network Open.* Available: https://jamanetwork.com/journals/jamanetworkopen/fullarticle/2767260?utm_source=For_The_Media&utm_medium=referral&utm_campaign=ftm_links&utm_term=061820 (Last visited 8/17/20).

Belawski, S. E., & Sojka, C. J. (2014). Intimate relationships. In L. Erickson-Schroth (Ed.), *Trans bodies, trans selves: A resource for the transgender community* (pp. 335–354). Oxford University Press.

Bell, S. N., & McClelland, S. I. (2018). When, if, how: Young women contend with orgasmic absence. *Journal of Sex Research, 55,* 679–691.

Belluck, P. (2019, August 19). Planned Parenthood refuses federal funds over abortion restrictions. *NY Times.* Available: https://www.nytimes.com/2019/08/19/health/planned-parenthood-title-x.html (Last viewed 8/2/20).

Belluck, P., & Carey, B. (2013, May 7). Psychiatry's new guide falls short, experts say. *New York Times,* p. A12.

Bem, S. L. (1983). Gender schema theory and its implications for child development: Raising gender-aschematic children in a gender-schematic society. *Signs, 8*(4), 598–616.

Benoit, C., Smith, M., Jansson, M., Magnus, S., Flagg, J., et al. (2017). Sex work and three dimensions of self-esteem: Self-worth, authenticity and self-efficacy. *Culture, Health & Sexuality.* https://doi.org/10.1080/13691058.2017.1328075

Beres, M. (2010). Sexual miscommunication? Untangling assumptions about sexual communication between casual sex partners. *Culture, Health & Sexuality, 12,* 1–14.

Beres, M. A., Senn, C. Y., & McCaw, J. (2014). Navigating ambivalence: How heterosexual young adults make sense of desire differences. *Journal of Sex Research, 51,* 765–776.

Berg, N., & Lien, D. (2006). Same-sex sexual behaviors: U.S. frequency estimates from survey data with simultaneous misreporting and non-response. *Applied Economics, 38,* 757–769.

Berg, R. C., Molin, S., & Nanavati, J. (2020). Women who trade sexual services from men: A systemic mapping review. *Journal of Sex Research, 57,* 104–118.

Bergan, M. E. (2011). *"There's no love here": Beach boys in Malindi, Kenya.* M.A. thesis, University of Bergen, Norway.

Bergeron, S., Corsini-Munt, S., Aerts, L., Rancourt, K., & Rosen, N. O. (2015). Female sexual pain disorders: A review of the literature on etiology and treatment. *Current Sexual Health Reports, 7,* 159–169.

Bergner, D. (2019, June 4). The struggles of rejecting the gender binary. *NY Times.* Available: https://www.nytimes.com/2019/06/04/magazine/gender-nonbinary.html (Last visited 2/20/20).

Bernstein, E. (2001). The meaning of purchase: Desire, demand and the commerce of sex. *Ethnography, 2,* 389–420.

Bernstein, E. (2012, November 13). The new rules of flirting. *Wall Street Journal,* pp. D1–D2.

Bernstein, E. (2015, May 5). What's your number? (we're not talking about phones). *Wall Street Journal.*

Bernstein, E. (2016, August 9). The power of fantasy in a happy relationship. *New York Times,* p. D2.

Berry, M. S., Johnson, P. S., & Collado, A. (2019). Sexual probability discounting: A mechanism for sexually transmitted infection among undergraduate students. *Archives of Sexual Behavior, 48,* 495–505.

Bersamin, M. M., Zamboanga, B. L., Schwartz, S. J., Donellan, M. B., Hudson, M., Weisskirch, R. S., et al. (2014). Risky business: Is there an association between casual sex and mental health among emerging adults? *Journal of Sex Research, 51,* 43–51.

Bersamin, M., Paschall, M. J., Saltz, R. F., & Zamboanga, B. L. (2012). Young adults and casual sex: The relevance of college drinking settings. *Journal of Sex Research, 40,* 272–281.

Besera, G., Moskosky, S., Pazol, K., et al. (2016, June 17). Male attendance at Title X family planning clinics—United States, 2003–2014. *Morbidity and Mortality Weekly Reports (MMWR), 65*(23), 602–605. Available: https://www.cdc.gov/mmwr/volumes/65/wr/mm6523a3.htm (Last visited 5/12/17).

Best, K. (2007, December 17). Kiss and tell: Smooches make or break a relationship. *Indianapolis Star,* p. E1.

Best, P. (2020). All middle school and high schoolers in Vermont will now have access to free condoms. *New York Post.* Available: https://nypost.com/2020/10/16/all-middle-and-high-schoolers-in-vermont-will-now-have-access-to-free-condoms/ (Last visited 11/23/2020).

Beyer, C., Baral, S. D., van Griensven, F., Goodreau, S. M., Chariyalertak, C., Wirtz, A. L., et al. (2012). Global epidemiology of HIV infection in men who have sex with men. *The Lancet, 380,* 367–377.

Bilefsky, D., & Anderson, C. (2017a, February 23). A paid hour a week for sex? Swedish town considers it. *New York Times.*

Bilefsky, D., & Anderson, C. (2017b, May 18). Swedish town rejects proposal to grant sex leave for workers. *New York Times.*

Billy, J. O. G., Grady, W. R., & Sill, M. E. (2009). Sexual risk-taking among adult dating couples in the United States. *Perspectives on Sexual and Reproductive Health, 41,* 74–83.

Bird, J. D., Morris, J. A., Koester, K. A., Pollack, L. M., Binson, D., & Woods, W. J. (2017). "Knowing your status and knowing your partner's status is really where it starts": A qualitative exploration of the process by which a sexual partner's HIV status can influence sexual decision making. *Journal of Sex Research, 54,* 784–794.

Biro, F. M., Pajak, A., Wolff, M. S., Pinney, S. M., Windham, G. C., Galvez, M. P., Greenspan, L. C., Kushi, L. H., & Teitelbaum, S. L. (2018). Age of menarche in a longitudinal US cohort. *Journal of Pediatric Adolescent Gynecology, 31*(4), 339–345. Available: https://www.ncbi.nlm.nih.gov/pubmed/29758276 (Last visited 4/16/20).

Bischof-Campbell, A., Hilpert, P., Burri, A., & Bischof, K. (2019). Body movement is associated with orgasm during vaginal intercourse in women. *Journal of Sex Research, 56*(3), 356–366.

Bischof-Campbell, K. (2012). Sexocorporal in the promotion of sexual pleasure. In *Pleasure and health (Proceedings of the Nordic Association for Clinical Sexology)* (pp. 59–68).

Biskupic, J. (2003, June 27). Gay sex ban struck down. *USA Today,* p. A1.

Biskupic, J. (2004, June 30). It may be up to parents to block web porn. *New York Times,* p. 6A.

Black, S. W., Kaminsky, G., Hudson, A., Owen, J., & Finchman, F. (2019). A short-term longitudinal investigation of hookups and holistic outcomes among college students. *Archives of Sexual Behavior, 48,* 1829–1845. Available: https://link.springer.com/article/10.1007/s10508-018-1330-4 (Last visited 5/5/20).

Blackwood, E. (1984). Sexuality and gender in certain Native American tribes: The case of cross-gender females. *Signs, 10,* 27–42.

Blair, K. L., & Pukall, C. F. (2014). Can less be more? Comparing duration vs. frequency of sexual encounters in the same-sex and mixed sex relationships. *Canadian Journal of Human Sexuality, 23,* 123–136.

Blais-Lecours, S., Vaillancourt-Morel, M., Sabourin, S., & Godbout, N. (2016). Cyberpornography: Time use, perceived addiction, sexual functioning, and sexual satisfaction. *Cyberpsychology, Behavior, and Social Networking, 18,* 649–655.

Blank, H. (2012). *Straight: The surprisingly short history of heterosexuality.* Beacon Press.

Bleakley, A., Ellithorpe, M. E., Hennessy, M., Khurana, A., Jamieson, P., & Weitz, I. (2017). Alcohol, sex and screens: Modeling media influence on adolescent alcohol and sex co-occurrence. *Journal of Sex Research, 54*(8), 1026–1037.

Blechman, E. A. (1990). *Emotions and the family: For better or for worse.* Erlbaum.

Blow, C. (2015, September 7). Sexual attraction and fluidity. *New York Times,* p. A17.

Blumstein, P., & Schwartz, P. (1983). *American couples.* McGraw-Hill.

Blunt-Vinti, H., Jozkowski, K. N., & Hunt, M. (2018). Show or tell? Does verbal and/or nonverbal communication matter for sexual satisfaction? *Journal of Sex & Marital Therapy, 45*(3), 206–217. Available: https://www.tandfonline.com/doi/pdf/10.1080/0092623X.2018.1501446?casa_token=kiizFwLrDGYAAAAA:2LDXnfRspCSdNvwsVN84I0iLGGQF-BORXHGlhNy0dv7s_nHeG656I05qeK0IMrGmMVhMw74Vx6LwzQA (Last visited 6/11/20).

Bogaert, A. F., Ashton, M. C., & Lee, K. (2018). Personality and sexual orientation: Extension to asexuality and the HEXACO model. *Journal of Sex Research, 55*(8), 951–961.

Bogart, L. M., Galvan, F. H., Wagner, G. J., & Klein, D. J. (2011). Longitudinal association of HIV conspiracy beliefs with sexual risk among Black males living with HIV. *AIDS and Behavior, 15,* 1180–1186.

Bogart, L. M., Walt, L. C., Pavlovic, J. D., Ober, A. J., Brown, N., & Kalichman, S. C. (2007). Cognitive strategies affecting recall of sexual behavior among high-risk men and women. *Health Psychology, 26,* 787–793.

Bonilla, L., & Porter, J. (1990). A comparison of Latino, Black, and non-Hispanic attitudes toward homosexuality. *Hispanic Journal of Homosexuality, 12,* 439–452.

Bonos, L., & Guskin, E. (2019, March 21). It's not just you: New data shows more than half of young people in America don't have a romantic partner. *The Washington Post.* Available: https://www.washingtonpost.com/lifestyle/2019/03/21/its-not-just-you-new-data-shows-more-than-half-young-people-america-dont-have-romantic-partner/ (Last visited 4/27/20).

Boorstein, M. (2020, June 26). Scandals, compensation programs lead Catholic clergy sex abuse complaints to quadruple in 2019. Available: https://www.washingtonpost.com/religion/2020/06/26/scandals-compensation-programs-lead-catholic-clergy-sex-abuse-complaints-quadruple-2019/. (Last visited: 2/24/2021).

Borneman, E. (1983). Progress in empirical research on children's sexuality. *SIECUS Report,* 1–5.

Borrello, G., & Thompson, B. (1990). A note regarding the validity of Lee's typology of love. *Journal of Psychology, 124*(6), 639–644.

Boskey, E. (2013). Sexuality in the DSM 5: Research, relevance, and reaction. *Contemporary Sexuality, 47*(1), 305.

Boskey, E. (2019). Top ten reasons to support sex education in schools. *VeryWell Health.* Available: https://www.verywellhealth.com/support-comprehensive-education-schools-3133083 (Last visited: 2/13/19).

Bostwick, H. (1860). *A treatise on the nature and treatment of seminal disease, impotency, and other kindred afflictions.* Burgess, Stringer.

Bostwick, W. B., & Dodge, B. (2019). Introduction to the special section on bisexual health: Can you see us now? *Archives of Sexual Behavior, 48,* 79–87.

Both, S., Lew-Starowica, M., Luria, M., Startorius, G., Maseroli, E., Tripodi, F., Lowenstein, L., Nappi, R. E., Corona, G., Reisman, Y., & Vignozzi, L. (2019). Hormonal contraception and female sexuality: Position statements from the European Society of Sexual Medicine (ESSM). *Journal of Sexual Medicine, 16*(11), 1681–1695. Available: https://pubmed.ncbi.nlm.nih.gov/31521571/ (Last visited 7/21/20).

Bouchard, K. N., Stewart, J. G., Boyer, S. C., Holden, R. R., & Pukall, C. F. (2019). Sexuality and personally correlates of willingness to participate in sex research. *The Canadian Journal of Human Sexuality, 28,* 26–37.

Bowerman, M. (2017, February 6). Survey: Sleeping together before a first date is A-OK, but cracked phones are a put-off. *USA Today.*

Bowleg, L., Teti, M., Massie, J. S., Patel, A., Malebranche, D. J., & Tschann, J. M. (2011). 'What does it take to be a man: What is a real man?' Ideologies of masculinity and HIV sexual risk among Black heterosexual men. *Culture, Health & Sexuality, 13,* 545–559.

Bowles, N., & Keller, M. H. (2019, December 7). Video games and online chats are 'hunting grounds' for sexual predators. *New York Times.* Available: https://www.nytimes.com/interactive/2019/12/07/us/video-games-child-sex-abuse.html (Last visited 1/21/20).

Bowles, N. (2017, November 12). As glare widens on harassers, men at office look in mirror. *New York Times,* p. A1.

Bowman, C. P. (2014). Women's masturbation: Experiences of sexual empowerment in a primarily sex-positive sample. *Psychology of Women Quarterly, 38,* 363–378.

Boyer, C. B., Shafer, M., Wibbelsman, C. J., Seeberg, D., Teitle, E., & Lovell, N. (2000). Associations of sociodemographic, psychosocial, and behavioral factors with sexual risk and sexually transmitted diseases in teen clinic patients. *Journal of Adolescent Health, 27,* 102–111.

Bradford, J. M. W., & Ahmed, J. G. (2014). The natural history of paraphilias. *Psychiatric Clinics in North America, 37,* xi–xv. https://doi.org/10-1061/j.psc.2-14.03.010

Bradshaw, C., Kahn, A. S., & Saville, B. K. (2010). To hook up or date: Which gender benefits? *Sex Roles, 62,* 661–669.

Brady, S. S., Tschann, M. M., Ellen, J. M., & Flores, E. (2009). Infidelity, trust and condom use among Latino youth in dating relationships. *Sexually Transmitted Diseases, 36,* 227–231.

Braithwaite, S. R., Coulson, G., Keddington, K., & Fincham, F. D. (2015). The influence of pornography on sexual scripts and hooking up among emerging adults in college. *Archives of Sexual Behavior, 44,* 111–123.

Brambilla, D. J., Matsumoto, A. M., Araujo, A. M., & McKinlay, J. E. (2009). The effect of diurnal variation on clinical measurement of serum testosterone and other sex hormone levels. *Journal of Clinical Endocrinology & Metabolism, 94*(3).

Braverman, E. R. (2011). *Younger (sexier) you.* Rodale.

Braverman, P., & Strasburger, V. (1994, January). Sexually transmitted diseases. *Clinical Pediatrics,* 26–37.

Brents, B. G., Jackson, C. A., & Hausbeck, K. (2010). *The state of sex: Tourism, sex, and sin in the new American heartland.* Routledge.

Brents, B., & Hausbeck, K. (2005). Violence and legalized brothel prostitution in Nevada. *Journal of Interpersonal Violence, 20,* 270–295.

Bringle, R. G., Winnick, T., & Rydell, R. J. (2013). The prevalence and nature of unrequited love. *SAGE Open,* 1–15. Available: https://journals.sagepub.com/doi/pdf/10.1177/2158244013492160 (Last visited 6/2/20).

British Columbia Ministry of Health. (2020). COVID-19: Guidance for sex workers (coronavirus COVD-19). Available: http://www.bccdc.ca/health-info/diseases-conditions/covid-19/prevention-risks/covid-19-and-sex. (Last visited: 2/11/2021).

Brizendine, L. (2010). *The male brain.* Crown.

Brodsky, A. (2017). "Rape-adjacent": Imagining legal responses to nonconsensual condom removal. *Columbia Journal of Gender and Law, 32*(2).

Brodwin, E. (2015, January 12). Here's why couples who live together shouldn't be in any rush to get married. *Business Insider.* Available: http://www.businessinsider.com/does-marriage-help-or-hurt-a-relationship-2015-1 (Last visited 12/11/2017).

Brody, J. E. (2020, February 24). Debating the value of PSA prostate screening. *NY Times.* Available: https://www.nytimes.com/2020/02/24/well/live/prostate-testing-PSA-cancer-screening.html (Last visited 10/20/20).

Brody, S. (2010). The relative health benefits of different sexual activities. *Journal of Sexual Medicine, 7,* 1336–1361.

Brooks, D. (2016, February 23). Three views of marriages. *New York Times,* p. A27.

Brotto, L. A., & Smith, K. B. (2014). Sexual desire and pleasure. In D. L. Tolman & L. M. Diamond (Eds.), *APA handbook of sexuality and psychology* (pp. 205–244). American Psychiatric Association.

Brotto, L. A., & Yule, M. (2017). Asexuality: Sexual orientation, paraphilia, sexual dysfunction or none of the above? *Archives of Sexual Behavior, 46*(3), 619–627.

Brotto, L. A., Chik, H. M., Ryder, A. G., Gorzalka, B. G., & Seal, B. N. (2005). Acculturation and sexual function in Asian women. *Archives of Sexual Behavior, 6,* 613–626.

Brown, E. (2021, February 22). Sexual assault against boys is a crisis. Available: https://www.washingtonpost.com/magazine/2021/02/22/why-we-dont-talk-about-sexual-violence-against-boys-why-we-should/?no_nav=true&tid=a_classic-iphone. Visited: 2/28/2021.

Brown, J. D. (2002). Mass media influences on sexuality. *Journal of Sex Research, 45,* 42–45.

Brown, T. N. T., Romero, A. P., & Gates, G. J. (2016). Food insecurity and SNAP participation in the LGBT community. Available: https://williamsinstitute.law.ucla.edu/press/press-releases/study-finds-lgbt-adults-experience-food-insecurity-and-snap-participation-at-higher-levels-than-non-lgbt-adults/ (Last visited: 10/9/2017).

Brunham, R. C., & Plummer, F. A. (1990). A general model of sexually transmitted epidemiology and its implications for control. *Medical Clinics of North America, 74,* 1339–1352.

Bryant, T. S., & Oliver, M. B. (Eds). *Media effects: Advances in theory and research.* Routledge.

Buber, M. (1958). *I and Thou.* Charles Schribner's Sons.

Buffardi, A. L., Thomas, K. K., Holmes, K. K., & Manhart, L. E. (2008). Moving upstream: Ecosocial and psychosocial correlates of sexually transmitted infections among young adults in the United States. *American Journal of Public Health, 98,* 1128–1136.

Bui, Q., & Miller, C. C. (2018, August 4). Data on mothers reveal schisms across America. *NY Times.* Available: https://www.nytimes.com/interactive/2018/08/04/upshot/up-birth-age-gap.html (Last visited 8/20/20).

Buisson, O., & Jannini, E. A. (2013). Pilot echographic study of the differences in clitoral involvement following clitoral or vaginal stimulation. *Journal of Sexual Medicine, 10,* 2734–2740.

Bullough, V. L. (1991). Transvestism: A reexamination. *Journal of Psychology and Human Sexuality,* 4(2), 53–67.

Bullough, V. L. (1994). *Science in the bedroom: A history of sex research.* Basic Books.

Bullough, V. L. (2004). Sex will never be the same: The contributions of Alfred C. Kinsey. *Archives of Sexual Behavior,* 33, 277–286.

Bulmer, M., & Izuma, K. (2018). Implicit and explicit attitudes toward sex and romance in asexuals. *Journal of Sex Research,* 55(8), 962–974.

Burghardt, J., Beutel, M., Hasenburg, A., Schmutzer, G., & Brahler, E. (2020). Declining sexual activity and desire in women: Findings from representative German surveys 2005 and 2016. *Archives of Sexual Behavior,* 46, 919–925.

Burkhill, S., Copas, A., Couper, M. P., Clifton, S., Prah, P., Datta, J., et al. (2016, February 11). Using the web to collect data on sensitive behaviors: A study looking at mode effects on the British National Survey on Sexual Attitudes. *PLoS ONE* 11(2), e0147983. https://doi.org/10.1371/journal.pone.0147983. Available: http://journals.plos.org/plosone/article?id=10.1371/journal.pone.0147983.

Busby, D. M., Chiu, H., Olsen, J. A., & Willoughby, B. J. (2012). Evaluating the dimensionality of pornography. *Archives of Sexual Behavior,* 46, 1723–1731.

Busby, D. M., Willoughby, B. J., Chiu, H., & Olsen, J. A. (2020). Measuring the multidimensional construct of pornography: A long and short version of the pornography usage measure. *Archives of Sexual Behavior,* 49, 3027–3039.

Buss, D. M. (1994.9/2003.9b). *The evolution of desire: Strategies of human mating* (Rev. ed.). Basic Books.

Buss, D. M. (2006). Strategies for human mating. *Psychological Topics,* 15, 239–260.

Buss, D. M. (1998). Sexual strategies theory: Historical origins and current status. *Journal of Sex Research,* 35, 19–31.

Buss, D. M. (1999). *Evolutionary psychology: The new science of the mind.* Allyn & Bacon.

Buss, D. M. (2000). *Dangerous passion: Why jealousy is as necessary as love and sex.* Simon & Schuster.

Buss, D. M. (2018). Sexual and emotional infidelity: Evolved gender differences in jealousy prove robust and replicable. *Perspectives on Psychological Science,* 13(2), 155–160. Available: https://journals.sagepub.com/doi/pdf/10.1177/1745691617698225?casa_token=ZUzQlRv_2VMAAAAA:nux1rxChPftF0lwE9jHM_IT8jTePILyEDK_vacXt3fTvPmxhT9jr2xkJ-O70inHtkx5HjVTmrNCIxg (Last viewed 6/2/10).

Buss, D. M. & Schmitt, D. P. (1993). Sexual strategies theory: An evolutionary perspective on human mating. *Psychological Review,* 100(2), 204–232.

Buss, D. M. & Schmitt, D. P. (2011). Evolutionary psychology and feminism. *Sex Roles,* 64, 204–232.

Buss, D. M. & Schmitt, D. P. (2011). Evolutionary psychology and feminism. *Sex Roles,* 64, 768–787.

Bussey, K., & Bandura, A. (1999). Social cognitive theory of gender development and differentiation. *Psychological Review,* 106, 676–713.

Bustos, M., Venkataramanan, R., & Caritis, S. (2018). Nausea and vomiting of pregnancy – What's new? *Autonomic Neuroscience,* 202, 62–72. Available: https://www.ncbi.nlm.nih.gov/pmc/articles/PMC5107351/ (Last visited 8/15/20).

Butler, J. (1993). *Bodies that matter: On the discursive limits of sex.* Routledge.

Butler, S. M., Smith, N. K., Collazo, E., et al. (2015). Pubic hair preferences, reasons for removal, and associated genital symptoms: Comparisons between men and women. *Journal of Sexual medicine,* 12(1), 48–58.

Byard, R. W., & Botterill, P. M. B. (1998). Autoerotic asphyxial death—Accident or suicide? *American Journal of Forensic Medicine and Pathology,* 19, 377–380.

Byers, E. S. (2005). Relationship satisfaction and sexual satisfaction: A longitudinal study of individuals in long-term relationships. *Journal of Sex Research,* 42(2), 113–118.

Byers, F. S., Henderson, J., & Hobson, K. M. (2009). University students' definitions of sexual abstinence and having sex. *Archives of Sexual Behavior,* 38, 665–674.

Byne, W. (2014). Forty years after the removal of homosexuality from the DSM: Well on the way but not there yet. *LGBT Health,* 1, 1–3.

Cabral, M. A., Schroeder, R., Armstrong, E. M., El Ayadi, A. M., Gurel, A. L., Chang, J., & Harper, C. C. (2018, October 30). Pregnancy intentions, contraceptive knowledge and educational aspirations among community college students. *Perspectives on Sexual and Reproductive Health,* 50(4), 181–188.

Cacioppo, S., Bianchi-Demicheli, F., Frum, C., Pfaus, J. G., & Lewis, J. W. (2012). The common neural bases between sexual desire and love: A multilevel kernel density fMRI analysis. *Journal of Sexual Medicine,* 9(4), 1048–1054.

Calam, R., Horne, L., Glasgow, D., & Cox, A. (1998). Psychological disturbance and child sexual abuse: A follow-up study. *Child Abuse and Neglect,* 22, 901–913.

Calderone, M. S. (1983). Childhood sexuality: Approaching the prevention of sexual disease. In G. Albee, et al. (Eds.), *Promoting sexual responsibility and preventing sexual problems.* University Press of New England.

Call, V., Sprecher, S., & Schwartz, P. (1995). The incidence and frequency of marital sex in a national sample. *Journal of Marriage and Family,* 57, 639–652.

Calzo, J. P. (2013). Hookup versus romantic relationship sex in college: Why do we care and what do we do? *Journal of Adolescent Health,* 52, 515–516.

Campbell, L., & Kohut, T. (2017). The use and effects of pornography in romantic relationships. *Current Opinion in Psychology,* 13, 6–10.

Campos-Outcalt, D., & Hurwitz, S. (2002). Female-to-female transmission of syphilis: A case report. *Sexually Transmitted Diseases,* 29, 119–120.

Campus Technical Assistance and Resource Project. (2016). Where we've been, where we're going: Mobilizing men and boys to prevent gender-based violence. Available: http://109.199.106.79/~center4cocc/resources/not-alone/Engaging_Men_Report_Final.pdf (Last visited: 10/11/2017).

"Can marijuana affect a man's sexual function?" (2020). International Society of Sexual Medicine. Available: https://www.issm.info/sexual-health-qa/can-marijuana-affect-a-mans-sexual-function/ (Last visited 9/18/20).

Cantor, D., Fisher, B., Chibnall, S., Harps, S., Townsend, R., Thomas, G., Lee, H., Kranz, V., Herbison, R., & Madden, K. (2020). Report on the AAU Campus Climate Survey on Sexual Assault and Misconduct. Association of American Universities. Available: https://www.aau.edu/sites/default/files/AAU-Files/Key-Issues/Campus-Safety/Revised%20Aggregate%20report%20%20and%20appendices%201-7_(01-16-2020_FINAL).pdf (Last visited: 11/26/2020).

Cantor, D., Townsend, R., & Sun, H. (2016). *Methodology report for the AAU campus climate survey on sexual assault and sexual misconduct: Fiscal year 2016.* Association of American Universities. Available: https://www.aau.edu/sites/default/files/%40%20Files/Climate%20Survey/Methodology_Report_for_AAU_Climate_Survey_4-12-16.pdf (Last visited: 10/6/2017).

Cao, S., Yin, X., Wang, Y., Zhow, H., Song, F., Lu, Z., et al. (2013). Smoking and risk of erectile dysfunction: Systematic review of observational studies with meta-analysis. *PLoS One,* 8(4), e60443. https://doi.org/10.1371/journal.pone.0060443

Caplan, A. L. (1992). Twenty years after: The legacy of the Tuskegee syphilis study. When evil intrudes. *Hastings Center Report, 22*(6), 29–32.

Capshew, J. H. (2012). *Herman B. Wells: The promise of the American university.* Indiana University Press.

Carael, M., Slaymaker, E., Lyerla, R., & Sarkar, S. (2006). Clients of sex workers in different regions of the world: Hard to count. *Sexually Transmitted Infections, 82*(Suppl-3), iii26–iii33.

Carbone, L., De Vivo, V., Saccone, G., D'Antonio, F., & Merrcorio, A. (2019). Sexual intercourse for induction of spontaneous onset of labor: A systematic review and meta-analysis of randomized controlled trials. *Journal of Sexual Medicine, 11,* 1787–1795.

Carnes, P. (1983). *Out of shadows.* CompCare.

Carnes, P. (1991). Progress in sex addiction: An addiction perspective. In R. T. Francoeur (Ed.), *Taking sides: Clashing views on controversial issues in human sexuality* (3rd ed.). Dushkin.

Caron, C. (2020, June 4). Gay couples can teach straight people a thing or two about arguing. *New York Times.* Available: https://www.nytimes.com/2020/06/01/parenting/relationship-advice-gay-straight.html (Last visited 7/3/20).

Caron, S. (2013). *The sex lives of college students: Two decades of attitudes and behaviors.* Maine College Press.

Carroll, A. E. (2016, May 9). Should you circumcise your baby boy? *NY Times.* Available: https://www.nytimes.com/2016/05/10/upshot/why-science-cant-help-you-much-in-deciding-on-circumcision.html (Last visited 2/10/20).

Carroll, J. L. (2010). *Sexuality now: Embracing diversity.* Wadsworth.

Carter, C. S., (2014). Oxytocin pathways and the evolution of human behavior. *Annual Review of Psychology, 65,* 17–39.

Carter, C. S., Pournajafe-Nazarloo, H., Kramer, K. M., Ziegler, T. E., White-Traut, R., Bello, D., & Schwertz, D. (2007). Oxytocin: Behavioral associations and potential as a salivary biomarker. *Annals of the New York Academy of Sciences, 1098,* 312–322.

Cassell, C. (2008). *Put passion first: Why sexual chemistry is the key to finding and keeping lasting love.* McGraw-Hill.

Castleman, M. (2004). *Great sex: A man's guide to the secret principles of total-body sex.* Rodale Books.

Catania, J. A., Dolcini, M. M., Orellana, R., & Narayanan. (2015). Nonprobability and probability-based sampling strategies in sexual science. *Journal of Sex Research, 52,* 396–411.

Cate, R. M., & Lloyd, S. A. (1992). *Courtship.* Sage.

Cates, J. R., Herndon, N. L., Schulz, S. L., & Darroch, J. E. (2004). *Our voices, our lives, our futures: Youth and sexually transmitted diseases.* School of Journalism and Mass Communication, University of North Carolina at Chapel Hill.

Center of Excellence for Transgender Care. (2017). *Guidelines for the primary and gender-affirming care of transgender and gender nonbinary people.* (2nd ed.). University of California, San Francisco. Available: http://transhealth.ucsf.edu/trans?page=guidelines-home (Last visited 12/6/17).

Centers for Disease Control and Prevention (CDC). (1981.15a). Pneumocystis pneumonia—Los Angeles. *Morbidity and Mortality Weekly Report, 30,* 250–252.

Centers for Disease Control and Prevention. (1992). 1993 revised classification system for HIV infection and expanded surveillance case definition for AIDS among adolescents and adults. *Morbidity and Mortality Weekly Report, 41,* 961–962.

Centers for Disease Control and Prevention. (1996). Surveillance report: U.S. AIDS cases reported through December 1995. *HIV/AIDS Surveillance Report, 7*(2), 1–10.

Centers for Disease Control and Prevention. (2007.15a). Sexually transmitted disease surveillance. Available: http://www.cdc.gov/std/stats/toc2006.htm (Last visited 10/15/08).

Centers for Disease Control and Prevention. (2010.15c). Scabies frequently asked questions. Available: http://www.cdc.gov/parasites/scabies/gen_info/faqs.html (Last visited 12/5/11).

Centers for Disease Control and Prevention. (2010.15e). Candidiasis. Available: http://www.cdc.gov/cxzved/divisions/dfbmd/diseases/candidiasis/index.htm (Last visited 12/5/11).

Centers for Disease Control and Prevention). (2010.16b). HIV transmission. Available: https://www.cdc.gov/hiv/basics/transmission.html (Last visited 12/13/11).

Centers for Disease Control and Prevention. (2011.15b). Chlamydia—CDC fact sheet. Available: http://www.cdc.gov/std/chlamydia/STDFact-Chlamyhdia.htm (Last visited 11/10/11).

Centers for Disease Control and Prevention. (2011.15c). Genital HPV infection—CDC fact sheet. Available: http://www.gov/std/HPV/STDFact-HPV.htm (Last visited 11/28/11).

Centers for Disease Control and Prevention. (2011.15f). Genital HPV infection—CDC fact sheet. Available: http://www.gov/std/HPV/STDFact-HPV.htm (Last visited 11/28/11).

Centers for Disease Control and Prevention. (2011.2a). CDC health disparities and inequalities report—United States, 2011. *Morbidity and Mortality Weekly Report, 60,* 1–116.

Centers for Disease Control and Prevention. (2013). Fact sheet for public health personnel. Available: https://npin.cdc.gov/publication/condoms-and-stds-fact-sheet-public-health-personnel (Last visited 11/29/2017).

Centers for Disease Control and Prevention. (2013.15b). Cervical cancer screening with the HPV test and the Pap test in women ages 30 and older. Available: http://www.cdc.gov/cancer/hpv/basic_info/screening/pap_test_result.htm (Last visited 12/12/14).

Centers for Disease Control and Prevention. (2014). Which STD tests should I get? Available: https://www.cdc.gov/std/prevention/screening reccs.ht (Last visited 10/1/2020).

Centers for Disease Control and Prevention. (2014.15b). *Sexually transmitted disease surveillance 2013.* Atlanta: U.S. Department of Health and Human Services.

Centers for Disease Control and Prevention. (2014.15c). HIV prevention. Available: http://www.cdc.gov/hiv/basics/prevention.html (Last visited 12/8/14).

Centers for Disease Control and Prevention. (2014.15i). *Sexually transmitted disease surveillance 2010.* U.S. Department of Health and Human Services.

Centers for Disease Control and Prevention. (2014.15l). Diseases characterized by urethritis and cervicitis. Available: http://www.cdc.gov/std/treatment/2010/urethritis-and-cervicitis.htm (Last visited 12/11/14).

Centers for Disease Control and Prevention. (2014.16a). About HIV/AIDS. Available: https://www.cdc.gov/hiv/basics/whatishiv.html (Last visited 12/16/14).

Centers for Disease Control and Prevention. (2014.16b). Opportunistic infections. Available: http://cdc.gov/hiv/living/opportunisticinfections.html (Last visited 12/29/14).

Centers for Disease Control and Prevention. (2014.16f). HIV surveillance by race/ethnicity (through 2012): Slide set. Available: http://www.cdc.gov/hiv/library/slideSets/index.html (Last visited 12/26/14).

Centers for Disease Control and Prevention. (2014.16g). HIV transmission. Available: http://cdc.gov/hiv/basics/transmission.html (Last visited 12/29/14).

Centers for Disease Control and Prevention. (2016a). Sexually transmitted disease surveillance, 2015. Available: https://www.cdc.gov/std/stats15/STD-Surveillance-2015-print.pdf (Last visited 8/31/17).

Centers for Disease Control and Prevention. (2016.6a). Sexual identity, sex of sexual contacts, and health-related behaviors among students in grades 9–12—United States and selected sites, 2015. *Morbidity and Mortality Weekly Report, 65*(9), 1–202.\

Centers for Disease Control and Prevention. (2016.15a). Condom fact sheet in brief. Available: https://www.cdc.gov/condomeffectiveness/brief.html (Last visited 11/30/2017).

Centers for Disease Control and Prevention. (2016.15c). Dental dam use. Available: https://www.cdc.gov/condomeffectiveness/Female-condom-use.html (Last visited 11/29/2017).

Centers for Disease Control and Prevention. (2016.15d). HPV (human papillomavirus) VIS. Available: https://www.cdc.gov/vaccines/hcp/vis/vis-statements/hpv.html (Last visited 12/14/2017).

Centers for Disease Control and Prevention. (2016.16b). 2016 conference on retroviruses and opportunistic infection. Available: https://www.cdc.gov/nchhstp/newsroom/2016/croi-2016.html#Graphics2 (Last visited 1/9/2018).

Centers for Disease Control and Prevention. (2017). HIV among African Americans. Available: https://www.cdc.gov/nchhstp/newsroom/docs/factsheets/cdc-hiv-aa-508.pdf (Last visited 12/04/17).

Centers for Disease Control and Prevention. (2017.6a). *Sexual activity and contraceptive use among teenagers in the United States, 2011–2015.* National Health Statistics Reports, No. 104. Available: https://www.cdc.gov/nchs/data/nhsr/nhsr104.pdf (Last visited 6/22/17).

Centers for Disease Control and Prevention. (2017.12g). STDs during pregnancy—CDC fact sheet (detailed). Available: https://www.cdc.gov/std/pregnancy/stdfact-pregnancy-detailed.htm (Last visited 10/3/17).

Centers for Disease Control and Prevention. (2017.13b). Health risks among sexual minority youth. Available: https://www.cdc.gov/healthyyouth/disparities/smy.htm (Last visited 12/5/17).

Centers for Disease Control and Prevention. (2017.15a). Genital HPV infection. Available: https://www.cdc.gov/std/hpv/hpv-Fs-July-2017.pdf (Last visited 10/22/2020).

Centers for Disease Control and Prevention. (2017.15a). STDs in record high, indicating an urgent need for prevention. Available: https://www.cdc.gov/media/releases/2017/p0926-std-prevention.html (Last visited 11/18/2017).

Centers for Disease Control and Prevention. (2017.15c). National notifiable infectious diseases and conditions: United States. Available: https://wwwn.cdc.gov/nndss (Last visited 11/18/2017).

Centers for Disease Control and Prevention. (2017.15d). Sexually transmitted diseases surveillance 2016. Available: https://www.cdc.gov/std/stats16/default.htm (Last visited 11/17/2017).

Centers for Disease Control and Prevention. (2017.15d). STDs in record high, indicating an urgent need for prevention. Available: https://www.cdc.gov/media/releases/2017/p0926-std-prevention.html (Last visited 11/18/2017).

Centers for Disease Control and Prevention. (2017.15i). Chlamydia—CDC fact sheet (detailed). Available: https://www.cdc.gov/std/chlamydia/stdfact-chlamydia-detailed.htm (Last visited 12/4/2017).

Centers for Disease Control and Prevention. (2017.15j). Gonorrhea—CDC fact sheet. Available: https://www.cdc.gov/std/gonorrhea/Gonorrhea-FS-June-2017.pdf (Last visited 12/5/2017).

Centers for Disease Control and Prevention. (2017.15k). Genital/vulvovaginal candidiasis (VVC). Available: http://www.cdc.gov/fungal/diseases/candidasis/genital/index.html (Last visited 12/16/14).

Centers for Disease Control and Prevention. (2017.15l). Syphilis—CDC fact sheet. Available: https://www.cdc.gov/std/syphilis/stdfact-syphilis.htm (Last visited 1/21/2018).

Centers for Disease Control and Prevention. (2017.15m). Genital HPV infection—CDC fact sheet. Available: https://www.cdc.gov/std/hpv/HPV-FS-July-2017.pdf (Last visited 12/2/2017).

Centers for Disease Control and Prevention. (2017.15n). What I should know about screening. Available: https://www.cdc.gov/cancer/cervical/basic_info/screening.htm (Last visited 12/6/2017).

Centers for Disease Control and Prevention. (2017.15v). Vaginal candidiasis. Available: https://www.cdc.gov/fungal/diseases/candidiasis/genital/index.html (Last visited 12/15/2017).

Centers for Disease Control and Prevention. (2017.15x). Scabies. Available: https://www.cdc.gov/parasites/scabies/fact_sheet.html (Last visited 12/15/2017).

Centers for Disease Control and Prevention. (2017.15y). Pelvic inflammatory disease—CDC fact sheet. Available: https://www.cdc.gov/std/PID/STDFact-PID.htm (Last visited 12/18/2017).

Centers for Disease Control and Prevention. (2017.15z). CDC fact sheet: Information for teens and young adults: Staying healthy and preventing STDs. Available: https://www.cdc.gov/std/life-stages-populations/std-fact-teens.htm (Last visited 12/12/2017).

Centers for Disease Control and Prevention. (2017.16a). About HIV/AIDS. Available: https://www.cdc.gov/hiv/basics/whatishiv.html (Last visited 1/3/2018).

Centers for Disease Control and Prevention. (2017.16b). Opportunistic infections. Available: https://www.cdc.gov/actagainstaids/basics/livingwithhiv/opportunisticinfections.html (Last visited 1/3/2018).

Centers for Disease Control and Prevention. (2017.16d). Prevention. Available: https://www.cdc.gov/hiv/basics/pevention.html (Last visited 1/16/18).

Centers for Disease Control and Prevention. (2017.16g). HIV and injection drug use. Available: https://www.cdc.gov/hiv/risk/idu.html (Last visited 1/10/2018).

Centers for Disease Control and Prevention. (2017.16i). HIV among African Americans. Available: https://www.cdc.gov/hiv/group/racialethnic/africanamericans/index.html (Last visited 1/11/2018).

Centers for Disease Control and Prevention. (2017.16m). Native Hawaiians and other Pacific Islanders. Available: https://www.cdc.gov/hiv/group/racialethnic/asians/index.html (Last visited 1/12/2018).

Centers for Disease Control and Prevention. (2017.16o). HIV among gay and bisexual men. Available: https://www.cdc.gov/hiv/group/msm/index.html (Last visited 1/12/2018).

Centers for Disease Control and Prevention. (2017.16r). HIV among youth. Available: https://www.cdc.gov/hiv/group/age/youth/index.html (Last visited 1/12/2018).

Centers for Disease Control and Prevention. (2017.16u). Prevention. Available: https://www.cdc.gov/hiv/basics/pevention.html (Last visited 1/16/18).

Centers for Disease Control and Prevention. (2018). Information for providers to share with male patients and parents regarding male circumcision and the prevention of HIV infection, sexually transmitted Infections, and other health outcomes. Available: https://www.cdc.gov/hiv/risk/male-circumcision.html (Last visited 9/9/2020).

Centers for Disease Control & Prevention. (2018.6a). Reproductive health: Teen pregnancy. Available: https://www.cdc.gov/teenpregnancy/about/index.htm (Last visited 4/18/20).

Centers for Disease Control & Prevention. (2018.6c). Youth risk behavior surveillance-United States, 2017. *Morbidity and Mortality Weekly Report (MMWR),* 67(8), 1–114. Available: https://www.cdc.gov/mmwr/volumes/67/ss/ss6708a1.htm (Last visited 4/16/20).

Centers for Disease Control & Prevention. (2018.11). STDs in adolescents and young adults. Available: https://www.cdc.gov/std/stats18/adolescents.htm (Last visited 7/23/20).

Centers for Disease Control & Prevention. (2018.12). What you need to know about marijuana use and pregnancy. Available: https://www.cdc.gov/marijuana/factsheets/pregnancy.htm (Last visited 8/17/20).

Centers for Disease Control & Prevention/National Vital Statistics (NCHS). (2019.7). Provisional number of divorces and annulments and rate: United States, 2000–2018. Available: https://www.cdc.gov/nchs/data/dvs/national-marriage-divorce-rates-00-18.pdf (Last visited 5/12/20).

Centers for Disease Control & Prevention. (2019.12a). Infant mortality. Available: https://www.cdc.gov/reproductivehealth/maternalinfant-health/infantmortality.htm (Last visited 8/21/20).

Centers for Disease Control & Prevention. (2019.12b). Vaccinating pregnant women. Available: https://www.cdc.gov/vitalsigns/maternal-vaccines/index.html (Last visited 8/18/20).

Centers for Disease Control & Prevention. (2019.12c). Zika virus: Pregnancy. Available: https://www.cdc.gov/zika/pregnancy/ (Last visited 8/18/20).

Centers for Disease Control and Prevention. (2019.12d). Preterm birth. Available: https://www.cdc.gov/reproductivehealth/maternalinfant-health/pretermbirth.htm (Last visited 10/7/17).

Centers for Disease Control & Prevention. (2019.12e). Infant mortality. Available: https://www.cdc.gov/reproductivehealth/maternalinfant-health/infantmortality.htm (Last visited 8/21/20).

Centers for Disease Control and Prevention. (2019.15a). *Sexually Transmitted Disease Surveillance 2018.* Available: https://www.cdc.gov/std/stats18/default.htm (Last visited: 9/4/20).

Centers for Disease Control and Prevention. (2019.15b). Annual reported cases of notifiable diseases and rates per 100,000, excluding U. S. Territories – United States, 2018. Available: https://wonder.cdc.gov/nndss/static/2018/annual/2018-table1.html (Last visited 9/4/20).

Centers for Disease Control and Prevention. (2019.15c). Vaginal candidiasis. Available: https://www.cdc.gov/fungal/diseases/candidiasis/genital/index.html (Last visited 9/22/2020).

Centers for Disease Control and Prevention. (2019.16a). What is HIV stigma. Available: https://www.cdc.gov/hiv/basics/hiv-stigma/index.html (Last visited: 10/7/2020).

Centers for Disease Control and Prevention. (2019.16b). HIV and Transgender Communities. Available: https://www.cdc.gov/hiv/pdf/policies/cdc-hiv-transgender-brief.pdf (Last visited: 10/16/2020).

Centers for Disease Control and Prevention. (2019.16c). HIV Prevention in the South. Available: https://www.cdc.gov/hiv/pdf/policies/cdc-hiv-prevention-south.pdf (Last visited 10/28/2020).

Centers for Disease Control and Prevention. (2019.16e). PEP. Available: https://www.cdc.gov/hiv/basics/pep.html (Last visited 10/28/2020).

Centers for Disease Control and Prevention. (2019.16f). Anal sex and HIV. Available: https://www.cdc.gov/hiv/risk/analsex.html (Last visited: 1/8/2020).

Centers for Disease Control and Prevention. (2020.2). Youth Risk Behavior Surveillance - United States, 2019. Available: https://www.cdc.gov/mmwr/volumes/69/su/pdfs/su6901-H.pdf (Last visited 9/12/20).

Centers for Disease Control & Prevention. (2020.12a). Before pregnancy. Available: https://www.cdc.gov/preconception/index.html (Last visited 8/14/20).

Centers for Disease Control & Prevention. (2020.12b). *First data released on maternal mortality in over a decade.* National Center for Health Statistics. Available: https://www.cdc.gov/nchs/pressroom/nchs_press_releases/2020/202001_MMR.htm (Last visited 8/15/20).

Centers for Disease Control & Prevention. (2020.12c). Data & statistics on birth defects. Available: https://www.cdc.gov/ncbddd/birthdefects/data.html (Last visited 8/17/20).

Centers for Disease Control & Prevention. (2020.12d). Alcohol use in pregnancy. Available: https://www.cdc.gov/ncbddd/fasd/alcohol-use.html (Last visited 8/17/20).

Centers for Disease Control & Prevention. (2020.12e). Smoking during pregnancy. Available: https://www.cdc.gov/tobacco/basic_information/health_effects/pregnancy/index.htm (Last visited 8/17/20).

Centers for Disease Control & Prevention. (2020.12f). *Key statistics from the National Survey of Family Growth - I listing.* Center for Health Statistics. Available: https://www.cdc.gov/nchs/nsfg/key_statistics/i_2015-2017.htm#impaired (Last visited 8/21/20).

Centers for Disease Control & Prevention. (2020.12g). Data on COVID-19 during pregnancy. Available: https://www.cdc.gov/coronavirus/2019-ncov/cases-updates/special-populations/pregnancy-data-on-covid-19.html (Last visited 9/1/20).

Centers for Disease Control & Prevention. (2020.12h). Update: Characteristics of symptomatic women of reproductive age with laboratory-confirmed SARS infection by pregnancy status – United States, January 22-October 3, 2020. Washington, DC: *Morbidity and Mortality Weekly Report (MMWR).* Available: https://www.cdc.gov/mmwr/volumes/69/wr/mm6944e3.htm?s_cid=mm6944e3_w (Last visited 11/4/20).

Centers for Disease Control & Prevention. (2020.12i). High blood pressure during pregnancy. Available: https://www.cdc.gov/bloodpressure/pregnancy.htm (Last visited 8/18/20).

Centers for Disease Control & Prevention. (2020.12j). ART success rates. Available: https://www.cdc.gov/art/artdata/index.html (Last visited 8/24/20).

Centers for Disease Control & Prevention. (2020.12k). Breastfeeding among U.S. children born 2010–2017, National Immunization Survey. Available: https://www.cdc.gov/breastfeeding/data/nis_data/results.html (Last visited 8/31/20).

Centers for Disease Control and Prevention. (2020.13a). National diabetes statistics report 2020. Available: https://www.cdc.gov/diabetes/pdfs/data/statistics/national-diabetes-statistics-report.pdf (Last visited 9/24/20).

Centers for Disease Control and Prevention. (2020.13b). What are the risk factors for breast cancer? Available: https://www.cdc.gov/cancer/breast/basic_info/risk_factors.htm (Last visited 9/24/20).

Centers for Disease Control and Prevention. (2020.13c). HPV-associated cervical cancer rates by race and ethnicity. Available: https://www.cdc.gov/cancer/hpv/statistics/cervical.htm (Last visited 9/25/20).

Centers for Disease Control and Prevention. (2020.15a). Hepatitis A questions and answers for the public. Available: https://www.cdc.gov/hepatitis/hcv/cfaq.htm#overview (Last visited 9/22/2020).

Centers for Disease Control and Prevention. (2020.15b). Hepatitis B overview. Available: https://www.cdc.gov/hepatitis/hbv/bfaq.htm#overview (Last viewed 9/22/2020).

Centers for Disease Control and Prevention. (2020.15c). Hepatitis C overview and statistics. Available: https://www.cdc.gov/hepatitis/hcv/cfaq.htm#overview (Last visited 9/22/2020).

Centers for Disease Control and Prevention. (2020.15d). Bacterial vaginosis. Available: https://www.cdc.gov/std/bv/stdfact-bacterial-vaginosis.htm (Last visited 9/22/2020).

Centers for Disease Control and Prevention. (2020.15e). Trichomoniasis – CDC fact sheet. Available: https://www.cdc.gov/std/trichomonas/stdfact-trichomoniasis.htm (Last visited 9/22/2020).

Centers for Disease Control and Prevention. (2020.15f). Parasites. Available: https://www.cdc.gov/parasites/index.html (Last visited 9/22/2020).

Centers for Disease Control and Prevention. (2020.15g). Just diagnosed: Next steps after testing for gonorrhea or chlamydia. Available: https://www.cdc.gov/std/prevention/NextSteps-GonorrheaOrChlamydia.htm (Last visited: 9/22/2020).

Centers for Disease Control and Prevention. (2020.16). Youth Risk Behavior Surveillance – United States, 2019. Available: https://www.cdc.gov/mmwr/volumes/69/su/pdfs/su6901-H.pdf (Last visited9/12/20).

Centers for Disease Control and Prevention. (2020.16a). HIV basics. Available: https://www.cdc.gov/hiv/basics/index.html (Last visited 10/7/2020).

Centers for Disease Control and Prevention. (2020.16b). HIV Surveillance Report. Available: https://www.cdc.gov/hiv/pdf/library/infographics/cdc-hiv-surveillance-vol-31-infographic.pdf (Last visited: 10/8/2020).

Centers for Disease Control and Prevention. (2020.16c). Diagnosis of HIV infection in the United States and Dependent Areas, 2018: Figures. Available: https://www.cdc.gov/hiv/library/reports/hiv-surveillance/vol-31/index.html (Last visited: 10/5/2020).

Centers for Disease Control and Prevention. (2020.16e). HIV and African Americans. Available: https://www.cdc.gov/hiv/group/racialethnic/africanamericans/index.html (Last visited: 10/11/2020).

Centers for Disease Control and Prevention. (2020.16f). HIV and Hispanics and Latinos. Available: https://www.cdc.gov/nchhstp/healthdisparities/hispanics.html (Last visited: 10/13/2020).

Centers for Disease Control and Prevention. (2020.16g). Asians and HIV. Available: https://www.cdc.gov/hiv/group/racialethnic/asians/index.html (Last visited: 10/12/2020).

Centers for Disease Control and Prevention. (2020.16h). HIV and Native Hawaiians and Other Pacific Islanders. Available: https://www.cdc.gov/hiv/pdf/group/racialethnic/nhopi/cdc-hiv-nhopi-factsheet-2020.pdf (Last visited: 10/13/2020).

Centers for Disease Control and Prevention. (2020.16i). HIV and American Indians and Alaska Natives. Available: https://www.cdc.gov/hiv/group/racialethnic/aian/index.html (Last visited 10/12/2020).

Centers for Disease Control and Prevention. (2020.16j). HIV and gay and bisexual men. Available: https://www.cdc.gov/hiv/group/racialethnic/aian/index.html (Last visited: 10/14/2020).

Centers for Disease Control and Prevention. (2020.16l). HIV and older Americans. Available: https://www.cdc.gov/hiv/pdf/group/age/olderamericans/cdc-hiv-older-americans.pdf (Last visited 10/27/2020).

Centers for Disease Control and Prevention. (2020.16m). PrEP. Available: https://www.cdc.gov/hiv/basics/prep.html (Last visited: 10/28/2020).

Centers for Disease Control & Prevention. (2021.12). Vaccination considerations for people who are pregnancy or breastfeeding. Available: https://www.cdc.gov/coronavirus/2019-ncov/vaccines/recommendations/pregnancy.html (Last visited 3/1/21).

Centers for Disease Control & Prevention. (2021.12a). Pregnant people. Available: https://www.cdc.gov/coronavirus/2019-ncov/need-extra-precautions/pregnant-people.html (Last visited 4/9/21).

Centers for Disease Control & Prevention. (2021.12b). Information about COVID-19 vaccines for people who are pregnant or breastfeeding. Available: https://www.cdc.gov/coronavirus/2019ncov/vaccines/recommendations/pregnancy.html (Last visited 4/9/21).

Centers for Disease Control and Prevention. (2021.18a). HIV risk among persons who exchange sex for money or nonmonetary items. Available: https://www.cdc.gov/hiv/group/sexworkers.html (Last visited: 2/16/2021).

Cesareanrates.org. (2020). Understanding Cesarean rates. Available: https://www.cesareanrates.org (Last visited 8/27/20).

Chambers, W. C. (2007). Oral sex: Varied behaviors and perceptions in a college population. *Journal of Sex Research, 44*, 28–42.

Champion, A. R., & Pedersen, C. L. (2015). Investigating differences between sexters and non-sexters on attitudes, subjective norms, and risky sexual behaviours. *The Canadian Journal of Human Sexuality, 24*(3), 205–214.

Chandra, A., Mosher, W. D., Copen, C., & Sionean, C. (2011). Sexual behavior, sexual attraction, and sexual identity in the United States: Data from the 2006–2008 National Survey of Family Growth. *National Health Statistics Report, 36.* Available: http://www.cdc.gov/nchs/data/nhsr/nhsr036.pdf (Last visited 6/29/11).

Charlton, B. M., Corliss, H. L., Spiegelman, D., Williams, K., & Austin, S. B. (2016). Changes in reported sexual orientation following US states recognition of same-sex couples. *American Journal of Public Health, 106*(12), 2202–2204.

Charnigo, R., Noar, S. M., Garnett, C., Crosby, R., Palmgreen, P., & Zimmerman, R. S. (2013). Sensation seeking and impulsivity: Combined associations with risky sexual behavior in a large sample of young adults. *Journal of Sex Research, 50*, 480–488.

Child Trends. (2018). Data point: Half of 20- to 29-year-old-women who gave birth in their teens have a high school diploma. Available: https://www.childtrends.org/half-20-29-year-old-women-gave-birth-teens-high-school-diploma (Last visited 4/18/20).

Child Trends. (2019). Teen births. Available: https://www.childtrends.org/indicators/teen-births (Last visited 9/20/20).

Chivers, M. L., Seto, M. C., Lalumière, M. L., & Grimbos, T. (2010). Agreement of self-reported and genital measures of sexual arousal in men and women: A meta-analysis. *Archives of Sexual Behavior, 39*, 5–56.

Chivers, M. L., Suschinsky, K. D., Timmers, A. D., & Bossio, J. A. (2014). Experimental, neuroimaging, and psychophysiological methods in sexuality research. In D. L. Tolman & L. M. Diamond (Eds.), *APA handbook of sexuality and psychology* (pp. 81–98). American Psychological Association.

Christopher & Dana Reeve Foundation. (2017a). Sexual health for men. Available: https://www.christopherreeve.org/living-with-paralysis/health/sexual-health/sexual-health-for-men (Last visited 11/21/17).

Christopher & Dana Reeve Foundation. (2017b). Sexual health for women. Available: https://www.christopherreeve.org/living-with-paralysis/health/sexual-health/sexual-health-for-women (Last visited 11/21/17).

CIA World Fact Book. (2019). Maternal mortality rates. Available: https://www.cia.gov/library/publications/resources/the-world-factbook/fields/353.html (Last visited 8/15/20).

Cipres, D., Rodriguez, A., Alvarez, J., Stern, L., Steinauer, J., et al. (2017). Racial/ethnic differences in young women's health-promoting strategies to reduce vulnerability to sexually transmitted infections. *Journal of Adolescent Health, 60*, 556–562.

Clark, S. K., Jeglic, E. L., Calkins, C., & Tatar, J. R. (2017). More than a nuisance: The prevalence and consequences of frotteurism and exhibitionism. *Sexual Abuse, 28*, 3–19.

Clark, T. D. (1977). *Indiana University: Midwestern pioneer: Vol. 3. Years of fulfillment.* Indiana University Press.

Claxton, S. E., DeLuca, H. K., & Manfred, H. M. (2015). The association between alcohol use and engagement in casual sexual relationships and experiences: A meta-analytic review of non-experimental studies. *Archives of Sexual Behavior, 44*, 837–856.

Cleveland Clinic. (2019). Heart disease & erectile dysfunction. Available: https://my.clevelandclinic.org/health/diseases/15029-heart-disease--erectile-dysfunction (Last visited 9/24/20).

Cobbina, J. E., & Oselin, S. S. (2011). It's not only the money: An analysis of adolescent versus adult entry into street prostitution. *Sociological Inquiry, 81*, 310–332.

Cohen, C. R., Lingappa, J. R., Baeten, J. M., Ngayo, M. O., Spiegel, C. A., Hong, T., et al. (2012). Bacterial vaginosis associated with increased risk of female-to-male HIV-1 transmission: A prospective cohort analysis among African couples. *PloS Medicine.* https://doi.org/10.1371/journal.pmed.1001251

Cohen, E. (2010). New Year's resolution: Have more sex. Available: http://com.site.printthis.clickability.como/pt/cpt?/action5cpt&title5New1Year$27s1resolution (Last visited 1/7/10).

Cohen, J. N., & Byers, E. S. (2014). Beyond lesbian bed death: Enhancing our understanding of the sexuality of sexual-minority women in relationships. *Journal of Sex Research,* 51, 893–903.

Coleman, E. (1986, July). Sexual compulsion vs. sexual addiction: The debate continues. *SIECUS Report,* 14(6), 7–11.

Coleman, E. (1987). Sexual compulsivity: Definition, etiology, and treatment considerations. *Journal of Chemical Dependency Treatment,* 1, 189–204.

Coleman, E. (1991). Compulsive sexual behavior: New concepts and treatments. *Journal of Psychology and Human Sexuality,* 4, 37–52.

Coleman, E. (1996). What sexual scientists know about compulsive sexual behavior. Society for the Scientific Study of Sexuality.

Coleman, E., Raymond, N., & McBean, A. (2003). Assessment and treatment of compulsive sexual behavior. *Minnesota Medicine,* 86(7), 42–47.

Coleman, L. M. (2001). Young people, "risk" and sexual behavior: A literature review. Report prepared for the Health Development Agency and the Teenage Pregnancy Unit. *Trust for the Study of Adolescence.*

Coleman, L. M., & Cater, S. M. (2005). A qualitative study of the relationship between alcohol consumption and risky sex in adolescents. *Archives of Sexual Behavior,* 34, 649–661.

Collado, A., Johson, P. S., & Loya, J. M. (2017). Discounting of condom-protected sex as a measure of high risk of sexually transmitted infection among college students. *Archives of Sexual Behavior,* 46, 2187–2195.

Collins, N. L., & Feeney, B. C. (2000). A safe haven: An attachment theory perspective on support seeking and caregiving in intimate relationships. *Journal of Personality and Social Psychology,* 76(6), 1053–1073.

"Condom use from a female perspective: Clue's study with KI-CURT." *Clue.* Available: https://helloclue.com/articles/sex/condom-survey (Last visited 1/30/20).

Congressional Research Service. (n.d.). H.R. 4137 - 104th Congress (1995-1996). Available: https://www.congress.gov/bill/104th-congress/house-bill/4137 (Last visited 3/6/2018).

Conley, T. D., Moors, A. C., Matsick, J. L., & Ziegler, A. (2013). The fewer the merrier?: Assessing stigma surrounding consensually non-monogamous romantic relationships. *Analyses of Social Issues and Public Policy (ASAP),* 13, 1–30.

Connell, J. (2019). Sexuality and COPD. *Healthline.* Available: https://www.healthline.com/health/copd/sex (Last visited 12/16/20).

Connell, R. W. (1995). *Masculinities.* University of California Press.

Conradi, C., Bradley, H. M., Broza, D., Buddhi, S., Chapman, E. L., et al. (2015). Community outbreak of HIV infection to injection drug use of the oxymorphone—Indiana, 2015. *Mortality and Morbidity Report,* 64, 443–444.

Cook, R. L., & Clark, D. B. (2005). Is there an association between alcohol consumption and sexually transmitted diseases? A systematic review. *Sexually Transmitted Diseases,* 32, 156–164.

Cooke, B., & Weathington, J. (2014). Human and animal research into sex-specific effects of child abuse. *Hormones and Behavior,* 65, 416–426.

Coontz, S. (2018, February 10). For a better marriage, act like a single person. *NY Times.* Available: https://www.nytimes.com/2018/02/10/opinion/sunday/for-a-better-marriage-act-like-a-single-person.html (Last visited 7/3/20).

Coontz, S. (2020, February 13). How to make your marriage gayer. *NY Times.* Available: https://www.nytimes.com/2020/02/13/opinion/sunday/marriage-housework-gender-happiness.html (Last visited 2/22/20).

Cooper, M. L. (2006). Does drinking promote risky sexual behavior? A complex answer to a simple question. *Current Directions,* 15, 19–23.

Coppens, V., Brink, S. T., Huys, W., Fransen, E., & Murrens, M. (2020). A survey of BDSM-related activities: BDSM experience correlates with age of first exposure, interest profile, and role identity. *Journal of Sex Research,* 57, 129–136.

Costa, R., Miller, G. F., & Brody, S. (2012). Women who prefer longer penises are more likely to have vaginal orgasms (but not clitoral orgasms): Implications for an evolutionary theory of vaginal orgasm. *Journal of Sexual Medicine.* https://doi.org/10.1111/j.1743-6109.2012.02917.x

Couper, M. P., Tourangeau, R., & Marvin, T. (2009). Taking the audio out of audio-CASI. *Public Opinion Quarterly,* 73, 281–303.

Coyne, S. M., Ward, L. M., Kroff, S. L., Davis, E. J., Holmgren, H. G., Jensen, A. C., Erickson, S. E., & Essig, L. W. (2019). Contributions of mainstream sexual media exposure to sexual attitudes, perceived peer norms, and sexual behavior: A meta-analysis. *Journal of Adolescent Health,* 64(4), 430–436.

Crosby, R. A., & Bounse, S. (2012). Condom effectiveness: Where we are now? *Sexual Health,* 9, 10–17.

Crosby, R. A., Casey, B. R., Vanderpool, R., Collins, T., & Moore, G. R. (2011). Uptake of free HPV vaccination among young women: A comparison of rural versus urban rates. *Journal of Rural Health,* 27, 380–384.

Crosby, R. A., DiClemente, R. J., & Salazar, L. F. (2006). *Research methods in health promotion.* Jossey-Bass.

Crosby, R. A., Milhausen, R. A., Yarber, W. L., Sanders, S. A., & Graham, C.A. (2008). Condom 'turn offs' among adults: An exploratory study. *International Journal of AIDS & STDs,* 19, 590–594.

Crosby, R. A., Sanders, S. A., Yarber, W. L., Graham, C. A., & Dodge, B. (2002). Condom use errors and problems among college men. *Sexually Transmitted Diseases,* 29, 552–557.

Crosby, R. A., Yarber, W. L., Graham, C. A., & Sanders, S. A. (2010). Does it fit okay? Problems with condom use as a function of self-reported fit. *Sexually Transmitted Infections,* 86, 36–38.

Cummings, J. (1987, June 8). Disabled model defies sexual stereotypes. *New York Times,* p. 17.

Cutler, A., McNamara, B., Qasba, N., Kennedy, H. P., Lundsberg, L., & Gariepy, A. (2018). "I just don't know": An exploration of women's ambivalence about a new pregnancy. *Womens Health Issues,* 28(1), 75–81. Available: https://www.ncbi.nlm.nih.gov/pmc/articles/PMC6223118/ (Last visited 9/21/20).

Cutler, W. (1999). Human sex-attractant pheromones: Discovery, research, development, and application in sex therapy. *Psychiatric Annals,* 29, 54–59.

Damon, W., & Rosser, B. R. S. (2005). Anodyspareunia in men who have sex with men. *Journal of Sex and Marital Therapy,* 31, 129–141.

Daniels, K., & Abma, J. C. (2018). Current contraceptive status among women aged 15-49: United States, 2015-2017. *NCHS Data Brief, No. 327.* Available: https://www.cdc.gov/nchs/products/databriefs/db327.htm (Last visited 7/16/20).

Daniels, K., & Abma, J. C. (2020). Current contraceptive status among women aged 15-49: United States, 2017-2019. *NCHS Data Brief, No. 388.* Available: https://www.cdc.gov/nchs/products/databriefs/db388.htm (Last visited 2/25/21).

Dank, M., Khan, B., Downey, P. M., Kotonias, C., Mayer, D., Owens, C., et al. (2014). Estimating the size and structure of the underground commercial sex economy in eight major U.S. cities. Available: https://www.urban.org/research/publication/estimating-size-and-structure-underground-commercial-sex-economy-eight-major-us-cities.

Dann, C. (2017, October 30). NBC.WSJ Poll: Nearly half of working women say they've experienced harassment. Available: https://www.nbcnews.com/politics/first-read/nbc-wsj-poll-nearly-half-working-women-say-they-ve-n815376 (Last visited 12/15/2017).

Darden, P. M., Thompson, D. M., Roberts, J. R., Hale, J. J., Pope, C., Naifeh, M., et al. (2013). Reasons for not vaccinating adolescents: National Immunization Survey of Teens, 2008–2010. *Pediatrics, 131*, 645–651.

Darkness to Light. (2015). Child sexual abuse statistics. Available: https://www.d2l.org/ (Last visited: 11/1/2017).

Das, A., Waite, L. J., & Laumann, E. O. (2012). Sexual expression over the life course. In L. M. Carpenter & J. DeLamater (Eds.), *Sex for life.* New York University Press.

Dastagir, A. E. (2019, September 30). # The MeToo Path. Now What? *USA Today.*

Davidson, J. K., & Darling, C. A. (1986). The impact of college-level sex education on sexual knowledge, attitudes, and practices: The knowledge/sexual experimentation myth revisited. *Deviant Behavior, 7*, 13–30.

Davies, A. P. C., & Shackelford, T. K. (2015). Comparisons of the effectiveness of mate-attraction tactics across mate pouching and general attraction and across types of romantic relationships. *Personality and Individual Differences, 85*, 140–144.

Davis, K. E., & Todd, M. J. (1985). Assessing friendship: Prototypes, paradigm cases and relationship description. In S. Duck & D. Perlman (Eds.), *Understanding personal relationships: An interdisciplinary approach.* Sage.

Davis, S. R., Davison, S. L., Donath, S., & Bell, R. J. (2005). Circulating androgen levels and self-reported sexual fluctuation in women. *Journal of the American Medical Association, 294*(17), 2167–2168.

Dawson, S. J., & Chivers, M. L. (2014). Gender differences and similarities in sexual desire. *Current Sexual Health Reports, 6*(4), 211–219.

Dawson, S. J., Huberman, J. S., Bouchard, K. M., Mcinnis, M. K., Pukall, C. F., & Chivers, M. L. (2019). Effects of Individual difference variables, gender and exclusivity of sexual attraction on volunteer bias in sexuality research. *Archives of Sexual Behavior, 48*, 2403–2417.

De Block, A., & Adriaens, P. R. (2013). Pathologizing sexual deviance: A history. *Journal of Sex Research, 50*, 276–298.

De Santisteban, P., & Gamez-Guadix, M. (2018). Prevalence and risk factors among minors for online sexual solicitations and interactions with adults. *Journal of Sex Research 55*(7), 939–950.

de Visser, R., Richters, J., Rissel, C., Grulich, A., Simpson, J., Rodrigues, D., & Lopes, D. (2019). Romantic jealousy: A test of social cognitive and evolutionary models in a population-representative sample of adults. *Journal of Sex Research, 47*(4), 498–507.

Dean, H. D., & Myles, R. L. (2013). Social determinants of sexual health in the USA among racial and ethnic minorities. In S. O. Aral, K. A. Fenton, & J. A. Lipshutz (Eds.), *The new public health and STD/HIV prevention* (pp. 273–291). Springer.

Debro, S. C., Campbell, S. M., & Peplau, L. A. (1994). Influencing a partner to use a condom: A college student perspective. *Psychology of Women Quarterly, 18*, 165–182.

Decker, M. R., Raj, A., Gupta, J., & Silverman, J. G. (2008). Sex purchasing and associations with HIV/STI among a clinic-based sample of U.S. men. *Journal of Acquired Immune Deficiency Syndromes, 48*, 355–365.

Dekker, R. (2020). The evidence on: Due dates. *Evidence Based Birth.* Available: https://evidencebasedbirth.com/evidence-on-due-dates/ (Last visited 8/14/20).

DeLamater, J. D., & Sill, M. (2005). Sexual desire in later life. *Journal of Sex Research, 42*(2), 138–149.

DeLamater, J. D., & Friedrich, W. (2002). Human sexual development. *Journal of Sex Research, 38*, 10–14.

Demand Abolition. (n.d.). Why prostitution shouldn't be legal. Available: https://www.demandabolitiion.org/resources/evidence-against-legalizing-prostitution (Last visited 9/6/2017).

Dempsey, A. F., Butchart, A., Singer, D., Clark, S., & Davis, M. (2011). Factors associated with parental intentions for male human papillomavirus vaccination: Results of a national survey. *Sexually Transmitted Diseases, 38*, 769–776.

Dewitte, M., & Mayer, A. (2019). Exploring the link between daily relationship quality, sexual desire, and sexual activity in couples. *Archives of Sexual Behavior, 47*, 1675–1686.

di Mauro, D. (1995). Executive summary. Sexuality research in the United States: An assessment of the social and behavioral sciences. Social Science Research Council. Available: Executive summary. Sexuality research in the United States: An assessment of the social and behavioral sciences. Social Science Research Council. (Last visited 8/2/18).

Diamond, L. (2008). *Sexual fluidity: Understanding women's love and desire.* Harvard University Press.

Diamond, L. A., Alley, J., Dickenson, J., & Blair, K. L. (2019). Who counts as sexually fluid? Comparing four different types of sexual fluidity in women. *Archives of Sexual Behavior.* Available: http://www.suarakita.org/wp-content/uploads/2019/12/Who-Counts-as-Sexually-Fluid-Comparing-Four-Different-Types-of-Sexual-Fluidity-in-Women.pdf (Last viewed 2/20/20).

Diamond, L. M., Dickenson, J. A., & Blair, K. L. (2017). Stability of sexual attractions across different time scales: The roles of bisexuality and gender. *Archives of Sexual Behavior, 46*(1), 193–204.

Diamond, L., Pardo, S., & Butterworth, M. (2011). Transgender identity and experience. In S. Schwartz, K. Luyckx, & V. Vignoles (Eds.), *Handbook of identity theory and research* (pp. 629–647). Springer.

Diaz, R. M. (1998). *Latino gay men and HIV: Culture, sexuality and risk behavior.* New York: Routledge.

Dick-Read, G. (1972). *Childbirth without fear* (4th ed.). Harper & Row.

Dieckmann, K. P., Anheuser, P., Schmidt, S., Soyka-Hundt, B., Pichlmeider, U., et al. (2015). Testicular prostheses in patients with testicular cancer—acceptance rate and patient satisfaction. *BMC Urology, 15.* Available: https://www.ncbi.nlm.nih.gov/pmc/articles/PMC4363351/ (Last visited 12/2/17).

Dindia, K. (1992). Sex differences in self-disclosure: A meta-analysis. *Psychological Bulletin, 112*, 106–124.

Dindia, K. (1994). The intrapersonal-interpersonal dialectical process of self-disclosure. In S. Duck (Ed.), *Understanding relationship processes IV: The dynamics of relationships* (pp. 27–57). Lawrence Erlbaum Associates, Inc.

Disability Statistics Annual Report. (2020). 2019 annual report of people with disabilities in America. Available: https://disabilitycompendium.org/sites/default/files/user-uploads/2019%20Annual%20Report%20—%20FINAL%20ALL.pdf (Last visited 9/24/20).

Dixson, B. J., Dixson, A. F., Bishop, P. J., & Parish, A. (2010). Human physique and attractiveness in men and women: A New Zealand–U.S. Comparative Study. *Archives of Sexual Behavior, 39*, 798–806.

Djerassi, C. (1981). *The politics of contraception.* Freeman.

Dodge, B., Reece, M., Herbenick, D., Schick, V., Sanders, S. A., & Fortenberry, J. D. (2010). Sexual health among U.S. Black and Hispanic men and women: A national representative study. *Journal of Sexual Medicine, 7*, 330–345.

Doherty, I. A., Schoenbach, V. J., & Adimora, A. A. (2009). Condom use and duration of concurrent partnerships among men in the United States. *Sexually Transmitted Infections, 36*, 265–272.

Doherty, S. (2020). The complicated relationship between drugs, sex and consent. Available: https://www.vice.com/en/article/5dmgnb/how-drugs-affect-sex-consent. (Last visited: 1/5/2021).

Dorey, G., Speakman, M. J., Feneley, R. C. L., Swinkels, A., & Dunn, C. D. R. (2005). Pelvic floor exercises for erectile dysfunction. *British Journal of Urology, 96,* 595–597.

Doring, N. (2020). How is the COVID-19 pandemic affecting our sexualities? An overview of the current media narratives and research hypotheses. *Archives of Sexual Behavior, 49,* 2765–2778.

DoSomething.org. (2017b). 11 facts about teen dads. Available: https://www.dosomething.org/facts/11-facts-about-teen-dads (Last visited 7/10/17).

Dotinga, R. (2015, November 18). Once-a-week sex makes couples happy. *WebMD.* Available: https://www.webmd.com/sex-relationships/news/20151118/once-a-week-sex-makes-for-happy-couples-study#1 (Last visited 7/26/18).

Downs, J. S., de Bruin, W. B., Murray, P. J., & Fischhoff, B. (2006). Specific STI knowledge may be acquired too late. *Journal of Adolescent Health, 38,* 65–67.

Drescher, J. (2014). Controversies in gender diagnoses. *LGBT Health, 1*(1), 10–14.

Dreznick, M. T. (2003). Heterosexual competence of rapists and child molesters: A meta-analysis. *Journal of Sex Research, 40,* 170–178.

Drigotas, S., Rusbult, C., & Verette, J. (1999). Level of commitment, mutuality of commitment, and couple well-being. *Personal Relationships, 6,* 389–409.

Drolet, M., Benard, E., Perez, N., & Brisson, M. (2019). Population-level impact and herd effects following the introduction of human papillomavirus vaccination programmes: Updated systematic review and meta-analysis. *Lancet, 394*(10197), 497–509.

Drucker, D. J. (2014). *The classification of sex: Alfred Kinsey and the organization of knowledge.* University of Pittsburgh Press.

Dubey, N., Hoffman, J. F., Schuebel, K., Yuan, Q., Martinez, P. E., Nieman, L. K., Rubinow, D. R., Schmidt, P. J., & Goldman D. (2017). The ESC/E(Z) complex, an effector of response to ovarian steroids, manifests an intrinsic difference in cells from women with premenstrual dysphoric disorder. *Molecular Psychiatry, 22,* 1172–1184. Available: https://www.nature.com/articles/mp2016229 (Last visited 1/30/20).

Dunn, K. M., Cherkas, L. F., & Spector, T. D. (2005). Genetic influences on variation in female orgasmic function: A twin study. *Biology Letters, 1,* 260–263.

Dworkin, S. L., & O'Sullivan, L. (2005). Actual versus desired initiation patterns among a sample of college men: Tapping disjunctures within traditional male sexual scripts. *Journal of Sex Research, 42,* 150–158.

Eagly, A. (1987). *Sex differences in social behavior: A social role interpretation.* Hillsdale, NJ: Erlbaum.

Earls, C. M., & Lalumière, M. L. (2009). A case study of preferred bestiality. *Archives of Sexual Behavior, 38,* 605–609.

Easton, J. A., & Shackelford, T. K. (2009). Morbid jealousy and sex differences in partner-directed violence. *Human Nature, 30,* 342–350.

Ebadi, S., & Moaveni, A. (2006). *Iran awakening: A memoir of revolution and hope.* Random House.

Edgar, R., & Freimuth, V. S. (1992). Strategic sexual communication: Condom use resistance and response. *Health Communications, 4,* 83–104.

Edmonson, C. (2021, February 26). House passes L.G.B.T.Q. legislation, but Senate prospects are bleak. *New York Times.*

Edwards, K. M., Turchik, J. A., Dardis, C. M., Reynolds, N., & Gidycz, C. A. (2011). Rape myths: History, individual and institutional-level presence, and implications for change. *Sex Roles, 65,* 761–773.

eHarmony. (2018). 64 percent of Americans say they're happy in their relationship. Available: https://www.prnewswire.com/news-releases/64-percent-of-americans-say-theyre-happy-in-their-relationships-300595502.html (Last visited 4/12/20).

eHarmony. (2019). 83 percent of Americans report being "happy" in their relationship. Available: https://www.prnewswire.com/news-releases/83-percent-of-americans-report-being-happy-in-their-relationships-300791440.html (Last visited 5/12/20).

Ehrensaft, D. (2017). Gender nonconforming youth: Current perspectives. *Adolescent Health, Medicine and Therapeutics, 8,* 57–67. Available: https://www.ncbi.nlm.nih.gov/pmc/articles/PMC5448699/ (Last visited 5/18/20).

Eileraas, K. (2011). Legal definitions of rape. In M. Z. Strange, C. K. Oyster, & J. E. Slone (Eds.), *Encyclopedia of women in today's world* (pp. 1205–1209). Sage.

Eisen, M. B., & Tibshirani, R. (2020, July 21). How to identify flawed research. *New York Times.*

Eisenberg, M. L., Galusha, D., Kennedy, W. A., & Cullen, R. R. (2018). The relationship between neonatal circumcision, urinary tract infection, and health. *World Journal of Men's Health, 36*(3), 176–182. Available: https://www.ncbi.nlm.nih.gov/pmc/articles/PMC6119846/ (Last visited 2/10/20).

Ellen, J. M., et al. (2006). Sex partner selection, social networks, and repeat sexually transmitted infections in young men: A preliminary report. *Sexually Transmitted Diseases, 33,* 18–21.

Elliott, L., & Brantley, C. (1997). *Sex on campus: The naked truth about the real sex lives of college students.* Random House.

Ellison, C. (1985). Intimacy-based sex therapy. In W. Eicher & G. Kockott (Eds.), *Sexology.* Springer-Verlag.

Ellison, C. (2000). *Women's sexualities.* New Harbinger.

EMarketer. (2019). U.S. Time spent with media 2019. Available: https://www.emarketer.com/content/us-time-spent-with-media-2019 (Last visited 1/17/20).

Emetu, R. E., Marshall, A., Sanders, S. A., Yarber, W. L., Milhausen, R., Crosby, R. A., & Graham, C. A. (2013). A novel self-guided, home-based intervention to improve condom use among young college men who have sex with men. *Journal of American College Health, 2014.*

Emmerink, P. M. J., Vanwesenbeeck, I., van den Eijnden, R. J. J. M., & ter Bogt, T. F. M. (2016). Psychosexual correlates of sexual double standard endorsement in adolescent sexuality. *Journal of Sex Research, 53*(3), 286–297.

Endocrine Society. (2016). New guideline spells out uses of menopausal hormone therapy and alternatives. Available: https://www.google.com/search?client=safari&rls=en&q=endocrine+society+and+recommendations+for+hormone+therapy&ie=UTF-8&oe=UTF-8 (Last visited 5/18/20).

Eng, T. R., & Butler, W. T. (Eds.). (1997). *The hidden epidemic: Confronting sexually transmitted diseases.* National Academies Press.

England, D. C. (2020). The history of marital rape laws. NOLO. Available: https://www.criminaldefenselawyer.com/resources/criminal-defense/crime-penalties/marital-rape.htm. (Last visited: 12/27/2020).

Epstein, M., Manhart, L. E., Hill, K. G., Bailey, J. A., Hawkins, J. D., Haggerty, K. P., & Catalano, R. F. (2014). Understanding the link between early sexual initiation and later sexually transmitted infection: Test and replication in two longitudinal studies. *Journal of Adolescent Health, 54,* 435–441.

Equality Now. (2019). FGM in the US. Author. Available: https://www.equalitynow.org/fgm_in_the_us_learn_more (Last visited 2/28/20).

Esterline, K. M., & Muehlenhard, C. L. (2017). Want to be seen: Young people's experiences with performative making out. *Journal of Sex Research, 54,* 1051–1063.

Fagan, P. J., Wise, T. N., Schmidt, C. W., & Berlin, F. S. (2002). Pedophilia. *Journal of the American Medical Association, 288,* 2458-2465.

Fahs, B. (2011). *Performing sex: The making and unmaking of women's erotic lives.* State University of New York Press.

Fairbrother, N., Hart, T. A., & Fairbrother, M. (2019). Open relationship prevalence, characteristics, and correlates in a nationally representative sample of Canadian adults. *Journal of Sex Research, 56*(6), 695-704.

Farley, M. (2015). Very inconvenient truths: Sex buyers, sexual coercion, and prostitution-harm-denial. *Logos: A Journal of Modern Society & Culture, 15,* 15-21.

Farley, M., Cotton, A., Lynn, J., et al. (2003). Prostitution and trafficking in nine countries: An update on violence and posttraumatic stress disorder. In M. Farley (Ed.), *Prostitution, trafficking and traumatic stress* (pp. 33-74). Haworth Press.

Farnam Street Media. (2020). How to spot bad science. Author. Available: https://fs.blog/2020/01/spot-bad-science/ (Last visited: 8/13/2020).

Farnsworth, C. H. (1992, January 14). Homosexual is granted refugee status in Canada. *New York Times,* p. A5.

Farvid, P., & Braun, V. (2017). Unpacking the "pleasures" and "pains" of heterosexual casual sex: Beyond singular understandings. *Journal of Sex Research, 54,* 73-90.

Federal Register. (2018, September 27). Obstetrical and gynecological devices; Reclassification of single-use female condom, to be renamed single-use internal condom. Author. Available: https://www.federalregister.gov/documents/2018/09/27/2018-21044/obstetrical-and-gynecological-devices-reclassification-of-single-use-female-condom-to-be-renamed (Last visited 7/23/20).

Fenigstein, A., & Preston, M. (2007). The desired number of sexual partners as a function of gender, sexual risks, and the meaning of "ideal." *Journal of Sex Research, 44,* 879-895.

Feray, J. C., & Herzer, M. (1990). Homosexual studies and politics in the 19th century: Karl Maria Kertbeny. *Journal of Homosexuality, 19*(1), 23-47.

Ferguson, C. J., & Hartley, R. D. (2009). The pleasure is momentary . . . the expense damnable? The influence of pornography on rape and sexual assault. *Aggression and Violent Behavior, 14,* 323-329.

Fetters. (2018, July 19). Americans have some pretty vanilla sexual fantasies. *The Atlantic.* https://www.theatlantic.com/family/archive/2018/07/sexual-fantasies-justin-lehmiller/565547/.

Fielder, R. L., & Carey, M. P. (2010). Predictors and consequences of sexual "hookups" among college students: A short-term prospective study. *Archives of Sexual Behavior, 39,* 1105-1119.

Fielder, R. L., Carey, K. B., & Carey, M. P. (2013). Are hookups replacing romantic relationships? A longitudinal study of first-year female college students. *Journal of Adolescent Health, 52,* 657-659.

Fielder, R. L., Walsh, J. L., Carey, K. B., & Carey, M. P. (2014). Sexual hookups and adverse health outcomes: A longitudinal study of first-year college women. *Journal of Sex Research, 51,* 131-144.

FIGO: International Federation of Gynecology and Obstetrics. (2017, April 13). Period syncing myth debunked. Available: https://www.figo.org/news/period-syncing-myth-debunked-0015541 (Last visited 1/30/20).

FindLaw. (2019). Statutory rape. Author. Available: https://criminal.findlaw.com/criminal-charges/statutory-rape.html (Last visited: 12/28/2020).

Firestone, R. W., Firestone, L. A., & Catlett, J. (2006). *Sex and love in intimate relationships.* American Psychological Association.

Fisher, D., & Howells, K. (1993). Social relationships in sexual offenders. *Sexual and Marital Therapy, 8,* 123-136.

Fisher, H. (2004.8a). Dumped! *Science and Technology.* Available: http://www.helenfisher.com/downloads/articles/03dumped.pdf (Last visited 6/2/20).

Fisher, H. (2004.8b). *Why we love: The nature and chemistry of romantic love.* Henry Holt.

Fisher, H. (2009). *Why him? Why her?* Henry Holt and Company.

Fisher, H. (2009a). Jealousy—The monster. Oprah.com. Available: http://www.oprah.com/relationships/Understanding-Jealousy-Helen-Fisher-PhD-on-Relationships (Last visited 8/14/17).

Fisher, H., & Garcia, J. (2017). Slow love: Courtship in the digital age. In R. J. Sternberg & K. Sternberg (Eds.), *The new psychology of love* (pp. 208-222). Cambridge University Press.

Fisher, H., Xu, X., Aron, A., & Brown, L. L. (2016). Intense, passionate, romantic love: A natural addiction? How the fields that investigate romance and substance abuse can inform each other. *Frontiers in Psychology, 7,* 687. Available: https://www.ncbi.nlm.nih.gov/pmc/articles/PMC4861725/ (Last visited 6/2/20).

Fisher, M. L., Worth, K., Garcia, J. R., & Meredith, T. (2012). Feelings of regret following uncommitted sexual encounters in Canadian university students. *Culture, Health & Sexuality, 14,* 45-57.

Fisher, T. D. (2007). Sex of experimenter and social norm effects on reports of sexual behavior in young men and women. *Archives of Sexual Behavior, 36,* 89-100.

Fisher, T. D. (2013). Gender roles and pressure to be truthful: The bogus pipeline modifies gender differences in sexual but not no-sexual behavior. *Sex Roles, 68,* 401-414.

Fisher, W. (1986). A psychological approach to human sexuality. In D. Byrne & K. K. Kelley (Eds.), *Alternative approaches to human sexuality.* Erlbaum.

Fisher, W. (1998). The sexual opinion survey. In C. M. Davis, W. L. Yarber, R. Bauserman, G. Schreer, & S. L. Davis (Eds.), *Handbook of sexuality-related measures.* Sage.

Fisher, W. A., & Barak, A. (2001). Internet pornography: A social psychological perspective on Internet sexuality. *Journal of Sex Research, 38,* 312-323.

Fisher, W. A., & Davis, C. M. (2007). *What sexual scientists know about pornography.* Society for the Scientific Study of Sexuality.

Fisher, W. A., Byrne, D., White, L. A., & Kelley, K. (1988). Erotophilia-erotophobia as a dimension of personality. *Journal of Sex Research, 25,* 123-151.

Fitzsimons, T. (2019, November 12). *OUT NEWS.* Nearly 1 in 5 hate crimes motivated by anti-LGBTQ bias, FBI finds. *NBC News.* Available: https://www.nbcnews.com/feature/nbc-out/nearly-1-5-hate-crimes-motivated-anti-lgbtq-bias-fbi-n1080891. (Last visited 12/21/2020).

Flora, C. (2016). "Just friends." *Scientific American: The Sexual Brain,* 98-103.

Flores, A. R. (2020, October 2). Victimization rates and traits of sexual and gender minorities in the United States: Results from the National Crime Victimization Survey, 2017. *Science Advances, 6*(40). Eaba6910.

Flores, A. R., Herman, J. L., Gates, G. J., & Brown, T. N. T. (2016, June 30). *How many adults identify as transgender in the United States?* The Williams Institute. Available: https://williamsinstitute.law.ucla.edu/press/press-releases/updated-estimates-show-1-4-million-adults-identify-as-transgender-in-the-us-doubling-estimates-from-a-decade-ago/ (Last visited 5/30/17).

Flores, D., & Barroso, J. (2017). 21st century parent-child sex communication in the United States: A process review. *Journal of Sex Research, 54*(4-5), 532-548.

Foldes, P., & Buisson, O. (2009). The clitoral complex: A dynamic sonographic study. *Journal of Sexual Medicine, 6,* 1223-1231.

Foley, S. (2015). Older adults and sexual health: A review of current literature. *Current Sexual Health Reports, 7,* 70-79.

Forbes, M. K., Eaton, N. R., & Krueger, R. F. (2017). Sexual quality of life and aging: A prospective study of a nationally representative sample. *Journal of Sex Research, 54*(2), 137–148.

Ford, C., & Beach, F. (1951). *Patterns of sexual behavior.* Harper & Row.

Forhan, S. E., Gottlieb, S. L., Sternberg, M. R., Xu, F., Datta, D., McQuillan, G. M., et al. (2009). Prevalence of sexually transmitted infections among female adolescents aged 14 to 19 in the United States. *Pediatrics,* 124, 1505–1512.

Fortenberry, J. D. (2019). Trust, sexual trust, and sexual health: An interrogative review. *Journal of Sex Research* 56(4–5), 425–439.

Fortenberry, J. D., Cecil, H., Zimet, G. D., & Orr, D. P. (1997). Concordance between self-report questionnaires and coital diaries for sexual behaviors of adolescent women with sexually transmitted infections. In J. Bancroft (Ed.), *Researching sexual behavior.* Indiana University Press.

Fortenberry, J. D., McFarlane, M., Bleakley, A., Bull, S., Fishbein, M., Grimley, D., et al. (2002). Relationship of stigma and shame to gonorrhea and HIV screening. *American Journal of Public Health,* 92, 378–381.

Foster, D. G., Higgins, J. A., Biggs, M. A., McCain, C., Holtby, S., & Brindis, C. D. (2012). Willingness to have unprotected sex. *Journal of Sex Research,* 49, 61–68.

Foster, J. D., Jonason, P. K., Shrira, H., Campbell, W. K., Shiverdecker, L. K., & Varner, S. C. (2014). What do you get when you make someone else's partner your own? An analysis of relationships formed via mate poaching. *Journal of Research in Personality,* 52, 78–90.

Frampton, J. R., & Fox, J. (2018, July–September). Social media's role in romantic partners' retroactive jealousy: Social comparison, uncertainty, and information seeking. *Social Media & Society,* 1–12. Available: https://journals.sagepub.com/doi/pdf/10.1177/2056305118800317 (Last visited 6/8/20).

Frascella, J., Potenza, M. N., Brown, L. L., & Childress, A. R. (2010). Shared brain vulnerabilities open the way for nonsubstance addictions: Caving addiction at a new joint? *Annals of the New York Academy of Sciences,* 1187, 294–315.

Frederick, D. A., & Haselton, M. G. (2007). Why is masculinity sexy? Tests of the fitness indicator hypothesis. *Personality and Social Psychology Bulletin,* 33, 1167–1183.

Frederick, D. A., Garcia, J. R., Gesselman, A. N., Mark, K. P., Hatfield, E., & Bohrnstedt, G. (2020). The happy American body 2.0: Predictors of affective body satisfaction in two U.S. national internet panel surveys. *Body Image,* 20, 70–84. Available: https://www.sciencedirect.com/science/article/pii/S174014451930213X (Last visited 9/16/20).

Frederick, D. A., Lever, J., Gillespie, B. J., & Garcia, J. R. (2017). What keeps passion alive? Sexual satisfaction is associated with sexual communication, mood setting, sexual variety, oral sex, orgasm, and sex frequency in a national U.S. study. *Journal of Sex Research,* 54, 186–201.

Fredrick, D. A., St. John, H. K., Garcia, J. R., & Lloyd, E. A. (2017, February 17). Differences in orgasm frequency among gay, lesbian, bisexual, and heterosexual men and women in a U.S. national sample. *Archives of Sexual Behavior,* 47(1), 273–288.

Freud, S. (1938). Three contributions to the theory of sex. In A. A. Brill (Ed.), *The basic writings of Sigmund Freud.* Modern Library.

Frey, J. D., Poudrier, G., Chiodo, M. V., & Hazen, A. (2016). A systematic review of metoidioplasty and radial forearm flap phalloplasty in female-to-male transgender genital reconstruction: Is the "ideal" neophallus an achievable goal? *Plastic and Reconstructive Surgery —Global Open,* 4(12), e1131.

Friedrich, W., Fisher, J., Broughton, D., Houston, M., & Shafran, C. (1998). Normative sexual behavior in children: A contemporary sample. *Pediatrics,* 101, e9.

Frisby, B. N., Dillow, M. R., Gaughan, S., & Nordlund, J. (2011). Flirtatious communication: An experimental examination of perceptions of social-sexual communication motivated by evolutionary forces. *Sex Roles,* 64, 682–694.

Frohlick, S. (2013). Intimate tourism markets: Money, gender, and complexity of erotic exchange in Costa Rican Caribbean town. *Anthropological Quarterly,* 86, 1330162.

Frost, D. M., & Meyer, I. H. (2009). Internalized homophobia and relationship quality among lesbians, gay men, and bisexuals. *Journal of Counseling Psychology,* 56, 97–109.

Fruhauf, S., Gerger, H., Schmidt, H. M., Munder, T., & Barth, J. (2013). Efficacy of psychological interventions for sexual dysfunction: A systematic review and meta-analysis. *Archives of Sexual Behavior,* 42, 915–933.

Fu, T. C., Hensel, D. J., Beckmeyer, J. J., Dodge, B., & Herbenick, D. (2019). Considerations in the measurement and reporting of withdrawal: Findings from the 2018 National Survey of Sexual Health and Behavior. *Journal of Sexual Medicine,* 16(8), 1170–1177. Available: https://pued.ncbi.nlm.nih.gov/31303571/ (Last visited 7/21/20).

Fu, T., Herbenick, D., Dodge, B., Owens, C., Sanders, S., Reece, M., & Fortenberry, J. D. (2019). Relationships among sexual identity, sexual attraction, and sexual behavior: Results from a nationally representative probability sample of adults in the United States. *Archives of Sexual Behavior,* 48, 1483–1493.

Fudge, M. C., & Byers, S. (2017). "I have a nice gross vagina": Understanding young women's genital self-perceptions. *Journal of Sex Research,* 54 (5), 351–361.

Fudge, M. C., & Byers, E. S. (2017). "I have a nice gross vagina": Understanding young women's genital self-perceptions. *Journal of Sex Research,* 54(3), 351–361.

Fugl-Meyer, K. S., Oberg, K., Lundberg, P. O., Lewin, B., & Fugi-Meyer, A. (2006). On orgasm, sexual techniques, and erotic perceptions in 18- to 74-yer-old Swedish women. *Journal of Sexual Medicine,* 3, 56–68.

Furr, J., Hebert, K., Wisenbaugh, E., & Gelman, J. (2018). Complications of genital enlargement surgery. *Journal of Sexual Medicine,* 15(2), 1811–1817. Available: https://www.jsm.jsexmed.org/article/S1743-6095(18)31256-6/fulltext (Last viewed 2/16/20).

Gagnon, J. (1977). *Human sexualities.* Scott, Foresman.

Gagnon, J. H. (1975). Sex research and social change. *Archives of Sexual Behavior,* 4, 112–141.

Gagnon, J. H., & Simon, W. (1973). *Sexual conduct: The origins of human sexuality.* Aldine.

Gallup, Inc. (2014). Same-sex marriage support reaches new high at 55%. Available: http://news.gallup.com/poll/169640/sex-marriage-support-reaches-new-high.aspx (Last visited 2/17/15).

Garcia, J. R., & Fisher, H. E. (2015). Why we hook up: Searching for sex or looking for love? In S. Tarrant (Ed.), *Gender, sex, and politics: In the streets and between the sheets in the 21st century* (pp. 238–250). New York: Routledge.

Garcia, J. R., Gesselman, A. N., Siliman, S. A., Perry, B. L., Coe, D., & Fisher, H. E. (2016). Sexting among singles in the USA: Prevalence of sending, receiving, and sharing sexual messages and images. *Sexual Health,* 13(5), 428–435.

Garcia, J. R., Lloyd, A. A., Wallen, K., & Fisher, H. E. (2014). Variation in orgasm occurrence by sexual orientation in a sample of U.S. singles. *Journal of Sexual Medicine,* 11(11), 2645–2652. Available: https://

onlinelibrary.wiley.com/doi/pdf/10.1111/jsm.12669?casa_token=psg7vS5 GjSoAAAAA:yT7BhL1GkriFN92d04KtW5sTMnXtSNGIaepDWBajn KUPWu6PhsUosOI0Vai7w2g11PiCvLFRTPLdapSu (Last visited 12/19/20).

Garcia, J. R., Massey, S. G., Merriwether, A. M., & Seibold-Simpson, S. M. (2013, August). *Orgasm experiences among emerging adult men and women: Gender, relationship context, and attitudes toward casual sex.* Poster presented at the annual meeting of the International Academy of Sex Research, Chicago, Illinois.

Garcia, J. R., Reiber, C., Massey, S. G., & Merriwether, A. M. (2012). Sexual hookup culture: A review. *Review of General Psychology,* 16, 161–176.

Garcia, J. R., Reiber, C., Merriwether, A. M., Heywood, L. L., & Fisher, H. E. (2010, March). *Touch me in the morning: Intimately affiliative gestures in uncommitted and romantic relationships.* Paper presented at the Annual Conference of the North Eastern Evolutionary Psychology Society, New Paltz, New York.

Garcia, M. A., & Umberson, D. (2019). Marital strain and psychological distress in same-sex and different-sex couples. *Journal of Marriage and Family,* 81(5), 1253–1268.

Garcia-Acero, M., Moreno-Nino, O., Suarez-Obando, F., Molina, M., Manotas, M. C., Prieto, J. C., Forero, C., Cespedes, C., Perez, J., Fernandez, N., & Rojas, A. (2020). Disorders of sex development: Genetic characterization of a patient cohort. *Molecular Medicine Reports,* 21(1), 97–106. Available: https://www.ncbi.nlm.nih.gov/pubmed/31746433 (Last visited 5/18/20).

Garrido, M., Sufrinko, N., Max, J., & Cortes, N. (2019). Where youth live, learn, and play matters: Tackling the social determinants of health in adolescent sexual and reproductive health. *Journal of Sexuality Education,* 13(3), 269–282.

Gates, G. J. (2015). Marriage and family: LGBT individuals and same-sex couples. *Marriage and Family,* 25(2), 67–87.

Gay Lesbian Alliance Against Defamation (GLADD). (2018). Tips for allies of transgender people. Available: https://www.glaad.org/transgender/allies (Last visited 2/23/20).

Gay, P. (1986). *The bourgeois experience: The tender passion.* New York: Oxford University Press.

Geary, D. C., Vigil, J., & Byrd-Craven, J. (2004). Evolution of human mate choice. *Journal of Sex Research,* 41, 27–42.

General Social Survey. (2019). Does respondent have marital partner? Available: https://gssdataexplorer.norc.org/trends/Gender%20&%20Marriage?measure=posslq (Last visited 4/28/20).

General Social Survey. (2019). General social surveys, 1972–2018: Cumulative codebook. Available: https://gss.norc.org/Documents/codebook/GSS_Codebook.pdf (Last visited 4/17/20).

Gentleman's Quarterly [GQ]. (2019, October 15). The state of masculinity now: A GQ survey. *The Editors of GQ.* Available: https://www.gq.com/story/state-of-masculinity-survey (Last visited 2/20/20).

George, W. H. (2019). Alcohol and sexual health behavior: "What we know and how we know it." *Journal of Sex Research,* 56(4–5), 409–424.

George, W. H., Davis, K. C., Norris, J., Heiman, J. R., Stoner, S. A., Schacht, R. L., Herndershot, C. S., & Kajumulo, K. F. (2009). Indirect effects of acute alcohol intoxication on sexual risk-taking: The roles of subjective and physiological sexual arousal. *Archives of Sexual Behavior,* 38, 498–513.

Gerard, M., Berry, M., Shtarkshall, R. A., Amsel, R., & Binik, M. (2020). Female multiple orgasm: An exploratory internet-based survey. *Journal of Sex Research.* https://doi.org/10.1080/00224499.2020.1743224

Gergen, K. J. (1985). The social constructionist movement in modern psychology. *American Psychologist,* 40, 266–275.

Gerressu, M., Mercer, C. H., Graham, C. A., Wellings, K., & Johnson, A. M. (2008). Prevalence of masturbation and associated factors in a British national probability survey. *Archives of Sexual Behavior,* 37, 266–278.

Gesselman, A. N., Ryan, R., Yarber, W. L., Vanterpool, K. B., Beavers, K. A., Grand, B. T., Wood, K., Graham, C. A., Milhausen, R., Sanders, S. A., & Crosby, R. A. (2020). An exploratory test of a couples-based condom-use intervention designed to promote pleasurable and safer penile-vaginal sex among university students. *Journal of American College Health.* https://doi.org/10/1080/07448481.2020.1818753

Gewirtz-Meydan, A., & Finzi-Dottan, R. (2017, February 6). Sexual satisfaction among couples: The role of attachment orientation and sexual motives. *Journal of Sex Research,* 55(2), 178–190.

Ghardi, J. R., Wittstein, I. S., Prasad, A., Sharkey, S., Dote, K., Akashi, Y. J., Cammann, V. L., Crea, F., Galiuto, L., Desmet, W., Yoshida, T., Manfredini, R., Eitel, I., Kosuge, M., Nef, H. M., Deshmukh, A., Lerman, A., Bossone, E., Citro, R., Ueyama, T., et al. (2018). International expert consensus document Takotsubo Syndrome (part I): Clinical characteristics, diagnostic criteria, and pathophysiology. *European Heart Journal,* 39, 2032–2046. Available: https://academic.oup.com/eurheartj/article/39/22/2032/5025412 (Last visited 7/5/20).

Gielen, A. C., Faden, R. R., O'Campo, P., Kass, N., & Anderson, J. (1994). Women's protective sexual behaviors: A test of the health belief model. *AIDS Education and Prevention,* 6, 1011.

Gilmore, M. R., Gaylord, J., Hatway, J., Hoppe, M. J., Morrison, D. M., Leigh, B. C., et al. (2001). Daily data collection of sexual and other health-related behaviors. *Journal of Sex Research,* 38, 35–42.

Glassenberg, A. N., Feinberg, D. R., Jones, B. C., Little, A. C., & DeBruine, L. M. (2010). Sex-dimorphic face shape preference in heterosexual and homosexual men and women. *Archives of Sexual Behavior,* 39, 1289–1296.

Golden, M. R., Dombrowski, J. C., Kerani, R. P., & Stekler, J. D. (2012). Failure of serosorting to protect African American men who have sex with men from HIV infection. *Sexually Transmitted Infections,* 39, 659–664.

Golden, M. R., Stekler, J., Hughes, J. P., & Wood, R. W. (2008). HIV serosorting in men who have sex with men: Is it safer? *Journal of Acquired Immune Deficiency Syndromes,* 49, 212–218.

Goldey, K. L., Push, A. R., Bell, S. N., & van Anders, S. M. (2016). Defining pleasure: A focus group of solitary and partnered sexual pleasure in queer and heterosexual women. *Archives of Sexual Behavior,* 45, 2137–2154.

Gonzalez-Lopez, G., & Vival-Ortiz, S. (2008). Latinas and Latinos, sexuality and society: A cultural sociological perspective. In H. Rodriguez, R. Saenz, and C. Menjivar (Eds.), *Latinas/os in the United States: Changing the face of America.* New York: Springer.

Goodman, A. (1993). Diagnosis and treatment of sexual addiction. *Journal of Sex and Marital Therapy,* 19, 225–251.

Gorbach, P. M., et al. (2009). Anal intercourse among young heterosexuals in three sexually transmitted disease clinics in the United States. *Sexually Transmitted Diseases,* 36, 193–198.

Gosink, P. D., & Jumbelic, M. I. (2000). Autoerotic asphyxiation in a female. *American Journal of Forensic Medicine and Pathology,* 21, 114–118.

Gottman, J., & Carrere, S. (2000, October). Welcome to the love lab. *Psychology Today,* 42–47.

Gottman, J., & Levenson, R. (2012). The 12-year study. Available: https://www.gottman.com/blog/the-12-year-study/ (Last visited 8/25/20).

Gould, S., & Mosher, D. (2017). Americans spent $8 billion on plastic surgery in 2016—here's the work they got done. *Business Insider.* Available: http://www.businessinsider.com/plastic-surgery-growth-statistics-facts-2016-2017-5 (Last visited 12/11/17).

Graham, C. A. (2019). The pill and women's sexuality. *BMJ*, 364, l335. Available: https://www.bmj.com/content/364/bmj.l335 (Last visited 7/22/20).

Graham, C. A., & Bancroft, J. (1997). A comparison of retrospective interview assessment versus daily ratings of sexual interest and activity in women. In J. Bancroft (Ed.), *Researching sexual behavior*. Indiana University Press.

Grant, J. M., Mottet, L. A., Tanis, J., Harrison, J., Herman, J., & Keisling, M. (2011). Injustice at every turn: A report of the National Transgender Discrimination Survey. National Center for Transgender Equality and National Gay and Lesbian Task Force. Available: http://www.thetaskforce.org/static_html/downloads/reports/reports/ntds_full.pdf (Last visited 12/6/17).

Grant, M. G. (2016, May 26). Amnesty International calls for an end to the 'Nordic Model' of criminalizing sex workers. *The Nation*.

Gray, P. B., & Garcia, J. R. (2013). *Evolution and human sexual behavior*. Cambridge, MA: Harvard University Press.

Gregor, T. (1985). *Anxious pleasures*. University of Chicago Press.

Grello, C., Welsh, D. P., & Harper, M. S. (2006). No strings attached: The nature of casual sex in college students. *Journal of Sex Research*, 43(3), 255–267.

Griffin, G. (1998). Understanding heterosexism—The subtle continuum of homophobia. *Women and Language*, 21, 11–21.

Griffith, J. D., Mitchell, S., Hart, C. L., Adams, L. T., & Gu, L. L. (2012). Pornography actresses: An assessment of the damaged goods hypothesis. *Journal of Sex Research*. https://doi.org/10.1080/00224499.2012.719168

Grimes, J. (2014). *Sexually transmitted disease*. Greenwood.

Grossman, J. M., Tracy, A. J., Charmaraman, L., Ceder, I., & Erkut, S. (2014). Protective effects of middle school comprehensive sex education with family involvement. *Journal of School Health*, 84, 739–747.

Grov, C., Wolff, M., Smith, M. D., Koken, J., & Parsons, J. T. (2014). Male clients of male escorts: Satisfaction, sexual behavior, and demographic characteristics. *Journal of Sex Research*, 51, 827–837.

Grower, P., & Ward, L. M. (2018). Examining the unique contribution of body appreciation to heterosexual women's sexual agency. *Body Image*, 27, 138–147. Available: https://pubmed.ncbi.nlm.nih.gov/30248567/ (Last visited 9/16/20).

Grubbs, J. B. (2020). Porn use is up, thanks to the pandemic. *The Conversation*. Available: from: https://theconversation.com/porn-use-is-up-thanks-to-the-pandemic-134972. (Accessed 2/4/2021).

Grulich, A. E., de Visser, R. O., Smith, A. M. A., Rissel, C. E., & Richters, J. (2003). Sex in Australia: Homosexual experience and recent homosexual encounters. *Australian and New Zealand Journal of Public Health*, 27, 155–163.

Gulgoz, S., Glazie, J. J., Enright, E. A., Alonso, D. J., Durwood, L. J., Fast, A. A., Lowe, R., Ji, C., Heer, J., Martin, C. L., & Olson, K. R. (2019, December 3). Similarity in transgender and cisgender children's gender development. *Proceedings of the National Academy of Sciences of the United States of America (PNA)*, 116(49), 24480–24485. Available: https://www.pnas.org/content/116/49/24480 (Last viewed 2/28/20).

Gunter, J. (2019, August 13). Why sexually transmitted infections can't shake their stigma. *New York Times*.

Gunter, J. (2019, September 19). Treating the incredible shrinking vagina. *NY Times*. Available: https://www.nytimes.com/2019/09/19/well/treating-the-incredible-shrinking-vagina.html (Last visited 12/18/20).

Gunter, J. (2019.3a). For the teen who no longer wants a period. *NY Times*. Available: https://www.nytimes.com/2019/11/12/well/for-the-teen-who-no-longer-wants-a-period.html (Last visited 1/30/20).

Gunter, J. (2019.3a). *The vagina bible: The vulva and the vagina – Separating the myth from the medicine*. Kensington Publishing Corp.

Gunter, J. (2019.3b). *The vagina bible: The vulva and the vagina – Separating the myth from the medicine*. Kensington Publishing Corp.

Gunter, J. (2019.3c) For the teen who no longer wants a period. *NY Times*. Available: https://www.nytimes.com/2019/11/12/well/for-the-teen-who-no-longer-wants-a-period.html(Last visited 1/30/20).

Guttmacher Institute. (2016b). American teens' sexual and reproductive health. Available: https://www.guttmacher.org/fact-sheet/american-teens-sexual-and-reproductive-health (Last visited 8/24/17).

Guttmacher Institute. (2016.11). Declines in teen pregnancy risk entirely driven by improved contraceptive use. Available: https://www.guttmacher.org/news-release/2016/declines-teen-pregnancy-risk-entirely-driven-improved-contraceptive-use (Last visited 7/20/20).

Guttmacher Institute. (2017). Contraceptive failure in the United States. Estimates from the 2006–2010 National Survey of Family Growth. Available: https://www.guttmacher.org/journals/psrh/2017/02/contraceptive-failure-united-states-estimates-2006-2010-national-survey-family (Last visited 7/3/17).

Guttmacher Institute. (2018). Infant abandonment. Available: https://www.guttmacher.org/state-policy/explore/infant-abandonment (Last visited 1/18/18).

Guttmacher Institute. (2019). Adolescent sexual and reproductive health in the United States. Available: file:///Users/barbarasayad/Desktop/Desktop/Adolescent%20Sexual%20and%20Reproductive%20Health%20in%20the%20United%20States%20%7C%20Guttmacher%20Institute.webarchive (Last visited 4/18/20).

Guttmacher Institute. (2019.11a). Unintended pregnancy in the United States. Available: https://www.guttmacher.org/fact-sheet/unintended-pregnancy-united-states (Last visited 7/16/20).

Guttmacher Institute. (2019.11b). Induced abortion in the United States. Available: https://www.guttmacher.org/fact-sheet/induced-abortion-united-states (Last visited 7/29/20).

Guttmacher Institute. (2019.11c). State policy trends 2019: A wave of abortion bans, but some states are fighting back. Available: https://www.guttmacher.org/article/2019/12/state-policy-trends-2019-wave-abortion-bans-some-states-are-fighting-back (Last visited 8/2/20).

Guttmacher Institute. (2020.6). Expanding the scope of sex education and the teen pregnancy prevention program: A work in progress. Available: https://www.guttmacher.org/article/2020/02/expanding-scope-sex-education-and-teen-pregnancy-prevention-program-work-progress (Last visited 4/22/20).

Guttmacher Institute. (2020.11a). Contraceptive use in the United States. Available: https://www.guttmacher.org/fact-sheet/contraceptive-use-united-states (Last visited 7/16/20).

Guttmacher Institute. (2020.11c). Contraceptive use among adolescents in the United States. Available: https://www.guttmacher.org/fact-sheet/contraceptive-use-among-adolescents-united-states (Last visited 7/20/20).

Guttmacher Institute. (2020.11d). An overview of abortion laws. Available: https://www.guttmacher.org/state-policy/explore/overview-abortion-laws (Last visited 8/2/20).

Gutzeit, O., Levy, G., & Lowenstein, L. (2020). Postpartum female sexual function: Risk factors for postpartum sexual dysfunction. *Sexual Medicine*, 9(1), 8–13. Available: https://www.ncbi.nlm.nih.gov/pmc/articles/PMC7042171/ (Last visited 10/7/20).

Ha, T., van den Berg, J. E. M., Engels, R. C. M. E., & Lichtwarck-Aschoff, A. (2012). Effects of attractiveness and status in dating desire in homosexual and heterosexual men and women. *Archives of Sexual Behavior*, 41, 673–682.

Hackney, A., Lane, A. R., Register-Mihalik, J., & O'Leary, C. B. (2017). Endurance exercise training and male sexual libido. *Medicine & Science in Sports and Exercise*, 49, 1383–1388.

Haelle, T. (2016, March 23). Probing the complexities of transgender mental health. *NPR.* Available: http://www.npr.org/sections/health-shots/2016/03/23/471265599/probing-the-complexities-of-transgender-mental-health (Last visited 5/31/17).

Hafford-Letchfield, T., Cocker, C., Rutter, D., Tinarwo, M., & McCormack, R. M. (2019). What do we know about transgender parenting?: Findings from a systematic review. *Health and Social Care in the Community,* 27(5), 1111–1115. Available: https://onlinelibrary.wiley.com/doi/full/10.1111/hsc.12759 (Last visited 8/27/20).

Hald, G. M., Kuyper, L., Adam, P., & de Wit, J. (2013). Does viewing explain doing? Assessing the association between sexually explicit materials use and sexual behaviors in a large sample of Dutch adolescents and young adults. *Journal of Sexual Medicine,* 10, 2986–2995.

Hale, C. J. (2013). 12 things no one told me about sex after rape. Available: https://thoughtcatalog.com/cj-hale/2013/06/12-things-no-one-told-me-about-sex-after-rape/ (Last visited: 11/1/2017).

Hales, C. M., Carroll, M. D., Fryar, C. D., & Ogden, C. L. (2020). Prevalence of obesity and severe obesity among adults: United States, 2017–2018, No. 360. *NCHS Data Brief.* Available: https://www.cdc.gov/nchs/products/databriefs/db360.htm (Last visited 8/18/20).

Hall, J. A. (2013). *The five flirting types.* Harlequin.

Hall, K. (2004). *Reclaiming your sexual self: How you can bring desire back into your life.* Wiley.

Hall, K. S., Sales, J. M., Komro, K., & Santelli, J. (2016). The state of sex education in the United States. *Journal of Adolescent Health,* 58(6), 595–597. Available: https://www.ncbi.nlm.nih.gov/pmc/articles/PMC5426905/ (Last visited 12/18/20).

Hall, S. A., Shackelton, R., Rosen, R., & Araujo, A. B. (2010). Risk factors for incident erectile dysfunction among community-dwelling men. *Journal of Sexual Medicine,* 7(2Pt1), 712–722.

Hamby, S., Finkelhor, D., & Turner, H. (2013). Perpetrator and victim gender patterns for 21 forms of youth victimization in the National Survey of Children's Experiences to Violence. *Victims and Violence,* 28, 915–939.

Hamilton, D. T., & Morris, M. (2010). Consistency of self-reported sexual behavior in surveys. *Archives of Sexual Behavior,* 39, 842–860.

Hammad, N., & van Hoff, J. (2020). "This is men, this is what I am, I am a man": The masculinities of men who pay for sex with women. *Journal of Sex Research,* 57, 650–6643.

Hampson, R. (2017, November 22–23). Fears fade in war on harassment. *USA Today,* p. 1A.

Han, J. J., Beltran, T. H., Song, J. W., Klarie, J., & Choi, S. (2017). Prevalence of genital human papillomavirus infection and human papillomavirus vaccination rates among U.S. adult men. *JAMA Oncology,* 3, 810–816.

Harding, S., & Norberg, K. (2005). New feminist approaches to social science methodologies: An introduction. *Signs: Journal of Women in Culture and Society,* 30, 2009–2015.

Harris, E. A., Hornsey, M. J., Larsen, H. F., & Barlow, F. K. (2019). Beliefs about gender predict faking orgasms in heterosexual women. *Archives of Sexual Behavior,* 48, 2419–2433.

Harte, C. B., & Meston, C. M. (2011). Recreational use of erectile dysfunction medications in undergraduate men in the United States: Characteristics and associated risk factors. *Archives of Sexual Behavior,* 40, 597–606.

Harvard Health Publishing. (2020). Erectile dysfunction. Available: https://www.health.harvard.edu/topics/erectile-dysfunction (Last visited 12/18/20).

Harvard Men's Health Watch. (2019). The growing problem of an enlarged prostate gland. *Harvard Health Publishing.* Available: https://www.health.harvard.edu/mens-health/the-growing-problem-of-an-enlarged-prostate-gland (Last visited 5/20/20).

Harvey, S. M., Oakley, L. P., Washburn, I., & Agnew, C. R. (2018). Contraceptive choice among young adults: Influence of individual and relationship factors. *Journal of Sex Research,* 55(9), 1106–1115.

Haseltine, K. (2017, August 4). Why we kiss on the lips. *Psychology Today.* Available: https://www.psychologytoday.com/us/blog/long-fuse-big-bang/201708/why-we-kiss-the-lips (Accessed: March 20, 2020).

Hatcher, R. A., Trussell, J., Nelson, A. L., Cates, W., Kowal, D., & Policar, M. S. (2011). *Contraceptive technology* (20th rev. ed.). Ardent Media.

Hatcher, R. A., Trussell, J., Stewart, F., Nelson, A. L., Cates, W., Guest, F., et al. (2007). *Contraceptive technology* (19th ed.). Ardent Media.

Hauck, G. (2019, June 28). Anti-LGBT hate crimes are rising the FBI says. *USA Today.* Available: https://www.usatoday.com/story/news/2019/06/28/anti-gay-hate-crimes-rise-fbi-says-and-they-likely-undercount/1582614001/ (Last visited: 12/21/2020).

Haupert, M. L., Pope, A. R. D., Garcia, J. R., & Smith, E. R. An inclusive gender identity measure. In R. R. Milhausen, J. K. Salaluk, T. D. Fisher, C. M. Davis, & W. L. Yarber (Eds.), *Handbook of sexuality-related measures* (pp. 353–355). Routledge.

Hawks, L., Woolhandler, S., Himmelstein, D. U., Bor, D. H., Gaffney, A., & McCormick, D. (2019, September 16). Association between forced sexual initiation and health outcomes among US women. *JAMA Internal Medicine,* 179(11), 1551–1558.

Hay, P. E., Kerry, S. R., Normansell, R., Horner, P., Reid, F., & Kerry, S. M. (2016). Which sexually active young female students are most at risk for pelvic inflammatory disease? *Sexually Transmitted Infections,* 92, 63–66.

Hazan, C., & Shaver, P. (1987). Romantic love conceptualized as an attachment process. *Journal of Personality and Social Psychology,* 52(3), 511–524.

He, F., Hensel, D. J., Harezlak, J., & Fortenberry, J. D. (2016). Condom use as a function of number of coital events in a new relationship. *Sexually Transmitted Diseases,* 43, 67–70.

Healthline. (2019). How to remove pubic hair safely at home and with a professional. Available: https://www.healthline.com/health/best-way-to-remove-pubic-hair (Last visited 1/28/20).

Healthline. (2019). Risk factors of having high or low estrogen levels in males. Available: https://www.healthline.com/health/estrogen-in-men (Last visited 2/12/20).

Helms, D. J., et al. (2008). Risk factors for prevalent and incident trichomonas vaginalis among women attending three sexually transmitted disease clinics. *Sexually Transmitted Diseases,* 35, 484–488.

Henderson, R. (2018, May 28). The science behind what Tinder is doing to your brain. *Psychology Today.* Available: https://www.psychologytoday.com/us/blog/after-service/201805/the-science-behind-what-tinder-is-doing-your-brain (Last visited 1/25/20).

Hensel, D. J., & Fortenberry, J. D. (2013). A multidimensional model of sexual health and sexual and prevention behavior among adolescent women. *Journal of Adolescent Health,* 52(2), 219–227.

Herbenick, D., Bowling, J., Fu, T., Dodge, B., Guerra-Reyes, L., & Sanders, S. (2017). Sexual diversity in the Unites States: Results from a nationally representative probability sample of adult women and men. *PLOS One,* 12(7). Available: https://journals.plos.org/plosone/article?id=10.1371/journal.pone.0181198 (Last viewed 6/9/20).

Herbenick, D., Fu, T. J., Dodge, B., & Baldwin, A. (2016, June). Female pleasure and orgasm: Results from a U.S. nationally representative survey. *Journal of Sexual Medicine,* 13(6), Supplement S242.

Herbenick, D., Reece, M., Hensel, D., Sanders, S., Jozkowski, K., & Fortenberry, J. D. (2011). Association of lubricant use with women's sexual pleasure, sexual satisfaction, and genital symptoms: A prospective daily diary study. *Journal of Sexual Medicine, 8,* 202–212.

Herbenick, D., Reece, M., Schick, V., & Sanders, S. A. (2013). Erect penis length and circumference dimensions of 1,661 sexually active men in the United States. *Journal of Sexual Medicine,* 11, 93–101.

Herbenick, D., Reece, M., Schick, V., Sanders, S. A., Dodge, B., & Fortenberry, J. D. (2010.2a, 2010.9a). Sexual behavior in the United States: Results from a national probability sample of men and women ages 14–94. *Journal of Sexual Medicine, 7,* 255–265.

Herbenick, D., Reece, M., Schick, V., Sanders, S. A., Dodge, B., & Fortenberry, J. D. (2010.2b, 2010.6). Sexual behaviors, relationships, and perceived health status among adult women in the United States: Results from a national probability sample of men and women. *Journal of Sexual Medicine, 7,* 277–290.

Herbenick, D., Reece, M., Schick, V., Sanders, S. A., Dodge, B., & Fortenberry, J. D. (2010.2c, 2010.14a). An event-level analysis of the sexual characteristics and composition among adults ages 18–59: Results from a national probability sample of men and women. *Journal of Sexual Medicine, 7,* 346–361.

Herdt, G., & McClintock, M. (2000). The magical age of 10. *Archives of Sexual Behavior,* 29(6), 587–606.

Herdt, G., & Polen-Petit, N. C. (2014). *Human sexuality: Self, society, and culture.* McGraw- Hill.

Herz, R. (2007). *The scent of desire: Discovering our enigmatic sense of smell.* William Morrow.

Herzer, M. (1985). Kertbeny and the nameless love. *Journal of Homosexuality,* 12, 1–26.

Hess, J. A., & Coffelt, T. A. (2012). Verbal communication about sex in marriage: Patterns of language use and its connection with relational outcomes. *Journal of Sex Research,* 49(6), 603–612.

Hicks, T. V., & Leitenberg, H. (2001). Sexual fantasies about one's partner versus someone else: Gender differences in incidence and frequency. *Journal of Sex Research,* 38, 43–50.

Higginbotham, E. B. (1992). African-American women's history and the metalanguage of race. *Journal of Women in Culture and Society,* 17, 251–274.

Higgins, J. A., & Smith, N. K. (2016). The sexual acceptability of contraception: Reviewing the literature and building a new concept. *Journal of Sex Research,* 53(4–5), 417–456.

Hill, B. J., Rahman, Q., Bright, D. A., & Sanders, S. A. (2010). The semantics of sexual behavior and their implications for HIV/AIDS research and sexual health: US and UK gay men's definitions of having "had sex." *AIDS Care,* 22, 1245–1251.

Hine, D. C. (1989). Rape and the inner lives of Black women in the Middle West: Preliminary thoughts on the culture of dissemblance. *Signs,* 14, 915.

Hirschfeld, M. (1991). *Transvestites: The erotic drive to cross dress.* Prometheus Books.

HIV.gov. (2020). U.S. Statistics. Available: https://www.hiv.gov/hiv-basics/overview/data-and-trends/statistics (Last visited: 10/11/2020).

Hobbs, M., Owen, S., & Gerber, L. (2016, September 5). Liquid love? Dating apps, sex, relationships, and the digital transformation of intimacy. *Journal of Sociology,* Available: https://www.researchgate.net/profile/Livia_Gerber/publication/308893318_Liquid_Love_manuscript_authors'_version/links/57f5990708ae8da3ce552c8e.pdf (Last visited 4/18/17).

Hock, R. R. (2007). *Human sexuality.* Pearson Education.

Hock-Long, L., Henry-Moss, D., Carter, M., Hatfield-Timajchy, K., Erickson, P. II, et al. (2013). Condom use with serious and casual heterosexual partners: Findings from a community venue-based survey of young adults. *AIDS Behavior,* 17, 900–913.

Hodgons, B., Kukkonen, T. M., Binik, Y. M., & Carrier, S. (2016). Using the dual control model to investigate the relationship between mood, genital and self-reported sexual arousal in men and women. *Journal of Sex Research,* 53(1), 1–15.

Hoffman, J. (2016, June 30). Doctors worry about women's preference for the cleanshaven 'Barbie doll look.' *New York Times,* A16.

Hoffman, J. (2020, October 7). "I won't be used as a guinea pig for white people". Available: https://www.nytimes.com/2020/10/07/health/coronavirus-vaccine-trials-african-americans.html (Last visited 10/20/2020).

Hoffman, J. (2020, October 29). People at still having sex so why are S.T.D. rates dropping? *New York Times.* Available: https://www.nytimes.com/2020/10/28/health/covid-std-testing.html (Last visited: 10/29/2020).

Hohman, M. (2020, July 1). FDA approves first non-hormonal contraceptive gel – here's how it works. *Today.* Available: https://www.today.com/health/fda-approves-first-non-hormonal-contraceptive-gel-here-s-how-t185616 (Last visited 7/28/20).

Holland, K. J., & French, S. E. (2012). Condom negotiation strategy use and effectiveness among college students. *Journal of Sex Research,* 49, 443–453.

Holleb, M. L. E. (2019). *The A–Z of gender and sexuality: From Ace to Ze.* Morgan Lev Edward Holleb.

Holman, D. M., Benard, V., Roland, K. B., Watson, M., Liddon, N., & Stokely, S. (2014). Barriers to human papillomavirus vaccination among US adolescents: A systematic review of the literature. *JAMA Pediatrics,* 168, 76–82.

Holmberg, D., & Blair, K. L. (2009). Sexual desire: Communication, satisfaction, and preferences of men and women in same-sex versus mixed-sex relationships. *Journal of Sex Research,* 46, 57–66.

Holmes, S. T., & Holmes, R. M. (2002). *Sex crimes.* Sage.

Holtzhausen, L., Ross, A., & Perry, R. (2016). Working on trauma—a systematic review of TF-CBT work with child survivors of sexual abuse. *Social Work,* 52, 511–524.

Hooker, E. (1957). The adjustment of the overt male homosexual. *Journal of Projective Psychology,* 21, 18–31.

Horan, S. M. (2015). Further understanding sexual communication: Honesty, deception, safety, and risk. *Journal of Social and Personal Relationships,* 33(4), 499–468.

HPV infections rampant. (2017, April 28). *The Week.* https://www.cancer.org/

Hucker, S. J. (2008). Sexual masochism: Psychopathology and theory. In D. R. Laws & W. T. O'Donohue (Eds.), *Sexual deviance: Theory, assessment, and treatment* (2nd ed.). Guilford Press.

Hucker, S. J. (2011). Hypoxyphilia. *Archives of Sexual Behavior,* 40, 1323–1326.

Hughes, S. M., & Kruger, D. J. (2011). Sex differences in post-coital behaviors in long- and short-term mating: An evolutionary perspective. *Journal of Sex Research,* 48, 496–505.

Hughes, S. M., Harrison, M. A., & Gallup, G. G. (2007). Sex differences in romantic kissing among college students: An evolutionary perspective. *Evolutionary Psychology,* 5, 612–663.

Hugosson, J. (2018). Stopping screening, when and how? *Translational Andrology and Urology,* (1), 46–53. Available: https://www.ncbi.nlm.nih.gov/pmc/articles/PMC5861277/ (Last visited 10/3/20).

Hull, E., Lorrain, D., Du, J., et al. (1999). Hormone-neurotransmitter interactions in the control of sexual behavior. *Behavioral Brain Research,* 105, 105–116.

Human Rights Campaign. (2016). Supporting and caring for transgender children. Available: https://www.hrc.org/resources/supporting-caring-for-transgender-children (Last visited 12/17/20).

Human Rights Campaign. (2017.13a). Explore: Health & aging. Available: https://www.hrc.org/explore/topic/health-and-aging (Last visited 12/5/17).

Human Rights Campaign. (2017.13b). Healthcare Equality Index. Available: https://assets2.hrc.org/files/assets/resources/HEI-2017.pdf?_ga=2.105218823.586201988.1512514981-1099071184.1512514981 (Last visited 12/5/17).

Human Rights Commission. (2011). Degrees of equality report: A national study examining workplace climate for LGBT employees (2009). Available: https://assets2.hrc.org/files/assets/resources/DegreesOfEquality_2009.pdf (Last visited: 10/13/2017).

Human Rights Watch. (2019). New health guidelines propel transgender rights. Available: https://www.hrw.org/news/2019/05/27/new-health-guidelines-propel-transgender-rights (Last visited 5/18/20).

Human Rights Watch. (2020). US Supreme Court ruling a victory for LGBT workers. Available: https://www.hrw.org/news/2020/06/15/us-supreme-court-ruling-victory-lgbt-workers (Last visited 12/17/20).

Humble, M. B., & Bejerot, S. (2016). Orgasm, serotonin reuptake inhibition, and plasma oxytocin in obsessive-compulsive disorder. Gleaning from a distant randomized clinical trial. *Sexual Medicine,* 4(3), 145–155.

Humphreys, L. (1975). *Tearoom trade: Impersonal sex in public places.* Aldine.

Hust, S. J. T., Marett, E. G., Ren, C., Adams, P. M., et al. (2014). Establishing and adhering to sexual consent: The association between reading magazines and college students' sexual consent negotiation. *Journal of Sex Research,* 51(3), 280–290.

Hutchinson, A., Begley, E. B., Sullivan, P., Clark, H. A., Boyett, B. C., & Kellerman, S. E. (2007). Conspiracy beliefs and trust in information about HIV/AIDS among minority men who have sex with men. *Journal of Acquired Immune Deficiency Syndromes,* 45, 503–506.

Hutchinson, K. B., Kip, K. E., & Ness, R. B. (2007). Condom use and its association with bacterial vaginosis and bacterial vaginosis-associated vaginal microflora. *Epidemiology,* 18, 702–708.

Hutson, M. (2016, March 16). Keeping up with the Joneses—in bed. *Scientific Mind.*

Huysamen, M., (2020). "There's massive pressure to please her": On the discourse production of men's desire to pay for sex. *Journal of Sex Research,* 57, 639–649.

Hyde, J. S., & DeLamater, J. D. (2008). *Understanding human sexuality* (10th ed.). McGraw-Hill.

Hyde, J. S., & DeLamater, J. D. (2020). *Understanding human sexuality* (14th ed.). McGraw-Hill.

Hyde, J. S., Bigler, R. S., Joel, D., Tate, C. C., & van Anders, S. (2018). The future of sex and gender in psychology: Five challenges to the gender binary. *American Psychologist,* 74(2), 171–193. Available: https://medschool.ucsd.edu/som/psychiatry/about/Diversity/Documents/Hyde%20et%20al%202019%20gender%20nonbinary.pdf (Last visited 2/23/20).

Ickovics, J. R., Beren, S. E., Grigorenko, E. L., Morrill, A. C., Druley, J. A., & Rodin, J. (2002). Pathways of risk: Race, social class, stress, and coping as factors predicting heterosexual risk behaviors for HIV among women. *AIDS and Behavior,* 6, 339–350.

Ijams, K., & Miller, L. D. (2000). Perceptions of dream-disclosure: An exploratory study. *Communication Studies,* 51, 135–148.

Imrie, S., Zaheh, S., Wylie, K., & Golomok, S. (2020). Children with trans parents: Parent-child relationship quality and psychological well-being. *Parenting.* Available: https://www.tandfonline.com/doi/pdf/10.1080/15295192.2020.1792194 (Last visited 8/27/20).

Institute of Medicine. (2001). *The health of lesbian, gay, bisexual, and transgender people: Building a foundation for better understanding.* National Academies Press.

Institute of Medicine. (2011). *The health of lesbian, gay, bisexual and transgender people: Building a foundation for better understanding.* National Academies Press. Available: https://www.ncbi.nlm.nih.gov/pubmed/22013611 (Last visited 12/6/17).

Institute of Medicine. (2011). Committee on Lesbian, Gay, Bisexual and Transgender Health Issues and Research Gaps and Opportunities: *The health of lesbian, gay, bisexual, and transgender people: Building a foundation for better understanding.* National Academies Press.

International Planned Parenthood Federation. (2019). Myths and facts about the Intra-Uterine Device (IUD). Available: https://www.ippf.org/blogs/myths-and-facts-about-intra-uterine-devices (Last visited 7/28/20).

Internet pornography law dies quietly in Supreme Court. (2009, January 22). *Herald Times,* p. E3.

Ioannidis, J. P. (2005). Contradicted and initially stronger effects in highly cited clinical research. *Journal of the American Medical Association,* 294, 218–228.

Ireland, L. (2019). *Who are the 1 in 4 American women who choose abortion?* University of Massachusetts Medical School. Available: https://www.umassmed.edu/news/news-archives/2019/05/who-are-the-1-in-4-american-women-who-choose-abortion/ (Last visited 7/16/20).

Ishii-Kuntz, M. (1997). Chinese American families. In M. K. DeGenova (Ed.), *Families in cultural context.* Mountain View, CA: Mayfield.

Ivey-Stephenson, A. Z., Demissie, Z., Crosby, A. E., Stone, D. M., Gaylor, E., Wilkins, N., Lowry, R., & Brown, M. (2020). Suicidal ideation and behaviors among high school students—Youth Risk Behavior Survey, United States, 2019. *Mortality and Morbidity Report,* 69, 1–15.

Jackson, S., & Scott, S. (2007). Embodying orgasm: Gendered power relations and sexual pleasure. *Women and Therapy,* 24, 99–110.

Jadva, V., Hines, M., & Golombok, S. (2008). Infants' preferences for toys, colors, and shapes: Sex differences and similarities. *Archives of Sexual Behavior,* 39, 1261–1273.

Jankowiak, W. R., Volsche, S. L., & Garcia, J. R. (2015). Is the romantic-sexual kiss a near human universal? *American Anthropologist,* 117, 535–539.

Jannini, E. A., Fisher, W. A., Bitzer, J., & McMahon, C. G. (2009). Is sex just fun? How sexual activity improves health. *Journal of Sexual Medicine,* 6, 2640–2648.

Janssen, E., McBride, K. R., Yarber, W., Hill, B. J., & Butler, S. M. (2008). Factors that influence sexual arousal in men: A focus group study. *Archives of Sexual Behavior,* 37(2), 252–265.

Janus, S., & Janus, C. (1993). *The Janus report on sexual behavior.* Wiley.

Jasienska, S., Lipson, P., Thune, I., & Ziomkiewicz, A. (2006). Symmetrical women have higher potential fertility. *Evolution and Human Behavior,* 27, 390–400.

Jawed-Wessel, S., & Sevick, E. (2017). The impact of pregnancy and childbirth on sexual behaviors: A systematic review. *The Journal of Sex Research,* 54(4–5), 411–423.

Jawed-Wessel, S., Santo, J., & Irwin, J. (2019, April). Sexual activity and attitudes as predictors of sexual satisfaction during pregnancy: A multilevel model describing the sexuality of couples in the first 12 weeks. *Archives of Sexual Behavior,* 48(3), 843–854. Available: https://link.springer.com/article/10.1007/s10508-018-1317-1 (Last viewed 8/17/20).

Jayson, S. (2007, July 9). Charles Atlas was right: Brawny guys get the girls. *USA Today,* p. D6.

Jayson, S. (2017, November 15). The power of #MeToo. *The Madison Courier,* p. A2.

Jensen, T. K., Priskorn, L., Holmboe, S. A., Nassan, F. L., Andersson, A. M., Dalgard, C., Petersen, H., Chavarrro, J. E., & Jorgensen, N. (2020). Associations of fish oil supplement use with testicular function in young men. *JAMA Network Open,* 3(1). Available: https://www.ncbi.nlm.nih.gov/pubmed/31951274 (Last visited 2/17/20).

Jewell, T. (2018). Can men get or spread bacterial vaginosis? *Healthline.* Available: https://www.healthline.com/health/bacterial-vaginosis-men (Last viewed 2/10/20).

Jin, S., Smith, D., Chen, R. Y., Ding, G., Yao, Y., et al. (2010). HIV prevalence and risk behaviors among male clients of female sex workers in Yunnan, China. *Journal of Acquired Immune Deficiency Syndromes, 53,* 124–130.

Joel, D., Tarrasch, R., Berman, Z., Mukamel, M., & Ziv., E. (2014). Queering gender: Studying gender identity in "normative" individuals. *Psychology & Sexuality,* 5, 261–321. Available: https://www.tandfonline.com/doi/abs/10.1080/19419899.2013.830640 (Last visited 12/16/20).

Johns Hopkins Medicine. (2019). Epidurals for labor: Fact Sheet. Available: https://anesthesiology.hopkinsmedicine.org/wp-content/uploads/2019/04/Epidural-Handout-11-20-2018.pdf (Last visited 8/27/20).

Joint United Nations Programme on AIDS and World Health Organization. (2005). AIDS epidemic update: December 2005. Available: http://data.unaids.org/publications/irc-pub06/epi_update2005_en.pdf (Last visited 2/27/18).

Joint United Nations Programme on HIV/AIDS. (2008). 2008 report on the global AIDS epidemic. Available: http://www.unaids.org/sites/default/files/media_asset/jc1510_2008globalreport_en_0.pdf (Last visited 2/27/18).

Joint United Nations Programme on HIV/AIDS. (2010). Global report: UNAIDS global report on the AIDS epidemic, 2010. Available: http://files.unaids.org/en/media/unaids/contentassets/documents/unaidspublication/2010/20101123_globalreport_en%5b1%5d.pdf (Last visited 2/27/2018).

Joint United Nations Programme on HIV/AIDS. (2017). Protecting the rights of sex workers. Available: http://www.unaids.org/en/resources/presscentre/featurestories/2017/june/20170602_sexwork (Last visited to: 9/11/2017).

Jonason, P. K., Li, N. P., & Cason, M. J. (2009). The "booty call": A compromise between men's and women's ideal mating strategies. *Journal of Sex Research,* 46, 460–470.

Jones, J. H. (1993). *Bad blood: The Tuskegee syphilis experiment* (Rev. ed.). Free Press.

Jones, J., & Mosher, W. D. (2013, December 20). Fathers' involvement with their children: United States, 2006–2010. *National Health Statistics Reports,* 71. https://www.cdc.gov/nchs/data/nhsr/nhsr071.pdf (Last visited 10/12/17).

Jones, K. G., Johnson, A. M., Wellings, K., Sonnenberg, P., Field, N., et al. (2015). The prevalence of, and factors associated with, paying for sex among men resident in Britain: Findings for the third National Survey of Sexual Attitudes and Lifestyles (Natsal-3). *Sexually Transmitted Infections,* 91, 116–123.

Jones, R. K., Lindberg, L. D., & Higgins, J. A. (2014). Pull and pray or extra protection? Contraceptive strategies involving withdrawal among US adult women. *Contraception,* 60(4), 416–421.

Jorgensen, M. J., Maindal, H. T., Larsen, M. B., Christensen, K. S., Andeson, B., & Olesen, F. (2015). Chlamydia trachomatis infection in young adults associated with concurrent partnerships and short gap between partners. *Infectious Diseases,* 47, 108.

Joyal, C. C., & Carpentier, J. (2017). "The prevalence of paraphilic interests and behaviors in the general population: A provincial survey." *Journal of Sex Research,* 54, 161–171.

Jozkowski, K. N., & Humphreys, T. P. (2014). Sexual consent on college campuses: Implications for sexual assault prevention. *The Health Educator,* 31, 31–36.

Jozkowski, K. N., & Peterson, Z. D. (2013). College students and sexual consent: Unique insights. *Journal of Sex Research,* 50, 517–523.

Jozkowski, K. N., & Sanders, S. A. (2012). Health and sexual outcomes of women who have experienced forced or coercive sex. *Women and Health,* 52, 101–118.

Julian, K. (2018). Why are young people having so little sex? *The Atlantic.* Available: https://www.theatlantic.com/magazine/archive/2018/12/the-sex-recession/573949/ (Last visited 1/25/20).

Kaestle, C. E. (2019). Sexual orientation trajectories based on sexual attractions, partners, and identity: A longitudinal investigation from adolescence through young adulthood using a U.S. representative sample. *Journal of Sex Research,* 56(7), 811–826.

Kaestle, C. E., & Allen, K. R. (2011). The role of masturbation in healthy sexual development: Perceptions of young adults. *Archives of Sexual Behavior,* 40, 983–994.

Kaestle, C. E., & Waller, M. W. (2011). Bacterial STDs and perceived risk among minority young adults. *Perspectives on Sexual and Reproductive Health,* 43, 158–163.

Kaestle, C. E., Halpern, C. T., Miller, W. C., & Ford, C. A. (2005). Young age at first intercourse and sexually transmitted infections in adolescents and young adults. *American Journal of Epidemiology,* 161, 774–778.

Kafka, M. P. (2010). The DSM diagnostic criteria for fetishism. *Archives of Sexual Behavior,* 26, 357–362.

Kaiser Family Foundation. (2012). National survey of teens and young adults on HIV/AIDS. Available: https://kaiserfamilyfoundation.files.wordpress.com/2013/01/8386-f.pdf (Last visited 1/22/2018).

Kaiser Family Foundation. (2017). National survey of young adults in HIV/AIDS. Available: https://www.kff.org/hivaids/report/national-survey-of-young-adults-on-hiv-aids/ (Last visited: 1/9/2018).

Kaiser Family Foundation. (2018.11). Emergency contraception. Available: https://www.kff.org/womens-health-policy/fact-sheet/emergency-contraception/ (Last visited 7/29/20).

Kaiser Family Foundation. (2019.11a). Oral contraceptive pills. Available: https://www.kff.org/womens-health-policy/fact-sheet/oral-contraceptive-pills/ (Last visited 7/21/20).

Kaiser Family Foundation. (2019.11b). Contraceptive implants. Available: https://www.kff.org/womens-health-policy/fact-sheet/contraceptive-implants/ (Last visited 7/29/20).

Kaiser Family Foundation. (2020.11). DMPA contraceptive injection: Use and coverage. Available: https://www.kff.org/womens-health-policy/fact-sheet/dmpa-contraceptive-injection-use-and-coverage/ (Last visited 7/22/20).

Kaiser Health News. (2019). AMA abortion lawsuit puts doctors in the thick of debate. Available: https://khn.org/news/ama-abortion-lawsuit-puts-doctors-in-the-thick-of-debate/ (Last visited 8/2/20).

Kann, L., Kitchen, S., Shanklin, S. L., Flint, K. H., Kawkins, J., Harris, W., et al. (2014). Youth risk behavior surveillance—United States, 2013. *Morbidity and Mortality Weekly Report, Surveillance Summaries,* 63(Supplement 4), 1–168.

Kantor, L. M. (2020). Pleasure and sex education: The need for broadening both the content and measurement. *American Journal of Public Health,* 110(2), 145–148. Praeger.

Kaplan, A. (1979). Clarifying the concept of androgyny: Implications for therapy. *Psychology of Women,* 3, 223–230.

Kaplan, H. S. (1974). *The new sex therapy.* Brunner/Mazel.

Kaplan, H. S., & Horwith, M. (1983). *The evaluation of sexual disorders: Psychological and medical aspects.* Brunner/Mazel.

Kaplan, M. S., & Krueger, R. B. (2010). Diagnosis, assessment, and treatment of hypersexuality. *Journal of Sex Research,* 47, 181–198.

Katz-Wise, S. L., & Hyde, J. S. (2014). Sexuality and gender: The interplay. In *APA handbook of sexuality and psychology* (pp. 29–62). American Psychological Association.

Katz-Wise, S. L., Rosario, M., Calzo, J. P., Scherer, E. A., Sarda, V., & Austin, S. B. (2017). Endorsement and timing of sexual orientation developmental milestones among sexual minority young adults in the growing up today study. *Journal of Sex Research, 54*(2), 172–185.

Kaya, A. E., & Caliskan, E. (2018). Women self-reported G-spot existence and relation with sexual function and genital perception. *Turkish Journal of Obstetrics and Gynecology,* 14(3), 182–187. Available: https://www.ncbi.nlm.nih.gov/pmc/articles/PMC6127477/ (Last visited 1/29/20).

Kearl, H. (2014). *Unsafe and harassed in public places: A national street harassment report.* Stop Street Harassment.

Keesling, B. (2006). *Sexual healing: The complete guide to overcoming common sexual problems* (3rd ed.). Hunter House.

Kelly, C., & Jensen, E. (2017, November 30). Sexual harassment claims lead to firings. *USA Today,* p. 1.

Kelly, G. F. (2013). *Sexuality today.* McGraw-Hill.

Kelly, M. P., Strassberg, D. S., & Kircher, J. R. (1990). Attitudinal and experiential correlates of anorgasmia. *Archives of Sexual Behavior,* 19(2), 165–167.

Kennair, L. E. O., Grontvedt, T. V., Mehnetoglu, M., Perilloux, C., & Buss, D. M. (2015). Sex and mating strategy impact the 13 basic reasons for having sex. *Evolutionary Psychological Science,* X, 207–219.

Kennedy, H. (1988). *The life and works of Karl Heinrich Ulrichs: Pioneer of the modern gay movement.* Alyson.

Kettrey, H. H. (2016). What's gender got to do with it? Sexual double standards and power in heterosexual college hookups. *Journal of Sex Research,* 53, 754–765.

Keuls, E. (1985). *Reign of the phallus: Sexual politics in ancient Athens.* University of California Press.

Khalil, A., von Dadelszen, P., Draycott, T., Ugwumadu, A., O'Brien, P., & Magee, L. (2020). Change in the incidence of stillbirth and preterm delivery during the COVID-19 pandemic. *Journal of the American Medical Association,* 324(7), 705–706. Available: https://jamanetwork.com/journals/jama/fullarticle/2768389 (Last visited 9/20/20).

Khan, A., & Khanum, P. A. (2000). Influence of son preferences on contraceptive use in Bangladesh. *Asia-Pacific Population Journal,* 15(3), 43–56.

Khandwala, Y. S., Baker, V. L., Shaw, G. M., Stevenson, D. K., Faber, H. K., Lu, Y., & Eisenberg, M. L. (2018) Association of paternal age with perinatal outcomes between 2007 and 2016 in the United States: Population based cohort study. *BMJ,* 363. Available: https://www.bmj.com/content/363/bmj.k4372 (Last visited 8/20/20).

Khazan, O. (2017, May 22). How people decide whether to have children. *The Atlantic.* Available: https://www.theatlantic.com/health/archive/2017/05/how-people-decide-whether-to-have-children/527520/ (Last visited 10/2/17).

Kidd, S. A., & Kral, M. J. (2002). Suicide and prostitution among street youth: A qualitative analysis. *Adolescence,* 37, 411–431.

Kimport, K. (2018). More than a physical burden: Women's mental and emotional work in preventing pregnancy. *Journal of Sex Research,* 55(9), 1096–1105.

King, P. A. (1992). Twenty years after. The legacy of the Tuskegee syphilis study. The dangers of difference. *Hastings Center Report,* 22(6), 35–38.

Kingston, D. A., & Yates, P. M. (2008). Sexual sadism: Assessment and treatment. In D. R. Laws & W. T. O'Donohue (Eds.), *Sexual deviance: Theory, assessment, and treatment* (2nd ed.). Guilford Press.

Kingston, S., & Thomas, T. (2019). No model in practice: A 'Nordic model' to respond to prostitution. *Crime, Law and Social Change,* 71, 423–439.

Kinsey, A., Pomeroy, W., & Martin, C. (1948). *Sexual behavior in the human male.* Saunders.

Kinsey, A., Pomeroy, W., Martin, C., & Gebhard, P. (1953). *Sexual behavior in the human female.* Saunders.

Kinsler, J. J., Glik, D., Buffington, S. D. C., Malan, H., Nadjat-Halem, C., Wainwright, N., & Papp-Green, M. (2018). A content analysis of how sexual behavior and reproductive health are being portrayed on prime-time television shows being watched by teens and young adults. *Journal of Health Communication,* 34(6), 644–651.

Kirby, D. (2007). *Emerging answers, 2007. Research findings on programs to reduce teen pregnancy and sexually transmitted diseases.* The National Campaign to Prevent Teen and Unplanned Pregnancy.

Kirby, D. (2008). The impact of abstinence and comprehensive sex and STD/HIV education programs on adolescent sexual behavior. *Sexuality Research and Policy,* 5(3), 18–27.

Kirkcaldy, R. D., Harvey, A., Papp, J. R., Holmes, K. K., Soge, O., del Rio, C., Hall, G., Papp, J., Bolan, G., & Weinstock, H. (2016). *Neisseria gonorrhoeae* antimicrobial resistance among men who have sex with men and men who have sex exclusively with women: The Gonococcal Isolate Surveillance Project, 2005–2010. *Annuals of Internal Medicine,* 158, 321–328.

Kirschbaum, A. L., & Peterson, Z. D. (2018). Would you say you "had masturbated" if. . . ?: The influence of situational and individual factors in labeling a behavior as masturbation. *Journal of Sex Research,* 55, 263–272.

Kirshenbaum, S. (2011). *The science of kissing.* Grand Central.

Kirzinger, A., Lopes, L., Wu, B., & Brodie, M. (2019). KFF Health Tracing Poll – March 2019: Public Opinion on the Domestic HIV Epidemic, Affordable Care Act, and Medicare-for-all. *Kaiser Family Foundation.* Available: https://www.kff.org/health-reform/poll-finding/kff-health-tracking-poll-march-2019/ (Last visited 10/28/2020).

Kirzinger, A., Munana, C., Brodie, M., Frederiksen, B., Weigel, G., Ranji, U., & Salganicoff, A. (2020). Public knowledge and attitudes about sexually transmitted infections: KFF polling and policy insights. *Kaiser Family Foundation.* Available: https://www.kff.org/womens-health-policy/issue-brief/public-knowledge-and-attitudes-about-sexually-transmitted-infections/ (Last visited 9/1/20).

Klaassen, M. J. F., & Peter, J. (2014). Gender (in)equality in Internet pornography: A content analysis of popular pornographic Internet videos. *Journal of Sex Research,* 52(7), 721–735.

Klass, P. (2016, September 6). "Is it too small?" *New York Times,* p. D4.

Klass, P. (2020, February 24). When a teenager's irregular periods are cause for concern. *NY Times.* Available: https://www.nytimes.com/2020/02/24/well/family/teenagers-irregular-menstrual-periods-PCOS.html (Last visited 10/16/20).

Klass, P. (2020, January 13). When heavy periods disrupt a teenager's life. *NY Times.* Available: https://www.nytimes.com/2020/01/13/well/family/teenagers-heavy-periods-menstrual-cycle-menstruation.html (Last visited 1/30/20).

Klebanoff, M. A., et al. (2010). Personal hygienic behaviors and bacterial vaginosis. *Sexually Transmitted Diseases,* 37, 94–99.

Klein, M. (2012). *Sexual intelligence: What we really want to know from sex—and how to get it.* Harper One.

Klein, M. (2016). *His porn, her pain: Confronting America's pornpanic with honest talk about sex.* Praeger.

Klein, V., Imhoff, R., Reininger, M., & Briken, P. (2019). Perceptions of sexual script deviation in women and men. *Archives of Sexual Behavior,* 48, 631–644. Available: https://link.springer.com/article/10.1007/s10508-018-1280-x (Last visited 5/14/20).

Kleinplatz, P. J., & Menard, A. D. (2020). *Magnificent sex: Lessons from extraordinary lovers.* Routledge.

Kleinplatz, P., & Moser, C. (2004). Toward clinical guidelines for working with BDSM clients. *Contemporary Sexuality,* 38, 1, 4.

Kohlberg, L. (1966). A cognitive-developmental analysis of children's sex-role concepts and attitudes. In E. E. Maccoby (Ed.), *The development of sex differences.* Stanford University Press.

Kohut, T., Baer, J. L., & Watts, B. (2016). Is pornography really about "Making Hate to Women"? Pornography users hold more egalitarian attitudes than nonusers in a representative American sample. *Journal of Sex Research,* 53(1), 1–11.

Kohut, T., Balzarini, R. N., Fisher, W. A., Grubbs, J. B., Campbell, L., & Prause, N. (2020). Surveying pornography use: A Shaky science resting on poor measurement foundations. *Journal of Sex Research,* 57, 722–742.

Kohut, T., Fisher, W. A., & Campbell, L. (2017). Surveying pornography use: A shaky science resting on poor measurement foundations. *Journal of Sex Research,* 57(6), 722–741.

Koken, J. A., Bimbi, D. S., Parsons, J. T., & Halkitis, P. N. (2004). The experience of stigma in the lives of male Internet escorts. *Journal of Psychology and Human Sexuality,* 16, 13–32.

Komisaruk, B. R., Whipple, B., Nasserzadeh, S., & Beyer-Flores, C. (2010). *The orgasm answer guide.* Johns Hopkins University Press.

Kontula, O. (2009). *Between sexual desire and reality.: The evolution of sex in Finland.* Vaestoliitto.

Kontula, O., & Haavio-Mannila, E. (2009). The impact of aging on human sexual activity and sexual desire. *Journal of Sex Research,* 46(1), 46–56.

Kontula, O., & Miettinen, A. (2016). Determinants of female sexual orgasms. *Socioaffective Neuroscience & Psychology,* 6, 31624.

Kosciw, J. G., Clark, C. M., Truong, N. L., & Zongrone. (2020). The 2019 National School Climate Survey. *GLSEN.* Available: https://www.glsen.org/sites/default/files/2020 11/NSCS19 111820.pdf (Last visited: 12/11/2020).

Kouldrat, Y., Pizzol, D., Cosco, T., Thompson, T., Carnaghi, M., Bertoldo, A., et al. (2017). High prevalence of erectile dysfunction in diabetes: A systematic review and meta-analysis of 145 studies. *Diabetes Medicine,* 34(9), 1185–1192.

Krakow, M., Beavers, A., Cosides, O., & Rositch, A. F. (2017). Characteristics of adolescents lacking provide-recommended human papillomavirus vaccination. *Journal of Adolescent Health,* 60, 619–622.

Kraus, S. W., et al. (2018). Compulsive sexual behavior disorder in the ICD-11. *World Psychiatry,* 17, 109–110.

Kraut-Becher, J. R., & Aral, S. O. (2003). Gap length: An importance factor in sexually transmitted diseases transmission. *Sexually Transmitted Infections,* 30, 221–225.

Krebs, C. P., Lindquist, C. H., Warner, T. D., Fisher, B. S., & Martin, S. L. (2009). College women's experiences with physically forced, alcohol- or other drug-enabled, and drug-facilitated sexual assault before and since entering college. *Journal of American College Health,* 57, 639–647.

Kreisel, K., Torrone, E., Bernstein, K., Hong, J., & Gorwitz, R. (2017). Prevalence of pelvic inflammatory disease in sexually experienced women of reproductive age—United States, 2013–2014. *Mortality and Morbidity Report,* 66, 80–83.

Kreklau, A., Vaz, I., Oehme, F., Strub, F., Brechbuhl, R., Christmann, C., & Gunthert, A. (2018) Measurements of a 'normal vulva' in women aged 15–84; A cross-sectional prospective single-centre study. *BJOG; An International Journal of Obstetrics and Gynaecology,* 125(13), 1656–1661. Available: https://obgyn.onlinelibrary.wiley.com/doi/10.1111/1471-0528.15387 (Last visited 2/7/20).

Krueger, E. A., Meyer, I. H., & Upchurch, D. M. (2018). Sexual orientation group differences in perceived stress and depressive symptoms among young adults in the United States. *LGBT Health,* 5(4), 242–249. Available: https://www.ncbi.nlm.nih.gov/pmc/articles/PMC5994153/ (Last visited 5/1/20).

Krueger, R. B. (2010a). The DSM diagnostic criteria for exhibitionism, voyeurism, and frotteurism. *Archives of Sexual Behavior,* 39, 325–345.

Krueger, R. B. (2010b). The DSM diagnostic criteria for sexual masochism. *Archives of Sexual Behavior,* 39, 346–356.

Kuehnle, K., & Drozd, L. (2012). *Parenting plan evaluations: Applied research for the family court.* Oxford University Press.

Kuper, L., Nussbaum, R., & Mustanski, B. (2011). Exploring the diversity of gender and sexual orientation identities in an online sample of transgender individuals. *Journal of Sex Research,* 49(2–3), 244–254.

Kuperberg, A., & Padgett, J. E. (2015). Dating and hooking up in college: Meeting contexts, sex, and variation by gender, partner's gender, and class standing. *Journal of Sex Research,* 52, 517–531.

Kvalem, I. L., Traeen, B., Markovic, A., & von Soest, T. (2019). Body image development and sexual satisfaction: A prospective study from adolescence to adulthood. *Journal of Sex Research,* 56(6), 791–801.

La France, B. H., Henningsen, D. D., Oates, A., & Shaw, C. M. (2009). Social-sexual interactions: Meta-analysis of sex differences in perceptions of flirtatiousness, seductiveness, and promiscuousness. *Communication Monographs,* 76, 263–268.

Lacey, R. S., Reifman, A., Scott, J. P., Harris, S. M., & Fitzpatrick, J. H. (2004). Sexual-moral attitudes, love styles and mate selection. *Journal of Sex Research,* 41(2), 121–128.

Ladas, A., Whipple, B., & Perry, J. (1982). *The G spot.* Holt, Rinehart & Winston.

Laframboise, S., & Anhorn, M. (2008). The way of the two spirited people. Available: http://www.dancingtoeaglespiritsociety.org/twospirit.php (Last visited 7/19/14).

Landry, S., Goncalves, M. K., & Kukkonen, T. M. (2016). Assessing differences in physiological subject response toward male and female oriented sexually explicit videos. *Canadian Journal of Human Sexuality,* 25, 208–215.

Lane, M., Ives, G. C., Sluiter, E. C., Waljee, J. F., Yao, T. H., Hu, H. M., & Kuzon, W. M. (2018). Trends in gender affirming surgery in insured patients in the United States. *PRS Global Open,* 6(4), 1738. Available: https://www.ncbi.nlm.nih.gov/pmc/articles/PMC5977951/ (Last visited 2/27/20).

Langston, C., Whitcomb, B. W., Purdue-Smithe, A. C., Sievert, L. L., Hankinson, S. E., et al. (2020). Association of parity and breastfeeding with risk of early natural menopause. *JAMA Network Open,* 3(1). Available: https://jamanetwork.com/journals/jamanetworkopen/fullarticle/2759124 (Last visited 8/31/20).

Larsson, I., & Svedin, C. G. (2002). Sexual experiences in childhood: Young adults' recollections. *Archives of Sexual Behavior,* 133(3), 263–274.

Laumann, E. O., Paik, A., & Rosen, R. C. (1999). Sexual dysfunction in the United States: Prevalence and predictors. *Journal of the American Medical Association,* 281, 537–544.

Laumann, E., Gagnon, J., Michael, R., & Michaels, S. (1994). *The social organization of sexuality.* University of Chicago Press.

Law, B. M. (2011). Hormones and desire. *American Psychological Association,* 42(3), 4. Available: http://www.apa.org/monitor/2011/03/hormones.aspx (Last visited 1/25/15).

Laws, D. R., & O'Donohue, W. T. (2008). Introduction. In D. R. Laws & W. T. O'Donohue (Eds.), *Sexual deviance: Theory, assessment, and treatment* (2nd ed.). Guilford Press.

Leapfrog Group. (2018). New report on maternity care in the U.S. shows encouraging progress reducing episiotomies, but none reducing C-sections. Available: https://www.leapfroggroup.org/news-events/new-report-maternity-care-us-shows-encouraging-progress-reducing-episiotomies-none (Last visited 8/27/20).

Lee, J. A. (1973). *The color of love.* New Press.

Lee, J. A. (1988). Love styles. In R. Sternberg & M. Barnes (Eds.), *The psychology of love.* Yale University Press.

Lefevor, G. T., Beckstead, A. L., Schow, R. L., Raynes, M., Mansfield, T. R., & Rosik, C. H. (2019). Satisfaction and health within four sexual identity relationship options. *Journal of Sex & Marital Therapy,* 45(5), 355–369.

Lefkowitz, E. S., Vasilenko, S. A., Wesche, R., & Maggs, J. L. (2019). Changes in diverse sexual and contraceptive behaviors across college. *Journal of Sex Research,* 56(8), 965–976.

Lehmiller, J. (2018). *Tell me what you want: The science of sexual desire and how it can help your sex life.* Hachette Go.

Lehmiller, J. J. (2014). *The psychology of human sexuality.* John Wiley & Sons.

Lehmiller, J. J., Garcia, J. R., Gesselman, A. N., & Mark, K. P. (2020). Less sex, but more sexual diversity: Changes in sexual behavior during the COVID-19 coronavirus pandemic. *Leisure Sciences.* Available: https://www.tandfonline.com/doi/full/10.1080/01490400.2020.1774016?casa_token=ZrEunxElvdsAAAAA%3AW-HGU3N4ZU3bZtgElgP3VvF3XhwzWyXHoqBxLdB7dCbGDHfMFu5XfhwxGb1D44-ho2NThH6i-TWJyA (Last visited 10/21/20).

Leitenberg, H., & Henning, K. (1995). Sexual fantasy. *Psychological Bulletin,* 117(3), 469–496.

Lenz, R., & Chaves, B. (1981). Becoming active partners: A couple's perspective. In D. Bullard & S. Knight (Eds.), *Sexuality and disability: Personal perspectives.* Mosby.

Lerum, K., & Dworkin, S. L. (2015). The power of (but not in?) sexual configurations theory. *Archives of Sexual Behavior,* 45, 495–499.

Letherby, G. (2003). *Feminist research in theory and practice.* Open University Press.

Lever, J. (1995, August 22). Lesbian sex survey. *The Advocate,* pp. 23–30.

Levine, E. C., Herbenick, D., Martinez, O., Fu, T. C., & Dodge, B. (2018). Open relationships, nonconsensual nonmonogamy and monogamy among U.S. adults: Findings from the 2012 national survey of sexual health and behavior. *Archives of Sexual Behavior,* 7, 1439–1450.

Levine, M. P., & Troiden, R. (1988). The myth of sexual compulsivity. *Journal of Sex Research,* 25(3), 347–363.

Ley, D., Prause, N., & Finn, P. (2014). The emperor has no clothes: A review of the "Pornography Addiction" model. *Current Sexual Health Reports.* https://doi.org/10.1007/s11930-014-0016-8

Lichtenstein, B., Hook, E. W., III, & Sharma, A. K. (2005). Public tolerance, private pain: Stigma and sexually transmitted infections in the American Deep South. *Culture, Health & Sexuality,* 7, 43–57.

Lieberman, L. D., Goldfarb, E. S., Kwiatkowski, S., & Santos, P. (2017). Does first sex really "Just happen?" A retrospective exploratory study of sexual debut among American adolescents. *American Journal of Sexuality Education,* 12(3), 237–256.

Linden, D. J. (2011). *The compass of pleasure: How our brains make fatty foods, orgasm, exercise, marijuana, generosity, vodka, learning, and gambling feel so good.* Penguin.

Lindley, L. L., Walsemann, K. M., & Carter, J. W. (2013). Invisible and at risk: STDs among young adult sexual minority women in the United States. *Perspectives on Sexual and Reproductive Health,* 45, 66–73.

Liong, M., & Cheng, G. H.-L. (2019). Objectifying or liberating? Investigation of the effects of sexting on body image. *Journal of Sex Research,* 56(3), 337–344.

Lips, H. (2007). *Sex and gender* (6th ed.). McGraw-Hill.

Lips, H. (2014). *Gender: The basics.* Routledge.

Liptak, A. (2020, July 8). Supreme Court upholds Trump administration regulation letting employers opt out of birth control coverage. *NY Times.* Available: https://www.nytimes.com/2020/07/08/us/supreme-court-birth-control-obamacare.html (Last visited 9/21/20).

Littara, A., Melone, R., Morales-Medina, J. C., & Iannitti, T. (2019). Cosmetic penile enhancement surgery: A 3-year single centre retrospective clinical evaluation of 355 cases. *Scientific Reports,* 9, 6323. Available: https://www.ncbi.nlm.nih.gov/pmc/articles/PMC6474863/ (Last visited 2/17/20).

Little, A. C., Apicella, C. L., & Marlowe, F. W. (2007). Preferences for symmetry in human faces in two cultures: Data from the UK and Hadza, an isolated group of hunter-gathers. *Proceedings of the Royal Society,* 274, 3113–3117.

Livingston, J. A., Testa, M., Windle, M., & Bay-Chen, L. Y. (2015). Alcohol involvement in first sexual intercourse experiences of adolescent girls. *Journal of Adolescence,* 43, 148–158.

Lloyd, E. A. (2006). *The case of the female orgasm: Bias in the science of evolution.* Harvard University Press.

Lloyd, J., Crouch, N. S., Minto, C. L., Liao, L. M., & Creighton, S. M. (2005). Female genital appearance: "Normality" unfolds. *BJOG: An International Journal of Obstetrics & Gynaecology,* 112(5), 643–646.

Locke, B. D., & Mahalik, J. R. (2005). Examining masculinity norms, problem drinking, and athletic involvement as predictors of sexual aggression in college men. *Journal of Counseling Psychology,* 52, 279–283.

Loewenstein, G., Krishnamurti, T., Kopisic, J., & McDonald, D. (2015). Does increased sexual frequency enhance happiness? *Journal of Economic Behavior & Organization,* 16, 206–218.

Lohmann, R. C. (2018). Changing teen sex trends. *U.S. News & World Report.* Available: https://health.usnews.com/wellness/for-parents/articles/2018-07-23/changing-teen-sex-trends (Last visited 4/16/20).

Lorenz, T. K., Heiman, J. R., & Demas, G. E. (2018). Interactions among sexual activity, menstrual cycle phase, and immune function in healthy women. *Journal of Sex Research,* 55(9), 1087–1095.

Luetke, M., Hensel, D., Herbenick, D., & Rosenberg. M. (2020) Romantic relationship conflict due to the COVID-19 pandemic and changes in intimate and sexual behaviors in a Nationally Representative Sample of American Adults. *Journal of Sex & Marital Therapy.* https://doi.org/10.1080/0092623X.2020

Luscombe, B. (2018, October 26). Why are we all having so little sex? *Time.* Available: https://time.com/5297145/is-sex-dead/ (Last visited 4/17/20).

Luster, J., Turner, A. N., Henry, J. P., & Gallo, M F. (2019). Association between pubic hair grooming and prevalent sexually transmitted infection among female university students. *PLoS ONE,* 14(9). Available: https://www.ncbi.nlm.nih.gov/pubmed/31483828 (Last visited 1/28/20).

Lynn, B. K., Lopez, J. D., Miller, C., Thompson, R. N., & Campian, E. C. (2019). The relationship between marijuana use prior to sex and sexual function in women. *Sexual Medicine,* 7, 192–197. Available: https://www.sciencedirect.com/science/article/pii/S2050116119300091 (Last visited 9/18/20).

Macapagal, K., Coventry, R., Arbeit, M. R., Fisher, C. B., & Mustanski, B. (2017). "I won't out myself just to do a survey": Sexual and gender minority adolescents' perspectives on the risks and benefits of sex research. *Archives of Sexual Behavior,* 46, 1393–1409.

MacNeil, S., & Byers, E. S. (2009). Role of sexual self-disclosure in the sexual satisfaction of long-term heterosexual couples. *Journal of Sex Research,* 46(1), 3–14.

Madsen, L., Parsons, S., & Grubin, D. (2006). The relationship between the five-factor model and *DSM* personality disorder in a sample of child molesters. *Personality and Individual Differences,* 40, 227–236.

Mah, K., & Binik, Y. M. (2002). Do all orgasms feel alike? Evaluating a two-dimensional model of the orgasm experience across gender and sexual context. *Journal of Sex Research,* 39(2), 104–113.

Mahay, J., Laumann, E., & Michaels, S. (2001). Race, gender, and class in sexual scripts. In E. Laumann & R. Michael (Eds.), *Sex, love and health in America* (pp. 197–238). Oxford University Press.

Maier, T. (2009). *Masters of sex*. Basic Books.

Malacad, B., L., & Hess, G. C. (2011). Sexual behavior research using the survey method: A critique of the literature over the last 6 years. *European Journal of Contraception and Reproductive Health Care, 16,* 328–335.

Male and female orgasm—different? (2013). *Go Ask Alice*. Available: http://www.goaskalice.columbia.edu/answered-questions/male-and-female-orgasm-%E2%80%94-different-0 (Last visited 12/12/17).

Mallory, A. B., Stanton, A. M., & Handy, A. B. (2019). Couples' sexual communication and dimensions of sexual function: A meta-analysis. *Journal of Sex Research, 56*(7), 882–898.

Manhart, L. E., Aral, S. O., Holmes, K. K., & Foxman, B. (2002). Sex partner concurrency: Measurement, prevalence, and correlates among urban 18–39-year-olds. *Sexually Transmitted Diseases, 29,* 133–143.

Manlove, J., Ryan, S., & Franzetta, K. (2003). Patterns of contraceptive use within teenagers' first sexual relationship. *Perspectives on Sexual and Reproductive Health, 35,* 246–255.

Mann, L. M., Llata, E., Flagg, E. W., Hong, J., Asbel, L., Carlos-Henderson, J., Kerani, R. P., Kohn, R., Pathela, P., Schumacher, C., & Torrone, E. A. (2019). Trends in the prevalence of anogenital warts among patients at sexually transmitted disease clinics—Sexually Transmitted Disease Surveillance Network, United States, 2010–2016. *Journal of Infectious Disease, 219*(9), 1389–1397.

Marazziti, D., Baroni, S., Giannaccini, G., Betti, L., Massimetti, G., Carmassi, C., & Catena-Dell'Osso, M. (2012). A link between oxytocin and serotonin in humans: Supporting evidence from peripheral markers. *European Neuropsychopharmacology, 22*(8), 578–583.

Marcantonio, T. L., Jozkowski, K. N., & Lo, W. (2018). Beyond "just saying no": A preliminary evaluation of strategies college students use to refuse sexual activity. *Archives of Sexual Behavior, 47,* 341–351.

Marcell, A. V., Morgan, A. R., Sanders, R., et al. (2017). The socioecology of sexual and reproductive health care use among young urban minority males. *Journal of Adolescent Health, 60,* 402–410.

Marcell, A., Gibbs, S. E., Choiriyyah, I., Sonenstein, F. L., Astone, N. M., Pleck, J. H., & Dariotis, J. K. (2016). National needs of family planning among U.S. men aged 15 to 44 years. *American Journal of Public Health, 106*(4), 733–739.

March of Dimes. (2017). Prescription opioids during pregnancy. Available: https://www.marchofdimes.org/pregnancy/prescription-opioids-during-pregnancy.aspx (Last visited 10/3/17).

March of Dimes. (2020.12). Quick facts: Prenatal care. Available: https://www.marchofdimes.org/peristats/ViewTopic.aspx?reg=99&top=5&lev=0&slev=1 (Last visited 8/15/20).

Margolies, L., Becher, M., & Jackson-Brewer, K. (1988). Internalized homophobia: Identifying and treating the oppressor within. In Boston Lesbian Psychologies Collective (Eds.), *Lesbian psychologies*. University of Illinois Press.

Marinovich, M. L., Hunter, K. E., Macaskill, P., & Houssami, N. (2018). Breast cancer screening using tomosynthesis or mammography: A meta-analysis of cancer detection and recall. *Journal of the National Cancer Institute, 110*(9), 942–949. Available: https://academic.oup.com/jnci/article/110/9/942/5068658 (Last visited 9/25/20).

Mark, K. P., & Murray, S. H. (2011). Gender differences in desire discrepancy as a predictor of sexual and relationship satisfaction in a college sample of heterosexual relationships. *Journal of Sex & Marital Therapy, 38*(2), 198–215.

Marrazzo, J. M., Thomas, K. K., Agnew, K., & Ringwood, K. (2010). Prevalence and risks for bacterial vaginosis in women who have sex with women. *Sexually Transmitted Infections, 37,* 335–339.

Marshall, B. L. (2012). Medicalization and the refashioning of age-related limits on sexuality. *Journal of Sex Research, 49,* 337–343.

Marshall, D. (1971). Sexual behavior on Mangaia. In D. Marshall & R. Suggs (Eds.), *Human sexual behavior*. Basic Books.

Marshall, W. L. (1993). The role of attachments, intimacy, and loneliness in the etiology and maintenance of sexual offending. *Sexual and Marital Therapy, 8,* 109–121.

Marshall, W. L., Marshall, L. E., & Serran, G. A. (2006). Strategies in the treatment of paraphilias: A critical review. *Annual Review of Sex Research, 17,* 162–182.

Martin, J. A., Hamilton, B. E., Osterman, M. J. K., & Driscoll, A. K. (2019). Births: Final data for 2018. *National Vital Statistics Reports, 68*(13). Available: https://www.cdc.gov/nchs/data/nvsr/nvsr68/nvsr68_13-508.pdf (Last visited 5/12/20).

Martinez, L. (May 2, 2019). Sexual assaults in military rise to more than 20,000, Pentagon survey says. *ABC News*. Available: https://abcnews.go.com/Politics/military-sexual-assault-numbers-increase-young-female-service/story?id=62762858. (Last visited: 2/23/2021).

Martinez, M. (2016, October 19). What to know about Nevada's legal brothels. Available: http://www.cnn.com/2015/10/14/us/lamar-odom-nevada-brothels/index.html (Last visited 8/25/2017).

Martins, Y., Preti, G., Crabtree, C. R., Runyan, T., Vainius, A. A., & Wysocki, C. J. (2005). Preference for human body odors is influenced by gender and sexual orientation. *Psychological Science, 16,* 694–701.

Martis, G. P. (1999). Tourism and the sex trade in St. Maarten and Curacao, the Netherlands Antilles. In K. Kempadoo (Ed.). *Sun, sex and gold: Tourism and sex work in the Caribbean*. (pp. 210–215). Rowman & Littlefield Publishers.

Martos, A. J., Wilson, P. A., & Meyer, I. H. (2017). Lesbian, gay, bisexual, and transgender (LGBT) health services in the Unites States: Origins, evolution, and contemporary landscape. *PLOS One*. Available: http://journals.plos.org/plosone/article?id=10.1371/journal.pone.0180544 (Last visited 12/5/17).

Masaro, C. L., Dahinten, V. S., Johnson, J., Ogilvie, G., & Patrick, D. M. (2008). Perceptions of sexual partner safety. *Sexually Transmitted Infections, 35,* 566–571.

Mass, M. K., Vasilenko, S. A., & Willoughby, B. J. (2018). A dyadic approach to pornography use and relationship satisfaction among heterosexual couples: The role of pornography acceptance and anxious attachment. *Journal of Sex Research, 55,* 772–782.

Masters, N. T., Casey, E., Wells, E. A., & Morrison, D. M. (2013). Sexual scripts among young heterosexually active men and women: Continuity and change. *Journal of Sex Research, 50*(5), 409–420.

Masters, W. H., & Johnson, V. E. (1970). *Human sexual inadequacy*. Little, Brown.

Masters, W. H., & Johnson, V. E. (1974). *The pleasure bond*. Little, Brown.

Match. (2016). Match releases new study on LGBTQ single population. Available: http://www.prnewswire.com/news-releases/match-releases-new-study-on-lgbtq-single-population-300273510.html (Last visited 7/17/17).

Match. (2019.8). Singles in America: Match releases ninth annual study on U.S. single population. Available: https://match.mediaroom.com/2019-07-30-Singles-in-America-Match-Releases-Ninth-Annual-Study-on-U-S-Single-Population (Last visited 7/8/20).

Matek, O. (1988). Obscene phone callers. In D. Dailey (Ed.), *The sexually unusual*. Harrington Park Press.

Mathews, S. J., Giuliano, T. A., Rosa, M. N., Thomas, K. H., & Swift, B A, (2020). Sexual Novelty Scale. In R. R. Milhausen, J. K. Sakaluk, T. D. Fisher, C. M. Fisher, & W. L. Yarber (Eds.), *Handbook of sexuality-related measures* (4th ed., pp. 510–513). Routledge.

Mathews, S. J., Giuliano, T. A., Rosa, M. N., Thomas, K. H., Swift, B. A., Ahern, N. D., Garcia, A. G., Smith, S. R., Niblett, C. M., & Mills, M. M. (2018). The battle against bedroom boredom: Development and validation of a brief measure of sexual novelty in relationships. *Canadian Journal of Human Sexuality, 26*, 277–287.

Mautz, B. S., Wong, B. B. M., Peters, R. A., & Jennions, N. (2013). Penis size interacts with body shape and height to influence male attractiveness. *Proceedings of the National Academy of Sciences,* 110, 6925–6930.

Mayo Clinic. (2017). Vaginitis. Available: https://www.mayoclinic.org/diseases-conditions/vaginitis/diagnosis-treatment/drc-20354713 (Last visited: 11/20/2020).

Mayo Clinic. (2017.15a). Cervicitis. Available: https://www.mayoclinic.org/diseases-conditions/cervicitis/symptoms-causes/syc-20370814 (Last visited: 12/18/2017).

Mayo Clinic (2018). Penis-enlargement products: Do they work? Available: https://www.mayoclinic.org/healthy-lifestyle/sexual-health/in-depth/penis/art-20045363 (Last visited 2/11/20).

Mayo Clinic. (2019.14). Mayo Clinic's approach to Peyronie's disease: Nonsurgical interventions. Available: https://www.mayoclinic.org/medical-professionals/urology/news/mayo-clinics-approach-to-peyronies-disease-nonsurgical-interventions/mac-20480520 (Last visited 1/12/20).

Mayo Clinic. (2019.12). Miscarriage. Available: https://www.mayoclinic.org/diseases-conditions/pregnancy-loss-miscarriage/symptoms-causes/syc-20354298 (Last visited 8/21/20).

Mayo Clinic. (2020). Peyronie's disease. Available: https://www.mayoclinic.org/diseases-conditions/peyronies-disease/diagnosis-treatment/drc-20353473 (Last visited: 6/29/2020).

Mayo Clinic. (2020.5). Ambiguous genitalia. Available: https://www.mayoclinic.org/diseases-conditions/ambiguous-genitalia/symptoms-causes/syc-20369273 (Last visited 5/18/20).

Mayo Clinic. (2020.15). Cervicitis. Available: https://www.mayoclinic.org/diseases-conditions/cervicitis/multimedia/cervicitis/img-20008354 (Last visited 10/22/2020).

Mayo Clinic. (2020.11a). Diaphragm. Available: https://www.mayoclinic.org/tests-procedures/diaphragm/about/pac-20393781 (Last visited 7/27/20).

Mayo Clinic. (2020.12a). Prenatal cell-free DNA screening. Available: https://www.mayoclinic.org/tests-procedures/noninvasive-prenatal-testing/about/pac-20384574 (Last visited 8/20/20).

Mayo Clinic. (2020.12b). Cesarean. Available: https://www.mayoclinic.org/tests-procedures/c-section/about/pac-20393655 (Last visited 8/31/20).

Mayo Clinic. (2020.13a). Pap smear. Available: https://www.mayoclinic.org/tests-procedures/pap-smear/about/pac-20394841 (Last visited 9/25/20).

Mayo Clinic. (2020.13b). Toxic shock syndrome. Available: https://www.mayoclinic.org/diseases-conditions/toxic-shock-syndrome/symptoms-causes/syc-20355384 (Last visited 10/16/20).

Mayo Clinic. (2020.13c). Vulvodynia. Available: https://www.mayoclinic.org/diseases-conditions/vulvodynia/diagnosis-treatment/drc-20353427 (Last visited 10/16/20).

Mayo Clinic. (2020.13d). Polycystic ovary syndrome (PCOS). Available: https://www.mayoclinic.org/diseases-conditions/pcos/symptoms-causes/syc-20353439 (Last visited 10/16/20).

Mayo Clinic. (2020.13e). Prostatitis. Available: https://www.mayoclinic.org/diseases-conditions/prostatitis/symptoms-causes/syc-20355766 (Last visited 10/16/20).

McAuliffe, T. L., DiFranceisco, W., & Reed, B. R. (2007). Effects of question format and collection mode on the accuracy of retrospective surveys of health risk behavior: A comparison with daily sexual activity diaries. *Health Psychology, 26*, 60–67.

McCabe, M. P., & Goldhammer, D. L. (2012). Demographic and psychological factors related to sexual desire among heterosexual women in a relationship. *Journal of Sex Research, 49*, 78–87.

McCabe, M. P., & Wauchope, M. (2005a). Behavioral characteristics of men accused of rape: Evidence for different types of rapists. *Archives of Sexual Behavior, 34*, 241–253.

McCabe, M. P., Sharlip, I. D., Lewis, R., Artalla, E., Balon, R., Fisher, A. D., et al. (2016). Incidence and prevalence of sexual dysfunction in women and men: A consensus statement from the Fourth International Consultation on Sexual Medicine 2015. *Journal of Sexual Medicine, 13*, 144–152.

McCallum, E. B., & Peterson, Z. D. (2012). Investigating the impact of inquiry mode on self-reported sexual behavior: Theoretical considerations and review of the literature. *Journal of Sex Research, 49*, 212–226.

McCarthy, B. W., & McCarthy, E. (2003). *Rekindling desire: A step-by-step program to help low-sex and no-sex marriages.* Brunner/Routledge.

McCarthy, B. W., & McCarthy, E. (2009). *Discovering your couple sexual style.* Routledge.

McConaghy, N. (1998). Pedophilia: A review of the evidence. *Australian and New Zealand Journal of Psychiatry, 32*, 252–265.

McCormick, N. (1996). Our feminist future: Women affirming sexuality research in the late twentieth century. *Journal of Sex Research, 33*(2), 99–102.

McCormick, N. B. (1979). Come-ons and put-offs: Unmarried students' strategies for having and avoiding sexual intercourse. *Psychology of Women Quarterly, 4*, 194–211.

McGrath-Lone, L., Marsh, K., Hughes, G., & Ward H. (2015). The sexual health of female sex workers compared with other women in England: Analysis of cross-sectional data from genitourinary medical clinics. *Sexually Transmitted Infections, 90*, 344–350.

McIntyre-Smith, A. (2010). *Understanding female orgasm: An information-motivation-behavioral skills analysis.* [Unpublished doctoral dissertation]. Western University, London, Ontario, Canada.

McIntyre-Smith, A., & Fisher, W. A. (2020). Clitoral self-stimulation scale. In R. R. Milhausen, J. K. Sakaluk, T. D. Fisher, C. M. Davis, & W. L. Yarber (Eds.), *Handbook of sexuality-related measures* (4th ed., pp. 510–513). Routledge.

McKeganey, N. (2006). Street prostitution in Scotland: The views of working women. *Drugs, Education, Prevention and Policy, 13*, 151–166.

McPhillips, K., Braun, V., & Gavey, N. (2001). Defining (hetero)sex: How imperative is the "coital imperative'? *Women's Studies International Forum, 24*, 229–240.

McWhirter, D. (1990). Prologue. In D. McWhirter, S. A. Sanders, & J. M. Reinisch (Eds.), *Homosexuality/heterosexuality: Concepts of sexual orientation* (p. 48). Oxford University Press.

Mead, M. (1975). *Male and female.* Morrow.

MedlinePlus. (2018). Estrogen and progestin (hormone replacement therapy). *U.S. National Library of Medicine.* Available: https://medlineplus.gov/druginfo/meds/a601041.html (Last visited 5/21/20).

MedlinePlus. (2020.13a). Cervical dysplasia. Available: https://medlineplus.gov/ency/article/001491.htm (Last visited 9/25/20).

MedlinePlus. (2020.13b). Endometriosis. Available: https://medlineplus.gov/endometriosis.html (Last visited 10/16/20).

MedlinePlus. (2020.5a). Turner Syndrome. Available: https://medlineplus.gov/genetics/condition/turner-syndrome/#frequency (Last visited 12/17/20).

MedlinePlus. (2020.5b). Androgen insensitivity syndrome. Available: https://medlineplus.gov/ency/article/001180.htm (Last visited 12/17/20).

MedlinePlus. (2020.5c). Congenital adrenal hyperplasia. Available: https://medlineplus.gov/genetics/condition/congenital-adrenal-hyperplasia-due-to-11-beta-hydroxylase-deficiency/ (Last visited 12/17/20).

MedlinePlus. (2020.5d). 5-alpha reductase deficiency. Available: https://medlineplus.gov/genetics/condition/5-alpha-reductase-deficiency/ (Last visited 12/17/20).

Medscape. (2019.13). Supplements for sex: What to know. Available: https://www.medscape.com/viewarticle/911644 (Last visited 9/24/20).

Meiu, G. P. (2015). 'Beach-Boys Elders' and 'Young Big-Men'" Subverting the temporalities of ageing in Kenya's Ethno-Erotic economics. *Ethnos,* 80, 472–469.

Men Can Stop Rape. (2011a). Bystander intervention. Available from: http://www.mencanstoprape.org/theories-that-shape-our-work (Last visited: 10/11/2017).

Men Can Stop Rape. (2011b). Who we are. Available from: https://www.mencanstoprape.org/images/stories/PDF/Handout_pdfs/men-can-stop-rape-factsheet-final.pdf (Last visited 3/15/2018).

Men, women lie about sex to match gender expectations. (2013, May 28). Ohio State University Research and Innovation Communications. Available: http://researchernews.osu.edu/archive/genderstar.htm

Mercer, C. H., Fenton, K. A., Copes, A. J., Wellings, K., Erens, B., McManus, S., et al. (2004). Increasing prevalence of male homosexual partnerships and practices in Britain, 1990–2000: Evidence from national probability surveys. *AIDS,* 18, 1453–1458.

Meston, C. M., & Buss, D. (2007). Why humans have sex. *Archives of Sexual Behavior,* 22, 477–507.

Meston, C. M., & Buss, D. M. (2009). *Why women have sex.* Henry Holt.

Meston, C. M., & O'Sullivan, L. F. (2007). Such a tease: Intentional sexual provocation within heterosexual interactions. *Archives of Sexual Behavior,* 36, 531–542.

Metz, M. E., & McCarthy, B. W. (2011). *Enduring desire: Your guide to lifelong intimacy.* Routledge.

Meyer, I. H., & Wilson, P. A. (2009). Sampling lesbian, gay and bisexual populations. *Journal of Counseling Psychology,* 56, 1, 23–31.

Meyer-Bahlburg, H. F. L. (2009). Variants of gender differentiation in somatic disorders of sex development: Recommendations for Version 7 of the World Professional Association for Transgender Health's *Standards of Care. International Journal of Transgenderism,* 11(4), 2226–2237.

Michael, R. T., Gagnon, J. H., Laumann, E. O., & Kolata, G. (1994). *Sex in America: A definitive study.* Little Brown.

Mikkola, M. (2019). *Pornography: A philosophical introduction.* Oxford University Press.

Mikulincer, M., & Shaver, P. R. (2008). Adult attachment and affect regulation. In J. Cassidy & P. R. Shaver (Eds.), *Handbook of attachment: Theory, research, and clinical applications* (pp. 503–531). The Guilford Press.

Miletski, H. (2000). Bestiality/zoophilia: An exploratory study. *Scandinavian Journal of Sexology,* 3, 149–150.

Miletski, H. (2002). *Understanding bestiality and zoophilia.* Ima Tek Inc.

Milhausen, R. R. (2004). *Factors that inhibit and enhance sexual arousal in college men and women.* [Unpublished doctoral dissertation]. Indiana University.

Milhausen, R. R., Crosby, R. A., & Yarber, W. L. (2008). Public opinion in Indiana regarding the vaccination of middle school students for HPV. *The Health Education Monograph,* 25(2), 21–27.

Milhausen, R. R., Graham, C. A., Sanders, S. A., Yarber, W. L., & Maitland, S. B. (2020). Validation of the sexual excitation/sexual inhibition inventory for women and men. *Archives of Sexual Behavior,* 39, 1091–1104.

Milhausen, R. R., Wood, J., Sanders, S. A., Crosby, R. A., Yarber, W. L., & Graham, C. A. (2011). A novel self-guided, home-based intervention to improve condom use among young college men who have sex with men: A pilot study. *Journal of Men's Health,* 8, 274–281.

Milhausen, R. R., Yarber, W., Sanders, S., & Graham, C. (2004, November). *Factors that inhibit and enhance sexual arousal in college men and women.* Paper presented at the annual meeting of the Society for the Scientific Study of Sexuality, Orlando, FL.

Milhausen, R., Sanders, S. A., Yarber, W. L., Graham, C. A., Vanterpool, K., & Kennedy, J. M. (2020, November 12). *Marriage in the time of COVID: A national study of martial quality, sexual behavior and reproductive health during the COVID-19 pandemic* (virtual paper presentation). Society for the Scientific Study of Sexuality Annual Conference.

Miller, L. (2000, October 17). Panel agrees: Rethink new porn laws. *USA Today,* p. D3.

Miner, M. H., Coleman, E., Center, B., Ross, M., & Simon Rosser, B. (2007). The compulsive sexual behavior inventory: Psychometric properties. *Archives of Sexual Behavior,* 36, 579–587.

Minichiello, V., Marino, R., & Browne, J. (2000). Commercial sex between men: A prospective diary-based study. *Journal of Sex Research,* 37(2), 151–160.

Minichiello, V., Scott, J., & Callander, D. (2013). New pleasures and old dangers: Reinventing male sex work. *Journal of Sex Research,* 50(3–4), 263–275.

Mitchell, K. R., Mercer, C. H., Plaubidis, G. B., Jones, K. G., Datta, J., Field, N., et al. (2013). Sexual function in Britain: Findings from the third National Survey of Sexual Attitudes and Lifestyles (Natsal-3). *The Lancet,* 382, 1817–1829.

Mitchell, K. R., Wellings, K. A., & Graham, C. (2012). How do men and women define sexual desire and sexual arousal? *Journal of Sex & Marital Therapy,* 40(1), 17–32.

Mitchell, R., King, M., Nazareth, I., & Wellings, K. (2001). Managing sexual difficulties: A qualitative investigation of coping strategies. *Journal of Sex Research,* 48, 325–333.

Moalem, S. (2009). *How sex works.* HarperCollins.

Moller, N. P., & Vossler, A. (2015). Defining infidelity in research and couple counseling: A qualitative study. *Sex & Marital Therapy,* 41(5), 487–497.

Molnar, A. (2013). Sexually explicit material affects behavior in young people less than thought. *Science News.* Available: http://www.eurekalert.org/pub_releases/2013-04/w-sem041813.php (Last visited 4/25/13).

Montagu, A. (1986). *Touching* (3rd ed.). Columbia University Press.

Montero, D. (May 6, 2018). Must read: Nevada's monopoly on vice may e easing with push to eliminate nearly half the state's brothels. *Los Angeles Times.* Available: https://www.latimes.com/nation/la-na-nevada-brothels-illegal-20180506-story.html (Last visited: 2/12/2021).

Montgomery-Graham, S., Kohut, T., Fisher, W., & Campbell, L. (2015). How the popular media rushes to judgement about pornography and relationships while research lags behind. *Canadian Journal of Human Sexuality,* 24, 243–256.

Monto, M. A. (2001). Prostitution and fellatio. *Journal of Sex Research,* 38, 140–145.

Moors, A. C. (2016). Has the American public's interest in information related to relationships beyond "the couple" increased over time? *Journal of Sex Research,* 54(6), 677–684.

Morgan, E. M. (2011). Associations between young adult's use of sexually explicit materials and their sexual preferences, behaviors, and satisfaction. *Journal of Sex Research,* 48, 520–530.

Morris, B. J., Krieger, J. N., & Klausner, J. D. (2017). CDC's male circumcision recommendations represent a key public health measure. *Global Health: Science and Practice,* 5(1), 15–27. Available: https://www.ghsp-journal.org/content/5/1/15 (Last visited 12/14/20).

Moser, C. (2015). Defining sexual orientation. *Archives of Sexual Behavior,* 45, 505–508.

Moser, C., & Kleinplatz, P. J. (2006). *DSM-IV-TR* and the paraphilias: An argument for removal. *Journal of Psychology & Human Sexuality,* 17, 93–109.

Moses, E., & Kelly, S. (2016). African American adolescent sexuality: Influences on sexual scripting and sexual risk behaviors. *Current Sexual Health Reports,* 8, 64–76.

Movement Advancement Project. (2017a). Non-discrimination laws. Available: http://www.lgbtmap.org/equality-maps/non_discrimination_laws (Last visited: 10/9/2017).

Movement Advancement Project. (2017b). Foster and adoption laws. Available: http://www.lgbtmap.org/equality-maps/foster_and_adoption_laws/ (Last visited 10/9/2017).

Movement Advancement Project. (2020a). Mapping LGBTQ equality: 2010 to 2020. Available: https://www.lgbtmap.org/2020-tally-report (Last visited: 12/22/2020).

Movement Advancement Project. (2020b). Equality maps snapshot: LGBTQ equality by state. Author. Available: https://www.lgbtmap.org/equality-maps/legal_equality_by_state. (Last visited: 12/21/2020).

Moynihan, R., & Mintzes, B. (2010). *Sex, lies & pharmaceuticals*. Greystone Books.

Muehlenhard, C. L. (2011). Examining stereotypes about token resistance to sex. *Psychology of Women Quarterly, 35*, 676–683.

Muehlenhard, C. L., & Peterson, Z. D. (2005). Wanting and not wanting sex: The missing discourse of ambivalence. *Feminism & Psychology, 15*, 15–20.

Muehlenhard, C. L., & Shippee, S. K. (2009). Men's and women's reports of pretending orgasm, *Journal of Sex Research, 46*, 1–16.

Muehlenhard, C. L., Humphreys, T. P., Jozkowski, K. N., & Peterson, Z. (2016). The complexities of sexual consent among college students: A conceptual and empirical review. *Journal of Sex Research, 53*, 457–487.

Muehlenhard, C. L., Peterson, Z. D., Humphreys, & Jozkowski, K. N. (2017). Evaluating the one-in-five statistic: Women's risk of sexual assault while in college. *Journal of Sex Research, 54*(4–5), 549–576.

Muehlenhard, C. L., Ponch, I. G., Phelps, J. L., & Giusti, L. M. (1992). Definitions of rape: Scientific and political implications. *Journal of Social Issues, 48*(1), 23–44.

Muglu, J., Rather, H., Arroyo-Manzano, D., Bhattacharya, S., Balchin, I., Khalil, A., Thilaganathan, B., Khan, K. S., Zamora, J., & Thangaratinam, S. (2019). Risks of stillbirth and neonatal death with advancing gestation at term: A systematic review and meta-analysis of cohort studies of 15 million pregnancies. *Plos Medicine.* Available: https://journals.plos.org/plosmedicine/article?id=10.1371/journal.pmed.1002838 (Last 8/21/20).

Muise, A., Giang, E., & Impett, E. A. (2014). Post sex affectionate exchanges promote sexual and relationship satisfaction. *Archives of Sexual Behavior, 43*, 1391–1402.

Muise, A., Maxwell, J. A., & Impett, E. A. (2018). What theories and methods from relationship research can contribute to sex research. *Journal of Sex Research, 55*(4–5), 540–562.

Muise, A., Schimmack, U., & Impett, E. A. (2015). Sexual frequency predicts greater well-being, but more is not always better. *Social Psychological and Personality Science, 7*, 295–302.

Munzy, C. A., Kapi, R., Austin, E. L., Brown, L., Hook, III, E. W., & Geisler, W. M. (2015). *Chlamydia trachomatis* infection in African American women who exclusively have sex with women. *International Journal of STD & AIDS, 27*, 978–983.

Murib, Z. (2020, February 25). A kind of anti-trans legislation is hitting the red states. *The Washington Post.* Available: https://www.washingtonpost.com/politics/2020/02/25/new-kind-anti-trans-legislation-is-hitting-red-states/ (Last visited 5/18/20).

Murphy, K. (2017, January 7). Yes, it's your parents' fault. *New York Times,* p. R2.

Murray, J. B. (2000). Psychological profile of pedophiles and child molesters. *Journal of Psychology: Interdisciplinary and Applied, 134*, 211–224.

Murray, S. H. (2019). *Not always in the mood: The new science of men, sex, and relationships.* Rowman & Littlefield.

Murray, S. H., Milhausen, R. R., Graham, C. A., & Kuczynski, L. (2017). A qualitative exploration of factors that affect sexual desire among men aged 30–65 in long-term relationships. *Journal of Sex Research, 54*(3), 319–330.

Murray, S. H., Milhausen, R. R., Graham, C. A., & Kuczynski, L. (2016). A qualitative exploration of factors that affect sexual desire among men aged 30–65 in long-term relationships. *Journal of Sex Research, 54*(3), 319–330.

Mushovic, I. (2011, September 1). Progress obscures gay inequality. *USA Today,* p. 7A.

Muskin, P. R., Clayton, A. H., Fisher, H. E., & Volpp, S. Y. (2017). Sex, sexuality, and serotonin. *Medscape.* Available: http://www.medscape.org/viewarticle/482059 (Last visited 8/11/17).

Nagel, J. (2003). *Race, ethnicity, and sexuality: Intimate intersection frontiers.* Oxford University Press.

Nagoski, E. (2015). *Come as you are.* New York: Simon & Schuster.

Nakano, M. (1990). *Japanese American women: Three generations, 1890–1990.* Mina Press.

Nanda, S. (1990). *Neither man nor woman: The Hijras of India.* Wadsworth.

Nassan, F. L., Jensen, T. K., Priskorn, L., Halldorsson, T. I., Chavarro, J. E., & Jorgensen, N. (2020). Association of dietary patterns with testicular function in young Danish men. *JAMA Open Network, 3*(2). Available: https://jamanetwork.com/journals/jamanetworkopen/fullarticle/2761546?utm_source=For_The_Media&utm_medium=referral&utm_campaign=ftm_links&utm_term=022120 (Last visited 8/25/20).

National Assessment of Educational Progress {NAEP}. (2017). NAEP mathematics report card. Available: https://www.nationsreportcard.gov/math_2017?grade=4 (Last visited 2/21/20).

National Association of Anorexia Nervosa and Associated Disorders {ANAD}. (n.d.) Eating disorder statistics. Available: https://anad.org/education-and-awareness/about-eating-disorders/eating-disorders-statistics/ (Last visited 9/16/20).

National Center for Education Statistics. (2016). Digest of education statistics. Available: https://nces.ed.gov/programs/digest/d16/tables/dt16_209.10.asp (Last visited 2/21/20).

National Center for Health Statistics. (2019). National Health Interview Survey. Available: https://www.cdc.gov/nchs/nhis/special_topics.htm. (Last visited: 12/11/2020).

National Center for Injury Prevention and Control. (2016a). Sexual violence on campus: Strategies for Prevention. Available from: https://www.cdc.gov/violenceprevention/pdf/campussvprevention.pdf (Last visited: 10/9/2017).

National Center for Injury Prevention and Control. (2016b). STOP SV: A technical package to prevent sexual violence. Available from: https://www.cdc.gov/violenceprevention/pdf/sv-prevention-technical-package.pdf (Last visited: 10/9/2017).

National Center for Missing & Exploited Children. (2011). What is sex tourism involving children? Available: http://www.missingkids.com/missingkids/servlet/PageServlet? LanguageCountry1en_US (Last visited 10/14/11).

National Center for Transgender Equality. (2016a). The report of the U.S. transgender survey. Available: http://www.transequality.org/sites/default/files/docs/usts/Executive%20Summary%20-%20FINAL%201.6.17.pdf (Last visited 6/1/17).

National Center for Transgender Equality. (2017, May 22). Breakthrough: Americans with Disabilities act can't exclude gender dysphoria. Available: http://www.transequality.org/blog/breakthrough-americans-with-disabilities-act-can-t-exclude-gender-dysphoria (Last visited 5/31/17).

National Coalition for Sexual Health. (2020, July 15). COVID-19 and sexual health. Available: https://nationalcoalitionforsexualhealth.org/sexual-health/NCSH_COVID19-and-Sexual-Health-Fact-Sheet.pdf (Last visited 2/15/21).

National Family Planning & Reproductive Health Association. (2020). Title X. Available: https://www.nationalfamilyplanning.org/title_x (Last visited 7/20/20).

National Health Service, Department of Health and Social Care. (2019). Sexual health for lesbian and bisexual women. Available: https://www.nhs.uk/live-well/sexual-health/sexual-health-for-lesbian-and-bisexual-women/ (Last visited 9/4/20).

National Health Service. (2018). Can you catch HIV from kissing? Available: https://www.nhs.uk/common-health-questions/sexual-health/can-you-catch-hiv-from-kissing/ (Last visited: 10/12/2020).

National Health Service. (2018). Female condoms. Available: https://www.nhs.uk/conditions/contraception/female-condoms (Last visited 9/15/20).

National Human Trafficking Resource Center. (2015). Sex trafficking. Available: https://humantraffickinghotline.org/type-trafficking/sex-trafficking (Last visited 2/3/15).

National Institute for Occupational Safety and Health [NIOSH]. (2020). Reproductive health and the workplace: Pesticides. Available: https://www.cdc.gov/niosh/topics/repro/pesticides.html (Last visited 8/17/20).

National Institute of Mental Health. (2016). Eating disorders. Available: https://www.nimh.nih.gov/health/topics/eating-disorders/index.shtml (Last visited 1/2/18).

National Institute on Aging. (2017.7a). What is menopause? Available: https://www.nia.nih.gov/health/what-menopause (Last visited 7/24/17).

National Institute on Alcohol Abuse and Alcoholism [NIAAA]. (2020). College drinking. Available: https://www.niaaa.nih.gov/sites/default/files/Collegefactsheet.pdf (Last viewed 9/18/20).

National Institute on Drug Abuse [NIDA]. (2019). Drug and alcohol use in college-age adults in 2018. Available: https://www.drugabuse.gov/drug-topics/trends-statistics/infographics/drug-alcohol-use-in-college-age-adults-in-2018 (Last viewed 9/18/20).

National Institute on Drug Abuse. (2020). Cocaine trends & statistics. Available: https://www.drugabuse.gov/drug-topics/cocaine/cocaine-trends-statistics (Last visited 9/18/20).

National Institutes of Health (NIH). (2016). NIH study links morning sickness to lower risk of pregnancy loss. Available: https://www.nih.gov/news-events/news-releases/nih-study-links-morning-sickness-lower-risk-pregnancy-loss (Last visited 10/3/17).

National Institutes of Health. (2020.5). Klinefelter syndrome. Available: https://rarediseases.info.nih.gov/diseases/8705/klinefelter-syndrome/ (Last visited 12/17/20).

"National sexuality education standards: Core content and skills, K–12." (2012). Journal of School Health. Available: http://www.futureofsexed.org/documents/josh-fose-standards-web.pdf (Last visited 8/19/14).

National Women's Health. (2019). Top ten things to know about today's sex drive drugs. Available: nwhn.org/addyitop10things/ (Last visited 9/27/20).

New York Health Department. (2020). Safer sex and COVID-19. Available: https://www1.nyc.gov/assets/doh/downloads/pdf/imm/covid-sex-guidance.pdf (Last visited 10/22/20).

New York University. (2020, March 30). Movement toward gender equality has slowed in some areas, stalled in others. Available: https://www.nyu.edu/about/news-publications/news/2020/march/movement-toward-gender-equality-has-slowed-in-some-areas–stalle.html (Last visited 5/14/20).

Newkirk II, V. R. (2016). A generation of bad blood. The Atlantic. Available: https://www.theatlantic.com/politics/archive/2016/06/tuskegee-study-medical-distrust-research/487439/ (Last visited: 12/28/2017).

Newport, F. (2018). In U.S., estimate of LGBT population rises to 4.5%. Gallup. Available: https://news.gallup.com/poll/234863/estimate-lgbt-population-rises.aspx (Last visited 4/27/20).

Niccolai, L. M., Farley, T. A., Ayoub, M. A., Magnus, M. K., & Kissinger, P. J. (2002). HIV-infected persons' knowledge of their sexual partners' HIV status. AIDS Education and Prevention, 14, 183–189.

Nicolini, Y., Tramacere, A., Parmigiani, S., & Dadomo, H. (2019). Back to stir it up: Erectile dysfunction in an evolutionary, developmental, and clinical perspective. Journal of Sex Research, 56, 378–390.

Nielson, C. M., et al. (2010). Consistent condom use is associated with lower prevalence of human papillomavirus infection in men. Journal of Infectious Diseases, 202, 445–451.

Noar, S. M., Morokoff, P. J., & Harlow, L. L. (2002). Condom negotiation in heterosexually active men and women: Development and validation of a condom influence strategy questionnaire. Psychology and Health, 17, 711–735.

Nonfoux, L., Chiaruzzi, M., Badiou, C., Baude, J., Tristan, A., Thioulouse, J., Muller, D., Prigent-Combaret, C., & Lina, G. (2018) Impact of currently marketed tampons and menstrual cups on Staphylococcus aureus growth and toxic shock syndrome toxin 1 production In Vitro. Applied and Environmental Microbiology. Available: https://aem.asm.org/content/84/12/e00351-18.full (Last visited 1/31/20).

Noorishad, P., Levaque, E., & Byers, S. (2019). More than one flavor: University students' specific sexual fantasies, interests, and experiences. Canadian Journal of Human Sexuality, 28, 143–158.

Nordic Model Now. (n.d.). What is the Nordic Model? Available from: https://nordicmodelnow.org/what-is-the-nordic-model (Last visited 9/13/2017).

North American Menopause Society. (2017.9). Androgens, antidepressants, and other drugs on which the jury's still out. Available: http://www.menopause.org/for-women/sexual-health-menopause-online/effective-treatments-for-sexual-problems/androgens-antidepressants-and-other-drugs-on-which-the-jury-s-still-out (Last visited 5/4/17).

North American Menopause Society. (2017a). Menopause FAQs: Understanding the symptoms. Available: http://www.menopause.org/for-women/expert-answers-to-frequently-asked-questions-about-menopause/menopause-faqs-understanding-the-symptoms (Last visited 7/25/17).

North American Menopause Society. (2020). Sexual health & menopause. Available: http://www.menopause.org/for-women/sexual-health-menopause-online/how-to-navigate-this-online-resource (Last visited 5/18/20).

North, A. (August 2, 2019). The movement to decriminalize sex work, explained. Available: https://www.vox.com/2019/8/2/20692327/sex-work-decriminalization-prostitution-new-york-dc. (Last visited: 2/16/2021).

Northrup, C., Schwartz, P., & Witte, J. (2013). The normal bar. Harmony.

Northrup, T. (2013). Examining the relationship between media use and aggression, sexuality, and body image. Journal of Applied Research on Children: Informing Policy for Children at Risk, 4(1), Article 3.

Nowosielski, K., Wrobel, B., & Kowalczyk, R. (2016). Women's endorsement of models of sexual response: Correlates and predictors. Archives of Sexual Behavior, 45(2), 291–302.

Nusbaum, M. R. (2002). Erectile dysfunction: Prevalence, etiology, and major risk factors. Journal of the American Osteopathic Association, 102(Suppl. 4), S1–S56.

Nuwer, R. (2016). The enduring enigma of female sexual desire. BBC News. Available: http://www.bbc.com/future/story/20160630-the-enduring-enigma-of-female-desire (Last visited 5/3/17).

Oakley, A. (1985). Sex, gender, and society (Rev. ed.). Harper & Row.

Office of the Assistant Secretary for Planning and Evaluation. (2014). Statutory rape: A guide to state laws and reporting requirements. Available: https://aspe.hhs.gov/report/statutory-rape-guide-state-laws-and-reporting-requirements (Last visited: 3/5/2018).

Office on Women's Health. (2018). Sexual assault on college campuses. U.S. Department of Health & Human Services. Available: https://www.womenshealth.gov/relationships-and-safety/sexual-assault-and-rape/college-sexual-assault (Last visited 2/21/20).

Office on Women's Health. (2019). Infertility. U.S. Department of Health and Human Services: Womenshealth.gov. Available: https://www.womenshealth.gov/a-z-topics/infertility (Last visited 6/1/21).

Office of Women's Health. (2019). Date rape drugs. Available: https://www.womenshealth.gov/a-z-topics/date-rape-drugs. (Last visited: 1/2/2021).

Olmstead, S. B., Negash, S., Pasley, K., & Fincham, F. D. (2013). Emerging adults' expectations for pornography use in the context of future committed relationships: A qualitative study. *Archives of Sexual Behavior, 42,* 625–635.

Olson-Kennedy, J. (2016). Mental health disparities among transgender youth: Rethinking the role of professionals. *JAMA Pediatrics, 170*(5), 423–424.

Opperman, E., Braun, V., Clark, V., & Rogers, C. (2014). "It feels so good it almost hurts"; Young adults' experiences of orgasm and sexual pleasure. *Journal of Sex Research, 51*(5), 503–515.

Oram, S., Abias, M., Bick, D., Boyle, A., French, R., et al. (2016). Human trafficking and health: A survey of male and female survivors in England. *Journal of the American Public Health Association, 106,* 1073–1078.

Oransky, I. (2020, July 29). Journal of retract homeopathy-COVID-19 paper, blames 'overflow of manuscripts'. Available: https://www.medscape.com/viewarticle/934808 (Last visited 8/13/2020).

Ordway, D. (2017, March 21). How to tell good research from flawed research: 13 questions journalists should ask. Available: https://journalistsresource.org/studies/society/news-media/good-research-bad-quality-journalism-tips/?utm_source=JR-email&utm_medium=email&utm_campaign=JR-email (Last visited: 8/13/2020).

Ordway, D. (2019, July 29). 53% of journalists surveyed weren't sure they could spot flawed research. Available: https://journalistsresource.org/studies/society/news-media/research-quality-news-annual-survey/ (Last visited 8/13/20).

Orenstein, P. (2016). *Girls & sex: Navigating the complicated new landscape.* HarperCollins.

Orenstein, P. (2019, February 24). It's not that men do not know what consent is. *New York Times.* Available: https://www.nytimes.com/2019/02/23/opinion/sunday/sexual-consent-college.html (Last visited: 1/5/2021).

Orenstein, P. (2020). *Boys & sex: Young men on hookups, love, porn, consent, and navigating the new masculinity.* HarperCollins.

Ortmann, D., & Sprott, R. N. (2013). *Sexual outsiders: Understanding BDSM sexualities and communities.* Rowman & Littlefield.

Osterberg, E. C., Gaither, T. W., Ward, M. A., et al. (2016, December 5). Correlation between pubic hair grooming and STIs: Results from a nationally representative probability sample. Sexually transmitted infections, 13. Available: http://escholarship.org/uc/item/0bq3f436?query=pubic%20hair%20removal%20and%20men#page-1 (Last visited 4/25/17).

Owen, J. J., Rhoades, G. K., Stanley, S. M., & Fincham, F. D. (2010). "Hooking up" among college students: Demographic and psychosocial correlates. *Archives of Sexual Behavior, 39,* 653–663.

Owen, J., & Fincham, F. D. (2011). Young adults' emotional reactions after hooking-up encounters. *Archives of Sexual Behavior, 40,* 321–330.

Owusu-Edusei, K., Chesson, H. W., Gift, T. L., Tao, G., Mahajan, R., et al. (2013). The estimated direct medical cost of selected sexually transmitted infections in the United States, 2008. *Sexually Transmitted Diseases, 40,* 197–201.

O'Callaghan, E., Shepp, V., Ellman, S. E., & Kirkner, A. (2019). Navigating sex and sexuality after sexual assault: A qualitative study of survivors and informal support provides. *Journal of Sex Research, 56,* 1045–1057.

O'Sullivan, L. F., & Vannier, S. A. (2016). Women's sexual desire and desire disorders from a developmental perspective. *Current Sexual Health Reports, 8,* 47–56.

Padden, K. (2014, June 17). "Why do we still have pubic and armpit hair?" (*Today I Found Out.*) Available: http://www.todayifoundout.com/index.php/2014/06/still-pubic-armpit-hair/ (Last visited 4/25/17).

Paik, A. (2010). "Hookups," dating, and relationship quality: Does the type of sexual involvement matter? *Social Science Research, 39,* 739–753.

Palmer, M. J., Clarke, L., Ploubidis, G. B., Mercer, C. H., Gibson, L. J., Johnson, A. M., Copas, A. J., & Wellings, K. (2017). "Is 'sexual competence' at first intercourse associated with subsequent sexual health status?" *Journal of Sex Research, 54*(1), 91–104.

Papp, L. M., Cummings, E. M., & Goeke-Morey, M. C. (2009). For richer, for poorer: Money as a topic of marital conflict in the home. *Family Relations, 58,* 91–103.

Parade. (2020, February 2). 351 of the most popular baby name ideas for 2020 – Plus four baby naming trends to follow. Available: https://parade.com/969021/marynliles/popular-baby-names/ (Last visited 2/21/20).

Parenthood. (2020.11c). Birth control shot. Available: https://www.plannedparenthood.org/learn/birth-control/birth-control-shot (Last visited 7/22/20).

Pariera, K. L., & McCormack, T. A. (2017). "Why can't we just have sex?": An analysis of anonymous questions about sex asked by ninth graders. *American Journal of Sexuality Education, 12*(3), 277–296. Available: https://www.tandfonline.com/doi/full/10.1080/15546128.2017.1359801 (Last visited 6/11/20).

Parker, J., & Burkley, M. (2009). Who's chasing whom? The impact of gender and relationship status on mate poaching. *Journal of Experimental Social Psychology, 45,* 1016–1019.

Parker, R. & Gagnon, J. (Eds.). (1995). *Conceiving sexuality: Approaches to sex research in a post-modern world.* Routledge.

Parker, R. J. (2020). *Killing the rainbow.* RJ Parker Publishing.

Parker-Pope, T. (2019, July 1). Should we all take the slow road to love? *NY Times.* Available: https://www.nytimes.com/2019/07/02/well/family/millennials-love-relationships-marriage-dating.html (Last visited 12/19/20).

Parry, N. (2016). As teen girls seek breast and genital surgery, experts emphasize education. *Medscape.* Available: https://www.medscape.com/viewarticle/864578 (Last visited 12/11/17).

Parsons, C. (2003, July 29). Sexual consent measure is signed. *Chicago Tribune,* pp. 1, 7.

Pascoal, P. M., Cardoso, D., & Henriques, R. (2015) Sexual satisfaction and distress in sexual functioning in a sample of the BDSM community: A comparison study between BDSM and non-BDSM contexts. *Journal of Sexual Medicine, 12,* 1052–1061.

Paul, B., & Shim, J. W. (2008). Gender, sexual affect, and motivations for Internet pornography use. *International Journal of Sexual Health, 20,* 187–199.

Paul, P. (2006). *Pornified: How pornography is transforming our lives, our relationships, and our families.* Times Books.

Peck, B., Manning, J., Tri, A., Skrzypczynski, D., Summers, M., & Grubb, K. (2016). What do people mean when they say they "had sex"? In J. Manning & C. M. Noland (Eds.), *Contemporary studies in sexuality and communication* (pp. 3012). Kendal Hunt.

Pediatric Academic Societies. (2018, May 5). Survey finds many adolescents are not talking to their doctors and parents about sex. *Medical Xpress.* Available: https://medicalxpress.com/news/2018-05-survey-adolescents-doctors-parents-sex.html (Last visited 4/20/20).

Peixoto, M. M., & Nobre, P. (2015). Prevalence of sexual problems and associated distress among gay and heterosexual men. *Sexual and Relationship Therapy, 30,* 221–225.

Peloquin, K., Brassard, A., Lafontaine, M. F., & Shaver, P. R. (2014). Sexuality examined through the lens of attachment theory: Attachment, caregiving, and sexual satisfaction. *Journal of Sex Research, 51*(5), 561–576.

Perel, E. (2006). *Mating in captivity.* Harper.

Perper, R. (2020, May 27). The 29 countries around the world where same-sex marriage is legal. *Business Insider.* Available: https://www.businessinsider.com/where-is-same-sex-marriage-legal-world-2017-11. (Last visited: 2/16/2021).

Perrin, P. B., Heesacker, M., Tiegs, T. J., Swan, A. W., et al. (2011). Aligning Mars and Venus: The social construction and instability of gender differences in romantic relationships. *Sex Roles*, 64(9–10), 613–628.

Perry, J. D., & Whipple, B. (1981). Pelvic muscle strength of female ejaculators: Evidence in support of a new theory of orgasm. *Journal of Sex Research*, 17(1), 22–39.

Pertot, S. (2007). *When your sex drives don't match*. Marlowe & Company.

Peter, J., & Valkenburg, P. M. (2006). Adolescents' exposure to sexually explicit online material and recreational attitudes toward sex. *Journal of Communication*, 56, 639–660.

Peterson, Z. D., & Muehlenhard, C. L. (2007). Conceptualizing the "wantedness" of women's consensual and nonconsensual sexual experiences: Implications for how women label their experiences with rape. *Journal of Sex Research*, 44, 72–88.

Pew Research Center. (2017). The share of Americans living without a partner has increased, especially among young adults. Available: https://www.pewresearch.org/fact-tank/2017/10/11/the-share-of-americans-living-without-a-partner-has-increased-especially-among-young-adults/ (Last visited 4/27/20).

Pew Research Center. (2017.7d). 5 facts on love and marriage in America. Available: http://www.pewresearch.org/fact-tank/2017/02/13/5-facts-about-love-and-marriage/ (Last visited 7/21/17).

Pew Research Center. (2018). How teens and parents navigate screen time and device distractions. Available: https://www.pewresearch.org/internet/2018/08/22/how-teens-and-parents-navigate-screen-time-and-device-distractions/ (Last visited 1/17/20).

Pew Research Center. (2019). Why is the teen birth rate falling? Available: https://www.pewresearch.org/fact-tank/2019/08/02/why-is-the-teen-birth-rate-falling/ (Last visited 4/18/20).

Pew Research Center. (2019.7a). Key findings on marriage and cohabitation in the U.S. Available: https://www.pewresearch.org/fact-tank/2019/11/06/key-findings-on-marriage-and-cohabitation-in-the-u-s/ (Last visited 4/30/20).

Pew Research Center. (2019.7b). Marriage and cohabitation in the U.S. Available: https://www.pewsocialtrends.org/2019/11/06/marriage-and-cohabitation-in-the-u-s/ (Last visited 5/11/20).

Pew Research Center. (2019.8). Key findings on marriage and cohabitation in the U.S. Available: https://www.pewresearch.org/fact-tank/2019/11/06/key-findings-on-marriage-and-cohabitation-in-the-u-s/ (Last visited 4/30/20).

Pew Research Center. (2019.12). Among 41 countries, only U.S. lacks paid parental leave. Available: https://www.pewresearch.org/fact-tank/2019/12/16/u-s-lacks-mandated-paid-parental-leave/ (Last visited 10/7/20).

Pew Research Center. (2020.8). Dating and relationships in the digital age. Available: https://www.pewresearch.org/internet/2020/05/08/dating-and-relationships-in-the-digital-age/ (Last visited 6/8/20).

Pew Research Center's Social and Demographic Trends. (2013). A survey of LGBT Americans: Attitudes, experiences and values in changing times. Available: http://www.pewsocialtrends.org/2013/06/12/a-survey-of-lgbt-americans (Last visited 9/11/14).

Peyser, E. (2020). Nevada sex workers are getting stiffed by COVID. *New York Magazine*. Available: https://nymag.com/intelligencer/2020/12/nevada-sex-workers-are-getting-stiffed-by-covid.html (Last visited: 1/12/2021).

Picchi, A. (2020, August 31). Paternity leave is ignored by corporate America – and that's a problem for women. *USA Today*. Available: https://www.usatoday.com/story/money/2020/08/31/lack-paternity-leave-problem-moms-and-dads-study-finds/5662562002/ (Last visited 9/1/20).

Pinkerton, S. D., Bogart, L. M., Cecil, H., & Abramson, P. R. (2002). Factors associated with masturbation in a collegiate sample. *Journal of Psychology and Human Sexuality*, 14, 103–121.

Pinkerton, S. D., Holtgrave, D. R., & Galletly, C. L. (2008). Infections prevented by increasing HIV serostatus awareness in the United States, 2001 to 2004. *Journal of Acquired Immune Deficiency Syndromes*, 47, 354–357.

Pittaro, M. (2019). What is sextortion and why should we be concerned? *Psychology Today*. Available: https://www.psychologytoday.com/us/blog/the-crime-and-justice-doctor/201901/what-is-sextortion-and-why-should-we-be-concerned (Last visited 1/24/20).

Pitts, R. A., & Greene, R. (2020). Promoting positive sexual health. *American Journal of Public Health*, 110(2), 149–150.

Planned Parenthood. (2017). Testicular cancer. Available: https://www.plannedparenthood.org/learn/cancer/testicular-cancer (Last visited 7/3/17).

Planned Parenthood. (2020.11a). One year after being forced out of Title X, Planned Parenthood continues to fight for patients. Available: https://www.plannedparenthood.org/about-us/newsroom/press-releases/one-year-after-being-forced-out-of-title-x-planned-parenthood-continues-to-fight-for-patients (Last visited 12/19/20).

Planned Parenthood. (2020.11b). Birth control pill. Available: https://www.plannedparenthood.org/learn/birth-control/birth-control-pill (Last visited 7/21/20).

Planned Parenthood. (2020.11d). Birth control patch. Available: https://www.plannedparenthood.org/learn/birth-control/birth-control-patch (Last visited 7/22/20).

Planned Parenthood. (2020.11e). Birth control ring. Available: https://www.plannedparenthood.org/learn/birth-control/birth-control-vaginal-ring-nuvaring (Last visited 7/23/20).

Planned Parenthood. (2020.11f). Birth control implant. Available: https://www.plannedparenthood.org/learn/birth-control/birth-control-implant-nexplanon (Last visited 7/23/20).

Planned Parenthood. (2020.11g). Condom. Available: https://www.plannedparenthood.org/learn/birth-control/condom (Last visited 7/23/20).

Planned Parenthood. (2020.11h). Internal condom. Available: https://www.plannedparenthood.org/learn/birth-control/internal-condomp.304 (Last visited 7/23/20).

Planned Parenthood. (2020.11i). Diaphragm. Available: https://www.plannedparenthood.org/learn/birth-control/diaphragm (Last visited 7/27/20).

Planned Parenthood. (2020.11j). Birth control sponge. Available: https://www.plannedparenthood.org/learn/birth-control/birth-control-sponge (Last visited 7/27/20).

Planned Parenthood. (2020.11k). Cervical cap. Available: https://www.plannedparenthood.org/learn/birth-control/cervical-cap (Last visited 7/27/20).

Planned Parenthood. (2020.11l). Spermicide. Available: https://www.plannedparenthood.org/learn/birth-control/spermicide (Last visited 7/27/20).

Planned Parenthood. (2020.11m). IUD. Available: https://www.plannedparenthood.org/learn/birth-control/iud (Last visited 12/28/20).

Planned Parenthood. (2020.11n). Fertility awareness. Available: https://www.plannedparenthood.org/learn/birth-control/fertility-awareness (Last visited 7/28/20).

Planned Parenthood. (2020.11o). Breastfeeding. https://www.plannedparenthood.org/learn/birth-control/breastfeeding (Last visited 7/28/20).

Planned Parenthood. (2020.11p). Sterilization. Available: https://www.plannedparenthood.org/learn/birth-control/sterilization (Last visited 7/28/20).

Planned Parenthood. (2020.11q). Vasectomy. Available: https://www.plannedparenthood.org/learn/birth-control/vasectomyp. 311 Add link & lettering (Last visited 7/29/20).

Planned Parenthood. (2020.11r). Emergency contraception. Available: https://www.plannedparenthood.org/learn/morning-after-pill-emergency-contraception (Last visited 7/29/20).

Planned Parenthood. (2020.11s). The abortion pill. Available: https://www .plannedparenthood.org/learn/abortion/the-abortion-pill (Last visited 7/30/20).

Planned Parenthood. (2020.11t). In-clinic abortion. Available: https://www .plannedparenthood.org/learn/abortion/in-clinic-abortion-procedures (Last visited 7/30/20).

Planned Parenthood. (2020.11u). Can you explain what pro-choice means and pro-life means? Available: https://www.plannedparenthood.org/ learn/teens/ask-experts/can-you-explain-what-pro-choice-means-and-pro-life-means-im-supposed-to-do-it-for-a-class-thanks (Last visited 9/21/20).

Platt, L., Grenfell, P., Meiksin, R., Elmes, J., Sherman, S. G., Sanders, T., Mwang, P., & Crago, A. (2018). Associations between sex work laws and sex workers' health: A systematic review and meta-analysis of quantitative and qualitative studies. *PLOS Medicine,* 15(12), e1002680.

Plaus, J. G., Quintana, G. R., Mac Cionnaith, C., & Parada, M. (2016). The whole versus the sum of some of the parts: Toward resolving the apparent controversy of clitoral versus vaginal orgasms. *Journal of Anxiety Disorders,* 23, 1011.

Pogrebin, L. C. (1983). *Family politics.* McGraw-Hill.

Polaris Project. (2020). 2019 Data Report. Available: https://polarisproject. org/wp-content/uploads/2019/09/Polaris-2019-US-National-Human-Trafficking-Hotline-Data-Report.pdf (Last visited: 2/11/2021).

Postpartum Depression.org. (2020). Postpartum depression statistics. Available: https://www.postpartumdepression.org/resources/statistics/ (Last visited 8/31/20).

Potts, M., & Short, R. V. (1999). *Ever since Adam and Eve: The evolution of human sexuality.* Cambridge, MA: Cambridge University Press.

Powell, E. (1996). *Sex on your own terms.* Minneapolis: CompCare.

Power to Decide (formerly The National Campaign to Prevent Teen and Unplanned Pregnancy). (2016). Survey Says: Parent Power. Washington, DC.

Prause, N., & Pfaus, J. (2015). Viewing sexual stimuli associated with greater sexual responsiveness, no erectile dysfunction. *Sexual Medicine,* 3, 90–98.

Prause, N., Park, J., Leung, S., & Miller, G. (2014). Women's preferences for penis size: A new research method using selection among 3D models. *Plos One,* 10(9). Available: https://www.ncbi.nlm.nih.gov/pmc/articles/ PMC4558040/ (Last visited 12/12/17).

Preidt, R. (2013). Is *'sex addiction' for real? Study says maybe not.* Retrieved August 5, 2013, from *Web*MD. Available: http://www.webmd.com/sex/ news/20130723/is-sex-addiction-for-real-says-maybe-not (Last visited 8/5/13).

Preiss, D. (2016, December 20). 15-year old girl found dead in a menstrual hut in Nepal. *NPR.* Available: http://www.npr.org/sections/goatsandsoda/ 2016/12/20/506306964/15-year-old-girl-found-dead-in-a-menstrual-hut-in-nepal (Last visited 5/2/17).

"Premenstrual syndrome." (2017). Office on Women's Health, Department of Health & Human Services. Available: https://www.womenshealth.gov- /a-z-topics/premenstrual-syndrome (Last visited 5/1/17).

Price, M., Kafka, M., Commons, M. L., Gutheil, T. G., & Simpson, W. (2002). Telephone scatologia—comorbidity with other paraphilias and paraphilia-related disorders. *International Journal of Law and Psychiatry,* 25, 37–49.

ProCon.org. (2018). Countries and their prostitution policies. Available: https://prostitution.procon.org/countries-and-their-prostitution-policies/ (Last visited: 2/16/2021).

"Prostitution Statistics". (2021). Available: https://havocscope.com/ prostitution-statistics/ (Last visited: 2/11/2021).

Qaseem, A., Horwitch, C. A., Vijan, S., Etxeandia-Ikobaltzeta, I., & Kansagara, D. (2020). Testosterone treatment in adult men with age-related low testosterone: A clinical guideline from the American College of Physicians. *Annals of Internal Medicine,* 172, 126–133. Available: https://www.acpjournals.org/doi/10.7326/M19-0882 (Last visited 5/21/20).

Queen, C. (2000, November 19). Sex in the city. *San Francisco Chronicle,* pp. 1, 4.

Quinnipiac Poll. (2017). 47% of U.S. women say they've been sexually assaulted, Quinnipiac national poll finds. Available: https://poll.qu.edu/ national/release-detail?Releaseid=2505 (Last visited: 12/15/2017).

Quist, M. C., Watkins, C. D., Smith, F. G., Little, A. C., DeBruine, L. M., & Jones, B. C. (2012). Sociosexuality predicts women's preferences for symmetry in men's faces. *Archives of Sexual Behavior,* 41, 1415–1421.

Rabin, R. C. (2019, July 16). A better way to manage your period? Try the menstrual cup, scientists say. *NY Times.* Available: https://www.nytimes. com/2019/07/16/health/menstrual-cup-periods-women.html (Last visited 1/30/20).

Radcliffe, J., Doty, N., Hawkins, L. A., Gaskins, C. S., Beidas, R., & Rudy, B. J. (2010). *AIDS Patient Care and STDs,* 24, 493–499.

Raffaelli, M., & Ontai, L. L. (2004). Gender socialization in Latino/a families: Results from two retrospective studies. *Sex Roles,* 50, 287–299.

Ragsdale, K., Bersamin, M. M., Schwartz, S. J., Zamboanga, B. L., & Grube, J. W. (2014). Development of sexual expectancies among adolescents: Contributions by parents, Peers and the media. *Journal of Sex Research,* 51(5), 551–560.

Rahmanian, E., Salari, N., Mohammadi, M., & Jalali, R. (2019). Evaluation of sexual dysfunction and female sexual dysfunction indicators in women with type 2 diabetes: A systematic review and meta-analysis. *Diabetology & Metabolic Syndrome,* 11(73). Available: https://dmsjournal.biome dcentral.com/articles/10.1186/s13098-019-0469-z (Last visited 9/24/20).

Randall, H. E., & Byers, E. S. (2003). What is sex? Students' definitions of having sex, sexual partner, and unfaithful sexual behavior. *Canadian Journal of Human Sexuality,* 12, 87–96.

Rape Network. (2000). Rape is a crime of silence. Available: http://www .rapenetwork.com/whatisrape.html (Last visited 11/16/00).

Rape, Abuse & Incest National Network. (2009b). Ways to reduce your risk of sexual assault. Available: http://rainn.org/get-information/sexual-assault-prevention (Last visited 9/18/14).

Rape, Abuse and Incest National Network. (2016a). How to respond if someone is pressuring you. Available: https://www.rainn.org/articles/ how-respond-if-someone-pressuring-you (Last visited: 1/18/2007).

Rape, Abuse and Incest National Network. (2016b). Your role in preventing sexual assault. Available: https://www.rainn.org/articles/your-role-preventing-sexual-assault (Last visited: 10/8/2017).

Rape, Abuse and Incest National Network. (2016d). Self-care after trauma. Available: https://www.rainn.org/articles/self-care-after-trauma (Last visited: 11/4/2017).

Rape, Abuse and Incest National Network. (2017). About sexual assault. Available: https://www.rainn.org/about-sexual-assault (Last visited: 12/12/2017).

Rape, Abuse & Incest National Network. (2021a). Street harassment. Available: rain.org/articles/street-harassment (Last visited: 1/2/2021).

Rape, Abuse, and Incest National Network. (2021b). Drug-facilitated Sexual Assault. (2020e). https://www.rainn.org/articles/drug-facilitated-sexu-al-assault (Last visited: 1/2/2021).

Rape, Abuse, and Incest National Network. (2021c). Your role in preventing sexual assault. Available: https://www.rainn.org/articles/your-role-preventing-sexual-assault (Last visited: 12/30/2020).

Rape, Abuse, and Incest National Network. (2021d). Steps to take to prevent sexual assault. Available: https://rainn.org/articles/steps-you-can-take-prevent-sexual-assault?_ga=2.30582076.266980624.1609361132-1808492836.1607546899 (Last visited: 12/30/2021).

Rape, Abuse, and Incest National Network. (2021e). How to respond if someone is pressuring you. Available: https://www.rainn.org/articles/how-respond-if-someone-pressuring-you (Last visited: 1/3/2021).

Rape, Abuse, and Incest National Network. (2021f). Staying safe on campus. Available: https://www.rainn.org/articles/staying-safe-campus (Last visited: 1/3/2021).

Rape, Abuse, and Incest National Network. (2021g). What does consent look like. Available; https://www.rainn.org/articles/what-is-consent (Last visited: 1/5/2021).

Rape, Abuse, and Incest National Network. (2021h). Self-care after trauma. Available from: https://www.rainn.org/sites/default/files/SelfCareOneP-ageRAINN.pdf (Last visited: 1/7/2021).

Rape, Abuse, and Incest National Network. (2021i). Warning signs for young children. Available: https://www.rainn.org/articles/warning-signs-young-children. (Last visited: 1/6/2021).

Rape, Abuse, and Incest National Network. (2021j). If you suspect a child is being harmed. Available: https://rainn.org/articles/if-you-suspect-child-being-harmed?_ga=2.34752225.1505248947.1610033412-1808492836.1607546899. (Last visited: 1/6/2021).

Rape, Abuse, and Incest National Network. (2021k). How can I protect my child from sexual assault? Available: https://www.rainn.org/articles/how-can-i-protect-my-child-sexual-assault (Last visited: 1/6/2021).

Rape, Abuse, and Incest National Network. (2021l). Talking to my child about sexual assault. Available: https://rainn.org/articles/talking-your-kids-about-sexual-assault?_ga=2.92014298.1505248947.1610033412-1808492836.1607546899 (Last visited: 1/6/2–21).

Rashidian, A. (2010). Understanding the sexual-selves of Iranian-American women: A qualitative study (unpublished doctoral dissertation). University of New England, Armidale, New South Wales, Australia.

Rathus, S. A., Nevid, J. S., Fichner-Rathus, L., McKay, A., & Milhausen, R. (2020). *Human sexuality in a world of diversity, 6th Canadian edition.* Pearson Canadian Incorporated.

Reardon, S. F., Fahle, E., Kalogrides, D., Podolsky, A., & Zarate, R. C. (2018). *Gender achievement gaps in U.S. school districts.* Stanford Center for Education Policy Analysis. Available; https://cepa.stanford.edu/content/gender-achievement-gaps-us-school-districts (Last visited 2/21/20).

Reczek, C. (2020). Sexual and gender minority families: A 2010 to 2020 decade in review. *Journal of Marriage and Family,* 82(1), 300–325. Available: https://onlinelibrary.wiley.com/doi/full/10.1111/jomf.12607 (Last visited 5/1/20).

Reece, M., Herbenick, D., Schick, V., Sanders, S. A., Dodge, B., & Fortenberry, J. D. (2010.2a). Condom use rates in a national probability sample of males and females ages 14 to 94 in the United States. *Journal of Sexual Medicine,* 7, 266–276.

Reece, M., Herbenick, D., Schick, V., Sanders, S. A., Dodge, B., & Fortenberry, J. D. (2010.2b). Sexual behaviors, relationships, and perceived health status among adult men in the United States: Results from a national probability sample. *Journal of Sexual Medicine,* 7, 291–204.

Reece, M., Herbenick, D., Schick, V., Sanders, S. A., Dodge, B., & Fortenberry, J. D. (2010.9a). Findings from the National Survey of Sexual Health and Behavior (NSSHB). *Journal of Sexual Medicine,* 7(Suppl. 5), 243–373.

Reece, R. (1988). Special issues in the etiologies and treatments of sexual problems among gay men. *Journal of Homosexuality,* 15, 43–57.

Rees, G., & Garcia, J. R. (2017). All I need is shoe: An investigation into the obligatory aspect of sexual object fetishism. *International Journal of Sexual Health,* 29(4), 303–312.

Rees, S., Silove, D., Chey, T., Steel, Z., Creamer, M., Teesson, M., et al. (2011). Lifetime prevalence of gender-based violence in women and the relationship with mental disorders and psychological function. *Journal of the American Medical Association,* 306, 513–521.

Regan, P. C., Levin, L., Sprecher, S., Christopher, F. S., & Cate, R. (2000). Partner preferences: What characteristics in their short-term sexual and long-term romantic partners? *Journal of Psychology & Human Sexuality,* 12, 1–21.

Regan, P. C., Shen, W., De La Pena, E., & Gosset, E. (2007). "Fireworks exploded in my mouth": Affective responses before, during, and after the very first kiss. *International Journal of Sexual Health,* 19(2), 1–16.

Regnerus, M., Price, J., & Gordon, D. (2017). Masturbation and partnered sex: Substitutes or complements. *Archives of Sexual Behavior,* 46, 2111–2121.

Rehor, J. E. (2015). Sensual, erotic, and sexual behaviors of women from the "kink" community. *Archives of Sexual Behavior,* 44, 825–836.

Reiber, C., & Garcia, J. R. (2010). Hooking up: Gender differences, evolution, and pluralistic ignorance. *Evolutionary Psychology,* 8, 390–404.

Reid, R. C., et al. (2012). Report of findings in a DSM-5 field trial for hypersexual disorder. *Journal of Sexual Medicine,* 9, 2868–2877.

Reiersol, O., & Skeid, S. (2006). The ICD diagnoses of fetishism and sadomasochism. *Journal of Homosexuality,* 50, 243–262.

Reimers, S. (2007). The BBC Internet study: General methodology. *Archives of Sexual Behavior,* 36, 147–161.

Reinberg, S. (2017, August 10). Only about one-third of American use condoms: CDC. *U.S. News & World Report.* Available: http://health.usnews.com/health-care/articles/2017-08-10/only-about-one-third-of-americans-use-condoms-cdc (Last visited 8/24/17).

Reiss, I. (1980). A multivariate model of the determinants of extramarital sexual permissiveness. *Journal of Marriage and Family,* 42, 395–411.

Reiss, I. (1989). Society and sexuality: A sociological explanation. In K. McKinney & S. Sprecher (Eds.), *Human sexuality: The societal and interpersonal context.* Ablex.

Reitman, V. (2004, September 12). Viagra users are getting younger and younger. *Indianapolis Star,* pp. J1, J4.

Resch, M., & Alderson, K. (2013). Female partners of men who use pornography: Are honesty and mutual use associated with relationship satisfaction? *Journal of Sex & Marital Therapy,* 40(5), 410–424.

Rettner, R. (2018). Why is the US one of the 'most dangerous' places in the developed world to give birth? *Live Science.* Available: https://www.livescience.com/63191-dangerous-childbirth-united-states.html (Last visited 8/15/20).

Reverby, S. M. (2009). *Examining Tuskegee: The infamous syphilis study and its legacy.* University of North Carolina Press.

Reynolds, A., & Caron, S. L. (2000). How intimate relationships are impacted when heterosexual men crossdress. *Journal of Psychology and Human Sexuality,* 12, 63–77.

Reynolds, G. (2015, June 28). The joy of (just the right amount) of sex. *The New York Times Magazine,* p. 18.

Reynolds, G. L., Fisher, D. G., & Rogala, B. (2015). Why women engage in anal intercourse: Results from a qualitative study. *Archives of Sexual Behavior,* 44, 983–995.

Richters, J., de Visser, R. O., Rissel, C. E., Grulich, A. E., & Smith, A. M. A. (2008). Demographic and psychological features of participants in bondage and discipline, "sadomasochism" or dominance and submission (BDSM). *Journal of Sexual Medicine,* 5, 1660–1668.

Rideout, V., & Robb, M. B. (2019). The common sense census: Media use by tweens and teens, 2019. *Common Sense Media.* Available: https://static1.squarespace.com/static/5ba15befec4eb7899898240d/t/5db-720c31d5972380170602b4/1572282565933/2019-census-8-to-18-full-report.FINAL.10_25_19.pdf (Last visited 1/21/20).

Rider, J. R., Wilson, K. M., Sinnott, J. A., Kelly, R. S., Mucci, L. A., & Giovannucci, E. L. (2016). Ejaculation frequency and risk of prostate cancer: Updated results with an additional decade of follow-up. *European Urology, 70*(6), 974–982.

Ridolfo, H., Miller, K., & Maitland, A. (2012). Measuring sexual identity using survey questionnaires: How valid are measures? *Sexuality Research and Social Policy, 9,* 113–124.

Rinehart, J. K., Nason, E. E., Yeater, E. A., & Miller, G. F. (2017). Do some students need special protection from research on sex and trauma? New evidence for your adult resilience in "sensitive topics" research. *Journal of Sex Research, 54,* 273–283.

Ritchwood, T. D., Ford, H., DeCoster, J., Sutton, M., & Lochman, J. E. (2015). Risky sexual behavior and substance use among adolescence: A meta-analysis. *Children and Youth Services Review, 52,* 74–88.

Robbins, C. L., Schick, V., Reece, M., Herbenick, D., Sanders, S. A., Dodge, B., & Fortenberry, J. D. (2011). Prevalence, frequency and associations of masturbation with partnered sexual behaviors among US adolescents. *Archives of Pediatric Medicine, 165*(12), 1087–1093.

Roberson, P. N. E., Olmstead, S. B., & Fincham, F. D. (2015). Hooking up during the college years: Is there a pattern? *Culture, Health & Sexuality, 17,* 576–591.

Roberts, J., Carr, L. W., Jones, A., Schilling, A., Mackay, D., & Potochny, J. D. (2019). A prospective approach to inform and treat 1340 patients at risk for BIA-ALCL. *Plastic and Reconstructive Surgery, 144*(1), 46–54.

Robinson, P. (1976). *The modernization of sex.* Harper & Row.

Robles, T. F., Trombello, J. M., Slatcher, R. B., & McGinn, M. M. (2013). Marital quality and health: A meta-analytic review. American Psychological Association: *Psychological Bulletin.* Available: http://richslatcher.com/papers/RoblesEtal_PsychBull_2013.pdf (Last visited 11/3/14).

Roen, K. (2019). Intersex or diverse sex development: Critical review of psychosocial health care research and indications for practice. *Journal of Sex Research, 56*(4), 511–528.

Romm, C. (2015, August 18). Why flibanserin is not the "Female Viagra". *The Atlantic.*

Ronan, W. (2020, November 17). New FBI hate crimes report shows increases in anti-LGBTQ attacks. Available: https://www.hrc.org/press-releases/new-fbi-hate-crimes-report-shows-increases-in-anti-lgbtq-attacks. (Last visited: 2/23/2021).

Roscoe, W. (1991). *The Zuni man/woman.* University of New Mexico Press.

Rose, T. (2004). *Longing to tell: Black women talk about sexuality and intimacy.* New York: Macmillan.

Rosen, R. C., Heiman, J. R., Long, J. S., Fisher, W. A., & Sand, M. A. (2016). Men with sexual problems and their partners: Findings from the International Survey of Relationships. *Archives of Sexual Behavior, 45,* 159–173.

Rosen, R. C., Miner, M. M., & Wincze, J. P. (2014). Erectile dysfunction: Integration of medical and psychological approaches. In Y. M. Binik & K. S. K. Hall (Eds.), *Principles and practices of sex therapy* (5th ed., pp. 61–81). Guilford Press.

Rosenfeld, J. (2019). 10 scientific benefits of kissing. Available: https://www.mentalfloss.com/article/501990/10-scientific-benefits-kissing (Last visited: 4/4/2020).

Rosin, H. (2014, April 29). When men are raped. Available: http://www.slate.com/articles/double_x/doublex/2014/04/male_rape_in_america_a_new_study_reveals_that_men_are_sexually_assaulted.html (Last visited 3/1/18).

Rosman, J., & Resnick, P. J. (1989). Sexual attraction to corpses: A psychiatric review of necrophilia. *Journal of the American Academy of Psychiatry and the Law, 17*(2), 153–163.

Ross, M. W., Essien, E. J., & Torres, I. (2006). Conspiracy beliefs about the origin of HIV/AIDS in four racial/ethnic groups. *Journal of Acquired Immune Deficiency Syndromes, 41,* 342–344.

Rosser, B. R. S., Kohli, N., Polter, E. J., Lesher, L., Capistrant, B. D., et al. (2019). The sexual functioning of gay and bisexual men following prostate cancer treatment: Results from the Restore Study. *Archives of Sexual Behavior, 49*(5), 1589–1600. Available: https://pubmed.ncbi.nlm.nih.gov/31016492/ (Last visited 10/3/20).

Rosser, S., Short, B. J., Thurmes, P. J., & Coleman, E. (1998). Anodyspareunia, the unacknowledged sexual dysfunction: A validation study of painful receptive anal intercourse and its psychosexual concomitants in homosexual men. *Journal of Sex and Marital Therapy, 24,* 281–292.

Rowen, T. S., Gaither, T. W., Awad, M. A., et al. (2016, August 16). Pubic hair grooming prevalence and motivation among women in the United States. *JAMA Dermatology, 152*(10), 1106–1113.

Rowland, D. L. (2012). *Sexual dysfunction in women.* Hogrefe Publishing.

Rudaysky, S. (2015, April 27). CDC: Indiana has "one of the worst" HIV epidemics. *Indianapolis Star.* Available from: https://www.usatoday.com/story/news/nation/2015/04/28/indiana-hiv-outbreak/26498117/ (Last visited 1/10/2018).

Ruggiero, S., Brandi, K., Mark, A., Paul, M., Reeves, M. F., Schalit, O., Blanchard, K., Key, K., & Chandrasekaran, S. (2020). Access to later abortions in the United States during COVID-19: Challenges and recommendations from providers, advocates and researchers. *Journal of Sexual and Reproductive Health Matters, 28*(1). Available: https://www.tandfonline.com/doi/full/10.1080/26410397.2020.1774185 (Last visited 7/30/20).

Rutkowska, A. Z., & Diamanti-Kandarakis, E. D. (2016). Polycystic ovary syndrome and environmental toxins. *Fertility & Sterility, 106*(4). Available: https://www.fertstert.org/article/S0015-0282(16)62728-0/pdf (Last visited 8/31/20).

Ryan, K. M. (2011). The relationship between rape myths and sexual scripts: The social construction of rape. *Sex Roles, 65,* 774–782.

Ryan, P. (2017, June 7). Can porn be feminist? These female directors say 'yes'. *USA Today,* p. 2D.

Rye, B. J., & Meaney, G. J. (2007). Voyeurism: Is it good as long as we do not get caught? *International Journal of Sexual Health, 19,* 47–56.

Sakaluk, J. K. (2016). Promoting replicable sexual science: A methodological review and call for metascience. *The Canadian Journal of Human Sexuality, 25,* 1–8.

Sakaluk, J. K., Todd, L. M., Milhausen, R., Lachowsky, N. J., & Undergraduate Research Group in Sexuality. (2014). Dominant heterosexual sexual scripts in emerging adulthood: Conceptualizations and measurement. *Journal of Sex Research, 51,* 516–531.

Saliares, E., Wilkerson, J. M., Sieving, R. E., & Brady, S. S. (2017). Sexually experienced adolescents' thoughts about sexual pleasure. *Journal of Sex Research, 54*(4–5), 604–618.

Salisbury, C. M. A., & Fisher, W. A. (2014). "Did you come?" A qualitative exploration of gender differences in beliefs, experiences, and concerns regarding female orgasm occurrence during heterosexual sexual interactions. *Journal of Sex Research, 51*(6), 616–631.

Salomon, L. J., Sotiriadis, A., Wulff, C. B., Obido, A., & Akolekar, R. (2019). Risk of miscarriage following amniocentesis or chorionic villus sampling: Systematic review of literature and updated metaanalysis. *Ultrasound in Obstetrics & Gynecology, 54*(4), 442–451. Available: https://obgyn.onlinelibrary.wiley.com/doi/full/10.1002/uog.20353 (Last visited 8/21/20).

Sanchez, Y. M. (1997). Families of Mexican origin. In M. K. DeGenova (Ed.), *Families in cultural context: Strengths and challenges in diversity.* Mayfield.

Sanders, S. A., Graham, C. A., Yarber, W. L., & Crosby, R. A. (2003). Condom use errors and problems among women who put condoms on their male partners. *Journal of American Medical Women's Association, 58,* 95–98.

Sanders, S. A., Hill, B. J., Yarber, W. L., Graham, C. A., Crosby, R. A., & Milhausen, R. A. (2010). Misclassification bias: Diversity in conceptualizations about having "had sex." *Sexual Health, 7,* 31–34.

Sanders, S. A., Reece, M., Herbenick, D., Schick, V., Dodge, B., & Fortenberry, J. D. (2010). Condom use during most recent vaginal intercourse event among a probability sample of adults in the United States. *Journal of Sexual Medicine, 7,* 362–373.

Sanders, S. A., Reinisch, J. M., & McWhirter, D. P. (1990). Homosexuality/heterosexuality: An overview. In D. P. McWhirter, S. A. Sanders, & J. M. Reinisch (Eds.), *Homosexuality/heterosexuality: Concepts of sexual orientation.* Oxford University Press.

Sanders, S. A., Yarber, W. L., Kaufman, E. L., Crosby, R. A., Graham, C. A., & Milhausen, R. R. (2012). Condom use errors and problems: A global view. *Sexual Health, 9,* 81–95.

Sanders, S., & Reinisch, J. (1999). Would you say you "had sex" if . . . ? *Journal of the American Medical Association, 281*(3), 275–277.

Sandfort, T. G., & de Keizer, M. (2001). Sexual problems in gay men: An overview of empirical research. *Annual Review of Sex Research, 12,* 93–120.

Sandnabba, N., Santtila, P., Alison, L., & Nordling, N. (2002). Demographics, sexual behavior, family background and abuse experiences of practitioners of sadomasochistic sex: A review of recent research. *Sexual and Relationship Theory, 17,* 39–55.

Sankofa, J. (n.d.). From margin to center: Sex work decriminalization is a radical justice issue. *Amnesty USA.* Available: https://www.amnyestyuse.org/from-margin-to-center-sex-work-decriminalization-is-a-racial-justice-issue/ (Last visited 9/6/2017).

Santelli, J. S., Kantor, L. M., Grilo, S. A., Speizer, I. S., Lindberg, L. D., Heitel, J., Schalet, A. T., Lyon, M. E., Mason-Jones, A., McGovern, T., Heck, C. J., Rogers, J., & Ott, M. A. (2017). Abstinence-only-until-marriage: An updated review of U.S. policies and programs and their impact. *Journal of Adolescent Health, 61*(3), 273–280. Available: https://www.ncbi.nlm.nih.gov/pubmed/28842065 (Last visited 4/18/20).

Santtila, P., Sandnabba, N. K., Alison, L., & Nordling, N. (2002). Investigating the underlying structure of sadomasochistically oriented behavior. *Archives of Sexual Behavior, 31,* 185–196.

Sarrel, P., & Masters, W. H. (1982). Sexual molestation of men by women. *Archives of Sexual Behavior, 11,* 117–131.

Satterwhite, C. L., Torrone, E., Meites, E., Dunne, E. F., Mahajan, R., Ocfemia, M. C., et al. (2013). Sexually transmitted infections among US women and men: Prevalence and incidence estimates. *Sexually Transmitted Diseases, 40,* 187–193.

Savin-Williams, R. (2017). *Mostly straight: Sexual fluidity among men.* Harvard University Press.

Savin-Williams, R. (2019). Developmental trajectories and milestones of sexual-minority youth. In S. Lamb & J. Gilbert (Eds.), *Cambridge handbooks in psychology. The Cambridge handbook of sexual development: Childhood and adolescence* (pp. 156–179). Cambridge University Press.

Savin-Williams, R. C. (2014). An exploratory study of the categorical versus spectrum nature of sexual orientation. *Journal of Sex Research, 51*(4), 446–453.

Scaccia, A. (2020). Facts about HIV: Life expectancy and long-term outlook. Available: https://www.healthline.com/health/hiv-aids/life-expectancy (Last visited: 10/7/2020).

Schaafsma, D., Kok, G., Stoffelen, J. M. T., & Curfs, L. M. G. (2015). Identifying effective methods for teaching sex education to individuals with intellectual disabilities: A systematic review. *Journal of Sex Research, 52*(4), 412–432.

Scheffey, K. L., Ogden, S. N., & Dichter, M. E. (2019). "The idea of categorizing makes me feel uncomfortable": University student perspectives on sexual orientation and gender identity labeling in the health care setting. *Archives of Sexual Behavior, 48,* 1555–1562.

Schiavi, M. C., Spina, V., Zullo, M. A., Colagiovanni, V., Luffarelli, P., Rago, R., & Palazzetti, P. (2020). Love in the time of COVID-19: Sexual function and quality of life analysis during the social distancing measures in a group of Italian reproductive-age women. *Journal of Sexual Medicine, 17,* 1407–1413.

Schick, V. R., Calabrese, S. K., & Herbenick, D. (2014). Survey methods in sexuality research. In D. L. Tolman & L. M. Diamond (Eds.), *APA handbook of sexuality and psychology* (pp. 81–98). American Psychological Association.

Schick, V. R., Rosenberg, J. G., Herbenick, D., Collazo, E., Sanders, S. A., & Reece, M. (2016). The behavioral definitions of "having sex with a man" and "having sex with a woman" identified by women who have engaged in sexual activity with both men and women. *Journal of Sex Research, 53,* 578–587.

Schmidt, P. (2011, September 18). Scholars of legal brothels offer a new take on the "oldest profession." *Chronicle of Higher Education.* Available: http://chronicle.com/article/Scholars-of-Brothels/129047 (Last visited 10/3/11).

Schmitt, D. P. (2003). Universal sex differences in the desire for sexual variety: Tests from 52 nations, 6 continents, and 13 islands. *Journal of Personality and Social Psychology, 85,* 85–104.

Schmitt, D. P., & Buss, D. M. (2001). Human mate poaching: Tactics and temptations for infiltrating existing partnerships. *Journal of Personality and Social Psychology, 80,* 894–917.

Schmucker, M., & Losel, F. (2008). Does sexual offender treatment work? A systematic review of outcome evaluations. *Psicothema, 20,* 10–19.

Schnarch, D. (2002). *Resurrecting sex.* HarperCollins.

Schneider, M. (2020, September 17). Gay marriages rise 5 years after Supreme Court ruling. *U.S. News and World Report.* Available: https://www.usnews.com/news/us/articles/2020-09-17/less-than-1-million-gay-couple-households-in-us-in-2019 (Last visited 12/18/20).

Schreiber, K. (2018, January 25). How sexually fluid are men and women, really? *Psychology Today.* Available: https://www.psychologytoday.com/us/blog/the-truth-about-exercise-addiction/201801/how-sexually-fluid-are-men-and-women-really (Last visited 2/20/20).

Schulze, C., Koon-Magnin, S., & Bryan, V. (2019). *Gender identity, sexual orientation & sexual assault: Challenging the myths.* Lynne Rienner Publishers.

Schumlich, E. J., & Fisher, W. A. (2018). Affirmative sexual consent? Direct and unambiguous consent is rarely included in discussions of recent sexual interactions. *Canadian Journal of Human Sexuality, 27,* 248–260.

Schwartz, C. (2016, February 7). Clicking for a therapist. *New York Times.*

Schwartz, J. (2007, January 27). Of gay sheep, modern science and the perils of bad publicity. *New York Times,* pp. A1, A16.

Schwartz, S. (2000). *Abnormal psychology: A discovery approach.* Mayfield.

Schwarzer, U., Sommer, F., Klotz, T., Braun, M., Reifenrath, B., & Engelmann, U. (2001). The prevalence of Peyronie's disease: Results of a large survey. *BJU International, 88,* 727–730.

Schwimmer, B. (1997). The Dani of New Guinea. Available: http://www.umanitoba.ca/faculties/arts/anthropology/tutor/case_studies/dani/ (Last visited 11/3/05).

Scorolli, C., Ghirlanda, S., Enquist, M., Zattoni, S., & Jannini, E. A. (2007). Relative prevalence of different fetishes. *International Journal of Impotence, 19,* 432–437.

Scott, D. (2010). *Extravagant abjection: Blackness, power, and sexuality in the African American literary imagination (sexual cultures).* New York: New York University Press.

Scott, R. H., Wellings, K., & Lindberg, L. (2020, February 3). Adolescent sexual activity, contraceptive use, and pregnancy in Britain and the U.S.: A multidecade comparison. *Journal of Adolescent Health.* Available: https://www.jahonline.org/article/S1054-139X(19)30887-0/fulltext (Last visited 4/17/20).

Sears, A. E. (1989). The legal case for restricting pornography. In D. Zillman & J. Bryant (Eds.), *Pornography: Research advances and policy considerations.* Erlbaum.

Seguin, L. J., & Milhausen, R. R. (2016). Not all fakes are created equal: Examining the relationships between men's motives for pretending orgasm and levels of sexual desire, and relationship and sexual satisfaction. *Sexual and Relationship Therapy, 32*, 159–175.

Seguin, L. J., Milhausen, R. R., & Kokkonen, T. (2020). Motives for feigning orgasms scale. In R. R. Milhausen, J. K. Sakialuk, T. D. Fisher, C. M. Davis, & W. L. Yarber (Eds.), *Handbook of sexuality-related measures.* (pp. 491–494). Routledge.

Seguin, L. J., Milhausen, R. R., & Kukkonen, T. (2015). The development and validation of the motives for feigning orgasms scale. *The Canadian Journal of Human Sexuality, 24*, 31–48.

Seguin, L. J., Rodrigue, C., & Lavigne, J. (2018). Consuming ecstasy: Representations of male and female orgasm in mainstream pornography. *Journal of Sex Research, 55*, 348–356.

Seligman, L., & Hardenberg, S. A. (2000). Assessment and treatment of paraphilias. *Journal of Counseling and Development, 78*, 107–113.

Selterman, D., Garcia, J. R., & Tsapelas, I. (2019). Motivations for extradyadic infidelity revisited. *Journal of Sex Research, 56*(3), 273–286.

Sendler, D., & Lew-Starowicz, M. Rethinking classification of zoophilia. *European Psychiatry.* https://doi.org/10.1016/j.eurpsy.2017.01.;1690

Senecal, M., Brisson, M., Maunsell, E., Ferenczy, A., Franco, E. L., Ratman, S., et al. (2011). Loss of quality of life associated with genital warts: Baseline analyses from a prospective study. *Sexually Transmitted Infections, 87*, 209–215.

Senn, C. Y., Eliasziw, M., Barata, P. C., Thurston, W., Newby-Clark, I. R., Radike, H., & Hobden, K. (2015). Efficacy of a sexual assault resistance program for university women. *New England Journal of Medicince, 372*, 2326–2335.

Seto, M. (2008). Pedophilia: Psychopathology and theory. In D. R. Laws & W. T. O'Donohue (Eds.), *Sexual deviance: Theory, assessment, and treatment* (2nd ed.). Guilford Press.

Sewell, K. K., & Strassberg, D. S. (2015). How do heterosexual undergraduate students define having sex? A new approach to an old question. *Journal of Sex Research, 52*, 507–516.

Sex Information & Education Council of Canada (SIECCAN). (2019). *Canadian guidelines for sexual health education.* Available: http://sieccan.org/wp-content/uploads/2019/08/Canadian-Guidelines-for-Sexual-Health-Education.pdf (Last visited 4/21/20).

Sexuality Information and Education Council of the United States (SIECUS). (2020). The SIECUS state profiles. Available: https://siecus.org/state-profiles-2019/ (Last visited 4/21/20).

Shackelford, T. K., Goetz, A. T., LaMunyon, C. W., Quintus, B. J., & Weekes-Shackelford, V. A. (2004). Sex differences in sexual psychology produce sex-similar preferences for a short-term mate. *Archives of Sexual Behavior, 33*, 405–412.

Shaeer, O., Shaeer, K., & Shaeer, E. (2012). The Global Online Sexuality Survey (GOSS): Female sexual dysfunction among Internet users in the reproductive group in the Middle East. *Journal of Sexual Medicine, 9*, 411–421.

Shahbaz, C., & Chirinos. (2017). *Becoming a kink aware therapist.* Routledge.

Shallcross, R., Dickson, J. M., Nunns, D., Taylor, K., & Kiemle, G. (2019). Women's experiences of vulvodynia: An interpretative phenomenological analysis of the journey towards diagnosis. *Archives of Sexual Behavior, 48*(3), 961–974.

Shaver, P. (1984). *Emotions, relationships, and health.* Sage.

Shaver, P., Hazan, C., & Bradshaw, D. (1988). Love as attachment: The integration of three behavioral systems. In R. Sternberg & M. Barnes (Eds.), *The psychology of love.* Yale University Press.

Shaw, M. L. (2020). FDA's revised blood donation guidance for gay men still courts controversy. *American Journal of Managed Care.* Available: https://www.ajmc.com/view/fdas-revised-blood-donation-guidance-for-gay-men-still-courts-controversy (Last visited: 12/11/2020).

Shen, X., Li, Y., Xu, S., Wang, N., Fan, S., Qin, X., Zhou, C., & Hess, P. E. (2017, October). Epidural analgesia during the second stage of labor: A randomized control trial. *Obstetrics & Gynecology, 130*(5), 1097–1103.

Shilts, R. (1987). *And the band played on: Politics, people, and the AIDS epidemic.* St. Martin's Press.

Shrage, L. (2015, August 10). When prostitution is nobody's business. *The New York Times,* Sunday Review, p. 2.

Shute, N. (2015, November 19). Is sex once a week enough for a happy relationship? *NPR Shots.*

Simon, C. (2018, July 13). Sex addiction classification is a medical condition, not a moral failure, *USA Today.*

Simon, W., & Gagnon, J. H. (1984). *Society, 22*, 53–60.

Simon, W., & Gagnon, J. H. (1986). Sexual scripts: Permanence and change. *Archives of Sexual Behavior, 15*, 97–120.

Simon, W., & Gagnon, J. H. (1987). A sexual scripts approach. In W. T. O'Donohue (Ed.), *Theories of human sexuality.* Plenum Press.

Singal, J. (2016, December 18). The phenomenon of "bud sex" between straight rural men. *New York Magazine.*

Singer, R., Crooks, N., Johnson, A. K., Lutnick, A., & Matthews, A. (2020). COVID-19 prevention and sex workers: A call to action. *Archives of Sexual Behavior, 49*, 2739–2741.

Singg, S. (2017). Health risks of zoophilia/bestiality. *Journal of Biological and Medical Sciences, 1*, e101.

Skoda, K., & Pedersen, C. L. (2019). Size matters after all: Experimental evidence that SEM consumption influences genital and body esteem in men. *Sage Journals, 9*(2), 1–11.

Skorska, M. N., Hodson, G., & Hoffarth, M. R. (2018). Experimental effects of degrading versus erotic pornography exposure in men on reactions toward women (objectification, sexism, discrimination). *The Canadian Journal of Human Sexuality, 27*, 261–276.

Slater, D. (2013, January 13). Darwin was wrong about dating. *New York Times,* pp. SR 7, 11.

Slowinski, J. (2007). Sexual problems and dysfunctions of men. In A. Owens & M. Tepper (Eds.), *Sexual health: State-of-the art treatments and research.* Praeger.

Smith, E. W. (2019, August 8). Is this sexuality scale still relevant in 2019? Available: https://www.yahoo.com/lifestyle/once-groundbreaking-sexuality-scale-still-160433733.html (Last visited 9/4/19).

Smith, L. M., Kaufman, J. S., Strumpf, E. C., & Lévesque, L. E. (2014). Effect of human papillomavirus (HPV) vaccination on clinical indicators of sexual behavior among adolescent girls: The Ontario Grade 8 HPV Vaccine Cohort Study. *Canadian Medical Association Journal.* https://doi.org/10.1503/cmaj.140900

Smith, L., Yang, L., Veronese, N., Soysal, P., Stubbs, B., & Jackson, S. E. (2019). Sexual activity is associated with greater enjoyment of life in older adults. *Sexual Medicine, 7*(11), 11–18.

Smith, M. D., Grov, C., Seal, D. W., & McCall, P. (2013). A social-cognitive analysis of how young men become involved in male escorting. *Journal of Sex Research, 50*, 1–10.

Smith, S. G., Zhang, X., Basile, K. C., Merrick, M. T., Wang, J., Kresnow, M., & Chen, J. (2018). The National Partner and Sexual Violence

Survey: 2015 Data Brief—Updated Release. Available: https://www.cdc.gov/violenceprevention/datasources/nisvs/index.html (Last visited: 11/22/2020).

Smith, S. J. (2015). Risky sexual behavior among young adult Latinos: Are acculturation and religiosity protective? *Journal of Sex Research,* 52(1), 43–54.

Snyder, H. N., & Sickmund, M. (2006). *Juvenile offenders and victims: 2006 national report.* U.S. Department of Justice.

Society for Assisted Reproductive Technology [SART]. (2020). Assisted reproductive technologies. Available: https://www.sart.org/topics/topics-index/assisted-reproductive-technologies/ (Last visited 8/25/20).

Solomon, J. (1998, March 16). An insurance policy with sex appeal. *Newsweek,* p. 44.

Sparling, S., & Cramer, K. (2015). Choosing the danger we think we know: Men and women's faulty perceptions of sexually transmitted infection risk with familiar and unfamiliar new partners. *Canadian Journal of Human Sexuality,* 243, 237–242.

Sports Illustrated. (2020). Swimsuit. Available: https://swimsuit.si.com/swim-daily/2020/02/12/si-swimsuit-2020-model-search-final-six-models (Last visited 4/16/20).

Sprecher, S. (1994). Two sides to the breakup of dating relationships. *Personal Relationships,* 1, 199–222.

Sprecher, S., & Toro-Morn, M. (2002). A study of men and women from different sides of earth to determine if men are from Mars and women are from Venus in their beliefs about love and romantic relationships. *Sex Roles,* 46(5–6), 131–147.

Sprott, R. A., & Hadcock, B. B. (2017). Bisexuality, pansexuality, queer identity, and kink identity. *Sexual and Relationship Therapy,* 33, 214–232.

Stack, L. (2019, October 19). Cases of S.T.D.s reach a record high. *New York Times.* Available: https://www.nytimes.com/2019/10/08/health/cdc-std-study.html (Last visited 10/22/2020).

Stanford Children's Health. (2020.12a). Medical genetics: Teratogens. Available: https://www.stanfordchildrens.org/en/topic/default?id-teratogens-overview-90-P09519 (Last visited 8/14/20).

Stanford Children's Health. (2020.12b). Episiotomy. Available: https://www.stanfordchildrens.org/en/topic/default?id=episiotomy-92-P07775 (Last visited 8/31/20).

Stanger-Hall, K. F., & Hall, D. W. (2011). Abstinence-only education and teen pregnancy rates: Why we need comprehensive sex education in the U.S. *PLos ONE,* 6(10).

Staples, R. (1991). The sexual revolution and the Black middle class. In R. Staples (Ed.), *The Black family* (4th ed.). Jenson Books.

Staples, R. (2006). *Exploring Black sexuality.* Rowman & Littlefield.

Staples, R., & Johnson, L. B. (1993). *Black families at the crossroads: Challenges and prospects.* Wiley.

Statista. (2019). Feminine hygiene market – Statistics & facts. Available: https://www.statista.com/topics/4889/feminine-hygiene-market/ (Last visited 2/28/20).

Statista. (2019.1a). Global digital population as of October 2019. Available: https://www.statista.com/statistics/617136/digital-population-worldwide/ (Last visited 1/21/20).

Statista. (2019.1b). Number of monthly active Facebook users worldwide as of 3rd quarter 2019. Available: https://www.statista.com/statistics/264810/number-of-monthly-active-facebook-users-worldwide/ (Last visited 1/21/20).

Statista. (2019.1c). Online dating in the United States – Statistics & facts. Available: https://www.statista.com/topics/2158/online-dating/ (Last visited 1/21/20).

Statista. (2020). Share of internet users in the United States who have used online dating sites or apps as of April 2017, by age group. Available: https://www.statista.com/statistics/706499/us-adults-online-dating-site-app-by-age/ (Last visited 1/21/20).

Steele, V. R., Staley, C., Fong, T., & Prause, N. (2013). Sexual desire, not hypersexuality, is related to neurophysiological responses elicited by sexual images. *Socioaffective Neuroscience & Psychology,* 3, 20770.

Steinberg, J. R. (2020). Decision rightness and relief predominate over the years following abortion. *Social Science and Medicine,* 248.

Stemple, L., & Meyer, I. H. (2014). The sexual victimization of men in America: New data challenge old assumptions. *American Journal of Public Health,* 104, e19–e26.

Sternberg, R. (1986). A triangular theory of love. *Psychological Review,* 93, 119–135.

Sternberg, R. J., & Barnes, M. L. (1989). *The psychology of love.* Yale University Press.

Sternberg, R., & Grajek, S. (1984). The nature of love. *Journal of Personality and Social Psychology,* 47, 312–327.

Stewart, L. E. (2014). Douching. In J. Grimes, K. Fagerberg, & L. Smith, (Eds.), *Sexually transmitted disease, Volume 1: A-H* (pp. 144–145). Greenwood.

Stop Street Harassment. (2017). Definitions. Available: http://www.stopstreetharassment.org/resources/definitions/ (Last visited: 10/7/2017).

Storms, M. D. (1980). Theories of sexual orientation. *Journal of Personality and Social Psychology,* 38, 783–792.

Storms, M. D. (1981). A theory of erotic orientation development. *Psychological Review,* 88, 340–353.

Strassberg, D. S., & Lowe, K. (1995). Volunteer bias in sex research. *Archives of Sexual Behavior,* 24(4), 369–382.

Strassburg, D. S., & Mackaronis, J. E. (2014). Sexuality and psychotherapy. In D. L. Tolman & L. M. Diamond (Eds.), *APA handbook of sexuality and psychology* (pp. 105–135). American Psychological Association.

Stritof, S. (2017). Marital rape. *The Spruce.* Available: https://www.thespruce.com/what-is-marital-rape-2300724 (Last visited 10/25/2017).

Struckman-Johnson, C., Struckman-Johnson, D., & Anderson, P. B. (2003). Tactics of sexual coercion: When men and women won't take no for an answer. *Journal of Sex Research,* 40, 76–86.

Stulhofer, A. (2006). How (un)important is penis size for women with heterosexual experience? [Letter to the Editor]. *Archives of Sexual Behavior,* 35, 5–6.

Stulhofer, A., & Ajdukovic, D. (2011). Should we take anodyspareunia seriously? A descriptive analysis of pain during receptive anal intercourse in young heterosexual women. *Journal of Sex & Marital Therapy,* 37, 346–358.

Sukel, K. (2016). Lust's reward. *Scientific American: Special Collection Explores the Sexual Brain,* 14–17.

Sumari-de Boer, I. M., Sprangers, M. A., Prins, J. M., & Nieuwkerk, P. T. (2012). HIV stigma and depressive symptoms are related to adherence and virological response to antiretroviral treatment among immigrant and indigenous HIV infected patients. *AIDS and Behavior,* 16, 1681–1689.

Sun, A. J., & Eisenberg, M. L. (2017). Association between marijuana use and sexual frequency in the United States: A population-based study. *Sexual Medicine,* 14(11), 1342–1347.

Supreme Court of the United States. (2003, June 26). John Geddes Lawrence and Tyron Garner, Petitioners *v.* Texas. Majority opinion. Available: https://www.oyez.org/cases/2002/02-102 (Last visited 2/1/20).

Sutherland, S. E., Rehman, U. S., Fallis, E. E., & Goodnight, J. A. (2015). Understanding the phenomenon of sexual desire discrepancy in couples. *Canadian Journal of Human Sexuality,* 24, 141–151.

Svoboda, E. (2008, January–February). Scents and sensibility. *Psychology Today.*

Swami, V., & Tovee, M. J. (2013). Men's oppressive beliefs predict their breast size preferences in women. *Archives of Sexual Behavior,* 42, 1199–1207.

Swanson, E. (2019). The textured breast implant crisis. *Annals of Plastic Surgery,* 82(6), 593-594. Available: https://www.ncbi.nlm.nih.gov/pmc/articles/PMC6530980/ (Last visited 2/28/20).

Swiatkowski, P. (2016). Magazine influence on body dissatisfaction: Fashion vs. health? *Cogent Social Sciences,* 2(1). Available: https://www.tandfonline.com/doi/citedby/10.1080/23311886.2016.1250702?scroll=top&needAccess=true (Last visited 1/19/20).

Symons, K., Vermeersch, H., & Van Houtte, M. (2014). The emotional experiences of early first intercourse: A multi-method method of study. *Journal of Adolescent Research,* 29(4), 533.

Szucs, L. E., Lowry, R., Fasula, A. M., Pampati, S., Copen, C. E., Hussaini, K. S., Kachur, R. E., Koumans, E. H., & Steiner, R. J. (2020). Condom and contraceptive use among sexually active high school students—Youth Risk Behavior Survey, United States, 2019. *Morbidity and Mortality Weekly Report (MMWR),* 69(1), 11-18.

Taberner, P. V. (1985). *Aphrodisiacs: The science and the myth.* University of Pennsylvania Press.

Tan, L. S., Chio, M. T. W., Sen, P., Lim, Y. K., Ng, J., Llancheran, A., et al. (2014). Assessment of psychological impact of genital warts among patients in Singapore. *Sexual Health,* 11, 313-318.

Tanfer, K., Cubbins, L. A., & Billy, J. O. G. (1995). Gender, race, class and self-reported sexually transmitted disease incidence. *Family Planning Perspectives,* 27, 196-202.

Tankard, J. M. (2009). Gay men attracted to masculine features. *Harvard Crimson.* Available: https://www.thecrimson.com/article/2009/11/6/faces-men-study-attraction-gay-masculine-harvard. (Last visited: 7/15/2020).

Tannen, D. (2016). He said, she said. *Scientific American: Special Collection Explores the Sexual Brain,* 92-97.

Tanner, L. (2005, July 17). Latest research findings: Research is often wrong. *Indianapolis Star,* p. A23.

Tao, G. (2008). Sexual orientation and related viral sexually transmitted disease rates among U.S. women aged 15 to 44 years. *American Journal of Public Health,* 98, 1007-1009.

Tashiro, T., & Frazier, P. (2003). "I'll never be in a relationship like that again": Personal growth following romantic relationship breakups. *Personal Relationships,* 10, 113-128.

Tepper, M. S., & Owens, A. F. (2007). Current controversies in sexual health: Sexual addiction and compulsion. In A. F. Owens & M. S. Tepper (Eds.), *Sexual health: State-of-the-art treatments and research.* Praeger.

Terris, M. K. (2018). Urethritis. *Medscape.* Available: https://emedicine.medscape.com/article/438091-overview (Last visited: 9/22/2020).

Testa, M., Brown, W. C., & Wang, W. (2019). Do men use more sexually aggressive tactics when intoxicated? A within-person examination of naturally occurring episodes of sex. *Psychology of Violence,* 9, 546-554.

Testa, M., Livingston, J. A., Wang, W. et al. (2020). Preventing college sexual victimization by reducing hookups: A randomized controlled trial of a personalized normative feedback intervention. *Prevention Science,* 21, 388-397.

Thakar, R. (2015). Is the uterus a sexual organ? Sexual function following hysterectomy. *Sexual Medicine Reviews,* 3(4), 264-278.

Thayer, L. (1986). *On communication.* Ablex.

The Nielson Total Audience Report; www.rbr.com/usp-content/uploads/Q1-2019-Nielson-Total-Audience-Report-Final.pdf.

The White House Council on Women and Girls. (2014). *Rape and sexual assault: A renewed call to action.* The White House.

Thigpen, J. W. (2009). Early sexual behavior in a sample of low-income, African-American children. *Journal of Sex Research,* 46, 67-69.

Thigpen, J. W. (2012). Childhood sexuality. In L. M. Carpenter & J. DeLamater (Eds.), *Sex for life.* New York University Press.

"Things you should (and shouldn't) do after sex". (2017). WebMD. Available: https://www.webmd.com/sex-relationships/ss/slideshow-sexual-hygiene (Last visited 4/4/2020).

Thomas, K., & Morgenson, G. (2016, April 10). The female Viagra, undone by a drug maker's dysfunction. *New York Times.*

Thomas, S. B., & Quinn, S. C. (1991). The Tuskegee syphilis study, 1932 to 1972: Implications for HIV education and AIDS risk education programs in the Black community. *American Journal of Public Health,* 81(11), 1498-1504.

Thurman, A. R., Holden, A. E. C., Shain, R. N., & Perdue, S. T. (2009). The male sexual partners of adult versus teen women with sexually transmitted infections. *Sexually Transmitted Diseases,* 36, 768-774.

Tiefer, L. (2001). A new view of women's sexual problems: Why new? Why now? *Journal of Sex Research,* 38(2), 89-110.

Tiefer, L. (2004). *Sex is not a natural act and other essays* (2nd ed.). Westview Press.

Timaeus, I. M., & Moultrie, T. A. (2020). Pathways to low fertility: 50 years of limitation, curtailment, and postponement of childbearing. *Demography,* 75, 267-296.

Tolman, D. L., & McClelland, S. I. (2011). Normative sexuality development in adolescence: A decade in review, 2000-2009. *Journal of Research on Adolescence,* 21(1), 242-255.

Tomassilli, J. C., Golub, S. A., Bimbi, D. S., & Parsons, J. T. (2009). Behind closed doors: An exploration of kinky sexual behaviors in urban lesbian and bisexual women. *Journal of Sex Research,* 46, 438-445.

Torrone, E., Papp, J., & Weinstock, H. (2014). Prevalence of *Chlamydia trachomatis* genital infection among persons aged 14-39 years—United States. *Mortality and Morbidity Weekly Report,* 63, 834-838.

Tovee, J., Tasker, K., & Benson, P. J. (2000). Is symmetry a visual cue to attractiveness in the human female body? *Evolution and Human Behavior,* 21, 191-200.

Toy Association. (2020). U.S. sales data. Available: https://www.toyassociation.org/ta/research/data/u-s-sales-data/toys/research-and-data/data/us-sales-data.aspx (Last visited 2/22/20).

Traen, B., Stulhofer, A., Jurin, T., & Hald, G. M. (2018). Seventy-five years old and still going strong: Stability and change in sexual interest and sexual enjoyment in elderly men and women across Europe. *International Journal of Sexual Health,* 30, 323-336.

Trevor Project. (2020). Asexual. Available: https://www.thetrevorproject.org/trvr_support_center/asexual/ (Last visited 4/30/20).

Tronstein, E. (2011). Genital shedding of herpes simplex virus among symptomatic and asymptomatic persons with HSV-2 infection. *Journal of the American Medical Association,* 305, 1411-1449.

Trotta, S. O. (2015). Sex after sexual assault: A guide for when it's tough. *Everyday Feminism.* Available: https://everydayfeminism.com/2015/01/sex-after-sexual-assault/ (Last visited: 11/2/2017).

Trussler, T., Hogg, R. S., Banks, P., Marchand, R., Robert, W., Gustaison, R., & Gilbert, M. (2010). *ManCount sizes-up the gaps: A sexual health survey of gay men in Vancouver.* Vancouver Costal Health.

Tschann, J. M., Flores, E., de Groat, C. L., Deardorff, J., & Wibbelsman, C. J. (2010). Condom negotiation strategies and actual condom use among Latino youth. *Journal of Adolescent Health,* 47, 254-262.

Twenge, J. M., Sherman, R. A., & Wells, B. E. (2015). Changes in American adults' sexual behavior and attitudes, 1972-2012. *Archives of Sexual Behavior,* 44, 2273-2285.

Twenge, J. M., Sherman, R. A., & Wells, B. E. (2017). Declines in sexual frequency among American adults, 1989-2014. *Archives of Sexual Behavior,* 46(8), 2389-2401.

Twenge, J. M., Sherman, R. A., & Wells, B. E. (2017). Sexual inactivity during young adulthood is more common among U.S. millennials and iGen: Age, period, and cohort effects on having no sexual partners after age 18. *Archives of Sexual Behavior,* 46, 433-440. Available: https://link.springer.com/article/10.1007/s10508-016-0798-z (Last visited 7/8/20).

Twinge, J. M., Sherman, R. A., & Wells, B. E. (2017). Common among U.S. millennials and iGen: Age, period, and cohort effects of having no sexual partners after age 18. *Archives of Sexual Behavior, 46*, 433–440. Available: https://link.springer.com/article/10.1007/s10508-016-0798-z (Last visited 4/17/20).

U.S. Attorney General's Commission on Pornography (AGCOP). (1986). *Final report.* U.S. Government Printing Office.

U.S. Census Bureau. (2019). Historical marital status tables. Available: https://www.census.gov/data/tables/time-series/demo/families/marital.html (Last visited 7/1/20).

U.S. Department of Education. (2016). U.S. Departments of Education and Justice release joint guidance to help schools ensure the civil rights of transgender students. Author. Available: https://www.ed.gov/news/press-releases/us-departments-education-and-justice-release-joint-guidance-help-schools-ensure-civil-rights-transgender-students (Last visited 6/13/17).

U.S. Department of Health & Human Services. (2017). Child maltreatment: 2015. Available: https://www.acf.hhs.gov/cb/resource/child-maltreatment-2015 (Last visited: 11/1/2017).

U.S. Department of Health & Human Services. (2019). *Trends in teen pregnancy and childbearing.* Office of Population Affairs. Available: https://www.hhs.gov/ash/oah/adolescent-development/reproductive-health-and-teen-pregnancy/teen-pregnancy-and-childbearing/trends/index.html (Last visited 4/20/20).

U.S. Department of Health and Human Services. (2000). The Development Disabilities Assistance and Bill of Rights Act of 2000. Available: https://www.acl.gov/sites/default/files/about-acl/2016-12/dd_act_2000.pdf (Last visited 2/4/18).

U.S. Department of Health and Human Services. (2011.15a). Healthy people, 2020: Lesbian, gay, bisexual and transgender health. Available: https://www.healthypeople.gov/2020/topics-objectives/topic/lesbian-gay-bisexual-and-transgender-health (Last visited 2/23/18).

U.S. Department of Health and Human Services. (2012). Fact Sheet: Sex Trafficking. Available: https://www.acf.hhs.gov/otip/resource/fact-sheet-sex-trafficking-english (Last visited: 9/11/2017).

U.S. Department of Justice. (2010). *Criminal victimization, 2009.* Bureau of Justice Statistics.

U.S. Department of Labor. (2020). Family and medical leave act. Available: https://www.dol.gov/agencies/whd/fmla (Last visited 8/31/20).

U.S. Equal Employment Opportunity Commission. (2009). Facts about sexual harassment FSE/4. Available: http://www.eeoc.gov/facts/fs-sex.html (Last visited 8/29/11).

U.S. Equal Employment Opportunity Commission. (2016). Select Task Force on the Study of Harassment in the Workplace. Available: https://eeoc.gov/task_force/harassment/report.

U.S. Equal Employment Opportunity Commission. (n.d.). Sexual harassment charges EEOC & FEPAs combined: FY 1997–FY 2011. Available: https://www.eeoc.gov/eeoc/statistics/enforcement/sexual_harassment.cfm (Last visited 8/2/18/).

U.S. Food and Drug Administration (FDA). (2017a). 5 things to know about breast implants. Available: https://www.fda.gov/ForConsumers/ConsumerUpdates/ucm338144.htm (Last visited 12/11/17).

U.S. Food and Drug Administration. (2017b). Silicone gel-filled breast implants. Available: https://www.fda.gov/MedicalDevices/ProductsandMedicalProcedures/ImplantsandProsthetics/BreastImplants/ucm063871.htm (Last visited 12/11/17).

U.S. Food & Drug Administration. (2019). Breast implants – Certain labeling recommendations to improve patient communication. Available: https://www.fda.gov/media/131885/download (Last viewed 2/7/20).

U.S. Food & Drug Administration. (2019.12). FDS approves first treatment for post-partum depression. Available: https://www.fda.gov/news-events/press-announcements/fda-approves-first-treatment-post-partum-depression (Last visited 8/31/20).

U.S. Food and Drug Administration. (2020.11a). Phexxi: Highlights of prescribing information. Available: https://www.accessdata.fda.gov/drugsatfda_docs/label/2020/208352s000lbl.pdf (Last visited 7/27/20).

U.S. Food and Drug Administration. (2020.11b). Essure permanent birth control. Available: https://www.fda.gov/medical-devices/implants-and-prosthetics/essure-permanent-birth-control (Last visited 7/28/20).

U.S. Merit Systems Protection Board. (1995). *Sexual harassment in the federal workplace: Trends, progress, continuing challenges.* Author.

U.S. Preventive Services Task Force. (2018.13). Prostate cancer: Screening. Available: https://www.uspreventiveservicestaskforce.org/uspstf/document/RecommendationStatementFinal/prostate-cancer-screening (Last viewed 10/2/20).

Ueda, P., Mercer, C. H., Ghaznavi, C., & Herbenick, D. (2020). Trends in frequency of sexual activity and number of sexual partners among adults aged 18 to 44 years in the US, 2000–2018. *JAMA Network Open, 3*(6). Available: https://jamanetwork.com/journals/jamanetworkopen/fullarticle/2767066 (Last visited 6/15/20).

UNAIDS. (2020.16a). Global HIV & AIDS statistics – 2020 fact sheet. Available: https://www.unaids.org/en/resources/fact-sheet (Last visited: 7/9/2020).

UNAIDS. (2020.16b). UNAIDS data 2020. Available: https://www.unaids.org/sites/default/files/media_asset/2020_aids-data-book_en.pdf (Last visited. 7/11/2020).

Ungar, L. (2015, August 19). "Little pink pill" gets FDA approval. *USA Today.*

United Nations Educational, Scientific and Cultural Organization (UNESCO). (2018). *International technical guidance on sexuality education: An evidence-informed approach* (Revised edition). Available: https://unesdoc.unesco.org/ark:/48223/pf0000260770 (Last visited 4/21/20).

United Nations General Assembly. (1993). Standard rules on the equalization of opportunities for persons with disabilities. Available: https://www.un.org/development/desa/disabilities/standard-rules-on-the-equalization-of-opportunities-for-persons-with-disabilities.html (Last visited 2/4/18).

United Nations International Labor Organization. (2017). *Global Estimates of Modern Slavery: Forced Labour and Forced Marriage.* Available: http://www.ilo.org/global/publications/books/WCMS_575479/lang--en/index.htm (Last visited: 1/2/2017).

United Nations International Labor Organizations. (2021). Force Labor, modern slavery and human trafficking. Available: https://www.ilo.org/global/topics/forced-labour/lang--en/index.htm. (Last visited: 2/11/2021).

United Nations. (2019). Contraceptive use by method, 2019. Available: https://www.un.org/development/desa/pd/sites/www.un.org.development.desa.pd/files/files/documents/2020/Jan/un_2019_contraceptiveusebymethod_databooklet.pdf (Last visited 7/28/20).

University of California, San Francisco Health (UCSF Health). (2019). Caring for yourself during pregnancy & beyond. Available: https://www.whattoexpect.com/pregnancy/epidural/ (Last visited 8/27/20).

University of Michigan. (2018). National poll on health aging: Let's talk about sex. Available: https://www.healthyagingpoll.org/sites/default/files/2018-05/NPHA-Sexual-Health-Report_050118_final2.pdf (Last viewed 5/19/20).

Urology Care Foundation. (2019). What is male infertility? Available: https://www.urologyhealth.org/urologic-conditions/male-infertility (Last visited 8/24/20).

Ussher, J. M., Perz, J., Rose, D., Kellett, A., & Dowsett, G. (2019). Sexual rehabilitation after prostate cancer through assistive aids: A comparison of gay/bisexual and heterosexual men. *Journal of Sex Research,* 56(70), 854–869.

Uuskula, A., Reile, R., Rezeberga, D., Karnite, A., Logminiene, Z., Padaiga, Z., et al. (2015). The prevalence of genital warts in the Baltic countries: Findings from national cross-sectional surveys in Estonia, Lativa and Lithuana. *Sexually Transmitted Infections,* 91, 55–60.

Valera, R., Sawyer, R., & Schiraldi, G. (2001). Perceived health needs of inner-city street prostitutes: A preliminary study. *American Journal of Health and Behavior,* 25, 50–59.

van Anders, S. (2015). Beyond sexual orientation: Integrating gender/sex and diverse sexualities via sexual configurations theory. *Archives of Sexual Behavior,* 44, 1177–1213. Available: https://link.springer.com/article/10.1007/s10508-015-0490-8 (Last visited 5/21/20).

van Lankveld, J. (2013). Does "normal" sexual functioning exist? *Journal of Sex Research,* 50(3–4), 205–206.

van Veen, M. G., Gotz, H. M., van Leeuwen, P. A., Prins, M., & van de Laar, M. J. W. (2010). HIV and sexual risk behavior among commercial sex workers in the Netherlands. *Archives of Sexual Behavior,* 39, 714–723.

VanderLaan, D. P., Petterson, L. J., Mallard, R. W., & Vasey, P. L. (2015). (Trans)gender role expectations and child care in Samoa. *Journal of Sex Research,* 52(6), 710–720.

Vannier, S. A., & Byers, S. A. (2013). A qualitative study of university students' perceptions of oral sex, intercourse and intimacy. *Archives of Sexual Behavior,* 42, 1573–1581.

Vannier, S. A., & O'Sullivan, L. F. (2010). Sex without desire: Characteristics of occasions of sexual compliance in young committed relationships. *Journal of Sex Research,* 47, 429–439.

Vanwesenbeeck, I. (2013). Prostitution push and pull: Male and female perspectives. *Journal of Sex Research,* 50, 11–16.

Vaughn, E. (2020). 7 women's health topics that we need to talk about in 2020. *NPR.* Available: https://www.npr.org/sections/health-shots/2020/01/02/793027826/7-womens-health-topics-we-need-to-talk-about-in-2020 (Last visited 1/30/20).

Veale, D., Miles, S., Bramley, S., Muri, G., & Hodsoll, J. (2015). Am I normal? A systematic review and construction of nomograms for flaccid and erect penis length and circumference in up to 15,521 men. *BJIU,* 115, 978–986. Available: https://onlinelibrary.wiley.com/doi/epdf/10.1111/bju.13010 (Last visited 2/15/20).

Vendituoli, M. (2014, July 4). In sexual-misconduct policies, difficulty arises in defining "yes." *Chronicle of Higher Education,* p. A10.

Vergano. (2013, April 9). The long and short of male attractiveness. *USA Today.*

Verner, S. (2017). Reconstruction decisions: "Living flat" after breast cancer. *Cure: Cancer Updates, Research & Education.* Available: https://www.curetoday.com/publications/cure/2017/breast-2017/reconstruction-decisions-living-flat-after-breast-cancer (Last visited 2/4/18).

Victims of Trafficking and Violence Protection Act of 2000. (2000). Available: http://www.state.gov/documents/organization/10492.pdf (Last visited 6/16/08).

Villarosa, L. (2017). America's hidden H.I.V. epidemic. *New York Times Magazine.* Available: https://www.nytimes.com/2017/06/06/magazine/americas-hidden-hiv-epidemic.html9 (Last visited 6/7/2017).

Viner, R. M., Gireesh, A., Stiglic, N., Hudson, L. D., Goodings, A. L., & Ward J. L. (2019). Roles of cyberbullying, sleep, and physical activity in mediating the effects of social media use on mental health and wellbeing among people in England: A secondary analysis of longitudinal data. *Lancet: Child & Adolescent Health,* 3(10), 685–696.

Voosen, P. (2013, September 13). Inside a revolution in mental health. *Chronicle Review,* B6–B9.

Vowels, L. M., & Mark, K. P. (2020). Strategies for mitigating sexual desire discrepancy in relationships. *Archives of Sexual Behavior,* 49, 1017–1028.

Wade, L. (2017). *American hookup: The new culture of sex on campus.* W. W. Norton & Company.

Wade, L. (2017). What's so cultural about hookup culture? *Sage Journals,* 16(1), 66–68. Available: https://journals.sagepub.com/doi/full/10.1177/1536504217696066 (Last visited 5/11/20).

Wagenaar, H., & Sietske, A. (2017). *Designing prostitution policy: Intention and reality in regulating the sex trade.* Policy Press.

Waite, L. J., Laumann, E. O., Das, A., & Schumm, P. L. (2009). Sexuality: Measures of partnerships, practices, attitudes, and problems in the National Social Life, Health, and Aging Study. *Journal of Gerontology: Social Sciences,* 65B(S1), i56–i66.

Wald, A., et al. (2005). The relationship between condom use and herpes simplex virus acquisition. *Annals of Internal Medicine,* 143, 707–713.

Waldman, M. (2020, August 4). Why pregnant women face special risks from COVID-19. *Science Magazine.* Available: https://www.sciencemag.org/news/2020/08/why-pregnant-women-face-special-risks-covid-19 (Last visited 8/18/20).

Wall, K. M., Stephenson, R., & Sullivan, P. S. (2013). Frequency of sexual activity with most recent male partner among young Internet-using men who have sex with men in the United States. *Journal of Homosexuality,* 60(10), 1520–1538. Available: https://www.ncbi.nlm.nih.gov/pmc/articles/PMC4667785/ (Last visited 5/30/20).

Walls, N. E. (2008). Toward a multidimensional understanding of heterosexism: The changing nature of prejudice. *Journal of Homosexuality,* 55, 20–70.

Walter, C. (2008, February). Affairs of the lips. *Scientific American.* Available: https://www.scientificamerican.com/article/affairs-of-the-lips-2012-10-23/ (Last viewed 8/2/18).

Walters, G. D., Knight, R. A., & Langstrom, N. (2011). Is hypersexuality dimensional? Evidence for the *DSM-5* from general population and clinical samples. *Archives of Sexual Behavior,* 40, 1309–1321.

Walton, M. T., Lykins, A. D., & Bhullar, N. (2016). Sexual arousal and sexual activity frequency: Implications for understanding hypersexuality. *Archives of Sexual Behavior,* 45, 777–782.

Wang, W. (2018). Who cheats more? The demographics of infidelity in America. *Institute for Family Studies.* Available: https://ifstudies.org/blog/who-cheats-more-the-demographics-of-cheating-in-america (Last visited 6/8/20).

Ward, H., & Day, S. (2006). What happens to women who sell sex? Report of a unique occupational cohort. *Sexually Transmitted Infections,* 82, 413–417.

Ward, L. M. (2016). Media and sexualization: State of empirical research, 1995–2015. *Journal of Sex Research,* 53(4–5), 560–577.

Ward, T., & Beech, A. R. (2008). An integrated theory of sex offending. In D. R. Laws & W. T. O'Donohue (Eds.), *Sexual deviance: Theory, assessment, and treatment* (2nd ed.). Guilford Press.

Watson, A., & McKee, A. (2013). Masturbation and the media. *Sexuality & Culture,* 17, 449–475.

Weare, S. (2018). From coercion to physical force: Aggressive strategies used by women against me in "Forced to Penetrate" cases in the United Kingdom. *Archives of Sexual Behavior,* 47, 2191–2205.

Webb, P. (1983). *The erotic arts.* New York: Farrar, Straus & Giroux.

WebMD. (1999). Why aren't men more involved? Available: https://www.webmd.com/sex/birth-control/features/why-arent-men-involved (Last visited 9/21/20).

WebMD. (2018). Hormone replacement therapy: Benefits and risks. Available: https://www.webmd.com/menopause/hrt-risks-benefits#1 (Last visited 5/18/20).

WebMD. (2019). Worried about precocious puberty? How to talk to your pediatrician. Available: https://www.webmd.com/children/developmental-stages#1 (Last visited 4/16/20).

WebMD. (2020). Date-rape drugs. Available: https://www.webmd.com/mental-health/addiction/date-rape-drugs#1. (Last visited: 1/2/2021).

WebMD. (2020.11a). Teenage pregnancy. Available: https://www.webmd.com/baby/teen-pregnancy-medical-risks-and-realities#1 (Last visited 9/20/20).

WebMD. (2020.11b). Annovera 0.15 mg–.013 mg/24 hr vaginal ring contraceptives. Available: https://www.webmd.com/drugs/2/drug-177561/annovera-vaginal/details (Last visited 7/23/20).

WebMD. (2020.12). Pregnancy tests. Available: https://www.webmd.com/baby/guide/pregnancy-tests#1 (Last visited 8/15/20).

WebMD. (2020.13). What is a hysterectomy? Available: https://www.webmd.com/women/qa/what-is-a-hysterectomy (Last visited 10/2/20).

Weeks, J. (1986). *Sexuality.* New York: Tavistock/Ellis Horwood.

Weinberg, M. S., Williams, C. J., & Moser, C. (1984). The social constituents of sadomasochism. *Social Problems, 31,* 379–389.

Weiner, L., & Avery-Clark, C. (2014). Sensate focus: Clarifying the Masters and Johnson model. *Social and Relationship Therapy.* https://doi.org/10.1080/14681994.2014.892920

Weisberg, D. K. (1990). *Children of the night.* Free Press.

Weitzer, R. (2005). New directions in research in prostitution. *Crime, Law and Social Change, 43,* 211–235.

Weitzer, R. (2010). The mythology of prostitution: Advocacy research and public policy. *Sex Research and Social Policy, 7,* 15–29.

Weitzer, R. (2012). *Legalizing Prostitution: From illicit vice to lawful business.* New York University Press.

Weller, C. (2017, May 13). 11 countries that desperately want people to have more sex. *Business Insider.* Available: from: http://www.businessinsider.com/countries-that-want-people-to-have-more-sex-2017-5 (Last visited: 12/29/2017).

Wells, B. (1986). Predictors of female nocturnal orgasm. *Journal of Sex Research, 23,* 421–427.

Wells, H. B. (1980). *Being lucky.* Indiana University Press.

Wells, T., Baguley, T., Sergeant, M., & Dunn, A. (2013). Perceptions of human attractiveness comprising face and voice cues. *Archives of Sexual Behavior, 42,* 805–811.

West, S. L., Vinikoor, L. C., & Zolnoun, D. (2004). A systematic review of the literature on female sexual dysfunction prevalence and predictors. *Annual Review of Sex Research, 15,* 40–172.

Westrom, L., Joesoef, R., Reynolds, G., & Hagdu, A. (1992). Pelvic inflammatory disease and infertility. *Sexually Transmitted Diseases, 19,* 1850192.

"What happens when people mix alcohol and sex?" (2020). *Medical News Today.* Available: https://www.medicalnewstoday.com/articles/alcohol-and-sex (Last visited 9/20/20).

What is considered child sexual abuse? (2014). StopItNow. Available: http://.stopitnow.org/warning_signs_csa_defintion (Last visited 10/8/14).

"What is PMS?" (2019). WebMD. Available: https://www.webmd.com/women/pms/what-is-pms#1 (Last visited 1/30/20).

Wheeler, J., Newring, K. A. B., & Draper, C. (2008). Transvestic fetishism: Psychopathology and theory. In D. R. Laws & W. T. O'Donohue (Eds.), *Sexual deviance: Theory, assessment, and treatment* (2nd ed.). Guilford Press.

When yes means yes. (2014, September 9). *New York Times,* p. A26.

Whipple, B. (2002). Review of Milan Zaviacic's book: The human female prostate: From vestigial Skene paraurethral glands and ducts to woman's functional prostate. *Archives of Sexual Behavior, 31,* 457–458.

Whipple, B., & Komisaruk, B. (1999). Beyond the G spot: Recent research on female sexuality. *Psychiatric Annals, 29,* 34–37.

Whipple, B., Knowles, J., & Davis, J. (2007). The health benefits of sexual expression. In M. S. Tepper & A. F. Owens (Eds.), *Sexual health: Vol. 1. Psychological foundations.* Praeger.

Whipple, B., Ogden, G., & Komisaruk, B. R. (1992). Physiological correlates of imagery-induced orgasm in women. *Archives of Sexual Behavior, 21*(2), 121–133.

Whyte, S., Brooks, R. C., & Torgler, B. D. (2018). Man, woman, "other": Factors associated with nonbinary gender identification. *Archives of Sexual Behavior, 47,* 2397–2406.

Widdice, L. E., Bernstein, D. J., Leonard, A. C., Marsolo, K. A., & Kahn, J. A. (2011). Adherence to the HPV vaccine dosing intervals and factors associated with completion of 3 doses. *Pediatrics, 127,* 77–84.

Widman, L., Choukas-Bradley, S., Helms, S. W., Golin, C. E., & Prinstein, M. J. (2014). Sexual communication between early adolescents and their dating partners, parents, and best friends. *Journal of Sex Research, 51*(7), 731–741.

Widom, C. S., & Kuhns, J. B. (1996). Childhood victimization and subsequent risk for promiscuity, prostitution, and teenage pregnancy: A prospective study. *American Journal of Public Health, 86*(11), 1607–1612.

Wiebe, E., & Just, A. (2019). How cannabis alters sexual experiences: A survey of men and women. *Journal of Sexual Medicine, 16,* 1758–1762.

Wiederman, M. W. (1999). Volunteer bias in sexuality research using college student participation. *Journal of Sex Research, 36,* 59–66.

Wiederman, M. W. (2005). The gendered nature of sexual scripts. *The Family Journal, 13,* 496–502.

Williams Institute. (2018.12). How many same-sex couples in the US are raising children? Available: https://williamsinstitute.law.ucla.edu/publications/same-sex-parents-us/ (Last visited 8/27/20).

Williams Institute. (2020). LGBT people and housing affordability, discrimination, and homelessness. Available: https://williamsinstitute.law.ucla.edu/publications/lgbt-housing-instability/ (Last visited 4/27/20).

Williams, C. J., & Weinberg, M. S. (2003). Zoophilia in men: A study of sexual interest in animals. *Archives of Sexual Behavior, 32,* 523–535.

Willis, M., & Jozkowski, K. N. (2018). Using smartphones to collect daily sexual behavior data from college students. *Journal of American College Health, 66,* 529–532.

Wilson, D. P., Regan, D. G., Heymer, K. J., Jin, F., et al. (2010). Serosorting may increase the risk of HIV acquisition among men who have sex with men. *Sexually Transmitted Diseases, 37,* 13–17.

Wing, S. E., Larson, T. V., Hudda, N., Boonyarattaphan, S., Fruin, S., & Ritz, B. (2020). Preterm birth among infants exposed to *in Utero* Ultrafine particles from aircraft emissions. *Environmental Health Perspectives, 128*(4). Available: https://ehp.niehs.nih.gov/doi/10.1289/EHP5732 (Last visited 8/18/20).

Wingood, G. M., DiClemente, R. J., Bernhardt, J. M., Harrington, K., Davies, S. L., Robillard, A., et al. (2002). A prospective study of exposure to rap music videos and African American female adolescents' health. *American Journal of Public Health, 93,* 437–439.

Wisch, R. (2019). Table of state animal sexual assault laws. *Animal Legal and Historical Center.* Available: https://www.animallaw.info/topic/table-state-animal-sexual-assault-laws (Last visited: 5/15/20).

Wisely, K. (2019). New study shows 50% of men act differently because of #Metoo era. *WishTV.com* Available: https://www.wishtv.com/fuel/

new-study-shows-50-of-men-act-differently-because-of-metoo-era/. (Last visited: 1/9/2021).

Witchel, S. F. (2019). Disorders of sex development. *Best Practice & Research Clinical Obstetrics & Gynaecolorgy,* 48, 90–102. Available: https://www.ncbi.nlm.nih.gov/pmc/articles/PMC5866176/ (Last visited 2/28/20).

Witte, S. S., El-Bassel, N., Gilbert, L., Wu, E., & Chang, M. (2010). Lack of awareness of partner STD risk among heterosexual couples. *Perspectives on Sexual and Reproductive Health,* 42, 49–55.

Wlodarski, R., & Dunbar, R. I. M. (2013). Examining the possible functions of kissing in romantic relationships. *Archives of Sexual Behavior,* 42(8), 1415–1423.

Wolf, R. (2014b, December 29, 2014). Heroine of gay-marriage movement feels pride in progress. *Indianapolis Star,* p. 4B.

Wolf, R., & Heath, B. (2015a, June 28, 2015). History made in 33 pages. *USA Today,* pp. B1, B3.

Wolf, R., & Heath, B. (2015b, June 27, 2015). Marriage for all. *USA Today,* p. B1.

Wolff, M., Wells, B., & Ventura-DiPersia, C. (2016). Measuring sexual orientation: A review and critique of U.S. data collection efforts and implications for health policy. *Journal of Sex Research,* 54(4–5), 507–531.

Womenshealth.gov. (2019). Infertility. Available: https://www.womenshealth.gov/a-z-topics/infertility (Last visited 8/21/20).

Wood, J. R., Milhausen, R. R., & Jeffrey, N. K. (2014). Why have sex? Reasons for having sex among lesbian, bisexual, queer, and questioning women in romantic relationships. *Canadian Journal of Human Sexuality,* 23, 75–88.

Working Group for a New View of Women's Sexual Problems. (2001). A new view of women's sexual problems. In E. Kaschak & L. Tiefer (Eds.), *A new view of women's sexual problems.* Haworth Press.

World Economic Forum. (2019). These 10 countries are closest to achieving gender equality. Available: https://www.weforum.org/agenda/2019/12/gender-gap-equality-women-parity-countries/ (Last visited 5/27/20).

World Health Organization (WHO). (2006). Defining sexual health: Report of a technical consultation on sexual health 28-31 January, 2002. Available: https://www.who.int/reproductivehealth/publications/sexual_health/defining_sh/en/ (Last visited 4/21/20).

World Health Organization. (2015). Gender. Fact Sheet No. 403. Available: http://www.who.int/mediacentre/factsheets/fs403/en/ (Last visited 5/26/17).

World Health Organization. (2017). Female genital mutilation. Available: http://www.who.int/mediacentre/factsheets/fs241/en/ (Last visited 6/10/17).

World Health Organization. (2017.12). 10 facts on breastfeeding. Available: https://www.who.int/features/factfiles/breastfeeding/en/ (Last visited 9/1/20).

World Health Organization. (2018). *International Classification of Diseases for Mortality and Morbidity Statistics, Eleventh Revision (ICD-11.* Available: https://www.who.int/classifications/icd/en/ (Last visited 6/20/20).

World Health Organization. (2018.3). Female genital mutilation. Available: https://www.who.int/news-room/fact-sheets/detail/female-genital-mutilation (Last visited 2/3/20).

World Health Organization. (2019). Sexually transmitted infections (STIs). Available: https://www.who.int/news-room/fact-sheets/detail/sexually-transmitted-infections-(stis) (Last visited 9/3/20).

World Health Organization. (2020). Gender and genetics. Available: https://www.who.int/genomics/gender/en/index1.html (Last visited 5/18/20).

World Professional Association for Transgender Health. (2012). Version 7. Standards of care for the health of transsexual, transgender, and gender nonconforming people. Available: https://s3.amazonaws.com/amo_hub_content/Association140/files/Standards%20of%20Care%20V7%20-%202011%20WPATH%20(2)(1).pdf (Last visited 12/7/17).

Wortman, L., & van den Brink, F. (2012). Body image and female sexual functioning and behavior: A review. *Journal of Sex Research,* 49(2), 184–211.

Wu, C., Zang, J., Gao, Y., Tan, A., Yang, X., Lu, Z., et al. (2012). The association of smoking and erectile dysfunction: Results from the Fangchenggang Area Male Health and Examination Survey (FAMHES). *Journal of Andrology,* 33, 59–65.

Wyatt, G. E., Williams, J. K., & Myers, H. F. (2008). African-American sexuality and HIV/AIDS: Recommendations for future research. *Journal of the National American Medical Association,* 100, 50–51.

Yarber, W. L. (1992). While we stood by . . . the limiting of sexual information to our youth. *Journal of Health Education,* 23, 326–335.

Yarber, W. L., & Sayad, B. W. (2010). Sexuality education for youth in the United States: Conflict, content, research and recommendations. *Kwartalnik Pedagogiczny,* 2(216), 147–164.

Yarber, W. L., Crosby, R. A., & Sanders, S. A. (2000). Understudied HIV/STD risk behaviors among a sample of rural South Carolina women: A descriptive pilot study. *Health Education Monograph Series,* 18, 1–5.

Yarber, W. L., Graham, C. A., Sanders, S. A., Crosby, R. A., Butler, S. M., & Hartzell, R. M. (2007). "Do you know what you're doing?" College students' experiences with male condoms. *American Journal of Health Education,* 38, 322–331.

Yarber, W. L., Milhausen, R. R., Beavers, K. A., Ryan, R., Sullivan, M. J., Vanterpool, K. B., et al. (2018). A pilot test of a self-guided, home-based intervention to improve condom-related sexual experiences, attitudes, and behaviors among young women. *Journal of American College Health,* 66, 421–428.

Yarber, W. L., Milhausen, R. R., Crosby, R. A., & Torabi, M. R. (2005). Public opinion about condoms for HIV and STD prevention: A midwestern telephone survey. *Perspectives on Sexual and Reproductive Health,* 37(3), 148–154.

Yarber, W. L., Sanders, S. A., Graham, C. A., Crosby, R. A., & Milhausen, R. R. (2007). Public opinion about what constitutes "having sex": A state-wide telephone survey in Indiana. Paper presented at the annual meeting of The Society for the Scientific Study of Sexuality, Indianapolis, IN.

Yarber, W. L., Torabi, M. R., & Veenker, H. C. (1989). Development of a three-component sexually transmitted diseases attitude scale. *Journal of Sex Education and Therapy,* 15, 36–49.

Yarber, W. L., Vanterpool, K., Merritt, B., & Kavaya, S. (2019). Partner responses to a partner's refusal to use male condoms (unpublished raw data).

Yeater, E. A., Miller, G., Rinehart, J. Kl., & Nason. E. (2012). Trauma and sex surveys meet minimal risk standards: Implications for institutional review boards. *Psychological Science,* 23, 780–787.

YouGov. (2017). YouGov NY, LBG 2017. Available: https://d25d2506sfb94s.cloudfront.net/cumulus_uploads/document/63uuj3b6pt/LGBTQ%20Results%202017.pdf (Last visited 4/27/20).

Young, A. (2019, November 14). Hospitals know how to protect mothers. They just aren't doing it. *USA Today.* Available: https://www.usatoday.com/in-depth/news/investigations/deadly-deliveries/2018/07/26/maternal-mortality-rates-preeclampsia-postpartum-hemorrhage-safety/546889002/ (Last visited 8/15/20).

Younger, J., Aron, A., Parke, S., Chatterjee, N., & Mackey, S. (2010). Viewing pictures of a romantic partner reduces experimental pain: Involvement of neural reward systems. *PloS One.* Available: http://

www.plosone.org/article/info%3Adoi%2F10.1371%2Fjournal.pone
.0013309 (Last visited 3/22/11).

Yuan, T., Fitzpatrick, T., Ko, N., Cai, Y., Chen, Y., Zhao, J., Li, L., Xu, J., Gu, J., Li, J., Hao, C., Yang, Z., Cai, W., Cheng, C. Y., Zhenzhou, L., Zhang, K., Wu, G., Meng, X., Grulich, A. E., Hao, Y., & Zou, H. (2019). Circumcision to prevent HIV and other sexually transmitted infections in men who have sex with me: A systematic review and meta-analysis of global data. *The Lancet,* 7, e436–4447.

Zamboni, B. D. (2019). A qualitative exploration of adult baby/diaper lover behavior from an online community sample. *Journal of Sex Research,* 56, 191–202.

Zattoni, F., Gul, M., Soligo, M., Morlacco, A., Motterle, G., Collavino, J., Barneschi, A. C., Moschini, M., & Dal Moro, F. (2020). The impact of COVID-19 pandemic on pornography habits: A global analysis of Google Trends. *Sexual Medicine Journal.* https://doi.org/10.1038/s41443-020-00380.

Zequi, S. C., Guimaraes, G. C., da Fonseca, F. P., de Matheus, W. E., Reis, J. C., da Aita, F. P., Glina, S., Fanni, V. S., Perez, L. O., Guidoni, L. R., Ortiz, V., Nogueira, L., Rocha, L., Cuck, G., de Costa, W., Moniz, R. R., Dantas, Jr, H., Soares, F. A., & Lopes, A. (2012). Sex with animals (SWA): Behavioral characteristics and possible association with penile cancer. *Journal of Sexual Medicine,* 9, 1860–1867.

Zhang, T., Sidorchuk, A., Sevilla-Cermeno, L., Vilaplana-Perez, A., Chang, Z., Larsson, H., Mataix-Cols, D., & Fernandez de la Cruz, L. (2019). Association of cesarean delivery with risk of neurodevelopmental and psychiatric disorders in the offspring: A systematic review and meta-analysis. *JAMA Network Open,* 2(80). Available: https://jamanetwork.com/journals/jamanetworkopen/fullarticle/2749054 (Last visited 8/31/20).

Zilbergeld, B. (1992). *The new male sexuality.* Bantam Books.

Zilbergeld, B. (1999). *Male sexuality* (Rev. ed.). Little, Brown.

Zinzow, H. M., & Thompson, M. (2015). A longitudinal study of risk factors for repeated sexual coercion and assault in U.S. college men. *Archives of Sexual Behavior,* 44, 213–222.

Zurbriggen E., Ramsey, L., & Jaworski, B. (2011). Self- and partner-objectification in romantic relationships: Associations with media consumption and relationship satisfaction. *Sex Roles,* 64, 449–462.

Zurbriggen, E. L., & Yost, M. R. (2004). Power, desire, and pleasure in sexual fantasies. *Journal of Sex Research,* 41, 288–300.

2020 Census: LGBTQ+. (2020). Available: https://www.census.gov/newsroom/press-kits/2020/2020-census-lgbtq.html (Last visited 4/27/20).

Name Index

Note: Page references followed by italicized "*f*" or "*t*" refer to figures or tables, respectively.

Bui, Q., 357
Buisson, O., 67, 420
Bull, S., 492
Bullough, V. L., 19, 47, 52, 59
Bulmer, M., 172, 201
Burghardt, J., 410, 417
Burkhill, S., 41
Burkley, M., 248
Burri, A., 420
Busby, D. M., 577
Buss, D. M., 86, 167, 209, 228, 240, 242, 244,
    247–249, 249t, 250t, 261, 294, 296, 416
Bussey, K., 138
Bustos, M., 351
Butchart, A., 476
Butler, J., 114
Butler, S. M., 39, 65, 242, 503
Butler, W. T., 451, 453, 460
Butterworth, M., 39
Buxbaum, M., 192
Byard, R. W., 304
Byers, E. S., 39, 69, 221, 222, 234, 263, 267,
    274, 379
Byers, S. A., 255, 272
Byne, W., 284
Byrd, J., Jr., 543
Byrd-Craven, J., 247
Byrne, D., 251

Cabral, M. A., 311
Cacioppo, S., 234
Cage, J., 120
Cai, W., 461
Cai, Y., 461
Calabrese, S. K., 34, 40
Calderone, M. S., 140
Caliskan, E., 67
Calkins, C., 295
Call, V., 267
Callander, D., 597
Calman, M., 299
Calzo, J. P., 148
Cammann, V. L., 208
Campbell, L., 213, 575, 577, 583, 587–589
Campbell, S. M., 509
Campbell, W. K., 249
Campian, E. C., 382
Campos-Outcalt, D., 453
Campus Technical Assistance and Resource
    Project, 556
Camus, A., 220, 491
Cantor, D., 531–534, 535f, 536, 537f, 539, 550,
    550f, 551, 551f, 552, 556
Cao, S., 426
Capistrant, B. D., 397
Caplan, A. L., 472
Capote, T., 140
Capshew, J. H., 52
Carael, M., 592
Carbone, L., 352
Cardoso, D., 301
Carey, B., 283
Caritis, S., 351
Carlos-Henderson, J., 475
Carmassi, C., 208
Carnaghi, M., 387
Carnegie Mellon University, 267
Carnes, P., 286
Caron, C., 222
Caron, S. L., 292, 427
Carpentier, J., 253, 287–291, 288f, 289f, 294–300
Carr, L. W., 84
Carrera, M., 160
Carrere, S., 222, 225

Carrier, S., 233
Carroll, A. E.., 90
Carroll, J. L., 297, 299
Carroll, M. D., 357
Carter, C. S., 221, 236
Carter, D., 378
Carter, J. W., 453, 455
Carter, M., 518
Casey, B. R., 476
Casey, E., 120, 242, 252
Cassell, C., 244, 416, 578
Castleman, M., 255, 415, 416, 421, 427, 437, 438,
    440, 442, 443, 448, 579, 582
Catalano, R. F., 454
Catania, J. A., 40, 222
Cate, R. M., 180
Catena-Dell'Osso, M., 208
Cater, S. M., 30
Cates, J. R., 486
Cates, W., 314, 315, 452
Catlett, J., 428
Catt, C. C., 599
Cecil, H., 41
Ceder, I., 52
Center, B., 286
Center of Excellence for Transgender Health, 405
Centers for Disease Control and Prevention, 59, 86,
    90, 98, 349, 353–358, 361, 361t, 363, 371,
    387, 390, 393, 405, 451–453, 452f–454f,
    457, 460, 461, 463, 465–470, 465f–470f,
    473–482, 475f, 485, 488, 490, 491,
    495–500, 497f–499f, 498, 502–508, 507f,
    510–517, 511f, 512f, 515f–517f, 522, 524,
    525, 525t, 529, 547, 566, 599
Centers for Disease Control and Prevention
    Reproductive Health Information
    Source, 342
Centers for Disease Prevention, 149t, 150f
Cesareanrates.org, 369
Cespedes, C., 129
Champion, A. R., 14
Chandra, A., 148
Chandrasekaran, S., 317
Chang, J., 311
Chang, M., 459, 518
Chang, Z., 369
Chapman, E. L., 505
Chariyalertak, C., 456
Charlton, B. M., 38
Charmaraman, L., 52
Charnigo, R., 30
Chatterjee, N., 234
Chavarro, J. E., 362
Chaves, B., 386
Chen, A., 228
Chen, J., 533, 546, 547f, 548, 549, 555, 563, 566
Chen, R. Y., 599
Chen, Y., 461
Cheng, C. Y., 461
Cheng, G. H.-L., 15
Cherkas, L. F., 420
Chesson, H. W., 451, 463
Chester, P., 594
Chey, T., 564
Chiaruzzi, M., 81
Chibnall, S., 531–534, 535f, 536, 537f, 550, 550f,
    551, 551f, 552, 556
Chief Scientific Advisor to Match, 185
Child Trends, 156, 314
Children of the Night, 605
Childress, A. R., 208
Chio, M. T. W., 475
Chiodo, M. V., 127
Chiu, H., 577

Chivers, M., 43
Chivers, M. L., 36, 233
Choi, S., 474
Choiriyyah, I., 312
Choukas-Bradley, S., 220
Chrisler, J. C., 342
Christensen, K. S., 455
Christian, J. C., 448
Christmann, C., 69
Christopher & Dana Reeve Foundation, 385
CIA World Factbook, 353
Cipres, D., 518, 519f
Citro, R., 208
Clark, A. E., 572
Clark, C. M., 541
Clark, D. B., 456
Clark, H. A., 477
Clark, K., 588
Clark, S. K., 295, 298, 476
Clark, T. D., 52
Clark, V., 422
Clarke, L., 154
Clark-Huckstep, A., 47, 51, 59
Claxton, S. E., 456
Clayton, A. H., 208
Clayton, H. B., 456
Cleveland Clinic, 387, 448
Clifton, S., 41
Clinton, B., 262, 538
Cobbina, J. E., 590, 593
Coburn, K., 539
Cocker, C., 365
Coe, D., 14
Coffelt, T. A., 222
Cohen, C. R., 477
Cohen, E., 279
Cohen, J. N., 274, 278
Colagiovanni, V., 451
Coleman, E., 286, 424
Coleman, L. M., 30
Collado, A., 459
Collavino, J., 578
Collazo, E., 39, 263
Collins, N. L., 206
Collins, P., 275
Collins, T., 476
Comfort, Alex, 240
Commons, M. L., 297
Communications Decency Act, 15
Conley, T. D., 492
Connell, J., 114, 387
Conradi, C., 505
Conron, K. L., 39
Constantinus Africanus, 243
Contraception Atlas, 342
Cook, M., 281
Cook, P. W., 281, 572
Cook, R. L., 456
Cooke, B., 568
Cooley, M., 295
Coontz, S., 121, 215
Cooper, M. L., 30, 213
Cooper, T., 251
Copas, A., 41
Copas, A. J., 154
Copeland, J., 324
Copen, C., 148
Copen, C. E., 515
Coppens, V., 300
Corinna, H., 163
Corliss, H. L., 38
Cornell University, 168, 171
Corona, G., 320
Corsini-Munt, S., 424

Subject Index

casual sex. See also "hooking up"
    and evolutionary mating perspectives, 247–250, 249t, 250t
caudate nucleus, 208
Caya (diaphragm), 328, 328f
CD4 cells
    function of, 493
    HIV infection of, 493, 493f, 494f
CD4 count, 491, 494
celibacy, 200–201
censorship, 6, 215, 586–590, 587f
Census Bureau, 170
Center of Excellence for Transgender Health, 405
Centers for Disease Control and Prevention (CDC), 59, 488
    on bacterial vaginosis, 477
    on chlamydia, 463, 467
    on condoms, 457
    on hepatitis, 477
    on HIV/AIDS, 490, 498–501, 500t, 504–506, 522, 523, 529
    on HPV, 474–476
    on male circumcision, 90
    on pregnancy and birth, 375
    on sexuality education, 514
    on sexual violence, 547
    on stalking, 533
    on STI notification, 451, 457, 485
    Youth Risk Behavior Survey of, 53–54, 150t
Centers for Disease Control and Prevention Reproductive Health Information Source, 342
Centers for Disease Control & Prevention, 405
cerebral palsy, 385
cervical cancer, 393–394, 393f
    detection and diagnosis of, 393–394, 393f
    HIV and, 491
    incidence of, 393
    risk factors for, 393, 474
    treatment of, 394
    vaccines against, 393, 460, 474, 475, 484, 487
cervical cap
    as contraception, 329, 329f
    as menstrual cup, 81
cervical dysplasia, 393–394, 393f
cervical intraepithelial neoplasia (CIN), 393–394, 491
cervical mucus method, 332–333
cervicitis, 481
cervix, 64
    anatomy of, 68–70
    in labor and delivery, 366
    mucous secretions of, 70, 79
    in pregnancy, 346f, 350
    self-examination of, 70
cesarean section, 369, 506
chancre, 464t, 470, 470f
chancroid, 451, 457, 479, 487
channeling, in gender-role learning, 115
cheating. See extrarelational sex
chickenhawks, 597
chickens, 597
child abuse prevention (CAP) programs, 571
childbearing decisions, 166
childbirth. See birth
"childbirth market," 367–372
child-free, 344
childhood/children
    curiosity and sex play in, 139–140, 140t
    effects of divorce on, 184
    expression of affection in, 142
    family context of, 141–142
    gender dysphoria in, 125
    gender identity development in, 109–110
    gender-role learning in, 113–118

HIV/AIDS in, 505–506, 514, 514f, 515
    masturbation in, 140–141
    protection from sexually explicit material in, 589–590
    psychosexual development of, 45
    with same-sex parents, 182
    sex trafficking of, 591
    sexual assault of, 549
    sexual interest in (See pedophilia)
    sexuality education for (See sexuality education)
    sexuality in, 138–142, 139f
    in sexually explicit material, 299, 586, 589–590
    as sex workers, 591, 593
    transgender, 124–125
    victimization in, 593
child marriage, 34f
child molestation, 298–299
Child Obscenity and Pornography Prevention Act, 589
Child Online Protection Act (COPA), 590
child pornography, 299, 586, 589
children
    outcomes of divorce on, 184
Children of the Night, 605
child sex trafficking, 591
child sexual abuse, 566–570
    contact or touching in, 566
    definition of, 566
    pedophilia and, 298–299 (See also pedophilia)
    prevention of, 569–570
    repressed memories of, 568
    and sex work, 593
    signs of, 567
    treatment for survivors of, 569
chlamydia, 465–467
    causative agent of, 465
    in men, 465t
    prevention of, 457
    race/ethnicity and, 465–467
    rates of, 465–467, 465f
    reporting of, 451, 451f, 453f, 465
    symptoms of, 465–466, 465t
    time from exposure to occurrence, 464t, 465t
    transmission of, 464t
    treatment of, 464t, 465t
    untreated, consequences of, 464t, 466
    in women, 464t, 466
Chlamydia trachomatis, 464t, 465
chorion, 346, 346f
chorionic villus sampling (CVS), 359–360, 359f
"Christina" (methamphetamine), 383
chromosome(s)
    release and combination of, 345–346
    sex, 99, 106
chromosome abnormalities, 129
chronic illness, 386–387
chronic lung disease, sexuality and, 387
chronic obstructive pulmonary disease (COPD), 387
Cialis, 397, 441, 441f
cigarettes. See smoking
cilia, 73, 85
CIN. See cervical intraepithelial neoplasia
circumcision
    male, 89, 96t
        debate over, 92
        and HIV/AIDS risk, 89, 90, 98, 502
        as initiation rite, 110
        procedure of, 89
        and sexually transmitted infections, 89, 98, 461, 462
cisgender, 5, 107
Civil Rights Act of 1964, 532
"the clap," 467. See also gonorrhea
cleanups, 599

Cleveland Clinic, 448
climacteric
    female (menopause), 192
    male (andropause), 192
clinical breast exam, 390, 391t
clinically normal behavior, 21
clinical research
    definition of, 36
    emphasis on pathological behavior in, 36
clitoral hood, 63, 63f, 70
clitoris
    anatomy of, 62–64
    construction of, in gender confirmation surgery, 125
    irritation or infection of, 426
    removal of, 36
    self-examination of, 70
    self-stimulation scale, 239
    sexual response of, 49, 63
    stimulation of, 49, 261, 269, 269f, 272, 418, 437
CMV (cytomegalovirus), 479
cocaine, 383, 504, 594
coercion, 548. See also sexual coercion
coercive paraphilia, 285, 293, 301
cognitive-behavioral therapy, 437–440
    couples approach in, 437
    for delayed ejaculation, 440
    for early ejaculation, 437–438, 438f
    for erectile disorder, 437–438
    for female orgasmic disorder, 437
    sensate focus in, 437, 438f
cognitive development theory, 114
cognitive social learning theory, 113–114
cohabitation, 178–179
    acceptance of, 177
    widespread acceptance of, 177
coitus, 274. See also sexual intercourse
coitus interruptus. See withdrawal, as contraception
college environment, 173, 175
college, sexual harassment in, 536–537
college students
    alcohol use by, 381
    condom-use mistakes of, 503
    evaluating STI status of partner, 459
    having sex, 167–168
    hooking up among, 174–177, 199
    kissing in, 270
    media influence on, 7
    oral sex in, 271–272
    sexual harassment of, 532–533, 535f, 537–538, 537f
    sexually explicit material viewed by, 576, 578, 583
    sexual orientation of, 172
    sexual turn-ons and turn-offs of, 436
    sexual violence against, 549–550, 550f, 559–560, 563f
    social setting of, 173f
    study of sexuality, 2–3
    survey research on, 54–55, 54f
    voyeurism in, 294
colostrum, 372
colposcopy, 394
combination antiretroviral therapy, 525
coming out
    in adolescence, 148–149
    definition of, 36
    degrees of, 171
    in early adulthood, 171
    media portrayals of, 11
    sampling and research on, 36
commercial sex act, 591
commitment
    in intimate love, 213
    and sexual intimacy, 153
    in triangular theory of love, 202–206, 202f

dental dams, 457
dependent variables, 43
Depo-Provera (DMPA), 320–321
  advantages of, 320
  disadvantages of, 320–321
  effectiveness of, 320
  prevalence of use, 310*f*
depression
  antepartum, 353
  child sexual abuse and, 568
  and erection difficulties, 418, 438
  postpartum, 372–373
  rape and, 563
  sexual dysfunction in, 411, 416
derogatory language, 148
DES (diethylstilbestrol), 390
descriptive research, 36
desire
  decline of, 428, 434
  developing bridges to, 433
  difficulty in studying, 250
  disorders of, 416–419
  Ellis on, 46
  erotophilia and, 251
  erotophobia and, 251
  female
    Ellis on, 46
    in established health principles, 89
    in established relationships, 242–243
    excessive, 285
    factors of, 112, 250–251
    medical enhancement of, 443, 443*f*
    and sexual variety, 247
    Finnish study of, 416, 416*f*, 417*f*
    fluidity in, 112
  male
    Ellis on, 46
    in established relationships, 89, 242–243
    excessive, 287
    factors of, 240, 242, 250–251
    inhibition of, 242–243
    process, 240
    and sexual variety, 247
  normal variance in, 416
  paraphilic, 287–289, 289*f*
  partners with different levels of, 415
  sexual orientation and, 250
  spontaneous, 433
development
  psychosexual, 45
  sex, disorders of (*See* disorders of sex development)
developmental disabilities, 388, 388*f*
Developmental Disabilities Assistance and Bill of
    Rights Act of 2000, 389
"deviant" sexual behavior, 24, 283
devices, to curb masturbation, 253, 253*f*
DHEA. *See* dehydroepiandrosterone
DHT. *See* dihydrotestosterone
diabetes mellitus, 387, 426
*Diagnostic and Statistical Manual of Mental
    Disorders (DSM)*
  on erectile disorder, 418
  on exhibitionism, 295
  on frotteurism, 297–298
  on gender dysphoria, 128
  on masochism, 303
  on paraphilia, 283–285
  on pedophilia, 298–299
  porn addiction missing from, 584
  on premenstrual dysmorphic disorder, 80
  on sadism, 302
  on sexual function difficulties, 408, 409, 409*t*
  on sexual pain disorders, 423–424
  on substance/medication-induced sexual
    dysfunction, 425

on transvestism, 291–292
  voyeurism in, 293–295
  on zoophilia, 293
diaphragm, 328, 328*f*
  advantages of, 328
  effectiveness of, 315*t*, 328
  as menstrual cup, 82
  possible problems with, 328
diary, sexual, 41
diethylstilbestrol (DES), 390
dieting, excessive, 378
digital media
  portrayals of sexuality in, 8–9
  time engaged with, 8, 9*f*
digital rectal exam (DRE), 397, 399
dihydrotestosterone, 132
dilation and evacuation (D&E), 337
dilation of cervix, 366
dildos, 431, 433*f*, 504
disability
  developmental, 388, 388*f*
  image of people with, 385, 385*f*
  myths about, 384
  physical, 385–386
  resources on, 405
  sexuality and, 384–389, 385*f*, 388*f*
  sexual rights of people with, 388–389
discipline, in BDSM, 301
Discovering Your Couple Sexual Style (McCarthy
    and McCarthy), 265–268
discrimination
  laws against, 180, 544–545, 545*f*
  against LGBTQ people, 149, 171, 541–544
  against people with HIV/AIDS, 492
  sexually explicit material and, 585
  stereotyping and, 33
  against transgender people, 132–133
  against women (*See* sexism)
  workplace, 537–539
disinhibition, 381
disorders of sex development (DSD),
    5, 128–129
  5-alpha reductase deficiency, 132
  androgen insensitivity syndrome, 130
  congenital adrenal hyperplasia, 130*t*, 135–136
  definition of, 128
  hypospadias, 130*t*, 132
  Klinefelter syndrome, 130–132, 130*t*, 131*f*
  resources on, 135–136
  Turner syndrome, 129–130, 130*t*
divorce, 184
  cohabitation after, 178–179
  consequences of, 184
  dating after, 184
  outcomes, on children, 184
  single parenting after, 184, 186
divorced people
  greater numbers of, 177
DMPA. *See* Depo-Provera
DOMA. *See* Defense of Marriage Act
domestic partnership, 179
dominatrix, 301
dopamine, 181, 208
double standard, 9, 17, 176
douching, 461
doulas, 372
Down syndrome, 357, 357*t*, 359, 385
drag queens, 292, 292*f*
dream analysis, 45
dreams, sexual, 253–256
dress and gender, 105
drinks, drugs placed in, 553
"the drip," 467. *See also* gonorrhea
Drug-Induced Rape Preventing and Punishment
    Act, 553

drug use
  in aftermath of sexual violence, 563
  child sexual abuse and, 568
  and fetal development, 354–355
  and HIV/AIDS, 384, 456, 492, 497*f*, 500*t*,
    504–505, 510–512, 512*f*, 515, 515*f*, 516,
    521, 523, 528, 599
  and sexual assault, 552
  and sexual function difficulties, 426
  and sexuality, 383–384, 383*f*
  and sexually transmitted infections, 453, 456
  and sex work, 594, 599, 600
"dry humping," 269, 269*f*
"dry orgasm," 243
DSD. *See* disorders of sex development
DSM-5, 283. *See also Diagnostic and Statistical
    Manual of Mental Disorders*
"dumped," 213
dysmenorrhea, 80–81
dyspareunia, 373, 423

"E" (drug), 553
early adulthood
  cohabitation in, 177, 179
  developmental concerns in, 165–166
  establishing sexual orientation in, 166, 168–173
  fertility/childbearing decisions in, 166
  love and intimacy, 166
  safer sex practices in, 166
  sexuality in, 166–180
  sexual philosophy in, 166
  singlehood in, 173–178
East Africa, gender identity in, 110
"easy lay," 553
eating disorders, 378
EC. *See* emergency contraception
ecstasy (drug), 384, 425, 553
ectoparasitic infestations, 463, 465*t*, 479–480
ectopic pregnancy, 357–358
edema, 351, 358
EEOC. *See* Equal Employment Opportunity
    Commission
effacement, 366
egg freezing, 363
egocentric fallacy, 34
eHarmony.com, 181
ejaculate, female, 68
ejaculation
  definition of, 95
  delayed, 423, 440
  emission stage of, 240–241
  expulsion stage of, 241–242
  in fellatio, 273
  frequency of, and prostate cancer, 396
  involuntary, 421
  in male sex work, 597
  orgasm with and without, 243
  premature, 421, 439–440
  process of, 88, 91, 94, 95
  in puberty, 144
  retrograde, 243
  in sexually explicit material, 578
  sperm in, 95
  spinal cord injuries and, 385
ejaculatory duct, 94, 95, 96*t*
ejaculatory inevitability, 241
Electra complex, 45
Electronic Frontier Foundation, 26
Ella, 335
Elle, 7, 7*f*
Ellis, Havelock, 43, 45–46, 45*f*
embryo, 346
  development of, 346–349, 346*f*–348*f*
  implantation, 345*f*, 346
  sexual differentiation of, 61, 62*f*

sexual health, 98, 376–405
  cancer and, 389–399
  definition of, 377
  disability and, 384–389, 385f, 388f
  resources, 405
sexual identity
  in early adulthood, 171
  media influence on, 2
sexual intercourse, 274–277
  aging and, 187
  behaviors before and after, 248
  definition of, 274
  in extradyadic sex involvement, 211
  first, in adolescence, 151–155, 155f
  forced, in sexual assault, 547
  as "having sex," 262–264
  in hierarchy of sexual behaviors, 429
  HIV transmission in, 501, 515, 520
  male sexual scripts on, 119–120
  Masters and Johnson on, 49
  during menstruation, 82
  pain during, 424
  positions for, 274–277, 274f–278f
  during pregnancy, 352
  prevalence of, 258f, 260t
  research on, 39
  safe sex behavior for, 483
  in sexually explicit material, 578, 579
  significance of, 274
  survey findings on, 51, 54, 55f, 56, 262
sexual interests
  culture and, 15–17
  definition of, 15
  paraphilic, 284
sexuality
  in adolescence, 142–161
  body image and, 378–380
  cancer and, 389–399
  in childhood, 138–142, 139f
  chronic illness, 386–387
  communication about, 214–215
  COVID-19, 401–403
  culture and, 15–20
  disability and, 384–389, 385f, 388f
  drug use and, 383–384, 383f
  in early adulthood, 166–180
  education, 157, 159
  gender equality and, 199
  "having sex," defining, 152–153
  human development, 151
  in infancy, 138–142
  Internet and access to, 7
  in late adulthood, 186–193
  law and, 601–603
  love and, 199–201
  in marriage and established relationships,
    155, 199
  meanings of, 31
  media portrayals of, 3–15
  and menstrual cycle, 82
  in middle adulthood, 180–184
  physical environment and, 199
  social context of, 4
  societal norms and, 20–24
  societal views of, 2–3
  student study of, 2–3
  time lines of, 166
  unrealistic image of, in sexually explicit
    material, 579
Sexuality and Disability (website), 405
sexuality education, 157, 159
  abstinence-only, 52, 157, 159
  CDC on, 514
  history of, 17, 157
  insufficient, 514

moral judgment of, 52, 151
  SIECUS guidelines for, 160, 183
  WHO guidelines for, 160
Sexuality Information and Education Council of the
    United States (SIECUS), 17, 160, 183, 603
sexualization of girls, 7, 144
sexual liberation, 16, 151
sexually explicit magazines, 575–576
sexually explicit material (SEM), 574–590
  censorship and law on, 586–590, 587f
  child protection from, 589–590
  children in, 299, 586, 589–590
  college students and, 578, 583
  consumption of, 576–578, 576t
  definition of, 575
  and discrimination, 585
  effects of, 581–586, 588–589
  erotica versus pornography, 574–575
  female empowerment via, 588
  gay and lesbian, 581
  gender and arousal from, 582
  mainstream, 578
  money-sex relationship and, 574
  motivation for using, 578
  objectification in, 579
  pornography catering to, 575–576
  power in, 579
  research on, 587–589
  resources on, 605
  romantic couples using, 583–584
  and sex addiction, 584, 588
  and sexual expression, 582, 584
  terminology of, 575
  themes, content, and actors in, 578–581
  therapeutic use of, 582
  violence in, 575, 579, 584–585
sexually explicit media, 575
sexually explicit videos (SEV)
  availability of, 575–576
  consumption of, 76t, 576
  definition of, 575
  effects of, 581–586, 588–589
  mainstream, 578
  motivation for using, 578
  themes, content, and actors in, 578–581
  use in romantic couples, 583–584
sexually transmitted infections (STIs), 89, 98,
    278, 449–488
  age and, 453
  alcohol and, 380, 455, 456
  asymptomatic nature of, 461
  avoiding, 482–484
  behavioral factors in, 454–457, 460
  biological factors, 461, 463
  "biological sexism" and, 452
  communication about, 219, 459, 484
  concurrent sexual relationships and, 455
  condoms and
    inconsistent and incorrect use of, 456, 457
    role in prevention, 324, 327
  consequences of, 463
  definition of, 450
  drug use and risk of, 384, 453, 456
  early initiation of sexual activity and, 454
  ectoparasitic, 463, 465, 465t, 479–480
  epidemic of, 450–463
  erroneous perception of partner's status and,
    459, 460
  factors contributing to spread of, 453–463
  health care access and, 460
  high-risk sexual behavior and, 384, 456
  high-risk sexual partners and, 455–456
  HIV transmission with other STIs, 456, 457, 463,
    465–473, 479
  incidence of, 450, 451

lack of knowledge and concern about, 456–457
  male circumcision reducing risk of, 461–463
  in men, 452–453
  mother-to-child transmission of, 357, 466,
    470, 472
  poverty/marginalization and, 460
  in pregnancy, 357
  prevalence of, 450, 451
  prevention of, 482–484, 518–522
    barrier methods and, 324
    female condoms and, 457
    internal condoms and, 327
    male condoms and, 324, 457, 474, 482–485
    safer sex practices and, 166
    stigma of, 492
    strategies for, 518–522
  race/ethnicity and, 453, 453f, 454f, 465–467, 473
  recognizing symptoms of, 484
  reporting of, 451–452
  resources on, 487
  safer and unsafe sex practices and, 483
  secrecy/moral conflict and, 460
  selection of, 483
  sequential sexual relationships and, 454–455
  sexual coercion and, 456
  in sex workers, 599, 601
  social factors in, 460
  stigma of, 460
  substance abuse and, 456, 486
  testing for, 484–486
  treatment of, 464t–465t, 483–486
  viral, 450, 464t–464t, 475–476
  in women, 452–453
"sexual marathon," 384
sexual masochism, 285t, 288f, 289f, 299–301, 303
sexual minority, 113
Sexual Novelty Scale (SNS), 290
sexual orientation, 6, 17–20, 148–149
  in adolescence, 148–149
  coming out, 11, 36, 148, 171
  definition of, 17
  and desire, 250
  establishing, in adulthood, 166, 168–173
  fluidity in, 112
  "gay sheep" research and, 32
  gender and, 113
  Kinsey on, 31, 47–48, 48f
  Kinsey scale, 31
  models of, 168–170, 168f
  mostly straight, 171–172
  origins of, 140
  sex research on, 39–40
  and sexual frequency, 200, 264–265, 265f
  sexual revolution and, 16–17
  survey findings on, 53, 55
  and transvestism, 291, 292
  varied, prevalence of, 172
sexual pain disorders, 423–425
sexual partners. See also sexual behavior
    with others
  after sexual assault, 565
  with different levels of desire, 415
  excessive need to please, 427
  exclusive, 482
  getting STI treatment for, 485
  high-risk, 455–456
  HIV-positive, 501, 502, 506, 521, 523–527
  in masochism, 301, 303, 303f
  notification
    in HIV/AIDS, 525, 527
    in STIs, 452f
  perception of STI status of, 459, 460
  talking about past, 219, 459, 483
  what men want from, 433
  what women want from, 433

street-based sex workers, 594–595
street harassment, 539–540, 539f
street hustlers, 596, 597f
stress, 426–427
stud farms, 596
Studies in the Psychology of Sex (Ellis), 45, 586
styles of love, 201–202, 202f
subjectively normal behavior, 21
submission, 300–302
substance abuse
  in adolescents, 55
  in aftermath of sexual violence, 568
  child sexual abuse and, 569
  and fetal development, 354–355
  and HIV/AIDS, 384, 456, 497, 499,
    499f, 500, 500t, 504–505, 510, 512,
    512f, 599
  and risk-taking, 30
  and sexual assault, 551
  and sexual function difficulties, 425
  and sexuality, 383–384, 383f
  and sexually transmitted infections, 456, 486
  and sexual violence, 551
  and sex work, 593–594
substance/medication-induced sexual
    dysfunction, 425
sudden infant death syndrome (SIDS), 361
sugar daddy, 597
suicide
  child sexual abuse and, 568
  in transgender people, 132
The Sunday Times, 32
Supreme Court. *See* U.S. Supreme Court
surgical abortion, 336–337, 337f
surrogate motherhood, 364
survey research, 36–41
  contemporary, 50–57
  on dating, 185
  definition of, 36
  example of, 37
  Internet, 40, 41f
  limitations of, 40
  sexual diary in, 41
survivor of sexual assault/violence, 531–532
sweating, vaginal, 236
swinging, 212
symmetry, and sexual attractiveness, 244–245
symptothermal method, 331, 333
syphilis, 469–473
  causative agent of, 469
  latent, 472
  in men, 469
  primary (stage I), 470
  race and, 452f, 453, 471–472, 472f
  rates of, 470
  reducing risk of, 457, 474
  reporting of, 451, 452f
  secondary, 472
  in STIs, 451, 452f
  symptoms of, 464t–465t, 470, 472
  time from exposure to occurrence, 464t, 465t
  transmission of, 470
  treatment of, 471
  Tuskegee experiment on, 471–472
  untreated, 472
  in women, 467, 468
syringes
  and hepatitis B transmission, 476
  and HIV transmission, 384, 499, 499f, 500, 500t,
    504–505, 512f, 599

tadalafil (Cialis), 441, 441f
tampons, 65, 67, 81, 82, 82f, 399
tantric sex, 277, 278
taste, 269

T cell(s), 493
  function of, 493
  HIV infection of, 493–494, 493f, 494f
  types of, 493
T-cell count, 491, 494
TCF. *See* Testicular Cancer Foundation
teachers, as socializing agents, 115–116
teenage fathers, 157
teenage mothers, 156–157, 157f
teenage pregnancy, 155–157
  and birth rates, 155–157
  decline in, 151, 155
  race and ethnicity and, 155–156, 155f, 162
  rates of, 155f
  resources on, 162–163
  unintended, 309, 314, 314f
Teen Mom (television show), 9, 157f
Teen Pregnancy Prevention Program (TPPP), 159
telephone interviewing, computer-assisted, 40
telephone scatologia, 285t
telephone scatologica, 297
television. *See also* media
  gay men, lesbian women, and bisexual and
    transgender people on, 11
  gender stereotypes on, 117–118
  portrayals of sexuality on, 8–9
  sexually explicit material on, 575
  standards and practices for, 9
  time spent viewing, 8, 9f
tenting of vagina, 236
teratogens, 353
testes
  anatomy of, 93, 93f, 94, 94f, 96t
  functions of, 93
  homologous sex organ of, 101f
  removal of, 398
  undescended, 94
testicular cancer, 398
  detection of, 98, 398
  incidence of, 398
  risk factors for, 398
  treatment of, 98, 398
Testicular Cancer Foundation (TCF), 405
testicular self-examination, 398
testosterone
  aging and, 192
  in female sexual response, 235
  for gender dysphoria, 126
  male cycles of, 98–99
  in male physiology, 96, 97, 97t
  in male sexual response, 235
  and paraphilia, 304
  personality effects of, 97
  in puberty, 142
  in science of love, 208
testosterone deficiency, 97, 98, 131, 235, 441
testosterone replacement therapy, 235
testosterone therapy (TT), 97–98
tests
  removal of, 126
texting, 14
The Theory of Everything (film), 384f
therapy, sex. *See* sex therapy
third gender, 19, 123. *See also* transgender people
third sex, 44
third trimester of pregnancy, 351, 351f
13 Reasons Why (television show), 9
threats, 548
3D ultrasound, 360
time from exposure to occurrence, 523–524
time lines, of sexual and reproductive
    events, 166f
"Tina" (methamphetamine), 383
Tinder, 13, 176
Title IX, 553

Title VII of the Civil Rights Act of 1964, 532
Title X Family Planning Program, 98, 313
tobacco. *See* smoking
Today Sponge, 328
tongue-lashing, 302
"tossing salad," 277
touching
  in child sexual abuse, 570
  in communication, 217
  in sexual battery, 551
  in sexual harassment, 533, 535, 536
  in sexuality, 268–269, 269f
toxic shock syndrome (TSS), 81, 328, 329, 399
toys, sex, 431–432, 500t, 504
traditional gender roles, 119–120, 267–268
traditional sexual style, 267–268
trafficking, sex, 590, 591
Trafficking Victims Protection Act (TVPA), 591
Trans Awareness Project, 136
transgender
  definition of, 6, 19, 110
  gender dysphoria *versus,* 127
  prevalence of, 123
  transvestism *versus,* 292
  as umbrella term, 124
transgender people, 127–132
  adolescent, 124–125, 148–149
  bathroom access for, 123
  children, 124–125
  coming out, 11, 171
  cultures accepting, 19
  on gender continuum, 123, 123f
  heterosexual bias against, 540–541
  HIV/AIDS in, 513–514
  media portrayals of, 11
  medical interventions for, 126–127
  prejudice and discrimination against, 132–133,
    175, 541–543
  resources for, 135–136
  rights of, 544–545, 545f, 602
  sex research on, 36
  sex therapy for, 443–445
  sexual harassment of, 540–546
  sexual identity of, 171
  as sex workers, 599
  understanding and supporting, 132–133
transition, in labor and delivery, 366, 367f, 368f
transmission
  circumcision preventing, 89, 90
  drug use and, 384
transsexual, 6
transvestism, 6, 285t, 291–292, 291f, 292f
  DSM classification of, 291–292
  gender and, 292
  Hirschfeld on, 46
  origin of term, 44
  prevalence of, 288f, 289f
  sexual orientation and, 291, 292
  transvestism in, 292
Treponema pallidum, 469
triangular theory of love, 202–206, 202f
tribidism, 269, 269f
Trichomonas vaginalis, 465t, 478
trichomoniasis, 457, 478–480
Trump, Donald, 538
trust
  and communication, 221–223
  definition of, 221
TSS. *See* toxic shock syndrome
tubal ligation, 315t, 333
tubal pregnancy, 357
tuberculosis, HIV-related, 491
tumors
  benign, 389
  malignant, 389